P9-DFQ-148

Edited by
ALEX BEN BLOCK
&
LUCY AUTREY WILSON

With a Preface by
GEORGE LUCAS

Introduction by
FRANCIS FORD COPPOLA

George Lucas's
Blockbusting

**A Decade-by-Decade
Survey of Timeless Movies
Including Untold Secrets
of Their Financial and
Cultural Success**

GEORGE
LUCAS

BOOKS

*it*books

AN IMPRINT OF HARPERCOLLINS*PUBLISHERS*

GEORGE
LUCAS

BOOKS

*it*books

FIRST EDITION

Designed by Timothy Shaner, NightandDayDesign.biz

Library of Congress Cataloging-in-Publication data is available
upon request.

ISBN 978-0-06-177889-6

10 11 12 13 14   OV/WCF   10 9 8 7 6 5 4 3

Contents

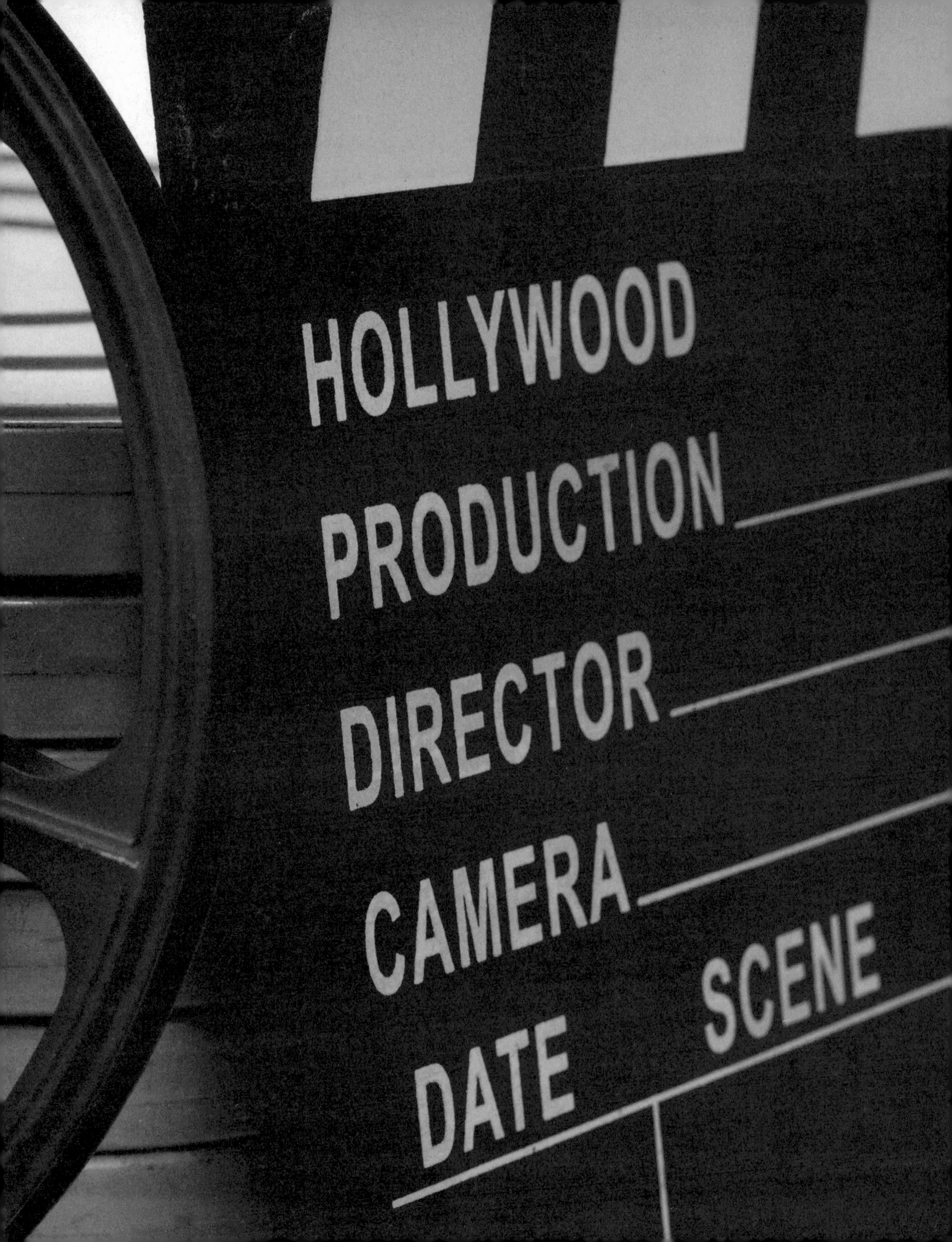
HOLLYWOOD
PRODUCTION
DIRECTOR
CAMERA
DATE
SCENE

Preface

When I went to film school at USC I didn't know anything about movies. We had a couple of theaters in Modesto, where I grew up, but other than that my exposure was very limited. The great thing about being in film school at that time was that there were filmmakers there who were interested in drama and high adventure, others who were interested in film as a director's medium, and still others who were interested in commercials and art films. As I learned about the craft and the business of filmmaking, I fell in love with the whole process. Here was a career that combined my interest in art and photography with my passion for storytelling and social issues.

That was back in the 1970s, a period of upheaval for the film business. Individuals were just starting to break out of the classic studio model, making their own artistic choices and affecting the kinds of films that were produced. As new as what was happening at the time may have seemed, it was really not so unique at all. It had happened before, and it's happening again.

Today's upheaval is both economic and technological. Just as the coming of age of the baby boomer audience in the seventies helped define the type of films that got made, digital technology is now making production far more democratic. As a result, creative power is again being pulled away from the studios and everyone is scrambling to figure out what's going to happen next.

Since the inception of moving pictures, the business of making movies has been changing and evolving to fit the times. Even beyond the rise and fall of studios, the ebb and flow of talent, and the changes in the technology of moviemaking itself, the production, distribution, and exhibition, of films have been influenced by the effects of war, changes in law and government, economic shifts, and cultural demographics. It's a fascinating big picture, and largely unexamined.

Blockbusting is an in-depth look at how 300 of the biggest and the best movies made it to the screen. It's a comprehensive view of our past, and a foreshadowing of our future. This is a book I wish I'd had when I was coming up in the industry, which is why I think it'll be a great tool for *anyone* interested in the art and business of making movies.

—*George Lucas*

Introduction

Just what is a "blockbuster" movie? Based on journalism's obsession with weekend grosses these days, you might think that it's solely about the money brought in at the box office worldwide. But by looking closely at some of the most successful movies ever released, *George Lucas's Blockbusting* answers the question in a subtle, yet more accurate way. A blockbuster movie is a combination of financial success, critical success, great storytelling, and timing. Blockbusting is determined by the impact it makes on the culture and its ability to stand the test of time.

Movie making combines many other art forms through a kind of alchemy. Clearly, the mixing of all the ingredients—human talent, storytelling, technical know-how, and a sense of timing—isn't easy. Filmmaking can be a grueling process requiring abundant amounts of energy and enthusiasm, so you have to be strong in your convictions. If you don't know enough about the technical aspects, you might find the camera operator, the grip, or someone else on the set calling the shots. If your sense of timing is off, you can waste millions of dollars making a movie few want to see. And you will have to collaborate with the people putting up the money whether you agree with them or not.

When I was directing *The Godfather* in 1971, Paramount did not like the cast I had chosen and they disapproved of how I was shooting the movie. I was often on the verge of getting fired. My story is hardly unique throughout the century or as long as movies have been made. Like *The Godfather,* it's a miracle some movies were ever released in their final form. Frank Capra had a hard time making *It Happened One Night* (1934) due to the interference of studio heavyweights Louis B. Mayer and Harry Cohn. *Citizen Kane* (1941) was nearly quashed by powerful newspaper publisher William Randolph Hearst, upon whose thinly disguised life the story was based. Hollywood tried twice to cast Bette Davis as the lead of *The African Queen* (1951) before Katharine Hepburn finally got the part, and *Psycho* (1960) was made only after Alfred Hitchcock agreed to finance it personally.

Talented people can be inspiring or difficult, more often they are both. But blockbuster movies cannot be made without them. This includes not only the stars but the producer and director who put them on the big screen. The achievements of the talented and successful filmmakers of the past inspire those who follow to reach new heights. They include the likes of F. W. Murnau, D. W. Griffith, Cecil B. DeMille, Frank Capra, Charles Chaplin, Walt Disney, John Ford, John Huston . . . and the list goes on. But there are other, lower-profile filmmakers who also serve as teachers. For me, that included Roger Corman, with whom I worked while I was a film student at UCLA.

The story is the foundation upon which all else is built in a blockbuster movie. It's what first intrigues a director, and attracts the best actors. The majority of the greatest movies ever made were based on fiction derived from popular novels, plays, or short stories. During the golden age of Hollywood we had such classics as *Gone with the Wind* (1939), the number-one film of all time in terms of box office success, based on Margaret Mitchell's bestseller. Before that came *David Copperfield* (1935), taken from the novel by Charles Dickens; *Captains Courageous* (1937), from the story by Rudyard Kipling; and *The Wizard of Oz* (1938), based on L. Frank Baum's classic book. Following *Gone with the Wind* came *The Grapes of Wrath* (1940) based on John Steinbeck's novel; *The Maltese Falcon* (1941) from the noir novel by Dashiell Hammett; *A Streetcar Named Desire* (1951) based on Tennessee Williams' play, and more. So it's no surprise that some of the biggest hits of the twenty-first century are *The Lord of the Rings* trilogy of films (2001–3) based on the fantasy books by J. R. Tolkien and the *Harry Potter* movies (2001 and still going strong) from the series of novels by J. K. Rowling. Not all great movies are based on fiction though. Some are also derived from history such as the biblical story behind *Ben Hur* (1959), the historical setting for *Cleopatra* (1963), and the profiles of real-life famous individuals such as *The Life of Emile Zola* (1937), *Lawrence of Arabia* (1962), and *Patton* (1970).

Although fewer in number, great original characters and ideas have sprung up directly for the screen from such storytelling filmmakers as Charles Chaplin, who first introduced his famous character in the short film *The Tramp* (1915); writer/actress Mae West, who wrote and starred in *She Done Him Wrong* (1933); *Sunset Boulevard* (1950) from writer/director Billy Wilder; Alfred Hitchcock's *North By Northwest* (1959), working with screenwriter Ernest Lehman; Martin Scorsese's *Taxi Driver* (1976) written by Paul Schrader; Woody Allen's *Annie Hall* (1977) with co-author Marshall Brickman; George Lucas's *Star Wars* movies (1977–2005); all the animated films from Pixar, and others.

The one characteristic that I believe is most important for success in the movie business is courage. An artist of any merit has doubts some of the time but one must stand behind one's ideas to be successful. When I look back, courage is what got me through the difficult times. For example, the script I wrote for *Patton* was considered controversial and exotic for its time because of the bizarre opening in which Patton stands in front of an American flag to give a speech. That opening was cited when my bosses went through the failings of the script. My option wasn't picked up and the script was filed away. Years later, and long after I was gone, it was resurrected by the story editor—and made faithfully. That controversial scene is now considered one of the better openings in movies and confirms the notion that it's often the things for which you are fired from that you receive "lifetime achievement" awards for years later.

Making movies has been a way for me to combine two life-long interests: literature and science. Filmmaking allows me to tell stories, try experimental techniques, and work to overcome a variety of technical challenges. I don't make movies based on what I think the audience wants to see, but to be successful a film does depend on the public's interest. Sometimes this interest is immediate. Sometimes it takes years to develop. Interest might come from the audience's desire to experience new tools like sound, color, special effects or 3-D, other times from changes in cultural values. Some movies are successful because of their timing in terms of technological breakthroughs, others because they hit a chord at a particular moment in time. *The Jazz Singer* (1927) never would have been such a big hit if not for its use of sound-on-film. *Snow White and the Seven Dwarfs* (1937) might not have worked as the first full-length animated film absent Technicolor. It's no surprise that films about war were popular in the 1940s with hits like *Mrs. Miniver* (1942) and *The Best Years of Our Lives* (1946) also taking Best Picture Oscars. To compete against television, 3-D movies were a hot fad in the 1950s (and now are back in considerably superior technical form to compete against cable and the Internet). The 1950s also brought CinemaScope and MGM Camera 65, without which *Ben Hur* (1959) might not have been such a giant box office success. Without the invention of the Nagra recorder in 1958, the ability to shoot and record sound easily on location might have made it impossible for such films as *Easy Rider* (1969) to be made. But if the baby boomers hadn't been coming into their own during this period, *Easy Rider* might never have been a hit.

It was a kind of timing that got me involved in *The Godfather*. I wasn't interested, but George Lucas said "Francis, you have got to do this. We have no money . . . They're going to chain up the Zoetrope doors and we're all going to be out on our ears." Although the need was there, I've still always felt you should only do a project where there's a possibility that you can fall in love with it, or at least a major aspect of it. When I started seeing the story as one about a king and his sons, none of whom had the talent or qualities of the king, I then saw it as a story of succession. And when that happened, I became much more interested. *The Godfather* became both a critical and box office success, to mine and everyone else's surprise.

What is truly amazing is that *despite* all of the difficulties, great movies are made. By including most of the great blockbusters of all time, *George Lucas's Blockbusting* is a great reference for anyone who loves movies.

—*Francis Ford Coppola*

Acknowledgments

This work is the combination of the efforts of many individuals over several years including the contributions of the feature film writers who provided the text on the 300 movies selected by George Lucas: Robert S. Birchard, Alex Ben Block, Louis Burklow, Douglas Burns, Bob Canning, Mark D'Anna, Gary Dretzka, Tom Dupree, Dina Gachman, David Kiehn, Michael Kogge, Scott Mazak, Frank McAdams, Christine McDermott, Rosaleen O'Byrne, Hayley Taylor Block, Daniel Wallace, and Sam Wasson. **Additional thanks** are due to the following people for their contributions to the decade text: Alex Ben Block for the majority of the writing; Lucy Autrey Wilson for the statistics research, lists, charts, and graphs; Ted Mundorff for the Exhibition Overview text from the 1950s through 2005; Bob Canning for his 1970s feature "How *Jaws* Heated Up Summer Movies"; Scott Mazak for his 1980s "Technology Spotlight on Industrial Light & Magic"; and David Kiehn for additional help with the decade text from the beginning through the 1920s. **Special thanks** as well to the one who loves film and film history and generously shared his rare knowledge. **Extra thanks** to the wonderful Hope Innelli at HarperCollins for her excellent edit. **More thanks** to all those who helped in the research and fact-checking: David Bergad, Mike Blanchard, Bonnie Chi, Rebecca Cline, Elizabeth Daley, Chrissie England, Peter Filichia, Sid Ganis, Madelyn Hammond, K.C. Hodenfield, Matthew Kennedy, Rick McCallum, Paul Matwiy, Russell Merritt, Patricia Prestinary, Howard Roffman, Michael Sragow, Steve Starkey, Randy Thom, Harold Vogel, Walter Much, and Robert Yehling.

Editors of the work include **Alex Ben Block,** an internationally known entertainment industry journalist, author, broadcaster, and show business historian. He was editor of two of Hollywood's top trade publications, *The Hollywood Reporter* and *Television Week,* which Block helped successfully relaunch. He was also an associate editor of *Forbes* magazine and a movie critic in Detroit, Miami, and Los Angeles. He is the author of *Outfoxed: The Inside Story of America's Fourth Television Network* and *The Legend of Bruce Lee.* He was featured on KPCC-FM's *Call Sheet* in Southern California and served as executive director of the Los Angeles Press Club. He oversaw programming for the American Pavilion at Cannes in 2008, and is currently editor-at-large for *The Hollywood Reporter* and show business historian for *Hollywood Today.* **Lucy Autrey Wilson** began her career with Lucasfilm in 1974, typing the script to the first *Star Wars* movie on an IBM Selectric typewriter. She then explored areas as diverse as construction, film, special effects, licensing, and merchandising. In the late 1980s, she launched an all-new *Star Wars* publishing program that grew to comprise more than 1,500 titles, including sixty-three *New York Times* bestsellers, before moving on to new challenges in nonfiction publishing. With a BA in English literature and an MBA in finance, she now combines her love of words and numbers by conducting the research and editorial work required to translate George Lucas's wide-ranging intellectual curiosity into books of all kinds. She currently serves as the director of publishing for George Lucas Books.

Note to the Reader

—From The Editors

There are 300 full-length feature films represented in this book. They are addressed in the order in which they were initially released in the United States. At least one movie per year, from 1913 through 2005, is included in the mix. You will encounter them in the Featured Films section of each chapter. These great movies, selected by George Lucas, are examined against the major production, distribution, exhibition, technology, and marketing changes that occurred by decade in the motion picture industry, thus providing a unique perspective on how that business has changed over time. A movie's success is not based solely on its profitability or the critical response it receives during its initial release but rather on its reception over time. For that reason, these 300 films are compared by their financial merits as well as their critical honors. Because the focus of this book is on the theatrical experience, the impact of TV and video is explored only on a case-by-case basis. To allow the reader to compare these great films on an apples-to-apples basis, all numbers reflecting revenue and cost appear both in their original values and in equivalent 2005 dollars.

A list of the 300 films George Lucas has selected appears in the Film Index on pages xx–xxix.

DATA TRACKED AND PRESENTED IN EACH DECADE THROUGHOUT

Key Financial Merits

All-Release domestic box office revenues

Production Cost

Top 300 Films position

Notes: (1) "All-Release" means the combined total of initial release revenue plus revenue from all known rereleases; (2) Production Cost, also known as the negative cost, generally applies to the initial release only; (3) the Top 300 Films position indicates the ranking of all feature-length theatrical films through 2005, not just of the 300 films featured in the book.

A list of the top 300 films ranked strictly by their All-Release equivalent 2005 dollar domestic box office revenue appears on pages xvi–xix.

Key Critical Honors

Academy Awards: all nominations and wins (1927–28 to 2005)

AFI 100 Years . . . 100 Movies Selection (10th Anniversary Edition, 2007; original, 1997)

National Film Preservation Board Selection (year of selection)
Golden Globe Awards: Best Picture win only (1944–2005)
New York Film Critics Circle Awards: Best Picture win only (1935–2005)
National Board of Review Awards: Best Film win only (1929–2005)
Film Daily Poll of Critics: Best Picture only (1922–1939)

Top Critically Acclaimed Lead Actors

To be included in this category, the actor must have won one or more of the following:
- An Academy Award for Best Actor
- An Honorary Award from the Academy (called a Special Award prior to 1948) for an uncategorized but noteworthy achievement in a given year or for an exceptional overall career achievement
- A Golden Globe Award (for Best Actor)
- A Cecil B. DeMille Award

Rankings are based on the number of lifetime Oscar nominations, the number of Oscar wins, the number of Golden Globe wins, whether the actor is in the top 25 AFI actor rankings, and by the number of the 300 Featured Films the actor starred in.

Top Directors

To be included in this category, the director must have directed at least one of the 300 Featured Films. Rankings are based on the cumulative All-Release domestic box office of each director's Featured Films initially released during the decade.

Decade-by-Decade Statistical Comparisons

General Statistics

Top 10 All-Release domestic box office movies of the decade (of all films released)
U.S. population (first year of each decade)
Average weekly U.S. movie attendance (first year of each decade)

Production Statistics

Average production costs by decade (Featured Films versus all films released)

Distribution Statistics

Annual U.S. box office gross revenues—first year of decade (all films released)
Number of new feature films released (all films released, not including reissues)

Exhibition Statistics

Average movie ticket price (first and last year of each decade)
Number of U.S. movie screens (first year of each decade)

NOTES ON ADJUSTING DOLLARS AND MAKING ESTIMATES

ADJUSTING REVENUES. Because of the time needed to complete the research and production of this book and due to the fact that the Motion Picture Association of America (MPAA) and the United States Bureau of Labor Statistics publish average annual ticket prices and consumer price index (CPI-U) percentages well after the end of each year, 2005 was selected as the most current year for which all dollars in the book could most accurately be converted. Revenues on movies released prior to 2005 are grossed up. Revenues on movies released after 2005 are adjusted down. Revenues are adjusted to 2005 dollars based on the change in average ticket price from the initial release year, or a subsequent rerelease year, to the average ticket price in 2005. When known, the revenues for some earlier films are also adjusted on the basis of the higher road show price, rather than the average ticket price, for those limited engagements. Because most movie revenue reporting was conducted on the basis of rentals (i.e., the share of the box office collected by the distributor) through the late 1980s, rentals are adjusted up to box office. When only rentals are known, box office revenues are estimated using a 25/75 ratio for the period of inception to 1919 (i.e., rentals are estimated to be 25 percent of the box office gross), 50/50 for the 1920s, and 45/55 from 1930 until the late 1980s, when reporting of rentals was discontinued. In the late 1980s when studios and trade magazines converted to reporting theatrical revenues in terms of box office, rentals are computed on the basis of 55/45 domestic (i.e., 55 percent of the domestic box office gross is estimated to be rentals) and 45/55 foreign.

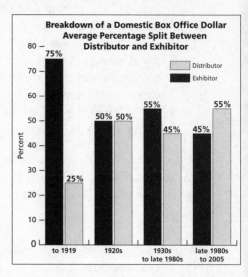

ESTIMATING THE NUMBER OF DAYS FOR PRINCIPAL PHOTOGRAPHY. The 300 Featured Films are compared on the basis of the number of days the movie took to film (i.e., the period of principal photography). When the exact number of days could not be obtained, they are estimated. If the start and end production dates are known, the number of shooting days is estimated using a six-day production week through 1956 (Monday through Saturday) and a five-day production week (Monday through Friday) after that. All estimated shooting days are marked "estimated."

ADJUSTING PRODUCTION COSTS. Production costs are adjusted to 2005 dollars based on the change in the CPI-U between the initial release year and 2005. Because the

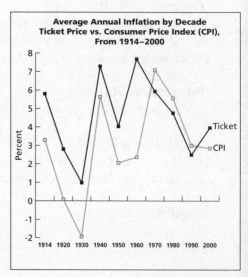

change in ticket prices does not follow the same inflation curve as the change in consumer prices, large variances exist between adjusted box office dollars and adjusted production costs, especially in the period before the 1970s. That means, in 2005 dollars, earlier films' production costs, as a percentage of their box office revenue, might appear much lower than the ratio between revenue and cost in unadjusted dollars.

ADJUSTING SALARIES. When available, comparative salaries, earnings, and profit participations are included. These are adjusted to 2005 dollars based on the change in the consumer price index between the year of payment and 2005.

SALARY COMPARISONS

CHANGING FEDERAL INDIVIDUAL INCOME TAX RATES. Salaries cited in each decade chapter are pretax. Net tax revenues would vary widely depending upon the year payments were received. The federal individual income tax rate table on page xiv, as an example, details the change in tax rates from 1913 to 2009, from a high of 94 percent in the 1940s to a low of 28 percent in the 1980s (based on the highest tax bracket for a married individual filing jointly).

Gains and losses on corporate stock paid out as additional compensation would follow separate tax rates. As an example, the Revenue Act of 1950 allowed corporations to give executives stock options, which when sold were taxed at a low capital gains rate of 25 percent versus the 91 percent highest tax rate that was applied to salaries in that same period.

NOTES ON GENRE (SILENT VERSUS SOUND) AND RUNNING TIMES

GENRE. Unless indicated as a "Silent Classic" in the genre field, all films are sound films.

RUNNING TIMES. When available, running times through the 1930s are given in number of feet, number of reels, and estimated minutes. After the 1930s, the times are listed only in minutes. Silent films up to approximately 1925 ran between 14 and 24 frames per second (fps), so film length in minutes varies from one account to another. Sound films from 1925 forward ran at approximately 24 fps, or approximately 90 feet per minute of sound film.

THE INDUSTRY AT A GLANCE, FROM INCEPTION TO 2005

General population, movie attendance, production, distribution, and exhibition statistics presented on a decade-by-decade basis throughout the book are condensed to provide a macro view of trends and events from the industry's start through 2005. See inserts on page 412.

FEDERAL INDIVIDUAL INCOME TAX RATES

Decade	Year(s)	MARRIED FILING JOINTLY	
		Maximum Marginal Tax Rate	Tax Bracket over Which Maximum Rate Applies
1910s			
	1913–1915 *(last law to change rates: Tariff Act of 10.3.1913)*	7%	$500,000
	1916–1917 *(Revenue Act of 1916)*	15%	$2,000,000
	1918–1919 *(Revenue Act of 1918)*	73%	$1,000,000
1920s			
	1920–1921	73%	$1,000,000
	1922–1923 *(Revenue Act of 1921)*	58%	$200,000
	1924 *(Revenue Act of 1924)*	46%	$500,000
	1925	25%	$100,000
	1926–1929 *(Revenue Act of 1926 and 1928)*	25%	$100,000
1930s			
	1930–1931 *(Revenue Act of 1928)*	25%	$100,000
	1932–1935 *(Revenue Act of 1932 and 1934)*	63%	$1,000,000
	1936–1939 *(Revenue Act of 1936 and 1938)*	79%	$5,000,000
1940s			
	1940 *(Revenue Act of 1940)*	79%	$5,000,000
	1941 *(Revenue Act of 1941)*	81%	$5,000,000
	1942–1943 *(Revenue Act of 1942)*	88%	$200,000
	1944–1945 *(Individual Income Tax Act of 1944 and Revenue Act of 1945)*	94%	$200,000
	1946–1948 *(Revenue Act of 1945 and 1948)*	91%	$200,000
	1949 *(Revenue Act of 1948)*	91%	$400,000
1950s			
	1950–1951 *(Revenue Act of 1950 and 1951)*	91%	$400,000
	1952–1953 *(Revenue Act of 1951)*	92%	$400,000
	1954–1959 *(Revenue Act of 1954)*	91%	$400,000
1960s			
	1960–1963 *(Internal Revenue Code of 1954)*	91%	$400,000
	1964 *(Revenue Act of 1964)*	77%	$400,000
	1965–1969 *(Revenue Act of 1964 and 1969)*	70%	$200,000

Decade	Year(s)	MARRIED FILING JOINTLY	
		Maximum Marginal Tax Rate	Tax Bracket over Which Maximum Rate Applies
1970s			
	1970–1976 *(Tax Reform Act of 1969)*	70%	$200,000
1980s			
	1980–1981 *(Revenue Act of 1978 and Economic Recovery Tax Act of 1981)*	70%	$215,400
	1982 *(Tax Equity and Fiscal Responsibility Act of 1982)*	50%	$85,600
	1983	50%	$109,400
	1984 *(Tax Reform Act of 1984)*	50%	$162,400
	1985	50%	$169,020
	1986 *(Tax Reform Act of 1986)*	50%	$175,250
	1987	38.5%	$90,000
	1988	28%	$149,250
	1989	28%	$155,320
1990s			
	1990 *(Omnibus Budget Reconciliation Act of 1990)*	28%	$162,770
	1991	31%	$82,150
	1992	31%	$86,500
	1993–1994 *(Omnibus Budget Reconciliation Act of 1993)*	39.6%	$250,000
	1995	39.6%	$256,500
	1996	39.6%	$263,750
	1997	39.6%	$271,050
	1998	39.6%	$278,450
	1999	39.6%	$283,150
2000s			
	2000	39.6%	$288,350
	2001 *(Economic Growth and Tax Relief Reconciliation Act of 2001)*	39.1%	$297,350
	2002	38.6%	$307,050
	2003 *(Jobs and Growth Tax Relief Reconciliation Act of 2003)*	35%	$311,950
	2004	35%	$319,100
	2005	35%	$326,450
	2006	35%	$336,550
	2007	35%	$349,700
	2008	35%	$357,700
	2009	35%	$372,950

Top 300 Films of All Time

All-Release Domestic Box Office
By Initial Year of Release, 1910–2005
Equivalent 2005 $s in Millions of $s

	Title	Year of Release	Equivalent in 2005 $s in Millions		Title	Year of Release	Equivalent in 2005 $s in Millions
1	Gone with the Wind*	1939	$1,407.7	31	Love Story*	1970	$447.6
2	Star Wars: Episode IV A New Hope*	1977	$1,085.1	32	Spider-Man*	2002	$445.4
3	The Sound of Music*	1965	$953.2	33	Independence Day*	1996	$444.0
4	E.T.: The Extra-Terrestrial*	1982	$889.4	34	Cleopatra*	1963	$435.7
5	The Ten Commandments*	1956	$829.2	35	Saturday Night Fever*	1977	$435.0
6	Titanic*	1997	$824.8	36	Home Alone*	1990	$434.0
7	Jaws*	1975	$802.9	37	Beverly Hills Cop*	1984	$432.8
8	Snow White and the Seven Dwarfs*	1937	$760.9	38	Butch Cassidy and the Sundance Kid*	1969	$426.5
9	Ben-Hur*	1959	$754.3	39	Close Encounters of the Third Kind*	1977	$424.1
10	The Exorcist*	1973	$722.9	40	Airport*	1970	$415.6
11	Doctor Zhivago*	1965	$622.4	41	This Is the Army	1943	$407.7
12	Star Wars: Episode V The Empire Strikes Back*	1980	$620.0	42	Batman*	1989	$403.5
13	The Sting	1973	$605.6	43	American Graffiti*	1973	$402.0
14	Star Wars: Episode VI Return of the Jedi*	1983	$597.6	44	The Lord of the Rings: The Return of the King*	2003	$398.4
15	Raiders of the Lost Ark*	1981	$554.7	45	101 Dalmations	1961	$395.3
16	Jurassic Park*	1993	$552.9	46	Thunderball*	1965	$395.2
17	Star Wars: Episode I The Phantom Menace*	1999	$540.3	47	It's a Mad, Mad, Mad, Mad World	1963	$389.4
18	Mary Poppins*	1964	$538.8	48	Spider-Man 2*	2004	$385.6
19	Around the World in 80 Days*	1956	$534.0	49	Bambi*	1942	$383.8
20	The Graduate*	1967	$525.0	50	National Lampoon's Animal House*	1978	$383.0
21	The Birth of a Nation*	1915	$522.0	51	The Passion of the Christ*	2004	$382.7
22	Grease*	1978	$520.5	52	Star Wars: Episode III Revenge of the Sith*	2005	$380.3
23	The Godfather*	1972	$505.9	53	Cinderella*	1950	$379.8
24	Forrest Gump*	1994	$505.6	54	Back to the Future*	1985	$374.7
25	The Lion King*	1994	$501.9	55	The Lord of the Rings: The Two Towers*	2002	$372.8
26	The Robe*	1953	$474.8	56	The Sixth Sense*	1999	$370.3
27	My Fair Lady*	1964	$474.2	57	Superman—The Movie*	1978	$367.7
28	Pinocchio*	1940	$465.2	58	Tootsie*	1982	$364.8
29	Shrek 2*	2004	$455.4	59	Smokey and the Bandit	1977	$364.3
30	Ghostbusters*	1984	$454.3				

	Title	Year of Release	Equivalent in 2005 $s in Millions		Title	Year of Release	Equivalent in 2005 $s in Millions
60	The Towering Inferno*	1974	$362.4	97	Quo Vadis*	1951	$312.4
61	The Bridge on the River Kwai*	1957	$362.3	98	Terminator 2: Judgment Day*	1991	$311.9
62	Blazing Saddles*	1974	$361.6	99	Dr. Seuss' How The Grinch Stole Christmas*	2000	$309.0
63	Sergeant York*	1941	$361.3	100	Toy Story 2*	1999	$307.8
64	Finding Nemo*	2003	$361.1	101	Swiss Family Robinson	1960	$307.2
65	Harry Potter and the Sorcerer's Stone*	2001	$359.0	102	Top Gun*	1986	$305.4
66	Peter Pan*	1953	$358.4	103	Ben-Hur: A Tale of the Christ*	1925	$305.2
67	Rocky*	1976	$352.8	104	Shrek*	2001	$303.1
68	The Lord of the Rings: The Fellowship of the Ring*	2001	$352.6	105	Guess Who's Coming to Dinner*	1967	$302.7
69	Goldfinger*	1964	$352.1	106	Crocodile Dundee*	1986	$302.0
70	The Jungle Book	1967	$351.1	107	Song of the South	1946	$301.9
71	Twister*	1996	$350.5	108	The Matrix Reloaded*	2003	$299.3
72	One Flew over the Cuckoo's Nest*	1975	$350.2	109	Saving Private Ryan*	1998	$292.8
73	West Side Story*	1961	$350.1	110	Lawrence of Arabia*	1962	$290.2
74	Men in Black*	1997	$350.1	111	Monsters, Inc.	2001	$289.8
75	The Greatest Show on Earth*	1952	$349.1	112	Harry Potter and the Goblet of Fire*	2005	$289.6
76	Duel in the Sun*	1947	$348.0	113	The Chronicles of Narnia: The Lion, the Witch, and the Wardrobe*	2005	$289.5
77	The Best Years of Our Lives*	1946	$345.3	114	Going My Way*	1944	$289.3
78	The Big Parade*	1925	$343.4	115	Tom Jones*	1963	$289.0
79	Indiana Jones and the Temple of Doom*	1984	$343.1	116	Harry Potter and the Chamber of Secrets*	2002	$288.7
80	Star Wars: Episode II Attack of the Clones*	2002	$342.4	117	The Fugitive*	1993	$284.7
81	Mrs. Doubtfire*	1993	$337.7	118	Meet the Fockers*	2004	$283.1
82	Aladdin	1992	$336.2	119	An Officer and a Gentleman	1982	$283.0
83	For Whom the Bell Tolls*	1943	$333.9	120	Mrs. Miniver	1942	$282.7
84	Ghost*	1990	$329.8	121	Gremlins	1984	$282.7
85	M*A*S*H*	1970	$328.6	122	Toy Story*	1995	$281.2
86	Lady and the Tramp	1955	$326.8	123	Dances with Wolves*	1990	$279.6
87	From Here to Eternity*	1953	$326.4	124	Samson and Delilah*	1949	$276.7
88	How the West Was Won*	1963	$325.3	125	Rain Man*	1988	$276.3
89	Pirates of the Caribbean: The Curse of the Black Pearl*	2003	$324.7	126	Armageddon*	1998	$275.5
90	The Bells of St. Mary's*	1945	$323.6	127	On Golden Pond*	1981	$273.7
91	Giant*	1956	$322.2	128	Earthquake	1974	$273.6
92	Fiddler on the Roof*	1971	$320.2	129	Rocky III	1982	$272.6
93	The Lost World: Jurassic Park	1997	$319.9	130	Rambo: First Blood Part II	1985	$271.6
94	The Poseidon Adventure*	1972	$317.6	131	The Jolson Story	1946	$271.3
95	Indiana Jones and the Last Crusade*	1989	$316.8	132	Batman Forever*	1995	$271.2
96	Fantasia*	1940	$314.8	133	Pretty Woman*	1990	$270.4
				134	Young Frankenstein	1974	$270.3
				135	The Incredibles	2004	$269.9

*These films also appear as Featured Films in this book.

	Title	Year of Release	Equivalent in 2005 $s in Millions		Title	Year of Release	Equivalent in 2005 $s in Millions
136	Home Alone 2: Lost in New York*	1992	$268.8	175	Who Framed Roger Rabbit*	1988	$240.4
137	Funny Girl*	1968	$268.7	176	There's Something About Mary	1998	$239.9
138	Three Men and a Baby*	1987	$268.6	177	The Dirty Dozen*	1967	$238.0
139	My Big Fat Greek Wedding*	2002	$266.4	178	Random Harvest	1942	$237.4
140	Cast Away*	2000	$264.6	179	The Valley of the Dolls	1967	$237.4
141	Mission: Impossible*	1996	$262.5	180	The Carpetbaggers	1964	$237.4
142	2001: A Space Odyssey*	1968	$261.9	181	Lethal Weapon 2*	1989	$236.6
143	Bonnie and Clyde*	1967	$261.1	182	Austin Powers in Goldmember	2002	$235.1
144	Austin Powers: The Spy Who Shagged Me (aka Austin Powers 2)	1999	$260.0	183	King Kong	1976	$234.9
145	The Longest Day*	1962	$259.5	184	War of the Worlds*	2005	$234.3
146	Bruce Almighty	2003	$258.0	185	Every Which Way but Loose	1978	$233.4
147	Harry Potter and the Prisoner of Azkaban	2004	$257.6	186	You Only Live Twice	1967	$230.1
148	Fatal Attraction*	1987	$256.8	187	Sayonara	1957	$230.1
149	Peyton Place	1957	$256.4	188	The Mummy Returns	2001	$228.8
150	Mission: Impossible II	2000	$256.2	189	X2: X-Men United	2003	$228.5
151	Rush Hour 2	2001	$256.1	190	Shane*	1953	$228.4
152	Patton*	1970	$255.4	191	South Pacific	1958	$228.0
153	The Goodbye Girl	1977	$253.8	192	To Sir, with Love	1967	$226.7
154	Apollo 13*	1995	$253.5	193	Platoon*	1986	$226.7
155	Liar Liar*	1997	$253.3	194	The Valley of Decision	1945	$226.3
156	Kramer vs. Kramer*	1979	$253.2	195	Since You Went Away	1944	$226.3
157	Robin Hood: Prince of Thieves*	1991	$252.0	196	Look Who's Talking	1989	$225.1
158	Spartacus*	1960	$251.9	197	Pearl Harbor	2001	$224.9
159	Beverly Hills Cop II*	1987	$251.9	198	True Lies	1994	$224.3
160	Signs	2002	$251.5	199	Heaven Can Wait	1978	$223.6
161	Batman Returns*	1992	$251.5	200	Lethal Weapon 3	1992	$223.5
162	Beauty and the Beast*	1991	$251.1	201	Meet Me in St. Louis*	1944	$223.3
163	Superman II*	1981	$249.4	202	Gladiator*	2000	$223.2
164	A Star Is Born	1976	$248.1	203	Jaws 2	1978	$222.5
165	Nine to Five*	1980	$246.1	204	The Santa Clause	1994	$221.7
166	The Song of Bernadette	1943	$245.6	205	Rocky IV	1985	$220.9
167	The Firm	1993	$245.2	206	The Caine Mutiny*	1954	$220.9
168	The Singing Fool	1928	$244.9	207	White Christmas*	1954	$219.9
169	Yankee Doodle Dandy*	1942	$244.3	208	The Waterboy	1998	$219.6
170	The Shaggy Dog	1959	$243.0	209	A Few Good Men*	1992	$218.8
171	Porky's*	1982	$241.8	210	A Bug's Life	1998	$218.8
172	Air Force One	1997	$241.5	211	King Kong	2005	$218.1
173	Stir Crazy	1980	$241.4	212	The Odd Couple	1968	$217.5
174	The Guns of Navarone*	1961	$240.5	213	Boom Town*	1940	$217.5
				214	What Women Want	2000	$217.4
				215	Guys and Dolls	1955	$217.3
				216	The Perfect Storm*	2000	$217.2
				217	Rocky II	1979	$216.7

	Title	Year of Release	Equivalent in 2005 $s in Millions		Title	Year of Release	Equivalent in 2005 $s in Millions
218	The Matrix*	1999	$216.3	259	Silver Streak	1976	$200.6
219	Tarzan	1999	$215.9	260	Oh God!	1977	$200.6
220	Unconquered	1947	$215.8	261	Thirty Seconds over Tokyo	1944	$200.3
221	Sister Act	1992	$215.6	262	The Flintstones	1994	$200.2
222	David and Bathsheba	1951	$215.2	263	The Deep	1977	$199.9
223	Jerry Maguire	1996	$215.0	264	Coming to America	1988	$199.9
224	Men in Black II	2002	$213.4	265	The Silence of the Lambs	1991	$199.0
225	Stage Door Canteen	1943	$213.2	266	Battle Cry	1955	$198.9
226	Terms of Endearment*	1983	$212.6	267	The Karate Kid, Part 2	1986	$198.9
227	All The President's Men*	1976	$212.5	268	Airplane!	1980	$198.9
228	Hooper	1978	$212.5	269	Meet the Parents	2000	$197.7
229	El Cid	1962	$211.0	270	Ransom	1996	$197.6
230	Reap the Wild Wind*	1942	$211.0	271	Welcome Stranger	1947	$197.5
231	Honey, I Shrunk the Kids	1989	$210.0	272	Doctor Dolittle	1998	$197.0
232	Psycho*	1960	$209.9	273	Stripes	1981	$196.9
233	Wedding Crashers	2005	$209.1	274	101 Dalmations (live action)	1996	$196.8
234	Hawaii	1965	$209.1	275	San Francisco*	1936	$196.7
235	The Parent Trap	1961	$209.0	276	Mister Roberts*	1955	$196.2
236	Pocahontas	1995	$208.6	277	Sleepless in Seattle	1993	$196.1
237	Star Trek: The Motion Picture	1979	$208.5	278	The Bible	1966	$196.0
238	Daddy Long Legs	1919	$208.3	279	The Mummy	1999	$195.9
239	Ocean's Eleven	2001	$207.7	280	Ice Age	2002	$194.6
240	Bullitt*	1968	$206.6	281	Anchors Aweigh	1945	$194.5
241	Charlie and the Chocolate Factory	2005	$206.5	282	The Rock	1996	$194.4
242	Big Daddy	1999	$206.3	283	Dark Passage	1947	$194.2
243	Apocalypse Now*	1979	$205.7	284	Madagascar	2005	$193.6
244	Batman Begins	2005	$205.3	285	Good Morning, Vietnam	1987	$193.3
245	The Absent-Minded Professor	1961	$205.3	286	Blue Skies	1946	$193.3
246	The King and I*	1956	$205.3	287	Rush Hour	1998	$192.9
247	Jurassic Park III	2001	$205.2	288	The Snows of Kilimanjaro	1952	$192.9
248	Teenage Mutant Ninja Turtles	1990	$205.0	289	The Day After Tomorrow	2004	$192.8
249	Planet of the Apes: AKA The Visitor	2001	$203.9	290	Runaway Bride	1999	$192.1
250	20,000 Leagues Under the Sea	1954	$203.5	291	Deep Impact	1998	$192.0
251	Sleeping Beauty	1959	$203.3	292	Easy Rider*	1969	$191.7
252	As Good As It Gets	1997	$202.9	293	Dumb and Dumber	1994	$191.6
253	Alien*	1979	$202.9	294	The Pride of the Yankees*	1942	$191.3
254	Irma La Douce	1963	$202.8	295	Airport II	1974	$190.7
255	The Way We Were	1973	$202.3	296	10	1979	$190.4
256	Midnight Cowboy*	1969	$202.2	297	The Omen	1976	$189.9
257	How to Marry a Millionarie	1953	$201.1	298	Who's Afraid of Virginia Woolf?*	1966	$189.5
258	The French Connection*	1971	$200.8	299	Good Will Hunting*	1997	$189.4
				300	Flashdance	1983	$189.1

These films also appear as Featured Films in this book.

Film Index

300 Films That Stand the Test of Time
Listed by the Decade in Which They Were First Released

The 1910s Featured Films

INITIAL RELEASE	FILM	DIRECTOR	U.S. DISTRIBUTOR
1913, Dec	The Sea Wolf	Hobart Bosworth	States Rights
1914, Feb	The Squaw Man	Oscar C. Apfel and Cecil B. DeMille	States Rights
1915, Mar	The Birth of a Nation	D. W. Griffith	States Rights
1916, Sept	Intolerance	D. W. Griffith	States Rights
1917, Oct	Cleopatra	J. Gordon Edwards	Fox Film Corp.
1918, Jan	Stella Maris	Marshall Neilan	Famous Players-Lasky and Artcraft Pictures
1919, Oct	Broken Blossoms	D. W. Griffith	United Artists

The 1920s Featured Films

INITIAL RELEASE	FILM	DIRECTOR	U.S. DISTRIBUTOR
1920, Sept	Way Down East	D. W. Griffith	United Artists
1921, Feb	The Kid	Charles Chaplin	First National
1921, Mar	The Four Horsemen of the Apocalypse	Rex Ingram	Metro
1922, Apr	Orphans of the Storm	D. W. Griffith	United Artists
1923, Sept	The Hunchback of Notre Dame	Wallace Worsley	Universal
1923, Dec	The Ten Commandments	Cecil B. DeMille	Paramount
1924, Dec	Greed	Erich von Stroheim	Metro-Goldwyn
1925, Jan	The Thief of Bagdad	Raoul Walsh	United Artists
1925, June	The Lost World	Harry O. Hoyt	First National
1925, Aug	The Gold Rush	Charles Chaplin	United Artists
1925, Sept	The Phantom of the Opera	Rupert Julian	Universal
1925, Nov	The Merry Widow	Erich von Stroheim	MGM
1925, Nov	The Big Parade	King Vidor	MGM
1925, Dec	Ben-Hur: A Tale of the Christ	Fred Niblo	MGM
1926, Dec	The General	Buster Keaton and Clyde Bruckman	United Artists
1927, Jan	Tell It to the Marines	George Hill	MGM
1927, Aug	Wings	William A. Wellman	Paramount
1927, Oct	The Jazz Singer	Alan Crosland	Warner Bros.
1928, Mar	The Crowd	King Vidor	MGM
1928, Nov	The Wind	Victor Sjostrom	MGM
1929, Jan	In Old Arizona	Raoul Walsh and Irving Cummings	Fox Film Corp.
1929, June	The Broadway Melody	Harry Beaumont	MGM
1929, Nov	The Hollywood Revue of 1929	Charles F. Reisner	MGM

The 1930s Featured Films

INITIAL RELEASE	FILM	DIRECTOR	U.S. DISTRIBUTOR
1930, Jun	The Big House	George W. Hill	MGM
1930, Aug	All Quiet on the Western Front	Lewis Milestone	Universal
1931, Feb	Cimarron	Wesley Ruggles	RKO
1931, Mar	City Lights	Charles Chaplin	United Artists
1931, Nov	Frankenstein	James Whale	Universal
1932, Feb	Shanghai Express	Josef von Sternberg	Paramount
1932, Apr	Grand Hotel	Edmund Goulding	MGM
1932, Nov	I Am a Fugitive from a Chain Gang	Mervyn LeRoy	Warner Bros.
1933, Jan	State Fair	Henry King	Fox Film Corp.
1933, Feb	She Done Him Wrong	Lowell Sherman	Paramount
1933, Mar	42nd Street	Lloyd Bacon	Warner Bros.
1933, Apr	King Kong	Ernest B. Schoedsack	RKO
1933, Nov	Little Women	George Cukor	RKO
1934, Feb	It Happened One Night	Frank Capra	Columbia
1934, May	The Thin Man	W. S. Van Dyke	MGM
1934, Oct	Cleopatra	Cecil B. DeMille	Paramount
1935, Jan	David Copperfield	George Cukor	MGM
1935, May	The Informer	John Ford	RKO
1935, Nov	Mutiny on the Bounty	Frank Lloyd	MGM
1935, Dec	Captain Blood	Michael Curtiz	First National Warner Bros.
1936, Feb	Modern Times	Charles Chaplin	United Artists
1936, Apr	Mr. Deeds Goes to Town	Frank Capra	Columbia
1936, Jun	San Francisco	W. S. Van Dyke	MGM
1936, Sept	The Great Ziegfeld	Robert Z. Leonard	MGM
1937, Jun	Captains Courageous	Victor Fleming	MGM
1937, Oct	The Life of Emile Zola	William Dieterle	Warner Bros.
1937, Dec	Snow White and the Seven Dwarfs	David Hand	RKO
1938, Feb	Bringing Up Baby	Howard Hawks	RKO
1938, Apr	In Old Chicago	Henry King	20th Century-Fox
1938, Aug	Alexander's Ragtime Band	Henry King	20th Century-Fox
1938, Sept	Boys Town	Norman Taurog	MGM
1939, Aug	The Wizard of Oz	Victor Fleming	MGM
1939, Oct	Mr. Smith Goes to Washington	Frank Capra	Columbia
1939, Dec	Gone with the Wind	Victor Fleming	MGM

The 1940s Featured Films

INITIAL RELEASE	FILM	DIRECTOR	U.S. DISTRIBUTOR
1940, Feb	Pinocchio	Ben Sharpsteen, Hamilton Luske, David Hand	RKO
1940, Mar	The Grapes of Wrath	John Ford	20th Century-Fox
1940, Aug	Boom Town	Jack Conway	MGM
1940, Nov	Fantasia	Ben Sharpsteen (prod supv) + 10 directors	RKO
1941, Jan	The Philadelphia Story	George Cukor	MGM
1941, Sept	Citizen Kane	Orson Welles	RKO
1941, Sept	Sergeant York	Howard Hawks	Warner Bros.
1941, Oct	The Maltese Falcon	John Huston	Warner Bros.
1941, Dec	How Green Was My Valley	John Ford	20th Century-Fox
1942, Mar	Reap the Wild Wind	Cecil B. DeMille	Paramount
1942, May	Yankee Doodle Dandy	Michael Curtiz	Warner Bros.
1942, July	The Pride of the Yankees	Sam Wood	RKO
1942, July	Mrs. Miniver	William Wyler	MGM
1942, Aug	Bambi	David Hand (supv dir)	RKO
1943, Jan	Casablanca	Michael Curtiz	Warner Bros.
1943, May	The Ox-Bow Incident	William A. Wellman	20th Century-Fox
1943, July	For Whom the Bell Tolls	Sam Wood	Paramount
1944, April	Double Indemnity	Billy Wilder	Paramount
1944, May	Going My Way	Leo McCarey	Paramount
1944, Dec	Meet Me in St. Louis	Vincente Minelli	MGM
1945, Nov	The Lost Weekend	Billy Wilder	Paramount
1945, Dec	The Bells of St. Mary's	Leo McCarey	RKO
1945, Dec	Spellbound	Alfred Hitchcock	United Artists
1946, Nov	The Best Years of Our Lives	William Wyler	RKO
1946, Dec	It's a Wonderful Life	Frank Capra	RKO
1947, May	Duel in the Sun	King Vidor	SRO
1947, Sept	Life with Father	Michael Curtiz	Warner Bros.
1947, Nov	Gentleman's Agreement	Elia Kazan	20th Century-Fox
1948, Jan	The Treasure of the Sierra Madre	John Huston	Warner Bros.
1949, Nov	All the King's Men	Robert Rossen	Columbia
1949, Nov	Battleground	William Wellman	MGM
1949, Dec	Samson and Delilah	Cecil B. DeMille	Paramount

The 1950s Featured Films

INITIAL RELEASE	FILM	DIRECTOR	U.S. DISTRIBUTOR
1950, Feb	The Third Man	Carol Reed	SRO
1950, Mar	Cinderella	Clyde Geronimi, Hamilton Luske, Wilfred Jackson	RKO
1950, Aug	Sunset Boulevard	Billy Wilder	Paramount
1950, Nov	All About Eve	Joseph L. Mankiewicz	20th Century-Fox
1951, Sept	A Streetcar Named Desire	Elia Kazan	Warner Bros.
1951, Nov	Quo Vadis	Mervyn LeRoy	MGM
1951, Nov	An American in Paris	Vincent Minelli	MGM
1951, Dec	The African Queen	John Huston	United Artists
1952, Jan	The Greatest Show on Earth	Cecil B. DeMille	Paramount
1952, Apr	Singin' in the Rain	Stanley Donen, Gene Kelly	MGM
1952, July	High Noon	Fred Zinnemann	United Artists
1952, Sept	The Quiet Man	John Ford	Republic
1953, June	Peter Pan	Clyde Geronimi, Hamilton Luske, Wilfred Jackson	RKO
1953, April	Shane	George Stevens	Paramount
1953, Sept	The Robe	Henry Koster	20th Century-Fox
1953, Sept	From Here to Eternity	Fred Zinnemann	Columbia
1954, June	The Caine Mutiny	Edward Dmytryk	Columbia
1954, July	On the Waterfront	Elia Kazan	Columbia
1954, Sept	Rear Window	Alfred Hitchcock	Paramount
1954, Nov	White Christmas	Michael Curtiz	Paramount
1955, April	East of Eden	Elia Kazan	Warner Bros.
1955, April	Marty	Delbert Mann	United Artists
1955, July	Mister Roberts	John Ford, Mervyn LeRoy	Warner Bros.
1955, Oct	Rebel Without a Cause	Nicholas Ray	Warner Bros.
1956, May	The Searchers	John Ford	Warner Bros.
1956, June	The King and I	Walter Lang	20th Century-Fox
1956, Oct	Around the World in 80 Days	Michael J. Anderson	United Artists
1956, Nov	The Ten Commandments	Cecil B. DeMille	Paramount
1956, Nov	Giant	George Stevens	Warner Bros.
1957, Sept	The Three Faces of Eve	Nunally Johnson	20th Century-Fox
1957, Dec	The Bridge on the River Kwai	David Lean	Columbia
1958, May	Vertigo	Alfred Hitchcock	Paramount
1958, Dec	Auntie Mame	Morton DaCosta	Warner Bros.
1959, Mar	Some Like It Hot	Billy Wilder	United Artists
1959, July	The Nun's Story	Fred Zinnemann	Warner Bros.
1959, July	North by Northwest	Alfred Hitchcock	MGM
1959, Nov	Ben-Hur	William Wyler	MGM

The 1960s Featured Films

INITIAL RELEASE	FILM	DIRECTOR	U.S. DISTRIBUTOR
1960, June	The Apartment	Billy Wilder	United Artists
1960, June	Psycho	Alfred Hitchcock	Paramount
1960, Oct	Spartacus	Stanley Kubrick	Universal
1961, Jul	The Guns of Navarone	J. Lee Thompson	Columbia
1961, Sept	The Hustler	Robert Rossen	20th Century-Fox
1961, Oct	West Side Story	Robert Wise	United Artists
1962, Oct	The Longest Day	Ken Annakin, Andrew Marton, Bernhard Wicki	20th Century-Fox
1962, Dec	Lawrence of Arabia	David Lean	Columbia
1962, Dec	To Kill a Mockingbird	Robert Mulligan	Universal
1963, Feb	How The West Was Won	John Ford, George Marshall, Henry Hathaway	MGM
1963, May	Dr. No	Terence Young	United Artists
1963, June	Cleopatra	Joseph L. Mankiewicz	20th Century-Fox
1963, Sept	Lilies of the Field	Ralph Nelson	United Artists
1963, Oct	Tom Jones	Tony Richardson	Lopert Pictures
1964, Jan	Dr. Strangelove, or How I Learned to Stop Worrying and Love The Bomb	Stanley Kubrick	Columbia
1964, Aug	Mary Poppins	Robert Stevenson	Buena Vista
1964, Oct	My Fair Lady	George Cukor	Warner Bros.
1964, Dec	Goldfinger	Guy Hamilton	United Artists
1965, Mar	The Sound of Music	Robert Wise	20th Century-Fox
1965, Dec	Thunderball	Terence Young	United Artists
1965, Dec	Doctor Zhivago	David Lean	MGM
1966, June	Who's Afraid of Virginia Woolf?	Mike Nichols	Warner Bros.
1966, Dec	A Man for All Seasons	Fred Zinnemann	Columbia
1967, June	The Dirty Dozen	Robert Aldrich	MGM
1967, Aug	Bonnie and Clyde	Arthur Penn	Warner Bros./Seven Arts
1967, Dec	Guess Who's Coming to Dinner	Stanley Kramer	Columbia
1967, Dec	The Graduate	Mike Nichols	Embassy
1968, April	2001: A Space Odyssey	Stanley Kubrick	MGM
1968, Sept	Funny Girl	Willian Wyler	Columbia
1968, Oct	Bullitt	Peter Yates	Warner Bros./Seven Arts
1969, May	Midnight Cowboy	John Schlesinger	United Artists
1969, June	The Wild Bunch	Sam Peckinpah	Warner Bros./Seven Arts
1969, July	Easy Rider	Dennis Hopper	Columbia
1969, Sept	Butch Cassidy and the Sundance Kid	George Roy Hill	20th Century-Fox

The 1970s Featured Films

INITIAL RELEASE	FILM	DIRECTOR	U.S. DISTRIBUTOR
1970, Jan	M*A*S*H	Robert Altman	20th Century-Fox
1970, Feb	Patton	Franklin Schaffner	20th Century-Fox
1970, Mar	Airport	George Seaton	Universal
1970, Sept	Five Easy Pieces	Bob Rafelson	Columbia
1970, Dec	Love Story	Arthur Hiller	Paramount
1971, Oct	The French Connection	William Friedkin	20th Century-Fox
1971, Nov	Fiddler on the Roof	Norman Jewison	United Artists
1971, Dec	A Clockwork Orange	Stanley Kubrick	Warner Bros.
1972, Mar	The Godfather	Francis Ford Coppola	Paramount
1972, July	Deliverance	John Boorman	Warner Bros.
1972, Dec	The Poseidon Adventure	Ronald Neame	20th Century-Fox
1973, Aug	American Graffiti	George Lucas	Universal
1973, Dec	The Sting	George Roy Hill	Universal
1973, Dec	The Exorcist	William Friedkin	Warner Bros.
1974, Feb	Blazing Saddles	Mel Brooks	Warner Bros.
1974, June	Chinatown	Roman Polanski	Paramount
1974, Dec	The Towering Inferno	Irwin Allen, John Guillermin	20th Century-Fox
1974, Dec	The Godfather Part II	Francis Ford Coppola	Paramount
1975, June	Jaws	Steven Spielberg	Universal
1975, Sept	The Rocky Horror Picture Show	Jim Sharman	20th Century-Fox
1975, Nov	One Flew over the Cuckoo's Nest	Milos Forman	United Artists
1976, Feb	Taxi Driver	Martin Scorsese	Columbia
1976, Apr	All the President's Men	Alan J. Pakula	Warner Bros.
1976, Nov	Rocky	John G. Avildsen	United Artists
1977, Apr	Annie Hall	Woody Allen	United Artists
1977, May	Star Wars: Ep IV A New Hope	George Lucas	20th Century-Fox
1977, Nov	Close Encounters of the Third Kind	Steven Spielberg	Columbia
1977, Dec	Saturday Night Fever	John Badham	Paramount
1978, June	Grease	Randal Kleiser	Paramount
1978, July	National Lampoon's Animal House	John Landis	Universal
1978, Oct	Midnight Express	Alan Parker	Columbia
1978, Dec	Superman—The Movie	Richard Donner	Warner Bros.
1979, May	Alien	Ridley Scott	20th Century-Fox
1979, Aug	Apocalypse Now	Francis Ford Coppola	United Artists
1979, Dec	Kramer vs. Kramer	Robert Benton	Columbia

The 1980s Featured Films

INITIAL RELEASE	FILM	DIRECTOR	U.S. DISTRIBUTOR
1980, May	Star Wars: Ep V The Empire Strikes Back	Irvin Kirshner	20th Century-Fox
1980, Sept	Ordinary People	Robert Redford	Paramount
1980, Nov	Raging Bull	Martin Scorsese	United Artists
1980, Dec	Nine to Five	Colin Higgins	20th Century-Fox
1981, Jun	Raiders of the Lost Ark	Steven Spielberg	Paramount
1981, Jun	Superman II	Richard Lester	Warner Bros.
1981, Sept	Chariots of Fire	Hugh Hudson	20th Century-Fox
1981, Dec	On Golden Pond	Mark Rydell	Universal
1982, Mar	Porky's	Bob Clark	20th Century-Fox
1982, Jun	E.T.: The Extra-Terrestrial	Steven Spielberg	Universal
1982, Dec	Tootsie	Sydney Pollack	Columbia
1983, May	Star Wars: Ep VI Return of the Jedi	Richard Marquand	20th Century-Fox
1983, Oct	The Right Stuff	Philip Kaufman	Warner Bros.
1983, Dec	Terms of Endearment	James L. Brooks	Paramount
1983, Dec	Silkwood	Mike Nichols	20th Century-Fox
1984, May	Indiana Jones and the Temple of Doom	Steven Spielberg	Paramount
1984, Jun	Ghostbusters	Ivan Reitman	Columbia
1984, Sept	Amadeus	Milos Forman	Orion
1984, Dec	Beverly Hills Cop	Martin Brest	Paramount
1985, Jul	Back to the Future	Robert Zemeckis	Universal
1985, Dec	The Color Purple	Steven Spielberg	Warner Bros.
1985, Dec	Out of Africa	Sydney Pollock	Universal
1986, May	Top Gun	Tony Scott	Paramount
1986, Sept	Crocodile Dundee	Peter Faiman	Paramount
1986, Dec	Platoon	Oliver Stone	Orion
1987, May	Beverly Hills Cop II	Tony Scott	Paramount
1987, Sept	Fatal Attraction	Adrien Lyne	Paramount
1987, Nov	Three Men and a Baby	Leonard Nimoy	Buena Vista
1988, Jun	Who Framed Roger Rabbit	Robert Zemeckis	Buena Vista
1988, Dec	Rain Man	Barry Levinson	United Artists
1989, May	Indiana Jones and the Last Crusade	Steven Spielberg	Paramount
1989, Jun	Dead Poets Society	Peter Weir	Buena Vista
1989, Jun	Batman	Tim Burton	Warner Bros.
1989, July	Lethal Weapon 2	Richard Donner	Warner Bros.
1989, Dec	Driving Miss Daisy	Bruce Beresford	Warner Bros.

The 1990s Featured Films

INITIAL RELEASE	FILM	DIRECTOR	U.S. DISTRIBUTOR
1990, Mar	Pretty Woman	Garry Marshall	Buena Vista
1990, Jul	Ghost	Jerry Zucker	Paramount
1990, Nov	Home Alone	Chris Columbus	'20th Century-Fox
1990, Nov	Dances with Wolves	Kevin Costner	Orion
1991, Jun	Robin Hood: Prince of Thieves	Kevin Reynolds	Warner Bros.
1991, Jul	Terminator 2: Judgment Day	James Cameron	TriStar
1991, Nov	Beauty and the Beast	Gary Trousdale, Kirk Wise	Buena Vista
1992, Jun	Batman Returns	Tim Burton	Warner Bros.
1992, Aug	Unforgiven	Clint Eastwood	Warner Bros.
1992, Nov	Home Alone 2: Lost in New York	Chris Columbus	20th Century-Fox
1992, Dec	A Few Good Men	Rob Reiner	Columbia
1993, Jun	Jurassic Park	Steven Spielberg	Universal
1993, Aug	The Fugitive	Andrew Davis	Warner Bros.
1993, Nov	Mrs. Doubtfire	Chris Columbus	20th Century-Fox
1993, Dec	Schindler's List	Steven Spielberg	Universal
1994, Jun	The Lion King	Roger Allers, Rob Minkoff	Buena Vista
1994, Jul	Forrest Gump	Robert Zemeckis	Paramount
1994, Oct	Pulp Fiction	Quintin Tarantino	Miramax
1995, May	Braveheart	Mel Gibson	Paramount
1995, Jun	Batman Forever	Joel Schumacher	Warner Bros.
1995, Jun	Apollo 13	Ron Howard	Universal
1995, Nov	Toy Story	John Lasseter	Buena Vista
1996, May	Twister	Jan de Bont	Warner Bros.
1996, May	Mission: Impossible	Brian De Palma	Paramount
1996, Jul	Independence Day	Roland Emmerich	20th Century-Fox
1996, Nov	The English Patient	Anthony Minghella	Miramax
1997, Mar	Liar Liar	Tom Shadyac	Universal
1997, Jul	Men in Black	Barry Sonnenfeld	Columbia
1997, Dec	Good Will Hunting	Gus van Sant	Miramax
1997, Dec	Titanic	James Cameron	Paramount
1998, Jul	Armageddon	Michael Bay	Buena Vista
1998, Jul	Saving Private Ryan	Steven Spielberg	DreamWorks
1998, Dec	Shakespeare in Love	John Madden	Miramax
1999, Mar	The Matrix	Andy and Larry Wachowski, Bruce Hunt	Warner Bros.
1999, May	Star Wars: Ep I The Phantom Menace	George Lucas	20th Century-Fox
1999, Jul	The Blair Witch Project	Daniel R. Myrick, Eduardo Sanchez	Artisan
1999, Aug	The Sixth Sense	M. Night Shyamalan	Buena Vista
1999, Nov	Toy Story 2	John Lasseter	Buena Vista

2000–2005 Featured Films

INITIAL RELEASE	FILM	DIRECTOR	U.S. DISTRIBUTOR
2000, May	Gladiator	Ridley Scott	DreamWorks
2000, June	The Perfect Storm	Wolfgang Petersen	Warner Bros.
2000, Nov	Dr. Seuss' How the Grinch Stole Christmas	Ron Howard	Universal
2000, Dec	Cast Away	Robert Zemeckis	20th Century-Fox
2001, May	Shrek	Vicky Jenson, Andrew Adamson	DreamWorks
2001, Nov	Harry Potter and the Sorcerer's Stone	Chris Columbus	Warner Bros.
2001, Dec	The Lord of the Rings: The Fellowship of the Ring	Peter Jackson	New Line
2001, Dec	A Beautiful Mind	Ron Howard	Universal
2002, Apr	My Big Fat Greek Wedding	Joel Zwick	IFC
2002, May	Spider-Man	Sam Raimi	Sony
2002, May	Star Wars: Ep II Attack of the Clones	George Lucas	20th Century-Fox
2002, Nov	Harry Potter and the Chamber of Secrets	Chris Columbus	Warner Bros.
2002, Dec	The Lord of the Rings: The Two Towers	Peter Jackson	New Line
2003, May	The Matrix Reloaded	Andy and Larry Wachowski	Warner Bros.
2003, May	Finding Nemo	Andrew Stanton, Lee Unkrich	Buena Vista
2003, Jul	Pirates of the Caribbean: The Curse of the Black Pearl	Gore Verbinski	Buena Vista
2003, Dec	The Lord of the Rings: The Return of the King	Peter Jackson	New Line
2004, Feb	The Passion of the Christ	Mel Gibson	Newmarket
2004, May	Shrek 2	Andrew Adamson, Kelly Asbury, Conrad Vernon	DreamWorks
2004, June	Spider-Man 2	Sam Raimi	Sony
2004, Dec	Meet the Fockers	Jay Roach	Universal
2005, May	Star Wars: Ep III Revenge of the Sith	George Lucas	20th Century-Fox
2005, June	War of the Worlds	Steven Spielberg	Paramount
2005, Nov	Harry Potter and the Goblet of Fire	Mike Newell	Warner Bros.
2005, Dec	The Chronicles of Narnia: The Lion, the Witch, and the Wardrobe	Andrew Adamson	Buena Vista

The Beginning to 1909

That's it. It's going to be the picture business for me.

—Gilbert M. "Broncho Billy" Anderson, after viewing
The Great Train Robbery with an audience in 1903

**GENERAL U.S.
STATISTICS, 1890–1910**

62,979,766
U.S. Population, 1890

76,212,168
U.S. Population, 1900

DECADE OVERVIEW

You have to understand what was happening in this country to see why movies were catching on. From 1900 to 1910, about nine or ten million immigrants poured in, and because nickelodeon movies were new, cheap, silent and set up no language difficulties, they became a popular pastime. —ADOLPH ZUKOR

MOTION PICTURE: A series of pictures projected on a screen in rapid succession with objects shown in successive positions slightly changed so as to produce the optical effect of a continuous picture in which the objects move.

MOVIE: A representation (as of a story) by means of motion pictures.

FILM: The Academy of Motion Picture Arts and Sciences, the American Film Institute, and the British Film Institute all define a feature as a film with a running time of 40 minutes or longer. The Centre national de la cinématographie in France defines it as a 35 mm film that is longer than 1,600 meters, which comes out to exactly 58 minutes and 29 seconds for sound films. The Screen Actors Guild gives a minimum running time of 80 minutes. A movie shorter than a feature film is a short film.

Inventing an Industry and an Art Form

No one person created motion pictures. There was active invention in both Europe and the United States. Although conventional wisdom suggests that Thomas Edison, inventor of the lightbulb and phonograph, was the father of film, that is only partially true. It was in his laboratory in West Orange, New Jersey, in the 1880s that movies were born, but many other players had contributed to that event.

One of the very first illusions of moving pictures was actually created in northern California by photographic pioneer Eadweard Muybridge. In 1879, under the sponsorship of former California governor and Central Pacific Railroad president Leland Stanford, Muybridge pioneered stop-action photography and invented the zoopraxiscope, a forerunner of the modern motion picture projector. The zoopraxiscope projected images off rotating glass disks to give the impression of motion. In February 1888 Muybridge visited Thomas Edison in New Jersey and proposed that they collaborate to combine the zoopraxiscope with the Edison phonograph. Edison agreed, but after a few experiments Muybridge felt there were too many drawbacks and abandoned the project. Edison was not so quick to give up. In October 1888, he filed for a caveat (a preliminary announcement of intentions) with the U.S. Patent Office for what he called a kinetoscope—a cylinder with photographic images arranged in a spiral pattern around it.

1

Edison then turned to his assistant Laurie Dickson to develop it. The kinetograph—the kineto-scope's motion picture camera—was the result of Dickson's efforts.

Dickson, whose full name was William Kennedy Laurie Dickson, was born in France in 1860 to parents of English and Scottish descent. He was nineteen years of age and an amateur photographer when he first wrote to Edison asking for work. Edison said no at first, but Dickson voyaged across the ocean anyway on his own savings, hanging around and eventually winning the coveted job as Edison's assistant. He was always talking about making movies, so Edison naturally enlisted his help on related projects. To create moving pictures, Dickson needed just the right film, so he turned first to John Carbutt and then to George Eastman.

Carbutt, an English photographer who came to America, founded the Keystone Dry Plate Works in 1879 with the intention of selling gelatin dry plates. Carbutt persuaded the Celluloid Manufacturing Company to produce a thin, almost transparent film by slicing a layer off a cel-luloid block and pressing it between heated polished plates to remove the slicing marks. Then, the celluloid strips were coated with a photosensitive gelatin emulsion. By 1888 Dickson was using a 15-inch-wide sheet of Carbutt's film for early Edison motion picture experiments with the kinetograph. There remained one challenge, however: the celluloid film base produced by this means was still considered too stiff for the needs of motion picture photography.

Meanwhile, inventor and manufacturer George Eastman had become interested in photog-raphy and had set out to simplify the process so it could be accessible to all. In 1881 he founded the Eastman Dry Plate Company and started to manufacture gelatin dry plates. By 1884 he had introduced flexible, paper-based photographic film. He wanted to "make the camera as conve-nient as the pencil." He received a patent for Kodak film in October 1884. Later, in 1888, he patented the Kodak roll-film camera.

Dickson used Eastman's more flexible roll film in the kinetograph in November 1890 dur-ing the making of the first movie, *Monkeyshines,* which was 5 seconds long. Edison saw great possibilities, but felt it was still not producing a strong enough image to project on a big screen. He decided to exhibit it in a coin-operated exhibition device instead: an upright cabinet with a peephole in which a film strip, approximately 50 feet in length and consisting of several im-ages, moved in an endless loop in front of an illuminated lens and behind a spinning wheel. The viewer got a brief look at 46 pictures per second. The spinning shutter gave the illusion of life-like motion. After some further experiments, Dickson settled on a strip of film that was 35 mm wide with sprocket holes on both sides that matched up to pins on a projecting device. This set the standard size of most movie film for years thereafter.

While development continued on a kinetoscope that could be mass-distributed, Dickson created the first film studio in a building that had a revolving stage. The building was called the "Black Maria" because it reminded some of a police lockup van. There Dickson set out to create movies of all kinds, including films celebrating popular entertainers and athletes. Over the next few years, he would capture images of many of the era's top stars, including William Frederick "Buffalo Bill" Cody, Annie Oakley, and the dancer Annabelle Whitford Moore.

Eager to repeat the success they had with the phonograph, which attracted customers will-ing to pay a nickel to hear a brief recording through earphones, the Edison Company sold the kinetoscope machines for $250 each and then granted territorial rights to buyers for its use within specific areas. The first kinetoscope parlor, featuring ten machines, opened in a neo-Greco-style building at 1155 Broadway (at 27th Street) in New York City on April 14, 1894, where the franchise was held by former Edison employee Alfred Tate and brothers Andrew and George Holland of Ottawa, Canada. The Hollands had bought phonographs from Edison when they first hit the market, so they were able to get in early on this latest invention. They quickly formed the Kinetoscope Company with partners Norman Raff and Frank Gammon. In August 1894 their company was granted exclusive rights for selling kinetoscopes within the United States and Canada for a three-year period. The kinetoscope was an immediate sensation, and soon more parlors opened all over the country. That success attracted competitors such as Charles Chinnock in the United States and Robert W. Paul in London, and soon the market became saturated. Within a few years, however, the kinetoscope fad waned, as the peephole machines were replaced by projection systems that could be watched by a group.

Meanwhile, Dickson had engaged in dealings with an Edison competitor. When Edison found out in April 1895, he confronted his assistant, and Dickson left Edison but not the industry. Almost immediately thereafter he formed the American Mutoscope and Biograph Company with three partners and designed a new system, purposely avoiding any of the Edison patents. It was extremely successful. That company later simplified its name to the Biograph Company in 1909 and became one of the major studios to participate in the early era of filmmaking, employing directors such as D. W. Griffith and Mack Sennett and movie stars such as Mary Pickford, the Gish sisters, and the "Biograph Girl," Florence Lawrence.

By 1896 the Lumière brothers and others had advanced film projector technology enough to interest Edison. When his sales representative Frank Harrison first told him about the Jenkins-Armat phantascope projector, Edison was thrilled. Although Charles Francis Jenkins of Dayton, Ohio, had been a stenographer for the U.S. government in Washington, D.C., he spent his spare time inventing a motion picture projector. By 1892 he could project small images on a wall or screen, but they were too small for public exhibition. In 1895 Jenkins went into partnership with Thomas Armat, a classmate of his at the Bliss School of Electricity in Washington. They showed their projector for the first time at the Cotton States Exposition in Atlanta, where Harrison saw it. A disagreement over ownership of the projector led to a rift between Jenkins and Armat. Eventually Jenkins sold his rights to Armat, who then sold the projector to Edison, who renamed it the Edison Vitascope and subsequently took credit for its invention. As Edison expanded his business, others were getting into the field too, including Vitagraph in New York, Sigmund Lubin in Philadelphia, and William Selig in Chicago.

Vitagraph, which was founded in New York City in 1896 by two British immigrants, J. Stuart Blackton and Albert E. Smith, would be the longest-lasting of the early film studios. Vitagraph's output was prolific, and by 1911 it had several studios in various parts of the country, including one in California. Its films were among the most popular silents produced and included stars such as Norma Talmadge and Florence Turner (the "Vitagraph Girl"). Rudolph Valentino began there as a bit player and went on to achieve tremendous fame later. Vitagraph was the only member of the Motion Picture Patents Company to survive the aftermath of the antitrust court decision against the Edison Trust, and continued to prosper into the 1920s; it was sold to Warner Bros. in 1925.

Sigmund Lubin, a German immigrant who had been trained as an optician, founded a film company under his own name in Philadelphia in 1882 and was selling films and his polyscope projector by 1902. Surviving a patent lawsuit by Edison in 1898, Lubin's company prospered for twenty years producing films on a variety of subjects, including African American stereotypes, boxing matches, comedies, crime, local views, news, and religious subjects. Lubin recognized early on that moving pictures were becoming part of everyday life and predicted "the time will come when . . . the moving picture will be delivered at home as is the morning newspaper of today."

William Selig prospered in the days of direct selling to exhibitors and exchanges as part of the General Film Company distribution system. When General Film proved inadequate to distribute features, it combined with the other major players of the day, first as part of V-L-S-E (Vitagraph-Lubin-Selig-Essanay) and later as part of K-E-S-E (Kleine-Edison-Selig-Essanay) to distribute its features. Selig established the first permanent motion picture studio in Los Angeles in October 1909. The decline of the Patent Company and General Film and the loss of European markets contributed to the cessation of his production company, Selig Polyscope, by 1918. However, William Selig kept his studio in east Los Angeles and rented it to Louis B. Mayer Productions. He continued producing sporadically into the 1930s.

Edison's kinetographic camera patent (which was finally granted in 1897) was for the United States only. Because Edison saw motion pictures as a gimmick, he skimped on paying an extra $150 to secure a worldwide patent for motion picture technology. That would prove to be a bad mistake. The threat to Edison from abroad was very real. In many ways, the initial development of the American cinema from the end of the nineteenth century until the outbreak of World War I was entwined with the development of a film industry in Europe, primarily in France with the Lumière brothers (Louis and Auguste), the Pathé brothers (Charles and Emile), Léon Gaumont, and Georges Méliès.

In the autumn of 1894 French photographer Antoine Lumière, inspired by an Edison peep show kinetoscope, took a length of film to show his sons Louis and Auguste, encouraging them to produce a system that would produce similar living pictures that could be projected onto a screen. By 1895 the brothers Lumière had a photographic supply factory in France that employed 300 people and was capitalized for 3 million French francs, a considerable sum at the time. They also had a portable camera and were sending cameramen around the world to film 1-minute scenes. They then arranged the first film to be shown to a paying public in December 1895 at the Salon Indien, in the basement of the Grand Café, Boulevard des Capucines, Paris. The owner refused an offer of 20 percent of the receipts and charged a flat rate of 30 francs a day. There was an afternoon preview to an invited audience, including Georges Méliès. For the first showing, only 33 tickets (in a room that seated 100) were sold at a price of 1 franc each. Ten different short films were shown on film strips 17 meters in length. One, called *Baby's Dinner*, featured Auguste Lumière and his wife trying to feed their baby without much success. Within three weeks, they were taking in 2,000 francs a day.

The arrival of the Lumière Cinématographe inspired Charles Pathé and his brother Emile to form the Société Pathé Frères in 1896 in Paris; a year later it became the Compagnie Générale de Cinématographes, Phonographes, et Pellicules with the two brothers as directors. The company flourished and developed both the manufacture of negative and positive film, the creation of factories and studios, and the making of cameras and projectors for sale worldwide. By 1907 two-thirds of the films shown in the United States were made in Europe. Pathé was already distributing a catalog of 1,500 films and was producing over 900,000 feet of film every day. Their films were seen that year in theaters in eighteen countries.

Léon Gaumont, a photographic equipment retailer, established the Gaumont Company in 1895. The success of its chronophotographe camera-projector, developed by Georges Demeny, allowed Gaumont to expand into film production, and by 1907 they were doing business in England, Germany, Russia, and the United States. In the late 1890s, their production facility in La Villette, France, Cité Elgé, was the largest in the world. Credited with producing the first animated movie, their British studio offshoot, Gaumont British, would later become known as the distributor and producer of Alfred Hitchcock's British films in the 1930s.

Fearful of competitors from Europe, Edison pushed ahead, and on April 23, 1896, the Vitascope movie projector was used in front of a paying audience for the first time as an attraction at Koster & Bial's Music Hall in New York's Herald Square. The film was projected on a screen within a gilt frame and amazed the audience. Edwin S. Porter, who had been hired by Edison as a camera and projector technician, later became one of Edison's primary directors. His first important film was the dramatic short *The Life of an American Fireman* in 1903. Porter followed that with the seminal action western *The Great Train Robbery* the same year. He went on to make many other short movies until establishing his own independent film company with other investors, the Rex Motion Picture Masterpiece Company, in 1909.

Although a short and not a feature, *The Great Train Robbery* was one of the very first blockbusters. It was the first film with a narrative fictional plot that captured the public imagination. For years after, when a nickelodeon opened, it usually premiered with *Train Robbery*. That formula was immediately copied, launching a new era in film. As the public tired of just seeing images move, the drive to create more movies with plots and stories began. While early American films were developing a more fictional narrative, the French took a more natural approach. Early French films featured street scenes, native dances, train arrivals, and military parades. The French were really the first documentary filmmakers.

Among the most innovative filmmakers of the earliest days was Georges Méliès, a French stage magician who had attended an early Lumière screening in Paris. In 1896 he began showing films regularly as part of his theatrical magic show, and by 1897 he had built Europe's first film studio in Montreuil, France, where he could make films indoors with the aid of artificial lighting. His most famous film, *A Trip to the Moon* (*Le voyage dans la lune*), was made in 1902. It was loaded with early special effects, visual tricks, camera handiwork, and whatever else it took to create illusions in one of the first science fiction and fantasy films ever. Méliès, who had become frustrated with the limits of what he could do onstage, found his calling in the wide-open possibilities of film.

Edison hated that his edge in the movie industry was getting away from him, so he decided to shut the door on his competitors. Beginning in 1908, Edison pressured ten companies to work together to monopolize the new motion picture business. Together they controlled patents and had the necessary funds to enforce those patents, sometimes in ruthless ways—such as with thugs who threatened anyone who dared to go against them. By pooling their interests, these member companies effectively cornered the market. Ultimately Kodak agreed to sell movie film stock only to them.

At first, the Motion Picture Patents Company (MPPC), otherwise known as the Edison Trust, enforced its will primarily in the eastern United States, most notably in New York and New Jersey, where most movie companies were based. Soon, however, the patent company members began moving west, attracted by the year-round warm weather. The independents followed, driving a migration to what became Hollywood.

Motion Picture Patents Companies, 1890–1909

American

Edison Manufacturing Company	Dissolved in 1926
Essanay	Stopped production in 1918
Biograph	Out of business by 1918
Kalem	Bought by Vitagraph in 1916
Lubin	Out of business by 1918
Selig	Out of business by 1918
Vitagraph	Sold to Warner Bros. in 1925

French

Gaumont	Part of the company absorbed by MGM in late 1920s
Méliès	Out of business by 1915 and bankrupt by 1923
Pathé	Spun off its interests to its American operation in 1914. Sold remnants of the American company to RKO in 1931

PRODUCTION SPOTLIGHT

Piracy, Trick Camera Work, Realistic Acting, and the Emergence of Genre Films

From the very inception of the motion picture industry, films have been the target of piracy, beginning with foreign movies, such as the French science fiction picture *Le voyage dans la lune,* which was among the first to be widely copied, illegally distributed, and exploited in the U.S. market. Often the pirates would put their own name on the newly struck prints, as if they had produced the pictures. These, of course, were blatant violations. However, the term *pirate* was also used to describe those who avoided paying the royalties demanded by the Edison Trust, which held patents on the lion's share of equipment used to make films. The offenders in this case were up-and-coming independent exhibitor-producers such as Carl Laemmle, William Fox, and Adolph Zukor who really did nothing more than make and show movies using unlicensed equipment to avoid the fees. Technically they were not pirates, just folks trying to keep costs down by filming on the sly or on locations far from the enforcers hired by the Edison Trust.

Whether stolen or original, movies throughout most of the nineteenth century consisted of simple scenes: images strung together or pictures from nature. That may have been enough for the era of coin-operated viewing machines and the first years of public exhibition, but by the turn of the century, audiences were getting bored. That is when Edwin Stanton Porter, a Pennsylvania native who had shown movies all over the world, introduced narrative to filmmaking in a way that would change the industry forever. He had at first returned home from his travels with the intent of manufacturing cameras and projectors, but instead he went to work for Thomas Edison in 1900. Using the knowledge he had gained as a touring projectionist to determine what audiences really liked, Porter became one of the most influential filmmakers of his time. His first films included comedies such as 1901's satirical *Terrible Teddy, the Grizzly King,* which made fun of Vice President Teddy Roosevelt. Like Méliès, Porter used illusions, tricks, and editing to create images in movies such as his 1902 *Jack and the Beanstalk.* His 1903 short *Life of an American Fireman* not only used innovative cuts and dissolves to help tell a complex story but also benefited from the use of stock footage, which Porter cut into his original footage. Porter's greatest movie was the 1903 release *The Great Train Robbery.*

Movie Censorship from the Beginning to 1909: A Brief History

Cities and states around the United States create local censorship boards to regulate the content in movies, which follow different rules and standards.

In addition to adding story lines to their moving pictures, which many had adapted from popular literature and plays, filmmakers of this time began presenting their work in varying genres including crime (*Raffles, the Amateur Cracksman*, 1905), animation (*Fantasmagorie,* 1908), and drama (*The Violin Maker of Cremona*, 1909).

A Trip to the Moon (*Le voyage dans la lune*)
Distributed by Edison and others, 1902
Directed by Georges Méliès
845 feet (13 minutes)

The First Cinemagician Is French

Marie-Georges-Jean Méliès was a thirty-four-year-old stage magician in Paris on December 28, 1895, when he was among the thirty-three people who attended the first showing at the Lumière brothers' new movie theater. What he saw changed his life. From then on he was dedicated to the motion picture art, using all of his skills as a magician and all of the stagecraft he had developed to make the first fantasy and science fiction movies. He would soon be referred to as a "cinemagician." As part of his cinema magic, Méliès was among the very first to use dissolves, close-ups, special effects, multiple exposures, stop-motion photography, time-lapse photography, stop tricks or substitutions, and hand-painted color in his movies. What separated Méliès from almost anyone else at the tail end of the nineteenth century was the fact that he was making movies primarily as a way to express his artistic ideas, not just as a way to further a gimmick that could capture images or take pictures of nature.

In late 1896, Méliès opened his own studio on the grounds of his family's property at Montreuil-sur-Bois. It looked a lot like a very large glass greenhouse. There was a carpentry workshop, a costume and scenery storage area, and a laboratory where film would be processed and then hand-painted frame by frame. Even as his enterprise grew, Méliès retained creative control. He not only directed all of the movies and adapted stage material to the screen but also managed the famed Théâtre Robert-Houdin in Paris. He was involved in editing as well as in designing costumes and sets and in creating effects. At the end of 1896, his company, Star Film, announced its motto: "The whole world within reach."

From 1897 until 1914, Méliès directed 531 films that ran from 1 to 40 minutes each. Most were variations on his magic stage shows, but with each one he became more clever about what he could accomplish on film. He was constantly looking for inspiration and new ways to use the medium. For instance, in 1896, as Méliès later recalled, he was struggling with a crude camera and film that would tear easily or get stuck. One day while in the center of Paris photographing outside of the opera, the camera jammed. By the time he resumed filming, the traffic and environment had changed. When he projected the result, he saw that he could use the trick of substitution for his illusions.

The idea for his greatest work, *A Trip to the Moon,* was taken from the Jules Verne novel *From the Earth to the Moon*. Elements of the story were also borrowed from the H. G. Wells book *The First Men on the Moon*. The production was the most expensive completed by Méliès at the time—10,000 francs (approximately $200). It was also his longest and most complex film, with several ambitious sets, numerous costumes, and elaborate special effects throughout. Méliès himself made clay models and plaster moldings for the moon creatures. He also wrote the scenario, drew storyboards for the film, acted in it, and directed it. In Méliès's studio, acrobats from the Folies Bergère portrayed the creatures, ballet dancers from the Châtelet were the stars in the night sky, and music hall singers were some of the space travelers. Méliès played the leader of the expedition. He couldn't get any theater actors to work in the film, as they considered movie acting undignified. Only later, when movies consistently paid better, did actors flock to his office. Throughout the production, Méliès made use of the trick effects he'd perfected in hundreds of previous films: scenes dissolve from one to the next, the night sky is double-exposed over the moonscape, creatures disappear in a puff of smoke, and miniature and full-size objects are combined to create an illusion of reality.

A Trip to the Moon was seen across Europe and the United States, but Méliès received little recognition or money from the American market. Despite a U.S. copyright, the film was duplicated illegally in America and sold to theaters under the copier's name. Méliès had placed his Star Film company logo, a five-pointed star, into the scenes so they would be visible throughout, but that didn't stop the duplicators, who simply painted them out of the new negatives.

Fred Balshofer, a pioneering American producer and director, worked briefly for the Lubin Film Company, where he copied *A Trip to the Moon* for perhaps the most brazen of these pirates, Sigmund Lubin, and recalled showing the film to one prospective buyer in particular. When the prospective client jumped up from his chair shouting, "Stop the machine," Balshofer and Lubin wondered what was wrong. They found out soon enough when the prospective buyer shouted, "I made that picture. I am George Méliès from Paris." Lubin jokingly told Méliès how Balshofer had labored hard to block out the trademark Méliès had painstakingly included, then laughed as he walked out of the room, leaving Méliès utterly speechless.

Méliès continued to make films and battle with the American market, but in the end he failed, losing everything at the outbreak of World War I. —*David Kiehn and Alex Ben Block*

The Great Train Robbery

Distributed by Edison, 1903
Directed by Edwin S. Porter
4 days of principal photography
740 feet (12 minutes)

1990 National Film Registry Selection

Getting on the Narrative Train

Edwin S. Porter's greatest movie came in 1903, when he shaped the story of the American West for audiences who had grown up on stage melodrama and dime novels with his movie

The Great Train Robbery. Delivered on a single reel, the innovative film used crosscut editing that allowed action to take place simultaneously in more than one place during the movie.

The film was inspired by a stage play of the same name. As Porter later recalled: "From laboratory examination of some of the popular story films of the French pioneer director Méliès—trick pictures like *A Trip to the Moon*—I came to the conclusion that a picture telling a story in continuity form might draw the customers back to the theaters." Porter's biggest problem was convincing Edison executives to finance the production; they felt it would cost too much. They finally gave permission as long as the budget didn't exceed $800.

Starring Gilbert M. Anderson, who would later become famous as Broncho Billy, *The Great Train Robbery* was a western that was actually shot in the East with location scenes in New Jersey. "I played a chap who ran away in the pasture and got shot, and the tenderfoot who did the jigging in the dancehall room—I couldn't dance, but that was me—then I was a robber, and after I fell off my horse. I did the train robbing part on foot; I played the man who held up the telegrapher."

Frank Hanaway, another robber hired because he could fall off a horse, performed that stunt on camera. Justus D. Barnes, the leader of the bunch, is the man who fires his gun point-blank at the camera in the final scene of the film.

The railroad car and office scenes both included a special effect; exterior shots in New Jersey matted in with a double exposure. Production was completed in four days.

At first glance Edison executives didn't know what to make of *The Great Train Robbery*. Porter suggested they preview it at Huber's Museum, the famous dime museum on East 14th Street. Anderson recalled: "I've seen some receptions to plays, but I've never seen such a reception to a picture in my life. They got up and shouted and yelled, and then when it was all over they yelled, 'Run it again! Run it again!' You couldn't get them out." Films were sold by the foot at that time. The price for new print was $111, but that was a bargain as the prints were played again and again until they fell apart.

The Great Train Robbery went on to be shown more times in more theaters than any film in history to date. When nickelodeons began in 1905 it was the film most likely to play on opening week, and it could still be seen in theaters as late as 1909. Even more importantly, it opened the door to a new kind of fictional and narrative filmmaking, in which story and plot were as important as location and cinematography. It proved the viability of commercial cinema and set the standard for the next decade of one-reel movies. It would be copied many times over during the century that followed, forever transporting audiences into a world of harrowing chase scenes and thrilling action adventure. —*David Kiehn and Alex Ben Block*

Raffles, the Amateur Cracksman

Distributed by Vitagraph, 1905
Directed by J. Stuart Blackton
5 days of principal photography
1,050 feet (18 minutes)

Film as Social Commentary

In 1905 Vitagraph was expanding production activity to complement its film exhibition business and its reputation for producing real-life newsreels, including some of the first from actual wars. Vitagraph's partners, Englishmen and former vaudevillians J. Stuart Blackton and Albert E. Smith and former film distributor William "Pop" Rock, hired Gilbert M. Anderson to produce and direct story films for the company. Anderson had begun his film career as an actor at the Edison studio in 1903 and graduated to story development and directing. It was Anderson who suggested making the movie *Raffles,* which was also the basis for a successful stage play touring the country at the time. Anderson knew a stage actor, J. Barney Sherry, who was ideal for the title role. Sherry was hired, and the partners began producing films as the Vitagraph Company of America.

The character of Raffles, the gentleman criminal, first appeared in *Cassell's Magazine* in England in 1898. During the next six years, author Ernest William Hornung (brother-in-law of Arthur Conan Doyle) wrote at least twenty-five more stories, which were first collected into an 1899 book called *The Amateur Cracksman*. The stories were social commentary and witty satire on Victorian England, and his character was the antithesis of Doyle's Sherlock Homes. Raffles was a gentleman who played cricket and lived well but made his money as a burglar. Holmes and Raffles, however, did share an ability to use disguises. The term "amateur cracksman" was meant to separate Raffles from lower-class professional criminals.

Production for the film began in early August 1905. The interior scenes were shot at Vitagraph's rooftop studio on the Morton Building at 116 Nassau Street in New York City and on location at a country house in Long Island. The open-air studio was less than ideal: a cloud of exhaust from a smokestack on the roof cast a shadow across every scene shot there. A bank robbery was staged for the film in front of the Knickerbocker Trust Company at Fifth Avenue and 34th Street, holding up traffic in every direction. When editing was finished in late August the film measured 1,050 feet, Vitagraph's longest film to date, running about 18 minutes.

Vitagraph sold prints of *Raffles* to any exhibitor who wished to buy them at a price of $126 each. It was still common for exhibitors to buy directly, but rental exchange agencies were soon established across the country in response to the public's growing interest in movies as nickelodeon theaters opened in big-city storefronts everywhere. Ten years after movies were first introduced to audiences in vaudeville auditoriums, the business was now starting to take hold. By 1906 there would be hundreds of nickelodeon theaters, and by 1907 thousands. In 1913 Vitagraph co-owner Albert E. Smith looked back at *Raffles, the Amateur Cracksman* as a turning point for the company: "On the strength of the success we had with this story and a few others that followed it, we bought a small plot of ground over in Brooklyn, and we built thereon a small studio." When Vitagraph sold itself to Warner Bros. in 1925, that two-block facility in Brooklyn was valued at more than $1 million. —*David Kiehn*

Fantasmagorie
Distributed by Gaumont, 1908
Directed by Emile Cohl
118 feet (2 minutes)

The First Animated Film

Emile Cohl (January 4, 1857–January 20, 1938) was the father of the animated cartoon. Born Emile Eugène Jean Louis Courtet, he was a French caricaturist. Cohl worked for Gaumont, one of the first major film companies, which had been founded in 1895 by Léon Gaumont. It was there in 1908 that Cohl created the first animated movie, called *Fantasmagorie*. Until then animation had been nothing more than bits, tricks, and pencil drawings jumping about. *Fantasmagorie* elevated the whole medium, showcasing its storytelling possibilities.

Cohl created a kind of light board effect by placing each of his drawings on an illuminated glass plate. He then traced the next drawing on top of that with the necessary changes. In all, he made 700 drawings, which, when shown successfully on film, produced consistent movement and allowed a short subject to have continuity. Working this way, Cohl was able to create the entire film by himself with only one camera assistant.

The action in *Fantasmagorie* is rapid, with characters blowing up like balloons, jumping in and out of boxes, fighting one another, and riding horses and elephants. Cohl was an advocate for a well-known, though short-lived, artistic movement of the time known as the Incoherents. While this picture was in fact incoherent, it was ultimately very influential. —*Alex Ben Block*

The Violin Maker of Cremona
Distributed by Biograph, 1909
Directed by D. W. Griffith
3 days of principal photography
963 feet (16 minutes)

Realistic Acting Makes Its Debut

In 1909 Biograph released the first film with realistic acting. It was influenced by the *film d'art* movement that began in France in 1908 with the Pathé Frères production of *The Assassination of the Duc du Guise,* released in the United States in February 1909. *Film d'art* represented a conscious effort to bring theatrical stagecraft to motion pictures. Because French films dominated the American market in the early nickelodeon era, this movement readily caught the attention of American filmmakers.

"Following the appearance of the Film d'art pictures," wrote actress Florence Lawrence, "nearly all of the Biograph [company] players asked [our director] Mr. Griffith to be allowed to do slow acting, only to be refused. He told us it was impossible since the buyers would not pay for a foot of film that did not have action in it."

The actors' wishes ultimately prevailed in the film *The Violin Maker of Cremona,* which provided seventeen-year-old Mary Pickford with her first leading screen role for Biograph. Pickford came to the Biograph studio looking for work in April 1909 after ten years in the theater and a stint on Broadway for producer David Belasco in *The Warrens of Virginia* (1907). Pickford refused to play in the exaggerated style demanded by the Biograph company, and it is generally thought that Griffith's decision to make *The Violin Maker of Cremona* in the *film d'art* style was influenced by Pickford's desire to perform in a more naturalistic style.

The film was based on a short verse play that would have been familiar to patrons of vaudeville theaters in the early 1900s. Its theatrical origins were evident in this adaptation, which was produced entirely at the Biograph studio, a converted brownstone located at 11 East 14th Street in New York, with painted flats for sets. Although Griffith is noted as the father of film technique, many of his early Biograph films are surprisingly devoid of any visual or editing pyrotechnics, nor do they exhibit the strong performances from actors that would distinguish his later work at Biograph.

Cinematographer G. W. Bitzer shot the film using the proprietary Biograph camera, which utilized an unperforated wide-format negative. The camera would punch a single pair of sprocket holes at the edges of each frame. In preparation for release, the film was reduction-printed to standard 35 mm, and the main title and subtitles, which were shot separately on 35 mm film, were then spliced into each release print.

The Violin Maker of Cremona was made at a time when producers sold prints to independently owned and operated film exchanges, and trade reviews amounted to little more than reprinting a studio-prepared synopsis, so it is impossible to know how well audiences responded. When the Biograph company went bankrupt in 1916, the receivers licensed a number of films for reissue through Unicorn Film Service, but an outraged Mary Pickford stopped their efforts when she bought the negatives to most of her Biograph films, purportedly to keep them out of circulation. —*Robert S. Birchard*

DISTRIBUTION OVERVIEW

I did not invent the cinema, but I industrialised it.
—CHARLES PATHÉ

Foreign Movie Distributors Dominate

In 1905, the same year the nickelodeon craze hit America, the only weakness, if any, in the burgeoning film business was its distribution. There were films but no dependable, regularly scheduled sources for movies. Films were sold outright by the foot. Orders were usually made by mail from a catalog published by the Montgomery Ward Company, Sears, Roebuck and Company, and others. The showman who ran the vaudeville theater would spend approximately $50 on a really popular movie and run it until patrons lost interest or until the celluloid print was in such tatters that it could no longer be run. The films that did survive were moved to newly formed "exchanges," where they were rented to other area exhibitors. The way most people saw movies by Biograph, Vitagraph, Lumière, or Lubin was in vaudeville theaters. Service companies (usually not the film's producers) would provide the projector operator and the film. Although a number of different film gauges were used by some camera and projection systems, by 1909 35 mm film with four holes per frame on each side of the film strip was recognized as the international standard for motion pictures.

It was in 1903 that Harry and Herbert Miles of San Francisco created the first of these movie exchanges. They bought films from exhibitors and rented them out for one-fifth of what they paid, fueling the Nickelodeon boom. By 1905 projectors could hold up to 1,000 feet of film, which ran at 60 feet per minute, providing a program that lasted fifteen or twenty minutes, just right for a "turn" in vaudeville. By 1907 there were as many as 150 exchanges operating across the United States, serving the entire country.

The exhibitors liked the new system of renting movies because it cut their costs and allowed them to change the program more frequently, which was very important by 1907, as consumers became easily bored by films they had seen before. It worked for the Miles brothers and others because they could send out the same print again and again to different theaters and make a profit.

Then came dating—not the boy-girl kind, but rather the very serious game of determining when to open a film. In the beginning, distributors released pictures as they became available. However, it soon became apparent that theaters would pay more for new films than they would for the right to repeat older films. That led the studios to create release schedules, which in turn allowed them to charge more for new films based on their drawing power. New releases were shipped in advance to exchanges across the country so they could open on the same date in all markets. Promotions could be launched around these dates and consumer anticipation built accordingly.

The power of the exchanges was also used to institute block booking, meaning that if a nickelodeon wanted a certain film, it also had to take other movies to help balance distribution of all the producer's films. The contract required the theater to take at least one print of every movie the producer made, sight unseen. It ensured that films were released soon after they were made.

This was to be the only era in U.S. film history in which movie distributors from a foreign country, predominately France, were dominant in the American market. During trial testimony in 1908, an Edison executive estimated that Pathé films represented 60 percent of all movies in circulation at that time. It wasn't because of cost that their films enjoyed such widespread distribution here; rather, it was because their movies were well made and often in color.

Brothers Charles and Emile Pathé had founded the company in 1897 with significant capital from industrialist investors. They made their first profits selling phonographs and cylinders that played on these machines. Soon they moved into movies. Emile oversaw the manufacturing, while Charles was concerned with production. They opened their first studio in 1898 in Vincennes, France. By 1904 Pathé had expanded operations into America as well. A sales office was set up in New York City and a manufacturing plant in New Jersey. By then they offered a catalog of more than 1,000 films for sale or rent. By 1905 Lumière had sold out to Pathé. In 1908, around the same time that it was working with Edison, Pathé created what later would be called a branch distribution system. It contracted for concessions, meaning that different entities had exclusive distribution rights for Pathé films in defined areas. In 1909 Pathé pioneered newsreels that gathered news, images, events, and sensations from all over the world. The newsreels were designed to allow contemporary audiences to view historic events.

EXHIBITION OVERVIEW

The word nickelodeon, *coined by a Pittsburgh theater owner, comes from combining the price of admission (five cents, or a nickel) with the Greek word for "theater."*

Major Film Studios Get Their Start in Exhibition

Beginning in 1905 there was a rapid expansion of nickelodeon movie theaters across the United States that would grow into a frenzy by the end of the decade. Most of these nickel theaters, however, were not created out of new or dedicated facilities. Instead, they sprang up in unoccupied storefronts, converted houses, restaurants, amusement parlors, and all sorts of auditoriums ranging in size from tiny to huge. By 1908 there were 123 theaters in New York City alone, all quickly becoming a vital part of their communities. These theaters not only offered movies but also hosted community events and special evenings with prizes and activities so they could effectively compete with other live stage entertainment.

But competition wasn't their only concern. Early theaters had to be very careful with the handling and storage of flammable nitrate film, and by the middle of the decade they also had the matter of censorship to contend with, as local theater owners could be held responsible for any immoral material shown. At first this wasn't an issue, since movies were just a series of images, a travelogue, or a reflection of nature. After 1905, however, as films became more narrative and sophisticated, there was a great deal more responsibility associated with showing them to the public.

Between 1900 and 1906, the Biograph company produced 1,035 Mutoscope attractions and 774 films made for theatrical distribution. By 1908 that trend had reversed. By 1920 the shift to narrative films ushered out the era of the nickelodeons and ushered in the era of new theaters designed and built specifically to show longer movies. Up until that time nickelodeons had been viewed as unsavory places, frequented by immigrants and the lower classes. As pictures became more popular, the middle and upper classes became interested too, and they demanded a better setting. From 1907 on, movie theaters responded by expanding into larger venues and offering more diverse films. These theaters would not only attract new audiences but also allow for an increase in ticket prices. By 1909 the price of admission would rise to a dime. These vaudeville and film hybrids, seen in auditoriums of 500 to 1,000 seats, opened the way for bigger business.

An exhibitor whose business flourished in the New York area during that time was Marcus Loew, the self-made son of Austrian Jewish immigrants who lived on the teeming Lower East Side. Max, as he was called, began his career selling newspapers before working in a mapmaking plant, selling gentlemen's clothing, and laboring in a fur factory. Finally, in 1905, he and Adolph Zukor formed a partnership to purchase penny arcades in Manhattan and Cincinnati. Loew went on to found Loew's, Inc., which would become the parent company of Metro-Goldwyn-Mayer (MGM) in the 1920s. Zukor would eventually take over Paramount.

The future titans of the Warner Bros. studio also had their start in the exhibition business when Harry, Albert, Sam, and Jack L. Warner opened a small nickelodeon business in Newcastle, Pennsylvania, in 1903.

Similarly, the growing exhibition business attracted Hungarian immigrant William Fox, who, like Max Loew, had worked as a newsboy and then in the fur and garment trade in New York. In 1904 Fox bought a failing penny arcade in Brooklyn and soon developed it into a chain of fifteen motion picture theaters throughout Brooklyn and Manhattan. He would go on to head the Fox Film Corporation.

In 1906 Carl Laemmle, the tenth of thirteen children in a middle-class Jewish family from Germany, invested his life savings in a nickelodeon in Chicago and launched another within two months. He would go on to co-found Universal Pictures.

The pattern continued in 1907 when Louis B. Mayer, who emigrated with his parents to New York from Russia as a child, bought a small, run-down motion picture theater in Haverhill, Massachusetts. He would go on to become head of production at MGM.

These career paths were very telling. While the profits from theaters throughout this time were substantial, exhibitors were still dependent on a steady supply of movies. But demands from the Edison Trust to pay royalties for every movie projector in every theater, among other rules, appeared very arbitrary, and expensive. That's when Loew, Fox, and others responded by expanding their operations into the production of movies as well, creating more vertical integration. Fox would later take a lead role in the litigation that brought down the Edison Trust, but by then he had shifted operations to the West Coast, setting the pattern for the next half century, in which business was conducted in New York while movie production was done in Los Angeles.

Soon it became clear that forming circuits of these vaudeville-style theaters provided a distinct advantage. One could book popular acts for a period of time long enough to play in all the theaters, providing them with greater leverage when they bought films from the producers. The competition among the circuits, of course, drove up the price of talent and film, so the largest operators banded together to form the Vaudeville Managers Association. The association then divided up the geographic territories among its members and set up a booking office through which all performers had to go. Five percent of the performers' pay was taken by the theaters as a fee for booking the talent in multiple venues. The ability to control the entire process served as a model for the new movie moguls, who saw that they too could control production, distribution, and exhibition. Thus the spadework was complete for what would become the Hollywood studio system, which lasted until the 1950s.

The 1910s

The Birth of a Nation was cinematic revolution—it was responsible for revolutions in every field affected by motion pictures.

—Kevin Brownlow from his book *The Parade's Gone By*
about D. W. Griffith's breakthrough film.

TOP 10 ALL-RELEASE MOVIES
DOMESTIC BOX OFFICE

By Initial Year of Release, 1910–1919

		Equivalent 2005 $s in Millions of $s
1	The Birth of a Nation	$522.0
2	Daddy Long Legs	$208.3
3	The Spoilers	$183.1
4	The Miracle Man	$160.3
5	Stella Maris	$102.6
6	Male and Female	$100.4
7	Intolerance	$98.3
8	Broken Blossoms	$96.8
9	Traffic in Souls	$88.8
10	Cleopatra	$85.5
	Total: $1,646.1	

GENERAL U.S. STATISTICS, 1910

92,228,496
U.S. Population

26 Million
Average Weekly
U.S. Movie Attendance

DECADE OVERVIEW

A Tale of Two Wars

The seminal event of the decade, of course, was World War I, which began in Europe in 1914, disrupting global production and distribution of silent films and shuttering the innovative European film industry. America joined the fight in 1917, leading to some shortages of domestic film supplies as well. Pioneering camera maker Bell and Howell turned resources toward developing military technology, while Kodak supplied film to the war efforts. But for much of the decade, it was a different fight that split the movie industry, a nasty legal and business battle—a patent war.

In 1910 the General Film Company was incorporated to bring order to the chaos of marketing films. Its stock was controlled by the Edison Manufacturing Company. Essentially, the General Film Company established a system of film exchanges and acted as sole distributor for the pictures of producers affiliated with the Motion Picture Patents Company (MPPC). Their monopolistic plan was to force unaffiliated independent exchanges to sell their businesses. If any independent exchange refused to do so, their supply of films would be cut off, forcing them to close. General Film would guarantee the sale of sixty-five prints of each film they produced at 11 cents a foot. Rather than simply selling prints outright, they would rent them using their new orderly tracking system. The income from these rentals would be divided with the producers after distribution expenses were deducted. Since the average one-reel dramatic film cost between $500 and $800 to produce, and the initial print sale through General Film guaranteed an income of approximately $7,000 with a percentage of film rentals to follow, it suddenly appeared as if the MPPC's producers had a license to mint money! In theory, this guaranteed return should have provided producers with more money to improve their motion pictures—and certainly some improvements in production values were made under the new arrangement—but as it turned out, the licensed producers opted instead to contain production costs in order to beat their competition.

Independent film exchange owners who refused to sell out to General Film, or who never even received offers to buy their businesses, were stuck. Unable to obtain films from MPPC, they had to rely on European movies to keep their exchanges operating. At the same time, U.S. audiences were showing a decided preference for American-made films, and there simply wasn't enough product coming from the few upstart independent producers such as the Independent Motion Picture Company (IMP), founded by Carl Laemmle, to satisfy their needs.

If MPPC hoped to stifle competition, it failed miserably. Forced by necessity to find new sources for films, several independent exchange operators set up their own production companies or encouraged others to jump into production. The years from 1910 to 1912 saw the formation of a number of new independents, including the American Film Manufacturing Company, controlled by exchange owner S. S. Hutchinson and silent partner John R. Freuler; the Rex Motion Picture Masterpiece Company, with former Edison director Edwin S. Porter at the helm;

the New York Motion Picture Company, founded by exchange owners Adam Kessel and Charles O. Baumann; the Reliance Film Company, formed in association with the Carleton Motion Picture Laboratory; the Majestic Film Company, established by exchange owner Harry Aitken; Powers Picture Plays, headed by Pat Powers; the Thanhouser Film Company, formed by theatrical producer Edwin Thanhouser; Champion, Pilot, Monopol, Comet, and dozens of others.

Seeking to cash in on the moving picture craze, the independents attempted to form their own umbrella distributor in 1911, the Motion Picture Distribution and Sales Company, but that entity soon collapsed due to the constant bickering of its member producers. In 1912 two new independent distributing companies emerged based on different organizational models. The Mutual Film Corporation, headed by Harry Aitken, was structured very much like General Film, acting as a distributor for independent companies, while the Universal Film Manufacturing Company, led by Carl Laemmle, Pat Powers, and Robert Cochrane, absorbed the interests of a number of independents in exchange for stock in Universal. While brand names such as Victor, Powers, and 101 Bison survived under the Universal banner, the individual companies ceased to exist. The producers releasing through Mutual maintained their own separate studios, while Universal created Universal City, "the strangest city in the world," to consolidate production facilities into one location near Los Angeles. Faced with growing competition, MPPC fought back on several fronts, raising budgets, improving production values, and filing lawsuits against its upstart rivals.

One important exchange owner was William Fox, whose Greater New York Film Rental Company was in MPPC's sights. Fox also owned a circuit of theaters around New York City. Not only did Fox refuse to sell his exchange, but in 1912 he also filed an antitrust suit in federal court against both MPPC and General Film. This legal action resulted in a clear victory. First, the U.S. Supreme Court canceled the patent on raw film stock, allowing the Eastman Kodak Company to break its

A Typical Prepatents Feature Film Sale

Region	Number of Prints Sold	Total Sale Price
New England States	2	$3,000
City and State of New York	3	$6,000
New Jersey	1	$1,200
Eastern Pennsylvania, Delaware, Maryland, D.C.	2	$3,000
Western Pennsylvania, Ohio, Kentucky, West Virginia	2	$2,750
Illinois and Indiana	2	$3,500
Kansas, North and South Dakota, Oklahoma	2	$2,200
Texas	2	$3,000
Oregon, Washington, Nevada	1	$2,000
California, Arizona, New Mexico	1	$3,000
Colorado, Wyoming, Utah	1	$1,750
Minnesota and Wisconsin	2	$2,500
Michigan	1	$2,000
Dominion of Canada	2	$2,000
Southern States not included above	3	$3,500
Total	27	$41,400

exclusive license with MPPC and permitting it to sell to independent producers. That important ruling was followed by a cancellation of the trust's patents in 1915 and, under the Sherman Antitrust Act, the end of the oligopoly in 1917. The breakup of the trust would energize the formation of the major Hollywood studios. William Fox, naturally, was a major beneficiary of the trust's demise. In 1913 he had set up his own releasing company, Box Office Attractions, and later created a company to produce feature films. By the middle of the decade he would combine the production, leasing, and exhibition operations of these two companies under one roof as the Fox Film Corporation.

In the early half of the decade before the antitrust case was decided, production and distribution were generally geared toward one-reel films with a running time of approximately 15 minutes, but audiences and filmmakers were beginning to show an interest in longer forms. Vitagraph produced a five-reel version of *The Life of Moses* in 1909, but because there was no mechanism for renting multireel films, the reels were released individually as five separate films. Early two-reel films such as D. W. Griffith's *Enoch Arden* (Biograph, 1911) and *The Danites* (Selig Polyscope, 1911), directed by Francis Boggs, were also released over two weeks as separate single-reel subjects. Some enterprising exhibitors, however, opted to combine these reels and show them as multireel attractions. When MPPC attempted to restrict films to the one-reel length, some filmmakers (notably D. W. Griffith at Biograph and G. M. Anderson at Essanay) began cranking their cameras at a much slower rate, 10 to 12 frames per second rather than the standard 16 fps, allowing them to cram more story into a single reel—but causing the action to race by on-screen if theater projectionists didn't slow their cranking speeds accordingly.

European producers, unhampered by the restrictions imposed by MPPC, were quicker to respond to the public's interest in longer films, and spectacles such as the Italian films *Quo Vadis?* (1912) and *Cabiria* (1914) found eager American audiences when they were imported into the United States. Penny arcade and nickelodeon operator Adolph Zukor established the Famous Players Film Company in 1912 with the release of one such long-length feature, *Queen Elizabeth*. Imported from France, this film starred famed stage actor Sarah Bernhardt. Zukor has often been cited as an independent rebel in the vein of Carl Laemmle or William Fox, but in fact he bought his way out of problems with the MPPC by agreeing to pay a $10,000 fee. Like so many others who first relied on foreign product, Adolph Zukor soon began producing his own films. Other newly organized independent producers who saw the artistic possibilities in feature-length films were Bosworth, Inc., headed by financier Frank A. Garbutt and actor-director Hobart Bosworth, and the Jesse L. Lasky Feature Play Company, with Lasky, Samuel Goldfish (later Goldwyn), and director Cecil B. DeMille among its principals.

Although these were profitable years for foreign producers, all of that would change as World War I escalated. Not only did production shut down throughout Europe, but the American satellite operations of companies such as Pathé, Gaumont, Méliès, Star Film, and Eclair were also closed, sold off, or spun off into separate U.S. companies unrelated to their European founders, leaving the way open for U.S. filmmakers to dominate world markets, a situation that continues today.

The transition of power, however, wasn't always easy. Longer films required higher production budgets, especially since many of the early features were based on popular theatrical plays and had cast well-known stage stars. Since established American distribution companies were not set up to handle longer films, feature producers were forced to return to the model that existed prior to the formation of MPPC, selling their pictures territory by territory. In theory, these "states rights" deals, as these were called, also generated royalty revenue. But in reality, all a producer could expect was average sales revenues of $35,000 to $45,000 from such regional sales (see table on page 20 for a typical sale). For this reason production budgets for early feature films were purposely kept low, in the $10,000 to $15,000 range. This proved to be a problem in particular for director D. W. Griffith, who was making a screen adaptation of Thomas Dixon's novel and play *The Clansman,* for Harry Aitken's Reliance-Majestic Company.

Inspired by Italian epics such as *Quo Vadis?* Griffith sought to turn *The Clansman* into the first American screen epic. His intent was to flesh out Dixon's lurid melodrama about the formation of the Ku Klux Klan with re-creations of Civil War battles and historic incidents such as Robert E. Lee's surrender at Appomattox and Abraham Lincoln's assassination. As costs mounted it was clear that Griffith was making something special, but it was not clear that the film, which would be retitled *The Birth of a Nation,* could ever make back its production cost. Aitken backed Griffith, but he was forced by his partners to pull the picture from the Mutual Film Corporation release schedule and create a separate company, the Epoch Producing Corporation, to handle the film's distribution. Stock in the new company was sold to finance "road show" marketing of the film. Under this arrangement, Epoch leased theaters in leading cities, launched its own publicity campaigns, and supplied the orchestra and musical score. Ticket prices at these specially licensed theatres were set far above the top prices in average movie theaters—for example, instead of paying the average 14-cent ticket price, moviegoers were charged as much as $2 per ticket to see *The Birth of a Nation* during its New York road show release in 1915. Thus Epoch was able to take 100 percent of the box office after expenses. The road show model essentially allowed the producer to take the cream off the top from returns in major territories before sending the film out into the states rights market (where the film was sold territory by territory). This same model would be followed for a number of other "big pictures" released in the teens, including Griffith's *Intolerance* (1916), Thomas H. Ince's *Civilization* (1916), and Cecil B. DeMille's *Joan the Woman* (1917).

Even less ambitious producers and directors were finding the transition to feature-length production challenging at this time. Although audiences seemed to accept limited sets and painted backdrops in short films, they demanded more of feature films. That ultimately led producers to pay more attention to such things as setting and decor. In 1914 Jesse L. Lasky went so far as to bring Broadway set designer Wilfred Buckland to Hollywood, where he became the first credited motion picture art director. But catering to the audience's demand for quality was putting too much pressure on budgets and threatening to make feature film production unprofitable.

It was then that W. W. Hodkinson, a former executive with the General Film Company, came to the rescue by forming Paramount Pictures and creating a model for feature film distribution. Established in 1914, Paramount constructed a national network of exchanges, and signed contracts with Famous Players, Bosworth, and Lasky to distribute their films exclusively. Paramount further agreed that for each film it would advance production costs of $17,500, provide a national advertising campaign, and split film rentals with the producers on a percentage basis. Soon after Paramount's arrival on the scene, Metro Pictures was formed to distribute the films of B. A. Rolfe Photoplays, Quality Pictures Corporation, Columbia Pictures (no relation to the current company of that name), and others. It was then too, as mentioned earlier, that William Fox reorganized his Box Office Attractions Company into the Fox Film Corporation to distribute the features he was producing as well as films from other outside producers.

W. W. Hodkinson believed strongly that production and distribution should be treated as separate operations. He was concerned that quality would suffer if production and distribution interests were combined, because the distribution arm would naturally be forced to take anything a studio made if it was tied directly to the producers. Adolph Zukor was of a different opinion. He believed that the financial risk of production necessitated that producers control distribution in order to ensure an outlet for their pictures.

A similar argument was raging within the Mutual Film Corporation. The American Film Company, Thanhouser, and several other companies were convinced that Mutual president Harry Aitken was giving preferential bookings to the films of his own Reliance-Majestic Company and the New York Motion Picture Corporation. The disagreement led to Aitkin's ouster. John R. Freuler was subsequently made president of Mutual, and Aitken set up the Triangle Film Corporation.

On paper Triangle was in a position to be the leading U.S. film company. Not only did it have top filmmakers D. W. Griffith, Thomas H. Ince, and Mack Sennett under contract, but Triangle also boasted star talent such as William S. Hart, Douglas Fairbanks, Lillian and Dorothy Gish, Dorothy Dalton, and Charles Ray. Aitken's attempt to capitalize on the successful distribution model for *The Birth of a Nation,* however, led to a different fate. He insisted that Triangle theaters play a bill consisting of a Griffith–Fine Arts feature, an Ince-Triangle-KayBee feature, and a Mack Sennett two-reel comedy at a $2 top ticket price. Unfortunately, audiences and exhibitors didn't find the Triangle program features to be sufficiently special to warrant the higher ticket prices. This was the beginning of the end for Triangle.

In 1916 Adolph Zukor's Famous Players Film Company, the Lasky Feature Play Company, and Bosworth merged to form Famous Players-Lasky Corporation, which voted to replace W. W. Hodkinson as president of Paramount and to absorb their former distributor to become an integrated production-distribution entity. Zukor then created Artcraft Pictures to sell the films of Mary Pickford at higher guarantees than the standard Paramount program contracts allowed. Artcraft soon raided Triangle and added Griffith, Ince, Sennett, Fairbanks, and William S. Hart to their roster. By 1918 Triangle had collapsed, and Artcraft combined with Paramount to establish the distribution model that would remain in place until the late 1940s, in which a slate of program pictures would be offered on a block-booking basis, and more desirable special attractions would be sold individually on their merits.

The member companies of MPPC began to fold their tents as legal pressures and the cost of feature production took their toll. Biograph went into bankruptcy in 1916. Kalem sold out to Vitagraph that same year. Edison, Essanay, and Selig shut down production in 1918. Lubin ceased production and reorganized as the Betzwood Film Company. Only Vitagraph would survive into the 1920s.

While it may have appeared at first to be an entirely new day in the motion picture business, the new distribution companies including Paramount, Mutual, Metro, and Fox proved to be just as demanding as MPPC and General Film. Exhibitors who wanted the Mary Pickford and Douglas Fairbanks specials were forced to book blocks of decidedly average Paramount pictures they had little interest in playing, while distribution fees, taken off the top before film rentals were reported, limited the profit participation possibilities for top-flight directors and stars.

To escape the growing power of a handful of distributors, Los Angeles exhibitor Thomas L. Tally, who had opened one of the first theaters specifically built to show movies, joined with West Virginia exhibitor John D. Williams and others in 1917 to merge twenty-six of the top theater companies showing first-run movies, creating the Associated First National Exhibitors Circuit with more than 200 theaters nationwide. Their motto was "The good guys get, by getting together." To jump-start production, First National raided other studios for stars, starting with Charlie Chaplin, whom they took away from Mutual by offering him greater creative control and a better release for his movies. First National gave him $125,000 for each film and an additional $15,000 if a production was longer than the usual two or three reels of film. The deal made Chaplin the first superstar. First National also stole away Mary Pickford and director D. W. Griffith from Paramount-Artcraft, throwing down the gauntlet to Adolph Zukor. In 1916 Pickford had signed a rich contract with Zukor for a salary of $10,000 a week, a $30,000 signing bonus, and a significant share of profits. But she jumped ship when First National offered an even more lucrative deal that paid her $350,000 per movie, a huge sum for the day, and ultimately gave her ownership of her pictures.

The ever-competitive Zukor decided he had to have his own first-run theater circuit too. After an attempt to merge with First National failed, Famous Players spent $10 million to build a national circuit that would remain among the premier exhibitors for the next three decades.

In 1919 Pickford and Chaplin joined with Douglas Fairbanks, director D. W. Griffith, and former Paramount president Hiram Abrams to form United Artists Corporation, allowing the partners to participate in profit sharing from the first box office dollar. This was the first attempt by a company to have the artists control all aspects of moviemaking and distribution.

When the decade began, movies were short, average weekly attendance was 26 million, and films were seen mostly in storefront nickelodeons. By the close of the decade, the feature film was firmly established, attendance had grown to 38 million, and there was a rush to build movie palaces that promised "an acre of seats in a garden of dreams." Audiences were reassured that they would get their money's worth in ambiance even if the picture on the screen wasn't quite a winner.

Major Movie Studios

Famous Players-Lasky . . . . Formed in 1916 by the merger of Famous Players (started in 1912 by Adolph
Corporation   Zuckor) and Jesse L. Lasky's Feature Play Company (started in 1913 by
                                     Samuel Goldfish, Cecil B. DeMille and Jesse L. Lasky)—will become
                                     Paramount Pictures, Inc., in 1936.

Fox Film Corporation. . . . . Formed in 1915 by the merger of William Fox's Greater New York Film Rental
                                     Company and Box Office Attractions Company—will become 20th
                                     Century-Fox Film Corporation in 1935.

Motion Picture Patents . . . . Incorporated in 1908 by the Edison Manufacturing Company and the
Company   American Mutoscope & Biograph Company—out of business by 1918.

The Universal Film . . . . Formed in 1912 by Carl Laemmle—will become Universal Pictures Company,
Manufacturing Company   Inc., in 1925.

Comparison of Three D. W. Griffith Directed Featured Films in the 1910s
Equivalent 2005 $s/(Unadjusted $s)

Film	Initial Release	Film Length	Days Principal Photography	Production Cost	Cost per Minute
The Birth of a Nation	1915	165 minutes	54	**$1.3 million** ($65,000)	**$7,617** ($394)
Intolerance	1916	194 minutes	200 estimated (9 months)	**$8.8 million** ($489,653)	**$45,223** ($2,524)
Broken Blossoms	1919	88 minutes	18	**$3.8 million** ($338,000)	**$43,360** ($3,841)

Breakdown of Two 1910s Films Initial Release
Equivalent 2005 $s/(Unadjusted $s) in Millions of $s

Film	Initial Release	Picture Length	Domestic Box Office	Domestic Rentals	Production Cost
Intolerance	1916	13–14 reels (194 minutes)	**$98.3** ($4.0)	**$24.6** ($1.0)	**$8.8** ($0.5)
Cleopatra	1917	11 reels (155 minutes)	**$85.5** ($2.0)	**$21.5** ($0.5)	**$4.5** ($0.3)

Note: Assumes 50 percent of *Intolerance* domestic rentals & box office at higher roadshow pricing.

Comparison of Three *Cleopatra* Films
Equivalent 2005 $s/(Unadjusted $s)

Star	Initial Release	Film Length	Days Principal Photography	Production Cost in Millions of $s	Domestic Theatrical Box Office in Millions of $s	Star Salary
Theda Bara	1917	155 minutes	not available	**$4.5** ($0.3)	**$85.5** ($2.0)	**$397,000** ($26,000 estimated)
Claudette Colbert	1934	95 minutes	44 estimated	**$12.3** ($0.8)	**$119.5** ($4.3)	**$729,000** ($50,000 estimated)
Elizabeth Taylor	1963	243 minutes	266	**$280.8** ($44.0)	**$435.7** ($57.8)	**$15.3 million** ($2,400,000 net after Fox lawsuit, including salary, overtime pay, living expenses and gross profit participation)

PRODUCTION SPOTLIGHT

Shorts, On-Location Filming, and Acting as Art

As the decade opened, the Edison Company was locked into the decision to produce short films that could each be shot in a week or less. Even if a movie was based on a well-developed story, such as *Frankenstein,* there was little time for plot in the typical 15-minute film. Once the power of the Edison Trust was broken and audiences began to experience longer films, there would be no turning back.

One of the earliest production houses to move west was Essanay, which had been founded in Chicago in 1907 by George K. Spoor and G. M. Anderson. The company's name was a result of combining *S* for Spoor and *A* for Anderson. In 1911 Essanay established a studio in northern California, where they pioneered two genres: westerns and slapstick comedy. Their westerns starred founder Anderson as "Broncho Billy"—one of the earliest being *Broncho Billy's Christmas Dinner.* Essanay reached the peak of its success in 1915 when Charlie Chaplin further defined his character the Tramp at their Niles, California, studio.

The acting and directing style D. W. Griffith advanced at Biograph with Mary Pickford in *The Violin Maker of Cremona* was built upon in the 1910s with Lillian Gish, who would first star in *An Unseen Enemy* in 1912 and go on from there to a star in the biggest blockbuster of the decade, *The Birth of a Nation.* This more developed acting style would go hand in hand with increasingly developed story lines as studios shifted the majority of their offerings from short films to featured films by the middle of the decade.

1910s Movie Censorship: A Brief History

In Mutual Film Corp. v. Industrial Commission of Ohio *(1915), the Supreme Court holds that movies are not protected by the First Amendment, allowing state and local boards (especially in Chicago and New York) to continue censoring films. The National Association for the Advancement of Colored People (NAACP) and others protest against* The Birth of a Nation *(1915), which is banned in places due to its controversial racial content.*

Frankenstein

Distributed by Edison, 1910
Directed by J. Searle Dawley
5 days of principal photography
975 feet (16 minutes)

A Typical Edison Short

When Thomas A. Edison, Inc., produced *Frankenstein* in 1910, the company was releasing at least three films a week. Two directors, J. Searle Dawley and Ashley Miller, were responsible for writing and directing those films. Miller specialized in comedy and Dawley in drama. They relied heavily on their literary and theatrical stage experience to develop material for their productions. The speed at which they were working didn't allow much time for research or reflection. Because of the film exchange system in existence at that time, the maximum length of a film was 1,000 feet and its running time was approximately 15 minutes. This hampered the telling of complex stories. So the key to successfully compressing Mary Wollstonecraft Shelley's novel, *Frankenstein, or, the Modern Prometheus,* into the movie's short span was to focus quite specifically on Dr. Frankenstein's redemption from evil through love. Dawley chose his actors from the stock company employed at the studio: leading man Augustus Phillips was cast as Dr. Frankenstein, character actor Charles Ogle as the monster, and Mary Fuller as Frankenstein's bride. None of these actors was given an individual credit on-screen.

The production was a challenge for two reasons: the necessity of special makeup for the monster, and the need for special effects. In those days makeup was done directly by the actor. Therefore Charles Ogle was responsible for his own appearance on-screen. He drew upon his experience as a stage actor of long standing in opera, drama, and the circus to create the monster with the aid of a wig, some ragged clothes, a theatrical makeup kit, and sheer force of personality. The camera tricks were a bit more difficult. They involved split screen, double exposure, and reverse filming. To make it appear on-screen as if the monster was formed in the midst of a flaming cauldron, they shot a dummy of the monster being burned, then incorporated that footage running in reverse. In an equally difficult scene where the monster disappears but his image remains in a mirror, the aperture of the camera was masked on one side while a dissolve was made to give the illusion of the monster fading away. The film was exposed again on the other side with the monster in the mirror. Use of such complex camera trickery in the early days of dramatic production was rare.

But those were the least of *Frankenstein*'s challenges. The film faced some censorship problems as well. Its tale of creation through science did not sit well with religious groups, so it was banned in some locations. Distribution of the film was conducted through the Edison-backed General Film Company exchange. Their system was extremely efficient, requiring as few as forty copies of each film to circulate around the United States, from first-run theaters in major cities to small-town theaters, all in the course of about six months. By the end of that time, millions of people had seen the movie and it had paid for itself many times over. It was easy enough to see that the greater the number of copies that could be distributed, the more money that could be made. Consequently, the Edison production staff was steadily increased to the point of being able to produce six films a week by 1912. *Frankenstein* was believed to be lost for many years until a collector in Wisconsin named Al Detlaff discovered a print in the 1970s. It has been viewed by several new generations since then. —*David Kiehn*

Broncho Billy's Christmas Dinner
Distributed by Essanay, 1911
Directed by Gilbert M. Anderson
3 days of principal photography
1,000 feet (15 minutes)

Movies Benefit from California Sunshine

Gilbert M. Anderson's Essanay company had been located in San Rafael, California, for six months before he decided to film a Christmas western for release in December 1911, only a month away. Generally, it took at least two months after a film was shot, developed, cut, and sent back to the main studio in Chicago for an Essanay picture to be released to theaters. But Anderson didn't waste any time on this one; he'd already made twenty-seven films in San Rafael, all of them one-reelers running about 15 minutes each.

To augment his mobile camera unit, Anderson's technicians outfitted a 70-foot railroad baggage car with a mobile laboratory that could process motion picture film and production stills on the spot. Anderson had learned that for westerns, it was more economical to shoot all of the "ride-throughs"—the scenes in which the horsemen charge cross-country—at one time. Sometimes he even would do this for multiple pictures at once.

This was the third movie featuring Broncho Billy in a series that would eventually total 140 films. Anderson was already recognized as an actor of merit from his work in 104 previous westerns, but now he brought something more to the screen: a continuing character with an appealing personality that audiences looked forward to seeing week after week. He would henceforth be known as "Broncho Billy" Anderson, the first movie star cowboy. By November 24, 1911, the film was nearly finished, with just a few shots left to complete. One of the last setups was in Fairfax, at the corner of Main Street and Bolinas Road, with leading lady Edna Fisher on the stagecoach as it was ready to "run away" with her alone on top. The horses were just supposed to appear spooked as cowboys fired their guns on the porch of the Fairfax Park Annex building, but this time the action spooked them for real. The coach took off with Edna and could not be stopped. She held on helplessly as it sped down the road, veering sharply onto Deer Creek Road, where it finally overturned. Edna was thrown 20 feet, fortunately sustaining only minor scrapes, bruises, and a sprained ankle. She continued to work on the film until it was finished later that day.

When *Broncho Billy's Christmas Dinner* was released on December 23, 1911, the incident with Edna and the horses was sensationalized in the press. While some viewers might have been enticed into theaters by the publicity alone, the movie's excellent quality spoke for itself. A review in the *New York Dramatic Mirror* stated: "There is a thrilling ride on a stage coach in this picture that is as exciting and realistic as anything of its character ever shown in pictures."

The profits from this film helped Anderson establish a studio in Niles, California, in 1913. By 1915 Anderson's annual income was $125,000 a year, extraordinary for the time. Because of his pioneering work—he had more than 400 films to his credit as an actor and director—Anderson was recognized with an Academy Award in 1958 "for his contributions to the development of motion pictures as entertainment." —*David Kiehn*

An Unseen Enemy

Distributed by General Film, 1912
Directed by D. W. Griffith
5 days of principal photography
1,000 feet (15 minutes)

Gish and Griffith Elevate Screen Acting to an Art

In 1912 nineteen-year-old Lillian Gish, who had already spent a decade as an actress and dancer on the stage, accompanied her sister, Dorothy, to New York City to visit their friend Gladys Smith, whose stage name was Mary Pickford. Smith was doing some acting for the "flickers" between theatrical engagements, and introduced the Gish sisters to director D. W. Griffith at the Biograph Company.

Griffith, a southerner and former playwright and actor who had become a film director, was producing hundreds of short films between 1908 and 1913 for Biograph. He immediately saw in Lillian Gish an innocence and charm perfect for his pictures.

Gish's first film for Griffith was *An Unseen Enemy,* in which she and her sister Dorothy are menaced by a thieving housekeeper after the death of their father, but resourcefully save the day in the end. The following year in *The Mothering Heart,* Lillian played a pregnant wife whose husband leaves her. She gives birth, but the baby dies. Instead of resorting to the typical histrionics of the era, Gish, under Griffith's direction, played her pain with restraint. Employing new pictorial techniques, including the close-up, also helped deliver emotional power in this film. Gish soon became known for using small gestures to provide a lot of information about her feelings and state of mind.

Gish and Griffith together raised film acting and directing to an art form with their revolutionary approach. Gish never considered

Index of Top Feature Film Directors Included in This Chapter	
1 D. W. Griffith	*The Birth of a Nation*
	Broken Blossoms
	Intolerance
2 Marshall Neilan	*Stella Maris*
3 J. Gordon Edwards	*Cleopatra*
4 Cecil B. DeMille	*The Squaw Man*
5 Hobart Bosworth	*The Sea Wolf*
See Note to the Reader for selection criteria.	

acting to be just a job; rather, she viewed it as a means to communicate a great deal more than words. Together Gish and Griffith showed that movies were a legitimate medium for artistic expression and could be used to convey far more than what could be relayed on a stage. Later Gish was given credit for inventing the real screen acting style that so many theater actors of her time scorned but which moviegoers so appreciated. Her sensitive performances elevated not only her movies but the whole concept of acting on film.

Gish eventually left Biograph in 1913 along with Griffith and most of his other regular players. Their greatest works were still ahead of them, but they had already changed movies forever. —*David Kiehn and Robert S. Birchard*

Actors of the 1910s: Comparison of Salaries and Profit Participations
Equivalent 2005 $s/(Unadjusted $s)

Actor	Film	Year	Salary
Mary Pickford	Various	1919	**$2,822,254** per picture excluding bonus ($250,000/each for three pictures plus $50,000 for her mother, plus a $100,000 bonus for each of the three 1919 films for First National: *Daddy Long Legs, The Hoodlum,* and *Heart o' the Hills*)
		1916	**$179,174**/week excluding bonus ($10,000/week for Artcraft Film Corp. Two-year deal signed in 1916 with Adolph Zukor plus a guaranteed bonus per film based on profits.)
		1915	**$38,672**/week ($2,000/week Famous Players)
		1914	**$19,530**/week ($1,000/week Famous Players)
		1913	**$9,864**/week ($500/week Famous Players)
		1911	**$5,480**/week ($275/week Majestic)
		1910	**$3,488**/week ($175/week Independent)
Charles Chaplin	Various	1916	**$179,174**/week excluding bonus ($10,000/week for Mutual Film plus $150,000 bonus)

U.S. INDUSTRY PRODUCTION STATISTICS, 1910s
Equivalent 2005 $s /(Unadjusted $s)

$3.0 Million ($197,225)
Average production cost of films featured in this chapter

$0.6 Million ($41,350)
Average production cost of all films released in 1910

DISTRIBUTION OVERVIEW

We . . . think that this step is positively and absolutely necessary to protect the great motion picture public from threatening combinations and trusts that would force upon them mediocre productions and machine-made entertainment.
—STATEMENT BY DOUGLAS FAIRBANKS, MARY PICKFORD, CHARLES CHAPLIN,
AND D. W. GRIFFITH ON THE FORMATION OF UNITED ARTISTS IN 1919

Major Movie Distributors

First National . . . . Formed in 1917. Later acquired by Warner Bros. in 1929.

General Film Company . . . . Incorporated in 1910 to distribute films produced by licensees of the Motion Picture Patents Company (MPPC). Transferred stock controlled by the Edison Manufacturing Company to Thomas A. Edison, Inc., in 1911 and sold the company in 1917. Distributed Edison, Essanay, Kalem, Lubin, Mina, Selig, and Vitagraph.

The Greater New York Film. . . . Formed in 1913 by William Fox then merged into Fox Film Corporation mid-decade.
   Rental Company

Metro Pictures Corp. . . . . Formed in 1915 to distribute the films of B. A. Rolfe Photoplays, Quality Pictures Corporation, Columbia Pictures. Later became part of MGM.

The Mutual Film Corp. . . . . Formed in 1912. Distributed American, Beauty, Broncho, Domino, Kay-Bee, Keysteon, Komic, Majestic, Princess, Reliance, Royal, and Thanhouser.

Paramount Pictures . . . . Formed in 1913 to distribute the films produced by Famous Players. Absorbed into Famous Players-Lasky Corp. in 1916.

United Artists . . . . Incorporated in 1919.

The Universal Film Corp. . . . . . . Formed in 1910 as the Motion Picture Distributing and Sales Company. Distributed Big U, "101," Bison, Eclair, Gold Seal, IMP, Joker, Laemmle, L-KO, Nestor, Powers, Rex, Sterling, and Victor brands.

TECHNOLOGY SPOTLIGHT

Color Them Black and White

There were early efforts to make movies in color using tinting, toning, and the labor-intensive hand-painting of individual frames, but that was not practical for most productions. The first patent for a color movie process had been filed in 1899 by Englishman Edward R. Turner. After Turner's sudden death in the middle of research and development, his system, named Kinemacolor, was further developed by American Charles Urban and Englishman C. Albert Smith.

By 1906 Kinemacolor had progressed to the point of exposing black and white negative film at 32 frames per second—twice the normal cranking speed of the time—through alternating red and green filters. The positive prints were then projected at the same rate through complementary green and red filters, creating a primitive color image on-screen. Because the red and green images were not exposed at the same time, color fringing often occurred when there was rapid or wide-ranging movement on-screen, ultimately making Kinemacolor an impractical format for wider use.

However, color imaging took a major step forward after the formation in 1912 of Kalmus, Comstock, and Wescott by Herbert Kalmus, Daniel Comstock —both graduates from the Massachusetts Institute of Technology (M.I.T.)—, and W. Burton Wescott, who had no degree but was considered by many to be a mechanical whiz. They reorganized as Technicolor Motion Picture Corporation in 1915 (the "Tech" in the name served as a reference to MIT).

Although Technicolor got off to a rocky start, they would soon smooth things out. Exhibitors found their first film, *The Gulf Between* in 1917, to be too difficult to correctly project. The sequencing of the images caused color fringing when objects moved; thus the projector had to be loaded so the film was in total sync with the color fly wheel. Improvements came with the release of the more commercial movie *Toll of the Sea* in 1922. Their finessed two-color system now exposed two images simultaneously on a single strip of film through orange and green filters. The frames were step-printed onto separate film rolls and tinted green and orange. These two tinted rolls were then cemented together to create the final release print. Focus and buckling problems were common in the early Technicolor days, and the fact that twice as much film was being used posed budgetary challenges, but a new direction was set and the door was opened to a new era of color movies.

MARKETING SPOTLIGHT

The Birth of Movie Marketing

As motion picture audiences grew, so too did the importance of the actors. The studios strove to emphasize them both on-screen and off. Offscreen, this meant the formation of publicity departments designed to create and broadcast an actor's personality; on-screen, filming techniques were developed to make the actor more desirable and easier to identify with. It was producer Carl Laemmle who originated the "publicity stunt," thus changing the movie marketing system dramatically. Laemmle had hired actress Florence Lawrence to join his IMP production company. Previously she had been with Biograph, where she gained recognition as the "Biograph Girl." Although accounts vary, most agree that Laemmle announced to the press that Lawrence had died in a streetcar accident in St. Louis. After news of her "death" had created a sufficient stir, he placed a full-page ad in papers to deny the story. The ad went so far as to state that the vicious rumor had been started by rivals who wished to discredit the star. He promised that an escort would accompany her to the premiere of her film in St. Louis. Of course, her appearance at the premiere caused a near-riot by eager fans.

Once stars became identifiable, the public's curiosity about them grew to be insatiable. Fan magazines arose in reaction, publishing photos, interviews, behind-the-scenes stories, and movie plot summaries. *Motion Picture Story* began in 1911 as a publication for theater owners, but within a year it hit the stands for public consumption. By 1914 circulation had grown to over 270,000. Following in 1912 was *Photoplay,* which at first published only film synopses but soon moved into biographies; by 1922 it had a circulation of more than 2 million.

Although fans were amenable to gossip and inside information about their idols, at this point no one wanted to hear about the stars' flaws and foibles. Scandals flourished later in the 1920s, but at the turn of the century, viewers seemed to prefer celebrities who were, in essence, perfected versions of themselves, someone they could consider a friend.

Theda Bara: The Manufactured Star

Theda Bara, who was viewed by many as the "wickedest woman on the screen," saw her career explode between 1915 and 1919. During that time she appeared in forty films produced and released by the Fox Film Corporation and was "moviedom's first wholly fabricated star personality," according to Robert Stanley in the book *The Celluloid Empire* (1978). Bara rose to fame overnight in *A Fool There Was,* a screen adaptation of the stage play by Porter Emerson Browne, which in turn was loosely based on Rudyard Kipling's poem "The Vampire." The film told the story of a woman whose lust and disregard for social convention could destroy any man who came into her clutches. The studio determined that it would help sell the product if the star was perceived to be as evil in real life as she was on-screen. So Al Selig and John Goldfrap, two former reporters hired by William Fox to publicize his movies, decided to create such a character. "We had every type of woman on the screen but an Arabian," they reasoned. They introduced their creation to the press to see if the newspapermen would catch on. The name Theda Bara, it was said, was an anagram for "Arab death."

"That's how the famous hoax press conference in Chicago came about," writes Eve Golden in *Vamp: The Rise and Fall of Theda Bara* (1996). "It all happened in early January 1915. . . . The details of the afternoon have long since become a part of Hollywood legend: the recitation of Theda's Egyptian childhood and French successes; the dramatic appearance of the languorous, fur-bedecked star; her brief chat with the press; and her famously overheard cry of 'give me air' after everyone else had left." To make sure everyone knew it was a hoax, Selig and Goldfrap even had young Louella Parsons stay around after the session to see Bara take off her disguise. That, however, didn't stop Bara from becoming the first overnight sensation or the movie's first sex star.

A Cincinnati newspaper got it right when they did their research and referred to Bara as a "local movie actress." She was born July 29, 1885, as Theodosia Goodman. Her father was a tailor. It wasn't until her fourth film, *The Devil's Daughter*, that the crew nicknamed Bara "The Vamp" for all the predatory females she had become known for playing. A reporter visiting the set overhead the comment and reported it to his readers, and a new word was added to the English language. At first it was only a descriptive noun, but it soon became an active verb as well as formerly proper young ladies sought to "vamp" their boyfriends into submission. Girls wanted to dress like the Vamp—a dark, mysterious look, with big eyes and heavy makeup. Bara was paid $75 a week for her first film. Four years later she was making $4,000 a week.

EXHIBITION OVERVIEW

The Arrival of Posh Movie Palaces

By 1913 there were 986 venues in New York City showing movies in some form—a mixture of small nickelodeons, converted storefronts, or theaters that had been partially or completely converted from live stage play and vaudeville venues. Some, such as Marcus Loew's Broadway Theater on 41st Street, and the Astor, where *Quo Vadis?* ran for twenty-two weeks, were large and elegant, but almost all suffered to an extent from having hard wooden opera seats, poor ventilation systems, and tiers of galleries supported by large columns that blocked the view of some patrons. Suddenly the race was on to build bigger, better theaters primarily to show movies. The first to open was the Wonderland Theater on Broadway and 45th Street, which seated 2,800, mixed movies with live vaudeville shows, and was conveniently located adjacent to a park with an indoor fair and amusement rides for kids.

Soon thereafter, Mitchell and Moe Mark came to New York from Buffalo, where they operated nickelodeons, with the hope of building the ultimate movie house. The brothers had traveled to Europe to study the great theaters of the Old World and then extended their study across America. This research led them to choose Thomas W. Lamb as their architect. Lamb was charged with designing the model for the movie palace of the future, which they would ultimately call the Strand Theater. The Strand was intended to be so grand that the Mark brothers could charge premium prices for the privilege of seeing movies there. The main auditorium was designed as a neo-Corinthian temple with gold leaf finishes throughout and a huge lit dome. There was a single balcony and a broad promenade with upholstering and Pullman-car-style plush seats, as well as wider armchairs upstairs. The orchestra was hidden, so the music seemed to rise out of nowhere. Along with crystal chandeliers and many other elegant touches, there were flowers everywhere.

To fulfill their dream, the Mark brothers wanted an impresario to orchestrate the environment and the entertainment. The hot name in exhibition at the time was Sam "Roxy" Rothapfel, who had turned the Regent Theater in Harlem into a huge success as part of a group called the Photoplay Theaters Company. Despite his ties to the group and its continuing expansion, Rothapfel left Photoplay to take charge of the Strand. He was given free rein to create a program of his own, and he did not let his new employers down. One of his innovations was to hire a small army of uniformed ushers who were trained both in discipline and in the nuances of fine service. On the day after the opening night in April 1914 the critic for the *New York Times* wrote: "Going to the new Strand Theater last night was very much like going to a Presidential reception, a first night at the opera or the opening of the horse show."

The first program featured a patriotic movie accompanied by the orchestra, which played equally patriotic music, followed by Hungarian Rhapsody No. 2. Then came the filmed scenes from a baseball game played earlier that morning in Brooklyn, which had been rushed through the lab for immediate screening. Then there was a short from Italy accompanied by a tenor singing "O sole mio" behind the screen. That was followed by a short Keystone Cops comedy that featured the "Mutual Girl," who also attended the opening. Then a quartet sang selections from the opera *Rigoletto*. Finally, the feature film *The Spoilers* was played. It ran roughly 2 hours and 15 minutes without any interruptions (at a time when movies were regularly stopped to change reels). There was no expense spared at the Strand, where Rothapfel had insisted on four projectors to ensure the seamless viewing of the films. There was also a special score to accompany the feature, another innovation at a time when orchestras typically played generic pieces during films.

Over the next six years, Rothapfel developed three more New York movie palaces—the Rialto, the Capitol, and the Rivoli—as other theater owners across the country rushed to copy his formula of excess for success.

U.S. INDUSTRY EXHIBITION STATISTICS, 1910s
Equivalent 2005 $s /(Unadjusted $s)

$6.41 ($0.10–$0.16)
Average movie ticket price (1910–1919)

10,000
Number of nickelodeon screens, 1910

THE SEA WOLF
States Rights, 1913

ALL-RELEASE EQUIVALENT 2005 $s
(Unadjusted $s) in Millions of $s

Domestic Box Office Revenues. . . . .$9.9/($0.2)
Production Cost . . . .$0.2/($0.01)
Principal Photography. . . . . .25 days estimated
8/14/1913–9/12/1913

Director . . . . Hobart Bosworth
Producer . . . . Hobart Bosworth
Production Company. . . . Bosworth, Inc.
Story by . . . . Based on the novel by
Jack London
Screenplay by . . . . Hobart Bosworth
Cast . . . . Hobart Bosworth, Herbert
Rawlinson, Viola Barry,
J. Charles Haydon, Jack London
Filming Locations . . . . . . Glen Ellen, Sausalito, and
Los Angeles, CA
Genre. . . . . Silent Classic, Drama
Format . . . . B&W
Initial Release . . . . 9/30/1913 premiere
(Los Angeles); 12/7/1913
general release
Rerelease. . . . . none
Running Time . . . . 105 minutes
7 reels
6,900 feet
MPAA Rating . . . . not rated

STANDING THE TEST OF TIME

ACADEMY AWARD Oscar Nominations and Wins

Predates Oscars

OSCAR TOTALS   Nominations 0   *Wins 0

AFI 100 YEARS 100 MOVIES SELECTION
2007 0   1997 0

TOP 300 FILMS POSITION . . . . .none
All-Release Domestic Box Office in Equivalent 2005 $s

National Film Preservation Board Selection. . . .none

OTHER AWARDS Best Picture Wins

	Year
Golden Globes	none
New York Film Critics.	none
National Board of Review	none
Film Daily Critics	none

His role of Wolf Larson exceeded my anticipations. It was magnificent.
—Jack London on Hobart Bosworth's performance

PLOT: Humphrey Van Weyden is rescued after a shipwreck in San Francisco Bay and made first mate by the rescue ship's captain, Wolf Larson, but a girl comes between them, resulting in Larson's death.

PRODUCTION: The Bosworth Company, named after actor-director Hobart Bosworth, was formed in July 1913 to produce a series of films based on Jack London's stories. This was the second time London had signed a contract with a film company to bring his stories to the screen. He'd previously made a deal with the Balboa Amusement Producing Corporation of Long Beach, California, but that contract expired before Balboa produced a single movie. When the owners of Balboa resumed their interest in London's work, they hired Bosworth to direct. But London was already too unhappy with Balboa and formally severed ties with them. Days later, Bosworth became associated with London and businessman Frank Garbutt, establishing Bosworth, Inc., specifically to produce the London films. Bosworth leased studio space at the Bradbury mansion, a rental facility used by independent producers, and quickly began work on the script. Hobart Bosworth and his company came to Jack London's ranch in Glen Ellen on August 14, 1913, to shoot the opening scene of the movie, in which London appears at his desk in a prologue to the story. The next day, London watched Bosworth stage crowd scenes in Sausalito for the ferryboat crash that leads to the meeting between Wolf Larson and Humphrey Van Weyden. Bosworth and his crew then returned to Los Angeles to shoot the rest of the film. By September 7, all but two scenes were done. A private screening was held at the end of the month at the Los Angeles Athletic Club, which was owned by Garbutt.

DISTRIBUTION: The release of the film was delayed by a legal conflict with a competing three-reel production hastily produced by Balboa in August after their agreement with London had expired. Negotiations between Balboa, Bosworth, and London dragged on for three months, until Balboa was finally forced to change the title of their film to *Cruise of the Hell Ship* and to exclude London's name from its advertising. *The Sea Wolf* was then distributed on a states rights basis by W. W. Hodkinson, who became one of the founders of Paramount Pictures in 1914. Unfortunately, the original negative of *The Sea Wolf* was destroyed in a vault fire at the Lubin laboratory, where release prints had been made, on June 13, 1914, making future distribution of this film quite difficult. Reviews for the film were mixed, generally praising Bosworth's performance but noting that the other actors left something to be desired. Herbert Rawlinson, as Humphrey Van Weyden, the one man to stand up to Wolf Larson, was barely mentioned except in a New York *Morning Telegraph* review on May 10, 1914, in which it was written that he was "mildly effective. But only mildly." Nevertheless, the film was thought to be a good start toward further productions of London's work. Seven more films were made, but London was disappointed in one of the last, *Martin Eden,* and the series ended. This film was remade by Famous Players-Lasky in 1920, by Ince Corp. in 1926, by Fox Film in 1930, by Warner Bros. in 1941, and by Allied Artists in 1958. In 1975 there was even an Italian production called *Legend of the Sea Wolf. —David Kiehn*

THE SQUAW MAN
States Rights, 1914

ALL-RELEASE EQUIVALENT 2005 $s
(Unadjusted $s) in Millions of $s

Domestic Box Office Revenues . . . . **$44.8**/($1.0)
Production Cost . . . . **$0.3**/($0.01)
Principal Photography . . . . **18** days
12/29/1913–1/20/1914

STANDING THE TEST OF TIME

ACADEMY AWARD Oscar Nominations and Wins

Predates Oscars

OSCAR TOTALS   Nominations 0   *Wins 0

AFI 100 YEARS 100 MOVIES SELECTION
2007 0   1997 0

TOP 300 FILMS POSITION . . . . .none
All-Release Domestic Box Office in Equivalent 2005 $s

National Film Preservation Board Selection . . . .none

OTHER AWARDS Best Picture Wins

	Year
Golden Globes	none
New York Film Critics	none
National Board of Review	none
Film Daily Critics	none

Director . . . . Oscar C. Apfel and Cecil B. DeMille

Producer . . . . Jesse Lasky, Samuel Goldfish, Cecil B. DeMille

Production Company . . . . Jesse L. Lasky Feature Play Company

Story by . . . . Based on the play *The Squaw Man* by Edwin Milton Royle

Screenplay by . . . . Cecil B. DeMille, Oscar Apfel

Cast . . . . Dustin Farnum, Red Wing, Winifred Kingston, Billy Elmer

Filming Locations . . . . . . Southern California, including San Pedro, San Fernando Valley, Hemet, Mount Palomar, West Adams district of Los Angeles and Universal ranch now Universal City

Genre . . . . Silent Classic, Western

Format . . . . B&W

Initial Release 2/23/1914

Rerelease . . . . none

Running Time . . . . 88 minutes
6 reels

MPAA Rating . . . . not rated

Have proceeded to California. Want authority to rent Barn in place called Hollywood.
—Telegram from Cecil B. DeMille to Jesse Lasky, 1913

PLOT: James Wynnegate leaves England, taking blame for the theft of charity funds (which was actually his cousin Sir Henry's crime), because Wynnegate harbors feelings for Sir Henry's wife. Settling in Wyoming, he is eventually reunited with the woman he loves.

PRODUCTION: The Jesse Lasky Feature Play Company producers were new to the movie business when they decided to produce a film based on the stage play *The Squaw Man*. Lasky had been packaging vaudeville acts; Samuel Goldfish, his brother-in-law, was a glove salesman; DeMille was a stage actor and playwright in the shadow of his older brother William. Goldfish had been encouraging Lasky to enter the movie business, but Lasky didn't see it as a viable opportunity until his friend DeMille talked of abandoning the theater for an adventure in revolutionary Mexico. Lasky suggested trying movies instead, and DeMille liked the idea. Despite their inexperience, they made some smart choices: they hired a famous stage actor, William Farnum, to star in their film; they chose a successful stage play, *The Squaw Man,* as their first production; and instead of filming in New York, where they were based, they decided to film in the West. Farnum and DeMille traveled with two invaluable men on their cross-country train ride: Oscar Apfel, a film director who had worked at Edison, Reliance, and Pathé and who would direct *The Squaw Man* under DeMille's supervision, and veteran cameraman Alfred Gandolfi, who had worked with Apfel at Pathé. During the trip Apfel and DeMille reworked the play into a shooting script. Their original destination was Flagstaff, Arizona, but when they got off the train the filmmakers were disappointed by the terrain. Farnum suggested they continue on to Los Angeles, where several film companies were already established, and that's exactly what they did. Taking rooms at the Alexandria Hotel in L.A., they were approached by two men, L. L. Burns and Harry Revier, who owned a film laboratory where the footage could be developed and printed. The lab was in a barn set up as a rental studio, and DeMille signed a lease to use the facility. From this base of operations, the remaining cast and crew were hired. Among the film's extras was Hal Roach, who became a director-producer for Harold Lloyd two years later and in the next decade brought fame to Laurel and Hardy. Southern California locations were used for a variety of scenes. By the end of January 1914, the film was completed. During a private screening for everyone connected to the production, the audience was in for a shock: the picture jumped and rolled, refusing to stay in frame. To save money, they had used nonstandard film stock with 65 perforations per foot rather than 64. It wasn't until the negative was taken to pioneer film producer Sigmund Lubin in Philadelphia that the problem was resolved and release prints were made.

DISTRIBUTION: The film was sold on a states rights basis by Sam Goldfish. Within just two weeks of the trade screening, he had sold territories in thirty-one of forty-eight states, and a week later only four states remained available. Those were soon sold as well. Although *The Squaw Man* was not the first Hollywood feature, as has sometimes been claimed, it was a significant film in the evolution of feature film production, and perhaps most importantly, it gave DeMille a start in his amazingly successful film career. —*David Kiehn*

THE BIRTH OF A NATION
(aka THE CLANSMAN)

States Rights, 1915

ALL-RELEASE EQUIVALENT 2005 $s

(Unadjusted $s) in Millions of $s

Domestic Box Office Revenues . . . . **$522.0**/($20.0)
Production Cost . . . . **$1.3**/($0.07)
Principal Photography . . . . **54** days estimated
7/4/1914–10/31/1914

Rerelease 1921, 1930
Running Time . . . . 165 minutes
NA reels
13,058 feet (3 hours first cut);
by March 3, 12,500 feet
MPAA Rating . . . . not rated

Director . . . . D. W. Griffith
Producer . . . . D. W. Griffith
Production Company . . . . Epoch Producing Corp.
Story by . . . . D. W. Griffith, based on the
novel by Thomas Dixon
Screenplay by . . . . Frank E. Woods (Scenario)
Cast . . . . Lillian Gish, Mae Marsh,
Henry Walthall
Filming Locations . . . . . . San Fernando Valley, Big Bear
Lake, Calabasas, Whittier,
Fullerton, Orange and the Fine
Arts Studio in California;
Imperial and Calexico, Mexico
Genre . . . . Silent Classic, War
Format . . . . B&W
Initial Release . . . . 2/8/1915 as *The Clansman*,
premiere (Los Angeles);
3/3/1915 general release as
The Birth of a Nation

STANDING THE TEST OF TIME

ACADEMY AWARD Oscar Nominations and Wins

Predates Oscars

OSCAR TOTALS   Nominations 0   *Wins 0

AFI 100 YEARS 100 MOVIES SELECTION
2007 0   1997 . . . #44
TOP 300 FILMS POSITION . . . . #21
All-Release Adjusted Domestic Box Office in Equivalent 2005 $s

National Film Preservation Board Selection 1992

OTHER AWARDS Best Picture Wins

	Year
Golden Globes	none
New York Film Critics	none
National Board of Review	none
Film Daily Critics	none

*Nothing so stupendous, so elaborate and so thrilling has ever before been produced
by an American director.*
—*Morning Telegraph* (New York), 1915

PLOT: The Civil War and reconstruction divides the Stoneman family of the North and their friends in the South, the Camerons, before they are joined together again in peace at the film's end.

PRODUCTION: D. W. Griffith was still working on *The Avenging Conscience* (1914) when he began preparations for *The Birth of a Nation,* inspired by *The Clansman,* a novel by Thomas Dixon recently produced as a play. Frank Woods, a former movie critic and scenario writer, brought the book to Griffith. The idea fired Griffith's imagination, and a deal was made with Dixon for the film rights. Even though *The Birth of a Nation* was conceived on a grand scale, Griffith only made notes to himself about the production and never wrote a script. He did, however, conduct six weeks of intensive rehearsals to work out how the story would be presented and who among his stock company of actors would play the roles. Griffith studied the history of the Civil War through documents, books, and photographs, striving for a visual authenticity that would evoke the look and feel of the times. For maximum effect, he even re-created the interior of Ford's Theater at the studio and had actors perform the lines of the play *Our American Cousin* on its stage just as they were spoken on the night of Lincoln's assassination. Filming began on location with battle scenes in the San Fernando Valley on July 4, 1914, so that these costly and complex shots could be finished as early as possible. Griffith didn't want them to be compromised later if the funding ran out. Funding was an ongoing problem: Griffith put in all the money he had; costumes and props were provided in exchange for a share in the film; Harry Aiken, president of the Mutual Film Company, put in $25,000 himself after Mutual's board of directors balked at using company funds; William Clune, owner of the largest theater in Los Angeles, paid $15,000 for a share; but that still wasn't enough. During a particularly difficult time, Griffith's cameraman Billy Bitzer handed over his life savings of $7,000. Creditors kept hounding Griffith for money, even as he continued to shoot. Filming was finally completed on October 31, 1914. Then Griffith spent three months editing while also supervising the musical score by Joseph Breil.

DISTRIBUTION: Griffith and Aiken formed the Epoch Producing Corporation to distribute the film, which premiered at Clune's Auditorium on February 8, 1915. Epoch sold territories on a states rights basis but also exhibited the film at selected theaters separately. The film made millions; Griffith himself earned more than $1 million during the first sixteen months of the initial run, and sold his share of Epoch to Aiken, who then continued to reap profits as sole owner. The film broke records in the big cities: it ran at Clune's for twenty-two weeks, the Colonial in Chicago for thirty-five weeks, and the Liberty in New York City for forty-five weeks. Long lines of people waiting to get into theaters were reported across the country. Even the controversy surrounding the film's portrayal of the Ku Klux Klan's vengeance against blacks failed to slow the crowds. —*David Kiehn*

INTOLERANCE
States Rights, 1916

ALL-RELEASE EQUIVALENT 2005 $s
(Unadjusted $s) in Millions of $s

Domestic Box Office Revenues. . . . . **$98.3**/($4.0)
Production Cost . . . .**$8.8**/($0.5)
Principal Photography. . . . . **9** months estimated
August 1915–April 1916

Director . . . . D. W. Griffith
Producer . . . . D. W. Griffith
Production Company. . . . Wark Producing Corp.
Story by . . . . D. W. Griffith
Screenplay by . . . . Anita Loos (Titles)
Cast . . . . Lillian Gish, Mae Marsh, Robert Harron, F. A. Turner
Filming Locations . . . . . . Fine Arts Studio back lot where Sunset Boulevard, Hollywood Boulevard, and Hillhurst converge
Genre. . . . . Silent Classic, Drama
Format. . . . . B&W with color tints and tones
Initial Release . . . . 9/5/1916 roadshow release
Rerelease. . . . . none
Running Time . . . . 216 minutes 13 reels
MPAA Rating . . . . not rated

STANDING THE TEST OF TIME

ACADEMY AWARD Oscar Nominations and Wins

Predates Oscars

OSCAR TOTALS   Nominations 0   *Wins 0

AFI 100 YEARS 100 MOVIES SELECTION
2007 . . . #49   1997. 0

TOP 300 FILMS POSITION . . . . .none
All-Release Adjusted Domestic Box Office in Equivalent 2005 $s

National Film Preservation Board Selection. . . . 1989

OTHER AWARDS Best Picture Wins

	Year
Golden Globes	none
New York Film Critics.	none
National Board of Review	none
Film Daily Critics	none

Intolerance opened last night . . . Lack of consecutive story is the picture's worst fault in fact it proved a disappointment as far as the first night audience was concerned.

—Telegram from Jesse L. Lasky to Cecil B. DeMille, 1916

PLOT: The theme of man's inhumanity to man is explored through four parallel stories in different historic ages and locations, including ancient Babylon, Judea in the time of Christ, France during the St. Bartholomew's Day massacre, and the United States in the early twentieth century.

PRODUCTION: *Intolerance* grew out of a never-released three-reel film *The Mother and the Law,* which D. W. Griffith made for the Reliance-Majestic Company. After *The Birth of a Nation,* Griffith reshot *The Mother and the Law* and expanded it into a five-reel feature for the Fine Arts wing of his newly organized Triangle Film Company, which was the successor to Reliance-Majestic. Perhaps because it was a modern-day melodrama, *The Mother and the Law* was deemed to be too "small" a picture to follow Griffith's twelve-reel triumph, *The Birth of a Nation,* and Griffith determined to expand the film. It was subtitled *Love's Struggle Throughout the Ages,* and Griffith intercut stories from four distinct historical epochs to create what he characterized as "a drama of comparisons." The structure of *Intolerance* seemed revolutionary, as the filmmaker juxtaposed the betrayal of Babylon by politically motivated pagan priests in 539 B.C. with the betrayal of Protestant Huguenots by politically determined French royalty in 1572, freely jumping from one era to another and treating these events as simultaneous rather than consecutive narratives. But it was not as much of a departure as it might seem. Griffith had already juggled three different story lines in the climax of *The Birth of a Nation,* though in that film the parallel stories occurred at the same historic moment in time. The bulk of *Intolerance* was shot over a period of nine months from mid-1915 into early 1916, but there were additional reshoots up to the moment of the film's release, and even after it opened Griffith added additional second-unit footage. When Griffith called *Intolerance* "a sun play of the ages," a fair amount of latter-day speculation arose as to what that meant. But it is no mystery, really. "Sun play" was just an infrequently used term for motion picture. Because of how slow film stocks of the time were, most movies, even interior scenes, were shot outdoors to take advantage of sunlight.

DISTRIBUTION: Although it has long been said that *Intolerance* cost $2 million to produce and was a colossal box office failure that haunted D. W. Griffith to the end of his career, that myth is entirely untrue. *Intolerance* was the most expensive American film made up until that point, costing a total of $489,653, and its performance at the box office was well below that of *The Birth of a Nation,* but it did recoup its cost and end with respectable overall numbers. Like *The Birth of a Nation, Intolerance* was first shown on a road show basis at higher prices and played ninety-six weeks in the top eleven U.S. cities. In 1919 Griffith took *Intolerance* apart to create two separate films: *The Mother and the Law,* a stand-alone version of the modern story Griffith first started shooting in 1914, and *The Fall of Babylon,* made from the Babylonian sequences with a happy ending tacked on. Another myth that circulated suggests that after the two films were fashioned, Griffith couldn't reassemble the original. This is also untrue. Several variations exist because Griffith often modified the film for specific venues and because the work went through extensive color-tinting and toning. Each release print was assembled by hand from hundreds of separate sequences. The most common version currently in circulation derives from a 1926 reedit by Griffith for a reissue that never occurred. —*Robert S. Birchard*

CLEOPATRA
Fox Film Corp., 1917

ALL-RELEASE EQUIVALENT 2005 $s
(Unadjusted $s) in Millions of $s

Domestic Box Office Revenues . . . .$85.5/($2.0)
Production Cost . . . .$4.5/($0.3)
Principal Photography . . . . not available

Director . . . . J. Gordon Edwards

Producer . . . . William Fox

Production Company . . . . Fox Film Corp.

Story by . . . . Original story by Adrian
Johnson adapted from the
1890 play *Cleopatre* by
Victorien Sardou and
Emile Moreau

Screenplay by . . . . Adrian Johnson (Scenario)

Cast . . . . Theda Bara, Fritz Leiber,
Thurston Hall, Albert Roscoe

Filming Locations . . . . . . Fox studio and various location
in California

Genre . . . . Silent Classic, Historical Drama

Format . . . . B&W with color tints and tones

Initial Release 10/14/1917

Rerelease 1920

Running Time . . . . 155 minutes (at 18 frames per
second)
11 reels

MPAA Rating . . . . not rated

STANDING THE TEST OF TIME

ACADEMY AWARD Oscar Nominations and Wins

Predates Oscars

OSCAR TOTALS   Nominations 0   *Wins 0

AFI 100 YEARS 100 MOVIES SELECTION
2007 0   1997 0

TOP 300 FILMS POSITION . . . . .none
All-Release Domestic Box Office in Equivalent 2005 $s

National Film Preservation Board Selection . . . .none

OTHER AWARDS Best Picture Wins

	Year
Golden Globes	none
New York Film Critics	none
National Board of Review	none
Film Daily Critics	none

*Theda Bara . . . wears some daring gowns which will occasion
many gasps from the spectators.*
—*Motography*, 1917

PLOT: This epic drama chronicles Cleopatra's love affairs with Julius Caesar, Marc Antony, and Harmachis (Pharon), a young priest of Isis, who has sworn to kill her.

PRODUCTION: Theda Bara, whose life story was manufactured by the studio to evoke an air of mystery, made her mark as a screen "vamp" in *A Fool There Was* (1915). Her box office popularity and the success of "big" pictures such as D. W. Griffith's *The Birth of a Nation* (1916) and *Intolerance* (1916) led exhibitor and producer William Fox to make this historical drama about the "greatest vamp of them all." Leading up to the film's release, the Fox publicity machine went into action, while a cooperative Theda Bara declared, "I felt the blood of the Ptolemys coursing through my veins." She also proclaimed with much fervor, "I live Cleopatra, I breathe Cleopatra, I am Cleopatra!" William Fox widely announced that *Cleopatra* was a $500,000 production, which would have made it the most expensive American motion picture to date. However, the actual production cost was just below $300,000, less than D. W. Griffith's *Intolerance* or Cecil B. DeMille's *Joan the Woman* (both 1916). Although Theda Bara's previous pictures had been made on the East Coast, at the Fox Film Corporation's rented studio facilities in New Jersey, the studio had recently expanded its West Coast operations, taking over the former Thomas Dixon Studio at Sunset Boulevard and Western Avenue in Los Angeles, so the decision to make *Cleopatra* in California was a logical one. A new glass stage was constructed on the lot especially for the film. In keeping with the studio's emphasis on the star, Bara wore a different costume in each sequence. It was said that the material for one of her costumes cost $1,000 a yard, but a wag noted that she wore only about 10 cents' worth in the picture. The Battle of Actium was staged at Balboa Beach. The Egyptian pyramids and the Sphinx were re-created at sand dunes in Ventura County. The city of Alexandria was built in Venice, California. Adrian Johnson's lengthy script was solid and historically accurate—except for those touches of mysticism that fans had come to expect from Theda Bara and the addition of a large-scale chariot race borrowed from the popular novel and stage hit, *Ben-Hur. Cleopatra* was director J. Gordon Edwards's (grandfather of filmmaker Blake Edwards) eleventh picture with the star.

DISTRIBUTION: By the time *Cleopatra* hit theaters in the fall of 1917 the cycle of big-budget epics that followed in the wake of *The Birth of a Nation* had just about run its course. Although *Cleopatra* did well, it was not a runaway hit. It did make a net profit of $60,077, and it was reissued in 1920 after Theda Bara had left the Fox studio, in part to satisfy promises to exhibitors for a production of *The Queen of Sheba,* which was to have starred Bara. Fox eventually made *The Queen of Sheba* in 1922 with Betty Blythe as the lead. The last known person to have seen Theda Bara's *Cleopatra* was Cecil B. DeMille, who screened a print in Hollywood in 1934 while he was in preparation for his own screen version of the story. After that screening the print was returned to the Fox vaults in Little Ferry, New Jersey, where it was destroyed, along with most of Fox's pre-1935 output, in a massive 1937 nitrate fire. —*Robert S. Birchard*

STELLA MARIS

Famous Players-Lasky Corp. and Artcraft Pictures Corp., 1918

ALL-RELEASE EQUIVALENT 2005 $s

(Unadjusted $s) in Millions of $s

Domestic Box Office Revenues . . . . **$102.6**/($2.4)
Production Cost . . . . **$2.2**/($0.2)
Principal Photography . . . . **30** days estimated
10/9/1917–11/12/1917

Director . . . . Marshall A. Neilan
Producer . . . . Marshall A. Neilan
Production Company . . . . Pickford Film Corp.
Story by . . . . Based on the novel by
William J. Locke
Screenplay by . . . . Frances Marion (Scenario)
Cast . . . . Mary Pickford
Filming Locations . . . . . . not available
Genre . . . . Silent Classic, Drama
Format . . . . B&W
Initial Release 1/21/1918
Rerelease . . . . none
Running Time . . . . 84 minutes
6 reels
MPAA Rating . . . . not rated

STANDING THE TEST OF TIME

ACADEMY AWARD Oscar Nominations and Wins

Predates Oscars

OSCAR TOTALS   Nominations 0   *Wins 0

AFI 100 YEARS 100 MOVIES SELECTION
2007 0   1997 0

TOP 300 FILMS POSITION . . . . none
All-Release Domestic Box Office in Equivalent 2005 $s

National Film Preservation Board Selection . . . none

OTHER AWARDS Best Picture Wins

	Year
Golden Globes	none
New York Film Critics	none
National Board of Review	none
Film Daily Critics	none

Well, she can't die soon enough.

—Producer Adolph Zukor talking to Mary Pickford
about her character Unity Blake

PLOT: In the film, set in Victorian times, Unity Blake, a servant girl beaten by the alcoholic wife of the kindhearted man Stella Maris loves, murders the wife and commits suicide so that Stella can live a happy life.

PRODUCTION: Mary Pickford bought a copy of the novel *Stella Maris* by William J. Locke to read during a train trip, and became so fascinated with Unity Blake that she decided to make a movie based on the character. Pickford boldly played two characters in this film: the beautiful, rich invalid Stella Maris, to appeal to her fans, and the unattractive Unity Blake, to satisfy herself. The Stella Maris character was no stranger to Pickford, as she had performed many variations of this attractive young woman in past films. However, the role of Unity Blake was something else; it represented a challenge this gifted actress couldn't resist. She smeared her hair with Vaseline to darken it and straighten her curls, then braided her hair and pinned it back. Her clothes were plain, her mouth was tightly drawn, and she stood awkwardly, one shoulder dropped and one hip high to give the impression that she had carried young children in her formative years. When her preparations were complete she walked about the studio pretending to be looking for work as a cleaning lady. No one recognized her, not even her favorite director, Marshall Neilan. That's when she knew she was ready to make the film. The movie fell under a deal Pickford had made in 1916 with Adolph Zukor and the Artcraft Film Corporation that allowed her to pick her own projects, directors, and supporting cast in order to make six films a year for $10,000 a week over the course of a two-year period and to receive half of the profits from her movies, or half a million dollars, whichever was greater. Artcraft was formed to produce and distribute Pickford's features because she had strongly objected to the practice of block booking, which often used her popular films to coerce exhibitors into buying other films they might not otherwise want. This was the third of five movies Mary Pickford made in a row with director Marshall Neilan, writer Frances Marion, and cinematographer Walter Stradling. To emphasize Unity's "ugliness," Pickford was photographed from what she deemed to be her "wrong side," the right side of her face. When being filmed as Stella Maris, she was photographed as usual on the left. Filming began in the fall of 1917 and was completed in a little over a month. Throughout this movie the public saw two sides of Pickford, but her transformation was so complete that if they hadn't seen the title credits opening the film, they might not have known that she was playing both roles.

DISTRIBUTION: As with all of Pickford's Artcraft pictures, this one made lots of money. Pickford was the most popular female star in the world at the time. She was so popular that Artcraft couldn't hold on to her—she left even before *Stella Maris* had opened. She made a deal with First National later that year giving her complete control over all of her productions and the ownership of her films. It was the next step toward complete control over distribution, which Pickford accomplished when she formed United Artists with Douglas Fairbanks, Charles Chaplin, and D. W. Griffith in 1919. —*David Kiehn*

BROKEN BLOSSOMS

United Artists, 1919

ALL-RELEASE EQUIVALENT 2005 $s

(Unadjusted $s) in Millions of $s

Domestic Box Office Revenues . . . . $96.8/($2.4)
Production Cost . . . . $3.8/($0.3)
Principal Photography . . . . **18** days
Dec 1918–Jan 1919

Director . . . . D. W. Griffith

Producer . . . . D. W. Griffith

Production Company . . . . D. W. Griffith Productions

Story by . . . . Based on the story "The Chink and the Child" by Thomas Burke in *Limehouse Nights*

Screenplay by . . . . D. W. Griffith

Cast . . . . Lillian Gish, Richard Barthelmess, Donald Crisp, Arthur Howard, Edward Piel, George Beranger, Norman "Kid McCoy" Selby

Filming Locations . . . . . . Shot entirely in studio Hollywood, CA

Genre . . . . Silent Classic, Romance

Format . . . . B&W with color tints and tones

Initial Release . . . . 5/13/1919 premiere (New York); 10/20/1919 general release

Rerelease . . . . none

Running Time . . . . 88 minutes (at 18 frames per second) 6 reels

MPAA Rating . . . . not rated

STANDING THE TEST OF TIME

ACADEMY AWARD Oscar Nominations and Wins

Predates Oscars

OSCAR TOTALS Nominations 0 *Wins 0

AFI 100 YEARS 100 MOVIES SELECTION
2007 0   1997 0

TOP 300 FILMS POSITION . . . . .none
All-Release Domestic Box Office in Equivalent 2005 $s

National Film Preservation Board Selection 1996

OTHER AWARDS Best Picture Wins

	Year
Golden Globes	none
New York Film Critics	none
National Board of Review	none
Film Daily Critics	none

I can't look at the damned thing; it depresses me so.

—D. W. Griffith to Lillian Gish after she asked
how the editing of *Broken Blossoms* was proceeding

PLOT: Cheng Huan, a young Chinese idealist, comes to London to convert the "heathen" British, but once there he becomes despondent and drug-addled. He meets an abused and beaten young English girl but her father, a prizefighter, violently objects.

PRODUCTION: After the relative box office failure of *Intolerance,* D. W. Griffith signed a contract to produce and direct a series of six-reel program pictures for Artcraft Pictures Corporation, a subsidiary of the Famous Players-Lasky Corporation. Griffith hired Sartov to assist his longtime cinematographer G. W. Bitzer, and Lillian Gish assumed the role of Lucy. Rose Smith, wife of film editor James Smith, suggested Richard Barthelmess for the role of Cheng Huan. He had gained notice in *War Brides* (1916) and had appeared opposite Lillian Gish's sister, Dorothy, in several Griffith-produced films. Early in 1919 Griffith signed an agreement to join with Douglas Fairbanks, Mary Pickford, and Charlie Chaplin to form United Artists Corporation, a development that would complicate the release of *Broken Blossoms.* Griffith developed his scenario not on paper but through an intensive six-week rehearsal schedule. He changed some elements of Thomas Burke's short story in his adaptation, giving Cheng Huan a history as a man of faith and setting him in a store in London that also served as his home, offering a reason for the disillusionment and opium addiction that envelop the character's life before he meets Lucy. In Burke's story the Chinese kills Battling Burrows by sticking a poisonous snake in his bed. Griffith simplified the action by having Cheng Huan plug Burrows with a pistol shot. *Broken Blossoms* was never intended to be anything more than a modestly budgeted program picture, and despite the lengthy rehearsals, the film itself was shot in a mere eighteen days. But it was evident as the picture was assembled that due to Henrik Sartov's innovative soft-focus photography, a commanding performance by Lillian Gish, and the tragic conclusion to the story, the end result would be something more than Griffith had anticipated. The most memorable images in the film were moments in which the abused Lucy, commanded to smile by her abusive father, uses her fingers to push up the corners of her mouth, and a terrifying scene in which Lucy, locked in a closet like a caged animal, awaits a beating as her father pounds at the door. Griffith's contract with Artcraft Pictures Corporation allowed the filmmaker the option to treat one of his program pictures as a special production to be released separately from the rest of the Artcraft program on its own merits as a road show attraction at advanced prices. *Broken Blossoms* was so designated and had its premiere in the George M. Cohan Theatre, a Broadway legit house.

DISTRIBUTION: Although D. W. Griffith still owed two pictures to Artcraft, United Artists was clamoring for product to feed into its new distribution system. Griffith persuaded Artcraft head Adolph Zukor to sell him the picture for $250,000 so that he could release it through UA, bringing the total cost of the film to about $338,000—a hefty figure for a six-reel film in that era. The board of United Artists agreed to borrow the money to allow Griffith to purchase the film. Fortunately, *Broken Blossoms* proved to be a hit, racking up $454,711.50 in rentals in its first two months of bookings. —*Robert S. Birchard*

The 1920s

In January 1928, producer Joe Schenck, Buster Keaton's brother-in-law, had sold Keaton's contract to MGM. The comedian was to get $3,000 a week for two pictures a year, with his production company receiving 25 percent of the net profits, and Keaton getting 25 percent of the production company's 25 percent ... Charlie Chaplin, among many others, told him not to acquiesce. 'They'll ruin you helping you. They'll warp your judgment. You'll get tired of arguing for things you know are right.' Keaton went along anyway. It was, he remembered, 'the worst mistake of my career.'

—Scott Eyman from his book, *Lion of Hollywood: The Life and Legend of Louis B. Mayer*

TOP 10 ALL-RELEASE MOVIES
DOMESTIC BOX OFFICE
By Initial Year of Release, 1920–1929

		Equivalent 2005 $s in Millions of $s
1	The Big Parade	$343.4
2	Ben-Hur: A Tale of the Christ	$305.2
3	The Singing Fool	$244.9
4	The Four Horsemen of the Apocalypse	$188.5
5	The Kid	$188.5
6	The Freshman	$175.4
7	The Broadway Melody	$171.4
8	The Gold Rush	$168.7
9	Madame DuBarry	$160.3
10	Way Down East	$160.3
		Total: $2,106.6

GENERAL U.S. STATISTICS, 1920

106,021,537
Total U.S. Population

38 Million
Average Weekly
U.S. Movie Attendance

DECADE OVERVIEW

Silent films had a language of their own; they aimed for the emotions, not the mind, and the best of them wanted to be, not a story, but an experience. —ROGER EBERT

Calm Between the End of World War I and the Stock Market Crash of 1929

The Roaring Twenties arrived more like a lamb than a lion for the motion picture business. Distributors lost much of their foreign revenue as overseas markets rebuilt after World War I (1914–18). But when the U.S. economy began to flourish again, so too did movies. Accompanying postwar prosperity, prohibition, and the Jazz Age was a deepening love affair between Americans, the movies, and the stars of the silver screen. The decade was also marked by the migration of fresh talent from Europe, such as German director F. W. Murnau; the advent of radio, which presented programming some feared would keep people at home nights instead of at the theaters; and the game changing innovation of sound, requiring movie production facilities and theaters to be remade for a new era.

By 1927, though, the movies were an American habit, with over 60 percent produced by the "majors," large vertically integrated companies that would continue to dominate the industry through the 1950s.

As ornate new theaters were built for the sound era, the old stigma that moviegoing was mainly for the lower classes and poor immigrants disappeared. Instead, middle- and upper-class audiences thronged to the new movie palaces, often decorated in Oriental, Baroque, or Moorish style. Once there, attendees were welcomed by a corps of uniformed ushers.

The movies that sold the most tickets best reflected the times, as many of the great silent war movies were released in the 1920s. Some of the pictures were sexy, daring, and openly exploitative. They often featured Rudolph Valentino, known as the "Latin Lover," or flappers and their boyfriends driving fast cars and drinking illegally obtained alcohol, referred to as "hooch," from hip flasks. A new morality had roared into the most fashionable quarters, as hemlines became shorter. Business boomed as orgies played on-screen. There was often a scene (set usually in a bathroom) where a star (such as Gloria Swanson) discreetly disrobed for the cameras. For the soap opera crowd, there were a new crop of romantic dramas from director Cecil B. DeMille and others about young married women who engaged in affairs out of boredom or frustration before returning to their spouses.

The on-screen antics seemed to mirror real-life Hollywood at times, such as in 1921 when comedian Fatty Arbuckle was charged with causing the death of actress Virginia Rappe at a party. Arbuckle had been signed by Paramount under the first multiyear, multimillion-dollar contract in Hollywood. Tried in the press by Hearst and in San Francisco by a politically motivated district attorney, Arbuckle was found innocent in his courtroom trial. Unfortunately, by

Top Five 1920s World War I Silent War Films
All-Release Domestic Box Office
Equivalent 2005 $s/(Unadjusted $s) in Millions of $s

Rank	Film	Initial Release	Domestic Box Office	Production Cost
1	*The Big Parade*	1925	$343.4/($10.2)	$4.7/($0.4)
2	*The Four Horsemen of the Apocalypse*	1921	$188.5/($5.0)	$8.7/($0.8)
3	*Wings*	1927	$138.5/($4.3)	$22.4/($2.0)
4	*What Price Glory?*	1926	$134.9/($4.0)	$9.1/($0.8)
5	*Tell It to the Marines*	1927	$89.0/($2.8)	$4.9/($0.4)

the time he was vindicated, his career had been destroyed. Handsome actor Wallace Reid, once known as "the screen's most perfect lover," became a drug addict after he was injured on a movie and given morphine so he could complete the picture. Reid died in a sanitarium in 1923. When movie director William Desmond Taylor was murdered in 1922, among those implicated was top screen comedienne Mabel Normand. Later, her chauffeur was a suspect in another death, the shooting of Courtland Dines. Amid highly charged emotions, religious and social groups voiced concerns that the theaters were exhibiting and promoting movies that displayed an unhealthy, immoral, and even dangerous lifestyle.

As thousands of new theaters opened their doors (nearly 20,000 by 1926) and moviegoing became a new American pastime, the need for more and better movies increased as well. To keep up, the major studios became self-contained factories that produced pictures in assembly-line fashion, which meant that they needed dependable formulas. They based these formulas on the movies that had most recently pleased the public. The studios signed contract players and kept huge crews of artists and technicians on salary to help capture, create, and sell the movies.

The ultimate arbiter of what the public wanted became the studio head. A handful of powerful moguls, most from an immigrant Jewish background, came to control the half dozen dominant studios. They personally picked every movie, deciding who would be in it and who would be behind the camera. They also decided whether the movies should have a happy ending to please audiences, or if the movie's ending should differ from the book, play, or legend the film was based on.

In the earliest days of cinema, the producers had refused to put the names of the actors on each movie, because they didn't want them to become so famous that they would demand more money. However, fans began to recognize favorite performers and clamor for them. Astute theater operators would post signs outside when a new movie came along, tagging a favored star in some way. The greatest early star of the cinema, Mary Pickford, was known among her fans as "the girl with the curls," or later as "America's sweetheart," which was somewhat ironic since Pickford was Canadian. Not only did actors now get screen credits, but the star system was bursting into being. Fans flocked to see individual stars, and soon cults grew around the most famous, most mysterious, or most notorious. There were magazines just for the fans of the stars, as studio publicity departments carefully controlled the image of their players. To reflect the new interest in movies and their stars, the Academy Awards were created. They were first presented in 1929 at a private dinner in the Blossom Room of the Hollywood Roosevelt Hotel, honoring the achievements between August 1927 and July 1928. Public interest proved so great, however, that the following year the Academy of Motion Picture Arts and Sciences permitted radio broadcasting of the event. Television would add a new dimension in 1953.

Not all stars survived the decade or the transition to sound, including Mary Pickford, whose career was over by 1933, even though she would live on into her eighties. However, a new generation of stars including Gary Cooper, Joan Crawford, and Greta Garbo appeared on the scene in the 1920s. These formidable actors were part of a new breed, able to give spoken words real meaning.

Throughout the decade, there were attempts at wide-screen presentation, including the silent epic *Napoleon*, which was released in 1927, marking the high point of the career of French filmmaker Abel Gance. Gance had created a projection system called Polyvision that used three strips of film shot by three different cameras simultaneously, which were then projected side by side, tripling the aspect ratio of the film, so as to effectively show a full battlefield.

In the 1920s block booking became a favored practice among producers and distributors, forcing exhibitors once again to take a company's entire lineup of films in order to book more desirable titles featuring more popular stars. Exhibitor outrage over block booking led to antitrust lawsuits against the studios in the 1930s, which would ultimately result in a consent decree that abolished the practice. Aware that their popular films had been used to leverage exhibitors into booking other films they didn't want, Mary Pickford and a group of other actors and filmmakers founded United Artists to offer pictures to any and all theaters based on their individual merits.

In addition to the many U.S.-produced films released in America, there continued to be foreign imports brought in by both the major distribution companies and by various independents. One such film was *The Cabinet of Dr. Caligari*, directed by German director Robert Wiene and released in the United States in 1921 by the Goldwyn Distributing Company. *Dr. Caligari* marked the beginning of the expressionist movement, wherein artists used minimal set materials to maximum effect and often haunting effects, and explored themes that were characteristically intellectual and dark in nature. Fritz Lang, an Austrian, also directed films in Germany during the early 1920s and had been the first choice of director for *The Cabinet of Dr. Caligari*. In October 1924 Lang came to the United States for a visit and conceived the idea for his later expressionist film *Metropolis*. This film took two years to complete and was the most expensive film ever produced in Germany. It was imported and released into the United States by Paramount in 1928. During the latter half of the decade, other European directors would make their mark on cinema as well, including F. W. Murnau, who was invited by Fox to come to Hollywood in 1927 to make *Sunrise: A Song of Two Humans*, his first American film, which has been called "the last high peak of German silent cinema."

By the time Black Friday walloped Wall Street in 1929, the American movie industry had never been healthier or more popular.

PRODUCTION SPOTLIGHT

The Movies Learn to Talk

Although the Warner brothers have historically been given the lion's share of credit for bringing sound to movies because of the publicity surrounding the release of Al Jolson's hit *The Jazz Singer* in 1927, they had long been in a race with Fox Film studio boss William Fox, who licensed the patents to a different sound system—the system that was ultimately adopted by nearly everyone else in the industry. Fox's system printed the sound as an optical track on the same strip of film used to record the picture. The Warner Bros. system, by contrast, required a more complicated synchronization between a record disc and the action on the screen. Although the system Fox championed won the battle, William Fox eventually lost his patents and rights in a peculiar Supreme Court ruling that essentially placed them in the public domain.

Sound also led to the formation of RKO Pictures, another major studio of the era. Once it was possible to add this further dimension to film, the doors opened for the arrival of the popular musicals released by MGM beginning in the latter part of the 1920s.

U.S. Theater Transition to Sound, 1925–1929

Year	Total Number of Theaters	Silent Theatres	Theaters Wired for Sound
1925	15,000	15,000	0
1926	19,489	19,489	0
1927	21,664	21,644	20
1928	22,304	22,204	100
1929	23,344	22,544	800

1920s Movie Censorship: A Brief History

The Motion Picture Producers and Distributors of America (MPPDA) is formed in 1922 to regulate movie content, led by former Postmaster General William H. Hays. Compliance is voluntary.

In 1926 the Women's Christian Temperance Union (WCTU) forms a Motion Picture Department to press for more governmental regulation of movies.

Top Five 1920s Sound Films
All-Release Domestic Box Office
Equivalent 2005 $s /(Unadjusted $s) in Millions of $s

Rank	Film	Initial Release	Domestic Box Office	Production Cost
1	*The Singing Fool*	1928	$244.9/($7.6)	$4.4/($0.4)
2	*The Broadway Melody*	1929	$171.4/($5.6)	$4.3/($0.4)
3	*Gold Diggers of Broadway*	1929	$155.1/($5.1)	$6.1/($0.5)
4	*Sunnyside Up*	1929	$133.7/($4.4)	$7.3/($0.6)
5	*The Jazz Singer*	1927	$126.5/($3.9)	$4.7/($0.4)

The Warner Brothers See a Demand for Talking Pictures

Among the studios that would dominate the early years of movies, Warner Bros. was the only family-run operation. Besides Sam, there was the oldest brother, Harry, who was president and supervised all operations; Albert, who ran the worldwide distribution network, based in New York; and Jack, who was head of production at the studio in California. Their father, Benjamin Warner, a cobbler by trade, had first come to America to escape persecution of the Jews by the czars of Russia. He was soon followed by his wife, Pearl, their oldest son, Harry, and a daughter, Anna. They lived in Baltimore at first, and then a series of other cities and towns, before finally settling in Youngstown, Ohio, where there was a welcoming Polish community. Ben opened a shop to repair shoes. By coincidence, all of his sons became interested in the movie business around the same time.

Sam, who was considered the family showman, more than hinted at his determination to get into the field as a teen when he convinced his father to pawn his watch so the boys could buy a used projector from a nickelodeon that had gone out of business. At first the brothers took their projector and played films during intermission in vaudeville theaters or in an empty social hall. In time, they opened their first nickelodeon in New Castle, Pennsylvania, where they struggled to buy movies at a price of roughly $25 for a 12-minute reel.

Jack Warner saw himself more as a performer and went on the road as a singer calling himself Leon Zuardo before returning to rejoin the family business.

Brother Abe, later to be known as Albert, saw a different opportunity. He realized that if he could buy up enough prints of movies, he could rent them to the other nickelodeons. He raised $2,000, traveled to New York, bought films, and then set up shop in Pittsburgh. At first the theater owners were hostile, but then they saw the value of renting twenty films (a ten-week supply) for $100 from the Warners' firm, the Duquesne Amusement Supply Company. Once the precedent was established, the brothers serviced theaters as far away as Portland, Oregon.

Life was good until the Warners ran into trouble in 1908. That's when Edison and others formed the Motion Picture Patents Company (MPPC), forcing them to shut their theater and film rental business. The brothers, who were nearly broke at the time, seemed finished. In 1913, a year after the U.S. federal government filed an antitrust suit against MPPC, they set up a company called Warner Features, which distributed the product of a number of independent producers and later distributed their own pictures. Their luck improved after Sam read a series of articles about America's ambassador to Germany just before the war started. Sam knew the ambassador's story would make a great movie, so he had Harry buy rights for $50,000, raising the money by selling shares in the movie. It was called *My Four Years in Germany* (1918) and went on to make the Warners more than $1 million in profit. Harry remained in New York while the other brothers moved to Los Angeles, where Sam and Jack began making movies that got the attention of critics. They excelled at making pictures that raised social awareness, such as *The Beautiful and Damned* (1922), based on a novel by a very young F. Scott Fitzgerald, and *Main Street* (1923), based on a book by Sinclair Lewis.

Their first blockbuster success arrived on four legs, thanks to an Alsatian dog that had been abandoned as a pup in the trenches by German soldiers during World War I. An American soldier found the dog and later trained him for the movies, naming him Rin Tin Tin. From the canine star's first film, *A Man from Hell's River* (1922), Rin Tin Tin was a hit.

In those years the film industry was growing rapidly, but it also had a new rival for the attention of the public: radio, which by the end of the decade would be in approximately 39 percent of all American homes. Many in the movie business saw radio as a competitor, thinking that if people were home listening to radio, they were not in theaters. That was especially true on nights when popular shows aired. Exhibitors reported the biggest dips in attendance during those hours. But Sam Warner believed it was better to join the opposition than be beaten by it. In 1925 he established a radio station, KWBC (for Warner Bros. Classics), in Los Angeles. He asked Jack to sing and stars of the Warner movies to appear as regular guests. It was also because of his contacts in radio that Sam heard about experiments being conducted for sound movies. Warner felt hampered from expanding further into sound movies, however, by the costly and unstable system of financing it was using to make its movies. Under this system, known as the franchise technique, the studio divided the country into twenty-eight zones, then sold rights to a package of five to ten films in each zone. Working this way meant that the buyer got a fixed percentage of the profits, leaving the Warners with lower margins than they had hoped for.

Harry Warner was looking to change the company's financing model and expand distribution in 1924 when he met Waddill Catchings, the top investment banker at the old-line Wall Street firm Goldman Sachs. Catchings was known for taking a chance on companies that he felt would grow. He was helping raise money at the time for Sears and the dime store chain Woolworth, which both went on to become huge successes. Warner went public to raise money and in 1925 used $1 million to buy movie industry pioneer Vitagraph, which had twenty-six distribution offices in the United States and two dozen more overseas, as well as studio facilities in Brooklyn, New York, and Hollywood, California. To pay for production, Catchings then arranged a $3 million revolving line of credit so that there would be a steady supply of capital for production and operations.

Warner quickly expanded with more exchanges in the United States and abroad, and within six months was equal in reach to the top distributors of the day, Famous Players-Lasky (Paramount) and Loew's, which owned Metro-Goldwyn-Mayer studios. To match its competitors, Warner also began to acquire movie theaters, with its flagship theater on Broadway in New York.

After seeing the new Western Electric system for recording and reproducing movies, Sam and Harry cooked up a way to profit quickly from the innovation. On June 25, 1925, Warner and Western Electric agreed to a one-year experiment. Sam Warner had the job of figuring out how to integrate the system into the studio's process of making movies. This required massive changes in the way things were done. The first films to use this technology were recordings of popular musical acts of the day. Warner moved quickly to sign contracts with a large number of entertainers and got the New York Philharmonic to record orchestral accompaniments for its movies. Then the company marketed the system and movies to vaudeville theaters, or combination houses (showing film and live acts), where they substituted the film of the act for the real thing, saving a lot of money. In each case, Western Electric got a contract to wire the theater. In December 1925, the experiment was deemed a success and negotiations began, resulting in a contract the following April by which Western Electric granted Warner's new subsidiary, Vitaphone Corporation, an exclusive license for sound film production and distribution.

In August 1926, Warner premiered Vitaphone at the Manhattan Opera House in New York City, a venue that had been wired for sound. The package presented included seven vaudeville shorts, mostly "serious" music such as opera, followed by the silent feature film *Don Juan,* with Vitaphone-recorded music in place of the usual orchestra. It was well received in New York and a dozen other cities across the United States. Despite this success, audiences, used to a full orchestral sound, complained it was inferior, adding to the misconception in Hollywood that the public didn't want sound. The top moguls of other companies made a pact among themselves in the middle of the decade not to put any sound movies out for at least one year, because they all knew that if sound came along, it would throw their budgets and production schedules into complete disarray. By the 1927–28 season, however, Warner began to shift production aggressively to sound. Among the first movies placed before the lights and microphones was *The Jazz Singer.* When it premiered on October 6, 1927, it was a sensation because star Al Jolson not only sang (as he had done in the *Plantation Act* short for Warner Bros. in 1926) but also spoke on film for the first time. While critics were generally lukewarm about the movie, audiences flocked to see the picture and to hear Jolson tell them, "You ain't heard nothing yet!" For the Warner brothers, it was a bittersweet moment. On the night before *The Jazz Singer* opened, Sam Warner, who had championed the development of sound, died suddenly at age forty of complications from a sinus infection.

By the fall of 1928, Warner Bros. had converted to a schedule of all talking movies, both features and shorts. Now it needed more movie theaters. So Catchings helped broker the acquisition of the Stanley theaters, all first-run houses in the mid-Atlantic region. Stanley owned part of First National, so Warner Bros. took over those theaters as well. Western Electric naturally followed, wiring each of these theaters for sound.

William Fox Creates a Better Sound System but Gets There Late

Warner Bros. had rushed the first talking feature into theaters, but Fox was never far behind in the race to bring sound to the movies. The Fox Film Corporation, directed by William Fox, had acquired Theodore Case and E. I. Sponable's sound film system, as well as some European sound-on-film patents. Fox, who called his system Movietone, decided to demonstrate the new realism of sound by sending crews all over the world to capture events never seen before by Western audiences. The resulting films were packaged and delivered as a news program between or before a feature film and were presented as Movietone News.

William Fox was born in Tulchva, Hungary, in 1879 and came to the United States as a toddler with his family. He dropped out of school in New York City and at age eleven got a job in a garment industry sweatshop; Fox later acquired his own garment company. He saved his money and eventually bought an arcade for $1,600. There were coin-operated machines downstairs, and movies were shown upstairs. The business was not all that he had hoped for, so Fox went to work fixing it up, refurbishing the space and adding a piano player who led sing-alongs during the intermissions.

Fox opened his first theater in 1904 and soon owned fifteen others throughout Brooklyn and other parts of New York City; eventually he expanded further, to twenty-five. However, Fox was bothered that the people who leased him movies made most of the profits. So he started his own distribution company, the Greater New York Film Rental Company.

When Edison formed MPPC, most exhibitors either paid the high fees and met their demands or went under. Not William Fox. He refused an offer by the trust to buy him out for $75,000 and asked for $750,000 instead. The trust canceled his license to show movies using the phony grounds that he had shown some of the movies in a house of prostitution. Fox fought back at every step, launching production of his own movies to keep his screens full. He also filed a $6 million lawsuit (which eventually would lead to the trust's demise), and the trust wound up paying him $300,000 to settle. That convinced Fox that he had to expand all of his operations and be self-sufficient. Through the end of the 1920s, Fox took a separate path from other studios, expanding his distribution around the world and building a new chain of theaters.

Fox always stood apart from most of Hollywood. He was bald and had a large nose, dark eyes, and a black moustache. He wore white shirts and sweaters, which he considered symbols of prosperity, and became an expert golfer, though he played with only one hand. As a child, Fox had fallen off a delivery truck. Because his family couldn't afford a good doctor, he received questionable medical care, which led to the removal of his elbow rendering his arm permanently useless.

Fox established Box Office Attractions in 1914, distributing the films of several independent producers. It became the Fox Film Corporation in 1915, the same year the studio launched its first star, Theda Bara. That year the studio earned $500,000. In 1916 Fox opened his first studio in Los Angeles, renting the old Selig Polyscope Company studio in the Edendale neighborhood of Los Angeles (later called Echo Park). He moved to a larger studio in 1917 at the corner of Sunset Boulevard and Western Avenue in Hollywood, on a lot that had been home to Thomas Dixon Productions. By 1924 Fox's net earnings had increased to over $2.5 million. With the stock market booming, Fox went public in 1925, raising $6 million through the sale of common stock. That allowed the company to increase movie budgets and expand their newsreel division, as well as continue their theater expansion program.

In 1925 Fox acquired one-third of West Coast Theaters, ensuring him access for his films in California. With Fox handling the financials and his wife decorating the theaters, they rapidly built movie palaces in Philadelphia, Washington, D.C., Brooklyn, Manhattan, St. Louis, Detroit, Milwaukee, Denver, San Francisco, Los Angeles, and elsewhere.

Fox was first attracted to sound movie technology when his executives pitched it as a way to strengthen the newsreel operation. The method they presented had been invented by Theodore Case, based on research he began as early as 1911 while still at Yale University. During World War I, Case worked on experiments that projected infrared light rays, which were used for the transmission of signals between ships. It was how convoys kept in line. Back home after the war, Case continued his experiments at what became the Case Research Laboratories in Auburn, New York, along with co-inventor Earl I. Sponable. Together they were able to develop a system so sensitive to light vibrations that little lines of sound could be photographed on celluloid strips alongside the image and sprocket holes.

Fox saw a talking picture for the first time in Parlor B of the Fox Movietone newsreel studio at 54th Street and Tenth Avenue. Also in attendance were Joy, Sponable, Case, Courtland Smith, and Jack Leo, who was to be responsible for any transition to sound at the California studios. The film shown was a close-up of a canary singing. Afterward, Fox accused Case and Sponable of using a ventriloquist hidden away somewhere in the building. Fox insisted the next demonstration be in his mansion in Woodmere, on Long Island, where he knew no one could trick him. Of course, it was no trick.

Fox agreed to make a deal for the Case patents but remained skeptical about the viability of sound movies until it could be perfected. He insisted on extensive experiments at the 54th Street studios. The test subjects included Beatrice Lillie, Ben Bernie, and Gertrude Lawrence. Sponable later lamented that if it hadn't been for Fox's hesitation, they could have beaten Warner Bros.' *The Jazz Singer* to market. As it was, Fox's newsreels enjoyed an advantage for the next few years until all other competitors converted to sound.

Fox quickly became the biggest cheerleader for sound, rapidly moving toward an all-sound system and hurrying to acquire more movie theaters to wire for sound. It was this rush to acquire theaters that later would cause Fox's debt problems and cost him his company, but at the time it seemed like a savvy business move.

Movietone premiered on May 2, 1926, at the Nemo Theater on Broadway in New York City. On hand to greet Fox and his wife that night was Courtland Smith, whom Fox had hired to oversee the new sound movie venture and exploit the Case patents. Smith was the brother-in-law of Arthur Brisbane, a powerful editorial columnist for the Hearst newspapers. It was Smith who developed the Movietone News and, later, unique theaters in major cities that played nothing but newsreels around the clock, a kind of CNN on the big screen.

On April 30, 1927, Fox showed his first sound newsreels at his corporate flagship theater, the Roxy in New York. It was a 4-minute reel of U.S. military cadets marching at West Point. It drew an enthusiastic response from the audience and the critics. In what could only be called a major publicity coup, a Fox Movietone camera was present at 8:00 a.m. on May 20, 1927, when Charles Lindbergh took off seeking to be the first to cross the Atlantic in an airplane. That same evening a packed house of 6,200 watched the footage and heard the sounds of the takeoff. The crowd gave the film a 10-minute standing ovation.

After Fox gave the green light, the studio rushed to build sound cameras, usually in enclosures to cloak the sound of their gears. The first Fox feature film with sound was *What Price Glory?* which was presented with a recorded symphonic score in November 1926. On October

28, 1927, the first all-sound newsreel was played at Fox's flagship theater, the Roxy, before a packed house. It provided viewers with the sights and sounds of Niagara Falls and of trains whistling and shooting steam behind them. There were also scenes from a rodeo and the Army-Navy football game. The first weekly Fox Movietone talking newsreel came out on December 3, 1927, and it was such a hit that the frequency was soon increased to twice a week and then three times a week.

By early 1928 Fox's Movietone Newsreels faced competition from Pathé, Paramount, Universal, and MGM, but Fox was, for a long time after, ahead in the race to shoot newsreel pictures around the world. In Hollywood, the first sound recording system developed by Fox Film Corp. cost $25,000. Each unit had to be moved by a half-ton truck. Not long after sound arrived at the studio, Fox's general manager, Winfield R. Sheehan (a former secretary to the New York police commissioner), came back to New York on a visit and observed the smaller, less cumbersome equipment developed for newsreels. He returned to Los Angeles and told his engineers to create equipment for feature production that was even smaller and lighter. Fox again pioneered with the movie *In Old Arizona* (1929), which was photographed and recorded in the vast expanses of the western United States. It showed the sweeping beauty of the land and captured the sounds of both the actors and nature.

Soon the other studios fell into line, choosing between paying royalties to Fox for the Case patents or using the RCA Photophone variable-area soundtrack. Within one year of the triumph of *The Jazz Singer,* Warner Bros. gave up on the Vitaphone system of sound on disc and made a deal to use the Case method.

In March 1928 Fox said a quarter of all features would be made with sound. By May he raised that to 100 percent, and he moved to wire as many theaters for sound as possible. Still, Fox did not release its first all-talking feature until early 1929, and by then all of the other major companies had also switched the bulk of their output to sound movies.

The Roaring Twenties were in full steam as William Fox reinvested his profits and borrowed even more money to expand. On October 28, 1928, Fox opened Movietone City, the first studio built from the ground up for sound production. There had been soundstages built at other studios previously, but it was Fox who turned the open spaces where Tom Mix movies had been made into a modern movie factory fully equipped for the sound era. It still stands today in the Westwood area of Los Angeles as the home of 20th Century-Fox and Fox Broadcasting, parts of Rupert Murdoch's News Corp. Fox rapidly acquired more theaters in New England, New York, New Jersey, California, Wisconsin, and the Pacific Northwest. By 1930 Fox had 532 U.S. theaters and another 450 outside of the country. It was second in size only to the Paramount-Publix theater circuit.

Fox also pioneered a 70 mm wide-screen process in the late 1920s, which he called Fox Grandeur, investing $2 million of his own in it. Just two years later he had produced several films in this format, as well as in their standard 35 mm versions. These were shown only in a few major cities with theaters equipped for the process. Although reaction was quite good, the format didn't catch on as well as he had hoped. This innovation occurred at a time when theaters were making the costly conversion to sound and couldn't possibly handle a new format as well. Efforts in this area were also thwarted when the Depression hit and the Academy of Motion Picture Arts and Sciences called a moratorium on all research into new wide-screen formats, making 35 mm the standard in 1931.

But in early 1929 Fox would go on to make his boldest move of all. Marcus Loew had died in 1927 and had been replaced as chairman of Loew's and MGM by Nicholas Schenck. The Loew family put his share up for sale at the market value of $28 million. That was too rich for most others, but Fox swooped in and paid a premium for the stock. On March 3, 1929, Fox held a press conference to announce that he would merge Fox with MGM-Loew's to create the largest movie production and distribution company in the world. In addition to Loew's stock, Fox had also acquired the shares held by Schneck, Loew's treasurer David Bernstein, and the Shuberts (who owned most Broadway theaters). A press release reported that 400,000 shares had traded hands for a sum of $50 million. This takeover was bitterly opposed by MGM studio head Louis B. Mayer, who looked down on Fox as being beneath MGM's high level. Fox bought another $70 million worth of stock on the open market, using money borrowed from a Wall Street bank. He then offered Mayer a $2 million deal to stay on, but Mayer continued to fight and used his long-standing personal relationship with newly elected U.S. president Herbert Hoover to lobby for his cause. As a result, Fox was stalled first by the U.S. Justice Department, which filed suit under the antitrust law to block the merger. Shortly thereafter the stock market crashed, making the value of the stock involved far less than before. Fox might have actually overcome this major obstacle had it not been for an auto accident that kept him sidelined for weeks when he most needed to be leading the battle to save the deal.

Fox tried to sell off assets late in 1929, but his debt situation only worsened. To raise money, he had to agree, against his best judgment, to transfer controlling ownership of Fox to a new trust in which his was only one of three votes. In 1930 Fox was forced out of the company he had built and headed for fifteen years. In 1931 Fox's successors made a deal with the Justice Department to sell all of its Loew's stock. Fox's sound patents were later challenged, and in an unusual ruling, the U.S. Supreme Court said the patents were no longer valid and that they were open to all.

In 1932 Fox Theaters Corp. went bankrupt for failure to pay a $410,000 note to Chicago Title and Trust, signed by Fox. Fox finally had to declare personal bankruptcy in 1936. Amid all this turmoil, Fox was told if he paid off a federal judge in Atlantic City, he would get favorable treatment, so he gave a bagman money. The attempted payoff was discovered, and Fox was found guilty in 1941 of bribery and sentenced to a year and a day in prison. He instantly became the invisible man in Hollywood. William Fox passed away in 1952 at the age of seventy-three, no longer a part of the industry he had built.

Sound Is Behind the Creation of RKO

Radio-Keith-Orpheum (RKO) was created because of the arrival of sound. In 1928, shut out of most of the sound business by Western Electric, RCA agreed to finance the creation of a vertically integrated movie company. It came about by the merger of the Film Booking Offices, a low-budget Hollywood studio controlled by Joseph P. Kennedy (father of President John F. Kennedy), the Keith-Albee-Orpheum Theaters, and the newly created RKO Distributing Corporation. It began life with approximately 100 movie theaters. RCA Photophone was used to equip the theaters with sound.

In October 1928 all of the interests were merged to create RKO. David Sarnoff was the first president. He also ran the NBC radio network. Soon Sarnoff made a deal to supply movies to 1,000 independent exhibitors, who would also buy sound equipment from RCA at better terms than those offered by Western Electric.

RKO ended the decade as the near equal of the other major studios, with some extra assets such as access to NBC and the RCA music divisions. In 1931 RKO Distributing took over Pathé to create a second company, the short-lived RKO-Pathé, which was later merged into Radio Pictures. As the Depression deepened, RKO could not meet all the mortgage payments on its theaters, and in 1933 it was forced to go bankrupt. Around 1937, the company was renamed RKO Radio Pictures. It would take six years to exit bankruptcy, and while the studio name would live on, RKO would never be as powerful again.

German Films Influence American Filmmakers and Bring Immigrant Talent to America

Out of the ashes of World War I, a vibrant film industry came back to life in Germany during the 1920s, centered mostly in Berlin. Because it was a time of economic depression and hyperinflation in Germany, filmmakers there couldn't compete with the lush, highly produced, and often extravagant Hollywood movies flooding their market. Instead they developed their own lean, dark vision. Arising from the artistic movement of the same name, German expressionism in film brought together the finest directors, technicians, and actors who not only embraced the irrational, the surrealistic, and the chaotic aspects of their ever-changing world but also combined new and imaginative technology and filming techniques to help deepen the audience's interaction with their movies.

The directors, writers, and producers were centered at the Ufa Studio, which had been created by the postwar Weimar Republic through consolidation of Decla, Nordisk, and most other film companies in Germany. Decla's owner, Erich Pommer, had been producer of *Das Cabinet des Dr. Caligari* (*The Cabinet of Dr. Caligari*), which has been cited as the first example of German expressionism. *Caligari* was about a man who tells his friend a story concerning a demented psychologist who manipulates a sleepwalker into killing people. When the man finishes his tale, doctors declare him crazy and take him away.

Also at Ufa, F. W. Murnau directed such films as *Nosferatu* (Germany release 1922, U.S. release 1929), *Last Laugh* (Germany release 1924, U.S. release 1925), and *Faust* (released in Germany and the U.S. in 1926). In *Last Laugh,* the camera was used in such as way that it had a point of view, as if the audience could see through the eyes of the character. It powerfully evoked the psychological state of the players. The camera's new mobility allowed for movement, tracking shots, pans, tilts, and zoom shots. *Faust,* too, was full of carefully composed shots, and featured breakthrough special effects. The lighting and use of shading was especially interesting. In one memorable moment, the giant black wings of Mephisto cast a shadow over a town about to be hit by plague. In 1925 Murnau received a four-year contract from Hollywood, where he made his masterpiece *Sunrise.*

Among the other talents who worked at Ufa and then came to America were Fritz Lang, who made *Metropolis* (Germany and U.S. release 1927), and Marlene Dietrich, who performed her first speaking role, sizzling on-screen, in *The Blue Angel* (Germany release and U.S. premiere 1930).

The Cabinet of Dr. Caligari
Distributed by Goldwyn, 1921
Directed by Robert Wiene
62 minutes

American Horror and Film Noir Movies are Influenced by 1920's German Expressionism Movies

Hans Janowitz and Carl Mayer met in Germany after World War I and cooked up the story of *Caligari* based upon their bizarre personal experiences—possibly witnessing a murderer run from the scene of his crime, dealing with an autocratic military psychiatrist, and seeing a supposedly hypnotized strongman make predictions at a fair. They fused their ideas and pumped out a scenario in six weeks. They then pitched their script to producer Erich Pommer at Decla Studios, who bought their odd story on the spot. Director Fritz Lang came aboard and proposed a framing device for the start and end of the film. When Lang dropped out to finish his movie *Spiders,* new director Robert Wiene formally accepted the framing idea despite the objections of the writers. As production loomed, Pommer brought in three top designers from Berlin art circles—Hermann Warm, Walter Reimann, and Walter Rohrig—to infuse the film's sets and costumes with the aesthetics of German expressionism.

Production began in December 1919 and wrapped by February 1920. Because of little money and limited power supplies during the postwar period, the film was shot entirely on studio soundstages to reduce costs. The designers created the film's nightmarish sets with paper, cardboard, and canvas. Shadow and light patterns were painted directly on the walls, floors, and backcloths. Crooked doorways, asymmetrical window frames, and elongated furniture were constructed to establish a mood of disharmony and insanity. To enhance that mood further, Wiene had the actors covered with thick white pancake makeup and directed them to act in a stylized and dreamlike manner. While filming the actors, Wiene kept the camera stationary in a series of somewhat theatrical medium long shots to privilege the surreal compositions and bizarre sets. During the final editing of the film, however, he applied some purely cinematic devices to enhance the storytelling—a few close-ups, some iris effects, and a short animated segment.

Pommer launched a massive promotional campaign weeks before the film's release. He plastered cryptic posters over the pillars, cafés, and subways of Berlin that enigmatically read, "You Must Become Caligari." The gimmick worked—the February 26, 1920, premiere at the Berlin Marmorhaus sold out, and the film went on to pack the house for most of its initial four-week run.

Eager to exploit a hit, the Goldwyn Distributing Company purchased American rights. The April 3, 1921, American premiere at the Capitol Theatre in New York was a huge gala event complete with a live staged prologue and epilogue. The Los Angeles premiere on May 7, 1921, at Miller's Theater, was somewhat less successful. The American Legion, playing on postwar anti-German sentiments and Hollywood's fears of foreign competition, staged a protest and forced the film to be withdrawn. Despite that hitch, critics unanimously hailed the film as an important experimental work of art. Its success has grown steadily since then—it has been credited with influencing both the horror films of the 1930s and the film noirs of the 1940s. Today it is universally accepted as the original cult classic. —*Scott Mazak*

Sunrise: A Song of Two Humans

Distributed by Fox Film Corp., 1927
Directed by F. W. Murnau
94 minutes

1989 National Film Registry Selection

William Fox Invites F. W. Murnau to America to Direct Fox Film Corporation's First Feature with a Movietone Soundtrack

After the successes of *Last Laugh* and *Faust,* Murnau was a hot property. American producer William Fox offered him a blank check to make any film he wished. Murnau snapped up the deal, gathered some of his closest German collaborators, and began planning his master-piece, which came to be called *Sunrise: A Song of Two Humans.* It was about a city woman who seduces a farmer into killing his wife. At the last moment, he refuses and begs his wife's for-giveness. After almost accidentally drowning, she agrees to accept his love once again. Murnau worked closely once more with writer Carl Mayer on the scenario, this time based on Hermann Sudermann's *The Excursion to Tilsit.* With the story in place, Rochus Gliese and his assistant, Edgar G. Ulmer, began designing the sets while Charles Rosher and Karl Struss handled the cinematography. Together the team churned out extensive storyboards and sketches, planning out every detail of lighting and camera placement before Murnau headed to Hollywood.

As filming approached, the production crew erected huge sets outside the Fox lot in West-wood, including an amusement park, a huge city set, and a mile-long streetcar track with a tram that ran on an automotive chassis. Crews also constructed a rural village set on the shore of California's Lake Arrowhead. Elaborate tracks for the cameras were suspended from ceil-ings and snaked around the ground as well. Struss was so dedicated to the project that he bought his own Bell and Howell electric motor camera and used it for filming. To heighten the illusion of depth, Murnau used forced perspective—floors sloped upward as they receded, large objects were placed in the foreground, and smaller objects, dolls, and little people were arranged in the background. Other tricks included use of rear-projection screens, a crude in-camera superimposition technique, and the addition of twenty-pound lead weights in actor George O'Brien's boots to give him a plodding, doom-laden gait. Given all these excesses, the production eventually ballooned dangerously over budget. At one point it took 300 laborers two weeks to painstakingly reattach fake leaves to a replanted tree, and a rain machine delay cost another three days. Finally, when Rosher was unable to shoot the perfect sunrise after waiting in a boat on the lake every morning for a week, he simply filmed a fake prop in the studio, removing layers of gauze from the lens to create a brightening effect.

Fox slated *Sunrise* to be its first feature with a Movietone soundtrack—it had a full orchestral score, sound effects, and a few snatches of lyrics from a record. The separate picture and track negatives were then printed together to form a "married" or "composite" print.

The premiere at New York's Times Square Theater on September 23, 1927, was a huge event. Unfortunately, it was quickly overshadowed by the opening of *The Jazz Singer* shortly thereafter on October 6, when the public thronged to see the latest gimmick, a talking picture. Despite the unlucky box office timing, the film was universally hailed by critics as the crowning achievement of the silent cinema. It garnered the first and only Unique and Artistic Picture Oscar at the first Academy Awards in 1929. Since then, its reputation has only grown—in 1967, *Cahiers du Cinema* named *Sunrise* the single greatest masterwork in the history of cinema. Further proof of its vaunted status came in 1989, when the Library of Congress voted it onto its first National Film Registry. —*Scott Mazak*

U.S. INDUSTRY PRODUCTION STATISTICS, 1920s
Equivalent 2005 $s /(Unadjusted $s)

$10.6 Million ($1.0 million)
Average production cost of films featured in this chapter

$1.1 Million ($108,000)
Average production cost of all films released in 1920

Index of Top Feature Film Directors Included in This Chapter

1	King Vidor	*The Big Parade*
		The Crowd
2	Charles Chaplin	*The Kid*
		The Gold Rush
3	Fred Niblo	*Ben-Hur: A Tale of the Christ*
4	D. W. Griffith	*Way Down East*
		Orphans of the Storm
5	Raoul Walsh	*In Old Arizona*
		The Thief of Bagdad
6	Rex Ingram	*The Four Horsemen*
		of the Apocalpyse
7	Harry Beaumont	*The Broadway Melody*
8	Cecil B. DeMille	*The Ten Commandments*
9	William A. Wellman	*Wings*
10	Alan Crosland	*The Jazz Singer*

See Note to the Reader for selection criteria.

Top 5 Critically Acclaimed Lead Actors of the 1920s

Rank	Actor Name
1	Charlie Chaplin
2	Buster Keaton
3	Warner Baxter
4	George Arliss
5	Emil Jannings

Rank	Actress Name
1	Lillian Gish
2	Norma Shearer
3	Mary Pickford
4	Janet Gaynor
5	Gloria Swanson

See Note to the Reader for selection criteria.

A Sampling of Movie Star Earnings, 1926
Equivalent 2005 $s/(Unadjusted $s)

Actor	Annual Earnings	Actor	Annual Earnings
Harold Lloyd	**$16.6 Million**/($1.5 million)	Douglas Fairbanks	**$11.0 Million**/($1.0 million)
Charles Chaplin	**$13.8 Million**/($1.25 million)	Mary Pickford	**$11.0 Million**/($1.0 million)

Actors of the 1920s: Comparison of Salaries and Profit Participations
Equivalent 2005 $s/(Unadjusted $s)

Actor	Film	Year	Salary
John Gilbert	*Hollywood Revue of 1929*	1929	**$2,855,263** Flat Fee ($250,000/per film guarantee in 1928)
Ramon Novarro	*Ben Hur: A Tale of the Christ*	1925	**$111,600**/week ($10,000/week)
Al Jolson	*The Jazz Singer*	1927	**$105,226**/week ($9,375/week for 8 weeks for total $75,000)
Lillian Gish	*The Wind*	1928	**$91,368**/week ($8,000/week for MGM)
Clara Bow	*Wings*	1927	**$56,121**/week ($5,000/week in 1929)
Buster Keaton	*Hollywood Revue*	1929	**$34,263**/week ($3,000/week in 1928)
Gary Cooper	*Wings*	1927	**$1,684**/week ($150/week)
Janet Gaynor	*Sunrise: A Song of Two Humans*	1927	**$1,122**/week ($100/week in 1926)

DISTRIBUTION OVERVIEW

Distributors Change Their Business Model

After the end of World War I, the major Hollywood studios rapidly extended their theatrical distribution systems, not only across the United States but around the world. In the silent era, there was no language barrier, so European films readily played in the United States and American films played overseas. From 1925 on, the five major U.S.-based movie distribution and exhibition companies, and three smaller players, had woven a network of offices and affiliates around the globe. By the late 1920s, they made up to 50 percent of their profits outside of the United States. Hollywood movies even outsold the local fare in England, France, Italy, and Japan.

The way distributors sold movies had also evolved. In the early days, the sale of movies was by the foot. Sale practices later evolved with the growth of exchanges, which first sold and then rented prints of movies. This practice continued during the Edison Trust era. The two most common ways movies were sold were either through states rights or as a road show production. States rights involved selling the movie to various theaters, which could play it as many times as they wished. A road show engagement meant that a movie had special appeal, so individual tickets could be sold at a higher than normal admission price through a select number of theaters, where the movie could run for weeks or even months. Neither of these two models proved satisfactory as the movie industry approached the studio era, when a steady supply of high-quality movies was available and the rapid marketing and exhibition of these movies was needed to finance even more production.

Major Movie Distributors, 1920s

BIG FIVE

Fox Film Corporation	Formed in 1915 when it merged with Greater New York Film Rental Company
Metro-Goldwyn-Mayer (MGM)	Established in 1924 by combining Metro Pictures Corporation, Goldwyn Picture Corporation, and Louis B. Mayer Pictures
Paramount	Changed its corporate name in 1927 from Famous Players-Lasky to Paramount Famous Lasky Corp
RKO Radio Pictures	Founded in 1928
Warner Bros.	Incorporated in 1923. Acquires Vitagraph in 1925 and First National in 1929

LITTLE THREE

Columbia	Incorporated in 1924
United Artists	Incorporated in 1919
Universal Pictures	Incorporated in 1925

The model that came to be adopted, and which remains in use today, was first proposed by William Wadsworth Hodkinson, a Utah movie exchange operator, who was an original founder of Paramount Pictures. Hodkinson envisioned a system for nationwide distribution that would give exhibitors a steady supply of films and producers a share of the profits. In return for a 35 percent distribution fee, the distributor got exclusive rights to a fully financed picture. The distributor gave the producer a cash advance to make the movie. The producer paid for prints, advertising, and marketing. This cut down on the studios' investment and risk while increasing the number of movies available to theaters.

In the 1920s, a typical movie's first run began in a handful of better downtown theaters, most of which were owned by a big company and were branded Paramount, Fox, Warner, MGM, or RKO. The dominance and simplicity of the deals meant that distribution staffs could be relatively small. They weren't really selling as much as servicing a specific territory or number of client exhibitors. After the first run of a week or a month, depending on the film's popularity, that movie, and that print of that movie, moved to a second-run theater, typically in an urban neighborhood within a preestablished geographical zone. After a time, that same print moved to a third run and on down into smaller towns and rural areas, until the movie had been fully exploited. During each run, there was a designated period of time required before the film could be sent to a lower-run theater (the "Clearance"). In some markets there might have been as many as eleven or twelve runs. A print was good for about 400 plays before it had to be replaced.

The dominance of the vertically integrated oligopoly of entertainment companies meant most producers went through them for distribution and access to theaters, although there was still a robust states rights market for lower-end product. This dominance allowed the companies to control their costs, demand high fees, and engage in anticompetitive practices such as block booking (selling multiple films at one time) and blind bidding (a process that prohibited them from seeing movies in advance).

U.S. INDUSTRY DISTRIBUTION STATISTICS, 1925
Equivalent 2005 $s/(Unadjusted $s)

$16,868 Million ($500 million)
Annual U.S. box office gross revenues

579
Number of new feature films released

TECHNOLOGY SPOTLIGHT

Willis O'Brien, Innovative Special Effects Giant

The creation of the monster in *King Kong* (1933) may be his best-known work, but Willis O'Brien's influence goes much deeper. He was a major innovator in the field of stop-motion photography, and his breakthroughs would forever change the movies. As a young man O'Brien was an illustrator, sculptor, and newspaper cartoonist; he also worked as a guide at Crater Lake in Oregon, showing around paleontologists seeking signs of prehistoric life in the hope of proving that dinosaurs once roamed the area. Later, when O'Brien was personally financing a test reel to sell himself and his projects to movie producers, he turned back to what he had learned about paleontology. He created a crude three-dimensional animation of a fight between a caveman and a dinosaur that ran less than a minute and a half. The movements were jerky and some of the clay models began to melt under the lights before the film's end, but the images were stunning to viewers of the age. One impressed producer gave O'Brien a $5,000 budget to make another short. This time he created *Dinosaur and the Missing Link* (1915). It was a story about a Neanderthal couple having prewedding problems. Thomas Edison saw that short and soon hired O'Brien to make additional shorts for his company Conquest Pictures. Among the movies O'Brien made for Edison was *R.F.D. 10,000 B.C.*, about a young man in love whose letter to his sweetheart is hijacked by his romantic rival, the postman. His work with Edison led to an offer from producer Herbert Dawley to do a full-length animated feature that would become *The Ghost of Slumber Mountain* (1918). Although O'Brien created 45 minutes of movie, it was cut down by the distributors to only 16 minutes (with pieces later showing up in other films). Still it was a big hit for the time, making $100,000. Dawley tried to take credit for the animation, but key players in the industry recognized the real talent.

In 1924 O'Brien was hired to create the three-dimensional stop-motion animation for *The Lost World*. Despite the film's success, O'Brien had problems getting other movies made, even though he was full of ideas, including a film about Atlantis, a sequel to *The Lost World* (which didn't happen because of studio management changes), and his version of *Frankenstein,* which would involve mixing live action and stop-motion. O'Brien also wanted to make a movie out of *Food of the Gods,* based on a book about giants by H. G. Wells. He even had an idea for a western in which the cowboys rode dinosaurs. That project finally got made as *The Valley of the Guanji* in 1969, with visual effects by Ray Harryhausen, who had worked for and studied under O'Brien and then went on to his own fame in animation.

O'Brien's final project of the silent era was *Creation,* about the appearance of a volcanic island and a submarine crew that discovers prehistoric creatures on it. O'Brien studied gorillas in zoos and the movement of many other large animals. He went to professional wrestling matches to see how giant creatures might battle and fall. He wanted his models to be a real as possible. In late 1931, after a year of work, with a script written and many models produced, RKO production head David O. Selznick asked producer Merian C. Cooper to look at the test footage and make a recommendation. While Cooper suggested pulling the plug on *Creation,* it ultimately opened the door to the creation of *King Kong.* To save money, Cooper saw he could use some of the *Creation* footage, including scenes of triceratops, tyrannosaurs, and pteranodons. In order to get the green light for *King Kong*, Cooper and O'Brien developed a new test reel, which was presented to the studio bosses with production sketches done by O'Brien, including the famous image of the giant gorilla atop the Empire State Building holding a woman in his hand as fighter planes attack. They got the go-ahead, and the rest is history. *King Kong* opened at both the Radio City Music Hall and its sister theater, the New RKO Roxy, on the same day in 1933 and smashed all records.

O'Brien never reached those heights again, partly due to personal tragedy. In 1933 his estranged and terribly ill wife killed their two sons and then tried to kill herself. Despite that, he worked on several more films, including *Mighty Joe Young* (1949), which won RKO Productions a special effects Oscar, primarily for the work of Willis and Harryhausen. O'Brien died in Los Angeles, nearly penniless, in 1962, but his name has lived on as one of the great special effects giants of cinema.

Dinosaur vs. Great Ape Movies
All-Release Domestic Box Office 1925–2005
Equivalent 2005 $s /(Unadjusted $s) in Millions of $s

Rank	Film	Initial Release	Distributor	Director	Domestic Box Office	Production Cost	Special Effects
1	*Jurassic Park*	1993	Universal	Steven Spielberg	$552.9 ($357.1)	$94.6 ($70.0)	Oscar winner Visual Effects
2	*The Lost World: Jurassic Park*	1997	Universal	Steven Spielberg	$320.0 ($229.1)	$93.7 ($77.0)	Oscar nominee Visual Effects
3	*King Kong*	1976	Paramount	John Guillermin	$234.9 ($78.1)	$82.4 ($24.0)	Oscar winner Visual Effects
4	*King Kong*	2005	Universal	Peter Jackson	$218.1 ($218.1)	$208.0 ($208.0)	Oscar winner Visual Effects
5	*Jurassic Park*	2001	Universal	Joe Johnston	$205.2 ($181.2)	$91.5 ($83.0)	not available
6	*King Kong*	1933	RKO	Ernest B. Schoedsack, Merian C. Cooper	$93.9 ($5.2)	$10.1 ($0.7)	Willis O'Brien Visual Effects
7	*The Lost World*	1925	1st National	Harry O. Hoyt	$87.7 ($2.6)	not available	Willis O'Brien Visual Effects
8	*The Lost World*	1960	20th Century-Fox	Irwin Allen	$34.7 ($4.1)	not available	Willis O'Brien Visual Effects

MARKETING SPOTLIGHT

I wanted to make a lot of money, and so I let them play me up as a lounge lizard, a soft, handsome devil whose only sin in life was to sit around and be admired by women.
—RUDOLPH VALENTINO

The Cult of the Movie Star: Rudolph Valentino, the "Latin Lover"

No star better symbolizes the emergence of the cult of celebrity in America than Rudolph Valentino, who became the first pop icon. His name will remain synonymous with great lovers of the silver screen forever. He was born Rodolfo Alfonso Raffaello Piero Filiberto Guglielmi in Castellaneta, Italy, where his family thought of him as a failure. His uncles sent him to America to "become a man." He landed in New York City, where, after bumming around, he became a professional dancer, met ladies of high society, and even became embroiled in a notorious divorce case. To escape that notoriety, he changed his name to Rudolph Valentino and made his way west with an opera company. He appeared in several movies during the 1910s, but it was his lead role in the Metro Picture film *The Four Horseman of the Apocalypse* (1921) that made Valentino a star.

He went on to make more than a dozen other films, including a Famous Players-Lasky feature, *The Sheik,* in 1921, establishing him as a new kind of leading man. His style was quite the opposite of the all-American blond athletic look that Douglas Fairbanks had made popular at the time. He was instead, the quintessential image of the Latin Lover, the sexy tango dancer, the passionate desert sheik.

In 1923 Valentino refused to make any more movies for Famous Players-Lasky, stating that his salary of $1,500 a week was too low. He pointed out that other top stars were receiving $10,000 a week. The studio sued and got an injunction stopping Valentino from making movies anywhere else. Valentino responded by going on a national tour as a dancer, which was very lucrative. He also published a book of poems and serialized his life story in a magazine. Valentino later returned to Famous Players for $7,500 a week.

In 1925 Valentino signed a new contract with United Artists that would finally give him the measure of creative control he had long wanted. The result were two of his most memorable movies: *The Eagle* (1925), based on a story by Russian author Alexander Pushkin, and *The Son of the Sheik* (1926), a sequel to his earlier hit.

The Son of the Sheik

Distributed by United Artists, 1926
Directed by George Fitzmaurice
70 minutes

2003 National Film Registry Selection

The Sheik Movie Sequel's Success Is Heightened by Death of Its Star

Shortly after Valentino's arrival at United Artists, UA president Joseph Schenck purchased the film rights to Edith M. Hull's novel *The Sons of the Sheik,* the sequel to her earlier best-selling novel *The Sheik,* which was the basis for the 1921 hit movie of the same name starring Valentino. Valentino wasn't thrilled about playing the Sheik character again. He had compared this character to a "lounge lizard," but he realized that this was what his public wanted. The studio knew that as well. The book had focused on twin sons, but those roles were combined for the movie to help simplify the story line. Valentino was especially pleased by the idea of playing both father and son in the film. Frances Marion's first draft of the screenplay was actually a satire of the book, but director George Fitzmaurice rejected it despite thinking that it was absolutely hilarious. Although Marion had to start all over, the result was worth the extra effort.

Valentino heard about the plans for a *Sheik* sequel while in Europe and bought his own costumes before his return. His previous film for UA, *The Eagle,* had been a great success, reviving his stalled career, and his leading lady, Hungarian-born actress Vilma Banky, was to co-star with him again. Valentino had wanted to work with George Fitzmaurice for years, and now that it was a reality he was very happy. Fitzmaurice, born in Paris, was ten years older than Valentino, had an artistic background, and believed strongly in the story as the foundation of a motion picture. (He was no doubt influenced by his wife, screenwriter Ouida Bergère.) He and Valentino worked well together, and even conferred on occasion in French when discussing the fine points of the production.

Many of *The Son of the Sheik*'s desert scenes were shot near Yuma, Arizona. Big wind machines whipped the sand around to create the appearance of a desert storm. Most scenes had to be shot in the early morning or late afternoon because of the tremendous heat of the day. As was the custom at the time, music was played on the set to inspire the actors, and Valentino requested Homer Grunn's *Desert Suite.* Valentino remained in good spirits despite the hardships, but Frances Marion remembered him as being "physically worn out and at times in nagging pain." Other location shooting was done at Guadalupe, California, where DeMille's *The Ten Commandments* had been filmed.

After previews in Santa Monica and Burbank, *The Son of the Sheik* premiered at Grauman's Million Dollar Theater in Hollywood on July 8, 1926, nearly two months before its official release. In that interval, Valentino accompanied the film to Chicago and New York for presentations, where it did tremendous business. While in New York, Valentino was taken ill with severe abdominal pains. He died there on August 23, 1926, at the age of thirty-one. His death set off a frenzy of national mourning. An estimated 100,000 people tried to pay respects to Valentino in New York City. Unprepared for the unprecedented turn-out, the New York police found themselves trying to quell a near riot. The outpouring of emotion from fans made all the headlines. A second funeral was held in Los Angeles where Valentino was buried at the Hollywood Forever Cemetery, "temporarily" in a crypt with screenwriter June Mathis. The move to another crypt was never made, and he has remained there ever since.

The close connection between Valentino's death and the film has given *The Son of the Sheik* a special status. His greatest legacy was as one of the first cinematic legends to live on long after his death. This would happen again later with beloved stars Marilyn Monroe and James Dean, but it was Valentino who began this phenomenon. His very name entered our vocabulary early on and was understood instantly to mean a great lover. This association remains even today, many years after he first set moviegoers' hearts a-flutter. *—David Kiehn*

Comparison of Six 1920s MGM Films Initial Release
Equivalent 2005 $s /(Unadjusted $s) in Millions of $s

Film	Year	Genre	Domestic Box Office	Domestic Rentals	Foreign Rentals	Production Cost	Domestic Print and Ad Costs
Ben-Hur: A Tale of the Christ	1925	Silent Classic, Biblical Epic	$294.1 ($8.7)	$147.1 ($4.4)	$169.6 ($5.0)	$44.3 ($4.0)	$42.1 ($3.8)
The Broadway Melody	1929	Musical	$171.4 ($5.6)	$85.7 ($2.8)	$47.6 ($1.6)	$4.3 ($.4)	$14.8 ($1.3)
The Big Parade	1925	Silent Classic, War	$336.7 ($10.0)	$168.3 ($5.0)	$38.5 ($1.1)	$4.3 ($.4)	$8.2 ($.7)
The Hollywood Revue	1929	Musical	$103.6 ($3.4)	$46.6 ($1.5)	$27.3 ($.9)	$4.9 ($.4)	$2.9 ($.3)
Tell It to the Marines	1927	Silent Classic, War	$89.0 ($2.8)	$40.1 ($1.3)	$13.1 ($.4)	$4.9 ($.4)	$1.6 ($.1)
The Merry Widow	1925	Silent Classic, Romance	$81.0 ($2.4)	$36.5 ($1.1)	$28.7 ($.9)	$6.6 ($.6)	$1.1 ($.1)

EXHIBITION OVERVIEW

Ornate New Movie Theaters on the Rise

One legacy of this decade was certainly the magnificent movie palaces created by Loew's, Publix, Fox, Warner, and other exhibitors. They awed audiences and brought in masses of patrons. It is what made the 1920s the era of presentation cinema in America.

The business models of the theater circuits at the time were clearly based on retailing techniques used by Sears, Woolworth, and other national chains. The most efficient was Publix Theaters, owned by Famous Players-Lasky, which was also a top producer; followed by Fox, MGM-Loew's, Warner Bros., and, beginning late in the 1920s, RKO. Publix used a budgeting system to control costs and increase economies of scale. All movies were booked from a central office, where they were carefully parceled out with national advertising. If a theater anywhere in the country was off budget on even one item, the manager had to file a written report with the home office explaining the variance in detail. In order to control the use of heating and air-conditioning, Publix required local managers to record the temperature and humidity in each part of the theater, from the balcony to the orchestra, every hour throughout the day and night. The company used the data to adjust environmental systems. Before they built a theater, Publix executives conducted studies and produced elaborate charts to show patterns of traffic, population, income, and leisure time habits. Publix couldn't rely just on Paramount movies to keep its theaters running at a high capacity level, so it negotiated favorable terms from other producers and distributors. Schedules were prepared six to eight weeks in advance, and regional managers were given an opportunity to flag films that might be controversial in their area. Publix sold not just its movies but also itself. It ran national advertising campaigns such as one with the ad slogan "You don't need to know what's playing at a Publix House. It's bound to be the best show in town."

The bargaining for movies wasn't particularly intense because that was all systemized as well. The five largest players created a system of zones and clearance areas in all cities and towns across America. There was a first-run zone that had a film exclusively for a week to a month before that same celluloid print was moved to a second-run theater (keeping down the cost of prints). The Publix contract with the distributor specified the admission price. Distributors regularly demanded that exhibitors block book a group of movies in advance without seeing them first. This kept the selling costs low and managed the risk inherent in production for the major distributors, since movies were presold. It also minimized the number of first-run theaters one of the big five needed to own in order to skim off the top of the market. By the late 1920s the big five vertically integrated entertainment companies owned 15 percent of the theaters but took in half to three-quarters of the profits.

U.S. INDUSTRY DISTRIBUTION vs. EXHIBITION
Number of New Feature Films Released
vs. Average Weekly Film Theater Attendance,
1925–1929

Year	Total Number of New Films Released	Number of Films Released by Majors	Number of Films Released by Independents	Number of Theater Attendees Millions of People
1925	579	442	137	46
1926	740	477	263	50
1927	743	510	233	57
1928	834	462	372	65
1929	707	393	314	80

U.S. INDUSTRY EXHIBITION STATISTICS, 1920s
Equivalent 2005 $s /(Unadjusted $s)

$6.41 ($0.16–$0.21)
Average movie ticket price (1920–1929)

15,000
Number of U.S. screens, 1925

WAY DOWN EAST
United Artists, 1920

ALL-RELEASE EQUIVALENT 2005 $s
(Unadjusted $s) in Millions of $s

Domestic Box Office Revenues. . . . . $160.3/($4.0)
Production Cost . . . . $7.8/($0.8)
Principal Photography. . . . . not available
Spring 1920

Director . . . . D. W. Griffith
Producer . . . . D. W. Griffith
Production Company . . . . D. W. Griffith Productions
Story by. . . . . Based on the play by Lottie Blair Parker and Joseph R. Grismer
Screenplay by . . . . Anthony Paul Kelly (Scenario)
Cast . . . . Lillian Gish, Richard Barthelmess
Filming Locations . . . . . . Griffith studio in Mamaroneck, NY, on location in Vermont
Genre. . . . . Silent Classic, Romance
Format. . . . . B&W
Initial Release 9/3/1920
Rerelease. . . . . none
Running Time . . . . 145 minutes
13 reels
12,500 feet
MPAA Rating . . . . not rated

STANDING THE TEST OF TIME

ACADEMY AWARD Oscar Nominations and Wins

Predates Oscars

OSCAR TOTALS   Nominations 0   *Wins 0

AFI 100 YEARS 100 MOVIES SELECTION
2007 0   1997 0

TOP 300 FILMS POSITION . . . . none
All-Release Domestic Box Office in Equivalent 2005 $s

National Film Preservation Board Selection. . . . none

OTHER AWARDS Best Picture Wins

	Year
Golden Globes	none
New York Film Critics.	none
National Board of Review	none
Film Daily Critics	none

We all thought privately that Mr. Griffith had lost his mind.
—Lillian Gish

PLOT: Anna Moore, a country girl tricked into a phony marriage that results in the birth of a baby that dies, finds work and refuge in a nearby farmhouse, but is cast out in the midst of a blizzard when her past is discovered. She is ultimately rescued by the farmer's son.

PRODUCTION: For his first production with United Artists, D. W. Griffith chose *Way Down East,* a melodramatic stage play produced on Broadway in 1898 by William Brady. Griffith bought the film rights from Brady for $175,000, the highest price ever paid for a property up until that time. Everyone was baffled by Griffith's choice; the play seemed hopelessly outdated. Anthony Paul Kelly was hired to write a scenario, but Griffith started rehearsals before the writing was finished, and the script was delivered in the seventh week with only one more week of rehearsals to go. The farm scenes and interiors were filmed at the Griffith studio in Mamaroneck, New York, but they were routine compared to the work ahead. The biggest challenge would be filming the blizzard at the climax of the movie. Griffith wanted the real thing and was prepared to wait until he got it. On March 6, 1920, a gale whipped the shore near the studio, and Lillian Gish braved the storm while cameraman Billy Bitzer captured it all, to Griffith's delight. Gish and the company also went to White River Junction, Vermont, to film the ice floe sequence. Gish decided it would be dramatic for her hair and hand to trail in the water. Co-star Richard Barthelmess said, "Not one, but twenty times a day, for two weeks, Lillian floated down on a cake of ice, and I made my way to her, stepping from one cake to another, to rescue her." A local newspaper reported: "Once a piece bearing the prostrate girl came to a jam at the end of open water and began to go under. Onlookers cried out in alarm and a real rescue was staged by the man whose part it was, during which this girl, lying in icy water, stuck to her cake and her acting and never turned a hair." Griffith and his cast went back to the studio, but assistant Elmer Clifton and other crew members stayed, waiting for the spring breakup of ice. When that finally occurred, the double for Barthelmess refused to go out on the scanty floes, so Clifton had to take over, making his way across the swiftly moving ice while cameramen followed him. Griffith edited the film down to 14,000 feet in July and August. After being previewed twice, it was cut down further to 12,500 feet.

DISTRIBUTION: Griffith drummed up some publicity for the film by demanding a $10 ticket price for the opening night in New York City. Curiosity about how he had fashioned the old play for the big screen brought the public into the theaters. The dramatic and thrilling climax to the movie fueled the rush to the box office and made *Way Down East* the most successful of Griffith's films, after *The Birth of a Nation*. It was exhibited on a road show basis in the best theaters with twenty units going nationwide, complete with symphonic orchestras. It played in two parts with an intermission. Gish appeared in some performances reading a prologue. It also got a wide release by United Artists. —*David Kiehn*

THE KID

First National, 1921

ALL-RELEASE EQUIVALENT 2005 $s

(Unadjusted $s) in Millions of $s

Domestic Box Office Revenues . . . . **$188.5**/($5.0)
Production Cost . . . . **$5.5**/($0.5)
Principal Photography . . . . **154** days estimated
7/21/1919–7/30/1920

Director . . . . Charles Chaplin
Producer . . . . Charles Chaplin
Production Company . . . . Charles Chaplin Productions
Story and
 Screenplay by . . . . Charles Chaplin
Cast . . . . Charlie Chaplin, Jackie Coogan,
Carl Miller, Edna Purviance,
Tom Wilson
Filming Locations . . . . . . Chaplin studio on La Brea
Avenue in Los Angeles
Genre . . . . Silent Classic, Comedy
Format . . . . B&W
Initial Release 2/6/1921
Rerelease 1972
Running Time . . . . 58 minutes
6 reels
5,300 feet
MPAA Rating . . . . not rated

STANDING THE TEST OF TIME

ACADEMY AWARD Oscar Nominations and Wins

Predates Oscars

OSCAR TOTALS   Nominations 0   *Wins 0

AFI 100 YEARS 100 MOVIES SELECTION
2007 0   1997 0

TOP 300 FILMS POSITION . . . . none
All-Release Domestic Box Office in Equivalent 2005 $s

National Film Preservation Board Selection . . . . none

OTHER AWARDS Best Picture Wins

	Year
Golden Globes	none
New York Film Critics	none
National Board of Review	none
Film Daily Critics	none

This is the most amazing person I ever met in my life.

—Charles Chaplin, talking about Jackie Coogan

PLOT: A baby abandoned by his unwed mother ends up in the care of a tramp for several years until the fortunes of the mother change for the better and she is reunited with the boy.

PRODUCTION: Chaplin was making *A Day's Pleasure,* one of the short films under his contract with First National, when he happened to see six-year-old Jackie Coogan and his father, Jack, performing onstage. Chaplin was inspired to create a film called *The Waif* with the boy in the title role but was disappointed to hear Coogan had been signed by Roscoe "Fatty" Arbuckle to a contract. When Chaplin learned it was actually the father who had been hired by Arbuckle, he immediately put young Jackie under contract and stopped production on *A Day's Pleasure* to fulfill his earlier vision for *The Waif,* which was eventually released as *The Kid.* Production began July 21, 1919, shooting in continuity with scenes of Edna Purviance as an unwed woman leaving the charity hospital with a baby in her arms. The pace of production moved swiftly until October, when First National impatiently requested Chaplin's next release. Chaplin realized that *The Waif* was evolving into a feature-length film, his first, and that he'd need more time to develop it properly, so he set the film aside and went back to working on *A Day's Pleasure,* finishing it in just three weeks. Work resumed on *The Kid* by mid-November, but in January Chaplin's problems with his marriage to Mildred Harris, his first wife, distracted him again. From February through April 1920 production stopped and started as he, his wife, and their lawyers negotiated the terms of a divorce. Filming was back on track that May with Chaplin and Coogan in the flophouse scenes. Although the film's happy ending was completed by July 30, 1920, difficulties were still to come. As the divorce proceedings intensified, Chaplin feared that his wife's lawyers would try to attach the film negative to the settlement and complicate his relationship with First National, already strained by the fact that a feature was being produced in the midst of a contract calling for a series of short films. The officials at First National wanted to pay Chaplin as if he had made three two-reelers, which would have amounted to less money for Chaplin than what he had already paid out of his own pocket. Believing that there was a conspiracy against him, Chaplin arranged to have the 278,000 feet of film shot for *The Kid* packed up into twelve crates, which he took with him to Salt Lake City. There the film was secretly edited in his hotel room. In November a divorce settlement was finally reached, followed by an agreement with First National executives, who seemed surprisingly unimpressed with *The Kid* after a private screening of it. A deal was struck, however, and *The Kid* went on to become First National's most profitable film, as well as Chaplin's—until *The Gold Rush.*

DISTRIBUTION: *The Kid* opened in New York on February 6, 1921. It became a hit not only in the United States but around the world. Audiences were moved by the relationship between the Tramp and the waif. The movie made a star out of Jackie Coogan and brought him acclaim as the greatest child actor of the silent era. Critics declared Chaplin's first feature film a blend of comedy and drama, and they began calling him "an artist." —*David Kiehn*

THE FOUR HORSEMEN OF THE APOCALYPSE

Metro, 1921

ALL-RELEASE EQUIVALENT 2005 $s

(Unadjusted $s) in Millions of $s

Domestic Box Office Revenues.........**$188.5**/($5.0)
Production Cost ....**$8.7**/($0.8)
Principal Photography...........**120** days estimated
7/19/1920–12/8/1920

Director	Rex Ingram
Producer	Richard Rowland
Production Company. . . .	Metro Pictures Corp.
Story by.	Based on the novel by Vincente Blasco Ibanez
Screenplay by	June Mathis
Cast	Rudolph Valentino, Alice Terry
Filming Locations	On location in and around Los Angeles, CA
Genre.	Silent Classic, War
Format.	B&W
Initial Release	3/6/1921 premiere (New York)
Rerelease.	none
Running Time	134 minutes 11 reels
MPAA Rating	not rated

STANDING THE TEST OF TIME

ACADEMY AWARD Oscar Nominations and Wins

Predates Oscars

OSCAR TOTALS   Nominations 0   *Wins 0

AFI 100 YEARS 100 MOVIES SELECTION
2007 0   1997 0

TOP 300 FILMS POSITION . . . . .none
All-Release Domestic Box Office in Equivalent 2005 $s

National Film Preservation Board Selection. . . . 1995

OTHER AWARDS Best Picture Wins

	Year
Golden Globes	none
New York Film Critics.	none
National Board of Review	none
Film Daily Critics	none

*The Four Horsemen of the Apocalypse is a living, breathing answer to those
who still refuse to take motion pictures seriously.*

—Robert Sherwood, *Life*, 1921

PLOT: Two branches of an Argentine family move to Europe, one side to France, the other to Germany. Both sides come into conflict during World War I.

PRODUCTION: *The Four Horsemen of the Apocalypse,* a novel by Vicente Blasco Ibáñez set amid the horrors of World War I, was a literary success when Richard Rowland, the president of Metro Pictures, bought the film rights to it for $20,000 against 10 percent of the gross. Despite the book's outstanding sales, the studio staff thought Rowland had made a mistake in buying a property they believed to be unfilmable. Rowland nevertheless pressed forward, assigning his most trusted studio writer, June Mathis, to get the story in shape for filming. Mathis became the driving force behind the scene, insisting on putting Rex Ingram, a modestly successful director, in charge of the film and hiring a largely unknown actor at the time, Rudolph Valentino, for the leading role. Mathis then worked with Ingram to guide Valentino's performance. Filming began on July 19, 1920. The old Gilmore Ranch in Hollywood was used for the South American scenes. The famous tango scene in the film, not part of the novel, was rehearsed for three days. Because of Valentino's experience as a dancer, Ingram saw this as a special moment in the movie and custom-fit the scene to Valentino's abilities. The castle and European village sets were constructed in the hills behind Griffith Park, where part of the Warner Bros. studio now stands. During the battle scenes in the village, fourteen cameras were used to capture the action. For the destruction of the village, an elaborate telephone switchboard system was used with lines running to more than a hundred points. On a signal, a roof would cave in with a burst of flame, or a shop storefront would tumble into the street. Although the battle scenes were an impressive part of the film, Ingram wisely felt the most important moments were the intimate scenes between Valentino and Alice Terry, his love interest, during the prelude to the war in France. To Ingram, who was a trained artist, attention to detail was all-encompassing, from the composition of the set to the close-ups of the lovers, and he would sketch out shot angles before filming them. John Seitz, his first cameraman, knew just what Ingram wanted after having worked with him on two prior pictures (Seitz would shoot nine of Ingram's remaining twelve films). If something didn't work in the editing, Ingram would reshoot until he was satisfied. Editing was completed by the end of December.

DISTRIBUTION: When the film opened at the Lyric Theater in New York on March 6, 1921, it was an immediate success. Rex Ingram was acclaimed as being among the first rank of his profession. Rudolph Valentino was a sensation. This film made his career. Metro immediately realized it had a hit on its hands, and Richard Rowland, on a trip to Europe, went about renegotiating his deal with the book's author. Blasco settled for a total sum of $190,000 for the story rights. When Rowland returned to New York, the worldwide rentals for *The Four Horseman* revealed that Metro would have owed Blasco $210,000 already. By the end of 1925 the figure would have climbed to $400,000. —*David Kiehn*

ORPHANS OF THE STORM
United Artists, 1922

ALL-RELEASE EQUIVALENT 2005 $s
(Unadjusted $s) in Millions of $s

Domestic Box Office Revenues......... **$75.4**/($2.0)
Production Cost .... **$10.4**/($1.0)
Principal Photography......... **2** months estimated
June 1921–November 1921

Director . . . . D. W. Griffith

Producer . . . . D. W. Griffith

Production Company . . . . D. W. Griffith Productions

Story by . . . . Based on the play *The Two Orphans* by Adolph D. Ennery

Screenplay by . . . . Marquis de Trolignac (Scenario)

Cast . . . . Lillian Gish, Dorothy Gish

Filming Locations . . . . . . Griffith's Mamaroneck studio in New York

Genre . . . . Silent Classic, Drama

Format . . . . B&W

Initial Release . . . . 12/28/1921 world premiere; 1/3/1922 roadshow (New York) at $2/top price; 4/30/1922 general release

Rerelease . . . . none

Running Time . . . . 150 minutes (with intermission) 12 or 14 reels 13,500 feet

MPAA Rating . . . . not rated

STANDING THE TEST OF TIME

ACADEMY AWARD Oscar Nominations and Wins

Predates Oscars

OSCAR TOTALS   Nominations 0   *Wins 0

AFI 100 YEARS 100 MOVIES SELECTION
2007 0   1997 0

TOP 300 FILMS POSITION . . . . .none
All-Release Domestic Box Office in Equivalent 2005 $s

National Film Preservation Board Selection . . . .none

OTHER AWARDS Best Picture Wins

	Year
Golden Globes	none
New York Film Critics	none
National Board of Review	none
Film Daily Critics	none

He [Griffith] was the hardest-working man I have ever known. During the years I worked for him, he spent sixteen hours a day and sometimes more on the job.

—Lillian Gish

PLOT: Two sisters arrive in Paris seeking a cure for the younger woman's blindness, but they are separated and subjected to abuse by their captors as the city is beset by revolution and mob rule.

PRODUCTION: After *Way Down East,* D. W. Griffith and Lillian Gish pursued separate projects. Following the failure of *Dream Street* (1921), Griffith became interested in making a film based on Goethe's *Faust* and asked Gish to come back to work on it. She had misgivings about it and instead suggested a film based on the play *The Two Orphans,* a melodrama first produced in 1882. After seeing a performance of it in New York together, Griffith bought the rights in May 1921 from Kate Claxton for $10,000. However, the copyright had expired and Claxton did not control the French original. Griffith widened the scope by setting it in Paris during the French Revolution and using elements from the Charles Dickens novel *A Tale of Two Cities.* Sets that replicated the royal palace, Notre Dame cathedral, the Bastille, the grand salon of Versailles, and the cobblestone streets of Paris were built on nearly fourteen acres of Griffith's Mamaroneck, New York, studio. That summer, Griffith also worked on getting money to produce the film. He finally secured a loan from the Central Union Trust Company for $340,000 against the film negatives and future receipts from *Way Down East, Dream Street,* and *Orphans of the Storm.* It was to be a deadly blow to the future of his studio. Making a period piece taxed the budget tremendously, but Griffith was creative. He shot the big mob scene at the guillotine with hundreds of extras on a Sunday so local residents could participate. They were given a box lunch and $1.25 for the day. They were thrilled. Filming went quickly, due as much to the weather as the budget. Griffith was determined to finish his outdoor scenes before winter and even took out an insurance policy to protect him if it snowed before November 20, the scheduled date of completion. Weather was also a factor when he shot the big mob scene. In those days of slow-speed film the maximum amount of sunlight was necessary to get the correct exposure. On that day the sky was overcast, but they couldn't afford to postpone. Griffith made his November deadline, but he still had to finish editing the film by Christmas. There was no time to reshoot the mob sequence. It had to be used as it was in the final cut.

DISTRIBUTION: The crowds were enthusiastic about the film, and many critics gave it rave reviews after its premiere in Boston on December 28, 1921, but it wasn't a big box office hit. In addition, expenses associated with presenting the film as a road show event, often with live appearances by the Gish sisters, were high. Despite how much money the picture generated, it still wasn't enough to keep Griffith's studio afloat. Griffith also had to contend with competing versions of the story, including an Italian production and another from Germany. He bought the German film to keep it off the market but couldn't stop the Italian release. Foreign rights were also a problem, as they were owned by William Fox, and Griffith had to pay Fox $85,000 to show the film in Europe. —*David Kiehn*

THE HUNCHBACK OF NOTRE DAME

Universal, 1923

ALL-RELEASE EQUIVALENT 2005 $s

(Unadjusted $s) in Millions of $s

Domestic Box Office Revenues. . . . . **$106.8**/($3.0)
Production Cost . . . . **$14.3**/($1.3)
Principal Photography. . . . .**146** days estimated
12/16/1922–6/3/1923

Director . . . . Wallace Worsley
Producer . . . . Carl Laemmle
Production Company. . . . Universal Pictures
Story by. . . . . Based on the novel by
Victor Hugo
Screenplay by . . . . Adaptation by Perley Poore
Sheehan, written by
Edward T. Lowe Jr.
Cast . . . . Lon Chaney, Ernest Torrence,
Patsy Ruth Miller
Filming Locations . . . . . . 100 percent in studio at
Universal Studios, CA
Genre. . . . . Silent Classic, Comedy
Format. . . . . B&W with color tinting
Initial Release . . . . 8/30/1923 premiere Carnegie
Hall (New York); 9/2/1923
Astor (New York); 9/6/1923
general release
Rerelease. . . . . none
Running Time . . . . 133 minutes
12 reels
12,000 feet
MPAA Rating . . . . not rated

STANDING THE TEST OF TIME

ACADEMY AWARD Oscar Nominations and Wins

Predates Oscars

OSCAR TOTALS   Nominations 0   *Wins 0

AFI 100 YEARS 100 MOVIES SELECTION
2007 0   1997 0

TOP 300 FILMS POSITION . . . . .none
All-Release Domestic Box Office in Equivalent 2005 $s

National Film Preservation Board Selection. . . .none

OTHER AWARDS Best Picture Wins

	Year
Golden Globes	none
New York Film Critics.	none
National Board of Review	none
Film Daily Critics	none

Well, it is the hardest part I ever played, that's all.

—Lon Chaney

PLOT: Quasimodo, the hunchbacked bell-ringer at the Cathedral of Notre Dame, foils a plot by the evil Jehan to possess the Gypsy girl Esmeralda, but does so at the cost of his life.

PRODUCTION: From the very start, Universal was most ambitious in its plans to adapt Victor Hugo's 1831 novel to the screen. The centerpiece of the film was a detailed, full-size reproduction of the Notre Dame cathedral with surrounding shops, houses, and cobblestone streets. These sets, which cost roughly $500,000 to build and decorate, covered 19 acres at Universal City. The only cost concession made was the decision not to build any higher than the tall arch over the cathedral's central entrance. A hanging miniature would be used for the top portion of the cathedral in long shots. To humanize the spectacle, Lon Chaney was hired to portray the one-eyed hunchback Quasimodo. Chaney had come a long way from his start as an extra at Universal in 1913 and by then was commanding $2,500 a week. When filming began on December 16, 1922, cameraman Robert Newhard, ASC, and lighting effects expert Harry D. Brown had solved the challenge of illuminating the expansive exterior sets with enough light for a proper exposure on the slow film used in those days. It required more than 450 light fixtures, including 52 sun arcs, of which there were only 56 in all of Hollywood. According to chief gaffer Earl Miller, "We needed every one for our night shots, and Universal arranged to rent all but one. Every night for seven long weeks all the sets in other studios were stripped of 24-inch sun arcs. They were loaded on trucks and hauled to Universal. We used them until 5 a.m., but had to return them to the proper studio and have them set up and ready to burn by 8 a.m." During the most elaborate of these setups, twenty-six cameras were used. It was grueling work, but Lon Chaney handled more than his fair share. He wore a twenty-pound plaster hump on his back and a leather harness that prevented him from standing upright. It took him three hours to apply his makeup, but, as he said to reporter Grace Kingsley, "the thing I dread most of all is not the putting on of the makeup, not even the wearing it, but the taking it off. See all the hair gone from my eyebrows? Pulled it out taking off my false eyebrows. And my eyelid is all burned from the application of strong glue. Also I'm sure I'm permanently warped about the shoulders from carrying that hump on my back." While the back pain was only temporary, the strain he endured in one eye from covering the other for six months of shooting was not; Chaney wore glasses for the rest of his life.

DISTRIBUTION: The film premiered at Carnegie Hall on August 30, 1923. Regular release began September 6. Chaney was praised across the board for his role, including a review in *Photoplay* that stated: "His performance transcends anything he has ever done, both in his makeup and in his spiritual realization of the character." In terms of revenue, *The Hunchback of Notre Dame* was one of the top films, after *The Covered Wagon* and *The Ten Commandments,* in 1923. —*David Kiehn*

THE TEN COMMANDMENTS
Paramount, 1923

ALL-RELEASE EQUIVALENT 2005 $s
(Unadjusted $s) in Millions of $s

Domestic Box Office Revenues . . . . **$153.1**/($4.3)
Production Cost . . . . **$16.9**/($1.5)
Principal Photography . . . . **81** days estimated
5/21/1923–8/16/1923

Director . . . . Cecil B. DeMille
Producer . . . . Adolph Zukor, Jesse L. Lasky
Production Company . . . . Famous Players-Lasky
Story by . . . . Jeanie Macpherson
Screenplay by . . . . Jeanie Macpherson (Scenario)
Cast . . . . cast in 2 parts; no stars
Filming Locations . . . . . . Paramount Studios, Hollywood,
CA; location shooting around
Santa Barbara and San
Francisco, CA
Genre . . . . Silent Classic, Biblical Epic
Format . . . . B&W with color tints and tones
and two-color Technicolor
sequences
Initial Release . . . . 12/4/1923 world premiere;
12/22/1923 (New York) at $2 for
full evening performance
Rerelease . . . . none
Running Time . . . . 136 minutes (at 20 fps)
14 reels
11,756 feet
MPAA Rating . . . . not rated

STANDING THE TEST OF TIME

ACADEMY AWARD Oscar Nominations and Wins

Predates Oscars

OSCAR TOTALS   Nominations 0   *Wins 0

AFI 100 YEARS 100 MOVIES SELECTION
2007 0   1997 0

TOP 300 FILMS POSITION . . . . none
All-Release Domestic Box Office In Equivalent 2005 $s

National Film Preservation Board Selection . . . . none

OTHER AWARDS Best Picture Wins

	Year
Golden Globes	none
New York Film Critics	none
National Board of Review	none
Film Daily Critics	1923

Although twenty-four hours have passed since I saw Ten Commandments *last night, I am still under the spell of the greatest motion picture that has ever been produced since very beginning of the feature photoplay."*
—Jesse L. Lasky to Adolph Zukor, October 1923

PLOT: In a prologue, based on the Book of Exodus in the Bible, Moses leads his tribe out of Egypt. In modern-day San Francisco, two brothers lead contrasting lives, one breaking all of the commandments with tragic results.

PRODUCTION: After disappointing results from *Adam's Rib* (1923), Cecil B. DeMille's previous film, DeMille decided that the idea for his next movie should come from the public, through a contest. First prize was $1,000. Thousands of letters poured into the studio. A lubricating oil manufacturing man from Lansing, Michigan, provided the theme DeMille would ultimately use at the beginning of his one-page story, "You cannot break the Ten Commandments—they will break you." Seven other entries suggested the Ten Commandments as the subject matter without providing a more specific idea for the plot, but DeMille decided to award each of them $1,000 because they had all had given him the title of the film: *The Ten Commandments*. Jeanie MacPherson, who began writing scenarios for DeMille in 1915 and continued with him until her death in 1946, wrote the treatment and screenplay in March and April 1923. Famous Players-Lasky assigned a budget of $750,000 for the production, and sets were built. Filming began with the prologue scenes on May 21, 1923, at the Guadalupe sand dunes in northern Santa Barbara County near Santa Maria, with impressive sets designed by Paul Iribe and Francis McComas. Everything was created on a massive scale, including sphinxes for the gate to the pharaoh's city. But the statues almost didn't arrive—during transport from Los Angeles they encountered a low bridge, and their heads had to be removed to clear passage and reattached before continuing on to the location. The prologue footage was shot in both black and white and color, after the fledgling Technicolor Motion Picture Corporation offered to let DeMille use their relatively new two-color process without risk. The fee for these services was to be paid only if he liked the results. DeMille approved the material and it was used in the final cut, along with tinted and toned scenes, and even some special stencil color footage. Thousands of extras were hired for the Exodus sequence, but with the changing spring weather of coastal fog and clouds slowing production, the costs mounted to more than $1 million. Paramount executives, particularly president Adolph Zukor, became uneasy. DeMille countered their efforts to curb expenses with an offer to buy the film himself for $1 million and was able to find investors to back him. Zukor was ready to sell, but another executive, Frank Garbutt, cautioned him, "Don't sell what you haven't seen." That ended the conflict, and production continued through to completion, with the modern story creating few difficulties. One further challenge to the production was in creating the parting waters of the Red Sea during the Exodus. That was accomplished by special effects cameraman Roy Pomeroy, combining live action and miniatures to produce a scene that is still impressive today.

DISTRIBUTION: The film's first public showing was, appropriately, at the Egyptian Theater in Hollywood on December 4, 1923. The movie's epic quality encouraged its exhibition on a road show basis. The movie did very well, fueled by praise from critics and the public, in addition to Christians who applauded DeMille's faithful rendering of the King James version of the Bible. *The Ten Commandments* became one of the biggest hits of the year, with $4.2 million in worldwide rentals against a final cost of $1.5 million. —*David Kiehn*

GREED

Metro-Goldwyn, 1924

ALL-RELEASE EQUIVALENT 2005 $s

(Unadjusted $s) in Millions of $s

Domestic Box Office Revenues . . . . **$21.6**/($0.6)
Production Cost . . . . **$6.3**/($0.6)
Principal Photography . . . . **198** days estimated
3/14/1923–10/6/1923

Rerelease . . . . none
Running Time . . . . 114 minutes
11 reels
10,607 feet
MPAA Rating . . . . not rated

Director . . . . Erich von Stroheim
Producer . . . . Louis B. Mayer
Production Company . . . . Metro-Goldwyn Pictures Corp.
Story by . . . . Based on the 1899 novel
McTeague by Frank Norris
Screenplay by . . . . Eric von Stroehim (Scenario and
adaptation by); June Mathis
(Titles)
Cast . . . . Gibon Gowland, ZaSu Pitts,
Jean Hershel, Chester Conklin,
Sylvia Ashton, Hughie Mack
Filming Locations . . . . . . In studio and at various
location around San Francisco
and Southern California
Genre . . . . Silent Classic, Comedy
Format . . . . B&W with color tints and tones
and Handschlegl stencil color
effects
Initial Release . . . . 12/4/1924 Cosmopolitan
Theater (New York); 1/26/1925
general release

STANDING THE TEST OF TIME

ACADEMY AWARD Oscar Nominations and Wins

Predates Oscars

OSCAR TOTALS   Nominations 0   *Wins 0

AFI 100 YEARS 100 MOVIES SELECTION
2007 0   1997 0

TOP 300 FILMS POSITION . . . . none
All-Release Domestic Box Office in Equivalent 2005 $s

National Film Preservation Board Selection 1991

OTHER AWARDS Best Picture Wins

	Year
Golden Globes	none
New York Film Critics	none
National Board of Review	none
Film Daily Critics	none

The screen must be life's mirror, part of the time, anyway. It is possible to tell a great story in motion pictures in such a way that the spectator forgets he is looking at beauteous little Gertie Gefelta, the producer's pet, and discovers himself intensely interested, just as if he were looking out a window at life itself.

—Erich von Stroheim

PLOT: A quack dentist bests his friend for the hand of a patient. When she wins a lottery, she becomes obsessed with the money. Her boyfriend kills her in a rage and later dies in the desert.

PRODUCTION: Erich von Stroheim gained attention as an actor playing "the hated Hun" in numerous films during World War I. He was an assistant director to D. W. Griffith and others. In 1918 he persuaded Universal Pictures head Carl Laemmle to allow him to direct and star in a film based on his own screenplay. The resulting film, *Blind Husbands,* proved to be a hit, and Stroheim followed it with *The Devil's Pass Key* (1919) and *Foolish Wives* (1922). *Foolish Wives* went over schedule and over budget, so much so that Universal ballyhooed the excessive cost as the first "million-dollar picture." However, on his next project, *Merry-Go-Round,* Stroheim ignored the budget and was fired by Carl Laemmle's young secretary, Irving Thalberg. Stroheim landed on his feet, signing a three-picture deal with the Goldwyn Company that paid him a $30,000 advance against a 25 percent share of the profits for each picture. As stipulated in the contract, each film was to cost no more than $175,000. Excess costs would be deducted from Stroheim's profit share. Each film also had to be between 4,500 and 8,500 feet in length. An edited version had to be delivered within fourteen weeks of its start date, and "none of the said pictures shall be of a morbid, gruesome or offensive character." Although it was announced that Stroheim's first Goldwyn production would be *The Merry Widow,* the project was postponed in favor of an adaptation of Frank Norris's naturalistic novel, *McTeague,* which had previously been filmed under the title *Life's Whirlpool* (Brady Picture Plays-World, 1916) by director Barry O'Neil. After Stroheim's adaptation of the novel was budgeted, it was determined that the cost would exceed $175,000, and the Goldwyn Company agreed to increase the release length to 12,000 feet and raise the budget to $347,000. However, Stroheim had a grander vision. His first assembly, shown privately in January 1924, was more than 40,000 feet and took over 9 hours to screen. His final director's cut was nearly 22,000 feet in length. He proposed releasing the film in two parts. In April 1924 the Goldwyn Company was merged with Metro Pictures (bought by theater chain owner Marcus Loew in 1919), creating Metro-Goldwyn—soon to become Metro-Goldwyn-Mayer. With the merger, Stroheim's nemesis Irving Thalberg returned as production head, with Louis B. Mayer as the new studio head. The studio demanded additional cuts, and Stroheim handed the film over to director Rex Ingram, who trimmed it to 18,000 feet. But Thalberg was not satisfied and had the film cut to eleven reels for release.

DISTRIBUTION: Although it has long been considered a classic of world cinema, even in its truncated eleven-reel version, *Greed* made a resounding thud at the box office on its initial release. No additional film footage has survived, but many critics have lamented the loss of Stroheim's longer version and several efforts have been made to re-create it. —*Robert S. Birchard*

THE THIEF OF BAGDAD

United Artists, 1925

ALL-RELEASE EQUIVALENT 2005 $s

(Unadjusted $s) in Millions of $s

Domestic Box Office Revenues . . . . **$106.8**/($3.0)
Production Cost . . . . **$20.6**/($1.8)
Principal Photography . . . . **8** months estimated

Director	Raoul Walsh
Producer	Douglas Fairbanks
Production Company	Douglas Fairbanks Pictures
Story by	Elton Thomas
Screenplay by	Lotta Woods
Cast	Douglas Fairbanks, Snitz Edwards, Charles Belcher
Filming Locations	Pickford-Fairbanks studio at 7200 Santa Monica Blvd., Hollywood, CA
Genre	Silent Classic, Adventure
Format	B&W with color tinting
Initial Release	3/18/1924 special presentation at the Liberty (New York) twice daily at $2.20 top; 1/1/1925 general release
Rerelease	none
Running Time	150 minutes 12 reels 11,230 feet
MPAA Rating	not rated

STANDING THE TEST OF TIME

ACADEMY AWARD Oscar Nominations and Wins

Predates Oscars

OSCAR TOTALS Nominations 0 *Wins 0

AFI 100 YEARS 100 MOVIES SELECTION
2007 0   1997 0

TOP 300 FILMS POSITION . . . . .none
All-Release Domestic Box Office in Equivalent 2005 $s

National Film Preservation Board Selection 1996

OTHER AWARDS Best Picture Wins

	Year
Golden Globes	none
New York Film Critics	none
National Board of Review	none
Film Daily Critics	none

These things have to be done properly, or not at all.

—Douglas Fairbanks, countering concerns about the cost of the production

PLOT: The thief of Bagdad goes on a spiritual quest to earn his happiness by finding a magic chest, giving him the power to defeat an invading Mongol army and win the hand of the princess he loves.

PRODUCTION: Douglas Fairbanks, now a producer as well as an actor, had been reluctant at first to attempt a picture on the grand scale of *Robin Hood* (1922), but with that film's undisputed success anything became possible. When he decided to produce a pirate movie, his staff began the research, writing, costume designs, and production schedule for the film. But he soon swept that project aside to film a fantasy of the Arabian Nights, inspired by the fifteenth-century tales of *A Thousand and One Nights*. He hired Dr. Arthur Woods to be the research director, William Cameron Menzies to design the massive sets, Mitchell Leisen to design the costumes, and Raoul Walsh to direct. Fairbanks didn't sit down to study all of the creative material generated, but he managed to understand the essence of what it was all about and fashion a story that Lotta Woods turned into a scenario. From there the staff produced a storyboard that was tacked to the office walls so the production could be charted and scheduled. When the massive sets were built Fairbanks thought they didn't have the ephemeral quality he was looking for; they seemed all too real. To solve the problem, four acres of cement were poured in the central plaza of the main structure, and the floor was painted black, then it was polished to a high gloss. The city's reflection in this wide expanse appeared dreamlike and set the tone for the look and spirit of the film. Eight months were spent making *The Thief of Bagdad*. It was a complicated venture, with huge sets, large crowds, and special effects. Fairbanks performed his stunts with amazing energy that must have been infectious on the set. He eluded his enemies by jumping from one gigantic urn to another. He climbed up and down ropes that sprang into the air, unsupported at the top. He fought giant monsters, rode a winged horse, and sped through the clouds on a magic carpet. He became invisible with the wave of a cloak and created mischief with the Mongols and palace guards. He made an army appear from puffs of smoke. The challenges for the cameraman and technical crew to make it all appear realistic were formidable. Fairbanks was able to leap from urn to urn with the aid of trampolines placed inside the containers, although it still took hours of practice to perform the stunt. Coy Watson, a specialist in using piano wire to suspend people and objects in the air, used this skill to execute the rope trick, manipulate the giant monsters, flap the wings of the horse galloping on a treadmill, and lift the magic carpet into the air.

DISTRIBUTION: *The Thief of Bagdad* premiered in New York on March 18, 1924, but didn't go into general release until January 1, 1925. During that interval it was shown at selected theaters in big cities for only two performances a day. Each program began with an elaborate stage performance that would set the mood. Thousands of people traveled from farms and small towns to see the film. The *New York Herald Tribune* declared: "It would be foolish to compare *The Thief of Bagdad* with any other production, for it is totally unlike anything that ever has been done." —*David Kiehn*

THE LOST WORLD
First National, 1925

ALL-RELEASE EQUIVALENT 2005 $s
(Unadjusted $s) in Millions of $s

Domestic Box Office Revenues . . . . **$87.7/**($2.6)
Production Cost . . . . not available
Principal Photography . . . .**80** days estimated
June 1924–Sept. 1924

Director . . . . Harry O. Hoyt under the
supervision of Earl Hudson

Producer . . . . Watterson R. Rothacker by
arrangement with Earl Hudson

Production Company . . . . First National Pictures

Story by . . . . Adapted from the novel by
Sir Arthur Conan Doyle

Screenplay by . . . . Marion Fairfax (Scenario)

Cast . . . . Bessie Love, Lloyd Hughes,
Lewis Stone, Wallace Beery

Filming Locations . . . . . . Brunton Studios, Hollywood, CA
(now part of Paramount
Studios on Melrose Ave.)

Genre . . . . Silent Classic, Sci-Fi

Format . . . . B&W, hand colored and tinted

Initial Release . . . . 2/2/1925 premiere (New York);
6/22/1925 general release

Rerelease . . . . none

Running Time . . . . 104 minutes
10 reels
9,700 feet

MPAA Rating . . . . not rated

STANDING THE TEST OF TIME

ACADEMY AWARD Oscar Nominations and Wins

Predates Oscars

OSCAR TOTALS   Nominations 0   *Wins 0

AFI 100 YEARS 100 MOVIES SELECTION
2007 0   1997 0

TOP 300 FILMS POSITION . . . . none
All-Release Domestic Box Office in Equivalent 2005 $s

National Film Preservation Board Selection 1998

OTHER AWARDS Best Picture Wins

	Year
Golden Globes	none
New York Film Critics	none
National Board of Review	none
Film Daily Critics	none

"Spiritist Mystifies World-Famed Magicians with Pictures of Prehistoric Beasts."
—*New York Times* headline reporting Sir Arthur Conan Doyle's presentation
to an American Society of Magicians dinner, 1922

PLOT: Professor Challenger leads an expedition to the Amazon in South America searching for evidence of prehistoric creatures to bring back to London, and also hoping to rescue a fellow explorer left behind on his last journey.

PRODUCTION: London film producer J. G. Wainwright bought an option on Sir Arthur Conan Doyle's novel *The Lost World* in 1919, but plans to bring the book to the screen remained in limbo for three years while how to create some of the story's prehistoric life forms and adventures was deliberated. This changed when Chicago producer Watterson Rothacker secured the rights. Rothacker had something Wainwright lacked: Willis O'Brien, who had been making stop-motion, model-animated films since 1919. When Conan Doyle showed a demonstration film O'Brien made to the American Society of Magicians, the demo caused an absolute sensation. Doyle let the audience believe that the events and creatures in the movie were real. He didn't disclose until the next day that they were actually created through movie magic. But by then, it was too late—news of the "Lost World" was on the front page of the *New York Times*, creating a burst of prerelease interest. It took time for the courts to settle various rights issues centered around the story and the animation technology, but Rothacker was able to sign an agreement on December 14, 1923, with First National to finance and distribute the film. Because of O'Brien's filmic wizardry, Ralph Hammeras was lured away from his own special effects company to produce the glass paintings and miniature sets, and twenty-year-old artist Marcel Delgado was hired to construct the forty-nine articulated dinosaur models used in the film so O'Brien could concentrate on the animation itself. Typically O'Brien would generate 20 or 30 seconds of usable footage a day using 18-inch models with metal skeletons and rubber skins he created. This was the first film in which actors had to react to things that would be added later, in postproduction. A major budget item was the rental of live animals for jungle scenes. There was a python, an alligator, spiders, termites, a bear cub, and a ring-tailed monkey. 2,000 extras, 200 automobiles, and six large buses that rolled along the street scene of London were employed. The jungle scenes included a river that was actually an open flowing sewer in Los Angeles and trees and foliage provided by the prop department. The film is most remembered for O'Brien's stop-motion animation of the dinosaurs. After each miniature set was assembled and the camera positioned, O'Brien was left alone to shoot the scene. O'Brien did all of the animating himself, except for a stampede with all forty-nine dinosaurs in motion on a 75-by-150-foot stage. It took a year of steady work at the Brunton Studio in Los Angeles for O'Brien to double-expose the animated shots with the live-action footage already filmed on the back lot by cinematographer Arthur Edeson, as well as shoot the many other intricate scenes of dinosaurs interacting. Further work was done by O'Brien and his crew at the old Biograph Studio in New York before the picture was completed.

DISTRIBUTION: *The Lost World* opened at the Astor Theater in New York on February 2, 1925, showing twice a day, but it didn't go into general release until June 22, 1925. The reason for the exclusive showing in New York was to maximize the word-of-mouth business: here was a unique film that shouldn't be missed. The public responded, and critics too were amazed by the lifelike actions of the monsters on-screen. —*David Kiehn*

THE GOLD RUSH
United Artists, 1925

ALL-RELEASE EQUIVALENT 2005 $s
(Unadjusted $s) in Millions of $s

Domestic Box Office Revenues . . . . **$168.7**/($5.0)
Production Cost . . . . **$10.3**/($1.0)
Principal Photography . . . . **170** days shooting;
235 days idle
2/8/1924–5/21/1925

Director . . . . Charles Chaplin
Producer . . . . Charles Chaplin
Production Company . . . . Charles Chaplin Production
Story by . . . . Based on the play *The Lucky Strike* by Charles Chaplin
Screenplay by . . . . Charles Chaplin
Cast . . . . Charlie Chaplin, Mack Swain, Tom Murray, Malcolm Waite, Henry Bergman, Georgia Hale
Filming Locations . . . . . . Chaplin studio on La Brea, Ave. Hollywood, CA; on location in Chatsworth, Sacramento, Los Angeles, Stockton, and Truckee, CA
Genre . . . . Silent Classic, Comedy
Format . . . . B&W
Initial Release . . . . 6/26/1925 premiere (Hollywood, CA); 8/16/1925 general release
Rerelease . . . . 1942 sound reissue (revenue not included above)
Running Time . . . . 72 or 74 minutes
9 or 10 reels
8,498, 8,555, or 9,760 feet
MPAA Rating . . . . not rated

STANDING THE TEST OF TIME

ACADEMY AWARD Oscar Nominations and Wins

Music (Music Score of a Dramatic or Comedy Picture): Max Terr

Sound Recording: RCA Sound, James Fields, Sound Director

Note: Awards for 1942 sound re-issue

OSCAR TOTALS Nominations **2** *Wins **0**

AFI 100 YEARS 100 MOVIES SELECTION
2007 . . . #58   1997 . . . #74

TOP 300 FILMS POSITION . . . . .none
All-Release Domestic Box Office in Equivalent 2005 $s

National Film Preservation Board Selection 1992

OTHER AWARDS Best Picture Wins

	Year
Golden Globes	none
New York Film Critics	none
National Board of Review	none
Film Daily Critics	1925

The picture I want to be remembered by.
—Charles Chaplin

PLOT: A lone prospector takes refuge from a storm with Big Jim Mackay, who has discovered gold but loses his memory of its location. Together they find the gold and share its wealth.

PRODUCTION: The quintessential film featuring Charlie Chaplin as the Little Tramp began on a Sunday morning in the fall of 1923, during a visit to Douglas Fairbanks and Mary Pickford. Chaplin was amusing himself by looking at stereo photos of the 1898 Klondike gold rush. One picture in particular struck his imagination: a view of Chilkoot Pass with miners lined up to the top of the snow-covered mountainside as they trekked to the gold fields. The scene was reinforced soon thereafter when Chaplin read a book about the Donner party, trapped in the snowbound Sierras in 1846. He wrote a play about a gold prospector, calling it *The Lucky Strike,* as the basis for his next film, and on December 3, 1923, copyrighted it. The filming of *The Gold Rush* began February 8, 1924, at the Chaplin studio on La Brea with scenes of the lone prospector confronted by Black Larsen at the miner's cabin. From February 20 to 24 Chaplin and cameraman Rollie Totheroh went to Truckee to scout locations for the winter exterior scenes. They returned in April with a full crew to shoot the scenes, including those inspired by the stereo pictures. Back again in Los Angeles, a small mountain setting was constructed on the lot using 239,577 board feet of lumber, 22,750 linear feet of chicken wire, 22,000 feet of burlap, 200 tons of plaster, 285 tons of salt, and 100 barrels of white flour, with four carts of confetti for the blizzard scenes. Shooting continued through the summer at the studio. At the end of September filming stopped because Chaplin was informed by his leading lady, Lita Grey, that she was pregnant. She was only sixteen. They were married in Guaymas, Mexico, that November. A new leading lady was required, and Chaplin found former Miss America contestant Georgia Hale to take over the role. Shooting resumed in January 1925, and principal photography was finished by May 21. Chaplin spent the next month editing the film. When finished, at nine reels, it was his longest film.

DISTRIBUTION: *The Gold Rush* premiered at Grauman's Egyptian Theater in Hollywood on June 26, 1925, and was a huge success. It became the highest-grossing movie comedy of the silent film era. The premiere was a spectacular affair. The live presentation before the movie featured a school of seals on an icy crag, joined by a group of dancing Eskimo girls. Additional performances included ice skating and a balloon act. Even the critics loved the film. The comments by Harriette Underhill of the *New York Herald Tribune* were typical: "Praising one of Mr. Chaplin's pictures is like saying that Shakespeare was a good writer. And yet we heard pie-faced persons coming out of the Strand after the performance was over saying, 'Do you know, I think Chaplin is a genius!' Well, so do we, but never has it been written so clearly in letters of fire as now." In 1942 Chaplin reissued the film using alternate takes, omitting all of the intertitles and narrating the film himself with a music score he composed. It was a hit all over again. —*David Kiehn*

THE PHANTOM OF THE OPERA
Universal, 1925

ALL-RELEASE EQUIVALENT 2005 $s
(Unadjusted $s) in Millions of $s

Domestic Box Office Revenues. . . . . **$103.9**/($3.1)
Production Cost . . . . **$11.2**/($1.0)
Principal Photography. . . . .**65** days estimated
10/19/1924–January 1925

Director . . . . Rupert Julian
Producer . . . . Carl Laemmle
Production Company. . . . Universal Pictures
Story by . . . . Adapted from the novel of the
same name by Gaston Leroux
Screenplay by . . . , ... Elliott Clawson (Scenario),
Walter Anthony (Titles)
Cast . . . . Lon Chaney, Mary Philbin,
Norman Kerry
Filming Locations . . . . . . Universal Studios, CA
Genre. . . . . Silent Classic, Drama
Format. . . . . B&W
Initial Release . . . . 9/6/1925 Astor (New York);
11/15/1925 general release
Rerelease. 1930
Running Time . . . . 101 minutes
10 reels
8,464 feet
MPAA Rating . . . . not rated

STANDING THE TEST OF TIME

ACADEMY AWARD Oscar Nominations and Wins

Predates Oscars

OSCAR TOTALS   Nominations 0   *Wins 0

AFI 100 YEARS 100 MOVIES SELECTION
2007 0   1997 0

TOP 300 FILMS POSITION . . . . .none
All-Release Domestic Box Office in Equivalent 2005 $s

National Film Preservation Board Selection. . . . 1998

OTHER AWARDS Best Picture Wins

	Year
Golden Globes	none
New York Film Critics	none
National Board of Review	none
Film Daily Critics	none

The cry that he let out just before he turned around seemed to come from all around the set. Not from him. It was almost inhuman.

—Mary Philbin

PLOT: In the 1870s, unlucky accidents befall the grand new Paris Opera House. The ghostly figure responsible mentors a promising young soprano in his lair underneath the structure, while harboring a frightening secret.

PRODUCTION: Irving Thalberg, a protégé of founder Carl Laemmle, had turned Universal around in the early twenties, but felt underappreciated and joined Louis B. Mayer at Loew's new Metro-Goldwyn studio, along with other disgruntled Universal artists, including Lon Chaney. Laemmle knew only Chaney could headline one of the biggest productions in Universal's history, so he negotiated for Chaney's loan from Metro-Goldwyn, which acquiesced because the picture could multiply the value of one of its top contract players. The mammoth Paris Opera House set would have to hold the weight of hundreds of extras in five tiers of boxes. So it was built on Universal's Stage 28 on a steel framework in concrete foundations, the first Hollywood set of its kind. So rugged was the construction that the set has never been struck; it remains on Stage 28 today. The son of deaf-mute parents, Chaney was a natural mime artist, perfect for the silent screen, but a notorious perfectionist and very difficult to work with. Director Rupert Julian was also known for his arrogant attitude, and the two men loathed each other, mostly communicating through intermediaries. Chaney directed most of his own scenes. He intended the Phantom makeup to be his tour de force, and his contract forbade the use of any Phantom photographs prior to the film's release. The Phantom's horrific visage is not a mask, but is based on Chaney's real face, with a wire device pushing his nostrils apart and celluloid disks exaggerating his cheekbones. He even kept the Phantom's appearance from co-star Mary Philbin; the famous unmasking scene took place very early in the schedule, and Philbin claimed her reaction upon seeing the skeletal makeup for the first time was genuine. Laemmle found the first rough cut too slow. He replaced Julian with action director Edward Sedgwick, who shot the chase scenes at the end and added a new subplot.

DISTRIBUTION: *Phantom*'s first rough cut was more than twice as long as the film we know today. After editing it for a San Francisco premiere, Laemmle recalled the print, removed the new subplot, and added some light moments with comedian Chester Conklin. When that didn't play, he reedited once again. After all this, the 1925 general release was missing at least 35 minutes of material from the premiere print, some of it critical to the story and now lost. Some scenes were shot for the new two-color Technicolor process, for which entirely different lighting was required. Chaney's makeup had the desired effect on moviegoers; some were so terrified that they left the theater or fainted. But unlike later movie exploitation, Universal kept this out of the newspapers, and actually settled several lawsuits out of court. In 1930 Universal released a new version of the film with most of the dramatic scenes that did not include Lon Chaney, completely reshot with dialogue. Although the soundtrack for the 1930 dialogue version survives, the picture elements for this sound version are not known to exist. The original 1925 cut of *The Phantom of the Opera* survives in 16 mm. The surviving 35 mm material is apparently a mute print of an international version originally released with a soundtrack, but distinctly different from either the 1925 cut or the part-talking domestic reissue version. —*Tom Dupree*

THE MERRY WIDOW

MGM, 1925

ALL-RELEASE EQUIVALENT 2005 $s

(Unadjusted $s) in Millions of $s

Domestic Box Office Revenues. . . . . **$81.0**/($2.4)
Production Cost . . . . **$6.6**/($0.6)
Principal Photography. . . . . **60** days estimated
12/1/1924–2/21/1925

Director . . . . Erich von Stroheim
Producer . . . . Louis B. Mayer
Production Company. . . . Metro-Goldwyn-Mayer Pictures
Story by. . . . . Adapted from Franz Lehar's operetta
Screenplay by . . . . Erich von Stroheim, Benjamin Glazer (Scenario & Adaptation), Marion Ainslee (Titles)
Cast . . . . Mae Murray, John Gilbert, Roy D'Arcy, Josephine Crowell, George Fawcett, Tully Marshall
Filming Locations . . . . . . MGM Studios, Culver City, CA
Genre. . . . . Silent Classic, Romance
Format. . . . . B&W
Initial Release . . . . 8/25/1925 premiere (New York); 11/15/1925 general release
Rerelease. . . . . none
Running Time . . . . 107 minutes
10 reels
10,027 feet
MPAA Rating . . . . not rated

STANDING THE TEST OF TIME

ACADEMY AWARD Oscar Nominations and Wins

Predates Oscars

OSCAR TOTALS   Nominations 0   *Wins 0

AFI 100 YEARS 100 MOVIES SELECTION
2007 0   1997 0
TOP 300 FILMS POSITION . . . . .none
All-Release Domestic Box Office in Equivalent 2005 $s

National Film Preservation Board Selection. . . .none

OTHER AWARDS Best Picture Wins

	Year
Golden Globes	none
New York Film Critics	none
National Board of Review	none
Film Daily Critics	none

Mr. von Stroheim, you are through.

—Louis B. Mayer to Erich von Stroheim during the making of *The Merry Widow*

PLOT: Sally O'Hara, a dancer on tour in the Balkans, marries the richest man in the land, who dies on their wedding night, and the royal family of the country, concerned that the fortune may be lost if she marries a foreigner, sends the crown prince to woo her.

PRODUCTION: Despite the difficulties with Erich von Stroheim's previous film, *Greed,* he remained under contract with MGM. It was assumed all along that after *Greed* von Stroheim would direct the Franz Lehar operetta *The Merry Widow*, and Mae Murray was selected to play the title role even though von Stroheim was opposed to it. The choice of the leading man was also studio-arranged, in this case rising star John Gilbert, whose next film would be *The Big Parade* (1925). Both stars clashed with von Stroheim, but it was Murray who gave him the most trouble. She asserted her authority by arriving on the set that first day with her own hairdresser, costumer, and cameraman. Filming began on December 1, 1924, on an MGM stage. Trouble began with John Gilbert when von Stroheim criticized him. Gilbert left the stage without a word, and oddly enough, it was Mae Murray who convinced the director to try to patch things up. After a talk between the two men, they made peace and got along well from then on. But as the picture continued, the tension between Murray and von Stroheim increased. As simple a scene as Murray dismounting from a horse became a test of wills, with von Stroheim cracking, "Who do you think you are?" and Murray answering, "The queen of MGM." The climactic confrontation came, however, during the shooting of "The Merry Widow Waltz." It was Murray's big scene, the centerpiece of the film, and von Stroheim dared to show the former Ziegfeld Follies dancer how to dance. This was too much for her. She screamed at him, "You dirty Hun. You think you know everything!" This time von Stroheim left the set and went home. Louis B. Mayer assigned director Monta Bell to take over, but most of the cast and crew refused to work for anyone besides von Stroheim. A meeting was arranged between Murray, von Stroheim, and Mayer that night. The next morning, a *Los Angeles Record* headline proclaimed: "Mae-Von Sign Peace." It was agreed that von Stroheim held absolute authority on the set as director, and production resumed. The film wrapped on February 21, 1925. On April 14, von Stroheim's contract with MGM was canceled by mutual consent.

DISTRIBUTION: *The Merry Widow* opened on August 25, 1925, in New York and became a hit with critics and the public alike. The film changed the opinion of many people who had disliked *Greed* intensely and its director even more. Richard Watts Jr., in the *New York Herald Tribune*, stated: "He is, in my opinion, the most important figure in motion pictures, not excepting Chaplin and Jannings." A *Film Daily* poll of the nation's film critics about the best film of the year put *The Merry Widow* in a tie for third place with *Don Q, Son of Zorro,* and behind *The Gold Rush* and *The Unholy Three.* —*David Kiehn*

THE BIG PARADE
MGM, 1925

ALL-RELEASE EQUIVALENT 2005 $s

(Unadjusted $s) in Millions of $s

Domestic Box Office Revenues . . . . **$343.4**/($10.2)
Production Cost . . . . **$4.7**/($0.4)
Principal Photography . . . . **45** days estimated
4/8/1925–5/29/1925

Running Time . . . . 141 minutes
12 reels
11,519 feet

MPAA Rating . . . . not rated

Director . . . . King Vidor
Producer . . . . Irving Thalberg (uncredited)
Production Company . . . . Metro-Goldwyn-Mayer Pictures
Story by . . . . Laurence Stallings
Screenplay by . . . . Harry Behn and (uncredited)
King Vidor
Cast . . . . John Gilbert, Renée Adorée,
Hobart Bosworth, Claire
McDowell, Claire Adams,
Robert Ober, Tom O'Brien,
Karl Dane, Rosita Marstini
Filming Locations . . . . . . The MGM lot and five Los
Angeles area locations: now
Elysian Park, Westwood, Los
Angeles International Airport,
Sepulveda Blvd., and Griffith Park
Genre . . . . Silent Classic, War
Format . . . . B&W with color tints and stencil
colored sequence
Initial Release . . . . 11/5/1925 roadshow release;
9/20/1927 general release
Rerelease . . . . 12/19/1931 sound reissue

STANDING THE TEST OF TIME

ACADEMY AWARD Oscar Nominations and Wins

Predates Oscars

OSCAR TOTALS   Nominations 0   *Wins 0

AFI 100 YEARS 100 MOVIES SELECTION
2007 0   1997 0

TOP 300 FILMS POSITION 77
All-Release Domestic Box Office in Equivalent 2005 $s

National Film Preservation Board Selection 1992

OTHER AWARDS Best Picture Wins
                                                                  Year
Golden Globes . . . . none
New York Film Critics . . . . none
National Board of Review . . . . none
Film Daily Critics . . . . none

*How wonderful it was to have a girl who could not speak English, and a man
who could not speak French—there was the excuse for all the pantomime you could want.*

—King Vidor

PLOT: As America enters World War I, three young men from varying backgrounds are brought together as soldiers and instant buddies, providing a lowly soldier's point of view on the horrors of war. One Yank falls for a French girl and returns to find her after the war.

PRODUCTION: Dissatisfied with the sort of "disposable" pictures he was making, director King Vidor told MGM producer Irving Thalberg he wanted to make a bigger picture that could play for an extended run in a deluxe theater. Vidor suggested three potential themes: "steel, wheat, or war." Thalberg preferred a war story and engaged the screenwriter Laurence Stallings, who had co-written the play *What Price Glory?* Stallings, a disabled veteran himself, delivered a five-page treatment but failed to expand upon it. Vidor and Harry Behn devised the screenplay from the bare bones provided by Stallings. They included scenes of graphic language and violence, to realistically portray Stallings's real-life experience in World War I (he lost a leg at Belleau Wood). "War had not been explored yet from the realistic GI viewpoint," Vidor noted in an interview later. "It was more based on songs like 'Over There' and songs of that sort." Although King Vidor wanted *The Big Parade* to be about an "average guy" who can only react to the events going on around him, the director insisted on creating scenes that told of an emotional truth, even if they were not necessarily realistic. He asked his second-unit director to go to Fort Sam Houston in San Antonio, Texas, to obtain footage of the army moving to the front. Vidor wanted the trucks, soldiers, and airplanes moving in a straight line. Army generals persuaded the second-unit director that in a war situation troops would not advance in a single straight line, and Vidor's instructions were ignored. The director persuaded producer Irving Thalberg that the scene needed to be reshot. Similarly, Vidor set his restaging of the battle of the Belleau Wood to the beat of a metronome amplified by an off-camera bass drummer pounding out the beat so it could be heard by the far-flung actors. Every footstep, movement, and body fall was timed to the beat, providing a measured, inevitable quality to the action, creating what he called a "ballet of death." Vidor used Signal Corps footage of troop and battle scenes as he laid out the flow of his film. Vidor also incorporated ideas after seeing them on film. One of the best-remembered scenes in *The Big Parade* did not concern battle action but was a quiet moment behind the front during which the American doughboy teaches the French farm girl how to chew gum. The scene was improvised when Vidor noticed that Donald Ogden Stewart, a writer visiting the set, was chewing gum. Vidor later lamented the loss of freedom to improvise that occurred after sound films came in.

DISTRIBUTION: *The Big Parade* was one of the most successful films of the silent era with a $3.5 million profit on its 1925 release. It played six straight months at Grauman's Egyptian Theater in Hollywood and ran eighty-six weeks at the Astor Theater in New York. It was reissued in 1931 with a recorded version of the film's original musical score written and compiled by William Axt and David Mendoza, but was only a modest success. —*Robert S. Birchard*

BEN HUR: A TALE OF THE CHRIST

MGM, 1925

ALL-RELEASE EQUIVALENT 2005 $s

(Unadjusted $s) in Millions of $s

Domestic Box Office Revenues . . . . **$305.2**/($9.1)
Production Cost . . . . **$44.8**/($4.0)
Principal Photography . . . . **120** days estimated
2/18/1925–August 1925

Rerelease . . . . 1/2/1932 sound reissue
Running Time . . . . 143 minutes
12 reels
11,693 feet

MPAA Rating . . . . not rated

Director . . . . Fred Niblo

Producer . . . . Louis B. Mayer, Samuel
Goldwyn, Irving Thalberg

Production Company . . . . Metro-Goldwyn-Mayer Pictures

Story by . . . . Based on the novel by
General Lew Wallace

Screenplay by . . . . June Mathis (Adaptation);
Katherine Hilliker,
H.H. Caldwell (Titles)

Cast . . . . Ramon Novarro, Francis X.
Bushman, May McAvoy,
Carmel Myers, Claire McDowell,
Kathleen Key, Frank Currier,
Betty Bronson

Filming Locations . . . . . . MGM Studios, Culver City, CA

Genre . . . . Silent Classic, Biblical Epic

Format . . . . B&W with color tints and
two-color Technicolor
sequences

Initial Release . . . . 12/30/1925 premiere roadshow
release (New York); 10/8/1927
general release

STANDING THE TEST OF TIME

ACADEMY AWARD Oscar Nominations and Wins

Predates Oscars

OSCAR TOTALS   Nominations 0   *Wins 0

AFI 100 YEARS 100 MOVIES SELECTION
2007 0   1997 0

TOP 300 FILMS POSITION 103
All-Release Domestic Box Office in Equivalent 2005 $s

National Film Preservation Board Selection 1997

OTHER AWARDS Best Picture Wins

	Year
Golden Globes	none
New York Film Critics	none
National Board of Review	none
Film Daily Critics	none

The technicians and players who worked on Ben-Hur *. . . established the production
as a sort of Dunkirk of the cinema: a humiliating defeat transformed,
after heavy losses, into a brilliant victory.*

—Kevin Brownlow, *The Parade's Gone By*

PLOT: Judah Ben-Hur (Ramon Novarro), unjustly blamed for throwing a brick at a Roman parade, is sentenced to a slave galley. His boyhood friend Messala (Francis X. Bushman) refuses to help. Judah returns to Rome, bests Messala in a chariot race, and discovers Christ.

PRODUCTION: Lew Wallace (1827–1905) was a general in the Mexican War and the Civil War and served as New Mexico's territorial governor. He also wrote several historical novels, most notably *Ben-Hur* in 1880, which became an international best seller. The novel was adapted for the stage in 1899 as *Ben-Hur: A Tale of the Christ*. It made a tortuous trip to the screen. In 1921 *Ben-Hur* theatrical producer Abraham Erlanger joined forces with producers Florenz Ziegfeld and Charles Dillingham to establish the Classical Cinematograph Corporation to purchase the screen rights to *Ben-Hur* for $600,000. They turned around and offered it to Hollywood for $1 million. Frank Godsol, who took over the Goldwyn Company in 1922, acquired the rights by promising to split box office receipts with Classical Cinematograph from dollar one. The Goldwyn Company started production in 1923 on location in Italy with Charles Brabin in the director's chair, George Walsh playing Judah Ben-Hur, and a budget of $750,000. Costs spiraled to over $2 million, and when Goldwyn merged with Loew's, Inc., to form Metro-Goldwyn-Mayer, new management fired Brabin and Walsh, scrapped all of Brabin's footage, and brought the unit back to Culver City, California, to essentially start from scratch. Before the *Ben-Hur* company left Europe, new director Fred Niblo reshot the sea battle scenes, which would essentially be the only Italian footage retained in the new version. The bulk of Brabin's footage was deliberately incinerated at Leghorn (Livorno), Italy. New sets were constructed in Culver City, including the Circus Maximus set for the story's centerpiece chariot race. The spectacular chariot race was overseen by second-unit director Reeves Eason, who had a rather schizophrenic career, dividing his time between directing poverty-row westerns and doing top-notch second-unit work on A pictures such as *Ben-Hur* and *The Charge of the Light Brigade* (1936). The race took two months to shoot and cost a reported $500,000. It involved thousands of extras—including Douglas Fairbanks and Mary Pickford—captured by forty cameras. In Lew Wallace's story, Ben-Hur and Messala are boyhood friends. George Walsh was much better suited in age and build for the role than Novarro, but surviving still pictures suggest that one of the reasons Walsh was replaced is that he was too similar in build to Francis X. Bushman, and it was difficult to tell them apart—especially in Brabin's aborted chariot race footage.

DISTRIBUTION: *Ben-Hur* grossed very well but was a commercial failure on its initial release, with a net loss of $698,000 due to production cost overruns and the heavy royalties paid to the rights holders of the novel and the theatrical adaptation. The 1932 sound reissue with recorded music and sound effects moved the film into the black, but the bulk of the business for the rerelease was in foreign venues. —*Robert S. Birchard*

105

THE GENERAL

United Artists, 1926

ALL-RELEASE EQUIVALENT 2005 $s

(Unadjusted $s) in Millions of $s

Domestic Box Office Revenues . . . . **$32.0**/($0.9)
Production Cost . . . . **$4.6**/($0.4)
Principal Photography . . . . **79** days estimated
6/8/1926–9/18/1926

Director . . . . Buster Keaton, Clyde Bruckman

Producer . . . . Joseph M. Schenck

Production Company . . . . Buster Keaton Productions

Story by . . . . Based on the novel *The Great Locomotive Chase* by William Pittenger

Screenplay by . . . . Buster Keaton, Clyde Bruckman

Cast . . . . Buster Keaton

Filming Locations . . . . . . On location in Cottage Grove, Oregon, the McKenzie River, Oregon; Santa Monica, Hollywood and Los Angeles, CA

Genre . . . . Silent Classic, Comedy

Format . . . . B&W

Initial Release . . . . 12/22/1926 premiere (Los Angeles)

Rerelease . . . . none

Running Time . . . . 77 minutes
8 reels
7,500 feet

MPAA Rating . . . . not rated

STANDING THE TEST OF TIME

ACADEMY AWARD Oscar Nominations and Wins

Predates Oscars

OSCAR TOTALS   Nominations 0   *Wins 0

AFI 100 YEARS 100 MOVIES SELECTION
2007 . . . #18   1997 0

TOP 300 FILMS POSITION . . . . none
All-Release Domestic Box Office in Equivalent 2005 $s

National Film Preservation Board Selection 1989

OTHER AWARDS Best Picture Wins

	Year
Golden Globes	none
New York Film Critics	none
National Board of Review	none
Film Daily Critics	none

Well, the moment you give me a locomotive and things like that to play with,
as a rule I find some way of getting laughs with it.

—Buster Keaton

PLOT: Northern Civil War spies steal a Southern army locomotive, disrupting supply lines as they head for Northern territory, but the train's engineer follows them, recaptures the train, and brings it back home.

PRODUCTION: Clyde Bruckman, a writer for Buster Keaton's company since Keaton's two-reeler days, gave Keaton a book by William Pittenger called *The Great Locomotive Chase*. Keaton immediately saw the possibilities for filming it, and, looking for authenticity, wanted to shoot on location in Tennessee. At first it appeared they'd be able to use the original "General" locomotive, on display at Chattanooga's Union Station, but when railway authorities heard the film was to be a comedy they withdrew their offer. Alternative locations were scouted, and ideal conditions were found at Cottage Grove, Oregon, where the company was welcomed. Keaton and company arrived in Cottage Grove on May 28, 1926, with eighteen train cars of equipment and a crew of sixty-five. Five hundred Oregon National Guard men were hired to play both the Union and Southern soldiers. Four or five train engines were acquired locally for the film, and that summer the little town of Cottage Grove came alive with activity. Keaton did his own stunts, which put him in significant danger several times during the shoot. Keaton cast his own father, Joe Keaton, as a Union general. Much of the production took place east of town, where a set of parallel tracks allowed traveling shots to be made with ease. A street set was built at this location to represent Marietta, Georgia, and was later reconfigured to be Chattanooga, Tennessee. In an unplanned moment, sparks from the stack of one of the wood-burning engines started a grass fire and the National Guard, led by Keaton, put it out. The highlight for the community was watching the burning train trestle collapse under the weight of an engine crossing the river, a scene reported to have cost $42,000 to stage, the most ever spent to create one scene until that time. On July 23, 4,000 people gathered seventeen miles outside of town to watch. Keaton gave the command to start the scene rolling, and when the train tumbled down into the river to his satisfaction he smiled. Two weeks later he and his company returned to Los Angeles to complete the film, shooting the interior and night scenes there and editing it.

DISTRIBUTION: The premiere was held in Los Angeles on December 22, 1926, in a slightly longer form than the release version. Keaton's films had been distributed by MGM since its formation in 1924. This changed when Joseph Schenck, president of Buster Keaton Productions, became president of United Artists. Schenck saw to it that United Artists would handle *The General* and provide additional funds to complete the movie. MGM's distribution capabilities were stronger than UA's, which was in part blamed for the drop in revenues compared with Keaton's previous releases. Reviews criticizing *The General* in 1926 are hard to believe now: "long and tedious," "the least funny thing Buster Keaton has ever done." In time that view was to change. Sound effects and a new score by Konrad Elfers were created for a foreign reissue of *The General* in the 1960s. —*David Kiehn*

TELL IT TO THE MARINES

MGM, 1927

ALL-RELEASE EQUIVALENT 2005 $s

(Unadjusted $s) in Millions of $s

Domestic Box Office Revenues . . . . **$89.0**/($2.8)
Production Cost . . . . **$4.9**/($0.4)
Principal Photography . . . . **48** days estimated
6/7/1926–8/3/1926

Director . . . . George Hill
Producer . . . . George Hill
Production Company . . . . George Hill Production
Story and
   Screenplay by . . . . Richard Schayer, Joseph
Farnham (Titles)
Cast . . . . Lon Chaney, William Haines,
Eleanor Boardman, Eddie
Gribbon, Carmel Myers
Filming Locations . . . . . . On location in Southern
California, the Marine base in
San Diego and MGM Studios,
Culver City, CA
Genre . . . . Silent Classic, War
Format . . . . B&W
Initial Release . . . . 12/23/1926 premiere
(New York); 1/29/1927
general release
Rerelease . . . . none
Running Time . . . . 103 minutes
9 reels
8,800 feet
MPAA Rating . . . . not rated

STANDING THE TEST OF TIME

ACADEMY AWARD Oscar Nominations and Wins
None

OSCAR TOTALS   Nominations 0   *Wins 0

AFI 100 YEARS 100 MOVIES SELECTION
2007 0   1997 0

TOP 300 FILMS POSITION . . . . .none
All-Release Domestic Box Office in Equivalent 2005 $s

National Film Preservation Board Selection . . . .none

OTHER AWARDS Best Picture Wins
                                                                    Year
Golden Globes . . . . none
New York Film Critics . . . . none
National Board of Review . . . . none
Film Daily Critics . . . . none

Lon Chaney's first appearance "au naturel" for many years and it makes one plead for more like it.

—*Motion Picture Magazine*, March 1927

PLOT: Sergeant O'Hara takes on the task of shaping up a new marine recruit who is treating his enlistment too lightly, as well as wooing a navy nurse the sergeant loves.

PRODUCTION: In early drafts of the scenario, dated February 20 and March 26, 1926, the leading role was that of a country boy, along the lines of parts played by Charles Ray at the height of his career. In the April 29 script, that character had been dropped in favor of the troublesome Skeet Burns, to be played by William Haines, and the sergeant who whips him into shape, played by Lon Chaney. With his fantastic makeup for *The Hunchback of Notre Dame* and *The Phantom of the Opera,* among many other films, Lon Chaney had become a master of transformation, the "Man of a Thousand Faces." So it was quite a change of pace for him to set aside his makeup kit to take on a role that didn't require it. Although Chaney didn't need to create a mask for Sergeant O'Hara, he did work hard to create a believable character. To that end, he met with General Smedley Butler, who was in command of the marine base in San Diego where much of *Tell It to the Marines* was filmed. Chaney wanted to know about marine life and conduct, and through his conversations with the general they became good friends. Chaney also won the admiration of the marine personnel with whom he worked on the base. The director of the film, George W. Hill, had worked his way up over the years from stagehand to cameraman, then director. Ira Morgan, the cameraman on *Tell It to the Marines,* had filmed on the *Broncho Billy* westerns in Niles in the 1910s before his feature work with King Vidor's breakthrough films and the big-budget Marion Davies dramas. Filming began on June 7, 1926. MGM received full cooperation from the U.S. Marine Corps during location filming at the base; scenes at sea were filmed on the USS *California,* where Chaney, William Haines, and Eddie Gribbon participate in firing one of the ship's five-inch guns. A battle with Chinese bandits was shot at the Iverson Ranch in Chatsworth, California. Interior scenes were filmed at the MGM studio in Culver City. Production ran smoothly and finished on August 3, 1926.

DISTRIBUTION: *Tell It to the Marines* premiered at the Embassy Theater in New York City on December 23, 1926, where it ran for thirteen weeks. This change-of-pace role for Chaney became a hit across the country, with positive reviews across the board. It was one of the highest-grossing films of 1927 and made a $664,000 profit, establishing it as one of MGM's most profitable movies for the year. Chaney made a rare public appearance at the film's Los Angeles premiere as a favor to his friend General Smedley. At that time, the Marine Corps gave him an honorary life membership, the first time an actor had ever received this gift. Critics praised Chaney for his believability as the marine sergeant, and the performance was probably an inspiration for the tough but sentimental sergeant characters in future military pictures. Chaney himself would eschew makeup again for roles as a gangster in *The Big City* (1928), a detective in *While the City Sleeps* (1928), and a railroad engineer in *Thunder* (1929). *—David Kiehn*

WINGS
Paramount, 1927

ALL-RELEASE EQUIVALENT 2005 $s

(Unadjusted $s) in Millions of $s

Domestic Box Office Revenues......... **$138.5**/($4.3)
Production Cost .... **$22.4**/($2.0)
Principal Photography........... **140** days estimated
9/7/1926–4/7/1927

Director .... William A. Wellman

Producer .... Lucien Hubbard

Production Company.... Paramount Famous Lasky Corp.

Story by............... John Monk Saunders

Screenplay by.......... Hope Loring, Louis D. Lighton (scenario); Julian Johnson (titles)

Cast .... Clara Bow, Charles Rogers, Richard Arlen, Gary Cooper, Jobyna Ralston, Julia Swayne Gordon

Filming Locations ...... Camp Stanley Army Reserve, Brooks Field, and Kelly Field, San Antonio, Texas; Paramount Studios, Hollywood, CA

Genre................. Silent Classic, War

Format............... B&W with tints and tones and some hand-colored scenes

Initial Release.......... 08/12/1927 premiere Criterion Theater (New York); 01/05/1929 general release

Rerelease............. none

Running Time.......... 139 minutes
13 reels
12,682 feet

MPAA Rating .... not rated

STANDING THE TEST OF TIME

ACADEMY AWARD Oscar Nominations and Wins

***OUTSTANDING PICTURE:** Paramount Famous Lasky

***ENGINEERING EFFECTS:** Roy Pomeroy

OSCAR TOTALS   Nominations **2**   *Wins **2**

AFI 100 YEARS 100 MOVIES SELECTION
2007 0   1997..... 0

TOP 300 FILMS POSITION ....none
All-Release Domestic Box Office in Equivalent 2005 $s

National Film Preservation Board Selection.... 1997

OTHER AWARDS Best Picture Wins

	Year
Golden Globes	none
New York Film Critics......................	none
National Board of Review..................	none
Film Daily Critics	none

So few people today have seen it,
but you still get great enthusiasm which
has been handed on, sincerely and honestly,
from people that did see it. With luck, this
will be a picture that will be remembered.
—William A. Wellman, 1964

PLOT: Two young Americans from the same small town fight in France during World War I, becoming inseparable combat pilots in the air—as well as rivals on the ground when it comes to the affections of the same girl.

PRODUCTION: In the mid-1920s Paramount sought an epic World War I story that could surpass MGM's *The Big Parade* (1925). Although flying was still somewhat of a novelty for the general population, the Great War had demonstrated the power and effectiveness of aerial combat, and Paramount decided on an aviation-themed story line. Screenwriter Byron Morgan, who in 1925 and 1926 had submitted original ideas for a story involving a World War I aviator, was the probable spark behind the film's script. In 1927 the studio paid Morgan $3,750 for all the material he had developed thus far and in exchange he waived claims to be mentioned in connection with the film. The story ultimately used was by a contract writer working for Jesse L. Lasky named John Monk Saunders—a World War I airman himself—who later turned his *Wings* movie story line into a book. Instead of a big-name director, the studio chose William Wellman, who had firsthand war experience as a combat flyer with the renowned Lafayette Flying Corps, which flew for the French Air Service during World War I but was made up mostly of American volunteers. To hedge its bet, Paramount attached popular new heartthrobs Charles "Buddy" Rogers and Richard Arlen, as well as the "It" girl, Clara Bow, to the project. Screenwriters Hope Loring and Louis Lighton managed to weave a somewhat familiar romantic element—a love triangle—into the aerial goings-on. Paramount sought cooperation from the U.S. government and received an enthusiastic response. The War Department provided $16 million worth of manpower and equipment: locations in San Antonio, Texas; aircraft; seasoned pilots; and thousands of soldiers who served as extras and also provided assistance to the production digging trenches and rigging explosives. At a cost of $2 million, *Wings* featured Paramount's highest production budget at the time, exceeding even the nearly $1.5 million spent on *The Ten Commandments* in 1923. Cameras, lugged aloft in special cradles attached to the planes or mounted on their fuselages, were wired with handheld control buttons so that the pilots could capture sequences as the planes engaged in aerial dogfights. Arlen, a former member of the Royal Canadian Flying Corps, and Rogers, a nonflyer hastily trained in Texas, performed some of their own flying. An accident claimed the life of one Air Corps pilot, and stunt flyer Dick Grace broke his neck in a stunt crash but fully recovered. The climactic re-creation of the Battle of St. Mihiel involved ten days of rehearsal, seventeen cameramen to capture the sequence, 3,500 troops, and scores of airplanes. According to Wellman, the entire battle sequence was filmed in just one day.

DISTRIBUTION: A benefit premiere was held May 19, 1927, at the Texas Theater in San Antonio for an aviators' memorial. The film's aerial sequences were initially projected in Magnascope, in which a special lens enlarged the picture to showcase the action. With Hollywood transitioning to talkies, *Wings* was given a musical score and sound effects for its January 1929 wide release. It was a hit, although it didn't do well enough to turn a profit against its significant costs. It became the first-ever winner of the Best Picture Oscar when the newly created Academy of Motion Picture Arts and Sciences handed out its first honors, for 1927–28. —*Douglas Burns*

THE JAZZ SINGER
Warner Bros., 1927

ALL-RELEASE EQUIVALENT 2005 $s

(Unadjusted $s) in Millions of $s

Domestic Box Office Revenues . . . . **$126.5**/($3.9)
Production Cost . . . . **$4.7**/($0.4)
Principal Photography . . . . **60** days estimated
June 1927–September 1927

Running Time . . . . 88 or 90 minutes
9 reels
8,117 feet
MPAA Rating . . . . not rated

Director . . . . Alan Crosland

Producer . . . . Jack Warner

Production Company . . . . Warner Bros. Pictures, Inc., the
Vitaphone Corporation

Story by . . . . Based on a short story by
Samson Raphaelson

Screenplay by . . . . Jack Jarmuth (Captions),
A.A. Cohn (Scenario)

Cast . . . . Al Jolson, May McAvoy,
Warner Oland

Filming Locations . . . . . . On location in Los Angeles
and San Francisco, CA and in
New York; in Studio at Warner
Bros. Studios, 5800 Sunset
Blvd., Los Angeles, CA

Genre . . . . Bio-Drama

Format . . . . B&W

Initial Release . . . . 10/6/1927 world premiere at
the Warner Theatre (New York);
2/4/1928 general release

Rerelease . . . . none

STANDING THE TEST OF TIME

ACADEMY AWARD Oscar Nominations and Wins

Writing (Adaptation): Alfred Cohn

***SPECIAL AWARD:** Warner Bros., for producing
The Jazz Singer, the pioneer outstanding talking
picture, which has revolutionized the industry

OSCAR TOTALS   Nominations **1**   *Wins 0+1

AFI 100 YEARS 100 MOVIES SELECTION
2007 0   1997 . . . #90

TOP 300 FILMS POSITION . . . . none
All-Release Domestic Box Office in Equivalent 2005 $s

National Film Preservation Board Selection 1996

OTHER AWARDS Best Picture Wins

	Year
Golden Globes	none
New York Film Critics	none
National Board of Review	none
Film Daily Critics	none

*The commercialization of sound-on-film, and the transformation of the industry
from silent films to talkies became a reality with the success of this film.*
—Tim Dirks

PLOT: The son of a Jewish cantor runs away in order to pursue his dream of becoming a jazz singer, returning many years later to New York to star in a Broadway show and attempt a reconciliation with his father.

PRODUCTION: In 1917 an undergraduate at the University of Illinois, Samson Raphaelson, saw the musical *Robinson Crusoe Jr.* and was struck by the performance of Al Jolson. Raphaelson saw a connection between Jolson's performance in blackface and the cantors from his religious childhood, and he wrote a short story, called "The Day of Atonement," about the life of a budding star. Raphaelson hit on the clash between Old World values and New World ambition. The story was published in *Everybody's Magazine* in 1922, and then Raphaelson adapted it into a play, *The Jazz Singer.* Jolson wanted to star in it, but Raphaelson felt it would play better as a straight drama, and cast George Jessel. It was an instant hit, running from 1925 to 1927. Warner Bros. acquired film rights for $50,000, and executive Darryl F. Zanuck urged the studio to use its new Vitaphone process. Warner signed Jessel to star, but when he demanded an additional $10,000 (because he thought the film would flop), Warner sought out Jolson. Using the Vitaphone process and sound was incredibly expensive and a huge risk for Warner Bros. They economized whenever possible, using sets from other films and having director Alan Crosland do his tracking shots out of the back of an old moving van in New York. According to his daughter, Harry Warner pawned his wife's jewelry and moved the family into a small apartment during production. The Jewish ghetto scenes were actual shots of a New York street taken through a window, and the theater in which Jolson sings was the Winter Garden, where he often performed. In total, the movie contains barely two minutes' worth of synchronized talking, most of it improvised. The rest of the dialogue is presented in printed subtitles. Originally Jolson was supposed to sing only his six songs, but he ad-libbed a few lines (as he would do onstage). After seeing the rushes, the studio sensed a hit and an additional scene was added where Jolson's character talks to his mother.

DISTRIBUTION: Later dubbed "the father of the talkies," Sam Warner died at age forty the day before the film debuted. The movie was an immediate sensation right from the premiere in New York City, which ended with the audience jumping to their feet, screaming out Jolson's name. It became a historic milestone and cinematic landmark. It sparked the sound revolution, turning Warner Bros. into a major studio. Although the film was ruled ineligible in the Best Picture category (it was thought unfair for a sound film to compete with silents), in May 1929 Zanuck (on behalf of his studio) was presented with a special Oscar, which he dedicated to Sam Warner. The film brought in $2.6 million in worldwide rentals and made a net profit of $1,196,750. Jolson's follow-up Warner Bros. feature film, *The Singing Fool* (1928), brought in over two times as much, with $5.9 million in worldwide rentals and a profit of $3,649,000, making them two of the most profitable films in the 1920s. —*Hayley Taylor Block*

THE CROWD
MGM, 1928

<table>
<tr><td colspan="2">ALL-RELEASE EQUIVALENT 2005 $s
(Unadjusted $s) in Millions of $s</td></tr>
</table>

Domestic Box Office Revenues. . . . . **$42.0**/($1.3)
Production Cost . . . . **$6.3**/($0.6)
Principal Photography. . . . . **75** days estimated
12/23/1926–3/21/1927

Director . . . . King Vidor

Producer . . . . Irving Thalberg (uncredited)

Production Company. . . . Metro-Goldwyn-Mayer Pictures

Story by. . . . . King Vidor and John V. A. Weaver

Screenplay by . . . . Joseph Farnham (Titles)

Cast . . . . Eleanor Boardman, James Murray, Bert Roach, Estelle Clark, Daniel G. Tomlinson, Dell Henderson, Lucy Beaumont, Freddie Burke Frederick, Alice Mildred Puter

Filming Locations . . . . . . not available

Genre. . . . . Silent Classic, Drama

Format . . . . B&W with color tints

Initial Release 3/3/1928

Rerelease. . . . . none

Running Time . . . . 86 or 98 minutes
9 reels
8,538 or 8,548 feet

MPAA Rating . . . . not rated

STANDING THE TEST OF TIME

ACADEMY AWARD Oscar Nominations and Wins

Unique and Artistic Picture: Metro-Goldwyn-Mayer
Directing: King Vidor

OSCAR TOTALS   Nominations **2**   *Wins **0**

AFI 100 YEARS 100 MOVIES SELECTION
2007 0   1997 0

TOP 300 FILMS POSITION . . . . .none
All-Release Domestic Box Office in Equivalent 2005 $s

National Film Preservation Board Selection. . . . 1989

OTHER AWARDS Best Picture Wins

	Year
Golden Globes	none
New York Film Critics.	none
National Board of Review	none
Film Daily Critics	none

[The Crowd was] an American rarity: a big-studio art film. In this silent film Vidor traces the sad life of a totally ordinary citizen, dreaming big, living small, in a brilliant expressionistic style. But his manner, which might have had a distancing effect, never interferes with the heartbreaking emotions this powerful film stirs.

—Richard Schickel

PLOT: Exploring the downward spiral of an average couple in the city, the film follows John Sims (James Murray) and Mary (Eleanor Boardman) as they wed, have children, grieve for their daughter who is killed in an accident, and watch life go on, swallowed up in the crowd.

PRODUCTION: Producer Irving Thalberg asked King Vidor if he had a follow-up to *The Big Parade* in mind. Vidor suggested another story about an average guy, this time in an everyday environment, who battles with life instead of a uniformed enemy, to be called *One of the Mob.* Thalberg thought this sounded too much like a gangster story, and Vidor suggested a change to *One of the Crowd.* According to Vidor, Thalberg came up with the shortened final title. Vidor and Thalberg agreed to cast an unknown in the lead, and Vidor found James Murray in the ranks of MGM extras. *The Crowd* is notable for its combination of naturalistic and expressionistic images. For one memorable shot of young John Sims coming up the stairs as he hears of his father's death, Vidor used an already-built stairway and painted the background in forced perspective. For the best-remembered scene in the film, the camera pans up the side of a skyscraper and moves in through an upper-story window, revealing John Sims working with his fellow employees at one of seemingly hundreds of perfectly matched desks. For this elaborate shot the skyscraper model was laid flat on the stage floor so the camera could roll above it. Through the window a still of the office was used for a match dissolve to the live-action scene of the workers getting ready to quit for the day at the striking of five o'clock. King Vidor often found inspiration in music for the mood of his films, and here he used Tchaikovsky's Sixth Symphony, the *Pathétique*, to provide an underlying structure for the narrative flow of his story. Production of *The Crowd* was complicated by the fact that Vidor had no suitable end for his story; apparently seven different endings were shot and tested. Early reviews and synopses disclose two of the possible endings. In one Mary returns home after having left. This ending was considered rather vague by a reviewer for *Variety.* In another ending John became successful again and the family was seen gathered around a Christmas tree as the picture faded out. The ending eventually used has Mary returning and the family going to the theater. As they laugh at the antics onstage the camera pulls back and they are lost in the crowd. Even as the film was released, it was being tinkered with. *Variety* reported the length of the film shown at its initial screening at the Capitol Theatre in New York to be 8,950 feet; viewers of subsequent screenings saw a different ending than the reviewer. The picture was also trimmed by some 400 feet before its general release.

DISTRIBUTION: For a rather downbeat story with no major stars, *The Crowd* did surprisingly well at the box office in major U.S. cities. The trade magazine *Motion Picture News* reported in its March 31, 1928, issue that "King Vidor's picture, *The Crowd,* is dominating at the Million Dollar [Theater in Los Angeles]." Although it was said to be a major influence on European directors and to have inspired Italian postwar neorealist cinema, *The Crowd* did rather tepid business overseas. Long out of circulation, the film became generally available for reappraisal in the 1970s. —*Robert S. Birchard*

THE WIND
MGM, 1928

ALL-RELEASE EQUIVALENT 2005 $s
(Unadjusted $s) in Millions of $s

Domestic Box Office Revenues . . . . **$26.1**/($0.8)
Production Cost . . . . **$5.5**/($0.5)
Principal Photography . . . . **50** days estimated
3/28/1927–5/24/1927

Director . . . . Victor Seastrom
Producer . . . . Irving Thalberg (uncredited)
Production Company . . . . Metro-Goldwyn-Mayer Pictures
Story by . . . . Based on a novel by
Dorothy Scarborough
Screenplay by . . . . Frances Marion, John Colton
(Titles)
Cast . . . . Lillian Gish, Lars Hanson,
Montagu Love, Dorothy
Cumming
Filming Locations . . . . . . At MGM studio and on location
near Bakersfield, CA
Genre . . . . Silent Classic, Western
Format . . . . B&W with Vitaphone score
and sound effects
Initial Release 11/11/1928
Rerelease . . . . none
Running Time . . . . 75 minutes
8 reels
6,721 feet
MPAA Rating . . . . not rated

STANDING THE TEST OF TIME

ACADEMY AWARD Oscar Nominations and Wins

None

OSCAR TOTALS   Nominations 0   *Wins 0

AFI 100 YEARS 100 MOVIES SELECTION
2007 0   1997 0

TOP 300 FILMS POSITION . . . . .none
All-Release Domestic Box Office in Equivalent 2005 $s

National Film Preservation Board Selection 1993

OTHER AWARDS Best Picture Wins

	Year
Golden Globes	none
New York Film Critics	none
National Board of Review	none
Film Daily Critics	none

I shall never forget the appearance of the crew during that picture. To protect their faces from the sun they all wore a heavy blackish makeup while their cracked and swollen lips were covered with some sort of white stuff.

—Miss Phyllis Moir, then secretary to Lillian Gish and later to Winston Churchill

PLOT: A girl from Virginia travels west to see her cousin. There she seeks out a man who wanted to marry her, only to discover that he already has a wife. She marries a farmer, but the other man won't leave her alone. She is driven nearly mad after being forced to kill him.

PRODUCTION: Lillian Gish read Dorothy Scarborough's novel in 1925 and recommended it to Metro-Goldwyn-Mayer. In basic plot and tone *The Wind* resembles W. Somerset Maugham's 1913 play *The Land of Promise,* which was filmed by Paramount in 1917 under its original title, and again in 1926 as *The Canadian.* Clarence Brown was originally slated to direct, but his extended Alaskan location schedule for the filming of *The Trail of '98* prevented him from doing *The Wind.* It became the final silent film for Gish, the medium's great star. Location scenes for *The Wind* were shot near Bakersfield, California, in the San Joaquin Valley. The men were housed in train cars on an unused siding, while Lillian Gish and the other women were put up in a Harvey hotel near the main line. Even though the company was shooting in the spring, temperatures hovered around 110 degrees. At one point Lillian Gish (or one of the crew members—accounts vary) severely burned her hand while attempting to open a car door. Eight wind machines were used to create the sandstorms required by the story. Victor Seastrom, who took over the project when Clarence Brown became unavailable, had worked with Gish on *The Scarlet Letter* the previous year, as had leading man Lars Hanson. Seastrom had started directing in 1912 in his native Sweden (there he is known as Victor Sjöström) before coming to Hollywood, where he directed the first MGM release, *He Who Gets Slapped.* Apparently the film was to have ended, as did the novel, with Letty driven mad by the wind as she wandered off into the storm. Irving Thalberg in Hollywood approved the film, but when it was screened for studio executives and sales staff in New York, they pointed out that test audiences did not like the dark ending. So several months after the completion of production Gish and others were called back for retakes that would add a happier ending, with Lige (Hanson) returning and Roddy's (Montagu Love) dead body permanently buried. Studio records do not indicate retake dates, but release of *The Wind* was held up for nearly eighteen months. When the picture did hit theaters, Metro-Goldwyn-Mayer opted to treat this adult drama as a straight-ahead western and suggested that exhibitors could stimulate juvenile interest by getting a "local store to make up a lariat and discolor it so that it has the appearance of having been used," then sponsoring a rope-spinning contest with "the lariat used by Lars Hanson in *The Wind*" as the prize.

DISTRIBUTION: *The Wind* hit theaters just as the demand for talkies was driving silent pictures from first-run theater screens. Even with a synchronized score and sound effects, the picture found a tepid reception from audiences and critics. The 1928 *Variety* review of *The Wind* dismissed the film: "Everything about the picture breathes quality. Yet it flops dismally." Although a failure in its day, with a net loss of $87,000, *The Wind* has become one of most frequently revived and revered American silent films. —*Robert S. Birchard*

IN OLD ARIZONA
Fox Film Corp., 1929

ALL-RELEASE EQUIVALENT 2005 $s
(Unadjusted $s) in Millions of $s

Domestic Box Office Revenues. . . . . **$73.5/($2.4)**
Production Cost . . . . **$3.6/($0.3)**
Principal Photography. . . . . **49** days estimated
9/9/1928–11/27/1928

Director . . . . Raoul Walsh, Irving Cummings
Producer . . . . Winfield Sheehan, studio head of production (uncredited)
Production Company . . . . Fox Film Corp.
Story by . . . . Based on the story "The Cabellero's Way" by O. Henry
Screenplay by . . . . Tom Barry
Cast . . . . Edmund Lowe, Warner Baxter, Dorothy Burgess
Filming Locations . . . . . . Fox studio Western Avenue in Hollywood, CA; on location: Bryce Canyon and Zion National Parks, UT
Genre. . . . . Western
Format. . . . . B&W
Initial Release . . . . 12/25/1928 premiere (Los Angeles); 1/20/1929 general release
Rerelease. . . . . none
Running Time . . . . 94 or 97 minutes
7 reels
8,724 feet
MPAA Rating . . . . not rated

STANDING THE TEST OF TIME

ACADEMY AWARD Oscar Nominations and Wins
Outstanding Picture - Fox
*ACTOR: Warner Baxter
Cinematography: Arthur Edeson
Directing: Irving Cummings
Writing: Tom Barry

OSCAR TOTALS Nominations 5 *Wins 1

AFI 100 YEARS 100 MOVIES SELECTION
2007 0   1997 0

TOP 300 FILMS POSITION . . . . none
All-Release Domestic Box Office In Equivalent 2005 $'S

National Film Preservation Board Selection. . . . none

OTHER AWARDS Best Picture Wins

	Year
Golden Globes	none
New York Film Critics.	none
National Board of Review	none
Film Daily Critics	none

Let me have the truck and I'll give you sound and the old action. We'll knock the public dead.

—Director Raoul Walsh to Fox production boss Winfield Sheehan

PLOT: The Cisco Kid manages to stay one step ahead of the law, but a lawman enlists his girl-friend in a scheme to trap him. He has to use all his skills to survive.

PRODUCTION: The first major western to use sound technology and the first important talkie to be filmed outdoors came about because Raoul Walsh, a former actor who had started directing for D. W. Griffith, figured out how to shoot a sound movie outside of a studio, despite bulky equipment. Walsh used a Fox Movietone News wagon, which allowed newsreels to get decent sound recordings outdoors. Fox's Winfield Sheehan sent him out to make a two-reeler. After some discussion, they decided to use the O. Henry story "The Caballero's Way," with Walsh playing the Cisco Kid. He took a crew to Bryce Canyon. Walsh struggled at first with directing a talkie; he could no longer use a megaphone, which he considered essential. Halfway through the second reel of film, Sheehan called. He had seen the first two days' shooting and was so excited that he demanded a five-reeler, a feature-length film. He told Walsh to "rewrite the script to fit. I don't care if you stay out there all year." Walsh regretted much of the subsequent padding he added to the story, saying, "Poor O. Henry. I hoped he would not turn over in his grave." Renting a stagecoach, Walsh shot some desert chase sequences to add to the film's length. Next, he moved the crew up to some boulder-strewn hills to shoot the Kid pulling a holdup. The rough terrain badly damaged the news truck. As Walsh would later record, "I think it was about then that the gods started laughing at me." The production was to return to the Fox back lot. Walsh set out with the crew in a caravan across the desert for the nearest train depot to Salt Lake City and on to Los Angeles. Riding beside the driver in the lead car (who Walsh suspected had drunk too much), they raced ahead of the other vehicles, nearly hitting some cattle and scattering a herd of deer. Then a large jackrabbit jumped at the windshield in front of Walsh. Crashing through the glass, the jackrabbit hit the director square in the face along with a shower of glass shards. Walsh's right eye was ruined. Sheehan sent Walsh to New York to meet with an eye specialist, but Walsh refused Sheehan's request to continue directing the film. Irving Cummings took over as director, while Warner Baxter replaced Walsh in the role of the Cisco Kid. Studio writers rewrote Walsh's script, but the film still bore his stamp. Long shots of him, in which his face is not distinguishable, were kept, as were the chase sequences through Bryce Canyon.

DISTRIBUTION: *In Old Arizona* was a hit, even if its slow pace makes it seem stiff and clichéd today. Baxter won the Best Actor Oscar for his performance, and the movie was voted one of the 10 Best Pictures of 1929 in a poll conducted by *Film Daily*. It brought in $1.3 million in world-wide rentals, 82 percent from the domestic market. The film also provided a role model for future singing cowboys, with Baxter crooning "My Tonia." It enabled Walsh to make the successful transition from a director of silent movies to a director of talkies. His follow-up directorial project, the 1929 film, *The Cockeyed World,* made more than $2.6 million in worldwide rentals. —*Louis Burklow*

THE BROADWAY MELODY
MGM, 1929

ALL-RELEASE EQUIVALENT 2005 $s
(Unadjusted $s) in Millions of $s

Domestic Box Office Revenues........ **$171.4**/($5.6)
Production Cost .... **$4.3**/($0.4)
Principal Photography........... **26** days estimated
10/23/1928–11/21/1928

Director .... Harry Beaumont

Producer .... Irving Thalberg, Lawrence Weingarten (both uncredited)

Production Company.... Metro-Goldwyn-Mayer Pictures

Story by .... Edmund Goulding

Screenplay by .... Sarah Y. Mason

Cast .... Bessie Love, Anita Page, Charles King

Filming Locations ...... MGM Studios, Culver City, CA

Genre .... Musical

Format .... B&W with two-color Technicolor sequences

Initial Release .... 2/1/1929 premiere (Los Angeles); 2/8/1929 at New York Astor for twice daily run; 6/6/1929 general release

Rerelease .... none

Running Time .... 105 minutes
10 reels
9,372 feet

MPAA Rating .... not rated

STANDING THE TEST OF TIME

ACADEMY AWARD Oscar Nominations and Wins

*OUTSTANDING PICTURE: Metro-Goldwyn-Mayer

Actress: Bessie Love

Directing: Harry Beaumont

OSCAR TOTALS   Nominations **3**   *Wins **1**

AFI 100 YEARS 100 MOVIES SELECTION
2007 0   1997 0

TOP 300 FILMS POSITION ....none
All-Release Domestic Box Office in Equivalent 2005 $s

National Film Preservation Board Selection....none

OTHER AWARDS Best Picture Wins

	Year
Golden Globes .... none	
New York Film Critics..................... none	
National Board of Review.................. none	
Film Daily Critics......................... none	

The New Wonder of the Screen!
ALL TALKING ALL SINGING ALL DANCING
Dramatic Sensation
—Ad copy for the first movie musical

PLOT: In this backstage musical about a vaudeville sister act, "Hank" Mahoney (Bessie Love) and her sister, Queenie (Anita Page), come to the big city looking for fame and find romantic heartbreak instead.

PRODUCTION: The release of *The Jazz Singer* in October 1927 caused a revolution in the movie business. By late 1928, films had to have some sort of sound—music and effects at the very least. There was no longer a market for purely silent pictures in the nation's first-run theaters. Talking sequences were hastily "goat-glanded" onto already completed silent pictures, and studios scrambled to turn out all-talking films. While MGM appeared slow to adapt, making silents with their top stars well into 1929, they were assessing the potential of sound in a slightly different way. Unsure that audiences would accept a musical, producer Irving Thalberg decided to conduct "an experiment," one that could be shot quickly and inexpensively. Based on a story by director Edmund Goulding, *The Broadway Melody* was written for vaudeville and Broadway stars the Duncan Sisters, but negotiations with the Duncans fell through. To write the dialogue, MGM hired Norman Houston and James Gleason, the latter a co-writer of the hit 1928 play *Is Zat So?* The songwriting team of Arthur Freed and Nacio Herb Brown, who had penned songs for local Los Angeles revues, composed the score for what became the first original talking musical for the screen. Charles King (not to be confused with the cowboy actor of the same name) was a Broadway performer with credits dating back to 1914. He was the perfect choice for this story's song and dance man. But it would be Bessie Love who stole the show. Love had been in films since 1916 but found herself out of work in 1928. An agent then persuaded her to pursue stage work. After appearing with a Fanchon and Marco prologue at Grauman's Egyptian Theater, she was tested by MGM and offered the role of Hank. Anita Page had scored big in *Our Dancing Daughters* for director Harry Beaumont, and bringing back that pairing added a touch of box office insurance. Bessie Love would recall that sound was so new, the company would make audio recordings of their rehearsals, then suggest adjustments in microphone position and sets to make sure that the final takes would be okay. By necessity, there were technical breakthroughs. At that time sound cameras were large and stationary, so Beaumont and cinematographer John Arnold invented what they referred to as a "coffin on wheels," a camera that was small enough to move around the room and effectively capture dance numbers. When Thalberg decreed that "The Wedding of the Painted Doll" scene was too staged and demanded that it be shot again, there was no money to rehire the orchestra and others. Instead, recording engineer Douglas Shearer found a way to play back the old soundtrack as the dancers filmed the scene yet again. That was the first playback system. The wedding scene was also filmed in two-color Technicolor but is only known to survive in black and white.

DISTRIBUTION: *The Broadway Melody* was a huge box office success, with a net profit of more than $1.6 million. And, of course, it led to a flood of movie musicals. It was voted one of the 10 Best Pictures of 1929 by *Film Daily*. It earned $4.4 million in worldwide rentals and was the first movie to spawn sequels (there were several until 1940). It became the first talking picture to win the Best Picture Academy Award. —*Robert S. Birchard*

121

THE HOLLYWOOD REVUE OF 1929
MGM, 1929

ALL-RELEASE EQUIVALENT 2005 $s
(Unadjusted $s) in Millions of $s

Domestic Box Office Revenues. . . . . **$103.6**/($3.4)
Production Cost . . . . **$4.9**/($0.4)
Principal Photography . . . . **34** days estimated
3/6/1929–4/13/1929

Director	Charles F. Reisner
Producer	Harry Rapf
Production Company	Metro-Goldwyn-Mayer Pictures
Story by	Joe Farnham (skit)
Screenplay by	Al Bonsberg, Robert Hopkins
Cast	Conrad Nagel, Jack Benny, John Gilbert, Norma Shearer, Joan Crawford, Bessie Love, Lionel Barrymore, Stan Laurel, Oliver Hardy, Anita Page, Marion Davies, Buster Keaton, Charles King
Filming Locations	MGM Studios, Culver City, CA
Genre	Musical
Format	B&W and color (two-strip Technicolor)
Initial Release	11/9/1929 initial release; 11/23/1929 general release
Rerelease	none
Running Time	113, 116 or 125 minutes 13 reels 11,669 feet
MPAA Rating	not rated

STANDING THE TEST OF TIME

ACADEMY AWARD Oscar Nominations and Wins

Outstanding Picture : Metro-Goldwyn-Mayer

OSCAR TOTALS   Nominations **1**   *Wins 0

AFI 100 YEARS 100 MOVIES SELECTION
2007 0   1997 0

TOP 300 FILMS POSITION . . . . .none
All-Release Domestic Box Office in Equivalent 2005 $s

National Film Preservation Board Selection . . . .none

OTHER AWARDS Best Picture Wins

	Year
Golden Globes	none
New York Film Critics	none
National Board of Review	none
Film Daily Critics	none

The first of the no-plot, all-star movie revues,
The Hollywood Revue of 1929 *came to the
screen with all of MGM's manifold resources
lavished upon it. The result was an
overproduced extravaganza that attempted
to out-Ziegfeld Ziegfeld in
the sheer scope of its presentation.*

—Clive Hirschhorn

PLOT: While there is no story to this all-star revue for MGM's stable of contract players, there is enough going on to prove that these stars could talk (and sing) with the best of them.

PRODUCTION: After *The Broadway Melody* wrapped principal photography in November 1928, MGM hired showman-songwriter Gus Edwards to oversee its musical shorts and announced a six-reel Movietone Revue. Talkies were just beginning to emerge, and all of the studios were anxious to show off their players' abilities to talk and sing. MGM then turned the Movietone concept into a feature-length minstrel show titled *The Revue of Revues,* directed by Christy Cabanne. In April 1929, with shooting almost completed, producers Irving Thalberg and Harry Rapf decided it was not glamorous enough and replaced Cabanne with Charles Reisner. Seeking to add luster, MGM added segments with Joan Crawford, Buster Keaton, Norma Shearer, John Gilbert, and just about every other star on the lot except Greta Garbo, whose contract stipulated that she appear only as the lead. Acting as emcees were Conrad Nagel and, in his film debut, Jack Benny. Their jokes revolved largely around the difference between stage performers and film actors. They kidded about Prohibition, sound in the movies, and a host of other current topics. They told in-jokes about the cast, and they especially enjoyed joshing the stars, teasing Norma Shearer about husband and producer Irving Thalberg. There were thirty acts, filmed almost entirely with a head-on camera aimed at a proscenium stage. New camera technology was also used. For instance, the opening number alternated between negative and positive film stock, with half of the dancers appearing in blackface while the other half appear white. There were also several inventive camera tricks, such as when a top star of the day, Bessie Love, was shrunken down in size so that she could make her grand entrance from within Jack Benny's pocket. There were also a couple of Technicolor sequences. One was a reprise of "Singin' in the Rain" (first filmed version) performed at the end by the whole cast. During another number, the studio had arranged for some theaters to have the smell of orange blossoms waft through the audience. Choreographer Sammy Lee created dance routines that were photographed from overhead. Marion Davies did a bit where she was made up to look like a cadet and was flanked by a platoon of very tall palace guards (because sponsor William Randolph Hearst enjoyed seeing her in male attire). Davies and Laurel and Hardy, all working on other projects, were required to shoot their segments on the graveyard shift. Studio publicist Pete Smith had the stars sign an affidavit (for the public) vouching for the authenticity of their voices, due to new dubbing techniques in use.

DISTRIBUTION: The film ranked in the top 10 box office hits of 1929 with a $1.1 million profit on worldwide rentals of $2.4 million. The premieres became circuses, with Grauman's Chinese Theater (Los Angeles) and the Capitol (New York) featuring live billboards (with scantily dressed women) that stopped traffic. MGM pitched it as a lavish theatrical presentation with two-a-day road show hard ticket releases, followed later by a general release. For years, the film was available only in its 82-minute TV release version; in the 1970s it was restored to almost its original 125-minute length. —*Hayley Taylor Block*

The 1930s

[Victor] Fleming was wanted very badly by Clark Gable and David Selznick. . . . [In January 1939, King Vidor was invited to take over The Wizard of Oz *to free up Fleming for* Gone with the Wind*] And I said I would. Victor Fleming was a good friend. . . . I took over, it was, as I remember, about two and a half weeks, three weeks possibly. Which included "Somewhere over the Rainbow" . . . and "We're Off to See the Wizard" . . . But I did not want any credit, and as long as Victor was alive, I kept quiet about it.*

—King Vidor

TOP 10 ALL-RELEASE MOVIES
DOMESTIC BOX OFFICE
By Initial Year of Release, 1930–1939

		Equivalent 2005 $s in Millions of $s
1	Gone with the Wind	$1,407.7
2	Snow White and the Seven Dwarfs	$760.9
3	San Francisco	$196.7
4	The Great Ziegfeld	$176.0
5	Boys Town	$175.1
6	The Wizard of Oz	$169.1
7	Alexander's Ragtime Band	$162.9
8	Whoopee!	$161.9
9	The Kid from Spain	$161.0
10	Saratoga	$150.6
		Total: $3,521.9

GENERAL U.S. STATISTICS, 1930

123,202,624
U.S. Population

90 Million
Average Weekly
U.S. Movie Attendance

DECADE OVERVIEW

The Golden Age of Hollywood

The 1930s was a decade defined by the global devastation of the Great Depression and the rumblings of World War II. Yet even as the movie industry was beset with economic problems, it was also being transformed by the spread of sound and the arrival of color. Both were meaningful tools in telling big stories such as *The Wizard of Oz* and *Gone with the Wind*. These two epics, released in 1939, highlighted a year of memorable films produced at the apex of the contract studio system, part of a period from 1927 into the 1950s known as the Golden Age of Hollywood.

This time was particularly fortuitous for screen performers who sounded as good on film as they looked. While a number of the stars of silent cinema—especially those from foreign countries—were having a difficult time making the transition to talking pictures, there were many others, including stage performers, playwrights, producers, and a new crop of attractive young actors, who were rising quickly to fire the popular imagination. Among those recruited from Broadway was Helen Hayes, who made her film debut in *The Sin of Madelon Claudet* in 1931, a performance that garnered her an Oscar for Best Actress.

Under the contract system, the studios controlled the talent. Stars rarely, if ever, enjoyed such privileges as a share in a film's profits the way they do today. Instead most were on salary and their pay ranges varied greatly. While Eddie Cantor and Will Rogers, for instance, were making $100,000 or more per picture in 1931, salaried actors such as Clark Gable were making $650 a week. Based on income tax returns, in 1935 Mae West was the second-highest-paid individual in America (after only William Randolph Hearst), collecting $480,833 from Paramount that year ($7.6 million in 2005 dollars).

The 1930s were also memorable for introducing twelve-time Oscar-nominated actress Katharine Hepburn to audiences. She would win her first Best Actress Oscar for *Morning Glory* (1933), and though she wouldn't win again until *Guess Who's Coming to Dinner* (1967), when she played opposite Spencer Tracy, we would see a lot of her famous co-star throughout the 1930s. Tracy won consecutive Best Actor Oscars for *Captains Courageous* (1937) and *Boys Town* (1938)—a feat that would not occur again until Tom Hanks won for *Philadelphia* (1993) and *Forrest Gump* (1994). One of the rare female top stars at Warner Bros., Bette Davis, would also win two Oscars for Best Actress during the 1930s: one for *Dangerous* (1935) and another for *Jezebel* (1938).

During the 1930s certain productions were shot in only a few days, while others took much longer. But production length had little correlation to profits. Director Victor Fleming took 86 days to shoot *The Wizard of Oz* and 140 days to shoot *Gone with the Wind*. *Wizard* lost money on its initial release, while *Gone with the Wind* became the number one box office film of all time. Charlie Chaplin spent 179 days filming *City Lights* (1931) and 147 days filming *Modern Times* (1936). Domestic rentals for *City Lights* totaled $2 million compared with only $1.4 million for *Modern Times*. On the other end of the spectrum, Lowell Sherman spent just 18 days shooting

She Done Him Wrong (1932), starring Mae West in an adaptation of her stage act. That film's rentals totaled $2 million in the United States and another $1 million throughout the rest of the world.

In the period between the two world wars, the international market was once again a major source of box office revenue for the studios. Although production resumed in Europe after the Great War, Hollywood films often dominated the box office wherever they played. Among the European film artists to rise during this time was Alfred Hitchcock. He had accepted a contract from David O. Selznick in 1939 and journeyed to America seeking greater creative freedom and a chance to work with the resources of the Hollywood studios. He would battle for control with Selznick, who was riding high on the success of *Gone with the Wind,* but ultimately it was Hitchcock who emerged on top.

As the decade began, movie attendance was down due to the high level of unemployment. Those who could no longer afford to go to the movies listened to film's archrival, the radio, instead. Theaters tried everything to lure in audiences. They lowered ticket prices, offered door prizes, and ran afternoon matinees and double features. But by the decade's end, more than 70 percent of all homes had at least one radio. It became film's primary competitor, but as some savvy studios had learned, radio was also a great promotional tool.

Many stars who began their careers in stage and vaudeville before moving into film played well on radio due to their voice training. One of the actors who exploited radio effectively was Orson Welles. He stunned the world with one of the most inspired radio scares of all time when he and his Mercury Theatre broadcast a version of *The War of the Worlds* on Halloween night in 1938. Although the program was identified as a fictional play at the beginning of the broadcast, thousands of people took it seriously, at least for a short time. The production was so convincing that it caused a major nationwide controversy. This key incident helped propel young Orson Welles to fame, earning him a contract with RKO that subsequently led to the creation of *Citizen Kane* (1941).

As radio's effects were being felt, the circuits with the most theaters suffered the gravest economic problems. Even as ticket sales wavered, exhibitors were being required to make huge capital investments to bring sound to the screen. This necessitated the participation of Wall Street and created a tale of two cities that would dominate the movie business for years thereafter: pictures were largely made in Los Angeles, while the home office, and control of the purse strings, remained in New York City.

After filing for bankruptcy in 1933, the biggest theatrical exhibition circuit, Paramount-Publix, turned to Wall Street for help. The public markets also kept Warner Bros. and MGM out of bankruptcy, raising millions but also turning over significant control to powerful investors. Universal Pictures and Fox Studios also went bankrupt, after which Fox was merged with Darryl F. Zanuck's much smaller 20th Century Pictures to become 20th Century-Fox. Meanwhile Columbia and United Artists downsized.

MGM emerged as the largest and most successful studio during the decade, as its exhibition business grew to dominate the first-run market in a number of key cities, especially in the heavily populated eastern United States. Louis B. Mayer ran the studio, but Irving Thalberg is cited as the creative genius who inspired the new level of dramas, musicals, and comedies that drove the company's success. Thalberg died in 1936 when he was only thirty-six years old, leaving behind many movie projects, including oversight of the highly successful comedy *Animal Crackers,* starring the Marx Brothers. Thalberg was remembered as a legend and as having set the gold standard for creative movie executives.

Another mark of the decade was the industry's high level of production. In addition to new films, there were many remakes of silent movies with sound. Amid the myriad features, shorts, newsreels, and cartoons there were A films with high budgets and well-known casts as well as B movies made for less, with younger and often unknown performers. It was from these B movies that genre films first developed, repeating successful cinematic formulas time and again.

Among the most popular genre films were monster movies. In fact, the decade inspired a bonanza of monster characters that would become cultural icons and spawn endless sequels in all media: *Dracula* (1931), *Frankenstein* (1931), *Dr. Jekyll and Mr. Hyde* (1932), *The Mummy* (1932), *Vampyr* (1932), *White Zombie* (1932), *Son of Kong* (1933), and *Werewolf of London* (1935). Over time some genre films became so popular they starred A-listers as well. There were screwball comedies to lighten the burden of hard economic times, including many short films featuring the Three Stooges, and other feature-length escapist fare such as westerns and horror movies. Then there were subgenres such as the prison drama, beginning with MGM's *The Big House* (1930). A year later the first of the Charlie Chan mysteries appeared, featuring a Caucasian actor in the title role made up to look Chinese.

Among the biggest stars of the decade was a little girl named Shirley Temple, who from age three until her teens made a string of hit pictures filled with family stories, music, excitement, singing, dancing, and comedy. She was the most famous child actor of her time, and even rated a tiny Oscar, but she was certainly not the only child actor. Short films featuring Our Gang, also known as the Little Rascals, were big hits as well.

The very earliest of the talking films suffered from technical gaffes or stiff acting by stage stars not yet accustomed to the film medium. From the advent of sound until 1932, all sound recording, including music and sound effects, had to be done at the time of production. However, in 1932, a system that allowed the mixing of sound during postproduction for the first time was developed and introduced.

During this decade, MGM boasted that it had more stars than the heavens, including Clark Gable and Joan Crawford, who teamed up for the movie *Dance, Fools, Dance* (1931)—a film that pushed the envelope with regard to screen sex. But that was soon to change. In 1930 the film industry, seeking to censor its own products before the government stepped in to do it for them, had agreed to implement the Production Code, which regulated what could and could not be shown on-screen. In 1934, under Joseph I. Breen, that code began to be enforced.

The labor movement also took root in Hollywood during the 1930s amid violence and recriminations between workers and studio bosses. However, thanks to legislation passed during

Roosevelt's New Deal, the unions were able to exercise their rights and organize first in the various movie production crafts, and then into guilds of writers, directors, and actors. The Academy of Motion Picture Arts and Sciences was originally envisioned by some of its organizers as an alternative to the labor unions, but instead became a place for various branches of movie production, distribution, and marketing to come together as a community. Later in the decade, scandals surfaced involving the largest of the craft unions, and several of the union leaders and one studio executive served prison time.

As the decade began, Fox was still pushing a new wide-screen 70 mm movie format for theaters. Among the films made in the Grandeur format was *The Big Trail* (1930). It marked the credited debut of young John Wayne, who would go on to become one of the medium's most prolific actors, first in B movies and then as a top film star. But the Grandeur format really didn't go much farther than that. While it didn't fail technically, it did become a victim of hard times. The studios got together under the newly formed Academy and decreed that a uniform standard was needed. Due to the economic crunch, they didn't want different systems to co-exist. They wanted one way to deliver movies that would be compatible all over the globe. Thus, the 35 mm movie strip became the Academy standard and remained so until the 1950s.

Technicolor introduced a three-strip color process in 1932, but movies were still mostly in black and white until the 1950s because color added more production expense and the distribution department didn't think it would make much difference in terms of consumer preference. They were wrong. Although there weren't many color movies available at the time, those that were dominated the awards ceremonies and the box office, led by the greatest box office success of the twentieth century, *Gone with the Wind*.

As the decade ended, the big five studios, and the little three that didn't own theaters, were going strong. There were threats from the government to break up companies involved in both production and exhibition, but the impact of the first legal volley by the U.S. Department of Justice, fired late in the decade, wouldn't be felt until the 1940s.

Monster Movies *Hannibal* vs. *Dracula*
All-Release Worldwide Box Office, 1931 and 2001
Equivalent 2005 $s /(Unadjusted $s) in Millions of $s

Film	Initial Release	Star	Domestic Box Office	Foreign Box Office	Worldwide Box Office	Production Cost	Cost as a Percentage of Worldwide Box Office
Dracula	1931	Bela Lugosi	$46.6 ($1.6)	$31.1 ($1.1)	$77.7 ($2.7)	$4.6 ($0.4)	13%
Hannibal	2001	Anthony Hopkins	$187.0 ($165.1)	$211.3 ($186.6)	$398.3 ($351.7)	$88.2 ($80.0)	23%

Comparison of Six MGM 1930s Movies
Initial Release Domestic vs. Foreign Rentals
Unadjusted $s

Film	Initial Release	Domestic Rentals	Domestic % of total	Foreign Rentals	Foreign % of total
Grand Hotel	1932	$1,235,000	48%	$1,359,000	52%
The Thin Man	1934	$818,000	57%	$605,000	43%
Mutiny on the Bounty	1935	$2,250,000	50%	$2,210,000	50%
San Francisco	1936	$2,868,000	54%	$2,405,000	46%
Captains Courageous	1937	$1,688,000	54%	$1,445,000	46%
Gone with the Wind	1939	$30,015,000	61%	$18,964,000	39%

Note: *Gone with the Wind* includes initial release plus four rereleases (1941, 1942, 1947 and 1954) since foreign rental revenues were available only cumulative through 1956.

Comparison of Two MGM *Mutiny on the Bounty* Films
Initial Release Domestic Box Office
Equivalent 2005 $s /(Unadjusted $s) in Millions of $s

Initial Release	Film Length	Principal Photography	Domestic Box Office	Production Cost	Net Profit/ –Loss	Salary
1935	132 minutes	84 days	$133.5 ($5.0)	$27.1 ($1.9)	$54.7 ($0.9)	Clark Gable $0.5 million (est. salary $2,500/week x 14 weeks for total flat fee $35,000)
1962	178 minutes	180 days estimated	$130.0 ($16.4)	$139.9 ($21.6)	–$83.2 (–$15.1)	Marlon Brando $8.1 million ($500,000 plus 10% gross + $10,000/week expenses + $5,000/day over schedule estimated total $1,250,000)

Top Five 1930s Clark Gable–Starring MGM Films
All-Release Domestic Box Office
Equivalent 2005 $s /(Unadjusted $s) in Millions of $s

Rank	Film	Initial Release	Domestic Box Office	Production Cost
1	*Gone with the Wind*	1939	**$1,407.7/($176.7)**	**$58.5/($4.2)**
2	*San Francisco*	1936	**$196.7/($8.3)**	**$18.2/($1.3)**
3	*Saratoga*	1937	**$150.6/($5.4)**	**$15.5/($1.1)**
4	*Test Pilot*	1938	**$150.6/($5.4)**	**$23.6/($1.7)**
5	*Mutiny on the Bounty*	1935	**$148.2/($5.7)**	**$27.1/($1.9)**

Snow White and the Seven Dwarfs
All-Release Domestic Box Office by Release Wave
Equivalent 2005 $s /(Unadjusted $s) in Millions of $s

Release Date	Release Wave	Domestic Box Office	Production Cost
12/21/1937	1	**$402.6/($14.4)**	**$20.2/($1.5)**
2/1/1944	2	**$28.9/$1.4)**	
2/1/1952	3	**$14.8/($1.1)**	
4/1/1958	4	not available	
6/1/1967	5	**$56.4/($10.6)**	
12/1/1975	6	**$73.0/($23.3)**	
7/15/1983	7	**$46.9/($23.0)**	
7/17/1987	8	**$74.4/($45.4)**	
7/2/1993	9	**$63.9/($41.3)**	
1937–2005		**$760.9/($160.7)**	**$20.2/($1.5)**

PRODUCTION SPOTLIGHT

The producer of motion pictures like every other person engaged in large-scale creative enterprise should have, above all, the faculty of foretelling public taste. . . . Box office returns tell the world at once whether he has touched the public with a success or missed it with a failure. Critics, good or bad, have insignificant influence on the box office.
—DARRYL F. ZANUCK

Change Brings Challenges

While sound was a great advancement and opened the door to a whole new level of story-telling, it also brought new technical challenges to every step of the production process, from the design and use of equipment to the nature of performance. The first sound equipment was large and immobile. To stifle the loud grinding of the camera's gears, both camera and cameraman were enclosed in a soundproof box that in some cases barely contained enough air for the cameraman to breathe. Gradual improvements occurred only because assertive filmmakers such as Rouben Mamoulian and Ernst Lubitsch demanded them.

Rouben Mamoulian Innovates with Technology

Mamoulian was an innovator in both theater and film. He was from an Armenian family, but he grew up in Russia. He moved to Moscow to study law; however, he loved the theater so

---

1930s Movie Censorship: A Brief History

Under pressure from the Women's Christian Temperance Union (WCTU) and others, the Motion Picture Producers and Distributors of America (MPPDA) puts in place tougher movie morality standards by creating the Production Code (also known as the Hays Code) in 1930. Movie producers continue to pay it little attention. The sexual suggestion in Monkey Business *(1931) and other Marx Brothers films is often the target of censors. Films starring Mae West, including* She Done Him Wrong *(1934) are also cited as the basis for strengthening the morals-focused Hays Code.*

The Catholic Legion of Decency is formed in 1934, and Joseph I. Breen becomes head of the new Production Code Administration (PCA), which begins to enforce the Hays Code. Breen holds that position for twenty years, during which the PCA is closely allied with the Legion of Decency. Movie production companies are essentially required to join the PCA and adhere to the code or be fined.

131

much that he took acting classes at night. He became a director and went on to win praise for his productions in London and then New York. He had a hit in 1926 with *Porgy on Broadway*, with an all African American cast, which was very rare at that time on the Great White Way. This success brought Mamoulian to the attention of Paramount. The studio signed him to direct movies adapted from plays and musicals at their facility located in Astoria, Queens, a borough of New York City. During the filming of his first feature, *Applause* (1929), Mamoulian was frustrated by the limitations of sound recording. He had wanted to move the camera around as directors had in silent films. So Mamoulian pestered his studio bosses until they found someone who could fix the problem. Instead of positioning a microphone in a single location, microphones were placed all around the set so Mamoulian was free to shoot in different directions. By trial and error he figured out the best positions for the recording equipment to be placed in each scene, making him one of the first directors of the era to achieve visual mobility while capturing sound. *Applause* also introduced the first double-channel soundtrack, allowing dialogue to overlap other sounds. Mamoulian was temperamental and chafed under the restrictions of the studio system, but he continued to improve the technology of the medium with each successive movie, including *City Streets* (1931) and *Love Me Tonight* (1932). He was also the first to direct a full-color, all-Technicolor movie, *Becky Sharp* (1935).

Ernst Lubitsch Uses Music as a Tool

Another immigrant who quickly mastered the new medium was German-born Ernst Lubitsch, who led the way in using music as a tool to advance the story in his films. He directed one of the first film musicals, *The Love Parade* (1929), which was nominated for six Academy Awards, and followed it with several others including *The Smiling Lieutenant* (1931) also starring the popular Maurice Chevalier. Lubitsch held another distinction too—in 1935 Paramount Pictures appointed him production manager, making him the first major director ever with the power to greenlight movies. The town sat up and took notice. *Time* magazine reported on February 18, 1935: "Never before in the history of the industry has so spectacular a director been considered sufficiently responsible to run a major studio.

Index of Top Feature Film Directors Included in This Chapter

1	Victor Fleming	*Gone with the Wind*
		The Wizard of Oz
		Captains Courageous
2	David Hand	*Snow White and the Seven Dwarfs*
3	Henry King	*Alexander's Ragtime Band*
		In Old Chicago
		State Fair
4	Frank Capra	*Mr. Smith Goes to Washington*
		It Happened One Night
		Mr. Deeds Goes to Town
5	W. S. Van Dyke	*San Francisco*
		The Thin Man
6	George Cukor	*Little Women*
		David Copperfield
7	Charles Chaplin	*City Lights*
		Modern Times
8	Robert Z. Leonard	*The Great Ziegfeld*
9	Norman Taurog	*Boys Town*
10	Lowell Sherman	*She Done Him Wrong*

See Note to the Reader for selection criteria.

The appointment caused Hollywood to rattle with astonishment. Director Lubitsch caustically suggested that the shock was due to the fact that he was "a picture-maker not a banker." Unfortunately, Lubitsch suffered from an inability to delegate work, which proved to be a big problem when he was charged with overseeing aspects of more than sixty movies, all of which needed attention at the same time. After only a year on the job as production chief, he was fired. Lubitsch returned to producing and directing his own work and still supervised other directors. In 1939 he fulfilled a long-held desire to work with Greta Garbo when he directed her in *Ninotchka*. They had long been friends, but this would be their only film together. The satirical comedy—sold under the slogan "Garbo Laughs!" —was co-written by Billy Wilder.

Gone with the Wind, 1939
Budget Breakdown
Equivalent 2005 $s /(Unadjusted $s)

Novel	$0.7 million/($50,000)
Studio department head labor	$4.6 million/$328,300)
Scarlett O'Hara search	$1.3 million/($92,000)
Stars, cast, and extra salaries	$6.6 million/($466,700)
Subtotal above-the-line	**$13.2 million/($937,000)**
Crew	$15.2 million/$1,080,600
Extras	$1.5 million/($108,500)
Sets (21)	$2.8 million/($197,900)
Wardrobe	$2.2 million/($153,800)
Raw film stock (474,538 feet × 3); picture negative developed 390,797 feet and printed 272,658 feet	$2.3 million/($167,100)
Soundtrack raw stock (535,000 feet); soundtrack developed 221,303 feet and printed 232,885 feet	$.2 million/($15,900)
Lighting, lumber, research, projection cost, transportation	$3.5 million/($250,900)
Location expenses and props	$2.1 million/($151,100)
Music	$1.4 million/($99,800)
Other	$14.1 million/($1,000,694)
Subtotal below-the-line	**$45.3 million/($3,226,294)**
Total production cost	**$58.5 million/($4,163,294)**

Top 15 War Films
All-Release Domestic Box Office, 1930–2005
Equivalent 2005 $s /(Unadjusted $s) in Millions of $s

Rank	Film	Distributor	War	Initial Release	Domestic Box Office	Production Cost
1	Gone with the Wind*	MGM	American Civil War	1939	$1,407.7/($176.7)	$58.5/($4.2)
2	Doctor Zhivago	MGM	Russian Revolution	1965	$622.4/($109.8)	$73.5/($11.9)
3	The Bridge on the River Kwai*	Columbia	WW II	1957	$362.3/($38.2)	$20.2/($2.9)
4	The Best Years of Our Lives*	RKO	WW II	1946	$345.3/($22.9)	$23.0/($2.3)
5	For Whom the Bell Tolls	Paramount	Spanish Civil War	1943	$333.9/($15.8)	$33.7/($3.0)
6	Mrs. Miniver*	MGM	WW II	1942	$316.5/($13.3)	$16.1/($1.3)
7	Saving Private Ryan	DreamWorks	WW II	1998	$292.8/($216.2)	$94.5/($78.0)
8	Lawrence of Arabia*	Columbia	WW I	1962	$290.2/($44.5)	$97.0/($15.0)
9	The Longest Day	20th Century-Fox	WW II	1962	$259.5/($34.2)	$55.6/($8.6)
10	The Guns of Navarone	Columbia	WW II	1961	$240.5/($28.9)	$45.7/($7.0)
11	The Dirty Dozen	MGM	WW II	1967	$238.0/($44.6)	$31.3/($5.4)
12	Platoon*	Orion	Vietnam	1986	$226.7/($138.0)	$11.6/($6.5)
13	Since You Went Away	United Artists	WW II	1944	$226.3/($11.4)	$22.2/($2.0)
14	Pearl Harbor	Buena Vista	WW II	2001	$224.9/($198.5)	$159.9/($145.0)
15	Apocalypse Now	United Artists	Vietnam	1979	$205.7/($83.5)	$83.4/($31.0)

*Academy Award winner for Best Picture.

She Done Him Wrong, 1933
Budget Breakdown
Equivalent 2005 $s /(Unadjusted $s)

Writers	**$92,661/($6,500)**
Directors (Lowell Sherman paid $12,000)	**$512,463/$35,948)**
Actors	**$726,295/($50,948)**
Subtotal above-the-line	**$1.3 million/($93,396)**
Technical	**$256,599/($18,000)**
Extras	**$167,502/($11,750)**
Sets	**$223,811/($15,700)**
Set dressing	**$71,277/($5,000)**
Wardrobe	**$152,576/($10,703)**
Lighting	**$54,456/($3,820)**
Props	**$14,255/($1,000)**
Miniatures and effects	**$7,128/($500)**
Sound	**$117,893/($8,270)**
Music and sound effects	**$154,814/($10,860)**
Negative film and sample print	**$156,810/($11,000)**
Other	**$1.4 million/($84,077)**
Subtotal below-the-line	**$2.8 million/($180,680)**
Total production cost	**$4.1 million/($274,076)**

U.S. INDUSTRY PRODUCTION STATISTICS, 1930s
Equivalent 2005 $s /(Unadjusted $s)

$16.1 Million ($1.2 million)
Average production cost of films featured in this chapter

$4.4 Million ($375,000)
Average production cost of all films released in 1930

Comic Revolutionaries Raise the Bar for Screen Comedy

When the first talkies were produced, Hollywood talent scouts were dispatched to Broadway to seek out talent who could talk as well as act. One of the hits running from December 1925 through August 1926 was *The Cocoanuts,* starring the madcap Marx Brothers, who, led by their mother, Minnie, had risen from poverty to become vaudeville stars and, in turn, one of the funniest and most influential comedy teams of all time. There was Groucho with his big cigar, walking bent over while talking, wisecracking and delivering asides that broke the fourth wall between the story and the viewer. There was Chico, who affected an immigrant Italian's thick accent while playing the piano brilliantly and looking for the next con to pull. There was Harpo, who played the comedic lecher who never spoke and whose antics included hilarious pantomimes and gags such as drawing a department store's worth of stuff from inside his jacket. Brothers Gummo and Zeppo dropped out along the way, later becoming successful Hollywood talent agents who represented several top stars of the 1930s and 1940s.

The brothers' agent, William Morris, offered Walter Wanger, head of production at Paramount studios, the rights to *The Cocoanuts* and the services of Groucho, Chico, Harpo, and Zeppo for $75,000. Wanger thought he had the deal of the century, but his boss, Adolph Zukor, turned up his nose at the idea. Zukor later made a deal negotiated by Chico for $100,000. That first film would be followed by another four pictures at Paramount. Anarchy had entered the movies, and comedy would never be the same.

These first Paramount pictures, more than any others, convey the brothers' freestyle, anything-goes brand of humor. They didn't ask permission; they just blew up comedic conventions and turned audiences upside down. Artists and filmmakers from Mel Brooks to Woody Allen and beyond have been influenced by their trademark anarchy—their free associations, spontaneous physical actions, sight gags, and clever chatter all bound up in some romantic, fantastic impossible dream.

Despite technical flaws and the brothers' own misgivings, *Cocoanuts* was an instant hit. But the first time the brothers saw a cut of the finished movie in a Paramount screening room they were outraged. They thought that the movie was a pale version of the Broadway play, not nearly as funny as the original work. They even tried to buy the negative so that they could have it destroyed—the same thing they had done earlier in their careers when they decided that they hated a silent film they shot. Paramount refused, of course, and in 1929 the film opened.

The brother's second film at Paramount was *Animal Crackers,* which was released in 1930, once again following their Broadway stage show. Like *Cocoanuts,* it was based on a book by George S. Kaufman adapted by Morrie Ryskind. This time, however, the studio was determined to keep a tighter rein on things. Director Victor Heerman was sent on the road with the Marx Brothers as they performed their play live, so he could note what worked best. He then pared the script down and made a much more tightly edited picture. While the director of *Cocoanuts* wanted to faithfully capture the play, Heerman preferred to focus on the brothers and their comedic personalities. He cut most of the musical numbers except for "Hooray for Captain Spaulding" and a love song. He kept the romantic subplot but moved everything else along briskly. *Animal Crackers* went over budget and over schedule, but it too became another hit.

The third Paramount film was *Monkey Business,* released in 1931. It was the first Marx Brothers movie that had not been based on a previously produced Broadway comedy hit and the first of their pictures to be made on the West Coast. Cartoonist and humorist S. J. Perelman and writer Will Johnstone came up with the idea of casting the brothers as stowaways on a ship. After several false starts, the script was penned by a group that included the brothers and the producer, in addition to Perelman and Johnstone. The writing took more than five months to complete. The success of this movie led to *Horse Feathers* in 1932, which critics have called the most surrealistic of all the Marx Brothers comedies, and then to *Duck Soup,* a comedy so anti-authoritarian that the dictator of Italy at the time, Benito Mussolini, banned the movie in his country because he believed it mocked him.

Duck Soup turned out to be the final Marx Brothers movie at Paramount. Its production was delayed until the brothers settled a lawsuit with the studio; their agent, Max Gordon, had negotiated a three-picture deal for which the brothers were to receive 50 percent of net profits over $400,000 on each picture, with the first $10,000 going to Gordon for brokering the deal, but disagreements over the net profit payments were responsible for a bitter contractual dispute. An early version of the script was titled "Cracked Ice," with Herman J. Mankiewicz supervising production once again and Ernst Lubitsch directing. Mankiewicz remained de facto producer without taking a credit. The movie was directed by Leo McCarey, the only top director to do a Marx Brothers movie. McCarey was assigned to the picture after the success of his vehicle for Eddie Cantor, *The Kid from Spain,* on which screenwriters Bert Kalmar and Harry Ruby had also worked. The title, *Duck Soup,* was an in-joke: slang for "something easy to do," also meaning "pushover" or "sucker." Its theme was in keeping with the animal theme of the earlier films, such as *Animal Crackers* and *Horse Feathers.* The screenplay leaned heavily on the brothers' vaudeville and radio routines, some of it adapted from an early 1930s radio show called *Flywheel, Shyster and Flywheel,* which starred Groucho and Chico. The movie was edited so that one bit appeared right after another at a frantic pace. It had little story but a lot of comedy routines, zany gags, silliness, and double entendres. A relatively short 70-minute satirical romp, it ruthlessly lampooned dictators, diplomats, and stuffed shirts. One of the most memorable comedic gems was the "mirror scene," in which Harpo, dressed as Groucho, pretending to be Groucho's reflection by inserting himself as a missing mirror. His movements are perfect, matching and mocking Groucho's every motion. The capper comes when Chico, also dressed as Groucho, barrels into both of them.

Unfortunately, *Duck Soup* was a critical and commercial flop upon its initial release. In the depth of the Great Depression, audiences didn't respond well to the political disrespect, cynicism, and antiwar message. At the time Roosevelt was trying to help America recover economically, Hitler was on the rise in Germany, and Mussolini was a popular figure in Italy. A quote by Groucho at the time proved very controversial as well. He said, "And remember while you're out there risking life and limb through shot and shell, we'll be in here thinking what a sucker you are." Shortly after its release, Paramount declined to renew their contract.

137

Not long after that, MGM production chief Irving Thalberg talked with Chico and Groucho about the prospect of working together. Thalberg felt that they were funny but told them that their movies weren't very good. He wanted to add structure and story and build the comedy around romance to help them appeal to women as well as men. It was also Thalberg's idea for the brothers to take the show on the road in script form and play in front of live audiences to get the timing on the material just right. He wanted them to find the big laughs. Having been the running joke for his small role in the movies, Zeppo quit the business to become an agent soon after the failure of *Duck Soup.* Thalberg offered to make the deal with the remaining three brothers, but when he suggested paying them a quarter less than what he would have paid if Zeppo had remained, Groucho retorted that they would be twice as funny without Zeppo. A deal was struck, and Thalberg oversaw the brothers' hugely successful reinvention in *A Night at the Opera* (1935) and in *A Day at the Races* (1937). After Thalberg's untimely death, the brothers went on to make *Room Service, At the Circus, Go West,* and their final film for MGM, *The Big Store,* using the formula Thalberg had helped to create. The brothers split up for several years after that.

Although they would work together again at a later date, mostly to pay Chico's gambling debts, their greatest days and most important movies were behind them. Chico's need for money led to several films released by United Artists, including *A Night in Casablanca* and their last film as a team, *Love Happy* (1949). The story for *Love Happy* had been created by Harpo, who had his only starring role in that final comedy. They also appeared together on *General Electric Theater,* hosted by Ronald Reagan. Harpo and Chico toured with a stage act, and Harpo did a number of TV guest appearances, including a most memorable gag with Lucille Ball. He also published his autobiography, *Harpo Speaks!* and in January 1963 uttered his first words onstage when he announced his retirement. He died after undergoing surgery in 1964. Chico, who suffered from arteriosclerosis, had passed away several years earlier, in 1961. And Groucho, who enjoyed a career in television as the host of *You Bet Your Life,* found new interest in his old age as an author and raconteur. He died on August 19, 1977, three days after Elvis.

What is drama but life with the dull bits cut out?
—ALFRED HITCHCOCK

Alfred Hitchcock: The Rise of the Director in Hollywood

The 39 Steps is considered by critics to be the greatest movie from Hitchcock's early years and the movie that launched his reputation as a master of screen suspense. The story of a Canadian who inadvertently gets involved in counterespionage and murder over the course of four frantic days was adapted by Hitchcock, his wife, Alma Reville, and screenwriter Charles Bennett from Scottish author John Buchan's popular 1915 spy novel. Although Buchan loudly complained that Hitchcock used only his title and roughly 10 percent of his story, upon seeing the film he admitted that it was better than his book. Hitchcock did his own storyboarding for the movie, to provide a sense of the editing and framing prior to filming, and he introduced what he called the "MacGuffin," a plot device that seems important to the characters but isn't really important to the audience. The atmospheric look of the film, according to Hitchcock, was influenced by Russian and German movies and was also attributed to the work of cinematographer Bernard Knowles and Austrian art director Oscar Werndorff. For his cast, Hitchcock turned to the London stage. Robert Donat became an international star based on his performance as Richard Hanney for the movie. For the female lead, Gaumont studio head Michael Balcon signed British actress Madeleine Carroll. Fearing that she might be too proper for the role, Hitchcock played a practical joke on the first day of shooting. In one scene, Carroll and Donat were to be handcuffed together. During rehearsal, Hitchcock left the set, announcing that he had an urgent matter to attend to and that he couldn't find the key to their cuffs. The actors remained locked together throughout the afternoon. By the time he returned, the stars had bonded. Hitchcock makes his cameo after the opening sequence of the movie as a man dumping some trash as Hannay and the woman rush from the theater. The movie was a hit with both critics and audiences as soon as it was released in London in June 1935 and in the United States in August 1935. It subsequently played all over the world to great acclaim. From its release until early in the next decade, many small theaters used it to fill in when no other films were available. It was known as a "mortgage lifter," because it could be relied upon to pull in ticket buyers.

After the success of *The Man Who Knew Too Much, The 39 Steps,* and his earlier films dating back to the silent era, Alfred Hitchcock consented to come to America to make movies. In 1939, following two years of entreaties by famed producer David O. Selznick and only three months before the release of Selznick's hit *Gone with the Wind,* Hitchcock finally agreed that the timing was right. Despite being the toast of British cinema, the director was itching to have access to Hollywood studio resources. In America, he would prove prolific, prophetic, and patriotic. He would also lead a change in the power structure of the movie industry, marking the rise of the director as the predominant creative force on the set, thereby reducing the role that the producer had played up until this point.

Although Selznick signed Hitchcock to a multipicture pact, the two were at odds from their very first film together, the 1940 drama *Rebecca,* based on a novel by Daphne du Maurier. Selznick had wanted Hitchcock to give the movie a real English feel. But Hitchcock had other ideas. The real problem was that each man thought he had the final say on things. Hitchcock felt battered during production; what was worse, he then had to watch Selznick dominate the postproduction process.

Hitchcock believed strongly that the director needed to be involved in every aspect of filmmaking, from choosing the source material to the final edit. He was completely unprepared for life in Selznick's world, where the producer ran things from initial idea to release. He was used to the English method, where each picture was hand-crafted. Selznick used his power to frustrate Hitchcock and leverage his control over the movie at every turn. The two would not work together again until 1945.

Hitchcock's second American movie, released in 1940, was *Foreign Correspondent.* It was based on a nonfiction book about an American reporter who, while chasing Nazi spies around England, is tied to a larger conspiracy across Europe, setting up the events of World War II. During and before production, fourteen writers worked on the script with producer Walter Wanger. Wanger had arranged for a "loan" from Selznick, who owned Hitchcock's contract. Hitchcock was determined to use the movie to send the public a message about the need to support England. At the time, America had not yet entered the war, and an isolationist sentiment was spreading. Hitchcock's message was most evident in the final scenes of the movie, when star Joel McCrea's character passionately pleads for the United States to support the British war effort during a radio broadcast. In the background the sound of bombs dropping on London can be heard. The movie opened three weeks before the bombing of London began, and only three days after the German Luftwaffe started blasting British airfields along the coast. At the 1941 Academy Awards, both *Rebecca* and *Foreign Correspondent* were nominated for Best Picture, with the Oscar going to *Rebecca,* which also won a Best Actress honor for Joan Fontaine, bringing her out of the shadow of her older sister, Olivia de Havilland.

Hitchcock directed two more films for release in 1941, one of which, *Suspicion,* marked his first time as a producer as well. It was also one of the first films he shot on location, substituting the coast of Santa Cruz, California, for the English coastline. His other film that year, also on a loan out to RKO, was *Mr. and Mrs. Smith,* his only comedy, which he said he made to please the star, Carole Lombard.

In 1942 Hitchcock was lent out to Universal to make *Saboteur,* the first of two consecutive films at the studio. It was the start of an enduring relationship between the director and Universal that would last through many movie and television projects until the end of his career, broken up sporadically by a four-picture deal at Warner Bros., a multipicture deal at Paramount, and a stint at MGM. His second film at Universal, *Shadow of a Doubt,* released in 1943, was his personal favorite. It is about a woman who comes to believe her beloved uncle is a serial killer. In it, Hitchcock uses overlapping dialogue and unusual close-ups, and plays on his fascination with the ways that people are killed.

In 1946 Hitchcock worked with Selznick again, this time on *Spellbound.* But by then circumstances had changed quite a bit. Hitchcock had become a major force in cinema, while Selznick had endured a mixed record. According to historians, *Spellbound* marks the end of an era when studio producers reigned and the beginning of an era when creative directors held more sway.

Through it all, Hitchcock developed his own unique style of production. He believed in extensive preproduction, creating storyboards for an entire movie before beginning principal photography. "For Hitchcock, filmmaking was what happened in his head, and then on paper, before shooting began. His movies were no accident, Art was the distillation of his design," noted Mary Corliss for a showing of Hitchcock's works by the Museum of Modern Art in New York City. It has often been said that Hitchcock would not even need to look through a viewfinder before shooting a scene. He would simply tell his crew to do exactly what he had specified in his detailed storyboards. He also used this practice as an excuse not to make any of the changes requested by his producers during a movie's production. In his 1994 book, *Tony Curtis: The Autobiography,* the actor wrote about the experiences of his wife at the time while working with Hitchcock: "When Janet [Leigh] was making *Psycho*, I'd go on the set and watch them work. Hitchcock had everything planned down to the smallest detail, and he came to the set each day absolutely prepared. Every shot in the movie was laid out on a storyboard. He would set up the stage and the cameras and show the cameraman the drawings, and they would match the shots exactly. That shower scene, for example, was pure geometry—this intricate combination of angles and body parts that rose up somehow in his brain. Then he just plugged the actors into the mathematical equation. Some actors didn't like it because it wasn't personal enough for them. They didn't think they had enough room to be creative. His singleness of purpose and concentration were too demanding for them. But we all know now how effective that method was." In truth, not every scene was storyboarded. One notorious example appeared in the movie *North by Northwest*. The famous scene involving the crop duster was improvised. There were no storyboards until after the film wrapped, when Universal's publicity department asked Hitchcock to concoct some for publicity purposes, which he did.

Hitchcock returned to wartime England in late 1943 and stayed there throughout much of 1944. While in his native country, he directed two short movies for the British Ministry of Information. One was *Bon Voyage* and the other *Aventure Malgache*. They were actually made for the Free French and were the only movies that Hitchcock ever made in the French language. Hitchcock also served as an advisor on a 1945 documentary on the Holocaust, with footage shot by the British troops who first entered the Nazi extermination camps. The film remained unreleased until 1985, when it was shown on the American TV show *Frontline*.

Hitchcock finally completed his contract with Selznick by making *The Paradine Case* (1948), a courtroom drama, which critics complained was too long. Now free of any studio obligations, Hitchcock began to produce and direct all of his own movies on a regular basis. He formed a production company with Sidney Bernstein called Transatlantic Pictures, which made only two movies, both flops, before folding. One of those was his first color movie, *Rope*, released in 1948. Hitchcock created suspense in a confined area, and also used very long takes, sometimes running up to ten minutes,

Top 10 Critically Acclaimed Lead Actors of the 1930s

Rank	Actor Name
1	Spencer Tracy
2	Clark Gable
3	Paul Muni
4	Fredric March
5	Cary Grant
6	Lionel Barrymore
7	Victor McLaglen
8	Charles Laughton
9	Wallace Beery
10	Robert Donat

Rank	Actress Name
1	Katharine Hepburn
2	Bette Davis
3	Claudette Colbert
4	Judy Garland
5	Greta Garbo
6	Vivien Leigh
7	Luise Rainer
8	Helen Hayes
9	Marie Dressler
10	Shirley Temple

See Notes to the Reader for selection criteria.

which was especially difficult using the bulky Technicolor camera. It was the first of four films Hitchcock would make with James Stewart. The other Transatlantic Picture was *Under Capricorn*.

Hitchcock went on to make a dozen more movies in the 1950s, including some of his most notable and successful films, such as *Rear Window, To Catch a Thief,* and *Vertigo,* under a profit-sharing contract at Paramount negotiated by his agent, Lew Wasserman (who went on to become president of MCA and Universal in the 1960s), as well as *North by Northwest* at MGM. He also became the host of a popular TV anthology series that ran from 1955 through 1965, a series that has lived on in reruns.

Hitchcock made sly little cameo appearances in each of his movies, and part of the fun for audiences was spotting the director. He became an iconic figure, identifiable only by the shadow version of his rotund figure. This famed director had come a long way from his birth in London, the son of a poultry dealer and fruit importer. He had been educated in Jesuit schools, attended the University of London, and worked for the telegraph company before getting a job in the film industry in 1920 designing title cards for silent movies.

Hitchcock continued to produce and direct masterpieces well into the 1960s, but even as his output slowed down, his mastery of the craft was evident, especially with such films as *Psycho, The Birds, Marnie,* and *Topaz.* The last film he directed was *Family Plot* (1976). He passed away in 1980 in Los Angeles.

General Corporate vs. Movie Business Salaries, 1937
Pretax* (1937 maximum individual tax rate 79 percent)
Equivalent 2005 $s /(Unadjusted $s)

Name	Job	Annual Earnings
Louis B. Mayer	Movie exec, Loew's, Inc. (MGM)	$17.6 million/($1,296,503)
J. Robert Rubin	Movie exec, Loew's VP	$9.4 million/($694,123)
William Randolph Hearst	Exec, Hearst Consolidated Publications	$6.8 million/($500,000)
Nicholas .M. Schenck	Movie exec, Loew's President	$6.6 million/($489,602)
Thomas J. Watson	President, IBM	$5.7 million/($419,938)
Eugene G. Grace	President, Bethlehem Steel	$5.4 million/($394,586)
George W. Hill	President, American Tobacco Co.	$5.2 million/($380,976)
Spryos P. Skouras	President, National Theatres Amusement Co.	$4.3 million/($320,054)
William S. Knudsen	President, General Motors Exec	$3.4 million/($247,210)
Owen D. Young	Chairman, General Electric	$3.2 million/($235,000)
Winthrop W. Aldrich	Chairman, Chase National Bank	$2.4 million/($175,000)

*Note: See tax rate table in Note to the Reader.

Actors of the 1930s: Comparison of Salaries and Profit Participations
Equivalent 2005 $s /(Unadjusted $s)

Actor	Film	Initial Release	Salary
Will Rogers	*State Fair*	1933	**$3.0 million** ($200,000)
Cary Grant	*Bringing up Baby*	1938	**$1.7 million** ($120,000 based on $75,000 base salary plus overages)
	She Done Him Wrong	1933	**$45,069 excluding reshoots** ($3,000 + $1,600 for reshoots)
Clark Gable	*Gone with the Wind*	1939	**$1.7 million including bonus** ($120,000 based on average $2,500/week plus bonus)
Katharine Hepburn	*Bringing up Baby*	1938	**$1.7 million** ($120,000 based on 72,500 per film fee plus overages)
Marlene Dietrich	*Shanghai Express*	1932	**$1.1 million** ($78,000)
Claudette Colbert	*It Happened One Night*	1934	**$728,731** ($50,000)
Mae West	*She Done Him Wrong*	1933	**$285,109** ($20,000)
Vivien Leigh	*Gone with the Wind*	1939	**$210,755** ($15,000 flat fee)
Adriana Caselotti (voice)	*Snow White and the Seven Dwarfs*	1939	**$189,875** ($14,000 flat fee)

A Sampling of Movie Star Earnings, 1936
Equivalent 2005 $s /(Unadjusted $s)

Actor	Annual Earnings	Actor	Annual Earnings
Gary Cooper	**$5.0 Million**/($370,214)	Claudette Colbert	**$4.8 Million**/($350,833)
Ronald Colman	**$4.9 Million**/($362,500)	Mae West	**$4.4 Million**/($323,333)

A Sampling of 1930s Director and Movie Star Salaries

In 1938, top actors were paid between $100,000 and $150,000 per picture. This included: Cary Grant, Claudette Colbert, Ronald Colman, Carole Lombard, Bing Crosby, Gary Cooper.

Bing Crosby made a deal with Paramount for nine pictures at $175,000 per picture which guaranteed him $1,575,000 for his services over a three-year period. He also reserved the right to make one film a year at any other studio at any price he could get.

In 1938 top directors were paid from $75,000 to $150,000 per picture. This included: John Ford, Frank Capra, Leo McCarey, Gregory La Cava.

DISTRIBUTION OVERVIEW

Monopolies Own Both the Studios and the Theaters

The major distributors of the decade were vertically integrated companies that both made and exhibited movies. The studio's ownership of theaters gave them control over how, where, and when films would play. The industry weathered a drop in attendance as the Great Depression hit early in the decade. Ticket prices fell, leading to a cutback in production. But movie-going returned to record levels by 1934, and production rose accordingly as movies became the most important form of entertainment. Theaters were still single-screen, so patrons waiting for the next show time looked at one sheets, preview cards, half sheets, and other forms of promotional material announcing forthcoming movies. On-screen trailers adopted an over-the-top tone, utilizing hard-sell tactics to entice people to upcoming movies. Control was in the hands of five companies, which inevitably led to price-fixing practices. In 1938 the U.S. Justice Department launched an investigation into what became known as the Paramount Case. The studio system was attacked by the government and pressured by labor unions even as Hollywood's movie "factories" produced an extraordinary number of high-quality films that culminated in a banner year for movies in 1939.

U.S. INDUSTRY DISTRIBUTION STATISTICS, 1930
Equivalent 2005 $s /(Unadjusted $s)

$21,328 Million ($732 million)
Annual U.S. box office gross revenues

595
Number of new feature films released

Major Movie Distributors, 1930s

BIG FIVE

Metro-Goldwyn-Mayer (MGM) . . . . Absorbed by Loew's, Inc., in 1936

Paramount . . . . In receivership in 1933. Reorganized in 1936 as Paramount Pictures

RKO Radio Pictures . . . . In receivership from 1933 to 1940

20th Century-Fox . . . . In receivership in 1933. Incorporated in 1935 as 20th Century-Fox following a merger with 20th Century Pictures

Warner Bros. . . . . Production head Darryl F. Zanuck leaves Warner Bros. to found 20th Century Pictures

LITTLE THREE

Columbia . . . . Harry Cohn becomes president in 1932

United Artists . . . . Alexander Korda becomes a full-fledged partner and stockholder in 1935 with Charlie Chaplin, Mary Pickford, Douglas Fairbanks, and Sam Goldwyn

Universal Pictures . . . . In receivership in 1933. Reorganized and incorporated in 1936 as Universal Pictures Co., Inc.

TECHNOLOGY SPOTLIGHT

Sound and Color at the Movies

During the 1930s, picture and sound technology made rapid advances. The Bell and Howell cameras used in the silent era were replaced by the much quieter Mitchell Company cameras necessitated by the making of sound films. RCA introduced the ribbon microphone, which was directional, eliminating a lot of extraneous noise. The arrival of sound raised other issues too: the sound-on-film systems adopted by most movie companies at the time (Fox, Paramount, Universal) required placing an optical strip alongside the visual image on a strip of 35mm film. Initially, the image size was decreased to make room for this optical strip, meaning it was no longer possible to have a 4-to-3 aspect ratio on-screen. Instead, the screen image was reduced to a more boxlike 1.15-to-1 aspect ratio. Technicians and directors complained that the size was inappropriate for dramatic content. Theater owners were also unhappy because most theaters were built for a 1.33-to-1 ratio. In

Width of Film Frame without Sound 4"

Height of Film Frame 3"

4/3 Aspect Ratio without sound strip = 1.33:1

Aspect Ratio with sound strip = 1.15:1

Sound Strip

145

1932 the Academy of Motion Picture Arts and Sciences voted to essentially re-create the former ratio by masking the top and bottom of the frame during shooting, and then projecting with special aperture plates, to achieve a 1.37-to-1 ratio. These specifications, known as the "Academy Standard," were used in most movies through 1953.

There had been films projected in color as early as the nineteenth century, but the era of color in mainstream feature films did not arrive until the 1930s. Technicolor, which had been working on color in film since 1915, achieved a breakthrough in 1932 with the development of a new three-color process that re-

	U.S. Theater Transition to Sound, 1930–1935		
Year	Total Number of Theaters	Silent Theaters	Theatres Wired for Sound
1930	23,000	14,140	8,860
1931	21,993	8,865	13,128
1932	18,715	4,835	13,880
1933	18,533	4,128	14,405
1934	16,885	2,504	14,381
1935	15,273	0	15,273

quired a special camera. Behind this camera's single lens was a beam splitter with two prisms, a reflecting mirror where the prisms joined, and a pair of apertures. The aperture in the rear captured the image through a green filter. The other aperture received the same image through a magenta filter that passed through red and blue light. Each color was imprinted on a strip of film and then combined into a matrix that became a dye-transfer print.

Walt Disney was the first to use the new color system in *Flowers and Trees,* an animated talking short in 1932 that was part of the Silly Symphony series. A year later Disney released *The Three Pigs* in color, and it was a hit along with its uplifting theme song, "Who's Afraid of the Big Bad Wolf?" but many in Hollywood were still afraid of big bad color. Some said it was just a distraction and that a good drama was better in black and white. Others avoided color because of the cost. It wasn't yet clear that audiences would demand it. Still, a handful of color films were produced, starting with two at RKO, *Becky Sharp* (1935) and *Dancing Pirate* (1936). Paramount made the first outdoor drama in full color with *The Trail of the Lonesome Pine* (1936). No studio or executive, however, embraced color earlier or with greater impact than Darryl F. Zanuck at Fox. Zanuck later said that he saw color as a way to differentiate his movies from competitors', especially certain prestige pictures and musicals. Zanuck had already experimented with color while still an executive at Warner Bros. There were two-strip Technicolor sequences in the 1929 Warner Bros. hit *Gold Diggers of Broadway,* as well as two other 1929 productions, the expensive star-studded review *The Show of Shows* and the musical operetta *The Desert Song.* At Warner in 1929, Zanuck was also involved with the first all-color, full-length talking picture, *On with the Show.* It was on this movie that Zanuck pioneered the dubbing of the voices, replacing those of star leads with those of better singers working off camera. When star Betty Comden sings, it is the voice of a studio singer that audiences hear. Zanuck even captured the first long shots of a dance sequence in that film utilizing a professional dancer in lieu of the star. After he took over as head of Fox Film Corp., Zanuck made the final sequence of the 1934 biographical drama *The House of Rothschild* in color. Then Zanuck turned his attention to *Ramona,* a period romantic drama that had been scheduled to be the studio's first color feature before Zanuck took charge. Zanuck replaced the scheduled stars (including Rita Hayworth) with Loretta

Young and Don Ameche, as well as the director with Henry King, who was to be Zanuck's go-to director on many more color features over the next few years. Zanuck followed with his next color feature the following year, *Wings of the Morning,* starring Henry Fonda, shot on location in 1936 in Ireland and Great Britain.

By 1938 other studios were shooting in color as well. MGM's first color feature was *Sweethearts,* and that same year Warner Bros. released four films in color, including *The Adventures of Robin Hood.* Color also got a boost in 1939 with the release of two giant hits, *The Wizard of Oz* and *Gone with the Wind,* both of which would be almost unthinkable without it. Still, most studios resisted because of the high costs involved; color movies didn't become common industry-wide until the 1950s, when the big screen was challenged for supremacy by television and the studios once again sought to differentiate their movies. It had been a long road.

MARKETING SPOTLIGHT

Studios Plant and Write News Stories

Sophisticated advertising and cross-promotion with radio boosted the ability to market movies as the talkies arrived. Studios had public relations departments to shape the image of contract players and protect the bosses. "Voluntary" studio censorship covered both movies and marketing. Every advertisement was submitted to the Advertising Advisory Council (AAC), a part of the Production Code Administration, before it could be distributed. That left the studios with ample latitude to sell their movies using ads as well as creative publicity efforts that included planting false stories along with fake names, doctored or staged photos, bogus biographies, and fabricated romances often intended to mask the nature of the stars' real-life romances. The studios often had prearranged deals with key newspapers, who wielded even more power in those days than the TV news or the Internet does today. For example, one of Hearst's popular dailies, the *Los Angeles Herald Examiner,* which was the studios' hometown afternoon paper, not only ran stories written by the studio PR departments but regularly withheld facts or refused to cover certain topics or people, in accordance with the studio execs' wishes. Hearst famously (as depicted in print and on film) used his influence to get publicity for his mistress, movie actress Marion Davies, but that influence still couldn't save her career. The most famous news controllers of the era, however, included Eddie Mannix and Howard Strickling of MGM, who earned the sobriquet "the Fixers" for their ability to manipulate coverage of stars' personal lives and legal entanglements.

Comparison of Three 1930s Films Initial Release
Equivalent 2005 $s /(Unadjusted $s) in Millions of $s

Film	Year	Domestic Box Office	Domestic Rentals	Foreign Rentals	Production Cost	Print and Ad Costs
The Wizard of Oz	1939	$126.8 ($4.6)	$57.1 ($2.0)	$27.0 ($1.0)	$38.9 ($2.8)	$8.9 ($0.6)
Mutiny on the Bounty	1935	$133.5 ($5.0)	$60.1 ($2.3)	$59.0 ($2.2)	$27.1 ($1.9)	$7.6 ($0.5)
San Francisco	1936	$163.4 ($6.4)	$73.5 ($2.9)	$61.7 ($2.4)	$18.2 ($1.3)	$5.9 ($0.4)

EXHIBITION OVERVIEW

Theaters Get Cooler, Exhibitors Centralize, Double Features Become More Widespread, and Candy Counters Are Introduced

To understand what happened to movie exhibitors in the 1930s, you have to look to Chicago, home of the largest animal stockyards in America. In 1917 movie theaters were cooled using fans that blew air over blocks of ice, but these systems were costly and not very effective. As a result, movie theaters in the South, Midwest, and most other warm climates would close for the summer months. At the same time, the meatpacking industry was making great advances in developing cooling systems that pumped carbon dioxide through pipes at high pressure. These systems were expensive and cumbersome but rapidly evolving. Barney Balaban learned about the advances in air-conditioning while working as a clerk at a cold storage company in Chicago. When he later went into the theater business with his brother-in-law, Sam Katz, and other family members, Balaban asked an engineering company called the Kroeschel Bros. Ice Machine Company if they could adapt the equipment used to cool huge meat lockers so that it could be used to cool movie theaters instead. These early improvisations had problems, but the Balaban & Katz theaters, which emerged as the leading regional exhibition circuit in the Midwest, kept making improvements on the system. Soon the public flocked to the comfort of the theaters instead in the heat of the Chicago summer. The result was consistently good ticket sales that didn't rely much on what movie was playing.

Theater circuits all over the country began to copy Balaban & Katz, not only for their use of cooling systems but for their other innovations as well. They quickly became one of the fastest-growing and most profitable exhibitor circuits, around having made the transition from storefront nickelodeons to modern movie palaces. All of their theaters offered the public extravagant amenities, a lavishly decorated atmosphere, live stage shows, and other special attractions in addition to the feature movie.

The Balaban family had been poor immigrants, but by 1908 they opened their first nickelodeon theater in Chicago's West Side ghetto. They continued to build and acquire theaters, branching out into film distribution. They owned a restaurant for a time called the Movie Inn, which served as a meeting place for people in the movie business. It was there that the Balaban brothers first met Samuel Katz. Katz had graduated from high school and attended college while working at a series of jobs, including playing the piano for a nickelodeon on Chicago's South Side. He fell in love with the movie business and in 1912 acquired his first theater. Katz had three theaters by 1916, when he merged with the Balabans. Together they decided to build a huge theater, which became the Central Park. When this theater opened in 1917 it boasted the first modern-era air-conditioning system, as described above. More theaters followed in the mid-1920s, including the Uptown, with 5,000 seats; the Norshore, with 3,000 seats; and the Oriental, with 4,000 seats. They were all hugely successful and allowed Balaban & Katz to expand into surrounding states by acquiring and building new theaters.

This was the beginning of a new era in exhibition—an era when regional chains were replaced by national circuits that used the modern methods of mass-market retailers to standardize and economize as they built whole theatrical empires. For the first years, Balaban & Katz didn't even have access to the best movies, but it didn't seem to matter. They had learned that they could succeed despite the movies by following five basic principles. First, they picked locations that were in high-traffic areas or near mass transit stations, including the first theaters built in suburban areas, where a more affluent population was growing. Second, they built theaters that were so grand they were part of the experience. Third, they provided a new level of service, including uniformed ushers to direct patrons to their seats. Fourth, they included live stage shows as well as filmed entertainment. Fifth, they provided air-conditioning, which in the summer months proved to be as big an attraction as the entertainment programming.

The architects consistently used by Balaban & Katz were the brothers George and C. W. Rapp, who started with them on the Central Park Theater. From 1917 until 1932, the Rapps were constantly building splendid, often ornate theaters with sophisticated lighting systems for the circuit. Their dazzling designs included images from Spain, France, and Italy and incorporated elements of the art deco style as well.

In addition, the services included free child care, smoking rooms, expansive elegant lobby areas, and organ music piped in while patrons were escorted by ushers through separate entryways and exits expressly created to move huge crowds quickly. There were often playgrounds and afternoon tea shows for ladies who shopped with small children. A nurse was always on hand with medical equipment.

At B&K theaters, ushers wore red uniforms, white gloves, and yellow epaulets on their jackets.

They were polite, even to rude ticket buyers, addressing patrons as "sir" or "ma'am." Ushers were chosen only if they met certain criteria—they had to be white, anywhere from seventeen to twenty-one years of age, roughly 5 feet 7 inches in height, and between 125 and 145 pounds. They also had to be enrolled in a local college. One of the usher's jobs was to fill out cards throughout the day noting the number of patrons in each part of the theater so the manager could direct incoming customers to available seating swiftly. They used early versions of calculating machines and telephones to provide updated information to management so they could effectively plan future programs.

By 1925 Hollywood studios were wooing Balaban & Katz, hoping to open and play as many of their movies there as possible. Katz was able to leverage this interest when making a deal with Adolph Zukor for Famous Players-Lasky to acquire Balaban & Katz—a deal that gave the circuit access to high-quality movies on a regular basis. Balaban & Katz used the power to book even better movies as yet another way to clobber their competitors, cementing their position as the dominant theater circuit in their markets. In the deal, Balaban got a large block of stock and became president of the newly merged combined company, while Zukor continued as the powerful chairman. Balaban oversaw the studio, while Sam Katz moved to New York to oversee the combined theater assets, which by 1927 had been renamed Paramount-Publix Theaters.

Katz quickly applied the five-point system developed by B&K to the entire Paramount and Publix circuit. It was the beginning of the true centralization of the movie theater business and the emergence of much larger national circuits. Balaban & Katz had effectively provided the blueprint for how theaters operated until after World War II. Under Katz, new scientific systems for tracking and managing every aspect of the business were developed. From his office atop the Paramount building in New York City, he and his staff used their centralized system to decide what carpets to put in each theater, what music to play, when the curtains should open, and what films to book. All major hires were made by the New York office, which provided local managers with written instructions on how to market movies in their area, articles written for the press, and schedules of live shows and movies. All of it had to be done on a tight budget. This, in effect, gave Katz unprecedented authority over what became the largest of the five major circuits operated by vertically integrated companies. Paramount and others used this power to force independent circuits to buy a whole year's output of movies in advance, sight unseen, a practice that would draw federal antitrust scrutiny.

By the 1930s, the Publix theater chain operated theaters from Chicago to Texas and from North Carolina to Iowa. Through its Famous Players circuit it also became the major circuit in Canada. The studio set up distribution offices across the country to service theaters in pre-established geographical zones with not only movies but also marketing and advertising materials and other support. These distribution offices set the terms for each movie's run and decided when it would move to second-run theaters and beyond. At each level, the cost of admission would be lower. Katz realized that to succeed, Paramount-Publix did not need to own all the theaters, just the biggest and best. This marked the beginning of Hollywood's strategic control of the major first-run theaters in the biggest cities. Such control allowed them to launch their movies, create a marketing profile, and, when they had a hit, milk the most out of it before allowing that movie to play in smaller markets.

When sound first came along, Katz even found a way to use it to save money. He had film recordings made of the top vaudeville acts and then played those films instead of hiring the live performers. The public didn't seem to notice or care. Despite these savings, the conversion to sound was expensive, and it came along just as the nation was hit by the Great Depression. Paramount-Publix, with more than a thousand theaters by 1931, had borrowed heavily to build its movie palaces, which was fine as long as attendance was strong. When attendance fell off due to the Depression, the company was forced into bankruptcy, ending the era of Adolph Zukor as chief executive.

The bankers brought in their own management team, but the studio still faltered, and by 1933 Balaban had been rehired to run the renamed Paramount Pictures, a job he would keep until 1966. After bankruptcy, the entire company was run more tightly. The armies of ushers disappeared from theaters, replaced by only a handful of attendants who directed patrons inside. To lure audiences back during the Depression, theaters began to offer double features, even triple features at times. Again, borrowing tactics from the retailing community, they offered special pricing and prizes, especially on slow nights such as Monday, and on Fridays when a new film arrived. There was Dish Night, for instance, when patrons could win sets of china to take home, and similar giveaways of linens, silk stockings, cooking utensils, and even items from the grocery store.

One of the big draws was Bank Night, when theaters would offer the most popular prize possible in hard times—cash. Bank Night was so big that for a few years it would disrupt attendance at local churches, baseball games, and other activities.

Air-conditioning had been so expensive in the 1920s that only the big movie palaces could afford it. At the 1933 World's Fair, however, Willis Carrier demonstrated a new system that almost all theaters bought to boost attendance.

The practice of double features became even more widespread in 1933 when the federal government, for a time, outlawed the use of games of chance.

To increase profits, theaters also developed what became the in-theater candy stand. Unlike ticket sales, exhibitors did not have to share concession sales with the movie makers; so while ticket sales provided the bulk of studio revenue, the candy counter pumped up the profits for exhibitors.

U.S. INDUSTRY DISTRIBUTION vs. EXHIBITION
Number of New Films Released
vs. Average Weekly Film Theater Attendance,
1930–1939

Year	Total Number of New Films Released	Number of Films Released by Majors	Number of Films Released by Independents	Number of Theater Attendees Millions of People
1930	595	362	233	90
1931	622	324	298	75
1932	685	318	367	60
1933	644	338	306	60
1934	662	361	301	70
1935	766	356	410	80
1936	735	362	373	88
1937	778	408	370	88
1938	769	362	407	85
1939	761	388	373	85

U.S. INDUSTRY EXHIBITION STATISTICS, 1930s
Equivalent 2005 $s /(Unadjusted $s)

$6.41 ($0.22–0.23)
Average movie ticket price (1930–1939)

23,000
Number U.S. screens, 1930

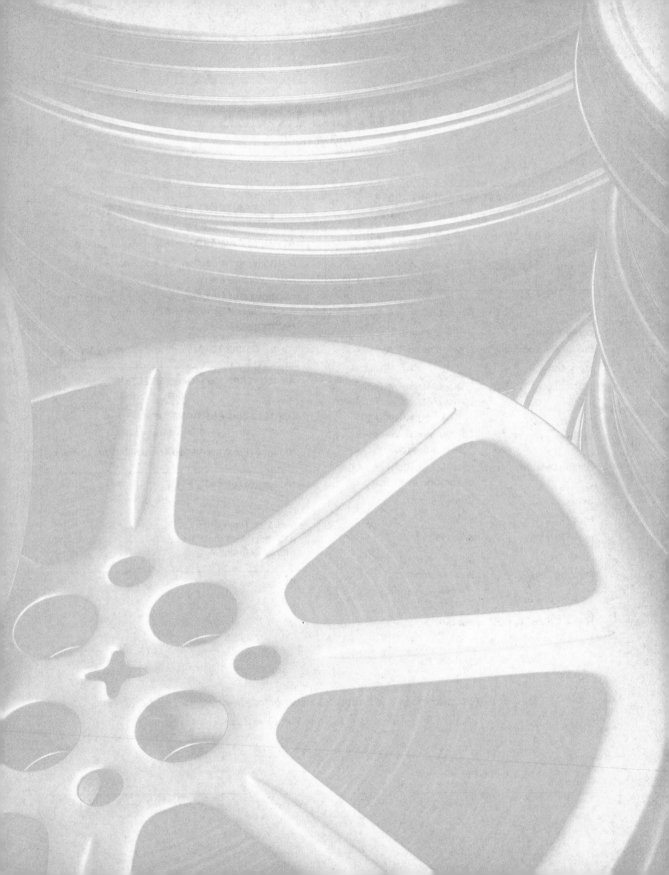

THE BIG HOUSE

MGM, 1930

ALL-RELEASE EQUIVALENT 2005 $s

(Unadjusted $s) in Millions of $s

Domestic Box Office Revenues . . . . **$84.2**/($2.9)
Production Cost . . . . **$4.8**/($0.4)
Principal Photography . . . . **31** days estimated
2/25/1930–4/1/1930

Director . . . . George Hill
Producer . . . . Irving Thalberg
Production Company . . . . Cosmopolitan Pictures
Story and
   Screenplay by . . . . Frances Marion (scenario);
                        Frances Marion, Joe Farnham,
                        Martin Flavin (dialogue)
Cast . . . . Chester Morris, Wallace Beery,
                        Robert Montgomery
Filming Locations . . . . . . MGM Studio, Culver City, CA;
                        on location Long Beach, CA
Genre . . . . Crime
Format . . . . B&W
Initial Release 6/14/1930
Rerelease . . . . none
Running Time . . . . 80 or 84 minutes
                        10 reels
                        7,901 feet
MPAA Rating . . . . not rated

STANDING THE TEST OF TIME

ACADEMY AWARD Oscar Nominations and Wins

Outstanding Production: Cosmopolitan

Actor: Wallace Beery

***SOUND RECORDING:** MGM Studio Sound Dept.
Douglas Shearer, Sound Director

***WRITING:** Frances Marion

      OSCAR TOTALS   Nominations **4**   *Wins **2**

AFI 100 YEARS 100 MOVIES SELECTION
                  2007 0   1997 0

TOP 300 FILMS POSITION . . . . .none
All-Release Domestic Box Office in Equivalent 2005 $s

National Film Preservation Board Selection . . . .none

OTHER AWARDS Best Picture Wins

	Year
Golden Globes	none
New York Film Critics	none
National Board of Review	none
Film Daily Critics	none

It is an insight into life in a jail that has never before been essayed on the screen.
—Mordaunt Hall, *New York Times*, 1930

PLOT: A young man sent to Sing Sing prison for manslaughter is put into a cell with two career criminals, one of whom escapes and falls in love with the young man's sister. A jailbreak leads to a prison riot and violent police reaction.

PRODUCTION: This seminal prison drama made during the dawn of talkies was an early example of MGM production chief Irving Thalberg's desire for strong material conveyed realistically. Director George William Hill, in creating his personal masterwork, painted a stark and brutally realistic depiction of prison life. Hill warned his cast that he would fire anyone he saw "acting" and also demanded that no one wear any makeup. The script was by Frances Marion, the highest-paid screenwriter in America from 1916 through 1930, the year she married George Hill. Before writing the script, she toured San Quentin, keeping a diary of conversations with prison officials and inmates and noting observations about atmosphere, personalities, and prison jargon. The studio originally proposed a key role for Lon Chaney, who, like Charlie Chaplin, had shunned talking films at first. But Chaney declined because he was already working on his first talkie, *The Unholy Three* (and would die less than two months after that film's release in August 1930 of a throat hemorrhage). Instead, Wallace Beery, who was newly signed to the studio, got the part. Thalberg knew that he was taking a risk in giving Beery a major starring role, just as he was taking a risk by casting George Montgomery, who had never carried a drama before, as the lead. Later, when the film played poorly at sneak previews, Thalberg stepped in to reedit it. Because he saw in the note cards that women complained the most, he changed the role of the female lead who falls for the career criminal, making her the sister of the jailed young man rather than his wife. His efforts paid off as subsequent audiences responded favorably to the movie. Hill was considered a great talent and directed a few more films (most notably *Min and Bill*) before committing suicide at his beach house in 1934. He was thirty-nine years old when he died. MGM spent lavishly on the sets for this film, re-creating the courtyard, mess hall, and tiers of cells. The art department, under Cedric Gibbons, successfully captured the oppressive atmosphere of the prison, making it seem like a medieval fortress. Even the sound by Douglas Shearer (brother of actress Norma Shearer, Thalberg's wife) was realistic, right down to the prisoners' stomping feet. Cinematographer Harold Wenstrom used innovative camera angles, dolly shots, and lighting techniques to great effect, and his command of the crane afforded a dramatic view as the camera ascended the spiral staircase to the prisoners' cells. The film is also notable for its innovative editing, including a memorable shot in which an empty mess hall slowly dissolves into an overcrowded room full inmates with sad faces and tin cups.

DISTRIBUTION: It was voted one of the 10 Best Pictures of 1930 in a poll by *Film Daily* critics and was one of the top 10 box office films of 1930, coming in behind Amos 'n' Andy's *Check and Double Check,* Howard Hughes's *Hell's Angels,* and *All Quiet on the Western Front.* Frances Marion's realistic script was acknowledged with an Oscar, as was Douglas Shearer's sound work (Shearer won on the same night his sister, Norma, got the Best Actress Oscar for *The Divorcee*). *The Big House* was the subject of a study guide in the New York City schools, published in the early 1930s. —*Alex Ben Block*

ALL QUIET ON THE WESTERN FRONT
Universal, 1930

ALL-RELEASE EQUIVALENT 2005 $s
(Unadjusted $s) in Millions of $s

Domestic Box Office Revenues . . . . **$97.1**/($3.3)
Production Cost . . . . **$15.2**/($1.3)
Principal Photography . . . . **99** Days
11/21/1929–3/24/1930

Running Time . . . . 140 minutes
14 reels
12,423 feet

MPAA Rating . . . . not rated

Director . . . . Lewis Milestone
Producer . . . . Carl Laemmle Jr.
Production Company . . . . Universal Pictures Corp.
Story by . . . . Based on the novel by
Erich Maria Remarue
Screenplay by . . . . Maxwell Anderson, George
Abbott, Del Andrews
Cast . . . . Louis Wolheim, Lew Ayres,
John Wray, Arnold Lucy
Filming Locations . . . . . . Universal Studios, Universal
City, CA; on location at
RKO-Pathé Studios in Culver
City, CA; Los Angeles,
Newport Beach, Laguna Beach,
Malibu Lake, and Sherwood
Forest, CA
Genre . . . . War
Format . . . . B&W
Initial Release 8/24/1930
Rerelease . . . . none

STANDING THE TEST OF TIME

ACADEMY AWARD Oscar Nominations and Wins

*OUTSTANDING PRODUCTION: Universal

Cinematography: Arthur Edeson

*DIRECTING: Lewis Milestone

Writing: George Abbott, Maxwell Anderson, Del
Andrews

OSCAR TOTALS   Nominations 4   *Wins 2

AFI 100 YEARS 100 MOVIES SELECTION
2007 0   1997 . . . . #54

TOP 300 FILMS POSITION . . . . none
All-Release Domestic Box Office in Equivalent 2005 $s

National Film Preservation Board Selection 1990

OTHER AWARDS Best Picture Wins
	Year
Golden Globes	none
New York Film Critics	none
National Board of Review	1930
Film Daily Critics	1930

*When shells demolish these underground quarters, the shrieks of fear, coupled with the
rat-tat-tat of machine guns, the bang-ziz of the trench mortars, and the whining of shells,
it tells the story of the terrors of fighting better than anything so far has done in
animated photography coupled with the microphone.*

—Mordaunt Hall, *New York Times*, 1930

PLOT: The futility of war is seen through the experiences of young German soldiers, first as schoolboys driven by a teacher's patriotic fervor, then in training, and finally as they face the horrors and senselessness of trench warfare, leaving them hungry, tired, and scared.

PRODUCTION: Universal Pictures stepped up with one of the first great antiwar films ever, produced during the brief reign of studio boss Carl Laemmle Jr., the twenty-three-year-old son of the company's founder. Universal, until that time, had been known for lower-budget movies, but young Laemmle wanted to improve the studio's reputation. It was considered risky to make a movie from the point of view of a German soldier, but Laemmle was undaunted. The film was based on the best-selling novel by Erich Maria Remarque, who drew on his actual experiences as a German soldier. The movie was conceived originally as a silent epic but was converted to sound as the importance of the new medium became increasingly evident. The transition sent the budget soaring to the then astronomical sum of $1.25 million. Production began in November 1929, eleven years to the day after the end of World War I. This was a symbolic gesture on Laemmle's part and was used extensively in creating publicity at the time. Sets sprawled across California ranch land as the 2,000 extras were directed in great battle scenes by Lewis Milestone, who had emigrated from Russia in 1917 to avoid being drafted into the czar's army, only to serve in World War I in the American army. Milestone later said he was strongly influenced by the Russian movie masters, especially Sergei Eisenstein. Milestone arranged to use a giant crane first developed by director Pál Fejös and cinematographer Hal Mohr for the 1929 movie *Broadway*. It allowed him to obtain many fluid battlefield shots and re-create the experience of a soldier in the depths of war. The film featured twenty-one-year-old Lew Ayres in a star-making turn. Although it was among the first epic talkies, the film was noted for its realistic soundtrack, presenting the authentic sounds of war for the first time. The trench scenes were shot at the Irvine Ranch, about 66 miles south of Los Angeles. A whole village was built on the Universal lot, which later became an attraction on the Universal tour. Working closely with Milestone throughout the production was famed stage director George Cukor, who was hired as a dialogue director responsible for rehearsing the actors and keeping a close watch on their accents.

DISTRIBUTION: The film was a critical success. *Variety* gave it a rave review, and *American Cinematographer* called it "one of the greatest war pictures ever filmed." It did very good business, although it was not the runaway hit Universal expected it to be. In America, former doughboys said it was very realistic. In Germany, where it caused riots and demonstrations, it was criticized as propaganda by the Nazi government of the 1930s and banned until after World War II. Even beyond Germany, it faced heavy censorship in almost every country in the world. Laemmle campaigned to win the Nobel Peace Prize for making the movie but was unsuccessful. —*Alex Ben Block*

CIMARRON

RKO, 1931

ALL-RELEASE EQUIVALENT 2005 $s

(Unadjusted $s) in Millions of $s

Domestic Box Office Revenues . . . . **$71.2**/($2.4)
Production Cost . . . . **$18.4**/($1.4)
Principal Photography . . . . **75** days estimated
8/27/1930–11/22/1930

Director . . . . Wesley Ruggles
Producer . . . . William LeBaron
Production Company . . . . Radio Pictures
Story by . . . . Based on the novel by
Edna Ferber
Screenplay by . . . . Howard Estabrook
Cast . . . . Richard Dix, Irene Dunne
Filming Locations . . . . . . Jasmin Quinn Ranch near
Bakersfield, CA
Genre . . . . Western
Format . . . . B&W
Initial Release . . . . 1/26/1931 premiere;
2/9/1931 general release
Rerelease . . . . none
Running Time . . . . 124 minutes
13 reels
11,182 feet
MPAA Rating . . . . not rated

STANDING THE TEST OF TIME

ACADEMY AWARD Oscar Nominations and Wins
*OUTSTANDING PRODUCTION: RKO Radio
Actor: Richard Dix
Actress: Irene Dunne
*ART DIRECTION: Max Ree
Cinematography: Edward Cronjager
Directing: Wesley Ruggles
*WRITING (Adaptation): Howard Estabrook

OSCAR TOTALS   Nominations **7**   *Wins **3**

AFI 100 YEARS 100 MOVIES SELECTION
2007 0   1997 0

TOP 300 FILMS POSITION . . . . .none
All-Release Domestic Box Office in Equivalent 2005 $s

National Film Preservation Board Selection . . . .none

OTHER AWARDS Best Picture Wins

	Year
Golden Globes	none
New York Film Critics	none
National Board of Review	1931
Film Daily Critics	1931

An elegant example of super film making and a big money picture. This is a spectacular western away from all others. It holds action, sentiment, sympathy, thrills and comedy—and 100 percent clean. Radio Pictures has a corker in Cimarron.

—*Variety,* 1931

PLOT: During the great 1889 Oklahoma land rush, Yancey is a bigger-than-life character who, with his wife, Sabra, helps civilize the frontier. When he disappears, she has to take over.

PRODUCTION: This was the most expensive and critically acclaimed film produced by the newly formed RKO Radio Pictures. RKO production chief William Le Baron, former managing editor of *Collier's* magazine, is credited as producer of *Cimarron* and more than two dozen other 1931 releases. LeBaron entered the movie business in 1919 as a writer with Cosmopolitan Productions in New York. In 1927 he took the job as vice president of production at Film Booking Offices (FBO), then run by Joseph P. Kennedy. After FBO merged to become RKO, LeBaron assumed his same job with his company's successor. *Cimarron* was LeBaron's fifth movie with star Richard Dix as associate producer or producer. The studio paid the popular author Edna Ferber a record price of $125,000 for the screen rights to her 1929 novel, one in a series of historical epics she wrote. RKO purchased it specifically as a vehicle for Dix, whose character, Yancey Cravat, was based on real-life lawyer Temple Houston, son of Sam Houston (whom Dix later portrayed in 1939's Republic Pictures release *Man of Conquest*). One of the extras was Nino Cochise, the actual grandson of the real Chief Cochise. The title of the film is taken from the Cimarron Territory, which for many years was an unsettled area in what is now Oklahoma. It had been home to Native Americans until 1886, when the United States opened 2 million acres of Indian land to homesteaders, causing a land rush. This was a production on as big a scale as the three-month Cecil B. DeMille *The Ten Commandments* shoot in 1923. The famous land rush scenes took a week to shoot and employed more than 5,000 extras, twenty-eight cameramen using forty-seven cameras, six still cameramen, twenty-seven assistants, and livestock spread over 40 acres. Great attention was paid to authenticity. Using Ferber's descriptions of what occurred, cinematographer Edward Cronjager planned every shot of the land rush sequence in advance. B. Reeves Eason, who had overseen the chariot races in *Ben-Hur,* was hired to work with director Wesley Ruggles on the land rush. There were eighteen days of retakes after principal production ended in November 1930. American Indians used in the movie were "made up white to appear coppery on the screen," according to a publicity release. The production was over budget by $354,114.

DISTRIBUTION: Critics immediately hailed the movie, but box office wasn't as strong as needed to cover the high production cost. RKO premiered it at the Globe Theater in New York City with a top ticket price of $2, which was very high at the time. Despite winning Best Picture, *Cimarron* lost $565,000 on its initial release and was considered a disappointment. The box office was hurt because it came out as the economic turmoil of the Great Depression depressed all ticket sales. Released in home video, the movie has not held up well. After the opening rush, it moves too slowly for modern audiences and suffers from melodramatic acting and outdated references to African Americans, American Indians, and the handicapped. It was the first and one of the few westerns to win an Academy Award as Best Picture (the next was *Dances with Wolves* in 1990). —*Alex Ben Block*

CITY LIGHTS (*SUBTITLED* "A COMEDY ROMANCE IN PANTOMIME")

United Artists, 1931

ALL-RELEASE EQUIVALENT 2005 $s

(Unadjusted $s) in Millions of $s

Domestic Box Office Revenues. . . . . **$120.8**/($4.5)
Production Cost . . . . **$19.3**/($1.5)
Principal Photography. . . . . **179** days shooting;
504 days idle
12/31/1927–1/22/1931

Director . . . . Charles Chaplin

Producer . . . . Charles Chaplin

Production Company. . . . Charles Chaplin Productions

Story and

Screenplay by . . . . Charles Chaplin

Cast . . . . Charlie Chaplin, Virginia
Cherrill, Florence Lee

Filming Locations . . . . . . On location in Los Angeles and
San Francisco, CA

Genre. . . . . Silent Classic - Comedy
(no dialogue incl. in
synchronized sound track)

Format. . . . . B&W

Initial Release . . . . 2/6/1931 roadshow release;
3/1/1931 general release

Rerelease. . . . . none

Running Time . . . . 86 or 87 minutes
9 reels

MPAA Rating . . . . not rated

STANDING THE TEST OF TIME

ACADEMY AWARD Oscar Nominations and Wins

None

OSCAR TOTALS   Nominations 0   *Wins 0

AFI 100 YEARS 100 MOVIES SELECTION
2007. . .#11   1997. . .#76

TOP 300 FILMS POSITION . . . . .none
All-Release Domestic Box Office in Equivalent 2005 $s

National Film Preservation Board Selection. . . . 1991

OTHER AWARDS Best Picture Wins

	Year
Golden Globes	none
New York Film Critics	none
National Board of Review	none
Film Daily Critics	none

*City Lights was Chaplin's first production after talking movies were introduced.
He avoided sound, wisely as it turns out, since the awkward sound equipment
of the early days would have trapped his films in soundstages and sets.*

—Roger Ebert

PLOT: In this slapstick-filled melodrama, Chaplin's famous character, the Little Tramp, falls for a beautiful blind girl who is selling flowers, and struggles to help her after she mistakes him for a wealthy duke.

PRODUCTION: Charles Chaplin, the first great screen comedian, was already a major star when he undertook what would become his longest production. He wrote the screenplay, edited thousands of feet of film, compiled the musical score, and produced and directed what some call his greatest film. He even invested his own money to make the picture, putting roughly $2 million at risk in production, marketing, and distribution costs. At the time it was made, talking films were so prevalent that Chaplin had been advised against releasing a silent movie. He trusted that his instinct was right and insisted that his most famous character, the Little Tramp, remain silent. The finished film included some sound effects and a complete musical score but no dialogue. For the role of the blind flower girl, Chaplin chose Virginia Cherrill, a recently divorced twenty-year-old from Chicago with no prior experience. Chaplin never viewed a lack of experience as a problem as long as his actors did what he told them to do. However, when Cherrill came to the set late one day, keeping Chaplin waiting, he fired her and began reshooting the film with Georgia Hale, his co-star in *The Gold Rush*. Soon afterward, however, he realized that Cherrill was already in too much of the film to edit her out or to reshoot her scenes entirely, and he reluctantly agreed to take her back, at double her salary. Cherrill had her own complaints: Chaplin was a notorious perfectionist. He filmed 342 takes of a scene in which the Little Tramp buys a flower from the blind girl before finally finding the ideal way to show that the blind girl thought the Tramp was a rich man.

DISTRIBUTION: The movie was an immediate critical and box office hit, grossing roughly $2 million in domestic rentals during its initial release. It was voted one of the 10 Best Pictures of the year by *Film Daily*. But that was no thanks to United Artists, whose management was skeptical that a silent film could still draw an audience. In the absence of their support Chaplin decided to take control of the film's distribution, opening the movie with special road show engagements. Such treatment had been reserved in the past for prestige films, but in this case, the limited showcase approach was the only way Chaplin could make the film's release an event on a budget. Chaplin leased New York City's George M. Cohan Theatre and hired his own staff to operate it. He oversaw every aspect of advertising, marketing, and distribution, billing the movie as "A Comedy Romance in Pantomime." When he thought UA was not spending enough on ads, he spent $30,000 more of his own money. During a twelve-week run at the Cohan Theatre, the movie grossed roughly half a million dollars in that one location alone. Over the course of his career, Charles Chaplin was nominated for three Academy Awards and won one. He also received two honorary Oscars. But despite the fact that *City Lights* is now considered to be his best film, it received no nominations for the 1931 Academy Awards. —*Alex Ben Block*

FRANKENSTEIN

Universal, 1931

ALL-RELEASE EQUIVALENT 2005 $s

(Unadjusted $s) in Millions of $s

Domestic Box Office Revenues . . . . **$54.4**/($1.9)
Production Cost . . . . **$3.7**/($0.3)
Principal Photography . . . . **35** days
8/24/1931–10/3/1931
Retakes 1 day 11/25/1931
Shot 6 1/2 script pages per day

Director . . . . James Whale

Producer . . . . Carl Laemmle Jr.

Production Company . . . . Universal Pictures

Story by . . . . Based on the novel Mary W. Shelley

Screenplay by . . . . Garrett Fort, Francis Edward Farogoh

Starring Cast . . . . Colin Clive, Mae Clarke, John Boles, Boris Karloff

Filming Locations . . . . . . On the Universal Studios back lot and on location in the Los Angeles, CA, area (Pasadena, San Fernando Valley, Lake Sherwood)

Genre . . . . Horror

Format . . . . B&W

Initial Release 11/21/1931

Rerelease . . . . 1937 (revenue not included above)

Running Time . . . . 67 or 70 minutes 8 reels

MPAA Rating . . . . not rated

STANDING THE TEST OF TIME

ACADEMY AWARD Oscar Nominations and Wins

None

OSCAR TOTALS   Nominations 0   *Wins 0

AFI 100 YEARS 100 MOVIES SELECTION
2007 0   1997 . . . . #87

TOP 300 FILMS POSITION . . . . none
All-Release Domestic Box Office in Equivalent 2005 $s

National Film Preservation Board Selection 1991

OTHER AWARDS Best Picture Wins

	Year
Golden Globes	none
New York Film Critics	none
National Board of Review	none
Film Daily Critics	none

James Whale was clearly influenced by Der Golem (1920), lifting many shots and concepts directly from that earlier film; in fact, the sequence with the little girl at the lake is very reminiscent of the climax of [German director Paul] Wegener's silent classic.

—John L. Flynn

PLOT: A scientist seeking to create life in his laboratory collects body parts from graveyards and on a stormy night brings a creature to life. When this creation proves to be violent, he plans to destroy it. But the monster escapes and terrorizes the German countryside.

PRODUCTION: In early 1931, Universal founder Carl Laemmle and his son, the newly installed production chief, needed a sequel to the 1931 hit *Dracula,* which had saved the studio from bankruptcy at the start of the Great Depression. They considered a Jekyll and Hyde story and a Sherlock Holmes mystery before giving the green light to *Frankenstein,* based on Mary Wollstonecraft Shelley's 1818 gothic novel and Dame Peggy Webling's successful play. The budget of approximately $60,000 quickly ballooned to more than $280,000. It had been first adapted for movies in 1910 by Thomas Edison as a silent short starring Charles Ogle as the monster. It was also made as silent films in 1915 and 1920. The monster's iconic flat head was created by makeup artist Jack Pierce and director James Whale on a special effects budget of $10,000, considered exorbitant at the time. The fantastic electrical sequences were designed by Kenneth Strickfaden, with later fans dubbing the equipment used to create these effects "Strickfadens." Initially, Universal cast Bela Lugosi, who had starred in *Dracula,* under French director Robert Florey, along with Bette Davis and Leslie Howard. Lugosi wanted to create his own makeup for the monster, but his design was rejected. After further screen tests, Lugosi refused the part, complaining there were no lines, and Davis and Howard also left. Universal then cast unknown Boris Karloff (born William Henry Pratt) in a role that made him an international star, and hired British-born Whale to direct. Karloff was uncredited in the opening sequence, where under "The Players" the monster is listed along with a question mark. Karloff's name, however, was included in the end credits. For the film's subsequent rerelease, Universal had to delete a scene where the monster throws a little girl into the lake, as it was deemed too violent by the Production Code Administration. This movie, which was the role model for all the gothic horror films that followed, was itself strongly influenced by 1920s German expressionist films. The entire production was on a fast track: shooting began on August 24, 1931 (with Universal using a set constructed for the 1930 film *All Quiet on the Western Front* to serve as the Bavarian village of Goldstadt), production ended in October, and the movie was in theaters by late November. Universal shot two endings, finally opting for the happy ending. Karloff later insisted it was not just censorship that led to the deletion of the scene at the lake. He recalled just before he died in 1969 that he too had urged the studio to cut the scene because it betrayed the character.

DISTRIBUTION: The movie was an immediate sensation. It drew $1.4 million in worldwide rentals in its first run versus $1.2 million for *Dracula,* which had opened in February 1931. Frankenstein's bolted-on head soon became part of pop culture. Over time, the film spawned close to a hundred sequels and reinventions. For a 1937 rerelease, more cuts were made to meet the Hays Code, including the line "In the name of God, now I know what it feels like to be God." In the video and DVD releases, however, those scenes have mostly been restored. —*Alex Ben Block*

SHANGHAI EXPRESS

Paramount, 1932

ALL-RELEASE EQUIVALENT 2005 $s

(Unadjusted $s) in Millions of $s

Domestic Box Office Revenues . . . . **$51.2**/($1.8)
Production Cost . . . . **$12.1**/($0.9)
Principal Photography . . . . **43** days estimated
10/12/1931–12/1/1931

Director	Josef von Sternberg
Producer	Adolph Zukor
Production Company	Paramount Publix
Story by	Based on a story by Harry Hervey
Screenplay by	Jules Furthman
Cast	Marlene Dietrich, Clive Brook, Anna May Wong, Warner Oland
Filming Locations	Paramount Studio in Hollywood, CA
Genre	Drama
Format	B&W
Initial Release	2/12/1932
Rerelease	none
Running Time	80 or 84 minutes 9 reels
MPAA Rating	not rated

STANDING THE TEST OF TIME

ACADEMY AWARD Oscar Nominations and Wins

Outstanding Production: Paramount Publix

*CINEMATOGRAPHY: Lee Garmes

Directing: Josef Von Sternberg

OSCAR TOTALS   Nominations 3   *Wins 1

AFI 100 YEARS 100 MOVIES SELECTION
2007 0   1997 0

TOP 300 FILMS POSITION . . . . .none
All-Release Domestic Box Office in Equivalent 2005 $s

National Film Preservation Board Selection . . . .none

OTHER AWARDS Best Picture Wins

	Year
Golden Globes	none
New York Film Critics	none
National Board of Review	none
Film Daily Critics	none

The screenplay, by Jules Furthman and an uncredited Howard Hawks, has a quality of wisecracking wit unusual in Sternberg's films: when someone asks Dietrich why she's going to Shanghai, she retorts, "To buy a new hat."

—Dave Kehr

PLOT: Two ladies of the evening—one Western (Shanghai Lily), one Chinese (Hui Fei)— travel by train across China at a time of civil war. When one of these ladies is sought by a warlord, another passenger tries to save her. He is a physician on an important medical mission, but he is also her former lover. While both are willing to make supreme sacrifices in the name of the other's safety, they and all the passengers on the train are ultimately saved when Hui Fei rises up to defeat the warlord.

PRODUCTION: Made before the Production Code created in 1930 was enforced, Dietrich pushes her sexiness to the edge in this fourth of seven collaborations with filmmaker Josef von Sternberg. He had first cast her in his 1930 German film *Der Blaue Engel* (released in the United States in 1931 as *The Blue Angel*). Dietrich was then twenty-nine and already a star of German cinema, theater, and cabaret. Sternberg took her to America, signed her to a Paramount-Publix contract, and made her an international sensation. Dietrich received $78,000 in salary for this movie. Sternberg had total authority over the picture. He had by then put together his own production unit at Paramount that included screenwriter Furthman, costume designer Travis Banton, art director Hans Dreier, and cinematographers Lee Garmes and Lucien Ballard. This was the final Sternberg collaboration with Garmes, who won an Oscar for his work on this film. Sternberg, who was an early film auteur, not only directed but also had a say in the writing, cinematography, and editing. This movie was based on a story by Harry Hervey, which the movie titles listed as a novel, although none was ever published. Paramount press materials credited Hervey as writer of the story "Sky over China," also known as "China Pass." Some in Hollywood called *Shanghai Express,* which deals with an eventful train journey between Peking and Shanghai, "*Grand Hotel* on wheels," for its assemblage of players and plots. This highly stylized film, with its emotionally charged love story and snappy dialogue, was shot so that the action and dialogue moved to the rhythms of the train as it made its treacherous trek. Although the production employs more than 1,000 extras and numerous locations, creating a sense of both the exotic and the teeming masses, the entire movie was shot either on soundstages at Paramount Pictures in Hollywood or at nearby locations in southern California. Production was an intense and stress-filled experience. Sternberg was known for shouting at everyone. He shouted so much that he lost his voice. Ultimately Sternberg hooked up a public address system so that he could be heard all over the set and stage. The Sternberg method of directing included him acting out all the roles; he then insisted that the actors do it exactly as he had.

DISTRIBUTION: *Shanghai Express* was Dietrich's biggest hit in America, bringing in $1.5 million in worldwide rentals. Due to the hard economic times, it was one of only a few Paramount pictures to turn a profit that season, with a net profit of $33,000. It was also one of the top 10 highest-grossing films of 1932. The Chinese government banned the movie and all other Paramount releases. In a negotiation involving the U.S. embassy, Paramount later made peace with the Chinese by promising not to make another film about similar issues. —*Alex Ben Block*

GRAND HOTEL
MGM, 1932

ALL-RELEASE EQUIVALENT 2005 $s
(Unadjusted $s) in Millions of $s

Domestic Box Office Revenues. . . . . **$76.5**/($2.7)
Production Cost . . . . **$9.9**/($0.7)
Principal Photography. . . . . **48** days
12/30/1931–2/19/1932
+ 6 days of retakes
from 3/21/1932–3/29/1932

Director . . . . Edmund Goulding
Producer . . . . Irving Thalberg, Paul Bern
Production Company. . . . Metro-Goldwyn-Mayer Pictures
Story by. . . . . Based on the novel *Menschen im Hotel* by Vicki Baum
Screenplay by . . . . William A. Drake
Cast . . . . Greta Garbo, John Barrymore, Joan Crawford, Wallace Beery, Lionel Barrymore
Filming Locations . . . . . . On the MGM Studio lot in Culver City, CA
Genre. . . . . Drama
Format. . . . . B&W
Initial Release . . . . 4/12/1932 premiere
Rerelease . . . . none
Running Time . . . . 105 or 115 minutes 12 reels
MPAA Rating . . . . not rated

STANDING THE TEST OF TIME

ACADEMY AWARD Oscar Nominations and Wins

*OUTSTADING PRODUCTION: Metro-Goldwyn-Mayer

OSCAR TOTALS   Nominations **1**   *Wins **1**

AFI 100 YEARS 100 MOVIES SELECTION
2007 0   1997 0

TOP 300 FILMS POSITION . . . . .none
All-Release Domestic Box Office in Equivalent 2005 $s

National Film Preservation Board Selection. . . . 2007

OTHER AWARDS Best Picture Wins

	Year
Golden Globes	none
New York Film Critics	none
National Board of Review	none
Film Daily Critics	1932

It is a production thoroughly worthy of all the talk it has created and the several motion-picture luminaries deserve to feel very proud of their performances, particularly Greta Garbo and Lionel Barrymore.

—Mordaunt Hall, *New York Times*, 1932

PLOT: The paths of five guests intersect over two days in the art deco Grand Hotel in Berlin. An aging Russian ballerina, a dashing baron, an ambitious stenographer, a dying bookkeeper, and a ruthless German businessman are all changed by their visit to the Grand Hotel.

PRODUCTION: Irving Thalberg, known as the boy wonder of Hollywood for his success as head of production at MGM, read a synopsis of a planned Broadway play, *The Grand Hotel,* and decided that it was the perfect vehicle for Hollywood's first all-star feature. It was based on a 1929 German-language novel, *Menschen im Hotel (People in a Hotel),* by Austrian-born American writer Vicki Baum, who had worked as a maid in a German hotel for six weeks, providing detailed observations. She also adapted it as a play in Berlin. Thalberg wanted his big star, Greta Garbo, to play the fading prima ballerina. He had MGM invest $15,000 in the play in return for movie rights. The play was a hit and ran for over a year, returning a profit to MGM. However, Thalberg had a problem: the big MGM stars balked. Garbo, at age twenty-seven, felt that she was too old to play a prima ballerina, and was unhappy that the part of the jewel thief who breaks into her room was given to John Barrymore instead of her real-life fiancé, John Gilbert. Joan Crawford worried her best scenes would be cut by censors and she would be lost among all the other stars. Wallace Beery objected that the role of the villainous businessman was too seedy a character but gave in when Thalberg said he could use a German accent to separate him from his earlier characters. Garbo was promised she would be billed just by her last name, which elevated her status as a star. Thalberg either twisted the arm of others or simply ordered them to report to the set. The movie was produced in January and February 1932 on the lot in Culver City for an A-level $695,341. The set design, by Cedric Gibbons, included a lavish lobby, with costumes by Adrian, a famous costumer of the day. Once filming began, the stars maneuvered to outdo each other. No one chewed scenery like Crawford, a temperamental diva who turned her small role as a sluttish clerk into a scene-stealing turn. When MGM did test screenings, Crawford so outshone Garbo that Thalberg felt it threw the balance of the movie off. So Garbo was brought back to add scenes that built up her character. Beery tried to ad-lib to upset Crawford, but she complained to Goulding, a British-born former actor with a reputation as a woman's director, and he told Beery to play the part as written.

DISTRIBUTION: *Grand Hotel* was a substantial hit, an event movie. On April 12, 1932, it opened with one of the first klieg-light-and-red-carpet premieres at Grauman's Chinese Theater in Hollywood. By the London opening, there were long lines for tickets. The movie made a profit of $951,659 on approximately $6 million in worldwide box office, with slightly more than half coming in from overseas. It included the line that would forevermore be associated with Garbo: "I want to be alone." MGM did a remake in 1945 as a musical, *Weekend at the Waldorf.* It was adapted for a Broadway play in 1989, once again without success. —*Alex Ben Block*

I AM A FUGITIVE FROM A CHAIN GANG

Warner Bros., 1932

ALL-RELEASE EQUIVALENT 2005 $s

(Unadjusted $s) in Millions of $s

Domestic Box Office Revenues . . . . **$40.3**/($1.4)
Production Cost . . . . **$3.3**/($0.2)
Principal Photography . . . . **31** days estimated
7/29/1932–9/2/1932

Director . . . . Mervyn LeRoy

Producer . . . . Hal B. Wallis (uncredited)

Production Company . . . . Warner Bros. Pictures

Story by . . . . Based on the novel *I Am a Fugitive from a Georgia Chain Gang* by Robert Elliott Burns

Screenplay by . . . . Howard J. Green, Brown Holmes, Sheridan Gibney

Cast . . . . Paul Muni, Glenda Farrell, Helen Vinson

Filming Locations . . . . . . Warner Bros. Studio, Burbank, CA

Genre . . . . Drama

Format . . . . B&W

Initial Release . . . . 11/10/1932 premiere (New York); 11/19/1932 general release

Rerelease . . . . none

Running Time . . . . 76 or 90 minutes

MPAA Rating . . . . not rated

STANDING THE TEST OF TIME

ACADEMY AWARD Oscar Nominations and Wins

Outstanding Production: Warner Bros.

Actor: Paul Muni

Sound Recording: Warner Bros. Studio Sound Dept., Nathan Levinson, Sound Director

OSCAR TOTALS Nominations **3** *Wins **0**

AFI 100 YEARS 100 MOVIES SELECTION
2007 0   1997 0

TOP 300 FILMS POSITION . . . . .none
All-Release Domestic Box Office in Equivalent 2005 $s

National Film Preservation Board Selection 1991

OTHER AWARDS Best Picture Wins

	Year
Golden Globes	none
New York Film Critics	none
National Board of Review	1932
Film Daily Critics	none

The movie and the book on which it was based . . . almost single-handedly led to the elimination of chain gangs from the South [and established] the Hollywood image of Southern sheriffs and prison wardens as mean, not-too-bright power abusers, an image still too familiar 60 years later.

—Kaye Lanning Minchew

PLOT: The film covers a decade in the life of James Allen, a World War I doughboy, who is involved in a petty robbery and sentenced to ten years' brutal hard labor in Georgia's prison system. He escapes, is returned, and escapes again, before finally being freed.

PRODUCTION: At a time when America seemed to want light entertainment, Warner Bros. took a risk by making a movie with strong social commentary. It was before the censors began enforcing the Production Code, so Warner was able to tell a realistic story, based on the real-life story of Robert E. Burns, who was living in hiding in New Jersey and dictated his account to his brother, a Catholic priest. It was serialized in *True Detective Magazine* in early 1931 and published as a novel in March 1932 by Vanguard Press. Darryl F. Zanuck, then Warner's head of production, optioned movie rights for $12,500 from Burns's brother, the Rev. Vincent G. Burns. Zanuck also hired Robert Burns (the real fugitive) as a consultant, under a deal that paid only his traveling expenses. Warner's East Coast story editor Jacob Wilk sent a memo to Zanuck on April 6, 1932, informing him that Robert Burns would visit, but that he would use the name Richard M. Crane to evade the Georgia authorities. The fugitive visited for several weeks, then returned to New Jersey, where almost a month after the film was released, he was arrested. However, this time the governor of New Jersey refused to extradite him, citing the cruel circumstances of his incarceration. Mervyn LeRoy was one of Hollywood's most heralded directors and was known for realistic films such as 1931's *Little Caesar. Fugitive* was shot mostly on the Warner lot in Burbank, California (with stock footage added), on a tight budget with a final cost of $228,000. The ending in particular was praised by critics for its stark simplicity. In reality, it was an accident: the lights on the set went out when a fuse blew during filming, but LeRoy kept the footage he shot that day in the movie anyway. The script did take major liberties in telling Burns's story. He was not a war hero but a shell-shocked mess. He did rob the lunch counter for $5.80. He was never an engineer but rather founded a real estate trade magazine, *Greater Chicago Magazine,* which he edited and published.

DISTRIBUTION: It was voted one of the 10 Best Pictures of 1933 by *Film Daily.* The film generated controversy over its portrayal of the southern penal system, but that controversy helped fuel the box office. Warner Bros.'s gamble paid off, and the studio began a whole series of movies with strong social themes. The success also helped save the studio financially. *Fugitive* was banned in Georgia for the first years after its release. There was also a backlash in other parts of the South, but the favorable reviews and booming box office soon became the bigger story. To try to assuage those in Georgia who claimed the film was filled with lies, the state is never named. The film brought in $1.6 million in worldwide rentals with a net profit of $870,000, making it one of the top films in 1932. The exposure helped put an end to the brutal Georgia system of forced labor. Ellis Arnall, who became governor of Georgia in 1945, finally pardoned Burns. In 1987 there was a TV movie called *The Man Who Broke 1,000 Chains,* billed as the true story. —*Alex Ben Block*

STATE FAIR

Fox Film Corp., 1933

ALL-RELEASE EQUIVALENT 2005 $s

(Unadjusted $s) in Millions of $s

Domestic Box Office Revenues . . . . **$74.8**/($2.7)
Production Cost . . . . **$8.9**/($0.6)
Principal Photography . . . . **46** days
11/1/1932–12/23/1932

Director . . . . Henry King

Producer . . . . Winfield Sheehan

Production Company . . . . Fox Film Corp.

Story by . . . . Based on the novel by Phil Stong

Screenplay by . . . . Paul Green, Sonya Levien

Cast . . . . Will Rogers, Janet Gaynor, Lew Ayres, Sally Eilers, Norman Foster, Louise Dresser

Filming Locations . . . . . . In studio at Fox Movietone City, Westwood Hills; external shots in Des Moines, Iowa and Corona, CA

Genre . . . . Musical

Format . . . . B&W

Initial Release 1/26/1933

Rerelease . . . . 1936 (revenue not included above)

Running Time . . . . 97–99 minutes
10 reels
8,894 feet

MPAA Rating . . . . not rated

STANDING THE TEST OF TIME

ACADEMY AWARD Oscar Nominations and Wins

Outstanding Production: Fox

Writing (Adaptation): Paul Green, Sonya Levien

OSCAR TOTALS   Nominations 2   *Wins 0

AFI 100 YEARS 100 MOVIES SELECTION
2007 0   1997 0

TOP 300 FILMS POSITION . . . . none
All-Release Domestic Box Office in Equivalent 2005 $s

National Film Preservation Board Selection . . . . none

OTHER AWARDS Best Picture Wins

	Year
Golden Globes	none
New York Film Critics	none
National Board of Review	none
Film Daily Critics	none

The public has grown accustomed to relying upon Will Rogers's pictures to provide unobjectionable humor for the entire family.

—Carl E. Milliken, MPPDA secretary, discussing the protests against the bedroom scene

PLOT: The film tells the story of a farming family who enters a temperamental prize hog in the Iowa State Fair, and the adventures and romances that ensue.

PRODUCTION: In 1931 Phil Stong, a novelist and reporter working for an ad firm, was encouraged by his wife to write his most famous novel, *State Fair,* about the local annual harvest festival. Stong's grandfather had been superintendent of the swine division at the Iowa State Fair, and Stong himself had covered the fair as a reporter. Stong used incidents and details from his own life. The novel came out in 1932 and was favorably reviewed. Stong received $15,000 from Fox for movie rights and was hired to work on the film. Fox contract director Henry King was assigned, and Spencer Tracy was originally cast in the lead. However, Tracy left to replace Charles Farrell in *Face in the Sky.* Many Fox players were cast, including Will Rogers (the highest-paid actor at that time), Janet Gaynor (the top box office attraction), and Lew Ayres (hot after *All Quiet on the Western Front* in 1930). Jason S. Joy, of the Motion Picture Producers and Distributors Association, convinced the producers to change one of the relationships in the novel from a sexual encounter to a romance leading to marriage. In the summer of 1932, King and Stong went to the Iowa State Fair and Exposition in Des Moines with a camera crew and filmed background material. Joe Valentine and Ed Hammeras captured background plates, the general atmosphere, and race sequences at the fair and on the midway using new Eastman Grayback Background Negative film stock. (The rest of the production was shot with Eastman Supersensitive Negative stock using two cameras wherever possible.) Fox also got permission to shoot at the I. V. Ashcroft farm near Corona, California, by agreeing to paint the farmhouse, put in a white picket fence, build chicken houses, and plant shrubs. Fox purchased three hogs at the fair, including the grand champion, Dike of Rosedale (Blue Boy). Rogers was told to be careful around Blue Boy but, undaunted, was found sleeping with the hog in its pen one day. A Fox supervisor asked if Rogers would like to take Blue Boy home, as he would make good eating, but Rogers said, "I just wouldn't feel right eatin' a fellow actor." Later, the hogs were given to the California state school system, presented by Rogers.

DISTRIBUTION: The film was a financial success for Fox and helped keep the studio in operation during the Depression years (1929–1940). It was chosen as one of the ten best films of 1933 by the National Board of Review and was fifth in the *Film Daily* poll of critics that year. The novel was reprinted in 1933 as a "Photoplay Edition," with stills from the film and a pictorial jacket designed as a promotional tie-in. Stong was able to buy his mother's family farm. In 1935 star Will Rogers died in a plane crash. That same year, the bedroom scene was cut to secure censor approval and the film was reissued on August 7, 1936. Subsequently, 20th Century-Fox produced remakes as musical films with songs by Richard Rodgers and Oscar Hammerstein II in 1945 and 1962. In 1976 CBS broadcast a 60-minute television movie based on the novel and films. —*Hayley Taylor Block*

SHE DONE HIM WRONG
Paramount, 1933

ALL-RELEASE EQUIVALENT 2005 $s
(Unadjusted $s) in Millions of $s

Domestic Box Office Revenues . . . . **$136.3**/($4.9)
Production Cost . . . . **$4.1**/($0.3)
Principal Photography . . . . **18** days
11/29/1932–12/22/1932

Director	Lowell Sherman
Producer	William LeBaron (Assoc.)
Production Company	Paramount Productions
Story by	Mae West
Screenplay by	Harvey Thew, John Bright
Cast	Mae West, Cary Grant, Gilbert Roland, Noah Berry, Rafaela Ottiano, David Landau, Rochelle Hudson
Filming Locations	Paramount Studio, Hollywood, CA
Genre	Comedy
Format	B&W
Initial Release	2/3/1933
Rerelease	none
Running Time	64 or 66 minutes 7 reels
MPAA Rating	not rated

STANDING THE TEST OF TIME

ACADEMY AWARD Oscar Nominations and Wins

Outstanding Production: Paramount

OSCAR TOTALS   Nominations **1**   *Wins 0

AFI 100 YEARS 100 MOVIES SELECTION
2007 0   1997 0

TOP 300 FILMS POSITION . . . . .none
All-Release Domestic Box Office in Equivalent 2005 $s

National Film Preservation Board Selection 1996

OTHER AWARDS Best Picture Wins

	Year
Golden Globes	none
New York Film Critics	none
National Board of Review	none
Film Daily Critics	none

To be convinced that she is a breeder of licentiousness and an exponent of pornography is to be unusually blind to her precise qualities as an actress.

—*New York Times* about Mae West, 1934

PLOT: Lady "Diamond" Lou is a singer in a Gay Nineties saloon on New York's Bowery. Although the saloon owner is a criminal and her benefactor, she stays out of trouble, even when an ex-boyfriend breaks out of jail and comes looking for her.

PRODUCTION: Mae West, who began her career at age five in vaudeville, had built her act around coarse humor (she was jailed once for eleven days on charges of obscenity). Her biggest stage hit was the bawdy 1928 play *Diamond Lil*, which West co-wrote. In 1930 West brought her play to Los Angeles, where Universal Pictures expressed interest in screen rights. However, they backed away after movie censors declared the play off-limits and even discouraged using West as a screenwriter. West's follow-up play, *The Constant Sinner*, didn't do very well, making her wonder if she was washed up at age thirty-nine. It was then that her pal George Raft suggested West come to Hollywood to play a small but juicy role in Paramount's 1932 gangster drama *Night After Night*. West balked at the part until they let her rewrite it. Her appearance left exhibitors clamoring for more, at a time when Paramount was losing $21 million a year. On October 19, 1932, studio head Adolph Zukor was told by censor Will H. Hays there was no way to make the play into a movie because "changing the title [of the play] is not enough." By November 21, Paramount's production head offered a compromise. The studio would make no mention in advertising or publicity that the film was based on West's notorious play *Diamond Lil* and the prostitute would be transformed into a pickpocket. Paramount also agreed to abide by the industry censor's warning to avoid "as far as possible . . . any feeling of sordid realism." Production began in November 1932 under the working title "Ruby Red." West was paid $25,000 for play rights and a $20,000 salary for what was her second film and first starring role. The movie reunited her with producer William LeBaron, who had first employed her in a 1911 play and had continued to keep in contact with her ever since. They shot in eighteen days, with eighteen principal cast members and ten chorus girls moving through 123 setups on ten sets. There were sixteen days in studio and two on location. West personally picked Cary Grant over studio objections, and the part ultimately made him a star. West didn't get along with co-writer John Bright (*The Public Enemy*, 1931) so when one censor suggested playing the whole thing as comedy, West had a viable excuse to cut Bright's lines and restore her own. Other former vaudevillians in the cast included Fuzzy Knight, Grace La Rue, and Rafaela Ottiano, who had been in the play's Broadway cast. After the film was shipped to theaters, on February 3, 1933, censors ordered all film exchanges to cut 100 feet of reel six, to eliminate most of West singing "Slow Motion Man." While this enraged Paramount execs, there was very little they could do.

DISTRIBUTION: The film was an immediate sensation, but controversy erupted over the sex, language, and humor it contained. It was voted one of the 10 Best Pictures of 1933 by *Film Daily*. The worldwide rentals of over $3 million kept the lights on at Paramount, which did not shy away from selling the movie's sex appeal. One tagline read: "Mae West gives a 'HOT TIME' to the nation." The backlash by the Catholic Legion of Decency and others led to even greater censorship that would last until the 1960s. It was the shortest movie ever nominated for Best Picture. —*Alex Ben Block*

42ND STREET

Warner Bros., 1933

ALL-RELEASE EQUIVALENT 2005 $s

(Unadjusted $s) in Millions of $s

Domestic Box Office Revenues . . . . **$89.1**/($3.2)
Production Cost . . . .**$6.6**/($0.4)
Principal Photography . . . . **43** days estimated
9/28/1932–11/16/1932

Director . . . . Lloyd Bacon

Producer . . . . Darryl Zanuck

Production Company . . . . Warner Bros. Pictures

Story by . . . . Based on the novel by
Bradford Ropes

Screenplay by . . . . Rian James, James Seymour

Cast . . . . Warner Baxter, Bebe Daniels,
Ruby Keeler, Dick Powell,
Ginger Rogers

Filming Locations . . . . . . Warner Bros. Studios, Burbank,
CA, and old Warner studio on
Hollywood Blvd.

Genre . . . . Musical

Format . . . . B&W

Initial Release . . . . 3/8/1933 premiere Strand
Theater (New York);
3/11/1933 general release

Rerelease . . . . none

Running Time . . . . 85 or 89 minutes

MPAA Rating . . . . not rated

STANDING THE TEST OF TIME

ACADEMY AWARD Oscar Nominations and Wins

Outstanding Production: Warner Bros.

Sound Recording: Warner Bros. Studio Sound Dept.,
Nathan Levinson, Sound Director

OSCAR TOTALS Nominations **2** *Wins 0

AFI 100 YEARS 100 MOVIES SELECTION
2007 0   1997 0

TOP 300 FILMS POSITION . . . . .none
All-Release Domestic Box Office in Equivalent 2005 $s

National Film Preservation Board Selection 1998

OTHER AWARDS Best Picture Wins

	Year
Golden Globes	none
New York Film Critics	none
National Board of Review	none
Film Daily Critics	none

No American film director explored the possibilities of the mobile camera more fully or ingeniously than Busby Berkeley. He was the Méliès of the musical, the corollary of Vertov in the exploration of the possibilities of cinematic movement.

—FilmReference.com

PLOT: In this unglamorized look at Broadway during the Great Depression, a demanding director puts singers and dancers through their paces. A starstruck ingénue gets her big break, the play is a hit, and she becomes a star.

PRODUCTION: Only six years after *The Jazz Singer* ushered in talking pictures, movie musicals were in a funk. After the success of *The Broadway Melody* in 1929, several others had flopped. Broadway choreographer Busby Berkeley was on the verge of returning to New York when Darryl F. Zanuck gave him a multiyear contract to choreograph musicals at Warner Bros., starting with *42nd Street*. Based on a novel by 1920s Broadway chorus dancer Bradford Ropes, the script by Rian James and James Seymour eliminated some of the grittier scenes but still provided realistic storytelling mixed with sentiment. Produced before the Hayes Office enforced censorship, there were bits of racy dialogue, sexually suggestive dances, and a scene in which a man carries the ingénue off to his bed. Although directed by Lloyd Bacon (after the first assigned director, Mervyn LeRoy, became unavailable), it was Berkeley's production numbers for songs such as "Shuffle off to Buffalo" and "Young and Healthy" that dazzled. He employed statuesque chorus girls in glamorous costumes, outrageous sets, multilevel architecture, and rotating or moving sets. Berkeley carried over, from working with producer Samuel Goldwyn, his policy of using only one camera, maintaining fluid movement, and frequently showing close-ups of the beautiful girls. His extravagant musical numbers and innovative camera angles, most notably his overhead shots with a moving camera, provided a changing kaleidoscope of images. The cast mixed veterans such as George Brent, Warner Baxter, and Bebe Daniels with new faces such as Ginger Rogers, Dick Powell, and Ruby Keeler (Mrs. Al Jolson in real life), who from this film became a star overnight, just like the character she played in the movie. Berkeley had served as a field artillery lieutenant during World War I, where he learned to drill, discipline, and choreograph large groups of people. He honed those skills on Broadway before coming to Hollywood. Berkeley argued later with those who saw great significance in his work. He said he was just driven to top himself again and again, and never repeat the past.

DISTRIBUTION: *42nd Street* was a big hit, with a $1.2 million profit on worldwide rentals of $2.3 million. It was named by *Variety* as one of the six best money pictures of the year, with *She Done Him Wrong, Tugboat Annnie, Gold Diggers of 1933, Little Women,* and *State Fair.* It was credited with reviving the movie musical genre. Before the end of the year Warner released two more musicals choreographed by Berkeley, *Gold Diggers of 1933* and *Footlight Parade.* To garner publicity for *42nd Street* prior to the opening, a train called the "42nd Street Special" went from Hollywood to New York doing publicity events along the way. Celebrities onboard included cowboy star Tom Mix and his horse along with chorus girls from the film. In 1980 the movie was adapted for Broadway and became a long-running hit musical. Turner Entertainment released a colorized version that was shown over the TBS cable network in 1986. —*Alex Ben Block*

KING KONG

RKO, 1933

<table>
<tr><td colspan="2">ALL-RELEASE EQUIVALENT 2005 $s
(Unadjusted $s) in Millions of $s</td></tr>
<tr><td>Domestic Box Office Revenues</td><td>$93.9/($5.2)</td></tr>
<tr><td>Production Cost</td><td>$10.1/($0.7)</td></tr>
<tr><td>Principal Photography</td><td>140 days estimated
8/10/1932–1/31/1933</td></tr>
</table>

Director	Merian C. Cooper, Ernest B. Schoedsack
Producer	Merian C. Cooper, Ernest B. Schoedsack (uncredited)
Production Company	Radio Pictures
Story by	Edgar Wallace, Merian C. Cooper
Screenplay by	James Creelman, Ruth Rose
Cast	Fay Wray, Robert Armstrong, Bruce Cabot
Filming Locations	RKO sound stages and 40-acre back lot in Culver City, CA
Genre	Action Adventure
Format	B&W
Initial Release	3/2/1933 world premiere; 4/7/1933 general release
Rerelease	1938, 1942, 1952, 1956, 1971 (rentals only available for initial & 1952 re-release)
Running Time	96, 100, or 110 minutes 11 reels 9,029 feet
MPAA Rating	not rated

STANDING THE TEST OF TIME

ACADEMY AWARD Oscar Nominations and Wins

None

OSCAR TOTALS   Nominations 0   *Wins 0

AFI 100 YEARS 100 MOVIES SELECTION
2007 . . . #41   1997 . . . #43

TOP 300 FILMS POSITION . . . . none
All-Release Domestic Box Office in Equivalent 2005 $s

National Film Preservation Board Selection 1991

OTHER AWARDS Best Picture Wins

	Year
Golden Globes	none
New York Film Critics	none
National Board of Review	none
Film Daily Critics	none

Animation will always remain animation because the action will never be perfectly smooth. Nevertheless, I think we have introduced such startling trick shots, and unusual value in King Kong *that everybody will want to see it.*

—Merian C. Cooper

PLOT: A film director recruits a young woman to sail to a mysterious Pacific island, where they find a giant ape, who falls for the girl. They return to New York to put their discovery on public display, but the ape escapes and is hunted down.

PRODUCTION: On an expedition to the Dutch East Indies, World War I aviator and adventurer Merian Caldwell Cooper saw his first movies being made and met Ernest Schoedsack, who became his collaborator. They teamed up for the documentary *Grass,* about the migratory habits of a tribe in Persia. It became a surprise hit for Paramount, which then financed *Chang,* their documentary on elephants. At Paramount, Cooper met producer David Selznick, who left to run RKO, taking Cooper along as his assistant. Cooper had seen gorillas in the wild and came up with an idea to make a movie about a large gorilla. Cooper assigned British writer Edgar Wallace to draft a screenplay but didn't like the result. Wallace died shortly after, but Cooper still gave him a screen credit. Cooper turned to Schoedsack's wife, Ruth Rose, to work on the script along with James Ashmore Creelman. Their working title was "The Eighth Wonder of the World," the story of a monster and a beautiful girl, based on the classic story of *Beauty and the Beast.* Cooper was also influenced by the 1925 film *The Lost World* with dinosaurs animated by Willis O'Brien using models by Marcel Delgado. In 1930 O'Brien and Delgado began working on *Creation.* In 1931 Selznick acquired both Cooper's idea and the *Creation* project, which he merged together. The $230,000 cost of abandoning *Creation* was absorbed into the *King Kong* budget. Cooper wanted to call the movie "Kong," the Malaysian word for gorilla, but Selznick thought it sounded oriental, so they added "King." The production used the jungle sets from a 1932 film, *The Most Dangerous Game.* The production, which cost $450,000, included technical innovations, including the use of rear screen projection, miniature models, and trick photography. O'Brien and Delgado built a series of Kong models, including an 18-inch version for long shots, as well as a full-size hand, foot, and face. The seven-foot-wide face, covered with thirty bearskins, had eighty-five motors operated by six men. The giant wall separating the villagers on the island from the monster was originally built for the 1927 film *King of Kings.* Bruce Cabot won his first starring role after meeting Cooper while a doorman at a club in Hollywood. It was Selznick's idea to cast Fay Wray and Robert Armstrong. After the premiere, Cooper went back and cut out a sequence in which giant spiders gobble up humans because it was too disturbing to the audience. The score by Max Steiner was acclaimed for capturing the emotion of the movie. It was one of the first American movies to include an extensive musical score.

DISTRIBUTION: After Selznick left for MGM, Cooper became RKO production chief on February 14, 1933. He orchestrated extensive promotions for *King Kong,* which premiered March 2 at the Radio City Music Hall and the new RKO Roxy in Radio City. It sold a record 50,000 tickets on the first day. After its general release April 7, it made $1.9 million in worldwide rentals, with a profit of $650,000. That helped save RKO from bankruptcy. —*Alex Ben Block*

LITTLE WOMEN
RKO, 1933

ALL-RELEASE EQUIVALENT 2005 $s
(Unadjusted $s) in Millions of $s

Domestic Box Office Revenues . . . . **$142.4**/($5.1)
Production Cost . . . . **$15.0**/($1.0)
Principal Photography . . . .**56** days estimated
6/28/1933–8/28/1933

Director . . . . George Cukor
Producer . . . . Merian C. Cooper (exec)
Production Company . . . . Radio Pictures
Story by . . . . Based on the novel by Louisa May Alcott
Screenplay by . . . . Sarah Y. Mason, Victor Heerman
Cast . . . . Katharine Hepburn, Joan Bennett, Paul Lukas, Edna May Oliver
Filming Locations . . . . . . Exteriors on the Warner Bros. Ranch, in Pasadena, CA, and at Lancaster's Lake in Sunland, CA. The exterior of the March house was on Providencia Ranch, Universal City, CA.
Genre . . . . Drama
Format . . . . B&W
Initial Release . . . . 11/16/1933 world premiere (New York); 11/24/1933 general release
Rerelease . . . . 1938 (not included above)
Running Time . . . . 107, 115, or 117 minutes 12 reels
MPAA Rating . . . . not rated

STANDING THE TEST OF TIME

ACADEMY AWARD Oscar Nominations and Wins

Outstanding Production: RKO Radio

Directing: George Cukor

*WRITING: (Adaptation : Victor Heerman, Sarah Y. Mason)

OSCAR TOTALS   Nominations **3**   *Wins **1**

AFI 100 YEARS 100 MOVIES SELECTION
2007 0   1997 0

TOP 300 FILMS POSITION . . . . .none
All-Release Domestic Box Office in Equivalent 2005 $s

National Film Preservation Board Selection . . . .none

OTHER AWARDS Best Picture Wins

	Year
Golden Globes	none
New York Film Critics	none
National Board of Review	none
Film Daily Critics	none

[The script was] something quite original for the time. It wasn't slicked up. The construction was very loose, very episodic, like the novel. Things happen, but they're not all tied together . . . the writers believed in the book, they understood its vitality, which is not namby-pamby in any way.

—George Cukor

PLOT: Four sisters struggle to keep up their spirits while their father is off fighting for the Union army in the Civil War. Romantic entanglements, marriages, and the return of their father add to the drama.

PRODUCTION: This was the final film put into production by David O. Selznick at RKO, and he lined up an all-star cast. He convinced his bosses to maintain the novel's period setting even though it made it more expensive. Selznick oversaw the start-up of the lavish production, including authentic New England sets meticulously re-created in California by Hobe Erwin, a famous designer of the era. Selznick then left for a producing deal at MGM (run by his father-in-law, Louis B. Mayer) in early 1933 (leading to the line "The Son-in-Law Also Rises"). He left behind his second in command, Merian C. Cooper, with whom he had worked at Paramount, and who was credited as executive producer on *Little Women.* After Selznick departed, George Cukor agreed to direct because it would allow him to fulfill a final work commitment at RKO. That reunited Cukor with Katharine Hepburn, whom he had directed in her debut, *A Bill of Divorcement.* Hepburn had just finished shooting 1933's *Morning Glory,* the role for which she would win her first Oscar as best actress. The lavish production for *Little Women* employed more than 4,000 people and involved months of preproduction, building detailed re-creations of New England locations from the book. More than 3,000 items, including costumes, appliances, and furniture, were authenticated by research. Hepburn had Walter Plunkett, the costume designer, copy a dress worn by her late maternal grandmother in a photographic tintype. Most of the scenes involving Joan Bennett had to be specially blocked out by Cukor so that her pregnancy did not show. Even though the temperature was over 100 degrees during production, real snow was created and spread for scenes set in winter. It was the third movie made from Louisa May Alcott's 1868 novel, based on her own experiences, and the first of those to utilize sound. During production, recently unionized sound technicians went on strike, and outside sound men were brought in, causing production delays when scenes had to be reshot. There were multiple versions of the script. The final, Oscar-winning adapted screenplay is by Victor Heerman, who had been a film director, and his wife, Sarah Y. Mason. Selznick would later hire costumer Walter Plunkett for *Gone with the Wind.* Louise Closser Hale was first cast as Aunt May, but she died July 26, 1933, and Edna May Oliver took the role.

DISTRIBUTION: From its November 1933 opening at Radio City Music Hall in New York City, the movie was a smash hit, despite the Great Depression. It broke opening week theater records at Radio City (over $100,000 gross). The film made a profit of $800,000 on its initial release. It was voted one of the 10 Best Pictures of 1934 by *Film Daily.* It was rereleased by RKO in July 1938. *Little Women* marked one of the first times a classic of literature was produced without a Hollywood rewrite to try to make it more commercial. Its success allowed Selznick and others to tap more literary works while staying true to the material. —*Alex Ben Block*

IT HAPPENED ONE NIGHT
Columbia, 1934

ALL-RELEASE EQUIVALENT 2005 $s
(Unadjusted $s) in Millions of $s

Domestic Box Office Revenues. . . . . **$123.9**/($4.4)
Production Cost . . . .**$4.7**/($0.3)
Principal Photography. . . . . **35** days estimated
11/13/1933–12/21/1933

Director . . . . Frank Capra
Producer . . . . Harry Cohn
Production Company. . . . Columbia Pictures
Story by. . . . . Based on a short story by
Samuel Hopkins Adams
Screenplay by . . . . Robert Riskin
Cast . . . . Clark Gable, Claudette Colbert,
Walter Connolly
Filming Locations . . . . . . In studio and on location at
Busch Gardens, Pasadena,
Santa Monica mountains,
Los Angeles and Thousand
Oaks, CA
Genre. . . . . Romantic Comedy
Format . . . . B&W
Initial Release 2/23/1934
Rerelease. 1948
Running Time . . . . 105 minutes
11 reels
9,431 feet
MPAA Rating . . . . not rated

STANDING THE TEST OF TIME

ACADEMY AWARD Oscar Nominations and Wins
***OUTSTANDING PRODUCTION:** Columbia
***ACTOR:** Clark Gable
***ACTRESS:** Claudette Colbert
***DIRECTING:** Frank Capra
***WRITING:** (Adaptation): Robert Riskin

OSCAR TOTALS   Nominations **5**   *Wins **5**

AFI 100 YEARS 100 MOVIES SELECTION
2007 . . . #46   1997 . . . #35

TOP 300 FILMS POSITION . . . . none
All-Release Domestic Box Office in Equivalent 2005 $s

National Film Preservation Board Selection. . . . 1993

OTHER AWARDS Best Picture Wins

	Year
Golden Globes	none
New York Film Critics.	none
National Board of Review	1934
Film Daily Critics	none

Amazingly enough, the news about It Happened One Night *was not that
it made the "classic" ranks, but that it ever got made at all.*

—Frank Capra

PLOT: A spoiled heiress's father hates the man she hopes to marry. He holds his daughter prisoner, but she escapes. She takes off for New York City on a bus, where she meets a smug reporter, to whom she takes an instant dislike until romance flowers.

PRODUCTION: Frank Capra was visiting a barber in Palm Springs, where he had gone to write the script *Lady for a Day* with frequent collaborator Robert Riskin (husband of Fay Wray), when he happened to pick up *Cosmopolitan* magazine and read a short story by Samuel Hopkins Adams called "Night Bus." Capra recalled thinking that it "had the smell of novelty." Capra had Columbia acquire film rights for $5,000, which was considered cheap even then. Shortly after, Columbia boss Harry Cohn told Capra he was being loaned out to MGM. Capra balked, but Cohn insisted because MGM's Irving Thalberg had offered Columbia a $50,000 bonus and the loan of an MGM star for another movie—so Capra had to go. Not long after, Thalberg became ill and headed for Europe to recuperate, leaving Louis B. Mayer in charge of MGM. Mayer dumped Thalberg's pet projects, including Capra's. Back at Columbia's "poverty row" studio in Hollywood, Capra decided to make a film of "Night Bus," but Cohn complained that two other recent bus movies had failed. When Capra insisted, Cohn agreed but demanded a title without the word *bus*. For the male lead, Capra wanted Robert Montgomery, but Cohn used his loan from MGM to get Clark Gable, whose assignment was meant as Mayer's punishment for daring to ask for more money. To Capra's surprise, Hollywood's top actresses turned down the female lead, including Myrna Loy, Constance Bennett, and Margaret Sullavan. Capra and Riskin did a rewrite to make the leads more likable, the girl less spoiled, and Gable's role more manly, switching him from an artist to a newspaper reporter. Cohn sent Capra to woo Claudette Colbert, who was leaving on a ski trip in four weeks. Capra told her he could finish before then, even though he believed it impossible. Colbert reluctantly agreed to do the project if Columbia would pay her $50,000, double her fee at Paramount, which made her the highest-paid cast member. Capra was one of Hollywood's most efficient filmmakers and was able to finish before Colbert's deadline.

DISTRIBUTION: *It Happened One Night* opened to favorable but not rave reviews and modest business. It was voted one of the 10 Best Pictures of 1934 by *Film Daily*. Then people discovered Capra's comedy, began talking about it, and started going to see it again. It became a national obsession, with theaters sold out for weeks at a time. Critics returned for another look and it became the sleeper hit of the year. It was the first film to sweep the top Academy Awards (which didn't happen again until 1975). That kept it playing in small towns for long after its initial release. Despite its success, Capra wasn't taken seriously by influential critics of his day who called his mix of comedy, sentiment, and social commentary "Capricorn." —*Alex Ben Block*

THE THIN MAN
MGM, 1934

ALL-RELEASE EQUIVALENT 2005 $s
(Unadjusted $s) in Millions of $s

Domestic Box Office Revenues . . . . $50.7/($1.8)
Production Cost . . . . $3.3/($0.2)
Principal Photography . . . . **16** days
4/10/1934–4/27/1934
Retakes-mid May 1934

Director . . . . W. S. Van Dyke

Producer . . . . Louis B. Mayer

Production Company . . . . Metro-Goldwyn-Mayer

Story by . . . . Based on the novel by Dashiell Hammett

Screenplay by . . . . Albert Hackett, Frances Goodrich

Cast . . . . William Powell, Myrna Loy, Maureen O'Sullivan

Filming Locations . . . . . . At MGM studios, with some interior scenes in the Bidwell Mansion, Chico, CA

Genre . . . . Comedy

Format . . . . B&W

Initial Release 5/25/1934

Rerelease . . . . none

Running Time . . . . 91 minutes
10 reels

MPAA Rating . . . . not rated

STANDING THE TEST OF TIME

ACADEMY AWARD Oscar Nominations and Wins

Outstanding Production: Metro-Goldwyn-Mayer

Actor: William Powell

Directing: W.S. Van Dyke

Writing (Adaptation): Fances Goodrich, Albert Hackett

OSCAR TOTALS Nominations **4** *Wins 0

AFI 100 YEARS 100 MOVIES SELECTION
2007 0   1997 0

TOP 300 FILMS POSITION . . . . none
All-Release Domestic Box Office in Equivalent 2005 $s

National Film Preservation Board Selection 1997

OTHER AWARDS Best Picture Wins

	Year
Golden Globes	none
New York Film Critics	none
National Board of Review	none
Film Daily Critics	none

William Powell is to dialogue as Fred Astaire is to dance. His delivery is so droll and insinuating, so knowing and innocent at the same time, that it hardly matters what he's saying.
—Roger Ebert, *Chicago Sun-Times,* 2002

PLOT: Witty socialites Nick and Nora Charles are in New York for Christmas when they are drawn into the mysterious disappearance of an inventor and the death of his mistress, who is found clutching his watch chain.

PRODUCTION: Author Dashiell Hammett, a former Pinkerton detective, first published *The Thin Man* serially in *Redbook* magazine. A hardcover edition followed in 1934. The story of urbane married sleuths was said to be based on Hammett's relationship with his lover, playwright Lillian Hellman. The "thin man" in the title is actually the murder victim, but the phrase later became associated with the actor who played Nick, William Powell. He had been brought into the project by W. S. "Woody" Van Dyke, a veteran director and fan of the detective genre (he had written detective novels himself), chosen by Louis B. Mayer for what was to be a low-budget B movie. Van Dyke wanted to reunite Powell with Myrna Loy, both of whom he had directed in 1934's *Manhattan Melodrama* for MGM. He felt they had real chemistry. But Mayer was against casting Loy, then twenty-nine, who had been typecast as Oriental vamps and the "other woman" in prior films. Mayer ultimately gave in to Van Dyke. The film revived Powell's career and made Loy a major star. The pair would go on to make another dozen films together. The movie was shot very quickly, with only a few sets and even fewer exterior shots. Van Dyke liked to work quickly and came to be known as "one-take Woody." It was also Van Dyke's practice to stick to the schedule, even while letting his actors improvise some scenes, the best of which he would include in the film. In this case he came in about a week ahead of schedule. Van Dyke told writers Frances Goodrich and Albert Hackett to concentrate the story on the amusing relationship between Nick and Nora and make the crime mystery secondary, which earned Van Dyke, Powell, Goodrich, and Hackett their first Oscar nominations. The assignment came naturally to them because they had that same kind of breezy relationship in real life. The movie's beloved dog, Asta, was actually portrayed by several different dogs. Powell and Loy were told by the dog's trainer not to make friends with the animals, or it would break their concentration. Loy later claimed one of the dogs, whose real name was Skippy, bit her.

DISTRIBUTION: The film, to the surprise of MGM and everyone involved, was an instant hit, making $1.4 million in worldwide rentals. It was voted one of the 10 Best Pictures of 1934 by *Film Daily.* It boosted the careers of Powell and Loy and set the stage for a series of sequels. They were *After the Thin Man* (1936), *Another Thin Man* (1939), *Shadow of the Thin Man* (1941), *The Thin Man Goes Home* (1944), and *The Song of the Thin Man* (1947). The movie also made a star of Asta, the wire-haired terrier. After this movie there was a nationwide rush to acquire wire-haired terriers. Over the years, it was the source for a radio series (1941 to 1950), an NBC TV series (1957–59), a TV movie called *Nick and Nora* in 1975, and a 1991 stage musical that closed after nine performances. —*Alex Ben Block*

CLEOPATRA

Paramount, 1934

ALL-RELEASE EQUIVALENT 2005 $s

(Unadjusted $s) in Millions of $s

Domestic Box Office Revenues . . . . **$119.5**/($4.3)
Production Cost . . . . **$12.3**/($0.8)
Principal Photography . . . . **44** days estimated
3/12/1934–5/2/1934
Montage and special effects
shots: 5/11/1934–6/12/1934
and 6/20/1934

Director . . . . Cecil B. DeMille

Producer . . . . Cecil B. DeMille, Adolph Zukor

Production Company . . . . Paramount Productions

Story and

  Screenplay by . . . . Waldemar Young, Vincent
Lawrence based on historical
material by Bartlett Cormack

Cast . . . . Claudette Colbert, Warren
William, Henry Wilcoxon

Filming Locations . . . . . . Paramount lot and on locations
in California

Genre . . . . Historical Drama

Format . . . . B&W

Initial Release . . . . 8/16/1934 premiere (New York);
10/5/1934 general release

Rerelease . . . . none

Running Time . . . . 95 minutes (preview length) or
101 or 102 minutes
11 reels, 9,191 feet
(preview); final length
9,046 feet

MPAA Rating . . . . not rated

STANDING THE TEST OF TIME

ACADEMY AWARD Oscar Nominations and Wins

Outstanding Production: Paramount

Assistant Director: Cullen Tate

*CINEMATOGRAPHY: Victor Milner

Film Editing: Anne Bauchens

Sound Recording: Paramount Studio Sound Dept.,
Franklin B. Hansen, Sound Director

OSCAR TOTALS   Nominations **5**   *Wins **1**

AFI 100 YEARS 100 MOVIES SELECTION

2007 0   1997 0

TOP 300 FILMS POSITION . . . . none
All-Release Domestic Box Office in Equivalent 2005 $s

National Film Preservation Board Selection . . . . none

OTHER AWARDS Best Picture Wins

	Year
Golden Globes	none
New York Film Critics	none
National Board of Review	none
Film Daily Critics	none

*One of the director's most ambitious spectacles. It has substantial, decorative settings, a wealth of
minor properties, an imposing array of histrionic talent and an army of extras.*

—Mordaunt Hall, *New York Times*, 1934

PLOT: The story of Cleopatra VII of Egypt begins with her exile to the desert and continues with her rolling out of a rug given as a gift to Julius Caesar, leader of the powerful Roman army. Before long it is Cleopatra who rules Caesar.

PRODUCTION: Director Cecil B. DeMille had been known for his large-scale historical dramas since his silent epic *Joan the Woman* in 1917. When he decided to make *Cleopatra,* he ordered the sixteen-volume French military survey of Egypt. It provided the blueprint for the style of his film. He then invested months of intense research, with great emphasis on realism in set decor and authentic props. This film represented an opportunity for DeMille to portray the golden age of Rome on a big canvas with all of its pomp, pageantry, extravagant lifestyles, opulence, depravity, and sin. The Hays Code had just been instituted when this was made, so DeMille was able to still use risqué images that later would have been prohibited. When DeMille had first cast Claudette Colbert, who was under contract to Paramount, in his 1932 film *The Sign of the Cross,* he was taken by her sophistication, beauty, and sense of humor. He felt that these attributes made her the ideal choice for Cleopatra. However, Colbert was in fragile health at the time—she had recently had appendicitis, brought on by the rigors of a jungle shoot in *Four Frightened People*—and her stand-in on *Cleopatra* had to be used for many rehearsals. Costumer Travis Banton had done his homework, researching historical Egyptian and Roman designs, but his priority on Colbert's costumes was to reveal as much of her figure as industry censors would permit in the last days before a toughened Production Code took effect on July 1, 1934. Since Colbert feared snakes, her scenes with the snake were put off until the very end. DeMille first saw English actor Henry Wilcoxon while in a projection booth at Paramount and cast him as Marc Antony in his first lead role. DeMille was a stickler for accurate details. At one point he saw that an extra was wearing a belt that was not historically accurate. Using his trademark megaphone, he demanded before the entire company that his secretary send a memo to the production department complaining about the error. In another case, DeMille learned that Romans cooled wine in snow, so rather than use marble dust for snow, as was typically done, he had his crew collect real frost by scraping it off the studio refrigeration pipes. He also insisted that Cleopatra have real grapes to eat even though they were out of season. The studio ordered ten crates of grapes. When they went bad, more grapes were flown in from Argentina. Even the asp that bites Cleopatra was real, having had its poison extracted before being used. While it was a lavish production, DeMille did incorporate some stock footage from his 1923 version of *The Ten Commandments* as part of a montage of action scenes with chariots and sword-wielding soldiers carrying shields.

DISTRIBUTION: After a huge, highly publicized premiere at the Paramount Theater on New York's Times Square on August 18, 1934, the movie became an immediate box office success in America. However, it wasn't as well received in Italy. *Variety* reported in 1935 that when the movie premiered in Rome, there were boos, catcalls, and derisive laughter. An Italian critic ravaged the movie as a "burlesque." —*Alex Ben Block*

DAVID COPPERFIELD
MGM, 1935

ALL-RELEASE EQUIVALENT 2005 $s
(Unadjusted $s) in Millions of $s

Domestic Box Office Revenues . . . . $96.2/($3.6)
Production Cost . . . . $15.3/($1.1))
Principal Photography . . . . 62 days estimated
9/17/1934–11/27/1934

Director . . . . George Cukor
Producer . . . . David O. Selznick
Production Company . . . . Metro-Goldwyn-Mayer
Story by . . . . Based on the novel by
Charles Dickens
Screenplay by . . . . Hugh Walpole, Howard
Estabrook
Cast . . . . W. C. Fields, Lionel Barrymore,
Maureen O'Sullivan
Filming Locations . . . . . . MGM Studios, Culver City, CA
Genre . . . . Drama
Format . . . . B&W
Initial Release 1/13/1935
Rerelease . . . . none
Running Time . . . . 129 or 133 minutes
MPAA Rating . . . . not rated

STANDING THE TEST OF TIME

ACADEMY AWARD Oscar Nominations and Wins
Outstanding Production: Metro-Goldwyn-Mayer
Assistant Director: Joseph Newman
Film Editing: Robert J. Kern

OSCAR TOTALS Nominations **3** *Wins **0**

AFI 100 YEARS 100 MOVIES SELECTION
2007 0   1997 0

TOP 300 FILMS POSITION . . . . none
All-Release Domestic Box Office in Equivalent 2005 $s

National Film Preservation Board Selection . . . . none

OTHER AWARDS Best Picture Wins

	Year
Golden Globes	none
New York Film Critics	none
National Board of Review	none
Film Daily Critics	1935

I think it's always a mistake to make too clever adaptations. Because [then the audience] really [doesn't] know what the vitality of the work that you're doing is.

—George Cukor

PLOT: A period drama set in Victorian England follows a boy named David Copperfield, whose father dies and whose mother remarries a very strict man. David survives a difficult childhood, finds his love, and becomes a writer.

PRODUCTION: In the mid-1930s there were four adaptations of books by English author Charles Dickens at three different studios. MGM made the two most lavish adaptations, *A Tale of Two Cities* and *David Copperfield*. Both were produced by David O. Selznick, who brought in director George Cukor for *Copperfield*. Selznick wanted to bring literary classics to the screen. He also felt a personal link to this material. His father, producer Lewis Selznick, had used this book to learn English when he first arrived from Russia, and also read pages from it to his sons in the evenings. Selznick bombarded Mayer, his father-in-law, with memos on the subject for a year. MGM executives opposed the period production, complaining that it was too highbrow for mass audiences. But Selznick used his contractual right and pressure on Mayer to get it made. The book had been written in 1849–50, first as a serial and then as a novel. Dickens later said it was his personal favorite. Howard Estabrook did several versions of the script. Cukor and Estabrook even went to England to soak up the Dickensian scene. But Selznick still didn't find Estabrook's script authentic, so he brought in English novelist Hugh Walpole to get the tone right. Selznick proposed making two movies at once, but that proved impractical. George Cukor, paid a hefty $113,585 to direct, went for highly stylized art direction, sets, and photography. Originally Selznick and Cukor wanted an all-English cast, with the movie shot in England. Instead, the biggest name was American star Lionel Barrymore, heavily made up and in a small role. Another recent Oscar winner, Charles Laughton, was cast as Micawber but soon dropped out, uncomfortable in a comic role. Selznick also said later he was concerned Laughton would put them over schedule with his illnesses and moods. Selznick replaced him by borrowing W. C. Fields from Paramount for his first serious acting role. The budget didn't allow them to shoot in England, but numerous English actors living in Hollywood were cast. MGM wanted to cast hot child actor Jackie Cooper, but Selznick and Cukor refused, instead launching an eight-month search that led to the casting of English child stage actor Freddie Bartholomew, despite concerns over embarrassing public behavior by the boy's father. Once production was under way, there were three units, led by the first unit with George Cukor directing. A second unit was under John Waters, and a third was under Slavko Vorkapich. A fourth was added during production, under the German director Leontine Sagan.

DISTRIBUTION: Theater owners complained about the unusually long running time of 2 hours 13 minutes, but those concerns disappeared when the film became a hit. It was billed as "Metro-Goldwyn-Mayer's Greatest Motion Picture," featuring a "star cast of 65 players!" It made a profit of $686,000 on world rentals of $3 million. It was one of MGM's biggest-grossing films of the year, after the Clark Gable–starring *Mutiny on the Bounty* and *China Seas*. —*Alex Ben Block*

THE INFORMER
RKO, 1935

ALL-RELEASE EQUIVALENT 2005 $s
(Unadjusted $s) in Millions of $s

Domestic Box Office Revenues . . . . **$27.0**/($1.0)
Production Cost . . . .**$3.5**/($0.2)
Principal Photography . . . .**28** days estimated
2/11/1935–3/14/1935

Director . . . . John Ford
Producer . . . . Cliff Reid
Production Company . . . . Radio Pictures
Story by . . . . Based on the 1925 novel by
Liam O'Flaherty
Screenplay by . . . . Dudley Nichols
Cast . . . . Victor McLaglen, Heather
Angel, Preston Foster, Margot
Grahame, Wallace Ford
Filming Locations . . . . . . Shot 100 percent in studio
Genre . . . . Drama
Format . . . . B&W
Initial Release . . . . 5/9/1935 premiere (New York);
5/24/1935 general release
Rerelease . . . . 1936, 1948 (not included
above)
Running Time . . . . 91, 95, or 97 minutes
10 reels
MPAA Rating . . . . not rated

STANDING THE TEST OF TIME

ACADEMY AWARD Oscar Nominations and Wins

Outstanding Production: RKO Radio

*ACTOR: Victor McLaglen

*DIRECTING: John Ford

Film Editing: George Hively

*MUSIC (Scoring): RKO Radio Studio Music Dept.,
Max Steiner, dept. head (Score by Max Steiner)

*WRITING (Screenplay): Dudley Nichols

OSCAR TOTALS   Nominations **6**   *Wins 4

AFI 100 YEARS 100 MOVIES SELECTION
2007 0   1997 0

TOP 300 FILMS POSITION . . . . .none
All-Release Domestic Box Office in Equivalent 2005 $s

National Film Preservation Board Selection . . . .none

OTHER AWARDS Best Picture Wins

	Year
Golden Globes	none
New York Film Critics	1935
National Board of Review	1935
Film Daily Critics	none

*A striking psychological study of a gutter Judas and a rawly impressive picture of the
Dublin underworld during the Black and Tan terror.*
—Andre Sennwald, *New York Times,* 1935

PLOT: In Dublin, Irish Communist Gypo Nolan turns in a comrade to the British authorities during the civil war of 1921–23, and later is caught by the IRA.

PRODUCTION: John Ford was drinking buddies with Irish author Liam O'Flaherty and took an option on *The Informer* in 1933. Before he got a green light from RKO in October 1934, the project was rejected by Fox, Columbia, MGM, Paramount, and Warner Bros. The studios believed that the depressing story about a pathetic lead character, with the potential for political fallout, wasn't worth the risk. According to Ford, it was the intervention of Joseph P. Kennedy, founder of RKO, with RCA president David Sarnoff in 1928 that got him the job. *The Informer* had been filmed previously in England in 1929 starring Cyril McLaglen but only had dialogue in the second half and was considered a commercial flop. RKO gave Ford a tight budget of $250,000 and forced the director to give up his salary for a share of profits. RKO wanted Richard Dix for the lead, but Ford refused. He wanted Victor McLaglen (brother of Cyril), who had starred in *The Lost Patrol* (1934). The movie was filmed on one big set built on two stages that had reproductions of Dublin streets. The thick fog that envelops much of the movie came out of Ford's interest in darkly shot German expressionist films and the film's small budget. The moody atmosphere helped hide the cheap plywood sets and added to the sense of stark realism. Ford worked on the screenplay over the course of six intense days with his frequent collaborator, Dudley Nichols, aboard Ford's schooner, *Araner,* sailing off the coast of Mexico. The critically acclaimed look was aided by cinematographer Joseph August. There are stories, many of which were later denied, about how Ford got McLaglen to give the performance of a lifetime by verbally abusing him, shifting schedules, doing takes of scenes when the actor thought it was a rehearsal, and regularly getting his actor drunk. Ford brought the film in under budget and ahead of schedule with a cost of just $242,756.

DISTRIBUTION: The movie did not do well on its initial Radio City Music Hall release but was discovered after the general release and played in theaters for a long time thereafter. It was voted one of the 10 Best Pictures of 1935 by *Film Daily*. It made a profit of $325,000 on worldwide rentals of $950,000 and impressed critics enough to become the first film to win Best Picture from the New York Film Critics Circle unanimously on the first ballot. Dudley Nichols became the first artist to refuse his Oscar because of a feud between the Screen Writers Guild and the Academy of Motion Picture Arts and Sciences. He later picked it up at the 1938 Oscars. Ford credited this film with the formation of the Directors Guild: late one night, as he was leaving the RKO studios, Ford saw extras enter a soundstage; a producer had ordered them to the set to shoot additional scenes of Ford's movie without his approval. That interference so angered Ford that he led the formation of the new guild. While the film passed muster with American censors, it faced cuts in Canada, Ireland, and especially England, where the government censors insisted on 129 cuts. —*Alex Ben Block*

MUTINY ON THE BOUNTY
MGM, 1935

ALL-RELEASE EQUIVALENT 2005 $s
(Unadjusted $s) in Millions of $s

Domestic Box Office Revenues . . . . **$148.2**/($5.7)
Production Cost . . . . **$27.1**/($1.9)
Principal Photography . . . . **84** days
5/13/1935–8/21/1935
+4 days reshooting

Director	Frank Lloyd
Producer	Irving Thalberg
Production Company	Metro-Goldwyn-Mayer
Story by	Based on the novel by Charles Nordhoff and James Norman Hall
Screenplay by	Talbot Jennings, Jules Furthman, Carey Wilson
Cast	Charles Laughton, Clark Gable, Franchot Tone
Filming Locations	MGM Studio, Culver City, CA; on location in Tahiti and Catalina Island, CA; in studio at MGM in CA
Genre	Action Adventure
Format	B&W
Initial Release	11/8/1935
Rerelease	1939, 1956
Running Time	130–132 minutes 13 reels
MPAA Rating	not rated

STANDING THE TEST OF TIME

ACADEMY AWARD Oscar Nominations and Wins

***OUTSTANDING PRODUCTION:** Metro-Goldwyn-Mayer

Actor: Glark Gable

Actor: Charles Laughton

Actor: Franchot Tone

Directing: Frank Lloyd

Film Editing: Margaret Booth

Music (Scoring): Metro-Goldwyn-Mayer Studio Music Dept., Nat W. Finston, dept. head (Score by Herbert Stothart)

Writing (Screenplay): Talbot Jennings, Jules Furthman, Carey Wilson

OSCAR TOTALS   Nominations **8**   *Wins 1

AFI 100 YEARS 100 MOVIES SELECTION
2007 0   1997 . . . #86

TOP 300 FILMS POSITION . . . . .none
All-Release Domestic Box Office in Equivalent 2005 $s

National Film Preservation Board Selection . . . .none

OTHER AWARDS Best Picture Wins

	Year
Golden Globes	none
New York Film Critics	none
National Board of Review	none
Film Daily Critics	1936

*[Irving] Thalberg pored over [the script] striving for every possible improvement.
He paced relentlessly up and down the office, slapping the side of his trousers
with a small baton he carried, probing the minds of the four men in the room.*

—Bob Thomas, *Thalberg*

PLOT: An eighteenth-century British ship embarks on a two-year scientific mission to Tahiti. Having endured all they can stand of their overbearing captain, the crew mutinies on the return voyage and sets the captain and his few loyalists adrift in a lifeboat. The captain makes his way to port, and many of the mutineers are captured and tried in England.

PRODUCTION: Irving Thalberg had been forced by health problems to switch from running MGM to just producing. Thalberg's showcase production was this second film version of *Mutiny on the Bounty,* after 1933's *In the Wake of the Bounty.* Both were based on the trilogy of books by Charles Nordhoff and James Norman Hall. Louis B. Mayer was opposed to the film due to concerns over risk, cost, the lack of important women's roles, and the fact that a mutineer was the story's hero. The project had come to Thalberg from Oscar-winning director Frank Lloyd (*Cavalcade,* 1933), who offered the rights if he could direct. Thalberg was personally involved in every aspect as it became the most expensive MGM movie since *Ben-Hur: A Tale of the Christ* in 1925. He intended to cast Wallace Beery, Clark Gable, and Robert Montgomery. Then he decided Beery was too American, so he recruited Charles Laughton. After Montgomery declined to reschedule his vacation, Franchot Tone took the role that launched his career. Thalberg initially hired Carey Wilson and John Farrow to write the script, but he didn't like their work. Next he had Talbot Jennings complete a draft. Then he had Jennings work with Robert Hopkins, who added comedy bits to balance the serious subject matter. Finally, Thalberg had Allen Rivkin do a rewrite, adding more comedy. The studio did extensive research to make sure everything was realistic, even checking British naval records. To ensure authenticity, they shot in Tahiti as well as on Catalina Island (a short boat ride from San Pedro, California) and on the MGM lot in Culver City. Two full-size ships, the *Bounty* and *Pandora,* were constructed and sailed 14,000 miles from California to Tahiti. They ran into heavy seas and were damaged, requiring expensive repairs. Problems pushed the budget up from $1,252,995 to $1,899,973. A barge full of equipment sank and a man was killed trying to save it. A shoot in Tahiti was ruined by underexposed film. Laughton was having difficulty at first with his role and for nearly two weeks called Thalberg at home every night. Then suddenly the calls stopped and Laughton gave a memorable performance. Clark Gable and Laughton didn't get along. Gable had not wanted to do the movie and objected strongly to shaving his "lucky moustache" because an English naval officer would be clean-shaven. Gable was talked into taking the role by producer Eddie Mannix, who pointed out that he would have the key romantic role.

DISTRIBUTION: MGM executives were nervous about the expensive picture, but this rousing sea adventure was an immediate hit and became the highest-grossing movie of 1935. It was in the top 10 of MGM's most profitable movies as of its initial release and went on to become the first remake to win a Best Picture Academy Award, boosting Thalberg's reputation. It made a profit of $914,027 on its 1935 theatrical release, $116,000 profit on its 1939 rerelease, and another $85,487 profit on its 1956 rerelease. —*Alex Ben Block*

CAPTAIN BLOOD
First National (WB), 1935

ALL-RELEASE EQUIVALENT 2005 $s
(Unadjusted $s) in Millions of $s

Domestic Box Office Revenues . . . . **$64.5**/($2.4)
Production Cost . . . . **$14.2**/($1.0)
Principal Photography . . . . **68** days estimated
8/7/1935–10/25/1935

Director . . . . Michael Curtiz

Producer . . . . Harry Joe Brown

Production Company . . . . Cosmopolitan

Story by . . . . Based on the novel *Captain Blood: His Odyssey* by Rafael Sabatini

Screenplay by . . . . Casey Robinson

Cast . . . . Errol Flynn, Olivia de Havilland, Lionel Atwill, Basil Rathbone

Filming Locations . . . . . . not available

Genre . . . . Action Adventure

Format . . . . B&W

Initial Release 12/28/1935

Rerelease . . . . 1951 (not included above)

Running Time . . . . 119 minutes
12 reels

MPAA Rating . . . . not rated

STANDING THE TEST OF TIME

ACADEMY AWARD Oscar Nominations and Wins

Outstanding Production: Cosmopolitan

Sound Recording: Warner Bros.–First National Studio Sound Department, Nathan Levinson, Sound Director

Warner Bros. write in nominations

Directing: Michael Curtiz

Music (Scoring): Warner Bros. – First National Studio Music Dept., Leo Forbstein, dept. head (Score by Erich Wolfgang Korngold)

Writing (Screenplay): Casey Robinson

OSCAR TOTALS   Nominations **5**   *Wins **0**

AFI 100 YEARS 100 MOVIES SELECTION
2007 0   1997 0

TOP 300 FILMS POSITION . . . . none
All-Release Domestic Box Office in Equivalent 2005 $s

National Film Preservation Board Selection . . . . none

OTHER AWARDS Best Picture Wins

	Year
Golden Globes	none
New York Film Critics	none
National Board of Review	none
Film Daily Critics	none

With a spirited and criminally good-looking Australian named Errol Flynn playing the genteel buccaneer to the hilt, the photoplay recaptures the air of high romantic adventure which is so essential to the tale.

—Andre Sennwald, *New York Times*, 1935

PLOT: Irish doctor Peter Blood is convicted of treason in seventeenth-century England for tending to a wounded friend. He is shipped off to a life of slavery in the West Indies. He escapes to become a successful pirate.

PRODUCTION: With MGM's 1935 *Mutiny on the Bounty* in the works, Jack L. Warner and his production head, Hal Wallis, at Warner Bros. wanted their own seafaring adventure and decided to remake *Captain Blood,* which had been produced as a silent film in 1924, based on the best-selling 1922 novel by Rafael Sabatini. Warner Bros. had acquired the rights to the original film when it took over Vitagraph in 1925, but once Hollywood had transitioned from silent to sound films beginning in the late 1920s, studios were cautious about producing expensive pirate adventures. Warner picked hardworking director Michael Curtiz to direct and cast Robert Donat, star of 1934's *The Count of Monte Cristo,* in the title role. Just before production, Warner and Donat got into an argument during a transatlantic call, and the veteran star dropped out. Warner felt the material and supporting cast were strong but knew they were taking a big risk by producing a swashbuckler without any big stars. Instead, at the urging of Curtiz, the lead went to unknown Errol Flynn. Flynn was an Australian born in Tasmania. He was signed by Warner sight unseen, based solely on his work in a British picture. Flynn, twenty-six years old, had only two brief U.S. screen appearances before then. The actor had been recommended to Curtiz by Flynn's wife at the time, actress Lili Damita. The female lead also went to an unknown, nineteen-year-old Olivia de Havilland (sister of actress Joan Fontaine). It was the role that made Flynn a star. *Captain Blood* was one of the first true action-adventure films of the sound era. Although it was planned that Curtiz would incorporate footage originally shot for the 1924 movie *The Sea Hawk* (acquired by Warner Bros. when it took over First National in 1929) as well as footage from the original 1924 film *Captain Blood,* none of this footage was used in the final cut of the 1935 film. During the making of the movie, Flynn collapsed and passed out. Warner thought he had been drunk and chewed him out. Two days later doctors said that he had suffered from an attack of blackwater fever, contracted while Flynn had been in the South Pacific. The exciting battle sequence, when the pirates, led by Blood, take the French ships, required one of the biggest technical teams working together with 2,500 extras. Six editors had to work overtime to cut 60,000 feet of exposed film to twelve reels to meet a Christmas release.

DISTRIBUTION: From its premiere in New York City right after Christmas in December 1935, the film was a success, winning plaudits from critics and audiences alike. It brought in almost $2.5 million in worldwide rentals initially, and in depressed 1935 it had a net profit of $660,000. The Academy gave the film two nominations, and Warner Bros. backed a write-in campaign that resulted in three more nominations. That led the Academy to change the rules and eliminate write-in nominations. Flynn wasn't the only overnight sensation: Basil Rathbone became the image of a cold-blooded pirate, and de Havilland's career took off as well. Flynn and de Havilland went on to appear in seven more films together. *—Alex Ben Block*

MODERN TIMES
United Artists, 1936

ALL-RELEASE EQUIVALENT 2005 $s
(Unadjusted $s) in Millions of $s

Domestic Box Office Revenues . . . . **$94.4**/($3.8)
Production Cost . . . . **$21.1**/($1.5)
Principal Photography . . . . **147** days shooting
263 days idle
10/11/1934–8/30/1935

Director . . . . Charles Chaplin
Producer . . . . Charles Chaplin
Production Company . . . . Charles Chaplin Film Corp.
Story and
   Screenplay by . . . . Charles Chaplin
Cast . . . . Charles Chaplin,
Paulette Goddard
Filming Locations . . . . . . Chaplin's own studio in
Hollywood and exteriors in
Southern California
Genre . . . . Silent Classic, Comedy
Format . . . . B&W (no dialogue, except that
coming from radio or TV,
included in synchronized sound
track although Chaplin sings a
song in gibberish at the end of
the film)
Initial Release . . . . 2/5/1936 premiere (New York);
2/21/1936 premiere
(Los Angeles)
Rerelease 2003
Running Time . . . . 87 minutes
10 reels
MPAA Rating . . . . not rated

STANDING THE TEST OF TIME

ACADEMY AWARD Oscar Nominations and Wins
None

    OSCAR TOTALS   Nominations 0   *Wins 0

AFI 100 YEARS 100 MOVIES SELECTION
2007 . . . #78   1997 . . . #81

TOP 300 FILMS POSITION . . . . .none
All-Release Domestic Box Office in Equivalent 2005 $s

National Film Preservation Board Selection 1989

OTHER AWARDS Best Picture Wins

	Year
Golden Globes	none
New York Film Critics	none
National Board of Review	none
Film Daily Critics	none

*He stands alone as the greatest entertainer of
modern times! No one on earth can
make you laugh as heartily or touch your heart
as deeply . . . the whole world laughs,
cries and thrills to his priceless genius!*
—UA's ad tagline for *Modern Times*, 1936

PLOT: A Depression-era satire on the modern mechanized world, *Modern Times* featured the Little Tramp (Charles Chaplin) as a worker on the assembly line in a futuristic factory where the machines rule. Charlie can't keep up, but he eventually escapes with a homeless girl.

PRODUCTION: Chaplin was horrified by automation, and this movie was as close as he would come to a political statement about class struggle and the perils of the modern world. His working title was "The Masses." Despite the seriousness of its subject matter, however, the film played worldwide and across generations because of its comedy. There is humor in a little man who can make fun of the rich and powerful. Chaplin was more of an anarchist, but his critics accused him of being a Communist. Yet no one hated this movie more than Hitler. There were reports later of a conspiracy by the Nazis to discredit Chaplin by pursing a plagiarism suit, charging that he stole his conveyer belt sequence from the 1931 film *À nous la liberté (Freedom for Us),* even though that director, René Clair, refused to be part of the suit. The case wasn't settled until World War II ended. This was supposed to have been Chaplin's first all-talking movie, and he did tests, but ultimately he felt that the universal appeal of the Tramp would be lost if he had to speak. So Chaplin insisted on making a silent film with a score and sound effects but no dialogue. After 683 days in production on *City Lights,* which was released in February 1931 (179 shooting days and 504 idle days), Chaplin took nearly a three-year break before beginning production in October 1934 on *Modern Times.* This would be the last time his character of the Tramp would appear. Chaplin spent over a year inside his own studio in Hollywood and shooting around southern California to produce the last great film without dialogue, which would be released almost eight years after *The Jazz Singer* (1927) had initiated the sound era. The soundtrack included an original musical score by Chaplin performed by an orchestra under the baton of Alfred Newman, featuring the romantic theme song "Smile." The factory was a parody of Henry Ford's highly efficient plants, which were among the first to run assembly lines. Co-star Paulette Goddard was his real-life wife. The film has a highly stylized look because Chaplin shot most of it at 18 frames per second (the same standard used for silent films), although he knew it would be shown at 24 frames (the standard used for talking pictures), which makes the slapstick comedy even more frantic.

DISTRIBUTION: The movie opens with the words "A story of industry, of individual enterprise, of humanity crusading in the pursuit of happiness." Audiences flocked to laugh at the Tramp, but critics were divided on the importance of the film, which brought in only $1.4 million in domestic rentals (compared with $2.5 million from *The Kid,* 1921; $2.5 million from *The Gold Rush,* 1925; and $2.0 million from *City Lights,* 1931). Those who praised the film were pleased that Chaplin did not become overtly political, while his critics, especially those on the left, were disappointed that he did not show unions or protest marches, which were common at the time. *Modern Times* was rereleased in 2003 with limited U.S. box office of $163,577. —*Alex Ben Block*

MR. DEEDS GOES TO TOWN
Columbia, 1936

ALL-RELEASE EQUIVALENT 2005 $s
(Unadjusted $s) in Millions of $s

Domestic Box Office Revenues . . . . $59.3/($2.3)
Production Cost . . . . $11.2/($0.8)
Principal Photography . . . . 47 days estimated
12/13/1935–2/5/1936

Director . . . . Frank Capra

Producer . . . . Frank Capra

Production Company . . . . Columbia Pictures

Story by . . . . Based on the short story
"The Opera Hat" by
Clarence Buddington Kelland

Screenplay by . . . . Robert Riskin

Cast . . . . Gary Cooper, Jean Arthur,
George Bancroft

Filming Locations . . . . . . Columbia studio
in Culver City, CA

Genre . . . . Romantic Comedy

Format . . . . B&W

Initial Release 4/12/1936

Rerelease . . . . none

Running Time . . . . 115 or 118 minutes
12 reels
10,617 feet

MPAA Rating . . . . not rated

STANDING THE TEST OF TIME

ACADEMY AWARD Oscar Nominations and Wins

Outstanding Production: Columbia

Actor: Gary Cooper

*DIRECTING: Frank Capra

Sound Recording: Columbia Studio Sound Dept.,
John Livadary, Sound Director

Writing (Screenplay): Robert Riskin

OSCAR TOTALS   Nominations 5   *Wins 1

AFI 100 YEARS 100 MOVIES SELECTION

2007 0   1997 0

TOP 300 FILMS POSITION . . . . .none
All-Release Domestic Box Office in Equivalent 2005 $s

National Film Preservation Board Selection . . . .none

OTHER AWARDS Best Picture Wins

	Year
Golden Globes	none
New York Film Critics	1936
National Board of Review	1936
Film Daily Critics	none

Never have I seen a performer with such a chronic case of stage jitters.
I'm sure she vomited before and after every scene.

—Frank Capra on directing Jean Arthur

PLOT: A greeting card poet from Vermont comes to New York for a $20 million inheritance. A female reporter falls for him. He forms a foundation to give money away, so a lawyer tries to get him declared insane. The poet triumphs.

PRODUCTION: After sweeping the Academy Awards with *It Happened One Night,* Frank Capra was concerned about expectations for his subsequent films. He did *Broadway Bill,* about a runaway heiress and a racehorse, but continued looking for something more substantial, movies that would "say something." He wanted to do *Lost Horizon,* but star Ronald Coleman wasn't available. He considered Russian classics and a Revolutionary War story but finally chose "The Opera Hat," a story serialized in the *American Magazine* in April and September 1935 by Clarence Buddington Kelland, a prolific former lawyer, magazine writer, and conservative political activist. It filled the bill for Capra, who wanted to make a social statement as well as a movie. Capra later defined his films beginning with this one as the rebellious cry of the individual against being trampled on by mass conformity. It was adapted for the screen by Robert Riskin, the seventh of their twelve collaborations. The script became classic Capra screwball comedy with romance and a broader philosophical theme, which Kelland was not happy about. In fact, Kelland would not permit the script to be published while he was alive. Beginning with this film, Capra refused to just take on any work produced by studio writers. He insisted on spending months tailoring the script for production. This established a trend for all top directors. He also got unusual autonomy to make the movie he wanted from notoriously difficult Columbia Pictures boss Harry Cohn. For the first time Capra was also given credit above the title, which was extremely unusual. Capra did have to work around Cohn's order that directors could print only one of their takes from each scene. Instead of shouting "cut" and stopping the camera after each take, he yelled "do it again" and kept rolling. Capra insisted that only one actor could play the lead, but Gary Cooper wasn't available for six months, causing a delay in production that added roughly $100,000 to the cost of the already pricey project. For the female lead, Capra wanted Carole Lombard, but she dropped out to do another film three days before production. Looking through dailies of other films being shot, Capra spied Jean Arthur, whom he cast in the role against the advice of Harry Cohn. Capra convinced Cohn by making him pay attention to her voice, not her face. She turned out to be very nervous and somewhat difficult, but Capra handled her with a gentle touch and got an excellent performance. Arthur had been in seventy movies dating back to the silent era, but this became her breakout role.

DISTRIBUTION: The movie opened at Radio City Music Hall in New York City and despite tepid reviews was a hit for Columbia. It was voted one of the 10 Best Pictures of 1936 by *Film Daily.* It grossed in excess of $1 million in domestic rentals during its initial theatrical run, which made it the top picture for Columbia that year and one of the ten highest-grossing movies of the year. It earned Capra the second of three Oscars as Best Director. Upon release, it was banned in Nazi Germany for using "non-Aryan actors." —*Alex Ben Block*

SAN FRANCISCO
MGM, 1936

ALL-RELEASE EQUIVALENT 2005 $s
(Unadjusted $s) in Millions of $s

Domestic Box Office Revenues . . . . **$196.7**/($8.3)
Production Cost . . . . **$18.2**/($1.3)
Principal Photography . . . .**45** days
2/14/1936–4/20/1936
+ 7 days retakes

Director . . . . W. S. Van Dyke
Producer . . . . John Emerson,
Bernard H. Hyman
Production Company . . . . Metro-Goldwyn-Mayer
Productions
Story by . . . . Robert Hopkins
Screenplay by . . . . Anita Loos
Cast . . . . Clark Gable, Jeanette
MacDonald, Spencer Tracy
Filming Locations . . . . . . Metro-Goldwyn-Mayer Studios,
Culver City, CA
Genre . . . . Disaster
Format . . . . B&W
Initial Release 6/26/1936
Rerelease 1939, 1948
Running Time . . . . 111 or 115 minutes
12 reels
MPAA Rating . . . . not rated

STANDING THE TEST OF TIME

ACADEMY AWARD Oscar Nominations and Wins

Outstanding Production: Metro-Goldwyn-Mayer
Actor: Spencer Tracy
Assistant Director: Joseph Newman
Directing: W. S. Van Dyke
***SOUND RECORDING:** Metro-Goldwyn-Mayer
Studio Sound Dept., Douglas Shearer, Sound
Director
Writing (Original Story): Robert Hopkins

OSCAR TOTALS   Nominations **6**   *Wins **1**

AFI 100 YEARS 100 MOVIES SELECTION
2007 0   1997 0

TOP 300 FILMS POSITION . . . . #275
All-Release Domestic Box Office in Equivalent 2005 $s

National Film Preservation Board Selection . . . . none

OTHER AWARDS Best Picture Wins

	Year
Golden Globes	none
New York Film Critics	none
National Board of Review	none
Film Daily Critics	none

*It is a shattering spectacle, one of the truly great cinematic illusions; a monstrous,
hideous, thrilling débâcle with great fissures opening in the earth, buildings crumbling,
men and women apparently being buried beneath showers of stone and plaster,
gargoyles lurching from rooftops, water mains bursting,
live wires flaring, flame, panic and terror.*

—Frank S. Nugent, *New York Times*, 1936

PLOT: A battling priest and a beautiful girl singer influence the life of a handsome rogue who runs the hottest nightspot on San Francisco's seedy Barbary Coast around the time of the terrible 1906 earthquake.

PRODUCTION: Robert E. "Hoppy" Hopkins was employed in the mid-1930s by MGM to rove among movie sets suggesting dialogue, jokes, and gags. "Hoppy" had an idea for a rousing disaster epic set around the 1906 San Francisco earthquake. He brought it to Jeanette MacDonald, who in March 1935 presented it to MGM producer Eddie Mannix and studio boss Louis B. Mayer. She wanted Clark Gable to star with her, but Gable wasn't available, nor did he want to work with MacDonald because she had broken her engagement with his friend Nelson Eddy after suffering a miscarriage. Still, MacDonald convinced MGM to delay at considerable expense until he was available. Gable's role was made more substantial, and ultimately Mayer forced him to take it. Herman J. Mankiewicz wrote the first script based on Hopkins's original story. Then Thalberg handed it to Anita Loos (*Gentlemen Prefer Blondes*), who created Blackie based on the real life of Wilson Mizner, a colorful friend who had died in 1933. She completed several drafts for Thalberg and director W. S. "Woody" Van Dyke II, a veteran of the silent film era. When production began on Valentine's Day, 1936, Gable showed up smelling like garlic. MacDonald had to kiss him anyway in take after take. She later complained to Mayer about it. MacDonald also refused to sing the title song, "San Francisco," as a torch song but when Van Dyke insisted, she made a $500 wager that the song would flop. The director paid tribute to his past by hiring silent-era stars Edgar Kennedy, King Baggott, Rhea Mitchell, and Jean Acker (Rudolph Valentino's first wife) for background roles and inviting D. W. Griffith to direct a scene when he visited the MGM set on the last day of production. MGM spent lavishly to re-create San Francisco only to destroy it in the earthquake scenes, flattening more than 25,000 buildings. Cedric Gibbons was the credited art director working in collaboration with associate art director A. Arnold "Buddy" Gillespie, special effects artist James Basevi, and John Hoffman, among others. Nathalie Bucknall and her MGM research team also authenticated hundreds of items.

DISTRIBUTION: Tragically, Thalberg died shortly before the film's release. The movie was an immediate hit, with $5.3 million in worldwide rentals and a profit of $2.2 million on the initial release alone. However, the Paramount Theater manager in San Francisco was concerned about local reaction, so he had a cameraman take shots of the city, paying tribute to what San Francisco had since become, and he ran this montage after the picture. Seeing the positive reaction it garnered, MGM added similar scenes at the end of the movie for the entire run. Considered anachronistic, the added scenes were deleted for a 1948 rerelease, but they were later restored for home video. After the movie and title song became hugely successful, MacDonald paid off her $500 bet to Van Dyke as promised. The movie was nominated for six Oscars but won only for Best Sound Recording. It might have won for special effects, but that category wasn't created until 1939. It was voted one of the 10 Best Pictures of 1936 by *Film Daily*. Two subsequent reissues were also profitable. —*Alex Ben Block*

THE GREAT ZIEGFELD
MGM, 1936

ALL-RELEASE EQUIVALENT 2005 $s
(Unadjusted $s) in Millions of $s

Domestic Box Office Revenues......... **$176.0**/($6.9)
Production Cost .... **$30.7**/($2.2)
Principal Photography............ **61** days estimated
9/25/1935–12/5/1935

Director .... Robert Z. Leonard
Producer .... Hunt Stromberg
Production Company.... Metro-Goldwyn-Mayer
Story and
  Screenplay by .... William Anthony McGuire
Cast .... William Powell, Myrna Loy, Luise Rainer, Frank Morgan, Fanny Brice, Virginia Bruce
Filming Locations ...... Metro-Goldwyn-Mayer Studios, Culver City, CA
Genre................ Musical
Format............... B&W
Initial Release 9/4/1936
Rerelease............. not available
Running Time .... 170 or 180 minutes
20 reels
16,292 feet
MPAA Rating .... not rated

STANDING THE TEST OF TIME

ACADEMY AWARD Oscar Nominations and Wins

*OUTSTANDING PRODUCTION: Metro-Goldwyn-Mayer

*ACTRESS: Luise Rainer

Art Direction: Cedric Gibbons, Eddie Imazu, Edwin B. Willis

*DANCE DIRECTION: "A Pretty Girl Is Like a Melody" number, Seymour Felix

Directing: Robert Z. Leonard

Film Editing: William S. Gray

Writing (Original Story): William Anthony McGuire

OSCAR TOTALS Nominations **7** *Wins **3**

AFI 100 YEARS 100 MOVIES SELECTION
2007 0   1997 0

TOP 300 FILMS POSITION .... none
All-Release Domestic Box Office in Equivalent 2005 $s

National Film Preservation Board Selection.... none

OTHER AWARDS Best Picture Wins

	Year
Golden Globes	none
New York Film Critics....................	none
National Board of Review	none
Film Daily Critics	none

So thoroughly Ziegfeldian is The Great Ziegfeld *. . . that it would be easy to pretend it had been produced by the Great Glorifier himself rather than by Hunt Stromberg.*
—Frank S. Nugent, *New York Times,* 1936

PLOT: This is a lavish musical biography of theatrical showman Florenz Ziegfeld Jr. (1869–1932), who rises from carnival barker to Broadway impresario. The action stops for elaborate production numbers, with hundreds of beautiful, scantily clad young dancers.

PRODUCTION: Approximately a year after the death of Florenz Ziegfeld, Universal Pictures acquired film rights to his life story from his widow, actress Billie Burke. She also became a technical advisor on the film, which led to a seven-year contract with MGM. William Anthony McGuire, a protégé of Ziegfeld's, spent a year writing the script and producing, with Edward Sutherland set to direct. However, as Universal's investment exceeded $225,000, much of it spent on luxurious sets, it became clear that the movie was too big for the financially troubled studio. So a deal was struck to sell it to MGM, which was then a much larger studio. Universal was paid $300,000, and production moved to MGM's Culver City lot. MGM retained McGuire's screenplay but replaced him as producer with Hunt Stromberg. Robert Z. Leonard was named to direct. In the era before TV, this film was designed to be a musical performance as well as a movie, but most critics thought it worked so well because of the strong central performances, especially those by William Powell, Myrna Loy, and Luise Rainer. There were rumors that Billie Burke personally chose Powell to play her late husband, even though they didn't look much alike. Producer Hunt Stromberg later said Powell had indeed captured the spirit of the role. Powell and Loy, who was cast as Billie Burke shortly before production began, had starred together in *The Thin Man* in 1934. Rainer, who played Ziegfeld's first wife, was a rising young star from Austria. Her part was small but included a dramatic scene on the phone with her ex-husband, which helped earn Rainer an Oscar as Best Actress. The cast was bolstered by former Ziegfeld stage stars (some of whom were Ziegfeld discoveries), including Ray Bolger, Ann Pennington, Harriet Hoctor, and Fanny Brice, who sang the song "My Man" from her stage act. The film's best-remembered musical number is built around the song "A Pretty Girl Is Like a Melody" and featured 180 performers on a spiraling "wedding cake" set that required 4,300 yards of silk rayon to drape and cost $220,000 to produce. A number of other former Ziegfeld stars added realism to the show business story. One who refused to participate was Marilyn Miller, who had had a great triumph on Broadway impersonating Billie Burke. She had also been rumored to be a Ziegfeld mistress but later split from him. Miller died the day before the movie premiered in New York City, at age thirty-seven.

DISTRIBUTION: *The Great Ziegfeld* was the most expensive MGM movie since *Ben-Hur* in 1925 (which had cost over $3.9 million to make and made a profit only after its 1932 sound reissue). Despite its high cost, *Ziegfeld* made a profit of $822,000 on $4.7 million in worldwide rentals. It was voted one of the 10 Best Pictures of 1936 by *Film Daily*. The premiere was at the Carthay Circle Theatre in Los Angeles, which had recently been renovated. —*Alex Ben Block*

CAPTAINS COURAGEOUS
MGM, 1937

ALL-RELEASE EQUIVALENT 2005 $s
(Unadjusted $s) in Millions of $s

Domestic Box Office Revenues . . . . **$104.5**/($3.8)
Production Cost . . . . **$22.3**/($1.6)
Principal Photography . . . . **125** days estimated
9/23/1936–2/15/1937

Director . . . . Victor Fleming

Producer . . . . Louis D. Lighton

Production Company . . . . Metro-Goldwyn-Mayer

Story by . . . . Based on the novel by
Rudyard Kipling

Screenplay by . . . . John Lee Mahin, Marc Connelly,
Dale Van Every

Cast . . . . Freddie Bartholomew, Spencer
Tracy, Lionel Barrymore

Filming Locations . . . . . . MGM studio, Culver City, CA;
location shooting (primarily
second-unit) in Monterey,
CA, and Gloucester,
Masschusetts; Port aux
Basques, Newfoundland,
and Shelburne, Nova Scotia,
Canada; the Florida Keys;
and Mazatlán, Mexico

Genre . . . . Drama

Format . . . . B&W

Initial Release 6/25/1937

Rerelease . . . . none

Running Time . . . . 115, 116, or 118 minutes
12 reels

MPAA Rating . . . . not rated

STANDING THE TEST OF TIME

ACADEMY AWARD Oscar Nominations and Wins

Outstanding Production: Metro-Goldwyn-Mayer

*ACTOR: Spencer Tracy

Film Editing: Elmo Veron

Writing (Screenplay): John Lee Mahin, Marc Connelly,
Dale Van Every

OSCAR TOTALS   Nominations **4**   *Wins **1**

AFI 100 YEARS 100 MOVIES SELECTION
2007 0   1997 0

TOP 300 FILMS POSITION . . . . none
All-Release Domestic Box Office in Equivalent 2005 $s

National Film Preservation Board Selection . . . . none

OTHER AWARDS Best Picture Wins

	Year
Golden Globes	none
New York Film Critics	none
National Board of Review	none
Film Daily Critics	none

Spencer [Tracy] behaved during production: he admired director Victor Fleming, a hard-drinking man's man who knew how to get along with the likes of Tracy and [Clark] Gable.

—Jane Ellen Wayne, *The Leadng Men of MGM*

PLOT: A spoiled brat is rescued at sea by a fishing boat on its way out for the season. The captain refuses to turn back, so the boy is forced to stay. With help from a Portuguese fisherman, he becomes a man.

PRODUCTION: MGM's adaptation of Rudyard Kipling's 1897 novel was one of three adaptations of Kipling stories released in 1937, only a year after the English novelist's death (others were *Elephant Boy* and *Wee Willie Winkie*). Director Victor Fleming, who got above-the-title treatment along with Kipling, was a former race car driver and chauffeur who became a cinematographer and then director in the silent era. His knack for big action and pulling performances out of stars made him popular throughout the 1930s. Irving Thalberg cast Spencer Tracy, but Tracy didn't want the role at first. He thought that the part was secondary to the boy's role and didn't want to get his hair curled. Fleming and Tracy's wife finally convinced him. Uncertain about the Portuguese accent, Tracy studied ethnic performances by Paul Muni (*The Story of Louis Pasteur,* 1935) and Edward G. Robinson. Kipling's spoiled boy of nineteen was made younger to suit twelve-year-old Freddie Bartholomew, appearing in his eleventh and most notable movie. Lionel Barrymore, as the captain, is seen standing unassisted for one of the last times, due to real-life degenerative arthritis. Mickey Rooney and Bartholomew were tutored each day aboard ship to keep up with their studies. In 1937 Bartholomew was also the subject of a court battle between his aunt, who raised him, and his long-absent parents, who came around when he became rich. The lawsuit was unsuccessful but expensive. After Katharine Hepburn saw Tracy in this film, she became determined to work with him, leading to their creative collaboration and long-term affair. Production was to begin on approximately September 14, 1936, but when Thalberg suddenly died on September 13, shooting was pushed back until later in the month. It was halted once more in January 1937 when Fleming underwent surgery, with Jack Conway taking over for a while. Most of the movie was shot on a soundstage—a "wet set," even though the later studio publicity suggested otherwise. Most of the location shots were done by the second unit—in waters off the coast of California, in the Florida Keys, and in Mazatlán, Mexico, where the storm scenes were done. Backgrounds and exteriors were also filmed in Canada (Port aux Basques, Newfoundland, and Shelburne, Nova Scotia) and Massachusetts (Gloucester). The production imported hundreds of live fish from Alaska, as well as frozen ones from Boston, to outfit an authentic fishing vessel. Fleming's recording of the songs live on the set (including "What Shall We Do with a Drunken Sailor," "Blow the Man Down," and others) was innovative at the time.

DISTRIBUTION: Critics acclaimed this film, with Howard Barnes of the *New York Herald Tribune* declaring it a screen "masterpiece." It was voted one of the 10 Best Pictures of 1937 by *Film Daily*. *Captains Courageous,* with $3.1 million in worldwide rentals and a profit of $357,350, was one of MGM's highest-grossing films of 1937, coming in behind the 1937 Clark Gable–Jean Harlow film *Saratoga*. At the premiere in Los Angeles, there were picketers dressed in black tie, part of an industry strike at the time. In 1955 it became the first MGM film shown on television. Turner Broadcasting broadcast a colorized version on the TNT cable network in 1989. —*Alex Ben Block*

THE LIFE OF EMILE ZOLA
Warner Bros., 1937

ALL-RELEASE EQUIVALENT 2005 $s
(Unadjusted $s) in Millions of $s

Domestic Box Office Revenues . . . . $92.9/($3.3)
Production Cost . . . . $9.5/($0.7)
Principal Photography . . . . 52 days estimated
3/8/1937–5/6/1937

Director . . . . William Dieterle

Producer . . . . Hal B. Wallis

Production Company . . . . Warner Bros.

Story by . . . . Heinz Herald, Geza Herczeg

Screenplay by . . . . Norman Reilly Raine, Heinz Herald, Geza Herczeg

Cast . . . . Paul Muni, Gale Sondergaard, Joseph Schildkraut, Gloria Holden

Filming Locations . . . . . . Warner Bros. Studio, Burbank, CA; some scenes in Laguna Beach, CA

Genre . . . . Bio-Drama

Format . . . . B&W

Initial Release . . . . 8/11/1937 world premiere; 10/2/1937 general release

Rerelease . . . . none

Running Time . . . . 123 minutes

MPAA Rating . . . . not rated

STANDING THE TEST OF TIME

ACADEMY AWARD Oscar Nominations and Wins

*OUTSTANDING PRODUCTION: Warner Bros.

Actor: Paul Muni

*ACTOR IN A SUPPORTING ROLE: Joseph Schildkraut

Art Direction: Anton Grot

Assistant Director: Russ Saunders

Directing: William Dieterle

Music (Scoring): Warner Bros. Studio Music Dept., Leo Forbstein, dept. head (Score by Max Steiner)

Sound Recording: Warner Bros. Studio Sound Dept., Nathan Levinson, Sound Director

Writing (Original Story): Heinz Herald, Geza Herczeg

*WRITING (Screenplay): Norman Reilly Raine, Heinz Herald, Geza Herczeg

OSCAR TOTALS   Nominations 10 *Wins 3

AFI 100 YEARS 100 MOVIES SELECTION
2007 0   1997 0

TOP 300 FILMS POSITION . . . . none
All-Release Domestic Box Office in Equivalent 2005 $s

National Film Preservation Board Selection 2000

OTHER AWARDS Best Picture Wins

	Year
Golden Globes	none
New York Film Critics	1937
National Board of Review	none
Film Daily Critics	1937

Warner has touched movie critics and fans on a nerve that had almost been atrophied by the average producers chronic cynicism—the nerve that quickens to serious social issues.

—*Fortune* magazine, 1937

PLOT: Emile Zola, a best-selling author in Paris, writes a celebrated editorial in defense of a Jewish French army officer convicted on false evidence and sent to Devil's Island. As a result, Zola is tried for treason and convicted.

PRODUCTION: The movie originated with a pitch by European playwrights Heinz Herald and Geza Herczeg to producer-director Ernst Lubitsch. Lubitsch, who was under contract to Paramount, sent them to Hal B. Wallis, head of production at Warner Bros., because he felt the only person to star was Paul Muni, who had an unprecedented contract at Warner that gave him approval over his films. Although it is the story of a famous French novelist who fought to free a Jew who was the victim of anti-Semitism and a massive military cover-up, there is no reference to Jews on-screen. At the time it was produced, there were obvious parallels to what Hitler was doing in Germany. In his novel *An Empire of Their Own: How the Jews Invented Hollywood,* author Neal Gabler has suggested there was reluctance by Jewish movie moguls to do anything that might single out the Jews for undue attention. A former star of the Yiddish theater, Muni prepared intensively for his roles. He was coming off an Oscar-winning performance in 1935's *The Story of Louis Pasteur.* Warner-based producer Henry Blanke took the idea to studio boss Jack Warner, who chose Norman Reilly Raine to do the screenplay. Muni was a perfectionist and insisted that his wife approve every take. There were reshoots even when the director William Dieterle was satisfied, but Mrs. Muni wasn't. To give Muni time to grow a real beard, production was adjusted so that they shot in the reverse order. Muni's beard was darkened as Zola got younger. Muni's makeup took three and a half hours to apply each morning. The studio constructed more than fifty different sets, including the Pantheon in Paris. Scenes of Devil's Island were shot on location near Laguna Beach, California. In February 1937, as production was about to start, Warner's legal department discovered that Lucie Dreyfus, wife of the late Alfred Dreyfus and a major character in the script, was still alive. The lawyers said that gave her the right to stop the movie or sue. A story editor later informed the legal department that Pierre Dreyfus, the couple's son, had had the script reviewed by the family. Some changes had been made at their request and, despite numerous liberties taken with the story, the family liked the movie and had signed off.

DISTRIBUTION: The movie premiered in August 1937 in New York City. It was a critical success and a solid performer at the box office. It became the first biography to win the Best Picture Oscar. Due to political sensitivity, it was not shown in France until 1952, which marked the fiftieth anniversary of Zola's death. An author of a biography of Zola accused Warner Bros. of plagiarism, and eventually the studio bought rights to his book for a small sum and listed it in the credits. There was also a claim by German playwright Hans Rehfisch that the movie stole from his play *The Dreyfus Affair,* and he received a settlement from the studio. In January 1998, French president Jacques Chirac presided over a memorial ceremony to honor the 100th anniversary of the publication of Zola's novel *J'Accuse. —Alex Ben Block*

SNOW WHITE AND THE SEVEN DWARFS

RKO, 1937

ALL-RELEASE EQUIVALENT 2005 $s

(Unadjusted $s) in Millions of $s

Domestic Box Office Revenues . . . . $760.9/($160.6)
Production Cost . . . . $20.2/($1.5)
Production Period . . . . 3+ years
Production meetings began August 1934
Animation began early 1936
First pencil test 2/19/1936

Director . . . . David Hand
Producer . . . . Walt Disney
Production Company . . . . Walt Disney Productions
Story by . . . . Based on the Grimm Fairy Tale
Screenplay by . . . . Adaptation by Ted Sears, Otto Englander, Earl Hurd, Dorothy Ann Blank, Richard Creedon, Dick Richard, Merrill de Maris, Webb Smith
Cast . . . . Adriana Caselotti, Harry Stockwell, Lucille LaVerne, Moroni Olsen, Billy Gilbert, Otis Harlan (uncredited voices)
Filming Locations . . . . . . Walt Disney Studios, Burbank, CA
Genre . . . . Animation
Format . . . . Color (Technicolor)
Initial Release 12/21/1937
Rerelease . . . . 1944, 1952, 1958, 1967, 1975, 1983, 1987 (50th anniversary restoration), 1993 (digital restoration)

Running Time . . . . 80, 82–83, or 85–86 minutes
10 reels
7,462 feet
MPAA Rating . . . . not rated

STANDING THE TEST OF TIME

ACADEMY AWARD Oscar Nominations and Wins

Music (Scoring): Walt Disney Studio Music Dept., Leigh Harline, dept. head (Score by Frank Churchill, Leigh Harline and Paul J. Smith)

*SPECIAL AWARD: 1938 to Walt Disney for *Snow White and the Seven Dwarfs,* recognized as a significant screen innovation which has charmed millions and pioneered a great new entertainment field for the motion picture cartoon

OSCAR TOTALS Nominations 1 *Wins 0+1

AFI 100 YEARS 100 MOVIES SELECTION
2007 . . . #34   1997 . . . #49

TOP 300 FILMS POSITION . . . . #8
All-Release Domestic Box Office in Equivalent 2005 $s

National Film Preservation Board Selection 1989

OTHER AWARDS Best Picture Wins

	Year
Golden Globes	none
New York Film Critics	none
National Board of Review	none
Film Daily Critics	1938

The first full-length animated feature, the turning point in Walt Disney's career, a milestone in film history, and, as more and more people realize with each passing year, a great film.

—Leonard Maltin

PLOT: A wicked queen attempts to murder Snow White, but her beautiful stepchild finds refuge in the forest with seven dwarfs. The queen eventually does poison her, but she is saved by a handsome prince.

PRODUCTION: When Walt Disney was fifteen and working as a newsboy in Kansas City, he attended a silent film version of *Snow White* made in 1916 by Famous Players, shown at the local convention center using four projectors on four separate screens. It made a strong impression. By the early 1930s, Disney was successfully producing short cartoons. However, he saw the future in making full-length animated features. For his first subject he returned to the story he had loved as a boy, a story that had originated in Europe during the Middle Ages and was first published by German brothers Jacob and Wilhelm Grimm in 1812. In 1934 Disney called together his creative team and spent four hours sharing his vision for the film, acting out each of the roles. Initially, he ran into opposition from his wife and brother Roy, who said that they couldn't afford it. During the more than three years it was in production, many in the movie industry referred to the venture as "Disney's Folly." Theater owners said no one would sit through a cartoon longer than 10 minutes. But Disney stood his ground, and further insisted on shooting the movie in color. When the budget rose from $250,000 to $1,488,423, he even mortgaged his own home and automobile. Disney had bet more than his company on the success of *Snow White*. Roughly two dozen songs were composed, but only eight are included in the movie. Disney also cut animated scenes that slowed the story, to the consternation of his animators. They had created approximately 250,000 detailed drawings during six months of effort, and although they had studied human anatomy before beginning work on the movie, Disney became dissatisfied with the early footage they were turning out. He wanted the human characters to look less cartoony, so he resorted to shooting live-action footage of actors performing the scenes and then tracing the action. This technique, called rotoscoping, was developed by animation producer Max Fleischer in 1915. Disney technicians also developed the multiplane camera, which separated foreground overlay art, animation cells, and backgrounds by several inches and created a more three-dimensional effect on-screen.

DISTRIBUTION: Disney disagreed with his distributor, United Artists, on how to release *Snow White*. They saw it as a romance, while he wanted it sold as a fairy tale for the whole family. It resulted in an early end to their distribution deal, as Disney switched to RKO Radio Pictures. It premiered in California on December 21, 1937, at the Carthay Circle Theatre in Los Angeles. The same industry people who had mocked Disney now gave his movie a standing ovation. It broke the house record at Radio City Music Hall in New York, became a global sensation, and was the top box office attraction of 1937. It was the highest-grossing film of all time until *Gone with the Wind* displaced it in 1939. It was the first American movie to release a soundtrack album. At the 1938 Academy Awards, child star Shirley Temple presented Disney with a special Oscar statuette and seven miniature statutes. —*Alex Ben Block*

BRINGING UP BABY
RKO, 1938

ALL-RELEASE EQUIVALENT 2005 $s
(Unadjusted $s) in Millions of $s

Domestic Box Office Revenues. . . . . **$53.2**/($1.9)
Production Cost . . . . **$15.2**/($1.1)
Principal Photography. . . . . **91** days
9/23/1937–1/6/1938

Director . . . . Howard Hawks
Producer . . . . Howard Hawks
Production Company. . . . RKO Radio Pictures
Story by. . . . . Based on a short story by
Hagar Wilde
Screenplay by . . . . Dudley Nichols, Hagar Wilde
Cast . . . . Katharine Hepburn,
Cary Grant, Charlie Ruggles,
Barry Fitzgerald
Filming Locations . . . . 20th Century-Fox Studios; on
location in Los Angeles,
Malibu, and Flintridge, CA
Genre. . . . . Romantic Comedy
Format. . . . . B&W
Initial Release 2/18/1938
Rerelease. 1940
Running Time . . . . 100 or 102 minutes
11 reels
MPAA Rating . . . . not rated

STANDING THE TEST OF TIME

ACADEMY AWARD Oscar Nominations and Wins

None

OSCAR TOTALS   Nominations 0   *Wins 0

AFI 100 YEARS 100 MOVIES SELECTION
2007 . . . #88   1997. . . #97

TOP 300 FILMS POSITION . . . . .none
All-Release Domestic Box Office in Equivalent 2005 $s

National Film Preservation Board Selection. . . . 1990

OTHER AWARDS Best Picture Wins

	Year
Golden Globes	none
New York Film Critics.	none
National Board of Review	none
Film Daily Critics	none

Now the moment you caricature something, you're accused of disliking it. But really you're just picking things that make a good caricature—the attitude of newspapermen, the attitude of scientists—and it's bound to make people think you're poking fun at them.

—Howard Hawks

PLOT: A mild-mannered paleontologist, who has to convince a philanthropist to donate money to his museum, gets entangled with a free-spirited woman who takes him to her Connecticut home with a pet leopard in tow. Their initial antagonism blossoms into romance amid madcap antics.

PRODUCTION: After a blowup at Goldwyn on the 1936 movie *Come and Get It,* Howard Hawks made a new deal at RKO with studio head Sam Briskin, whom the versatile director knew from Columbia Pictures. Hawks was to be paid $130,000 per year for two years to direct up to three films per year and 10 percent gross profit participation once receipts exceeded 1.75 times the negative cost or up to 25 percent of the gross once receipts exceeded the cost by 3 times. Hawks first film was to have been *Gunga Din,* but the project stalled over casting. Briskin wanted Hawks to do a story like *Iron Horse* (1924), but Hawks chose a short story by New York writer Hagar Wilde that had appeared in the April 10 issue of *Collier's* magazine. It was acquired for $1,004. Wilde had worked in Hollywood for Howard Hughes and found the experience distasteful and unpleasant. But she returned to California to work with Hawks and screenwriter Dudley Nichols (*The Informer*) for a few weeks, fleshing out her characters and adding to certain scenes. Because Pandro Berman, whose RKO film unit was making the most profit, was unswerving in his belief in Katharine Hepburn, there was never any real doubt she would play Susan, the dizzy heiress. The Huxley role was offered to Robert Montgomery and Ray Milland, among others. But MGM wouldn't loan out Montgomery, and Milland turned it down. After having appeared with Katharine Hepburn in the notorious box office flop *Sylvia Scarlett* (1935), Gary Grant was reluctant to appear in *Bringing Up Baby,* but Howard Hawks, and a $75,000 paycheck, persuaded Grant to change his mind. Hawks had Grant model his character's look on comic Harold Lloyd. The little terrier (George) had been Asta in *The Thin Man* (1934). For scenes with the leopard, Russell Metty and Vernon Walker filmed two separate takes of the same action, one with the animal and the other with only actors. The two takes were combined in the lab to make it look as if they were all together in the scene. Hawks felt Hepburn was overacting early in the production. "The great trouble is people trying to be funny," Hawks observed. "If they don't try to be funny, then they are funny." The film ended 40 days over schedule and $329,120 over budget, partly due to the salary overages payable to Cary Grant and Katharine Hepburn.

DISTRIBUTION: Although the film garnered good reviews in the press, it was an erratic box office performer. Katharine Hepburn had a profit participation deal, but the film never went into profits, losing $365,000 on its theatrical release. The real shock was its poor performance in New York's Radio City Music Hall, where it was yanked after only one week. Katharine Hepburn was characterized, along with Joan Crawford, Greta Garbo, Marlene Dietrich, and others, by Harry Brandt, president of the Independent Theatre Owners of America, as being "box office poison." Hawks was fired. Hepburn was offered the choice of taking a role she didn't want at RKO or buying out her contract, which she did for $220,000. She would return to Broadway in *The Philadelphia Story,* buy the film rights, and return in triumph to Hollywood. —*Alex Ben Block*

IN OLD CHICAGO
20th Century-Fox, 1938

ALL-RELEASE EQUIVALENT 2005 $s
(Unadjusted $s) in Millions of $s

Domestic Box Office Revenues . . . . **$121.6**/($4.4)
Production Cost . . . . **$21.1**/($1.5)
Principal Photography . . . . **56** days estimated
6/14/1937–8/31/1937

Director . . . . Henry King

Producer . . . . Darryl F. Zanuck

Production Company . . . . 20th Century-Fox

Story by . . . . Niven Busch

Screenplay by . . . . Lamar Trotti, Sonya Levien

Cast . . . . Tyrone Power, Alice Faye,
Don Ameche, Alice Brady

Filming Locations . . . . 20th Century Fox studio in
Westwood Hills, CA; on
location at Oakdale,
CA, and near Yuma, AZ

Genre . . . . Musical, Disaster

Format . . . . B&W

Initial Release . . . . 1937 world premiere;
4/15/1938 general release

Rerelease . . . . none

Running Time . . . . 111 or 115 minutes roadshow
release; 94 minutes
general release
12 reels
10,002 feet

MPAA Rating . . . . not rated

STANDING THE TEST OF TIME

ACADEMY AWARD Oscar Nominations and Wins

Outstanding Production: 20th Century-Fox

*ACTRESS IN A SUPPORTING ROLE: Alice
Brady

*ASSISTANT DIRECTOR: Robert Webb

Music (Scoring): 20th Century-Fox Studio Music
Dept., Louis Silvers, dept. head

Sound Recording: 20th Century-Fox Studio Sound
Dept., E.H. Hansen, Sound Director

Writing (Original Story): Niven Busch

OSCAR TOTALS Nominations 6 *Wins 2

AFI 100 YEARS 100 MOVIES SELECTION
2007 . . . . . 0 1997 0

TOP 300 FILMS POSITION . . . . .none
All-Release Domestic Box Office in Equivalent 2005 $s

National Film Preservation Board Selection . . . .none

OTHER AWARDS Best Picture Wins

	Year
Golden Globes	none
New York Film Critics	none
National Board of Review	none
Film Daily Critics	none

*The archetypal Zanuck movie of the late thirties. A massive melodrama about the
supposed birth of modern Chicago, it had only the flimsiest basis in fact.
But it was a lively show with colorful performances . . . and one
spectacular episode: the burning of Old Chicago.*
—Mel Gussow, *Don't Say Yes Until I Finish Talking*

PLOT: Two sons of Margaret O'Leary grow up on opposite sides of the law, and their lifelong rivalry heats up as Mrs. O'Leary's cow starts the 1871 fire that burns down much of the old city of Chicago.

PRODUCTION: In the year after MGM had great success with its disaster epic *San Francisco,* 20th Century-Fox production head Darryl F. Zanuck wanted to make a romantic saga, set against the famous nineteenth-century Chicago fire, that would star Clark Gable and Jean Harlow. Gable wasn't available, but Zanuck made a deal for Harlow in return by allowing Tyrone Power to make *Madame X* for MGM. However, when Harlow died on June 7, 1937, that deal was scrapped. Zanuck hired two different writers, Niven Busch and Richard Collins, to write separate scenarios. Collins based his story on the 1872 novel *Barriers Burned Away* by E. P. Roe, but the story by Busch became the basis for the script by Sonya Levien and Lamar Trotti. While Zanuck insisted on historical accuracy, much of it was fiction. Production Code Administration head Joseph Breen wrote a five-page letter detailing why the original script was objectionable and "not acceptable." Breen's big concern was the depiction of prostitutes. Zanuck agreed to changes. With Gable unavailable, Zanuck turned to Fox contract player Tyrone Power, whose breakout role had been 1936's *Lloyd's of London.* For Tyrone's chorus girl love interest, Zanuck turned to Alice Faye, a former big-band singer who had been signed to Fox in 1934 and had stared in such films as *Sing, Baby, Sing* (1936), *You Can't Have Everything* (1937), and *Wake Up and Live* (1937). The cast was rounded out with Don Ameche as the crusading brother and Alice Brady, who won an Oscar as Mrs. O'Leary. The fire scene, which runs about 20 minutes, was staged on the Fox back lot over the course of three days at a cost of about $500,000, adding to what was the most expensive movie Fox had produced to that date. The budget for costumes alone was $80,000.

DISTRIBUTION: Critics carped that it was bad history but acknowledged that it was hugely entertaining. Audiences agreed, making it a 1938 top 5 box office hit. It was voted one of the 10 Best Pictures of 1938 by *Film Daily.* It received an initial road show release, with a 111-minute version of the film shown in two parts. The 80-minute first section introduced the characters and established the rambling, corrupt town. In the 31-minute second section, the devastating fire consumes the city, with a mix of actual scenes, models, and process shots. The film went into general release in a 94-minute version and brought in worldwide rentals of $3.1 million, earning a tidy net profit of $625,000, but it couldn't beat *San Francisco.* Zanuck squashed an internal conflict over credit for the hit movie. Special effects director H. Bruce "Lucky" Humberstone had taken an ad in the *Hollywood Reporter* proclaiming that he had directed the critically acclaimed fire scene. Director Henry King was concerned this would diminish his chances of an Oscar nomination for Best Director. In a memo, Zanuck apologized to King for Humberstone's billing and noted that the main part of the fire and the rest of the picture were directed by King. However, Zanuck advised King not to run trade advertising to counter the misimpression because it would make him look "sore." Neither King nor Humberstone was nominated, although the film received a Best Picture nomination. —*Alex Ben Block*

ALEXANDER'S RAGTIME BAND
20th Century-Fox, 1938

ALL-RELEASE EQUIVALENT 2005 $s
(Unadjusted $s) in Millions of $s

Domestic Box Office Revenues . . . . **$162.9**/($5.8)
Production Cost . . . . **$18.4**/($1.3)
Principal Photography . . . . **60** days estimated
1/31/1938–4/9/1938

Director . . . . Henry King
Producer . . . . Darryl F. Zanuck
Production Company . . . . 20th Century-Fox
Story by . . . . Irving Berlin
Screenplay by . . . . Kathryn Scola, Lamar Trotti
Adaptation by Richard Sherman
Cast . . . . Tyrone Power, Alice Faye,
Don Ameche, Ethel Merman,
Jack Haley, Jean Hersholt
Filming Locations . . . . 20th Century-Fox Studios,
Beverly Hills, CA
Genre . . . . Musical
Format . . . . B&W
Initial Release 8/19/1938
Rerelease . . . . none
Running Time . . . . 105 or 106 minutes
12 reels
9,569 feet
MPAA Rating . . . . not rated

STANDING THE TEST OF TIME

ACADEMY AWARD Oscar Nominations and Wins

Outstanding Production: 20th Century-Fox
Art Direction: Bernard Herzbrun, Boris Leven
Film Editing: Barbara McLean
*MUSIC (Scoring): Alfred Newman
Music (Song): "Now It Can Be Told," Music and Lyrics by Irving Berlin
Writing (Original Story): Irving Berlin

OSCAR TOTALS   Nominations **6**   *Wins **1**

AFI 100 YEARS 100 MOVIES SELECTION
2007 0   1997 0

TOP 300 FILMS POSITION . . . . .none
All-Release Domestic Box Office in Equivalent 2005 $s

National Film Preservation Board Selection . . . .none

OTHER AWARDS Best Picture Wins

	Year
Golden Globes	none
New York Film Critics	none
National Board of Review	none
Film Daily Critics	none

Alexander's Ragtime Band is the first film musical to realize that the history of American popular music is the history of America. Irving Berlin is a historian; to hear his songs is to read that history.

—Film historian Gerald Mast

PLOT: The story follows a society boy in the early 1900s, who changes his name to pursue a career in ragtime instead of "serious" music. It details his musical successes and failures and the up-and-down romance he has with his lead singer over several decades.

PRODUCTION: Irving Berlin was America's most famous popular songwriter in the thirties. Fox's Darryl Zanuck wanted to be the first to offer a movie score mixing old and new works by a single composer. He proposed a biopic based on Berlin's life. Berlin was extremely sensitive to criticism and was adamantly opposed to the idea of the film being about his life. Zanuck suggested that Berlin "invent a fictitious story incorporating incidents from his life," and Berlin agreed. Berlin and Richard Sherman expanded a story by Berlin into a 114-page treatment. Zanuck was disappointed and assigned a team of in-house dramatists to work on it through many revisions. They took the film title from Berlin's 1911 song. The film had originally been conceived as a vehicle for Fred MacMurray but was eventually assigned to Tyrone Power. After toying with the idea of having Barbara Stanwyck play Powell's romantic foil, Zanuck cast Alice Faye. He also cast Don Ameche as Alexander's buddy, reuniting the trio who had worked together on *In Old Chicago,* which was released earlier in 1938. Fox went all out on the production, creating eighty-five lavish sets and stunning costumes. Though the story covers twenty-five years, none of the characters ages, which was deemed (according to the *Variety* 1938 review) "flattering to listeners who are young again." Berlin supervised the musical elements using more than 30 of his original songs (out of some 600 he had composed), including three new numbers: "Now It Can Be Told," "My Walking Stick," and "Marching Along with Time." The film allowed Zanuck to continue the sort of hit musicals Fox Film Corporation and 20th Century Pictures had produced prior to their 1935 merger, such as the Janet Gaynor–starring *Sunnyside Up* (Fox, 1929) and the Maurice Chevalier–starring *Follies Bergère de Paris* (20th Century, 1934).

DISTRIBUTION: Between the preview in Los Angeles on May 24, 1938, and the national release in August, there were sporadic openings across the United States. Berlin was dogged by persistent speculations questioning the legitimacy of his cultural claim. A lawsuit later charged Berlin and Zanuck with "stealing" songs and the story idea, though the suit was ultimately dismissed. Berlin's English publisher threatened to hold up the foreign release of the film because he still owned the English rights to many of the songs in the score and Fox had refused to pay him. Once the confusion cleared, however, the film blossomed into a commercial success, with a profit of $978,000 on worldwide rentals of $3.6 million. It was voted one of the 10 Best Pictures of 1938 by *Film Daily.* Its popularity added to Berlin's prestige in Hollywood. It was one of Fox's biggest-grossing films of 1938, the same year Fox's top star, Shirley Temple, could be seen on-screen in three musicals (*Rebecca of Sunnybrook Farm, Little Miss Broadway,* and *Just Around the Corner*). —*Hayley Taylor Block*

BOYS TOWN
MGM, 1938

<table>
<tr><td colspan="2">ALL-RELEASE EQUIVALENT 2005 $s
(Unadjusted $s) in Millions of $s</td></tr>
<tr><td>Domestic Box Office Revenues</td><td>$175.1/($6.3)</td></tr>
<tr><td>Production Cost</td><td>$10.7/($0.8)</td></tr>
<tr><td>Principal Photography</td><td>55 days estimated
6/6/1938–8/8/1938</td></tr>
</table>

Director	Norman Taurog
Producer	John W. Considine Jr.
Production Company	Metro-Goldwyn-Mayer Corp.
Story by	Dore Schary, Eleanor Griffin
Screenplay by	John Meehan, Dore Schary
Cast	Spencer Tracy, Mickey Rooney
Filming Locations	On location in Omaha, NE
Genre	Bio-Drama
Format	B&W
Initial Release	9/9/1938
Rerelease	none
Running Time	93 or 96 minutes 9 reels
MPAA Rating	not rated

STANDING THE TEST OF TIME

ACADEMY AWARD Oscar Nominations and Wins

Outstanding Production: Metro-Goldwyn-Mayer

*ACTOR: Spencer Tracy

Directing: Norman Taurog

*WRITING (Original Story): Dore Schary, Eleanore Griffin

Writing (Screenplay): John Meehan, Dore Schary

OSCAR TOTALS   Nominations **5**   *Wins **2**

AFI 100 YEARS 100 MOVIES SELECTION

2007 0   1997 0

TOP 300 FILMS POSITION . . . . .none
All-Release Domestic Box Office in Equivalent 2005 $s

National Film Preservation Board Selection . . . .none

OTHER AWARDS Best Picture Wins

	Year
Golden Globes	none
New York Film Critics	none
National Board of Review	none
Film Daily Critics	none

This picture is dedicated to him [Father Edward Flanagan] and his splendid work for homeless, abandoned boys, regardless of race, creed or color.
—Opening inscription in the film

PLOT: In Omaha, Nebraska, a priest, Father Flanagan, starts a shelter for wayward boys. Among them is Whitey, who gets in trouble, almost forcing the home to close. Eventually Whitey straightens out, and later Father Flanagan is recognized for his efforts.

PRODUCTION: Dore Schary, who would go on to run MGM, was a freelancer in the mid-1930s when he sold a script to the studio based on the real-life experiences of a Nebraska priest. MGM agreed to pay Boys Town $5,000 for the rights to the story and permission to film there. Father Flanagan refused at first, but then agreed after seeing a script that he liked. Studio head Louis B. Mayer picked Norman Taurog, who had just had a hit with *The Adventures of Tom Sawyer,* to direct, because he was known for his work with child actors such as his nephew (by marriage) Jackie Cooper. MGM child stars Cooper and Freddie Bartholomew were considered for the role of Whitey before Mickey Rooney got the part. It was Father Flanagan who wanted Spencer Tracy to portray him, but the famed actor declined, ostensibly because he had played a priest two years earlier in *San Francisco* and didn't want to be typecast (despite having appeared in six other films in the interim). Later reports also suggest that Tracy was hesitant because he was an alcoholic and was on a binge at the time. Tracy finally agreed to the role, which resulted in his becoming the first (and few) actors to win the Best Actor Oscar in consecutive years. Tracy spent a week with Father Flanagan before production to watch how he interacted with the boys. The location portion of the production took place at the end of June and early July, when construction was going on at Boys Town. Although there were some trees to buffer the sound, the noise still carried across the flat landscape. Some of the extras would be sent to ask the workmen, including those blasting out tree stumps, to stop while a scene was being shot.

DISTRIBUTION: At Father Flanagan's request, there was a gala premiere at Boys Town. About 30,000 fans turned out in Omaha on September 7, 1938, with the stars arriving by train. To promote the movie, MGM opened the 1938 season of a radio show it sponsored on NBC with a preview featuring Spencer Tracy, Mickey Rooney, and Father Flanagan. The film quickly became a smash hit nationwide, making a profit of over $2 million on worldwide rentals of $4 million. It was voted one of the 10 Best Pictures of 1938 by *Film Daily.* It did cause one problem: the public thought Father Flanagan had made so much money from the movie that donations to the institution dropped. MGM donated another $250,000 to build a dormitory at Boys Town. Spencer Tracy issued a statement clarifying the meager Boys Town gain and asked the public to keep contributing. MGM also agreed to pay Boys Town $100,000 to make a sequel. Most of the stars returned for *Men of Boys Town,* where, once again, the real boys were cast as extras. The 1941 sequel was also successful, with a profit of nearly $1.3 million. —*Alex Ben Block*

THE WIZARD OF OZ

MGM, 1939

Director . . . . Victor Fleming

Producer . . . . Mervyn LeRoy

Production Company . . . . Metro-Goldwyn-Mayer

Story by . . . . Based on the novel by
L. Frank Baum

Screenplay by . . . . Noel Langley, Florence Ryerson,
Edgar Allan Wolfe,
Noel Longley

Cast . . . . Judy Garland, Frank Morgan,
Ray Bolger, Bert Lahr,
Jack Haley, Margaret Hamilton

Filming Locations . . . . MGM Studios, Culver City, CA

Genre . . . . Musical

Format . . . . Color (Technicolor)

Initial Release . . . . 8/12/1939 world premiere
(Wisconsin); 8/15/1939 premiere
(Los Angeles, CA); 8/17/1939
premiere (New York);
8/25/1939 general release

Rerelease 1949, 1955

Running Time . . . . 97 or 101 minutes
10 reels
9,167 feet

MPAA Rating . . . . not rated

STANDING THE TEST OF TIME

ACADEMY AWARD Oscar Nominations and Wins

Outstanding Production: Metro-Goldwyn-Mayer

Art Direction: Cedric Gibbons, William A. Horning

Cinematography: Hal Rosson (not an official
nomination)

*MUSIC (Original Score): Herbert Stothart

*MUSIC (Song): "Over the Rainbow," Music by
Harold Arlen, Lyrics by E. Y. Harburg

Special Effects: A. Arnold Gillespie, Douglas Shearer

OSCAR TOTALS   Nominations 6   *Wins 2

AFI 100 YEARS 100 MOVIES SELECTION
2007 . . . #10   1997 . . . . #6

TOP 300 FILMS POSITION . . . . none
All-Release Domestic Box Office in Equivalent 2005 $s

National Film Preservation Board Selection 1989

OTHER AWARDS Best Picture Wins

	Year
Golden Globes	none
New York Film Critics	none
National Board of Review	none
Film Daily Critics	none

*The biggest reason for the film's success is that,
more than any other American motion picture,
The Wizard of Oz managed to combine the best
elements of the stage and cinema into a fable
about self-discovery that somehow still enthralls
both children and adults.*

—James Plath

PLOT: Kansas farm girl Dorothy Gale (Judy Garland) goes to a magical land called Oz, where she journeys with the Scarecrow (Ray Bolger), the Tin Man (Jack Haley), and the Cowardly Lion (Bert Lahr) to Emerald City to see the Wizard (Frank Morgan), who shows her how to get home.

PRODUCTION: MGM's Louis B. Mayer wanted a movie to rival Walt Disney's huge hit *Snow White and the Seven Dwarfs.* Both producer Mervyn LeRoy and his assistant Arthur Freed have taken credit for bringing L. Frank Baum's 1900 book, *The Wonderful Wizard of Oz,* to Mayer. The movie rights belonged to producer Samuel Goldwyn, who acquired them for $40,000 as a vehicle for Eddie Cantor, with W. C. Fields as the Wizard. Cantor declined, saying the story was not his type. After *Snow White* was released in December 1937, Goldwyn got offers from five studios in three days. MGM won the bidding and cast Judy Garland. It was LeRoy's first producing job at MGM since moving over from Warner Bros., and he also wanted to direct, but Mayer said no. The first director assigned was Norman Taurog, who left for another picture, replaced by Richard Thorpe, who shot the first couple of weeks. Then MGM fired him and brought in George Cukor, who fiddled with makeup and costumes, including those for Dorothy, before leaving for another assignment. Finally, Victor Fleming took over and, together with uncredited writer John Lee Mahin, adjusted the script. One device that aided storytelling was the mixing of sepia-tinted footage into what was mostly a Technicolor movie. The real world is portrayed as dark and drab, while Oz, in contrast, is full of brilliant colors. A portion of the soundtrack was prescored because the songs, most by E. Y. Harburg and Harold Arlen, were integral to the story. Some songs and entire musical numbers were shot but eventually cut. Other songs were added later, including "Over the Rainbow." In fact, Mayer considered cutting this song after early previews but was convinced to leave it in when Freed threatened to quit if it didn't stay in the movie. Margaret Hamilton, who played the Wicked Witch of the West, suffered first- and second-degree burns on her face and hands during a scene where she takes off from Munchkinland amid smoke and fire. To record the Munchkins, MGM sound chief Douglas Shearer and musical arranger Ken Darby had devised a system of recording dialogue and songs at a slow speed, which, when played back at normal speed, gave the voices a high-pitched sound. Although the cast of Munchkins grew to more than 116 little people and a dozen children, the speaking voices of only two little people ended up on the final soundtrack.

DISTRIBUTION: MGM spent $2.8 million to produce the movie and $630,750 on prints and ads, including $250,000 on a magazine ad campaign and premieres in Oconomowoc, Wisconsin, and at Grauman's Chinese Theater in Hollywood. MGM players Judy Garland and Mickey Rooney went on an East Coast publicity tour, which included a New York premiere of Oz. It was voted one of the 10 Best Pictures of 1939 by *Film Daily.* The movie made just over $3 million in worldwide rentals during its initial release but had a net loss of $1,137,230. It recouped its initial loss with a net profit of $1,148,396 on the 1949 rerelease on worldwide rentals of $1,796,528. A 1955 reissue brought in only $930,776, but $577,332 was pure profit. The next year MGM sold it to TV, where it has been playing annually ever since. *—Alex Ben Block*

MR. SMITH GOES TO WASHINGTON
Columbia, 1939

ALL-RELEASE EQUIVALENT 2005 $s
(Unadjusted $s) in Millions of $s

Domestic Box Office Revenues. . . . . **$92.9**/($3.3)
Production Cost . . . .**$26.7**/($1.9)
Principal Photography . . . .**80** days estimated
4/3/1939–7/7/1939

Director . . . . Frank Capra

Producer . . . . Frank Capra

Production Company. . . . Columbia Pictures

Story by . . . . Lewis R. Foster

Screenplay by . . . . Sidney Buchman

Cast . . . . Jean Arthur, James Stewart, Claude Rains, Edward Arnold

Filming Locations . . . . In studio at Columbia, Hollywood, CA; on location in Washington, D.C.

Genre. . . . . Drama

Format. . . . . B&W

Initial Release 10/19/1939

Rerelease. . . . . none

Running Time . . . . 125–126 minutes
13 reels 11,866 feet

MPAA Rating . . . . not rated

STANDING THE TEST OF TIME

ACADEMY AWARD Oscar Nominations and Wins

Outstanding Production: Columbia

Actor: James Stewart

Actor in a Supporting Role: Harry Carey

Actor in a Supporting Role: Claude Rains

Art Direction: Lionel Banks

Directing: Frank Capra

Film Editing: Gene Havlick, Al Clark

Music (Scoring): Dimitri Tiomkin

Sound Recording: Columbia Studio Sound Dept., John Livadary, Sound Director

***WRITING** (Original Story): Lewis R. Foster

Writing (Screenplay): Sidney Buchman

OSCAR TOTALS Nominations **11** *Wins 1

AFI 100 YEARS 100 MOVIES SELECTION
2007 . . . #26   1997 . . . #29

TOP 300 FILMS POSITION . . . . .none
All-Release Domestic Box Office in Equivalent 2005 $s

National Film Preservation Board Selection 1989

OTHER AWARDS Best Picture Wins

	Year
Golden Globes	none
New York Film Critics.	none
National Board of Review	none
Film Daily Critics	none

Buy it. Quick! In my name, Chet! Call Wasserman at MCA. See if Stewart and Arthur are available. . . . Hey, we can call it not Mr. Deeds, *but* Mr. Smith Goes to Washington.

—Frank Capra, the first time he read a synopsis of the film

PLOT: A political novice and local Boy Scout hero is appointed to the U.S. Senate by political bosses who expect him to do their bidding, but once there he fights political corruption, stages a filibuster, and eventually triumphs.

PRODUCTION: Newspaperman turned Hollywood gag writer Lewis R. Foster wrote a short story called "The Gentleman from Montana." Several studios shied away due to the political content. Paramount and MGM submitted Foster's story to the Production Code's Joseph Breen, who in 1938 warned them against it: "It looks to us like one that might well be loaded with dynamite, both for the motion picture industry, and for the country at large." Breen objected to the unflattering portrayal of "our system of government." Despite that, Frank Capra at Columbia sparked to the story and saw it as a sequel to his successful movie, *Mr. Deeds Goes to Town.* There was discussion about Gary Cooper reprising his role from *Deeds,* but Capra quickly wanted Jimmy Stewart and Jean Arthur, whom he had directed in the 1938 Best Picture Oscar winner *You Can't Take It with You.* His longtime collaborator Robert Riskin had left, so Capra turned to screenwriter Sidney Buchman. Capra, Buchman, a cameraman, and a photographer went on a research trip to Washington, D.C., where they toured, sketched ideas for sets, shot photos, and met with experts. While James Stewart was an established actor, this film made him a star. In the scenes where Stewart was in the final hours of the filibuster, he didn't sound hoarse enough, so Capra had Stewart's throat swabbed twice a day with a mercury chloride solution, which swelled and irritated his vocal chords. The production used the New York street set at Warner Bros. for scenes in which as many as 1,000 or more extras were employed. In an early cut the final portion of the movie was much longer. It included Smith going back to his home state for a parade, the end of the Taylor machine, Smith riding his motorcycle to visit Senator Paine, and Smith visiting his mother, all of which were cut after comments from a preview audience.

DISTRIBUTION: Major critics and the public loved this movie, but many politicians and members of the press in Washington were offended. It was voted one of the 10 Best Pictures of 1939 by *Film Daily.* At a premiere in Washington, D.C., put on by the National Press Club, Capra was referred to as "that Hollywood jerk," and needed the help of friends to spirit him away from the hostile crowd. Senate majority leader Alben W. Barkley, among others, denounced the movie as "a grotesque distortion" of the Senate. Hollywood radio personality Jimmie Fidler reported that other movie studios offered Columbia $2 million to shelve the picture before it caused problems in Washington, where they were lobbying for favorable legislation. The U.S. ambassador in London, Joseph Kennedy, urgently cabled Columbia chief Harry Cohn that he must stop distribution because the film "ridiculed democracy" and "might be construed as propaganda favoring the Axis powers." Cohn answered by sending Kennedy a stack of clippings that praised Smith as a hero. Shortly after, when the Nazis said they would ban all foreign films for the duration of the war, most French chose to see this as their final film, many crying as Smith stood in front of the statue of Abraham Lincoln and the word *liberty.* —*Alex Ben Block*

GONE WITH THE WIND
MGM, 1939

ALL-RELEASE EQUIVALENT 2005 $s
(Unadjusted $s) in Millions of $s

Domestic Box Office Revenues . . . . . . **$1,407.7**/($176.7)
Production Cost . . . . **$58.5**/($4.2)
Principal Photography . . . . **140** days estimated
1/29/1939–7/1/1939

Director . . . . Victor Fleming

Producer . . . . David O. Selznick

Production Company . . . . Selznick International Pictures

Story by . . . . Based on the novel by Margaret Mitchell

Screenplay by . . . . Sidney Howard

Cast . . . . Clark Gable, Leslie Howard, Olivia de Havilland, Vivien Leigh

Filming Locations . . . . . . In Studio at Selznick International Studios and MGM Studios, Culver City, CA; on Location in California: Agoura Hills, Los Angeles, Pasadena, Chico, Big Bear Lake, Calabasas, Malibu, Hollywood, Simi Valley

Genre . . . . Historical Drama, War

Format . . . . Color (Technicolor)

Initial Release . . . . 12/15/1939 roadshow release; 1/17/1941 wide release

Rerelease 1941, 1942, 1947, 1954, 1961, 1967, 1974, 1989, 1998

Running Time . . . . 220 minutes, 20,300 feet

MPAA Rating . . . . not rated

AFI 100 YEARS 100 MOVIES SELECTION
2007 . . . . #6   1997 . . . . #4

TOP 300 FILMS POSITION . . . . #1
All-Release Domestic Box Office in Equivalent 2005 $s

National Film Preservation Board Selection 1989

STANDING THE TEST OF TIME

ACADEMY AWARD Oscar Nominations and Wins

*OUTSTANDING PRODUCTION: Selznick International Pictures

Actor: Clark Gable

*ACTRESS: Vivien Leigh

Actress in a Supporting Role: Olivia de Havilland

*ACTRESS IN A SUPPORTING ROLE: Hattie McDaniel

*ART DIRECTION: Lyle Wheeler

*CINEMATOGRAPHY: Ernest Haller, Ray Rennahan

*DIRECTING: Victor Fleming

*FILM EDITING: Hal C. Kern, James E. Newcom

Music (Original Score): Max Steiner

Sound Recording: Samuel Goldwyn Studio Sound Dept., Thomas T. Moulton, Sound Director

Special Effects: John R. Cosgrove, Fred Albin, Arthur Johns

*WRITING (Screenplay): Sidney Howard

*SPECIAL AWARD: to William Cameron Menzies for outstanding achievement in the use of color for the enhancement of dramatic mood in the production of *Gone with the Wind*

*SCIENTIFIC OR TECHNICAL AWARD (Class III): to Don Musgrave and Selznick International Pictures, Inc., for pioneering in the use of coordinated equipment in the production *Gone with the Wind*

OSCAR TOTALS   Nominations **13**   *Wins **8+2**

OTHER AWARDS Best Picture Wins

	Year
Golden Globes	none
New York Film Critics	none
National Board of Review	none
Film Daily Critics	none

PLOT: On the eve of the Civil War, Scarlett O'Hara, the headstrong daughter of an Irish immigrant plantation owner, is secretly in love with Ashley Wilkes, who is to marry Melanie Hamilton. Then Scarlett meets Rhett Butler, a savvy cynical businessman and soldier, who falls in love with her.

PRODUCTION: Kay Brown, East Coast story editor for Selznick International, in 1936 read an advance copy of the 1,037-page novel by first-time author Margaret Mitchell and immediately saw it as a movie. She airmailed the script and a synopsis to her boss, David O. Selznick, pleading for him to buy the rights. Selznick felt it was too long for a movie. Then John Hay "Jock" Whitney, chairman of Selznick International, said he would buy the rights himself. That triggered Selznick to spend $50,000, the most ever paid for a first novel. When the book became a best seller, Selznick announced production plans. Selznick's father-in-law, Louis B. Mayer, wanted it for MGM. There were competing offers from Warner Bros. and United Artists. After much vacillating, Selznick made a deal with Mayer. He would get MGM's Gable as star and $1.25 million toward production in return for distribution rights and 50 percent of the profits. Gable was paid $120,000. They considered many actresses for Scarlett, including Katharine Hepburn, Loretta Young, and Lana Turner. Selznick's brother Myron, a talent agent, brought in English actress Vivian Leigh, who was quietly signed at a $15,000 salary even as the search continued. There were four directors, most notably George Cukor, whom Selznick fired after about a month of the seven-month shoot for being too slow and lacking a feel for the story. He was replaced by Victor Fleming, fresh from directing *The Wizard of Oz,* who directed roughly half the film. An estimated 4,400 people were involved with making the movie. Ten writers contributed to the screenplay, including Charles MacArthur, John Van Druten, and F. Scott Fitzgerald. The credited writer, Sidney Howard, was killed in August 1939 during production, and became the first posthumous winner of an Oscar. There were 2,848 costumes, including 1,230 Confederate uniforms. Vivian Leigh wore thirty-eight hairstyles. There were 1,000 horses and 375 other animals (dogs, mules, oxen, cows, pigs, chickens, ducks, geese, and peacocks) and 450 vehicles (wagons, hearses, fire equipment, carriages, ambulances, and gun caissons).

DISTRIBUTION: The film was a huge hit, and within a few months it became the biggest-grossing movie of all time. There was a highly publicized world premiere on December 15, 1939, at the Loew's Grand Theater in Atlanta, with a parade that attracted 1.5 million spectators and a grand ball attended by Leigh, Gable, de Havilland, Selznick, Margaret Mitchell, and other celebrities. The movie initially played road show engagements in large cities. It was released nationally at standard ticket prices on January 17, 1941. Selznick insisted on the printing of a booklet given to exhibitors that provided details on how the film should be projected, including the proper illumination level and how long to run the overtures. Selznick earned $4 million but sold all of his rights in 1942 to Whitney for $400,000 (which Whitney later sold back to MGM for $2.4 million). Between 1941 and 1998 the film was rereleased theatrically nine times. In 1954 it was reissued in a wide-screen version. For a 1967 rerelease, it was blown up to 70mm. In 1989 a fiftieth-anniversary edition from Turner Entertainment involved a complete audio and video restoration. —*Alex Ben Block*

The 1940s

Snow White and the Seven Dwarfs may have provided Disney with his finest moment, but Pinocchio is probably his greatest film. It shares in all the qualities that made the first feature such a success and adds to them a technical brilliance that has never been surpassed.

—Christopher Finch, *The Art of Walt Disney*

TOP 10 ALL-RELEASE MOVIES DOMESTIC BOX OFFICE

By Initial Year of Release, 1940–1949

		Equivalent 2005 $s in Millions of $s
1	Pinocchio	$465.2
2	This Is the Army	$407.7
3	Bambi	$383.8
4	Sergeant York	$361.3
5	Duel in the Sun	$348.0
6	The Best Years of Our Lives	$345.3
7	For Whom the Bell Tolls	$333.9
8	The Bells of St. Mary's	$323.6
9	Fantasia	$314.8
10	Song of the South	$301.9
		Total: $3,585.5

GENERAL U.S. STATISTICS, 1940

132,164,569
U.S. Population

80 Million
Average Weekly
U.S. Movie Attendance

DECADE OVERVIEW

Is it possible to make pictures which have purpose and significance and yet show a proper return at the box office? I believe it is. —DARRYL F. ZANUCK

A Time of Change

During the fourth decade of the twentieth century the movie business was impacted by the global events of World War II (1939–45) and then later in the decade by a pair of seminal events specific to the industry. One such event was the arrival of commercial television, beginning with NBC. This new entertainment medium offered consumers an alternative way to receive and enjoy visual content, different in many respects from what print, live theater, and movies offered. The other event was a federal antitrust action that forced movie studios to divest themselves of their movie theaters, which were, in many instances, the predominant source of their annual profits. This effectively ended the era of the vertically integrated studio.

At the outset of the forties there were five major and three lesser movie companies dominating the production, distribution, and exhibition of movies worldwide. Almost all were based in Hollywood or nearby, with head offices in New York. The majors were MGM-Loew's, which had the greatest revenues and most hits during the decade, along with 20th Century-Fox, Warner Bros., Paramount, and RKO. Each of these companies owned theaters as well as production means. The next tier included Universal, Columbia, and United Artists. Because none of these three companies owned theaters, they were that much more dependent on the success of their movies.

Unlike events in the 1930s, when the Great Depression caused studios that owned numerous theaters, such as Paramount, to suffer from overcapacity, the war efforts of the 1940s actually benefited the bigger theater circuits. As of their January 4, 1947, fiscal year end, Paramount reported record income of $200.8 million, as approximately 90 million Americans went to the movies each week. Moviegoing accounted for a full quarter of all leisure time spent in the country that year.

The mid-1940s also marked a high point for the studio system, with such bosses as Louis B. Mayer at MGM, Darryl F. Zanuck at 20th Century-Fox, Harry Cohn at Columbia, and Jack Warner at Warner Bros. performing at the top of their game. In fact, in 1947 Louis B. Mayer was the highest-paid executive in America. It was then too that the first power agents emerged, capitalizing on the studios' increased productivity by assembling packages of actors, directors, and screenplay writers for a commission.

Although studios were called "dream factories" during these successful years, the assembly-line nature of the work made them anything but dreamy. The pressure to keep production stages and movie screens filled was constant. Even stars were expected to work on four to six movies a year and could be "loaned out" to other studios to fulfill minimum picture obligations and earn their guaranteed compensation.

Control over talent was so extensive that studio publicists worked with or paid off police and reporters to spin or suppress news stories about their star contract players. Performers who successfully captured public attention became the engine driving the next wave of pictures to exhibitors. There was one instance, however, that nearly caused the cozy relationship between the press and Hollywood to implode. When newspaper baron William Randolph Hearst suspected Orson Welles of mocking him in his film *Citizen Kane*, Hearst set out to destroy both Welles and the movie. Despite his papers' negative reviews, the public embraced the movie and the genre it spawned. Some call *Citizen Kane* the first of a new generation of noir movies—dark, serious films that thrilled and bubbled with suspense. In fact, *Citizen Kane* was followed shortly thereafter by some of the greatest film noir classics ever, including Hitchcock's *Notorious,* with Cary Grant and Ingrid Bergman, and *Dark Passage,* starring Humphrey Bogart and Lauren Bacall.

While the major studios owned only a fraction of all theater screens at this time, those they did own were predominantly first-run screens, where a movie's reputation was almost always established. It was in first-run theaters that movies were deemed either successes or failures. This was yet another example of the control studios exerted throughout the decade.

Some relief in this control occurred around the midpoint of the decade, when the studios' absolute right to fine and endlessly suspend contract employees who resisted doing their bidding for them was challenged in the courts. In 1944 the actress Olivia de Havilland won a ruling that prohibited studios from adding length to her contract each time they suspended her, making the term of her servitude under that contract endless. From then on contracts were limited to seven years.

Around this same time, there were intense battles for union jurisdiction, especially among those representing the many different types of craftspeople involved in filmmaking, from carpenters to cinematographers. For several years pickets were a common sight at the gates of the major studios.

By contrast, a common sight at theaters during the early years of the decade were huge crowds of movie fans streaming in to see the epic Civil War film *Gone with the Wind*. Although this movie was initially released in 1939, the impact of David O. Selznick's sweeping drama was felt for the first eighteen months of the forties as well. Much of its run was in road show engagements, meaning that it opened in select theaters in the largest cities first. This film dominated the box office as no other movie ever had before, breaking all ticket sales records.

The other war dominating the 1940s, of course, was World War II. From the start, the U.S. government treated the movie industry as if it were part of the war effort, which meant that there were some material shortages and restrictions in effect, hampering costume, prop, and set construction, but generally studios were able to keep movie production going. Things intensified after Pearl Harbor, as nearly 40 percent of actors, executives, and others involved in the filmmaking industry quit or took leaves of absence to personally do their part. Some made movies specifically for the government; many studios made films with patriotic themes for the general public; Hollywood's finest directors, including Frank Capra, John Ford, John Huston, and William Wyler, made movies in support of the allies; and both on-screen and in person, stars actively sold war bonds, toured USO facilities, or met with soldiers. Studios, led by Warner Bros., donated generously to wartime causes. For a time theater marquees were dimmed or dark, and the use of klieg lights at movie premieres was banned.

More pictures with serious subjects were released during this time than in all the prior decades. If escapism had been the goal of movies in the 1930s, the forties brought much more sober and realistic fare. Movies such as *Mrs. Miniver* and *Casablanca* are examples of this phenomenon. Still, there were comedies, led by the team of Bob Hope and Bing Crosby, and musicals with stars such as Betty Grable, who became the pinup girl for American soldiers, boosting the morale of our armed forces in their own unique way. Remarkably, throughout it all, studios reported robust profits.

Although it was not yet considered one of the majors, Disney emerged during the forties as a true leader in family programming, especially animation. Under the guidance of Walt Disney, it began the decade by releasing *Pinocchio* and the groundbreaking animated musical *Fantasia,* which included the first multichannel soundtrack. While *Pinocchio* was initially hurt by the closing of the European markets in the wake of the Nazi takeover of the continent, the film, over a number of rereleases in later years, became a huge hit.

After the war ended, there were boom times throughout America again, and even more successes for Hollywood. A new crop of all-color musicals were produced, as were comedies and quality dramas including producer Samuel Goldwyn's *The Best Years of Our Lives* and the Frank Capra–directed *It's a Wonderful Life.*

Attendance in movie theaters reached an all-time high in 1946, held steady for the three years following, and then began an annual decline that would not level off until the early 1970s. Production also declined, which led to a decrease in the number of releases by each company as television ate into their audience. While there had been an average of 501 U.S.-produced films and 200 imported films released per year in the 1930s, the average would drop to 407 U.S.-produced films and 86 imports per year in the 1940s.

But television was not the only threat to the film industry at the time. The Cold War had begun between the U.S.-led West and the Soviet Union. There was paranoia in America about internal sympathizers with what was called the "Red menace." Even some of Hollywood's biggest stars were accused of having a Communist connection. Being a beloved actor, director, producer, or the scribe of an Oscar-winning script, in some instances, didn't always protect a person. Accusations of being a Communist could instantly destroy a career. Actual blacklists were circulated among the studios, listing people who could not work in movies because of their supposed politics. Most of the allegations against these people were based on nothing more than innuendo. Congressional hearings were held in Washington, D.C., Los Angeles, and elsewhere to root such people out. The House Un-American Activities Committee (HUAC) demanded that witnesses name names of suspected Communists under the threat that the entire industry could be denounced as sympathizers. A group of Hollywood writers, producers, and directors who refused to testify were indicted and became known as the Hollywood Ten. A number of stars flew to Washington, D.C., to protest the "Red scare" tactics, to no avail. The industry continued to make movies, some with a degree of self-consciousness and self-censure that surely impacted the results. Among the films released during that time, there was a share with anti-Communist themes.

By the end of the decade, the movie industry was once more becoming as international as it had been before World War II. However, the studios were not making as much money from these foreign territories as they had earlier. In the parts of Europe most devastated by the war, distributors were not permitted to take their receipts out of the region. Instead, they had to reinvest the money in that country, building facilities or making new movies.

By the end of the decade, with theater attendance in the United States dropping while television set sales were rising, the studios began to see that they had a problem they needed to contend with. They began to downsize, shedding thousands of workers and scaling back production on their own lots. Even big stars found themselves suddenly out of work.

In April 1948, producer Alexander Korda licensed the right to air twenty-four of the movies from his library on a New York City television station, marking the first sale of movies to TV. Up until that time, most studios had initially refused to sell content to TV, viewing the new medium as a fierce competitor. Others immediately understood the importance of Korda's actions. Paramount, for instance, followed his lead, becoming the first to sell movies to a station in Los Angeles, a station that also became the first to carry paid movie advertising.

With the advent of television news, production of theatrical newsreels, which required longer lead times to develop, had to change or wind down. Instead of going for breaking news stories, theatrical newsreels soon became entertainment news vehicles, promoting upcoming films and covering star appearances at premieres and other noteworthy events.

By the spring of 1948, RKO, now under the ownership of multimillionaire Howard Hughes, became the first of the major studios to sign an agreement with the government to sell its movie theaters. On February 25, 1949, Paramount Pictures signed a consent decree to separate its movie theaters from its production and distribution businesses. This process would be known after that as the Paramount decree. Later in 1949, Warner Bros. and Fox also agreed to sell their theaters. The end of the forties was truly the end of an era for movies.

The Hollywood Ten

Alvah Bessie . . . . .Screenwriter for WB and other studios. He was nominated for an Oscar for writing *Objective, Burma!*, 1945, before being blacklisted and imprisoned in 1950.

Herbert J. Biberman . . . . .American director of B movies in the 1930s, he was blacklisted and sentenced to six months in prison in 1950. His primary accusers were Budd Schulberg [Oscar winner for Writing (story & screenplay) *On The Waterfront*, 1954] and Edward Dmytryk.

Lester Cole .Screenwriter and co-founder of the Screen Writers Guild in 1933. He served a year in prison after being blacklisted in 1947.

Edward Dmytryk . . . . .Nominated for an Oscar for directing *Crossfire*, 1947, then sentenced to a year in prison for contempt of Congress in 1948. Following his imprisonment, he was blacklisted but directed three films in the United Kingdom. He returned to the United States in 1951, this time as a "friendly" witness, and his name was dropped from the blacklist. His most notable film was *The Caine Mutiny*, 1954.

Ring Lardner Jr. . . . . .Oscar winning screenwriter for *Woman of the Year*, 1942 (co-author credit), he spent a year in prison and was blacklisted until the mid-1960s. His big comeback was the screenplay to *M*A*S*H,* for which he won his second Oscar in 1970.

John Howard Lawson . . . . .Screenwriter and co-founder of the Screen Writers Guild in 1933. He was nominated for an Oscar for original story for *Blockade*, 1938, then sentenced to a year in prison and blacklisted in 1948.

Albert Maltz . . . . .Nominated for an Oscar for the screenplay *Pride of the Marines*, 1945, and winner, that year, of a Special Award Oscar for the short *The House I Live In*. He was blacklisted and sentenced to one year in jail in 1947. In 1950, his screenplay for *Broken Arrow* was nominated for an Oscar, under the name of Michael Blankfort. In 1991, the WGA restored the screenplay credit to Maltz.

Samuel Ornitz . . . . .An early organizer and board member of the Screen Actors Guild. Although he hadn't had a screen credit in two years, in 1947 he was called to testify before HUAC then spent a year in prison for contempt of Congress.

Adrian Scott . . . . .Screenwriter/producer, his name was provided to the HUAC by Edward Dmytryk. He was sentenced to a year in prison, blacklisted, and never worked in films again.

Dalton Trumbo. . . . . .Nominated for an Oscar for the screenplay *Kitty Foyle*, 1940. In 1943 he was cited for contempt of Congress and served a ten-month jail term. He wrote the Oscar winning story *Roman Holiday*, 1953 (under the "front" Ian McLellan Hunter), and the Oscar winning story *The Brave One*, 1956 (under the "alias" Robert Rich).

PRODUCTION SPOTLIGHT

War and Escapism: Film Noir and the Actors Studio

On June 13, 1942, the White House under President Franklin D. Roosevelt announced the creation of the United States Office of War Information (OWI). As part of the Victory Program, it was designed to help achieve total mobilization for the war effort. Popular radio commentator Elmer Davis was appointed as the first head of OWI, with a mandate to launch publicity campaigns that would get the American message across at home and abroad. The OWI also coordinated government information campaigns and was a direct connection to the media (print and radio) as well as to the motion picture industry. It was OWI's job to sell the war, to win the hearts and minds of those it addressed, and to make sure it was American propaganda that was disseminated. Its mandate also included making people aware of enemy spies and encouraging women to go to work in support of the war effort.

Through the Bureau of Motion Pictures (BMP), the OWI issued guidelines to Hollywood studios in the form of questions such as "Will this picture help win the war?" "What war information problem does it seek to clarify, dramatize, or interpret?" "If it is an 'escape' picture, will it harm the war effort by creating a false picture of America, her allies, or the world we live in?" "Does the picture tell the truth or will the young people of today have reason to say they were misled by propaganda?"

The BMP office in Hollywood was run by former newsman Lowell Mellett and his deputy, Nelson Poynter. They put out a call for all studios to submit scripts to them in advance for consultation on a voluntary basis. While this outraged some and smacked of more censorship, most studios found ways to accommodate the request. Mellett, Poynter, and others essentially passed judgment on the war-related content of each movie brought before them. In their *Government*

1940s Movie Censorship: A Brief History

In 1942 the United States Office of War Information (OWI) is formed and regulates political movie content through its Bureau of Motion Pictures (BMP). The Production Code Administration and BMP don't always agree. Where the PCA censors unsuccessfully demand changes to the story of the affair in Casablanca, *the BMP praises the film for its positive American political message.*

William Hays resigns as head of the Motion Picture Producers and Distributors of America (MPPDA) and is succeeded by former head of the U.S. Chamber of Commerce, Eric Johnston. Johnston renames the MPPDA the Motion Picture Association of America (MPAA).

Information Manual for the Motion Picture Industry, they urged depictions of a united America where workers and employers were standing together and making sacrifices for the war effort. They asked that combat films include a multiethnic cast of characters to show the diversity of America. All American allies in the war, such as England, France, and even Russia, were to be portrayed favorably. Nationalist China was to be shown as a liberal society. And even the Soviet Union was to be shown as "a heroic ally." The manual even added: "Yes, we Americans reject Communism, but we do not reject our Russian ally."

The 1942 movie *Little Tokyo,* which dealt with Japanese internment, upset the BMP and led to a crackdown on Hollywood. Still, many of the movie moguls were immigrant Jews, who were deeply disturbed by what was going on in Europe, so they willingly worked with the government. Every studio except Paramount submitted all their scripts to the BMP. Poynter or one of his crew had standing appointments at the studios' offices each week to discuss their views. This was not all done out of patriotism. OWI had a relationship with the Office of Censorship, which controlled the approval of movies to be released outside the United States. In some cases, when a country was liberated, OWI went in and exhibited movies that it had approved, and then held the proceeds in its accounts. This money wasn't released to the studios until the bureau was happy with their behavior.

No studio would make a movie that could not play both domestically and internationally, so although the OWI and BMP requests were voluntary, they were widely followed until the time the OWI office was closed in 1944. One of the films the BMP liked a great deal was Warner Bros.' *Casablanca.* Among other things, the official report praised the picture because "America is shown as the haven of the oppressed and homeless. Refugees want to come to the United States because here they are assured of freedom, democratic privileges and immunity from fear. The love and esteem with which this country is regarded by oppressed peoples should make audiences aware of their responsibilities as Americans to uphold this reputation and fight fascism with all that is in them." Another film inspired by the war effort was *Hollywood Canteen* in 1944, which was Hollywood's response to *Stage Door Canteen* of 1943, featuring several Broadway stars. These were extravaganzas, loaded with big-name actors and filled with wispy plots that were meant to convey a sense of patriotism. The BMP also acted as a movie distributor for some films such as *Liberation of Rome, Message from Malta, Wings Up, Recognition of the Japanese Zero Fighter,* and *Dover.*

No film was better propaganda or did more box office than *This Is the Army* (1943), which started out as a stage show. It was the creation primarily of songwriter and composer Irving Berlin. On a visit to his old military base, the former sergeant came up with the idea of restaging his play *Yip Yip Yaphank,* about the military. His idea was approved by Gen. George Marshall, who felt it would be good for wartime morale. The show opened on Broadway on July 4, 1942, and was a big hit. It was then taken on the road, playing across the country and finishing on the West Coast, where many members of the cast segued to the motion picture version. Warner Bros. won the bidding war for film rights, paying $250,000. All profits, as well as the salaries of producers Jack Warner and Hal Wallis, director Michael Curtiz, and screenwriter Casey Robinson, went to the Army Emergency Relief Fund. The movie, which premiered with a charity event costing $55 per ticket, played road show engagements for much of its release. It became one of the biggest-grossing films of the decade.

From Pearl Harbor in December 1941 until late in 1944, the studios were challenged by shortages, even though the government considered movies a necessary war industry. For instance, in May 1942, the War Production Board placed a ceiling of $5,000 on new construction for each movie. The government suggested instead that studios rely more on process shots and the use of miniatures. These rules were especially tough on independents, which did not have the same stockpiles of material as the majors. In 1943 the rule was modified, giving studios quarterly budgets so that they could decide more freely where and how to use those resources. Among the films that resulted were 1942's *Wake Island,* 1943's *Guadalcanal Diary,* 1943's *Bataan,* 1944's *Winged Victory* and *Thirty Seconds over Tokyo,* and 1945's *Operation Burma.* By late 1944, there was gasoline rationing on the West Coast, which eliminated most location shooting.

Congress cut funding for the OWI in 1943. That resulted in the closing of the BMP office in Hollywood in 1944. After that, the OWI operated mostly overseas, working to undermine enemy morale. Among other things, it created the Voice of America radio service, which continued on even after the OWI was disbanded by an executive order in August 1945 and its foreign work was turned over to the State Department.

Of course, Hollywood didn't just make war movies during the war. There was also great demand for escapist fare to take ticket buyers' minds as far away from the troubles of the day as possible. These films included comedies starring such teams as Bing Crosby and Bob Hope, and Abbott and Costello. They also included bigger and even more sensational musicals. The huge hit of 1944 was the musical comedy *Going My Way,* starring Bing Crosby. In 1945 musicals were again among the top-grossing movies. The most popular of these were *Anchors Aweigh,* with Gene Kelly and Frank Sinatra in his big-screen debut; *The Dolly Sisters,* starring Betty Grable; *Thrill of a Romance,* with Esther Williams; and the Walter Lang–directed musical remake of *State Fair. The Jolson Story* was a big hit in 1946, as were *Blue Skies,* with Bing Crosby and Fred Astaire; *The Harvey Girls,* with Angela Lansbury and Judy Garland; and *The Ziegfeld Follies,* starring William Powell, with additional appearances by an array of stars, including Judy Garland, Fred Astaire, Red Skelton, and Lucille Ball. At MGM, producer Arthur Freed was an important proponent of these escapist musicals. He put Broadway director and choreographer Busby Berkeley behind the camera for the 1942 hit *For Me and My Gal.* In 1944 he brought in former Broadway director Vicente Minnelli to make *Meet Me in St. Louis.* Freed was also behind 1947's *Summer Holiday,* 1948's *The Pirate,* Busby Berkeley's 1949 film *Take Me out to the Ball Game*, and, also in 1949, Stanley Donen's *On the Town,* starring Gene Kelly. Danny Kaye starred in the 1947 musical comedy *The Secret Life of Walter Mitty,* and Judy Garland was the star of *In the Good Old Summertime* in 1949.

As the war ended, there was also a surge of movies in the film noir style. These films were shaped by the horrors of war and followed in the wake of downbeat crime dramas. They were dark, with an oppressive visual style, and strayed far from the Hollywood convention of a happy ending. These movies explored themes of paranoia, betrayal, suspicion, greed, and desire in a world where morality was no longer the mandate. Some say *Citizen Kane* was the first

Breakdown of a 1940 Production Dollar
Casablanca, **1940**

Play	2%
All writers	5%
Director	7%
Star salaries	13%
Subtotal above-the-line	**27%**
Set builders	1.7%
Camera crew	1.0%
Makeup and hairdressers	0.9%
Cutters	0.4%
Film stock	0.8%
Developing and printing film stock	1.0%
Studio overhead	21.5%
Other	45.6%
Subtotal below-the-line	**73%**
Total	**100%**

Percentages computed from dollar budget breakdown on page 241.

film noir ever made, while others credit the early American works of Alfred Hitchcock. Other notable noir directors of the era included Billy Wilder, Fritz Lang, Otto Preminger, and Robert Siodmak. The growth of film noir was attributed to the emergence of crime novels in both the United States and France, such as *The Blue Dahlia, The Dark Corner, The Postman Always Rings Twice, Gilda, The Killers,* and *The Big Sleep.*

The forties had ushered in more realistic movies, and as the decade came to a close, there was also a movement for more realistic acting. In 1947 a group of actors and directors including Lee Strasberg and others formed the Actors Studio in New York City. Among the first teachers was director Elia Kazan. Famous early graduates included Marlon Brando, Paul Newman, Montgomery Clift, Rod Steiger, James Dean, Eva Marie Saint, Geraldine Page, Carroll Baker, Kim Stanley, Shirley Knight, and Joanne Woodward, as well as playwrights Edward Albee and Tennessee Williams. Strasberg had helped form the Actors Studio to pass on the concepts of Konstantin Stanislavski and the Moscow Art Theatre. Stanislavski had spent years developing an approach to realistic acting that was meant to provide "creative inspiration" even to those who were not very artistic. Its influence was seen in Method acting in such classics as the 1950s films *On the Waterfront* and *A Streetcar Named Desire.* The Method went on to influence the generations that followed.

U.S. INDUSTRY PRODUCTION STATISTICS, 1940s
Equivalent 2005 $s/(Unadjusted $s)

$20.4 Million ($1.9 million)
Average production cost of films featured in this chapter

$4.2 Million ($300,000)
Average production cost of all films released in 1940

Top 10 Critically Acclaimed Lead Actors of the 1940s

Rank	Actor Name
1	Gary Cooper
2	Laurence Olivier
3	James Stewart
4	Fredric March
5	Bing Crosby
6	James Cagney
7	Ronald Colman
8	Orson Welles
9	Ray Milland
10	Fred Astaire

Rank	Actress Name
1	Ingrid Bergman
2	Greer Garson
3	Olivia de Haviland
4	Jennifer Jones
5	Jane Wyman
6	Barbara Stanwyck
7	Joan Crawford
8	Loretta Young
9	Joan Fontaine
10	Ginger Rogers

See Note to the Reader for selection criteria.

Index of Top Feature Film Directors Included in This Chapter

1	William Wyler	*Mrs. Miniver*
		The Best Years of Our Lives
2	Leo McCarey	*Going My Way*
		The Bells of St. Mary's
3	Michael Curtiz	*Yankee Doodle Dandy*
		Casablanca
		Life with Father
4	Sam Wood	*For Whom the Bell Tolls*
		The Pride of the Yankees
5	Ben Sharpsteen, Hamilton Luske, David Hand	*Pinocchio*
6	David Hand	*Bambi*
7	Howard Hawks	*Sergeant York*
8	Cecil B. DeMille	*Samson and Delilah*
		Reap the Wild Wind
9	King Vidor	*Duel in the Sun*
10	Ben Sharpsteen (Production Supervisor + 10 Directors)	*Fantasia*

See Note to the Reader for selection criteria.

Comparison of Five MGM 1940s Movies
Initial Release Domestic vs. Foreign Splits

Unadjusted $s

Film	Initial Release	Domestic Rentals	Domestic % of Total	Foreign Rentals	Foreign % of Total
The Philadelphia Story	1941	$2,374,000	73%	$885,000	27%
Mrs. Miniver	1942	$5,358,000	60%	$3,520,000	40%
Meet Me in St. Louis	1944	$5,016,000	76%	$1,623,630	24%
Easter Parade	1948	$4,144,000	70%	$1,774,134	30%
Battleground	1949	$4,722,000	72%	$1,807,243	28%

Eleven of the Top 15 Noir Films Are Released in the 1940s, 20 Percent Directed by Alfred Hitchcock

Top 15 Noir Films
All-Release Domestic Box Office, 1920–2005
Equivalent 2005 $s/(Unadjusted $s) in Millions of $s

Rank	Film	Distributor	Initial Release	Domestic Box Office	Director
1	Dark Passage	Warner Bros.	1947	$194.2/($13.3)	Delmer Daves
2	Leave Her to Heaven	20th Century-Fox	1945	$186.5/($12.2)	John M. Stahl
3	Spellbound	United Artists	1945	$168.7/($11.1)	Alfred Hitchcock
4	Notorious	RKO	1946	$162.8/($10.7)	Alfred Hitchcock
5	The Postman Always Rings Twice	MGM	1946	$135.7/($8.9)	Tay Garnett
6	Double Indemnity	Paramount	1944	$111.3/($5.6)	Billy Wilder
7	Suspicion	RKO	1941	$102.6/($4.0)	Alfred Hitchcock
8	The Big Sleep	Warner Bros.	1946	$101.7/($6.7)	Howard Hawks
9	The Dark Mirror	Universal	1946	$93.3/($6.1)	Robert Siodmak
10	Detective Story	Paramount	1951	$84.9/($6.2)	William Wyler
11	Scarlet Street	Universal	1946	$84.8/($5.6)	Fritz Lang
12	Sunset Boulevard	Paramount	1950	$72.8/($5.2)	Billy Wilder
13	The Third Man	SRO	1950	$67.4/($5.4)	Carol Reed
14	The Maltese Falcon	Warner Bros.	1941	$57.0/($2.2)	John Huston
15	Touch of Evil	Universal	1958	$55.2/($27.9)	Orson Welles

Academy Award winner for Best Picture: none.

Three of the Top 15 Bio-Drama Films Are Released in the 1940s

Top 15 Bio-Drama Films
All-Release Domestic Box Office 1920–2005
Equivalent 2005 $s/(Unadjusted $s) in Millions of $s

Rank	Film	Distributor	Initial Release	Domestic Box Office	Production Cost
1	Sergeant York	Warner Bros.	1941	$361.3/($14.5)	$31.8/($2.4)
2	Lawrence of Arabia*	Columbia	1962	$290.2/($44.5)	$97.0/($15.0)
3	Patton*	20th Century-Fox	1970	$255.4/($61.7)	$63.5/($12.6)
4	The Pride of the Yankees	RKO	1942	$191.3/($8.5)	not available
5	A Beautiful Mind*	Universal	2001	$189.0/($170.7)	$86.0/($78.0)
6	Boys Town	MGM	1938	$175.1/($6.3)	$10.7/($0.8)
7	Coal Miner's Daughter	Universal	1980	$160.1/($67.2)	not available
8	A Man for All Seasons*	Columbia	1966	$151.3/($28.3)	$12.1/($2.0)
9	The Great Caruso	MGM	1951	$137.3/($10.1)	$13.9/($1.9)
10	Joan of Arc	RKO	1948	$132.7/($9.1)	$40.5/($5.0)
11	8 Mile	Universal	2002	$128.8/($116.8)	$44.5/($41.0)
12	Chariots of Fire*	Warner Bros.	1981	$128.6/($59.0)	$12.1/($6.0)
13	The Eddy Duchin Story	Columbia	1956	$128.0/($11.8)	not available
14	The Jazz Singer	Warner Bros.	1927	$126.5/($3.9)	$4.7/($0.4)
15	Walk the Line	20th Century-Fox	2005	$119.5/($119.5)	$28.0/($28.0)

*Academy Award Winner for Best Picture.

The Show Business of Walt Disney

Walter Elias Disney was not like the other moguls who arose during the era of the studio system, nor were his company's strategies similar to those of competitors such as Warner Bros., Paramount, and MGM. Most of these other studios were run by outspoken Jewish immigrants who lived a flamboyant lifestyle. Walt Disney, on the other hand, was a Protestant from the Midwest who preferred his privacy. Disney's success did not come by building the careers of living, breathing stars or, for many years, even by controlling his own distribution like all the other majors. Instead, what Walt Disney delivered was first-rate entertainment boosted by his keen interest in innovation. His fascination with sound and color informed everything his company did, from making movies to selling them and screening them effectively before audiences. His biggest star never called in sick because he was a wisecracking animated mouse with a high-pitched squeaky voice (which Disney provided himself for many years).

Disney was a visionary driven by a deeply personal passion for the work. To get away from home, Disney served as a Red Cross ambulance driver in France just after World War I ended. He painted signs for the canteen and designs for the trucks. When he returned home, Disney got a job as an artist at Kansas City Film Ad where he worked on short cartoons known as Newman Laugh-O-Grams. These cartoon shorts played before the feature at local theaters. Disney raised enough capital to establish his own company in 1922, retaining the Laugh-O-Gram name. One purchaser went bankrupt, however, and without sufficient revenue from other sales, Disney was forced to close that studio in 1923 after making a combination live-action/animated film called *Alice's Wonderland.* With that film in hand as a sample, Disney set off for Los Angeles, California, where his brother, Roy, was recuperating from tuberculosis. Two months after his arrival, at age twenty-one, Walt, in partnership with his brother, made a deal with Margaret J. Winkler, a New York–based states rights distributor, to produce one cartoon per month for her based on *Alice's Wonderland.* By 1927 Disney was concentrating his energies on the production side of the business, leaving the animation to his staff. He subsequently signed a one-year contract with Charles Mintz, who had married Margaret Winkler in 1924. Disney's next cartoon, *Oswald the Lucky Rabbit,* was very successful, but the Oswald name belonged to Mintz, who used that fact to hire away Disney's best animators and take over production of the Oswald series. That infuriated Disney so much that he set out to find other collaborators and create new cartoon heroes. As the result of collaboration between Disney and animator Ub Iwerks, Mickey Mouse was born in 1928.

The Disney brothers, Walt and Roy, started work on the first Mickey Mouse cartoons without a distributor just as *The Jazz Singer* opened. While some in Hollywood were conflicted about silent versus sound movies, Disney saw the value of the new technology immediately and decided that for the Mickey animations to have real impact he needed to add sound. The first Mickey cartoon, *Steamboat Willie* (1928), had a soundtrack that mixed traditional tunes such as "Yankee Doodle" and "Dixie" with sound effects including washboards and bells, all synchronized to make the sounds fit the action. The Disneys still had no distributor, however. The manager at Manhattan's Colony Theater in New York offered Disney a two-week run for the short film. It was a sensation, and due to its success, Disney was able to negotiate a distribution agreement with Pat Powers's company, Celebrity Pictures, which wanted the cartoons to help promote its Powers Cinephone system. Believing that Disney likely would not renew the distribution agreement, Powers offered Ub Iwerks a series of his own, which Iwerks promptly accepted. Iwerks sold his partnership with the Disney brothers for $2,920 and left. Just as Mintz had done earlier, Powers had underestimated Walt Disney. Iwerks was replaced with a stable of new animators, and a new distribution agreement was struck with Columbia Pictures.

Now that he had successfully utilized new sound technology, Disney began exploring color. Most of the systems he saw were unsatisfactory and inconsistent in quality. Then Technicolor came out with its three-strip color system in 1932. Roy Disney resisted the transition to color because he thought it would raise costs too much, but Walt insisted. So Disney made a two-year deal for the exclusive use of Technicolor in animation, forcing competitors such as Max Fleischer to use the two-color process Cinecolor, which Walt considered inferior. Disney's sound and color film, *Flowers and Trees,* part of the Silly Symphony series, was released in July 1932. It was the first commercially released film of any kind in the new Technicolor and was a critical and commercial success, raising interest in the entire Silly Symphony series. It received the first Oscar for Best Short Subject: Cartoons. After that, all Silly Symphony cartoons were produced in color. However, Disney kept making Mickey Mouse cartoons in black and white until 1935 because he wasn't convinced that they needed the additional boost.

Disney also brought a new level of efficiency to the making of animated films, a long and labor-intensive process. He organized his company between those who wrote gags and those who executed the animation. He innovated the storyboarding of his entire project in advance. Disney set up his own training program for artists, most of whom were recent art school graduates. They studied the movement of everything from people to animals to bubbles breaking. He wanted them to see every nuance so those nuances could be reproduced just as they appear in life.

In *The Three Little Pigs,* an eight-minute color cartoon, Disney gave each of the characters in the classic fairy tale their own personality, including the villainous wolf. Disney refused to license popular music for a high fee, so he created his own. Members of the staff contributed to both the melody and lyrics. His employee Frank Churchill, a former organist at silent movie theaters, wrote his first song for the film, called "Who's Afraid of the Big Bad Wolf?" That song became a huge popular hit.

The success of *The Three Little Pigs* convinced Disney to produce the first full-length animated feature, even though a chorus of naysayers said no one would sit through a long cartoon. He selected *Snow White and the Seven Dwarfs* as his first project. It would take longer (four years) and cost more (roughly $1.5 million) than expected. Along the way Disney would mortgage everything he owned to keep the project going, prompting some to call it "Disney's Folly." Disney adapted the Grimm Brothers' story, adding comedy touches and music and developing minor characters, including the dwarfs. Snow White and the prince are made to look and act as human as possible, while all of the other players look and sound like cartoon characters. Frank Churchill composed the score, including the hits "Whistle While You Work" and "Someday My

Prince Will Come." The manager of Radio City Music Hall was shown an incomplete version and booked it immediately. It was a huge critical and commercial hit. Radio City held it over for five more weeks. By the end of 1938, it had grossed more than $8 million in worldwide rentals and was ranked at the time as the second-highest-grossing film after the 1925 epic *Ben-Hur*.

Disney immediately plunged into more animated features while continuing his short subject program. In 1940 he released his second full-length cartoon, the classic Italian story *Pinocchio*. The same year the innovative *Fantasia*, which starred Mickey Mouse as the Sorcerer's Apprentice, came out. Due to extenuating circumstances, both films lost money on their initial releases. *Pinocchio* suffered from the fact that the war was forcing the close of overseas markets, and *Fantasia* was a box office disappointment due not only to limited foreign revenues but also to the costly distribution of Fantasound in most domestic theaters. Both would find added life, however, in rereleases every few years for decades thereafter.

Disney released two more feature-length cartoons in short order, *Dumbo* in 1941 and *Bambi* in 1942. In 1949 he released his first true-life adventure, *Seal Island*. He would continue to make such live-action nature shorts, featuring stories built around images of real animals in their native habitat as captured by his cameramen. *The Living Desert* (1953) and *The Vanishing Prairie* (1954), both documentaries, won special Academy Awards. Disney also found new revenue from licensing and merchandising. It began in the 1930s, as Walt Disney later recalled in an account of the company's history: "A fellow kept hanging around my hotel waving $300 at me and saying that he wanted to put the mouse on paper tablets for school children. As usual, Roy and I needed money, so I took the $300." That led to all kinds of licensed products, from watches to figurines to books. Mickey Mouse was also the star of a daily cartoon in newspapers.

Disney's studios were also committed to the war effort for several years in the 1940s. At the request of the State Department, Disney made films set in South America, where the U.S. government sought to counter a perceived pro-Nazi sentiment, with such films as *Saludos Amigos* in 1943 and *The Three Caballeros* in 1944. The company also produced propaganda and training films for the military. After the war, the studio was quickly up and running again with new civilian productions. In 1946 the first full-length live-action/animated film, *Song of the South,* was released. Then, to free up frozen funds in the United Kingdom, Disney made the live-action family feature *Treasure Island* (1950) in Britain. He also returned to animated features with *Cinderella* and made his first TV special that Christmas.

After having distributed its movies through Columbia, RKO, and others, Disney finally took over its own theatrical domestic distribution in the 1950s to gain greater control of his product's destiny. This move also significantly increased revenues. Disney mixed new animation with rereleases, which were very profitable since the cost of making the movie was already covered. In 1955 he released the animated *Lady and the Tramp* and in 1959 *Sleeping Beauty*. There were also new live-action films such as *20,000 Leagues Under the Sea* in 1954 and *The Shaggy Dog* in 1959.

Disney pioneered the use of Audio-Animatronics, first at Disneyland's enchanted Tiki Room in 1963, and then at the 1964 New York World's Fair, the same year *Mary Poppins* was released to great acclaim.

As television arrived, Disney refused to join other studios in selling or licensing his movie library for exhibition via the new medium. Unlike those who refused out of fear, Disney refused because he had a strategy. He knew his kid-friendly features could be profitably re-released every seven years or so, if they didn't appear on TV in the interim. That didn't mean Disney wasn't a fan of TV. In fact, he used his willingness to produce for TV to fuel another longtime dream, creating a new generation of theme parks. Disney enjoyed taking his daughters to parks, but he generally found these parks to be dirty and uninviting. He especially disliked how rude the people in service positions often were. He wanted to build a theme park that would be clean and family-friendly, enticing children and adults alike. Nobody thought it was a good idea at first. All of Disney's bankers and independent backers refused to put money toward this dream, even as Walt and Roy traveled around personally making presentations. They finally struck gold at the American Broadcasting Company, then run by Leonard Goldenson. ABC, at the time, was ranked a distant third behind CBS and NBC in the race to attract an audience to its shows. Goldenson wanted Disney product, so ABC loaned Disney the money to build the first park. The deal was structured in such a way that Disney could buy out ABC later if it wanted to, which it ultimately did in 1955 for $19 billion. The loan allowed Disney to build his dream theme park in Anaheim, California, a short drive from Los Angeles. On October 27, 1954, the Walt Disney anthology series, called *Disneyland,* premiered on ABC, and was hosted by Walt himself. In 1961 it would change its name to *The Wonderful World of Disney.* In time, this show became one of the longest-running TV anthology series in history. *The Mickey Mouse Club* began as a five-day-a-week series on ABC in 1955, offering a mix of talented child performers, cartoons, and short comedy and drama sequences. It was an instant sensation. Soon Americans were wearing Mickey Mouse ears. The show, along with the Disney miniseries *Davy Crockett* (begun as part of the Disneyland series in 1954 and 1955), also generated a whole new licensing and merchandising business, creating thousands of products, most aimed at children. In July 1955 the Disneyland theme park opened and, despite some early problems, the 160-acre fantasy land was another hit. It became America's best-known, best-attended, and most profitable amusement park.

In 1959, when NBC was just introducing color to television, they pursued Disney for content. After four seasons on the air, ABC and Disney could not come to terms on a renewal of *The Mickey Mouse Club,* so it was canceled. Disney then made a deal with NBC where the full color version of the show *Disneyland* moved in 1961 under the new name *The Wonderful World of Disney.*

Disney passed away on December 15, 1966, but his company continues on. He refused to call himself an artist, insisting instead that he was in show business. However, Walt Disney did create art, and he also inspired many others to mix their art with commerce, leaving a lasting legacy. He was known to say, "If you can dream it, you can do it. . . . Always remember that this whole thing was started with a dream and a mouse."

Actors of the 1940s: Comparison of Salaries and Profit Participations
Equivalent 2005 $s/(Unadjusted $s)

Actor	Film	Initial Release	Salary
James Cagney	*Yankee Doodle Dandy*	1942	**$7.8 million including p/p*** ($650,000 total including p/p: $150,000/per film salary + 10% p/p over $1.5 million)
Katharine Hepburn	*The Philadelphia Story*	1940	**$3.0 million including story rights** ($225,000 total including $75,000/salary + $150,000 profit on story rights bought for $25,000 and sold to MGM for $175,000)
Gary Cooper	*For Whom the Bells Toll*	1943	**$2.3 million** (Estimated total $200,000 paid at $12,500/week)
James Stewart	*It's a Wonderful Life*	1946	**$1.8 million** ($175,000 per film fee)
Myrna Loy Teresa Wright	*The Best Years of Our Lives*	1946	**$1.5 million each** ($150,000/per film fee each)
Barbara Stanwyck Fred MacMurray	*Double Indemnity*	1944	**$1.5 million each** ($150,000/per film fee each)
Irene Dunne	*Life with Father*	1947	**$1.3 million** ($150,000/per film fee)
Joseph Cotten	*Duel in the Sun*	1946	**$1.3 million** ($150,000/per film fee)

*Profit participation.

A Sampling of Movie Star Earnings, 1946
Equivalent 2005 $s/(Unadjusted $s)

Actor	Annual Earnings	Actor	Annual Earnings
Ginger Rogers	**$2.9 Million**/($292,159)	Lana Turner	**$2.3 Million**/($226,000)
Barbara Stanwyck	**$2.6 Million**/($256,666)	Betty Grable	**$2.1 Million**/($205,000)

General Corporate vs. Movie Business Salaries, 1947
Pretax* (1947 maximum individual tax rate 91 percent)
Equivalent 2005 $s/(Unadjusted $s)

Name	Job	Annual Earnings
Louis B. Mayer	Managing director of production, MGM	**$15.8 million**/Annual Earnings, 1947; **$20.7 million** lump sum settlement/ $1.8 million in 1947 (highest paid executive in America). Terminated 8/31/51 with a lump sum settlement of $2,750,000 paid 12/14/51
Charles P. Skouras	Owner, National Theaters	**$7.1 million**/($810,000 salary plus bonus)
Vincent Riggio	President, American Tobacco Co.	**$4.2 million**/($484,202)
E. H. Little	President, Colgate-Palmolive-Peet Co.	**$3.1 million**/($350,000)
A.A. Somerville	VP, R.T. Vanderbilt Co. (chemicals)	**$2.8 million**/($319,398)
Seton Porter	President, National Distillers Products Corp.	**$2.7 million**/($310,000)
William Randolph Hearst	Newspapers	**$2.6 million**/($300,000)
Theodore Seltzer	President, Bengue, Inc. (Ben-Gay)	**$2.6 million**/($295,613)
Eugene Grace	President, Bethlehem Steel	**$2.6 million**/($293,279)
G.A. Bryant	President, Austin Co. (a Cleveland building firm)	**$2.4 million**/($270,789)

*Note: See tax rate table in Note to Reader.

A Sampling of Director/Producer Earnings, 1946
Equivalent 2005 $s/(Unadjusted $s)

Director/Producer	Annual Earnings
Leo McCarey (Director)	**$3.6 Million**/($355,426)
Walter Wanger (Producer)	**$2.8 Million**/($282,899)

Casablanca, 1943 Budget Breakdown
Equivalent 2005 $s /(Unadjusted $s)

Play	$0.2 million/($20,000)
All writers	$0.6 million/($53,000)
Director, Michael Curtiz	$0.8 million/($73,400)
Stars, salaries	$1.6 million/($134,334)
(Humphrey Bogart, $36,667; Ingrid Bergman, $25,000; Claude Rains, $22,000; Paul Henreid and Conrad Veidt, $25,000/ea; Marcel Dalio, $667)	
Subtotal above-the-line	$3.2 million/($280,734)
Set builders	$0.2 million/($18,000)
Camera crew	$0.1 million/($10,873)
Makeup and hairdressers	$0.1 million/($9,100)
Cutters	$0.1 million/($4,630)
Film stock	$0.1 million/($8,000)
Developing and printing film stock	$0.1 million/($10,500)
Studio overhead	$2.5 million/($223,822)
Other	$5.3 million/($473,341)
Subtotal below-the-line	$8.5 million/($1,039,000)
Total production cost	$11.7 million/($1,039,000)

DISTRIBUTION OVERVIEW

Sex, Censorship, and the Relentless Rules of the Hays Office

Among the greatest challenges to distributing movies successfully in the 1930s and 1940s was the intense censorship that the industry had imposed on itself. This voluntary agreement to hold all scripts to a certain moral standard caused incalculable agony for many writers, directors, and studio executives, who often saw censors cut the most dramatic portions or the most realistic elements from their films. Guidelines had existed since the very beginning, but it was only a few months before the stock market crash of 1929 that the movie industry kicked censorship into high gear.

Sex had been increasingly present in movies until the Hays Code (also called the Production Code), established in 1930, created a formula studios had to adhere to, called the "law of compensating values." This document dictated that while there could be sex in a movie, it could never be condoned. In the end, those who indulged in any conduct that was perceived to be evil had to be punished. The Hays office provided reams of rules dealing with the use of profanity, vulgarity, obscenity, blasphemy, and racy costume design. Each script was scrutinized and notes were sent to the studio, most citing violations of the spirit of the code. Some words were forbidden from being uttered on-screen, including *fairy, madam, pansy, tart, nuts, hell, damn*, and *chippie*. The rule against obscenity in songs meant that many works by the biggest composers were banned, including at times some of Cole Porter's. Even use of the phrase "Oh God" was banned as blasphemy. A lot of time was spent discussing costumes that exposed the female body. There was to be no showing of women's breasts in a sexual manner. There was an exception to that rule in the racist society that imposed these values: African native women could dance about topless. It was also unacceptable to show a prisoner electrocuted or a baby being born. There could be no mention of prostitution or social and sexual diseases. For fear that moviegoers might copy such actions, filmmakers were not allowed to show murder techniques in detail, even in the context of a murder mystery.

Even the biggest movies of the era faced censorship battles, including *Gone with the Wind* in 1939, any film starring Mae West or the Marx Brothers, *Casablanca* in 1943, and *For Whom the Bell Tolls* also in 1943. In a memo sent to studio boss Jack Warner on May 19, 1942, regarding *Casablanca,* censor Joseph Breen demanded that a change be made in the script: "We cannot approve the suggestion that Captain Renault makes a practice of seducing the women to whom he grants visas. Any such inference of illicit sex could not be approved."

Breen and the Hays Office not only censored on their own behalf but also showed studios where foreign or state censors would disagree with a scene. In England, a husband and wife had to be depicted sleeping in twin beds rather than in one bed together. That was applied in the United States as well. Women could not show they had a navel; divorced couples had to reunite; all criminals were caught and punished; and war was always to be fought by Americans for a glorious cause.

The greatest directors, from Alfred Hitchcock to Billy Wilder, as well as the top playwrights and studio executives, all spent a great deal of time and effort figuring out how to get around code restrictions. In addition, there was a process in place for studios to appeal a Hays order if they were vehemently opposed to the requested changes. If denied the Seal of Approval from the Production Code Administration, the producers could appear before a board in New York City composed of the presidents of the studios, four independent film producers, and six theater owners. However, few appeals were ever made because studios knew that the odds were stacked against them. Some clever filmmakers found that they could get around the code at times by making musicals with outrageously skimpy costumes, as Busby Berkeley did, or by making provocative costumes part of a religious epic, as Cecil B. DeMille would do. If a producer dared release his movie without the seal, it was barred from most theaters and all military bases. It also faced boycotts and attacks from religious organizations and women's groups. It was considered a near miracle when a great movie made it through the approval process without having been damaged by it all.

Major Movie Distributors, 1940s

BIG FIVE

Metro-Goldwyn-Mayer (MGM). . . .Run by production head, VP, and General Manager Louis B. Mayer.

Paramount .Run by chairman of the board Adolph Zukor and President Barney Balaban.

RKO Radio Pictures . . . . .Sold to Howard Hughes in 1948.

20th Century-Fox. . . . . .Run by chief of production Darryl F. Zanuck.

Warner Bros.. . . . . .Run by production head VP Jack Warner.

LITTLE THREE

Columbia. .Run by president Harry Cohn.

United Artists. . . . . .Stockholders Sam Goldwyn and Alexander Korda pull out of UA in the early 40s.

Universal Pictures . . . . .Merges with International Pictures in 1946.

U.S. INDUSTRY DISTRIBUTION STATISTICS, 1940s
Equivalent 2005 $s/(unadjusted $s)

$19,631 Million ($735 Million)
Annual U.S. box office gross revenues

673
Number of new feature films released

TECHNOLOGY SPOTLIGHT

Color Movies and the Invention of Pan-Cake Makeup

Max Factor Sr. began his career as a makeup artist for the Russian Royal Ballet before emigrating to the United States in 1904. He settled in Los Angeles, California, during the same period of time that the major motion picture companies were moving there. Because Max Factor & Co. (founded in 1909) was so conveniently located, studios naturally turned to them with their makeup problems. In 1914 Max Factor Sr. created the first makeup specifically intended for motion pictures—a thinner greasepaint than what had been used for live theater productions. Later, in 1930 Lip Gloss was introduced. Even the word "makeup" was coined by Max Factor, although it wasn't until 1981 that the Academy of Motion Picture Arts and Sciences gave out its first Oscar in an award category with that name.

Despite all of this innovation, it was the introduction of Technicolor film in the 1930s and 1940s that really put the Max Factor company on the map. Because the old makeup used for black and white film made actors' faces appear too green or red when filmed in full color, Factor embarked upon months of laboratory research and experimentation to create an entirely new type of makeup—resulting in a solid cake form called "Pan-Cake Makeup." After registering the name with the U.S. Patent Office in 1937, the popularity of Pan-Cake Makeup spread. It was no longer worn only by motion picture stars when they were on screen, but it was also used by them in their off-screen appearances too. This made other women want to wear it as well. Almost overnight, it became one of the fastest-growing, largest-selling single makeup items in the history of cosmetics.

After Max Sr. died in 1938, his son Frank Factor (Max Factor Jr.) and other members of his family expanded the private company. In 1973 Max Factor & Co. merged with Norton Simon Industries, and in 1976 Max Factor Jr. resigned. He was the last of Max Factor's immediate family to work for the company. The Max Factor brand is now owned by Proctor & Gamble, although in 2009 P&G announced that it will discontinue the brand in the United States so that the company can focus its marketing on its more successful Cover Girl brand.

MARKETING SPOTLIGHT

Clash of the Filmmaker and the Newspaper Baron

One of the greatest battles over the distribution of a movie was the battle that occurred with the release of *Citizen Kane*, a film written, directed by, and starring the twenty-four-year-old wunderkind Orson Welles in his first Hollywood effort. He was given total creative freedom by RKO, which at the time was desperate for a hit. The film that Welles made, adapted from a script by Herman J. Mankiewicz, was later chosen by the American Film Institute as the greatest ever, but it did not enjoy the same kind of acclaim, or even significant box office success, when released in 1941, on the eve of World War II. That was due, in part, to the efforts of William Randolph Hearst—one of the most powerful newspaper barons of the age—to destroy it.

There was great curiosity at an advance screening of the movie because Welles had been touted by the studio as the "boy wonder." The audience included gossip columnist Louella Parsons, who hated the movie, deeming it an irresponsible attack on a great man—her boss, Hearst. After Parsons reported back to him, the seventy-six-year-old Hearst set out to not only shut down the movie but also destroy Welles. Reportedly, Hearst was particularly incensed that the film's newspaper magnate, clearly modeled after him, was depicted as having an affair with a younger woman and trying to use his influence to help her career. At the time, Hearst was having an affair with actress Marion Davies and was indeed using his money and influence to help her career. Many Hollywood executives, including Louis B. Mayer of MGM, took Hearst's side. They led an attempt to buy the movie from RKO and burn it. Hearst also decreed that none of his powerful newspapers, including the biggest-circulation daily in New York City, was ever to mention Welles, his movie, or any movie released by RKO again.

Hearst planted stories that put down Welles, and tried to intimidate theater owners into not showing the movie. He used blackmail and threats, and even spurred an FBI investigation of Welles. Hearst also made veiled threats that he would expose scandals about Welles's private life. He made blunt references to Welles being a Communist and asked why he didn't enlist in the military. The message had impact. When Welles's name was read at the Academy Awards as a nominee in the Best Screenplay category, some in the crowd booed.

Welles, who courted controversy his whole life, threatened to sue Hearst and RKO for suppressing his film. Behind the scenes, bankers for RKO joined forces with bankers important to the Hearst empire to convince the old newspaper mogul to back off. By then, however, the damage had been done. When the movie opened, the Hearst papers all gave it horrid reviews and told readers to avoid it. The film was also shot in a documentary style that put off some viewers who were used to more traditional entertainment. As a result, the movie had tepid box office returns on its initial run. It was only years later that the greatness of *Citizen Kane* was acknowledged.

Comparison of AFI Favorite Movies

Top 5 Favorite Movies
AFI 100 Years 100 Movies 10th Anniversary Edition, 2007
Equivalent 2005 $s /(Unadjusted $s) in Millions of $s

Rank	Film	Initial Release	All-Release Domestic Box Office
1	*Citizen Kane* (not in top 5 movies in 1941)	1941	**$59.4** ($3.8)
2	*The Godfather* (#1 movie in 1972)	1972	**$505.9**/($135.0)
3	*Casablanca* (not in top 5 movies in 1942)	1942	**$169.6**/($9.3)
4	*Raging Bull* (not in top 5 movies in 1980)	1980	**$55.9**/($23.5)
5	*Singin' in the Rain* (not in top 5 movies in 1952)	1952	**$98.0**/($7.4)

Note: *The Godfather* is the only film in AFI's top 5 that was number one at the domestic box office and is part of a franchise (three or more films).

The Godfather Franchise
All-Release Worldwide Box Office
Equivalent 2005 $s /(Unadjusted $s) in Millions of $s

Film	Initial Release	Domestic Box Office	Foreign Box Office	Production Cost	Worldwide Print and Ad Costs
The Godfather	1972	**$505.9**/($135.0)	**$415.1**/($110.1)	**$33.6**/($7.2)	**$90.2**/($19.3)
The Godfather Part II	1974	**$161.2**/($47.5)	**$142.3**/($45.5)	**$56.3**/($14.2)	**$53.6**/($14.0)
The Godfather Part III	1990	**$101.2**/($66.7)	**$69.3**/$45.5)	**$85.8**/($57.4)	**$72.4**/($49.3)
Total		**$768.3**/($249.2)	**$626.7**/($201.1)	**$175.7**/($78.8)	**$216.2**/($82.6)

Comparison of Four 1940s Films
and Two 1930s Films Rereleased in the 1940s
Initial Release or Rerelease Domestic Box Office
Equivalent 2005 $s/(Unadjusted $s) in Millions of $s

Film	Initial Release	Domestic Box Office	Domestic Rentals	Foreign Rentals	Production Cost	Print and Ad Costs
Duel in the Sun	1947	$348.0 (23.9)	$156.6 ($10.8)	not available	$63.5 ($7.3)	$17.5 ($2.0)
Samson and Delilah (includes road show release)	1949	$230.0 ($20.4)	$103.5 ($9.2)	not available	$26.2 ($3.2)	$14.8 ($1,8)
Meet Me in St. Louis	1944	$223.3 ($11.1)	$100.5 ($5.0)	$29.7 ($1.6)	$20.9 ($1.99)	$7.6 ($.7)
Mrs. Miniver	1946	$282.7 ($11.9)	$127.2 ($5.4)	$83.6 ($3.5)	$16.1 ($1.3)	$5.8 ($.5)
The Wizard of Oz (initial release 1939)	1949	$31.2 ($2.2)	$14.1 (1.0)	$11.0 ($.8)	not available	$1.6 ($.2)
San Francisco (initial release 1936)	1948	$20.9 (1.4)	$9.4 ($0.6)	$5.3 ($0.4)	not available	$0.5 ($0.1)

American Age 12–30 Comprise 55% of Total Moviegoing Audience vs. 35% of Total U.S. Population

Motion Picture Theater Attendance by
Age vs. U.S. Population by Age

Movie Attendance Age Range	Percentage of Total Movie Audience	U.S. Population Age Range	Percentage of Total U.S. Population
5–11	10%	5–9	8%
12–17	20%	10–19	18%
18–30	35%	20–29	17%
31–45	20%	30–44	22%
45+	15%	45+	27%

EXHIBITION OVERVIEW

Divestiture Speeds the Death of the Studio System

The linchpin of the studio system was its control of everything from development to exhibition—until the courts ruled against several of the studios as illegal monopolies. The Paramount consent decree of 1949 forced the five major studios that owned theaters in addition to production and distribution means to divest themselves of their theater holdings. It also brought about major changes in the way movies were selected by theaters and sold by distributors, and an end to many other predatory practices.

By 1938 the studios were aware that the administration of President Franklin D. Roosevelt was about to charge them as an illegal monopoly, so studio chiefs went for a chat with FDR on June 25. In attendance on the studio side were Barney Balaban (Paramount), George Schaefer (Paramount), Harry Cohn (Columbia), Sidney Kent (20th Century-Fox), Nicholas Schenck (Loew's-MGM), Nate Blumberg (Universal), Albert Warner (Warner Bros.), Leo Spitz (RKO), and Will Hays, president of the MPPDA. As a result of the White House meeting, the industry leaders announced a new plan that would allow them to self-regulate the way movies were sold to independent and competing theaters. The plan also addressed the way movies were booked and exhibited, again attempting to conduct reform on a voluntary basis.

However, in July 1938, just one month after this meeting, the U.S. Department of Justice filed a lawsuit against the majors and select independent exhibitors. In 1939 the Justice Department also filed suit against other independent exhibitors, charging that they too engaged in monopolistic practices. The industry's response to the suits was reflected by the comments of Sidney Kent, who had been elected leader of the voluntary action committee. He said that the "most intelligent and satisfactory solution to our problems eventually will be reached through self-regulation rather than through litigation." The studios argued that block booking and vertical integration were needed or the business would not be economically viable. They pointed to their experience during the Great Depression, when many sustained large losses and some had to declare bankruptcy and be reorganized. The government insisted that any settlement would require an end to block booking of movies and a mandate to separate production from exhibition, so the suit continued.

On June 30, 1940, the trial commenced in federal court in New York City. After two weeks of preliminary activity, the trial was suspended and a settlement was reached. After two intense days of negotiations in October 1940, both sides agreed to what was known as the consent decree of 1940. The government backed off its demand that the studios sell their theaters, and in return, the studios agreed to restrict block booking to packages of no more than five films at a time. The block booking of short subjects was prohibited completely. The five major companies that owned theaters also agreed to end blind bidding and provide trade screenings of movies for exhibitors in all thirty-one theatrical markets. They also agreed not to expand ownership of theaters without federal approval. The government retained the right to reinstate the lawsuit if after three years they were not satisfied with the compliance of the decree.

The 1940 compromise did not satisfy many independent producers, who felt that the studios still had too much of a monopoly. So the Society of Independent Motion Picture Producers (SIMPP) was created by Mary Pickford, Sam Goldwyn, Walt Disney, David O. Selznick, Walter Wanger, and others to do battle. When the SIMPP filed suit against Paramount Theaters in Detroit in 1942, they became the first producers to sue exhibitors. Some politicians and officials in the Justice Department also felt that the studios had gotten off too easily. But after Pearl Harbor, the movie industry was declared too vital to the war effort, because of its ability to tell the Allies' story around the world, to be interfered with. As a result, any planned legal action against them was put off while the country mobilized for World War II. By late in the summer of 1943, when the war effort had progressed and the 1940 decree had expired, the Justice Department renewed its case against the studios. The studios could no longer plead poverty. During the war years many of them had racked up record profits, especially Paramount, which owned the greatest number of theaters and benefited the most from the boom in attendance during the war.

In 1945 the Justice Department brought its case to federal court in the Southern District of New York, demanding separation of production from exhibition. Oddly, however, the court did not rule for that. Instead it determined that the major companies were in violation of the Sherman Antitrust Act. The court prohibited block booking, cooperative ownership or pooling of theaters, and the fixing of minimum admission prices. It also mandated the creation of a system for competitive bidding by all exhibitors. To the ire of the Justice Department, however, the studios didn't have to divest themselves of their theater assets. Both sides appealed. Meanwhile, the years 1946–48 marked the highest attendance yet at American theaters. Paramount reported a profit of $39 million for 1946, more than twice that of second-place Fox. Despite the profits, the studios complained that the war and its aftermath had eliminated much of their foreign revenue, which was now half what it had been before the war.

The 1938 Antitrust Suit

The suit filed by the U.S. government on July 20, 1938, against five major defendants [Paramount Pictures, Loew's Inc. (MGM), Radio-Keith-Orpheum Corp. (RKO), Warner Bros. Pictures, Inc., and 20th Century-Fox Film Corp.] calling for the divorcement of theaters addressed several issues as follows:

1 Fixed admission prices (price-fixing)
2 Clearance (guaranteed days between runs)
3 Formula deals (allocated playing time and film rentals)
4 Franchises (restricting opportunities of small exhibitors to license films in competition)
5 Block booking (forcing exhibitor to take other features with film desired)
6 Discriminations
7 Joint ownership (studios share interest in some circuits and/or theaters)
8 Horizontal conspiracy
9 Monopoly power
10 Pooling agreements

In May 1948 the U.S. Supreme Court upheld the verdict but rejected competitive bidding as unworkable. It sent the question of divestiture back to the lower courts, and in 1949 a district court finally ruled for separation of production and exhibition.

Paramount and RKO were the first to sign consent decrees agreeing to split their theater assets from their other units. RKO did it because the Howard Hughes regime had plunged the company so far toward bankruptcy that it needed to liquidate what it could. Although Paramount appeared to have the most to lose—under president Barney Balaban, it was the biggest, most profitable studio, with more than 3,000 employees in the mid-1940s—it was the first to sign the decree, thinking that it had a backup plan: Balaban saw the future in television and was already deeply invested in the new medium.

There is a myth that Hollywood after World War II ignored TV's potential and missed the boat on controlling the medium. While some companies did indeed hold back, others such as Paramount under Balaban's leadership moved quickly to develop a TV-centric strategy. There was no time to waste. Average movie attendance was falling: from 90 million in 1946, it would be half that ten years later. Although Paramount was known for its conservative management style, Balaban had invested a then hefty sum of $400,000 in television as early as 1938. He backed DuMont, a pioneering TV set manufacturer, which in the 1940s was briefly a fourth TV network. Dumont sought Paramount programming to compete with RCA Corp.'s NBC. But Balaban had an even bigger vision. Paramount obtained a license from the Federal Communications Commission (FCC) to experiment in television and debuted W9XBK in Chicago in 1940 and W6XYZ in Los Angeles in 1942. After the FCC began giving out permits for commercial television on July 1, 1941, many of the original call signs changed. W9XBK eventually became WBKB and W6XYZ became KTLA. All over the country, Paramount-controlled theater circuits filed with the FCC for TV station licenses in local markets including Detroit, Dallas, Des Moines, and Tampa. The FCC took note of Paramount's aggressive growth and passed a rule limiting ownership by any one company to five TV stations. However, that move alone is not what did in Balaban's TV push. Under the 1934 law that created the FCC, the commission can refuse licenses to anyone convicted of monopolistic practices. After Paramount had already agreed to spin off its theaters, thinking it could now switch to TV, the FCC ruled that the anti-trust violation made Paramount ineligible to hold a TV license. That effectively barred all of the studios from owning some or all of the first generation of TV networks and local stations, which eventually proved to be a hugely lucrative business.

In time, the Paramount decision resulted in significant growth in independent production, as many who learned their craft at the studios went out on their own. Powerful agents arose to represent these talented directors, actors, cinematographers, writers, and others. Studios hired independent producers who raised some or all of their own financing, freeing the studios to focus more on sales, distribution, and marketing. Everyone from actors and directors to cinematographers and costume designers were now hired project by project. Curiously, divestiture padded the bottom line of exhibition for a time. The newly independent circuits, bent on making money instead of servicing the studios' agenda, dumped unprofitable theaters, picked better movies, raised ticket prices, and became that much more profitable even as attendance fell. Divestiture also brought about unintended consequences. Once there were truly independent theaters, movies from abroad and outside of the mainstream found screen time. This diversity of sexual, social, and ethical views made it impossible to impose the old-fashioned moral strictures dictated earlier by the Hollywood code. This, of course, led to the end of the censorship of movies.

Consent Decree Results

Big Five Studio Defendants	Number of Wholly Owned Theaters (out of 18,076 in 1945)	New Theater Ownership
Paramount Pictures	1,395 (plus 361 owned with 1 or more other defendants)	Forms independent company United Paramount Theaters in 12/31/1949 to take over theater operations.
20th Century-Fox	636	Forms National Theatres, Inc., in 5/1/1952. Incorporates as 20th Century-Fox Film Corp in 7/22/1952 excluding theaters. As of 9/27/1952 National Theatres takes over all theatre assets from Fox.
Warner Bros.	501	Forms Stanley Warner Corp. in 1/30/1953 to take over theatres formerly operated by Warner Theaters.
Metro-Goldwyn-Mayer	135	Separates theater assets in 3/12/1959 when Loew's Theatres, Inc., takes over MGM's U.S. and Canadian theater operations.
RKO Radio Pictures	109 (had 163 prior to bankruptcy 1933–1940)	Agrees to sell its remaining theaters in 3/28/1949

U.S. INDUSTRY EXHIBITION STATISTICS, 1940s
Equivalent 2005 $s/(Unadjusted $s)

$6.41 ($0.24 to $0.46)
Average movie ticket price (1940–1949)

19,032
Number of U.S. screens, 1940

U.S. INDUSTRY DISTRIBUTION vs. EXHIBITION
Number of New Films Released
vs. Average Weekly Film Theater Attendance,
1940–1949

Year	Total Number of New Films Released	Number of Films Released by Majors	Number of Films Released by Independents	Number of Theater Attendees Millions of People
1940	673	363	310	80
1941	598	379	219	85
1942	533	358	175	85
1943	427	289	138	85
1944	442	270	172	85
1945	377	234	143	85
1946	467	252	215	90
1947	486	249	237	90
1948	459	248	211	90
1949	479	234	245	70

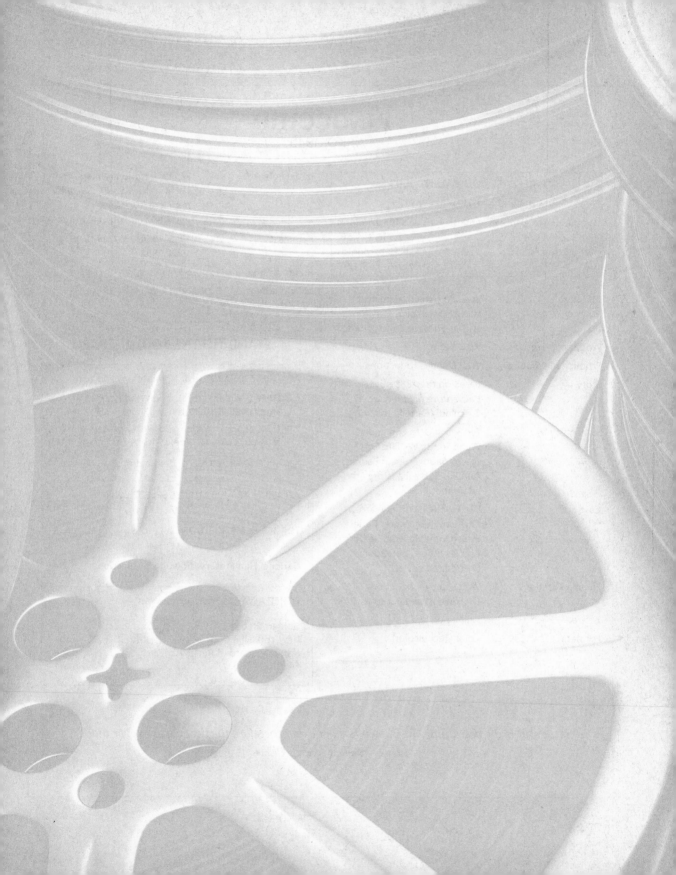

PINOCCHIO
RKO, 1940

ALL-RELEASE EQUIVALENT 2005 $s
(Unadjusted $s) in Millions of $s

Domestic Box Office Revenues . . . . **$465.2**/($84.3)
Production Cost . . . . **$36.8**/($2.6)
Production Period . . . .**3 years 10 months**
1/3/1936–11/3/1939

Director . . . . Ben Sharpsteen, Hamilton
Luske (supervising directors),
and David Hand (uncredited)

Producer . . . . Walt Disney

Production Company . . . . Walt Disney Productions

Story by . . . . Based on the 1883 novel
L'avventure di Pinocchio by
C. Collodi (Carlo Lorenzini)

Screenplay by . . . . Ted Sears, Otto Englander,
Webb Smith, William Cottrell,
Joseph Sabo, Erdman Penner,
Aurelius Battaglia (story
adaptation)

Cast . . . . Dickie Jones, Cliff Edwards,
Christian Rub, Walter Catlett,
Evelyn Venable, Frankie Darro,
Charles Judels, Don Bodie
(uncredited voices)

Filming Locations . . . . . . Walt Disney Productions
(Hollywood and Burbank, CA)

Genre . . . . Animation

Format . . . . Color (Technicolor)

Initial Release . . . . 2/7/1940 world premiere, Center
Theatre (New York); 2/9/1940
premiere ((Los Angeles);
2/23/1940 general release

Rerelease 1945, 1954, 1962, 1971, 1978,
1984, 1992

Running Time . . . . 87 minutes

MPAA Rating . . . . not rated

STANDING THE TEST OF TIME

ACADEMY AWARD Oscar Nominations and Wins

* **MUSIC** (Original Score): Leigh Harline, Paul J.
Smith, Ned Washington

* **MUSIC** (Song): "When You Wish Upon a Star,"
Music by Leigh Harline; Lyrics by Ned Washington

OSCAR TOTALS   Nominations **2**   *Wins **2**

AFI 100 YEARS 100 MOVIES SELECTION
2007 0   1997 0

TOP 300 FILMS POSITION . . . . **#28**
All-Release Domestic Box Office in Equivalent 2005 $s

National Film Preservation Board Selection 1994

OTHER AWARDS Best Picture Wins

	Year
Golden Globes	none
New York Film Critics	none
National Board of Review	none
Film Daily Critics	none

It is still is the best thing Mr. Disney has done and therefore the best cartoon ever made.
—Frank S. Nugent, *New York Times*, 1940

PLOT: Pinocchio, a wooden puppet created by the kindly woodcarver Geppetto, is brought to life by the Blue Fairy and, with the help of a cricket as his conscience, must prove himself worthy of becoming a real boy.

PRODUCTION: Fanciful characters, a storybook setting, ensnaring temptations, and wish fulfillment: *L'avventure di Pinocchio,* written by Italian author Carlo Lorenzini under the pen name C. Collodi, was first serialized in an Italian newspaper in 1881, and was published in novel form in 1883. Walt Disney saw the timeless tale as superlative fodder for a full-length animated film, and with the runaway success of *Snow White and the Seven Dwarfs,* the *Pinocchio* project was fast-tracked as one of three ambitious follow-ups (along with *Bambi* and *Fantasia*). First came a reworking of the story. In Collodi's book, Pinocchio is self-centered, ill-mannered, and delinquent. When his external conscience—a moralizing, unnamed cricket—attempts to point out the young puppet's misguided ways, he is squashed with a mallet. Pinocchio himself suffers a number of grievous misfortunes: his feet are burned, he is held captive or jailed several times, a giant ogre prepares to devour him, and he is hanged from a tree. Disney assigned a team of writers to make the Pinocchio character more innocent, naive, and well-intentioned, yet gullible. Despite the lessons learned from *Snow White, Pinocchio* proved a difficult undertaking. As a puppet brought to life, Pinocchio emerged as a rather stilted, expressionless character without any endearing, boyish qualities. The talking cricket—now named Jiminy—remained an unattractive insect. Adhering too closely to Collodi's original concepts had produced unsatisfactory results, so in June 1938 Walt halted the project. Six months of work was scrapped, and the animation team refocused on making the leading characters more engaging. Twelve animators assigned to the Pinocchio character labored for eighteen months to create features that possessed more rounded, human qualities. Rejecting all previous renderings of Jiminy Cricket, Walt assigned a young animator, Ward Kimball, to the task of reimagining this character. The final result was a diminutive, charming creature who would croon two memorable songs in the film: "When You Wish upon a Star" and "Give a Little Whistle." New characters included Figaro the kitten and Cleo the goldfish; Collodi's "terrible shark" became the equally terrifying Monstro the whale. The startling depth in backgrounds was achieved by extensive use of an improved multiplane camera, which shot through four to five glass layers of painted scenes. It is estimated that only 300,000 of the 2 million drawings done for the project were used in the final film.

DISTRIBUTION: The outbreak of World War II, five months prior to *Pinocchio*'s release, negatively impacted the film. On its initial release *Pinocchio* brought in only $1.6 million in domestic rentals (compared with *Snow White*'s $4.2 million) and $1.9 million in foreign rentals (compared with *Snow White*'s $4.3 million). However, its legacy prevailed. The popular Jiminy Cricket went on to host a number of Disney shorts, and the Oscar-winning "When You Wish upon a Star" became the company's unofficial signature anthem. A healthy slate of theatrical reissues would eventually redeem *Pinocchio* at the box office. Its arrival on home video formats, starting in 1985, has only added to its popularity and timeless appeal. —*Douglas Burns*

THE GRAPES OF WRATH
20th Century-Fox, 1940

ALL-RELEASE EQUIVALENT 2005 $s
(Unadjusted $s) in Millions of $s

Domestic Box Office Revenues . . . . **$65.3**/($2.4)
Production Cost . . . . **$10.5**/($0.8)
Principal Photography . . . . **37** days estimated
10/5/1939–11/16/1939

Director . . . . John Ford
Producer . . . . Darryl F. Zanuck
Production Company . . . . 20th Century-Fox Film Corp.
Story by . . . . Based on the novel by
John Steinbeck
Screenplay by . . . . Nunnally Johnson
Cast . . . . Henry Fonda, Jane Darwell,
John Carradine, Charlie
Grapewin, Russell Simpson,
O. Z. Whitehead
Filming Locations . . . . . . California: 20th Century-Fox
Studios (studio and backlot);
Lasky Mesa, San Fernando
Valley, Lamont, Irvine Ranch,
Tustin, Iverson Ranch,
Chatsworth, Needles; Arizona:
Topock, Petrified Forest
National Park; New Mexico:
Gallup, Laguna Pueblo,
Santa Rosa
Genre . . . . Drama
Format . . . . B&W
Initial Release . . . . 1/24/1940 premiere (New York);
3/15/1940 general release
Rerelease 1947
Running Time . . . . 129 minutes
MPAA Rating . . . . not rated

STANDING THE TEST OF TIME

ACADEMY AWARD Oscar Nominations and Wins

Outstanding production: 20th Century-Fox
Actor: Henry Fonda
*ACTRESS IN A SUPPORTING ROLE: Jane
Darwell
*DIRECTING: John Ford
Film Editing: Robert Simpson
Sound Recording: 20th Century-Fox Studio Sound
Department, E.H. Hansen, Sound Director
Writing (Screenplay): Nunnally Johnson

OSCAR TOTALS   Nominations 7   *Wins 2

AFI 100 YEARS 100 MOVIES SELECTION
2007 . . . #23   1997 . . . #21

TOP 300 FILMS POSITION . . . . .none
All-Release Domestic Box Office in Equivalent 2005 $s

National Film Preservation Board Selection 1989

OTHER AWARDS Best Picture Wins

	Year
Golden Globes	none
New York Film Critics	1940
National Board of Review	1940
Film Daily Critics	none

*Before all else, it is the story of the family, the
way it reacts, how it is shaken by a serious
problem which overwhelms it. It is not a social
film on this problem, it's a study of a family.*

—John Ford

PLOT: Tom Joad (Henry Fonda) discovers that the hard life does not end after his release from prison. Dust storms have withered the farmlands, so the family joins a migration to California with other Okies.

PRODUCTION: Against the advice of many at Fox, production head Darryl F. Zanuck bought the movie rights to John Steinbeck's controversial Pulitzer Prize–winning novel, *The Grapes of Wrath,* for $70,000. John Steinbeck said later that if he had known Chase National Bank held a majority of the studio's stock, he wouldn't have sold his book to 20th Century-Fox. But unexpectedly, Chase's chairman gave Zanuck his blessing, since his wife loved the novel and had gotten him hooked on it as well. Zanuck still proceeded with caution, hiding the production under a false working title, "Highway 66," and ordering only three copies of the screenplay made. While Steinbeck authorized screenwriter Nunnally Johnson to "tamper" with his book, Johnson added only a few new scenes, most notably the one where the Joads stop to buy a nickel loaf of bread. John Ford received the script while filming *Drums Along the Mohawk* and agreed to direct it because the Joads' journey seemed to parallel his own family's plight in Ireland during the potato famine. Zanuck and Ford cast Henry Fonda in the much-coveted role of Tom Joad with the stipulation that he star in seven other Fox films. Beulah Bondi was Ford's choice to play Ma, but Zanuck argued for the earthy Jane Darwell, already under contract at Fox. After only four weeks of preproduction, Ford and cinematographer Gregg Toland started shooting on a tight schedule, mostly on Fox studio sets. They referenced the famous photographs of the Farm Security Administration to make the picture look as bleak and harsh as a documentary. Toland used deep-focus photography and low-key lighting to emphasize shadows and darkness, techniques that would inspire film noir. Without the usual makeup or diffusion, Ford's actors came across on celluloid as hard-edged, dirty Dust Bowlers. Otto Brower's second unit traveled the Okies' route for footage of the actual sites. Zanuck wanted the sound to match the authenticity of the picture and invested in a six-man crew to drive to Oklahoma and capture the noise of a real jalopy. While those expensive effects were never used, Zanuck's choice of an accordion version of "Red River Valley" became the movie's theme song. Ford claimed he also let Zanuck direct Ma's final, uplifting soliloquy when the producer deemed Ford's original ending of Tom walking away too depressing.

DISTRIBUTION: Premiering in New York about two months after production was finished, *The Grapes of Wrath* went on to be one of Fox's biggest pictures of 1940 (although it brought in less than Walter Lang's musical *Tin Pan Alley*). Steinbeck loved the "hard, straight picture," finding it "harsher than the book," while the *New York Times* called it "one of cinema's masterworks." The film prompted songwriter Woody Guthrie to pen his song "Tom Joad." The FBI would later investigate Ford, Steinbeck, and others involved in the film for suspicious Communist activity. Ironically, the House Un-American Activities Committee singled out *The Grapes of Wrath* as an exemplary film that showcased America's ills yet was made by people whose loyalty to their homeland remained unquestioned. —*Michael Kogge*

BOOM TOWN

MGM, 1940

ALL-RELEASE EQUIVALENT 2005 $s

(Unadjusted $s) in Millions of $s

Domestic Box Office Revenues. . . . . **$217.5**/($8.1)
Production Cost . . . . **$27.9**/($2.1)
Principal Photography . . . . **92** days estimated
3/1/1940–6/17/1940

Director . . . . Jack Conway

Producer . . . . Sam Zimbalist

Production Company . . . . Metro-Goldwyn-Mayer

Story by . . . . Based on the story "A Lady
Comes to Burkburnett," by
James Edward Grant

Screenplay by . . . . John Lee Mahin

Cast . . . . Clark Gable, Spencer Tracy,
Claudette Colbert,
Hedy Lamarr, Frank Morgan,
Lionel Atwill

Filming Locations . . . . . . MGM studio and on location in
Bakersfield, CA

Genre . . . . Drama

Format . . . . B&W

Initial Release 8/30/1940

Rerelease . . . . none

Running Time . . . . 116 minutes

MPAA Rating . . . . not rated

STANDING THE TEST OF TIME

ACADEMY AWARD Oscar Nominations and Wins

Cinematography: Harold Rosson

Special Effects: Photographic Effects by A. Arnold
Gillespie; Sound Effects by Douglas Shearer

OSCAR TOTALS   Nominations **2**   *Wins 0

AFI 100 YEARS 100 MOVIES SELECTION
2007 0   1997 0

TOP 300 FILMS POSITION . . . . #213
All-Release Domestic Box Office in Equivalent 2005 $s

National Film Preservation Board Selection . . . . none

OTHER AWARDS Best Picture Wins

	Year
Golden Globes	none
New York Film Critics	none
National Board of Review	none
Film Daily Critics	none

I was deadly serious all during the making. . . . I needed this one and it had to be good.
Clark was kind to me all during the film. Spencer was aloof but worked hard.
When a picture is going good, everyone feels it. We felt all during the filming
we had a good one. And it was. The reviews were a smash.

—Hedy Lamarr

PLOT: Two oil wildcatters in Burkburnett, Texas, hit a gusher, go into business together despite their dislike for each other, and find themselves fighting further over a woman.

PRODUCTION: MGM decided to do an adventure film that would capture the spirit and excitement of America in the early 1900s when oil was discovered in West Texas. They were inspired by James Edward Grant's story "A Lady Comes to Burkburnett," which was published in *Cosmopolitan* magazine in 1939. They assigned Jack Conway to direct and John Lee Mahin to write the screenplay. Mahin, who had worked with Clark Gable on the 1932 film *Red Dust,* brought the script to Gable to read. Gable was making more than $4,000 a week at MGM, having just starred in *Gone with the Wind.* When he agreed to take the part, MGM cast him with Spencer Tracy for the third time, after their successes in *San Francisco* (1936) and *Test Pilot* (1938). The female lead was written for Myrna Loy, but MGM cast Claudette Colbert, which brought a flurry of publicity for the first Gable-Colbert reunion since the Oscar-winning performances in *It Happened One Night* six years earlier. Hedy Lamarr, whom studio head Louis B. Mayer had brought from Vienna, Austria, and was grooming for stardom, lobbied hard for the supporting female role to prove herself as an actress. Much of the film was shot on location in Bakersfield, California. Gable was familiar with the subject of oil and felt at home on set, having spent his teenage years working as a rigger in the Oklahoma oil fields with his wildcatter father, William Gable. He even used his father as a model for his character, Big John McMasters. When filming their fight scenes, Gable insisted on doing his own stunt work, though Tracy used a double. In one scene, Tracy's double accidentally landed a blow to Gable's face, cutting his lip and breaking his dentures, stopping shooting for a week. Gable and Tracy had enjoyed working with each other, but by the time of this film Tracy had grown tired of playing the best friend who watched while Gable won the girl (and got top billing). Tracy wanted to be a star in his own right. He was irritable and withdrawn throughout production and distanced himself from everyone on the set. He referred to Colbert as "Frenchie" or "Froggie," which she disliked, and his relationship with Lamarr was as combative in real life as on the screen. In one scene you can see Tracy repeatedly and aggressively poking Lamarr in the chest in an improvisation. Many wondered if Gable, the king of Hollywood, and Lamarr, billed as the world's most beautiful woman, would strike sparks, but Gable had just married the love of his life, Carole Lombard (who would die in a plane crash two years later) and was a faithful husband throughout.

DISTRIBUTION: *Boom Town* was the biggest moneymaker of 1940 and one of the top films of the decade. A prerelease news item in the *Hollywood Reporter* said that MGM had decided to run the film on a single bill and increase the admission price. The studio's justification for this policy was that with so many stars, it was actually "four films in one." This was the final film featuring Gable and Tracy together. MGM paired up Gable and Lamarr immediately after in *Comrade X.* —*Hayley Taylor Block*

FANTASIA

Walt Disney Productions (road show), 1940; RKO (general release), 1942

ALL-RELEASE EQUIVALENT 2005 $s

(Unadjusted $s) in Millions of $s

Domestic Box Office Revenues . . . . **$314.8**/($63.4)
Production Cost . . . . **$31.8**/($2.3)
Production Period . . . . **3.3** years estimated
Mid-1937–November 1940

Rerelease 1942, 1944, 1946, 1953, 1956,
1963, 1969, 1977, 1982, 1985,
1990

Running Time . . . . 124 minutes

MPAA Rating . . . . not rated

Production Supervisor . . Ben Sharpsteen

Directors . . . . James Algar, Samuel Armstrong,
Ford Beebe, Norman Ferguson,
Jim Handley, T. Hee, Wilfred
Jackson, Hamilton Luske,
Bill Roberts, Paul Satterfield

Producer . . . . Walt Disney

Production Company . . . . Walt Disney Productions

Story by . . . . Joe Grant, Dick Huemer (Story
Direction)

Cast . . . . Deems Taylor, Leopold
Stokowski and the Philadelphia
Symphony Orchestra, Mickey
Mouse

Filming Locations . . . . . . Walt Disney Productions
(Hollywood and Burbank, CA)

Genre . . . . Animation

Format . . . . Color (Technicolor)/Fantasound
(initial road show version)

Initial Release . . . . 11/13/1940 world premiere,
Broadway Theatre (New York);
1/29/1941 premiere (Los
Angeles, CA) road show
version; 4/10/1942 RKO general
release; cut to 81 minutes, with
a standard soundtrack

STANDING THE TEST OF TIME

ACADEMY AWARD Oscar Nominations and Wins

*SPECIAL AWARD: Walt Disney, William E. Garity,
J.N.A. Hawkins and the RCA Manufacturing
Company for their outstanding contribution to
the advancement of the use of sound in motion
pictures

*SPECIAL AWARD: Leopold Stokowski (and his
associates) for their unique achievement in the
creation of a new form of visualized music

OSCAR TOTALS   Nominations **0**   *Wins 0+2

AFI 100 YEARS 100 MOVIES SELECTION
2007 0   1997 . . #58

TOP 300 FILMS POSITION . . . . **#96**
All-Release Domestic Box Office in Equivalent 2005 $s

National Film Preservation Board Selection 1990

OTHER AWARDS Best Picture Wins

	Year
Golden Globes	none
New York Film Critics	none
National Board of Review	none
Film Daily Critics	none

Fantasia is timeless. It may run ten, twenty, thirty years. Fantasia *is an idea in itself.
I can never build another* Fantasia. *I can improve. I can elaborate. That's all.*

—Walt Disney, 1940

PLOT: Colorful, diverse animated interpretations accompany a concert of classical musical selections, including Bach's Toccata and Fugue in D Minor, Tchaikovsky's *Nutcracker Suite,* Stravinsky's *Rite of Spring,* Beethoven's Pastoral Symphony, and others.

PRODUCTION: Mickey Mouse needed a hit. Though the pie-eyed cartoon brainchild of Walt Disney was still popular, his animated antics had begun to take a backseat to those of Donald Duck, Goofy, and Pluto. Accordingly, in 1937 Walt Disney decided to star Mickey in the mythical tale of the Sorcerer's Apprentice. It had been interpreted in 1797 as the ballad "Der Zauberlehrling" by Johann Wolfgang von Goethe and as a musical by French composer Paul Dukas in 1897. When famed conductor Leopold Stokowski agreed to orchestrate the music for this production, he encouraged Disney to consider a collection of animated visualizations of musical themes. Walt enthusiastically agreed and work began on the project as a short, but as production costs reached an alarming $125,000, Walt decided it would be a feature-length movie instead. During the fall of 1938, Disney, Stokowski, and celebrated music critic Deems Taylor joined Disney story directors Dick Huemer and Joe Grant to choose the music from a diverse selection of compositions. With the original track from the "Sorcerer's Apprentice" sequence already completed in Los Angeles, Stokowski would conduct the Philadelphia Symphony Orchestra for the remaining seven sequences. Disenchanted with the audio quality in theaters, Walt asked his sound department and RCA engineers to devise a system on par with the best concert halls. Thus was born Fantasound—a process of recording music using multiple microphones, then playing it back on an equal number of speakers, creating a breakthrough stereophonic effect. But even more spectacular was Fantasia's total cost: $2.28 million. Expenses for music alone reached $400,000, with the initial Fantasound system (for New York's Broadway Theater) costing an additional $85,000. Eleven more installations were built at $30,000 apiece so that the film could play in twelve theaters across the country simultaneously. A press book at the time noted that the film involved 508 new characters, 103 musicians, 751 artists, and 600,000 celluloid drawings.

DISTRIBUTION: While film critics heralded *Fantasia* as something stunningly unique, classical music critics were more reserved. Audiences were perplexed, some complaining that the film was not the usual "Disney fare" or that the "Night on Bald Mountain" sequence had frightened their children. The intricacies of the Fantasound setup required that the film be road-shown, but some theater owners balked at installing the system. Consequently, Disney abandoned its plans to road-show the picture in seventy-six major American cities over a two-year period and the movie was handed over to the studio's normal distributor, RKO Radio Pictures. RKO promptly cut the film to 81 minutes and it entered general release with a standard soundtrack, often on the lower half of a double bill with a western. Financially, Fantasia was a failure. Yet numerous reissues of the film—restored to a running time of two hours—kept *Fantasia* alive. By its 1969 reissue, it was achieving cult status among the college screening circuit for its "psychedelic" qualities. It received a rerecorded, state-of-the-art Dolby digital soundtrack in 1982, and in December 1999 the Disney company produced a companion film, *Fantasia/2000,* containing the original "Sorcerer's Apprentice" sequence and seven new ones. *—Douglas Burns*

THE PHILADELPHIA STORY

MGM, 1941

ALL-RELEASE EQUIVALENT 2005 $s

(Unadjusted $s) in Millions of $s

Domestic Box Office Revenues. . . . .**$135.5**/($5.3)
Production Cost . . . .**$12.5**/($0.9)
Principal Photography. . . . . **48** days estimated
7/5/1940–8/14/1940
Eight-week shoot

Director . . . . George Cukor
Producer . . . . Joseph L. Mankiewicz
Production Company. . . . Metro-Goldwyn-Mayer
Story by . . . . Based on the Broadway play
by Philip Barry
Screenplay by . . . . Donald Ogden Stewart
Cast . . . . Cary Grant, Katharine Hepburn,
James Stewart, Ruth Hussey
Filming Locations . . . . . . MGM Studios, Culver City, CA
Genre. . . . . Romance
Format. . . . . B&W
Initial Release 1/17/1941
Rerelease. 1955
Running Time . . . . 112 minutes
MPAA Rating . . . . not rated

STANDING THE TEST OF TIME

ACADEMY AWARD Oscar Nominations and Wins

Outstanding Production: Metro-Goldwyn-Mayer
*ACTOR: James Stewart
Actress: Katharine Hepburn
Actress in a Supporting Role: Ruth Hussey
Directing: George Cukor
*WRITING (Screenplay): Donald Ogden Stewart

OSCAR TOTALS   Nominations **6**   *Wins **2**

AFI 100 YEARS 100 MOVIES SELECTION
2007 . . . #44   1997. . . #51

TOP 300 FILMS POSITION . . . .**none**
All-Release Domestic Box Office in Equivalent 2005 $s

National Film Preservation Board Selection. . . . 1995

OTHER AWARDS Best Picture Wins

	Year
Golden Globes	none
New York Film Critics	none
National Board of Review	none
Film Daily Critics	none

*The film is a quick-witted translation of the play, essentially a parlor drama with witty,
Oscar Wilde–like banter and glib repartee.*

—Dan Jardine

PLOT: In this romantic screwball comedy, a wealthy Philadelphia socialite, Tracy Lord, is about to embark on her second marriage when a newspaper reporter and photographer arrive, having blackmailed the bride's father into letting them report on the wedding.

PRODUCTION: Playwright Philip Barry's *The Philadelphia Story,* inspired by the real-life hijinks of heiress Hope Montgomery Scott, originated on Broadway in late March 1939 and ran for a full year. The female lead, Tracy Lord, was played by Katharine Hepburn, who had suffered several commercial failures and been labeled "box office poison" by *The Independent Film Journal.* With the success of the play Hepburn struck out on her own, buying the film rights from Barry for $25,000 and bringing the property to MGM, stipulating in the contract that the film could be made only if Hepburn reprised her stage role. The final deal gave her approval of director, co-stars, and script supervision and a salary of $75,000 plus $175,000 for the film rights to the story. With producer Joseph Mankiewicz, she was able to handpick the cast. Hepburn wanted Clark Gable as C. K. Dexter Haven and Spencer Tracy as Macauley Connor before she even met them, but as both actors were busy with other projects, Cary Grant and James Stewart, also big stars, were cast instead. Grant was actually given a choice of which of the two male leads he wanted to play. Screenwriter Donald Ogden Stewart and director George Cukor were signed. Cukor had already directed Hepburn in four films. Filming took eight weeks and no retakes were required—even during the scene where James Stewart hiccups when drunk, in which Cary Grant is seen looking down and grinning. Stewart had improvised the hiccup, putting Grant in a position where he had to compose himself quickly and not break out laughing. Stewart was uncomfortable with some of the dialogue, notably in the swimming pool scene, where he was required to wear a dressing gown. At the time, Stewart remarked that had he been required to play the scene in just a swimming costume, it would have ended his career. Hepburn, on the other hand, was quite comfortable around the pool and actually did the pool dive without the use of a stunt double. Stewart was also extremely nervous before shooting the scene where Connor passionately recites his poetry to Tracy. As luck would have it, Noël Coward was visiting the set that day, and when Cukor asked Coward to offer encouragement to Stewart, Coward offhandedly said something to the effect of "Did I mention I think you're a fantastic actor?" Shortly thereafter, Stewart filmed the scene without a hitch and went on to win the Academy Award for Best Actor.

DISTRIBUTION: The film was released on January 17, 1941, in the United States. *The Philadelphia Story* opened to enormous acclaim and made over $3 million in worldwide rentals, with a net profit of $1.3 million. Cary Grant donated his $100,000 salary to British war relief. *The Philadelphia Story* was rereleased in 1955 and then on DVD in 2002 by Warner Home Video with a special edition that followed in 2005. It was remade in 1956 as the musical *High Society* starring Bing Crosby, using classic songs by Cole Porter; that film marked the last performance by Grace Kelly before she became princess of Monaco. —*Christine McDermott*

CITIZEN KANE
RKO, 1941

ALL-RELEASE EQUIVALENT 2005 $s
(Unadjusted $s) in Millions of $s

Domestic Box Office Revenues. . . . .$59.4/($3.8)
Production Cost . . . .$10.4/($0.8)
Principal Photography. . . . . .71 days estimated
7/30/1940–10/21/1940

Director . . . . Orson Welles

Producer . . . . Orson Welles

Production Company . . . . RKO Radio Pictures, Inc.,
Mercury Productions, Inc.

Story and Screenplay by . Herman J. Mankiewicz,
Orson Welles

Cast . . . . Joseph Cotton, Dorothy
Comingore, Everett Sloane,
Ray Collins, George Coulouris,
Agnes Moorehead,
Paul Stewart, Ruth Warrick,
Erskine Sanford, William
Alland, Orson Welles

Filming Locations . . . . . . Shot primarily at RKO-Pathe
(AKA Selznick International)
studio in Culver City, CA

Genre. . . . . Bio-Drama

Format. . . . . B&W

Initial Release . . . . 5/1/1941 road show premiere,
Palace on Broadway (New
York); 5/6/1941 (Chicago);
5/8/1941 (Los Angeles);
9/5/1941 general release

Rerelease. . . . . 1956 limited release; 5/1/1991
50th Anniversary U.S. rerelease
by Paramount with newly
restored print by original editor
Robert Wise. Turner, who had
acquired the film from RKO was
colorizing it but found a clause
in Welles's original RKO
contract calling for a film in
black and white.

Running Time . . . . 120 minutes

MPAA Rating . . . . not rated

STANDING THE TEST OF TIME

ACADEMY AWARD Oscar Nominations and Wins

Outstanding Motion Picture: Mercury

Actor: Orson Welles

Art Direction/Set Decoration: (B&W) Perry Fergusno,
Van Nest Polglase; Al Fields, Darrell Silvera

Cinematography (B&W): Gregg Toland

Directing: Orson Welles

Film Editing: Robert Wise

Music (Music Score of a Dramatic Picture): Bernard
Herrmann

Sound Recording: RKO Radio Studio Sound Dept.,
John Aalberg, Sound Director

***WRITING** (Original Screenplay): Herman
J. Mankiewicz, Orson Welles

OSCAR TOTALS   Nominations **9**   *Wins 1

AFI 100 YEARS 100 MOVIES SELECTION
2007 . . . . #1   1997. . . . #1

TOP 300 FILMS POSITION . . . . .none
All-Release Domestic Box Office in Equivalent 2005 $'S

National Film Preservation Board Selection. . . . 1989

OTHER AWARDS Best Picture Wins

	Year
Golden Globes	none
New York Film Critics.	1941
National Board of Review	1941
Film Daily Critics	none

Citizen Kane *is not about*
Louella Parsons's boss.

—Orson Welles

PLOT: A newsreel journalist investigates the life of powerful newspaper magnate Charles Foster Kane by interviewing those who knew him best, revealing a megalomaniacal bully who died unhappy and alone amidst breathtaking wealth.

PRODUCTION: Orson Welles was the enfant terrible of American theater and a national sensation after his stunning 1938 radio broadcast *The War of the Worlds.* RKO president George Schaefer offered him a film contract allowing him complete creative control, an arrangement he would never again enjoy. Welles worked on two aborted projects for RKO before settling on an idea co-created with Herman Mankiewicz, which became *Citizen Kane.* Not only was Welles new to the cinema, but most of his actors, stage and radio players chosen from his Mercury Theatre company, would also be making their film debuts. Just before shooting, Welles spent weeks on the sets, learning about the procedure of filmmaking. *Citizen Kane,* originally titled *The American,* was known as "RKO 281" during production. Welles took his independence very seriously: at one point, when RKO executives insisted on visiting the set, Welles shut down production and organized a crew baseball game until the studio people left in frustration. The most experienced member of the crew was cinematographer Gregg Toland, whose pioneering work was so admired by Welles that the two men shared equal billing on a title card at the end. Among the innovations Toland devised were a clever method to keep fore-, mid-, and background characters all in sharp focus; the use of wide-angle lenses to reveal ceilings; and daring off-kilter camera setups. Another key collaborator was composer Bernard Herrmann, who had previously worked on Welles's radio projects.

DISTRIBUTION: Newspaper publisher William Randolph Hearst, widely believed to be the inspiration for Welles's unsympathetic title character, offered RKO $800,000 to destroy the negative and prints before release. When he was refused, Hearst waged war on the production, banning any mention of RKO products in his newspapers and radio stations and threatening to air long-suppressed Hollywood scandals. The studio found it difficult to get bookings, as competing distributors vitally needed to advertise in Hearst media. After postponing its release by almost two months, RKO screened *Citizen Kane* only in its own theaters or in rented independent houses. Partly because of this opposition, and partly because audiences were unaccustomed to its challenging narrative structure, *Citizen Kane* was a box office failure, losing $150,000 and costing Welles his creative autonomy at age twenty-six. The film soon disappeared into the studio vaults. However, critical reaction was immediately favorable, with several reviewers terming *Citizen Kane* one of the finest films of all time, though other intimidated journalists remained silent on the subject. In 1946 the film was released in Europe and met with similar acclaim, especially from critics and filmmakers who were newly discovering American films and would go on to create the influential French New Wave. Despite this European interest, *Citizen Kane* continued to languish in America until the late fifties, when RKO began licensing its film catalog to television. With both Hearst and the *Kane* controversy long dead, a new generation was able to appreciate the film for its own sake. Today, it is considered one of the towering masterpieces of cinema history. —*Tom Dupree*

SERGEANT YORK

Warner Bros., 1941

ALL-RELEASE EQUIVALENT 2005 $s

(Unadjusted $s) in Millions of $s

Domestic Box Office Revenues . . . . **$361.3**/($14.5)
Production Cost . . . . **$31.8**/($2.4)
Principal Photography . . . . **70** days
                                        2/3/1941–5/1/1941
70 days principal + **20** days second-unit battle scenes

Director . . . . Howard Hawks

Producer . . . . Jesse L. Lasky, Hal B. Wallis

Production Company . . . . Warner Bros. Pictures, Inc.

Story by . . . . Based on the book *Sergeant York: His Own Life Story and War Diary* by Alvin C. York and Tom Skeyhill

Screenplay by . . . . John Huston, Howard Koch, Abem Finkel, Harry Chandlee

Cast . . . . Gary Cooper, Walter Brennan, Joan Leslie, Ward Bond, Margaret Wycherly, George Tobias

Filming Locations . . . . . . Warner studio ranch, Simi Valley and other Southern California location, and behind York's real life farm house in Pall Mall, Tennessee

Genre . . . . Bio-Drama

Format . . . . B&W

Initial Release . . . . 7/2/1941 world premiere; 9/27/1941 general release

Rerelease 1949

Running Time . . . . 134 minutes

MPAA Rating . . . . not rated

STANDING THE TEST OF TIME

ACADEMY AWARD Oscar Nominations and Wins

Outstanding Motion Picture: Warner Bros.

*ACTOR: Gary Cooper

Actor in a Supporting Role: Walter Brennan

Actor in a Supporting Role: Margaret Wycherly

Art Direction/Interior Decoration: John Hughes/ Fred MacLean

Cinematography (B&W): Sol Polito

Directing: Howard Hawks

*FILM EDITING: William Holmes

Music (Music Score of a Dramatic Picture): Max Steiner

Sound Recording: Warner Bros. Studio Sound Dept., Nathan Levinson, Sound Director

Writing (Original Screenplay): Abem Finkel, Harry Chandlee, Howard Koch, John Huston

OSCAR TOTALS   Nominations **11**   *Wins **2**

AFI 100 YEARS 100 MOVIES SELECTION
                              2007 0   1997 0

TOP 300 FILMS POSITION . . . . **#63**
All-Release Domestic Box Office In Equivalent 2005 $'S

National Film Preservation Board Selection . . . . none

OTHER AWARDS Best Picture Wins
	Year
Golden Globes	none
New York Film Critics	none
National Board of Review	none
Film Daily Critics	none

I said, "OK, you come on over to the studio with me and anytime I say, 'Isn't that right, Mr. Cooper?' you just say 'Yes.'" So we went over . . . and I said, "We'll do the picture if you'll let us alone. Isn't that right, Mr. Cooper?" He said, "Yes." . . . And I said, "We're going to change the story. We're going to get a new writer. Isn't that right, Mr. Cooper?" And he said, "Yes." And we got all those things.

—Howard Hawks

PLOT: The true story of Tennessee farmer Alvin York, who went from religious pacifist to the greatest hero of World War I. On his return he is awarded the Congressional Medal of Honor but only wants to go back home.

PRODUCTION: Jesse L. Lasky, then head of production at Famous Players-Lasky, watched from his Broadway office as Alvin C. York was honored with a ticker tape parade in 1919. Lasky sought film rights to his story, but York refused and returned to Tennessee. He declared at the time: "This uniform ain't for sale." During the next two decades Lasky, who had moved to Fox and then Warner Bros., kept coming back to York. In 1928 he finally acquired the rights to York's autobiography, *Sergeant York: His Own Life Story and War Diary.* York was known during the 1930s as an isolationist; however, with a new war brewing, Lasky was finally able to convince him that it was important to tell his story. York participated under three conditions: (1) his profits were to be contributed to a Bible school, (2) the actress who played his wife couldn't smoke cigarettes in real life, and (3) only Gary Cooper could portray him. Cooper, however, who wasn't eligible for military service due to an old hip injury, didn't want the role at first. He only agreed after a personal plea from York and the hiring of Cooper's pal Howard Hawks to direct. Cooper was under contract to Samuel Goldwyn, Lasky's former brother-in-law, and negotiations were difficult. They finally did a swap for Warner player Bette Davis, who appeared in Goldwyn's 1941 film *Little Foxes.* The film was given an initial budget of $1 million and a shooting schedule of 48 days. Production got under way with the working title "The Amazing Life of Sergeant York." As art director, John Hughes supervised construction of the 123 sets required. Warner Bros. considered shooting on location, but the logistics were too difficult. So they created a mountain set on the Warner ranch resembling the Three Forks of the Wolf area of the Tennessee Valley. It had 121 cedar, pine, and oak trees and a 200-foot-long stream. It revolved, providing sixteen different camera angles. The sets, including a country store and church, were estimated to have cost $1 million. During a visit to the set York saw Cooper smoking a cigarette and threatened to halt production, but he was talked out of it.

DISTRIBUTION: The premiere was at the Astor Theater in New York City on July 2, 1941, timed to capitalize on the Independence Day weekend theme of patriotism as war raged in Europe and Asia. Despite the over-the-top propaganda tone, most critics embraced it and audiences immediately loved it. *Film Daily* called it one of the best pictures of the year. Warner Bros. was initially able to charge a higher than usual admission of 75 cents to $1.10 per ticket in exclusive runs in major cities through Labor Day. The film then gradually played in more markets, becoming the number one film in the United States by the fall. It was the biggest-grossing movie of 1941. With worldwide rentals of $7.8 million in its initial release, the movie made a net profit of over $3 million. York died on September 2, 1964, and was buried with full military honors. —*Alex Ben Block*

THE MALTESE FALCON

Warner Bros., 1941

ALL-RELEASE EQUIVALENT 2005 $s

(Unadjusted $s) in Millions of $s

Domestic Box Office Revenues . . . . **$57.0**/($2.2)
Production Cost . . . . **$5.1**/($0.4)
Principal Photography . . . . **36** days estimated
6/9/1941–7/18/1941
Retakes 8/8/1941 and 9/10/1941

Director . . . . John Huston
Producer . . . . Hal B. Wallis
Production Company . . . . Warner Bros. Pictures, Inc.
Story by . . . . Based on the novel by
Dashiell Hammett
Screenplay by . . . . John Huston
Cast . . . . Humphrey Bogart, Mary Astor,
Gladys George, Peter Lorre,
Barton MacLane, Lee Patrick,
Sidney Greenstreet
Filming Locations . . . . . . Warner Bros. Studio,
Burbank, CA
Genre . . . . Film Noir
Format . . . . B&W
Initial Release 10/18/1941
Rerelease . . . . none
Running Time . . . . 100 minutes
MPAA Rating . . . . not rated

STANDING THE TEST OF TIME

ACADEMY AWARD Oscar Nominations and Wins

Outstanding Motion Picture: Warner Bros.
Actor in a Supporting Role: Sydney Greenstreet
Writing (Screenplay): John Huston

OSCAR TOTALS   Nominations **3**   *Wins **0**

AFI 100 YEARS 100 MOVIES SELECTION
2007 . . . #31   1997 . . . #23

TOP 300 FILMS POSITION . . . . none
All-Release Domestic Box Office in Equivalent 2005 $s

National Film Preservation Board Selection 1989

OTHER AWARDS Best Picture Wins

	Year
Golden Globes	none
New York Film Critics	none
National Board of Review	none
Film Daily Critics	none

I decided on a radical procedure: to follow the book rather than depart from it. . . .
The fact was that Falcon *has never really been put on-screen.*

—John Huston

PLOT: When detective Sam Spade's partner is killed, he is drawn into a plot to steal a priceless statuette whose value is measured in lives lost. He searches for the killer while also solving the mystery of the falcon.

PRODUCTION: Dashiell Hammett's novel *The Maltese Falcon* had been released as a film in 1931 starring Richard Cortez as Sam Spade, so there was little enthusiasm when Warner Bros. planned another adaptation. The studio wanted George Raft, but he turned it down, refusing to do a remake. Geraldine Fitzgerald passed to do a play. But first-time director John Huston got his first choice for Spade, Humphrey Bogart. One of Warner's most dependable heavies, Bogart had become a leading man in films such as *They Drive by Night,* released in July 1940, and *High Sierra,* released in January 1941. Huston and Bogart called on Mary Astor to play Brigid. She was thrilled: "She [Brigid] was attractive, charming, appealingly feminine and helpless, and a complete liar and murderess." Next, Huston gathered a unique supporting cast. Sydney Greenstreet, an English stage actor, was nervous about his first film role, but Huston said, "I had only to sit back and take delight in him and his performance." Peter Lorre, the Hungarian-born actor whom Huston considered to be "one of the finest and most subtle actors I have ever worked with," hinted at Joel Cairo's homosexuality without setting off censors. Elisha Cook Jr. lived in a retreat in the high Sierra. He received word by courier of his casting as Wilmer. Huston meticulously scripted each scene and camera angle before photography began. Associate producer Henry Blanke told him to remember every time he shot a scene that each scene is the most important. Huston considered this "the best advice any young director could have." Early on, producer Hal Wallis found a problem in the dailies: the movie did not have "the punchy, driving kind of tempo that this picture requires." The director promised the story would soon be "turning like a pinwheel." The scenes that merited Wallis's disapproval were reshot to everyone's satisfaction. The production moved along so briskly that the cast and director regularly took leisurely lunches at the Lakeside Country Club, where they teased each other mercilessly. Those lunches also provided a chance to unwind, as the film's numerous long dialogue scenes required a great deal of precision and concentration. Bogart later called June 20, 1941, the turning point of his career. That day, he shot the first scene in which he kisses Brigid. It was his first "genuine clinch" with a woman in a movie. His nervousness forced seven takes. Huston credited Bogart with the last line of the film, "The stuff that dreams are made of," which elevated the film from mystery to doomed romance. The shoot was completed two days early and under budget.

DISTRIBUTION: A September preview caused Warner to demand that the opening scene be reshot to simplify some story elements. When released wide the next month, the film was considered a B picture by the studio, but the response was so positive that it quickly acquired A status. Jack Warner also had a new, unconventional leading man. The only person unhappy with the film was Dashiell Hammett. Having sold the rights to his novel for $8,500, he discovered the character of Sam Spade had been part of the bargain. He never earned another penny from the film rights to his most famous creation. —*Louis Burklow*

HOW GREEN WAS MY VALLEY

20th Century-Fox, 1941

ALL-RELEASE EQUIVALENT 2005 $s

(Unadjusted $s) in Millions of $s

Domestic Box Office Revenues . . . . $129.1/($5.4)
Production Cost . . . . $16.7/($3.1)
Principal Photography . . . . .56 days estimated
6/9/1941–8/14/1941

Director	John Ford
Producer	Darryl F. Zanuck
Production Company	20th Century-Fox Film Corp.
Story by	Based on the book by Richard Llewellyn
Screenplay by	Philip Dunne
Cast	Walter Pidgeon, Maureen O'Hara, Donald Crisp, Anna Lee, Roddy McDowall, John Loder, Sara Allgood
Filming Locations	The Fox ranch in the Malibu Hills
Genre	Drama
Format	B&W
Initial Release	10/28/1941 world premiere; 12/26/1941 general release
Rerelease	none
Running Time	118 minutes
MPAA Rating	not rated

STANDING THE TEST OF TIME

ACADEMY AWARD Oscar Nominations and Wins

*OUTSTANDING MOTION PICTURE: 20th Century-Fox

*ACTOR IN A SUPPORTING ROLE: Donald Crisp

Actress in a Supporting Role: Sara Allgood

*ART DIRECTION/INTERIOR DECORATION: Richard Day, Nathan Juran/Thomas Little

*CINEMATOGRAPHY: Arthur Miller

*DIRECTING: John Ford

Film Editing: James B. Clark

Music (Music Score of a Dramatic Picture): Alfred Newman

Sound Recording: 20th Century-Fox Studio Sound Dept., E. H. Hansen, Sound Director

Writing (Screenplay): Philip Dunne

OSCAR TOTALS   Nominations **10**   *Wins 5

AFI 100 YEARS 100 MOVIES SELECTION
2007 0   1997 0

TOP 300 FILMS POSITION . . . . .none
All-Release Domestic Box Office in Equivalent 2005 $s

National Film Preservation Board Selection 1990

OTHER AWARDS Best Picture Wins

	Year
Golden Globes	none
New York Film Critics	none
National Board of Review	none
Film Daily Critics	none

That How Green Was My Valley *was ever made speaks volumes about the kind of studio boss Darryl Zanuck was. He was not solely driven by bottom line profits, even though his favorite saying was "time is money." Zanuck loved the art and process of great filmmaking.*

—Maureen O'Hara

PLOT: Through the nostalgic eyes of young Huw Morgan, we observe the decline of a Welsh mining village and the effects of industrialization on its inhabitants.

PRODUCTION: When Darryl Zanuck read Richard Llewellyn's best seller *How Green Was My Valley,* he thought he had finally found his *Gone with the Wind.* His projected four-hour Technicolor epic would star Katharine Hepburn and Tyrone Power and be shot all on location in Wales. He brought on William Wyler to direct, and together they devoted three months to preparing the film. It was then that the studio got cold feet and pulled the plug. Wyler's signature extravagance was beginning to get too expensive, the story was becoming more and more ambitious every day, and the whole idea of a movie about labor unrest seemed dangerous—to say nothing of their discomfort with Wyler's unconventional casting. Roddy McDowall recalls, "Wyler was in the projection room running four different tests of children and the last one was mine. The casting director stood up and put his hand in front of the projector light and said, 'You don't want to see this kid. He's bandy-legged, he's not attractive, and he has a turned eye.' . . . But Willie said, 'As long as we're here, let's see it.' " It was after viewing McDowall's screen test that screenwriter Philip Dunne decided his script would not follow Huw's development to manhood, as originally planned, but rather stick closely to his youth ("They'll never forgive us if we let that boy grow up," he said) and like that, Tyrone Power was out. As far as the New York office was concerned, this was the last straw. The execs canceled the production, and Zanuck, who insisted Dunne's script was the best he had ever read, was distraught. For a time, it looked like *How Green Was My Valley* was done for good. But Zanuck was determined—and then he thought of John Ford. He could shoot the picture for a reasonable budget. The new director made several notable changes to Wyler's original cast (ex-lover Katharine Hepburn would have to go), but he retained thirteen-year-old McDowall for the part of Huw. Due to the war in Europe, production remained in the United States. Art director Richard Day constructed his Wales as a monumental set spanning 80 acres of Los Angeles coast. To enhance the feeling of authenticity, Ford had real blocks of coal brought in—some weighing upward of one ton each—so that he could film the actors really chipping away at the mines. In addition, Ford wanted genuine coal residue to be spread over the Santa Monica hillsides, but practicality reigned and he was denied. Instead, the hills were painted black with twenty thousand gallons of paint. To make the illusion more convincing (and to save on costs), Zanuck's Technicolor dreams were exchanged for a more forgiving black and white.

DISTRIBUTION: On worldwide rentals of $4.9 million, the movie made a net profit of $2.2 million on its initial release. *Lux Radio Theater* revived the original narrative only a year after the film's release with a series of three broadcast dramatizations, the first of which starred Walter Pidgeon, Maureen O'Hara, Donald Crisp, Sara Allgood, and Roddy McDowall in reprises of their on-screen roles. It won Best Picture and Best Director against *Citizen Kane,* the film the AFI now considers to be the greatest American picture ever made. —*Sam Wasson*

REAP THE WILD WIND

Paramount, 1942

ALL-RELEASE EQUIVALENT 2005 $s

(Unadjusted $s) in Millions of $s

Domestic Box Office Revenues . . . . **$211.0**/($8.9)
Production Cost . . . . **$24.4**/($2.0)
Principal Photography . . . . **70** days estimated
6/2/1941–8/19/1941
Second Unit 4/28/1941–8/31/1941
Picture reopened 9/9/1941–9/12/1941

Initial Release . . . . 3/18/1942 premiere
(Hollywood)
Rerelease . . . . none
Running Time . . . . 124 minutes
MPAA Rating . . . . not rated

Director . . . . Cecil B. DeMille
Producer . . . . Cecil B. DeMille
Production Company . . . . Paramount Pictures, Inc.
Story by . . . . Based on the novel by Thelma Strabel
Screenplay by . . . . Alan LeMay, Charles Bennett, Jesse Lasky Jr.
Cast . . . . Ray Milland, John Wayne, Paulette Goddard, Raymond Massey, Robert Preston, Susan Hayward, Lynne Overman
Filming Locations . . . . . . Paramount Studio, Hollywood, CA; Santa Monica Pan Pacific Marine Museum; Key West, FL; the "Old New York" set at the 20th Century-Fox; the water tank at the United Artists studio; the Columbia Ranch in Burbank, CA; Charleston, SC; and Miami and New Iberia, FL
Genre . . . . Drama
Format . . . . Color (Technicolor)

STANDING THE TEST OF TIME

ACADEMY AWARD Oscar Nominations and Wins

Art Direction/Set Decoration: Hans Dreier, Roland Anderson/George Sawley

Cinematography (Color): Victor Milner, William V. Skall

***SPECIAL EFFECTS:** Photographic Effects by Gordon Jennings, Farciot Edouart, William L. Pereira; Sound Effects by Louis Mesenkop

OSCAR TOTALS   Nominations **3**   *Wins **1**

AFI 100 YEARS 100 MOVIES SELECTION
2007 0   1997 0

TOP 300 FILMS POSITION . . . . #230
All-Release Domestic Box Office in Equivalent 2005 $s

National Film Preservation Board Selection . . . . none

OTHER AWARDS Best Picture Wins

	Year
Golden Globes	none
New York Film Critics	none
National Board of Review	none
Film Daily Critics	none

Those who read the book and see the picture, will discover certain radical differences. . . .
For that, no apology is necessary, if you believe in dramatic license.
Miss Strabel wrote a narrative; I have made a play.

—Cecil B. DeMille, foreword to 1942 novel *Reap the Wild Wind*

PLOT: An adventure and love triangle set in the Florida Keys in the 1840s, where a rare woman ship salvager faces an unscrupulous rival, who may be sabotaging ships. She rescues a ship captain and falls for him, but it ends with tragic results.

PRODUCTION: It started with the serialization of a novel by Thelma Strabel in the *Saturday Evening Post* in 1940, but DeMille discarded most of the original plot in favor of a story using his favorite theme of two rivals in love, one not completely good, the other not entirely bad. For Loxi, DeMille's "ideal casting" list included Vivien Leigh, Katharine Hepburn, Joan Fontaine, and Lana Turner. He gave the part to Paulette Goddard, who had sought the female lead in *Gone with the Wind*, allowing audiences to see what she might have brought to Scarlett. DeMille sought George Brent for the role of Stephen Tolliver, but Paramount executive Y. Frank Freeman persuaded him to use Paramount contract player Ray Milland, considered a better box office bet. Hattie McDaniel was tapped to play Maum Maria, but her $8,000 fee and billing requirement scrapped the deal. Louise Beavers landed the role for $3,150. DeMille had to convince John Wayne to play a villain, one of the few times he was the bad guy. Cecil B. DeMille stayed close to home, just as he had ever since he became the host of the Monday night CBS radio program *Lux Radio Theater* in 1936. He'd shoot mostly on Paramount studio soundstages in Hollywood, while second-unit director Richard Rosson was sent on location to shoot most of the exterior scenes with doubles substituting for the lead actors. Some scenes were filmed near the Pacific Ocean, not far from L.A., and others near Key West, Florida. DeMille was noted for using conceptual art and storyboards, and he often referred to these images while setting shots and adjusting lighting. The photography for this movie features vibrant colors produced with three-strip Technicolor. Although the film was over budget throughout production, DeMille was never one to economize in his use of raw film stock. He shot a hefty 27 feet of film for every foot that ended up on the screen. The most expensive scene took place underwater with Milland, Wayne, and a giant squid. DeMille wanted a real squid but had to settle for a giant mechanical version with hydraulic pistons that made the 30-foot tentacles move. It was operated from an electrical keyboard, while DeMille directed over a loudspeaker and communicated with his actors, Milland and Wayne, over phone lines rigged into their diving helmets.

DISTRIBUTION: The premiere was held on March 18, 1942, at the newly remodeled Paramount Theater (formerly and, now again, known as El Capitan). It was also a celebration of the thirtieth anniversary of Paramount and DeMille's thirtieth year making movies. Critical reaction was enthusiastic, as was the box office. The April 11, 1942, review in *Liberty* magazine gave the film four stars for showmanship but added, "It makes no pretense of being a co-ordinated artistic achievement. That isn't DeMille's field. He has preferred here, as so often in the past, to pack a picture full of spectacle, excitement, color and comedy." On February 18, 1944, Paramount took out a trade ad announcing that gross film rentals were over $3.8 million. —*Robert S. Birchard*

YANKEE DOODLE DANDY
Warner Bros., 1942

ALL-RELEASE EQUIVALENT 2005 $s
(Unadjusted $s) in Millions of $s

Domestic Box Office Revenues . . . . $244.3/($10.3)
Production Cost . . . . $18.4/($1.5)
Principal Photography . . . . 57 days estimated
12/3/1941–2/10/1942

Director . . . . Michael Curtiz
Producer . . . . Jack L. Warner, Hal B. Wallis
Production Company . . . . Warner Bros. Pictures
Story by . . . . Robert Buckner
Screenplay by . . . . Robert Buckner, Edmund Joseph
Cast . . . . James Cagney, Joan Leslie, Walter Huston, Richard Whorf, Irene Manning
Filming Locations . . . . . . Warner Bros. studio, Burbank, CA
Genre . . . . Musical
Format . . . . B&W
Initial Release . . . . 5/29/1942 world premiere (New York); 6/6/1942 general release
Rerelease . . . . none
Running Time . . . . 126 minutes
MPAA Rating . . . . not rated

STANDING THE TEST OF TIME

ACADEMY AWARD Oscar Nominations and Wins

*ACTOR: James Cagney

Actress in a Supporting Role: Walter Huston

Directing: Michael Curtiz

Film Editing: George Amy

*MUSIC (Scoring of a Musical Picture): Ray Heindorf, Heinz Roemheld

*SOUND RECORDING: Warner Bros. Studio Sound Dept., Nathan Levinson, Sound Director

Writing (Original Motion Picture Story): Robert Buckner

OSCAR TOTALS   Nominations **8**   *Wins **3**

AFI 100 YEARS 100 MOVIES SELECTION
2007 . . . #98   1997 . . #100

TOP 300 FILMS POSITION . . . . **#169**
All-Release Domestic Box Office in Equivalent 2005 $s

National Film Preservation Board Selection 1993

OTHER AWARDS Best Picture Wins

	Year
Golden Globes	none
New York Film Critics	none
National Board of Review	none
Film Daily Critics	none

Curtiz . . . wore his coat of many colors rather well, and he was most unhappy when off the set. I used to say there was no such person as Curtiz, but only Curtiz the director. I understand they would actually take the camera from him to keep him from going on for 24 hours of straight shooting.

—James Cagney

PLOT: Celebrating patriotism and "Americana," this film is the fictionalized musical biography of composer, singer, dancer, and Broadway star George M. Cohan, who dominated American musical theater in the early twentieth century.

PRODUCTION: In 1941 George M. Cohan, seriously ill with cancer, shopped a film about his life. The story was a natural for the movies, especially with the threat of world war on the horizon. After several deals fell through (including one where Fred Astaire was to star), a friend suggested Cagney. Although the quintessential tough guy on-screen, Cagney had starred in vaudeville and could sing and dance. Unhappy with his one-dimensional image and having twice been publicly accused of being a Communist, Cagney was eager to play the patriotic role. He was signed at Warner Bros. (where he got $150,000 per picture, complete script approval, plus profit participation), and his younger brother, William, who managed his career, was associate producer. William brought the idea to Jack L. Warner and a deal was struck shortly thereafter, granting Cohan final approval on the film. Writer Robert Buckner took his screenplay from Cohan's memoirs and personal meetings over six months. Cohan insisted that many things be fictionalized or omitted, such as his opposition to Actors Equity and the fact that he had been married twice. The Cagneys believed that Buckner deferred too much to Cohan and that the script lacked humor. They asked the famous "script doctors," twin brothers Julius J. Epstein and Philip G. Epstein, to rewrite it, but the studio turned the revisions over to Edmund Joseph, whose work never satisfied the Cagneys. Ultimately, the Epsteins worked on the script without screen credit. Michael Curtiz, who had directed Cagney in *Angels with Dirty Faces* (1938), was brought on to direct. Cagney began rehearsals two months prior to shooting with choreographer Johnny Boyle, who had staged the original dances for Cohan. Production began on December 3, a few days before the bombing of Pearl Harbor. Then, two weeks into shooting, Cagney announced that he would not re-sign with the studio when his contract expired. Eager to appease him, Warner Bros. let Cagney make the film as he wished, sparing no expense. The studio built 285 separate sets, and Curtiz directed beautifully staged musical numbers. Although he was foul-mouthed and cynical on set, Curtiz was so moved by the scene in which Cohan bids farewell to his dying father that he ruined a take with his sobs. It was the first time that a living U.S. president (FDR, played by Jack Young) was portrayed in a motion picture.

DISTRIBUTION: Cohan was too ill to leave his New York apartment during filming but approved the script. It was originally set to premiere July 4, 1942, on Cohan's birthday, but with his health deteriorating, the release was pushed up to May 29 (Memorial Day). It became the second-biggest box office hit of 1942 (after *Mrs. Miniver*) and was praised by critics, making a profit of $3.4 million on worldwide rentals of $6.5 million. The war gave added meaning to the flag-waving patriotism in the picture. Cohan died in November 1942. Cagney left Warner Bros. and won his sole Oscar for the role (which he always recalled as his favorite). He was the first actor to win an Oscar for a musical role. Due to war priorities, Cagney's Oscar was made out of plaster. It is said that the morning after the Oscars, Cagney gave the award to his brother as a gesture of appreciation. —*Alex Ben Block*

THE PRIDE OF THE YANKEES

RKO, 1942

ALL-RELEASE EQUIVALENT 2005 $s

(Unadjusted $s) in Millions of $s

Domestic Box Office Revenues. . . . . **$191.3**/($8.5)
Production Cost . . . . not available
Principal Photography. . . . . **50** days estimated
2/11/1942–April 1942

Director	Sam Wood
Producer	Samuel Goldwyn
Production Company. . . .	Samuel Goldwyn Productions
Story by.	Paul Gallico
Screenplay by.	Jo Swerling, Herman J. Mankiewicz
Cast	Gary Cooper, Teresa Wright, Babe Ruth, Walter Brennan
Filming Locations	Pelham Parkway (Bronx, NY); Wrigley Field, Chicago; Yankee Stadium (Bronx); University of Southern California
Genre.	Bio-Drama
Format.	B&W
Initial Release	7/14/1942 premiere (New York); 8/18/1942 premiere (Los Angeles)
Rerelease	1949
Running Time	127 minutes
MPAA Rating	not rated

No attempt is made to inject color into the characterization of Gehrig. He's depicted for what he was, a quiet, plodding personality who strived for and achieved perfection in his profession.

—*Variety*

STANDING THE TEST OF TIME

ACADEMY AWARD Oscar Nominations and Wins

Outstanding Motion Picture: Samuel Goldwyn Productions

Actor: Gary Cooper

Actress: Teresa Wright

Art Direction/Set Decoration (B&W): Perry Ferguson/Howard Bristol

Cinematography (B&W): Rudolph Maté

*FILM EDITING: Daniel Mandell

Music (Music Score of a Dramatic or Comedy Picture): Leigh Harline

Sound Recording: Samuel Goldwyn Studio Sound Dept., Thomas T. Moulton, Sound Director

Special Effects: Photographic Effects by Jack Cosgrove, Ray Binger; Sound Effects by Thomas T. Moulton

Writing (Original Motion Picture Story): Paul Gallico

Writing (Screenplay): Jo Swerling, Herman J. Mankiewicz

OSCAR TOTALS   Nominations **11** *Wins 1

AFI 100 YEARS 100 MOVIES SELECTION
2007 0   1997 0

TOP 300 FILMS POSITION . . . . **#294**
All-Release Domestic Box Office in Equivalent 2005 $s

National Film Preservation Board Selection. . . . none

OTHER AWARDS Best Picture Wins

	Year
Golden Globes	none
New York Film Critics.	none
National Board of Review	none
Film Daily Critics	none

PLOT: The film recounts the story of baseball's "Iron Man," Lou Gehrig, a gentle man who rose from humble beginnings to baseball stardom. When diagnosed with amyotrophic lateral sclerosis (ALS), he faced death with courage and dignity.

PRODUCTION: Initially, Samuel Goldwyn had been reluctant to produce the film, believing that baseball films were "box office poison." When newsreel footage of Lou Gehrig's 1939 retirement speech was released, Gehrig was suddenly seen as much more than just a great baseball player: he was an American hero who faced a tragic illness with outstanding valor. It was then that Samuel Goldwyn, at the suggestion of his story editor Niven Busch (married to Teresa Wright, who played Eleanor Gehrig in the movie), decided to make the biopic. Because the film was made during World War II and targeted a predominantly female home-front audience, *The Pride of the Yankees* was intended as not just a baseball movie or the story of a first-generation immigrant who achieved fame in the "land of opportunity," but rather a human story—and above all, a love story. Gary Cooper (who slightly resembled Gehrig and shared some of his quiet and humble qualities) was the obvious choice to star in the film. He resisted at first, but when Goldwyn threatened to sue him, Cooper agreed. This film completed Cooper's obligations under a six-film contract with Goldwyn. Walter Brennan was cast as sportswriter Sam Blake, loosely based on writer Fred Lieb, one of Gehrig's closest friends. Some of Gehrig's Yankee teammates, including Bill Dickey, Bob Meusel, Mark Koenig, and Babe Ruth, along with veteran sportscaster Bill Stern, were recruited to give the film greater authenticity, and to delight baseball fans. Gary Cooper, who was neither a baseball fan nor an athlete, required a lot of help to look passable on-screen as a ballplayer. As it turned out, Cooper was right-handed where Gehrig had been a lefty, making the task of authenticity even more difficult. To address this, the type was set in reverse on the uniforms the actors wore in all baseball scene close-ups. Cooper would also hit the ball and run to third instead of first; then the prints would be reversed during the film's edit. In addition, Joseph "Lefty" O'Doul was recruited to improve Cooper's batting style. Cooper, at age forty-one, was out of shape and had suffered from previous injuries while making films. To keep him from looking too old, cinematographer Rudolph Mate shot him in the young Gehrig scenes with lighting from below to mask any wrinkles. As Gehrig aged in the story, the lighting effect was gradually eliminated. During the filming of the movie, Eleanor Gehrig (who also consulted on the script) came to the set and lent Teresa Wright the actual bracelet that Lou had given her on their fourth anniversary. The bracelet was made of seventeen metal medallions celebrating milestones in Gehrig's career, including seven World Championships and six All-Star appearances, and is now in the Baseball Hall of Fame. To underscore the romantic focus of the film, Irving Berlin's love song "Always," a favorite of Lou and Eleanor Gehrig as well as Sam Goldwyn, permeates the film.

DISTRIBUTION: The movie opened in New York approximately one year after Gehrig's death, on July 14, 1942, and brought in more than $4.2 million in worldwide rentals on its initial release. Widely acclaimed, it turned out to be the highest-grossing film that Goldwyn had produced to date. —*Christine McDermott*

MRS. MINIVER
MGM, 1942

ALL-RELEASE EQUIVALENT 2005 $s
(Unadjusted $s) in Millions of $s

Domestic Box Office Revenues . . . . $282.7/($11.9)
Production Cost . . . . $16.1/($1.3)
Principal Photography . . . . .80 days estimated
11/5/1941–2/10/1942

Director . . . . William Wyler
Producer . . . . Sidney Franklin
Production Company . . . . Metro-Goldwyn-Mayer
Story by . . . . Based on the 1939 book by Jan
Struther
Screenplay by . . . . Arthur Wimperis, George
Froeschel, James Hilton,
Claudine West
Cast . . . . Greer Garson, Walter Pidgeon,
Teresa Wright, Dame May
Whitty, Reginald Owen,
Henry Travers, Richard Ney,
Henry Wilcoxon
Filming Locations . . . . . . Metro-Goldwyn-Mayer Studios,
Culver City, CA
Genre . . . . War
Format . . . . B&W
Initial Release . . . . 6/04/1942 premiere, Radio City
Music Hall, (New York);
7/22/1942 Carthay Circle
Theater, (Los Angeles);
7/23/1942 general release
Rerelease . . . . none
Running Time . . . . 134 minutes
MPAA Rating . . . . not rated

STANDING THE TEST OF TIME

ACADEMY AWARD Oscar Nominations and Wins

***OUTSTANDING MOTION PICTURE:** Metro-Goldwyn-Mayer

Actor: Walter Pidgeon

Actor in a Supporting Role: Henry Travers

***ACTRESS:** Greer Garson

Actress in a Supporting Role: Dame May Whitty

***ACTRESS IN A SUPPORTING ROLE:** Teresa Wright

***WRITING** (Screenplay): Arthur Wimperis, George Froeschel, James Hilton, Claudine West

***CINEMATOGRAPHY:** Joseph Ruttenberg

***DIRECTING:** William Wyler

Film Editing: Harold F. Kress

Sound Recording: Metro-Goldwyn-Mayer Studio Sound Dept., Douglas Shearer, Sound Director

Special Effects: Photographic Effects by A. Arnold Gillespie, Warren Newcombe; Sound Effects by Douglas Shearer

OSCAR TOTALS   Nominations **12** *Wins 6

AFI 100 YEARS 100 MOVIES SELECTION
2007 0   1997 0

TOP 300 FILMS POSITION . . . . #120
All-Release Domestic Box Office in Equivalent 2005 $s

National Film Preservation Board Selection . . . . none

OTHER AWARDS Best Picture Wins

	Year
Golden Globes	none
New York Film Critics	none
National Board of Review	none
Film Daily Critics	none

Mrs. Miniver *is that almost impossible feat, a great war picture that photographs the inner meaning, instead of the outward realism, of World War II.*

—*Time,* 1942

PLOT: Clem and Kay Miniver, a middle-class British couple with three children, find their comfortable way of life disappearing as the grim, encroaching realities of World War II descend on their homeland and in particular their idyllic rural village.

PRODUCTION: Actress Greer Garson fainted upon exiting Louis B. Mayer's office. She had just endured a meeting at which the MGM mogul begged, cajoled, and insisted that she star in *Mrs. Miniver*—a part Norma Shearer had rejected. To convince the reluctant actress, Mayer had given a sweeping performance of the script appealing heavily to Garson's British patriotism "To this day, I still think Louis Mayer played Mrs. Miniver better than I did," Garson later quipped. Garson had enjoyed the best-selling book by Jan Struther that relayed the cheerful adventures of an English housewife and her family on the eve of World War II. But upon purchasing the film rights from Struther for $32,500, MGM producer Sidney Franklin had his team of British writers spend six months refashioning the buoyant story into a terse, dramatic account of Britain's grim wartime situation, reflecting the current reality. Struther's tale ended in September 1939, which is the point at which Franklin's screenwriters started their version of the story. Adding to Garson's angst was the hiring of director William Wyler, whose reputation as a perfectionist often resulted in numerous takes. Borrowed from the Goldwyn studio, Wyler was bent on awakening an indifferent America to Britain's desperate plight. "This is a hell of a time to escape from reality," he had said. "We're in an all-out war—a people's war—it's the time to face it." Unable to shoot at Metro's Denham studio north of London because of the war, the movie was shot completely at MGM in Culver City under Louis B. Mayer's watchful eye—a development that did not bode well for Wyler. Art director Cedric Gibbons was irritated with Wyler's interference and Garson had walked off the set one day following a row with the strong-willed director. After Wyler was summoned to Mayer's office and presented with a list of grievances, the on-set confrontations subsided a bit. Wyler's most vexing problem, however, was the film's final patriotic sermon, delivered by the village vicar (Henry Wilcoxon). Although the sequence had already been filmed, Wyler was convinced that it needed to be rewritten and reshot, but Wilcoxon had already enlisted in the U.S. Navy (Pearl Harbor had been attacked during the *Mrs. Miniver* shoot). Upon the grant of a two-day leave, Wilcoxon and Wyler were finally able to hammer out a revised speech overnight and have the new footage in the can by noon the next day.

DISTRIBUTION: Wyler's decision paid off—Wilcoxon's climactic address was so stirring that President Franklin Roosevelt had it printed as leaflets, air-dropped over Europe, and broadcast via radio on Voice of America. Likewise, British prime minister Winston Churchill proclaimed that *Mrs. Miniver* was "more powerful to the war effort than the combined work of six military divisions." *Mrs. Miniver*'s galvanizing effect on Americans spawned a record-breaking ten-week run at Radio City Music Hall and garnered a $5.4 million take in domestic rentals (making *Mrs. Miniver* 1942's top grosser), with a $4.8 million profit on worldwide rentals of $8.9 million. —*Douglas Burns*

BAMBI
RKO, 1942

<table>
<tr><td colspan="2" align="center">ALL-RELEASE EQUIVALENT 2005 $s</td></tr>
<tr><td colspan="2" align="center">(Unadjusted $s) in Millions of $s</td></tr>
<tr><td>Domestic Box Office Revenues</td><td>$383.8/($101.6)</td></tr>
<tr><td>Production Cost</td><td>$20.9/($1.7)</td></tr>
<tr><td>Production Period</td><td>5.2 years</td></tr>
<tr><td colspan="2" align="center">December 1936–February 1942</td></tr>
</table>

Director . . . . David Hand (Supervising Director)

Producer . . . . Walt Disney

Production Company . . . . Walt Disney Productions

Story by . . . . Based on the book by Felix Salten

Screenplay by . . . . Larry Morey (story adaptation); Perce Pearce (story direction)

Cast . . . . Bambi (voiced by Bobby Stewart, Donnie Dunagan, Hardie Albright, John Sutherland), Thumper (Peter Behn, Tim Davis, Sam Edwards), Flower (Stan Alexander, Tim Davis, Sterling Holloway), Faline (Cammie King, Ann Gillis)

Filming Locations . . . . . . Walt Disney Productions (Hollywood and Burbank, CA)

Genre . . . . Animation

Format . . . . Color (Technicolor)

Initial Release . . . . 8/8/1942 world premiere (London, England); 8/13/1942 U.S. premiere, Radio City Music Hall (New York); 8/21/1942 general release

Rerelease 1947, 1957, 1966, 1975, 1982, 1988

Running Time . . . . 69 minutes

MPAA Rating . . . . not rated

STANDING THE TEST OF TIME

ACADEMY AWARD Oscar Nominations and Wins

Music (Music Score of a Dramatic or Comedy Picture): Frank Churchill, Edward Plumb

Music (Song): "Love Is a Song," Music by Frank Churchill; Lyrics by Larry Morey

Sound Recording: Walt Disney Studio Sound Dept., Sam Slyfield, Sound Director

OSCAR TOTALS   Nominations **3**   *Wins **0**

AFI 100 YEARS 100 MOVIES SELECTION
2007 0   1997 0

TOP 300 FILMS POSITION . . . . #49
All-Release Domestic Box Office in Equivalent 2005 $s

National Film Preservation Board Selection . . . . none

OTHER AWARDS Best Picture Wins

	Year
Golden Globes	none
New York Film Critics	none
National Board of Review	none
Film Daily Critics	none

It would be churlish to rebuke an effort that has caught so much startling beauty or that so often touches the heart with a humor that is both inventive and wise.

—Theodore Strauss, *New York Times*, 1942

PLOT: Bambi, a fawn born in the forest, grows to maturity with his animal friends while experiencing the wonders and cycles of nature as well as the joys and dangers of life, including love, loss, and a life-threatening encounter with humans.

PRODUCTION: With *Snow White and the Seven Dwarfs* nearing completion in late 1936, Walt Disney sought additional properties for animation. He had read *Bambi: A Life in the Woods,* a Book-of-the-Month Club hit by Austrian writer Felix Salten, and thought the novel, published in 1923 and translated for American readers in 1928, would be ideal. When he discovered that MGM producer-director Sidney Franklin (*The Good Earth, Mrs. Miniver*) had already optioned the rights as a possible live-action project, the two men entered lengthy discussions. Franklin eventually relinquished the rights in April 1937, conceding that Disney's animation medium "would do greater justice to the yarn." Franklin's involvement was subsequently acknowledged via an on-screen dedication in Bambi's opening credits, praising his "inspiring collaboration." With two additional animated features (*Pinocchio* and *Fantasia*) and a slate of cartoon shorts in production, Disney's studio on Hyperion Avenue in Los Angeles was out of space; the *Bambi* unit was moved to a rented building on North Seward Street in Hollywood. Additional characters were added to Salten's story, including Thumper the Rabbit and Flower the Skunk. Walt soon realized that Bambi would present more challenges than *Snow White* or *Pinocchio*. There were no human characters and the story's tone was far more serious. To ensure that the animals and their environment remained authentic, Walt dispatched artist Maurice Day on a five-month trip to Maine with orders to photograph, sketch, and paint forests, wildlife, plant life and other imagery to use as references. The Maine Development Commission also sent two live fawns to California for the animators to study. A full-blown studio "zoo" ensued as birds, squirrels, chipmunks, raccoons, rabbits, and two skunks (named Herman and Petunia) were added to the menagerie. Originally planned as the company's second animated feature film, *Bambi* fell behind schedule. The company's move in December 1939 to Burbank and a crippling animators' strike in 1941, lasting more than 100 days, slowed the production. What's more, on December 7, 1941, following the attack on Pearl Harbor, army troops moved onto the Disney lot, establishing a support base for local antiaircraft installations to protect the nearby Lockheed aircraft plant. The war also depleted the studio's male workforce—one-third of Walt's animators were drafted while most of the remaining staff switched over to producing military training films. Yet production on *Bambi* endured, shepherded along by four of Disney's legendary "Nine Old Men"—Frank Thomas, Milt Kahl, Oliver Johnston, and Eric Larson. Final inking and painting was completed in January 1942 and final scenes went to the Camera Department the following month. The finished film consisted of 110,000 frames.

DISTRIBUTION: Bambi underperformed both in the United States and overseas in its initial 1942 release, in part due to wartime restrictions. Worldwide rentals of $3,449,353 barely recouped the film's nearly $2 million production cost. However, six subsequent theatrical reissues through 1988 have catapulted *Bambi* into the top echelon of Disney animated films; it is also a top seller on home video formats. *—Douglas Burns*

CASABLANCA
Warner Bros., 1943

ALL-RELEASE EQUIVALENT 2005 $s
(Unadjusted $s) in Millions of $s

Domestic Box Office Revenues . . . . **$169.6**/($9.3)
Production Cost . . . . **$11.7**/($1.0)
Principal Photography . . . . **61** days estimated
5/25/1942–8/31/1942

Director . . . . Michael Curtiz
Producer . . . . Hal B. Wallis
Production Company . . . . Warner Bros. Pictures, Inc.
Story by . . . . From a play by Murray Burnett, Joan Alison
Screenplay by . . . . Julius J. Epstein, Philip G. Epstein, Howard Koch
Cast . . . . Humphrey Bogart, Ingrid Bergman, Paul Henreid, Claude Rains, Conrad Veidt, Sidney Greenstreet, Peter Lorre
Filming Locations . . . . . . Nearly 100 percent at Warner Bros. studio, Warner Bros. lot, and Van Nuys Airport (the final scene only)
Genre . . . . Drama, War
Format . . . . B&W
Initial Release . . . . 11/26/1942 world premiere (New York); 1/23/1943 general release
Rerelease 1949, 1992
Running Time . . . . 102 minutes
MPAA Rating . . . . not rated

STANDING THE TEST OF TIME

ACADEMY AWARD Oscar Nominations and Wins

*OUTSTANDING MOTION PICTURE: Warner Bros.

Actor: Humphrey Bogart

Actor in a Supporting Role: Claude Rains

Cinematography (B&W): Arthur Edeson

*DIRECTING: Michael Curtiz

Film Editing: Owen Marks

Music (Music Score of a Dramatic or Comedy Picture): Max Steiner

*WRITING (Screenplay): Julius J. Epstein, Philip G. Epstein, Howard Koch

OSCAR TOTALS Nominations **8** *Wins **3**

AFI 100 YEARS 100 MOVIES SELECTION
2007 . . . . #3   1997 . . . . #2

TOP 300 FILMS POSITION . . . . .none
All-Release Domestic Box Office in Equivalent 2005 $s

National Film Preservation Board Selection 1989

OTHER AWARDS Best Picture Wins

	Year
Golden Globes	none
New York Film Critics	none
National Board of Review	none
Film Daily Critics	none

I suspect that with enough time and effort a picture could be got from this very obvious imitation of Grand Hotel.
—Robert Lord of Warner Bros.

PLOT: Expatriate American Rick Blaine owns the most popular nightclub in Vichy-controlled Casablanca, Morocco. One night, in walks the very girl who broke his heart in Paris just before the German occupation and turned him into a bitter cynic.

PRODUCTION: Four days after the Japanese attack on Pearl Harbor, Warner Bros. story analyst Stephen Kamot reported on an unproduced stage play, *Everybody Comes to Rick's,* by Murray Burnett and Joan Alison. By the end of the month, producer Hal Wallis had paid $20,000 for the film rights and changed the piece's title to *Casablanca.* No one involved with the production treated it as anything other than the dozens of modest-budget, low-expectation films they were used to working on. Facilitated by actors who could be moved around like chess pieces—Ronald Reagan and George Raft were considered for the male lead, Ann Sheridan for the love interest, and then-unknown Lena Horne for a gender-switched Sam—the Hollywood studio system created a masterpiece. With its high six-figure budget, *Casablanca* was not a particularly expensive film to produce. Neither was it a bargain-basement B movie. It was, however, a film that benefited from good fortune every step of the way. The perfect Warner contract players were available—the studio controlled most of the film's major actors except Ingrid Bergman, who was under contract to David O. Selznick—and its best contract director, Michael Curtiz, accepted too. After Julius and Philip Epstein abandoned their more comic take on the project, screenwriter Howard Koch was able to step in, hurriedly writing in a more melodramatic style while the production was under way. Because of this last-minute work, the actors did not know how the story would turn out until just before they prepared to shoot the final scenes. For example, the last few pages of Koch's script turned Claude Rains's character into a patriotic rogue rather than the villain Rains had been playing all along. Naturally, there were quite a number of delays due to cast members not knowing their lines, which in some cases had been handed to them only the night before. Another important addition to the mix was veteran composer-conductor Max Steiner, also on the Warner staff, who contributed a lush, romantic score that emphasized the torrid love affair at the film's center.

DISTRIBUTION: The movie premiere, held on Thanksgiving Day 1942 as the Allies landed in North Africa, was followed by a parade up Fifth Avenue in New York, where the Free French flag was unfurled for the first time in the United States since the fall of the Nazi-supported Vichy government. However, the film didn't take off until its general release in 1943, when a much-anticipated Roosevelt-Churchill summit was scheduled for the real-life Casablanca, newly liberated by Eisenhower's North Africa campaign. It was the January 1943 release that turned the picture into a sensation and vaulted it to success at the Academy Awards. Its combined 1942–43 take was a $4 million profit on $6.9 million in worldwide rentals. In later years, Humphrey Bogart's star rose even higher in retrospect, and by the sixties *Casablanca* had attained the eminence of an all-time Hollywood classic, with continuing engagements in art and revival houses. Bogart's trench-coat-clad character became iconic, widely imitated, and parodied, even famously misquoted in the title of Woody Allen's play *Play It Again, Sam.* But by then it had become part of Americana. —*Tom Dupree*

THE OX-BOW INCIDENT
20th Century-Fox, 1943

ALL-RELEASE EQUIVALENT 2005 $s
(Unadjusted $s) in Millions of $s

Domestic Box Office Revenues . . . . **$32.9**/($1.5)
Production Cost . . . . **$6.4**/($0.6)
Principal Photography . . . . **46** days estimated
6/29/1942–8/20/1942

Director . . . . William A. Wellman

Producer . . . . Lamar Trotti

Production Company . . . . 20th Century-Fox Film Corp.

Story by . . . . Based on the novel by
Walter Van Tilburg Clark

Screenplay by . . . . Lamar Trotti

Cast . . . . Henry Fonda, Dana Andrews,
Mary Beth Hughes,
Anthony Quinn

Filming Locations . . . . . . Primarily at 20th Century-Fox
studio, CA; some exteriors at
Iverson Ranch in Chatsworth
and around in Lone Pine, CA.

Genre . . . . Western

Format . . . . B&W

Initial Release 5/21/1943

Rerelease . . . . none

Running Time . . . . 74 minutes

MPAA Rating . . . . not rated

STANDING THE TEST OF TIME

ACADEMY AWARD Oscar Nominations and Wins

Outstanding Motion Picture: 20th Century-Fox

OSCAR TOTALS   Nominations **1**   *Wins 0

AFI 100 YEARS 100 MOVIES SELECTION
2007 0   1997 0

TOP 300 FILMS POSITION . . . . .none
All-Release Domestic Box Office in Equivalent 2005 $s

National Film Preservation Board Selection 1998

OTHER AWARDS Best Picture Wins

	Year
Golden Globes	none
New York Film Critics	none
National Board of Review	1943
Film Daily Critics	none

I went to all the producers for whom I had worked and got turned down.
Zanuck was the only one with the guts to do an out-of-the-ordinary story
for the prestige rather than the dough.

—William Wellman

PLOT: Based on the report of a fatal shooting and cattle rustling, a posse is thrown together and subsequently lynches three innocent men for a murder that has not been committed.

PRODUCTION: Walter Van Tilburg Clark was an English teacher in upstate New York when he wrote his first novel, *The Ox-Bow Incident*. Published in 1940, it drew immediate literary acclaim. Movie rights were acquired in 1941 by former Paramount producer Harold Hurley, who almost made a deal with United Artists. He later sold rights to director William Wellman, who paid $500 more than Hurley had originally paid for the rights. Wellman then took the story, which had cost him $6,500 of his own money (marking the only time Wellman ever spent his own funds on a movie), to everyone he knew, but no one in Hollywood would touch the project because they were afraid of its dark story line. In the context of the times, the story was viewed as an intimation that the kind of evil Hitler wreaked on Europe could inhabit even a small western town. Although he had had a falling-out with Zanuck two years earlier, Wellman called him and said, "I've got the greatest story I've ever had in my life. I want to read it to you." Zanuck agreed. He told Wellman that he didn't think the film would make any money, but he wanted the studio to have it, provided Wellman agreed to make two more pictures for Fox. Zanuck then brought in prolific screenwriter Lamar Trotti to write the script and produce. The scenes were filmed on a very low budget. Most of the movie was shot on soundstages, with some location shots filmed around California. Zanuck was in the army during shooting and helped with the production from London, where he was stationed, as much as he could. Sara Allgood was initially cast as Jennie "Ma" Grier, but was later replaced by Florence Bates, who was then injured in a horseback-riding scene. Bates was replaced by Jane Darwell, who is seen in the movie. In August 1942, production shut down for approximately ten days because of wartime limits on new construction materials. During the hiatus, previously used sets were torn down and the material was recycled, mostly to build the mountain pass set. The studio boasted that the Ox-Bow Valley setting was "the largest set ever constructed" by Fox, covering some 26,703 feet. The final cost was only $569,000.

DISTRIBUTION: The Production Code Administration strongly protested the script, especially the scenes that show the sheriff as having been responsible for the lynching. The censors asked for changes that would illustrate some retribution for the ringleader, requesting that the character commit suicide. With those changes, a rare movie depicting a lynching was allowed. Henry Fonda, who had a military deferment, enlisted in the U.S. Navy immediately upon completing the film. The movie was kept out of circulation by the apprehensive studio for almost a year due to its pessimistic and somber message. Although one of only a handful of westerns nominated for a Best Picture Oscar, and a darling of the critics, the film did not perform well. It ended its initial run with a net loss of $5,400 on worldwide rentals of only $891,000. A version was made for television in 1955 starring Robert Wagner and Cameron Mitchell. —*Dina Gachman*

FOR WHOM THE BELL TOLLS
Paramount, 1943

ALL-RELEASE EQUIVALENT 2005 $s
(Unadjusted $s) in Millions of $s

Domestic Box Office Revenues . . . . **$333.9**/($15.8)
Production Cost . . . . **$33.7**/($3.0)
Principal Photography . . . . **141** days estimated
11/21/1941–12/9/1941
6/18/1942–6/19/1942
7/2/1942–10/31/1942
1/20/1943–2/10/1943

Director . . . . Sam Wood

Producer . . . . Sam Wood

Production Company . . . . Paramount Pictures

Story by . . . . Based on the novel by
Ernest Hemingway

Screenplay by . . . . Dudley Nichols

Cast . . . . Gary Cooper, Ingrid Bergman,
Akim Tamiroff, Arturo de
Cordova, Joseph Calleia, Katina
Paxinou, Vladimir Sokoloff

Filming Locations . . . . . . On location: Sonora Highlands;
in studio: Paramount lot

Genre . . . . War

Format . . . . Color (Technicolor)

Initial Release 7/14/1943

Rerelease 1957

Running Time . . . . 170 minutes

MPAA Rating . . . . not rated

STANDING THE TEST OF TIME

ACADEMY AWARD Oscar Nominations and Wins

Outstanding Motion Picture: Paramount

Actor: Gary Cooper

Actor in a Supporting Role: Akim Tamiroff

Actress: Ingrid Bergman

*ACTRESS IN A SUPPORTING ROLE: Katina
Paxinou

Art Direction/Interior Decoration: Hans Dreier,
Haldane Douglas/Bertram Granger

Cinematography: Ray Rennahan

Film Editing: Sherman Todd, John Link

Music (Music Score of a Dramatic or Comedy Picture):
Victor Young

OSCAR TOTALS   Nominations 9   *Wins 1

AFI 100 YEARS 100 MOVIES SELECTION
2007 0   1997 0

TOP 300 FILMS POSITION . . . . #82
All-Release Domestic Box Office in Equivalent 2005 $s

National Film Preservation Board Selection . . . . none

OTHER AWARDS Best Picture Wins

	Year
Golden Globes	none
New York Film Critics	none
National Board of Review	none
Film Daily Critics	none

*Hemingway told Ingrid Bergman, "After I'd seen the first five minutes I couldn't stand it
any longer so I walked out. . . . It took me five visits to see that movie."*
—Frank McAdams, *The American War Film: History and Hollywood*

PLOT: Robert Jordan, a freelance demolitions expert, joins a group of Spanish partisans during the Spanish Civil War and falls in love with an idealistic woman before going on a suicide mission.

PRODUCTION: In 1937 Nobel Prize–winning writer Ernest Hemingway went to report on the Spanish Civil War. He sided with the Republicans, who by 1939 had been defeated. Hemmingway returned to America and took up residence in Key West, Florida, with regular trips to Cuba, writing a novel based on his experiences in both locales. The title comes from Meditation XVII of *Devotions upon Emergent Occasions,* a metaphysical poem by Jacobean poet John Donne. It was published in 1940, and Paramount purchased screen rights for a reported $100,000 in December 1940. That sparked a letter-writing campaign by the Legion of Decency and others, contending the novel was "pro-Red and immoral." Cecil B. DeMille planned a film based on the novel, and Jeanie MacPherson worked on the script for it from October 28, 1940, to May 13, 1941. However, at the instigation of John Hay Whitney, DeMille turned the project over to Paramount to work on another film (which, ultimately, was never made). In 1941 Louis Bromfield wrote the first draft of a new script, working 48 days for $25,000. Dudley Nichols (who received sole screenplay credit) worked on the script from October 16, 1941, to July 18, 1942, for $51,000 and took much of the politics out of the screenplay, concentrating on the love affair and action. Before Gary Cooper was cast, others mentioned were Spencer Tracy, Paul Muni, Henry Fonda, and Franchot Tone. Frances Farmer, Michele Morgan, and Olivia de Havilland were considered for Maria. Hemingway influenced casting, requesting Cooper and Bergman. Because of the war, Paramount set up the production in California, using the Sierra Nevada to stand in for Spain. Vera Zorina was initially cast as Maria but was replaced by Ingrid Bergman, fresh off the Warner Bros. lot, where she had just completed *Casablanca.* Initial studio production began November 21, 1941, working from Louis Bromfield's draft. Dudley Nichols was called in to do a rewrite working from October 16, 1941, to July 18, 1942. Filming in the Sierra Nevada mountain range began June 18, 1942. The cast and crew were put up in Sonora. Production designer William Cameron Menzies (*Gone with the Wind*) had the task of developing special effects along with Paramount process photographer Farciot Edouart. Stand-ins had a firm call for 7:30 a.m., with actual shooting beginning around noon each day (for maximum mountain sunlight). It was a difficult location shoot. By October 31, 1942, the day of the scene at the town square and city hall, the production was 46 days behind schedule, and the budget had been revised several times. Reshooting continued from January 20, 1943, to February 10, 1943. In May 1943 Sam Wood okayed a special machine gun effect for the final scene. In the last sequence Gary Cooper's horse falls and breaks a leg. The stunt horse was brown, while Cooper's film horse was gray, so they painted the stunt horse gray. Gary Cooper's salary was $12,500 per week for twelve weeks, prorated for extensions. Ingrid Bergman received $8,000 per week.

DISTRIBUTION: Despite the early furor over the novel being "pro-Red and immoral," the film opened to strong and favorable reviews and brought in $11 million in worldwide rentals in its initial release. *—Frank McAdams*

DOUBLE INDEMNITY
Paramount, 1944

ALL-RELEASE EQUIVALENT 2005 $s
(Unadjusted $s) in Millions of $s

Domestic Box Office Revenues. . . . . **$111.3**/($5.6)
Production Cost . . . .**$10.3**/($0.9)
Principal Photography. . . . .**51** days estimated
9/27/1943–11/24/1943
Retakes in Dec/Jan due
to scratches in negative

Director . . . . Billy Wilder
Producer . . . . Joseph Sistrom
Production Company. . . . Paramount Pictures
Story by. . . . . Based on the novel by
James M. Cain
Screenplay by . . . . Billy Wilder, Raymond Chandler
Cast . . . . Fred MacMurray, Barbara
Stanwyck, Edward G. Robinson
Filming Locations . . . . . . In and around Los Angeles
Genre. . . . . Film Noir
Format . . . . B&W
Initial Release 4/24/1944
Rerelease . . . . none
Running Time . . . . 106 minutes
MPAA Rating . . . . not rated

STANDING THE TEST OF TIME

ACADEMY AWARD Oscar Nominations and Wins

Best Motion Picture: Paramount

Actress: Barbara Stanwyck

Cinematography (B&W): John Seitz

Directing: Billy Wilder

Music (Music Score of a Dramatic or Comedy Picture): Miklos Rozsa

Sound Recording: Paramount Studio Sound Dept., Loren L. Ryder, Sound Director

Writing (Screenplay): Billy Wilder, Raymond Chandler

OSCAR TOTALS   Nominations 7   *Wins 0

AFI 100 YEARS 100 MOVIES SELECTION
2007 . . . #29   1997. . #38

TOP 300 FILMS POSITION . . . . .none
All-Release Domestic Box Office in Equivalent 2005 $s

National Film Preservation Board Selection. . . . 1992

OTHER AWARDS Best Picture Wins

	Year
Golden Globes	none
New York Film Critics	none
National Board of Review	none
Film Daily Critics	none

It's the only picture I ever saw made from my books that had things in it
I wish I had thought of. Wilder's ending was much better than my ending.

—James M. Cain, author of the 1935 novel *Double Indemnity*

PLOT: Insurance salesman Walter Neff is seduced by his client's wife. They take out a big policy on her husband together. They commit what seems like the perfect murder until another insurance executive inspects the claim.

PRODUCTION: Billy Wilder acquired film rights for James M. Cain's *Double Indemnity* after he became aware that a secretary in his office had been reading the manuscript in the bathroom. Paramount bought it for Wilder despite a warning from the censors that the story violated the Production Code. Wilder's writing partner, Charles Brackett, thought the novella too sordid and refused to collaborate. Paramount instead hired local Los Angeles author Raymond Chandler for his similar hard-boiled style. The thirteen weeks it took Wilder and Chandler to write the script strained the limits of each man's sanity. The fifty-five-year-old novelist hated listening to lectures on writing from the much younger Wilder. He detested how Wilder would pace around the room, swinging a cane, while dictating lines, or how he'd stop working to answer phone calls from countless girlfriends. For his part, Wilder couldn't stand Chandler's blunt rudeness, his constant drinking and smoking, and his incessant demands that Wilder apologize for his own quirks. Things turned so sour between them that Wilder would hide in the bathroom for long periods of time. Casting was just as difficult. Everyone from Cagney to Peck turned down the lead role, for fear that playing a murderer would damage their career. George Raft wanted Neff to pull out an undercover police badge at the end. Wilder's nemesis at Paramount, Y. Frank Freeman, pushed actor Fred MacMurray to take the part only because it might punish the actor for having played contractual hardball. MacMurray, who was hesitant at first, later said it was the best role he ever took. Despite his struggles with Chandler, Wilder knew he had something special in *Double Indemnity*. "Keep quiet," he declared on set, "history is being made." He insisted the film look as seedy as its story, opting to shoot on location in Los Angeles whenever possible. Cinematographer John Seitz blew aluminum particles in the air to make the Dietrichson house seem like a dusty tomb. Costume designer Edith Head dressed Barbara Stanwyck in a platinum blond wig and an ankle bracelet to look sleazy and cheap. A frantic moment when Wilder was running late inspired the famous car stall after the murder, now a Hollywood cliché. Wilder believed the original ending he shot, a sequence where Neff chokes to death in a prison gas chamber, to be one of his best scenes. But against the wishes of everyone involved in the production, he cut it, deeming the last exchange between Keyes and Neff more elegant.

DISTRIBUTION: Wilder's heart sank when he heard the whistles during the April 1944 preview in Westwood, then realized they were meant for Stanwyck's sexy entrance. It didn't seem to matter that she played a murderess; advertisers wanted her face to sell everything from diamonds to bedspreads. Smoke shops posted window cards of Neff lighting Keyes's cigar, while the trade magazine *Boxoffice* recommended that insurance agencies take the entire staff to a screening. Cain thought the film better than his novella, and even Chandler, years later, admitted that of the films he'd worked on, his favorite was the one he wrote for "an odd little director with a touch of genius, Billy Wilder." —*Michael Kogge*

GOING MY WAY
Paramount, 1944

ALL-RELEASE EQUIVALENT 2005 $s
(Unadjusted $s) in Millions of $s

Domestic Box Office Revenues . . . . $289.3/($14.4)
Production Cost . . . . $11.1/($1.0)
Principal Photography . . . . .58 days estimated
8/16/1943–10/22/1943

Director . . . . Leo McCarey
Producer . . . . Leo McCarey
Production Company . . . . Paramount Productions
Story by . . . . Leo McCarey
Screenplay by . . . . Frank Butler, Frank Cavett
Cast . . . . Bing Crosby, Barry Fitzgerald,
Frank McHugh, James Brown,
Gene Lockhart
Filming Locations . . . . . . On location in Los Angeles;
most shot in studio
Genre . . . . Musical
Format . . . . B&W
Initial Release . . . . 4/27/1944 on military bases;
5/3/1944 general release
Rerelease . . . . none
Running Time . . . . 130 minutes
MPAA Rating . . . . not rated

STANDING THE TEST OF TIME

ACADEMY AWARD Oscar Nominations and Wins

***BEST MOTION PICTURE:** Paramount

***ACTOR:** Bing Crosby

Actor: Barry Fitzgerald

***ACTOR IN A SUPPORTING ROLE:** Barry
Fitzgerald

Cinematography (B&W): Lionel Lindon

***DIRECTING:** Leo McCarey

Film Editing: Leroy Stone

***MUSIC** (Song): "Swinging on a Star," Music by
James Van Heusen; Lyrics by Johnny Burke

***WRITING** (Original Motion Picture Story):
Leo McCarey

***WRITING** (Screenplay): Frank Butler,
Frank Cavett

OSCAR TOTALS   Nominations **10** *Wins 7

AFI 100 YEARS 100 MOVIES SELECTION
2007 0   1997 0

TOP 300 FILMS POSITION . . . . **#114**
All-Release Domestic Box Office in Equivalent 2005 $s

National Film Preservation Board Selection 2004

OTHER AWARDS Best Picture Wins

	Year
Golden Globes	1945
New York Film Critics	1944
National Board of Review	none
Film Daily Critics	none

I think probably seventy-five percent of each day's shooting was made up on the set by Leo.
—Bing Crosby

PLOT: A progressive young priest tries to breathe new life into the run-down parish of an elderly, conservative Irish pastor, while bringing the religious institution out of debt and improving the lives of delinquent street kids by turning them into a choir.

PRODUCTION: In 1942 director, writer, and producer Leo McCarey was under contract to RKO. He had an idea for a buddy film about two priests (working title "The Padre"), drawing from McCarey's own real-life experiences. He based the characters on his friend Father Martin O'Malley and his favorite aunt, Sister Mary Benedict. McCarey originally approached Spencer Tracy to play the younger priest, but MGM was concerned that Tracy was being typecast. After considering James Cagney, McCarey went to his friend Bing Crosby. This raised eyebrows because the drama was already considered a hard sell and Crosby was perceived as merely a popular singer and comedian. However, McCarey always had faith in Crosby's acting and had promised to cast him as a lead in one of his films someday. Crosby was under contract at Paramount. In order to borrow Crosby from Paramount, RKO had to allow McCarey to write and direct another film, based on the same character, which would become *Going My Way*. ("The Padre" would later become *The Bells of St. Mary's*, which, though written first, came out after *Going My Way*, serving as a sequel). Paramount was nervous about the film's prospects and required that McCarey waive his salary in lieu of a share of the profits. Carl "Alfalfa" Switzer from the *Our Gang* comedies was cast in the choir, and the Metropolitan Opera's star Rise Stevens played the part of O'Malley's childhood friend, opera star Genevieve Linden. McCarey, in his usual way of directing, threw out much of the screenplay and improvised new scenes and dialogue on the set, where a close bond developed between cast and crew. According to Crosby, McCarey would arrive in the morning, with no one having any idea what they would be doing that day, and immediately go to the piano and play ragtime for an hour or two while he thought up new scenes. He was most interested in capturing the real responses of the actors than flashy editing and glamorous photography. The hallmark of his style was his use of the two-shot, which allowed two actors to carry out a scene for several minutes without a break in continuity, leaving room for improvisation.

DISTRIBUTION: The film's debut, intended to support the war effort, was at sixty-five different military bases on April 27, 1944. Despite controversy over depictions of priests drinking, the film instantly charmed audiences and critics and became a huge hit. It was the top-grossing film of the year and won respect for Crosby as an actor, marking his rise to the pinnacle of his career. Crosby's recording of "Swinging on a Star" became one of his biggest hits. McCarey's share of profits gave him the highest reported income in the United States that year, $1,113,035. Barry Fitzgerald became the only actor to be nominated for both Best Actor and Best Supporting Actor for the same role in the same year. (The Academy changed the rules so it never could happen again.) Afterward, McCarey and his associates (among them Bing Crosby and Hal Roach Jr.) formed Rainbow Productions, Inc., to produce the sequel at RKO, *The Bells of St. Mary's*, starring Crosby and Ingrid Bergman. —*Hayley Taylor Block and Alex Ben Block*

MEET ME IN ST. LOUIS

MGM, 1944

ALL-RELEASE EQUIVALENT 2005 $s

(Unadjusted $s) in Millions of $s

Domestic Box Office Revenues . . . . $223.3/($11.1)
Production Cost . . . . $20.9/($1.9)
Principal Photography . . . . 70 days
                                              12/7/1943–4/7/1944

Director . . . . Vincente Minelli

Producer . . . . Arthur Freed

Production Company . . . . Metro-Goldwyn-Mayer

Story by . . . . Based on the New Yorker story by Sally Benson

Screenplay by . . . . Irving Brecher, Fred F. Finklehoffe

Cast . . . . Judy Garland, Margaret O'Brien, Mary Astor

Filming Locations . . . . . . MGM studio

Genre . . . . Musical

Format . . . . Color (Technicolor)

Initial Release 12/31/1944

Rerelease . . . . none

Running Time . . . . 113 minutes

MPAA Rating . . . . not rated

STANDING THE TEST OF TIME

ACADEMY AWARD Oscar Nominations and Wins

Cinematography (Color): George Folsey

Music (Scoring of a Musical Picture): Georgie Stoll

Music (Song): "The Trolley Song," Music and Lyrics by Ralph Blane and Hugh Martin

Writing (Screenplay): Irving Brecher, Fred F. Finkelhoffe

OSCAR TOTALS Nominations **4** *Wins 0

AFI 100 YEARS 100 MOVIES SELECTION
                         2007 0   1997 0

TOP 300 FILMS POSITION . . . . **#201**
All-Release Domestic Box Office in Equivalent 2005 $s

National Film Preservation Board Selection 1994

OTHER AWARDS Best Picture Wins

	Year
Golden Globes	none
New York Film Critics	none
National Board of Review	none
Film Daily Critics	none

At the sneak previews some MGM execs said, "We didn't expect anything; there was no story. We were wrong about that!"

—Irving Brecher, co-screenwriter

PLOT: A St. Louis family with four beautiful daughters deals with the father's transfer to New York just before the 1904 World's Fair. The transition is especially heartbreaking for the seventeen-year-old daughter, who has a crush on the boy next door.

PRODUCTION: Sally Benson published a story in twelve installments in the *New Yorker* between June 21, 1941, and May 23, 1942, under the umbrella title "5135 Kensington," which was the address of the fictional Smith family. MGM outbid Paramount for the rights, and producer Arthur Freed, who headed a production unit, had Benson work on the screenplay. Benson also published the stories as a novel. Freed saw it as a source for a nostalgic turn-of-the-century family movie, to make up for having lost the rights to the play *Life with Father* to Warner Bros. Freed wanted George Cukor to direct, but Cukor went off to do war training films. So Freed turned to Vincente Minnelli, due to his unique production design for *The Wizard of Oz*. At first, Judy Garland had no interest in the film, but Minnelli and writer Irving Brecher thought she would be perfect as Esther Smith. They convinced Garland to read the original *New Yorker* stories and then presented Irene Sharaff's exquisite costume sketches. Most importantly, Garland was promised that Minnelli's direction would not let the irrepressible charm of young Margaret O'Brien upstage her. Production commenced with Minnelli's direction, a rude awakening for Garland. Perfectionist that he was, Minnelli did take after take. Garland, now in her early twenties, was tired of playing juvenile roles, and Minnelli was unhappy with what he saw as her parodic characterization of the young Esther. Often demanding hysterically that Freed intercede and change directors, Garland gradually began to appreciate Minnelli's vision, especially the flattering way in which he framed her in every scene. Her appreciation of the way she appeared in daily rushes may have been a contributing factor to the Garland-Minnelli engagement during production. (They married June 15, 1945, and divorced in 1952.) "The Trolley Song" scene was done in just one take, and seeing the film today, it proves that Minnelli was superb at capturing not only the era but also St. Louis's grand expectations of the upcoming world's fair. Today, Judy Garland's problems are well known, but at the time, she missed 13 days of shooting, bringing production to a total of 70 days (and a final cost of $1,884,539), as opposed to the originally budgeted 58 days (and a budget of $1,650,604). However, the street and homes built specifically on what became known as "St. Louis Street" were used by MGM and/or rented out continually for the next twenty-seven years.

DISTRIBUTION: The public had eagerly awaited the debut of *Meet Me in St. Louis,* which had been highly publicized with the tagline "The Trolley Song' Picture." Not only was the film a resounding success at the box office, but industry praise was overwhelming, with *Variety* and *The Hollywood Reporter* going so far as to say it was the role that gave Garland "true stature" as an actress. It made a profit of $2.4 million on worldwide rentals of $6.6 million, making it one of the top films of 1944 and one of the all-time biggest-grossing musical films through 2005. Over the years, the movie has become more widely associated with the Christmas season, mainly due to Garland's poignant performance of "Have Yourself a Merry Little Christmas." Released via Warner Home Video in 2004, the film continues to touch hearts and memories even today. —*Christine McDermott*

THE LOST WEEKEND

Paramount, 1945

ALL-RELEASE EQUIVALENT 2005 $s

(Unadjusted $s) in Millions of $s

Domestic Box Office Revenues......... **$152.6**/($10.0)
Production Cost .... **$13.6**/($1.3)
Principal Photography............. **63** days estimated
10/1/1944–10/5/1944 NY shoot
10/23/1944–12/30/1944
Paramount Studio shoot
Reshoots April 1945

Director .... Billy Wilder

Producer .... Charles Brackett

Production Company.... Paramount Pictures

Story by .... Based on the novel by
Charles R. Jackson

Screenplay by .... Charles Brackett, Billy Wilder

Cast .... Ray Milland, Jane Wyman

Filming Locations ...... Paramount Studio, Los Angeles,
CA; New York City

Genre................ Drama

Format............... B&W

Initial Release .... 10/5/1945 world premiere
(London, England); 11/16/1945
U.S. general release

Rerelease............. none

Running Time .... 101 minutes

MPAA Rating .... not rated

STANDING THE TEST OF TIME

ACADEMY AWARD Oscar Nominations and Wins

*BEST MOTION PICTURE: Paramount

*ACTOR: Ray Milland

Cinematography (B&W): John F. Seitz

*DIRECTING: Billy Wilder

Film Editing: Doane Harrison

Music (Music Score of a Dramatic or Comedy Picture):
Miklos Rozsa

*WRITING (Screenplay): Charles Brackett, Billy
Wilder

OSCAR TOTALS   Nominations 7   *Wins 4

AFI 100 YEARS 100 MOVIES SELECTION
2007 0   1997 0

TOP 300 FILMS POSITION ....none
All-Release Domestic Box Office in Equivalent 2005 $s

National Film Preservation Board Selection....none

OTHER AWARDS Best Picture Wins

	Year
Golden Globes	1946
New York Film Critics......................	1945
National Board of Review	none
Film Daily Critics	none

Not only did I know it was going to make a good picture, I also knew that the guy who was going to play Don Birnam—Ray Milland, the drunk—was going to get the Academy Award. Because for the people who are watching pictures, if you are a cripple, if you stammer, if you are a hunchback, if you are an alcoholic, they think that is acting.

—Billy Wilder

PLOT: Don Birnam plans to spend a weekend in the country with his brother and work on his novel rather than drink himself into a stupor. But brotherhood and the bottle don't mix, and what is supposed to be a quick afternoon sip at the local bar becomes the bender into hell.

PRODUCTION: Lured by the title, Wilder picked up *The Lost Weekend* by Charles R. Jackson at a railway kiosk in Chicago and couldn't put it down. He phoned writing partner Charles Brackett immediately after he disembarked, six in the morning Los Angeles time, to urge Paramount to buy the film rights. Y. Frank Freeman, head of Paramount's West Coast production, had passed on the book previously. Luckily for Wilder, Freeman was out of the office, and his production chief, Buddy De Sylva, purchased the rights for $50,000. Freeman was not happy when he found out, and he stonewalled every attempt to make the picture. It took a nod from Paramount's president, Barney Balaban, to get it greenlighted. Wilder and Brackett banged out the first draft of the script in two months, as opposed to the four to six months it usually took them. Perhaps their speed was born from personal experience with alcoholism: Wilder had just finished working with hard drinker Raymond Chandler on *Double Indemnity,* and Brackett's wife was a stay-at-home lush. But 1944 was only twelve years from the end of Prohibition, and a film that featured drunks and prostitutes could very well be rejected under the Production Code. To the ire of the censors, Wilder and Brackett submitted their script piecemeal and started production before the board had approved all pages. Wilder refused to use miniatures and insisted on shooting in New York City. He wanted his "Odyssey of a drunk" to have the greatest verisimilitude. Cinematographer John Seitz used the fastest film available and hid his cameras in the back of bakery trucks and piano packing crates to achieve a documentary style. Unaware of the production, gossip rags reported Milland's wild nights in New York. Back at Paramount, Wilder requested that a replica of the New York bar P. J. Clarke's be built for the interior scenes. The set was so faithful that actor-wit Robert Benchley would arrive daily from another set and order a bourbon. In his most extensive use of special effects, Wilder had technicians construct an artificial bat for one of the whiskey-induced hallucinations. Paramount would later advertise the film with images from the grotesque sequence of the bat swooping down and eating the mouse.

DISTRIBUTION: Wilder was humiliated when a Santa Barbara preview audience laughed at *The Lost Weekend*. The studio buckled and paid Charles Jackson $500 for a revised ending. Rumors flew around town that the liquor industry offered $5 million if Paramount would destroy the negative. With his film well over budget, a discouraged Wilder shot the final sequence in April, then accepted a U.S. military commission and left for Germany. Y. Frank Freeman wrote off *The Lost Weekend* as a total loss. He promised it would never be released. While in Germany, Wilder received letters of praise from people who had attended private industry screenings. Word of mouth spread that the film was a lost treasure. The buzz convinced Balaban to change course, and in October 1945 Paramount tested the picture in London, where it became a sensation. A month later, the studio finally released it in America, and suddenly "losing a weekend" meant going on a bender. The House of Seagram even found a way to exploit the film's success, lecturing in an Oscar ad that "some men should not drink!" —*Michael Kogge*

THE BELLS OF ST. MARY'S
RKO, 1945

ALL-RELEASE EQUIVALENT 2005 $s
(Unadjusted $s) in Millions of $s

Domestic Box Office Revenues. . . . . **$323.6**/($17.7)
Production Cost . . . . **$17.7**/($1.6)
Principal Photography . . . . **59** days
3/1/1945–5/14/1945
Additional retakes
9/5/1945–9/22/1945

Director . . . . Leo McCarey
Producer . . . . Leo McCarey
Production Company . . . . Rainbow Productions
Story by . . . . Leo McCarey
Screenplay by . . . . Dudley Nichols
Cast . . . . Bing Crosby, Ingrid Bergman,
Henry Travers, William Gargan
Filming Locations . . . . . . RKO Studios, Paramount back
lot
Genre . . . . Drama
Format . . . . B&W
Initial Release 12/6/1945
Rerelease . . . . 1959 by Republic Pictures
Running Time . . . . 126 minutes
MPAA Rating . . . . not rated

STANDING THE TEST OF TIME

ACADEMY AWARD Oscar Nominations and Wins

Best Motion Picture: Rainbow Productions
Actor: Bing Crosby
Actress: Ingrid Bergman
Directing: Leo McCarey
Film Editing: Harry Marker
Music (Music Score of a Dramatic or Comedy Picture):
Robert Emmett Dolan
Music (Song): "Aren't You Glad You're You?," Music
by James Van Heusen; Lyrics by Johnny Burke
*SOUND RECORDING: RKO Radio Studio Sound
Dept., Stephen Dunn, Sound Director

OSCAR TOTALS   Nominations **8**   *Wins **1**

AFI 100 YEARS 100 MOVIES SELECTION
2007 0   1997 0

TOP 300 FILMS POSITION . . . . #89
All-Release Domestic Box Office in Equivalent 2005 $s

National Film Preservation Board Selection . . . . none

OTHER AWARDS Best Picture Wins

	Year
Golden Globes	none
New York Film Critics	none
National Board of Review	none
Film Daily Critics	none

I was determined I had to persuade David, and I did.
—Ingrid Bergman

PLOT: Father O'Malley and Sister Benedict are sent to St. Mary's, a shabby Catholic school on its last legs, and set about getting it up on its feet again.

PRODUCTION: On the heels of the financial smash of his *Going My Way,* director Leo McCarey thought to revive the character of Father O'Malley with another mild-mannered tale of priest and parish. Irene Dunne, McCarey's favorite actress, might have played Sister Benedict were it not for the determination of RKO (where McCarey was under contract) to have Ingrid Bergman, one of the top box office draws of the day. Unfortunately, the star was contracted to David O. Selznick, who maintained that sequels had only limited remunerative potential. What's more, he was concerned that the role in question would take his leading lady too far from her comfort zone, the romantic heroine. Bergman, however, was interested; Selznick had no choice but to at least appear compliant. He proceeded cautiously, continually raising Bergman's loan-out price, which to his befuddlement, McCarey would always meet, and when he did, Selznick would raise the price yet again. The stalemate was finally broken when the actress arranged to read the script, fell in love with it, and insisted that if Selznick didn't agree to a price, she would go back to Sweden for good. She just had to have the part. So, Selznick settled (for a sum of $175,000, as well as an agreement from RKO to return to him the screen rights to *A Bill of Divorcement* and *Little Women,* two Cukor pictures he had produced over a decade before). It was one of the largest, most lucrative loan-out negotiations in Hollywood history. This was also the first movie by the short-lived Rainbow Productions, Inc., formed by Leo McCarey, Bing Crosby, Hal Roach Jr., and others (which was later sold to Paramount in December 1947). *The Bells of St. Mary's* was early into shooting on the evening of March 15, 1945—the night Mc-Carey's *Going My Way* took home seven Oscar statuettes, including one for Crosby, two for McCarey (writer and director—an Oscar first), and Best Picture. In addition, Ingrid Bergman, their current co-collaborator, won Best Actress for her performance in *Gaslight.* All this added up to the kind of free publicity that made McCarey's set the most popular and closely watched in town. McCarey, beloved by many, was committed to approaching his material with an eye to accuracy, and his fervor was catching. Bergman threw herself into the role, devoting much of her schedule to research and training. She met with Leo McCarey's aunt, the nun on whom her part was based, and was observed by a real-life priest the director had installed as a technical advisor on the set. It was a pleasant production.

DISTRIBUTION: This was that rare sequel that did even better at the box office than the original, bringing in a $3.7 million profit on $11.2 million in worldwide rentals. Although *The Bells of St. Mary's* was critically acclaimed and received eight Academy Award nominations, it won only one Oscar, for Best Sound. It became the top domestic box office film of 1945. Nine years later, in 1954, the picture's rights reverted back to money-savvy McCarey, who endeavored to rerelease it through Paramount. In 1959 Republic Pictures Corporation reissued it. The same year, CBS broadcast a forgettable made-for-TV remake starring Robert Preston and Claudette Colbert. —*Sam Wasson*

SPELLBOUND
United Artists, 1945

ALL-RELEASE EQUIVALENT 2005 $s
(Unadjusted $s) in Millions of $s

Domestic Box Office Revenues . . . . **$168.7**/($11.1)
Production Cost . . . . **$18.4**/($1.7)
Principal Photography . . . . **57** days
7/10/1944–September 1944

Director . . . . Alfred Hitchcock
Producer . . . . David O. Selznick
Production Company . . . . Selznick International Pictures, Vanguard Films, Inc.
Story by . . . . Francis Beeding from his novel, *The House of Dr. Edwardes*
Screenplay by . . . . Ben Hecht
Cast . . . . Ingrid Bergman, Gregory Peck, Michael Chekhov, Leo G. Carroll
Filming Locations . . . . RKO studio, Culver City, CA
Genre . . . . Film Noir
Format . . . . B&W
Initial Release . . . . 10/31/1945 premiere (New York); 12/18/1945 general release
Rerelease . . . . none
Running Time . . . . 111 minutes
MPAA Rating . . . . not rated

STANDING THE TEST OF TIME

ACADEMY AWARD Oscar Nominations and Wins

Best Motion Picture: Selznick International Pictures
Actor in a Supporting Role: Michael Chekhov
Cinematography (B&W): George Barnes
Directing: Alfred Hitchcock
***MUSIC** (Music Score of a Dramatic or Comedy Picture): Miklos Rozsa
Special Effects: Photographic Effects by Jack Cosgrove

OSCAR TOTALS Nominations 6 *Wins 1

AFI 100 YEARS 100 MOVIES SELECTION
2007 0   1997 0

TOP 300 FILMS POSITION . . . . .none
All-Release Domestic Box Office in Equivalent 2005 $s

National Film Preservation Board Selection . . . .none

OTHER AWARDS Best Picture Wins

	Year
Golden Globes	none
New York Film Critics	none
National Board of Review	none
Film Daily Critics	none

It's a love story, and it's a story about murder, about quiet murders, not the dark alley variety, but murders over a breakfast table. . . . Spellbound is a story about murders over a glass of milk.
—Alfred Hitchcock

PLOT: The new administrator of a mental hospital falls in love with a beautiful psychiatrist, but the doctor begins to suspect that the man she loves is not who he claims to be, and that the real administrator may have been murdered.

PRODUCTION: David O. Selznick purchased the rights to the 1929 novel by John Palmer and Hilary St. George Sanders (under the pseudonym Francis Beeding) for $40,000. He was committed to producing the first major film to deal with psychoanalysis, and hired noted scribe Ben Hecht as screenwriter and his own analyst as the picture's technical advisor. In June 1944 Hitchcock had Hecht beef up the love story for intended stars Joseph Cotton and Dorothy McGuire. Instead, Ingrid Bergman, fresh from her Oscar-winning performance in *Gaslight*, was cast in the female lead opposite newcomer Gregory Peck, and Michael Chekhov, a nephew of the Russian playwright, in the supporting role originally slated for Paul Lukas. Hitchcock wanted Bernard Hermann to write the score, but Miklós Rózsa got the assignment. He employed the theremin, a tremolo-producing electronic instrument, which he had used earlier that year in *The Lost Weekend*. The nightmare sequence, designed by surrealist Salvador Dalí, and directed by William Cameron Menzies, originally ran longer, but when Selznick ordered it trimmed, Menzies demanded that his name be removed from the credits. Selznick also axed a prologue deemed too clinical in test screenings, replacing it with a pithy Shakespearean quote: "The fault . . . is not in our stars, but in ourselves." Additionally, Selznick disliked Hitchcock's title suggestions, "The Guilt Complex," "The Mind of Dr. Edwardes," and "Hidden Impulse." He preferred *Spellbound*, as did women who were polled during a preview. For the effect achieved during the scene in which Chekhov gives Peck a drugged glass of milk, a giant glass pail was brought up to the camera as gallons of milk were spilled from it into a trough below. For the climactic ending, when murderer Leo G. Carroll aims a pistol at Bergman, a large-scale model hand and gun were placed a few feet from the camera, to keep both in focus simultaneously. The hand was rotated so that the gun's muzzle filled the screen before the gun went off with a shocking red stencil color burst lasting only four frames, one-sixteenth of a second—the culmination of a week's preparation and nineteen takes. Censors objected to the suicide, but Selznick personally convinced them that it was crucial. Censors also felt that the costume worn by a mental patient (played by Rhonda Fleming) was too revealing. Her scenes were reshot with redesigned costumes.

DISTRIBUTION: Hitchcock first became an on-screen salesman pitching *Spellbound* to theater audiences in a trailer that no longer exists. In it, he plays with the concept of psychoanalysis by asking, "Did it ever occur to you that the person seated next to you at this moment might be a potential murderer . . . ? What do you know about . . . what actually goes on in his mind . . . ? Has he ever opened the locked doors of his mind and revealed the things that are hidden there . . . ? *Spellbound* deals with methods by which the individual is forced to open those closed doors . . . all of them." Hitchcock would use elements of this same script nineteen years later to pitch *Marnie*, which dealt with similar Freudian themes. —*Bob Canning*

THE BEST YEARS OF OUR LIVES

RKO, 1946

ALL-RELEASE EQUIVALENT 2005 $s

(Unadjusted $s) in Millions of $s

Domestic Box Office Revenues . . . . **$345.3**/($22.9)
Production Cost . . . . **$23.0**/($2.3)
Principal Photography . . . . **100** days estimated
4/15/1946–8/9/1946

Director . . . . William Wyler

Producer . . . . Samuel Goldwyn

Production Company . . . . Samuel Goldwyn Productions

Story by . . . . MacKinlay Kantor from
Glory for Me

Screenplay by . . . . Robert E. Sherwood

Cast . . . . Fredric March, Myrna Loy,
Teresa Wright, Dana Andrews,
Virginia Mayo, Cathy
O'Donnell, Hoagy Carmichael

Filming Locations . . . . . . Shot 60 percent on location:
Hollywood and Los Angeles,
CA; Ontario International
Airport, Ontario, CA; shot 40
percent in studio at Samuel
Goldwyn Studios, Hollywood,
CA

Genre . . . . Drama, War

Format . . . . B&W

Initial Release . . . . 11/21/1946 premiere, Astor
Theater (New York);
12/18/1946 (Chicago);
12/25/1946 (Boston and
Los Angeles); 7/3/1948
general release

Rerelease . . . . 2/2/1954 (reformatted for
widescreen)

Running Time . . . . 172 minutes

MPAA Rating . . . . not rated

STANDING THE TEST OF TIME

ACADEMY AWARD Oscar Nominations and Wins

***BEST MOTION PICTURE:** Samuel Goldwyn
Productions

***ACTOR:** Fredric March

***ACTOR IN A SUPPORTING ROLE:** Harold
Russell

***DIRECTING:** William Wyler

***FILM EDITING:** Daniel Mandell

***MUSIC** (Music Score of a Dramatic or Comedy
Picture): Hugo Friedhofer

Sound Recording: Samuel Goldwyn Studio Sound
Dept., Gordon Sawyer, Sound Director

***WRITING** (Screenplay): Robert E. Sherwood

***SPECIAL AWARD:** to Harold Russell for bringing
hope and courage to his fellow veterans through
his appearance in *The Best Years of Our Lives*

OSCAR TOTALS Nominations **8** *Wins **7+1**

AFI 100 YEARS 100 MOVIES SELECTION
2007 . . . #37   1997 . . . #37

TOP 300 FILMS POSITION . . . . #76
All-Release Domestic Box Office in Equivalent 2005 $s

National Film Preservation Board Selection 1989

OTHER AWARDS Best Picture Wins

	Year
Golden Globes	1947
New York Film Critics	1946
National Board of Review	none
Film Daily Critics	none

I don't care if it doesn't make a nickel. I just want every man, woman, and child in America to see it.
—Sam Goldwyn

PLOT: Three World War II veterans from differing walks of life—an air force major, an army sergeant, and a disabled sailor—meet while returning home and find their lives become entwined as they face readjustment to civilian life.

PRODUCTION: As a mother with a son serving in World War II, Frances Goldwyn, wife of film mogul Samuel Goldwyn, read with interest an article in the August 7, 1944, issue of *Time* magazine titled "The Way Home," about soldiers returning stateside from battle. She suggested to Sam that the readjustments facing returning veterans could be motion picture material. He seemed disinterested at first. However, that same month he had his story editor, Kay Brown, register two titles: *Home Again* and *The Way Home.* By September, Goldwyn was fully hooked, sharing his enthusiasm with writer MacKinlay Kantor: "Returning soldiers! Every family in America is a part of this story." Goldwyn offered Kantor $20,000—$7,500 for a screenplay treatment, and the balance for the story. Kantor decided to write the novel—now called *Glory for Me*—centering around three servicemen who become friends while returning to the same fictitious hometown of Boone City (modeled after Cincinnati, Ohio). To script, Goldwyn hired Robert E. Sherwood (*Rebecca*) and tagged William Wyler, a recently returned air force veteran, as director. For the cast, Goldwyn mined his supply of contract players: Dana Andrews, Virginia Mayo, Cathy O'Donnell, and Teresa Wright. When Fred MacMurray and Olivia de Havilland turned down the roles of Al and Milly Stephenson, agent Leland Hayward recommended two of his clients, Fredric March and Myrna Loy. Both signed on. Farley Granger was to play Homer Parrish, who returned a drooling, convulsing spastic. All involved found the character unsettling. Wyler recalled seeing a rehabilitation documentary in which Harold Russell, a nonactor who had lost both hands above the wrists in an explosives accident, performed everyday chores with a pair of prosthetic hooks. Russell ended up with the role and won two Oscars for his natural, inspirational performance. With the first rehearsal one day away, Wyler suddenly developed cold feet, insisting that the script wasn't ready. Goldwyn reminded him that the cast and crew, now drawing their full salaries, were prepped and ready to go. "They'll be here every day until you show up," Goldwyn warned, "and you'll pay the difference." Wyler relented. Filming took place at the Goldwyn Studios, with exteriors filmed at various locations nearby. Wyler discovered an airplane "graveyard" at Ontario Airport, east of Los Angeles, and used the site for an evocative scene in which Dana Andrews wanders among row upon row of abandoned, cannibalized aircraft.

DISTRIBUTION: Goldwyn and Wyler, worried about the film's length, hoped that sneak-preview audiences might indicate where to make cuts. However, at every screening, the audience sat in rapt attention for the entire film, bursting into applause at the end. The film remained uncut. Goldwyn was aiming for a January 1947 opening, but Wyler convinced him that an earlier release could possibly garner some Academy Award nominations for 1946. Wyler was correct: *The Best Years of Our Lives* was nominated in eight categories and won seven Oscars. The film made a $5 million profit on worldwide rentals of $14.8 million. —*Douglas Burns*

IT'S A WONDERFUL LIFE
RKO, 1946

ALL-RELEASE EQUIVALENT 2005 $s
(Unadjusted $s) in Millions of $s

Domestic Box Office Revenues . . . . **$106.8**/($7.3)
Production Cost . . . . **$31.8**/($3.2)
Principal Photography . . . . **90** days
4/15/1946–8/2/1946

Director . . . . Frank Capra
Producer . . . . Frank Capra
Production Company . . . . Liberty Films, Inc.
Story by . . . . Based on Philip Van Doren Stern's Christmas card and the short story, "The Greatest Gift"
Screenplay by . . . . Frances Goodrich, Albert Hackett, Frank Capra
Cast . . . . James Stewart, Donna Reed, Lionel Barrymore, Henry Travers
Filming Locations . . . . . . In Studio: RKO lot, Culver City, CA; on Location: RKO Ranch, Encino, CA, and Beverly Hills High School, Beverly Hills, CA
Genre . . . . Drama
Format . . . . B&W
Initial Release . . . . 12/21/1946 (New York); 12/24/1946 (Los Angeles); 1/7/1947 general release
Rerelease . . . . 1990 (UK only)
Running Time . . . . 125 minutes
MPAA Rating . . . . not rated

STANDING THE TEST OF TIME

ACADEMY AWARD Oscar Nominations and Wins

Best Motion Picture: Liberty Films
Actor: James Stewart
Directing: Frank Capra
Film Editing: William Hornbeck
Sound Recording: RKO Radio Studio Sound Dept., John Aalberg, Sound Director

OSCAR TOTALS Nominations 5 *Wins 0

AFI 100 YEARS 100 MOVIES SELECTION
2007 . . . #20   1997 . . . #11

TOP 300 FILMS POSITION . . . . none
All-Release Domestic Box Office in Equivalent 2005 $s

National Film Preservation Board Selection 1990

OTHER AWARDS Best Picture Wins

	Year
Golden Globes	none
New York Film Critics	none
National Board of Review	none
Film Daily Critics	none

I thought it was the greatest film I had ever made—a film to tell the weary, the disheartened, and the disillusioned; the wino, the junkie, the prostitute; those behind prison walls and those behind Iron Curtain, that no man is a failure!

—Frank Capra

PLOT: A down-on-his-luck family man, contemplating suicide, is visited by his guardian angel, who convinces him that his life is important and meaningful to those who know and love him.

PRODUCTION: Frank Capra, the man who won Oscars for three classic pictures, returned to Hollywood from serving in the U.S. Army during World War II, only to discover that most studios thought his "blue-sky optimism," or "Capracorn," was well past its expiration date. That's when he formed an independent production company with director-friends William Wyler and George Stevens. Based on the triumvirate's promise of three films each, their enterprise, Liberty Films, found a home at RKO. In 1945 the studio bought the rights to the short story "The Greatest Gift" for $10,000 as a vehicle for Cary Grant. But three unsatisfactory scripts later, the project was shelved and Grant started work on *The Bishop's Wife*. Capra paid RKO $50,000 for the story (which began as the writer's personalized Christmas card), and for the hero and villain, Capra got James Stewart and Lionel Barrymore. With few exceptions, the rest of the supporting cast was made up entirely of players from his prewar films. Four acres of RKO's Encino Ranch became Bedford Falls. Snow scenes were planned for twenty-eight days of the initial 84-day shooting schedule, but as Stewart trudged through studio snow banks (white-painted cornflakes), the noise was practically deafening. Capra wanted to record the sound live, so a new snow effect was developed using 6,000 gallons of fire retardant foamite, sugar and water that was pumped through a wind machine. When a 90-degree-plus heat wave hit, the fake snow melted, pushing the film six days over schedule and almost $1 million over budget.

DISTRIBUTION: Wyler had begun directing *The Best Years of Our Lives* at RKO the same day that Capra began *It's a Wonderful Life,* but Wyler's film premiered in November to universally ecstatic reviews and excellent box office, while Capra's opened in December to mixed reviews and unspectacular returns. Then, Oscar pitted *The Best Years of Our Lives* against *It's a Wonderful Life* for Best Picture, Best Director, and Best Actor, and Wyler's film won them all, plus four more, while Capra went home empty-handed. Additionally, when the Communist witch-hunts began in earnest in 1947, the FBI found Barrymore's portrayal of an evil capitalist to be "subversive Bolshevik propaganda" and Stewart's put-upon common man "a common trick used by the Communists." With *It's a Wonderful Life* an underachiever and the FBI mounting an "innuendo campaign," a financially strapped and humiliated Capra wanted to unload Liberty Films. The partnership was dissolved and Liberty sold to Paramount (Capra's 32 percent share was roughly $994,000 before taxes). In the ensuing years, the film became a football in a shuffle of corporate assets. After the initial twenty-eight-year copyright period expired, *Life* lapsed into the public domain. The film suddenly exploded onto countless TV stations every holiday season, and in the 1980s, the film was slapped onto videotape by dozens of cheesy companies, sold cut-rate, and put out in two colorized versions. Capra complained, "They splashed it all over with Easter-egg colors and they ruined it." Aaron Spelling Productions, which owned Philip Van Doren Stern's underlying story, reasserted its exclusive right to use some of the background music (such as Irving Berlin's "This is the Army, Mr. Jones"), and licensed the exclusive TV broadcast rights to NBC in the early 1990s. —*Bob Canning*

DUEL IN THE SUN
Selznick Releasing Organization, 1947

ALL-RELEASE EQUIVALENT 2005 $s
(Unadjusted $s) in Millions of $s

Domestic Box Office Revenues . . . . **$348.0**/($23.9)
Production Cost . . . . **$63.5**/($7.3)
Principal Photography . . . .**91** days
2/28/1945–November 1945

Director . . . . King Vidor

Producer . . . . David O. Selznick

Production Company . . . . Vanguard Films

Story by . . . . Based on the novel by
Niven Busch

Screenplay by . . . . David O. Selznick; adaptation
by Oliver H. P. Garrett

Cast . . . . Jennifer Jones, Joseph Cotten,
Gregory Peck, Lionel
Barrymore, Herbert Marshall,
Lillian Gish, Walter Huston,
Charles Bickford

Filming Locations . . . . . . Tucson, AZ; Lasky Mesa and
Sonora, CA

Genre . . . . Western

Format . . . . Color (Technicolor)

Initial Release . . . . 12/31/1946 premiere
(Los Angeles); 5/8/1947
general release

Rerelease . . . . none

Running Time . . . . 138 minutes

MPAA Rating . . . . not rated

STANDING THE TEST OF TIME

ACADEMY AWARD Oscar Nominations and Wins

Actress: Jennifer Jones

Actress in a Supporting Role: Lillian Gish

OSCAR TOTALS   Nominations **2**   *Wins 0

AFI 100 YEARS 100 MOVIES SELECTION
2007 0   1997 0

TOP 300 FILMS POSITION . . . . **#75**
All-Release Domestic Box Office in Equivalent 2005 $s

National Film Preservation Board Selection . . . .none

OTHER AWARDS Best Picture Wins

	Year
Golden Globes	none
New York Film Critics	none
National Board of Review	none
Film Daily Critics	none

I know that when I die, the stories will read, "David O. Selznick, producer of Gone with the Wind, *died today." I'm determined to leave them something else to write about.*

—David O. Selznick

PLOT: A beautiful half-Indian woman in frontier Texas is taken in by wealthy Anglos, but she cannot achieve her father's dream of becoming a real lady as the two wealthy sons fight for her hand.

PRODUCTION: In 1944 RKO bought the rights to Niven Busch's novel *Duel in the Sun,* planning to star John Wayne and Hedy Lamarr. The rights were obtained despite objections by Production Code Administration head Joseph Breen, voiced to William Gordon at RKO three months previously. Breen saw the novel as "a story of illicit sex and murder for revenge without the full compensating moral values required by the [Motion Picture] Code." Busch, who was also the producer, wanted to borrow Jennifer Jones from David O. Selznick's company, but Selznick had no intention of loaning his wife out to a first-time producer. Later in November, Selznick purchased the rights and enlarged its scale to showcase Jones. He wrote the screenplay and hired native Texan King Vidor to direct. He created the lurid, over-the-top ending in which Pearl and Lewt shoot each other, then die in each other's arms. He also added the backstory about Pearl's parents to better "explain" the main character. Vidor brought his own unique take to the material as well. Although he was an experienced Hollywood veteran, Vidor made films that were sympathetic toward the poor and downtrodden, denounced racism and the inhumanity of war, and still managed to work as rousing action-adventure tales of the West. In *Duel in the Sun* Vidor saw a story of injustice to a woman whose only sin was to have come from a mixed-race marriage. The production was troubled from the start. Inclement weather delayed shooting in Arizona and California. A strike by the Teamsters, Screen Actors Guild, and International Association of Theatrical Stage Employees shut down production in April 1945. Another shutdown occurred that November when Jones became ill. These setbacks added to the cost, and it quickly became the most expensive movie made until that time. The film's primary problems were between director and producer. Determined to protect his wife's stardom, Selznick constantly sent notes to Vidor. Vidor's mounting frustration finally led him to snap. He walked off the set shortly before the end of production. Selznick convinced William Dieterle, noted primarily for biopics, to replace Vidor long enough to complete the movie. Selznick still gave Vidor sole directing credit. An appeal to the Directors Guild by Dieterle was unsuccessful.

DISTRIBUTION: Even after concluding production, the film's troubles were not over. United Artists canceled its deal to distribute the film because Selznick had sold off abandoned projects to Fox and RKO. MGM also declined to release the film, so a new distribution company, Selznick Releasing Organization, was formed. The need to meet Production Code requirements caused Selznick to recut the film two times in 1947 before it could pass most local censor boards (it did not pass in Memphis; consequently *Duel* didn't play in the Bluff City until 1959). Taking advantage of a then-unprecedented multimillion-dollar budget for prints and advertising, Selznick used a saturation booking policy, playing multiple screenings in each city. The reviews were not kind, and the film acquired an unwanted nickname, "Lust in the Dust," but controversy and the sexy plot sold a great number of tickets, making it the top film of 1947. —*Louis Burklow*

LIFE WITH FATHER

Warner Bros., 1947

ALL-RELEASE EQUIVALENT 2005 $s

(Unadjusted $s) in Millions of $s

Domestic Box Office Revenues........	**$163.7**/($11.2)
Production Cost	**$41.2**/($4.7)
Principal Photography...........	**102** days estimated
	4/11/1946–8/12/1946

Director	Michael Curtiz
Producer	Robert Buckner
Production Company	Warner Bros. Pictures
Story by	Based on the play by Russel Crouse and Howard Lindsay (based on the book by Clarence Day Jr.)
Screenplay by	Donald Ogden Stewart
Cast	William Powell, Irene Dunne, Elizabeth Taylor, Edmund Gwenn, ZaSu Pitts, Jimmy Lydon
Filming Locations	Warner Studio back lot, CA
Genre	Comedy
Format	Color (Technicolor)
Initial Release	8/14/1947 world premiere (Skowhagen, MN); 8/15/1947 (New York); 9/13/1947 general release
Rerelease	none
Running Time	118 minutes
MPAA Rating	not rated

STANDING THE TEST OF TIME

ACADEMY AWARD Oscar Nominations and Wins

Actor: William Powell

Art Direction/Set Decoration (Color): Robert M. Haas/George James Hopkins

Cinematography (Color): Peverell Marley, William V. Skall

Music (Music Score of a Dramatic or Comedy Picture): Max Steiner

OSCAR TOTALS   Nominations **4**   *Wins **0**

AFI 100 YEARS 100 MOVIES SELECTION

2007 0   1997 0

TOP 300 FILMS POSITION . . . . none
All-Release Domestic Box Office in Equivalent 2005 $s

National Film Preservation Board Selection . . . . none

OTHER AWARDS Best Picture Wins

	Year
Golden Globes	none
New York Film Critics	none
National Board of Review	none
Film Daily Critics	none

Being two different people in one day unnerved me to no end!

—Irene Dunne

PLOT: Disguised as a simple family story set in New York's Gilded Age, this character-focused comedy proves that although straitlaced Father assumes he rules the roost with an iron fist, it is truly Mother who knows best.

PRODUCTION: Clarence Day Jr.'s 1935 memoir *Life with Father,* along with a 1932 prequel, *God and My Father,* and a 1937 sequel, *Life with Mother,* became the basis in 1939 of Broadway's longest-running nonmusical play. It was scripted by Howard Lindsay and Russel Crouse. As the play gained popularity a bidding war began for film rights. Eventually, Jack Warner outbid Louis B. Mayer for the rights, paying $500,000 and agreeing to a generous cut of profits and script approval. Hungarian-born Michael Curtiz pushed to direct Irene Dunne despite Warner's assumption that Bette Davis would star as Mother. Curtiz feared Davis did not have the necessary warmth for the character. His choice had always been Irene, yet she dismissed it as a boring family story. Virtually minutes before the part was offered to Mary Pickford, Dunne called Curtiz and accepted the role. MGM loaned William Powell to Warner to play Clarence Day Sr. Re-creating 1890s Madison Avenue on the Warner back lot was expensive and immediately put the film over budget. Costs continued to rise, and the movie soon exceeded its allotted six weeks. Curtiz pushed for additional sets: Delmonico's restaurant, the Days' church, and the family home. The studio gave Curtiz six more weeks, but production eventually ran sixteen weeks beyond what had been originally scheduled, with the director assuming all responsibility. In reality, Curtiz was shooting around William Powell's cancer treatments and refused to betray Powell's confidence. The censors insisted that the play's final line, in which Mr. Day says he is "going to be baptized, dammit!" be rewritten for the film. While the Day family were all redheads, the cast was not. Just as color was being applied to the principals, a city water main broke, shutting off water needed for the rinse. Everyone would have gone bald had Perc Westmore not removed the dye with cold cream and "saved the Days." Clarence Day Jr. had been on his sickbed as he finished the book and didn't live to see the play or movie. As part of the sale of rights to Warner, Day's widow had to be brought to Hollywood to serve as technical advisor, along with Lindsay and Crouse. Not a word of the play's text could be changed without their permission. Irene Dunne eased the situation when she became fast friends with Mrs. Day, and even wore some of her actual jewelry in the movie.

DISTRIBUTION: With much fanfare the movie premiered in the same year the play ended its run. Irene Dunne objected to William Powell's star billing. Eventually half of the prints would give Dunne top billing, the other half Powell. To determine which name would appear first at the New York premiere, they flipped a coin. No matter what the billing, the movie became a worldwide hit with $6.5 million in worldwide rentals, from *Pappa och vi* in Sweden to *Vita col padre* in Italy, although it booked a net loss of $350,000. Sadly, this charming film had just one domestic and worldwide release due to legal snafus with the Day estate. In 1975 it fell into the public domain. —*Christine McDermott*

GENTLEMAN'S AGREEMENT
20th Century-Fox, 1947

ALL-RELEASE EQUIVALENT 2005 $s
(Unadjusted $s) in Millions of $s

Domestic Box Office Revenues. . . . . **$126.3**/($8.7)
Production Cost . . . . **$17.5**/($2.0)
Principal Photography. . . . . **60** days
5/24/1947–8/19/1947

Director	Elia Kazan
Producer	Darryl F. Zanuck
Production Company. . . .	20th Century-Fox Film Corp.
Story by.	Based on the serialized story by Laura Z. Hobson
Screenplay by	Moss Hart
Cast	Gregory Peck, Dorothy McGuire, John Garfield, Celeste Holm, Anne Revere
Filming Locations	New York City; Darien, CT
Genre.	Romance
Format.	B&W
Initial Release	11/11/1947
Rerelease	none
Running Time	118 minutes
MPAA Rating	not rated

STANDING THE TEST OF TIME

ACADEMY AWARD Oscar Nominations and Wins
*BEST MOTION PICTURE: 20th Century-Fox
Actor: Gregory Peck
Actress: Dorothy McGuire
*ACTRESS IN A SUPPORTING ROLE: Celeste Holm
Actress in a Supporting Role: Anne Revere
*DIRECTING: Elia Kazan
Film Editing: Harmon Jones
Writing (Screenplay): Moss Hart

OSCAR TOTALS   Nominations **8**   *Wins **3**

AFI 100 YEARS 100 MOVIES SELECTION
2007 0   1997 0

TOP 300 FILMS POSITION . . . . .none
All-Release Domestic Box Office In Equivalent 2005 $s

National Film Preservation Board Selection. . . .none

OTHER AWARDS Best Picture Wins

	Year
Golden Globes	1948
New York Film Critics.	1947
National Board of Review	none
Film Daily Critics	none

Although I had directed four films, I wasn't a filmmaker yet, because I didn't respect the work to the end.
—Elia Kazan

PLOT: A magazine writer learns the true meaning of prejudice when, in order to write an article, he goes undercover and pretends to be Jewish.

PRODUCTION: Laura Hobson's story, on which the film is based, was serialized in *Cosmopolitan* before being published as a book. Also in advance of the book's publication, Fox's Darryl F. Zanuck paid $75,000 for the movie rights. When other studio chiefs, who were mostly Jewish, heard about this film, they warned Zanuck and Kazan against making it, but Zanuck refused to listen to their advice. He did, however, recognize that the film had to be a success. If it failed, the board at Fox would not soon forget. Moss Hart was so excited about the story that he told his agent he would write the script for minimum pay, which he did. But as he soon realized, the main challenge with Hobson's story was that it had no real climax to translate dramatically to the screen. Hart asked for Hobson's help in creating the missing climax, and luckily their collaboration worked. During the rehearsal period, Kazan was forced to give many of his notes to Gregory Peck over the phone because Peck was running a theater in La Jolla, California, at the time. From what Kazan has said, Peck's serious nature made it difficult to direct him. Kazan once attempted to get Peck to punch a wall in frustration during a scene, but no matter how hard he tried, Peck could not bring himself to do it. Nevertheless, Kazan claimed that the "production was perfectly managed by Zanuck" and the director felt little tension on set. It was in *Gentleman's Agreement,* that the word *Jew* was said on-screen for the first time, rather than just being implied by visual stereotypes. Laura Hobson's best-selling book came out while the film was shooting, not before, as many people would believe.

DISTRIBUTION: Despite the controversy surrounding the movie, it was one of Fox's highest-grossing films of 1947 after *Forever Amber* and the Betty Grable picture *Mother Wore Tights.* Kazan has said that when the editing was two-thirds finished he "dropped it . . . in Zanuck's lap" and had very little to do with the editing or scoring of the film. He felt his work was done, and he trusted the producer to guide it through postproduction. To compensate Moss Hart for the low pay he received for the script, Fox bought him an expensive new car once the film proved to be a success. After the film's release, Peck was blackballed—denied entry into many of the "restricted" clubs in Los Angeles—for several years because the public associated him with the film. The movie broke new ground for its time, but Kazan and many others looked back on it as too safe. Speaking about the film in the 1970s, Kazan called it "too polite." The movie was rejected by Spain's quasi-religious film censorship board. It was finally shown in that country in 1949 under a new title. In 1948 *Lux Radio Theater* did a radio play based on the movie, with Gregory Peck, Anne Baxter, and Jeff Chandler. —*Dina Gachman*

THE TREASURE OF THE SIERRA MADRE

Warner Bros., 1948

ALL-RELEASE EQUIVALENT 2005 $s

(Unadjusted $s) in Millions of $s

Domestic Box Office Revenues . . . . **$74.5**/($5.1)
Production Cost . . . . **$30.8**/($3.8)
Principal Photography . . . . **111** days
3/17/1947–7/22/1947

Director . . . . John Huston
Producer . . . . Henry Blanke
Production Company . . . . Warner Bros. Pictures
Story by . . . . Based on the novel by B. Traven
Screenplay by . . . . John Huston
Cast . . . . Humphrey Bogart,
Walter Huston, Tim Holt,
Bruce Bennett
Filming Locations . . . . . . Tampico and mountain country
surrounding Jungapeo, Mexico
Genre . . . . Drama
Format . . . . B&W
Initial Release 1/24/1948
Rerelease . . . . none
Running Time . . . . 126 minutes
MPAA Rating . . . . not rated

STANDING THE TEST OF TIME

ACADEMY AWARD Oscar Nominations and Wins

Best Motion Picture: Warner Bros.

*ACTOR IN A SUPPORTING ROLE: Walter Huston

*DIRECTING: John Huston

*WRITING (Screenplay): John Huston

OSCAR TOTALS   Nominations **4**   *Wins **3**

AFI 100 YEARS 100 MOVIES SELECTION
2007 . . . #38   1997 . . . #30

TOP 300 FILMS POSITION . . . . none
All-Release Domestic Box Office in Equivalent 2005 $s

National Film Preservation Board Selection 1990

OTHER AWARDS Best Picture Wins

	Year
Golden Globes . . . . none	
New York Film Critics	1948
National Board of Review . . . . none	
Film Daily Critics . . . . none	

I know you for what you are . . . Oh, you're not putting anything over
on me . . . I'm doing this to save my life.

—Dobbs (Humphrey Bogart) to Curtin (Tim Holt)

PLOT: Three Americans set out to prospect for gold in the remote mountains of Mexico but end up fighting for their lives and discovering what is truly important in life.

PRODUCTION: In 1941 Warner Bros. bought the rights to B. Traven's novel *The Treasure of the Sierra Madre* for its young writer-director John Huston to adapt. The project was put on hold while Huston served in World War II. After his return in 1946, Huston wrote a script and sent it to the book's author, who lived in Mexico. Back came a twenty-page reply with detailed suggestions on set construction, lighting, and other elements. Anxious to meet Traven, Huston secured a tentative promise to see him at a Mexico City hotel. Huston waited for almost a week. One morning, he awoke to find a man at his bedside. The man handed him a card identifying himself as Hal Croves, a translator who was a great friend of Traven's. If Huston wanted to meet with Traven, he would have to do it through Croves. The two men spent a great deal of time together discussing the story. Huston could never decide if the man was actually Traven, but he had a detailed knowledge of the novels. Huston had already cast two of the roles in his mind as he wrote. Humphrey Bogart would play paranoid prospector Fred C. Dobbs and Walter Huston, his father, would be the "part-goat" old prospector Howard. Huston felt his father had a great influence on his life and saw this role as a chance to honor him. For his part, Bogart recognized early on that the elder Huston would steal the picture from him but was philosophical about the prospect: "He's probably the only performer in Hollywood to whom I'd gladly lose a scene." After some discussion of Ronald Reagan and Zachary Scott as Curtin and Cody, respectively, Huston cast actors he considered much more suited to the roles, Tim Holt and one-time Tarzan Bruce Bennett. For Gold Hat, the Mexican bandit leader, he picked a part-time actor, Alfonso Bedoya. According to the director, Bedoya was actually frightened of the men playing his fellow thieves (one of whom had once been a real-life bandit), and they took any and all opportunities to hit him when the cameras were off. *Treasure of the Sierra Madre* was the first American film to be shot entirely outside of the United States. The shoot was marked by Bogart's one and only argument with Huston. Wanting to enter his yacht *Santana* in a race to Honolulu, Bogart was anxious to wrap production, but Huston would not alter his schedule. One day he asked Bogart, Holt, and his father to reshoot a dialogue scene. Unhappy about the extra take, Bogart went along, but that night at dinner he started grumbling about the boat race. Finally, Huston decided he had heard enough from his star. Reaching out, he grabbed Bogart's nose between his first two fingers and twisted it. Later, a chastened Bogart approached Huston and begged him, "Let things be with us as they always have been." The feud was over.

DISTRIBUTION: The critical and popular response was highly positive, although it made only 70 percent of what Huston's follow-up Bogart movie, *Key Largo* (1948), made. Today *Treasure of the Sierra Madre* is often referred to as Huston's best film and has maintained the esteem it had upon its release. It is one of three Huston-Bogart collaborations on the AFI 100 Years . . . 100 Movies list with *The Maltese Falcon* (1941) and *The African Queen* (1951). —*Louis Burklow*

ALL THE KING'S MEN

Columbia, 1949

ALL-RELEASE EQUIVALENT 2005 $s

(Unadjusted $s) in Millions of $s

Domestic Box Office Revenues. . . . .**$74.3**/($5.3)
Production Cost . . . .**$8.2**/($1.0)
Principal Photography. . . . . .55 days
11/29/1948–1/28/1949

Director . . . . Robert Rossen

Producer . . . . Robert Rossen

Production Company. . . . Robert Rossen Productions

Story by . . . . Based on the play *Proud Flesh* and novel by Robert Penn Warren

Screenplay by . . . . Robert Rossen

Cast . . . . Broderick Crawford, Mercedes McCambridge Joanne Dru, John Ireland, John Derek

Filming Locations . . . . . . On location in Northern California: Fairfield, Stockton, Suisun, University of the Pacific

Genre. . . . . Drama

Format. . . . . B&W

Initial Release . . . . 11/8/1949 premiere (New York); 11/16/1949 (Los Angeles)

Rerelease . . . . none

Running Time . . . . 109 minutes

MPAA Rating . . . . not rated

STANDING THE TEST OF TIME

ACADEMY AWARD Oscar Nominations and Wins

*BEST MOTION PICTURE: Robert Rossen Productions

*ACTOR: Broderick Crawford

Actor in a Supporting Role: John Ireland

*ACTRESS IN A SUPPORTING ROLE: Mercedes McCambridge

Directing: Robert Rossen

Film Editing: Robert Parrish, Al Clark

Writing (Screenplay): Robert Rossen

OSCAR TOTALS   Nominations **7**   *Wins 3

AFI 100 YEARS 100 MOVIES SELECTION
2007 0   1997 0

TOP 300 FILMS POSITION . . . . .none
All-Release Domestic Box Office in Equivalent 2005 $s

National Film Preservation Board Selection. . . . 2001

OTHER AWARDS Best Picture Wins

	Year
Golden Globes	1950
New York Film Critics.	1949
National Board of Review	none
Film Daily Critics	none

Mr. Rossen has assembled in this starkly unprettified film a piece of pictorial journalism that is remarkable for its brilliant parts.

—Bosley Crowther, *New York Times*, 1949

PLOT: Loosely based on Louisiana's notorious governor Huey "Kingfish" Long, it's the story of the dramatic political ascent and decline of Willie Stark, a small-town lawyer turned governor and power broker during the 1930s.

PRODUCTION: In 1939 Robert Penn Warren, the country's first poet laureate, published his play *Proud Flesh,* examining Machiavellian politics and idealism corrupted by power based on his observations of Louisiana governor Huey Long. In 1946 Warren reworked the material as a novel, *All the King's Men,* which became a best seller and won the Pulitzer Prize. Columbia Pictures acquired movie rights for $250,000 and made a deal with Robert Rossen to write the screenplay, produce, and direct, all for $25,000. During production, Rossen was subpoenaed by the House Un-American Activities Committee, but before he was blacklisted he worked on several films, including this one. Studio boss Harry Cohn wanted Spencer Tracy as Stark, but Rossen, influenced by the neorealistic films of Italy, was determined to avoid the usual trappings of Hollywood productions. Rossen had seen character actor Broderick Crawford on Broadway in *Of Mice and Men* and wanted him as Stark. The studio argued for a star but after his screen test agreed on Crawford, who was so eager to play the role that he cut his usual fee in half. Rossen filmed some scenes straight from the book but did change the focus from the Jack Burden character to Stark. Rossen shot in a noir style, which created an appropriately dark, conspiratorial mood, often using experimental dialogue, having the characters repeat the same sentence many times for different effects. The film was shot outdoors in all sorts of weather, which gave a sense of the passing of time. Burnett Guffey's cinematography added a vivid and menacing presence that influenced urban gangster films of the fifties. Rossen also used a documentary-like style for the scenes during Stark's campaign for immediacy. To achieve authenticity, Rossen cast townsfolk from Stockton, California, where they were filming, in all the minor roles (a railroad brakeman played Pa Stark, the city's sheriff played the sheriff, and the local preacher played the preacher). Rossen shot the extras in the big crowd scene before Stark's assassination with four cameras at once to get their unrehearsed reactions. As the rushes came in, the studio executives became alarmed because the photography had none of the usual polish of Columbia films, and there were scenes being shot that were not in the finished script. However, Cohn had faith in the project (he related to the character of Stark) and brought in the additional resource of film editor Robert Parrish to help trim the movie.

DISTRIBUTION: Rossen believed the film had a good chance at an Oscar, so Cohn released it in Los Angeles before the year-end deadline. Rossen himself paid for publicity, though little was needed. The film was a critical success, winning the Best Picture award of the New York Film Critics Circle and going into the Oscars as the favorite. (Cohn declined to attend, telling Rossen, "It's your show.") Soon after the film's release, Rossen was blacklisted in Hollywood until 1953, when he agreed to name names and was able to resume his career. —*Hayley Taylor Block*

BATTLEGROUND

MGM, 1949

ALL-RELEASE EQUIVALENT 2005 $s

(Unadjusted $s) in Millions of $s

Domestic Box Office Revenues . . . . **$155.5**/($11.3)
Production Cost . . . . **$13.2**/($1.6)
Principal Photography . . . . **52** days
4/5/1949–6/3/1949

Director . . . . William A. Wellman

Producer . . . . Dore Schary

Production Company . . . . Metro-Goldwyn-Mayer

Story and
 Screenplay by . . . . Robert Pirosh

Cast . . . . Van Johnson, John Hodiak,
 Ricardo Montalban,
 George Murphy

Filming Locations . . . . . . MGM Studio, Culver City, CA

Genre . . . . War

Format . . . . B&W

Initial Release 11/9/1949

Rerelease 1954

Running Time . . . . 118 minutes

MPAA Rating . . . . not rated

STANDING THE TEST OF TIME

ACADEMY AWARD Oscar Nominations and Wins

Best Motion Picture: Metro-Goldwyn-Mayer

Actor in a Supporting Role: James Whitmore

*CINEMATOGRAPHY (B&W): Paul C. Vogel

Directing: William A. Wellman

Film Editing: John Dunning

*WRITING (Story and Screenplay): Robert Pirosh

OSCAR TOTALS   Nominations **6**   *Wins **2**

AFI 100 YEARS 100 MOVIES SELECTION

2007 0   1997 0

TOP 300 FILMS POSITION . . . . .none

All-Release Domestic Box Office in Equivalent 2005 $s

National Film Preservation Board Selection . . . .none

OTHER AWARDS Best Picture Wins

	Year
Golden Globes	none
New York Film Critics	none
National Board of Review	none
Film Daily Critics	none

*When [director] Wellman saw us at the end of the training schedule he felt
that we were ready as an infantry squad.*

—John Hodiak

PLOT: A squad from the 101st Airborne encounters fierce combat and freezing weather when they are surrounded by Germans in the Belgian town of Bastogne during the Battle of the Bulge.

PRODUCTION: Before the war Robert Pirosh worked in Hollywood as a comedy writer. Pirosh was with the 35th Infantry Division at Bastogne during the Ardennes offensive. He kept a diary during that time. Back in Hollywood in 1947, at RKO, Pirosh got development executive Dore Schary's approval of a sixty-page outline. Director Fred Zinnemann was deluged with cast and crew offers. However, studio head Howard Hughes felt that the script was too grim and that the public was tired of movies about the infantry. Hughes wanted to develop an Army Air Force film instead. Schary left RKO and was soon hired by Louis B. Mayer at MGM. He convinced a reluctant Mayer to put *Battleground* into development with William Wellman as director. Wellman and Pirosh began rewriting the script using Lt. Col. Harry Kinnard, a Bulge veteran, as technical advisor. Because of contract negotiations Robert Taylor, Bill Williams, Robert Ryan, and Keenan Wynn were forced to leave the project. Cast replacements included Van Johnson as Holley, John Hodiak as Jarvess, and James Whitmore as Sergeant Kinnie. A "bookend flash-back" through Jarvess's POV was scrapped in favor of a straight-line story. Wellman and Kinnard arranged to have soldiers from the 101st Airborne conduct an eleven-day "boot camp" to prepare the actors. A close-order "jive drill" sequence, choreographed by several black drill instructors, was approved by the Production Code office. The jive drill would open the film with a cadence chant. Colonel Kinnard supervised the boot camp, March 21 to April 1. While the Production Code office approved the cadence chant, a controversy came up revolving around the word *nuts,* which was on the code's list of prohibited words. Since *nuts* was General McAuliffe's actual response to the German surrender offer, the word was allowed. Production began April 5 and went to June 3, 1949, in Culver City. Screenwriter Pirosh and director Wellman had a falling-out, resulting in Pirosh being barred from the set. Soundstages were dotted with trees shipped from northern California. Chemical "snow" was used daily, blown by wind machines to duplicate the brutal Belgian winter. The dialogue of the soldiers was "homogenized" because of the Production Code's dogma on profanity.

DISTRIBUTION: *Battleground* was the sleeper hit of 1949 with critics and audiences. It received six Oscar nominations with two wins. It brought in $6.5 million in worldwide rentals in its initial release, 72 percent from the domestic market. Dore Schary's tenacious belief in the film increased his influence with MGM and began L. B. Mayer's decline, with Schary succeeding him in 1951. The year 1949 proved to be a benchmark in the war film genre with *Battleground, 12 o'Clock High,* and *Sands of Iwo Jima* taking their places as classics. —*Frank McAdams*

SAMSON AND DELILAH

Paramount, 1949

ALL-RELEASE EQUIVALENT 2005 $s

(Unadjusted $s) in Millions of $s

Domestic Box Office Revenues. . . . . $276.7/($25.6)
Production Cost . . . . $26.2/($3.2)
Principal Photography. . . . . 70 days
10/4/1948–12/22/1948
Reshoots January 18,
20, and 21, 1949

Director	Cecil B. DeMille
Producer	Cecil B. DeMille
Production Company	Paramount
Story by	Based on the history of Samson and Delilah in the Holy Bible, Judges 13–16
Screenplay by	Jesse L. Lasky Jr., Fredric M. Frank
Cast	Hedy Lamarr, Victor Mature, George Sanders, Henry Wildoxen, Angela Lansbury
Filming Locations	Lone Pine, CA; Paramount Studios, Hollywood, CA
Genre	Biblical Epic
Format	Color (Technicolor)
Initial Release	12/21/1949 road show premiere, Paramount and Rivoli Theaters (New York); 02/02/1950 Paramount Theaters, (Los Angeles and Hollywood, CA); 3/28/1951 general release
Rerelease	1959, 1968
Running Time	128 minutes
MPAA Rating	not rated

STANDING THE TEST OF TIME

ACADEMY AWARD Oscar Nominations and Wins

*ART DIRECTION/SET DECORATION: Hans Dreier, Walter Tyler/Sam Comer, Ray Moyer

Cinematography: George Barnes

*COSTUME DESIGN: Edith Head, Dorothy Jeakins, Elois Jenssen, Gile Steele, Gwen Wakeling

Music (Music Score of a Dramatic or Comedy Picture): Victor Young

Special Effects: Cecil B. DeMille Productions

OSCAR TOTALS   Nominations **5**   *Wins **2**

AFI 100 YEARS 100 MOVIES SELECTION
2007 0   1997 0

TOP 300 FILMS POSITION . . . . #124
All-Release Domestic Box Office in Equivalent 2005 $s

National Film Preservation Board Selection. . . . none

OTHER AWARDS Best Picture Wins

	Year
Golden Globes	none
New York Film Critics	none
National Board of Review	none
Film Daily Critics	none

> . . . A lusty action story with a heavy coating of torrid-zone romance. Cecil B. DeMille has again dipped into the Bible for his material, made appropriately dramatic revisions in the original, and turned up with a DeMille-size smash.
>
> —*Daily Variety*, 1950

PLOT: Samson, a respected and feared Hebrew leader bestowed with superhuman strength, falls for a Philistine woman but is seduced by her femme fatale sister, Delilah. Subsequently scorned, she betrays him and shears him of his God-given strength.

PRODUCTION: *Samson and Delilah* ultimately reached the screen fourteen years after Cecil B. DeMille first expressed an interest in the story. In 1935 DeMille commissioned Harold Lamb to write a screenplay and bought the rights to Vladimir Jabotinsky's 1930 Samson novel *The Judge and the Fool,* which had been translated from German. A year later, DeMille also purchased the screen rights to the 1877 French opera *Samson et Dalila,* and although he continued gathering research, other film commitments—*The Buccaneer, Union Pacific, Northwest Mounted Police,* and *Reap the Wild Wind,* among others—intervened. In 1948 DeMille returned to the project, but current Paramount executives were leery of the costs involved and weren't sure postwar audiences were interested in Bible stories. DeMille, undaunted, was able to convince them that the tale could be told as a great love story, backing his pitch with a rendering created by artist Dan Sayre Groesbeck that emphasized Samson's massive strength and Delilah's seductive appeal. The project was given the go-ahead. After Palestine was nixed as a location, a second-unit crew was dispatched to North Africa to shoot background footage and gather authentic props. They reportedly filmed in "twenty localities, from Algiers to Casablanca," including the Moroccan town of Moulay Idris, the nearby archeological site of Volubilis, and the town of Bou-Saada in northeastern Algeria. Back in California, DeMille considered popular Paramount player Betty Hutton for the role of Delilah. Other reported contenders were Rita Hayworth, Jean Simmons, and Lana Turner, but Austrian beauty Hedy Lamarr was the final choice. DeMille made some effort to groom Mr. Universe of 1947, Steve Reeves, for the role of Samson, but after two auditions he concluded that it wouldn't work. Burt Lancaster was also a possibility, but his youthful looks and a bad back ruled against him. Instead, DeMille borrowed Victor Mature from 20th Century-Fox, the studio that, in 1941, had signed the handsome "beefcake" actor as a potential screen partner for their "cheesecake" glamour star, Betty Grable. Angela Lansbury landed the role of Semadar after fellow Brit Phyllis Calvert, initially cast, fell ill and had to withdraw. *Samson and Delilah*'s climactic collapse of the Temple of Dagon was a special effects triumph combining full-size sets filled with people and a detailed miniature of the entire temple populated with tiny dolls. Only the feet of the statue of Dagon were built full-size for closer shots. The wide shots were all miniatures.

DISTRIBUTION: Months prior to the film's release, Paramount sent actor Henry Wilcoxon and press agent Richard Condon on a twenty-five-city tour, armed with 400 pounds of promotional materials. Their mission was to meet with six groups of "public opinion leaders" in each city—women's clubs, churches and religious groups, school officials, fashion designers, manufacturers and retailers, and the media, including film exhibitors. With this $1 million promotional effort and DeMille's pat formula of biblical spectacle mixed with a dash of sex, *Samson and Delilah* had returned a net profit of nearly $5.6 million by December 1969. —*Douglas Burns*

The 1950s

I was the first actor after Marlon [Brando] to have a non-binding contract, which gives you enormous advantages. You could work at other studios, and do a picture for somebody else that was much better.

—Charlton Heston

TOP 10 ALL-RELEASE MOVIES
DOMESTIC BOX OFFICE
By Initial Year of Release, 1950–1959

		Equivalent 2005 $s in Millions of $s
1	*The Ten Commandments*	$829.2
2	*Ben-Hur*	$754.3
3	*Around the World in 80 Days*	$534.0
4	*The Robe*	$474.8
5	*Cinderella*	$379.8
6	*The Bridge on the River Kwai*	$362.3
7	*The Greatest Show on Earth*	$349.1
8	*Lady and the Tramp*	$326.8
9	*From Here to Eternity*	$326.4
10	*Peter Pan*	$323.3
		Total: $4,660.0

GENERAL U.S. STATISTICS, 1950

151,325,798
U.S. Population

60 Million
Average Weekly
U.S. Movie Attendance

DECADE OVERVIEW

I came out here with one suit and everybody said I looked like a bum. Twenty years later Marlon Brando came out with only a sweatshirt and the town drooled over him. That shows how much Hollywood has progressed. —Humphrey Bogart

Dalton Trumbo was one of the Unfriendly Ten. He stood on his rights under the First Amendment, the right of every American to free speech. He went to jail for a year. Now, almost ten years later, he still couldn't set foot on any studio lot . . . The blacklist was still in place. —Kirk Douglas

An Industry in Turmoil

The fifties was a decade that rocked the motion picture industry to its core. The biggest companies were literally split in half by a government consent decree that forced producers to sell their movie theater divisions, thus ending half a century of vertical integration and changing the economics of the movie industry considerably. Amid the postwar American economic boom, the migration to new suburbs, waves of Cold War paranoia, and Hollywood blacklisting, the arrival of the 1950s saw the collapse of studio control over every aspect of moviemaking, the release of contract players, and the end of movie theaters as the only place to see a picture. Everything had been changed by the commercial debut of television. It had quickly reached into millions of homes, changing how people consumed entertainment and sending movie theater ticket sales into freefall. At first the motion picture industry tried to give television the cold shoulder. They scrambled to address the new suburban culture, particularly the car culture, building drive-ins in addition to other theaters. But the studios were still losing ground. Only a few smaller companies such as Walt Disney and Republic sold content to TV initially (despite a lawsuit levied by cowboy star Roy Rogers in an attempt to block the deal). By the midpoint of the decade, however, faced with financial ruin, even the biggest companies were making deals with TV. RKO ultimately sold its library of 740 features and 1,100 shorts in 1955. One year later Columbia Pictures sold its feature films to its television subsidiary Screen Gems. It was also in 1956 that *The Wizard of Oz* was first shown on TV. It would go on to become an annual broadcasting event. Soon movie studios such as Warner Bros. were also producing for television. Despite their participation in the competing medium of TV, studios still clamored to protect their core business. In a bid to bring fans back to theaters, they launched new in-theater formats—the first since the 1930s—including CinemaScope, VistaVision, Cinerama, and three-dimensional movies. The movie business was also becoming much more international at this time, with native film industries booming in Italy and France, among other European countries. In 1956 the Academy of Motion Picture Arts and Sciences began giving out an award for Best Foreign Language Film of the year.

U.S. TV and Radio Household Media Use, 1940–1965

	Number of Households with TV Sets (000)	Percentage of all Households with TV Sets	Percentage of all Households with Radios
1940	—	—	73%
1946	8	—	—
1947	14	—	—
1948	172	—	—
1949	940	2%	—
1950	3,875	8%	91%
1955	30,700	67%	—
1960	45,750	88%	94%
1965	52,700	92%	—

U.S. INDUSTRY PRODUCTION STATISTICS, 1950s
Equivalent 2005 $s/(Unadjusted $s)

$25.3 Million ($3.5 million)
Average production cost of films featured in this chapter

$8.9 Million ($1.1 million)
Average production cost of all films released in 1950

PRODUCTION SPOTLIGHT

In Hollywood until the 1950s, the final decisions, great and small,
were made by the front offices, or by surrogates of those exalted founts of wisdom.
The head of the studio or the vice president in charge of production had his way.
No writer, no star, no director of that period had the final say. —GARSON KANIN

TV Changes Everything

In the fall of 1955, *Warner Bros. Presents* became the first television program produced by a first-rank Hollywood studio, followed closely by shows produced by 20th Century-Fox on CBS and MGM on ABC. By 1960 there were TV shows from all the majors. Warner Bros. also began producing series such as *Cheyenne, Maverick,* and *77 Sunset Strip.* In 1953 the Academy Awards were televised for the first time, drawing record ratings. With the merger of the American Federation of Labor and the Congress of Industrial Organizations into the AFL-CIO in 1955 and the increasing clout of the various Hollywood guilds, average production went from a six-day week to a five-day week. The first generation of movie moguls were gone or on their way out: Darryl F. Zanuck left Fox in the 1950s (although he would return in 1962), Louis B. Mayer was fired from MGM in 1951, and Harry Cohn, head of Columbia, died in 1958. As the era of the studio contract player system ended, new deals were being negotiated by powerful talent agents, driving up the cost of big-budget pictures. The Screen Actors Guild (SAG) negotiated royalties from the TV broadcast of films, as did the Directors Guild of America (DGA) and the Writers Guild of America (WGA). B movies disappeared, but a new kind of low-budget film from companies such as American International Pictures appealed to a younger crowd with

1950s Movie Censorship: A Brief History

References to Blanche DuBois's infidelities are excised from the original 1951 version of A Streetcar Named Desire. The African Queen *(1951) is also the focus of censor objections. In the 1952 case* Burstyn v. Wilson, *the Supreme Court strikes down a ban on the short film* The Miracle, *by Italian director Roberto Rossellini. For the first time, the courts hold that motion pictures are entitled to some First Amendment protection.*

The Legion of Decency and the MPAA begin to clash. Hollywood studio authority over the content of films collides with major changes in general American mores and customs. In 1956 the Legion approves the depiction of drug use in Otto Preminger's The Man with a Golden Arm, *but the MPAA does not. The MPAA approves Elia Kazan's film* Baby Doll, *but the Legion condemns it for its erotic content.*

stories about rebellious teens, bikers, surfers, social protest, and science fiction. New antiheroes emerged from performances by Marlon Brando and James Dean, while the screen sensuality of Ava Gardner, Kim Novak, and Marilyn Monroe changed views of sexuality and brought greater realism to acting. The movies discovered rock and roll, and saw the rise of Elvis Presley, first in music and then on the big screen, before he was drafted by the U.S. Army late in the decade. By the mid-fifties, the studios also ended the ban prohibiting movie stars from appearing on television. Stars began showing up in everything from comedies to dramas, simultaneously promoting movies and boosting their careers. Soundstages that had been used exclusively for movies were turned over to TV production, while many major movies were shot on location, bringing fresh visuals, more realistic perspectives, and improved production technology to the process. Although color had been available to moviemakers since the 1930s, it was only with the advent of TV that color became more common in film. The studios saw it as a clear way to trump black and white TV. By 1955 more than half the theatrical releases in the United States were in color.

Index of Top Feature Film Directors Included in This Chapter

1	Cecil B. DeMille	*The Ten Commandments*
		The Greatest Show on Earth
2	William Wyler	*Ben-Hur*
3	Hamilton Luske, Clyde Geronimi, Wilfred Jackson	*Cinderella*
4	George Stevens	*Giant*
		Shane
5	Fred Zinnemann	*From Here to Eternity*
		The Nun's Story
		High Noon
6	Michael Anderson	*Around the World in 80 Days*
7	Mervyn LeRoy	*Quo Vadis*
		Mister Roberts
8	Henry Koster	*The Robe*
9	Elia Kazan	*A Streetcar Named Desire*
		On the Waterfront
		East of Eden
10	David Lean	*The Bridge on the River Kwai*

See Note to the Reader for selection criteria.

I have sometimes likened the producer to the restorer of a broken mosaic . . .
Some parts of the mosaic can be supplied by historians. The missing parts . . .
the producer must supply; but the integrity of the whole work demands that
what the producer supplies must fit in with what history knows.
—CECIL B. DEMILLE ON *THE TEN COMMANDMENTS*

Six of the Top 15 Biblical Epic Films
Are Released in the 1950s

Top 15 Biblical Epic Films
All-Release Domestic Box Office 1920–2005
Equivalent 2005 $s/(Unadjusted $s) in Millions of $s

Rank	Film	Initial Release	Domestic Box Office	Production Cost
1	The Ten Commandments	1956	$829.2/($89.1)	$95.3/($13.3)
2	Ben-Hur*	1959	$754.3/($85.8)	$106.7/($15.9)
3	The Robe	1953	$474.8/($37.8)	$30.1/($4.1)
4	The Passion of the Christ	2004	$382.2/($370.3)	$31.0/($30.0)
5	Ben-Hur: A Tale of the Christ (Silent)	1925	$305.2/($9.1)	$44.8/($4.0)
6	Samson and Delilah	1949	$276.7/($25.6)	$26.2/($3.2)
7	David and Bathsheba	1951	$215.2/($15.8)	not available
8	The Bible	1966	$196.0/($33.3)	$108.5/($18.0)
9	The Ten Commandments (Silent)	1923	$153.1/($4.3)	$16.9/($1.5)
10	The Prince of Egypt (Animated)	1998	$138.4/($101.3)	$89.9/($75.0)
11	King of Kings	1961	$131.9/($16.7)	$32.9/($5.0)
12	Demetrius and the Gladiators	1954	$108.1/($9.4)	$32.7/($4.5)
10	Solomon and Sheba	1959	$103.l/($12.2)	$33.6/($0.5)
14	The Greatest Story Ever Told	1965	$97.3/($15.3)	$124.0/($20.0)
15	King of Kings (Silent)	1927	$92.4/($5.3)	$14.2/($1.3)

*Academy Award winner for Best Picture.

Sword-and-Sandal Movie Comparison

MGM's 1959 wide-screen premiere of *Ben-Hur* receives twelve Academy Award nominations and eleven wins, while the DreamWorks 2000 release of *Gladiator* picks up twelve nominations and five wins.

Comparison of *Ben-Hur* vs. *Gladiator* Movies
Initial Release Worldwide Box Office
Equivalent 2005 $s/(Unadjusted $s) in Millions of $s

	Ben-Hur, 1959	*Gladiator*, 2000
Domestic box office	**$704.2**/($74.7)	**$223.2**/($187.7)
Foreign box office	**$608.6**/($72.2)	**$321.0**/($269.9)
Worldwide box office	**$1,312.8**/($146.9)	**$544.2**/($457.6)
Domestic rentals	**$316.9**/($33.6)	**$122.8**/($103.2)
Foreign rentals	**$273.9**/($32.5)	**$144.4**/($121.5)
Worldwide rentals	**$590.8**/($66.10)	**$267.2**/($224.7)
Production cost	**$106.7**/($15.9)	**$116.8**/($103.0)
Prints and ads	**$98.4**/($14.7)	**$59.5**/($52.5)
Distribution fee	**$155.7**/($16.5)	**$94.6**/($79.5)
Negative interest	not available	**$16.9**/($14.9)
P&L	**$230.0**/($19.5)	**−$20.6**/(−$25.2)
Film length and number of days	**217** minutes	**154** minutes
Principal photography	**200** days estimated	**89** days estimated

Notes:

Ben-Hur unadjusted $s based on actuals. Inflation numbers do not take into consideration possible initial road show release with higher than average ticket prices in 1959 so adjusted $s may be inflated. Box office estimated assuming rentals are 45% of total.

Gladiator assumptions: Domestic rentals estimated at 55 percent of domestic box office, 45 percent of foreign box office; distribution fee estimated based on 30 percent domestic rentals/40 percent foreign rentals; prints based on number of engagements at peak domestic release × 2 (to estimated number of screens) × $1,500/per print cost); ad costs from *Hollywood Reporter*. Combined prints and ads total is domestic only; Negative interest based on number of days from start of production 2/1/1999 through release May 2000) × 9.5 percent prime in 2000 + 25% or 11.88 percent on $103 million; negative cost includes estimated $5.0 million salary paid Russell Crowe ($5.7 in 2005 $s). Does not include revenues from DVD sales or the costs of gross participants.

Youth Films Are Popular but Don't Make the Big Bucks

While youth films and visual gimmicks such as 3-D were getting a lot of attention, the top live-action blockbusters of the decade were still traditional big-budget studio movies led by biblical-era epics *The Ten Commandments, Ben-Hur,* and *The Robe,* along with wide-screen spectacles such as *Around the World in 80 Days, The Greatest Show on Earth,* and *The Bridge on the River Kwai.*

Comparison of James Dean and Marlon Brando 1950s Films
All-Release Domestic Box Office
Equivalent 2005 $s/(Unadjusted $s)
Domestic Box Office and Production Cost in Millions of $s

Film	Initial Release	Male Star	Domestic Box Office	Production Cost	Salary Paid to Male Star
A Streetcar Named Desire	1951	Marlon Brando	$130.5 ($10.3)	$13.5 ($1.8)	$648,300 ($80,000)
On the Waterfront	1954	Marlon Brando	$109.9 ($9.6)	$6.6 ($0.9)	$914,300 ($125,000)
Guys and Dolls	1955	Marlon Brando	$217.3 ($20.0)	$40.1 ($5.5)	$1,452,000 ($200,000)
Sayonara	1957	Marlon Brando	$230.1 ($23.3)	not available	$2,154,000 excluding p/p* ($300,000 + 10% profits)
East of Eden	1955	James Dean	$122.8 ($11.1)	$11.7 ($1.6)	$72,600 ($10,000 approximately at $1,200/week)
Rebel without a Cause	1955	James Dean	$113.0 ($10.2)	$10.9 ($1.5)	$90,800 ($12,500 approximately at $1,250/week)
Giant	1956	James Dean	$322.2 ($31.3)	$35.9 ($5.0)	$164,000 ($22,500 approximately at $1,500/week)

*Profit participation.

Actors of the 1950s: Comparison of Salaries and Profit Participations
Equivalent 2005 $s/(Unadjusted $s)

Actor	Film	Initial Release	Salary
William Holden	*The Bridge on the River Kwai*	1957	**$20.9 million** ($3 million including p/p* on $30 million in world rentals based on 10% gross p/p in lieu of salary. Paid at $50,000/year)
	Sunset Boulevard	1950	**$172,324/($21,000)**
Yul Brynner	*Solomon and Sheba*	1959	**$4,026,804/($600,000)**
Cary Grant	*North by Northwest*	1959	**$3,041,003 excluding p/p** ($450,000 + % of gross p/p + $5,000 per day for extra work)
Marilyn Monroe	*Some Like It Hot*	1959	**$2,027,336 excluding p/p** ($300,000 + 10% gross p/p after $4 million)
Audrey Hepburn	*The Nun's Story*	1959	**$1,677,835 excluding p/p** ($250,000 + p/p)
Elizabeth Taylor	*Giant*	1956	**$1,256,526/($175,000)**
Humphrey Bogart	*The African Queen*	1951	**$938,942 excluding p/p** ($125,000 + p/p)
Burt Lancaster	*From Here to Eternity*	1953	**$877,753/($120,000)**
Orson Welles	*The Third Man*	1950	**$810,373/($100,000)**
Tony Curtis and Jack Lemmon	*Some Like It Hot*	1959	**$675,779** ($100,000/ea + 5% gross p/p after $1 million over breakeven)
Gloria Swanson	*Sunset Boulevard*	1950	**$410,294/($50,000)**
Charlton Heston	*The Ten Commandments*	1956	**$359,007/($50,000 total paid at $2,000/week for 25 weeks)**
Kim Novak	*Vertigo*	1958	**$19,113/week/**($2,750/week)
Eva Marie Saint	*North by Northwest*	1959	**$13,516/week/**($2,000/week)

*Profit participation.

A Sampling of Director Salaries
Equivalent 2005 $s/(Unadjusted $s)

Director	Film	Initial Release	Salary
William Wyler	*Ben-Hur*	1959	**$6.7 million including p/p*** ($1.0 million including $350,000 fee + 8% gross p/p)
Alfred Hitchcock	*North by Northwest*	1969	**$1.7 million** ($250,000 + 10% net p/p & ownership)
	Vertigo	1958	**$1.0 million** ($150,000 + 10% & ownership)
	Rear Window	1954	**$1.0 million** ($150,000 + 10% & ownership)
Billy Wilder	*Some Like It Hot*	1959	**$1.4 million** ($200,000 + 17.5%–20% p/p)
	Sunset Boulevard	1950	**$0.7 million** ($90,000) for directing; **$1.7 million** ($211,416) for screenplay
John Ford	*Mister Roberts*	1955	**$1.3 million** ($175,000)

*Profit participation.

Comparison of Two *The Ten Commandments* Films Initial Release
Directed by Cecil B. DeMille
Equivalent 2005 $s/(Unadjusted $s) in Millions of $s

Initial Release	Production Cost	Domestic Film Rental	Foreign Film Rental	Worldwide Box Office (estimated)
1956	**$95.3** ($13.3)	**$339.9** ($31.3)	**$247.5** ($23.9)	**$1,305.3** ($122.7)
1923	**$16.9** ($1.5)	**$77.3** ($2.2)	**$71.2** ($2.0)	**$295.6** ($8.3)

A Sampling of Producer Earnings, 1950
Equivalent 2005 $s/(Unadjusted $s)

Producer	Annual Earnings
Darryl Zanuck (production head at 20th Century-Fox)	$2.1 Million/($260,000)

Note: Annual salary prior to 50 percent pay cut in 1951.

Top 10 Critically Acclaimed Lead Actors of the 1950s

Rank	Actor Name
1	Gary Cooper
2	Marlon Brando
3	Humphrey Bogart
4	Alec Guinness
5	William Holden
6	Charlton Heston
7	Jose Ferrer
8	Ernest Borgnine
9	David Niven
10	Gene Kelly

Rank	Actress Name
1	Ingrid Bergman
2	Deborah Kerr
3	Audrey Hepburn
4	Susan Hayward
5	Vivien Leigh
6	Joanne Woodward
7	Grace Kelly
8	Rosalind Russell
9	Anna Magnani
10	Simone Signoret

See Note to the Reader for selection criteria.

DISTRIBUTION OVERVIEW

Formats Change to Enhance the Viewing Experience

As the studios stumbled, they sharply cut production, dropping the number of major-company new movie releases from 263 in 1950 to 184 in 1960. The independent studios also reduced their numbers, dropping from 359 new movie releases in 1950 to 203 in 1960. At the same time, new marketing and advertising techniques were introduced that reflected the rise of sophisticated new agencies and the research that was available in the postwar years. For the first time TV was being used to advertise and promote select movies. Essentially, the studios were seeking ways to differentiate the theater experience from what consumers could get for free in their living rooms. In 1952 Cinerama became the first wide-screen process to hit theaters, utilizing three 35mm projectors, special lenses, and a special screen. The demonstration film made to show off the process, *This Is Cinerama,* became a surprise runaway hit. In 1953 20th Century-Fox announced that all subsequent film releases would utilize a wide-screen process called CinemaScope. This process compressed a wide-screen image onto standard 35mm film. When the image was projected through an anamorphic lens, it returned to wide-screen specifications. Fox also made theaters install stereophonic sound to complement the enhanced visuals. At first the new systems caused some confusion. Warner Bros. shut down for ninety days to determine which of the competing formats to use, while MGM, United Artists, Columbia Pictures, and Disney all committed to CinemaScope. Paramount had VistaVision, its own wide-screen process, claiming that CinemaScope lacked clarity of image. There was also new interest in special effects at this time, not only for science fiction but also to enhance epics such as 1956's *The Ten Commandments,* the last film directed by Cecil B. DeMille.

U.S. INDUSTRY DISTRIBUTION STATISTICS, 1950s
Equivalent 2005 $s/(Unadjusted $s)

$19,174 Million ($1,376 Million)
Annual U.S. box office gross revenues

622
Number of new feature films released

Major Movie Distributors, 1950s

Buena Vista . . . . New distribution company established by the Walt Disney Company in 1954

Columbia. President Harry Cohn dies in 1958

MGM . . . . Production head Louis B. Mayer is fired in 1951. Separation of theater assets from production and distribution assets takes place on March 12, 1959

Paramount Pictures . . . . Organized on January 1, 1950, to take over the production and distribution activities of the former Paramount Pictures, Inc. Adolph Zuckor retires in 1959.

RKO Radio Pictures . . . . GenCorp buys RKO Pictures from Howard Hughes for $25 million in 1955 then sells the movie portion of the business in 1958

20th Century-Fox. . . . . Incorporated on July 22, 1952, excluding theaters. Production head Darryl F. Zanuck leaves to become an independent producer in 1956

United Artists Corp. . . . . Arthur Krim and Robert Benjamin assume management in 1951

Universal Pictures . . . . Decca Records acquires a controlling interest in 1952

Warner Bros. . . . . Warner Bros. Pictures, Inc., takes over the production and distribution assets of Warner Bros. Pictures, Inc., on February 28, 1953

TECHNOLOGY SPOTLIGHT

Cinerama Launches Giant Screen Era

The making of the travelogue *This Is Cinerama* was so low-budget and under the radar that entrepreneur, showman, and producer Mike Todd personally acted as location scout during a shoot in Europe, while his twenty-one-year-old son Michael junior directed test scenes in Venice. Those demonstration shots became the first half of the movie.

As the premiere neared, the elder Todd declared personal bankruptcy, partly due to gambling losses. Although he held as much stock in Cinerama as his partner, broadcaster Lowell Thomas, and more than Fred Waller, who had spent seventeen years developing Cinerama, Todd had to relinquish his voting rights or face losing all his stock. Instead, Todd sold his position in the company he helped found on the eve of this landmark blockbuster premiere. Mike Todd Jr. later recalled: "Instead of crying or moaning about it, or starting a lawsuit, Dad figured, 'Well, all right, I'm getting screwed, but I'll show them. There's a better way to do this.'" Todd senior, who tragically died in a plane crash six years later, left to found Todd AO, a competing process.

However, it was Cinerama (an anagram for *American*) that came first and set the standard for all the rest. On September 30, 1952, three projectors lit images on a huge curved screen in the Broadway Theater in Manhattan. The next day, in the *New York Times,* appeared the first front-page movie article ever. In it Bosley Crowther described the reaction of the crowd: " . . . The astonished first night audience tore the theater apart with cheers." The next day all the executives who had ignored Waller's ideas were calling him directly. Todd was replaced at Cinerama by producer Merian C. Cooper, who had overseen the hit *King Kong* for RKO in 1933. A spate of wide-screen competitors emerged. The beleaguered movie industry saw it as their salvation—as something audiences couldn't get on TV. That belief was reinforced when, playing for only thirteen weeks in one theater, the documentary *This Is Cinerama* became the fifth-highest-grossing movie of 1952, beating the popular Humphrey Bogart and Katharine Hepburn film *The African Queen* at the box office.

There had been prior attempts at wide-screen exhibition beginning as early as in the 1920s with D. W. Griffith's Widescope, Paramount's Magnafilm, MGM's Fanthom Screen, and William Fox's Grandeur. And French director Abel Gance used three cameras for the climax of his five-hour 1927 film *Napoleon.* However, during the 1930s, in the wake of the Depression, plunging ticket sales, and rising censorship, an Academy committee had declared a moratorium on wide-screen productions. For the next two decades, there was only 35 mm.

Cinerama was quickly followed by big-screen competitors CinemaScope, VistaVision, Super Panavision, and others.

Aspect ratio—*the width of an image divided by its height.*
—CINEMASOURCE.COM

Wide-Screen Becomes the New Norm

Four main categories of wide-screen filming and projection:
1. Using film wider than the standard 35 mm
2. Using a special anamorphic lens that "squeezes" the image in filming and "unsqueezes" it in projection
3. Using more than one camera and more than one projector
4. Masking the top and bottom of conventional film during projection to produce the effect of width
—EPHRAIM KATZ, *THE FILM ENCYCLOPEDIA*

The original shape of film was 4 wide by 3 high, decided in the late nineteenth century by Thomas Edison. For every 4 feet across, the projected image would go up 3 feet (4 divided by 3 results in an aspect ratio of 1.33:1, meaning the image's width is 1.33 times greater than its height). This aspect ratio was officially adopted in 1917 by the Society of Motion Picture Engineers and was used by the film industry almost exclusively until the early 1950s. TVs in the 1940s and 1950s matched this aspect ratio so that theatrical movies could be satisfactorily viewed on television.

During the 1930s, the addition of a sound strip onto the film strip reduced the image size, resulting in an aspect ratio of 1.37:1. In 1932 the Academy of Motion Picture Arts and Sciences voted to maintain the 1.33:1 ratio by reducing the height of the image.

Beginning in the 1950s, as a means of differentiating themselves from television films, motion pictures were shot and projected in wider sizes. Some processes, such as Cinerama, required that theaters have three projectors and a special curved screen. Others, such as CinemaScope, used camera lenses that squeezed the image size first, then unsqueezed it when projected with another special lens. Still other systems used larger film stock or ran the film strip horizontally through the camera.

By the 1960s, CinemaScope, with an aspect ratio of 2.35:1, had become the new standard, although other ratios existed. Cinerama continued through the 1960s, mainly as a brand name for films shot with one camera in 70mm Ultra Panavision or Super Technirama 70 and projected onto Cinerama's curved screen with a single projector. As the new formats spread, most theaters quietly did away with the Cinerama curved screens in favor of a solid flat screen. Today wide-screen dominates American filmmaking in a variety of aspect ratios.

Popular Theatrical Aspect Ratios and Some Sample Films

Format	Aspect Ratio	Sample Film, Release Year
Academy Standard The same aspect ratio as early TV. When sound was introduced it reduced the image size by the space taken up by the sound strip to 1.37:1.	1.33:1	Silent movies to early 1930s
Cinerama Originally developed by Fred Waller of Paramount's special-effects department, it required three special cameras. The three strips of film were then projected in sync onto a huge deeply curved screen with three projectors but were separated by two visible vertical lines where the images came together.	2.60:1	*This is Cinerama*, 1952 (documentary) *The Wonderful World of the Brothers Grimm*, 1962 *How the West Was Won*, 1963
Academy Flat or Academy Standard 35 mm film with sound that is shot with the image unsqueezed then framed (via a crop, matte, or other device) and shown theatrically wider than it would be on a standard television screen. This format is also referred to as **"Spherical."**	1.37:1 1.66:1 (output 1950s USA then mostly Europe) 1.85:1 (output mostly USA)	*Shane*, 1953 (1st to use 1.66:1 ratio- shot 1.37:1 but projected with top and bottom cropped) *Psycho*, 1960 *Dr. No*, 1963 *Tom Jones*, 1963 *Bonnie and Clyde*, 1967 *Easy Rider*, 1969 *Godfather* movies beginning 1972 (1.85:1)

Format	Aspect Ratio	Sample Film, Release Year
CinemaScope Created by 20th Century-Fox, this process uses an anamorphic lens that optically captures an image twice as wide as the film by squeezing it, then unsqueezing it when projected with a special lens. By the mid-1960s, widescreen anamorphic films shot with Panasonic lenses were referred to as **"Panavision."**	2.35:1 2.55:1	*The Robe,* 1953 *East of Eden,* 1955 *The Bridge on the River Kwai,* 1957 *The Apartment,* 1960 *The Graduate,* 1967 *Star Wars* movies beginning 1977 *Dances with Wolves,* 1990 *The Passion of the Christ,* 2004
VistaVision Developed by Paramount Pictures as an alternative to Fox's anamorphic CinemaScope system. In shooting VistaVision, the film is run horizontally, as in a still camera, providing a film area twice that of a CinemaScope camera.	1.50:1 1.85:1 2.35:1	*White Christmas,* 1954 *The Searchers,* 1956 *The Ten Commandments,* 1956 *Vertigo,* 1958 *North by Northwest,* 1959 *One Eyed Jack,* 1961 (last U.S. use of VistaVision)

Todd-AO
Co-created by Michael Todd, one of the original Cinerama partners. Process uses a single camera shooting 65 mm negative, which is then printed onto 70 mm film to accomodate the sound track. Earlier versions used a frames per second (fps) rate of 30 rather than the standard 24 fps.
	2.20:1
	2.35:1
		Epics and Musicals of the 1950s and 1960s, including:
		    Oklahoma, 1955 (30 fps)
		    Around the World in 80 Days, 1956 (30 fps)
		    Cleopatra, 1963
		    The Sound of Music, 1965
		    Airport, 1970

Technirama Invented by Technicolor, using a 35 mm camera with film running horizontally and an anamorphic (squeeze) lens. The name **Super Technirama 70** was used on films where the shooting was done in Technirama, and at least some prints were made on 70 mm stock by unsqueezing the image.	2.20:1 2.35:1	*Sayonara,* 1957 *Auntie Mame,* 1958 *Solomon and Sheba,* 1959 *Spartacus,* 1960 (70 mm)
MGM Camera 65 Created by MGM with Panavision this process used 65 mm film with a special anamorphic lens that squeezed the image 1.25x.	2.76:1	*Ben Hur,* 1959 *Mutiny on the Bounty,* 1962
Super Panavision 70 The Panavision company's system to compete with Todd-AO and Super Technirama 70.	2.20:1 2.35:1	*West Side Story,* 1961 *The Longest Day,* 1962 *Lawrence of Arabia,* 1962 *Indiana Jones* movies beginning with *Raiders,* 1981
Ultra Panavision 70 After *Mutiny on the Bounty,* Panavision acquired MGM's camera equipment division, as well as the rights to the Camera 65 system it had developed for MGM and renamed the technology Ultra Panavision.	2.76:1	*It's a Mad, Mad, Mad, Mad World,* 1963 *The Greatest Story Ever Told,* 1965 (both films presented in 70mm Cinerama)

With Multiple Screen Formats Comes Multiple Color Print Processes

Technicolor: The Technicolor Corporation, which was founded in 1915, developed a trademark for the most widely used motion picture color process in Hollywood from the 1920s to the 1950s. Two-color Technicolor was used for early films, followed by three-strip Technicolor, then Technicolor as it is known today. Sample films: *Gone with the Wind,* 1939; *Cinderella,* 1950; *The Greatest Show on Earth,* 1952; *Spartacus,* 1960, *Guess Who's Coming to Dinner* 1967; *The Wild Bunch,* 1969; *Star Wars: Episode I A New Hope,* 1977; *Kramer vs. Kramer,* 1979; *Amadeus,* 1984.

DeLuxe: The company now called Deluxe began as the camera and film department at the William Fox Film Corporation in Fort Lee, New Jersey, in 1915. Beginning in the 1950s, the brand name DeLuxe was used on film that 20th Century-Fox processed through Deluxe's labs. The Rank Group in the United Kingdom (which owned Odeon Cinemas and Pinewood Studios until 2000) purchased Deluxe in 1989, then sold it to MacAndrews & Forbes Holdings, Inc., in 2006. Sample films: *Star Wars: Episode V The Empire Strikes Back,* 1980; *Star Wars: Episode VI Return of the Jedi,* 1983; *Indiana Jones and the Temple of Doom,* 1984; *Braveheart,* 1995.

Eastmancolor: In the 1950s, Eastman Kodak introduced its own single-strip color negative and print stock, which was inferior to Technicolor but was cheaper and faster to process. They also allowed the processing of their film in labs chosen by the studios, who could call the processed film anything they wanted. Sample films with Eastmancolor credits: *Around the World in 80 Days,* 1956; *The Guns of Navarone,* 1961; *The Rocky Horror Picture Show,* 1975; *Midnight Express,* 1978.

    Metrocolor: A process used by MGM using Eastman Kodak film. Sample films: *How the West Was Won,* 1963; *2001: A Space Odyssey,* 1968; *The Exorcist,* 1973; *Raiders of the Lost Ark,* 1981; *Terms of Endearment,* 1983.

    Warnercolor: A process used by Warner Bros. using Eastman Kodak film in the 1950s for its more modestly budgeted films. Sample films: *Mister Roberts,* 1955; *Rebel Without a Cause,* 1955; *A Clockwork Orange,* 1971.

Color by CFI: Consolidated Film Industries (CFI) was initially incorporated in New York in 1924 and built itself up to become a leading film laboratory in the Los Angeles area. The lab processed negatives and made prints for motion pictures and television. It was acquired by Technicolor in 2000. Sample films: *Platoon,* 1986; *Terminator 2: Judgment Day,* 1991; *Titanic,* 1997; *Dr. Seuss' How the Grinch Stole Christmas,* 2000.

MARKETING SPOTLIGHT

Saul Bass Unifies Key Art and Creates Narrative Credit Sequences

In 1953 when director and independent producer Otto Preminger decided that United Artists' advertising campaign made his controversial comedy *The Moon Is Blue* appear to be pornographic, he turned to independent graphic designer Saul Bass, who created an iconic central image for the film. Bass portrayed the characters kissing as they perched on a crescent blue moon. He would go on to reinvent key art—the central image of a movie used for promotional purposes—and develop the first holistic approach to presenting a motion picture. Before Bass's arrival, posters and opening credits had been very functional. They often featured a panorama of characters, a clever gag, or a visual bit. Bass also created imaginative title sequences that were more like little experimental films with great psychological and emotional impact. He saw that the graphic arts could be as artistically important as the fine arts.

Bass worked with Alfred Hitchcock on *Vertigo, North by Northwest, Psycho,* and others. He also worked with Robert Aldrich on *The Big Knife,* Billy Wilder on *The Seven Year Itch,* Mike Todd on *Around the World in 80 Days,* and others throughout his four decades in the business. But it was Bass's early collaborations with Otto Preminger that marked an important shift in movie marketing. For *Carmen Jones,* a 1954 musical based on a Bizet opera with an all-black cast, Bass created a rose within a flame as the film's icon. Upon looking at it, Bass and Preminger wondered how it might appear in motion. An animated version was made and ultimately became the opening credit sequence of the film.

The most important collaboration, from a historical perspective, was on the 1955 film *The*

Comparison of Three 1950s Films Initial Release
Equivalent 2005 $s/(Unadjusted $s) in Millions of $s

Film	Initial Release	Domestic Box Office	Domestic Rentals	Foreign Rentals	Production Cost	Print and Ad Costs
Around the World in 80 Days	1956	$518.8 ($48.4)	$233.5 ($21.8)	$114.5 ($11.1)	$43.1 ($6.0)	$45.1 ($6.3)
The Robe	1953	$474.8 ($37.8)	$209.7 ($16.7)	$118.3 ($9.4)	$30.1 ($4.1)	$21.6 ($3.0)
Quo Vadis	1951	$303.9 ($22.3)	$152.0 ($11.1)	$212.4 ($15.6)	$57.3 ($7.6)	$20.4 ($2.7)

Man with the Golden Arm. Movie theater owners wanted a poster featuring the film's popular star, Frank Sinatra, but Preminger went with Bass's iconic image of an addict's arm extended into a twisted hand. Bass expanded that into an animated three-minute opening title sequence that played under a jazz score. The animation depicts a black paper cutout of the arm moving to the music. That sequence not only became a sensation but also launched a new generation of key art.

"Motion picture photography was always about ten years behind," Bass recalled late in his career. "That's what distinguished my initial work in films. I was bringing to bear the visual standards that I had developed in the graphic field. That was very startling, and that's what made the work I did then look so wild."

EXHIBITION OVERVIEW

General Cinema Exemplifies the Rise of the Independent Regional Exhibitor

The postwar baby boom was a time of great change in the world of theatrical motion picture exhibition. As a result of the consent decree in the 1940s, the studios were forced to spin off their theater holdings. Then the rise of television began to undermine the once faithful movie-going audience. The old downtown theaters, which were the show palaces for generations, fell into disrepair as ownership changed. No longer were there fully uniformed ushers waiting for customers in the cavernous lobbies. Ticket sales started to decline significantly. Admissions totaled $1.37 billion in 1950 but had fallen to $984 million by 1960. Most notably, young couples just starting their families began leaving the urban areas for a place called suburbia. This gave rise to a new kind of entrepreneur: the regional theater owner.

Independent regional theater owners existed prior to the 1950s, but the studios controlled the product and maintained a release strategy that opened their top product in their own theaters. The government-mandated change in studio ownership of theaters gave the regional independent theater owner the opportunity to grow and prosper in this new environment. These exhibitors included such visionaries as Philip and Richard Smith (Boston), William Forman (Los Angeles), John Danz (Seattle), Ben Marcus (Milwaukee), Raymond Syufy (Vallejo, California), Michael Naify (San Francisco), Stan Durwood (Kansas City), Ted Mann (Minneapolis), and Sumner Redstone (Boston).

Philip Smith's General Cinema Corporation became one of the leading exhibition companies in the United States, rising from a small company born in 1922 to one that would have 175 theaters in twenty-four states by 1997. Smith's vision was centered on shopping malls. He opened the first mall theater in 1951 at Shoppers' World in Framingham, Massachusetts, and eventually built theaters in more malls than any other exhibitor in the country. Smith was the first to recognize the importance of the mall, the new suburban downtown that accommodated automobiles with offers of ample free parking. Rather than take over old theaters, General Cinema primarily built new theaters in new areas. In the 1960s and into the early 1970s they even employed ushers and a doorman to greet and seat customers. This return to old showmanship helped propel General Cinema's success for the next twenty years. As Philip and his son Richard (who became CEO in 1961 after Philip's death) grew the company, it became increasingly important to get first-run films for their theaters. They wanted the same films in their suburban mall theaters as were appearing in the older first-run downtown theaters. Distributors including Buena Vista (Disney), Columbia, and Paramount agreed with General Cinema's vision and sold pictures to them on a day-and-date basis. This was the beginning of the mass general releases we see today, where films can open on as many as six thousand (or more) screens on day one.

After becoming successful by building in smart locations, General Cinema continued to expand by buying other exhibition circuits. Revenues grew, not only from the increased number of screens but also from the growing concession sales; General Cinema even became the largest independent bottler of Pepsi-Cola. But when General Cinema started buying noncore businesses and cutting costs in the theater division, the tide began to change. Those decisions eventually led to the company's bankruptcy and sale to AMC Theatres in 2002. Sadly, General Cinema's life cycle was typical of many of the theater companies that would come to a close by the turn of the century.

U.S. INDUSTRY EXHIBITION STATISTICS, 1950s
Equivalent 2005 $s/(Unadjusted $s)

$6.41 ($0.46 to $0.68)
Average movie ticket price (1950–1959)

19,106
Number of U.S. screens, 1950

THE THIRD MAN

Selznick Releasing Organization, 1950

ALL-RELEASE EQUIVALENT 2005 $s

(Unadjusted $s) in Millions of $s

Domestic Box Office Revenues . . . . $67.4/($5.4)
Production Cost . . . . not available
Principal Photography . . . . 80 days estimated
10/22/1948–12/11/1948
(Vienna); 12/15/1948–
3/31/1949 (Studio)

Director . . . . Carol Reed
Producer . . . . Carol Reed
Production Company . . . . Selznick Enterprises, London
Film Production
Story by . . . . Graham Greene
Screenplay by . . . . Graham Greene
Cast . . . . Joseph Cotten, Valli, Orson
Welles, Trevor Howard
Filming Locations . . . . . . Shot on location in Vienna,
Austria; in studio in the UK at
Isleworth and Shepperton
Genre . . . . Film Noir
Format . . . . B&W
Initial Release . . . . 8/31/1949 premiere (London,
UK); 2/2/1950 U.S. release
Rerelease . . . . 1999 with a new internegative
and completely re-mastered
sound negative
Running Time . . . . 104 minutes UK/ 93 minutes U.S.
MPAA Rating . . . . not rated

STANDING THE TEST OF TIME

ACADEMY AWARD Oscar Nominations and Wins
*CINEMATOGRAPHY: Robert Krasker
Directing: Carol Reed
Film Editing: Oswald Hafenrichter

OSCAR TOTALS   Nominations 3   *Wins 1

AFI 100 YEARS 100 MOVIES SELECTION
2007 0   1997 . . . #57
TOP 300 FILMS POSITION . . . . none
All-Release Domestic Box Office in Equivalent 2005 $s

National Film Preservation Board Selection . . . . none

OTHER AWARDS Best Picture Wins

	Year
Golden Globes	none
New York Film Critics	none
National Board of Review	none
Film Daily Critics	none

Yes I suffered a lot of opposition going to Vienna . . . In those days, one didn't take actors on location. But here's an example of the way finance does dominate the business. If you've got five weeks on location, you know you've got to get all your shots in that period. We had a day and a night unit. . . . We worked from eight p.m. to five a.m. then went to bed, got up at ten a.m. worked with the day unit until four . . . That way we got double the work done in the same time.

—Carol Reed

PLOT: An American writer of westerns tries to decipher the mysterious disappearance and accidental death of an old school friend in post–World War II Vienna.

PRODUCTION: London Film founder and executive producer Alexander Korda, a Hungarian émigré, wanted to film in Vienna (then occupied by U.S., British, and French forces) to tap reserves of currency in Austria that were difficult to get out. Korda hired writer Graham Greene and director Carol Reed to shoot *The Fallen Idol* (1948). During production, Korda decided to do another film with the same team. Drawing on his own history, Greene conceived the idea for *The Third Man*. Greene and his family had long been involved with the British intelligence services, where Greene's boss had been Harold "Kim" Philby, who turned out to be a notorious spy. The movie was based on Philby's earlier exploits in Vienna. In April 1948, David O. Selznick signed a four-picture deal with Korda to provide financing in return for U.S. distribution rights. Greene started by writing a treatment for *The Third Man* (published as a novella in 1950). Selznick originally wanted to pair Noël Coward and Cary Grant. When Grant wanted too much money, Selznick favored Robert Mitchum, but Mitchum went to jail on marijuana charges. Reed pushed for Orson Welles instead of Noël Coward, and the production became only more tumultuous from there. Selznick not only battled with Korda, Greene, and Reed over casting but fought their choices of locations and approach too. Reed wanted documentary-style realism, shot on location in Vienna and London; Selznick did not. At the time, Selznick was taking the drug Dexedrine, an amphetamine that Reed also became hooked on, in order to work twenty-hour days. Much of the photography was done at night by the first unit. Studio work took place in London at Isleworth and Shepperton, with sets by Korda's brother. Reed and Krasker devised an expressionistic style of shooting with wide-angle lenses, distortion, and harsh lighting that produced the necessary tension and irony for the tale (their black and white cinematography won the picture's only Oscar). After one day, Welles refused to film in the sewers, so sets were built at Shepperton instead. However, Reed used casting assistant director Guy Hamilton to double for Welles in long shots. Reed felt that Greene's indeterminate ending would strike the audience as cynical, and wanted a more downbeat approach; finally Greene conceded. The entire score was performed on the zither by Anton Karas, whom Reed discovered in an Austrian beer hall.

DISTRIBUTION: The film won the Grand Prix at Cannes 1949 and was one of the top 10 films released in 1950 in the United States. "The Harry Lime Theme" sold half a million records in three months. Selznick and Korda disagreed about the U.S. release: Korda had the only negative of the film, and demanded a renegotiation of their contract so that he would share in the U.S. box office. It was finally presented as "A Selznick Release," and Korda got two on-screen credits. There are two different versions of the film. Selznick eliminated 11 minutes for the U.S. version to make Martins (the American) more likable, fearing that American audiences might liken Lime's dialogue to Communist propaganda and that censors wouldn't accept the nudity and violence. He also replaced introductory narration done by Carol Reed with a version read by Joseph Cotten. It is the number one favorite British film of the twentieth century, as selected by the British Film Institute (BFI) in 1996. —*Hayley Taylor Block*

CINDERELLA

RKO, 1950

ALL-RELEASE EQUIVALENT 2005 $s

(Unadjusted $s) in Millions of $s

Domestic Box Office Revenues........ **$379.8**/($86.6)
Production Cost ....**$23.5**/($2.9)
Production Period ....**2+** years
Early 1948–late
September 1949

Director . . . . Wilfred Jackson, Hamilton
Luske, Clyde Geronimi

Producer . . . . Walt Disney

Production Company . . . . Walt Disney Productions

Story by . . . . From the original "Cinderella"
story by Charles Perrault

Screenplay by . . . . William Peet, Ted Sears, Homer
Brightman, Kenneth Anderson,
Erdman Penner, Winston
Hibler, Harry Reeves,
Joe Rinaldi

Cast . . . . Ilene Woods, Eleanor Audley,
Verna Felton, William Phipps
(voices)

Filming Locations . . . . . . Walt Disney Studio, Burbank,
CA

Genre . . . . Animation

Format . . . . Color (Technicolor)

Initial Release . . . . 2/15/1950 limited release;
3/04/1950 wide release

Rerelease 1957, 1965, 1973, 1981, 1987

Running Time . . . . 74 minutes

MPAA Rating . . . . not rated

STANDING THE TEST OF TIME

ACADEMY AWARD Oscar Nominations and Wins

Music (Scoring of a Musical Picture): Oliver Wallace,
Paul J. Smith

Music (Song): "Bibbidi-Bobbidi-Boo," Music and
Lyrics by Mack David, Al Hoffman, and Jerry
Livingston

Sound Recording: Walt Disney Studio Sound Dept.,
C. O. Slyfield, Sound Director

OSCAR TOTALS   Nominations **3**   *Wins **0**

AFI 100 YEARS 100 MOVIES SELECTION
2007 0   1997 0

TOP 300 FILMS POSITION . . . . **#53**
All-Release Domestic Box Office in Equivalent 2005 $s

National Film Preservation Board Selection . . . . none

OTHER AWARDS Best Picture Wins

	Year
Golden Globes	none
New York Film Critics	none
National Board of Review	none
Film Daily Critics	none

Cinderella *is beguiling proof that Walt Disney
still knows his way around fairyland. With just
the right wizard's brew of fancy and fun, sugar
and spice, he makes an old, old story seem as
innocently fresh as it must to the youngest
moppet hearing it for the first time.*

—Time, *1950*

PLOT: Cinderella, a young girl mistreated and tormented by her cruel stepmother and stepsisters, is transformed into a vision of loveliness and dispatched to the royal ball by her fairy godmother, where she catches the eye of the kingdom's marriage-minded prince.

PRODUCTION: Roy Disney, Walt's brother and business partner, summed up the company's situation in the post–World War II era: "After the war was over, we were like a bear coming out of hibernation. We were skinny and gaunt and we had no fat on our bones. Those were lost years for us." Indeed, the company had barely survived, managing to sustain its famed animation department with ongoing cartoon shorts, films produced for the war effort (*Victory Through Air Power, Four Methods of Flush Riveting*), and several films aimed at promoting the United States' Good Neighbor Policy toward South America (*Salidos Amigos, The Three Caballeros*). Despite modest revenues, Disney was in debt to Bank of America to the tune of $4.3 million. For its immediate postwar offerings, Disney dabbled in live-action storytelling highlighted by animated sequences (*Song of the South, So Dear to My Heart*) and several "package" pictures—feature-length films comprising animated shorts strung together, such as *Make Mine Music, Fun and Fancy Free,* and *Melody Time.* Box office results were, again, mixed. Nevertheless, Walt was determined to keep the company's full-length feature film legacy alive, and had three projects under consideration: *Cinderella, Alice in Wonderland,* and *Peter Pan.* Of the three, *Cinderella* showed the most promise. The timeless fairy tale, with its origins dating back to the Greek historian Strabo in the first century B.C., had become popular with French author Charles Perrault's version published in 1697. As a fledgling animator in 1922, Disney produced a seven-minute Laugh-O-Gram featuring an animated *Cinderella* short; in 1933, when he was more established in Hollywood, he considered the story for a Silly Symphony cartoon. By 1948 Walt finally had both the money and a proven *Snow White*-esque story line—a girl in trouble—to embark on what many considered his biggest risk. Ten directing animators were assigned to *Cinderella,* including Walt's core group of artists, known as the "Nine Old Men." To aid the animators in their work, close to 90 percent of the story was first filmed using live actors, in black and white, on sets with makeshift props. Close to two years were spent building the story line and shooting the live-action film used as a working model; animation for the final feature took six months. As with other Disney animated films, new characters were added to bolster the story: Jacques and Gus the mice; Bruno the dog; and the slinking, conniving cat Lucifer.

DISTRIBUTION: The gamble paid off. *Cinderella* opened to smash business, becoming the first outright hit for the Disney company since 1937's *Snow White and the Seven Dwarfs.* The film grossed over $4 million in domestic rentals during its initial run, making it one of the top 10 pictures of 1950. Several of *Cinderella*'s songs became top *Your Hit Parade* entries. As the first Disney film to have its songs published and copyrighted by the newly created Walt Disney Music Company, *Cinderella*'s box office as well as revenues from record sales, music publishing, and other merchandise gave Walt Disney Productions the cash flow to continue its animated feature film efforts as well as substantially reduce its debt. —*Douglas Burns*

SUNSET BOULEVARD
Paramount, 1950

ALL-RELEASE EQUIVALENT 2005 $s
(Unadjusted $s) in Millions of $s

Domestic Box Office Revenues..........$72.8/($5.2)
Production Cost ....$14.2/($1.8)
Principal Photography.....................**54** days
4/18/1949–6/18/1949
6 additional days retakes

Director . . . . Billy Wilder

Producer . . . . Charles Brackett

Production Company. . . . Paramount Pictures

Story and

  Screenplay by . . . . Charles Brackett, Billy Wilder, and D. M. Marshman Jr.

Cast . . . . William Holden, Gloria Swanson, Erich von Stroheim

Filming Locations . . . . . . Paramount, Paramount back lot. The Alto-Nido apartments were real apartments near Paramount Studios, the interior of Schwab's Drug Store was recreated, the exterior of Desmond's mansion was a 1920's-era home on Wilshire Boulevard, which at the time was owned by J. Paul Getty's ex-wife. Paramount installed a pool. It has since been demolished.

Genre. . . . . Film Noir

Format. . . . . B&W

Initial Release 8/4/1950

Rerelease. . . . . none

Running Time . . . . 110 minutes

MPAA Rating . . . . not rated

STANDING THE TEST OF TIME

ACADEMY AWARD Oscar Nominations and Wins

Best Motion Picture: Paramount

Actor: William Holden

Actor in a Supporting Role: Erich von Stroheim

Actress: Gloria Swanson

Actress in a Supporting Role: Nancy Olson

*ART DIRECTION/SET DECORATION: Hans Dreier, John Meehan/Sam Comer, Ray Moyer

Cinematography (B&W): John F. Seitz

Directing: Billy Wilder

Film Editing: Arthur Schmidt, Doane Harrison

*MUSIC (Music Score of a Dramatic or Comedy Picture): Franz Waxman

*WRITING (Story and Screenplay): Charles Brackett, Billy Wilder, D. M. Marshman Jr.

OSCAR TOTALS   Nominations **11** *Wins 3

AFI 100 YEARS 100 MOVIES SELECTION
2007 . . . #16   1997 . . . #12

TOP 300 FILMS POSITION . . . . .none
All-Release Domestic Box Office in Equivalent 2005 $s

National Film Preservation Board Selection. . . . 1989

OTHER AWARDS Best Picture Wins

	Year
Golden Globes	1951
New York Film Critics.	none
National Board of Review	1950
Film Daily Critics	none

If only every picture could've gone so smoothly! I wanted Swanson, I got her. I wanted von Stroheim, I got him. I wanted to DeMille, I got him. I wanted Queen Kelly, I got it. I wanted Paramount, I got it. Even when I didn't get the casting I wanted, it turned out to be right.

—Billy Wilder

PLOT: A struggling screenwriter needs his big break, or the finance men will take his car away. His luck seems to turn when he stumbles upon a silent-film queen, who hires him to rewrite her screenplay, *Salome*—a job that will cost him his life.

PRODUCTION: When Billy Wilder first arrived in Los Angeles, Sunset Boulevard was just a country road. But its name stuck in his head, and as Hollywood legend has it, he scribbled an idea on a scrap of paper about a faded film star who believes she's back in the movies after newsreel cameras photograph her arrest for a murder. D. M. Marshman Jr., a former *Life* magazine journalist who played cards with Wilder, suggested that the murdered man be the star's young lover. Wilder and collaborator Charles Brackett hired Marshman as a cowriter. When they had no luck pursuing Greta Garbo, they considered Mae West, Pola Negri, and Mary Pickford to play Norma Desmond. But then George Cukor recommended Gloria Swanson, a 1925 superstar, who was hosting a talk show in New York. Although insulted that she had been asked for a screen test, Swanson accepted the role on Cukor's insistence for $50,000, which Wilder called "one of the great bargains in film history." Montgomery Clift backed out three weeks before production, deeming the role of the screenwriter too close to his own love affair with an older woman. Gene Kelly couldn't get out of his contract at MGM, and Wilder's *Double Indemnity* star Fred MacMurray declined. They finally chose William Holden. Wilder gave cinematographer John Seitz great latitude to shoot in a film noir style. For some shots Seitz sprinkled dust in front of the lens to suggest a musty atmosphere. But it was associate art director John Meehan who came up with the way to shoot the famous floating corpse scene. Wilder requested that the viewer see the body from a fish's perspective so Meehan, recalling an article he had read in a fishing magazine, placed a mirror at the bottom of the pool and filmed the body in reflection. Swanson ultimately resented the fact that Norma Desmond became her trademark role, because the skills of makeup artist Wally Westmore and costume designer Edith Head had made her look far older than her fifty-two years. The casting of Erich von Stroheim as Desmond's butler and ex-husband proved fortuitous because Erich had directed Swanson previously in *Queen Kelly* (the film was released in France in 1932 and in the United States in 1985). Wilder was able to use some of the footage from that film in *Sunset Boulevard* as footage from one of Norma Desmond's old films.

DISTRIBUTION: The first preview in the college town of Evanston, Illinois, had the audience howling with laughter and delayed the film's release until late summer. But after Wilder cut the opening scene, where a dead Joe Gillis talks to other corpses at the morgue, *Sunset Boulevard* became the most anticipated film of the year. *Newsweek* even put Gloria Swanson on its cover six weeks before the film's release. The movie made MGM boss Louis B. Mayer so mad he chided Wilder before a group of celebrities: "You have disgraced the industry that made and fed you. You should be tarred and feathered and run out of Hollywood." Its opening broke nonholiday records at the Radio City Music Hall in New York, and the seven-week run earned the theater's sixth-largest gross. Andrew Lloyd Webber adapted the film for his Broadway musical in the 1990s, when Glenn Close starred onstage as Norma Desmond. —*Michael Kogge*

ALL ABOUT EVE

20th Century-Fox, 1950

ALL-RELEASE EQUIVALENT 2005 $s

(Unadjusted $s) in Millions of $s

Domestic Box Office Revenues.........	**$89.8**/($6.4)
Production Cost	**$11.3**/($1.4)
Principal Photography....................	**48** days
	4/11/1950–6/7/1950

Director	Joseph L. Mankiewicz
Producer	Darryl F. Zanuck
Production Company....	20th Century-Fox Film Corp.
Story by..............	Based on the short story "The Wisdom of Eve" by Mary Orr
Screenplay by	Joseph Mankiewicz
Cast	Bette Davis, Anne Baxter, George Sanders, Celeste Holm
Filming Locations	New York City and Westchester County, NY; New Haven, CT (second unit work); Curran Theatre, San Francisco, CA, and 20th Century-Fox Studios, West Los Angeles, CA (principal photography)
Genre.................	Drama
Format..............	B&W
Initial Release	10/13/1950 Roxy Theater (New York); 11/9/1950, Grauman's Chinese Theater (Hollywood, CA)
Rerelease..............	10/6/2000 (limited rerelease for 50th anniversary)
Running Time	138 minutes
MPAA Rating	not rated

STANDING THE TEST OF TIME

ACADEMY AWARD Oscar Nominations and Wins

*BEST MOTION PICTURE: 20th Century-Fox

*ACTOR IN A SUPPORTING ROLE: George Sanders

Actress: Anne Baxter

Actress: Bette Davis

Actress in a Supporting Role: Celeste Holm

Actress in a Supporting Role: Thelma Ritter

Art Direction/Set Decoration: Lyle Wheeler, George W. Davis/Thomas Little, Walter M. Scott

Cinematography: Milton Krasner

*COSTUME DESIGN: Edith Head, Charles LeMaire

*DIRECTING: Joseph L. Mankiewicz

Film Editing: Barbara McLean

Music (Music Score of a Dramatic or Comedy Picture): Alfred Newman

*SOUND RECORDING: 20th Century-Fox Studio Sound Dept., Thomas T. Moulton, Sound Director

*WRITING (Screenplay): Joseph L. Mankiewicz

OSCAR TOTALS Nominations **14** *Wins 6

AFI 100 YEARS 100 MOVIES SELECTION
2007 . . . #28   1997 . . . #16

TOP 300 FILMS POSITION ....none
All-Release Domestic Box Office in Equivalent 2005 $s

National Film Preservation Board Selection.... 1990

OTHER AWARDS Best Picture Wins

	Year
Golden Globes	none
New York Film Critics......................	1951
National Board of Review..................	none
Film Daily Critics..........................	none

. . . Probably the wittiest, the most devastating, the most adult and literate motion picture ever made that had anything to do with the New York stage.

—Leo Mishkin, *New York Morning Telegraph*, 1950

PLOT: Broadway star Margo Channing comes to realize that Eve Harrington, a younger woman she has taken under her wing, has surreptitiously been ingratiating herself to Margo's friends, associates, and an influential critic in order to further her own theatrical ambitions.

PRODUCTION: "Superb starring role for Susan Hayward." So wrote writer-director Joseph L. Mankiewicz in a 1949 memo to Darryl F. Zanuck, head of 20th Century-Fox, regarding Mary Orr's short story "The Wisdom of Eve," which had appeared in the May 1946 issue of *Cosmopolitan* magazine. Orr's article was based on actress Elisabeth Bergner, who, while performing onstage in *The Two Mrs. Carrolls* in 1943–44, had hired an enthusiastic young fan to be her personal assistant, only to discover that the girl was an aspiring actress planning to use her new position—and employer—to further her own theatrical career.

Mankiewicz, fresh from his Oscar-winning film *A Letter to Three Wives,* was interested in fashioning his next movie around an aging actress, and felt that the scheming, manipulative young girl in Orr's story could be an important element in his new film's story line. In the memo to Zanuck, Mankiewicz wrote that Orr's story "fits in with an original idea [of mine] and can be combined." Zanuck was sold: He purchased the film rights to "The Wisdom of Eve" from Orr for $5,000. The film project was tagged with the tentative title of "Best Performance." In his screenplay, Mankiewicz changed the main character's name to Margo Channing (from Margola Cranston) and kept Eve Harrington, Lloyd and Karen Richards, and Miss Caswell. Margo's husband was eliminated, and a love interest, Bill Sampson, was added, as were the characters of Addison DeWitt, Max Fabian, Birdie Coonan, and Phoebe. Susan Hayward was out as Margo (Zanuck felt she was "too young"); Claudette Colbert was in. However, fate intervened when Colbert suffered a ruptured disc and was forced to withdraw. Bette Davis, finishing up *Payment on Demand* for RKO, received a call from Zanuck: could she start shooting the following week? Davis jumped at the chance to claim the prestigious role, one that would forever after be closely associated with the actress. Shooting began April 11, 1950, at the Curran Theatre in San Francisco, which was rented for two weeks while dark. From San Francisco, the company moved to Stage 9 at 20th Century-Fox in Los Angeles for over a month of shooting interiors. The project commanded early attention in the press when Bette Davis and Gary Merrill, each of whom was married to another, fell in love during the first week of shooting. Journalists and gossip columnists scrambled to report every new on- and off-set romantic tidbit, and within a month after *Eve* wrapped, the couple married. Mankiewicz delivered a rough cut of the film to Zanuck on June 24, 1950.

DISTRIBUTION: Zanuck attempted a road-show-type policy for *Eve*'s New York release, only admitting patrons into theaters at the start of each scheduled screening. Following a week of outcry from moviegoers who were used to entering the theater at any time, the policy was dropped and ticket sales increased by 25 percent. *All About Eve* would reap a modest $2.9 million in domestic rentals, but critical acclaim was overwhelming: the film garnered a stunning fourteen Academy Award nominations, a record that stood for forty-seven years until it was tied in 1997 by *Titanic*. In 1970 *All About Eve* was adapted into a successful Broadway musical, *Applause,* with Lauren Bacall in the role of Margo Channing. —*Douglas Burns*

A STREETCAR NAMED DESIRE

Warner Bros., 1951

ALL-RELEASE EQUIVALENT 2005 $s

(Unadjusted $s) in Millions of $s

Domestic Box Office Revenues . . . . $130.5/($10.3)
Production Cost . . . . $13.5/($1.8)
Principal Photography . . . . 56 days estimated
8/14/1950–10/17/1950

Director . . . . Elia Kazan
Producer . . . . Charles K. Feldman
Production Company . . . . Charles K. Feldman Group
Story by . . . . Based on the play by Tennessee Williams adapted by Oscar Saul
Screenplay by . . . . Tennessee Williams
Cast . . . . Vivien Leigh, Marlon Brando, Kim Hunter, Karl Malden
Filming Locations . . . . . . On location in Los Angeles, CA; New Orleans, LA; in studio at Warner Studios, Bros. CA
Genre . . . . Drama
Format . . . . B&W
Initial Release . . . . 9/29/1951 (Los Angeles)
Rerelease . . . . October 1958 (by 20th Century-Fox); 1/7/1970 (by United Artists); October 1993 (by Warner Bros.)
Running Time . . . . 125 minutes
MPAA Rating . . . . not rated

STANDING THE TEST OF TIME

ACADEMY AWARD Oscar Nominations and Wins

Best Motion Picture: Charles K. Feldman, Producer

Actor: Marlon Brando

*ACTOR in a SUPPORTING ROLE: Karl Malden

*ACTRESS: Vivien Leigh

*ACTRESS in a SUPPORTING ROLE: Kim Hunter

*ART DIRECTION/SET DECORATION: Richard Day/George James Hopkins

Cinematography: Harry Stradling

Costume Design: Lucinda Ballard

Directing: Elia Kazan

Music (Music Score of a Dramatic or Comedy Picture): Alex North

Sound Recording: Warner Bros. Studio Sound Dept., Col. Nathan Levinson, Sound Director

Writing (Screenplay): Tennessee Williams

OSCAR TOTALS   Nominations **12**   *Wins 4

AFI 100 YEARS 100 MOVIES SELECTION
2007 . . . #47   1997 . . . #45

TOP 300 FILMS POSITION . . . . none
All-Release Domestic Box Office in Equivalent 2005 $s

National Film Preservation Board Selection 1999

OTHER AWARDS Best Picture Wins

	Year
Golden Globes	none
New York Film Critics	1951
National Board of Review	none
Film Daily Critics	none

Hollywood had no choice but to admit that his film, more than any other, had altered the system as practiced for decades. It was a far cry from the prepackaged, presold three-picture-a-year deals . . . all designed and executed for the stars by full time studio employees.

—Peter Manso, *Brando: A Biography*

PLOT: In this film, set in the French Quarter of New Orleans, Blanche DuBois, a fragile and neurotic woman, visits her pregnant sister and husband on a desperate search for someplace in the world to call her own after having been exiled from her own hometown.

PRODUCTION: Elia Kazan directed the Broadway production of Tennessee Williams's play *A Streetcar Named Desire* in 1947, with unknowns Marlon Brando (whom he had found at the Actors Studio) and Jessica Tandy playing the leads, with Kim Hunter and Karl Malden in the supporting cast. The theatrical production won the Pulitzer Prize and the New York Drama Critics' Circle award for Best Play. However, no major studio wanted to produce a film version due to the nature of the content. Even Kazan resisted the idea of directing the film adaptation at first, explaining that he didn't like to work on the same project twice. It was only after Williams implored him to take on the assignment that Kazan signed on. Although he hired a screenwriter to "open the play up," he soon realized that this play was a classic and shouldn't be altered, with the exception of minor changes. Talent agent and lawyer Charles K. Feldman bought the property to produce and got Warner Bros. to release it. Nine members of the Broadway cast repeated their roles, but Warner Bros. insisted that Vivien Leigh play Blanche DuBois instead of Jessica Tandy to add "star power" to the film. Leigh had played Blanche in the first London production, under the direction of her then-husband, Sir Laurence Olivier. Leigh initially felt uneasy when she joined the tight New York cast in rehearsals. Kazan used those feelings of alienation to enrich her performance. (Leigh suffered from bipolar disorder and later had difficulties distinguishing her real life from that of Blanche DuBois.) Although Kazan and Brando originally disliked Leigh, they soon came around and the cast worked smoothly. Kazan placed a mockup of the set in the corner of the soundstage so that while the shots were being set up, the actors could rehearse as if they were in a play. He also shot the film, mainly from eye level, with an old-fashioned studio camera that was nailed down. The lack of camera tricks enabled him to concentrate on the stories and performances more. He made the set walls movable, so that as the film progresses the Kowalski apartment actually gets smaller, to suggest that the walls are closing in on Blanche. The music, by Alex North, was very different from the usual action-based score, reflecting the psychological dynamics of the characters. By the time the film was made, New Orleans no longer had streetcars, but authorities were able to lend the production the original streetcar named Desire for the opening sequence. Also difficult to find at that time were fitted T-shirts, so a regular T-shirt was bought, washed several times, and resewn to fit tightly on Brando.

DISTRIBUTION: The movie got critical raves and was a box office hit, bringing in $3.9 million in domestic rentals in its initial release. Kazan was furious that scenes had been cut without his approval due to demands from the Catholic Legion of Decency, despite his having conducted a script reading for Joseph Breen's office and making changes prior to production. The movie made Brando a star, although he was the only one of the four actors nominated not to win an Academy Award. The film was unique in that it was distributed via three separate studios: every seven years, when rights reverted back to the Charles K. Feldman Group, they licensed it to a different distributor. —*Hayley Taylor Block*

QUO VADIS

MGM, 1951

ALL-RELEASE EQUIVALENT 2005 $s

(Unadjusted $s) in Millions of $s

Domestic Box Office Revenues. . . . . **$312.4**/($23.5)
Production Cost . . . . **$57.3**/($7.6)
Principal Photography . . . . **129** days
5/22/1950–11/2/1950

Director . . . . Mervyn LeRoy

Producer . . . . Sam Zimibalist

Production Company . . . . Metro-Goldwyn-Mayer

Story by . . . . Based on the epic poem by
Henryk Sienkiewicz

Screenplay by . . . . John Lee Mahin, S. B. Behrman,
Sonya Levien

Cast . . . . Robert Taylor, Deborah Kerr,
Leo Genn, Peter Ustinov

Filming Locations . . . . . . Produced in Italy at Cinecittà
Studios, Rome

Genre. . . . . Historical Drama

Format. . . . . Color (Technicolor)

Initial Release . . . . 11/4/1951 road show release;
12/25/1953 general release

Rerelease 1964

Running Time . . . . 171 minutes

MPAA Rating . . . . not rated

STANDING THE TEST OF TIME

ACADEMY AWARD Oscar Nominations and Wins

Best Motion Picture: Sam Zimbalist, Producer

Actor in a Supporting Role: Leo Genn

Actor in a Supporting Role: Peter Ustinov

Art Direction/Set Decoration: William A. Horning,
Cedric Gibbons, Edward Carfagno/Hugh Hunt

Cinematography: Robert Surtees, William V. Skall

Costume Design: Herschel McCoy

Film Editing: Ralph E. Winters

Music (Music Score of a Dramatic or Comedy Picture):
Miklós Rózsa

OSCAR TOTALS   Nominations **8**   *Wins **0**

AFI 100 YEARS 100 MOVIES SELECTION
2007 0   1997 0

TOP 300 FILMS POSITION . . . . #97
All-Release Domestic Box Office in Equivalent 2005 $s

National Film Preservation Board Selection . . . . none

OTHER AWARDS Best Picture Wins

	Year
Golden Globes	none
New York Film Critics.	none
National Board of Review	none
Film Daily Critics	none

If you delay another year, I'll be too old for the role.

—Peter Ustinov, in a telegram to Mervyn LeRoy and Sam Zimbalist

PLOT: Around A.D. 64, Marcus Vinicius, a patrician Roman returning from war in the time of Emperor Nero, falls in love with Lygia, a Christian hostage of state, who becomes caught between her love for a warrior and her love for God.

PRODUCTION: As early as 1925, MGM showed interest in making a movie from *Quo Vadis: A Narrative of the Time of Nero,* a Polish historical epic written by Henryk Sienkiewicz, first published as a newspaper serial in 1895 and then as a novel in 1896, contributing to the author winning the Nobel Prize for literature in 1905. The title is from John 16:5, translated from Latin as "Whither goest Thou, Lord?" The first mention of a film version to appear in the Hollywood trades occurred in 1935, with a rumor that Marlene Dietrich and Wallace Beery would star as Poppaea and Nero. In 1942 producer Arthur Hornblow Jr. said it would be his first MGM feature. He wanted Alfred Lunt for Nero but was turned down, so he approached first Orson Welles and then Charles Laughton, who had played Nero a decade earlier in Paramount's *Sign of the Cross.* But it was not meant to be. The war placed certain budgetary and logistical restrictions on the project, and production was put off. Five years later, Louis B. Mayer assigned John Huston to direct and Gregory Peck to star, but Charles Feldman, who was slated to produce, was held up on *Fabiola,* Peck came down with an eye infection, and John Huston lost interest. It wasn't until Dore Schary took Mayer's empty seat atop Metro's throne that interest was revived in the property. Anxious to upstage the growing threat of television, the new studio chief set up *Quo Vadis* to be the perfect antidote to the small screen. What he wanted to create—and director Mervyn LeRoy and producer Sam Zimbalist agreed to—was the greatest movie spectacle of all time, with more than 200 speaking parts, 120 lions, an unruly bull, and upward of 30,000 extras (including Sophia Loren in her film debut). Some 2,000 of them were scattered about the set—a massive replica of ancient Rome—as it caught fire on cue and blazed to ash. But Rome wasn't burned in a day. What required three months to prepare took three weeks to destroy. LeRoy's inferno played on as many as four color cameras—a Cinecittà Studios first—to ensure that a second take wouldn't be needed. When he received the raw footage, editor Ralph Winters must have gasped: he had 580,000 feet of film on his hands.

DISTRIBUTION: *Quo Vadis* received the MGM publicity treatment par excellence. The studio spent $2.7 million on prints and ads—35 percent of what the film had cost to make. They arranged approximately a hundred promotional tie-ins, which, according to a *Hollywood Reporter* news item, was something of a world record. Today we might remember *Quo Vadis* not for its box office returns (at its release it was MGM's highest grosser since *Gone with the Wind*) nor for its critical reception (the papers were less than ebullient) but for the picture's influence on the filmmaking fashions of the day. Suddenly, antiquity was the rage. After *Quo Vadis* came Columbia's *Salome,* Universal's *Sign of the Pagan,* and Warner Bros.' *Helen of Troy,* all within a matter of years. —*Sam Wasson*

AN AMERICAN IN PARIS

MGM, 1952

ALL-RELEASE EQUIVALENT 2005 $s

(Unadjusted $s) in Millions of $s

Domestic Box Office Revenues. . . . . **$113.7**/($8.3)
Production Cost . . . . **$20.5**/($2.7)
Principal Photography. . . . . **52** days
8/1/1950–1/8/1951
Retakes April 1951

Director	Vincente Minnelli
Producer	Arthur Freed
Production Company	Metro-Goldwyn-Mayer
Story and Screenplay by	Alan Jay Lerner
Cast	Gene Kelly, Leslie Caron, Oscar Levant, Georges Guetary, Nina Foch
Filming Locations	70 percent on MGM studio soundstages; 15 days shot on location in Paris, France
Genre.	Musical
Format.	Color (Technicolor)
Initial Release	10/4/1951 premiere (New York); 11/9/1951 general release
Rerelease.	1992
Running Time	113 minutes
MPAA Rating	not rated

STANDING THE TEST OF TIME

ACADEMY AWARD Oscar Nominations and Wins

*****BEST MOTION PICTURE:** Arthur Freed, Producer

*****ART DIRECTION/SET DECORATION:** Cedric Gibbons, Preston Ames/Edwin B. Willis, Keogh Gleason

*****CINEMATOGRAPHY:** Alfred Gilks; Ballte Photography by John Alton

*****COSTUME DESIGN:** Orry-Kelly, Walter Plunkess, Irene Sharaff

Directing: Vincent Minnelli

Film Editing: Adrienne Fazan

*****MUSIC:** Johnny Green Saul Chaplin

*****WRITING** (Story and Screenplay): Alan Jay Lerner

OSCAR TOTALS   Nominations **8**   *Wins **6**

AFI 100 YEARS 100 MOVIES SELECTION
2007 0   1997. . . #68

TOP 300 FILMS POSITION . . . . .none
All-Release Domestic Box Office in Equivalent 2005 $s

National Film Preservation Board Selection. . . . 1993

OTHER AWARDS Best Picture Wins

	Year
Golden Globes	1952
New York Film Critics.	none
National Board of Review.	none
Film Daily Critics.	none

The real reasons to see An American in Paris *are for the Kelly dance sequences, the closing ballet, the Gershwin songs, [and] the bright locations.*

—Roger Ebert

PLOT: Gene Kelly is an ex–GI following his dream of being a painter in Paris. He falls for a radiant Leslie Caron, romancing her through humorous plot twists and enchanting dance sequences.

PRODUCTION: Gene Kelly and Vincente Minnelli were the driving forces behind this multiple Oscar winner. Studio executives didn't quite understand the concept, so Kelly and Minnelli arranged screenings of the French film *The Red Shoes* (1948) and a 1934 cartoon, *La joie de vivre,* both of which included extensive dancing. It was a tough sell to MGM executives and was the last MGM film approved by longtime studio head Louis B. Mayer. Arthur Freed, representing MGM, negotiated the film rights for the musical piece "An American in Paris, Tone Poem for Orchestra" with Ira Gershwin, the brother of deceased composer and pianist George Gershwin, during one of their friendly pool games. MGM paid $158,750 for the rights and an additional fee of $56,250 to Ira for consultation on new lyrics. Freed wanted Alan Jay Lerner to write the story, even though he was still working on the score for MGM's musical *Royal Wedding* (released March 1951). Lerner, a playwright and lyricist whose first success was the 1947 Broadway musical *Brigadoon,* began writing the screenplay in December 1949, finishing the final draft in a twelve-hour marathon on the night before his wedding, March 12, 1950. The only filming not done on MGM soundstages were the exterior shots of famous Parisian landmarks opening the film with Gene Kelly's introductory narration about his lifelong desire to paint in the City of Lights. Minnelli, now noted for films of extraordinarily rich visual beauty, was a painter himself and strove to give the film's dance sequences an otherworldly appearance. This was painstakingly accomplished by copying styles of various famous French painters and turning the MGM soundstages into rich (and expensive) venues for the innovative modern-dance musical scenes, all choreographed by Kelly. Often overlooked, because of the cherished Gershwin music and romantic dance sequences, is the Walter Plunkett–Orry-Kelly black and white ball scene, which so overloads the screen with details that it is virtually impossible to absorb it all in just one viewing.

DISTRIBUTION: Premiered in New York on October 4, 1951, MGM attempted to prepare audiences in advance for the unexpected music and dance styles featured in the film. These were not the traditional "good-time, tap-dancing, discovery of young love" stories for which the Freed unit was famous. The trailer and tag lines were a tip-off: as audiences were barraged with works of famous French artists, sensual dance sequences, panoramas of Paris, and strategically oversized captions and taglines, including "Adventures of an Ex-GI in the City of Romance! Arts Students' Biggest Ball! Most Daring Ever Filmed! Screen's Most Spectacular Musical!" Previous U.S. censorship issues revolving around the "benefactress" relationship between the characters played by Nina Foch and Gene Kelly had been resolved, although a 1955 memo indicated that censors in French Indochina banned the film because it depicted friendly Franco-American relations and glorified France. The film made a $2 million profit on worldwide rentals of $17.9 million. In 1992 MGM and Turner Interment released an updated version in approximately thirty theaters across the United States. This new print was a re-restoration due to a 1978 fire at the Eastman Archives in New York that destroyed two reels of the original 35 mm negative. —*Christine McDermott*

THE AFRICAN QUEEN

United Artists (domestic); Romulus Films (foreign), 1951

ALL-RELEASE EQUIVALENT 2005 $s

(Unadjusted $s) in Millions of $s

Domestic Box Office Revenues. . . . . **$127.6**/($9.6)
Production Cost . . . . not available
Principal Photography. . . . .**120** days estimated
May 1951–August 1951

Director . . . . John Huston
Producer . . . . S. P. Eagle (Sam Spiegel)
Production Company. . . . Horizon Enterprises, Inc.,
Romulus Films, Ltd.
Story by . . . . Based on C. S. Forester's novel
Screenplay by . . . . James Agee, John Huston
Cast . . . . Humphrey Bogart,
Katharine Hepburn
Filming Locations . . . . . . On location in the Belgian
Congo, Africa; in studio at
Isleworth Studios in England
Genre. . . . . Drama
Format. . . . . Color (Technicolor)
Initial Release . . . . 12/26/1951 world premiere
(Los Angeles); 2/20/1952 (New
York); 3/21/1952 general release
Rerelease. . . . . .none
Running Time . . . . 106 minutes
MPAA Rating . . . . not rated

STANDING THE TEST OF TIME

ACADEMY AWARD Oscar Nominations and Wins
*ACTOR: Humphrey Bogart
Actress: Katharine Hepburn
Directing: John Huston
Writing (Screenplay): James Agee, John Huston

   OSCAR TOTALS   Nominations **4**   *Wins **1**

AFI 100 YEARS 100 MOVIES SELECTION
2007 . . . #65   1997. . . #17

TOP 300 FILMS POSITION . . . . .none
All-Release Domestic Box Office in Equivalent 2005 $s

National Film Preservation Board Selection. . . . 1994

OTHER AWARDS Best Picture Wins

	Year
Golden Globes	none
New York Film Critics.	none
National Board of Review	none
Film Daily Critics	none

Whether C. S. Forester had his salty British tongue in his cheek when he wrote his extravagant story of romance and adventure . . . we wouldn't be able to tell you. But it is obvious—to us, at least—that director John Huston was larking when he turned the novel into a film.

—Bosley Crowther, *New York Times*, 1952

PLOT: An unlikely romance develops in Africa between an Anglican missionary lady and the rough-hewn skipper of a tramp steamer as they try to escape the kaiser's soldiers.

PRODUCTION: Columbia originally bought the 1935 C. S. Forester novel as a vehicle for Charles Laughton and Elsa Lanchester. Later, Warner Bros. bought it for Bette Davis and David Niven. It was offered to Bette Davis again in 1947, but due to the birth of her daughter that same year, she had to pull out. On tour with *As You Like It* for the theater guild (1950–51) Katharine Hepburn became interested and was ultimately cast. This was the first produced screenplay for critic James Agee, who suffered a heart attack while on the project. John Huston recruited novelist Peter Viertel to help him finish the script (and revise Allnut's dialogue after Bogart stumbled over the character's Cockney accent). Producer Sam Spiegel paid dearly to get the cast he wanted and to meet Huston's grandiose aspirations, which included shooting on location, even in extreme conditions. The director flew more than 25,000 miles scouting locations. He choose a camp near Biondo, on the Ruiki River, in what was then the Belgian Congo. Spiegel attempted to save money by doing without crew members whose duties overlapped those of other technicians and craftsmen. He would recruit locals or ask the stars to help out. Hepburn, for a time, doubled as the wardrobe mistress, while Bogart's wife, Lauren Bacall, helped cook and set up camp. Filming in jungle conditions was no picnic, as cast and crew were required to fend off blood flukes, crocodiles, soldier ants, wild boars, stampeding elephants, poisonous snakes, malaria, and dysentery, all in equatorial heat. Hepburn became annoyed with the boys-will-be-boys behavior of Bogart, Huston, and their cronies. While the men drank booze and smoked cigars incessantly, Hepburn got dysentery from the water. "All I ate was baked beans, canned asparagus and Scotch whiskey," Bogart recalled. "Whenever a fly bit Huston or me, it dropped dead." The steamer was authentic. The *L/S Livingston* had been a working vessel for forty years. Because of cramped quarters, parts of the boat were re-created on a large raft for close-ups. Bogart, too, for all his macho reputation, was none too keen to serve as a host to live leeches for one of the most memorably queasy scenes ever filmed. He preferred rubber leeches, but Huston called in a leech wrangler, who arrived in London with a tank full of the squirming bloodsuckers. They compromised by placing rubber leeches on Bogart and live leeches on the breeder's chest for close-ups. Like Forester, the filmmakers also debated how *The African Queen* should end. Ultimately, the unlikeliest scenario was chosen, and it proved to be a crowd-pleaser.

DISTRIBUTION: Audiences flocked to see *The African Queen,* although box office results from Horizon Pictures and Romulus Films, both based in England, have remained vague. Walt Disney modeled Disneyland's Jungle Cruise attraction after the tramp steamer in the film. In 1953 Viertel recycled his memories of the shoot for the novel *White Hunter, Black Heart.* Nearly forty years later, Clint Eastwood would direct and star in an adaptation of that book, for which Viertel also wrote the screenplay. The boat used in *The African Queen* is now docked next to a Holiday Inn on Key Largo and has been added to the U.S. National Register of Historic Places. —*Gary Dretzka*

THE GREATEST SHOW ON EARTH

Paramount, 1952

ALL-RELEASE EQUIVALENT 2005 $s

(Unadjusted $s) in Millions of $s

Domestic Box Office Revenues . . . . **$349.1**/($31.6)
Production Cost . . . . **$28.6**/($3.9)
Principal Photography . . . . **78** days estimated
2/5/1951–5/26/1951

Director . . . . Cecil B. DeMille

Producer . . . . Cecil B. DeMille

Production Company . . . . Cecil B. DeMille Productions

Story by . . . . Fredric M. Frank, Theodore
St. John, Frank Cavett

Screenplay by . . . . Fredric M. Frank, Barré Lyndon,
Theodore St. John

Cast . . . . Betty Hutton, Cornel Wilde,
Charlton Heston, Dorothy
Lamour, Gloria Grahame,
James Stewart

Filming Locations . . . . . . Sarasota, FL; Philadelphia, PA;
Washington, D.C.; Paramount
Studios, Hollywood, CA
Sarasota, FL 2/5/1951–3/8/1951;
Studio 3/19/1951–3/31/1951
and 4/9/1951–5/11/1951;
Washington and Philadelphia
5/16/1951–5/26/1951

Genre . . . . Drama

Format . . . . Color (Technicolor)

Initial Release . . . . 1/10/1952 world premiere,
Radio City Music Hall,
(New York); 2/21/1952
premiere (Los Angeles);
7/9/1952 general release

Rerelease 1954, 1960

Running Time . . . . 153 minutes

MPAA Rating . . . . not rated

STANDING THE TEST OF TIME

ACADEMY AWARD Oscar Nominations and Wins

***BEST MOTION PICTURE:** Cecil B. DeMille,
Producer

Costume Design: Cecil B. DeMille

Directing: Cecil B. DeMille

Film Editing: Anne Bauchens

***WRITING** (Motion Picture Story): Frederic M.
Frank, Theodore St. John, Frank Cavett

OSCAR TOTALS Nominations **5** *Wins **2**

AFI 100 YEARS 100 MOVIES SELECTION
2007 0   1997 0

TOP 300 FILMS POSITION . . . . **#74**
All-Release Domestic Box Office in Equivalent 2005 $s

National Film Preservation Board Selection . . . . none

OTHER AWARDS Best Picture Wins

	Year
Golden Globes	1953
New York Film Critics	none
National Board of Review	none
Film Daily Critics	none

*Show has been called by many sources as the single worst film to ever win the top
prize at the Academy Awards, but I must disagree. It's arguably the corniest,
to be certain, but the worst? Not at all.*

—David Cornelius

PLOT: Follows a headstrong yet dedicated circus manager as he confronts tightfisted financiers, a rivalry between two aerialists, unexpected romantic problems, determined con men, and a clown with a secret past as a renowned performing troupe embarks on its annual tour.

PRODUCTION: In April 1948, producer David O. Selznick announced a film set amidst the famed Ringling Bros. and Barnum and Bailey Circus. When Selznick was unable to secure funding, a bidding war for the rights erupted among Paramount, MGM, and 20th Century-Fox. Paramount won, and at a July 24, 1949, press conference, producer-director Cecil B. DeMille and John Ringling North, president of the circus, launched the project. "This is not to be a history of the circus," DeMille noted. "We will tell the story of the circus and its people in relation to all other people." North added that he hoped his favorite actress, Ann Sheridan, would be among the film's cast (ultimately, she wasn't). Paramount paid the circus $250,000 for use of their facilities and the rights to the title *The Greatest Show on Earth,* which was the circus's slogan. Over the next year, a number of writers worked at fashioning an original screen story and script that would be acceptable to DeMille, a known stickler for realism and attention to detail. In 1950, when a story line was finally approved, DeMille and a small entourage intercepted the Ringling Brothers Circus in Milwaukee and accompanied the ensemble during a northern tour. It was a research trip for DeMille: he peered through a viewfinder at the performers and animals from all angles, climbed rope ladders to reach aerialist platforms, and observed the daily tasks of trainers and roustabouts. Early candidates for the pivotal manager role included Kirk Douglas and Burt Lancaster (a former circus acrobat), but DeMille ultimately chose Charlton Heston after seeing him in the 1950 film *Julius Caesar.* James Stewart, who had always wanted to portray a clown, approached DeMille and was given the unique role of Buttons, who plays a doctor on the lam from the FBI and is seen only in clown makeup during the film. Other roles were filled by a mix of Paramount contract players (Betty Hutton, Dorothy Lamour), independent contractors (Cornel Wilde, Gloria Grahame), and approximately 1,450 circus performers. Principal photography began in Sarasota, Florida, where more than 50,000 residents turned out for the filming of the parade. The circus big top cost $100,000, costumes another $200,000. After six weeks, the crew returned to the Paramount lot for two months, then rejoined the circus in Washington, D.C., and accompanied it to Philadelphia, Pennsylvania. The film was shot intermittently through May 1951, but production was halted for ten days so that DeMille and his technical staff could observe the circus's opening in New York's Madison Square Garden.

DISTRIBUTION: Many critics may have hated or dismissed *The Greatest Show on Earth* as typical DeMille "schmaltz," but audiences flocked to the epic in droves—it would become Paramount's biggest moneymaker at the time, though it would be—bested by *The Ten Commandments* in 1956. Initially a road show engagement limited to fifty "situations" between January and Easter week of 1952, the film then entered wide release for the summer. *Daily Variety* gave it the top spot for 1952 with rentals of $12 million. By May 1953, *Variety* was reporting that the Best Picture winner had amassed $18.35 million in worldwide rentals. —*Douglas Burns*

SINGIN' IN THE RAIN
MGM, 1952

ALL-RELEASE EQUIVALENT 2005 $s
(Unadjusted $s) in Millions of $s

Domestic Box Office Revenues . . . . **$98.0**/($7.4)
Production Cost . . . . **$18.7**/($2.5)
Principal Photography . . . . **132** days estimated
6/18/1951–11/21/1951
Additional shooting December 1951

Director . . . . Gene Kelly, Stanley Donen

Producer . . . . Arthur Freed

Production Company . . . . Metro-Goldwyn-Mayer

Story and
Screenplay by . . . . Adolph Green, Betty Comden

Cast . . . . Gene Kelly, Donald O'Connor,
Debbie Reynolds, Jean Hagen,
Millard Mitchell, Cyd Charisse

Filming Locations . . . . . . Metro-Goldwyn-Mayer Studios,
Culver City, CA

Genre . . . . Musical

Format . . . . Color (Technicolor)

Initial Release . . . . 3/27/1952 world premiere,
Radio City Music Hall
(New York); 4/9/1952
premiere, Pantages Theatre
(Los Angeles); 4/11/1952
general release

Rerelease . . . . 1975, 1992 (40th anniversary
rerelease), 2002 (50th
anniversary rerelease)

Running Time . . . . 103 minutes

MPAA Rating . . . . not rated

STANDING THE TEST OF TIME

ACADEMY AWARD Oscar Nominations and Wins

Actress in a Supporting Role: Jean Hagen
Music (Scoring of a Musical Picture): Lennie Hayton

OSCAR TOTALS   Nominations **2**   *Wins **0**

AFI 100 YEARS 100 MOVIES SELECTION
2007 . . . . #5   1997 . . . #10

TOP 300 FILMS POSITION . . . . .none
All-Release Domestic Box Office in Equivalent 2005 $s

National Film Preservation Board Selection 1989

OTHER AWARDS Best Picture Wins

	Year
Golden Globes	none
New York Film Critics	none
National Board of Review	none
Film Daily Critics	none

Concocted by Arthur Freed with showmanship know-how, it glitters with color,
talent and tunes, and an infectious air that will click with ticket buyers in all types of situations.
—*Daily Variety,* 1952

PLOT: The advent of "talkies" in Hollywood throws Monumental Pictures into a chaotic frenzy when the studio realizes that Lina Lamont, the female half of the studio's popular romantic team of Lockwood and Lamont, has a voice that would curdle milk.

PRODUCTION: Producer Arthur Freed, a former Tin Pan Alley songwriter who had become MGM's foremost producer of musicals, came up with an idea: a musical showcasing many of the existing songs that he and partner Nacio Herb Brown had co-written. Louis B. Mayer liked the idea and approved a budget of $1,880,090. Assigned to the project were Stanley Donen and Gene Kelly, who had co-directed the successful MGM hit *On the Town,* released in 1949. Also assigned were *On the Town*'s song- and screenwriters, Betty Comden and Adolph Green, who were asked to concoct a story around the musical material. Comden and Green came across an unproduced MGM outline titled "Excess Baggage" that could possibly be used as a foundation for the story. Since some of the selected songs had appeared in films made shortly after Hollywood's painful transition to talkies, they based their original screen story on this turbulent cinematic milestone. The title was borrowed from a popular 1929 Freed-Brown hit song, "Singin' in the Rain." Cliff "Ukulele Ike" Edwards had performed the song in *The Hollywood Revue of 1929,* and it had been sung by both Jimmy Durante (*Speak Easily,* 1932) and Judy Garland (*Little Nellie Kelly,* 1940). Freed had hoped to pair Kelly with his *An American in Paris* sidekick, Oscar Levant, but both Donen and Kelly insisted that the role of Cosmo Brown be filled by a dancer. Donald O'Connor, borrowed from Universal, got the part. For the role of the story's young, aspiring actress-singer, Kathy Selden, Louis B. Mayer cast "Miss Burbank of 1948," eighteen-year-old Debbie Reynolds—a promising MGM contract player who had done a spirited rendition of "Aba Daba Honeymoon" in the 1950 film *Two Weeks with Love.* Once signed, Reynolds was shunted off to three months' worth of dancing lessons. Prerecording of the musical numbers began May 22, 1951, and included two songs not by Freed and Nacio, "Moses" and "Fit as a Fiddle." Principal photography, utilizing MGM soundstages and the studio's multiple back lots, began on June 18. But three days later Louis B. Mayer was ousted as head of MGM—a position he had held for twenty-seven years—and replaced by production chief Dore Schary, who had clashed with Mayer on a number of occasions. The film's "Broadway Melody" ballet sequence, shot in late fall of 1951, required two months of rehearsal, two of the largest soundstages, and was $85,000 over budget, at a total cost of $605,960. *Singin' in the Rain*'s final overall cost, which was well over its approved budget, was $2,540,800.

DISTRIBUTION: Following two late December sneaks in California—one in Riverside and another in Pacific Palisades—two musical numbers were cut: Gene Kelly's solo version of "All I Do Is Dream of You" and Debbie Reynolds's solo rendition of "You Are My Lucky Star." It premiered at 103 minutes two weeks prior to Easter in 1952, to highly favorable reviews and an initial four-day tally of $95,000. The film's theatrical run ultimately garnered domestic rentals of $3.3 million ($7.7 million worldwide) and landed the film in the top 10 highest-grossing films released in 1952. It has remained a staple of TV and video, with some critics calling it the greatest musical film of all time. —*Douglas Burns*

HIGH NOON

United Artists, 1952

ALL-RELEASE EQUIVALENT 2005 $s

(Unadjusted $s) in Millions of $s

Domestic Box Office Revenues . . . . **$100.9**/($7.6)
Production Cost . . . . **$5.5**/($0.8)
Principal Photography . . . . **28** days estimated
9/5/1951–10/6/1951

Director . . . . Fred Zinnemann

Producer . . . . Stanley Kramer, Carl Foreman
(uncredited)

Production Company . . . . Stanley Kramer Productions

Story by . . . . Based on the short story
"The Tin Star" by John W.
Cunningham in *Collier's*,
12/6/1947

Screenplay by . . . . Carl Foreman

Cast . . . . Gary Cooper, Thomas Mitchell,
Lloyd Bridges, Katy Jurado,
Grace Kelly, Otto Kruger,
Lon Chaney, Henry Morgan

Filming Locations . . . . . . Motion Picture Center,
Hollywood, CA and on location
at the Columbia Ranch in
Burbank and in Sonora, CA

Genre . . . . Western

Format . . . . B&W

Initial Release . . . . 7/24/1952 (New York);
7/30/1952 general release

Rerelease . . . . none

Running Time . . . . 85 minutes

MPAA Rating . . . . not rated

STANDING THE TEST OF TIME

ACADEMY AWARD Oscar Nominations and Wins

Best Motion Picture: Stanley Kramer, Producer

***ACTOR:** Gary Cooper

Directing: Fred Zinnemann

***FILM EDITING:** Elmo Williams, Harry Gerstad

***MUSIC** (Music Score of a Dramatic or Comedy
Picture): Dimitri Tiomkin

***MUSIC** (Song): "High Noon (Do Not Forsake Me,
Oh My Darlin')," Music by Dimitri Tiomkin; Lyrics
by Ned Washington

***WRITING** (Screenplay): Carl Foreman

OSCAR TOTALS   Nominations **7**   *Wins **4**

AFI 100 YEARS 100 MOVIES SELECTION
2007 . . . #27   1997 . . . #33

TOP 300 FILMS POSITION . . . . none
All-Release Domestic Box Office in Equivalent 2005 $s

National Film Preservation Board Selection 1989

OTHER AWARDS Best Picture Wins

	Year
Golden Globes	none
New York Film Critics	1952
National Board of Review	none
Film Daily Critics	none

*This for me was not a political film . . . I came to think of it as a question
of conscience . . . A man's character is his destiny.*

—Fred Zinnemann

PLOT: A frontier marshal, leaving town and law enforcement after having just gotten married, delays his departure to deal with a group of killers coming to town, and finds that he has to fight off the gang all by himself.

PRODUCTION: As early as 1949, announcements that John W. Cunningham's short story "The Tin Star" would receive the Hollywood treatment turned up regularly in the trades and even in the *New York Times,* which reported that Screen Plays Corp., Stanley Kramer's company at the time (formed with Herbert Baker and Carl Foreman in 1947), would produce an adaptation. Kramer had already established himself as a filmmaker specializing in offbeat material. Foreman, screenwriter on the 1949 films *Champion* and *Home of the Brave* and the 1950 film *The Men,* drafted a script that turned the western genre's conventions upside down. There was little action and no sweeping landscape. The film was designed to be a tight, claustrophobic story that emphasized how its characters had to deal with their own consciences. A clear subtext connects the movie's story line to the time it was being made, which was during the 1951–52 hearings by the House Un-American Activities Committee (HUAC). These hearings sought to prove Communist infiltration of American movies, leading to a blacklist that ended many careers. Carl Foreman was served a subpoena by the committee but refused to name names. Two days after principal photography commenced, *Daily Variety* listed Kramer as the film's only producer. A few days later, Kramer informed Foreman by letter that he had been relieved of his co-producing duties and that he should stay off the lot at Columbia Pictures, the studio where Kramer had just signed a deal with Harry Cohn, although Kramer spent the rest of 1951 finishing *High Noon,* his last independent production. This marked the only time in all of his movies that Kramer did not take an on-screen producer credit; under the words "The End" appears "A Stanley Kramer Production," the closest thing to such a credit. Another of Kramer's untraditional moves was to hire a foreign-born director, Fred Zinnemann, to direct. A native of Vienna, Zinnemann used new approaches, including those pioneered by Italian neorealists. He considered the film's politics "non-existent[,] and I would believe they were non-existent for Coop." Gary Cooper, cast as Will Kane, had been a friendly witness for HUAC. The official take on *High Noon* was that it was a story of conscience, pure and simple. The movie was produced quickly and cheaply, following Zinnemann's credo that time was, in his words, "an enemy." The film's running time matches the time in which the story plays out, approximately 85 minutes, creating a high degree of tension that culminates in one of the few long shots as the camera pulls away from Kane to reveal him alone in the street.

DISTRIBUTION: Hollywood's most outspoken anti-Communist, John Wayne, was dismayed by *High Noon,* calling it "the most un-American thing I've ever seen in my whole life." Despite that view, the movie found quick success when released in 1952. *High Noon* is also the film often cited by American presidents and presidential candidates as a favorite. It was screened three times at the White House for Dwight D. Eisenhower, a noted western novel fan. Reportedly, when the outlaws set fire to the barn where Kane hides, the president shouted, "Run!" Bill Clinton cited it as his favorite movie and, shortly before he left office, told an interviewer he would recommend the movie to George W. Bush. —*Louis Burklow*

THE QUIET MAN

Republic, 1952

ALL-RELEASE EQUIVALENT 2005 $s

(Unadjusted $s) in Millions of $s

Domestic Box Office Revenues . . . . **$112.8**/($8.4)
Production Cost . . . . **$12.9**/($1.8)
Production Period . . . . **48** days
Early June 1951–late August 1951

Director . . . . John Ford

Producer . . . . John Ford, Merian C. Cooper

Production Company . . . . Argosy Pictures

Story by . . . . Based on the short story "The Quiet Man" by Maurice Walsh in *The Saturday Evening Post*, February 11, 1933

Screenplay by . . . . Frank S. Nugent

Cast . . . . John Wayne, Maureen O'Hara

Filming Locations . . . . . . Connemara (near Galway), Lettergesh Beach, Oughtebrand, Teeracht, and Cong, County Mayo, Ireland; Republic Studios in Studio City, Los Angeles, CA (interiors)

Genre . . . . Romantic Comedy

Format . . . . Color (Technicolor)

Initial Release . . . . 6/6/1952 world premiere (London and Dublin); 8/21/1952 U.S. premiere (New York); 9/14/1952 general release

Rerelease . . . . none

Running Time . . . . 129 minutes

MPAA Rating . . . . not rated

STANDING THE TEST OF TIME

ACADEMY AWARD Oscar Nominations and Wins

Best Motion Picture: John Ford and Merian C. Cooper, Producers

Actor in a Supporting Role: Victor McLaglen

Art Direction/Set Decoration: Frank Hotaling/John McCarthy Jr., Charles Thompson

*CINEMATOGRAPHY: Winton C. Hoch, Archie Stout

*DIRECTING: John Ford

Sound Recording: Republic Studio Sound Dept., Daniel J. Bloomberg, Sound Director

Writing (Screenplay): Frank S. Nugent

OSCAR TOTALS   Nominations **7**   *Wins **2**

AFI 100 YEARS 100 MOVIES SELECTION
2007 0   1997 0

TOP 300 FILMS POSITION . . . . none
All-Release Domestic Box Office in Equivalent 2005 $s

National Film Preservation Board Selection . . . . none

OTHER AWARDS Best Picture Wins

	Year
Golden Globes	none
New York Film Critics	none
National Board of Review	1952
Film Daily Critics	none

Everything's all green. Tell the cameraman to take the green filter off.

—Herbert J. Yates upon first seeing the dailies

PLOT: An American returns to the Irish town of his birth searching for his happiness and finds himself unable to escape his past.

PRODUCTION: It was surprising in 1950 when top Hollywood director John Ford signed a deal with Republic, which produced westerns and B pictures under president Herbert J. Yates, who had also founded the largest film processing laboratory, Consolidated. As the son of Irish immigrants, Ford had long wanted to bring *The Quiet Man* to the screen. He acquired the rights to the story in 1936, but nothing came of it. He tried again in 1947, and only got to make it after promising Yates that first he would direct *Rio Grande* (1950). It was a big hit, and Ford was able to use its success to win Yates's assent to making *The Quiet Man* next. Ford brought together his "repertory company," a group of actors he used again and again. John Wayne, the star he created in *Stagecoach* in 1939, was the title character. Maureen O'Hara, whom Ford considered the only actress who could stand up to Wayne, was his sole choice for Mary Kate Danaher. Ford stalwarts Victor McLaglen, Mildred Natwick, and Ward Bond were also featured. Ford's own brother Francis, who introduced him to the movie business in the 1910s, had a small role (despite the fact that the brothers no longer spoke; Francis showed up, did his scenes, and left without a word from his brother). Despite Herbert Yates's misgivings (he referred to it as Ford's "phony art-house movie"), the project finally went into production in 1951. Filming in Ireland lasted eight weeks, with the cast being housed during the shoot at Ashford Castle. Despite the fact that it was a dry, sunny summer on the Emerald Isle, cinematographer Winton Hoch complained of a haze that forced him to use booster lights to cut through the mist. The result was an idyllic look to each scene that uses the lush green countryside to best effect. John Wayne got his first chance to direct on this film. When Ford came down with a cold, Wayne directed the horse race sequence and other scenes in his absence. This pleased the director; as one of Wayne's managers said, "Ford had a love for Wayne, as much love as Ford could give." The film clocked in at 129 minutes, but Yates wanted it cut to two hours. When the final cut was screened for the studio executives, they saw Francis Ford's and McLaglen's characters begin to fight as the end credits appear. When the disappointed executives asked why the film ended before the fight did, Ford replied he had not been able to find anything to cut, so he just chopped off the end. The movie was subsequently released at a length of 129 minutes.

DISTRIBUTION: The film premiered in London and Dublin, then in New York shortly before the national opening. The reviews seconded Ford's view that he had made "the sexiest picture ever, with honesty, good taste and humor." Ford won his fourth (and last) Best Director Oscar as well as three awards at the Venice Film Festival. *The Quiet Man* became Republic's most acclaimed film and its biggest moneymaker ever. In addition, it provided a tremendous boost to the Irish tourism industry. —*Louis Burklow*

PETER PAN

RKO, 1953

ALL-RELEASE EQUIVALENT 2005 $s

(Unadjusted $s) in Millions of $s

Domestic Box Office Revenues........ **$358.4**/($82.2)
Production Cost .... **$29.3**/($4.0)
Production Period .... **2+ years**
May 1949–June 1951

Initial Release . . . . 2/5/1953 world premiere,
Roxy Theatre (New York)

Rerelease 1958, 1969, 1976, 1982, 1989

Running Time . . . . 76 minutes

MPAA Rating . . . . not rated

Director . . . . Hamilton Luske, Clyde
Geronimi, Wilfred Jackson

Producer . . . . Walt Disney

Production Company . . . . Walt Disney Productions

Story by . . . . Adapted from the stage play
Peter Pan by Sir James M. Barrie

Screenplay by . . . . Ted Sears, Erdman Penner,
Bill Peet, Winston Hibler,
Joe Rinaldi, Milt Banta,
Ralph Wright, Bill Cottrell

Cast . . . . Bobby Driscoll (Peter Pan),
Kathryn Beaumont (Wendy
Darling), Hans Conried
(Capt. Hook/Mr. Darling),
Bill Thompson (Mr. Smee)
(voices)

Filming Locations . . . . . . Walt Disney Productions
(Burbank, CA)

Genre . . . . Animation

Format . . . . Color (Technicolor)

STANDING THE TEST OF TIME

ACADEMY AWARD Oscar Nominations and Wins

None

OSCAR TOTALS   Nominations **0**   *Wins **0**

AFI 100 YEARS 100 MOVIES SELECTION
2007 0   1997 0

TOP 300 FILMS POSITION . . . . #66
All-Release Domestic Box Office in Equivalent 2005 $s

National Film Preservation Board Selection . . . . none

OTHER AWARDS Best Picture Wins

	Year
Golden Globes	none
New York Film Critics	none
National Board of Review	none
Film Daily Critics	none

*The movie avoids much of the cute picture-postcard look that has oversweetened
some of Disney's previous films. Ornamented with some bright and lilting tunes,
it is a lively feature-length Technicolor excursion into a world that glows
with an exhilarating charm and a gentle joyousness.*

—*Time,* 1953

PLOT: Peter Pan, the hero of Wendy, John, and Michael Darling's imaginative bedtime stories, materializes and whisks the children out of their London home and off to Never Land, where they embark on fanciful adventures and battle the notorious Captain Hook.

PRODUCTION: Walt Disney had a special fondness for Scottish novelist and playwright James M. Barrie's adventure-fantasy *Peter Pan*, which had premiered on the London stage in 1904 and subsequently was novelized by Barrie in 1911, titled *Peter and Wendy*. As a twelve-year-old in Marceline, Missouri, Disney had seen a touring stage company's production of Barrie's work, and also had been cast as "the boy who would not grow up" in a school play. Disney remained enthralled with the story after seeing Paramount's 1924 silent film version starring Betty Bronson in the lead role. In 1939, realizing its potential as an animated feature, Walt was able to obtain the film rights from the Great Ormond Street Hospital in London, the establishment to which Barrie bequeathed all rights in 1929. Storyboards were begun on the project in 1940, and by 1941 a basic story structure was completed. However, America's entry into World War II sidelined the ambitious project. Slow to recover from the war years, the Disney company could not afford to undertake a prolonged, multimillion-dollar project. Thus, production work on *Peter Pan* didn't resume until May 1949. It was decided that, much like *Cinderella,* a "working model"—a live-action version of the story—was needed to aid the animators in their character development. This filmed version, shot in black and white on studio soundstages with a minimum of props, included dancer Roland Dupree as Peter Pan and popular radio star Hans Conried as the villainous Captain Hook. Actress-dancer Margaret Kerry was cast as Tinker Bell, and it was Kerry—not the widely rumored Marilyn Monroe—who became the reference model for the temperamental sprite. Character voices for the ensuing animated feature included Conried, reprising his role of Hook, and Kathryn Beaumont, fresh from providing the voice of Alice in Disney's *Alice in Wonderland,* as the voice of Wendy Darling. Disney's production would also be the first Peter Pan ever in which Peter was portrayed by a male actor. Disney contract star Bobby Driscoll was selected to provide the voice of the title character, following his impressive work in such company films as *Song of the South* (1946), *So Dear to My Heart* (1948), and *Treasure Island* (1950). *Peter Pan*'s animation team consisted of ten directing animators, including Walt's core team, dubbed the "Nine Old Men." It would be the last time the famed team would work together on a single film project. They were a prolific group—once completed, the final film consisted of 500,000 individual drawings.

DISTRIBUTION: *Peter Pan* opened to positive reviews and robust box office, landing in the number five spot on the list of top-grossing films for 1953 with $7 million in domestic rentals (approximately $195.5 million in domestic box office in 2005 dollars). Five subsequent theatrical rereleases, and its home video debut in 1990, have kept Peter Pan a perpetual moneymaker for the Disney company. In 2002 an animated sequel, *Return to Never Land,* racked up a worldwide box office gross of close to $110 million. —*Douglas Burns*

SHANE

Paramount, 1953

ALL-RELEASE EQUIVALENT 2005 $s

(Unadjusted $s) in Millions of $s

Domestic Box Office Revenues......**$228.4**/($19.6)
Production Cost ....**$24.2**/($3.3)
Principal Photography...................**75** days
7/15/1951–10/19/1951

Director .... George Stevens

Producer .... George Stevens

Production Company.... Paramount Pictures

Story by .... Based on the novel by
Jack Schaefer

Screenplay by .... A. B. Guthrie Jr.

Cast .... Alan Ladd, Jean Arthur,
Van Heflin, Brandon De Wilde,
Jack Palance

Filming Locations ...... Big Bear Lake, CA; Grand Teton
National Park and Jackson
Hole, WY; Iverson Ranch,
Chatsworth, CA; Paramount
Studios, Hollywood, CA

Genre................. Western

Format............... Color (Technicolor)

Initial Release .... 4/23/1953 (New York); 6/4/1953
(Los Angeles)

Rerelease............. April 1959, February 1966

Running Time .... 118 minutes

MPAA Rating .... not rated

STANDING THE TEST OF TIME

ACADEMY AWARD Oscar Nominations and Wins

Best Motion Picture: George Stevens, Producer

Actor in a Supporting Role: Brandon De Wilde

Actor in a Supporting Role: Jack Palance

*CINEMATOGRAPHY: Loyal Griggs

Directing: George Stevens

Writing (Screenplay): A. B. Guthrie, Jr.

OSCAR TOTALS   Nominations **6**   *Wins **1**

AFI 100 YEARS 100 MOVIES SELECTION
2007 . . . #45   1997 . . . #69

TOP 300 FILMS POSITION .... **#190**
All-Release Domestic Box Office in Equivalent 2005 $s

National Film Preservation Board Selection.... 1993

OTHER AWARDS Best Picture Wins

	Year
Golden Globes	none
New York Film Critics	none
National Board of Review	none
Film Daily Critics	none

You know, the one thing I wanted to do with Shane was to show if you point a
.45 at a man and pull the trigger, you destroy an upright figure.

—George Stevens

PLOT: A stranger rides into a small Wyoming town and finds himself in the middle of a range war. Hiring on with a family of homesteaders, Shane takes on the cattle barons but finds he cannot escape his own past as a gunfighter.

PRODUCTION: George Stevens's son George junior read Jack Schaefer's novel based on Wyoming's Johnson County War of 1892 and recommended it to his father. At the suggestion of Howard Hawks, Stevens hired author A. B. Guthrie Jr. (his novel *The Big Sky* was made into a movie by Hawks in 1952) to write the script despite the fact that Guthrie had never written any screenplays. Stevens had started in movies as a seventeen-year-old cameraman and made mostly lighthearted films before going off for service in World War II, where he shot actual footage of the liberation of Europe. When he returned, he pursued more thoughtful works that challenged American complacency beginning with *A Place in the Sun* (1951), which was followed by *Something to Live For* (1952) and then *Shane*. Stevens's postwar movies featured an outsider not at peace with his or her life. When Paramount first acquired Schaefer's novel in 1949, the studio considered both Alan Ladd and Ray Milland for the title role. When Stevens came on board, he wanted Montgomery Clift as *Shane* and William Holden as Joe Starrett, but Clift turned it down. When Holden also became unavailable, Stevens asked for a list of available actors under contract to Paramount. From that list, he chose Ladd for Shane, Van Heflin for Joe, and Jean Arthur for Marian. Stevens doggedly worked at perfecting the look of the film, using the drawings of William Henry Jackson and the paintings of Charles M. Russell. Artist Joe de Young worked with him on making the costumes and decor look as true to the period as possible, even traveling around the West for research. When the production chose an area near Jackson Hole, Wyoming, Stevens had frontier town and cemetery sets built side by side so that he could shoot them in one long shot. Although budgeted for 45 days, Stevens took 75 days to shoot the film while keeping costs low. Once in Wyoming, he shot in all kinds of weather and lighting conditions to enhance the realism of the picture. A climactic fistfight between Ladd and Heflin was choreographed by Stevens; the resulting blows struck by each man feel realistic enough to make viewers flinch while not being sure which character to root for. Stevens also experimented with ways to show the extreme violence of people being shot. Each gunshot sounds like a miniature explosion. He also rigged actors with a block and pulley system to jerk them backward violently as if from a bullet's impact. At one point, the Production Code office asked the director to tone down Wilson's shooting of Torrey, in which he is thrown into the mud. Stevens considered the scene vital to his story, did not change it, and got the scene past censors.

DISTRIBUTION: *Shane* was the first flat wide-screen color western to be produced and was projected in a 1.66:1 aspect ratio in its opening at Radio City Music Hall in New York and Grauman's Chinese Theater in Hollywood. *Variety* reported that the "widescreen projection did contribute . . . to a sense of the bigness." Audiences approved of the large scale. It was a top domestic box office western at its release, after King Vidor's 1947 *Duel in the Sun.* —*Louis Burklow*

THE ROBE

20th Century-Fox, 1953

ALL-RELEASE EQUIVALENT 2005 $s

(Unadjusted $s) in Millions of $s

Domestic Box Office Revenues........**$474.8**/($37.8)
Production Cost ....**$30.1**/($4.1)
Principal Photography............**57** days estimated
2/24/1953–4/30/1953
(additional shooting began 5/26/1953)

Director . . . . Henry Koster
Producer . . . . Frank Ross
Production Company. . . . 20th Century-Fox
Story by . . . . Based on the novel by
Lloyd C. Douglas
Screenplay by . . . . Philip Dunne; adaptation by
Gina Kaus
Cast . . . . Richard Burton, Jean Simmons,
Victor Mature, Michael Rennie
Filming Locations . . . . . . On location in California at Ray
Corrigan Ranch, Simi Valley,
Iverson Ranch, Chatsworth, Los
Angeles, and San Francisco's
Palace of Fine Arts; in Studio at
Fox studio in Century City, CA
Genre. . . . . Biblical Epic
Format. . . . . Color (Technicolor)
Initial Release 9/16/1953
Rerelease. . . . . none
Running Time . . . . 135 minutes
MPAA Rating . . . . not rated

STANDING THE TEST OF TIME

ACADEMY AWARD Oscar Nominations and Wins

Best Motion Picture: Frank Ross, Producer

Actor: Richard Burton

*ART DIRECTION/SET DECORATION: Lyle
Wheeler, George W. Davis/Walter M. Scott,
Paul S. Fox

Cinematography: Leon Shamroy

*COSTUME DESIGN: Charles LeMaire, Emile
Santiago

OSCAR TOTALS   Nominations 5   *Wins 2

AFI 100 YEARS 100 MOVIES SELECTION
2007 0   1997 0

TOP 300 FILMS POSITION . . . . #26
All-Release Domestic Box Office in Equivalent 2005 $s

National Film Preservation Board Selection. . . . none

OTHER AWARDS Best Picture Wins

	Year
Golden Globes	none
New York Film Critics	none
National Board of Review	none
Film Daily Critics	none

Hollywood will rise or fall on the success of The Robe.

—Darryl F. Zanuck

PLOT: A story chronicling the rise of Christianity through the lives of fictional and real characters, including the Roman centurion Marcellus (who presided over Christ's crucifixion), as they come into contact with the robe Christ handed down from the cross.

PRODUCTION: In 1942 producer Frank Ross bought film rights to author Lloyd C. Douglas's novel *The Robe* even before it was completed, for $100,000. Ross then made a joint financing and distribution deal with RKO Radio Pictures. For a number of reasons, including wartime shortages of material, the project was stalled. In December 1951, RKO sued Ross for their investment of $960,000, paid out for three scripts, miniatures, costumes, and sets. The estate of novelist Douglas also entered the suit, claiming that it had the option to repurchase the rights to *The Robe* if Ross did not produce the film. In April 1952 Ross countersued, claiming that Howard Hughes (who had bought RKO in 1948) had made it impossible for him to produce by "threats, intimidations," and other actions. The lawsuit was settled in May 1952 when Darryl Zanuck had 20th Century-Fox acquire rights in a deal that paid RKO up to $950,000 out of profits. Zanuck was seeking another religious epic after the success in 1951 of *David and Bathsheba*. As producer, Ross received $40,000 and 20 percent of any net profits. Zanuck hired Fox veteran Henry Koster to direct and Leon Shamroy to do cinematography. Zanuck offered the role of Marcellus to Tyrone Power in an attempt to get him to renew his contract, but Power chose to star on the stage instead. Koster and Ross assembled a talented but lesser-known cast, headed by Welsh-born Broadway star Richard Burton (in his third film of a three-picture deal with Fox). The studio began doing film tests in standard-ratio 35mm film, but when shooting was about to commence, Zanuck decided to make *The Robe* the first film in the wide-screen anamorphic process CinemaScope. Rather than travel to Rome and Palestine, exteriors were shot at San Francisco's Palace of Fine Arts and on forty-one sets across Fox's back lot. The crucifixion set alone took fifteen workers, sixty carpenters, and twelve artists, who spent six weeks building the base of Golgotha, covering it with dirt, and painting the panoramic backdrop. The sets, locations, and costumes cost $500,000. Koster hired his second assistant director, Donald C. Klune, to play the role of Jesus (whose face is never shown). Klune would sign all the extras' vouchers and finish the paperwork while still in costume; however, the studio told him to eat lunch in his dressing room, as they thought it would be inappropriate for "Jesus" to eat in the commissary.

DISTRIBUTION: Bidding for the premiere in New York was fierce, with the Astor, Victoria, and Bijou theaters all offering unheard-of guarantees of $500,000 against 90 percent of the box office take. However, Zanuck opted for the Roxy, which had the necessary seating capacity and a 68-by-24-foot screen. It was the year's top-grossing film, beating out the military drama *From Here to Eternity*. It made Burton a huge star and sparked a succession of religious films. It brought in $16.7 million in domestic rentals, $9.4 million in foreign rentals, and made a net profit of $8.1 million. Fox began producing a sequel, *Demetrius and the Gladiators* (1954), with Victor Mature reprising his role in *The Robe*, even before filming on *The Robe* wrapped, making *The Robe* the only biblical epic with a sequel. *Demetrius* was not nearly as successful. —*Hayley Taylor Block*

FROM HERE TO ETERNITY

Columbia, 1953

ALL-RELEASE EQUIVALENT 2005 $s

(Unadjusted $s) in Millions of $s

Domestic Box Office Revenues......... $326.4/($26.0)
Production Cost .... $14.6/($2.0)
Principal Photography............ 51 days estimated
3/7/1953–5/5/1953

Director .... Fred Zinnemann
Producer .... Buddy Adler
Production Company.... Columbia Pictures
Story by.............. Based on the 1951 novel by James Jones
Screenplay by......... Daniel Taradash
Cast .... Burt Lancaster, Montgomery Clift, Deborah Kerr, Frank Sinatra, Donna Reed
Filming Locations ...... Schofield Barracks, Halona Cove, Kuhio Beach Park, Waikiki Beach, and Honolulu, Oahu, HI; Columbia Studios, Hollywood, CA
Genre................ Military Drama
Format............... B&W
Initial Release......... 8/5/1953 world premiere, Capitol Theater (New York); 9/30/1953 premiere (Los Angeles)
Rerelease............. 12/5/2003 (limited 50th anniversary rerelease: five theaters for one week)
Running Time.......... 118 minutes
MPAA Rating .... not rated

STANDING THE TEST OF TIME

ACADEMY AWARD Oscar Nominations and Wins

*BEST MOTION PICTURE: Buddy Adler, Producer
Actor: Montgomery Clift
Actor: Burt Lancaster
*ACTOR IN A SUPPORTING ROLE: Frank Sinatra
Actress: Deborah Kerr
*ACTRESS IN A SUPPORTING ROLE: Donna Reed
*CINEMATOGRAPHY: Burnett Guffey
Costume Design: Jean Louis
*DIRECTING: Fred Zinnemann
*FILM EDITING: William Lyon
Music (Music Score of a Dramatic or Comedy Picture): Morris Stoloff, George Duning
*SOUND RECORDING: Columbia Studio Sound Dept., John P. Livadary, Sound Director
*WRITING (Screenplay): Daniel Taradash

OSCAR TOTALS   Nominations **13** *Wins **8**

AFI 100 YEARS 100 MOVIES SELECTION
2007 0   1997... #52

TOP 300 FILMS POSITION .... #86
All-Release Domestic Box Office in Equivalent 2005 $s

National Film Preservation Board Selection.... 2002

OTHER AWARDS Best Picture Wins

	Year
Golden Globes	none
New York Film Critics.......................	1953
National Board of Review...................	none
Film Daily Critics	none

Rapturously received from the moment it was released in 1953, From Here to Eternity remains, half a century later, a singular cinematic experience, one of the landmarks of American film.

—Kenneth Turan

PLOT: In the months leading up to the Japanese attack on Pearl Harbor, military personnel stationed at Schofield Barracks on the Hawaiian island of Oahu find themselves enveloped by boredom, isolation, corruption, and romantic entanglements.

PRODUCTION: All of Hollywood was laughing, and reportedly the joke went something like this: "Q: Why would Harry Cohn buy a dirty book like *From Here to Eternity*?" "A: He thinks everybody talks that way." Cohn, the fiery, profane head of Columbia Pictures, had paid $82,000 for James Jones's racy, 850-page novel—an "unfilmable" work laden with profanities, violence, and sexual situations. Industry pundits agreed: the project—dubbed "Cohn's Folly"—would never be granted location filming permits by the U.S. military, nor would it get past the Production Code censors. Undaunted, Cohn assigned Buddy Adler (*No Sad Songs for Me*) as producer and brought Jones aboard to adapt his own novel. When Jones's work proved problematic, screenwriter Daniel Taradash (*Golden Boy*) was approached; he accepted with the stipulation that he receive 2.5 percent of the film's profits. Taradash then made an impassioned plea for Fred Zinnemann (*High Noon*) as director. Cohn protested that Zinnemann was an "art-house director," but was ultimately persuaded by Taradash's fervor. Burt Lancaster was top choice for the role of Sergeant Milt Warden, but Edmond O'Brien was also signed in the event Lancaster's deal fell through. Cohn favored Columbia contract players Aldo Ray or John Derek for the role of Robert E. Lee Prewitt; Zinnemann threatened to walk unless Montgomery Clift was cast instead. Frank Sinatra, whose career was floundering at that point, begged Cohn for the role of Private Angelo Maggio, even offering to pay for it. Eli Wallach had already agreed to play Maggio, but when he opted to do a Broadway play, Sinatra won the role by default. Joan Crawford, approached for the part of the adulterous Army wife Karen Holmes, declined—reportedly over cameraman and wardrobe issues. When Deborah Kerr's agent recommended the genteel actress as a replacement, Cohn responded with a string of expletives. But Adler and the others thought casting Kerr against type was brilliant. Likewise, former Iowa farm girl Donna Reed—a Columbia contract player who had attracted attention when she appeared in Aldo Ray's *Eternity* screen test—was cast against type as Lorene, the social club "hostess." Taradash's toned-down script cleared the Production Code office. The U.S. Army insisted on two changes: Maggio's beatings at the hands of the stockade sergeant could not be shown, and the corrupt Captain Holmes must be punished for his actions (in the book he was promoted). With those revisions made, Adler was permitted to shoot at Schofield Barracks in Hawaii, where the story took place.

DISTRIBUTION: Cohn had set *Eternity*'s budget at $2 million. Including prints and advertising, the final cost was $2,406,000. The film's premiere in New York triggered around-the-block lines and around-the-clock screenings, with the Capitol Theatre closing only briefly in the early morning hours so custodians could tidy up. *From Here to Eternity* soon became Columbia's highest-grossing picture at the time, bringing in almost $12 million in domestic rentals. It went on to become the second-highest-grossing film of 1953, behind *The Robe*. On Oscar night, "Cohn's Folly" tied *Gone with the Wind*'s long-standing record of eight Academy Award wins. The last laugh definitely belonged to Harry Cohn. —*Douglas Burns*

THE CAINE MUTINY

Columbia, 1954

ALL-RELEASE EQUIVALENT 2005 $s

(Unadjusted $s) in Millions of $s

Domestic Box Office Revenues . . . . $220.9/($19.3)
Production Cost . . . . $17.4/($2.4)
Principal Photography . . . . .68 days estimated
6/3/1953–8/24/1953

Director . . . . Edward Dmytryk

Producer . . . . Stanley Kramer

Production Company . . . . Stanley Kramer Productions, Columbia Pictures

Story by . . . . Based on the novel by Herman Wouk

Screenplay by . . . . Stanley Roberts

Cast . . . . Humphrey Bogart, José Ferrer, Van Johnson, Fred MacMurray, Robert Francis, May Wynn

Filming Locations . . . . . . In California on location: Los Angeles, San Francisco, Yosemite National Park; in Hawaii on location: Pearl Harbor

Genre . . . . Drama

Format . . . . Color (Technicolor)

Initial Release . . . . 6/24/1954 (New York)

Rerelease . . . . none

Running Time . . . . 125 minutes

MPAA Rating . . . . not rated

STANDING THE TEST OF TIME

ACADEMY AWARD Oscar Nominations and Wins

Best Motion Picture: Stanley Kramer, Producer

Actor: Humphrey Bogart

Actor in a Supporting Role: Tom Tully

Film Editing: William A. Lyon, Henry Batista

Music (Music Score of a Dramatic or Comedy Picture): Max Steiner

Sound Recording: Columbia Studio Sound Dept., John P. Livadary, Sound Director

Writing (Screenplay): Stanley Roberts

OSCAR TOTALS   Nominations **7**   *Wins **0**

AFI 100 YEARS 100 MOVIES SELECTION
2007 0   1997 0

TOP 300 FILMS POSITION . . . . #206
All-Release Domestic Box Office in Equivalent 2005 $s

National Film Preservation Board Selection . . . . none

OTHER AWARDS Best Picture Wins

	Year
Golden Globes	none
New York Film Critics	none
National Board of Review	none
Film Daily Critics	none

[The film is] a disappointment in my career, to tell the truth. I insist it could have been a classic . . . Stanley Roberts' original script was about 190 pages, even without the romantic subplot . . . It should have remained that— a 3½- or 4-hour picture—and it would have been perfect.

—Edward Dmytryk

PLOT: In 1943 the minesweeper USS *Caine* gets a new by-the-book skipper. At sea his bizarre demands lead his officers to take away his command, raising charges of mutiny that play out during a court-martial.

PRODUCTION: During the three long years between publication of the 1951 novel *The Caine Mutiny: A Novel of World War II* and the start of production, author Herman Wouk adapted the court-martial sequence into a Broadway play, *The Caine Mutiny Court-Martial.* Despite strong public interest, major studios were reluctant to turn the story into a film, knowing the Department of Defense would demand revisions in exchange for cooperation. Instead, independent producer Stanley Kramer optioned the novel for $60,000. After the best seller won the Pulitzer Prize, the U.S. Navy finally eased its stand. When the producers agreed to include a disclaimer after the opening credits, assuring audiences there had never been a mutiny on a U.S. Navy vessel, the U.S. Navy provided ships, planes, combat boats, and access to Pearl Harbor and Bay Area naval facilities. If filmed as written, Herman Wouk's 500-page screenplay treatment would have lasted 15 hours. Veteran screenwriter Stanley Roberts rewrote Wouk's treatment into 190 minutes. After studio boss Harry Cohn demanded that a love scene be added, Roberts left the production. Michael Blankfort put the finishing touches on the script but was not credited because he was associated with other blacklisted artists. Kramer chose Edward Dmytryk to direct, even though he was one of the Hollywood Ten and had been blacklisted and incarcerated (although he later gave names). Columbia had originally wanted Richard Widmark to play Queeg, and Dick Powell also voiced interest in the role, but Kramer convinced the studio to hire Bogart after he reduced his asking price to get the part. Cohn also insisted in the contract that the film be made for $2 million and not be longer than two hours. According to Edward Dmytryk, "One penny beyond that, or a minute beyond two hours' length, and Columbia had the right to take over the film for editing." The destroyer-minesweeper USS *Thompson* doubled for the USS *Caine,* and the decommissioned aircraft carrier USS *Kearsarge* was used in the scene where officers tried to convince Admiral Halsey of Queeg's problems. Because the contrast in appearance and prestige between the two ships was made intentionally obvious, viewers would appreciate Wouk's ability to depict "the pressure cooker of life aboard a Navy minesweeper, and what might happen when rigidity, power and the pressures of war become too much for the crew."

DISTRIBUTION: *The Caine Mutiny* was a big hit, grossing $8.7 million in U.S. rentals during its initial run, putting it among Columbia's fifteen biggest hits. It covered the losses incurred by Kramer on previous projects for the studio. It was the top-grossing of films starring Bogart, followed by *Dark Passage* (1947), *Casablanca* (1942), *The African Queen* (1951), and *Key Largo* (1948). —*Gary Dretzka*

ON THE WATERFRONT

Columbia, 1954

ALL-RELEASE EQUIVALENT 2005 $s

(Unadjusted $s) in Millions of $s

Domestic Box Office Revenues . . . . $109.9/($9.6)
Production Cost . . . . $6.6/($0.9)
Principal Photography . . . . **36** days
September 1953–December 1953

Director . . . . Elia Kazan
Producer . . . . Sam Spiegel
Production Company . . . . Horizon-American
Story and
  Screenplay by . . . . Budd Schulberg
Cast . . . . Marlon Brando, Eva Marie
Saint, Karl Malden, Lee J. Cobb,
Rod Steiger
Filming Locations . . . . . . Shot entirely on location in
Hoboken, NJ
Genre . . . . Drama
Format . . . . B&W
Initial Release 7/28/1954
Rerelease . . . . none
Running Time . . . . 108 minutes
MPAA Rating . . . . not rated

STANDING THE TEST OF TIME

ACADEMY AWARD Oscar Nominations and Wins

*__BEST MOTION PICTURE:__ Sam Spiegel, Producer
*__ACTOR:__ Marlon Brando
Actor in a Supporting Role: Lee J. Cobb
Actor in a Supporting Role: Karl Malden
Actor in a Supporting Role: Rod Steiger
*__ACTRESS IN A SUPPORTING ROLE:__ Eva Marie
Saint
*__ART DIRECTION:__ Richard Day
*__CINEMATOGRAPHY:__ Boris Kaufman
*__DIRECTING:__ Elia Kazan
*__FILM EDITING:__ Gene Milford
Music (Music Score of a Dramatic or Comedy Picture):
Leonard Bernstein
*__WRITING__ (Story and Screenplay): Budd Schulberg

OSCAR TOTALS   Nominations **12** *Wins 8

AFI 100 YEARS 100 MOVIES SELECTION
2007 . . . #19   1997 . . . . #8
TOP 300 FILMS POSITION . . . . none
All-Release Domestic Box Office in Equivalent 2005 $s

National Film Preservation Board Selection 1989

OTHER AWARDS Best Picture Wins

	Year
Golden Globes	1955
New York Film Critics	1954
National Board of Review	1954
Film Daily Critics	none

On the Waterfront *was my own story; every day I worked on that film,
I was telling the world where I stood and my critics to go and fuck themselves.*

—Elia Kazan

PLOT: The story of an ex-prizefighter who inadvertently participates in the murder of a fellow longshoreman while working on the docks for the local gang boss, and then falls in love with the victim's sister and testifies publicly.

PRODUCTION: In 1949 Malcolm Johnson's Pulitzer Prize–winning series of articles "Crime on the Waterfront" awakened America to the widespread corruption and crime on the New York waterfront. Playwright Arthur Miller wrote a screenplay about the Brooklyn waterfront titled *The Hook,* for Elia Kazan to direct. The film was never produced, due to pressure from the studios for Miller to change the villains to Communists to be more "pro-American." Miller refused, and Kazan began collaborating with writer Budd Schulberg, who like Kazan had testified before the House Un-American Activities Committee (HUAC) as a "friendly" witness. Schulberg spent two years studying the New York waterfront, interviewing longshoreman and union leaders, and even mortgaged his farm to keep working on the project. They submitted the finished screenplay to Darryl F. Zanuck at 20th Century-Fox, who turned it down because he was doing only Cinemascope. All the majors passed until Sam Spiegel set up a deal with Columbia and convinced Marlon Brando, who had cooled on Kazan after HUAC, to join the film. Brando had originally refused the part, and Spiegel had then offered it to Frank Sinatra, who sued Spiegel in the amount of $500,000 for breach of contract when Brando ultimately took the part. (They later settled amicably.) Brando was paid $125,000. Although the other leads, Lee J. Cobb, Rod Steiger, and Karl Malden, were all Hollywood veterans, they cast Eva Marie Saint (who had a successful career in TV) as the female lead in her debut feature film. Kazan believed that postwar audiences demanded great realism, and he was able to achieve that authenticity by shooting over thirty-six days on location in Hoboken, New Jersey, in the cargo holds of ships, workers' slum dwellings, bars, alleys, and rooftops. He also cast real-life, professional ex-heavyweight boxers as some of the labor boss's chief bodyguards in the film. Many real longshoremen from Hoboken were used as extras as well. While shooting the film, Brando had it written into his contract that he would be allowed to leave the set early every day to see his analyst because he was dealing with the death of his mother. Steiger complained that Kazan favored Brando, and was greatly angered by Brando's leaving the set early, forcing Steiger to play his close-ups to a stand-in. The film paralleled Kazan's life, and he used it as an attempt to vindicate himself politically and justify his informant actions with HUAC.

DISTRIBUTION: Columbia disliked the film when they originally saw it, so Spiegel decided to give it a lift by getting Leonard Bernstein to score. The naturalistic, well-acted film powerfully conveyed a message about society's ills. Combining Boris Kaufman's gritty black and white cinematography and Brando's stellar performance, Kazan's vision was realized, and the film became a modest success. From a budget of just under $1 million, the film made $4.2 million in domestic rentals and was nominated for twelve Academy Awards, winning eight. It also was the fourth of four consecutive nominations for Brando. Although the part of Edie Doyle was properly a lead, producer Spiegel listed Saint as a supporting actress in the hopes of getting her a nomination. It worked, and she won the Oscar. —*Alex Ben Block and Hayley Taylor Block*

REAR WINDOW
Paramount, 1954

ALL-RELEASE EQUIVALENT 2005 $s
(Unadjusted $s) in Millions of $s

Domestic Box Office Revenues . . . . $154.5/($22.8)
Production Cost . . . . $14.5/($2.0)
Principal Photography . . . . **40** days estimated
8 weeks from 11/27/1953–1/13/1954

Director . . . . Alfred Hitchcock

Producer . . . . Alfred Hitchcock

Production Company . . . . Patron, Inc., Paramount
Pictures

Story by . . . . Cornell Woolrich
(from a short story)

Screenplay by . . . . John Michael Hayes

Cast . . . . James Stewart, Grace Kelly,
Wendell Cory, Thelma Ritter,
Raymond Burr

Filming Locations . . . . . . One huge confined set at
Paramount Studios,
Hollywood, CA

Genre . . . . Thriller

Format . . . . Color (Technicolor)

Initial Release . . . . 8/1/1954 premiere (New York);
9/1/1954 general release

Rerelease . . . . September 1962 (Paramount),
9/30/1983, 1/21/2000
(Universal)

Running Time . . . . 112 minutes

MPAA Rating . . . . not rated

STANDING THE TEST OF TIME

ACADEMY AWARD Oscar Nominations and Wins

Cinematography (Color): Robert Burks

Directing: Alfred Hitchcock

Sound Recording: Paramount Studio Sound Dept.,
Loren L. Ryder, Sound Director

Writing (Screenplay): John Michael Hayes

OSCAR TOTALS   Nominations **4**   *Wins 0

AFI 100 YEARS 100 MOVIES SELECTION
2007 . . . #48   1997 . . . #42

TOP 300 FILMS POSITION . . . . none
All-Release Domestic Box Office in Equivalent 2005 $s

National Film Preservation Board Selection 1997

OTHER AWARDS Best Picture Wins

	Year
Golden Globes	none
New York Film Critics	none
National Board of Review	none
Film Daily Critics	none

*Well, the poor man. It's the climax of peeping tomism, isn't it? "Why did you do it?" he says.
"If you hadn't been a peeping tom, I would have gotten away with it." Stewart can't answer.
What can he say? He's caught. Caught with his plaster down.*

—Alfred Hitchcock

PLOT: During a heat wave, a bored, wheelchair-bound photographer, stuck in his Greenwich Village apartment for weeks, spies on his neighbors across a courtyard, and becomes obsessed with a man he suspects of murdering and dismembering his wife.

PRODUCTION: In the spring of 1953, Alfred Hitchcock asked Lew Wasserman, his agent at MCA, to buy him the rights to the screen treatment for *Rear Window,* based on Cornell Woolrich's 1942 short story "It Had to Be Murder." The treatment was written by respected stage director Joshua Logan, who planned to direct. Hitchcock asked John Michael Hayes, an acquaintance, and a writer of radio suspense dramas, also represented by MCA, to do a new treatment. It was to be the first film under an eight-film contract with Paramount, with the copyright returned to Hitchcock after a period of time. Hitchcock insisted that the protagonist have a love interest and asked Hayes to add one with Grace Kelly in mind. After spending a week with her on the set of *Dial M for Murder*, Hayes was won over by her sly humor, sophistication, and sexiness. Based on Hayes's treatment, James Stewart agreed to star. Hiring thirty-seven-year-old actor Raymond Burr as the villain was one of Hitchcock's private jokes, as he knew the actor could be made up to look like fifty-two-year-old producer David O. Selznick, with whom Hitchcock often bitterly clashed. The part of the composer went to actor-songwriter Ross Bagdasarian ("Come on-a My House," "The Witch Doctor"), who would eventually win two Grammy Awards as David Seville, the creator of Alvin and the Chipmunks. The production created the largest indoor set built at Paramount Studios (Stage 18), modeled after an apartment-courtyard at New York's Christopher Street at West 10th Street. It measured 98 feet wide by 185 feet long by 40 feet high (about four stories tall). It consisted of 31 apartments, eight of which were completely furnished, and had electricity and running water. The soundstage floor had to be excavated (approximately 25 feet) and furniture usually stored underneath was warehoused elsewhere. Stewart's second-floor apartment was actually at street level. One thousand arc lights were used to replicate sunlight. Thanks to extensive prelighting of the set, the crew could make the switch from day to night in less than 45 minutes, reducing shooting time by about half. However, the heat buildup from the lights once activated the sprinkler system. The sound coming from the street, alleyway, apartments and courtyard is diegetic, meaning that all the speech, music, and other ambience come naturally from within the world of the film. During shooting, Hitchcock never left Stewart's apartment. The actors across the courtyard took his direction wearing flesh-colored earpieces. Censors had many objections, including the "illicit" Stewart-Kelly relationship and the "peep show" sexuality of the character called Miss Torso. Hitchcock made minor concessions, but he got away with many of these elements verbatim.

DISTRIBUTION: Stewart pioneered the "back-end deal" at a cash-strapped Universal with *Winchester '73* (1950), in which he worked for a share of the movie's profits, which turned out to be very lucrative for him. This shrewd practice continued with *Rear Window.* The movie was distributed by Paramount from 1954 through the 1962 rerelease. Once the rights reverted to Hitchcock, he made a new distribution agreement with Universal, which rereleased the film in 1983 and again in 2000. —*Bob Canning*

WHITE CHRISTMAS

Paramount, 1954

ALL-RELEASE EQUIVALENT 2005 $s

(Unadjusted $s) in Millions of $s

Domestic Box Office Revenues . . . . **$219.9**/($19.6)
Production Cost . . . . **$27.4**/($3.8)
Principal Photography . . . . **68** days estimated
9/21/1953–12/10/1953

Director . . . . Michael Curtiz

Producer . . . . Robert Emmett Dolan

Production Company . . . . Paramount Productions

Story and
Screenplay by . . . . Norman Krasna, Norma
Panama, Melvin Frank

Cast . . . . Bing Crosby, Danny Kaye,
Rosemary Clooney, Vera-Ellen,
Dean Jagger

Filming Locations . . . . . . Paramount Studios, Hollywood,
CA; Twentieth Century-Fox
Studios, West Los Angeles, CA

Genre . . . . Musical

Format . . . . Color (Technicolor)

Initial Release . . . . 10/14/1954 premiere, Radio City
Music Hall (New York);
10/27/1954 premiere
(Los Angeles); November 1954
wide release

Rerelease 1961

Running Time . . . . 120 minutes

MPAA Rating . . . . not rated

STANDING THE TEST OF TIME

ACADEMY AWARD Oscar Nominations and Wins

Music (Songs): "Count Your Blessings Instead of
Sheep," Music and Lyrics by Irving Berlin

OSCAR TOTALS Nominations **1** *Wins 0

AFI 100 YEARS 100 MOVIES SELECTION
2007 0   1997 0

TOP 300 FILMS POSITION . . . . **#207**

All-Release Domestic Box Office in Equivalent 2005 $s

National Film Preservation Board Selection . . . . none

OTHER AWARDS Best Picture Wins

	Year
Golden Globes	none
New York Film Critics	none
National Board of Review	none
Film Daily Critics	none

*It's impossible to overemphasize how much this was Bing's picture. His word was always
the tie-breaker. There was never a raised voice, but Bing set the tone. He was in charge.*

—Rosemary Clooney

PLOT: Wallace and Davis, a popular song-and-dance duo, team up with a fledgling sister act in an attempt to help their former World War II commander, the owner of a Vermont ski lodge, who has fallen on hard financial times.

PRODUCTION: A stunningly successful Christmas song from a twelve-year-old film provided Paramount executives the impetus to wrap an entire film around the tune in question—"White Christmas"—and cast the most popular star in America at the time, Bing Crosby. The song "White Christmas," by Irving Berlin, was first performed by Crosby on the radio Christmas Day, 1941, and sold as a record on May 29, 1942. When included in the 1942 Paramount film *Holiday Inn,* starring Crosby and Fred Astaire, "White Christmas" won the Best Song Oscar. Paramount wanted to reteam Crosby and Astaire, but Astaire bowed out and was replaced by Donald O'Connor. However, O'Connor contracted Q fever, a serious bacterial infection, and although the studio waited six months, he was still too weak to perform. He was replaced by Danny Kaye. Rounding out the cast were songstress Rosemary Clooney (recently signed to a seven-year contract) and former MGM dancer Vera-Ellen. Director Michael Curtiz (*Casablanca*), fresh from a twenty-seven-year stint at Warner Bros., took the helm as director. The film's score included such Berlin standards as "Mandy," "Blue Skies," and the lucrative title tune, as well as such new compositions as "Sisters," "Count Your Blessings Instead of Sheep," and "Love, You Didn't Do Right by Me." In the movie, Vera-Ellen's singing was dubbed by Trudy Stevens or Clooney. There was no official soundtrack, but two albums were released in 1954. Decca had the soundtrack rights, but Clooney sang for Columbia, so Decca's album had Peggy Lee singing Clooney's part. Columbia released an album of Clooney singing the title tune and seven other tunes from the film. *White Christmas* was filmed almost entirely on various soundstages at Paramount Studios in Hollywood. The Pine Tree, Vermont, railroad station was a set at 20th Century-Fox. "We shot the train station stuff at [20th Century-]Fox. That was the only studio in town that had a train station." Clooney also recalled that the cast and crew enjoyed the luxury of plenty of preparation time: "Six weeks' rehearsal—that's almost unheard of." With television encroaching on the popularity of theatrical films, Paramount executives decided that *White Christmas* would be the first film presented in the company's revolutionary VistaVision wide-screen process, Paramount's response to Fox's CinemaScope. Only a few VistaVision prints were actually released, including the engagement at Radio City Music Hall in New York, since it required special projection equipment. Other engagements were in standard 35 mm.

DISTRIBUTION: The presence of an oft-heard song over a decade old, and the fact that 1942's *Holiday Inn* covered similar territory, didn't deter audiences from lining up outside Radio City Music Hall in New York for the film's premiere engagement. Box office figures were merry and bright: *White Christmas* brought in over $8 million in domestic rentals during its initial run. It became one of the top-grossing films of 1954, and a big hit when released to TV, where it remains a perennial holiday favorite. As for the song itself, it was the all-time best-selling single for more than fifty years until it was finally displaced, in 1997, by Elton John's "Candle in the Wind" with new lyrics honoring the late Princess Diana. —*Douglas Burns*

EAST OF EDEN

Warner Bros., 1955

ALL-RELEASE EQUIVALENT 2005 $s

(Unadjusted $s) in Millions of $s

Domestic Box Office Revenues......... **$122.8**/($11.1)
Production Cost .... **$11.7**/($1.6)
Principal Photography............**63** days estimated
5/27/1954–8/9/1954

Director	Elia Kazan
Producer	Elia Kazan
Production Company....	Warner Bros. Pictures
Story by	Based on the novel by John Steinbeck
Screenplay by	Paul Osborn
Cast	Julie Harris, James Dean, Raymond Massey, Burl Ives, Richard Davalos
Filming Locations	On Location in Monterey, Mendocino, Salinas, CA; in studio at Warner Brothers Burbank Studios, 4000 Warner Boulevard, Burbank
Genre................	Drama
Format...............	Color (Technicolor)
Initial Release	3/9/1955 world premiere (New York); 4/9/1955 general release
Rerelease.............	none
Running Time	115 minutes
MPAA Rating	not rated

STANDING THE TEST OF TIME

ACADEMY AWARD Oscar Nominations and Wins

Actor: James Dean

*ACTRESS IN A SUPPORTING ROLE: Jo Van Fleet

Directing: Elia Kazan

Writing (Screenplay): Paul Osborn

OSCAR TOTALS   Nominations **4**   *Wins **1**

AFI 100 YEARS 100 MOVIES SELECTION
2007 0   1997 0

TOP 300 FILMS POSITION ....none
All-Release Domestic Box Office in Equivalent 2005 $s

National Film Preservation Board Selection. . . .none

OTHER AWARDS Best Picture Wins

	Year
Golden Globes	1956
New York Film Critics......................	none
National Board of Review...................	none
Film Daily Critics	none

This was really a very personal film, one of the most personal I've ever made . . .
I was very like Cal, so East of Eden *was for me a kind of self-defense.*
It was about people not understanding me.

—Elia Kazan

PLOT: An updated retelling of the biblical story of twin brothers, Cal (Cain) and Aron (Abel), and their rivalry for love and acceptance just before the United States' entry into World War I.

PRODUCTION: After his success with *On the Waterfront,* Elia Kazan wanted to make a film that was important to him both personally and socially. He found it in John Steinbeck's best-selling 1952 novel (inspired by the fourth chapter of Genesis, the story of Cain and Abel). Kazan thought the last part of the book would make a good film. Steinbeck and Kazan had become friends when Steinbeck wrote the screenplay for *Viva Zapata!* (1952). Kazan convinced Steinbeck to let Paul Osborn write the screenplay and got Jack Warner to fund the film, promising Kazan final cut and a producer credit as well. Kazan had been thinking of casting Marlon Brando in the lead role, but Osborn suggested James Dean, whom he had seen in a play in New York. At first, Kazan disliked Dean, but after meeting with him he decided "he was Cal," and Steinbeck agreed. For Dean's first starring role, Kazan took him to California (on his first plane ride) for screen tests disguised as wardrobe tests. They visited Dean's father on the way, and Kazan observed the tense father-son relationship, which he used in his film. Raymond Massey, cast as the father, disliked Dean at first too, especially his Brando-style Method realism. He never knew what Dean would do next. Kazan used this dynamic as well to intensify their antagonistic on-screen relationship. A replica of the town of Salinas was built at the studio, which spared no expense after the success of Kazan's *A Streetcar Named Desire.* This was Kazan's first film in color, which presented some problems. Despite these other challenges, Kazan and cameraman Ted McCord broke the rules of Cinemascope to achieve groundbreaking dramatic effects. They often tipped the camera and pushed it in close, using the distortion to help the drama. Kazan also put objects in the foreground, blocking off a third of the large frame, to keep the picture changing. He emphasized the color green, using the studio's Eastmancolor process to make the color more saturated and grainy. From the very start, Kazan worked closely with Dean, knowing the young actor required his personal attention. He would spar with him on set, have him run around before shooting, and even got him drunk on Chianti before one difficult scene. A couple of weeks before Eden wrapped, Kazan noticed Dean getting a swelled head as word of his performance spread. Kazan moved Dean into a dressing room across from his to keep an eye on him. He also forbade him from riding his new Triumph T-110 motorcycle until shooting had finished. Kazan said, "I kept my eye on him night and day, so we'd be sure to get through the goddamn picture."

DISTRIBUTION: The studio held a preview. As word got around, a bunch of kids showed up to the screening. When Dean appeared, the girls started screaming and Kazan knew a star had been born. The film was originally released in showcase venues with a four-track magnetic soundtrack. *East of Eden* was the only James Dean film released before his death in September 1955. Dean received a posthumous Best Actor Oscar nomination. —*Hayley Taylor Block*

MARTY

United Artists, 1955

ALL-RELEASE EQUIVALENT 2005 $s

(Unadjusted $s) in Millions of $s

Domestic Box Office Revenues . . . . **$73.7**/($6.7)
Production Cost . . . . **$2.5**/($0.3)
Principal Photography . . . . **19** days
9/7/1954–November 1954

Director . . . . Delbert Mann

Producer . . . . Harold Hecht

Production Company . . . . Hecht and Lancaster's Steven
Productions

Story by . . . . Based on the 1953 TV play by
Paddy Chayefsky

Screenplay by . . . . Paddy Chayefsky

Cast . . . . Ernest Borgnine, Betsy Blair,
Esther Minciotti

Filming Locations . . . . . . Exteriors in the Bronx; interiors
at Goldwyn studios in
Hollywood; Waverly Ballroom
scenes in Downtown
Los Angeles

Genre . . . . Drama

Format . . . . B&W

Initial Release 4/11/1955

Rerelease . . . . none

Running Time . . . . 91 minutes

MPAA Rating . . . . not rated

STANDING THE TEST OF TIME

ACADEMY AWARD Oscar Nominations and Wins

*BEST MOTION PICTURE: Harold Hecht,
Producer

*Actor: Ernest Borgnine

Actor in a Supporting Role: Joe Mantell

Actress in a Supporting Role: Betsy Blair

Art Direction/Set Decoration: Edward S. Haworth,
Walter Simonds/Robert Priestley

Cinematography (Black-and-White): Joseph LaShelle

*Directing: Delbert Mann

*Writing (Screenplay): Paddy Chayefsky

OSCAR TOTALS   Nominations **8**   *Wins 4

AFI 100 YEARS 100 MOVIES SELECTION
2007 0   1997 0

TOP 300 FILMS POSITION . . . . .none
All-Release Domestic Box Office in Equivalent 2005 $s

National Film Preservation Board Selection 1994

OTHER AWARDS Best Picture Wins

	Year
Golden Globes	none
New York Film Critics	1955
National Board of Review	1955
Film Daily Critics	none

*You spill your guts into the typewriter, which is why you can't stand to see what you write
destroyed or degraded into a hunk of claptrap by picture butchers.*

—Paddy Chayefsky

PLOT: It looks like Marty will be a bachelor for life. He's timid and overweight, and he lives with his mother. And then, one Saturday night, Marty meets Clara. She's timid too.

PRODUCTION: Bronx-born producer Harold Hecht had his eye on *Marty* ever since he saw it on television in 1953. Considering his reputation as a producer with partner Burt Lancaster, and old-neighborhood memories of young Paddy (back to 1947), Hecht had every reason to believe he could secure the property. But Paddy Chayefsky wasn't taking. The writer didn't want his intimate character piece destroyed by the Hollywood suits—he'd been down this road before— and respectfully declined. Hecht, adamant, returned with a counteroffer that Chayefsky, reconsidering, fashioned into a small coup of creative control. His terms were as follows: he was to write the script and the rewrites, and also oversee casting, and Delbert Mann, the director of the television adaptation, was to return for the movie. Oh, and one more thing: Chayefsky wanted to co-direct. That way, he thought, if Mann was fired during filming (this was, after all, his first feature film), he would be ready to step in. Hecht acquiesced, and the author was granted everything. Early on, United Artists executives considered Brando and Jackie Gleason for the title role, but Chayefsky and Mann wanted Rod Steiger, who had played Marty in the TV original. After Steiger declined, Ernest Borgnine's name was offered. Chayefsky and Mann didn't see Borgnine as a romantic lead until they rehearsed him in a small motel. The very next day, he got the part. Soon thereafter, actress Betsy Blair was chosen for Clara, but when Harold Hecht got wind of her leftist leanings, he had second thoughts. Maybe they should have cast Cloris Leachman after all. Or Nancy Marchand, who had originated the role. But Chayefsky was firm: no film of his would buckle under HUAC pressures. Blair would stay. And she did. Production began with three days of Bronx exteriors and moved to the Goldwyn soundstages in Hollywood in mid-September 1954. That's when Paddy Chayefsky, after arriving on what should have been a finished set, found out his movie had been shut down. A serious bout of financial mismanagement on the part of Hecht-Lancaster revealed an empty production account. *Marty* was bankrupt. It looked like the film would never be finished. Then Bankers Trust stepped in and agreed to a loan that allowed Hecht-Lancaster, under United Artists, to form Steven Productions. A few weeks later, production resumed. The entire film was shot in nineteen days.

DISTRIBUTION: When *Marty,* miraculously, was completed, UA executives decided to release it as the second feature in a double bill. It looked like *Marty* was too arty for the big business crowds, and the future Best Picture winner, the modest black-and-white love story with no star power, no action, and a lot of dialogue, was slated for second fiddle. There was even talk of shelving it for good. Instead it opened at one cinema in Manhattan with little publicity. UA hired a window decorator to sketch the ad. He created a tubby-looking fellow modeled on Chayefsky that became the film's poster. Reviews were fantastic, including one by influential columnist Walter Winchell. It became the first American movie to win the Palme d'Or at Cannes. From there on out, *Marty* was in business. —*Sam Wasson*

MISTER ROBERTS
Warner Bros., 1955

ALL-RELEASE EQUIVALENT 2005 $s
(Unadjusted $s) in Millions of $s

Domestic Box Office Revenues . . . . **$196.2**/($17.8)
Production Cost . . . . **$17.1**/($2.4)
Principal Photography . . . . **61** days estimated
9/1/1954–11/10/1954

Rerelease . . . . none
Running Time . . . . 123 minutes
MPAA Rating . . . . not rated

Director . . . . John Ford, Mervyn LeRoy

Producer . . . . Leland Hayward

Production Company . . . . Orange Productions

Story by . . . . Based on the 1946 novel by Thomas Heggen and the 1948 stage play by adapted by Thomas Heggen and Joshua Logan

Screenplay by . . . . Frank Nugent, Joshua Logan

Cast . . . . Henry Fonda, James Cagney, William Powell, Jack Lemmon, Betsy Palmer, Ward Bond, Phil Carey

Filming Locations . . . . . . Midway Island; Honolulu and Kaneohe Bay, Oahu, Hawaii; Warner Bros. Studios, Burbank, CA

Genre . . . . Comedy (war)

Format . . . . Color (WarnerColor)

Initial Release . . . . 7/14/1955 premiere, Radio City Music Hall (New York); 7/20/1955 premiere, Paramount, Wiltern, and Pantages Theaters (Los Angeles); 7/30/1955 general release

STANDING THE TEST OF TIME

ACADEMY AWARD Oscar Nominations and Wins

Best Motion Picture: Leland Hayward, Producer

*ACTOR IN A SUPPORTING ROLE: Jack Lemmon

Sound Recording: Warner Bros. Studio Sound Dept., William A. Mueller, Sound Director

OSCAR TOTALS   Nominations **3**   *Wins **1**

AFI 100 YEARS 100 MOVIES SELECTION
2007 0   1997 0

TOP 300 FILMS POSITION . . . . **#276**
All-Release Domestic Box Office in Equivalent 2005 $s

National Film Preservation Board Selection . . . . none

OTHER AWARDS Best Picture Wins

	Year
Golden Globes	none
New York Film Critics	none
National Board of Review	none
Film Daily Critics	none

The movie went out, and it was a blockbuster. But I've said it before and I'll say it again, it was not the picture that Josh and Leland and I had dreamed it might be.

—Henry Fonda

PLOT: Douglas Roberts is an officer aboard the plodding U.S. Navy cargo ship USS *Reluctant*, which has been bypassed by the action of World War II and instead sails "from tedium to apathy and back again, with an occasional side trip to monotony."

PRODUCTION: Born in Iowa in 1918, writer Thomas Heggen served in the U.S. Navy during World War II as communications officer aboard an attack transport, the USS *Virgo*. He began writing a series of amusing stories about his fellow sailors, their beloved cargo officer, and shipboard life under the command of a tyrannical, eccentric captain. A cousin urged Heggen to rework the anecdotes into a novel, and the result—*Mr. Roberts*—was published in 1946, becoming a best seller. Agent and theatrical producer Leland Hayward (*A Bell for Adano, State of the Union*) bought the rights to the novel, hiring Heggen and writer-director Joshua Logan (*Annie Get Your Gun*) to collaborate on a stage production. The smash hit play, with Henry Fonda cast in the title role, opened on Broadway on February 18, 1948, and went on to win five Tony Awards, including Best Play, Best Director (Logan), Best Producer (Hayward), Best Author (Logan and Heggen), and Best Actor (Fonda). Warner Bros. purchased the film rights in 1953, with Hayward attached as producer and Logan and Frank Nugent (*The Quiet Man*) hired to write the screenplay (*Roberts* author Heggen had been found dead in his bathtub, a probable suicide, in 1949). Marlon Brando and William Holden were approached for the lead role, but once John "Pappy" Ford was tapped as director, he insisted on its originator, Fonda. Screen newcomer Jack Lemmon and veterans James Cagney and William Powell rounded out the principal cast. For exteriors, the studio was granted permission by the U.S. Navy to utilize the light cargo ship USS *Hewell*, and Ford returned to the place where he had been wounded during World War II, Midway Island. Following four weeks of filming at Midway, the troupe moved to Hawaii for an equal number of weeks. From Hawaii, they returned to Warner Bros. in California for interior shots.

Rough seas abounded. First Leland Hayward was hospitalized for a series of internal hemorrhages. Then, despite seven previous film projects together, friction developed between Fonda and Ford. Fonda, well acquainted with the Roberts character and story, took exception to script deviations Ford and Nugent had implemented. "I didn't like it," Fonda recalled. "Josh [Logan] and Tom Heggen had written an excellent play, and very subtly, the dialogue had been changed around. Not a helluva lot, but enough to lose the laughs and nuances of frustration and pain." During a tense meeting to address the problem, Ford, his ire fueled by alcohol, slugged Fonda. He immediately apologized, but an uneasy atmosphere subsequently prevailed. After the company returned to California, Ford suffered a ruptured gallbladder and underwent emergency surgery. Hayward replaced him with Mervyn LeRoy (*Quo Vadis*), who directed the film's interior segments at Warner Bros. "Mervyn LeRoy didn't miss a beat," recalled Fonda.

DISTRIBUTION: *Mister Roberts* sailed onto movie screens buoyed by enthusiastic reviews and receptive audiences. For PR, Fonda, Cagney, and Lemmon reenacted several scenes on Ed Sullivan's popular *Toast of the Town* television variety show. It returned a net profit of $4.5 million on worldwide rentals of $9.9 million, putting it in the top 5 domestic films of 1955. —*Douglas Burns*

REBEL WITHOUT A CAUSE
Warner Bros., 1955

ALL-RELEASE EQUIVALENT 2005 $s
(Unadjusted $s) in Millions of $s

Domestic Box Office Revenues . . . . **$113.0**/($10.2)
Production Cost . . . . **$10.9**/($1.5)
Principal Photography . . . . **51** days estimated
3/28/1955–5/25/1955

Director . . . . Nicholas Ray
Producer . . . . David Weisbart
Production Company . . . . Warner Bros. Pictures
Story by . . . . Nicholas Ray
Screenplay by . . . . Stewart Stern
Cast . . . . James Dean, Natalie Wood, Sal Mineo
Filming Locations . . . . . . On location: Los Angeles, Hollywood, Los Feliz, Mendocino, Santa Monica, CA.; Ocala, FL; in studio at Warner Bros. Studio in Burbank, CA
Genre . . . . Drama
Format . . . . Color (WarnerColor)
Initial Release 10/27/1955
Rerelease 1956
Running Time . . . . 111 minutes
MPAA Rating . . . . not rated

STANDING THE TEST OF TIME

ACADEMY AWARD Oscar Nominations and Wins

Actor in a Supporting Role: Sal Mineo
Actress in a Supporting Role: Natalie Wood
Writing (Motion Picture Story): Nicholas Ray

OSCAR TOTALS   Nominations **3**   *Wins **0**

AFI 100 YEARS 100 MOVIES SELECTION
2007 0   1997 . . . #59

TOP 300 FILMS POSITION . . . . none
All-Release Domestic Box Office in Equivalent 2005 $s

National Film Preservation Board Selection 1990

OTHER AWARDS Best Picture Wins

	Year
Golden Globes	none
New York Film Critics	none
National Board of Review	none
Film Daily Critics	none

In my opinion James Dean directed Rebel Without a Cause, *from blocking all the scenes, setting the cameras, starting the scene and saying "cut."*

—Dennis Hopper

PLOT: In a twenty-four-hour time period, a teenage delinquent in a new town gets blamed for the death of the local gang leader and hides out in an abandoned house, where he forms a bond with two other teenage outcasts.

PRODUCTION: In the early 1950s, with teenagers and juvenile delinquency in the news, Nicholas Ray told his Hollywood agent, Lew Wasserman, he wanted to do a movie "about the young people next door," not the street toughs portrayed in other teen films. Ray did research at juvenile hall in Los Angeles and wrote an intense seventeen-page treatment. Wasserman then made a deal at Warner Bros., eager to tap the youth market. Warner suggested that Ray adapt Dr. Robert Lindner's best seller, *Rebel Without a Cause: The Story of a Criminal Psychopath,* which the studio had been trying to develop for several years. The film was the first to show the world through the eyes of teenagers. Ray channeled his own alienation and confusion (his father was an alcoholic and his teenage son had had an affair with his second wife) into the story. Leon Uris and Irving Shulman wrote drafts of the screenplay that Ray vetoed. Even playwright Clifford Odets provided ideas. Stewart Stern, a recent graduate of the University of Iowa writing program, developed the final script, completed just four days before production. Ray began shooting in gritty black and white, but after Dean became a sensation in *East of Eden,* Warner Bros. upgraded and switched to color. This would help distinguish the film from *Blackboard Jungle* as well. Ray rolled with the switch to color, discarding some scenes already shot, but it put him behind schedule. His methodic style exacerbated the problem, causing him to get further and further behind. Ray wanted James Dean (who had just worked with Ray's mentor, Elia Kazan) for the lead, but Dean accepted only after *Giant* was delayed by Elizabeth Taylor's pregnancy. Ray also cast former child actors Natalie Wood and Sal Mineo. At first, Ray thought Wood was too wholesome for the role (even though Ray, forty-three, was having an affair with the sixteen-year-old). But Wood, who desperately wanted the part, finally convinced him. She had been in a car accident with Dennis Hopper (whom she was also sleeping with) and someone in the hospital called her a "goddamn juvenile delinquent." (Ray later cast Hopper in the film, but gave all his lines to another actor when he found out about Hopper and Wood.) To convince Warner Bros. that Wood could play the part, Ray had a vocal coach and a costume designer make her look older and sexier. Seeking authenticity, Ray cast real-life gang member Frank Mazzola, whom he also hired as technical advisor for the fight scenes. Ray formed a great rapport with the teenagers and did improvisations before shooting. Ray also used color coding to define and evoke the emotional lives of the characters (for example, Dean's red jacket signified the audacity of rebellion). Dean, the Method actor, insisted on using real switchblades for a fight scene, but then was badly cut. Dean also injected himself into the direction, even suggesting script revisions. Ray, who was never very forceful, treated Dean as a friend and let him have his way, which added to the slow pace. The finished production was eleven days over schedule.

DISTRIBUTION: Released right after James Dean's untimely death in a car crash, *Rebel* made slightly less than *East of Eden,* which came out in April. The film's portrayal of teenage culture helped define its generation. —*Hayley Taylor Block*

THE SEARCHERS
Warner Bros., 1956

ALL-RELEASE EQUIVALENT 2005 $s
(Unadjusted $s) in Millions of $s

Domestic Box Office Revenues........ **$118.3**/($10.9)
Production Cost .... **$26.9**/($3.8)
Principal Photography..................... **49** days
6/16/1955–7/13/1955

Director .... John Ford

Producer .... Merian C. Cooper (executive producer), Patrick Ford (associate producer)

Production Company.... C. V. Whitney Pictures, Inc.

Story by.............. Based on the novel by Alan Le May

Screenplay by......... Frank S. Nugent

Cast .... John Wayne, Jeffrey Hunter, Vera Miles, Ward Bond, Natalie Wood

Filming Locations ...... Aspen and Gunnison, CO; Edmonton, Alberta, Canada; Mexican Hat and Monument Valley, UT; Bronson Caves, Bronson Canyon, Griffith Park, Los Angeles, CA; and RKO-Pathe Studios, Culver City, CA

Genre................ Western

Format............... Color (WarnerColor)

Initial Release 5/26/1956

Rerelease............. none

Running Time .... 119 minutes

MPAA Rating .... not rated

STANDING THE TEST OF TIME

None

OSCAR TOTALS   Nominations **0**   *Wins **0**

AFI 100 YEARS 100 MOVIES SELECTION
2007 ... #12   1997 ... #96

TOP 300 FILMS POSITION .... none
All-Release Domestic Box Office in Equivalent 2005 $s

National Film Preservation Board Selection.... 1989

OTHER AWARDS Best Picture Wins

	Year
Golden Globes	none
New York Film Critics....................	none
National Board of Review.................	none
Film Daily Critics......................	none

"I should like to do a tragedy, the most serious in the world, that turned into the ridiculous.
—John Ford before making *The Searchers*

PLOT: A Civil War veteran spends years in an obsessive search for his two nieces, kidnapped by Comanche Indians after their family was massacred.

PRODUCTION: After the release of the Ford-directed drama *The Long Gray Line* in February 1955 and the war comedy *Mister Roberts* in July 1955, John Ford was ready for another western. He joined with screenwriter Frank S. Nugent to adapt Alan Le May's novel *The Searchers* for a movie he believed would be "good for my health, spirit and morale."

Ford and Nugent turned the book's hero, Ethan Edwards, into a dark, isolated antihero. A much more traditional western hero in the novel, Ford's Ethan is a haunted, racist, repressed figure living on the outskirts of polite society. It didn't seem like a role for Ford's frequent collaborator John Wayne, but he wanted the part. As with many of his films, Ford staffed both cast and crew with old friends and family: his son Patrick was an associate producer on the movie, while son-in-law Ken Curtis was a cast member. John Wayne's son Patrick also acted. Natalie Wood and her younger sister, Lana, were cast as Debbie at different ages. Olive Carey and Harry Carey Jr., the widow and son of Ford's friend, silent western star Harry Carey, had roles in the film. *The Searchers* would be the first film financed by C. V. Whitney Pictures. A famous millionaire sportsman, "Jock" Whitney had once been a partner of David O. Selznick's in projects such as *Gone with the Wind*. He also was friends with Ford's producing partner Merian C. Cooper. Their partnership allowed the film to start production less than five months after Ford and Nugent first conceived the idea. As with eight of his other westerns, Ford shot a great deal of the film in Monument Valley, Utah, where he began his shoot June 16, 1955. Despite the fact that he had done location shoots there for almost twenty years, Ford utilized the landscape differently. This time he referenced the realistic portraits of cowboy artist Charles Russell to shape the look of his film. *The Searchers* was photographed by Winton C. Hoch in Technicolor and VistaVision, a wide-screen process that ran a 35 mm filmstrip horizontally through the camera. Production was in two separate shoots during the winter and summer of 1955. Pat Ford organized the first stage of shooting, which began in March in the snows of Gunnison, Colorado. Although officially considered second-unit footage, these scenes involving Ethan and actors playing cavalrymen and Comanches were directed by John Ford and photographed by Hoch. Principal photography, which took forty-nine shooting days, finished three days ahead of schedule. The rest of the interiors were shot at the RKO-Pathé Studio in Culver City.

DISTRIBUTION: *The Searchers* was another box office success for Ford and Wayne, making more than any of their other collaborations until the 1963 U.S. release of *How the West Was Won*. But critics tended to be a bit disdainful of the film at the time of its release, some even referring to it as meandering and confusing. Wayne also was accused by some reviewers of acting like a lunatic. The film did not receive a single Oscar nomination. Only in subsequent decades has the film won the admiration of the critics. —*Louis Burklow*

THE KING AND I
20th Century-Fox, 1956

ALL-RELEASE EQUIVALENT 2005 $s
(Unadjusted $s) in Millions of $s

Domestic Box Office Revenues. . . . .$205.3/($18.8)
Production Cost . . . .$33.0/($4.6)
Principal Photography. . . . . .57 days estimated
11/21/1955–1/28/1956

Director . . . . Walter Lang

Producer . . . . Charles Brackett

Production Company . . . . 20th Century-Fox

Story by. . . . . Based on the novel *Anna and the King of Siam* by Margaret Landon

Screenplay by . . . . Ernest Lehman

Cast . . . . Deborah Kerr, Yul Brynner, Rita Moreno

Filming Locations . . . . . . 20th Century-Fox studio lot

Genre. . . . . Musical

Format. . . . . Color (DeLuxe)

Initial Release . . . . 6/29/1956 (New York)

Rerelease . . . . 1961 in "Grandeur 70"

Running Time . . . . 133 minutes

MPAA Rating . . . . not rated

STANDING THE TEST OF TIME

ACADEMY AWARD Oscar Nominations and Wins

Best Motion Picture: Charles Brackett, Producer

***ACTOR:** Yul Brynner

Actress: Deborah Kerr

***ART DIRECTION/SET DECORATION:** Lyle R. Wheeler, John DeCuir/Walter M. Scott, Paul S. Fox

Cinematography (Color): Leon Shamroy

***COSTUME DESIGN:** Irene Sharaff

Directing (Color): Walter Lang

***MUSIC** (Scoring of a Musical Picture): Alfred Newman, Ken Darby

***SOUND RECORDING:** 20th Century-Fox Studio Sound Dept., Carl Faulkner, Sound Director

OSCAR TOTALS   Nominations **9**   *Wins 5

AFI 100 YEARS 100 MOVIES SELECTION
2007 0   1997 0

TOP 300 FILMS POSITION . . . . #246
All-Release Domestic Box Office in Equivalent 2005 $s

National Film Preservation Board Selection . . . .none

OTHER AWARDS Best Picture Wins

	Year
Golden Globes	1957
New York Film Critics	none
National Board of Review	none
Film Daily Critics	none

I am convinced that this is our best work. I have a kind of humble feeling of not knowing how we did it. It has more wisdom as well as heart than any other musical play by anybody. It will remain "modern" long after any of our other plays.

—Oscar Hammerstein II to Richard Rogers

PLOT: In 1862, after the death of her military husband, a schoolteacher sails for Bangkok with her young son to teach English to the sixty-seven children of King Mongkut of Siam.

PRODUCTION: The 1946 hit movie *Anna and the King of Siam,* which starred Irene Dunne and Rex Harrison, was based on the best-selling novel, which in turn was adapted from the memoirs of Anna Leonowens. Broadway superstar Gertrude Lawrence was enamored of the film and felt it would make an excellent stage musical as a vehicle for herself, so she brought it to the attention of her friends Richard Rodgers and Oscar Hammerstein II. By coincidence, the wives of both songwriters had read Margaret Landon's book and had already pitched the idea to them. An instant smash, the musical opened on March 29, 1951, and closed March 20, 1954, after 1,246 performances and five Tony Awards, including Best Musical and Best Actress. Ernest Lehman (*Sabrina*) was assigned to write the screenplay. Art directors Lyle Wheeler and John DeCuir spent $750,000 designing forty sets, each significantly more opulent than the play's award-winning sets. To adapt his stage choreography for the screen, Jerome Robbins was brought to Hollywood for the first time, and Irene Sharaff, whose costumes won a Tony, was hired for the film version. Marlon Brando was briefly considered for the role of the king, but cooler heads prevailed, and Tony Award winner Yul Brynner re-created the role, now considered "monumental" by film historians, "as much a part of our collective consciousness as the Statue of Liberty," according to one noted critic. The heartbreaking challenge, however, was in the recasting of Anna, after Gertrude Lawrence, its contractually guaranteed star, died of cancer during the run of the show at age fifty-four. Maureen O'Hara and singer Dinah Shore were candidates for the role, but at Brynner's suggestion, Deborah Kerr became his co-star. During postproduction, the sound reels were accidentally destroyed, and the entire cast had to redub all their lines.

DISTRIBUTION: The film was shot in a much-ballyhooed new process called CinemaScope 55 ("More Than Your Eyes Have Ever Seen"). It was, instead, exhibited in standard 35 mm CinemaScope, with four-channel stereo rather than the six-channel stereo originally hyped. Ultimately, CinemaScope 55 was never seen by the moviegoing public. Regardless, *The King and I* became one of the highest-grossing films of the year. In 1961 Fox reissued the film using 70 mm prints optically converted from the 55 mm negative, calling this hybrid process Grandeur 70. But it was, in reality, an optical reduction, not a blowup. One can only imagine what the Thai ambassador to the United Nations truly thought of the film when he accepted producer Charles Brackett's invitation to attend the New York premiere, because the Thai government considered *Anna and the King of Siam* and *The King and I* grossly inaccurate and insulting to its history. To this day, the book and both movies are still banned in Thailand.

Nevertheless, the property remains the classic cash cow. Brynner starred in a short-lived sitcom version in the 1970s, and in the 1977 and 1985 Broadway revivals. A 1998 production ran for 780 performances, winning four Tonys, including Best Musical Revival. Productions frequently tour throughout Europe and are especially popular in Australia and Japan. An animated version was released in 1999, as was a nonmusical drama starring Jodie Foster. Long live the king. —*Bob Canning*

AROUND THE WORLD IN 80 DAYS

United Artists, 1956

ALL-RELEASE EQUIVALENT 2005 $s

(Unadjusted $s) in Millions of $s

Domestic Box Office Revenues . . . . **$534.0**/($51.5)
Production Cost . . . . **$43.1**/($6.0)
Principal Photography . . . . **127** days estimated
8/9/1955–12/20/1955

Running Time . . . . 175 minutes
MPAA Rating . . . . not rated

Director . . . . Michael Anderson
Producer . . . . Michael Todd
Production Company . . . . The Michael Todd Co.
Story by . . . . Based on the 1873 novel *Le Tour du Mond en Quatre-Vingts Jours* by Jules Verne
Screenplay by . . . . S. J. Perelman, James Poe, John Farrow
Cast . . . . David Niven, Cantinflas, Robert Newton, Shirley MacLaine
Filming Locations . . . . . . 140 locations, plus RKO-Pathé Studios, Culver City CA; RKO Studios, Hollywood CA; Universal-International, 20th Century-Fox, Warner Bros., Columbia, Elstree Studios, London
Genre . . . . Comedy
Format . . . . Color (Eastmancolor)
Initial Release . . . . 10/17/1956 premiere, New York Rivoli Theatre (New York, where it played for three consecutive years); 12/22/1956 premiere (Los Angeles); 1959 general release in regular 35 mm widescreen format
Rerelease 1968

STANDING THE TEST OF TIME

ACADEMY AWARD Oscar Nominations and Wins

*BEST MOTION PICTURE: Michael Todd, Producer

Art Direction/Set Decoration: James W. Sullivan, Ken Adam/Ross J. Dowd

*CINEMATOGRAPHY: Lionel Lindon

Costume Design: Miles White

Directing: Michael Anderson

*FILM EDITING: Gene Ruggiero, Paul Weatherwax

*MUSIC: Victor Young

*WRITING (Screenplay – adapted): James Poe, John Farrow, S. J. Perelman

OSCAR TOTALS   Nominations **8**   *Wins **5**

AFI 100 YEARS 100 MOVIES SELECTION
2007 0   1997 0

TOP 300 FILMS POSITION . . . . #19
All-Release Domestic Box Office in Equivalent 2005 $s

National Film Preservation Board Selection . . . none

OTHER AWARDS Best Picture Wins

	Year
Golden Globes (Drama)	1957
New York Film Critics	1956
National Board of Review	1956
Film Daily Critics	none

Around the World was the greatest experience of my whole life. I had the concept of making it as a fairy tale for adults. Look at the people's faces in the theatre; you'll see they look like children.

—Mike Todd

PLOT: A nineteenth-century Englishman tries to win a £20,000 wager by traveling around the world in eighty days. However, he and his valet are pursued by a detective who believes the gentleman has robbed the Bank of England.

PRODUCTION: Mike Todd purchased the rights to the Jules Verne novel for $100,000 from film producer Alexander Korda, who had given up plans to shoot the epic. Coincidentally, Todd had produced a flop Broadway musical in 1946 based on the same property, starring and directed by Orson Welles. He was now determined to film a wide-screen extravaganza, but he was not enamored of Cinerama's three-screen/three-projector process (which he helped develop). He contacted Brian O'Brien, VP of optical research at American Option Company, for help in creating "Cinerama outta one hole." Soon the 70 mm Todd-AO process was introduced, its 128° bug-eye lens closely approximating Cinerama's 146° view without the distracting on-screen dividing lines. Todd had always envisioned David Niven in the lead as Phileas Fogg and although Fogg's manservant, Passepartout was a diminutive Frenchman in the original book, Todd pursued Cantinflas, a diminutive Mexican also known as "Mexico's Charlie Chaplin" to play the part instead. In a canny business move, Todd expanded Passepartout's role, elevating it to that of action-hero and drawing upon the Mexican superstar's popularity to generate huge ticket sales in Latin America. Todd also created an entirely new concept in casting: the cameo. Filling bit parts were dozens of familiar character actors and a number of stars such as Frank Sinatra and Marlene Dietrich. Also making an appearance in the film's prologue was esteemed newsman Edward R. Murrow. Murrow's segment was shown in the 1.37:1 format, and as the intro drew to a close, the theater's curtains parted to reveal the impressive Todd-AO presentation. Generally, Todd kept process shots to a minimum. Filming took place on at least seven back lots and in some 140 locations (including Iraq and Afghanistan). In Bangkok, Todd borrowed the royal barge belonging to his friend the king of Thailand for a day's shooting. *Oklahoma!*, the first film to use the Todd-AO process, had to shoot a separate 35 mm version for theaters not equipped with Todd-AO projectors and the specially sized curved screens. To circumvent this, Todd had two simultaneous versions shot using two identical Todd-AO cameras side by side, one running at 30 fps for the 70 mm version, and the other running at 24 fps for the 35 mm reduction print. The iconic hot air balloon never appeared in the original novel, but Jules Verne was not the showman Michael Todd was. Todd insisted that he had created a "show," complete with an intermission and entr'acte, rather than a movie. At his insistence, theaters reserved seats, passed out playbills, and banned the sale of popcorn.

DISTRIBUTION: As part of a distribution deal, negotiated near postproduction, UA gave Todd $4 million for 10 percent, and a friend of Todd's got 1.8 percent for a $250,000 emergency loan when money ran out during the western sequence that Todd himself had directed. UA lost control of the film to Todd's widow, Elizabeth Taylor, after the final CBS-TV airing. In 1983 Warner Bros. acquired the rights from Taylor and released the film theatrically in a reedited 143-minute version, and later on video. —*Bob Canning*

THE TEN COMMANDMENTS
Paramount, 1956

ALL-RELEASE EQUIVALENT 2005 $s
(Unadjusted $s) in Millions of $s

Domestic Box Office Revenues . . . . **$829.2**/($89.1)
Production Cost . . . . **$95.3**/($13.3)
Principal Photography . . . . **160** days estimated
10/14/1954–12/3/1954 (Egyptian unit)
3/28/1955–8/13/1955 (Hollywood unit)

Running Time . . . . 220 minutes
19,994 feet
24 reels

MPAA Rating . . . . not rated

Director . . . . Cecill B. DeMille

Producer . . . . Cecil B. DeMille

Production Company . . . . Motion Picture Associates

Story by . . . . Based on *Prince of Egypt* by
Dorothy Clark Wilson, *Pillar of Fire* by the Rev. J. H. Ingraham, and *On Eagle's Wings* by the Rev. G. E. Southon, in accordance with the Holy Scriptures

Screenplay by . . . . Aeneas MacKenzie, Jesse L. Lasky Jr., Jack Gariss, Fredric M. Frank

Cast . . . . Aeneas MacKenzie, Jesse L. Lasky Jr., Jack Gariss, Fredric M. Frank

Filming Locations . . . . . . Egypt and Paramount Studios, Los Angeles, CA; Locations in Egypt included Beni Yousaff, near Cairo; Aswan near the Nile River; St. Catherine's Monastery; Abu Ruwash, Luxor, and Kharga

Genre . . . . Biblical Epic

Format . . . . Color (Technicolor)

Initial Release . . . . 11/8/1956 premiere (New York)

Rerelease . . . . 1966, 1972, 1990 (restored print)

STANDING THE TEST OF TIME

ACADEMY AWARD Oscar Nominations and Wins

Best Motion Picture: Cecil B. DeMille, Producer

Art Direction/Set Decoration: Hal Pereria, Walter, H. Tyler, Albert Nozaki/Samuel M. Comer, Ray Moyer

Cinematography: Loyal Griggs

Costume Design: Edith Head, Ralph Jester, John Jensen, Dorothy Jeakins, Arnold Friberg

Film Editing: Anne Bauchens

Sound Recording: Paramount Studio Sound Department, Loren L. Ryder, Sound Director

*SPECIAL EFFECTS: John Fulton

OSCAR TOTALS   Nominations **7**   *Wins 1

AFI 100 YEARS 100 MOVIES SELECTION
2007 0   1997 0

TOP 300 FILMS POSITION . . . . #5
All-Release Domestic Box Office in Equivalent 2005 $s

National Film Preservation Board Selection 1999

OTHER AWARDS Best Picture Wins

	Year
Golden Globes	none
New York Film Critics	none
National Board of Review	none
Film Daily Critics	none

Our intention was . . . to be worthy of the Divinely inspired story created three thousand years ago—the five Books of Moses.

—Cecil B. DeMille

PLOT: Raised as an Egyptian prince, Moses is eventually banished before learning that he is a Jew and that he has a divine mission. On the orders of God, he leads his people out of bondage seeking the promised land.

PRODUCTION: After the box office success of *Samson and Delilah* in 1949, Cecil B. DeMille decided to remake his 1923 biblical epic, *The Ten Commandments*. DeMille jettisoned the "modern story" from the silent version in favor of an expanded narrative of the life of Moses, which is not detailed in the Bible. DeMille and his writers filled the missing narrative with elements of sex, intrigue, and spectacle that added box office appeal. Work on the script went on for three years and involved extensive research, employing a team of scholars and historians. Chief researcher Henry Noerdlinger's 1956 book said they studied 950 books, 984 periodicals, 1,286 clippings, and 2,964 photographs, and consulted libraries all over the world. DeMille was able to realize his dream of filming in the original Middle Eastern locations but still used designs from the 1923 film. The sets in Egypt took more than six months to construct. *The Ten Commandments* was shot in Technicolor and Paramount's wide-screen VistaVision. Charlton Heston, under contract to DeMille for three pictures, received $2,000 a week, with his ten-week guarantee upped to twenty-five weeks. Heston agreed to work for free after twenty-five weeks if still needed. On the recommendation of Paramount's casting department, DeMille went to Broadway to see Yul Brynner onstage in *The King and I* and offered him the role of Rameses. That delayed production two years, as the stage producers would not release Brynner before 1955. Brynner received $7,500 a week for a ten-week guarantee. Edward G. Robinson was cast, even though his career had stumbled after he testified before Congress during the 1950s Red scare. Production began in Egypt in October 1954 with DeMille and a crew of eighty Hollywood technicians. The desert heat was so intense that each day the film negative was packed in ice and immediately flown back to Los Angeles, where it was developed and flown back to Egypt so DeMille could view dailies. The movie used more than 7,000 extras (the most ever as of that date) and about 5,000 animals. While shooting at the Gates of Tanis set, near Giza, DeMille suffered a heart attack. He recovered sufficiently to continue, but the Egyptian shoot was cut short. Production resumed at the Paramount studio in Hollywood four months later. For the scene of the parting of the Red Sea, supervised by John P. Fulton (who also did effects for the 1923 version), there were two water tanks covering a 300-by-300-foot square area of the Paramount back lot and part of the RKO back lot. At the critical moment 360,000 gallons of water was poured out in two minutes. Then the film was run backward and the actors were superimposed over the shots of the water.

DISTRIBUTION: Critical reaction to *The Ten Commandments* was mixed. However, the public flocked to see it, first in special reserved-seat road show engagements at higher than normal prices, then in neighborhood theaters. It grossed its first $60 million playing in only eighty theaters. It played at the Criterion in New York City for seventy weeks. Beyond theatrical reissues, it became a staple of network television at Easter time. —*Robert S. Birchard*

GIANT

Warner Bros., 1956

ALL-RELEASE EQUIVALENT 2005 $s

(Unadjusted $s) in Millions of $s

Domestic Box Office Revenues	**$322.2**/($31.3)
Production Cost	**$35.9**/($5.0)
Principal Photography	145 days
	5/21/1955–10/12/1955

Director	George Stevens
Producer	George Stevens, Henry Ginsberg
Production Company	Warner Bros.
Story by	Based on the 1952 novel by Edna Ferber
Screenplay by	Fred Guiol, Ivan Moffat
Cast	Elizabeth Taylor, Rock Hudson, James Dean
Filming Locations	Charlottesville and Keswick, VA; Marfa and Valentine, TX; Lockheed Air Terminal (Burbank Airport) and Warner Bros. Studio, Burbank, CA
Genre	Western
Format	Color (WarnerColor)
Initial Release	10/10/1956 premiere, Roxy Theater (New York); 10/17/1956 premiere, Grauman's Chinese Theatre (Los Angeles); 11/24/1956 general release
Rerelease	1963, 1970, 1996 (limited)
Running Time	201 minutes
MPAA Rating	not rated

STANDING THE TEST OF TIME

ACADEMY AWARD Oscar Nominations and Wins

Best Motion Picture: George Stevens and Henry Ginsberg, Producers

Actor: James Dean

Actor: Rock Hudson

Actress in a Supporting Role: Mercedes McCambridge

Art Direction/Set Decoration: Boris Leven/Ralph S. Hurst

Costume Design: Moss Mabry, Marjorie Best

*DIRECTING: George Stevens

Film Editing: William Hornbeck, Philip W. Anderson, Fred Bohanan

Music (Music Score of a Dramatic or Comedy Picture): Dimitri Tiomkin

Writing (Screenplay – Adapted): Fred Guiol, Ivan Moffat

OSCAR TOTALS Nominations **10** *Wins 1

AFI 100 YEARS 100 MOVIES SELECTION
2007 0   1997 . . . #82

TOP 300 FILMS POSITION . . . . #91
All-Release Domestic Box Office in Equivalent 2005 $s

National Film Preservation Board Selection 2005

OTHER AWARDS Best Picture Wins

	Year
Golden Globes	none
New York Film Critics	none
National Board of Review	none
Film Daily Critics	none

He loved the idea of telling a story . . . and, in Giant, *he saw an opportunity to have a big canvas and deal with a lot of themes that were interesting to him.*

—George Stevens Jr., son of director George Stevens

PLOT: On the vast southwestern Texas plains, two generations of the wealthy cattle-ranching Benedict family cope with household discord, conflicting ideals, racial intolerance, and the sudden, life-changing discovery of oil on their land.

PRODUCTION: Texans hated the novel *Giant*. Edna Ferber's 1952 best seller took aim at the Lone Star State's nouveau riche oil barons, their colorful excesses, and their cavalier exploitation of both the land and the underprivileged laborers who worked it. Upon its publication, one Houston critic suggested that, should its author ever set foot in Texas again (Ferber had ventured forth to gather research), she should be met with a "necktie party." Director George Stevens (*A Place in the Sun*, *Shane*) saw Ferber's book as an opportunity to focus on the subject he loved best: the American people. With a viable screenplay from Fred Guiol and Ivan Moffat (collaborators with Stevens on both *A Place in the Sun* and *Shane*), the package was sold to Warner Bros. and initially budgeted at $1,850,000 (later revised to $2,549,000). Texas was included for on-location shooting. "The story's so hot, and Texans object so hotly, we'll have to shoot it with a telephoto lens, across the border, from Oklahoma," Stevens quipped. For the principal leads, Stevens opted for a young cast that could be "aged" with makeup as the story progressed. Elizabeth Taylor, twenty-three, was signed at $175,000 for fourteen weeks; Rock Hudson, twenty-nine, was borrowed from Universal at $100,000 for ten weeks; and a charismatic Actors Studio newcomer, James Dean, twenty-four, was signed at $1,500 a week with a ten-week guarantee. Exterior location shooting began on May 21, 1955, at the Belmont estate and Keswick railway depot near Charlottesville, Virginia, with both locations doubling for Maryland. On June 6, the filmmakers came to Marfa and Valentine, Texas, shooting for 70 days on the Worth Evans Ranch and nearby locations. The towering Gothic façade of the Benedict mansion was built at Warner Bros. and shipped via six railway flatcars to Texas. Rather than bar the curious from his set, Stevens welcomed the skeptical Texas citizenry, predicting (correctly) that they could become goodwill ambassadors for his film. Scores of locals flocked to the site to watch the daily activity and to participate in an outdoor barbecue sequence. From Texas, the production returned to Warner Bros. for the remaining interiors. *Giant* wrapped principal photography on October 12, 1955—to the relief of studio head Jack Warner, who was seething over its lengthy shooting schedule (which came in 44 days past its end date) and alarming budget escalations (the final cost was a stunning $5 million).

DISTRIBUTION: Jack Warner's distress was understandable. On September 30, just days after completing his scenes, James Dean was dead—killed when his Porsche Spyder collided with another vehicle near Cholame, California. Stevens's yearlong task of editing 860,000 feet of film sailed past two expected 1956 delivery dates—February 12 and May 7. And, despite Warner's plea for a two-hour run time, the final film ran 3 hours 20 minutes. The anguish was worth it. Texans may have dismissed Ferber's novel, but they—along with the rest of America—flocked to Stevens's movie. Its initial release generated $12 million in North American box office rentals, becoming, at the time, the most successful picture in Warner Bros.' history in unadjusted dollars and number three in 2005 dollars, just after *This Is the Army* (1943) and *Sergeant York* (1941). *—Douglas Burns*

THE THREE FACES OF EVE
20th Century-Fox, 1957

ALL-RELEASE EQUIVALENT 2005 $s

(Unadjusted $s) in Millions of $s

Domestic Box Office Revenues. . . . . **$32.2**/($3.1)
Production Cost . . . . **$12.2**/($1.8)
Principal Photography. . . . .**31** days
2/5/1957–3/25/1957

Director . . . . Nunnally Johnson
Producer . . . . Nunnally Johnson
Production Company. . . . 20th Century-Fox Film Corp.
Story by . . . . Based on a 17 page article first published in the *Journal of Abnormal and Social Psychology* in 1954 and later in a book published in 1957 by Corbett H. Thigpen, M.D., and Hervey M. Cleckley, M.D.
Screenplay by . . . . Nunnally Johnson
Cast . . . . Joanne Woodward, David Wayne, Lee J. Cobb
Filming Locations . . . . . . Some location exterior shots in Savannah, GA, and the Medical College of Georgia in Augusta, GA
Genre. . . . . Drama
Format. . . . . B&W
Initial Release . . . . 9/18/57 premiere, Miller Theater (Augusta, GA)

Rerelease. . . . . none
Running Time . . . . 91 minutes
MPAA Rating . . . . not rated

STANDING THE TEST OF TIME

ACADEMY AWARD Oscar Nominations and Wins

*ACTRESS: Joanne Woodward

OSCAR TOTALS   Nominations **1**   *Wins **1**

AFI 100 YEARS 100 MOVIES SELECTION
2007 0   1997 0

TOP 300 FILMS POSITION . . . . .none
All-Release Domestic Box Office in Equivalent 2005 $s

National Film Preservation Board Selection. . . .none

OTHER AWARDS Best Picture Wins

	Year
Golden Globes	none
New York Film Critics.	none
National Board of Review	none
Film Daily Critics	none

Again, as in so many of my films, I was given an off-beat subject, a psychological subject. I read the script thoroughly, and oddly enough I backed out of treating each episode with a different photographic technique. I told Nunnally Johnson that Joanne Woodward must play the whole thing, that we couldn't help her with lighting.

—Stanley Cortez, cinematographer

PLOT: A quiet southern housewife is diagnosed with multiple personality disorder and studied by a therapist who attempts to help her.

PRODUCTION: Nunnally Johnson brought the story to Fox before the book was published, since he had heard about the actual case history of the Georgia housewife Christine "Chris" Costner-Sizemore, who had developed split personality disorder as a child when confronted with death in her family and other traumatic incidents. Her case was documented by her doctors, Corbett Thigpen and Hervey Cleckley. The doctors kept exhaustive notes and video footage of the real "Eve," and both Johnson and Joanne Woodward used this material during preproduction. Costner-Sizemore was paid approximately $7,000, while Dr. Corbett Thigpen, to whom Costner-Sizemore had signed over all rights to her story, received approximately $1 million. The role of Eve was originally offered to Judy Garland, who was so excited about it she told Johnson they must cut their wrists and mingle their blood as a promise that she'd get the part. Shortly after, Garland backed out, and Johnson found Woodward, who was known from a few TV appearances. Orson Welles, after reading the script, declared that whoever played Eve would get an Oscar. Most of the filming took place over two months in the spring of 1957 and came in under budget. The costume designer, Renié (*Cleopatra*), created "transition dresses" to help Woodward as she slipped between Eve's three different personalities. For example, when she became Eve Black, the sultry, seductive personality, the same dress was made slightly tighter and more revealing. These were subtle costume changes that were mainly for the benefit of Woodward. Johnson claimed that Woodward was incredibly easy to direct and that he mainly just stayed out of the actress's way. *The Three Faces of Eve* was the first movie that cinematographer Stanley Cortez shot in CinemaScope.

DISTRIBUTION: Johnson wanted the film to appear realistic, almost like a documentary. To add authenticity, he decided to have an introduction, delivered to the audience, from "distinguished journalist and commentator" Alistair Cooke, to add an air of reality. Johnson wrote Cook's lines, including his frequent voice-overs, during postproduction. Johnson feuded with Fox's head of production, Buddy Adler, who wanted to have a title song for the film—a practice that was popular during the time. Johnson refused, and eventually got Adler to relent. Although in the budget range of 1950s movies such as *East of Eden* (1955) and *Peyton Place* (1957), *The Three Faces of Eve* failed to live up to those movies at the box office. It has, however, increased in popularity with time. It also marks the first time that multiple personality disorder was depicted in film. Years later, Woodward went on to play the doctor in the 1976 TV movie *Sybil*, about multiple personality disorder. Costner-Sizemore, prevented from revealing her identity at the time, didn't like the book or movie, saying they were unrealistic. For one thing, she actually had more than 20 multiple personalities, not just three. She also felt that the portrayal by her therapists exploited her. In 1989 she sued to recover legal rights to her own life story and won. —*Dina Gachman*

THE BRIDGE ON THE RIVER KWAI
Columbia, 1957

ALL-RELEASE EQUIVALENT 2005 $s
(Unadjusted $s) in Millions of $s

Domestic Box Office Revenues........ **$362.3**/($38.2)
Production Cost .... **$20.2**/($2.9)
Principal Photography........... **165** days estimated
11/26/1956–5/11/1957

Director............... David Lean
Producer.............. Sam Spiegel
Production Company.... Horizon Pictures
Story by.............. Based on the novel by Pierre Boulle
Screenplay by......... Pierre Boulle, Carl Foreman, Michael Wilson
Cast................. William Holden, Alec Guinness, Jack Hawkins
Filming Locations ...... Sri Lanka
Genre................. War
Format............... Color (Technicolor)
Initial Release......... 10/2/1957 world premiere (London); 12/18/1957 U.S. premiere, Palace Theater (New York)
Rerelease 1964
Running Time......... 161 minutes
MPAA Rating .... not rated

STANDING THE TEST OF TIME

ACADEMY AWARD Oscar Nominations and Wins
***BEST MOTION PICTURE:** Sam Spiegel, Producer
***ACTOR IN A LEADING ROLE:** Alec Guinness
Actor in a Supporting Role: Sessue Hayakawa
***CINEMATOGRAPHY:** Jack Hildyard
***DIRECTING:** David Lean
***FILM EDITING:** Peter Taylor
***MUSIC** (Scoring): Malcolm Arnold
***WRITING** (Screenplay – based on material from another medium): Pierre Boulle, Carl Foreman, Michael Wilson

OSCAR TOTALS   Nominations **8**   *Wins **7**

AFI 100 YEARS 100 MOVIES SELECTION
2007... #36   1997... #13
TOP 300 FILMS POSITION .... **#61**
All-Release Domestic Box Office in Equivalent 2005 $s

National Film Preservation Board Selection.... 1997

OTHER AWARDS Best Picture Wins
	Year
Golden Globes	1958
New York Film Critics.......................	1957
National Board of Review...................	1957
Film Daily Critics.........................	none

I swore I would never work for Columbia again. A year later I was on a plane to Ceylon to make Bridge on the River Kwai—*for Columbia!*

—William Holden

PLOT: When prisoners in a World War II Japanese POW camp are forced to construct a strategic railway bridge in Burma, the British colonel leading the men envisions an exemplary structure—oblivious to the fact that he is aiding the enemy.

PRODUCTION: Published in France in 1952, Pierre Boulle's popular novel *Le pont de la rivière Kwai* caught the eye of Carl Foreman, the Oscar-nominated American screenwriter (*High Noon*) living in exile in London after being blacklisted in Hollywood. Foreman, who wrote under pseudonyms, optioned the book and first approached Alexander Korda, who declined to produce because the British colonel "was either insane or a traitor." Then came a chance meeting with Sam Spiegel, who agreed and cut a deal with Columbia Pictures. After considering John Ford, Howard Hawks, and others, Spiegel decided on Englishman David Lean as director. Lean promptly did an extensive rewrite. Calder Willingham (*Paths of Glory*) also took an unsuccessful stab at the script before Spiegel assigned it to another blacklisted writer, Michael Wilson (*A Place in the Sun.*) Construction on the film's centerpiece—the bridge—was nearing completion on the island of Ceylon (now Sri Lanka), even before Spiegel had a cast. Laurence Olivier said no to the role of Colonel Nicholson. Alec Guinness likewise declined—he was committed to a play, and had clashed with Lean on *Oliver Twist* nine years earlier. Spiegel persisted, and Guinness finally said yes. Spiegel wanted Humphrey Bogart, but Columbia mogul Harry Cohn nixed that. Cary Grant was considered, but Spiegel feared audiences would associate Grant with romantic comedy. With the clock ticking, William Holden said yes. He received $300,000 plus 10 percent of the gross receipts, payable at a maximum sum of $50,000 per year—an extremely lucrative deal for Holden. Jungle sequences were shot in the Ceylon interior, at Kitulaga. The prison camp set was seven miles from the capital city, Colombo. The final sequence was the climactic scene of the film—the blowing up of the bridge as a Japanese troop train crosses. But as Lean's multiple cameras began rolling and the train headed across the structure, there was no detonation. A crewmember had forgotten to alert the explosives experts to proceed. The crewless train toppled off the rails after striking an electrical generator. Heavy-duty jacks were brought in to right the train, and a second attempt went off without a hitch. Nerves were frayed once again when this crucial footage was lost en route to London. Luckily, it was discovered two weeks later at the airport in Cairo, Egypt.

DISTRIBUTION: *The Bridge on the River Kwai* made its U.S. debut on December 18, 1957. Audiences flocked to Lean's "war is insanity" epic in droves, and the film made over $15 million in rentals in its initial domestic theatrical run. After its eight Oscar nominations and Best Picture win, it played through 1958. Although the *Variety* review noted that author Boulle, who spoke no English, did an "excellent job of screenwriting," the reality was the movie was written by blacklisted writers Michael Wilson and Carl Foreman. On December 11, 1984, the Academy Board of Governors voted posthumous Oscars to Wilson and Foreman, and their screenwriting credit was restored by the WGA in 2000. It is number eleven on the BFI list of the top 100 British films of the twentieth century. —*Douglas Burns*

VERTIGO

Paramount, 1958

ALL-RELEASE EQUIVALENT 2005 $s

(Unadjusted $s) in Millions of $s

Domestic Box Office Revenues . . . . **$78.8**/($14.0)
Production Cost . . . . **$16.8**/($2.5)
Principal Photography . . . . **68** days estimated
9/30/1957–12/19/1957

Director	Alfred Hitchcock
Producer	Alfred Hitchcock
Production Company	Alfred J. Hitchcock Productions, Inc., Paramount Pictures
Story by	Pierre Boileau, Thomas Narcejac from their novel *D'Entre les Morts*
Screenplay by	Alec Coppel, Samuel Taylor
Cast	James Stewart, Kim Novak
Filming Locations	Northern California: San Francisco, Big Basin Redwoods State Park, Big Basin, Pebble Beach, San Juan Bautista; Los Angeles: Paramount Studios 16 days on location, 60 days in studio excluding retakes
Genre	Thriller
Format	Color (Technicolor)
Initial Release	5/9/1958 world premiere (San Francisco); 5/28/1958 general release
Rerelease	1983, 1996
Running Time	120 minutes
MPAA Rating	not rated

STANDING THE TEST OF TIME

ACADEMY AWARD Oscar Nominations and Wins

Art Direction/Set Decoration: Hal Pereira, Henry Bumstead/Sam Comer, Frank McKelvy

Sound: Paramount Studio Sound Dept., George Dutton, Sound Director

OSCAR TOTALS   Nominations **2**   *Wins **0**

AFI 100 YEARS 100 MOVIES SELECTION
2007 . . . . #9   1997 . . . #61

TOP 300 FILMS POSITION . . . . none
All-Release Domestic Box Office in Equivalent 2005 $s

National Film Preservation Board Selection 1989

OTHER AWARDS Best Picture Wins

	Year
Golden Globes	none
New York Film Critics	none
National Board of Review	none
Film Daily Critics	none

Alarmingly close to allegorical autobiography . . . Hitchcock seems [to be] the great exponent of male sadism.

—John Russell Taylor, *The Life and Times of Alfred Hitchcock*

PLOT: Still in love with a woman who he believes committed suicide, a detective hired to protect another woman meets his lover's look-alike, obsessively molds her into the reincarnation of his lover, and discovers she took part in the murder.

PRODUCTION: Paramount paid $25,275 for the French novel *D'entre les morts (From Among the Dead)*, by Pierre Boileau and Thomas Narcejac. Pulitzer Prize–winning playwright Maxwell Anderson was assigned to do the screen adaptation. When the adaptation and his suggested title, *Illicit Darkening*, proved to be unusable, Hitchcock hired Angus MacPhail. Due to MacPhail's alcoholism, he quit after writing only fifteen pages. Alec Coppel made many improvements on the Anderson version, but Hitchcock was still not satisfied. He hired Samuel Taylor at a fee of $20,000 per week for six weeks to rewrite the Coppel script. Filming was delayed when Hitchcock had to undergo gallbladder surgery. Vera Miles, who was set to play the role of Madeline/Judy, became pregnant, so he turned to Kim Novak. Novak, however, held out for more money from Columbia (her home studio). In the end Paramount paid $250,000 for her to do *Vertigo* and the next picture with Jimmy Stewart. Eventually, Novak's weekly salary went from $1,250 to $2,750. Hitchcock molded her into the character he wanted, advising her on what to wear and how to speak, in a life-imitating-art fashion. Composer Bernard Herrmann believed that Hitchcock should have set the film in a steamy, sensual city such as New Orleans and that Scottie should have been played by Charles Boyer rather than Stewart. But what better location than San Francisco, a city full of hills, for a film about vertigo? What also distinguishes the movie is the way Stewart's everyman persona becomes all the more disconcerting when his long-suppressed lustful desires manifest themselves. Oscar-winning composers Jay Livingston and Ray Evans ("Que Sera Sera") wrote a title song that was recorded by Billy Eckstine, but Hitchcock found it inappropriate and cut it from the film. The "vertigo effect" (sometimes called "contra-zoom" or "trombone shot") was created by uncredited second-unit cameraman Irmin Roberts with a simultaneous combination of zooming in and tracking backward. A stuntman filmed the scene using an upside-down model of the bell tower staircase when several on-set attempts did not work. The cost for just a couple of seconds of screen-time was $19,000. All of the interiors and some of the exteriors were re-created in the studio. For example, although 900 Lombard (Scottie's residence) is a real exterior, all of the dialogue shot at the house's door was done on a soundstage.

DISTRIBUTION: *Vertigo* premiered at San Francisco's Stage Door Theatre on May 9, 1958. It opened at New York's Capitol Theatre and in L.A. at the Paramount on May 28 to unenthusiastic critical response (typical was *Time* magazine's: " . . . [a] Hitchcock-and-bull story"). It cost $2,479,000 (not including Hitchcock's or Stewart's salaries or their undisclosed percentage of the film's grosses) and made $2.8 million in domestic rentals. Of the budget, Paramount put up $2,004,722.49, and Hitchcock Productions paid $443,307. Hitchcock's contract gave Paramount a seven-year lease on five of his films, after which rights would revert to Hitchcock. There was another release after the rights reverted to Hitchcock in the late 1960s through Universal and then a sale to TV. Hitchcock then took it out of circulation until a major 1983–84 Hitchcock re-release program, followed by a 1996 restoration. —*Bob Canning*

AUNTIE MAME
Warner Bros., 1958

ALL-RELEASE EQUIVALENT 2005 $s
(Unadjusted $s) in Millions of $s

Domestic Box Office Revenues........**$180.8**/($18.3)
Production Cost ....**$21.8**/($3.2)
Principal Photography............**70** days estimated
4/1/1958–June 1958

Director .... Morton daCosta

Producer .... Morton daCosta

Production Company .... Warner Bros. Pictures

Story by .... Jerome Lawrence and Robert E. Lee (from their stage adaptation of Patrick Dennis's novel)

Screenplay by .... Betty Comden, Adolph Green

Cast .... Rosalind Russell, Forrest Tucker, Coral Browne, Fred Clark, Roger Smith, Patric Knowles, Peggy Cass

Filming Locations ...... 100 percent in Warner Bros. Studios, Burbank, CA

Genre .... Comedy

Format .... Color (Technicolor)

Initial Release .... 11/27/1958 premiere; 12/27/1958 general release

Rerelease .... none

Running Time .... 143 minutes

MPAA Rating .... not rated

STANDING THE TEST OF TIME

ACADEMY AWARD Oscar Nominations and Wins

Best Motion Picture: Warner Bros.

Actress: Rosalind Russell

Actress in a Supporting Role: Peggy Cass

Art Direction/Set Decoration: Malcolm Bert, George James Hopkins

Cinematography (Color): Harry Stradling Sr.

Film Editing: William Ziegler

OSCAR TOTALS   Nominations **6**   *Wins 0

AFI 100 YEARS 100 MOVIES SELECTION
2007 0   1997 0

TOP 300 FILMS POSITION ....none
All-Release Domestic Box Office in Equivalent 2005 $s

National Film Preservation Board Selection .... none

OTHER AWARDS Best Picture Wins

	Year
Golden Globes	none
New York Film Critics	none
National Board of Review	none
Film Daily Critics	none

The stage play was more like a movie script in its pile-up of pictorial business and its multiplicity of scenes. The invitation to expansion was hand-engraved in the play.

—Bosley Crowther, *New York Times*

PLOT: During the Depression, an orphan goes to live with his father's sister. The boy experiences many madcap adventures thanks to his aunt's unconventional lifestyle, but conflicts arise with the straitlaced trustee of his father's will.

PRODUCTION: In the titular role of Mame Dennis, Rosalind Russell became the toast of Broadway, which served to reenergize her above-the-title name recognition, at least on the Great White Way. (Based solely on her ecstatic out-of-town reviews in Washington, D.C., she was invited to dine alone at the White House with President and Mrs. Dwight Eisenhower.) But the question remained: did her name still ring Hollywood's box office chimes? Eve Arden was under contract to Warner Bros. and had been considered for the lead role, after wowing audiences and critics in a West Coast tour of the play. However, Russell was also a principal investor in the show (with a 13.43 percent share), so she eventually edged Arden out. Vivian Vance (Ethel Mertz on *I Love Lucy*) auditioned for the part of Mame's boozy best friend, Vera Charles, but the part eventually went to British stage actress Coral Browne. Filming began on Warner's Soundstage 18 on April 1, 1958. The picture's nickname could have been "Auntie Maim." Browne, who flew in from London on the second day of shooting, went directly to the makeup department to have her dark brown tresses bleached platinum blond so as to stand out more distinctly from Russell, who had black hair. Unfortunately, most of Browne's hair fell out in clumps overnight, and she reported for work the next day almost completely bald. Costume designer Orry-Kelly quickly came up with a solution: a turban. (Ironically, there is an exchange in the play/movie in which Vera tells Mame, "You should keep your hair natural like mine," and Mame replies, "If I kept my hair natural like yours, I'd be bald.") On June 10, in a party scene in which the guests are all drinking a fiery cocktail called a "Flaming Mame," Russell was required to give actor Willard Waterman a friendly slap on the back. This caused the burning alcohol-Sterno concoction in his cup to spill onto his hand, blistering him and burning a hole in the carpet and the dress of actress Lee Patrick, who was seated in front of him. The Oscar nomination for art/set direction was well earned, because Russell's character remodeled her Beekman Place duplex as often as her hairdos and costumes, and the set had to be dressed and decorated six times, once to include goldfish swimming inside a formidable light fixture hanging from the hallway ceiling. For the episodic scene changes, first-time director Morton DaCosta had Warner electrician Frank Flanagan work out a series of unique fadeouts whereby only Russell's face was left in view. Flanagan's process was done on the spot, as the lights were faded out with each episode break. The technique became known as the "Flanagan fade."

DISTRIBUTION: As of the end of the fiscal year in August 1958, Warner Bros. was in dire financial straits, showing a net loss of $1,023,808, owing to a series of bombs. The success of *Auntie Mame,* with a net profit of $3.4 million on worldwide rentals of $9.5 million, contributed to the studio's $15,875,230 net profit by August 1959. In 1966 it inspired *Mame,* a stage musical with a score by Jerry Herman, which was a hit. That was followed by the 1974 film remake starring Lucille Ball, which was a flop. —*Bob Canning*

SOME LIKE IT HOT
United Artists, 1959

ALL-RELEASE EQUIVALENT 2005 $s

(Unadjusted $s) in Millions of $s

Domestic Box Office Revenues . . . . **$157.1**/($16.7)
Production Cost . . . .**$18.7**/($2.8)
Principal Photography . . . .**69** days estimated
8/4/1958–11/6/1958

Director . . . . Billy Wilder

Producer . . . . Billy Wilder

Production Company . . . . Ashton Productions, The Mirisch Company

Story by . . . . Based on the German film *Fanfaren der Liebe*, story by Robert Thoeren and Michael Logan

Screenplay by . . . . Billy Wilder, I. A. L. Diamond

Cast . . . . Marilyn Monroe, Tony Curtis, Jack Lemmon, George Raft, Edward G. Robinson Jr.

Filming Locations . . . . . . On location in San Diego, CA, and at The Goldwyn Studio in Los Angeles, CA

Genre . . . . Comedy

Format . . . . B&W

Initial Release . . . . December 1958 world premiere; 3/29/1959 general release

Rerelease . . . . none

Running Time . . . . 123 minutes

MPAA Rating . . . . not rated

STANDING THE TEST OF TIME

ACADEMY AWARD Oscar Nominations and Wins

Actor: Jack Lemmon

Art Direction/Set Decoration: Ted Haworth/ Edward G. Boyle

Cinematography (B&W): Charles Lang Jr.

***COSTUME DESIGN** (B&W): Orry-Kelly

Directing: Billy Wilder

Writing (Screenplay – based on material from another medium): Billy Wilder I. A. L. Diamond

OSCAR TOTALS   Nominations **6**   *Wins 1

AFI 100 YEARS 100 MOVIES SELECTION
2007 . . . #22   1997 . . . #14

TOP 300 FILMS POSITION .none
All-Release Domestic Box Office in Equivalent 2005 $s

National Film Preservation Board Selection 1989

OTHER AWARDS Best Picture Wins

	Year
Golden Globes	1960
New York Film Critics	none
National Board of Review	none
Film Daily Critics	none

You mean you're going to have machine guns, bullets, dead bodies—and then gags?
You can't make it work, Billy. Blood and jokes do not mix.

—David O. Selznick, as told by Billy Wilder

PLOT: Two down-on-their-luck musicians flee Prohibition-era Chicago after witnessing the St. Valentine's Day massacre. To hide, they dress in drag and join an all-girls jazz band on a trip to Florida, where they both fall for the beautiful lead singer.

PRODUCTION: Screenwriter Robert Thoeren, an old friend of Billy Wilder's from Berlin, suggested Wilder remake the German musical *Fanfaren der Liebe* (*Fanfares of Love,* 1951), as his next project after the serious *Witness for the Prosecution*. While Wilder and co-writer I. A. L. Diamond believed the original film was too Germanic, its premise of musicians willing to disguise themselves as women to earn a living inspired them. But in 1950s America, a drag comedy by itself likely would have been too controversial. Wilder's idea to make the musicians on the run from the mob proved to be the ironclad foundation of the story. United Artists wanted Frank Sinatra and Anthony Perkins to star in the picture, but Sinatra stood Wilder up at a lunch meeting and Perkins had a previous commitment. After Tony Curtis and Jack Lemmon were cast, Wilder arranged for famous female impersonator Barbette to teach them how to act like women. Though his experience directing Marilyn Monroe in *The Seven Year Itch* was a nightmare, Wilder cast her after she sent him a conciliatory letter. Industry veterans called *Some Like It Hot* "Wilder's folly." Not only was the film's basic conception culturally contentious, but Marilyn Monroe's constant lateness and excessive absences (she was late on 29 days and called in sick for 13 days) cost the production $200,000. Her on-set antics brought Wilder to the brink of a nervous breakdown and contributed to his back problems. Monroe drank alcohol every day, couldn't remember her lines, and refused to listen to Wilder's direction unless her acting coach, Paula Strasberg (wife of acting teacher Lee Strasberg), approved it. When she objected to filming in black and white, Wilder's preference, Wilder fibbed that the women's makeup on Lemmon and Curtis looked too phony in color. Goldwyn Studios housed most of the film except the scenes at the Florida resort, which Wilder shot at the Victorian-era Hotel Coronado near San Diego. Wilder also reached back to his early days as a journalist and hired Matty Malneck, a violinist for the Paul Whiteman band, about which Wilder had written, to arrange the jazz tunes that Sugar Kane sang. When Tony Curtis felt that he needed to add an affectation to make his character, Shell Oil Jr., stand out from his other roles of Joe and Josephine, his mock imitation of a Cary Grant accent won Wilder's blessing. As usual, Wilder and Diamond wrote much of the film as it went along in production. The famous last line, an offhand remark by Diamond in a story session, served as a temporary substitute until they came up with something better. They never did.

DISTRIBUTION: Despite mixed reaction at some early previews, Wilder stuck by his cut of the film and eliminated only one scene. To build hype for the film, Marilyn Monroe's face was postered on the front cover of *Life*. Excitement for the film was fueled further by gossip about the star. Although the film opened to a slow start in March 1959, it picked up steam, ranking number three in domestic rentals of pictures released in 1959, despite receiving a B rating from the Legion of Decency. In 1972 David Merrick staged *Sugar* on Broadway, a musical adaptation. —*Michael Kogge*

THE NUN'S STORY
Warner Bros., 1959

ALL-RELEASE EQUIVALENT 2005 $s
(Unadjusted $s) in Millions of $s

Domestic Box Office Revenues . . . . **$121.5**/($12.9)
Production Cost . . . .**$23.5**/($3.5)
Principal Photography . . . .**100** days estimated
1/28/1958–6/30/1958

Director	Fred Zinnemann
Producer	Henry Blanke
Production Company	Warner Bros.
Story by	Based on the book by Kathryn Hulme
Screenplay by	Robert Anderson
Cast	Audrey Hepburn, Peter Finch, Dame Edith Evans, Dame Peggy Ashcroft
Filming Locations	Filmed on location in Brugge, Belgium; Democratic Republic of Congo; and in studio at Cinecittà Studios in Rome, Italy
Genre	Drama
Format	Color (Technicolor)
Initial Release	7/4/1959
Rerelease	none
Running Time	149 minutes
MPAA Rating	not rated

STANDING THE TEST OF TIME

ACADEMY AWARD Oscar Nominations and Wins

Best Motion Picture: Henry Blanke, Producer

Actress: Audrey Hepburn

Cinematography: Franz Planer

Directing: Fred Zinnemann

Film Editing: Walter Thompson

Music (Music Score of a Dramatic or Comedy Picture): Franz Waxman

Sound: Warner Bros. Studio Sound Dept., George R. Groves, Sound Director

Writing (Screenplay – based on material from another medium): Robert Anderson

OSCAR TOTALS   Nominations **8**   *Wins 0

AFI 100 YEARS 100 MOVIES SELECTION
2007 0   1997 0

TOP 300 FILMS POSITION . . . . none
All-Release Domestic Box Office in Equivalent 2005 $s

National Film Preservation Board Selection . . . . none

OTHER AWARDS Best Picture Wins

	Year
Golden Globes	none
New York Film Critics	none
National Board of Review	1959
Film Daily Critics	none

Whether one liked the picture or not is perhaps not important. The important thing was that I felt it would be wrong to try to influence the audience for or against the institution of religious life. That's why in the end, when the nun left the convent, I had no music, no comment of any sort.

—Fred Zinnemann

PLOT: The story of a nun whose faith and vows are tested during her time working in the Belgian Congo and upon the outbreak of World War II.

PRODUCTION: In 1956 Kathryn C. Hulme wrote *The Nun's Story,* based on the experiences of her best friend, Marie-Louise Habets, a Belgian nurse and an ex-nun she had met in 1945 at camp for displaced persons in Germany. The book became a best seller and was translated into twelve languages. Gary Cooper sent the book to director Fred Zinnemann, who was immediately interested. However, the studios thought no one would want to see a film about a nun, and that it might upset the Catholic Church. Zinnemann wanted Audrey Hepburn, one of the few major stars untainted by scandal. With Hepburn signed, Warner agreed to do the film. Zinnemann spent months preparing the cast and doing research. Hepburn spent so much time with Habets and Hulme people referred to them as the "3-H Club." Zinnemann, who was not Catholic, purposely cast non-Catholics in the film and also hired "vocational consultants" (Dominican and Jesuit priests) to avoid offending anyone. The logistics of filming in Europe and the Congo were challenging. The bishop of Bruges refused permission to shoot at Habets's Sisters of Charity convent in Ghent, but Warner negotiated the use of a similar French convent. Franz Planer's photography and Marjorie Best's costumes provided a good deal of atmosphere. During production, Hepburn ate only simple convent-type meals and would not look at herself in mirrors. She even asked to have a phonograph turned off because a nun wouldn't be allowed to listen to it. They shot in the Belgian Congo for two months. Food was flown in from Brussels twice a week. They spent four days with the British missionary Dr. Stanley Browne, shooting in his leper colony on the Congo River. Zinnemann planned an elaborate shot (involving three men sinking in quicksand at a cost of $40,000), but it was scrubbed when the river fell two feet overnight. Interiors were shot in Rome at the Cinecittà Studios Experimental Center. Art director Alexandre Trauner created a replica convent, Michelangelo's "Pietà," and other statues. They were forced to shoot around Hepburn, who had kidney stones, partly due to dehydration in the Congo. Real nuns were not allowed to be photographed, so they hired twenty dancers from the ballet corps of the Rome Opera, who were drilled by two Dominican nuns.

DISTRIBUTION: Warner Bros. felt the final cut was too long and downbeat, with too much detail of the nun's life. Composer Franz Waxman was upset because 80 percent of the music he recorded had been deleted by Zinnemann. This included music from the end because Zinnemann didn't want to impose any interpretation. Eventually all but 15 percent of the music was put back, though Zinnemann was allowed to have the silent ending (a first for Warner Bros.). The film opened at Radio City Music Hall and was one of the top films in 1959. Zinnemann and Hepburn both won New York Film Critics Circle awards, but *Ben-Hur*'s sweep of the Academy Awards (eleven wins out of twelve nominations) meant zero Oscar wins for the picture. The movie was Hepburn's most successful until *My Fair Lady* (1964). —*Hayley Taylor Block*

NORTH BY NORTHWEST
MGM, 1959

ALL-RELEASE EQUIVALENT 2005 $s
(Unadjusted $s) in Millions of $s

Domestic Box Office Revenues. . . . . **$125.1**/($13.3)
Production Cost . . . .**$29.2**/($4.3)
Principal Photography. . . . . **82** days estimated
8/27/1958–12/18/1958

Director . . . . Alfred Hitchcock

Producer . . . . Alfred Hitchcock

Production Company. . . . Metro-Goldwyn-Mayer Corp.

Story and
   Screenplay by . . . . Ernest Lehman

Cast . . . . Gary Grant, Eva Marie Saint,
James Mason, Jessie Royce
Landis, Leo G. Carroll

Filming Locations . . . . . . New York City; Glen Cove,
Long Island; Chicago; Rapid
City, SD; E. Bakersfield, CA; Los
Angeles, MGM Stage 5

Genre. . . . . Thriller

Format. . . . . Color (Technicolor)

Initial Release . . . . 7/17/1959 world premiere
(Chicago); 7/28/1959
general release

Rerelease . . . . 1999 UK and Germany only

Running Time . . . . 136 minutes

MPAA Rating . . . . not rated

STANDING THE TEST OF TIME

ACADEMY AWARD Oscar Nominations and Wins

Art Direction/Set Decoration (color): William A.
Horning, Robert Boyle, Merrill Pye/ Henry Grace,
Frank McKelvy

Film Editing: George Tomasini

Writing (Story and Screenplay – written directly for
the screen): Ernest Lehman

OSCAR TOTALS   Nominations **3**   *Wins 0

AFI 100 YEARS 100 MOVIES SELECTION
2007 . . . #55   1997 . . . #40

TOP 300 FILMS POSITION . . . . none
All-Release Domestic Box Office in Equivalent 2005 $s

National Film Preservation Board Selection. . . . 1995

OTHER AWARDS Best Picture Wins

	Year
Golden Globes	none
New York Film Critics.	none
National Board of Review.	none
Film Daily Critics	none

*A thriller so improbable that it becomes quite brilliant in evading
even the most fantastic of audience guesses.*
—Almar Haflidason, BBC

PLOT: A Manhattan ad exec, mistaken for a nonexistent spy, is kidnapped by enemy agents. His escape brings about a UN assassination and a cross-country chase that culminates on the face of Mt. Rushmore.

PRODUCTION: Scriptwriter Ernest Lehman, who was hired by Hitchcock to adapt the book *The Wreck of the Mary Deare* for the screen, found himself at an impasse and couldn't continue. Unperturbed, Hitchcock recalled a real-life case related to him by journalist Otis L. Guernsey Jr. in which some secretaries at a British embassy invented a nonexistent agent and successfully tricked the Germans into looking for him. Expanding on that idea, Hitchcock wanted to include the assassination of a foreign dignitary at the United Nations and a chase across Mt. Rushmore. Inspired, Lehman completed sixty-five pages, and with these Hitchcock was able to sell MGM on the project. It was the only film Hitchcock made for MGM. Jimmy Stewart had been mentioned for the lead (when the lead character was to be a salesman by profession), Yul Brynner for the lead villain, and Cyd Charisse for the femme fatale, but Cary Grant, James Mason, and Oscar winner Eva Marie Saint eventually landed the roles. The film was budgeted for $3,071,314. Filming at the United Nations was prohibited, but Hitchcock outwitted UN security by shooting the master shot of Grant, as Roger Thornhill, heading toward the building. The camera was hidden in a carpet cleaning truck across the street, and the real security guards are captured on film watching Grant as he walks across the courtyard. Hitchcock's modus operandi included molding his leading lady into his notion of the ideal woman for the film. In Saint's case, he instructed her to lower her voice, not to use her hands, and to look directly into Grant's eyes every time she spoke to him. When it came to clothes, Hitchcock's actresses always reflected his dictatorial sense of style. For this picture, he nixed virtually all of the costumes designed by MGM's wardrobe department, and instead took Saint to Bergdorf Goodman on Fifth Avenue, where he chose her outfits for the film directly off the models' backs. For the sequence in which Grant is chased across a cornfield by a crop duster, the swooping plane was shot from a ditch. Grant was subsequently photographed on a soundstage in a ditch in front of a process screen. When filming of the movie's finale, in which Grant and Saint are pursued by murderous villains against the backdrop of Mount Rushmore, was prevented by rangers for the Department of the Interior because they feared the desecration of a national monument, the set was reproduced in concrete at MGM with a 30-by-150-foot backdrop of the stone visage of the four presidents. Great care was taken by Hitchcock, the cast, and the crew so as not to appear disrespectful of the monument. The picture went five days over schedule and ran $1,273,896 over budget. Grant was paid $450,000 plus a percentage of the gross profits. He also received $5,000 for each day the film went over schedule (Saint was paid $2,000 per day) for a total of $315,000 in penalty fees for having to work nine weeks past the time his contract called for.

DISTRIBUTION: From its premiere at Radio City Music Hall in New York City, it was a big hit. It went on to be the fourth-biggest-grossing movie of 1959. —*Bob Canning*

BEN-HUR
MGM, 1959

ALL-RELEASE EQUIVALENT 2005 $s
(Unadjusted $s) in Millions of $s

Domestic Box Office Revenues........ **$754.3**/($85.8)
Production Cost .... **$106.7**/($15.9)
Principal Photography.......... **200** days estimated
5/20/1958–1/7/1959
Sound retakes 7/7/1959
Sound closed 8/17/1959

Director . . . . William Wyler
Producer . . . . Sam Zimbalist
Production Company. . . . Metro-Goldwyn-Mayer Corp.
Story by . . . . Based on the 1880 novel
Ben-Hur: A Tale of The Christ,
by General Lew Wallace
Screenplay by . . . . Karl Tunberg
Cast . . . . Charlton Heston, Jack Hawkins,
Haya Harareet, Stephen Boyd,
Hugh Griffith, Martha Scott,
Cathy O'Donnell, Sam Jaffe
Filming Locations . . . . . . Cinecittà Studios, Rome; MGM
Studios; and additional exterior
settings throughout Italy
Genre. . . . . Biblical Epic
Format. . . . . Color (Technicolor)
Initial Release . . . . 11/18/1959 70 mm wide-screen
premiere (New York);
11/24/1959 general release
Rerelease. . . . . 1969 (recut shorter version)
Running Time . . . . 217 minutes
MPAA Rating . . . . not rated

*Why don't you go after DeMille or somebody
like that? I've never done a spectacle,
that's not my style at all.*

—William Wyler to producer Sam Zimbalist

STANDING THE TEST OF TIME

ACADEMY AWARD Oscar Nominations and Wins

*BEST MOTION PICTURE: Sam Zimbalist,
Producer

*ACTOR: Charlton Heston

*ACTOR IN A SUPPORTING ROLE: Hugh Griffith

*ART DIRECTION/SET DECORATION: William
A. Horning, Edward Carfagno/Hugh Hunt

*CINEMATOGRAPHY: Robert L. Surtees

*COSTUME DESIGN: Elizabeth Haffenden

*DIRECTING: William Wyler

*FILM EDITING: Ralph E. Winters, John D. Dunning

*MUSIC (Music Score of a Dramatic or Comedy
Picture): Miklós Rózsa

*SOUND: Metro-Goldwyn-Mayer Studio Sound
Department, Franklin E. Milton, Sound Director

*SPECIAL EFFECTS: Visual Effects by A. Arnold
Gillespie, Robert MacDonald; Audible Effects
by Milo Lory

Writing (Screenplay – based on material from
another medium): Karl Tunberg

OSCAR TOTALS Nominations **12** *Wins **11**

AFI 100 YEARS 100 MOVIES SELECTION
2007 . . #100   1997 . . . #72

TOP 300 FILMS POSITION . . . . #9
All-Release Domestic Box Office in Equivalent 2005 $s

National Film Preservation Board Selection. . . . 2004

OTHER AWARDS Best Picture Wins

	Year
Golden Globes (Drama).	1960
New York Film Critics.	1959
National Board of Review.	none
Film Daily Critics.	none

PLOT: After Judah Ben-Hur is banished to slavery for refusing to provide the Romans with names of Jews who oppose Roman rule, he vows to regain his freedom and avenge himself. He survives and manages to return to Jerusalem.

PRODUCTION: The mid-fifties were tough for MGM. The onetime powerhouse of American entertainment was going broke. Dwarfed by television and choking under the consent decrees of 1948 as well as the antitrust regulations of 1952, the aging movie factory found itself on the precipice of obsolescence. If they had any intention of recovering, they were going to have to roll the dice. And so Metro attempted the ultimate in studio filmmaking: a wide-screen mega-epic. Inspired by the success of Cecil B. DeMille's 1956 remake of *The Ten Commandments,* MGM decided to revive *Ben-Hur,* a property that had been a box office hit when they released it in 1925 (although it had a negative P&L until its sound reissue in 1932). Producing would be Sam Zimbalist, the man who turned out *Quo Vadis* for MGM in 1951. His director of choice, surprisingly, was William Wyler, who was known for "sophisticated" pictures. Wyler was incredulous, but Zimbalist insisted. "The more I thought about it," Wyler remembers, "the more I saw the possibilities." Soon he was won over (at the time, the British Film Institute reported that Wyler received "the largest sum ever paid any individual connected with a single film in the history of the medium," which amounted to 8 percent of the gross and an up-front payment of $350,000). Charlton Heston, with whom Wyler collaborated on *The Big Country,* soon followed. After years of preparation, everything was finally in place. Even before the cameras rolled, the production budget was rumored to be the highest of all time. And the actual building hadn't even begun. *Ben-Hur*'s set was so spectacular it became a bona fide tourist attraction. Half a square mile of Italy's Cinecittà Studios was converted into the Jerusalem of long ago, complete with an eighteen-acre chariot arena, the largest set ever built by Hollywood. New Panavision lenses were developed specifically for the production, enabling director of photography Bruce Surtees to shoot certain scenes in very wide shots without losing sharp focus; more than eighty horses were brought in from around the world to run in the chariot race, and more than 7,000 extras cheered from the bleachers. It would take the filmmakers five weeks to complete just the chariot race sequence. The shoot was so grueling that Henry Henigston, the man who had been managing the production for years before it even went before the cameras, had doctors worried for his life and was advised to leave the set immediately. The real tragedy was Sam Zimbalist, who left the location with chest pains, collapsed, and died only forty minutes later. He had been working at MGM since 1927.

DISTRIBUTION: The marketing blitz was outrageous. Swords for kids, gowns for ladies, tiaras, towels, candy bars, and paperback books all hit shelves. As the most extravagant film ever made, the picture was its own advertisement. Exhibitors jumped on MGM's chariot. In tandem with the film's Los Angeles premiere, the Culver City Chamber of Commerce declared November 24, 1959, "Ben-Hur Day," and from there everything looked up. Box office was more beautiful than predicted (the film was the fastest and biggest grosser at the time). The movie made a net profit of $19.5 million on its initial release and added another $10.1 million on its 1969 re-release. At last, MGM was back in the black. —*Sam Wasson*

FILM INDUSTRY AT A GLANCE

From Inception to 2005

Contained within each chapter of this book are U.S. film industry statistics. These numbers provide a snapshot of the general state of the business by decade and reflect what was going on in production, distribution, marketing, and exhibition for each ten-year period in film history.

By contrast, the charts and graphs contained on these pages, provide an illustrated view of those combined statistics, thus supplying, at a glance, an overview of the major trends that have effected the industry from its inception to the present.

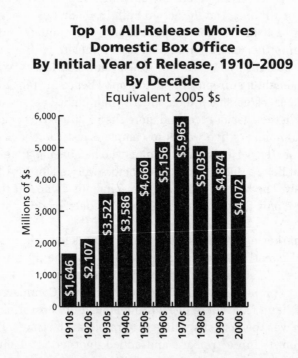

**Top 10 All-Release Movies
Domestic Box Office
By Initial Year of Release, 1910–2009
By Decade**
Equivalent 2005 $s

**TOP 10 ALL-RELEASE MOVIES
DOMESTIC BOX OFFICE
By Initial Year of Release, 1910–2009**
Equivalent 2005 $s in Millions of $s

Movie		Initial Release	U.S. Distributor	Domestic Box Office
1	Gone with the Wind	1939	MGM	$1,407.7
2	Star Wars: Episode IV A New Hope	1977	20th Century-Fox	$1,085.1
3	The Sound of Music	1965	20th Century-Fox	$953.2
4	E.T.: The Extra-Terrestrial	1982	Universal	$889.4
5	The Ten Commandments	1956	Paramount	$829.2
6	Titanic	1997	Paramount	$824.8
7	Jaws	1975	Universal	$802.9
8	Snow White and the Seven Dwarfs	1937	RKO Radio	$760.9
9	Ben-Hur	1959	MGM	$754.3
10	The Exorcist	1973	Warner Bros.	$722.9

Average Weekly U.S. Movie Attendance
First Year of Decade

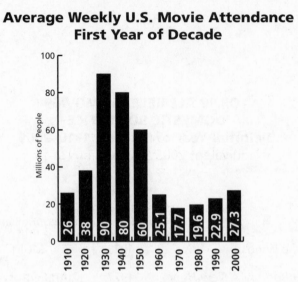

Total U.S. Population vs. Average Weekly
U.S. Movie Attendance
First Year of Decade

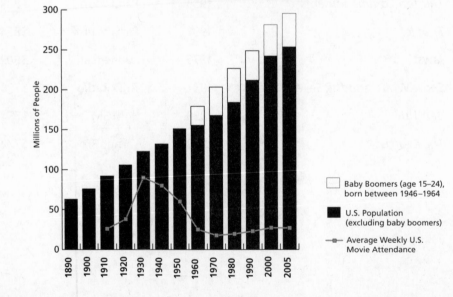

Average Production Costs
Featured Films vs. All Films
Equivalent 2005 $s

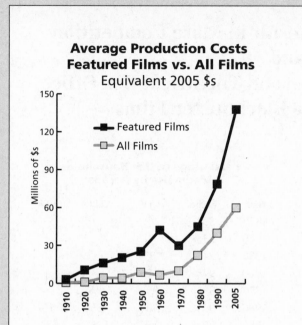

U.S. Industry
Annual U.S. Box Office
Gross Revenues
Equivalent 2005 $s

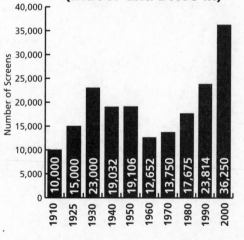

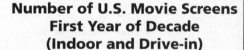

U.S. Industry
Number of New Feature
Films Released
First Year of Decade

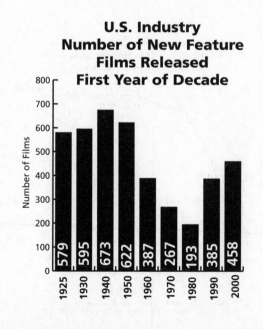

Number of U.S. Movie Screens
First Year of Decade
(Indoor and Drive-in)

415

More Media Channels Result in More Competition
and
More Revenue Sources Beyond Theatrical Box Office
Especially for Big Blockbuster Films

Changing Percentage of Distributor Revenue by Source, 1980–2003

Year	Theatrical	Video/ DVD	TV (Pay and Free)
1980	53%	3%	44%
1985	25%	20%	55%
1990	26%	29%	45%
1995	21%	41%	38%
2000	19%	37%	44%
2004	17%	47%	36%

Percentage of U.S. Households Media Use by Decade

Year	Radio	TV	Cable	VCR
1930	39%			
1940	73%			
1950	91%	8%		
1960	94%	88%		
1970	99%	95%	4%	
1980	99%	98%	15%	1%
1990	99%	98%	52%	67%
2000	99%	98%	69%	85%
2004	99%	98%	68%	91%

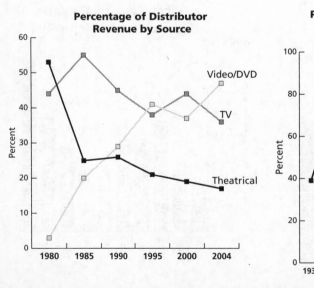

Percentage of Distributor Revenue by Source

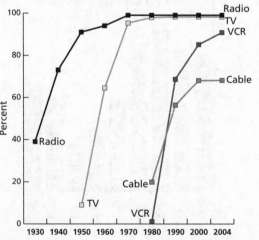

Selected Communications Media Percentage of U.S. Households with Radio, TV, Cable, and VCR

416

More Screens Mean Higher Print and Ad Costs Especially for Big Blockbuster Films

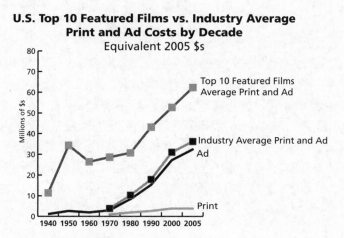

U.S. Top 10 Featured Films vs. Industry Average Print and Ad Costs by Decade

Equivalent 2005 $s

Top 10 Featured Films Average Print and Ad

Industry Average Print and Ad

Ad

Print

Motion Picture Top 10 Featured Films Domestic Print and Ad Costs
vs.
Industry Average Domestic Print and Ad Costs by Decade
Equivalent 2005 $s
(Unadjusted $s) in Millions of $s

Year	Industry Average Print Costs	Industry Average Advertising Costs	Industry Average Print and Ad Costs	Top 10 Featured Film Print and Ad Averages
1940	not available	**$1.1**/($0.08)		**$11.4**/($1.2)
1950	not available	**$2.6**/($0.3)		**$34.3**/($4.9)
1960	not available	**$1.9**/($0.3)		**$26.4**/($4.3)
1970	**$0.9**/($0.2)	**$2.9**/($0.6)	**$3.8**/($0.8)	**$28.6**/($8.8)
1980	**$1.9**/($.8)	**$8.4**/($3.5)	**$10.3**/($4.3)	**$30.7**/($17.0)
1990	**$2.6**/($1.7)	**$15.3**/($10.2)	**$17.9**/($12.0)	**$43.2**/($34.9)
2000	**$3.8**/($3.3)	**$27.2**/($24.0)	**$31.0**/($27.3)	**$52.7**/($46.5)
2005	**$3.8**/($3.8)	**$32.4**/($32.4)	**$36.2**/($36.2)	**$62.3**/($57.6)

The 1960s

My three Ps: passion, patience, perseverance. You have to do this if you've got to be a filmmaker. You have to have passion if you're going to deal with this subject. Patience, because it's going to take a long time to get there. And perseverance: keep at it, keep at it. Down the line, put your foot in the door of any organization to get in, and then you can find out how you can work your way up within the organization to achieve what you want to achieve.

—Director Robert Wise

TOP 10 ALL-RELEASE MOVIES DOMESTIC BOX OFFICE
By Initial Year of Release, 1960–1969

		Equivalent 2005 $s in Millions of $s
1	The Sound of Music	$953.2
2	Doctor Zhivago	$622.4
3	Mary Poppins	$538.8
4	The Graduate	$525.0
5	My Fair Lady	$474.2
6	Cleopatra	$435.7
7	Butch Cassidy and the Sundance Kid	$426.5
8	101 Dalmations	$395.3
9	Thunderball	$395.2
10	It's a Mad, Mad, Mad, Mad World	$389.4
	Total:	**$5,155.7**

GENERAL U.S. STATISTICS, 1960

179,323,175
Total U.S. Population

24,020,004
U.S. Population
Age 15–24

25.1 Million
Average Weekly
U.S. Movie Attendance

DECADE OVERVIEW

A Period of Cultural Change

Amid unprecedented postwar prosperity, some 35 million of the total 70 million American baby boomers entered their formative teen years in the tumultuous sixties, driving a decade of extraordinary social, political, legal, economic, and cultural change. It was an equally revolutionary period for movie studios, many of which were swallowed up by entertainment corporations with a broader agenda than the vertically integrated conglomerates that had dominated since the 1920s. Increasingly, sophisticated TV advertising methods were revolutionizing movie marketing, although newspapers remained the dominant ad medium. A series of movies based on the fictional British secret agent James Bond launched a new generation of sexy, funny, character-driven action-adventures, with striking credit sequence imagery and a modern marketing approach. Although movie attendance was continuing to drop, the under-thirty generation attended cinemas more frequently than any other age group and returned to see favorite films more than once. They were not only a potent force behind the success of some of the biggest films of the day, such as *The Sound of Music,* which appealed to moviegoers of all ages, but they were also the force behind the success of more youth-oriented films featuring antiheroes such as *Bonnie and Clyde.*

Seven out of eight ticket buyers (who paid an average of $1 for each movie admission) in the mid–1960s had television at home, frequently color TVs. Moviegoing was no longer a habit; it was an option. As a result, movie production and attendance plummeted throughout the first three-quarters of the decade. Increasingly it was movies aimed at young people that clicked, especially those with social themes young audiences identified with, such as *The Graduate*. By late in the decade the emphasis on youth affected every aspect of popular culture. The antiestablishment low-budget megahit *Easy Rider* symbolized the rise of this youth culture. While Mom and Dad were at home watching TV, the kids still sought opportunities to be in public among peers. They were served by a new generation of suburban venues with plenty of parking. American Multi-Cinema (AMC), a Kansas City exhibitor, opened the first multiscreen venue, accelerating the decline of big-city movie palaces. The drive-in as a place to watch movies reached its nadir, led by General Cinema, which went public in 1960 as General Drive-In. Wide-screen theatrical presentations, begun in the 1950s, continued in the 1960s, but the viewer was more likely to experience them on flat screens rather than curved ones. There was an increase in foreign-language films as well as low-budget, high-concept movies about

U.S. Movie Screen Snapshot
The Rise and Fall of
the Drive-in

First Year of Decade	Total Screens	Indoor Theatres	Drive-in Theaters
1950	19,106	16,904	2,202
1960	16,991	12,291	4,700
1970	13,750	10,000	3,750
1980	17,675	14,171	3,504
1990	23,814	22,904	910
2000	36,250	35,567	683
2005	37,740	37,092	648

kids at the beach, lots more Elvis singing and swaying his hips, and a new independent American cinema symbolized by artists such as filmmaker John Cassavetes. The last vestiges of the Production Code evaporated, and the industry, under pressure from parents and elected officials, created its own ratings system. Lower-cost movie cameras and projectors in 8 mm and 16 mm became available, spawning the home movie craze. Many of those kids went on to attend colleges that were beginning to take film studies seriously, incubating a generation of filmmakers that would explode on the scene in the 1970s.

> ## The Number One and Number Two
> ## Musical Films
> ## Are Released in the 1960s
> ## Both Starring Julie Andrews

Top 15 Musical Films
All-Release Domestic Box Office, 1920–2005
Equivalent 2005 $s/(Unadjusted $s) in Millions of $s

Rank	Film	Initial Release	Domestic Box Office	Production Cost
1	The Sound of Music*	1965	$953.2/($158.9)	$49.7/($8.0)
2	Mary Poppins	1964	$538.8/($101.8)	$27.8/($4.4)
3	Grease	1978	$520.5/($207.3)	$18.0/ ($6.0)
4	My Fair Lady*	1964	$474.2/($76.0)	$102.8/($16.3)
5	This Is the Army	1943	$407.7/($18.4)	$21.1/($1.9)
6	West Side Story*	1961	$350.1/($50.9)	$45.7/($7.0)
7	Fiddler on the Roof	1971	$320.2/($86.0)	$43.4/($9.0)
8	Going My Way*	1944	$289.3/($14.4)	$11.1/($1.0)
9	The Jolson Story	1946	$271.3/($17.8)	$28.0/($2.8)
10	Funny Girl	1968	$268.7/($56.1)	$78.6/($14.0)
11	The Singing Fool	1928	$244.9/($7.6)	$4.4/($0.4)
12	Yankee Doodle Dandy	1942	$244.3/($10.3)	$18.4/($1.5)
13	South Pacific	1958	$228.0/($24.8)	$37.9/($5.6)
14	Meet Me in St. Louis	1944	$223.3/($11.1)	$20.9/($1.9)
15	White Christmas	1954	$219.9/($19.6)	$27.4/($3.8)

*Academy Award winner for Best Picture.

Comparison of the Number One All-Time Highest Box Office Western with the Number Three Lowest Cost–Highest Revenue Movie
By Release Wave
Equivalent 2005 $s/(Unadjusted $s) in Millions of $s

	Butch Cassidy and the Sundance Kid		American Graffiti	
Release Wave	Release Date	Domestic Box Office	Release Date	Domestic Box Office
1	9/24/1969	$322.4/($71.4)	8/1/1973	$350.9/($96.3)
2	2/27/1974	$104.1/$30.7)	5/26/1978	$51.1/($18.7)
Total		$426.5/($102.1)		$402.0/($115.0)

The Number One Western Film Is Released in the 1960s

Top 15 Western Films
All-Release Domestic Box Office 1920–2005

Equivalent 2005 $s/(Unadjusted $s) in Millions of $s

Rank	Film	Initial Release	Domestic Box Office	Production Cost
1	Butch Cassidy and the Sundance Kid	1969	$426.5/($102.1)	$35.2/($6.6)
2	Duel in the Sun	1947	$348.0/($23.9)	$63.5/($7.3)
3	How the West Was Won	1963	$325.3/($43.2)	$94.4/($14.6)
4	Dances with Wolves*	1990	$279.6/($184.2)	$28.4/($19.0)
5	Shane	1953	$228.4/($19.6)	$24.2/($3.3)
6	The Outlaw	1943	$172.1/($11.3)	$33.9/($3.0)
7	Unforgiven*	1992	$156.2/($101.2)	$48.7/($35.0)
8	Maverick	1994	$155.9/($101.6)	not available
9	The Alamo	1960	$149.9/($17.8)	$79.2/($12.0)
10	Jesse James	1939	$144.6/($5.2)	$16.2/($1.1)
11	True Grit	1969	$142.9/($31.7)	not available
12	The Covered Wagon	1923	$142.4/($4.0)	$6.9/($0.6)
13	Red River	1948	$140.8/($9.7)	$27.6/($3.4)
14	Little Big Man	1970	$129.5/($33.3)	$50.3/($10.0)
15	Vera Cruz	1954	$122.8/($11.1)	$21.8/($3.0)

*Academy Award winner for Best Picture.

PRODUCTION SPOTLIGHT

Pushing the Limits as Never Before

In 1963, as U.S. film production fell to its lowest level in half a century, the most expensive movie in film history until that time opened on an unprecedented wave of advertising, publicity, and gossip. It cost $44 million to produce. Despite the hype that fed on the private lives of stars Elizabeth Taylor and Richard Burton, *Cleopatra* was razzed by critics and sold fewer tickets than anyone anticipated. It did eventually turn a small profit, but by then, the dragged-out production had already claimed its first victim: half of the historic 20th Century-Fox lot in West Los Angeles was sold off to create Century City, providing the studio with just enough cash to avoid bankruptcy. The film's disappointing box office results hastened the end of big-budget historical epics and reflected a harsh new economic reality in Hollywood.

With studios unsure about what kind of movies to make and the old censorship rules on the rocks, a handful of filmmakers emerged who pushed the limits in terms of language, subject, and realistic images. This new boldness was expressed by producer, writer, and director Billy Wilder in his 1960 film *The Apartment,* starring Jack Lemmon, which took a frank approach to the subject of sex outside of marriage. Lemmon would later star in the Blake Edwards–directed *Days of Wine and Roses* (1962), a hard-hitting message picture about the relationship between

---

1960s Movie Censorship: A Brief History

Jack Valenti, former assistant to President Lyndon Johnson, becomes head of the Motion Picture Association of America (MPAA) in 1966 and begins to revise the Production Code. He recognizes a need to adjust the ratings system to reflect societal changes, after confronting censorship issues related to the movie Who's Afraid of Virginia Woolf? *(the first film with the code SMA, for Suggested for Mature Audiences) and* Blow Up *in 1966 (which is released by Michelangelo Antonioni without an MPAA seal).*

In 1968 the MPAA institutes a nationwide system of voluntary film ratings to be guided and monitored by three organizations: National Association of Theater Owners (NATO), Motion Picture Association of America (MPAA), and International Film Importers and Distributors of America (IFIDA). Although voluntary, most theater owners will show only films that have an MPAA rating. All rating categories are trademarked except for X.

G: General Audiences
M: Mature audiences (later revised to PG: Parental Guidance Suggested)
R: Restricted (children under 16 to be with an adult)
X: No one under 17 admitted

Index of Top Feature Film Directors Included in This Chapter

an alcoholic businessman and his wife. In 1961 director Elia Kazan's *Splendor in the Grass* featured the first on-screen open-mouth kiss in the United States. Elizabeth Taylor would earn her two Best Actress awards in the decade, first with *Butterfield 8* (1960), as an amoral but highly paid prostitute, and then as the boozy wife in *Who's Afraid of Virginia Woolf?* (1966). In 1962 director Stanley Kubrick dealt with pedophilia in *Lolita*. That same year *To Kill a Mockingbird* told the story of a black man falsely accused of raping a white woman, at a time when race relations in America were changing rapidly. Director Otto Preminger dealt with homosexuality more openly on-screen than ever before in 1962's *Advise and Consent*, while Sidney Lumet's 1965 drama *The Pawn Broker* became the first mainstream film to contain frontal nudity.

Many of the most daring movies came to the United States from overseas. Federico Fellini's 1960 Italian-language drama *La dolce vita* broke taboos in telling the story of a playboy gossip columnist in Italy.

Late in the decade, after the establishment of a new movie ratings system, the creative doors opened even wider, especially in the depiction of violence. The 1968 crime drama *The Boston Strangler* graphically told the story of a mass murderer. No film defined the antihero worship as much as Warren Beatty's 1967 *Bonnie and Clyde,* which punctuated its period gangster tale with visceral visual violence that brought criticism from critics even as the movie became a huge hit.

U.S. INDUSTRY PRODUCTION STATISTICS, 1960s
Equivalent 2005 $s/(Unadjusted $s)

$42.3 Million ($6.9 million)
Average production cost of films featured in this chapter

$6.6 Million ($1.0 million)
Average production cost of all films released in 1960

Bloody Horror Classics Are a Hit with the Youth Market

Roger Corman, who began directing in 1955, was one of the most prolific filmmakers in history, having produced or directed nearly 300 movies. Two of his best-known films, *The Little Shop of Horrors* and *House of Usher,* were both released in 1960. *Little Shop* was shot in only 2 days, so Corman was delighted when American International Pictures gave him 15 days to shoot their horror thriller *House of Usher.* James H. Nicholson and Samuel Z. Arkoff founded their releasing company in 1954 and renamed it American International Pictures in 1956. It was known for its low-budget exploitation films. *House of Usher,* however, was a big risk for them, with a $250,000 budget, their biggest ever, and it was their first picture made in color and CinemaScope. But the Corman-directed 85-minute movie, starring Vincent Price, made $1 million in its first six months in theaters. Corman went on to direct six more films for AIP, all based on Edgar Allan Poe stories, which were very popular with the youth market.

Working on Roger Corman films proved to be a great training ground for some of the next generation's superstar filmmakers. Francis Ford Coppola, for instance, worked as Corman's assistant in the early 1960s, and Corman produced Coppola's first movie, *Dementia 13,* in 1963. In the 1970s Martin Scorsese directed *Boxcar Bertha* for Corman, and in the 1980s Corman hired James Cameron as a model maker on his movie *Battle Beyond the Stars.*

Top 10 Critically Acclaimed Lead Actors of the 1960s

Rank	Actor Name
1	Gregory Peck
2	Peter O'Toole
3	Richard Burton
4	John Wayne
5	Burt Lancaster
6	Albert Finney
7	Anthony Quinn
8	Rod Steiger
9	Sidney Poitier
10	Warren Beatty

Rank	Actress Name
1	Katharine Hepburn
2	Elizabeth Taylor
3	Julie Andrews
4	Maggie Smith
5	Vanessa Redgrave
6	Anne Bancroft
7	Barbra Streisand
8	Sophia Loren
9	Julie Christie
10	Marilyn Monroe

See Note to the Reader for selection criteria.

Joseph E. Levine: A New Breed of Independent Producer

As the studios looked to partners, a new breed of independent producer, such as flamboyant wheeler-dealer Joseph E. Levine, took charge, bringing together stars, stories, and crew in films he packaged and produced in return for studio financing. Rising out of the poverty of the Great Depression, Levine bought his first movie theater in New Haven, Connecticut. He moved into distribution in New England and launched Embassy Pictures in the late 1940s. He rolled out nationally in 1956 with *Godzilla, King of the Monsters!* He Americanized this Japanese hit (otherwise known as *Gojiro*) by hiring well-known actor Raymond Burr to appear in insert sequences that effectively explained the action to U.S. audiences.

Levine was a master of publicity and poured on the advertising, creating a surprise success. He also paid $120,000 for the rights to a low-budget Italian period action film, *Hercules,* then spent an additional $1.1 million for advertising. Distributed in the United States in 1958 by Warner Bros., the Joseph E. Levine presentation grossed approximately $20 million in worldwide box office. With this success, Levine launched his own productions, showing surprising taste. He was the passionate producer behind *The Graduate,* released in 1967 (which won Mike Nichols an Oscar for directing), and *The Lion in Winter,* released in 1968 (which won Oscars for Katharine Hepburn as Best Actress, its score, and its screenplay), among other notable films.

In the mid-1960s Levine hit his stride. He was seen at premieres, the Cannes Film Festival, and all over Hollywood making deals. While he didn't use a studio logo on his movies in the early years, he did begin his films with "Joseph E. Levine Presents" and ended them with "An Embassy Pictures Release." He was the producer or executive producer of five films in 1964 alone. That was also the year Levine received the Hollywood Foreign Press Association's Cecil B. DeMille Award in recognition of his lifetime achievement in motion pictures.

Levine had hits and misses, but his highs, including *The Graduate,* put him on top. He soon sold Embassy for a huge profit to the Avco conglomerate in the late sixties and then left in 1974 to focus on one film at a time. The great work of his later years was the war epic *A Bridge Too Far* (1977). He bet on his own gut instinct time and again. "Joe is a loner and Board decisions are not his way of operating," wrote Sir Richard Attenborough in the foreword to Levine's opulent self-published coffee-table book about their film *A Bridge Too Far.* "I tend to lead too much with my heart instead of my head anyway," Levine wrote in that same 1977 book. "And sometimes, I guess, I even scare people because I use four letter words . . . That's the way I've always lived my life . . . There is one four letter word I used all the time we were making this film. It's

Top 5 Independently Produced and Distributed Films, 1920–2005				
Initial Release Domestic Box Office				
Equivalent 2005 $s/(Unadjusted $s) in Millions of $s				
Film Title	**Initial Release**	**Independent Distributor**	**Domestic Box Office**	**Production Cost**
The Graduate	1967	Embassy Pictures	**$525.0**/($98.3)	**$17.5** ($3.0)
The Passion of the Christ	2004	Newmarket Films	**$382.2**/($370.3)	**$31.0** ($30.0)
Duel in the Sun	1947	Selznick Releasing Organization (SRO)	**$348.0**/($23.9)	**$63.5** ($7.3)
My Big Fat Greek Wedding	2002	IFC Films	**$266.4**/($241.4)	**$5.4** ($5.0)
The Blair Witch Project	1999	Artisan Entertainment	**$177.3**/($140.5)	**$.04** ($.04)

called, work . . . No one involved with this project was ever afraid of the word work. Eighteen hours a day, weekends, night shooting, everyone worked. And worked hard." And nobody worked harder than Joseph E. Levine.

The 1960s Had Fewer Independent U.S. Produced Movies Released

Year	Total Number of Feature Films Released in the U.S.	Number of Major Studio Feature Films Released	Number of Independent Feature Films Released
1930	509	356	153
1940	477	348	129
1950	383	242	141
1960	154	119	35
1970	267 (+39 reissues)	185	82
1980	193 (+42 reissues)	161	32
1990	385 (+25 reissues)	169	216
2000	458 (+17 reissues)	191	267
2005	535 (+14 reissues)	190	345

A Sampling of Director Salaries, 1960s
Equivalent 2005 $s/(Unadjusted $s)

Director	Film	Initial Release	Salary
David Lean	Lawrence of Arabia	1962	$8.9 million incl p/p* ($1.1 million p/p + $200,000 salary)
Mike Nichols	The Graduate	1967	$2.9 million/($500,000)
	Who's Afraid of Virginia Woolf?	1966	$1.5 million/($250,000)
Billy Wilder	The Apartment	1960	$1.3 million + 17.5% p/p after recoupment of 3x cost/ ($200,000 + p/p)
Joseph L. Mankiewicz	Cleopatra	1963	$1.0 million + other/($150,000 + Fox agreed to pay $3 million–half to Mankiewicz and half to his NBC network partner) to buy-out Figaro, his production company
Stanley Kubrick	Spartacus	1960	$1.0 million/($150,000)

*Profit participation.

Actors of the 1960s: Comparison of Salaries and Profit Participations
Equivalent 2005 $s/(Unadjusted $s)

Actor	Film	Initial Release	Salary
Elizabeth Taylor	Who's Afraid of Virginia Woolf?	1966	**$6,630,556 excluding p/p*** ($1,100,000 + 10% gross p/p)
	Cleopatra	1963	**$6,382,353 excluding p/p** [$1,000,000 (+ $125,000/ week for 16 weeks + $50,000/ week for additional weeks + $3,000/week expenses + 10% gross p/p. Final take approx. $7 million including p/p)]
Peter Sellers	Dr. Strangelove	1964	**$6,300,000** ($1,000,000 for 3 roles)
Audrey Hepburn	My Fair Lady	1964	**$6,300,000 excluding p/p** [$1,000,000 (+ 5% gross p/p after $1 million over breakeven]
Steve McQueen	Bullitt	1968	**$5,612,069** ($1,000,000)
Richard Burton	Who's Afraid of Virginia Woolf?	1966	**$4,520,833** ($750,000)
	Cleopatra	1963	**$1,595,588** ($250,000 excluding overages)
Paul Newman	Butch Cassidy and the Sundance Kid	1969	**$3,991,144** ($750,000)
Julie Andrews	The Sound of Music	1965	**$1,395,000** ($225,000)
Shirley MacLaine and Jack Lemmon	The Apartment	1960	**$1,155,000** ($175,000)
Barbra Streisand	Funny Girl	1968	**$1,122,000** ($200,000)
Dustin Hoffman	The Graduate	1967	**$264,000** ($17,000)

*Profit participation.

Sexy Spy Becomes International Hit

In 1953, after heroic service for the British intelligence service, former journalist, banker, and spy Ian Fleming bought a gold-plated typewriter and moved into an estate in Jamaica he dubbed Goldeneye. There he wrote his first novel, *Casino Royale,* about a sophisticated but sensitive spy named James Bond, who was licensed to kill by the British secret service. The books found a growing audience over time. Movie rights were acquired by Albert "Cubby" Broccoli and Harry Salzman, who on October 5, 1962, released the sixth Bond novel published in the United Kingdom as the first Bond movie, *Dr. No,* starring Sean Connery as a cool, sexy spy. It was an immediate box office success, despite critical misgivings, and spawned a series of sequels over the next four decades. After four more films, Connery quit and was replaced by Australian model George Lazenby, who completed one movie as the famed character. Then Connery returned for one more, and was followed by Roger Moore (who made seven Bond movies), Timothy Dalton (who made two), and Pierce Brosnan (who made four). Brosnan was subsequently replaced by Daniel Craig. Each film had an archvillain and one or more "Bond girls," beginning with Ursula Andress as Honey Ryder in *Dr. No.* The first Bond film to gross $100 million worldwide was *Goldfinger,* released in 1964, the same year Fleming died of a heart attack. Broccoli produced Bond movies until his death in 1996. His heirs carry on, and the films have grown into a series of box office blockbusters.

James Bond Franchise Films
All-Release Worldwide Box Office
Equivalent 2005 $s/(Unadjusted $s) in Millions of $s

Rank	Film	Initial Release	Bond Actor	Worldwide Box Office	Production Cost	Salary
1	*Thunderball*	1965	Sean Connery	**$848.1** ($141.2)	**$41.9** ($6.8)	**$4.7** ($0.8)
2	*Goldfinger*	1964	Sean Connery	**$820.4** ($124.9)	**$18.6** ($3.0)	**$3.2** ($0.5)
3	*Casino Royale*	2006	Daniel Craig	**$581.5** ($594.2)	**$145.3** ($150.0)	**$3.3** ($3.4)
4	*From Russia with Love*	1964	Sean Connery	**$543.8** ($78.9)	**$12.6** ($2.0)	**$1.6** ($0.3)
5	*Moonraker*	1979	Roger Moore	**$535.0** ($210.3)	**$91.5** ($34.0)	not available
6	*The Spy Who Loved Me*	1977	Roger Moore	**$533.0** ($185.4)	**$45.1** ($14.0)	not available
7	*GoldenEye*	1995	Pierce Brosnan	**$518.5** ($351.9)	**$76.9** ($60.0)	**$5.1** ($4.0)

Rank	Film	Initial Release	Bond Actor	Worldwide Box Office	Production Cost	Salary
8	*Quantum of Solace*	2008	Daniel Craig	**$514.2** ($576.0)	**$181.4** ($200.0)	**$8.1** ($8.9)
9	*You Only Live Twice*	1967	Sean Connery	**$514.2** ($101.0)	**$59.9** ($10.3)	**$4.4 excluding p/p*** ($0.8 + 25% net merch royalty
10	*Die Another Day*	2002	Pierce Brosnan	**$465.4** ($431.9)	**$154.2** ($142.0)	**$17.9** ($16.5)
11	*Tomorrow Never Dies*	1997	Pierce Brosnan	**$463.2** ($338.9)	**$133.9** ($110.0)	**$10.0** ($8.2)
12	*Live and Let Die*	1973	Roger Moore	**$460.3** ($126.4)	**$30.8** ($7.0)	not available
13	*For Your Eyes Only*	1981	Roger Moore	**$449.4** ($194.9)	**$60.2** ($28.0)	not available
14	*Dr. No*	1963	Sean Connery	**$448.8** ($59.5)	**$7.0** ($1.1)	**$0.6** ($0.1)
15	*Diamonds Are Forever*	1971	Sean Connery	**$442.5** ($116.0)	**$34.7** ($7.2)	**$5.8 excluding p/p** ($1.2 + 12.5% of gross)
16	*The World Is Not Enough*	1999	Pierce Brosnan	**$439.5** ($361.8)	**$158.3** ($135.0)	**$13.5** ($12.4)
17	*Octopussy*	1983	Roger Moore	**$373.8** ($183.7)	**$53.9** ($27.5)	**$7.8** ($4.0)
18	*The Man with the Golden Gun*	1974	Roger Moore	**$334.0** ($98.5)	**$27.7** ($7.0)	not available
19	*The Living Daylights*	1987	Timothy Dalton	**$313.5** ($191.2)	**$68.8** ($40.0)	**$5.2** ($3.0)
20	*On Her Majesty's Secret Service*	1969	George Lazenby	**$291.5** ($64.6)	**$37.3** ($7.0)	**$0.6** ($0.1)
21	*A View to a Kill*	1985	Roger Moore	**$275.2** ($152.4)	**$54.5** ($30.0)	**$9.1** ($5.0)
22	*License to Kill*	1989	Timothy Dalton	**$250.9** ($156.2)	**$56.7** ($36.0)	**$7.9** ($5.0)
Total Worldwide Box Office				**$10,416.6** ($4,839.8)	**$1,550.9** (1,057.8)	
Total Domestic Box Office				**$3,530.2** ($1,552.6)		

Note: Excludes *Never Say Never Again* (1983), not considered an "official" Bond film.

*Profit participation.

429

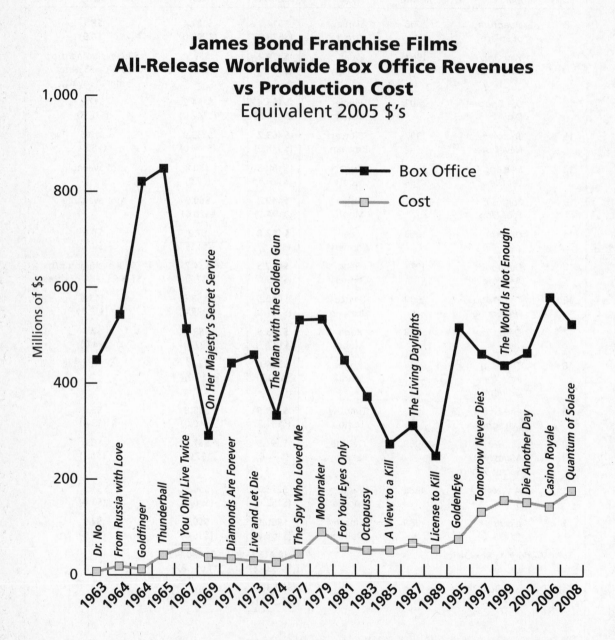

James Bond Franchise Films
All-Release Worldwide Box Office Revenues
vs Production Cost
Equivalent 2005 $'s

DISTRIBUTION OVERVIEW

TV Becomes Important as an Additional Movie-Release Channel

The major studios dominated, but their customer base of theaters and ticket sales was rapidly dwindling and there was new competition from smaller, fast-moving independent producers. Some, such as American International Pictures, made lots of low-budget exploitation fare that could be advertised to the youth audience, who might see it in a boxy suburban theater or at a drive-in; others, such as filmmaker John Cassavetes, released the occasional movie themselves in what developed into a distribution track for art house cinema.

For the majors there was now a secondary market for movies—television. With U.S. household TV penetration nearing 100 percent and strong bidding among the three national broadcasters—CBS, NBC, and ABC—prices popped. When the RKO library was sold to TV in 1955, it was licensed at a fee of $10,000 per title. But by 1968 the fee was consistently over $800,000 per movie. The bidding wars first began in 1961, when NBC licensed past theatrical titles from 20th Century-Fox, and launched the first weekly movie night on a major network. Prices shot up quickly. In 1966 ABC paid Columbia $2 million for *The Bridge on the River Kwai*. Its telecast made Nielsen history, drawing 60 million viewers and beating out Ed Sullivan's popular variety show. Ford, as sole sponsor, showcased its new lineup of cars. This spawned a side industry for the studios, who went into high gear making lower-budget movies for initial distribution on television. The made-for-television movie (MFT) trend began soon after MCA made a deal with NBC to produce 90-minute movies in Universal City. The movies were shot in 6 to 25 days for about $500,000 per hour compared to the 50 to 70 days it took for most theatrical films to be made. The producers made their investment back on the first sale of multiple viewings to a network, and added the asset to its celluloid library.

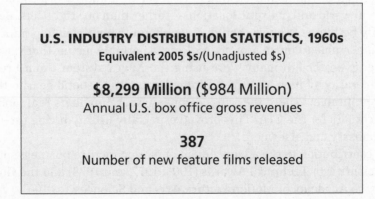

U.S. INDUSTRY DISTRIBUTION STATISTICS, 1960s
Equivalent 2005 $s/(Unadjusted $s)

$8,299 Million ($984 Million)
Annual U.S. box office gross revenues

387
Number of new feature films released

Major Movie Distributors, 1960s

Buena Vista	Founder Walt Disney dies in 1966
Columbia	Thwarts a foreign ownership takeover attempt in 1966
MGM	Sold to Edgar Bronfman Sr. in 1967 then to Kirk Kerkorian in 1969
Paramount Pictures	Sold to Gulf and Western in 1966
20th Century-Fox	Darryl F. Zanuck regains control and names his son Richard as vice president in 1962
United Artists Corp.	Merged with Transamerica in 1967
Universal Pictures	Sold to MCA in 1962. Lew Wasserman takes over as chairman in 1969
Warner Bros.	Sold to Seven Arts Productions in 1967. Acquired by Kinney National Service and headed by Steven J. Ross in 1969

TECHNOLOGY SPOTLIGHT

Cold War Activities Indirectly Support Motion Picture Sound Advancements

Following the breakup of the studio system in the early 1950s, many of the old studio sound departments were dismantled. The invention of the Nagra recorder by Stefan Kudelski in 1958 could not have come at a better time. Born in Poland, Kudelski was educated in Switzerland, and his Nagra recorder was famous for its Swiss engineering—it was built to operate in cold weather or humid conditions and could withstand being dropped. By the 1960s, with smaller movie cameras and a portable Nagra recording system, it was now possible for the new breed of independent directors and sound designers to shoot film and record sound wherever they wanted—in the real world and in exotic locations—rather than on studio lots. Before the Nagra, which could easily be hung off one's shoulder, sound equipment weighed hundreds of pounds and was very cumbersome to move around. Making it portable meant that it was now possible to film anywhere. Even though many were using the Nagra system, from French New Wave advocates to a generation of new American filmmakers, selling sound gear to the movie industry was not very profitable. Where the Swiss company Nagra made its real money was producing miniature recorders for the CIA. This proved especially useful during the Cold War to spy on the Russian embassy and elsewhere.

To honor his contribution to the advancement of motion picture business sound, Stefan was awarded three Scientific or Technical Awards (1965, 1977, and 1978) and the Gordon E. Sawyer Award (1990) by the Academy of Motion Picture Arts and Sciences.

MARKETING SPOTLIGHT

Movie Marketing Acquires a British Accent

When it came to 1960s popular culture, Britannia ruled the world. In 1963, as American movie production was falling to an all-time low and U.S. foreign-language movie distribution was at a historic high, the bawdy British comedy *Tom Jones* was a huge hit, the Beatles were climbing the music charts, and a new kind of fashion that had begun in swinging England was all the rage. The brash, bold, youthful, anything-goes British attitude soon seeped into film design and advertising.

One of those attracted to the sizzling British scene was American Maurice Binder. Although Binder had been successfully creating movie preview trailers and designing screen titles in the United States since the 1950s, he headed overseas to work for the London branch of the New Jersey–based company National Screen Service.

When the studios began dumping their in-house advertising, promotion, and publicity departments to save money, some of that work went to Madison Avenue advertising agencies, where "organization men" turned threads of scientific marketing research into ad concepts reflecting what consumers wanted most. National Screen was one of the ad companies to successfully fill the creative void at the studios. They created, printed, distributed, and delivered marketing materials to theaters, gaining a near monopoly on this business until the late twentieth century, when express delivery changed the game significantly.

It was while working for National Screen in London that Binder met producers Harry Salzman and Cubby Broccoli, partners in the first major James Bond movie, *Dr. No.* Salzman and Broccoli hired Binder to make the movie's marketing materials eye-catching and youthful. People had become used to television graphics, and the producers wanted to capture that same hip sensibility for their films.

Binder accomplished what they asked of him, creating nontraditional graphics and titles with a fresh, modern look. Abstract elements mixed with outrageous imagery and playful animation. In the opening sequence of the movie the audience found themselves staring into a gun sight. Binder had devised a most clever and dramatic way to drive their attention to what he and the filmmakers deemed most important, creating what would be a lasting first impression of the movie. For the second Bond movie, *From Russia with Love,* Salzman and Broccoli brought Binder back, but they also hired another Yank expatriate, Robert Brownjohn, an influential figure in the New York and London graphic design scene throughout the 1950s and 1960s. The roving gun sight that Binder had introduced in *Dr. No* remained, but the concept was further shaped to include a "short hook"—a trick borrowed from television in which a quick but powerful sequence such as a car crash, explosion, or a murder was used to keep people from switching channels. In this case, however, the short hook was used to enhance style. It set up the entire action-packed opening sequence, which remains a trademark of *Bond* films to this day. These opening sequences represented a change in the way movies were positioned with audiences.

433

Comparison of Seven 1960s Films Initial Release
Equivalent 2005 $s /(Unadjusted $s) In Millions of $s

Film	Initial Release	Domestic Box Office	Domestic Rentals	Foreign Rentals	Production Cost	Domestic Print and Ad Costs
The Sound of Music	1965	$880.1 ($138.7)	$434.1 ($68.4)	$293.3 ($46.2)	$49.7 ($8.0)	$56.8 ($9.2)
The Dirty Dozen	1967	$238.0 ($44.6)	$107.1 ($20.1)	$59.7 ($11.2)	$31.3 ($5.4)	$48.0 ($8.2)
2001: A Space Odyssey	1968	$178.0 ($36.4)	$80.1 ($16.4)	$26.9 ($5.5)	$58.0 ($10.3)	$38.5 ($6.9)
Cleopatra	1963	$435.7 ($57.8)	$166.6 ($22.1)	$137.1 ($18.2)	$280.8 ($44.0)	$33.9 ($5.3)
West Side Story	1961	$285.3 ($36.1)	$128.4 ($16.2)	$123.6 ($15.6)	$45.7 ($7.0)	$28.1 ($4.3)
The Longest Day	1962	$244.7 ($30.9)	$110.1 ($13.9)	$145.4 ($19.3)	$55.6 ($8.6)	$19.2 ($3.0)
Butch Cassidy and the Sundance Kid	1969	$322.4 ($71.4)	$131.7 ($29.2)	$35.7 ($7.9)	$35.2 ($6.6)	$11.9 ($2.2)

The movie poster and trailer no longer had to tell the whole story. Instead, they could be used as a sales tool—a teaser to dazzle and focus the audience on a few key, buzzworthy elements of the film. In this way the early Bond marketing materials broke the mold and set the standard for a new approach to movie marketing and advertising.

EXHIBITION OVERVIEW

Stanley H. Durwood and the Rise of AMC Entertainment

AMC Entertainment, Inc., through its subsidiary American Multi-Cinema, Inc., was destined to become the largest theatrical exhibition company in the world, in terms of revenue, and one of the largest motion picture exhibitors in the United States, in terms of the number of theater screens it operated. This was all due to AMC's visionary founder, Stan Durwood. Durwood started out as a second-generation exhibitor in Kansas City. In 1963 he was approached by a developer who made it possible for Durwood to turn his idea of a multiplex into reality. His seemingly simple concept was to house multiple auditoriums in a single location so that he could screen more than one movie at a time. Durwood always credited himself as the first to build a multiplex even though General Cinema already had converted its Framingham location into a two-screen theater. To support Durwood's claim, a company historian would argue that Durwood was in fact the first to actually design and build a multiple-screen theater. Durwood is also credited with being the first to have cup holders built into the armrests in auditoriums.

During the next few decades, AMC Theatres would expand out of Kansas City to become a national chain of multiplex theaters; after 1997 the company would add megaplex theaters. The original AMC prototypes were four- or six-screen auditoriums that were run very inexpensively. Instead of operating the usual projection booths with a union projectionist, Durwood installed an automated system allowing the theater manager to start and stop the movies from the lobby area. By the mid-1980s this theater prototype expanded to include eight to twelve screens. By 1986 AMC boasted 200 buildings with 1,100 screens.

In 1995 AMC opened a theater called The Grand in Dallas, Texas. The Dallas market had not been known for generating big box office numbers with the exception of one General Cinema theater in the Northpark Mall. But The Grand became an overnight phenomenon due to AMC's installation of stadium seating, which replaced the gentle 15° floor slope with a 30° slope created by stepping up every row from the bottom to the top in equal measure. This groundbreaking change improved sightlines for visitors and reduced the chance that tall people would block the view of short people behind them. A short time later, AMC opened another stadium-seated theater in San Diego, California. Their opening box office numbers confirmed that their success was no fluke and that stadium seating had in fact set a new future standard for theaters. Since most exhibition companies had just completed building and/or refurbishing sprees before the multiplex concept took hold, many soon found that their new theaters were already outdated. Bankruptcy loomed for many of these theater owners. Every market that opened a new stadium theater would force an old slope-floor theater out of business or give it no alternative but to operate as a subrun theater, which meant it played films only after the film's initial theatrical run. Some companies were stubborn and resistant to change. United Artists Theaters, for example, decided that slope floors were fine and did not adjust its building plans. The company closed shortly thereafter. Others reacted quickly and embraced the new design. Pacific Theatres was under construction in Chatsworth, California, with a twenty-one-auditorium megaplex that had been designed with a slope floor. After the AMC San Diego opening, construction was halted, the theater was redesigned, and it opened successfully as the Winnetka Theatre. Technically, stadium seating was not a completely new concept if one considers the historical theater palaces that date back to the Greeks and Romans. However, Stan Durwood can take credit for changing the design of megaplex seating to the model that is still used in theaters today.

*The news that the Roxy Theater [in New York City] has finally been sold
to a large realty firm that apparently intends to demolish it and use the property
for extending an adjacent hotel is one more indication of the dilemma of the famous
movie palaces along Broadway. These days there are simply more people who will
pay money to sleep in hotels than will pay money to sleep in theaters.*
—BOSLEY CROWTHER, *NEW YORK TIMES*, 1960

Luster Fades on Golden Age Movie Palaces

Billed when it opened in June 1929 as "the world's finest theater," the Fox Theater at 1350 Market Street in San Francisco closed its doors in 1963, a victim of the times, as customers migrated to the suburbs. It was one of many fading single-screen theaters in downtown areas shuttered during the decade. Some theaters throughout the nation were similarly demolished, while others were converted to performing arts centers. However, the Fox Theater stands out from all the others built during the golden age of the motion picture palace, which spanned the years from roughly 1919, when New York's Capitol opened with 5,000 seats, to 1932, when Radio City Music Hall opened. Other exhibitors may have built one or two great theaters, but William Fox built a whole majestic chain of them, including ones in Detroit, Brooklyn, St. Louis, Atlanta, and San Francisco. "Never again . . . would there be anything as lavish. Radio City Music Hall would be larger, but its ultra-modern interior could not compare with the masses of decoration and were plastered into the auditoriums of these five Fox's," wrote Preston J. Kaufmann in *Fox, the Last Word*.

U.S. INDUSTRY EXHIBITION STATISTICS, 1960s
Equivalent 2005 $s/(Unadjusted $s)

$6.41 ($0.76 to $1.42)
Average movie ticket price (1960–1969)

12,652
Number of U.S. screens, 1960
(9,150 indoor and 3,502 drive-in)

THE APARTMENT

United Artists, 1960

ALL-RELEASE EQUIVALENT 2005 $s
(Unadjusted $s) in Millions of $s

Domestic Box Office Revenues . . . . **$125.6**/($14.9)
Production Cost . . . . **$19.8**/($3.0)
Principal Photography . . . . **50 days**
November 1959–February 1960

Director . . . . Billy Wilder

Producer . . . . Billy Wilder

Production Company . . . . The Mirisch Company

Story and
Screenplay by . . . . Billy Wilder, I. A. L. Diamond

Cast . . . . Jack Lemmon, Shirley MacLaine, Fred MacMurray

Filming Locations . . . . . . New York City, including Central Park, the Majestic Theatre and Columbus Avenue; interiors at Samuel Goldwyn Studios in Hollywood, CA

Genre . . . . Drama

Format . . . . B&W

Initial Release . . . . 6/15/1960 premiere (New York); 6/21/1960 general release

Rerelease . . . . none

Running Time . . . . 125 minutes

MPAA Rating . . . . not rated

STANDING THE TEST OF TIME

ACADEMY AWARD Oscar Nominations and Wins

*BEST MOTION PICTURE: Billy Wilder, Producer

Actor: Jack Lemmon

Actor in a Supporting Role: Jack Kruschen

Actress: Shirley MacLaine

*ART DIRECTION/SET DECORATION (B&W): Alexander Trauner/Edward G. Boyle

Cinematography (B&W): Joseph LaShelle

*DIRECTING: Billy Wilder

*FILM EDITING: Daniel Mandell

Sound: Samuel Goldwyn Studio Sound Dept. Gordon E. Sawyer, Sound Director

*WRITING (Story and Screenplay – written directly for the screen): Billy Wilder, I. A. L. Diamond

OSCAR TOTALS Nominations **10** *Wins 5

AFI 100 YEARS 100 MOVIES SELECTION
2007 . . . #80   1997 . . . . #93

TOP 300 FILMS POSITION . . . . none
All-Release Domestic Box Office in Equivalent 2005 $s

National Film Preservation Board Selection 1994

OTHER AWARDS Best Picture Wins

	Year
Golden Globes (Comedy)	1961
New York Film Critics	1960
National Board of Review	none
Film Daily Critics	none

*My customary answer to people who ask, "What is the theme of your movie?"
is, "You can't eat soup with a fork."*

—Billy Wilder

PLOT: An insurance accountant lets senior executives use his apartment for illicit affairs. But after finding his big boss's mistress in his bed trying to commit suicide, he realizes his mistake and soon thereafter falls in love with the girl.

PRODUCTION: When Billy Wilder first saw director David Lean's *Brief Encounter* (1945), he wondered about the man who let his friend use his apartment for an affair. The idea stayed with Wilder for many years, but he didn't pursue it for fear of censorship. Finally, the success of *Some Like It Hot* (1959) showed that the American audience might be prepared for the dark underside of interoffice relations. Wilder decided to move ahead when a 1950s Hollywood scandal mirrored the plot: a talent agent conducted his affair with a well-known actress in his assistant's bachelor pad. Wilder and co-writer I. A. L. Diamond took the incident a step further and had the young assistant lend out his apartment to advance his career. During writing, Wilder changed the program for Buddy and Fran's date at the Majestic Theater to *The Music Man,* after watching and despising a production of *The Sound of Music.* Two days before production, Paul Douglas, the actor cast as big boss J. D. Sheldrake, suffered a fatal heart attack. Wilder convinced Fred MacMurray to take the role of the philandering boss. Though the first weeks of shooting occurred on location in New York, the cold weather forced much of the footage to be reshot at Goldwyn Studios. Notorious for filming only what he wanted, Wilder claimed that it took merely a week to edit the picture and that only 1,000 feet were left on the cutting room floor. One of Wilder's favorite films, King Vidor's *The Crowd* (1928), inspired the opening sequence of the lone worker lost in a huge corporate canvas. On a small studio set, art director Alexander Trauner utilized smaller desks, little people, and the technique of forced perspective to make the office workplace seem to continue on into infinity. Adding to the huge $400,000 sets, IBM loaned the production more than $2.5 million worth of office equipment. Wilder furnished Buddy's apartment with his own bentwood double bed, art from his personal collection, and his wife's fur coat to keep costs down. Wilder and Diamond finished the second half of the script during production, tailored to the actors' performances. According to Shirley MacLaine, they didn't finish the script until four days before the shooting of the last scene. Her character's final sequence of dashing back to Buddy's apartment was made up of her running past the same three houses from different angles.

DISTRIBUTION: To promote *The Apartment,* Wilder placed a trade paper ad having fun with Columbia's campaign for *Suddenly, Last Summer*: it read "Suddenly, Last Winter—he knew his apartment was being used for something evil." The movie premiered at Grauman's Chinese in Hollywood on June 21, 1960, and set an opening-day record at New York's Plaza Theatre. It also did well overseas, even reaching behind the Iron Curtain. Communists heralded the film as an attack on capitalism, to which Wilder responded: "[The story] could happen anywhere, in Hong Kong, in Tokyo, Rome, Paris, London. But there is one place where it could not have happened, and that is Moscow . . . in Moscow nobody has his own apartment." The film's plot was the basis for the Broadway hit *Promises, Promises* (1968–69). —*Michael Kogge*

PSYCHO
Paramount, 1960

ALL-RELEASE EQUIVALENT 2005 $s
(Unadjusted $s) in Millions of $s

Domestic Box Office Revenues. . . . . . . **$209.9**/($24.9)
Production Cost . . . . **$5.3**/($0.8)
Principal Photography. . . . . **36** days estimated
11/30/1959–2/1/1960

Director . . . . Alfred Hitchcock

Producer . . . . Alfred Hitchcock

Production Company . . . . Alfred J. Hitchcock Productions, Shamley Productions

Story by . . . . Based on the novel by Robert Bloch

Screenplay by . . . . Joseph Stefano

Cast . . . . Anthony Perkins, Janet Leigh

Filming Locations . . . . . . Primarily at Universal Studio; locations shots at Golden State Freeway and Harry Maher's Used Car Lot in North Hollywood, CA

Genre. . . . . Thriller

Format. . . . . B&W

Initial Release . . . . 6/16/1960 premiere (New York)

Rerelease. . . . . none

Running Time . . . . 109 minutes

MPAA Rating . . . . not rated

STANDING THE TEST OF TIME

ACADEMY AWARD Oscar Nominations and Wins

Actress in a Supporting Role: Janet Leigh

Art Direction/Set Decoration (B&W): Joseph Hurley, Robert Clatworthy/ George Milo

Cinematography (B&W): John L. Russell

Directing: Alfred Hitchcock

OSCAR TOTALS   Nominations **4**   *Wins 0

AFI 100 YEARS 100 MOVIES SELECTION
2007 . . . #14   1997 . . . #18

TOP 300 FILMS POSITION . . . . **#232**
All-Release Domestic Box Office in Equivalent 2005 $s

National Film Preservation Board Selection. . . . 1992

OTHER AWARDS Best Picture Wins

	Year
Golden Globes (Comedy)	none
New York Film Critics.	none
National Board of Review	none
Film Daily Critics	none

That game with the audience was fascinating. I was directing the viewers. You might say I was playing them, like an organ.

—Alfred Hitchcock

PLOT: After embezzling $40,000 from her employer, Marion Crane is driving to meet her lover when heavy rain forces her to stop at the remote Bates Motel. Upon meeting a troubled young man there, her journey takes a shocking and unexpected turn.

PRODUCTION: Alfred Hitchcock first became aware of Robert Bloch's novel *Psycho,* itself inspired by the grisly Wisconsin case of Ed Gein, from a favorable newspaper review. He bought the film rights anonymously for $9,000, although the project was more exploitative than his previous films. Unfortunately, Paramount, where Hitchcock had a seven-year distribution deal, had grave misgivings about the material: it was considered vulgar and rife with potential censorship problems. The studio agreed to distribute and promote *Psycho* only if Hitchcock would finance it personally through his company, Shamley Productions. He agreed in return for 60 percent of the gross. To hold costs down, he enlisted a crew coming primarily from his successful television series (1955–65) and filmed at Revue Studios on the Universal lot, where the series was housed. Hitchcock said he used black and white because in color the shower sequence would have been too gory. Black and white was also less expensive. The Revue crew was accustomed to working much faster than a feature film unit, but Hitchcock still took the time to get what he wanted. *Psycho*'s most famous sequence, the shower scene, lasts less than a minute on-screen but required seven days and more than seventy camera setups to film. Although Hitchcock liked to plan his shots in advance and work from storyboards for each camera setup, he largely ignored graphic designer Saul Bass's drawings for the famed shower sequence. As the film appears on-screen, one would be hard pressed to match any of Hitchcock's shots or edits of that scene with the shots and continuity suggested in the storyboards. It put the film 9 days over its 27-day shooting schedule. As with most films shot in 35mm, Hitchcock used 50mm lenses, but he did so in a way that resulted in an unsettling voyeuristic effect. *Psycho*'s thematic intimacy manifested itself in other ways too. It was the first American film to show an actress clad only in undergarments, the first time moviegoers had ever seen a flushing toilet, and the opening scene—which depicts two lovers lying together in bed—was, though far from explicit, groundbreaking for the time. After viewing the first rough cut, Hitchcock was convinced it would flop. His longtime collaborator, composer Bernard Herrmann, suggested an inventive use of the string section only, creating one of the greatest film scores of all time.

DISTRIBUTION: *Psycho*'s initial release is still legendary for being the first to refuse admittance after the picture began. Because a key character does not survive *Psycho*'s halfway point, Hitchcock realized latecomers might be puzzled if they didn't see the performer. He even enforced his policy with security guards in the largest cities. Exhibitors complained at first but relented when tardy audience members found themselves waiting in long lines outside—a sure sign that *Psycho* was a hit. The immediate critical reaction, however, was mostly negative. Over the years that changed, and *Psycho* is now considered a classic of the suspense thriller genre. A February 1964 *New York Times* article reported that *Psycho* was the second most profitable black and white film in Hollywood history after *The Birth of a Nation* (1915). —*Tom Dupree*

SPARTACUS
Universal, 1960

ALL-RELEASE EQUIVALENT 2005 $s
(Unadjusted $s) in Millions of $s

Domestic Box Office Revenues . . . . $251.9/($34.2)
Production Cost . . . . $79.2/($12.0)
Principal Photography . . . . 167 days estimated
1/27/1959–7/12/1959

Director . . . . Stanley Kubrick
Producer . . . . Edward Lewis
Production Company . . . . Bryna Productions, Universal International Films
Story by . . . . Based on the novel by Howard Fast
Screenplay by . . . . Dalton Trumbo
Cast . . . . Kirk Douglas, Laurence Olivier, Jean Simmons, Charles Laughton, Peter Ustinov, John Gavin, Tony Curtis
Filming Locations . . . . . . Hearst Castle in San Simeon (Crassus's villa), Thousand Oaks (Appian Way), Spain (battle scenes), Barham Boulevard/101 Freeway (Spartacus/Antoninus end scene), Universal studio lot
Genre . . . . Action Adventure
Format . . . . Color (Technicolor)
Initial Release . . . . 10/6/1960 premiere (New York); 10/7/1960 general release
Rerelease . . . . 1967, 1991 restored version
Running Time . . . . 196 minutes
MPAA Rating . . . . not rated

STANDING THE TEST OF TIME

ACADEMY AWARD Oscar Nominations and Wins

***ACTOR IN A SUPPORTING ROLE:** Peter Ustinov
***ART DIRECTION/SET DECORATION:** Alexander Golitzen, Eric Orbom/Russell A. Gausman, Julia Heron
***CINEMATOGRAPHY:** Russell Metty
***COSTUME DESIGN:** Valles, Bill Thomas
Film Editing: Robert Lawrence
Music (Music Score of a Dramatic or Comedy Picture): Alex North

OSCAR TOTALS   Nominations 6   *Wins 4

AFI 100 YEARS 100 MOVIES SELECTION
2007 . . . #81   1997 0

TOP 300 FILMS POSITION . . . . #158
All-Release Domestic Box Office in Equivalent 2005 $s

National Film Preservation Board Selection . . . . none

OTHER AWARDS Best Picture Wins

	Year
Golden Globes	1961
New York Film Critics	none
National Board of Review	none
Film Daily Critics	none

Here was Kubrick with his wide eyes and his pants hiked up looking like a kid of seventeen. It was as if they were asking, "Is this some kind of joke?"

—Kirk Douglas, on the crew's reaction after meeting their new director

PLOT: As the Roman Republic begins to collapse, the gladiator-turned-general Spartacus (Kirk Douglas) amasses an army of his fellow slaves to rise up against their Roman masters and blaze a path through Italy back to their homes.

PRODUCTION: Just as his character had to survive the gladiator pits, executive producer Kirk Douglas had to duel with United Artists' *The Gladiators* to make his version of the Spartacus story. Though the films were based on different novels, they shared the same historical material. To win, Douglas put *Spartacus* on the fast track, quickly assembling a top cast and rolling cameras before the script was completed. Douglas and producing partner Edward Lewis hired blacklisted writer Dalton Trumbo to adapt the novel, using Lewis's name so as not to stir up right-wing McCarthyites. Leading roles went to British actors to play Romans and to Americans to play the slaves, who would wear the "cow do," a kind of crew-cut ponytail that Hollywood hairstylist Jay Sebring invented for the film. A young Saul Bass contributed more than just the breathtaking titles: Douglas and Universal gave him free rein to develop the battle sequences and gladiator school. Stanley Kubrick was playing poker when Douglas called him to take over the troubled production. Universal had insisted on Anthony Mann, but after two weeks of arguing over performances, Douglas paid the director his full salary and let him go. Kubrick, then thirty years old, did not immediately win the crew's respect. He insisted on perfection from the extras and ordered camera coverage that exceeded anything the crew had ever done before. To test if the leading actress, Sabina Bethmann, could bring more emotion to her role of Varinia, Kubrick told her that she was dismissed. When she froze instead of reacting, he promptly let her go. He replaced her with Jean Simmons in the role. He insisted on a brutal realism in the war scenes and persuaded Douglas to add the final battle between the Romans and the slaves. The panoramic shots of the approaching Roman army took Kubrick a full week to shoot with the Spanish military. The character scenes shot at Hearst Castle and on the Universal lot were no less difficult. It irked Charles Laughton that rival Laurence Olivier's salary was five times his own. The competition between the two actors became so fierce that Olivier required someone else to feed him his lines. Nine months were spent on the film's sound design, which included the recording of 76,000 screaming fans at a Notre Dame–Michigan State football game.

DISTRIBUTION: The anti-Red press fumed when Douglas revealed that Trumbo wrote the screenplay. They saw the film as Communist propaganda and urged moviegoers to boycott. But by this time, much of the McCarthy hysteria had died down. President John F. Kennedy buoyed support by slipping into a public screening in Washington, D.C., to watch it. Douglas originally wanted the premiere to be held in the Baths of Caracalla when the Olympics were finished. Universal needed more time for publicity, so Spartacus opened in October. Anthony Hopkins dubbed Olivier's voice for a 1991 rerelease that restored scenes cut by the censors, incorporating one that suggested Crassus's bisexuality. Kubrick himself never thought of Spartacus as part of his oeuvre, since he hadn't seen it through from conception. —*Michael Kogge*

THE GUNS OF NAVARONE
Columbia, 1961

ALL-RELEASE EQUIVALENT 2005 $s
(Unadjusted $s) in Millions of $s

Domestic Box Office Revenues........ **$240.5**/($28.9)
Production Cost .... **$45.7**/($7.0)
Principal Photography...........**100** days estimated
2/9/1960–10/11/1960

Director . . . . J. Lee Thompson

Producer . . . . Carl Foreman

Production Company. . . . Open Road Films

Story by . . . . Based on the novel by Alistair MacLean

Screenplay by . . . . Carl Foreman

Cast . . . . Gregory Peck, David Niven, Anthony Quinn, Stanley Baker, Anthony Quayle, Irene Papas, Gia Scala

Filming Locations . . . . . . Produced in England; on location in Rhodes, Greece, and Iverson Ranch, Chatsworth, CA; in Studio at Shepperton, Elstree studios, U.K.

Genre. . . . . War

Format . . . . Color (Eastmancolor)

Initial Release 7/1/1961

Rerelease. . . . . none

Running Time . . . . 159 minutes

MPAA Rating . . . . not rated

STANDING THE TEST OF TIME

ACADEMY AWARD Oscar Nominations and Wins

Best Motion Picture: Carl Foreman, Producer

Directing: J. Lee Thompson

Film Editing: Alan Osbiston

Music (Music Score of a Dramatic or Comedy Picture): Dimitri Tiomkin

Sound: Shepperton Studio Sound Dept., John Cox, Sound Director

***SPECIAL EFFECTS:** Visual Effects by Bill Warrington; Audible Effects by Vivian C. Greenham

Writing (Screenplay – based on material from another medium): Carl Foreman

OSCAR TOTALS   Nominations **7**   *Wins **1**

AFI 100 YEARS 100 MOVIES SELECTION
2007 0   1997 0

TOP 300 FILMS POSITION . . . . **#174**
All-Release Domestic Box Office in Equivalent 2005 $s

National Film Preservation Board Selection. . . . none

OTHER AWARDS Best Picture Wins

	Year
Golden Globes (Drama).	1962
New York Film Critics	none
National Board of Review	none
Film Daily Critics	none

There's a hint of moral dilemma when it becomes necessary for a girl partisan to be killed, but the problem is easily solved by allowing a female compatriot to do the job.
—Penelope Gilliatt, *London Observer*, 1961

PLOT: A British commando unit is formed in 1943 to rescue 1,200 Allied soldiers and to destroy a garrison of German heavy artillery set on perilous cliffs.

PRODUCTION: Working within the British film industry after being blacklisted in the United States, Carl Foreman, under contract to Columbia Pictures, acquired the screen rights to Alistair MacLean's 1957 best seller. Foreman's adaptation differed from the novel, emphasizing more heroic qualities in the characters. It was to be a full location shoot with physical challenges, including a dangerous scaling of cliffs and a storm sequence at sea. Two cast members were actual World War II veterans, David Niven and Anthony Quayle. William Holden was initially cast as Captain Keith Mallory but was rejected after he asked for $750,000 plus 10 percent of the gross and negotiations fell apart. Gregory Peck signed on instead for $350,000 plus a smaller percentage. David Niven replaced Kenneth Moore. Alexander Mackendrick came aboard as director. Shooting began as scheduled but director problems emerged as the footage was viewed. It was determined by producer Carl Foreman that the action challenge was too much for Mackendrick, so he halted production on March 10 and called for replacement candidates. The studio submitted three names, all British: Michael Anderson, J. Lee Thompson, and Guy Hamilton. Their previous action films were screened. Foreman, with studio approval, settled on J. Lee Thompson, a former Royal Air Force pilot who had less than a week to prepare. Thompson hit the ground running, starting March 15. "Soon we saw that we were in good hands," reflected Peck, although the production ran into more difficulties. The sea storm sequence, insufficiently budgeted, caused Quinn to injure his back, and then Niven became gravely ill. Thompson was a tiny man and often held a sketchpad. He refused to read the script until it was time to shoot the scene, and then he would make one arbitrary decision after another. A character would smoke, grab a knife, fool with sticks of dynamite. In a 1998 interview Peck said, "We all played it tongue in cheek. We couldn't have played it dead straight." J. Lee Thompson later said, "It had its basis in truth. There were German guns in the straits between Turkey and Greece. They were tremendous guns and we couldn't get any naval ships past them. In real life they [the commandos] didn't succeed. The guns eventually fell because Germany fell." When the film went over budget and over schedule, Foreman granted that the production was in trouble but assured the studio that the film would be completed and judged a success.

DISTRIBUTION: Word filtered from Europe to Hollywood that Columbia had a major release in the offing. The studio decided to release the film in the United Kingdom first, assuming that it would be a hit with critics and audiences, setting up advance word in the United States. The gamble paid off. Although the film received seven Academy Award nominations, the actors were bypassed. It was one of the highest-grossing films released in 1961 and is considered one of Peck's most financially rewarding, because he had a percentage of the gross. —*Frank McAdams*

THE HUSTLER
20th Century-Fox, 1961

ALL-RELEASE EQUIVALENT 2005 $s
(Unadjusted $s) in Millions of $s

Domestic Box Office Revenues . . . . $70.3/($8.4)
Production Cost . . . . $13.1/($2.0)
Principal Photography . . . . **52** days
3/6/1961–5/15/1961

Director . . . . Robert Rossen
Producer . . . . Robert Rossen
Production Company . . . . Rossen Enterprises
Story by . . . . Based on the novel by Walter Tevis
Screenplay by . . . . Robert Rossen, Sidney Carroll
Cast . . . . Paul Newman, Jackie Gleason, Piper Laurie, George C. Scott
Filming Locations . . . . . . Los Angeles, New York
Genre . . . . Drama
Format . . . . B&W
Initial Release 9/25/1961
Rerelease . . . . none
Running Time . . . . 135 minutes
MPAA Rating . . . . not rated

STANDING THE TEST OF TIME

ACADEMY AWARD Oscar Nominations and Wins

Best Motion Picture: Robert Rossen, Producer

Actor: Paul Newman

Actor in a Supporting Role: Jackie Gleason

Actor in a Supporting Role: George C. Scott

Actress: Piper Laurie

***ART DIRECTION/SET DECORATION:** Harry Horner/Gene Callahan

***CINEMATOGRAPHY:** Eugen Schüfftan

Directing: Robert Rossen

Writing (Screenplay – based on material from another medium): Sidney Carroll, Robert Rossen

OSCAR TOTALS   Nominations **9**   *Wins 2

AFI 100 YEARS 100 MOVIES SELECTION
2007 0   1997 0

TOP 300 FILMS POSITION . . . . none
All-Release Domestic Box Office in Equivalent 2005 $s

National Film Preservation Board Selection 1997

OTHER AWARDS Best Picture Wins

	Year
Golden Globes	none
New York Film Critics	none
National Board of Review	none
Film Daily Critics	none

With Paul interesting things happened. Starting from the character . . . he finds himself questioning the entire universe. And so the first time you rehearse with him, he has so many things to do, so many problems to resolve, that you think there will be no coming out of them ever.

—Robert Rossen

PLOT: Arrogant, small-time pool hustler Fast Eddie (Paul Newman) yearns to beat the reigning champ, Minnesota Fats (Jackie Gleason), but the challenge proves tougher than Eddie imagined.

PRODUCTION: The novel by Walter Tevis that the film is based on was optioned to several people, including Frank Sinatra, before Robert Rossen optioned the rights. No one was able to figure out how to effectively translate the book for the screen and bring drama to a story about the game of pool until Rossen got hold of it. Paul Newman committed to the role of Fast Eddie after reading only half of the script. Once the ball was rolling, the actors had two solid weeks of rehearsal time before shooting began. Newman and Gleason were coached by top pool player Willie Mosconi, winner of fourteen world championships between 1941 and 1957. Newman, who claimed to have never picked up a pool cue before this film, had a pool table installed in his house before and during shooting. The filmmakers chose the Ames Billiard Academy in New York City because of its size and authentic age and character. Even so, the art department spent two weeks making the location look more worn down and lived in, to fit the mood of the film. Willie Mosconi coached the actors during shooting by often shouting instructions to them from the sidelines. His voice was later cut out in sound editing. Gleason, a seasoned pool player, did most of his own playing. During production, the studio decided to change the title to *Sin of Angels,* but later changed it back to *The Hustler.* Fox executives were nervous about the film—they had low expectations about how it would perform. At the time, Fox was hemorrhaging money on the *Cleopatra* production, adding to fears about other projects. The apartment where many of Piper Laurie and Paul Newman's scenes were shot was built on a stage at Fox Studios in New York. During the shoot, Rossen decided to start with the pool competition scenes within the first few weeks and to shoot them in sequence to ensure the best performances from the cast. The movie was shot in black and white and Cinemascope by German cinematographer Eugen Schüfftan, who won one of the two Oscars.

DISTRIBUTION: Against the wishes of 20th Century-Fox, the film was edited in New York City as Robert Rossen had requested. When the film came out in the United States, many people assumed that Fast Eddie and Minnesota Fats were real people, when in fact they were fictional characters. Subsequently two well-known pool players changed their names to Fast Eddie and Minnesota Fats, causing more confusion. Two decades after *The Hustler,* Newman reprised his role as Fast Eddie in Martin Scorsese's *The Color of Money* (1986) with Tom Cruise. Newman's character makes a reference to *The Hustler* in the later film when he says that someone "retired" him at pool a long time ago, referring to Gleason's character, Minnesota Fats. Paul Newman did win an Oscar for his portrayal of Fast Eddie, but it was in *The Color of Money* and not for his work in *The Hustler.* —*Dina Gachman*

WEST SIDE STORY
United Artists, 1961

ALL-RELEASE EQUIVALENT 2005 $s
(Unadjusted $s) in Millions of $s

Domestic Box Office Revenues........**$350.1**/($50.9)
Production Cost ....**$45.7**/($7.0)
Principal Photography...........**110** days estimated
8/10/1960–February 1961

Director	Robert Wise, Jerome Robbins
Producer	Robert Wise
Production Company	Mirisch Pictures, B and P Enterprises
Story by	Arthur Laurents (based loosely on Shakespeare's play *Romeo & Juliet*)
Screenplay by	Ernest Lehman
Cast	Natalie Wood, Richard Breymer, Russ Tamblyn, Rita Morena, George Chakiris
Filming Locations	On location in Mahanttan, New York; in studio at Samuel Goldwyn Studios, Los Angeles, CA
Genre	Musical
Format	Color (Technicolor)
Initial Release	10/18/1961 world premiere and initial road show release; 9/1/1962 general release
Rerelease	1968, 1971, 1989
Running Time	155 minutes
MPAA Rating	not rated

STANDING THE TEST OF TIME

ACADEMY AWARD Oscar Nominations and Wins

*BEST MOTION PICTURE: Robert Wise, Producer

*ACTOR IN A SUPPORTING ROLE: George Chakiris

*ACTRESS IN A SUPPORTING ROLE: Rita Moreno

*ART DIRECTION/SET DECORATION: Boris Leven/Victor A. Gangelin

*CINEMATOGRAPHY: Daniel L. Fapp

*COSTUME DESIGN: Irene Sharaff

*DIRECTING: Robert Wise, Jerome Robbins

*FILM EDITING: Thomas Stanford

*MUSIC (Scoring of a Musical Picture): Saul Chaplin, Johnny Green, Sid Ramin, Irwin Kostal

*SOUND: Todd-AO Sound Dept., Fred Hynes, Sound Director; and Samuel Goldwyn Studio Sound Dept., Gordon E. Sawyer, Sound Director

Writing (Screenplay – based on material from another medium): Ernest Lehman

OSCAR TOTALS Nominations **11** *Wins **10**

AFI 100 YEARS 100 MOVIES SELECTION
2007 . . . #51   1997 . . . #41

TOP 300 FILMS POSITION . . . . **#72**
All-Release Domestic Box Office in Equivalent 2005 $s

National Film Preservation Board Selection. . . . 1997

OTHER AWARDS Best Picture Wins

	Year
Golden Globes (Musical)	1962
New York Film Critics	1961
National Board of Review	none
Film Daily Critics	none

To make it acceptable for kids to be dancing in the streets.

—Robert Wise, when asked what the biggest challenge as a filmmaker was with regard to *West Side Story*

PLOT: The forbidden love story of Maria and Tony is set against the teeming slums of 1950s Manhattan, where racial tensions created open warfare between the members of rival teen gangs from different ethnic and cultural backgrounds.

PRODUCTION: In 1949 writer Arthur Laurents and choreographer Jerome Robbins wanted to do a Broadway musical that would be a modern-day *Romeo and Juliet.* They intended it to be about an Italian Catholic boy who falls for a Jewish Holocaust survivor on the teeming East Side of New York City, set around Easter and Passover, to be called *East Side Story.* In 1954, however, with a wave of Puerto Rican immigration into the city, Laurents changed the boy to a Polish Catholic and the girl to a Puerto Rican. In 1955 Steven Sondheim came aboard to write songs and lyrics. The play opened September 26, 1957, and ran for 734 performances but was beat out for the Best Musical Tony by *The Music Man,* which played twice as many performances. Its dark themes and social realism were a break with the lighter musicals typical of the time. The language and gang culture were controversial. United Artists film producer Walter Mirisch was an admirer and paid the play's producer, Harold Prince, $375,000 plus 10 percent of the movie gross for the rights. Choreographer Jerome Robbins and composer Leonard Bernstein, whose breakthrough score blended jazz, avant-garde, Broadway, and Latin music, also received a percentage of profits. Jerome Robbins was to be co-director of the movie, concentrating on musical and dance aspects, while Robert Wise, who had been Orson Welles's editor on *Citizen Kane* and was far more experienced, having already directed twenty-seven films, focused on the dramatic scenes. Conflicts arose soon after production began. Robbins's painstaking direction of the dances put the production behind schedule. When the movie was a third done and already $300,000 over budget, the studio dropped Robbins, who had choreographed only four numbers. He still got screen credit. Wise fought for realistic location shooting in New York, adding both cost and authenticity to the movie. The interior filming was on Goldwyn Studio soundstages in Los Angeles, where thirty-five sets were built six feet off the ground to allow low angle shots. Although six members of the original Broadway cast appeared in the movie, most were considered too old to play teens. Singing by the leads, Natalie Wood and Richard Beymer, was dubbed in postproduction. Woods, who early on tried to get Beymer fired due to his weak voice and lack of dance skills, was ultimately voiced by Marni Nixon, while Jimmy Bryant sang for Beymer. Of the principal cast, only George Chakiris did all of his own singing. Wise's direction set new standards for musical movies, which had previously consisted of long shots of song and dance numbers. By contrast, Wise played with quick edits and varied his angles, serving his goal of presenting the characters more realistically. The costuming was trend-setting. It was the first example of gangs identified by colors, in this case by the low-cut sneakers each wore.

DISTRIBUTION: *West Side Story* opened at the Rivoli Theater in New York on October 18, 1961, and was critically acclaimed. It played a road show engagement for sixty-eight weeks and became the highest-grossing movie of the year. The soundtrack album sold more copies than any previous movie musical. With its three rereleases, it took in over $105 million in worldwide box office ($720 million in 2005 dollars). —*Hayley Taylor Block*

THE LONGEST DAY

20th Century-Fox, 1962

ALL-RELEASE EQUIVALENT 2005 $s

(Unadjusted $s) in Millions of $s

Domestic Box Office Revenues........ **$259.5**/($34.2)
Production Cost .... **$55.6**/($8.6)
Principal Photography.......... **200** days estimated
June 1961–April 1962

Director	Ken Annakin, Andrew Marton, Bernhard Wicki
Producer	Darryl F. Zanuck
Production Company	Darryl F. Zanuck Productions
Story by	Based on the book by Cornelius Ryan
Screenplay by	Cornelius Ryan; additional episodes written by Romain Gary, James Jones, David Pursall, Jack Seddon
Cast	John Wayne, Robert Mitchum, Henry Fonda, Robert Ryan, Rod Steiger, Robert Wagner, Richard Beymer, Mel Ferrer, Jeffrey Hunter, Paul Anka, Sal Mineo
Filming Locations	On Location: Normandy, Corsica; in Studio: 20th Century-Fox, CA
Genre	War
Format	B&W
Initial Release	10/3/1962 road show release; 3/22/1963 reserve seating release
Rerelease	1969
Running Time	180 minutes
MPAA Rating	not rated

STANDING THE TEST OF TIME

ACADEMY AWARD Oscar Nominations and Wins

Best Picture: Darryl F. Zanuck, Producer

Art Direction/Set Decoration: Ted Haworth, Leon Barsacq, Vincent Korda/Gabriel Bechir

***CINEMATOGRAPHY:** Jean Bourgoin, Walter Wottitz, Henri Persin (Persin's name was later deleted)

Film Editing: Samule E. Beetley

***SPECIAL EFFECTS:** Visual Effects by Robert MacDonald; Audible Effects by Jacques Maumont

OSCAR TOTALS   Nominations **5**   *Wins **2**

AFI 100 YEARS 100 MOVIES SELECTION
2007 0   1997 0

TOP 300 FILMS POSITION . . . . #145
All-Release Domestic Box Office in Equivalent 2005 $s

National Film Preservation Board Selection . . . . none

OTHER AWARDS Best Picture Wins

	Year
Golden Globes	none
New York Film Critics	none
National Board of Review	1962
Film Daily Critics	none

*[Cornelius] Ryan is now in Paris ironing out the wrinkles in the script . . .
It is the most expensive and difficult undertaking I have ever attempted in my life.*

—Darryl F. Zanuck

PLOT: The epic retelling of the Normandy invasion from the perspective of both the Allies and the Germans.

PRODUCTION: Raoul J. Levy, a French producer, acquired the first option on Cornelius Ryan's 1959 best seller. When financing fell through, Darryl Zanuck stepped up and bought out Levy's option. In a break with previous war films, Zanuck enlisted technical advisors of four nationalities: French, British, German, and American. Three directors would be used along with five credited screenwriters. Associate producers Elmo Williams and Frank McCarthy began working on logistics. McCarthy began lobbying the Department of Defense for extras, ships, planes, and landing craft. British Spitfire and German Messerschmitt fighter planes had to be built. More than 500,000 rounds of blank cartridges were needed. There were 162 international speaking parts; French and German actors spoke in their own language with subtitles. Zanuck kept demanding rewrites as the production date loomed. William Holden abruptly left the film and was replaced by John Wayne, who asked for, and got, $250,000 for his appearance. McCarthy was able to use the U.S. Sixth Fleet's amphibious maneuvers at Saleccia Beach in northern Corsica. A reinforced Marine Corps battalion was outfitted with camouflaged net helmets and World War II–type leggings. The Americans were joined by a flotilla of French vessels, resulting in a combined fleet of 22 ships that would substitute for the 5,000 that were actually used on D-Day. Henry Grace, an MGM set designer, was cast as General Eisenhower because of his remarkable likeness. British actor Richard Todd, a Normandy veteran, was cast as Major John Howard, defender of the Orne River bridge. Eddie Albert, a decorated Navy veteran, was cast as Colonel Thompson. British actor Christopher Lee, an RAF veteran, was turned down for a role because he didn't look military enough. Trevor Reid was cast as British field marshal Bernard Montgomery because of his likeness. The production began with the landing sequence in Corsica. When the marines left the Higgins boats and trudged through the water, many were seasick and had already thrown up. The assault on the cliffs at Pointe du Hoc, on the right side of Omaha Beach, was filmed at the actual location. The sheer cliffs dropped eighty feet down to a gravel beach. There was no need to cast Adolf Hitler: the Führer was intentionally off camera, on the phone, or asleep. Later, Richard Burton and Roddy McDowall came in from the set of *Cleopatra* for their cameo parts. Local citizens from the town of Ste.-Mère-Eglise were used as extras for the harrowing nighttime sequence where German soldiers were shooting American paratroopers out of the sky. Red Buttons hung in a parachute for four nights on the church steeple. Many of the actual bunkers on the cliffs above the Normandy beach were used in the film.

DISTRIBUTION: The film opened to strong trade reviews and took in $33.2 million in worldwide rentals, resulting in a net profit of $4.2 million during its initial release. The premiere festivities were held in Manhattan over two days, complete with a star-drenched banquet and a Broadway parade that featured the Fordham University marching band. *The Longest Day* set a docudrama precedent for productions designed to portray historical incidents, telling the story from several perspectives. It is one of the highest-grossing war films worldwide of all time. —*Frank McAdams*

LAWRENCE OF ARABIA
Columbia, 1962

ALL-RELEASE EQUIVALENT 2005 $s
(Unadjusted $s) in Millions of $s

Domestic Box Office Revenues. . . . . . . **$290.2**/($44.5)
Production Cost . . . . **$97.0**/($15.0)
Principal Photography. . . . .**125** days estimated
5/15/1961–9/29/1961 Jordan
12/8/1961–7/4/1962 Spain
7/14/1962–8/18/1962 Morocco

Director . . . . David Lean

Producer . . . . Sam Spiegel

Production Company. . . . Horizon Pictures

Story by. . . . . Based on the writings of
T. E. Lawrence

Screenplay by . . . . Robert Bolt, Michael Wilson

Cast . . . . Peter O'Toole, Alec Guinness,
Anthony Quinn, Jack Hawkins,
Jose Ferrer, Anthony Quayle,
Claude Rains, Arthur Kennedy,
Omar Sharif

Filming Locations . . . . . . Morocco, Spain; England,
Jordan; Wales; and California;
Shepperton Studios,
Shepperton, Surrey, England

Genre. . . . . Bio-Drama

Format. . . . . Color (Technicolor)

Initial Release . . . . 12/10/1962 premiere (UK);
12/16/1962 premiere (New
York); 12/21/1962 premiere
(Los Angeles); February 1963
general release, after initial
road show engagements

Rerelease. 1971, 1989, 1994, 2002

Running Time . . . . 222 minutes (initial release
1962); 202 minutes (general
release 1963); restored 70 mm
format 217 minutes (released
theatrically 1989)

MPAA Rating . . . . not rated

STANDING THE TEST OF TIME

ACADEMY AWARD Oscar Nominations and Wins

*BEST PICTURE: Sam Spiegel, Producer

Actor: Peter O'Toole

Actor in a Supporting Role: Omar Sharif

*ART DIRECTION/SET DECORATION: John Box,
John Stoll/Dario Simoni

*CINEMATOGRAPHY: Fred A. Young

*DIRECTING: David Lean

*FILM EDITING: Anne Coates

*MUSIC (Music Score – substantially original):
Maurice Jarre

*SOUND: Shepperton Studio Sound Dept., John
Cox, Sound Director

Writing (Screenplay – based on material from
another medium): Robert Bolt, Michael Wilson
(then-blacklisted co-author Michael Wilson was
given credit by The Academy in 1995)

OSCAR TOTALS   Nominations **10** *Wins 7

AFI 100 YEARS 100 MOVIES SELECTION
2007 . . . . #7   1997 . . . . #5

TOP 300 FILMS POSITION . . . . #110
All-Release Domestic Box Office in Equivalent 2005 $s

National Film Preservation Board Selection. . . . 1991

OTHER AWARDS Best Picture Wins

	Year
Golden Globes (Drama).	1963
New York Film Critics.	none
National Board of Review.	none
Film Daily Critics.	none

We were a great team . . . but I couldn't go on with Sam [Spiegel] . . .)
I couldn't trust him.

—David Lean after quarreling with Spiegel in 1963 over Lean's share of the film's profits

PLOT: A scholarly young British officer sent to evaluate the Arab revolt against the Turks becomes a charismatic guerrilla leader who temporarily unifies the Arab factions.

PRODUCTION: Thomas Edward Lawrence had resisted attempts to film his life story through his death in 1935. In a 1952 letter to Columbia studio head Harry Cohn, director David Lean wrote about Lawrence's autobiography, *Seven Pillars of Wisdom,* "I can't think of a better subject for my first film in America." Competing scripts led both Lean and Columbia to back out, but when producer Sam Spiegel acquired the rights in 1960, the project came together. Six days later, Columbia announced that Marlon Brando would play Lawrence and Lean would direct. Brando dropped out and Albert Finney turned down the part before Lean found Peter O'Toole, whom he saw in *The Day They Robbed the Bank of England.* Spiegel was less enthusiastic, but tests soon convinced him. Spiegel and Lean had been working on the script with Michael Wilson, but after three drafts Wilson withdrew. He had wanted to examine sociopolitical aspects of international relations during World War I, while Lean was more interested in a psychological study of a unique character. Playwright Robert Bolt was brought in to replace Wilson. Although much of the structure remained from Wilson's script, Bolt received sole screenwriting credit. Only in a 1989 restoration of the film did both men get on-screen credit for the work. The first scene to be shot was a simple one: two men, Lawrence and Tafas, riding across the desert on camels. It took Lean nearly a month to shoot. The scale of the scene was enhanced by the new Super Panavision 70 film, with a 65mm negative. Since the camera was heavy and not very mobile, it was mounted on a miniature locomotive with a crane attached. A four-wheel-drive camera car called the CAM-EL (camera elevator) had its own darkroom. With further delays, the film had grown so large and behind budget that additional second units had to be brought in. One second-unit director was André de Toth, a Hungarian-born Hollywood director of westerns and thrillers who shot in Spain and later Morocco.

DISTRIBUTION: To ensure postproduction wrapped up quickly, Spiegel arranged for the film to be shown in the presence of Queen Elizabeth on December 10, 1962, a Monday. On Sunday it was screened for the film crew. No one had seen the film from beginning to end before. When both audiences saw it, they were swept away. Even in the midst of a newspaper strike that cut down on ads, there were long lines at the New York theater premiere. The road show opening, helped by Lawrence's seven Oscars and glowing press notices, was a box office smash: it played for a year in London, Madrid, and throughout the United States. As selected by the British Film Institute in 1996, it is the number three film in the top 100 British films of the twentieth century. —*Louis Burklow*

TO KILL A MOCKINGBIRD
Universal, 1962

ALL-RELEASE EQUIVALENT 2005 $s
(Unadjusted $s) in Millions of $s

Domestic Box Office Revenues......... **$126.6**/($16.0)
Production Cost .... **$12.9**/($2.0)
Principal Photography............ **65** days estimated
March 1962–May 1962

Director	Robert Mulligan
Producer	Alan J. Pakula
Production Company....	Universal-International Films, Pakula-Mulligan Productions, Brentwood Production
Story by..............	Based on the novel by Harper Lee
Screenplay by	Horton Foote
Cast	Gregory Peck, Mary Badham, Phillip Alford, John Megna, Frank Overton, Rosemary Murphy, Robert Duvall
Filming Locations	On location in Monroeville, AL; in studio at Universal Studios, Universal City, CA
Genre................	Drama
Format...............	B&W
Initial Release	12/25/1962
Rerelease.............	none
Running Time	129 minutes
MPAA Rating	not rated

STANDING THE TEST OF TIME

ACADEMY AWARD Oscar Nominations and Wins

Best Picture: Alan J. Pakula, Producer

*ACTOR: Gregory Peck

Actress in a Supporting Role: Mary Badham

*ART DIRECTION/SET DECORATION: Alexander Golitzen, Henry Bumstead/Oliver Emert

Cinematography (B&W): Russell Harlan

Directing: Robert Mulligan

Music: (Music Score – substantially original): Elmer Bernstein

*WRITING (Screenplay – based on material from another medium): Horton Foote

OSCAR TOTALS   Nominations **8**   *Wins 3

AFI 100 YEARS 100 MOVIES SELECTION
2007 . . . #25   1997 . . . #34

TOP 300 FILMS POSITION ....none
All-Release Domestic Box Office in Equivalent 2005 $s

National Film Preservation Board Selection.... 1995

OTHER AWARDS Best Picture Wins

	Year
Golden Globes	none
New York Film Critics....................	none
National Board of Review.................	none
Film Daily Critics........................	none

[Harper's story] has become as much a part of the American myth as Huckleberry Finn *and* Tom Sawyer. *I think the triumph of the film is that it captured the soul of that book.*

—Alan J. Pakula

PLOT: A widowed lawyer in 1930s rural Alabama defends a young black man accused of raping a white woman. The story is told through the eyes of his six-year-old tomboy daughter.

PRODUCTION: Robert Mulligan, movie director and one of the foremost directors of TV dramas such as *Playhouse 90,* formed Pakula-Mulligan Productions in 1962 with producer Alan J. Pakula to film Harper Lee's semiautobiographical novel about her small-town southern life and racial unrest. The character Dill was based on Lee's real-life neighbor Truman Capote. Lee's sole novel won the Pulitzer Prize in 1960, a critical time at the beginning of the civil rights movement. Although the book was a best seller, studios felt it wouldn't work as a film. They said it had no real story. Mulligan sent the book to Gregory Peck, who loved it and identified with the story. He felt it was something he "had to do." Peck met with Lee's father, attorney Amasa Lee, her model for Atticus Finch, who was amused that his tomboy daughter had grown up to be a Pulitzer Prize winner. Peck studied Lee's father's mannerisms, which became part of his character. Mulligan wanted Horton Foote to write the screenplay, but Foote resisted, concerned about adapting a work he loved. Mulligan introduced Lee to Foote, and Foote ultimately agreed. Mulligan searched in the South for "real children" for the roles of Scout and Jem. Philip Alford, who had some theater experience, agreed to audition only because it meant he could skip school. Mary Badham had no previous acting experience. Because the town of Monroeville, Alabama, where Lee's story takes place, had grown after World War II, Henry Bumstead, the production designer, found a San Fernando Valley town about to be destroyed that looked to him like the 1930s South. He moved all the houses to a back lot in Hollywood. Robert Duvall, cast in his first role as the reclusive Boo Radley, stayed out of the sun for six weeks and dyed his hair blond for the role. The title sequence captured the secret world of childhood with a series of small objects and toys (which have important and symbolic meanings in the film) seen through the eyes of a child who is humming quietly to herself. Elmer Bernstein, who had worked with Mulligan on a previous film, developed the lyrical score, which he was inspired to write while imagining what a child would play at the piano. Mulligan conceived the set as a place where the children could feel as if they were in their own backyard. Lee visited the set the first day of shooting and was stunned that it looked so much like her hometown. She started crying during the first scene because Peck reminded her of her father, who had passed away before filming began. Mulligan said the courtroom scene (which took 2–3 weeks to film) was the most difficult. Producer Alan J. Pakula got a note from the studio, after they had seen the film dailies, saying they were worried Peck didn't look glamorous enough.

DISTRIBUTION: *To Kill a Mockingbird* was praised for taking a piece with potential for melodrama, violence, and hatred and giving it nuance. Even Harper Lee agreed that the film lost nothing of the spirit of her original novel. It was Gregory Peck's favorite work and the movie for which he is best remembered. During filming, Peck formed close friendships with the cast, including Mary Badham (Scout), to whom he became a surrogate father, and Brock Peters, who delivered Peck's eulogy in 2003. —*Hayley Taylor Block*

HOW THE WEST WAS WON
MGM, 1963

ALL-RELEASE EQUIVALENT 2005 $s
(Unadjusted $s) in Millions of $s

Domestic Box Office Revenues........ **$325.3**/($43.2)
Production Cost .... **$94.4**/($14.6)
Principal Photography.....................**189** days
5/26/1961–11/30/1961

Director . . . . John Ford (*The Civil War*),
George Marshall (*The Railroad*),
Henry Hathaway (*The Rivers,
The Plains, The Outlaws*)

Producer . . . . Bernard Smith

Production Company . . . . Cinerama, Inc.,
Metro-Goldwyn-Mayer

Story by . . . . James R. Webb

Screenplay by . . . . James R. Webb

Cast . . . . Carroll Baker, Lee J. Cobb,
Henry Fonda, Carolyn Jones,
Karl Malden, Gregory Peck,
George Peppard, Robert
Preston, Debbie Reynolds,
James Stewart, Eli Wallach,
John Wayne, Richard Widmark;
narrated by Spencer Tracy

Filming Locations . . . . . . South Dakota, Illinois,
Colorado, Kentucky, Arizona,
Utah, Oregon, California, and
at MGM Studio in Culver City,
CA

Genre . . . . Western

Format . . . . Color (Technicolor for Cinerama
prints; Metrocolor for 70 mm
and 35 mm prints)

Initial Release . . . . 11/01/1962 world premiere
Casino Cinerama Theatre
(London); 2/20/1963 U.S.
premiere Warner Hollywood
Theater (Hollywood, CA)

Rerelease . . . . 1969–70, 2003 (limited), 2005
(limited)

Running Time . . . . 162 minutes (plus overture and
intermission music)

MPAA Rating . . . . not rated

STANDING THE TEST OF TIME

ACADEMY AWARD Oscar Nominations and Wins

Best Picture: Bernard Smith, Producer

Art Direction/Set Decoration: George W. Davis,
William Ferrari, Addison Hehr/Henry Grace,
Don Greenwood Jr., Jack Mills

Cinematography: William H. Daniels, Milton Krasner,
Charles Lang Jr., Joseph LaShelle

Costumer Design: Walter Plunkett

*FILM EDITING: Harold F. Kress

Music (Music Score – substantially original): Alfred
Newman, Ken Darby

*SOUND: Metro-Goldwyn-Mayer Studio Sound
Dept., Franklin E. Milton, Sound Director

*WRITING (Story and Screenplay – based on
material from another medium): James R. Webb

OSCAR TOTALS   Nominations **8**   *Wins **3**

AFI 100 YEARS 100 MOVIES SELECTION
2007 0   1997 0

TOP 300 FILMS POSITION . . . .**#87**
All-Release Domestic Box Office in Equivalent 2005 $s

National Film Preservation Board Selection 1997

OTHER AWARDS Best Picture Wins

	Year
Golden Globes	none
New York Film Critics	none
National Board of Review	none
Film Daily Critics	none

PLOT: Set against a backdrop of intriguing historical events and life-threatening conflicts, three generations of the pioneering Prescott family experience the development and expansion of the American West in an odyssey that spans fifty years.

PRODUCTION: In 1959 *Life* magazine published a seven-part series, "How the West Was Won," with the first installment as the cover story of the magazine's April 6 issue and the final chapter appearing on May 18. Readers were enthralled: it is estimated that 25 million people read the series during its run. One of those readers was entertainer Bing Crosby, who purchased the rights to the series to serve as the foundation of a record album of pioneer-era songs. The album was recorded and distributed by Crosby's own record label under the same title. Crosby then realized the material's potential as either a television series (ultimately deemed too expensive) or an epic motion picture. Metro-Goldwyn-Mayer agreed and purchased the rights from Crosby, who signed over his share of any potential profits to benefit St. John's Hospital of Santa Monica, California. For a production of such scope, MGM partnered with Fred Waller and his Cinerama Corporation. Waller had labored for sixteen years developing his latest wide-screen process—utilizing a three-lens camera and three projectors on a curved theater screen—that mimicked the full range of human vision. Cinerama (an anagram of *American*) debuted on September 30, 1952, with the premiere of *This Is Cinerama*, which stunned audiences and became a top-grossing film of 1952. Hollywood studios, however, balked at the expense, and only a handful of travelogues (*Cinerama Holiday, Seven Wonders of the World,* and others) followed—until Metro agreed to simultaneously shoot both *The Wonderful World of the Brothers Grimm* and *How the West Was Won* in "Waller's Wonder," Cinerama. Three directors—John Ford, George Marshall, and Henry Hathaway—were assigned to the epic, budgeted at an astonishing $15 million. Filming in Cinerama generated mixed reactions from the filmmakers. Hathaway, having studied the Cinerama process in depth, became adept at working around its limitations. Ford, however, complained about having to dress such large sets, since Cinerama captured a much wider view than the standard single-camera process. "Every time the camera is moved 10 feet," joked actor Robert Preston to a reporter, "they have to dress another 200 acres." Close-up shots with the massive camera required positioning just inches from the actors' faces, unnerving some of the cast as well.

DISTRIBUTION: In late 1962, with most domestic Cinerama venues tied up with engagements of *Brothers Grimm* and *The Best of Cinerama,* MGM executives decided to hold off on the U.S. release of *How the West Was Won* until 1963. Business was robust, with the film garnering $19.4 million in domestic rentals. It would be the last three-strip Cinerama dramatic film to be made. Since no single-camera version was filmed simultaneously, there were two annoying and distracting dividing lines that were noticeable when the film was projected on flat, non-Cinerama theater screens. This was just one of the format's limitations. All told, "Waller's Wonder" was visually thrilling, but still impractical and cumbersome. *—Douglas Burns*

DR. NO

United, Artists 1963

ALL-RELEASE EQUIVALENT 2005 $s
(Unadjusted $s) in Millions of $s

Domestic Box Office Revenues......... **$121.2**/($16.1)
Production Cost .... **$7.0**/($1.1)
Principal Photography............**55** days estimated
1/16/1962–3/30/1962

Director .... Terence Young

Producer .... Harry Saltzman,
Albert R. Broccoli

Production Company.... Eon Productions

Story by.............. Based on the novel by
Ian Fleming

Screenplay by......... Richard Maibaum, Johanna
Harwood, Berkely Mather

Cast .... Sean Connery, Ursula Andress,
Joseph Wiseman, Jack Lord,
Bernard Lee

Filming Locations ...... On location in Jamaica,
Trinidad and Tobago, and
London; in studio at Pinewood
Studios, Buckinghamshire, UK

Genre................. Action Adventure

Format............... Color (Technicolor)

Initial Release .... 10/5/1962 (London); 5/8/1963
(U.S.)

Rerelease............. none

Running Time .... 111 minutes

MPAA Rating .... not rated

STANDING THE TEST OF TIME

ACADEMY AWARD Oscar Nominations and Wins

None

OSCAR TOTALS   Nominations 0   *Wins 0

AFI 100 YEARS 100 MOVIES SELECTION
2007 0   1997 0

TOP 300 FILMS POSITION .... none
All-Release Domestic Box Office in Equivalent 2005 $s

National Film Preservation Board Selection.... none

OTHER AWARDS Best Picture Wins

	Year
Golden Globes .... none
New York Film Critics..................... none
National Board of Review .... none
Film Daily Critics......................... none

It [Dr. No] was a miracle. When you look back on it we were just damn lucky and everything worked. It was just one of those things. It could have gone exactly the other way, and they'd have been sunk without a trace.

—Terence Young

PLOT: The British secret service sends James Bond to the West Indies to investigate the disappearance of another British agent and his secretary. The impeccably groomed and sophisticated secret agent has been accorded the designation 007, which means he's licensed to kill.

PRODUCTION: Plans for adapting Ian Fleming's modestly popular espionage novels into a film series began as early as the late 1950s, but it wasn't until Canadian producer Harry Saltzman optioned the novels—with the exception of *Casino Royale*—from Ian Fleming in 1960 that things began to work. Saltzman teamed with New Yorker Albert R. "Cubby" Broccoli and made a six-picture deal with United Artists in 1961. Although *Dr. No* was the sixth of the fourteen Bond novels, it became the first to reach the screen. There were at least five different scripts on *Dr. No,* including one in which the villain was a monkey. Broccoli was upset that after he had paid a lot of money for Fleming's novel, the book's story wasn't even part of the script. So director Terence Young worked with Joanna Harwood, his continuity girl on a previous picture, to make the screenplay more like the novel. By the time *Dr. No* began production, book sales were soaring thanks to President John F. Kennedy, who said it was what he currently had on his nightstand. Considered for the role of 007 were Roger Moore, Rex Harrison, Trevor Howard, Max Von Sydow, Patrick McGoohan, and a twenty-eight-year-old model, Peter Anthony, who had won a casting contest but couldn't act. Broccoli had seen Sean Connery in Disney's *Darby O'Gill and the Little People* (1958) and had to convince a reluctant UA that he was their lead actor. Terence Young spotted Ursula Andress in late 1961, and the producers hired her just before filming began in Jamaica. *Dr. No* had a modest budget, even in 1962. When cost overruns threatened to push the budget $100,000 over its $1 million limit, United Artists even weighed suspending production. (In 2005 dollars, *Dr. No*'s production cost was less than 5 percent of the $154.2 million spent on *Die Another Day,* 2002.) Filming was done on location, mainly in Jamaica, through February 26, 1962, then moved to Pinewood Studios until March 30, when principal photography ended. While Peter Hunt edited Young's footage, Broccoli commissioned Monty Norman to write the calypso-flavored score. But Noel Rodgers, then head of music at UA, called in composer John Barry to overhaul the theme tune, which he did by letting guitarist Vic Flick loose. The resulting distinctive twangy guitar has been heard in every one of the Bond films since.

DISTRIBUTION: *Dr. No* was released in Great Britain and other European markets in 1962 ahead of its U.S. debut in May 1963. Although the U.S. release was negatively affected by the political climate in the wake of the Cuban missile crisis, *Dr. No* had an advantage in that it arrived premarketed. Despite condemnation by the powerful Catholic League of Decency, the books were best sellers and had been serialized in *Playboy.* Ranked thirteenth in adjusted worldwide box office out of the twenty-one "official" Bond films released through 2006, *Dr. No* paved the way for every other movie in the franchise. In June 2005 the catch phrase "Bond. James Bond" was honored as one of the greatest quotations in cinema history by the American Film Institute. *Dr. No* is number forty-one on the list of the top 100 British films of the twentieth century as selected by the British Film Institute. —*Gary Dretzka*

CLEOPATRA
20th Century-Fox, 1963

ALL-RELEASE EQUIVALENT 2005 $s
(Unadjusted $s) in Millions of $s

Domestic Box Office Revenues . . . . **$435.7**/($57.8)
Production Cost . . . . **$280.8**/($44.0)
$31.1 actual cost net of
insurance reimbursement
Principal Photography . . . . **266** days (Italian
production) 9/25/1961–7/26/1962
10 month shoot + several weeks
of reshoots in Spain and London
UK production (not included above)
September 1960–November 1960

Director . . . . Joseph L. Mankiewicz
Producer . . . . Walter Wanger
Production Company . . . . MCL Films, 20th Century-Fox,
Walwa Films
Story by . . . . Based on histories by Plutarch,
Suetonius, Appian, and other
ancient sources and *The Life
and Times of Cleopatra* by
C. M. Franzero
Screenplay by . . . . Joseph L. Mankiewicz, Ranald
MacDougall, Sidney Buchman
Cast . . . . Elizabeth Taylor, Richard
Burton, Rex Harrison
Filming Locations . . . . . . In studio at Pinewood Studios,
London, UK; in studio at
Cinecittà Studios, Rome, Italy;
on Location: Spain: Almería,
Andalucía; Italy: Anzio, Rome,
Lazio, Ischia Island, Naples,
Campania; Egypt; Malibu, CA
Genre . . . . Historical Drama
Format . . . . Color (DeLuxe)
Initial Release . . . . 6/12/1963 premiere (New York)
Rerelease . . . . none

Running Time . . . . 243 minutes
MPAA Rating . . . . not rated

STANDING THE TEST OF TIME

ACADEMY AWARD Oscar Nominations and Wins

Best Picture: Walter Wanger, Producer

Actor: Rex Harrison

*ART DIRECTION/SET DECORATION: John
DeCuir, Jack Martin Smith, Hilyard Brown,
Herman Blumenthal, Elven Webb, Maurice
Pelling, Boris Juraga/Walter M. Scott,
Paul S. Fox, Ray Moyer

*CINEMATOGRAPHY: Leon Shamroy

*COSTUME DESIGN: Irene Sharaff, Vittorio Nino
Novarese, Renie

Film Editing: Dorothy Spencer

Music (Music Score – substantially original): Alex
North

Sound: 20th Century-Fox Studio Sound Dept., James
P. Corcoran, Sound Director; and Todd-AO Sound
Dept., Fred Hynes, Sound Director

*SPECIAL EFFECTS: Emil Kosa Jr.

OSCAR TOTALS   Nominations 9   *Wins 4

AFI 100 YEARS 100 MOVIES SELECTION
2007 0   1997 0

TOP 300 FILMS POSITION . . . . #34
All-Release Domestic Box Office in Equivalent 2005 $s

National Film Preservation Board Selection . . . . none

OTHER AWARDS Best Picture Wins

	Year
Golden Globes	none
New York Film Critics	none
National Board of Review	none
Film Daily Critics	none

*I can't afford the luxury of more talk. Interest on the $35 million the picture has consumed
amounts to $7,000 a day. Completing work on it will cost a couple million more.*
—Darryl F. Zanuck

PLOT: The life story of Egypt's Queen Cleopatra in the years leading up to the founding of the Roman Empire focuses on her love affairs with Julius Caesar and, after he is stabbed to death, with his successor, Marc Antony.

PRODUCTION: As theater attendance dropped with the rise of television, 20th Century-Fox was in financial trouble. Because it had endured a string of flops, studio president Spyros P. Skouras, a Greek immigrant and former movie exhibitor, called for a spectacle that couldn't be matched on the small screen. He and independent producer Walter Wanger joined forces in 1958 to remake the 1917 version of *Cleopatra,* which had starred Theda Bara. The plan included a budget under $2 million with a 64-day shooting schedule. In mid-1959 Wanger asked for more money, and the budget was boosted to $5 million. Rouben Mamoulian was the first director assigned to the project. Elizabeth Taylor's high-profile casting resulted in the first $1 million salary for a female star. Because the Summer Olympics were in Rome, filming began in England. After a brief start, Taylor became so sick that they had to shut down production, scrapping everything. Mamoulian was fired and left on January 18, 1961, after sixteen weeks of production, $7 million in costs, and 10 minutes of usable film. The insurance company footed the bill. Once Taylor recovered she was granted approval of director. She gave Fox two choices: George Stevens or Joseph Mankiewicz. Stevens was busy with *The Greatest Story Ever Told,* and so Mankiewicz got the job. Mankiewicz moved the set to the Cinecittà Studios, outside of Rome. Peter Finch and Stephen Boyd bowed out, and Rex Harrison came on as Caesar, followed by Richard Burton, who was bought out of his Broadway *Camelot* contract by Fox. The new plan called for 26,000 costumes, including 65 for Taylor alone at a cost of $194,800; 10,000 spears and 15,000 bows and quivers were also constructed for the 6,000 extras. Although married to others, on-screen lovers Elizabeth Taylor and Richard Burton began a torrid and highly public offscreen affair during the shoot, which intensified the negative publicity swirling around the film. With *Cleopatra* costs mounting, Darryl F. Zanuck took over as studio boss, forcing Skouras to take the ceremonial post of chairman. Wanger was forced out, and Zanuck gave Mankiewicz three months to finish the film. Principal photography wrapped on July 26, 1962, with 120 miles of exposed film to be edited. Mankiewicz was fired during editing, but Zanuck hired him back to reshoot the opening battle scenes with Caesar in Spain, which looked too cheap in the rough cut.

DISTRIBUTION: Mankiewicz wanted *Cleopatra* to be released as two separate films, called *Caesar and Cleopatra* and *Antony and Cleopatra,* each two to three hours in length. Zanuck refused. Instead, the studio released a single four-hour epic. Fox hyped *Cleopatra* with a hefty domestic ad budget of $2.6 million. With an estimated 10,000 onlookers, the movie premiered in New York on June 12, 1963, with opening-night tickets going for $100 per person. By the end of its big-screen life, *Cleopatra* had played in 8,500 theaters, roughly half of all the movie theaters in America in 1963. Although the movie was Fox's highest-grossing film of 1963, the studio did not make its money back until 1966, when ABC paid $5 million to air the film twice on TV. —*Dina Gachman*

LILIES OF THE FIELD

United Artists, 1963

ALL-RELEASE EQUIVALENT 2005 $s
(Unadjusted $s) in Millions of $s

Domestic Box Office Revenues . . . . $50.3/($6.7)
Production Cost . . . . $1.5/($0.2)
Principal Photography . . . . 13 days
Summer 1962

Director . . . . Ralph Nelson

Producer . . . . Ralph Nelson

Production Company . . . . Rainbow Productions

Story by . . . . Based on the novel by
William E. Barrett

Screenplay by . . . . James Poe

Cast . . . . Sidney Poitier, Lilia Skala,
Stanley Adams

Filming Locations . . . . . . Tucson, AZ

Genre . . . . Drama

Format . . . . B&W

Initial Release . . . . 9/25/1963 (Denver, CO)

Rerelease . . . . none

Running Time . . . . 94 minutes

MPAA Rating . . . . not rated

STANDING THE TEST OF TIME

ACADEMY AWARD Oscar Nominations and Wins

Best Picture: Ralph Nelson, Producer

*ACTOR: Sidney Poitier

Actress in a Supporting Role: Lilia Skala

Cinematography (B&W): Ernest Haller

Writing (Screenplay – based on material from
another medium): James Poe

OSCAR TOTALS   Nominations 5   *Wins 1

AFI 100 YEARS 100 MOVIES SELECTION
2007 0   1997 0

TOP 300 FILMS POSITION . . . . none
All-Release Domestic Box Office in Equivalent 2005 $s

National Film Preservation Board Selection . . . . none

OTHER AWARDS Best Picture Wins

	Year
Golden Globes	none
New York Film Critics	none
National Board of Review	none
Film Daily Critics	none

The real star of Lilies of the Field *was the man whose creative force, whose integrity and professional commitment, husbanded the entire project into being, Ralph Nelson.*

—Sidney Poitier

PLOT: West Homer Smith, a black construction worker, is held on a remote farm in the Arizona desert by a collective of Catholic nuns who believe he was sent by God to build them a church.

PRODUCTION: When he was turned down by Harry Belafonte, director Ralph Nelson approached Sidney Poitier to star in his dream project, an adaptation of William Edmund Barrett's novel *Lilies of the Field*. After Poitier agreed, Nelson turned to studio financiers, and was denied everywhere. It seemed he was asking for the impossible: a story about a sexless relationship between a black man and a German nun. Who would buy it? Nelson's agent, Fred Ingels, managed to squeeze a measly $250,000 out of United Artists, which was doubtful that Poitier could carry a film on his own—that is, without a white co-star. Nevertheless, UA offered the sum on the condition that Nelson be held personally responsible for whatever financial troubles were incurred during production. The director accepted. To make ends meet, Poitier agreed to a major salary cut in favor of a piece of the profits, but still, Nelson was far from full financing. That's when he mortgaged his house. Now everything was on the line. There was no margin for error. Because there wasn't enough money to pay the actors for rehearsal, the company agreed to secret run-throughs (unbeknownst to the unions) for an entire week before filming began. The shooting schedule Nelson and production manager Joe Popkin devised allowed for only 14 days of production. Poitier biographer Aram Goudsouzian describes an atmosphere of communal frenzy: "Nelson cut every conceivable cost. He shot interiors inside actual buildings, not on soundstages. He hired his secretary and construction workers as extras. He cast himself as a contractor, and he changed his character's name to Harold Ashton to match the construction equipment." Miraculously, the whole thing took thirteen days to shoot—that's one day ahead of schedule.

DISTRIBUTION: Though he despised publicity tours, Poitier consented to make the rounds on behalf of *Lilies of the Field*. It was a good cause, after all, and he had a big stake in the box office. He appeared at special screenings all over the country, gathering the attention of both civil rights advocates and their opponents. The film was released to mostly glowing critical reaction and went on to make a profit, but its greatest moment was yet to come. On the night of the Academy Awards, Sidney Poitier defeated Albert Finney (*Tom Jones*), Rex Harrison (*Cleopatra*), and Paul Newman (*Hud*) to win the Oscar for Best Actor. It was the first Best Actor Oscar awarded to a black person. After his name was called, Poitier's ears were filled with applause. "The applause continued for an additional five or six seconds," he remembers, "just enough time for me to pluck from my mind the opening line to a speech I had never seriously thought I would be called upon to deliver. As the applause died down I was ready. I began, 'It has been a long journey to this moment.'" Poitier's remark was as relevant to his collaborators as it was to the cause of civil rights. After all, Nelson's movie was more than a triumph of human determination—it was a triumph of determined humanism. —*Sam Wasson*

TOM JONES

Lopert Pictures (domestic); United Artists (foreign), 1963

ALL-RELEASE EQUIVALENT 2005 $s
(Unadjusted $s) in Millions of $s

Domestic Box Office Revenues........$289.0/($38.7)
Production Cost . . . . $7.0/($1.1)
Principal Photography.... 75 days estimated 15 weeks
from June 1962 to August 1962

Director . . . . Tony Richardson
Producer . . . . Tony Richardson
Production Company. . . . Woodfall Film Productions
Story by. . . . . Based on the novel by Henry Fielding
Screenplay by . . . . John Osborne
Cast . . . . Albert Finney, Susannah York, Hugh Griffith, Edith Evans, Joan Greenwood
Filming Locations . . . . . . England: Cranborne Manor, estates in Somerset; Nettlecombe girl's school; Devon; Weymouth, Dorset; Southwark district, London; Londonderry House at Hyde Park Corner (Lady Bellamy's House)
Genre. . . . . Comedy
Format. . . . . Color (Eastmancolor)
Initial Release . . . . 6/26/1963 premiere (London); 10/7/1963 premiere (New York)
Rerelease. 1989
Running Time . . . . 131 minutes; 121 minutes director's cut
MPAA Rating . . . . not rated

STANDING THE TEST OF TIME

ACADEMY AWARD Oscar Nominations and Wins
*BEST PICTURE: Tony Richardson, Producer
Actor: Albert Finney
Actor in a Supporting Role: Hugh Griffith
Actress in a Supporting Role: Diane Cilento
Actress in a Supporting Role: Dame Edith Evans
Actress in a Supporting Role: Joyce Redman
Art Direction/Set Decoration: Ralph Brinton, Ted Marshall, Jocelyn Herbert/Josie MacAvin
*DIRECTING: Tony Richardson
*MUSIC (Music Score – substantially original): John Addison
*WRITING (Screenplay – based on material from another medium): John Osborne

OSCAR TOTALS   Nominations 10 *Wins 4

AFI 100 YEARS 100 MOVIES SELECTION
2007 0   1997 0

TOP 300 FILMS POSITION . . . . #115
All-Release Domestic Box Office in Equivalent 2005 $s

National Film Preservation Board Selection. . . . none

OTHER AWARDS Best Picture Wins

	Year
Golden Globes (Comedy)	1964
New York Film Critics.	1963
National Board of Review	1963
Film Daily Critics	none

The prognosis was not good. The head of British distribution for United Artists saw the finished cut. He pronounced disaster. . . . But then . . . Lines were forming around London Pavilion. Rock 'n' roll had just broken through in England with the first impact of the Beatles. The sixties were starting to swing, and Tom Jones became part of the "revolution."

—Tony Richardson

PLOT: The illegitimate foundling Tom Jones (Albert Finney) is raised as a second son by kindly Squire Allworthy until his wanton ways with the ladies get him duly banished from the Allworthy estate and the heart of his truly beloved, Sophie Western (Susannah York).

PRODUCTION: After years of directing gritty British working-class dramas, Tony Richardson eagerly headed for greener pastures. The English countryside was never more colorful than in Henry Fielding's *Tom Jones,* the wild, picaresque novel Richardson had read and loved while at Oxford. With its bawdy scenes and comic inventiveness, many deemed the novel to be unfilmable and Columbia Pictures demanded that Richardson's production company, Woodfall Films, pony up much of the costs. But as principal photography neared, Richardson shopped the project to United Artists to secure a bigger budget. The young executive David Picker saw a potential grosser and gave detailed instructions to UA board members about how to read John Osborne's ribald script. The following day, the board sealed a deal that elated Richardson and left Columbia crying foul. In the new agreement, Woodfall Films would earn an incredible 75 percent of the profits after UA's production costs were absorbed. *Tom Jones* lived up to its reputation as a nearly impossible undertaking. Richardson sought to capture the most genuine eighteenth-century England ever seen on film in a modern cinematic style that matched the irreverence of the book. Bemoaning the void of creativity on studio soundstages, he insisted that his first color film be shot entirely on location in a pastel color scheme. His vision required that cinematographer Walter Lassally experiment with floodlights, odd filters, silk nets from 1920s Parisian hats, and a laboratory desaturation process John Huston had used on *Moby Dick* to maintain constant lighting and colors in the outdoors. Meanwhile, the set turned into a daily battlefield after a drunken Hugh Griffith horsewhipped lead actor Albert Finney too vigorously and received a punch in the face in return. The hounds also refused to behave. None would devour the dead deer at the end of the hunt because the night before a local hunters' fraternity overfed the starving dogs in protest of what they believed to be a film against blood sports. Even the cooked chickens seemed in on the mischief, as their bones proved too soft to break during the famous gorging scene. The prop department had to glue matchsticks together to create a wishbone that cracked.

DISTRIBUTION: The rough cut of *Tom Jones* impressed neither director nor studio. Richardson and editor Anthony Gibbs used every editing trick in their arsenal to stitch together scenes they considered threadbare. Most critics agreed with their assessment and United Artists prepared for a flop but when *Tom Jones* opened in June 1963 at the London Pavilion, hordes of young mods embraced it, making the film a smashing success. It remained at the Pavilion longer than any other film in the theater's history. *Tom Jones* had touched the cultural zeitgeist, embodying the personal and sexual liberation of the times. United Artists feared a British costume drama might turn off Americans, so the studio released it slowly in metropolitan markets throughout the winter of 1963–64. *Tom Jones* built a following accordingly, seducing first Oscar voters and then the national audience, to earn one of the largest American grosses for a non-road-show release. It is number fifty-one on the BFI's top 100 British films list. —*Michael Kogge*

465

DR. STRANGELOVE, OR HOW I LEARNED TO STOP WORRYING AND LOVE THE BOMB

Columbia, 1964

ALL-RELEASE EQUIVALENT 2005 $s

(Unadjusted $s) in Millions of $s

Domestic Box Office Revenues . . . . **$77.0**/($11.4)
Production Cost . . . . **$11.3**/($1.8)
Principal Photography . . . .**85** days estimated
1/28/1963–5/26/1963

Director . . . . Stanley Kubrick

Producer . . . . Stanley Kubrick

Production Company . . . . Hawk Films

Story by . . . . Based on the novel *Red Alert* by Peter George

Screenplay by . . . . Stanley Kubrick, Terry Southern, Peter George

Cast . . . . Peter Sellers, George C. Scott, Slim Pickens

Filming Locations . . . . . . London Airport and Shepperton Studio in the UK

Genre . . . . Black Comedy

Format . . . . B&W

Initial Release 1/30/1964

Rerelease . . . . 7/13/1964 (1 engagement 4 weeks in release)

Running Time . . . . 93 minutes (cut from 102 minutes)

MPAA Rating . . . . not rated

STANDING THE TEST OF TIME

ACADEMY AWARD Oscar Nominations and Wins

Best Picture: Stanley Kubrick, Producer

Actor: Peter Sellers

Directing: Stanley Kubrick

Writing (Screenplay – based on material from another medium): Stanley Kubrick, Peter George, Terry Southern

OSCAR TOTALS Nominations 4 *Wins 0

AFI 100 YEARS 100 MOVIES SELECTION
2007 . . . #39   1997 . . . #26

TOP 300 FILMS POSITION . . . . .none
All-Release Domestic Box Office in Equivalent 2005 $s

National Film Preservation Board Selection 1989

OTHER AWARDS Best Picture Wins

	Year
Golden Globes	none
New York Film Critics	none
National Board of Review	none
Film Daily Critics	none

What could be more absurd than the very idea of two megapowers willing to wipe out all of human life because of an accident, spiced up by political difference that will seem as meaningless to people a hundred years from now as the theological conflicts of the Middle Ages appear to us today?

—Stanley Kubrick

PLOT: When a paranoid U.S. general launches a preemptive nuclear strike against the Soviet Union, the world depends on Group Captain Lionel Mandrake, American president Merkin Muffley, and the ex-Nazi Dr. Strangelove (all played by Peter Sellers) to thwart Armageddon.

PRODUCTION: As the young Stanley Kubrick started to have a family of his own, he contemplated moving to Australia to be as far away from a U.S.-USSR nuclear war as possible. His fears led him to imagine what such a scenario might be like, so he and producing partner James B. Harris optioned Peter George's novel *Red Alert* for a bargain $3,500. Though Kubrick worked with George on developing a serious screenplay, the wisecracks he and Harris traded about catering the War Room inspired him to turn the story into a farce. In the month before production commenced, Kubrick and gonzo writer Terry Southern beat out comedic scenes in the backseat of a Bentley limo. Production designer Ken Adam relied on aviation magazines to model the B-52 bomber because NASA and the U.S. military refused to provide what was considered classified information. The bomber's authenticity later stunned U.S. Air Force personnel. Kubrick wanted John Wayne to play the B-52 pilot Major "King" Kong, but after Wayne rejected the part and Sellers failed to nail a Texas twang, he selected Slim Pickens, who came straight from his ranch in full cowboy regalia. Kubrick shot *Dr. Strangelove* in England to cut costs and to accommodate Sellers, who was going through a divorce and could not leave the country. The London airport stood in for the U.S. military base, while the sequence of Americans soldiers firing at each other was filmed on Shepperton's back lot. Director of photography Gilbert Taylor, whom Kubrick hired only after he'd correctly answered technical questions from *American Cinematographer*, flew into the Arctic to capture background footage for the B-52. For the production stills, Kubrick arranged to have the crime photographer Arthur Fellig, known around the world as "Weegee," brought in to shoot on special assignment. Kubrick approached the actors as he did all things technical, requesting take after take until he found something interesting. While the other actors griped that Kubrick brought out their hammiest performances, Sellers loved the freedom Kubrick gave him to improvise, which resulted in Strangelove's notorious Hitler salute. Kubrick planned to end the film with a pie-throwing contest, but after 2,000 shaving-cream pies were tossed, he ordered the War Room cleaned, the costumes laundered, and a new ending shot. He was not convinced that what was fun for the cast would be funny to the audience.

DISTRIBUTION: Columbia Pictures scheduled the critics' preview for November 23, 1963, but canceled after the news of John F. Kennedy's assassination broke. The studio required one of Major Kong's lines to be rerecorded from "a fella could have a pretty good time in Dallas" to "a fella could have a pretty good time in Las Vegas." Studio executives thought little of the picture, and the VP of production deemed it a disgrace. Nonetheless, the film generated much discussion in newspapers about the inanity of the Cold War and went on to become Columbia's biggest breadwinner in 1964. The mythical War Room became such an indelible image in American political theater that upon inauguration, Ronald Reagan requested to see it. Perhaps more importantly, *Dr. Strangelove*'s success gave Kubrick the power he needed to make his next films the way he wanted to make them. —*Michael Kogge*

MARY POPPINS

Buena Vista, 1964

ALL-RELEASE EQUIVALENT 2005 $s

(Unadjusted $s) in Millions of $s

Domestic Box Office Revenues........**$538.8**/($101.8)
Production Cost ....**$27.8**/($4.4)
Principal Photography........... **89** days estimated
5/6/1963–9/6/1963

Director	Robert Stevenson
Producer	Walt Disney, Bill Walsh
Production Company	Walt Disney Productions
Story by	Based on the *Mary Poppins* novels by P. L. Travers
Screenplay by	Bill Walsh, Don DaGradi
Cast	Julie Andrews, Dick Van Dyke, David Tomlinson, Glynis Johns
Filming Locations	Walt Disney Studios, Burbank, CA
Genre	Musical
Format	Color (Technicolor)
Initial Release	8/27/1964 premiere (Hollywood, CA); 8/29/1964 general release
Rerelease	1966 (limited), 1973, 1980
Running Time	139 minutes
MPAA Rating	G–General Audiences (rated in 1972)

AFI 100 YEARS 100 MOVIES SELECTION

2007 0   1997 0

TOP 300 FILMS POSITION .... #18

All-Release Domestic Box Office in Equivalent 2005 $s

National Film Preservation Board Selection .... none

STANDING THE TEST OF TIME

ACADEMY AWARD Oscar Nominations and Wins

Best Picture: Walt Disney and Bill Walsh, Producers

*ACTRESS: Julie Andrews

Art Direction/Set Decoration: Carroll Clark, William H. Tuntke/Emile Kuri, Hal Gausman

Cinematography: Edward Colman

Costume Design: Tony Walton

Directing: Robert Stevenson

*FILM EDITING: Cotton Warburton

*MUSIC (Music Score – substantially original): Richard M. Sherman, Robert B. Sherman

Music (Scoring of Music – adaptation or treatment): Irwin Kostal

*MUSIC (Song): "Chim Chim Cher-ee," Music and Lyrics by Richard M. Sherman and Robert B. Sherman

Sound: Walt Disney Studio Sound Dept., Robert O. Cook, Sound Director

*SPECIAL VISUAL EFFECTS: Peter Ellenshaw, Eustace Lycett, Hamilton Luske

Writing (Screenplay – based on material from another medium): Bill Walsh, Don DaGradi

OSCAR TOTALS   Nominations **13**   *Wins 5

OTHER AWARDS Best Picture Wins

	Year
Golden Globes	none
New York Film Critics	none
National Board of Review	none
Film Daily Critics	none

PLOT: Mary Poppins, a "practically perfect" nanny, soars out of the London skies, bringing magical and unexpected changes to the household of an aloof banker, his distracted wife, and their two mischievous children.

PRODUCTION: The film considered by many to be Walt Disney's crowning achievement was more than twenty years in the making. In the late 1930s, Walt found his daughter Diane engrossed in a book of stories about a magical British nanny, Mary Poppins. Disney recognized the property, first published in 1934, as potential movie material. However, author P. L. Travers, living in New York to escape a war-torn London, was adamant: her *Mary Poppins* stories were not for sale to Hollywood. Subsequent attempts by Disney to obtain the rights, in 1944 and 1946, were equally futile. Finally, in 1959, Walt met with Travers in person during a trip to England and made a deal. Agreeing to $100,000 and 5 percent of the gross, Travers also insisted on script approval, wary of her character becoming a "cartoon character."

Robert Stevenson (*Jane Eyre, Old Yeller*) was assigned to direct, while writers Bill Walsh and Don DaGradi began adapting six adventures from the *Poppins* book into a fluid screenplay. The songwriting team of Richard and Robert Sherman was given the task of creating music and songs for the film. For the title role, Walt considered Mary Martin, Bette Davis, and Angela Lansbury. But after several studio staffers saw Julie Andrews perform a number from *Camelot* on TV's *The Ed Sullivan Show,* they enthusiastically suggested the British actress to Walt. Andrews was interested, but had a stipulation: if Warner Bros. cast her as Eliza Doolittle in the upcoming film version of *My Fair Lady* (a role Andrews had originated onstage), the *Poppins* deal was off. When Jack Warner, who wanted a more "commercial" star for Eliza, signed Audrey Hepburn instead, and Walt finally had his Mary. To maintain authenticity, the United Kingdom was tapped for most of the remaining *Poppins* cast—David Tomlinson, Glynis Johns, Reginald Owen, Hermione Baddeley, Arthur Treacher, Elsa Lanchester, and two child actors who had starred in Disney's *The Three Lives of Thomasina,* Karen Dotrice and Matthew Garber. To avoid a complete absence of American talent, Disney signed popular TV sitcom star Dick Van Dyke and veteran comedian Ed Wynn. Jane Darwell (Ma Joad in 1940's *The Grapes of Wrath*) was cast as the Bird Woman, in what would be her final movie. The entire *Poppins* production was filmed in Burbank, California, utilizing all four soundstages on the Disney lot. English artist Peter Ellenshaw produced more than a hundred matte paintings of London and its environs to fill out scenes and provide backdrops, and fourteen top Disney animators created the animated sequences and characters.

DISTRIBUTION: During the *Mary Poppins* premiere at Grauman's Chinese Theater in Hollywood, a dismayed P. L. Travers viewed the film and then approached Walt Disney with a number of objections. "When do we start cutting it?" she asked. Walt explained that script approval applied to just that—the script—and not the final film. "We aren't going to change a thing," he concluded. In its initial run, *Poppins* garnered an astounding $44 million in worldwide rentals and became the company's first Best Picture Oscar contender. Several rereleases and its undying popularity on home video formats have made it one of Disney's greatest film successes. —*Douglas Burns*

MY FAIR LADY
Warner Bros., 1964

ALL-RELEASE EQUIVALENT 2005 $s
(Unadjusted $s) in Millions of $s

Domestic Box Office Revenues........$474.2/($76.0)
Production Cost ....$102.8/($16.3)
Principal Photography........... 89 days estimated
8/13/1963–12/17/1963
(production shut down
1 ½ days to honor President
Kennedy assassination on 11/22/1963)

Director .... George Cukor
Producer .... Jack L. Warner
Production Company.... Warner Bros. Pictures
Story by.............. Based on the Broadway musical play by George Bernard Shaw
Screenplay by .... Alan Jay Lerner
Cast .... Audrey Hepburn, Rex Harrison
Filming Locations ...... Warner Bros. Studio, Burbank, CA
Genre................ Musical
Format............... Color (Technicolor)
Initial Release .... 10/21/1964 premiere (New York); 10/28/1964 premiere (Los Angeles)
Rerelease............ 1973, 1994
Running Time .... 170 minutes
MPAA Rating .... G

STANDING THE TEST OF TIME

ACADEMY AWARD Oscar Nominations and Wins

*BEST PICTURE: Jack L. Warner, Producer

*ACTOR: Rex Harrison

Actor in a Supporting Role: Stanley Holloway

Actress in a Supporting Role: Gladys Cooper

*ART DIRECTION/SET DECORATION: Gene Allen, Cecil Beaton/George James Hopkins

*CINEMATOGRAPHY: Harry Stradling

*COSTUME DESIGN: Cecil Beaton

*DIRECTING: George Cukor

Film Editing: William Ziegler

*MUSIC (Scoring of Music – adaptation or treatment): Andre Previn

*SOUND: Warner Bros. Studio Sound Dept., George R. Groves, Sound Director

Writing (Screenplay–based on material from another medium): Alan Jay Lerner

OSCAR TOTALS   Nominations **12** *Wins **8**

AFI 100 YEARS 100 MOVIES SELECTION
2007 0   1997...#91

TOP 300 FILMS POSITION .... #27
All-Release Domestic Box Office in Equivalent 2005 $s

National Film Preservation Board Selection....none

OTHER AWARDS Best Picture Wins

	Year
Golden Globes (Musical)...................	1965
New York Film Critics.......................	1964
National Board of Review..................	none
Film Daily Critics.........................	none

In my business I have to know who brings people and their money to a movie theatre box office. I knew Audrey Hepburn had never made a financial flop.

—Jack Warner

PLOT: In this musical, an arrogant professor, Henry Higgins, wagers that he can turn an uneducated flower seller, Eliza Doolittle, into a refined Victorian lady, and ends up falling for her in the process.

PRODUCTION: Film producer Gabriel Pascal acquired the rights to produce film versions of several of Shaw's plays, *Pygmalion* included. Shaw's tale derived from Latin poet Ovid's story (in the *Metamorphoses*). Alan Jay Lerner agreed to write a musical adaptation of the play. He and writing partner Frederick Loewe quickly realized that the play seemed incapable of obeying the rules for the construction of a musical. Richard Rodgers and Oscar Hammerstein II had attempted to adapt *Pygmalion* but felt that Shaw's intellectual dialogue didn't work as a musical. They abandoned the project for two years, and then Gabriel Pascal died. When Lerner read Pascal's obituary, he thought about *Pygmalion* again. He and Loewe reunited and everything fell into place. They changed the ending so that Eliza ends up with Higgins, which in the original play was ambiguous. However, they left Shaw's dialogue largely intact, working under the notion that Higgins must be played by a great actor, not a great singer. They adopted the idea that Higgins should talk on pitch rather than sing outright, more an expression of ideas than emotions. When the Broadway production needed financing, Columbia Records President Goddard Leiberson convinced his parent company CBS to invest $250,000 for rights to the cast album. The acclaimed play ran on Broadway from 1956 to 1962. When Jack Warner saw the Broadway premiere, he immediately began making plans for the most lavish movie musical in history, paying a record $5.5 million for screen rights, plus 5 percent of the gross to the Shaw estate. Rex Harrison had starred with Julie Andrews on Broadway to great acclaim, but Warner cast Harrison with Audrey Hepburn, who was considered a bigger draw. Vincente Minnelli was the studio's first choice for director, but he wanted too much money, so Jack Warner hired George Cukor. Almost the entire studio prepped for the elaborate stage design. The set was created on a single soundstage, with a pit below. Preproduction took three months. Art director Cecil Beaton designed the extravagant sets and costumes for the movie, as he had done for the 1956 Broadway musical. Exotic beads, jewels, and furs were flown in from all over the world. They turned out over 1,000 costumes, with 250 individually researched costumes for one scene alone. Audrey Hepburn's singing was dubbed by Marni Nixon, despite Hepburn's lengthy preparation. Rex Harrison refused to prerecord his musical numbers, so they implanted a wireless microphone (one of the first ever) in Harrison's neckties. However, this meant that his words were completely aligned with his movement while everyone else's looked off because they had lip-synched. To remedy the situation, the studio had to lengthen and shorten Harrison's notes in places so that he was in sync with all of the others.

DISTRIBUTION: The film was a huge success, the top domestic box office film of 1964. The cast album became the industry's biggest LP of all time, selling 2.5 million copies. Hepburn failed to receive an Oscar nomination but, ironically, Julie Andrews was awarded a Best Actress Oscar for Disney's *Mary Poppins*. During her acceptance speech, her voice dripping with sarcasm, Andrews thanked Jack Warner "for making this possible" (by not hiring her). —*Hayley Taylor Block*

471

GOLDFINGER
United Artists, 1964

ALL-RELEASE EQUIVALENT 2005 $s
(Unadjusted $s) in Millions of $s

Domestic Box Office Revenues . . . . **$352.1**/($51.1)
Production Cost . . . .$18.6/($3.0)
Principal Photography . . . . .95 days estimated
1/20/1964–7/21/1964
Location shoots 1/20/1964–3/8/1964
Cast shoots 3/9/1964–7/21/1964

Initial Release . . . . 9/17/1964 (London); 12/22/1964 (U.S.)

Rerelease 1966, 1969, 1972

Running Time . . . . 108 minutes

MPAA Rating . . . . not rated

Director . . . . Guy Hamilton

Producer . . . . Harry Saltzman, Albert R. Broccoli

Production Company . . . . Eon Productions, Ltd.

Story by . . . . Based on the novel by Ian Fleming

Screenplay by . . . . Richard Maibaum, Paul Dehn

Cast . . . . Sean Connery, Honor Blackman, Gert Frobe, Shirley Eaton, Tania Mallet, Harold Sakata

Filming Locations . . . . . . On Location: Mexico, Switzerland, UK; and Kentucky, Washington, D.C., and Florida in the U.S; in studio at Pinewood, UK

Genre . . . . Action Adventure

Format . . . . Color (Technicolor)

STANDING THE TEST OF TIME

ACADEMY AWARD Oscar Nominations and Wins

SOUND EFFECTS: Norman Wanstall

OSCAR TOTALS   Nominations **1**   *Wins 1

AFI 100 YEARS 100 MOVIES SELECTION
2007 0   1997 0

TOP 300 FILMS POSITION . . . . **#68**
All-Release Domestic Box Office in Equivalent 2005 $s

National Film Preservation Board Selection . . . .none

OTHER AWARDS Best Picture Wins

	Year
Golden Globes	none
New York Film Critics	none
National Board of Review	none
Film Daily Critics	none

Of all the Bonds, Goldfinger *is the best, and can stand as a surrogate for the others. If it is not a great film, it is a great entertainment, and contains all the elements of the Bond formula that would work again and again.*

—Roger Ebert

PLOT: British secret agent James Bond investigates a sinister gold bullion dealer, Auric Goldfinger, who's suspected by the Bank of England of smuggling precious metals and gems to unfriendly nations. Bond discovers an international plot to wipe out America's gold reserves.

PRODUCTION: Published in March 1959, *Goldfinger* was the seventh of Fleming's James Bond novels, and carried the working title "The Richest Man in the World." After two moderately budgeted successes—*Dr. No* and *From Russia with Love*—*Goldfinger* had a budget more than those of the first two combined. This freed the filmmakers to create a new template for the franchise, which included an elaborately staged set piece intended to precede the opening credits. Terence Young, director of the first two movies in the series, was involved early in the preproduction process but was replaced by Guy Hamilton after Young and the producers couldn't come together on a contract. Orson Welles was sought to play the villain but wanted too large a salary. Theodore Bikel and Titos Vandis also were strongly considered before German actor Gert Fröbe agreed to terms. A contract dispute may also have cost Jack Lord the recurring role of Felix Leiter, which went to Cec Linder. Concerned about government and studio censors, the film's producers had considered changing Pussy Galore's name to Kitty Galore, but, by then, British newspapers had already begun to refer to Honor Blackman as "Pussy." In Fleming's novel the character was a lesbian, but that element was left out of the screenplay. The set for the Fontainebleu Hotel pool scene, built at Pinewood Studios, would be the last visited by Fleming, who died on August 12, 1964. Due to his commitment to Alfred Hitchcock's *Marnie,* Sean Connery joined the production in March 1964, after it had already begun in Florida. The sequences in which Bond was shown to be in America were, instead, shot at Pinewood Studios. *Goldfinger* marks the first appearance of several trademark Bond touchstones: his stated preference for a martini that is "shaken, not stirred"; the first appearance of the Q Branch workshop and its gadget-testing gags; the first of three title songs sung by Shirley Bassey; his silver birch Aston Martin DB5; the first opening-credits sequence actually to show the actor who's playing James Bond; and, by nearly bisecting 007 with a laser beam, it also introduced audiences to futuristic weaponry. Jill Masterson's incongruously glamorous death by skin suffocation—however unlikely, scientifically—required that Shirley Eaton undergo two hours of makeup application and that a doctor be on the set in case anything went wrong.

DISTRIBUTION: *Goldfinger* burst out of the gate, earning back its cost in just two weeks and bringing in a net profit of $31.7 million on $51.1 million in worldwide rentals. It was the first title in the franchise to open in London and New York in the same year. The truest indication of Bond's commercial power was reflected in the resulting popularity of the product placements. Sales of the Aston Martin DB5, for instance, increased by 50 percent after having been featured in the movie. Leslie Bricusse, Anthony Newley, and John Barry's brassy title song, as recorded by British superstar Shirley Bassey, was the first Bond theme to become a top 10 hit. Although no filming was allowed at Fort Knox, *Goldfinger*'s 3-D model is on permanent exhibition at the base's museum. *Goldfinger* is number seventy in the BFI's top 100 British films of the twentieth century. —*Gary Dretzka*

THE SOUND OF MUSIC
20th Century-Fox, 1965

ALL-RELEASE EQUIVALENT 2005 $s
(Unadjusted $s) in Millions of $s

Domestic Box Office Revenues........**$953.2**/($158.9)
Production Cost ....**$49.7**/($8.0)
Principal Photography...........**114** days estimated
3/26/1964–8/20/1964 6 weeks budgeted
actual shoot took 11 weeks – 25 days over schedule
reshoots in Los Angeles 7/6/1964–9/1/1964

Director	Robert Wise
Producer	Robert Wise
Production Company....	Argyle Enterprises Production
Story by..............	Howard Lindsay, Russell Crouse (suggested by *The Story of the Trapp Family Singer*s)
Screenplay by.........	Ernest Lehman
Cast	Julie Andrews, Christopher Plummer
Filming Locations	Filmed in the Austrian Alps and near Salzberg, Austria; in Bavaria Germany and at the Fox Studio in California (period spent in Salzberg, Austria from 4/22/1964–7/2/1964)
Genre.................	Musical
Format...............	Color (DeLuxe)
Initial Release.........	3/2/1965 premiere Rivoli Theater (New York); 3/10/1965 premiere Fox Wilshire Theater (Los Angeles)
Rerelease.............	1973, 1990
Running Time.........	174 minutes
MPAA Rating	G

STANDING THE TEST OF TIME

ACADEMY AWARD Oscar Nominations and Wins

*BEST PICTURE: Robert Wise, Producer

Actress: Julie Andrews

Actress in a Supporting Role: Peggy Wood

Art Direction/Set Decoration: Boris Leven/ Walter M. Scott, Ruby Levitt

Cinematography: Ted McCord

Costume Design: Dorothy Jeakins

*DIRECTING: Robert Wise

*FILM EDITING: William Reynolds

*MUSIC (Scoring of Music – adaptation or treatment): Irwin Kostal

*SOUND: 20th Century-Fox Studio Sound Dept., James P. Corcoran, Sound Director, and Todd-AO Sound Dept., Fred Hynes, Sound Director

OSCAR TOTALS   Nominations **10** *Wins 5

AFI 100 YEARS 100 MOVIES SELECTION
2007 . . . #40   1997 . . . #55

TOP 300 FILMS POSITION .... **#3**
All-Release Domestic Box Office in Equivalent 2005 $s

National Film Preservation Board Selection.... 2001

OTHER AWARDS Best Picture Wins

	Year
Golden Globes (Musical).....................	1966
New York Film Critics.....................	none
National Board of Review..................	none
Film Daily Critics........................	none

The Sound of Music just happened to come out when the world was hungry for this kind of warm, emotional family entertainment.

—Robert Wise

PLOT: A spirited nun leaves the convent to be a governess for the seven children of a widowed naval captain with whom she falls in love during the Nazi occupation of Germany.

PRODUCTION: In 1959 Howard Lindsay and Russel Crouse wrote a musical based on Maria Augusta Trapp's 1949 autobiography, *The Story of the Trapp Family Singers,* which was made into a popular German film, *Die Trapp Familie* (1956). They originally intended to use songs that the real Trapp family sang, but when Mary Martin, who originated the role of Maria on Broadway, asked Richard Rodgers and Oscar Hammerstein II to write a song for her character, they ended up writing a whole new score. The musical was a huge success, and 20th Century-Fox bought the film rights for $1.25 million against 10 percent of the gross in June 1960. Fox also purchased a six-year option to the U.S. release of *Die Trapp Familie* and *Die Trapp Familie in Amerika*. They were edited into one movie, dubbed in English, and released in America as *The Trapp Family* in 1961. Fox's contract stated that any new film version of *The Sound of Music* could not be released until January 1, 1965, when the stage version would have exhausted its Broadway run and touring engagements. Zanuck wanted to get the project started, so screenwriter Ernest Lehman was hired in December 1962. *West Side Story*'s director, Robert Wise, initially passed but later cleared his schedule and agreed to the job. Julie Andrews was cast after Wise saw advance footage of *Mary Poppins*. She signed a two-picture contract with Fox for a flat fee of $225,000 per picture and no share in the profits. Sean Connery, Yul Brynner, and Bing Crosby, among others, were considered for Captain von Trapp, but Wise wanted Christopher Plummer, who he felt would give the role an edge. Wise auditioned and tested dozens of children in Los Angeles, New York, and London. It wasn't until two weeks into rehearsals that they found Charmian Carr (later Charmian Farnan), who debuted as the eldest daughter, Liesel. Carr became a mother figure to the other children. The entire interior of the Trapp estate was built at the Fox studio in Los Angeles. Rehearsals began there on February 10, 1964, and on March 26, 1964, the first scene was shot. Location shooting in Salzberg began April 22 and stretched beyond the budgeted 6 weeks due to incessant rain. By the time the company wrapped production in Salzberg they were 25 days behind schedule and over budget. They returned to Los Angeles for some additional shooting between July 6 and September 1. The film was ready to preview in January 1965, and the audience reaction was overwhelmingly positive.

DISTRIBUTION: *The Sound of Music* marked a dramatic financial turnaround for 20th Century-Fox. Although East Coast critics were negative, their reviews didn't stop people from going to see the movie. From its initial two-theater run, it opened into twenty-five theaters for four weeks as a road show with a 70mm print and six-track stereophonic sound. The road show release then expanded to 131 theaters and by December 1965 the film had been number one at the box office for thirty weeks. It remained in road show for two years. Until *Gone with the Wind*'s October 1967 reissue, *The Sound of Music* was the number one domestic box office movie of all time in adjusted dollars. It dropped into third place after the *Star Wars* 1997 reissue. The RCA soundtrack album sold more than 20 million copies. —*Hayley Taylor Block*

THUNDERBALL
United Artists, 1965

ALL-RELEASE EQUIVALENT 2005 $s
(Unadjusted $s) in Millions of $s

Domestic Box Office Revenues........ **$395.2**/($63.6)
Production Cost .... $41.9/($6.8)
Principal Photography............ **84** days estimated
2/16/1965–7/9/1965

Director	Terence Young
Producer	Kevin McClory
Production Company....	Eon Productions
Story by	Ian Fleming, Kevin McClory, Jack Whittingham
Screenplay by	Richard Maibaum, John Hopkins
Cast	Sean Connery, Claudine Auger, Adolfo Celi
Filming Locations	On Location: Paris, France; Nassau, The Bahamas; in studio: Pinewood Studios, London, UK
Genre.................	Action Adventure
Format...............	Color (Technicolor)
Initial Release	12/9/1965 (Tokyo); 12/21/1965 (New York); 12/29/1965 (UK)
Rerelease.............	1968, 1970, 1972
Running Time	125 minutes
MPAA Rating	not rated

STANDING THE TEST OF TIME

ACADEMY AWARD Oscar Nominations and Wins

*SPECIAL VISUAL EFFECTS: John Stears

OSCAR TOTALS   Nominations **1**   *Wins **1**

AFI 100 YEARS 100 MOVIES SELECTION
2007 0   1997 0

TOP 300 FILMS POSITION .... **#46**
All-Release Domestic Box Office in Equivalent 2005 $s

National Film Preservation Board Selection.... none

OTHER AWARDS Best Picture Wins

	Year
Golden Globes	none
New York Film Critics....................	none
National Board of Review.................	none
Film Daily Critics........................	none

Now Mr. Fleming's superhero ... has not only power over women, miraculous physical reserves, skill in perilous maneuvers and knowledge of all things great and small, but he also has a much better sense of humor than he has shown in his previous films. And this is the secret ingredient that makes Thunderball *the best of the lot.*

—Bosley Crowther, *New York Times*, 1965

PLOT: Agent 007 is ordered to quash a heinous extortion scheme, in which £100 million would be transferred to a SPECTRE account in exchange for a promise not to detonate a pair of nuclear warheads stolen from a RAF Vulcan strategic bomber.

PRODUCTION: Originally intended to be the first of the *James Bond* films, *Thunderball* became stalled in a legal battle that would take decades to settle. In the late 1950s, Ian Fleming collaborated with Kevin McClory and Jack Whittingham on an original story and screenplay titled "James Bond, Secret Agent," destined either for the big screen or television. After the movie failed to be made, Fleming appropriated the story and fleshed it out as a novel. In 1963, after producer Harry Saltzman bought the film rights to all of the Bond novels from Fleming and went into partnership with Albert R. Broccoli, McClory initiated legal action against Fleming. Ultimately, he won the right to adapt a film from *Thunderball,* but couldn't find backing in Hollywood. He reluctantly went to Saltzman and Broccoli to propose collaborating on the project. The heavy emphasis on underwater action derived from an idea by McClory to shoot the entire film using special cameras developed at Todd-AO, his previous employer. Otherwise, *Thunderball* was built using the same template as nearly every other episode in the franchise, including casting a beautiful femme fatale, who in this case was a former Miss France. They had wanted Raquel Welch, but 20th Century-Fox production chief Richard D. Zanuck was able to call in a favor from Broccoli, who released Welch from her contract so she could star in *Fantastic Voyage* instead. The production made full use of the islands and turquoise waters of the Bahamas. The extensive use of underwater photography required a much longer than normal shooting schedule. It also meant Connery and other cast members would have to share scenes with actual sharks (stuntman Bill Cumming was paid a $450 bonus to jump into the villain's shark-infested pool). Typical of the *Bond* franchise, *Thunderball* introduced audiences to such gadgets as the rocket-propulsion jet pack, which had been developed for military use in difficult terrain; a compact rebreather used to keep bubbles from giving away the location of a scuba diver; water cannons on Bond's Aston Martin; and various underwater vehicles. Dionne Warwick had recorded "Mr. Kiss Kiss Bang Bang" for use as the theme song, but it was replaced by Tom Jones's rendition of "Thunderball."

DISTRIBUTION: *Thunderball* was the first of the Bond films to be released during the same week in New York and London, if only because the producers couldn't meet a deadline that would have allowed a London premiere in September. As a result of the 1963 lawsuit settlement and the agreement struck between Eon Productions (Saltzman and Broccoli's company) and McClory, McClory and Whittingham's names were added to the credits and the rights to the film reverted back to McClory after ten years. In 1983 McClory executive produced a second *Thunderball* adaptation, *Never Say Never Again,* which benefited from the return of Connery in the lead role. It has never been considered a true Bond film. Nineteen eighty-three would also see the release of Eon Productions' *Octopussy,* starring Roger Moore as 007. A decade later, Sony and McClory would attempt another adaptation of the same property, but a suit by MGM/UA thwarted any advancement of that project. —*Gary Dretzka*

DOCTOR ZHIVAGO
MGM, 1965

ALL-RELEASE EQUIVALENT 2005 $s
(Unadjusted $s) in Millions of $s

Domestic Box Office Revenues........**$622.4**/($109.8)
Production Cost .... **$73.5**/($11.9)
Principal Photography................... **232** days
12/28/1964–10/7/1965

Director . . . . David Lean
Producer . . . . Carlo Ponti
Production Company. . . . Sostar S. A., Metro-Goldwyn-Mayer British Studios, Ltd.
Story by . . . . Based on the novel by Boris Pasternak
Screenplay by . . . . Robert Bolt
Cast . . . . Geraldine Chaplin, Julie Christie, Tom Courtenay, Alec Guinness, Siobhan McKenna, Ralph Richardson, Omara Sharif, Rod Steiger, Rita Tushingham
Filming Locations . . . . . . Alberta, Canada (stock railroad footage); on location in Madrid, Canillas, Málaga, Soria, Castilla, León, and Granada, Spain; Helsinki, Joensuu, Punkaharju, Punkasalmi, and Pyhäselkä, Finland
Genre. . . . . Historical Drama
Format. . . . . Color (Metrocolor)
Initial Release . . . . 12/22/1965 premiere (New York); January 1966 reissued 17 minutes shorter
Rerelease. 1972
Running Time . . . . 197 minutes original release; 180 minutes cut version
MPAA Rating PG-13

STANDING THE TEST OF TIME

ACADEMY AWARD Oscar Nominations and Wins

Best Picture: Carlo Ponti, Producer

Actor in a Supporting Role: Tom Courtenay

*ART DIRECTION/SET DECORATION: John Box, Terry Marsh/Dario Simoni

*CINEMATOGRAPHY (Color): Freddie Young

*COSTUME DESIGN: Phyllis Dalton

Directing: David Lean

Film Editing: Norman Savage

*MUSIC (Music Score – substantially original): Maurice Jarre

Sound: MGM British Studio Sound Dept.

*WRITING (Screenplay – based on material from another medium): Robert Bolt

OSCAR TOTALS Nominations **10** *Wins **5**

AFI 100 YEARS 100 MOVIES SELECTION
2007 0   1997 . . . #39

TOP 300 FILMS POSITION . . . . **#11**
All-Release Domestic Box Office in Equivalent 2005 $s

National Film Preservation Board Selection. . . .none

OTHER AWARDS Best Picture Wins

	Year
Golden Globes (Drama).	1966
New York Film Critics.	none
National Board of Review	none
Film Daily Critics	none

If you think about it, Doctor Zhivago *really has the same formula as* Gone with the Wind. *It's a big love story on the background of civil war. It leaves you with the same sort of feeling.*

—Omar Sharif

PLOT: In the years surrounding the 1917 Bolshevik Revolution in Russia, surgeon-poet Yuri Zhivago, destined to love two women, is torn between fidelity and passion, while struggling to retain his individualism amid the excesses of the revolution.

PRODUCTION: Russian poet Boris Pasternak worked on his epic novel, *Doctor Zhivago* (based partly on his own experiences), for ten years. It was rejected by Soviet authorities, but in 1957 it was smuggled out and published in Milan. It was awarded the Nobel Prize for literature in 1958 (though Pasternak renounced the honor so he could continue living in Russia). Pasternak died in 1960, and his love, Olga (on whom Lara was based), was forced to spend time in the Soviet work camps. Producer Carlo Ponti bought the rights for his wife, Sophia Loren, to star. MGM agreed to finance if David Lean would direct. Lean was coming off the success of *Bridge on the River Kwai* and *Lawrence of Arabia* (both won Best Picture and Best Director Oscars), so he was eager for the change that a love story represented. However, he didn't want Loren, whom he thought was 'too tall' for the part. Lean and British playwright Robert Bolt spent a year turning the 700-page novel into a 284-page script. Lean pressed for Peter O'Toole to star, but O'Toole declined after the grueling experience of *Lawrence of Arabia.* Omar Sharif, who also worked on Lawrence, asked Lean to consider him for the role of Pasha. Instead, Lean offered him the title role. Geraldine Chaplin was cast after Lean saw her on a magazine cover, and Alec Guinness was cast because Lean considered him his good-luck charm. Lean took a location-scouting trip spanning 10,000 miles before settling on locations in Spain. (Since the book had been banned in Russia, shooting there was not an option.) More than 800 workers spent roughly eighteen months creating a replica of Moscow in a Madrid suburb. The snowy winter scenes were shot in Finland near the Soviet border. *Zhivago* was a demanding film to shoot because all four seasons were represented which caused the long production to grow into one of the twenty most expensive movies made up until that time. Freddie Young reluctantly agreed to do the cinematography after Lean had a falling-out with Nicolas Roeg. To create the ice palace, the crew covered a house with hot beeswax, then splashed it with freezing water. To reflect seasonal changes, leaves on trees were painted by hand at night. In one scene, a woman was badly injured when she fell under a real locomotive train. By the time shooting finished in early October 1965, Lean had less than three months to edit 31 hours of footage, having promised MGM a Christmas release. He worked day and night for ten weeks with his chief film editor, Norman Savage. Maurice Jarre (who had won an Oscar for *Lawrence*) composed and recorded the underscore in the same short ten-week period. After Lean rejected his first three efforts, Jarre wrote the Oscar-winning "Lara's Theme," after which the rest of the scoring went smoothly.

DISTRIBUTION: Reviews for the 197-minute release in New York in December 1965 were largely negative, so Lean withdrew the first print and spent three weeks recutting. MGM, meanwhile, proceeded with a massive publicity campaign in advance of *Zhivago*'s national release. The cut version that went into wide release in early 1966 proved critic-proof and the film became a huge hit. It is number twenty-seven on the BFI's list of the top 100 British films of the twentieth century. —*Hayley Taylor Block*

WHO'S AFRAID OF VIRGINIA WOOLF?

Warner Bros., 1966

ALL-RELEASE EQUIVALENT 2005 $s

(Unadjusted $s) in Millions of $s

Domestic Box Office Revenues . . . . **$189.5**/($32.2)
Production Cost . . . . **$45.2**/($7.5)
Principal Photography . . . . **100** days estimated
7/26/1965–12/13/1965

Director . . . . Mike Nichols
Producer . . . . Ernest Lehman
Production Company . . . . Chenault Production
Story by . . . . Based on the play by
Edward Albee
Screenplay by . . . . Ernest Lehman
Cast . . . . Elizabeth Taylor, Richard Burton,
George Segal, Sandy Dennis
Filming Locations . . . . On location: Cambridge, MA,
Dijon Street; Red Basket, 151
College Highway,
Southampton, MA; Smith
College, Northampton, MA; in
studio: Warner Bros. Studios,
Burbank, CA
Genre . . . . Drama
Format . . . . B&W
Initial Release 6/22/1966
Rerelease . . . . none
Running Time . . . . 131 minutes
MPAA Rating . . . . not rated

STANDING THE TEST OF TIME

ACADEMY AWARD Oscar Nominations and Wins

Best Picture: Ernest Lehman, Producer
Actor: Richard Burton
Actor in a Supporting Role: George Segal
*ACTRESS: Elizabeth Taylor
*ACTRESS IN A SUPPORTING ROLE: Sandy
Dennis
*ART DIRECTION/SET DECORATION: Richard
Sylbert/George James Hopkins
*CINEMATOGRAPHY (B&W): Haskell Wexler
*COSTUME DESIGN: Irene Sharaff
Directing: Mike Nichols
Film Editing: Sam O'Steen
Music (Original Music Score): Alex North
Sound: Warner Bros. Studio Sound Dept., George R.
Groves, Sound Director
Writing (Screenplay – based on material from
another medium): Ernest Lehman

OSCAR TOTALS   Nominations **13** *Wins 5

AFI 100 YEARS 100 MOVIES SELECTION
2007 . . . #67   1997 0

TOP 300 FILMS POSITION . . . . **#298**
All-Release Domestic Box Office in Equivalent 2005 $s

National Film Preservation Board Selection . . . . none

OTHER AWARDS Best Picture Wins

	Year
Golden Globes	none
New York Film Critics	none
National Board of Review	none
Film Daily Critics	none

One of the things I think that animated this movie the most was that here were, let's see,
one, two, three, four stage people—Richard, George, Sandy and me—and . . .
we were all awed by Elizabeth's knowledge of film acting . . . because of the
great surprise of her being able to handle all this verbal material.

—Mike Nichols

PLOT: A middle-aged New England professor and his wife invite a young couple—a new professor and his naive wife—over for a nightcap, during which the hosts become increasingly abusive toward each other and their guests.

PRODUCTION: Mike Nichols used his success as a Broadway director (*Barefoot in the Park*) to launch his movie-directing career with Edward Albee's 1962 Pulitzer Prize–winning play *Who's Afraid of Virginia Woolf?* The title was taken from graffiti Albee had seen on a bar mirror, which he said meant "Who's afraid of the big bad wolf . . . who's afraid of living life without false illusions?" Warner Bros. had purchased screen rights in the early 1960s from Albee for $500,000, intending Bette Davis and James Mason to star. However, when they brought in producer and screenwriter Ernest Lehman, fresh from *The Sound of Music,* he wanted Elizabeth Taylor, a bigger star at the time. Taylor's contract gave her the right of approval over director, co-star, cameraman, hairdresser, and costume designer, along with $1.1 million and 10 percent of the gross. Although Nichols had never directed, he was Elizabeth Taylor's first choice. Lehman saw Nichols as someone who would add prestige to the film and a director who could handle the tempestuous couple in the script. After Jack Lemmon and Glenn Ford declined the role of abusive professor, Burton was hired for a $750,000. Taylor, who saw this role as her *Hamlet,* was actually a controversial choice, as she was considered too young and pretty for the part. She put on about thirty pounds and did hours in makeup to help her look older. Nichols insisted on shooting in black and white, to get the right tone. Lehman, who also wrote the screenplay for $250,000, penned seven versions. Albee later claimed much of his dialogue was restored by Nichols, Burton, and Taylor unbeknownst to Lehman. They had three weeks of rehearsals and then shot mostly at the studio on a closed set. Still, the cost escalated because Nichols worked very slowly and methodically. Studio boss Jack Warner insisted on cinematographer Haskell Wexler who lit each shot with a rich depth of field, creating striking close-ups and daring hand-held tracking shots. Although Nichols told Wexler to make certain Elizabeth Taylor "didn't look so good," Taylor would greet Wexler with a kiss every morning to make certain she still looked pretty good at all times.

DISTRIBUTION: Before the film could be released, the studio and filmmakers had to get approval of the vulgar language and strong themes from the Motion Picture Association of America. To secure this approval, Warner Bros. made some minor deletions and put a special warning at the start of the movie, which also had to appear on all advertising. The censors insisted on removing the words "screw you" but allowed "goddamn you," "screw," "bugger," and "hump the hostess" in the movie. Upon its release it was only the fifth movie to receive 13 or more Oscar nominations after *Gone with the Wind* (1939), *All About Eve* (1950), *From Here to Eternity* (1953) and *Mary Poppins* (1964). Wexler was the last to win an Oscar for black-and-white cinematography before color and black-and-white cinematography became a single category. —*Hayley Taylor Block*

A MAN FOR ALL SEASONS

Columbia, 1966

ALL-RELEASE EQUIVALENT 2005 $s
(Unadjusted $s) in Millions of $s

Domestic Box Office Revenues . . . . **$151.3**/($28.3)
Production Cost . . . . $12.1/($2.0)
Principal Photography . . . . **66** days estimated
5/4/1966–8/5/1966

Director . . . . Fred Zinnemann
Producer . . . . Fred Zinnemann
Production Company . . . . Highland Films
Story by . . . . Based on the play by
Robert Bolt
Screenplay by . . . . Robert Bolt
Cast . . . . Paul Scofield, Wendy Hiller,
Leo McKern, Robert Shaw,
Orson Welles, Susannah York,
Nigel Davenport, John Hurt,
Corin Redgrave
Filming Locations . . . . Produced in England; location
scenes filmed in Oxfordshire,
Hampshire, and Surrey;
additional footage shot in
Shepperton Studios
Genre . . . . Drama
Format . . . . Color (Technicolor)
Initial Release . . . . 12/12/1966 premiere
(New York); 12/14/1966
general release
Rerelease . . . . none
Running Time . . . . 120 minutes
MPAA Rating . . . . not rated

STANDING THE TEST OF TIME

ACADEMY AWARD Oscar Nominations and Wins

*BEST PICTURE: Fred Zinnemann, Producer

*ACTOR: Paul Scofield

Actor in a Supporting Role: Robert Shaw

Actress in a Supporting Role: Wendy Hiller

*CINEMATOGRAPHY: Ted Moore

*COSTUME DESIGN: Elizabeth Haffenden,
Joan Bridge

*DIRECTING: Fred Zinnemann

*WRITING (Screenplay – based on material from
another medium): Robert Bolt

OSCAR TOTALS   Nominations 8   *Wins 6

AFI 100 YEARS 100 MOVIES SELECTION
2007 0   1997 0

TOP 300 FILMS POSITION . . . . .none
All-Release Domestic Box Office in Equivalent 2005 $s

National Film Preservation Board Selection . . . .none

OTHER AWARDS Best Picture Wins
	Year
Golden Globes (Drama)	1967
New York Film Critics	1966
National Board of Review	1966
Film Daily Critics	none

Fred Zinnemann was a jewel. A calm, rational man, quietly authoritative and in perfect control of the myriad aspects of filmmaking. He had a simplicity in his understanding of A Man for All Seasons *which reflected the simplicities and the complex resoluteness of Sir Thomas More without apparent effort or contrivance.*

—Paul Scofield

PLOT: Henry VIII's wish to divorce the wife who has not borne him a male heir is carefully considered and then opposed by his chancellor, Sir Thomas More, who refuses to grant his king public absolution.

PRODUCTION: In the mid-sixties, when *A Man for All Seasons* was getting ready to shoot, its director, Fred Zinnemann, and its genre, the costume drama, were yesterday's news. Zinnemann was a vestige of the old guard, and his material, a period film adapted from the stage, was seen as more than a little anachronistic in light of Hollywood's recent flirtation with liberal broadmindedness. Zinnemann was also coming off the box office flop *Behold a Pale Horse.* The studio was understandably nervous about the film's box office potential. The fact that the film was to be based on Robert Bolt's hit play, which grew out of a 1954 radio broadcast, was of little consolation to Columbia, which furnished the production with a relatively small budget and, as a result, pretty much left Zinnemann to his movie. When the film's original producer, Mike Frankovich, found himself lost in the production chaos of *Casino Royale,* he promptly dropped the project into the hands of executive producer William N. Graff. Suddenly Zinnemann found himself with an even longer leash, and he ran with it. Although the movie's executive producer wanted Laurence Olivier for the lead, Zinnemann insisted upon casting Paul Scofield (who played More onstage), even though Scofield was almost unknown to the moviegoing world. Because of the fear that Scofield wasn't a big enough name to draw in audiences, Richard Burton was approached as well, but he turned the part down. Alec Guinness was considered for Cardinal Wolsey before Orson Welles was cast. Bolt pushed for John Huston to play Norfolk, but he declined. To keep the budget down, all the actors took less than their usual salary. In the end, Zinnemann called it "the easiest film I have ever made." Even the weather seemed to cooperate. It actually snowed when the script called for it, and there was a recurrent gust of wind—as if it knew just when to blow—that gave perfect emphasis to a scene between Scofield and Robert Shaw. Production designer John Box craftily constructed a replica of Hampton Court for the meager sum of £5,000, and costumers Elizabeth Haffenden and Joan Bridge were granted permission to forsake authenticity in favor of the absolute basics. Even Vanessa Redgrave was cashkind. For her brief appearance as Anne Boleyn, she gladly (and gracefully) worked without pay.

DISTRIBUTION: *A Man for All Seasons* was, against all odds, a big international hit. Paul Scofield in particular won praise, along with an Oscar as Best Actor. Although bested at the worldwide box office in 1966 by *Hawaii* and *The Bible,* among others, with its modest budget *A Man for All Seasons* had the highest return over production cost of any film that year. In 1988 Charlton Heston, who had lobbied for the lead in Zinnemann's production, finally got it. When the actor became actor-director for his made-for-TV remake of Bolt's now legendary play, he cast himself as Thomas More alongside John Gielgud as Cardinal Wolsey and Vanessa Redgrave, whom he promoted from Anne Boleyn to the role of Lady Alice More. The second filming is closer to Bolt's original, restoring the figure of the Common Man—a kind of Greek chorus—who in the feature film was divided into several different characters. It is forty-third on the BFI's list of the top 100 British films of the twentieth century. —*Sam Wasson*

THE DIRTY DOZEN
MGM, 1967

ALL-RELEASE EQUIVALENT 2005 $s
(Unadjusted $s) in Millions of $s

Domestic Box Office Revenues . . . . **$238.0**/($44.6)
Production Cost . . . .**$31.3**/($5.4)
Principal Photography . . . .**100** days estimated
4/25/1966–10/13/1966

Director . . . . Robert Aldrich
Producer . . . . Kenneth Hyman
Production Company . . . . M. K. H. Productions, Metro-Goldwyn-Mayer
Story by . . . . Based on the novel by E. M. Nathanson
Screenplay by . . . . Nunnally Johnson, Lukas Heller
Cast . . . . Lee Marvin, Ernest Borgnine, Charles Bronson, Jim Brown, John Cassavetes, Richard Jaeckel, George Kennedy, Trini Lopez, Ralph Meeker, Robert Ryan, Telly Savalas, Clint Walker, Robert Webber
Filming Locations . . . . On Location in Buckinghamshire, north of London; in studio at Elstree Studios
Genre . . . . War
Format . . . . Color (Metrocolor)
Initial Release 6/16/1967
Rerelease . . . . none
Running Time . . . . 149 minutes
MPAA Rating . . . . not rated

STANDING THE TEST OF TIME

ACADEMY AWARD Oscar Nominations and Wins

Actor in a Supporting Role: John Cassavetes
Film Editing: Michael Luciano
Sound: MGM Studio Sound Dept.
*SOUND EFFECTS: John Poyner

OSCAR TOTALS   Nominations **4**   *Wins 1

AFI 100 YEARS 100 MOVIES SELECTION
2007 0   1997 0

TOP 300 FILMS POSITION . . . . **#177**
All-Release Domestic Box Office in Equivalent 2005 $s

National Film Preservation Board Selection . . . . none

OTHER AWARDS Best Picture Wins

	Year
Golden Globes	none
New York Film Critics	none
National Board of Review	none
Film Daily Critics	none

The film . . . glorifies its savagery, sacrificing an intelligent distaste for the approval of a dim witted segment of the populace who will pay for vivid violence.

—Paine Knickerbocker, *San Francisco Chronicle*, 1967

PLOT: A rogue army major must select and train twelve condemned felons to jump into occupied France on the eve of the Normandy invasion and execute high-ranking German officers.

PRODUCTION: In 1959 photographer Russ Meyer met magazine writer and editor E. M. (Mick) Nathanson, who told him about a naval aviators book he was collaborating on. It featured a tough squadron leader who had whipped a group of ne'er-do-well pilots into a superb fighting unit. Meyer thought they sounded just like the "Dirty Dozen," a group of soldier-prisoners being trained for a secret mission he had filmed in England two months before the Normandy invasion. The short anecdote inspired Nathanson to write a novel. He made a publishing deal with Random House, then set off on a research trip that included a visit to the Pentagon law library. With the manuscript still incomplete, MGM purchased an option for $10,000. When the novel was published, MGM purchased screen rights for $75,000 with another $10,000 to be paid in the event the novel became a book club selection, which occurred in the spring of 1965. The studio assigned William Perlberg as producer, with George Seaton as director. Two screenplays were written. Later, when Kenneth Hyman was named as producer with Robert Aldrich directing, Nunnally Johnson was signed for the adaptation, with Lukas Heller doing a rewrite. John Wayne turned down the role of Reisman before it went to Lee Marvin. The Production Code censors complained about "Reisman's use of prostitutes for the men." Robert O'Brien, CEO of MGM at the time, objected to Pinkley (Donald Sutherland) hoodwinking Colonel Breed (Robert Ryan) by impersonating a general. A production breakdown, with approved locations, was completed on April 15, 1966. The prostitute and hoodwinking sequences remained, with Aldrich's approval. Shooting began on April 25 north of London. It soon ran over budget and behind schedule, but Aldrich built camaraderie with the actors. A sequence that did not appear in the novel was added, depicting high-ranking Nazi officers and their women in a cellar as gasoline is poured through the ventilation shafts and topped off with hand grenades to ensure a mass execution. The grisly sequence provided audiences with a graphic contrast to the Third Reich gas chambers and stood as a strong director's statement. When Trini Lopez walked out before his jump sequence into France was completed, Aldrich had him written out. His character, jumps, but ends up hung in a tree with a broken neck. Later Lopez requested to return to the film, but Aldrich said no "your character is dead." Aldrich wanted film audiences to see war in its actuality: man at his best and worst, with vicious good needed to conquer evil.

DISTRIBUTION: Released during the so-called Summer of Love, this war film opened to long lines and seemed to strike a chord with the counterculture crowd. Audiences loved that the heroes were all societal outcasts, which was clear when John Cassavetes was nominated for an Academy Award for his role as social degenerate Victor Franko. Feeling that his contributions to the screenplay were not properly recognized, Lukas Heller challenged his second-position credit before the Writers Guild arbitration panel. His claim was rejected. The film's grosses bailed MGM out of red ink. Today the term "Dirty Dozen" has become a universal cliché, giving birth to many Ramboesque characters. The movie also spawned a later television series. —*Frank McAdams*

BONNIE AND CLYDE

Warner Bros./Seven Arts, 1967

ALL-RELEASE EQUIVALENT 2005 $s

(Unadjusted $s) in Millions of $s

Domestic Box Office Revenues . . . . **$261.1**/($48.9)
Production Cost . . . . **$14.6**/($2.5)
Principal Photography . . . . **60** days estimated
10/1966–12/1966

Director . . . . Arthur Penn
Producer . . . . Warren Beatty
Production Company . . . . Tatira-Hiller Production
Story and
  Screenplay by . . . . David Newman, Robert Benton
Cast . . . . Warren Beatty, Faye Dunaway,
Michael J. Pollard, Gene
Hackman, Estelle Parsons,
Denver Pyle, Dub Taylor,
Evans Evans, Gene Wilder
Filming Locations . . . . On location in various cities in
Texas and in studio at Warner
Bros., Burbank, CA
Genre . . . . Crime
Format . . . . Color (Technicolor)
Initial Release 8/13/1967
Rerelease 1968
Running Time . . . . 111 minutes
MPAA Rating . . . . not rated

STANDING THE TEST OF TIME

ACADEMY AWARD Oscar Nominations and Wins

Best Picture: Warren Beatty, Producer

Actor: Warren Beatty

Actor in a Supporting Role: Gene Hackman

Actor in a Supporting Role: Michael J. Pollard

Actress: Faye Dunaway

*ACTRESS IN A SUPPORTING ROLE: Estelle
Parsons

*CINEMATOGRAPHY: Burnett Guffey

Costume Design: Theadora Van Runkle

Directing: Arthur Penn

Writing (Story and Screenplay – written directly for
the screen): David Newman, Robert Benton

OSCAR TOTALS   Nominations **10** *Wins **2**

AFI 100 YEARS 100 MOVIES SELECTION
2007 . . . #42   1997 . . . #27

TOP 300 FILMS POSITION . . . . **#143**
All-Release Domestic Box Office in Equivalent 2005 $s

National Film Preservation Board Selection 1992

OTHER AWARDS Best Picture Wins

	Year
Golden Globes	none
New York Film Critics	none
National Board of Review	none
Film Daily Critics	none

*Young people understood this movie instantly. They saw Bonnie and Clyde as rebels like themselves.
It was a movie that spoke to a generation in a way none of us had really expected.*

—Arthur Penn

PLOT: A bored, small-town waitress and an ex-con fall in love during a violent, legendary crime spree in the Midwest during the Great Depression.

PRODUCTION: When Robert Benton, art director at *Esquire* magazine, met journalist David Newman they discovered that they both admired the French New Wave cinema, and in 1963 they decided to write a screenplay together in that fashion. As a child in Texas, Benton had heard about 1930s bank robbers Clyde Barrow and Bonnie Parker. They wrote a seventy-five-page treatment envisioning the infamous couple not as just outlaws but as social outcasts deserving sympathy. They sent it to François Truffaut, who couldn't get studio backing and soon moved on to another project. Truffaut passed a copy to Jean-Luc Godard, who was interested but put it off because he could not shoot immediately. Major studios didn't like the scene in which Clyde invites his pal C. W. Moss (a composite of two Barrow gang members) to join in a sexual ménage à trois. Actor Warren Beatty, then twenty-eight, and his girlfriend, Leslie Caron, heard about the script from Truffaut. Caron persuaded Beatty to buy it so that they could star together. (Caron terminated their relationship when Beatty didn't hire her to play Bonnie). Beatty paid the writers $10,000 for an option and a further $75,000 when it went into production. Beatty then persuaded Arthur Penn to direct, and finally sold it to Warner Bros., even though the studio believed gangster films were out of style. Warner, seeing little potential, paid first-time producer Beatty $200,000 plus an unprecedented 40 percent of the gross, instead of his usual salary. Newcomer Faye Dunaway was cast as Bonnie, after Natalie Wood, Tuesday Weld, Jane Fonda, and others declined. Although the script deviated significantly from historical records, Penn still felt that it was too sophisticated. He added some slapstick humor and country music to lighten it up. Robert Towne, a Hollywood script doctor, did rewrites. Goldman changed Clyde's bisexuality to impotence but, to fulfill Beatty's sex symbol image, had him consummate his love for Bonnie before the end. The gory finale was shot in a rapid-fire, slow motion montage, which went way beyond prior Hollywood screen violence. Penn used four cameras at different speeds (24, 48, 72, and 96 fps). The death scene had to be done in one take because they only had one car and one load of squibs (bags of red liquid, fired from inside an actor's clothes).

DISTRIBUTION: Jack Warner disliked the cut Beatty showed him. Beatty asked to buy the film, but the studio refused and put *Bonnie and Clyde* into limited release on August 13, 1967. It sold few tickets and was denounced by film critics for glamorizing violence and sexual ambiguity. By late fall, Warner pulled it from theaters. However, film critic Pauline Kael praised the movie in an influential 9,000-word review for the *New Yorker*. It also opened in London and became a phenomenon in Europe. Several major critics reversed themselves and printed rave reviews. On December 8, 1967, *Time* magazine put *Bonnie and Clyde* on the cover, praising it as a harbinger of a New Cinema. Beatty forced Warner Bros. to do a test release in twenty-five theaters in early 1968 and it was a hit. Warner rereleased it in February 1968 in more than 350 theaters with great success. It became one of the top-grossing movies of 1968. —*Hayley Taylor Block*

GUESS WHO'S COMING TO DINNER
Columbia, 1967

ALL-RELEASE EQUIVALENT 2005 $s
(Unadjusted $s) in Millions of $s

Domestic Box Office Revenues . . . . **$302.7**/($56.7)
Production Cost . . . . **$23.4**/($4.0)
Principal Photography . . . . **51** days
3/20/1967–5/29/1967

Director . . . . Stanley Kramer
Producer . . . . Stanley Kramer
Production Company . . . . Columbia Pictures
Story and
 Screenplay by . . . . William Rose
Cast . . . . Spencer Tracy, Sidney Poitier, Katharine Hepburn
Filming Locations . . . . San Francisco, CA; mostly shot on the set of the Drayton home, on a sound-stage; exteriors for the San Francisco house were shot in Pasadena, CA; background mattes created images of San Francisco Bay, the Golden Gate Bridge, and other landmarks
Genre . . . . Drama
Format . . . . Color (Technicolor)
Initial Release 12/11/1967
Rerelease . . . . none
Running Time . . . . 108 minutes
MPAA Rating . . . . not rated

STANDING THE TEST OF TIME

ACADEMY AWARD Oscar Nominations and Wins

Best Picture: Stanley Kramer, Producer
Actor: Spencer Tracy
Actor in a Supporting Role: Cecil Kellaway
*ACTRESS: Katharine Hepburn
Actress in a Supporting Role: Beah Richards
Art Direction/Set Decoration: Robert Clatworthy/ Frank Tuttle
Directing: Stanley Kramer
Film Editing: Robert C. Jones
Music (Scoring of Music – adaptation or treatment): DeVol
*WRITING: (Story and Screenplay – written directly for the screen): William Rose

OSCAR TOTALS Nominations **10** *Wins **2**

AFI 100 YEARS 100 MOVIES SELECTION
2007 0   1997 . . . #99

TOP 300 FILMS POSITION . . . . #105
All-Release Domestic Box Office in Equivalent 2005 $s

National Film Preservation Board Selection . . . . none

OTHER AWARDS Best Picture Wins

	Year
Golden Globes	none
New York Film Critics	none
National Board of Review	none
Film Daily Critics	none

*I can't explain why I was never able to say to Spencer Tracy what I wanted to say . . .
what a great actor he was.*

—Stanley Kramer

PLOT: When their only child introduces her black fiancé to them, her parents are delightfully yet poignantly forced to reexamine their philosophies of life, love, and liberalism.

PRODUCTION: With seven Oscars and a 1961 Irving G. Thalberg Award, Stanley Kramer had a reputation for being one of Hollywood's most prolific producer-directors of "message movies." One morning during a walk in Beverly Hills, comedy writer William Rose, with whom Kramer had done *It's a Mad, Mad, Mad, Mad World*, told a story about a liberal white South African whose daughter falls for a black man. Kramer immediately sparked to the idea but wanted to set it in America. He almost immediately envisioned it as the perfect "situation" movie for Spencer Tracy. Katharine Hepburn was on board after Kramer cast her niece Katharine Houghton as well. Sidney Poitier agreed when he learned of Tracy and Hepburn's participation. All the stars knew in advance was that the script would be a comedy-drama concerned with young love, contemporary racial prejudice, and the joys and challenges of marriage in general. They were told that the film would be shot entirely in San Francisco and they also knew the subject was controversial, as interracial marriage remained illegal in seventeen states at the time the film went into production in 1966. The biggest challenge for the filmmakers became Tracy's failing health. No company would provide production insurance. As this was their ninth film together and their offscreen relationship was still flourishing, Hepburn put her salary in escrow to cover production insurance costs. In William Rose's Oscar-winning screenplay, Kramer purposely sought to turn the ethnic stereotype upside down by making Poitier's character an idealized version of perfection, so that the only reason one would object to the marriage would be racial. William Rose actually wrote two scripts to accommodate Spencer Tracy's failing health. One included Tracy's character and the other did not. When principal photography commenced, Tracy was physically able to work for only a few hours at a time, usually mornings. Oddly, this made things easier on Sidney Poitier. Although he was an Academy Award winner himself (*Lilies of the Field*, 1963), Poitier was still so intimidated by Tracy and Hepburn that Kramer allowed him to deliver his lines to empty chairs with eye-level markers. The bust of Tracy in his home office had actually been hand-crafted by Hepburn a few years earlier, and her tears during Tracy's final monologue were real. Given the true state of his rapidly deteriorating heart, she knew it was their last on-screen pairing and that she was losing her loving companion of more than twenty-five years.

DISTRIBUTION: Released by Columbia as "A Love Story of Today" with accompanying posters and trailers featuring the interracial couple, *Guess Who's Coming to Dinner* was an immediate success. In equivalent 2005 dollars, it was Columbia's third-highest domestic box office film to date after *The Bridge on the River Kwai* (1957) and *From Here to Eternity* (1953). The film was still in theaters at the time of the Reverend Dr. Martin Luther King's assassination (April 4, 1968), and so the memorable line "Who do you think you are, Martin Luther King?" said to Poitier by Isabel Sanford, who played Tillie, the family's opinionated maid, was removed. Although it was restored for the DVD version, the video release did not carry the original line. Spencer Tracy died seventeen days after completion of principal photography. —*Christine McDermott*

THE GRADUATE

Embassy, 1967

ALL-RELEASE EQUIVALENT 2005 $s

(Unadjusted $s) in Millions of $s

Domestic Box Office Revenues........ **$525.0**/($98.3)
Production Cost .... **$17.5**/($3.0)
Principal Photography...........**100** days estimated
March 1967–August 1967

Director	Mike Nichols
Producer	Lawrence Turman
Production Company	Embassy Pictures
Story by	Based on the novel by Charles Webb
Screenplay by	Calder Willingham, Buck Henry
Cast	Anne Bancroft, Dustin Hoffman, Katharine Ross
Filming Locations	Beverly Hills, on the Sunset Strip and on the USC campus in Los Angeles, CA; various Berkeley locations and the famous Ambassador Hotel in Los Angeles, CA; the Robinson's house in La Verne, CA
Genre	Romantic Comedy
Format	Color (Technicolor; Panavision)
Initial Release	12/16/1967
Rerelease	1997
Running Time	105 minutes
MPAA Rating	R

STANDING THE TEST OF TIME

ACADEMY AWARD Oscar Nominations and Wins

Best Picture: Lawrence Turman, Producer

Actor: Dustin Hoffman

Actress: Anne Bancroft

Actress in a Supporting Role: Katharine Ross

Cinematography: Robert Surtees

*DIRECTING: Mike Nichols

Writing (Screenplay – based on material from another medium): Calder Willingham, Buck Henry

OSCAR TOTALS   Nominations **7**   *Wins **1**

AFI 100 YEARS 100 MOVIES SELECTION
2007 . . . #17   1997 . . . . #7

TOP 300 FILMS POSITION . . . . **#20**

All-Release Domestic Box Office in Equivalent 2005 $s

National Film Preservation Board Selection 1996

OTHER AWARDS Best Picture Wins

	Year
Golden Globes (Comedy)	1968
New York Film Critics	none
National Board of Review	none
Film Daily Critics	none

Wonderful director, Nichols. He had no plan, but he had a lot of options that he knew he was going to discover in the editing room. He was doing what I think an artist is supposed to do: he was painting, he was just feeling his way.

—Dustin Hoffman

PLOT: A biting satire about nebbish Benjamin Braddock, an aimless recent college graduate, who is seduced by and has a secretive affair with a middle-aged friend of his family—and then falls in love with the woman's daughter.

PRODUCTION: Producer Lawrence Turman read about Charles Webb's 1963 novel in the *New York Times Book Review* and optioned it for $1,000 against $20,000 if the film was made. Turman paid the $1,000 out of his own pocket and hired Mike Nichols without meeting him based on having liked his direction of *Barefoot in the Park* on Broadway. Various screenwriters came and went: Playwright William Hanley was paid $500 to write a draft. Calder Willingham did another version based on Webb's novel but refused to work with Nichols on a rewrite (he got a credit only after demanding a Writers Guild arbitration). Peter Nelson also did a version, but neither Nichols nor Turman liked it. Finally Nichols suggested Buck Henry (one of the writers of the popular TV series *Get Smart*). To facilitate the eccentric last-minute casting of Dustin Hoffman, in a role originally intended for a WASPy blonde, producers changed the Braddocks into Beverly Hills Jews. Warren Beatty was the producers' first choice for Benjamin, but he declined in favor of making *Bonnie and Clyde*. Robert Redford wanted the part but was judged too conventionally handsome to play the shy, inexperienced graduate. Six actors were tested, including Jack Nicholson. Burt Ward was cast but was under contract to play Robin on the *Batman* TV series and couldn't get a release. The part of Mrs. Robinson was first offered to Doris Day, who turned it down, finding the material offensive. It went to Anne Bancroft (only six years older than Hoffman), whom Turman had admired on Broadway. Director Mike Nichols, working with veteran cinematographer Robert Surtees, wisely decided to keep the focus predominantly on Benjamin's point of view. Bravura shots such as the opening, tight on Benjamin's face as he negotiates a people-mover at Los Angeles International Airport, have since become part of the language of film. Nichols and Surtees sought to create a stylized effect, weaning the viewer away from the obviously studio-bound setups that had dominated films for decades. Extensive planning went into getting the scene of Benjamin jumping off a diving board into Mrs. Robinson's bed just right. Turman credits Nichols for changing the final wedding scene so that the ceremony was concluded before Benjamin breaks in and shouts to Elaine. Nichols thought the melancholy harmonies of Simon and Garfunkel were perfect for the film, and commissioned Paul Simon to write three original songs. By the time the film was edited, Simon had delivered only one. He played a few notes of a second song in progress, "Mrs. Roosevelt." Nichols said, "It's now about Mrs. Robinson." The resulting soundtrack album, which also used already-existing Simon and Garfunkel music, went to number one on the charts.

DISTRIBUTION: *The Graduate* tapped into the zeitgeist of a new generation and was an immediate sensation: co-screenwriter Buck Henry recalled visiting theaters that not only were so full but people were "sitting on the steps, breaking the fire laws." It was so successful that Embassy Pictures head Joseph E. Levine gave novelist Webb an additional $10,000 in thanks. The single word of advice one adult gives Benjamin, "Plastics," became an instant symbol of corporate shallowness and hypocrisy. A play adapted from the movie was a hit in London in 2000 and on Broadway in 2002. —*Tom Dupree*

2001: A SPACE ODYSSEY
MGM, 1968

ALL-RELEASE EQUIVALENT 2005 $s
(Unadjusted $s) in Millions of $s

Domestic Box Office Revenues . . . . **$261.9**/($58.5)
Production Cost . . . . **$58.0**/($10.3)
Principal Photography . . . . **135** days estimated
12/29/1965–7/7/1966

Director . . . . Stanley Kubrick

Producer . . . . Stanley Kubrick

Production Company . . . . Polaris Production, Metro-Goldwyn-Mayer Production

Story and
  Screenplay by . . . . Stanley Kubrick, Arthur C. Clarke

Cast . . . . Keir Dullea, Gary Lockwood

Filming Locations . . . . MGM British Studios at Borehamwood (most scenes); Shepperton Studios, London; Monument Valley, UT; Arizona deserts Outer Hebrides/South Harris, Western Isles, Scotland; African deserts; Switzerland; Germany

Genre . . . . Sci-Fi

Format . . . . Color (Metrocolor)

Initial Release . . . . 4/2/1968 premiere (Washington, D.C.); 5/10/1968 premiere (London); also presented in UK in Cinerama for limited road show engagement

Rerelease 1971, 1977, 2001

Running Time . . . . 160 minutes (U.S.) release 141 minutes (UK version)

MPAA Rating . . . . G

STANDING THE TEST OF TIME

ACADEMY AWARD Oscar Nominations and Wins

Art Direction: Tony Masters, Harry Lange, Ernie Archer

Directing: Stanley Kubrick

*SPECIAL VISUAL EFFECTS: Stanley Kubrick

Writing (Story and Screenplay – written directly for the screen): Stanley Kubrick, Arthur C. Clarke

OSCAR TOTALS   Nominations **4**   *Wins **1**

AFI 100 YEARS 100 MOVIES SELECTION
2007 . . . #15   1997 . . . #22

TOP 300 FILMS POSITION . . . . **#142**
All-Release Domestic Box Office in Equivalent 2005 $s

National Film Preservation Board Selection 1991

OTHER AWARDS Best Picture Wins

	Year
Golden Globes	none
New York Film Critics	none
National Board of Review	none
Film Daily Critics	none

STANLEY KUBRICK DR STRANGELOVE PATHS OF GLORY
ETC INTERESTED IN DOING FILM ON ETS STOP
INTERESTED IN YOU STOP ARE YOU INTERESTED
QUERY THOUGHT YOU WERE RECLUSE STOP

FRIGHTFULLY INTERESTED IN WORKING WITH
ENFANT TERRIBLE STOP CONTACT MY AGENT STOP
WHAT MAKES KUBRICK THINK IM A RECLUSE QUERY

—Cables between Stanley Kubrick and Arthur C. Clarke that initiated their collaboration

PLOT: Scientists excavate a mysterious alien monolith under the lunar surface. It seems to be transmitting a low-level signal toward the planet Jupiter, so the starship *Discovery,* crewed by five astronauts and the HAL 9000 computer, is dispatched to investigate.

PRODUCTION: After destroying the Earth in *Dr. Strangelove,* it seemed fitting that director Stanley Kubrick would look for life elsewhere in the universe. He began watching every science fiction film and devoured the best novels of the genre, searching for a collaborator. A conversation with Roger Caras, Columbia's publicist, led him to writer Arthur C. Clarke. The two immediately hit it off. Kubrick selected Clarke's short story "The Sentinel" to adapt into a novel because he thought the screenplay form was inadequate to express his vision. "If you can describe it," he told Clarke, "I can film it." Little did Clarke realize that describing Kubrick's ideas in novel form would take nearly four years, right up until the time the film was released, and that hundreds of his written pages would go unused in the movie. While Clark wrote the novel, Kubrick shot the film almost entirely on set in London, trying to keep pace with the rapid developments of the American-Soviet space race. As a result, the film's budget skyrocketed from $4.5 to $10.3 million, with a staggering $6.5 million going toward 205 visual effects shots. To achieve the utmost realism, Kubrick had the effects team employ silent-film techniques that exposed the negative a dozen times instead of using blue screens and traveling mattes. Former NASA film technician Douglas Trumbull shot rolling artwork through a slit to create the hallucinogenic star gate effect. For the *Discovery*'s "Ferris wheel," the Vickers Engineering Group built a huge centrifuge at a cost of $750,000 that could fit actors and cameras inside. After the art department spent $50,000 and still failed to devise a prehistoric set that matched the authenticity of the ape costumes designed by Stuart Freeborn, Andrew Birkin, the production tea boy, took a night train on his own to Liverpool and photographed the nearby dunes to serve as a better design reference. Kubrick was so impressed with the boy's resourcefulness that he hired him as an effects coordinator and special assistant. Later, as Kubrink tinkered with the final cut of the movie, he made one last surprise move. Rather than use the new music commissioned from renowned composer Alex North, Kubrik decided to stick with his temporary sound track consisting of classical works. North, however, was not made aware of the fact that Kubrik did not use his music until the crescendo of Richard Strauss's "Thus Spake Zarathustra" shocked him at the premiere.

DISTRIBUTION: Most critics found *2001* turgid and pretentious, yet their reviews didn't stop young people from flocking to the theaters for the "ultimate trip." Confident that he had a hit, Kubrick spent $20,500 to buy 500 shares of MGM stock. The initial returns in 1968 put the film $800,000 in the red and seemed to have curbed Kubrick's swagger, much to the delight of some executives and critics who craved seeing him fall. But the long haul proved the director's intuition correct. By 1972 the film had earned over $58 million in U.S. box office and reversed its critical fate, becoming a favorite of film icons such as Federico Fellini, who found the death of HAL 9000 particularly sad. —*Michael Kogge*

FUNNY GIRL
Columbia, 1968

ALL-RELEASE EQUIVALENT 2005 $s
(Unadjusted $s) in Millions of $s

Domestic Box Office Revenues . . . . **$268.7**/($56.1)
Production Cost . . . . **$78.6**/($14.0)
Principal Photography . . . . **82** days estimated
8/7/1967–12/1/1967

Director . . . . William Wyler
Producer . . . . Ray Stark
Production Company . . . . Rastar Productions
Story by . . . . Based on the musical play by Isobel Lennart
Screenplay by . . . . Isobel Lennart
Cast . . . . Barbra Streisand, Omar Sharif, Kay Medford, Anne Francis, Walter Pidgeon
Filming Locations . . . . . . In studio: Warner Bros. lot, Burbank, CA; on location: New York City, NY; Hoboken, NJ; San Marino and Santa Monica, CA
Genre . . . . Musical
Format . . . . Color (Technicolor)
Initial Release . . . . 9/8/1968 (New York)
Rerelease 1973, 2001
Running Time . . . . 155 minutes
MPAA Rating . . . . G

STANDING THE TEST OF TIME

ACADEMY AWARD Oscar Nominations and Wins

Best Picture: Ray Stark, Producer

*ACTRESS: Barbra Streisand (tie)

Actress in a Supporting Role: Kay Medford

Cinematography: Harry Stradling

Film Editing: Robert Swink, Maury Winetrobe, William Sands

Music (Song – Original for the Picture): "Funny Girl" (Music by Jule Styne; Lyrics by Bob Merrill)

Music: Adaptation score by Walter Scharf

Sound: Columbia Studio Sound Dept.

OSCAR TOTALS   Nominations **8**   *Wins 1

AFI 100 YEARS 100 MOVIES SELECTION
2007 0   1997 0

TOP 300 FILMS POSITION . . . . **#137**
All-Release Domestic Box Office in Equivalent 2005 $s

National Film Preservation Board Selection . . . . none

OTHER AWARDS Best Picture Wins

	Year
Golden Globes (Musical)	1969
New York Film Critics	none
National Board of Review	none
Film Daily Critics	none

Barbra was insecure and nervous about the new medium at first. She was a bit obstreperous in the beginning, but things were ironed out when she discovered some of us knew what we were doing. Sometimes, she would argue for her way. If I was set on my way, that's the way we did it. She was not difficult in that sense. She was very cooperative.

—William Wyler

PLOT: A musical biography loosely based on singer-comedienne Fanny Brice's rise to fame and her love affair with and turbulent marriage to gambler Nick Arnstein.

PRODUCTION: Other than Barbra Streisand, who had played the part of Fanny Brice on Broadway and in the West End 798 times, no one knew the character better than producer Ray Stark. Brice, who died in 1951, was Stark's mother-in-law. Having long desired to dramatize the life of this legendary Ziegfeld and Broadway star, Stark put together the stage musical and chose Streisand to play the lead. On December 1, 1965, Streisand signed a four-picture deal with Stark to ensure that she'd be cast in the film version. Yet, in a classic case of Hollywood cluelessness when it came to casting, Columbia was resistant to having the twenty-six-year-old neophyte as the leading lady in its lavish and expensive film, and insisted instead on Shirley MacLaine for box office security. Stark was adamant about Streisand filling the role, and her screen test proved him right, as it greatly impressed studio executives. Streisand, in turn, won her own casting battle. For a time, Frank Sinatra was considered a strong contender for the role of Nick Arnstein, but Streisand had veto power, and the role was offered to Marlon Brando, Tony Curtis, Rock Hudson, and Gregory Peck, all of whom turned it down. Omar Sharif was eventually cast, based in part on his success in the title role of *Doctor Zhivago* two years earlier. After first-choice director Sidney Lumet left the picture over creative differences with Stark and Streisand, Oscar-winning filmmaker William Wyler was offered the directing reins. Wyler initially declined, as he was deaf in one ear and felt he could not effectively direct a musical. However, after meeting the persuasive young actress, he agreed to helm the movie anyway. It was his first and only musical. The initial day of filming began two months after the June 1967 Arab-Israeli War (also known as the Six-Day War) ended. The Cairo press rebuked Egyptian Omar Sharif for his on- and offscreen romance with a Jew, and Stark took full advantage of the publicity. He played up the couple, thereby creating early international buzz for the movie. There is a popular misconception that "Rat-Tat-Tat-Tat," which stopped the show nightly onstage, was replaced with the comic ballet "The Swan" because the former was "too dated" for the movie version. In fact, the song was replaced because its Yiddish-accented lyrics (such as "I'm Pri-vit Schvartz from Rock-a-vay") and the red, white, and blue bagels hanging from Streisand's gunbelt were considered "too Jewish" for 1960s mainstream America. Streisand had also wanted to show more range by proving that she could dance.

DISTRIBUTION: Critics were virtually unanimous in their praise of Streisand, who eclipsed all others in the film, including Sharif. Some critics felt Sharif was "miscast," with one (Roger Ebert) complaining that he came off like "a cigar-store Indian." Regardless, *Funny Girl* was the highest-grossing domestic box office film of 1968. Seven years later a sequel, *Funny Lady,* "a big, messy flop of a movie" (Ebert again), was released, but not even Streisand, by then a star, could save it. In 2001 the film was fully restored in six-track digital sound and dye-transfer Technicolor. Streisand's signature greeting to Sharif, "Hello, gorgeous," was voted number eighty-one in AFI's 2005 list of the 100 most memorable movie lines. —*Bob Canning*

BULLITT
Warner Bros./Seven Arts, 1968

ALL-RELEASE EQUIVALENT 2005 $s
(Unadjusted $s) in Millions of $s

Domestic Box Office Revenues........ **$206.6**/($42.2)
Production Cost ....$30.9/($5.5)
Principal Photography............70 days estimated
February 1968–May 1968

Director . . . . Peter Yates
Producer . . . . Philip D'Antoni
Production Company . . . . Seven Arts Production, Solar Productions
Story by . . . . Based on the novel *Mute Witness* by Robert L. Pike
Screenplay by . . . . Alan R. Trustman, Harry Kleiner
Cast . . . . Steve McQueen, Robert Vaughn, Jacqueline Bisset, Don Gordon, Robert Duvall
Filming Locations . . . . San Francisco, CA
Genre . . . . Crime
Format . . . . Color (Technicolor)
Initial Release 10/17/1968
Rerelease . . . . none
Running Time . . . . 113 minutes
MPAA Rating . . . . M

STANDING THE TEST OF TIME

ACADEMY AWARD Oscar Nominations and Wins
*FILM EDITING: Frank P. Keller
Sound: Warner Bros.-Seven Arts Studio Sound Dept.

OSCAR TOTALS   Nominations **2**   *Wins **1**

AFI 100 YEARS 100 MOVIES SELECTION
2007 0   1997 0

TOP 300 FILMS POSITION . . . . **#240**
All-Release Domestic Box Office in Equivalent 2005 $s

National Film Preservation Board Selection 2007

OTHER AWARDS Best Picture Wins

	Year
Golden Globes	none
New York Film Critics	none
National Board of Review	none
Film Daily Critics	none

What we did in the streets with automobiles, I don't think will be done for a long, long time.
—Steve McQueen

PLOT: A San Francisco police detective is assigned to protect an underworld informant who is scheduled to testify against the mob. When the informant is killed by Mafia hit men, the cop decides to investigate the case on his own.

PRODUCTION: Movie agent John Flaxman owned the rights to Robert L. Pike's 1963 novel *Mute Witness,* whose protagonist was sixty-five-year-old New York City police detective Lieutenant Clancy. He asked Alan R. Trustman, who wrote *The Thomas Crown Affair* (Steve McQueen's previous film), to script an adaptation. Trustman changed the hero's name to Lt. Frank Bullitt, made him roughly thirty years younger, and reset the action in San Francisco. Flaxman sold the rights to independent producer Phil D'Antoni, who then pitched the screenplay to McQueen and partner Robert Releya's Solar Productions. *Bullitt* was to be Solar's first in a lucrative six-picture deal with Warner Bros. McQueen insisted that Peter Yates direct the movie, as the actor had been impressed with a previous film he had helmed featuring an authentic car chase through London. McQueen was also instrumental in getting his friend Robert Vaughn, fresh from *The Man from U.N.C.L.E.,* for the co-starring role as the crooked politician. Reality was of key importance to McQueen, who convinced newly elected San Francisco mayor Joseph Alioto to open up the city for filming. In exchange, Solar agreed to pay hired extras from poverty areas at full union scale. Studio execs were not happy and ordered Solar back to Burbank to complete the movie, including the car chase. McQueen refused, and Warner killed the rest of their six-picture deal, but *Bullitt* went forward in San Francisco as originally planned. San Francisco General Hospital was used in several sequences with real-life doctors and nurses as extras. A gun-toting foot chase was staged inside San Francisco International Airport and on Runway No. 5 involving a real Pan American Airlines jet. However, permission to film the car chase on the Golden Gate Bridge was denied. For his first American film, Yates used a lightweight Arriflex camera for the handheld footage inside the cars during the landmark chase through some thirty noncontiguous streets. Famed stuntman Bill Hickman played a bad guy driving a Dodge Charger, chased by McQueen in a Mustang. Lalo Schifrin, who wrote the film's jazz-flavored score, pointed out that the power of the chase would have been diluted by background music. Consequently, sound crews recorded full sets of sound effects for each car out in the desert (to avoid any extraneous sounds) so that every snap, crackle, and pop of the torturous chase would be heard, setting a standard for all film chases to follow. Another of the film's technological innovations was created when the Mafia stoolie, holed up in his hotel room, is peppered with bullets. Again, in the name of reality, Yates wanted more than a crushed "ketchup sachet" to indicate a bullet's entry into the human body. So the victim is seen being lifted off his feet, jerked through the air, and slammed against a wall, leaving "a nebula of blood." Used for this revolutionary effect were an electronically ignited plasma-filled baggie, lurch cables, and jolt harnesses. This is, of course, standard operating procedure these days.

DISTRIBUTION: *Bullitt* was an immediate hit and finished in the top three domestic box office hits for 1968, coming in behind *Funny Girl* and *The Odd Couple.* —*Bob Canning*

497

MIDNIGHT COWBOY

United Artists, 1969

ALL-RELEASE EQUIVALENT 2005 $s	
(Unadjusted $s) in Millions of $s	
Domestic Box Office Revenues	**$202.2**/($44.8)
Production Cost	**$19.2**/($3.6)
Principal Photography	**80** days estimated March 1968–July 1968

Running Time . . . . 113 minutes
MPAA Rating . . . . X (later changed to R)

Director . . . . John Schlesinger

Producer . . . . Jerome Hellman

Production Company . . . . Jerome Hellman Productions, Florin Productions

Story by . . . . Based on the novel by James Leo Herlihy

Screenplay by . . . . Waldo Salt

Cast . . . . Dustin Hoffman, Jon Voight, Sylvia Miles, John McGiver, Brenda Vaccaro

Filming Locations . . . . Filmways Studio, 246 E. 127th St., East Harlem, N.Y.; various New York City locales including Times Square and 114 E. 72nd St. (Sylvia Miles's apartment), Lincoln Tunnel; New Jersey; in Florida: Hollywood, Miami, Miami Beach; in Texas: Big Springs, Stanton, and Sweetwater

Genre . . . . Drama

Format . . . . B&W and Color (DeLuxe)

Initial Release 5/25/1969

Rerelease . . . . none

STANDING THE TEST OF TIME

ACADEMY AWARD Oscar Nominations and Wins

*BEST PICTURE: Jerome Hellman, Producer

Actor: Dustin Hoffman

Actor: Jon Voight

Actress in a Supporting Role: Vylvia Miles

*DIRECTING: John Schlesinger

Film Editing: Hugh A. Robertson

*WRITING (Screenplay – based on material from another medium): Waldo Salt

OSCAR TOTALS   Nominations 7   *Wins 3

AFI 100 YEARS 100 MOVIES SELECTION
2007 . . . #43   1997 . . . #36

TOP 300 FILMS POSITION . . . . #256
All-Release Domestic Box Office in Equivalent 2005 $s

National Film Preservation Board Selection 1994

OTHER AWARDS Best Picture Wins

	Year
Golden Globes	none
New York Film Critics	none
National Board of Review	none
Film Daily Critics	none

Collaborating with all the creative people involved in making a movie is a real challenge. Everything is fine at the outset, but as work on the production progresses, egos assert themselves and tempers can flare.

—John Schlesinger

PLOT: Freewheeling loser Joe Buck takes a bus to New York seeking quick riches as a gigolo for older women. He meets sickly petty criminal Ratzo Rizzo, and to survive, the pair develop an unusual friendship.

PRODUCTION: English model-designer Kaffe Fassett gave fellow Brit John Schlesinger a copy of James Leo Herlihy's novel *Midnight Cowboy*. He took it on vacation to Morocco and returned with a passion to make it as a movie. Schlesinger contacted American producer Jerome Hellman, who acquired book rights in March 1966. Hellman pitched a movie budgeted at $750,000 all over Hollywood but was turned down. Then David Picker of United Artists offered a $1 million budget, specifying that it had to be shot in black and white to save money. UA offered creative freedom, but Hellman still warned Picker that they planned a very realistic movie. Picker said that if necessary UA would release it under its Lopert banner, as they had done with Billy Wilder's *Kiss Me Stupid*, although that would make it far more difficult to book theaters and to get attention. To write the script, they approached Truman Capote, Gore Vidal, and Francis Coppola before hiring young playwright Jack Gelbert. They hated his script and turned to formerly blacklisted writer Waldo Salt, who worked closely with Schlesinger. Hellman loved Salt's script but saw the budget rising. He asked UA for $2.5 million. Picker agreed to $2.2 million if Schlesinger, Hellman, and Salt would defer salary in lieu of profits (a deal that would make them rich). As production was about to begin, UA said they could shoot in color. Hellman wanted "natural color effects" just like what Francis Coppola had achieved in his indie film *You're a Big Boy Now*. Hellman insulated Schlesinger as the budget climbed to $3.6 million. Hoffman fought for and won the role of Ratso by doing an in-character audition, taking Schlesinger on a tour of Times Square. For Joe Buck, Schlesinger rebuffed Warren Beatty and Robert Redford, while considering Roger Ewing, Alan Alda, Alex Cord, Michael Parks, and Michael Sarrazin before being charmed by Jon Voight, who then spent weeks on back roads in Texas working on his accent. Rehearsals with actors were improvisational. Schlesinger recalled the New York shoot as an unhappy experience, working with people taking graft and "robbing the production." Schlesinger battled over the editing with Hugh Robertson and brought in Jim Clark to cut the flashbacks. John Barry had composed a haunting theme, but they wanted more. Bob Dylan was commissioned to write a song but left them hanging. They approached Harry Nilsson and heard his track—"Everybody's Talkin'," written by Fred Neil—and that was it. Dylan eventually offered "Lay, Lady, Lay" but too late. Filming in New York was interrupted for a day because of the funeral of Robert F. Kennedy.

DISTRIBUTION: *Midnight Cowboy* was a blockbuster despite mixed reviews. The film got the first adult or X rating for nudity, homosexuality, and language. Hellman soon saw it as a "scarlet letter," which limited the theaters they could book. When nominated as Best Picture, the Academy didn't want an X-rated nominee, so the MPAA offered an R if Schlesinger would slice a single frame from an oral sex scene. He refused. After *Midnight Cowboy* won Best Picture, it was rerated R without any changes. —*Alex Ben Block*

THE WILD BUNCH

Warner Bros./Seven Arts, 1969

ALL-RELEASE EQUIVALENT 2005 $s

(Unadjusted $s) in Millions of $s

Domestic Box Office Revenues . . . . **$43.1**/($10.0)
Production Cost . . . . **$31.9**/($6.0)
Principal Photography . . . . **81** days
3/25/1968–6/30/1968

Director . . . . Sam Peckinpah
Producer . . . . Phil Feldman
Production Company . . . . Warner Bros./Seven Arts
Story by . . . . Walon Green, Roy N. Sickner
Screenplay by . . . . Walon Green, Sam Peckinpah
Cast . . . . William Holden, Ernest
Borgnine, Robert Ryan,
Warren Oates, Jaime Sanchez,
Ben Johnson
Filming Locations . . . . Location scenes filmed in
Parras, Mexico
Genre . . . . Western
Format . . . . Color (Technicolor)
Initial Release . . . . 6/18/1969 premiere
(Los Angeles)
Rerelease 1995
Running Time . . . . 134 or 148 minutes
MPAA Rating . . . . R

STANDING THE TEST OF TIME

ACADEMY AWARD Oscar Nominations and Wins

Music [Original Score: for a motion picture (not a musical)]: Jerry Fielding

Writing (Story and Screenplay – based on material not previously published or produced): Story by Walon Green, Roy N. Sickner; Screenplay by Walon Green, Sam Peckinpah

OSCAR TOTALS   Nominations **2**   *Wins **0**

AFI 100 YEARS 100 MOVIES SELECTION
2007 . . . #79   1997 . . . #80

TOP 300 FILMS POSITION . . . . none
All-Release Domestic Box Office in Equivalent 2005 $s

National Film Preservation Board Selection 1999

OTHER AWARDS Best Picture Wins

	Year
Golden Globes	none
New York Film Critics	none
National Board of Review	none
Film Daily Critics	none

We are telling a tale of hardened veterans of western outlawry.
The brutal tale must be told honestly.

—Sam Peckinpah

PLOT: A posse of aging outlaws attempts to have one more moment of glory before the Wild West changes forever.

PRODUCTION: The story is based on a true border incident that occurred in 1913: U.S. outlaws hijacked a train full of ammunition that was being sent to Pancho Villa. Walon Green and Roy Sickner (an ex-stuntman) created the initial script, and Peckinpah brought it to producer Phil Feldman. Soon after, Peckinpah began lengthy rewrites. Peckinpah told executives that Lee Marvin was interested, which sparked their interest, but at the last minute Marvin backed out to do *Paint Your Wagon*. The role then went to William Holden. Peckinpah had been banned from studio films for three years due to budget overruns and was making his comeback with what was to be a low-budget movie. Costume designer Gordon Dawson had only five weeks to fit the actors, create their wardrobe, and age the clothes as Peckinpah requested. The film was originally scheduled for 70 days of shooting, at a budget of $3,451,420. The tough, 81-day shoot took place in the dusty, hot conditions of Mexico, and Peckinpah said, "Getting out of the studio was the best thing that ever happened to us," because the actors and the crew got the feeling of the era in which the film took place. Most of the film was shot in and around Parras, Mexico. Peckinpah responded to the rugged, virgin character of the landscape, but the heat, sand-storms, and tension got to many crew members. Peckinpah did not use storyboards and came on set instead with a few crude sketches on the back of script pages. During the first six days they shot 25,290 feet of film. The Mexican government cooperated fully, and more than 1,000 locals were used as extras. The prop department flew in 12,000 red harvester ants and a dozen gray scorpions from Hollywood for the production. They also used roughly 90,000 rounds of ammunition and more than 3,000 squibs for the battle sequences. The film boasts forty speaking parts. As many as six cameras ran at times. It took three weeks to shoot the final gun battle. The film went over schedule and cost nearly $3 million more than budgeted. Interspersing various speeds of slow-motion footage with regular-speed footage was emotionally impactful. The film also boasted 3,642 cuts—the most of any feature up to that time. Wary of using a score that sounded too pristine, they recorded in Mexico with Mexican guitar music, giving it a less polished sound.

DISTRIBUTION: At a test screening of the rough cut in Kansas City, more than thirty people left the theater, sickened by the violence. Some critics assailed the film because of this violence, while others appreciated its honest depiction of the era. Audiences immediately responded. Years later, when the film was about to be rereleased in theaters, the MPAA slapped an NC-17 rating on the film, even though it received an R rating initially. After a yearlong battle, the filmmakers got their R rating back and were able to release it again. When the home video market opened up in the early 1980s, *The Wild Bunch* was one of the first twenty films released on video by Warner Bros. —*Dina Gachman*

EASY RIDER
Columbia, 1969

ALL-RELEASE EQUIVALENT 2005 $s
(Unadjusted $s) in Millions of $s

Domestic Box Office Revenues........ **$191.7**/($42.5)
Production Cost .... **$1.9**/($0.4)
Principal Photography............**30** days estimated
February 1968–April 1968

Director .... Dennis Hopper

Producer .... Peter Fonda

Production Company.... Pando-Raybert Productions

Story and
  Screenplay by .... Dennis Hopper, Peter Fonda, Terry Southern

Cast .... Peter Fonda, Dennis Hopper, Jack Nicholson

Filming Locations....... On location in Nevada, Louisiana, Arizona, and California

Genre................ Drama

Format............... Color (Technicolor)

Initial Release .... 5/13/1969 Cannes Film Festival opening; 7/14/1969 premiere Beekman Theater (New York)

Re-Release .... 1994, 35th anniversary (limited), 2004

Running Time .... 94 minutes

MPAA Rating .... R

STANDING THE TEST OF TIME

ACADEMY AWARD Oscar Nominations and Wins

Actor in a Supporting Role: Jack Nicholson

Writing (Story and Screenplay – based on material not previously published or produced): Peter Fonda, Dennis Hopper, Terry Southern

OSCAR TOTALS   Nominations 2   *Wins 0

AFI 100 YEARS 100 MOVIES SELECTION
2007 . . . #84   1997 . . . #88

TOP 300 FILMS POSITION . . . . **#292**
All-Release Domestic Box Office in Equivalent 2005 $s

National Film Preservation Board Selection. . . . 1998

OTHER AWARDS Best Picture Wins

	Year
Golden Globes	none
New York Film Critics	none
National Board of Review	none
Film Daily Critics	none

Having a meeting for Dennis [Hopper] was like having an audience. There was no way he was going to listen to anybody else. It was all about his speeches. So when they get to New Orleans, there was war. Lots of people have never spoken to each other again, lots of hard feelings.

—Bill Hayward

PLOT: After smuggling drugs from Mexico to L.A., two dropouts from sixties society, Wyatt and Billy, ride cross-country on motorcycles in search of freedom and a little fun at Mardi Gras. They see the country for what it is, but the country doesn't always see them for who they are. Along the way they meet some colorful characters before arriving at an apocalyptic end.

PRODUCTION: The low-budget road movie that changed Hollywood began in September 1967 with Peter Fonda, drunk and stoned, at Showrama, an industry convention in Toronto, promoting *The Trip* for American International Pictures (AIP). From the podium, he saw a poster of another AIP movie, *Wild Angels,* featuring Fonda and Bruce Dern in leather with motorcycles. In a flash, Fonda envisioned a hit movie, a "modern western," with "two cats riding across the country." Late that night he phoned pal Dennis Hopper in L.A., waking him. Hopper immediately wanted to direct. Fonda said he'd produce, and both would star. The working titles were "The Losers" and "Mardi Gras." Hopper brought in his brother-in-law Bill Hayward, forming Pando Productions (even as Hayward divorced Hopper's sister, Brooke). Fonda convinced Terry Southern to write the script for scale (approximately $350 a week) instead of his usual $100,000 fee. Southern came up with the title, a term for a man who lives off prostitutes. Fonda had a deal with AIP, but it didn't like the druggy antiheroes and wanted Hopper to direct or star, not both. So pal Jack Nicholson steered them to Raybert Productions (which produced the hit TV show *The Monkees*), run by Bob Rafelson and Bert Schneider. They greenlighted the film under their deal with Columbia Pictures on a skimpy $365,000 budget. Raybert got a third of any profits, with Pando and Columbia splitting the rest. Raybert gave them an initial $40,000 to do the Mardi Gras scenes as a test. With less than a week to prepare for Mardi Grasthey scrambled for 16mm cameras, cast, and crew. Hopper famously began on day one screaming that he was in charge, alienating many. Despite defections, they shot 16 hours of film in five days. Principal photography included grueling cross-country travel and frequent creative fights between Hopper and Fonda, who for much of the shoot barely spoke. Back in L.A., Hopper assembled a four-hour version that was eventually edited down to 90 minutes by Nicholson, Fonda and credited editor Donn Cambern. Furious at first, Hopper later admitted he loved the final cut. Crosby, Stills, and Nash were commissioned to create the score, but it was scrapped in favor of the temporary track which used cuts from music by such artists as the Byrds, Jimi Hendrix, and Steppenwolf.

DISTRIBUTION: Hopper and Fonda screened *Easy Rider* for friends throughout 1968, leading to an invitation to compete at the Cannes Film Festival, where in May 1969 the world premiere was met by stunned silence followed by a standing ovation. Hopper won best director honors. The American premiere was July 10, 1969, at New York's Museum of Modern Art. It soon became a box office phenomenon: a low-budget film that broke all the rules and became the third-highest grosser of 1969, with over $19 million in rentals on initial release. It was hailed over time as the start of an innovative new American cinema and became a cultural touchstone for the sixties generation. —*Alex Ben Block*

BUTCH CASSIDY AND THE SUNDANCE KID
20th Century-Fox, 1969

ALL-RELEASE EQUIVALENT 2005 $s
(Unadjusted $s) in Millions of $s

Domestic Box Office Revenues	**$426.5**/($102.1)
Production Cost	**$35.2**/($6.6)
Principal Photography	**77 days**
	9/16/1968–1/8/1969

Director	George Roy Hill
Producer	John Foreman
Production Company	Campanile Productions
Story and Screenplay by	William Goldman
Cast	Paul Newman, Robert Redford, Katharine Ross
Filming Locations	Filmed on location in Mexico, Wyoming, Colorado; and Utah filming started on the railway between Durango and Silverton, CO
Genre	Western
Format	Color (DeLuxe)
Initial Release	9/23/1969 (New Haven, CT)
Rerelease	1974
Running Time	110 minutes
MPAA Rating	M

STANDING THE TEST OF TIME

ACADEMY AWARD Oscar Nominations and Wins

Best Picture: John Foreman, Producer

*CINEMATOGRAPHY: Conrad Hall

Directing: George Roy Hill

*MUSIC (Original Score): Burt Bacharach

*MUSIC (Song): "Raindrops Keep Fallin' on My Head"

Sound: William Edmondson, David Dockendorf

*WRITING (Story and Screenplay – based on material not previously published or producer): William Goldman

OSCAR TOTALS Nominations **7** *Wins 4

AFI 100 YEARS 100 MOVIES SELECTION
2007 . . . #73   1997 . . . #50

TOP 300 FILMS POSITION . . . . **#38**
All-Release Domestic Box Office in Equivalent 2005 $s

National Film Preservation Board Selection 2003

OTHER AWARDS Best Picture Wins

	Year
Golden Globes	none
New York Film Critics	none
National Board of Review	none
Film Daily Critics	none

I think it's a good film. It was a hell of a lot of hard work doing it and actually even more fun. And if the audiences don't dig it I think I'll go out of my f—king mind!

—George Roy Hill

PLOT: Butch Cassidy and Sundance, leaders of an outlaw gang during the civilizing of the West, rob a train once too often, causing a special posse to trail them all the way to South America.

PRODUCTION: Based on the real-life exploits of outlaws Butch Cassidy and Sundance, screenwriter William Goldman wrote a comedic western "buddy movie" with a contemporary feel. Although the script was based on fact, many studios wanted a more typical western. Goldman enjoyed the myth-shattering possibilities of his story and held out until Fox made an unprecedented $350,000 bid in October 1967. George Roy Hill signed on to direct, and Paul Newman was cast as Butch Cassidy (though everyone but Hill thought he should play Sundance). Hill then cast Robert Redford as Sundance (though studio head Darryl Zanuck wanted Marlon Brando or Warren Beatty). The original shooting script called for a 70-day shoot with 7 days for the second unit. The budget was set at $7.4 million. They rehearsed for two weeks at Fox, but Hill kept the scenes loose and open for improvisation. Newman and Redford, both knowledgeable about film, were allowed to make contributions, but Hill had difficulty communicating with Katharine Ross. (He later banned her from the set when she was not performing.) The original script was darker, but once they started shooting, they determined that the film should be more comedic. Before the shoot, Hill did great amounts of research, watching fifty westerns. He hired Conrad Hall for his outdoor photography and regularly consulted with him to get the best photographic effects. Hall achieved the kind of washed-out, desaturated color that Hill wanted for the film by overexposing two or three stops. Hall also frequently shot with backlight and as much dust and smoke as possible. They used black-and-white lighting techniques even after the film's switch to color (such as in Sundance's first visit with Etta). They also used reverse lighting to make the daytime shots look like nighttime. Hill hired Burt Bacharach to write a semi-modern, anachronistic, upbeat score, instead of a traditional western one. However, there were less than 12 minutes of music in the whole film because Hill didn't like to score scenes that contained dialogue. Because many of the shots were expensive and dangerous (one of the stunt men fractured his pelvis), hours were spent staging each scene. A special car had to be built for the horses to jump from in the scene when the posse arrives. In addition to that, it cost more than $1,000 per jump per stunt rider. The train robbery scenes were also extremely expensive to capture. Shot on a narrow-gauge period train in Colorado with more than 165 people on set, those scenes cost between $30,000 and $35,000 a day.

DISTRIBUTION: Although initially panned by critics because of its pop interpretation of the West, *Butch Cassidy and the Sundance Kid* became one of the top-grossing films of all time, generating $11.9 million in net profit on its initial release. It made the two outlaws legends and established the prototype for the "buddy film." It struck a chord with Vietnam-era audiences, tired of the idealized western. The character of Sundance redefined the western hero and became one of Redford's most popular roles, as well as the source of the name for his independent film festival. In 1979 a prequel was filmed, called *Butch and Sundance: The Early Days.* —*Hayley Taylor Block*

The 1970s

Well, the political environment and the cultural environment [in the 1960s and early 1970s] that was the most extreme in San Francisco actually existed everywhere in this country, especially among young people. It was just more extreme and . . . more radical [in San Francisco] which suited us [at American Zoetrope] fine because we wanted that. We really wanted to shake up the status quo in terms of the esthetics of how movies were made and what they were about and that was very much in tune with where we were.

—George Lucas

TOP 10 ALL-RELEASE MOVIES DOMESTIC BOX OFFICE
By Initial Year of Release, 1970–1979

		Equivalent 2005 $s in Millions of $s
1	Star Wars: Episode IV A New Hope	$1,085.1
2	Jaws	$802.9
3	The Exorcist	$722.9
4	The Sting	$605.6
5	Grease	$520.5
6	The Godfather	$505.9
7	Love Story	$447.6
8	Saturday Night Fever	$435.0
9	Close Encounters of the Third Kind	$424.1
10	Airport	$415.6
	Total:	**$5,965.2**

GENERAL U.S. STATISTICS, 1970

203,302,031
U.S. Population

35,441,369
U.S. Population
Age 15–24

17.7 Million
Average Weekly
U.S. Movie Attendance

DECADE OVERVIEW

Auteur—a film director whose practice accords with the auteur theory.
Auteur theory—a view of filmmaking in which the director is considered the primary creative force in a motion picture.

The once proud studio system, already a leaky vessel, was listing badly (circa early 1970s), and the conglomerates were circling beneath the chop, looking for dinner. Although Hollywood watchers looked on gloomily as studio after studio became no more than an appetizer for some company whose primary business was insurance, zinc mining or funeral homes, there was a ray of sunshine. The same upheavals that had left the studios bruised and battered made room for fresh blood in the executive suites.
—PETER BISKIND, *EASY RIDERS, RAGING BULLS*

Auteur Filmmakers and the Blockbuster Complex

As the decade began, the baby boom generation became ever more crucial to the survival of movies. The most active ticket buyers were largely young and single. Because this specific demographic didn't see movies as a habit, they required a new level of marketing. They demanded to see more on the big screen than what they saw on TV—they wanted spectacle, realistic violence, comedies with contemporary mores, strong sexual content, and exercises in nostalgia. Feature production faltered as studios scrambled to find financing and scripts that would appeal to a more targeted audience than in the past.

The quarter-century-long decline in movie theater attendance that began with the arrival of television hit rock bottom as the 1970s arrived. While the fighting in Vietnam raged on and antiwar protests were mounted at home, a national economic recession hit Hollywood hard. Despite hits such as Fox's *Butch Cassidy and the Sundance Kid* (1969), Universal's *Airport* (1970), and Paramount's *Love Story* (1970), the studios collectively lost $600 million in 1969–70. The few successes they did have were hard to repeat. The last vestiges of the studio system were about to be disassembled. MGM, in Culver City, under new ownership by Las Vegas mogul Kirk Kerkorian, sold chunks of its back lot for real estate development in 1974. Universal and Columbia, which had risen to the ranks of major studios, entered the decade near bankruptcy. In the greatest management upheaval since the arrival of sound, new leadership took power at Warner Bros., MGM, United Artists, and Paramount. RKO was gone, but at least National General and Cinerama Releasing, movie divisions tied to broadcast networks, had a burst of activity.

In 1971, surprisingly, it was conservative Republican president Richard Nixon who heard the pleas of the movie industry for help and arranged a series of special tax breaks to help stimulate business. Over the next five years the resulting tax shelters and tax-leveraged investments became hugely important to Hollywood and financed a great number of movies. By the time tax shelters were phased out by Congress in late 1976, two other important revenue sources emerged, pay TV and cable, both of which would significantly change the business and the way people saw movies.

The biggest hit in the early years of the decade was Paramount's *The Godfather,* a sprawling gangster saga from director Francis Ford Coppola. It began a long run of hits for Paramount Pictures, which would share the leadership for biggest box office and most hits throughout the decade with Warner Bros.

A new generation of filmmakers, many coming out of university film programs, connected with the youth audience, a feat that mystified the corporate studio bosses. As a result, the studios acted more like banks than producers for a few years, providing an unusual degree of creative freedom to a group of directors who aspired to be auteurs.

At mid-decade, Spielberg's much-delayed production *Jaws* redefined the meaning of a blockbuster in the modern era. It was the first studio-planned national wide release, with a TV saturation ad campaign, licensing, and merchandising. It was also the first summer blockbuster, setting a precedent for all other summer blockbusters to follow. Two years later, *Star Wars* grossed $2.6 million at the domestic box office between its opening on Wednesday, May 25, 1977, and the following Monday (Memorial Day). It subsequently went on to gross more than $221 million in domestic box office by the end of its initial release, having started in only 32 theaters, peaking in 1,098 theaters by week thirteen, and ending its initial run at week sixty-one.

The record domestic box office for *Star Wars* in 1977, along with hits such as *Smokey and the Bandit, Saturday Night Fever,* and *Close Encounters of the Third Kind,* helped rocket industrywide gross ticket sales that year past $2.3 billion. More ways to make money surfaced, as did more profit participants to share in the successes. A new breed of powerful talent agents and big-name stars soon became central to gathering all of the elements needed to make the most important movies, because big productions needed "bankable" stars. That led to record salaries for actors in demand, including Robert Redford, Dustin Hoffman, Jack Nicholson, Clint Eastwood, Barbra Streisand, and especially Marlon Brando, who commanded $3.7 million plus 11.3 percent of the U.S. gross and 5.6 percent of the foreign gross to appear for fifteen minutes in *Superman* (1978) and $1 million plus 11.3 percent of the gross to appear in *Apocalypse Now* (1979).

Disaster genre movies also became popular. Thanks primarily to director Irwin Allen, five of the top 15 disaster movies of all time were released in the 1970s.

During the latter part of the decade, intoxicated by the success of *Jaws* and *Star Wars,* Hollywood developed a blockbuster complex. The new studio mantra was to invest huge sums of money into a few "tent-pole" movies. That meant the hits had to pay for the mistakes. These high expectations sent production costs soaring, raised star salaries to new levels, and escalated the cost of advertising and promoting each movie even more. At the same time, increases in the consumer price index were exceeding the rising cost of admissions, meaning that labor and other production costs for most movies were increasing at a higher rate than box office ticket prices. This was in stark contrast to conditions in the 1960s, when ticket prices outpaced inflation. By the end of the decade, however, blockbuster movies were paying off due to fact that they were selling a greater number of tickets.

While the 1970s started on a low note, with production and box office down, the movie industry had successfully revived itself by the second half of the decade. The baby boom generation had fully embraced the medium. Popular movies could now make huge sums of money from exhibition worldwide. This led to the establishment of "franchises"—multiple movies spawned by an initial hit. Franchises went beyond the earlier practice of making sequels. These were often series of films, some planned two or three pictures in advance. Many continued into the decades that followed including *Star Wars* and *Alien* at 20th Century-Fox and *Superman* at Warner Bros. The James Bond franchise, begun in the 1960s, continued at United Artists as Roger Moore took over the role of 007 in 1973 and did four of his seven Bond films during the 1970s. As the decade ended, the movie business was booming—even if it was one big hit at a time.

People chase fire engines, flock to car crashes. People thrive on tragedy. It's unfortunate, but in my case, it's fortunate. The bigger the tragedy, the bigger the audience.
—IRWIN ALLEN

One-Third of the Top 15 Disaster Films Are Released in the 1970s

Top 15 Disaster Films
All-Release Domestic Box Office 1920–2005
Equivalent 2005 $s /(Unadjusted $s) in Millions of $s

Rank	Film	Initial Release	Domestic Box Office	Production Cost
1	Titanic*	1997	$824.8/($600.8)	$243.4/($200.0)
2	Independence Day	1996	$444.0/($306.2)	$93.4/($75.0)
3	Airport	1970	$415.6/($100.5)	$50.3/($10.0)
4	The Towering Inferno	1974	$362.4/($107.1)	$56.5/($14.3)
5	Twister	1996	$350.5/($241.7)	$114.5/($92.0)
6	The Poseidon Adventure	1972	$317.6/($84.6)	$23.4/($5.0)
7	Armageddon	1998	$275.5/($201.6)	$167.7/($140.0)
8	Earthquake	1974	$273.6/($80.7)	$27.7/($7.0)
9	Apollo 13	1995	$253.5/($172.1)	$89.7/($70.0)
10	War of the Worlds	2005	$234.3/($234.3)	$132.0/($132.0)
11	The Perfect Storm	2000	$217.2/($182.6)	$158.8/($140.0)
12	San Francisco	1936	$196.7/($8.3)	$18.2/($1.3)
13	The Day After Tomorrow	2004	$192.8/($186.7)	$129.2/($125.0)
14	Deep Impact	1998	$192.0/($140.5)	$89.9/($75.0)
15	Airport II	1974	$190.7/($56.2)	$15.8/($4.0)

*Academy Award winner for Best Picture.

The only major filmmaker who seemed vaguely interested was Sam Peckinpah, but with his particular approach the story's body count would have encompassed half of North America.
—PETER BART ON PARAMOUNT'S ATTEMPT AT FINDING A DIRECTOR OTHER THAN
FRANCIS FORD COPPOLA FOR *THE GODFATHER*

Forty Percent of the Top 15 Crime Films Are Released in the 1970s

Top 15 Crime Films
All-Release Domestic Box Office 1920–2005
Equivalent 2005 $s /(Unadjusted $s) in Millions of $s

Rank	Film	Initial Release	Domestic Box Office	Production Cost
1	The Sting*	1973	$605.6/($169.0)	$24.2/($5.5)
2	The Godfather*	1972	$505.9/($135.0)	$33.6/($7.2)
3	The Fugitive	1993	$284.7/($183.9)	$59.5/($44.0)
4	Bonnie and Clyde	1967	$261.1/($48.9)	$14.6/($2.5)
5	A Few Good Men	1992	$218.8/($141.3)	$83.5/($60.0)
6	Ocean's Eleven	2001	$207.7/($183.4)	$99.2/($90.0)
7	Bullitt	1968	$206.6/($42.2)	$30.9/($5.5)
8	The French Connection*	1971	$200.8/($51.7)	$8.7/($1.8)
9	Pulp Fiction	1994	$162.9/($107.9)	$10.5/($8.0)
10	The Godfather Part II*	1974	$161.2/($47.5)	$56.3/($14.2)
11	The Getaway	1972	$146.6/($38.9)	$15.7/($3.4)
12	Another 48 Hrs.	1990	$135.0/($89.1)	$59.8/($40.0)
13	Ocean's Twelve	2004	$128.7/($125.5)	$113.7/($110.0)
14	Dragnet	1954	$120.8/($10.6)	$3.6/($0.5)
15	A Clockwork Orange	1971	$116.2/($30.0)	$10.6/($2.2)

*Academy Award winner for Best Picture.

I believe implicitly that every young man in the world is fascinated with either sharks or dinosaurs. I grew up spending my summers on Nantucket, fishing and swimming, so whereas some kids were into dinosaurs, I was naturally into sharks. I've been lucky enough to follow that obsession into adulthood.
—Peter Benchley, author of the novel *Jaws*

The Number One Thriller Film Is Released in the 1970s

Top 15 Thriller Films
All-Release Domestic Box Office 1920–2005
Equivalent 2005 $s /(Unadjusted $s) in Millions of $s

Rank	Film	Initial Release	Domestic Box Office	Production Cost
1	*Jaws*	1975	$802.9/($260.0)	$44.1/($12.2)
2	*The Exorcist*	1973	$722.9/($232.7)	$53.9/($13.0)
3	*The Sixth Sense*	1999	$370.3/($293.5)	$46.9/($40.0)
4	*Fatal Attraction*	1987	$256.8/($156.6)	$24.1/($14.0)
5	*Signs*	2002	$251.5/($228.0)	$67.3/($62.0)
6	*The Firm*	1993	$245.2/($158.3)	$56.8/($42.0)
7	*Jaws 2*	1978	$222.5/($81.8)	$84.0/($28.0)
8	*Psycho*	1960	$209.9/($24.9)	$5.3/($0.8)
9	*The Silence of the Lambs**	1991	$199.0/($130.7)	$28.7/($20.0)
10	*Ransom*	1996	$197.6/($136.5)	$87.1/($70.0)
11	*Hannibal*	2001	$187.0/($165.1)	$88.2/($80.0)
12	*The Hunt for Red October*	1990	$184.9/($122.0)	$52.3/($35.0)
13	*What Lies Beneath*	2000	$184.9/($155.5)	$90.7/($80.0)
14	*Basic Instinct*	1992	$181.8/($117.7)	$68.2/($49.0)
15	*The Blair Witch Project*	1999	$177.3/($140.5)	$0.04/($0.03)

*Academy Award winner for Best Picture.

PRODUCTION SPOTLIGHT

The Success of the New Auteur Film Director Brings Corporate America to Hollywood

The first half of the decade was marked by the rise of a new breed of motion picture artist and film school graduate inspired by the French New Wave cinema, which declared that the director was an auteur, or sole "author" of the movie. It was a theory put forward in the early 1970s by French filmmaker François Truffaut, who wrote in the magazine *Cahiers du Cinema* that directing should be a way to express a personal artistic vision. At the time the studios were losing money and unable to reach the important baby boomer audience. There was an unprecedented changing of the guard in the studio executive suites. They didn't know what kind of movies to make. The talk in the *New York Times* was all about Japanese cinema, the French New Wave, and films such as Michelangelo Antonioni's *Blow Up,* with an impenetrable plot and full frontal nudity. These films seemed to speak to the disaffected youth of the world. Into this void came a new generation of writers, directors, producers, actors, cinematographers, and other film artists whom the press came to call the New Hollywood. For the most part they were graduates of film schools and steeped in the counterculture. Desperate to reach the baby boomers, who now made up over 17 percent of the U.S. population, Hollywood gave these young filmmakers an unusual degree of freedom for the first few years. Since they were young, it was believed that they knew how to reach the youth audience. This approach didn't always work, but at least the first half of the 1970s flowered with quirky, original movies, often with new levels of sex and violence, that looked as though they were made by independents but were in reality firmly rooted in the studios. For a few brief years the movie business was changed. Where it had always been producer-driven, now it revolved around the cult of the director. At the same time, many studios took advantage of new camera technology, moving filming off the lot and shooting on location instead, which was usually less expensive than building sets. The location shoots also provided a new level of realism that fit in with the modern subjects, open attitudes, and antiestablishment themes of many of these movies.

1970s Movie Censorship: A Brief History

A few major films are released with an X rating: Midnight Cowboy *in 1969,* A Clockwork Orange *in 1971, and* Last Tango in Paris, *1973. Since the X rating is not a trademark of the MPAA, the porn industry begins to self apply it to their films in the 1970s. The result is that few theater owners will show X-rated films and even fewer will advertise them.*

The godfather of the New Hollywood was Francis Ford Coppola, the producer and director who set out to use his *Godfather* movie profits to start a new kind of high-tech studio where the artists would be in charge. Among his protégés was a young George Lucas, a USC film school grad who directed his first feature film, *THX 1138,* for American Zoetrope, which he co-founded with Coppola in northern California rather than set up shop in Hollywood. They collaborated again two years later on Lucas's landmark boomer drama *American Graffiti,* a low-budget film that so enraptured youth, it became a blockbuster. *American Graffiti,* one of the lowest-cost, highest-revenue movies ever released, combined with the huge global success of *Star Wars,* made George Lucas the top box office director of the decade. Second place went to his friend Steven Spielberg, with *Jaws* and *Close Encounters.* Upon the success of *Jaws* and *Star Wars,* the short-lived era of New Hollywood came to an end, accompanied by the failure of many of the auteur-driven movies. The blockbuster had become the new Hollywood paradigm. The huge amounts of cash generated by the megahits attracted more corporations to own and invest in Hollywood, bringing an increased emphasis on marketing and research. Along with the new ownership, the corporations and conglomerates brought in Ivy League MBAs and tax shelter money. Like the old moguls, the MBAs knew they couldn't pick a hit, but they did think that they could create the right elements for success. The new goal was to make big-budget, star-driven movies that could be described in one line on a movie poster. They were called high-concept movies.

Many of the new megamovies were like the B movies of the past, but remade with A-movie budgets, production values, and stars. This steadily drove the average cost to make a studio movie up from $2 million in 1970 to $9.4 million by 1980 and the average cost to make a block-buster movie three to five times that. New life was given to genre films: classic horror with William Friedkin's *The Exorcist,* gangster dramas with *The Godfather,* romance with *Love Story,* westerns with 1969's *The Wild Bunch,* thrillers with *Jaws,* disaster movies with *Airport,* private-eye movies with *Chinatown,* and science fiction with *Star Wars.*

U.S. INDUSTRY PRODUCTION STATISTICS, 1970s
Equivalent 2005 $s /(Unadjusted $s)

$30.0 Million ($8.4 Million)
Average production cost of films featured in this chapter

$10.1 Million ($2.0 Million)
Average production cost of all films released in 1970

Index of Top Feature Film Directors Included in This Chapter

1	George Lucas	*Star Wars*
		American Graffiti
2	Steven Spielberg	*Jaws*
		Close Encounters of the Third Kind
3	William Friedkin	*The Exorcist*
		The French Connection
4	Francis Ford Coppola	*The Godfather*
		Apocalypse Now
5	George Roy Hill	*The Sting*
6	Randal Kleiser	*Grease*
7	Arthur Hiller	*Love Story*
8	John Badham	*Saturday Night Fever*
9	George Seaton	*Airport*
10	John Landis	*National Lampoon's Animal House*

Top 10 Critically Acclaimed Lead Actors of the 1970s

Rank	Actor Name
1	Jack Nicholson
2	Dustin Hoffman
3	Jack Lemmon
4	Marlon Brando
5	Gene Hackman
6	Jon Voight
7	George C. Scott
8	Richard Dreyfuss
9	Harrison Ford
10	John Travolta

Rank	Actress Name
1	Jane Fonda
2	Ellen Burstyn
3	Diane Keaton
4	Faye Dunaway
5	Glenda Jackson
6	Sally Field
7	Liza Minnelli
8	Louise Fletcher
9	Ali MacGraw
10	Patty Duke

See Note to the Reader for selection criteria.

Actors of the 1970s: Comparison of Salaries and Profit Participations
Equivalent 2005 $s /(Unadjusted $s)

Actor	Film	Initial Release	Salary
Marlon Brando	*Superman—The Movie*	1978	**$11,924,257** excluding p/p* ($3,700,000 salary + gross profit participation for total $14 million)
	Apocalypse Now	1979	**$2,995,399** excluding p/p ($1,000,000 salary + 11.3% of the gross)
	The Godfather	1972	**$964,444** ($200,000)
Sylvester Stallone	*Rocky*	1976	**$6,864,675** including p/p ($2,000,000 total including $20,000 actor salary + $35,000 writing fee + 6.75% net p/p)
Robert Redford	*The Sting*	1973	**$2,199,324** ($500,000)
Al Pacino	*The Godfather II*	1974	**$2,000,000** excluding p/p ($500,000 + gross p/p)
	The Godfather	1972	**$163,529** ($35,000)
Steve McQueen	*The Towering Inferno*	1974	**$5,900,000** excluding p/p ($1,500,000 + 10% participation)
Paul Newman	*The Towering Inferno*	1974	**$4,000,000** excluding p/p ($1,000,000 + 10% participation)
William Holden	*The Towering Inferno*	1974	**$3,971,095** ($750,000)
Harrison Ford	*Star Wars*	1977	**$2,094,802** ($650,000)
	American Graffiti	1973	**$2,200**/week ($500/week)
Jean Seberg	*Airport*	1970	**$755,026** excluding expenses ($150,000 + $1,000/week expenses for 16 weeks)
Gene Hackman	*The French Connection*	1971	**$361,667** including bonus ($50,000 salary + $25,000 bonus total $75,000)
Diane Keaton	*The Godfather*	1972	**$163,529** ($35,000)
Robert De Niro	*Taxi Driver*	1976	**$120,132** ($35,000)
Sigourney Weaver	*Alien*	1979	**$81,000** ($30,000)

*Profit participation.

A Sampling of Director Salaries
Equivalent 2005 $s /(Unadjusted $s)

Director	Film	Initial Release	Salary
Francis Ford Coppola	*The Godfather Part II*	1974	**$4.0 million** ($1.0 million to write, direct, and produce)
	The Godfather	1972	**$0.8 million** ($175,000)
Steven Spielberg	*Close Encounters of the Third Kind*	1977	**$3.2 million** ($1.0 million)
Richard Donner	*Superman—The Movie*	1978	**$3.0 million** ($1.0 million)
William Friedkin	*The Exorcist*	1973	**$2.2 million** excluding p/p* ($500,000 + p/p)
	The French Connection	1971	**$0.8 million** excluding p/p ($175,000 + p/p)
George Lucas	*Star Wars*	1977	**$0.6 million** excluding net p/p ($200,000 + p/p)
	American Graffiti	1973	**$0.2 million** exluding net p/p ($50,000 + p/p)
Robert Altman	*M*A*S*H*	1970	**$0.4 million** ($75,000)
John G. Avildsen	*Rocky*	1976	**$0.2 million** exluding p/p ($50,000 + p/p)

*Profit participation.

Economics is the most inhibiting factor for a director making a film. Most creative people, with the exception of actors and directors, create alone and in silence. With actors and directors it's a little like taking your clothes off in front of a mob of people. There are hundreds of technicians; if we are on a street, there are horns honking and the clock is ticking away. Every time the director says, "Let's try it this way" and not "Let's do it this way," he is spending money at enormous rates. The average Hollywood studio company out on location spends anywhere between $30,000 and $50,000 a day.
—SYDNEY POLLACK

Attracting Baby Boomers with Youth-Oriented Low-Cost Movies, Disaster Pics, Violence, Sex, and Gross-Out Comedy

Hollywood's goal, as the seventies arrived, was to captivate the exploding baby boom generation, just growing into their teen years, with youth-oriented pictures such as *Bonnie and Clyde* in 1967 and *Easy Rider* in 1969, films that were inexpensive to make yet brought huge returns. The baby boomers would emerge as the most loyal moviegoing audience of all time, across all demographic groups, but the studios found it hard to re-create this magic as the decade began.

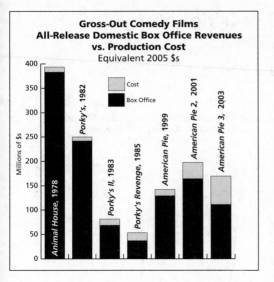

**Gross-Out Comedy Films
All-Release Domestic Box Office Revenues
vs. Production Cost**
Equivalent 2005 $s

In the early 1970s, some of the biggest successes were more typical studio movies, such as the series of high-budget disaster pictures, starting with *Airport* in 1970 and followed by *The Poseidon Adventure* in 1972. The successful 1974 Universal release *Earthquake* was accompanied by an in-theater system that made the floor vibrate when the big one hit. Essentially, Sensurround positioned heavy bass speakers around the theater, causing vibrations synchronized to the movie's plot. The problem was that the vibrations bled into adjacent auditoriums, and in some older buildings they impacted the integrity of the architecture. In Hollywood, Grauman's Chinese Theater had to place netting above the heads of ticket buyers in case any of the numerous ornaments were shaken from the walls or ceiling. Sensurround was a great publicity gimmick, though. Even before there was stereo TV, NBC ran *Earthquake* with a simulcast on a local FM station that allowed viewers to re-create the effect in their own home.

The easing of censorship soon led to a change in what was acceptable on film, increasing concerns about the rise of more violent movies. One 1971 release that became a lightning rod for controversy over violent content was Stanley Kubrick's *A Clockwork Orange*. Many critics were especially outraged that Kubrick's movie invited viewers to laugh at violence and rape. The

Comparison of Gross-Out Comedy Films
All-Release Domestic Box Office

Equivalent 2005 $s /(Unadjusted $s) in Millions of $s

Film	Initial Release	Domestic Box Office	Production Cost
National Lampoon's Animal House	1978	$383.0/($141.6)	$10.4/($3.5)
American Pie	1999	$129.4/($102.6)	$12.7/($10.8)
American Pie 2: Secret Disguise	2001	$164.3/($145.1)	$33.1/($30.0)
American Pie 3: American Wedding	2003	$111.2/($104.6)	$58.4/($55.0)
Total *American Pie* Franchise		$404.9/($352.3)	$104.2/($95.8)
Porky's	1982	$241.8/($111.3)	$8.1/($4.0)
Porky's II: The Next Day	1983	$68.7/($33.8)	$12.7/($6.5)
Porky's Revenge	1985	$37.0/($20.5)	$16.3/($9.0)
Total *Porky's* Franchise		$347.5/($165.6)	$37.2/($19.5)

The #2 All-Release Highest Box Office Movie Opens in the 1970s

Comparison of #1 (*Gone with the Wind*) & #2 (*Star Wars: Ep IV A New Hope*)

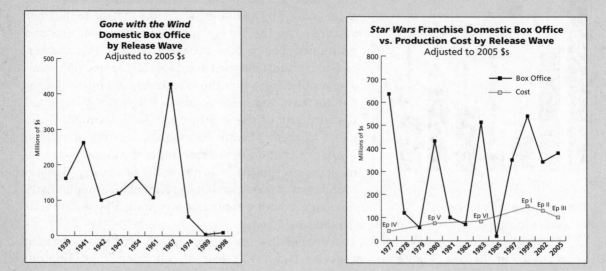

Gone with the Wind
All-Release Domestic Box Office

Equivalent 2005 $s /(Unadjusted $s) in Millions of $s

Release Date	Release Wave	Domestic Box Office	Production Cost
12/15/1939	1	$161.9/($21.5)	$58.5/($4.2)
1/17/1941	2	$262.1/($10.2)	
3/31/1942	3	$100.2/($4.2)	
4/1/1947	4	$119.8/($8.2)	
7/2/1954	5	$162.8/($14.2)	
3/10/1961	6	$107.3/($12.9)	
10/4/1967	7	$427.3/($80.7)	
8/23/1974	8	$53.2/($15.7)	
1/31/1989	9	$3.9/($2.4)	
6/25/1998	10	$9.2/($6.8)	
Total		$1,407.7/($176.8)	$58.5/($4.2)

Star Wars Franchise
All-Release Domestic Box Office
Equivalent 2005 $s /Unadjusted $s) in Millions of $s

Film	Release Date	Release Wave	Domestic Box Office	Production Cost
Star Wars: Episode IV	5/25/1977	1	$636.1/($221.3)	$41.9/($13.0)
	7/21/1978	2	$119.9/$43.8)	
	8/15/1979	3	$57.1/($22.5)	
	4/10/1981	4	$39.8/($17.2)	
	8/13/1982	5	$39.2/($18.0)	
	1/31/1997	6	$193.1/($138.3)	
	Subtotal		$1,085.2/($461.1)	$41.9/($13.0)
Star Wars: Episode V	5/21/1980	1	$432.2/($181.4)	$75.8/($32.0)
	7/31/1981	2	$61.7/($26.8)	
	11/19/1982	3	$31.7/($14.5)	
	2/21/1997	4	$94.4/($67.6)	
	Subtotal		$620.0/($290.3)	$75.8/($32.0)
Star Wars: Episode VI	5/25/1983	1	$513.8/($252.5)	$83.7/($42.7)
	3/29/1985	2	$20.3/($11.3)	
	3/14/1997	3	$63.5/($45.5)	
	Subtotal		$597.6/($309.3)	$83.7/($42.7)
Star Wars: Episode I	5/19/1999	1	$540.0/($428.2)	$149.5/($127.5)
Star Wars: Episode II	5/16/2002	1	$342.4/($310.7)	$130.3/($120.0)
Star Wars: Episode III	5/19/2005	1	$380.3/($380.3)	$101.4/($101.4)
Total			$3,565.8/($2,179.9)	$582.6/($436.6)

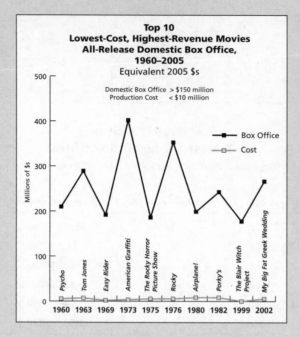

**Top 10
Lowest-Cost, Highest-Revenue Movies
All-Release Domestic Box Office,
1960–2005**
Equivalent 2005 $s

Domestic Box Office > $150 million
Production Cost < $10 million

Top 10 Blockbuster Movies
Lowest Production Cost (< $10 million)
Highest Revenue (Domestic Box Office > $175 million)
All-Release Domestic Box Office, 1960–2009

Equivalent 2005 $s /(Unadjusted $s) in Millions of $s

Rank	Film	Initial Release	Domestic Box Office	Production Cost
1	*The Blair Witch Project*	1999	**$177.3/($140.5)**	**$.04/($0.04)**
2	*Easy Rider*	1969	**$191.7/($42.5)**	**$1.9/($0.4)**
3	*American Graffiti*	1973	**$402.0/($115.0)**	**$3.3/($0.8)**
4	*Psycho*	1960	**$209.9/($24.9)**	**$5.3/($0.8)**
5	*My Big Fat Greek Wedding*	2002	**$266.4/($241.4)**	**$5.4/($5.0)**
6	*The Rocky Horror Picture Show*	1975	**$185.9/($120.9)**	**$5.4/($1.5)**
7	*Rocky*	1976	**$352.8/($117.2)**	**$5.5/($1.6)**
8	*Tom Jones*	1963	**$289.0/($38.2)**	**$7.0/($1.1)**
9	*Porky's*	1982	**$242.8/($111.3)**	**$8.1/($4.0)**
10	*Airplane!*	1980	**$198.9/($83.5)**	**$8.3/($3.5)**

film had received an X rating and was blamed in the press for vicious copycat crimes, especially in the United Kingdom. As a result, Kubrick had the movie withdrawn from distribution there for many years. After Kubrick's death in 1999, his wife said that he had become a recluse because of death threats he received during the *Clockwork Orange* controversy.

By late in the decade, the gross-out comedy genre had emerged, most notably with *National Lampoon's Animal House,* released in 1978, a movie about a party-animal frat house at fictitious Faber College.

In the vanguard of the new "personal" style of filmmaking ushered in by Easy Rider, *BBS [for Bert Schneider, Bob Rafelson, and Steve Blauner, the partners] was probably the first major American producing entity to adopt an auteurist line as a matter of state policy. "We do not care what the story content of a film is," Bert Schneider declared in 1970, "who the stars are, or if there are stars involved. We are concerned only with who is making the film. If his energy and personality project something unique, he is given the freedom and help to express himself. We'll gamble that the films will express those personal qualities."*
—STEPHEN FARBER AND MARC GREEN, *HOLLYWOOD DYNASTIES*

We have no obligation to make a statement. But to make money, it is often important to make history, to make art or to make some significant statement.
—MICHAEL EISNER IN A 1980S MEMO TO HIS STAFF

Paramount Perfects the High-Concept Movie

From 1974 until 1984, Paramount Pictures had stable management under chairman Barry Diller and president Michael Eisner and was consistently at or near the top of the list among major studios competing for box office market share, second only to Warner Bros. as the most successful studio of the 1970s.

Paramount achieved a steady record of success with such memorable seventies films as *The Godfather, Chinatown, Saturday Night Fever,* and *Grease.* The studio had been acquired in 1966 by Gulf and Western chairman Charles Bludhorn, who ran a multifaceted conglomerate. He hired Diller away from ABC, and a year later Diller brought in Eisner, who had also been at ABC. The former network executives brought a tough-minded, bottom-line-oriented, fast-paced approach to the business of moviemaking. Diller and Eisner's team included Dawn Steele, Jeffrey Katzenberg, Don Simpson, and Larry Gordon, each of whom at times headed production. For most of the 1970s, Paramount also led the industry in TV production and distribution with hits such as *Happy Days, Taxi,* and *Laverne and Shirley.*

Paramount made a few big star-driven movies, but for the most part it took a different approach. The story and marketing concept were the stars of the movie. Around Hollywood, the Paramount team came to be known as the "killer Dillers" for their smart, tough negotiations and highly marketable movies. Eisner preached movies that had big ideas and low costs, declining to sign expensive holding deals with talent or directors because he felt the material would attract them when the time came. Filmmakers had to be passionate about their projects and be willing to repeatedly fight for the script, cast, money, and attention.

Paramount's policy was to keep down costs by developing movies in-house. They rarely turned to high-powered agent packages that might include script, talent, and filmmakers, ready to shoot. That didn't preclude Eisner from having a close relationship with the biggest talent agent of the era, Michael Ovitz of the Creative Artists Agency. To Eisner, the quality of the story was paramount. He wanted compelling characters and a satisfying resolution for the audience—a clear determination of who won and who lost. He looked for universal themes presented in three "acts" that could be marketed in a sentence. Eisner's approach was dubbed "high concept," but it was really an attempt to manufacture potential blockbusters. "We cannot expect numerous hits, but if every film has an original and imaginative concept, then we can be confident that something will break through," wrote Eisner in a memo to his executives at Paramount.

To create blockbusters, Paramount marketing ramped up its television advertising, promotion, and publicity, and where possible it expanded into merchandising and licensing, including producing a series of hit soundtrack albums. Eisner and Diller passed on some movies that later became hits, but year after year they ranked among the top movie distributors by market share. "It isn't the movies you pass on that make the difference, but the ones you make," Eisner often said. Although he was fanatical about keeping costs down, Eisner was willing to take some risks. In 1980 he pushed aside Diller's concerns about the cost to make what was then a very rich deal with producer George Lucas, director Steven Spielberg, and star Harrison Ford for *Raiders of the Lost Ark,* creating a profitable movie franchise. With a $22 million production cost, *Raiders* became one of Paramount's biggest-budget projects (in unadjusted dollars) since *Star Trek* in 1979 ($45 million) and *King Kong* in 1976 ($24 million).

Paramount management remained intact until the untimely death of Bludhorn in 1983. His successor, Martin Davis, felt Diller and Eisner were taking too much credit and too big a share of the profits for themselves. So in 1984 he pushed them out. Diller joined 20th Century-Fox, where he later founded the Fox TV network with Rupert Murdoch. Eisner became CEO of the Walt Disney Company and went on to great success there for many years. Katzenberg followed Eisner to Disney. He was later forced out by Eisner and went on to form DreamWorks SKG with Steven Spielberg and David Geffen.

DISTRIBUTION OVERVIEW

The Start of Pay TV and Home Video as Venues After Theatrical Release

While pay TV and cable were not significant sources of revenue for the studios in the 1970s, the structure for change was established. In 1974 one of the first pay TV systems, the Z Channel in Los Angeles, was delivered over analog cable systems and via microwave. It featured on-air film festivals, independent movies, rare classics, foreign films, the director's personal cut of a movie, and even late-night European soft-core porn movies. However, the Z Channel was gone by the end of the decade, as a pair of pay TV giants who delivered content via satellite divided up the market, with HBO landing as the largest, followed by Showtime.

The first HBO signal had been transmitted to 365 subscribers in Wilkes-Barre, Pennsylvania, in 1972. At the time, HBO (then a division of Time, Inc.) had to beg Hollywood for movies to show. HBO pioneered the satellite delivery of its service in the middle 1970s. Ten years later HBO reached 15 million homes worldwide, and by 1981 it was Hollywood's largest single buyer of movies. The channel originally ran full-length movies uncut within a year of their release to theaters. HBO soon began adding original programming as well, for both the primary services and a sister channel called Cinemax that played somewhat older movies and more exploitation fare.

The first videotape cassette system for TVs was invented in 1972 but didn't live to see the 1980s. Avco, a large conglomerate that had purchased Embassy Pictures from Joseph E. Levine, introduced Cartrivision as a combination player, recorder, and receiver. It was the first to offer prerecorded tapes of movies, based on a license with Columbia Pictures. By the second half of the decade, Avco was gone, but Sony was selling the Betamax video recorder for home use.

In 1977 Michigan businessman Andre Blay pioneered independent home video distribution in Farmingdale, a Detroit suburb. Blay's company, Magnetic Video, became the first to widely license, market, and distribute movies on the half-inch tape format, for both Betamax and a second system, VHS, the format that would eventually come to dominate. Blay made a breakthrough when Steve Roberts, president of 20th Century-Fox TV, licensed fifty of their best-selling movies to Magnetic Video—which initially sold them through a direct sales company, Video Club of America. In 1977 George Atkinson purchased Magnetic Video titles and offered them in his store in Los Angeles, Video Station, becoming the first video rental retailer. To raise money, Atkinson charged $50 for an annual membership and $100 for a lifetime membership, which allowed the member to rent a video for $10 a day. Atkinson was threatened with legal action but was able to establish that under U.S. copyright law he had the right to rent and resell videos he had legally purchased. Over his first five years, he franchised more than 400 Video Station stores across the United States.

The studios faced a setback in 1979, when Universal, Fox, Columbia, and Paramount tried to create a joint venture for a new cable network, to be called Premier. The studios got about a 45 percent return from theatrical revenues but only about 20 percent of pay TV revenues, so they wanted to create their own entity to raise their take by millions. Premier was effectively stopped four months after it was first announced when a Justice Department injunction was issued under then President Jimmy Carter. The government claimed Premier would be anticompetitive and would engage in price-fixing and boycotting other groups and companies. Premier had promised to release movies nine months before they would be available to competitors HBO or Showtime.

Major Movie Distributors, 1970s

Buena Vista . . . . E. Cardon "Card" Walker becomes president of the Walt Disney Company in 1971

Columbia Pictures . . . . Run by president David Begelman from 1973 to 1978 when he is fired for embezzlement

MGM. . . . . Owner Kirk Kerkorian sells off real estate and other assets

Paramount Pictures . . . . Run by Paramount's parent company Gulf and Western's chairman Charles Bluhdorn, Paramount Pictures chairman Barry Diller, and president Michael Eisner

20th Century-Fox. . . . . After Darry Zanuck leaves in 1971, run by production head Alan Ladd Jr. In 1978 corporate control passes to investors Marc Rich and Marvin Davis

United Artists Corp . . . . Owned by Transamerica. In 1973 UA becomes the exclusive distributor of MGM product. In 1978 chairman Arthur Krim and President Robert Benjamin leave to form Orion Pictures

Universal Pictures . . . . Run by MCA Universal chairman Lew Wasserman

Warner Bros . . . . Renamed Warner Communications, Inc., in 1971 with Warner Bros. film subsidiary headed by Ted Ashley

U.S. INDUSTRY DISTRIBUTION STATISTICS, 1970s
Equivalent 2005 $s /(Unadjusted $s)

$5,910 Million ($1,429 Million)
Annual U.S. box office gross revenues

267
Number of new features released

TECHNOLOGY SPOTLIGHT

Dolby Sounds Like a Good Idea for Movies

No aspect of movie technology was more revolutionized during the decade than sound, from how it was recorded to how it was delivered in a movie theater auditorium. And no company had greater impact on the improved sound than Dolby Laboratories, founded in 1965 by engineer Ray Dolby, who had been part of the group at Ampex Corp. in Redwood City, California, that produced the first videotape recorder in 1956.

Ray Dolby's breakthrough was a noise reduction system for single or multitrack audio recording, which he also applied to movie sound beginning in the mid-1970s. Dolby had seen that optical movie soundtracks, like magnetic tape, were limited by noticeable background noise. Although the Academy mono standard, which can faithfully reproduce frequencies from 60 to 8,000 hertz, or a range of seven octaves, was a 100 percent improvement over the telephone, which can only reproduce from 300 hertz to 3,000 hertz, or just over three octaves, Dolby saw an opportunity for improvement. His system, which can reproduce 30 to 16,000 hertz, or nine octaves, filtered out much of that noise, resulting in a 28 percent improvement over Academy mono. Progress came slowly at first. Part of it was a standards issue. Since the 1930s, the movie industry had used a standard theater playback response known as the "Academy" characteristic. It made it possible to play any 35 mm projector but limited the ability to improve the sound output on an optically printed strip of film. Hampering sound quality even more was the fact that many theaters still had mono speakers, which exhibitors were slow to replace. Change did ultimately occur, but it did so in stages. In 1971, Dolby noise reduction was first used on all premixes and masters of the movie *A Clockwork Orange,* while a conventional optical soundtrack was used on the release prints.

In 1975 Dolby introduced a 35 mm stereo optical release print format called Dolby Stereo. In the space on a movie strip where the optical soundtrack had been printed, there were now two soundtracks carrying four channels of sound capable of surrounding the listener. The format also distinguished itself by offering a choice of mono or multitrack playback, with higher-quality sound. The new format was not only universal but also cost roughly the same as mono prints. Theaters also found that converting to Dolby systems, which involved installing some new equipment, was no more expensive than maintaining their prior systems.

Shortly thereafter the first Dolby-encoded stereo optical soundtrack was used in the film *Lisztomania*. This allowed for LCR (left, center, right) encoding, which was later perfected in the 1976 movie *A Star Is Born,* when true LCRS (left, center, right, surround) encoding was first used. Public awareness spiked after Dolby Stereo surround sound was showcased in two highly popular 1977 movies, *Star Wars* and *Close Encounters of the Third Kind.* Research soon evidenced that ticket buyers would seek out theaters with better sound. This drove most exhibitors to finally convert to stereo sound systems. In turn, studios were motivated to improve sound capture and production in collaboration with Dolby. Over the following decade, more than 6,000 theaters were equipped by Dolby Laboratories with upgraded systems, and the Dolby Stereo logo became a familiar on-screen presence. While it was the big movies that adapted Dolby Stereo surround sound technology first, it soon became an industry standard for most optical soundtracks.

MARKETING SPOTLIGHT

Marketing and Production Costs Rise

Attempts to build blockbusters by making every picture an event was proving to be very expensive and not always successful for the studios. This was compounded by the rising cost of labor and other goods. Where average ticket prices rose 63 percent between 1970 and 1979, from $1.55 to $2.52, the cost of making and marketing a movie were disproportionately higher, with production costs rising 121 percent and marketing costs increasing 189 percent over the decade. With this rise in marketing expenditures, the allocation of ad dollars shifted as well. In 1970 the largest single category of ad expenditures was in newspapers, which received roughly $187 million of the $208 million spent during this time. Network and local TV ad sales by movie companies were roughly $20 million. By 1980 newspapers were still tops, with approximately $486 million of the $704 million spent, but network and local TV stations had jumped to about $206 million. It was a trend that would continue for years to come, with print getting less and electronic media getting more of the movie marketing dollars. In addition to higher expenses going to paid advertising, the studios rolled out enhanced publicity, promotion, and partner licensing programs.

U.S. INDUSTRY, 1970s
PRODUCTION COSTS vs. ADVERTISING COSTS
Equivalent 2005 $s /(Unadjusted $s)

$10.1 Million ($2,000,000)	Average production cost of all films released in the 1970s	**$2.9 Million** ($580,000)	Average advertising cost of all films released in the 1970s
$22.3 Million ($9,400,000)	Average production cost of all films released in the 1980s	**$8.4 Million** ($3,544,000)	Average advertising cost of all films released in the 1980s
121%	Percentage change adjusted for inflation	189%	Percentage change adjusted for inflation

Comparison of Eight 1970s Films Initial Release
Equivalent 2005 $s /(Unadjusted $s) in Millions of $s

Film	Initial Release	Domestic Box Office	Domestic Rentals	Foreign Rentals	Production Cost	Domestic Print and Ad Costs
Star Wars: Ep IV A New Hope	1977	$636.1 ($221.3)	$365.1 ($127.0)	$406.7 ($141.5)	$41.9 ($13.0)	$53.2 ($16.5)
Alien	1979	$200.8 ($78.9)	$102.0 ($40.1)	$27.5 ($10.8)	$29.1 ($10.8)	$51.1 ($19.0)
The Godfather*	1972	$504.1 (133.7)	$322.7 ($85.6)	$158.4 ($42.0)	$33.6 ($7.2)	$47.7 ($10.2)
Apocalypse Now	1979	$200.4 ($78.8)	$96.6 ($38.0)	$1.7 ($0.7)	$83.4 ($31.0)	$37.0 ($13.8)
Fiddler on the Roof	1971	$293.7 ($75.6)	$132.2 ($34.0)	$41.7 ($11.1)	$43.4 ($9.0)	$21.7 ($4.5)
Rocky	1976	$352.8 ($117.2)	$168.5 ($56.0)	$60.7 ($21.1)	$5.5 ($1.6)	$19.3 ($5.6)
One Flew over the Cuckoo's Nest	1975	$350.2 ($112.0)	$185.3 ($59.3)	$107.0 ($35.6)	$16.0 ($4.4)	$18.5 (5.1)
M*A*S*H	1970	$278.5 ($67.3)	$125.3 ($30.3)	$29.5 ($7.1)	$14.6 ($2.9)	$11.4 ($2.3)

*Note: Worldwide unadjusted print and ad costs total $19.3.

EXHIBITION OVERVIEW

Distributor-Exhibitor Relationships Change

In the 1970s modern exhibition was beginning to blossom. New theaters not only were replacing aging facilities but also were being built in brand-new communities and in malls. The new theater model shifted from buildings with single auditoriums to buildings with multiple auditoriums, known as multiplexes.

Each major film studio maintained distribution offices, known as branches, in nearly thirty cities throughout the United States. The branch offices were located in small and large cities alike—Des Moines to Dallas to Washington, D.C. The distribution and shipping of film was done through these branches.

In the early 1970s, most film distribution was conducted through a close relationship between the distribution salesman and the exhibition film buyer. The buyer represented the theater owner but was essentially in bed with the distributor, meaning that the buyer would ensure that the theater played all that distributor's films. But when the number of theater screens exceeded the number of available films, practices began to change. While existing relationships and loyalties remained strong, securing the right to exhibit a film in a specific market now occurred as a result of a bidding process. During this auction process, exhibitors competed for rights on the basis of written bids. A typical exhibitor's bid included a guaranteed amount of money that would be paid prior to the opening of the film, the weekly percentage share, the advertising contribution, the minimum and maximum amount of time the film would play in the theater, and a list of competing theaters that had to be prohibited from exhibiting the film at the same time.

In the past, exhibitors had not been required to guarantee the amount of money they would pay for a film, nor were they obligated to guarantee the number of days or weeks the film would play in a particular market. Historically, exhibitors had settled with the distributor after the film had played. This ensured a fair split between exhibitor and distributor no matter how the film performed. The new practice of selling via bidding added enormous risk for exhibitors. If a film did not perform, exhibitors would be out the amount of money they had guaranteed. Under these new arrangements, they were also denied the ability to terminate a poorly performing film and open a new one. In other words, the exhibitor was stuck if the film was a bust. To make matters worse, the bidding process often occurred prior to the distributor screening the film (this was known as blind bidding). When the distributors cried foul, legislation requiring the studio to screen the film to exhibitors prior to accepting bids was ultimately enacted in many states.

Theater owners began to look for relief as losses mounted. By 1976 the practice of splitting emerged, meaning that multiple competing exhibitors discussed and agreed upon which film would play in which theaters. In many cases, distributors were compliant with this development because all of their films got played. In other cases, distributors wanted to select which

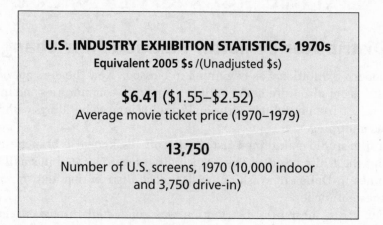

U.S. INDUSTRY EXHIBITION STATISTICS, 1970s
Equivalent 2005 $s /(Unadjusted $s)

$6.41 ($1.55–$2.52)
Average movie ticket price (1970–1979)

13,750
Number of U.S. screens, 1970 (10,000 indoor and 3,750 drive-in)

theaters their film played. In 1977 the government declared that splitting was illegal. General Cinema, the largest theater circuit at that time, publicly declared that although it was "disappointed" by the ruling, it would discontinue the practice of splitting. Other exhibitors were not as tractable and continued the practice while pointing to past court cases and even initiating a lawsuit in Virginia.

The government steadfastly enforced the decision and subsequently filed against four exhibitors in Milwaukee, Wisconsin, in 1980. This legal battle not only continued between distribution, exhibition, and the government well into the late 1980s but also has significantly shaped the way business would be conducted decades later.

New Era of Wide Release Impacts Theater Owner's Share of Box Office

As the blockbuster complex took hold with the success of *Jaws* and *Star Wars*, the traditional balance of power between movie distributors and exhibitors shifted. For decades the key to launching a movie was booking the right few theaters, which gave the owners of those theaters

---

1970s MOVIE GOER
Money Spent on Movie Ticket vs. Food
(Unadjusted $s)

Average ticket price	$1.55
Average spent on food	$0.22
47% on candy	
29% on popcorn	
24% on soft drink	
Total	$1.77

1970s THEATER OWNER
Money Made on Movie Ticket vs. Food

Average operating profit from box office revenue and concessions sales (pretax)	3.5 cents
Percentage of profit attributable to film	60%
Percentage attributable to food	40%

the leverage to negotiate favorable terms for the rental of that movie. By the last years of the decade, distributors were dealing with hundreds of theaters on opening weekend. The distributor, not the exhibitor, now called the shots. As a result, the percentages of box office receipts that went back to the studio rose from just over 31 percent in 1970 to nearly 46 percent in 1977. This gave the distributors new power and changed the theater's economic model. Now most ticket sales went back to the distributor, while the owner of the theater made more of his profits at the concession stand.

Timeline of Key Events That Shaped Distributor and Exhibitor Business Practices

1938—The United States took action, under the Sherman Antitrust Act, against five majors, Paramount, Loew's (MGM), RKO, Warner, and Fox, and three minors, United Artists, Columbia, and Universal, finally decreeing in 1940 that they could not own theaters. In accordance with the decrees, the companies named were to divest themselves of approximately 3,000 theaters, just over 17 percent of the 18,000 theaters in the United States. Since this time, distribution and exhibition of motion pictures have been directed by the Antitrust Division of the Department of Justice and argued by distributors and exhibitors alike.

1963—National General, a theater chain, asks permission to enter into production. Judge Palmieri (the federal judge holding jurisdiction over the consent decrees since the original *United States v. Paramount* case in 1948–52) grants the request under the condition that theaters are sold the film(s) on a theater-by-theater basis. This condition attempts to protect non–National General theaters from being excluded in the licensing of the movie(s).

1969—National General seeks to extend permission to stay in production. The court subsequently adds two more provisions. The first enjoins National General "from engaging in a policy of preferring to exhibit in its own theaters features produced or distributed by it to exhibiting features of competing distributors." The second requires National General to maintain records with respect to why pictures play in a National General theater instead of in a competing theater and why such pictures play instead of a feature from a competing distributor.

1977—On April 1, the Department of Justice announces that all split agreements by exhibitors, with or without the consent of distributors, violate antitrust laws. Splits or splitting is a practice that allows for competing exhibitors to collectively select which theater an upcoming film was going to play in. This practice eliminates head-to-head competition for the same film in the same film zone. After hearing the Justice Department's stance, General Cinema, the largest theater circuit, announces with regret that it will cease the practice. This announcement is nicknamed the "April Fool's decision." Many exhibitors believe the Department of Justice is wrong, and so they continue the practice. In August, a lawsuit is filed by Greenbrier Cinemas, a Virginia exhibitor, challenging the government's position.

1978—The Department of Justice investigates how United Artists (the studio, not the circuit) distributed *A Bridge Too Far* (1977). UA takes the position that it was not required to submit the picture to all theaters for bidding or negotiation. UA distributes all films to its previously declared customers and does not allow other theaters to negotiate for its product.

1980—On May 6, the Department of Justice files a civil law suit against United Artists Theaters and three other exhibitors in Milwaukee, Wisconsin, charging them with illegal allocation of feature films (splitting). This day also marks the start of the Greenbrier trial, which would ultimately result in a win for those who were pro-splitting.

How *Jaws* Heated Up Summer Movies

In the early 1970s, the only movies that got a simultaneous wide release were big-budget turkeys that the studios wanted to play off quickly before word about their failings got out. Good movies didn't open during the summer either. Studios viewed the hot weather months as a time when people were too busy traveling or frolicking outdoors and not typically inclined to go to the movies. The "important" films generally opened late in the year (e.g., *Ben-Hur,* which opened in November 1959), or in the spring (e.g., *The Sound of Music,* which opened in March 1965). TV advertising was considered too expensive for film ads. What we now know as marketing departments were then called publicity departments because it was mainly a publicity-driven business. There were movie trailers but not a lot of other advertising. But that would all change with *Jaws.*

Universal Pictures was originally planning a Christmas 1974 release for *Jaws,* but production problems and budget overruns sabotaged the schedule. When Universal executives finally tested the movie, they were heartened by the strong reaction from audiences, so they decided to give it the widest release in history, on what became 490 screens, backed by an unprecedented $700,000 TV ad campaign. They also decided on a summer opening to tie in with the beach theme of the movie. It turned out to be the perfect way to lure in the booming youth audience. There had been a few prior movies that had opened during the summer months and done well, but almost all were scheduled then by accident. They included *Bonnie and Clyde* (1967), *Easy Rider* (1969), and *American Graffiti* (1973). And while Columbia had tried to drive ticket sales for the July 1975 opening of the Charles Bronson movie *Breakout* with significant advertising dollars, the plan had not quite worked as hoped. So Universal was looking to ramp up the marketing for *Jaws* to levels never before seen. Three nights before the film was scheduled to open nationwide, the studio saturated the networks during peak primetime hours with a barrage of thirty-second trailers. When it opened on June 20, *Jaws* became a national sensation. Universal went into wide release at the end of July. Over 67 million Americans flocked to see the film, buying over $200 million worth of tickets. It broke the previous records set by *The Godfather* and *The Exorcist,* and with that big splash *Jaws* launched the era of the summer blockbuster movie. Every year since, studios have used the summer as a springboard for movies targeting teens who are out of school and able to see their favorite films repeatedly. Fox's *The Omen* followed suit in the summer of 1976, and by the time *Star Wars* enjoyed its pre–Memorial Day release in May 1977, it appeared as if tent-pole pictures were vying for a running start even before summer began.

Film marketing has come a long way since *Jaws*'s modest $7.7 million opening weekend, but clearly it was the shark that raised the stakes for everyone thereafter.

75 Percent of the Top 20 All-Release Domestic Box Office Films Released 1975–2005 Are Released in the Summer

Top 20 Movies
All-Release Domestic Box Office, 1975–2005
Equivalent 2005 $s in Millions of $s

Rank	Film	Initial Release	Domestic Box Office
1	Star Wars: Ep IV A New Hope	May 1977	$1,085.1
2	E.T.: The Extra Terrestrial	June 1982	$889.4
3	Titanic	December 1997	$824.8
4	Jaws	June 1975	$802.9
5	Star Wars: Ep V The Empire Strikes Back	May 1980	$620.0
6	Star Wars: Ep VI Return of the Jedi	May 1983	$597.6
7	Raiders of the Lost Ark	June 1981	$554.7
8	Jurassic Park	June 1983	$552.9
9	Star Wars: Ep I The Phantom Menace	May 1999	$540.3
10	Grease	June 1978	$520.5
11	Forrest Gump	July 1994	$505.6
12	The Lion King	June 1994	$501.9
13	Shrek 2	May 2004	$455.4
14	Ghostbusters	June 1984	$454.3
15	Spider-Man	May 2002	$445.4
16	Independence Day	July 1996	$444.0
17	Saturday Night Fever	December 1977	$435.0
18	Home Alone	November 1990	$434.0
19	Beverly Hills Cop	December 1984	$432.8
20	Close Encounters of the Third Kind	November 1977	$424.1

Franchise Films Originating in the 1970s

Equivalent 2005 $s in Millions of $s

Rank	Franchise	Number of Films in Franchise	All-Release Worldwide Box Office
1	Star Wars	6	$6,872.9
2	Jaws	4	$2,238.9
3	Rocky	6	$2,060.6
4	Superman	5	$1,797.0
5	The Godfather	3	$1,395.1
6	Alien	5	$1,139.2

Star Wars

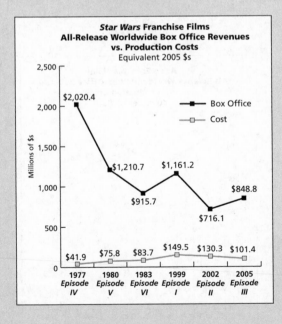

Star Wars Franchise Films
All-Release Worldwide Box Office Revenues
vs. Production Costs
Equivalent 2005 $s

Jaws

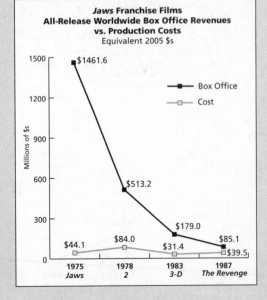

Jaws Franchise Films
All-Release Worldwide Box Office Revenues
vs. Production Costs
Equivalent 2005 $s

Rocky

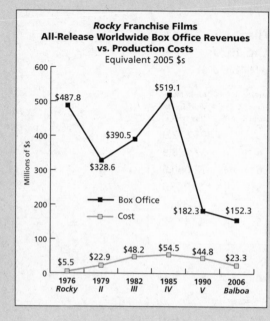

***Rocky* Franchise Films**
All-Release Worldwide Box Office Revenues
vs. Production Costs
Equivalent 2005 $s

Superman

***Superman* Franchise Films**
All-Release Worldwide Box Office Revenues
vs. Production Costs
Equivalent 2005 $s

The Godfather

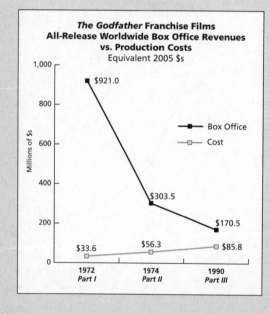

***The Godfather* Franchise Films**
All-Release Worldwide Box Office Revenues
vs. Production Costs
Equivalent 2005 $s

Alien

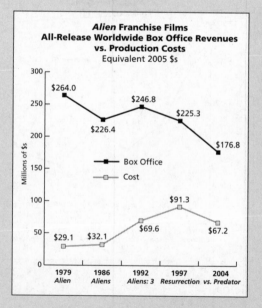

***Alien* Franchise Films**
All-Release Worldwide Box Office Revenues
vs. Production Costs
Equivalent 2005 $s

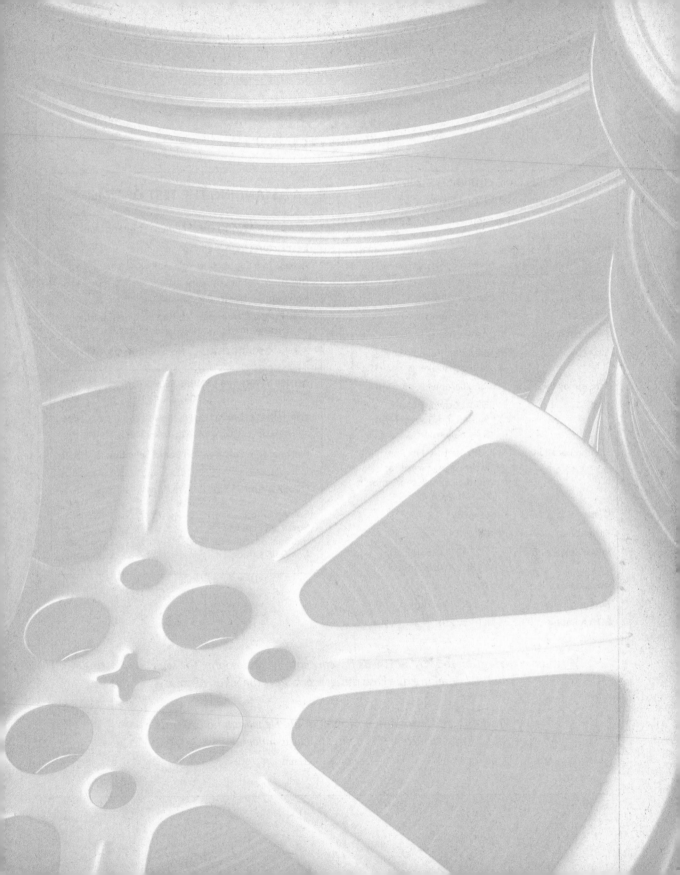

M★A★S★H

20th Century-Fox, 1970

ALL-RELEASE EQUIVALENT 2005 $s

(Unadjusted $s) in Millions of $s

Domestic Box Office Revenues . . . . **$328.6**/($81.1)
Production Cost . . . . **$14.6**/($2.9)
Principal Photography . . . . **42** days
4/14/1969–6/11/1969

Director . . . . Robert Altman

Producer . . . . Ingo Preminger

Production Company . . . . Aspen Productions

Story by . . . . Based on the novel by Richard Hooker

Screenplay by . . . . Ring Lardner Jr.

Cast . . . . Elliott Gould, Donald Sutherland, Tom Skerritt, Sally Kellerman

Filming Locations . . . . . . 20th Century-Fox Ranch in Malibu, CA, except for football game scene, shot at Griffith Park, CA

Genre . . . . Comedy

Format . . . . Color (DeLuxe)

Initial Release . . . . 1/25/1970 (New York); 2/18/1970 (Los Angeles)

Rerelease 1973

Running Time . . . . 113 or 116 minutes

MPAA Rating . . . . R (now PG)

STANDING THE TEST OF TIME

ACADEMY AWARD Oscar Nominations and Wins

Best Picture: Ingo Preminger, Producer

Actress in a Supporting Role: Sally Kellerman

Directing: Robert Altman

Film Editing: Danford B. Greene

*WRITING (Screenplay – based on material from another medium): Ring Lardner Jr.

OSCAR TOTALS   Nominations 5   *Wins 1

AFI 100 YEARS 100 MOVIES SELECTION
2007 . . . #54   1997 . . . #56

TOP 300 FILMS POSITION . . . . **#84**
All-Release Domestic Box Office in Equivalent 2005 $s

National Film Preservation Board Selection 1996

OTHER AWARDS Best Picture Wins

	Year
Golden Globes	1971
New York Film Critics	none
National Board of Review	none
Film Daily Critics	none

My main contribution to M★A★S★H was the concept, the philosophy, the style, the casting, and then making all those things work. Plus the jokes, of course.

—Robert Altman

We didn't understand Bob Altman at all. He was obviously nuts, what he was doing. It was wonderful.

—Donald Sutherland

PLOT: *M*A*S*H* chronicles the antics of three surgeons at a mobile army surgical hospital as they struggle to maintain their sanity and good humor against the backdrop of brutal violence in the Korean War.

PRODUCTION: In 1968 screenwriter Ring Lardner came across the Korean War novel *MASH*, by Richard Hooker. Lardner, who had previously been blacklisted in Hollywood because of his suspected involvement with the Communist Party, responded to the strong antiestablishment undertones of the story and was convinced it could be sold as a movie. He took the idea to his former agent, Ingo Preminger, who in turn approached 20th Century-Fox executive Richard Zanuck. Upon reading the book, Zanuck agreed to let Preminger produce the film with Lardner signing on to write the screenplay. With the United States' escalating problems in Vietnam, Fox sensed that the film could be a timely and lucrative property if the sensitive subject matter was handled properly. They shied away from offering the directorial job to older, more established directors in favor of a younger talent such as Arthur Penn or Stanley Kubrick. But more than seventeen directors turned down their offers. Preminger then approached relative newcomer Robert Altman, who was skeptical of the project at first but ultimately accepted, because he "saw in it the opportunity to do something [he] had been working on for about five years, which was a World War II farce." Altman, sensing an opportunity to make a subversive statement about the Vietnam War, took an unusual approach to directing the film. He encouraged his cast to improvise scenes rather than work directly from the script. His goal was to focus attention on the acerbic wit and personality of the ensemble, with the hopes of creating a realist, documentarylike experience of the war. However, not everyone shared his vision. Actors Donald Sutherland and Elliot Gould had their agents speak with the studio in the hopes of getting Altman fired. Screenwriter Ring Lardner was furious with the seemingly endless ramble of overlapping and often unintelligible dialogue, little of which was in his original screenplay. And, after seeing an early cut of the film, Fox executives were so displeased with the graphic hospital scenes and seeming lack of a plot that they considered pulling the plug on the film altogether. But Altman and producer Ingo Preminger persisted, showing the finished film to a test audience in September 1969. The screening was a raucous success, and the film was released as planned on January 25, 1970. Altman had brought the film in at a cost of $2.9 million, under its $3.4 million budget.

DISTRIBUTION: Thanks in no small part to its obvious relevance to the Vietnam War, *M*A*S*H* was an immediate critical and commercial success, bringing in a net profit of $17.8 million in its initial release. Younger audiences tended to applaud the film's undermining of authority and wartime politics, while critics and older viewers alike praised it for its satirical representation of military red tape and bureaucracy. The film went on to gross more than $96.9 million in worldwide box office (including the 1973 rerelease) and won an Oscar for Ring Lardner. However, the most lucrative aspect of the film was the 1971 television series it inspired. Created by Gene Reynolds and Larry Gelbart, *M*A*S*H* ran for twelve seasons and remains in syndication to this day. —*Mark D'Anna*

PATTON

20th Century-Fox, 1970

ALL-RELEASE EQUIVALENT 2005 $s

(Unadjusted $s) in Millions of $s

Domestic Box Office Revenues........ **$255.4**/($61.7)
Production Cost .... **$63.5**/($12.6)
Principal Photography..................... **82** days
2/3/1969–5/21/1969
Retakes 6/11/1969

Director	Franklin J. Schaffner
Producer	Frank McCarthy
Production Company. . . .	20th Century-Fox Film Corp.
Story and. . . . . Screenplay by	Francis Ford Coppola, Edmund H. North
Cast	George C. Scott, Karl Malden, Michael Bates, Edward Binns, Lawrence Dobkin, John Doucette
Filming Locations	Spain: Almería, Andalucía, Castilla y León, La Granja, Pamplona, Basque region, Segovia, Sevilla Studios, Madrid; England: Over Peover, Knutsford, Cheshire; Morocco: Rabat, Casablanca, Volubilis, Meknès; Greece: Crete
Genre.	Bio-Drama
Format.	Color (DeLuxe)
Initial Release	2/4/1970 premiere (New York)
Rerelease.	none
Running Time	173 minutes
MPAA Rating	M

STANDING THE TEST OF TIME

ACADEMY AWARD Oscar Nominations and Wins

*BEST PICTURE: Frank McCarthy, Producer

*ACTOR: George C. Scott (refused award)

*ART DIRECTION/SET DECORATION: Urie McCleary, Gil Parrondo/Antonio Mateos, Pierre-Louis Thevenet

Cinematography: Fred Koenekamp

*DIRECTING: Franklin J. Schaffner

*FILM EDITING: Hugh S. Fowler

Music (Original Score): Jerry Goldsmith

*SOUND: Douglas Williams, Don Bassman

Special Visual Effects: Alex Weldon

*WRITING (Story and Screenplay – based on factual material or material not previously published or produced): Francis Ford Coppola, Edmund H. North

OSCAR TOTALS   Nominations **10**   *Wins **7**

AFI 100 YEARS 100 MOVIES SELECTION
2007 0   1997 . . . #89

TOP 300 FILMS POSITION . . . . **#152**
All-Release Domestic Box Office in Equivalent 2005 $S

National Film Preservation Board Selection 2003

OTHER AWARDS Best Picture Wins

	Year
Golden Globes	none
New York Film Critics	none
National Board of Review	1970
Film Daily Critics	none

We set out to do a character study in some depth. We did not set out to present an argument.

—Franklin Schaffner

PLOT: Firebrand General George S. Patton must fight a war on two fronts: the first against his worthy nemesis, the Nazi general Erwin Rommel, the second against his own hubris and consequently Allied faith in his command.

PRODUCTION: For more than nineteen years, former brigadier general Frank McCarthy struggled to set up a motion picture about his World War II boss, General George S. Patton. He had the blessing of Fox's Darryl F. Zanuck, but lost that of the Patton family when the studio inadvertently sought their approval soon after Mrs. Patton's funeral in 1953. The rejection stalled the film for years until McCarthy snapped up the rights to two bestselling books about Patton. No screenwriter could draft exactly what McCarthy and Zanuck wanted, so in 1965 McCarthy hired twenty-six year-old Francis Ford Coppola, fresh from his writing credit on the WWII film, *Is Paris Burning?* Although Coppola's own soldierly experience was limited to playing a tuba in military school, he pored over the research and composed a script that McCarthy felt confident enough to show to Hollywood's leading men. But Coppola's characterization of Patton didn't seem to suit Burt Lancaster, Lee Marvin, or Rod Steiger, and another writer was commissioned for a more conventional take. Coppola's version was later resurrected by the story editor. Ulcers and arguments with George C. Scott forced director William Wyler to exit. McCarthy then brought Franklin J. Schaffner on board because of his skill with the large scope of *Planet of the Apes* (1968). For *Patton* Schaffner was to oversee seventy-one physical locations in six countries, and employ more than 54 tanks, ten World War II–era warplanes, and a contingent of the Spanish army. After devouring thirteen biographies, wearing out old newsreels of the general, and working extensively with the makeup team to match Patton's exact nose, eyebrows, hair, teeth, and facial moles, Scott's devotion and perfectionism turned to major anxiety. But when he finally stood before the camera, the nervousness disappeared, and he achieved what Darryl Zanuck considered a "performance that has never been surpassed in film history."

DISTRIBUTION: *Patton* was the second —after *The Bible* (1966)—and last film shot in the panoramic 70mm of Dimension 150 with every single visual effect staged for real. Because of the image quality, Fox released the nearly three-hour epic as a special road show event. The nation's division over Vietnam worried the studio, though *Patton* won over both hawks and doves. The "silent majority" believed the film honored the old warrior ethos at a time when America was most desperate for a hero. President Nixon hailed the film as his all-time favorite and screened it the night before he ordered the invasion of Cambodia. The antiwar movement, on the other hand, saw the film as an indictment against such monomania and warmongering. *Patton* marched onwards to seize the fourth best gross of $28 million in domestic rentals in 1970 (after *Love Story, Airport* and *M*A*S*H*) and soundly declared victory at the Academy Awards. George C. Scott famously refused to accept his Oscar, calling the ceremony a "meat parade," preferring instead to watch hockey at his farm in upstate New York. —*Michael Kogge*

AIRPORT

Universal, 1970

ALL-RELEASE EQUIVALENT 2005 $s

(Unadjusted $s) in Millions of $s

Domestic Box Office Revenues. . . . . . . **$415.6**/($100.5)
Production Cost . . . . **$50.3**/($10.0)
Principal Photography. . . . .**80** days estimated
January 1969–May 1969

Director . . . . George Seaton
Producer . . . . Ross Hunter
Production Company. . . . Ross Hunter Productions,
Universal Pictures
Story by . . . . Based on the novel by
Arthur Hailey
Screenplay by . . . . George Seaton
Cast . . . . Burt Lancaster, Dean Martin,
Jean Seberg, Jacqueline Bisset,
George Kennedy, Helen Hayes,
Van Heflin, Maureen Stapleton,
Barry Nelson, Lloyd Nolan,
Dana Wynter, Barbara Hale
Filming Locations . . . . . . Minneapolis-Saint Paul
International Airport, MN;
Universal Studios, Universal
City, CA
Genre . . . . Disaster
Format . . . . Color (Technicolor)
Initial Release . . . . 3/5/1970 premiere, Radio City
Music Hall (New York)
Rerelease. . . . . none
Running Time . . . . 137 minutes
MPAA Rating . . . . G

STANDING THE TEST OF TIME

ACADEMY AWARD Oscar Nominations and Wins

Best Picture: Ross Hunter, Producer

*ACTRESS IN A SUPPORTING ROLE: Helen Hayes

Actress in a Supporting Role: Maureen Stapleton

Art Direction/Set Decoration: Alexander Golitzen, E. Preston Ames/Jack D. Moore, Mickey S. Michaels

Cinematography: Ernest Laszlo

Costume Design: Edith Head

Film Editing: Stuart Gilmore

Music (Original Score): Alfred Newman

Sound: Ronald Pierce, David Moriarty

Writing (Screenplay – based on material from another medium): George Seaton

OSCAR TOTALS Nominations **10** *Wins 1

AFI 100 YEARS 100 MOVIES SELECTION

2007 0   1997 0

TOP 300 FILMS POSITION . . . .**#40**

All-Release Domestic Box Office in Equivalent 2005 $s

National Film Preservation Board Selection. . . .none

OTHER AWARDS Best Picture Wins

	Year
Golden Globes	none
New York Film Critics	none
National Board of Review	none
Film Daily Critics	none

They weren't great, but they weren't supposed to be . . . I gave the public what they wanted—a chance to dream, to live vicariously, to see beautiful women, jewels, gorgeous clothes, melodrama.

—Ross Hunter on his movies

PLOT: In this star-studded disaster epic, a major metropolitan airport confronts various workplace crises and personal dramas, including a fierce blizzard, a mischievous stowaway, and a transatlantic flight with a suicidal bomber on board.

PRODUCTION: The airliner-in-peril genre had been established earlier with such films as 1939's *Five Came Back* (and a 1956 remake, *Back from Eternity*), *No Highway in the Sky* (1951), *The High and the Mighty* (1954), *Zero Hour!* (1957), and *The Crowded Sky* (1960), but Universal's *Airport* would launch a new cycle of big-budget, star-driven disaster movies. There was much speculation about the casting of characters from this wildly popular 1968 novel by British writer Arthur Hailey, who was no stranger to aviation drama, as he had been a pilot with the Royal Air Force during World War II. Producer Ross Hunter, a schoolteacher-turned-actor-turned-producer, was known for his glossy, slick melodramas and bouncy romantic comedies at Universal, including *Magnificent Obsession, Tammy and the Bachelor, Imitation of Life,* and *Thoroughly Modern Millie.* Screenwriter and director George Seaton was given a then-whopping production budget of $10 million to make what would be his last big movie after a long career as an actor in radio, a screenwriter, and a director. Leading the film's cast were Burt Lancaster and Dean Martin, who were paid a percentage of the box office receipts in addition to their salaries. Jean Seberg received $150,000 plus $1,000 a week in expenses for sixteen weeks. Her contract also guaranteed her no less than fourth billing (her name appeared third). Helen Hayes, the "First Lady of the American Theater," was signed as the impish stowaway—a role for which she would win her second Best Actress Oscar. The nonhuman "star," of course, was the Boeing 707 jetliner used to depict the Trans Global Airlines craft. The plane was leased from the Flying Tigers air cargo line and painted with the fictional Trans Global Airlines logo and tail emblem. Seaton was denied permission to shoot at Los Angeles International or Chicago's O'Hare Airport, so the Minneapolis–St. Paul International Airport doubled for Chicago's fictitious Lincoln International Airport. Hoping to shoot the film's crucial blizzard sequences in a real snowfall, the filmmakers were dismayed to discover that most of the region's fifty-one inches of snow had already fallen and was lying around in six-foot-high drifts. This forced the use of plastic "snow," whipped into blizzardlike torrents by six wind machines hastily imported from the studio back in California. Later, when additional exterior storm scenes were needed, a parking lot at Universal Studios was used as the airport "runway," again using the mock TGA airliner and ubiquitous fans and plastic snowflakes. All interiors, including the 707 passenger cabin, were shot on soundstages at Universal. George Seaton subsequently came down with the flu, which developed into pneumonia, so uncredited director Henry Hathaway (*The Lives of a Bengal Lancer, True Grit*) stepped in to cover for the ailing director.

DISTRIBUTION: Despite generally unfavorable reviews—even star Burt Lancaster called it "the biggest piece of junk ever made"—*Airport* quickly became the second-highest-grossing picture of 1970 after *Love Story.* It spawned three sequels—*Airport 1975, Airport '77,* and *The Concorde—Airport '79,* and it triggered a string of disaster epics (*The Poseidon Adventure, Earthquake, The Towering Inferno, The Hindenburg, When Time Ran Out,* and others) throughout the 1970s and beyond. *—Douglas Burns*

FIVE EASY PIECES

Columbia, 1970

ALL-RELEASE EQUIVALENT 2005 $s

(Unadjusted $s) in Millions of $s

Domestic Box Office Revenues . . . . **$81.8**/($19.8)
Production Cost . . . . **$8.1**/($1.6)
Principal Photography . . . . **38** days estimated
11/10/1969–1/3/1970

Director . . . . Bob Rafelson
Producer . . . . Bob Rafelson, Richard Wechsler
Production Company . . . . BBS Productions
Story by . . . . Bob Rafelson, Adrien Joyce
Screenplay by . . . . Adrien Joyce
Cast . . . . Jack Nicholson, Karen Black
Filming Locations . . . . . . On location in California: Bakersfield, Kern County, Shafter, Taft; Canada: Vancouver Island, British Columbia; Oregon: Eugene, Florence, Portland; Illinois: Franklin Park; Washington: San Juan Islands, Seattle
Genre . . . . Drama
Format . . . . Color (Technicolor)
Initial Release . . . . 9/11/1970 premiere (New York); 9/12/1970 general release
Rerelease . . . . none
Running Time . . . . 96 minutes
MPAA Rating . . . . R

STANDING THE TEST OF TIME

ACADEMY AWARD Oscar Nominations and Wins

Best Picture: Bob Rafelson and Richard Wechsler, Producers

Actor: Jack Nicholson

Actress in a Supporting Role: Karen Black

Writing (Story and Screenplay – based on factual material or material not previously published or produced): Stoy by Bob Rafelson, Adrien Joyce; Screenplay by Adrien Joyce

OSCAR TOTALS   Nominations **4**   *Wins **0**

AFI 100 YEARS 100 MOVIES SELECTION
2007 0   1997 0

TOP 300 FILMS POSITION . . . . .none
All-Release Domestic Box Office in Equivalent 2005 $s

National Film Preservation Board Selection 2000

OTHER AWARDS Best Picture Wins

	Year
Golden Globes	none
New York Film Critics	1970
National Board of Review	none
Film Daily Critics	none

Blending the road movie with social critique, the film offers a brutally enlightening picture of America during the Vietnam era. Bobby is the embodiment of the time and the country: part drifter, part redneck, part patrician.

—Channel 4 Film

PLOT: After losing his beloved mother, a gifted young pianist leaves his effete family and embarks on a search for meaning in a world split apart by mainstream conformity and countercultural upheaval. When his father suffers a debilitating stroke, Bobby Dupea is asked by his sister to give up his blue-collar conceits and return home to say goodbye. He reluctantly agrees but is shanghaied by his waitress girlfriend into bringing her along for the ride.

PRODUCTION: Written under the name Adrien Joyce, Carole Eastman's Oscar-nominated screenplay was informed by events in the life of director-producer Bob Rafelson, who, before going to college and co-creating *The Monkees,* left home to experience life on the road. To make ends meet, he worked in a rodeo, as a deck hand, on an ocean liner, as a jazz drummer, and, like the character Bobby Dupea in *Five Easy Pieces,* on an oil rig. His collaborator on *The Monkees* TV series and on the movie *Head* was indie godfather Bert Schneider. Their company, BBS Productions (named from the first initials of Bert Schneider, Bob Rafelson, and Steve Blauner), would finance the projects of filmmakers who were not yet able to find work inside the studio system. Jack Nicholson was a close friend and collaborator of both Rafelson and Schneider, having worked earlier with them—and Karen Black, his co-star in this movie—on *Easy Rider.* The $1.6 million allotted to the project was small, even by 1970 standards. Even so, it was Rafelson's intention to make a film that was an existential character study shot almost entirely on location in the dusty oil patches of Bakersfield and amidst the lush greenery of the Pacific Northwest. The finished product hewed closely to Eastman's script, with the exception of the film's opening and closing scenes. Originally, the opening credits were accompanied by snapshots and home movies, revealing key elements of Bobby's boyhood and musical education. That version also helped explain why the boy would elect to leave home and give up a promising career. And at one point, *Five Easy Pieces* was to end more definitively, with Bobby dying in an automobile accident. The famous chicken salad scene, in which a waitress refuses to accommodate Bobby's simple request for plain toast, was played exactly as written in the screenplay and is one of the most memorable exchanges in movie history. To this day, director Henry Jaglom—a close friend of the principals—claims it was inspired by an incident in his life.

DISTRIBUTION: Rafelson's wildly inventive debut feature, *Head* (1968), was launched without any sort of meaningful marketing campaign. (Columbia was baffled by it, while influential critics dismissed anything pertaining to *The Monkees* out of hand.) Thus, the success of *Five Easy Pieces* depended on a familiarity with Nicholson's Oscar-nominated supporting role in *Easy Rider,* welcoming reviews, and positive word of mouth, which it got. The film also benefited from a soundtrack that juxtaposed Tammy Wynette's classic "Stand By Your Man" and "D-I-V-O-R-C-E" with beautifully played chamber music (the title referred to a book of piano lessons for beginners). Rafelson and Nicholson intended *Five Easy Pieces* to be the first in an extended trilogy of films focusing on dysfunctional families. Rafelson's often antagonistic relationship with mainstream Hollywood—along with poor box office response to such challenging art house fare as *The King of Marvin Gardens* and *Stay Hungry*—would eventually short-circuit any chance for Rafelson to call his own shots on big-budget projects. —*Gary Dretzka*

LOVE STORY
Paramount, 1970

ALL-RELEASE EQUIVALENT 2005 $s
(Unadjusted $s) in Millions of $s

Domestic Box Office Revenues........$447.6/($108.2)
Production Cost ....$11.4/($2.3)
Principal Photography...........100 days estimated
September 1969–March 1970

Director .... Arthur Hiller

Producer .... Howard G. Minsky

Production Company.... The Love Story Company

Story and
  Screenplay by .... Erich Segal

Cast .... Ali MacGraw, Ryan O'Neal,
John Marley, Ray Milland

Filming Locations ...... On location: Cambridge,
MA; Manhattan and
Long Island, NY

Genre................. Romance

Format............... Color (Movielab)

Initial Release 12/17/1970

Rerelease.............. none

Running Time .... 99 minutes

MPAA Rating .... PG

STANDING THE TEST OF TIME

ACADEMY AWARD Oscar Nominations and Wins

Best Picture: Howard G. Minsky, Producer

Actor: Ryan O'Neal

Actor in a Supporting Role: John Marley

Actress: Ali MacGraw

Directing: Arthur Hiller

***MUSIC** (Original Score): Francis Lai

Writing (Story and Screenplay – based on factual
material or material not previously
published or produced): Erich Segal

OSCAR TOTALS   Nominations 7   *Wins 1

AFI 100 YEARS 100 MOVIES SELECTION
2007..... 0   1997..... 0

TOP 300 FILMS POSITION .... #31
All-Release Domestic Box Office in Equivalent 2005 $s

National Film Preservation Board Selection....none

OTHER AWARDS Best Picture Wins

	Year
Golden Globes (Drama)...................	1971
New York Film Critics....................	none
National Board of Review.................	none
Film Daily Critics.......................	none

*I thought we were making a nice little movie. That's how it was regarded by
everyone . . . Nobody could have—or would have— predicted
how much of a phenomenon it would become.*

—Arthur Hiller

PLOT: A young man and a young woman, both smart and beautiful, fall in love. He's rich, she's poor, which causes some parental friction. No matter, their love is too strong. They get married. Then she gets cancer and dies.

PRODUCTION: Yale classics professor Erich Segal wrote a romantic drama based on his life at Harvard with his Radcliffe girlfriend. Every studio turned it down. Still, Segal and his William Morris agent, Howard Minsky, persevered. Minsky quit agenting to work full-time as a producer and promoter. It was Minsky who got the script to Ali McGraw in New York and had her commit before he convinced Paramount production chief Robert (Bob) Evans, who then sold it to his bosses at Gulf and Western with the help of a short film by his pal Mike Nichols. After a long search, Ryan O'Neal was cast as the male lead. Known for TV work on *Peyton Place*, O'Neal was one of six actors tested. Eight actors turned down the role: Michael Douglas, Jon Voight, Michael Sarrazin, Michael York, Keith Carradine, Peter Fonda, and Beau and Jeff Bridges. Just before production, Paramount threatened to pull the plug unless Hiller cut $25,000 off his salary, already below his usual rate. Hiller agreed but got a percentage of profits instead, which ultimately paid him a great deal more. Paramount was taken over by international conglomerate Gulf and Western in 1966 and by the end of the 1960s had suffered a series of flop movies. As a result, Evans could budget only $2 million for Segal's story, and that came with a warning from his boss, Stanley Jaffe: "Over $2 million, Evans, it's from your pocket." On location in New York and Massachusetts, Hiller watched every penny. He finished principal photography slightly under budget and returned to Hollywood to assemble the picture. When they saw it, Hiller and the editor felt a few extra shots were needed for character development. After refusing at first, Paramount acquiesced, but would authorize only $15,000 for reshoots. Evans, who had made Ali McGraw his third wife a month after principal photography began, agreed to pay for some of the extra shooting out of his pocket. After fretting about a blizzard back east, Hiller, McGraw, and O'Neal arrived for the two-day shoot, where handheld cameras were employed to capture scenes in the snow. Back at the studio, after an initial test preview, something still wasn't working. Hiller realized that he needed to move the scene where the heroine's illness is revealed to a point later in the picture, after her character is more established. It provided the needed touch. The final cost came in at $2,260,000.

DISTRIBUTION: At the suggestion of a William Morris literary agent, Segal turned the screenplay into a 131-page novel in little more than a month. Amid low expectations, it was published just before the film's release. It became the top-selling fiction book of 1970 and was translated into twenty languages. That helped make the movie an immediate hit and the year's top-grossing film, with nearly $49 million in domestic rentals. There was an unsuccessful sequel, *Oliver's Story*, produced eight years later. The broadcast premiere in 1972 marked the shortest time between theatrical and TV up until that time. —*Hayley Taylor Block*

THE FRENCH CONNECTION

20th Century-Fox, 1971

ALL-RELEASE EQUIVALENT 2005 $s

(Unadjusted $s) in Millions of $s

Domestic Box Office Revenues . . . . **$200.8**/($51.7)
Production Cost . . . . **$8.7**/($1.8)
Principal Photography . . . .**75** days
11/30/1970–3/11/1971 in New York
3/24/1971–3/27/1971 in France

Director . . . . William Friedkin
Producer . . . . Philip D'Antoni
Production Company . . . . D'Antoni Productions, Inc.,
Schine-Moore Productions
Story by . . . . Based on the book by
Robin Moore
Screenplay by . . . . Ernest Tidyman
Cast . . . . Gene Hackman, Fernando Ray,
Roy Scheider
Filming Locations . . . . . . Manhattan, Bedford
Stuyvesant, NYC, Brooklyn,
and Queens in New York;
Washington, D.C.; Marseille,
France
Genre . . . . Crime
Format . . . . Color (DeLuxe)
Initial Release 10/7/1971
Rerelease . . . . none
Running Time . . . . 104 minutes
MPAA Rating . . . . R

STANDING THE TEST OF TIME

ACADEMY AWARD Oscar Nominations and Wins

***BEST PICTURE:** Philip D'Antoni, Producer

***ACTOR:** Gene Hackman

Actor in a Supporting Role: Roy Scheider

Cinematography: Owen Roizman

***DIRECTING:** William Friedkin

***FILM EDITING:** Jerry Greenberg

Sound: Theodore Soderberg, Christopher Newman

***WRITING** (Screenplay – based on material from
another medium): Ernest Tidyman

OSCAR TOTALS   Nominations **8**   *Wins **5**

AFI 100 YEARS 100 MOVIES SELECTION
2007 . . . #93   1997 . . . #70

TOP 300 FILMS POSITION . . . . #258
All-Release Domestic Box Office in Equivalent 2005 $s

National Film Preservation Board Selection 2005

OTHER AWARDS Best Picture Wins

	Year
Golden Globes (Drama)	1972
New York Film Critics	none
National Board of Review	none
Film Daily Critics	none

It's a blue-collar film that blue-collar audiences thought real.
The cops were not the squeaky clean, "only the facts, ma'am,"
Jack Webb types from Dragnet. *They held court on the streets.*

—William Friedkin

PLOT: Two New York City detectives unravel a complicated plan to smuggle more than $32 million worth of pure heroin from France, and make the biggest drug bust in U.S. law enforcement history.

PRODUCTION: Although it was based on the nonfiction book *The French Connection: A True Account of Cops, Narcotics, and International Conspiracy* by Robin Moore, director William Friedkin was mainly interested in the characters involved in the historic 1960s drug bust. While producer Philip D'Antoni shopped the package around to the studios, Friedkin toured the back alleys of New York with Eddie "Popeye" Egan and Sonny "Cloudy" Grosso, the real-life detectives portrayed in the book, to watch actual cops in action. After the major studios passed, National General Pictures agreed to finance the picture, but then balked at the proposed $2.5 million budget. Friedkin and D'Antoni went through two screenwriters before settling on *New York Times* crime reporter Ernest Tidyman. They paid Tidyman $5,000 for two weeks to write a new script based on the characters Egan and Grosso. However, the film still hovered in limbo until Richard Zanuck of 20th Century-Fox unexpectedly put it on the fast track. Because D'Antoni's option had expired and author Robin Moore signed off his rights to drinking partner G. David Schine on a cocktail napkin, Fox had to pay Schine $5,000 for the napkin (and the rights) and give him participation in the profits. Jackie Gleason was considered for the lead but rejected, and Paul Newman was too expensive. Friedkin auditioned New York writer Jimmy Breslin but found he couldn't drive or act. Gene Hackman got the lead role only to spar with Friedkin throughout the production. Hackman despised Eddie Egan and had trouble making his character, Jimmy "Popeye" Doyle, as brutal and racist as Friedkin wanted him to be. His neurotic, obsessed performance, propelled to the limits of rage by Friedkin, won Hackman an Academy Award. Friedkin relied on his documentary roots to bring out the grit and dirt of New York. He told camera operator Ricky Bravo to just run onto the scene and film what he saw through the eyepiece. To top the car chase in D'Antoni's last film, *Bullitt,* Friedkin and cinematographer Owen Roizman shot from the back of a 1970 Pontiac, while Hackman and stunt driver Bill Hickman sped through the streets at 90 mph, usually without permission.

DISTRIBUTION: *The French Connection* opened in only a few theaters in October 1971. Fox widened the release when they realized that they had a hit on their hands. People phoned their local cinemas to find out what time during the earlier showing the car chase began, so they could catch it twice. Friedkin was delighted that the final gunshot provoked discussion, although he claimed he threw it in just to end the film "with a bang." Popeye Doyle's single-minded pursuit of justice at all costs triggered a controversy about the role of the police in society, with some Italian critics designating *The French Connection* as the most pro-fascist film ever made. Friedkin nearly missed attending the Oscars when, in typical Popeye Doyle fashion, his Rolls-Royce broke down, forcing him to hitch a ride from a construction worker. Fox sold the film for TV as part of a package of movies and allocated $1.5 million of the revenue to Friedkin's film. Friedkin fought the studio until it agreed to double the TV allocation to $3 million. —*Michael Kogge*

FIDDLER ON THE ROOF

United Artists, 1971

ALL-RELEASE EQUIVALENT 2005 $s
(Unadjusted $s) in Millions of $s

Domestic Box Office Revenues........ **$320.2/($86.0)**
Production Cost .... **$43.4/($9.0)**
Principal Photography............**90** days estimated
August 1970–January 1971

Director .... Norman Jewison

Producer .... Norman Jewison

Production Company.... Mirisch-Cartier Productions

Story by.............. Based on short stories by Sholem Aleichem and the 1964 Broadway musical

Screenplay by .... Joseph Stein

Cast .... Topol, Norma Crane, Paul Mann, Molly Picon, Leonard Frey, Rosalind Harris, Michele Marsh, Neva Small

Filming Locations ...... On location: Gorica, Zagreb, Lekenik, and Mala, Croatia; in studio: Pinewood Studios, London

Genre................. Musical

Format............... Color (Panavision)

Initial Release 11/2/1971

Rerelease............. 1979

Running Time .... 181 minutes (original release in two segments with an intermission, later trimmed to 149 minutes for 1979 rerelease)

MPAA Rating .... G

STANDING THE TEST OF TIME

ACADEMY AWARD Oscar Nominations and Wins

Best Picture: Norman Jewison, Producer

Actor: Topol

Actor in a Supporting Role: Leonard Frey

Art Direction/Set Decoration: Robert Boyle, Michael Stringer/Peter Lamont

*CINEMATOGRAPHY: Oswald Morris

Directing: Norman Jewison

*MUSIC (Scoring: Adaptation and Original Song Score): Adaptation Score by John Williams

*SOUND: Gordon K. McCallum, David Hildyard

OSCAR TOTALS   Nominations **8**   *Wins **3**

AFI 100 YEARS 100 MOVIES SELECTION
2007 0   1997..... 0

TOP 300 FILMS POSITION .... #92
All-Release Domestic Box Office in Equivalent 2005 $s

National Film Preservation Board Selection....none

OTHER AWARDS Best Picture Wins

	Year
Golden Globes (Musical)....................	1972
New York Film Critics......................	none
National Board of Review..................	none
Film Daily Critics.........................	none

Tevye: "As the Good Book says, if you spit in the air, it lands in your face."

—From the screenplay

PLOT: Tevye, a Jewish peasant and milkman in prerevolutionary Russia, copes with the day-to-day problems of shtetl life, his Jewish traditions, his wife and daughters, and state-sanctioned pogroms.

PRODUCTION: Based on short stories by Ukrainian writer Sholem Aleichem, the Harold Prince production opened on Broadway in September 1964, immediately winning audiences with its simple story of the traditions that bind a family. Toronto-born director Norman Jewison, who had directed musicals on TV and stage, was brought on for the film by executives who mistakenly thought he was Jewish because his name was Jewison. To prepare for the movie, Jewison spent time in Israel and immersed himself in the Jewish Orthodox community. Many of the men in the film were chosen because of their lineage and look, as well as their association with the Yiddish theater. Although the popular comic Zero Mostel had performed the role of Tevye on Broadway, Jewison looked for someone who could more realistically portray an Eastern European Jew. He heard that Israeli Chaim Topol was playing Tevye at Her Majesty's Theatre in London, so in 1967 Jewison flew there to see him. He was very impressed, but Topol was only thirty-five, so every morning the makeup department would have to age him considerably for the part. Jewison considered Hanna Meron for Golda, but when she lost a leg in a terrorist attack in Munich, he cast Norma Crane. Before production, Crane was diagnosed with breast cancer, the disease from which she would die in 1973. The Russians refused to cooperate because the film contained anti-czarist sentiment. There was pressure from Hungary and Romania to deny filming as well. Consequently, most of the film was shot on location in Yugoslavia, under the rule of Marshal Tito, who loved movies and wasn't too supportive of the Soviet Union. (They later held a special screening just for him.) The film was shot mainly in Croatia, just outside the capital, Zagreb, where they were able to find areas that had remained undeveloped. It was a perfect stand-in for 1910 Anatevka. They built the whole village in an abandoned square. However, most of the interior shots and some exterior shots were done at the Pinewood studios in London. They recorded all of the music first, then shot everything to the music. The cadenza was recorded by Isaac Stern, and the rest was played by the London Orchestra, which John Williams put together and conducted. The actor who played the fiddler was actually a Russian dancer who specialized in a dance form called "eccentric dance." The choreography was by Jerome Robbins's assistant Tom Abbott, assisted by Sammy Bayes. It followed Robbins's stage dances as closely as possible. They shot the film from summer to winter, because Jewison wanted it to get progressively colder and bleaker. To help achieve the earthy look Jewison was striving for, Academy Award–winning cinematographer Oswald Morris shot the entire film with a woman's brown pantyhose placed over the lens.

DISTRIBUTION: *Fiddler* had the highest domestic box office of 1971 (it was second in worldwide box office after *Diamonds Are Forever*), with more than $100 million in unadjusted worldwide box office on its initial release. The soundtrack album was also a huge seller. The 1979 rerelease was not as successful, with the $3.8 million print and ad costs almost as high as the $4.3 million in worldwide rentals. —*Hayley Taylor Block*

A CLOCKWORK ORANGE
Warner Bros., 1971

ALL-RELEASE EQUIVALENT 2005 $s
(Unadjusted $s) in Millions of $s

Domestic Box Office Revenues . . . . **$116.2**/($30.0)
Production Cost . . . . **$10.6**/($2.2)
Principal Photography . . . . **100** days estimated
October 1970–April 1971

Director . . . . Stanley Kubrick
Producer . . . . Stanley Kubrick
Production Company . . . . Hawk Films Ltd.
Story by . . . . Based on the novel by Anthony Burgess
Screenplay by . . . . Stanley Kubrick
Cast . . . . Malcolm McDowell, Warren Clarke, James Marcus, Michael Tarn
Filming Locations . . . . . . A British production at Pinewood Studios, Iver Heath and EMI-MGM Studios, Boreham Wood, Elstree, England; on location in and around London
Genre . . . . Crime
Format . . . . Color (Warnercolor)
Initial Release 12/19/1971
Rerelease . . . . 1972, R-rated version in select markets
Running Time . . . . 137 minutes
MPAA Rating . . . . X (and R-rated cut)

STANDING THE TEST OF TIME

ACADEMY AWARD Oscar Nominations and Wins

Best Picture: Stanley Kubrick, Producer

Directing: Stanley Kubrick

Film Editing: Bill Butler

Writing (Screenplay – based on material from another medium): Stanley Kubrick

OSCAR TOTALS   Nominations **4**   *Wins **0**

AFI 100 YEARS 100 MOVIES SELECTION
2007 . . . #70   1997 . . . #46

TOP 300 FILMS POSITION . . . . none
All-Release Domestic Box Office in Equivalent 2005 $s

National Film Preservation Board Selection . . . . none

OTHER AWARDS Best Picture Wins

	Year
Golden Globes	none
New York Film Critics	1971
National Board of Review	none
Film Daily Critics	none

Everyone is fascinated by violence. After all, man is the most remorseless killer who ever stalked the earth. Our interest in violence in part reflects the fact that on the subconscious level we are very little different from our primitive ancestors.

—Stanley Kubrick

PLOT: The government of near-future Britain has developed a therapy to relieve criminals of their violent behavior. After a murderous rampage, juvenile delinquent Alex DeLarge (Malcolm McDowell) becomes a candidate to be cured. But just how far will Alex and the government go to end the violence?

PRODUCTION: Thinking he had brain cancer, Anthony Burgess had published seven novels by the end of 1962, hoping to provide for his wife after his death (he ultimately died of lung cancer in 1993). One of those seven novels was *A Clockwork Orange*. While working with Stanley Kubrick on *Dr. Strangelove*, Terry Southern gave a copy of Burgess's book to the director in the hopes that Kubrick would make a film from Southern's screenplay adaptation. A few years later, Kubrick decided to pen the film himself and asked Warner Bros. to buy the rights for $200,000. Although he was able to leverage the critical success of *2001* into a lucrative three-year deal with Warner Bros. that included final cut privileges, the studio was less generous this time around. Fearing that the film's ultraviolence and sexual content would guarantee an X rating, the maximum investment it would make was $2 million. Kubrick accepted, knowing that he had to cast cheaply. He found his star in Malcolm McDowell, who at twenty-eight would play a much older Alex than the fourteen-year-old depicted in the book. Abandoning parts of his own screenplay, Kubrick would rip out whole passages from Burgess's novel and consult the actors on the set about the best way to improvise the scenes. For Alex's rape of Mrs. Alexander, Kubrick asked McDowell to perform a song-and-dance routine. The only song the actor could remember was one from childhood, "Singin' in the Rain." A phone call and an hour later, Kubrick had secured the rights. Since the budget was tight, production designer John Barry built only four sets, and housed the Korova Milkbar in a warehouse. Kubrick shot the rest of the film on location in London, using wireless lapel mics, source lighting, fast lenses, and a handheld camera. The young composers Walter Carlos and Rachel Elkind always had dreamed of working with Kubrick, so they sent a tape of their electronic music to his agent. Kubrick liked what he heard and commissioned them to synthesize electronic versions of Beethoven and other classics.

DISTRIBUTION: The MPAA rated *A Clockwork Orange* with an X, but this did not stop Warner from getting the film on the covers of *Time* and *Newsweek*. The movie opened in New York City in December 1971 and played throughout the year. A recut R-rated version was distributed at the end of 1972 to venues that refused to play X-rated films. It was damned by public watchdogs and a juvenile crime wave across Europe and America was attributed to the film's influence. Arthur Bremer, who attempted to assassinate George Wallace during the 1972 U.S. presidential campaign, wrote in his diary that when he saw the film he imagined shooting the governor. Young men in droog costumes, acting like Alex, terrorized the streets of London to such a degree that in 1974, Stanley Kubrick banned his own film from being screened in England for some years. It is number eighty-one in the British Film Institute's top 100 British films of the twentieth century, as selected in 1996. —*Michael Kogge*

THE GODFATHER
Paramount, 1972

ALL-RELEASE EQUIVALENT 2005 $s
(Unadjusted $s) in Millions of $s

Domestic Box Office Revenues........**$505.9**/($135.0)
Production Cost ....**$33.6**/($7.2)
Principal Photography...........**77** days estimated
3/29/1971–8/6/1971

Director .... Francis Ford Coppola
Producer .... Albert S. Ruddy
Production Company.... Paramount Pictures
Story by.............. Mario Puzo, based on the novel of the same name
Screenplay by .... Mario Puzo, Francis Ford Coppola
Cast .... Marlon Brando, James Caan, Richard Castellano, Richard Conte, Robert Duvall, Sterling Hayden, Diane Keaton, John Marley, Al Pacino
Filming Locations ...... On location in New York (Staten Island, Bronx, Manhattan, Queens, Long Island); California (Hollywood, Los Angeles); New Jersey; Las Vegas, Nevada; Sicily, Italy
Genre................ Crime
Format................ Color (Technicolor)
Initial Release .... 3/15/1972 premiere (New York); 3/24/1972 general release
Rerelease............. 1977, 1997
Running Time .... 175 minutes
MPAA Rating .... R

STANDING THE TEST OF TIME

ACADEMY AWARD Oscar Nominations and Wins
***BEST PICTURE:** Albert S. Ruddy, Producer
***ACTOR:** Marlon Brando
Actor in a Supporting Role: James Caan
Actor in a Supporting Role: Robert Duvall
Actor in a Supporting Role: Al Pacino
Costume Design: Anna Hill Johnstone
Directing: Francis Ford Coppola
Film Editing: William Reynolds, Peter Zinner
Sound: Bud Grenzbach, Richard Portman, Christopher Newman
***WRITING** (Screenplay – based on material from another medium): Mario Puzo, Francis Ford Coppola

OSCAR TOTALS Nominations **10** *Wins **3**

AFI 100 YEARS 100 MOVIES SELECTION
2007 .... #2   1997.... #3

TOP 300 FILMS POSITION .... **#23**
All-Release Domestic Box Office in Equivalent 2005 $s

National Film Preservation Board Selection.... 1990

OTHER AWARDS Best Picture Wins

	Year
Golden Globes (Drama).....................	1973
New York Film Critics.....................	none
National Board of Review.................	none
Film Daily Critics.........................	none

Every film creates its own identity, and it's possible to rivet an audience without the obvious tools. I was more surprised than anyone that this picture seemed to work the way it did.

—Francis Ford Coppola

PLOT: The youngest son of a powerful New York crime chieftain returns from heroic service in World War II to find himself slowly but inexorably drawn into the family's dark business.

PRODUCTION: In the spring of 1968, Paramount executive Robert Evans optioned Mario Puzo's novel treatment for $12,500 against $75,000 if it became a book. The studio initially envisioned *The Godfather* as a relatively inexpensive film; Puzo's script brought the action to the present day. They hired lesser-known director Francis Ford Coppola, whom they expected to be malleable, and began second-guessing him almost immediately. Coppola insisted on retaining the novel's forties setting and shooting in New York, but his first major battle was for Marlon Brando in the title role. The actor was in a career decline and was rumored to be difficult on the set, so Coppola filmed a "makeup test" at Brando's home, during which the forty-seven-year-old actor gradually transformed himself on camera. This ultimately satisfied the studio brass. As was his custom, Coppola held open casting calls for certain roles. Two notables who came "off the street" were Abe Vigoda as Tessio and Salvatore Corsitto as the undertaker whose monologue opens the film—a scripting suggestion by an early reader who noted the arresting opening of Coppola's script for *Patton*. The resolute Coppola worked under tremendous duress. The studio claimed displeasure with the first week's rushes—even though they included the film's iconic restaurant double murder—and he began to hear rumblings that he might be dismissed. The period setting had significantly increased the budget, yet he was shooting at a blistering pace. The lavish outdoor wedding reception at the beginning was completed in only 2½ days, the crime bosses' "boardroom" meeting in one. When Coppola insisted on location work in Sicily, Paramount's strident objections nearly claimed his job again, but the director prevailed. In keeping with its dramatic theme, *The Godfather* was a Coppola family affair. The director's father, Carmine, composed tarantellas and other incidental Italian music for both wedding receptions depicted in the film. The infant seen in the climactic baptism scene was played by Coppola's newborn daughter Sofia. Paramount's Robert Evans also objected to Coppola's choice of Nino Rota for the score but after a test screening with Rota's music dropped in, Evans relented. Other filmmakers also provided help: some inserts were shot by Coppola's friend and protégé George Lucas and Robert Towne helped write the intimate scene between Brando and Al Pacino just before the Godfather's death. One final scene, where Pacino's character proposes to Diane Keaton's Kay Adams, was shot locally during editing in Ross, California rather than in New England where the scene was set.

DISTRIBUTION: *The Godfather*'s distribution plan was innovative and precedent-setting, with Paramount collecting over $25 million from exhibitors even before the premiere. In addition, the distributor/exhibitors split was 90/10 for the first twelve weeks of release. The movie opened in five theaters in the New York area before moving to 316 theaters nationwide. Soon it was breaking records. By September, in unadjusted dollars, the film had overtaken the previous all-time box office champions, *Gone with the Wind* and *The Sound of Music.* —*Tom Dupree*

DELIVERANCE

Warner Bros., 1972

ALL-RELEASE EQUIVALENT 2005 $s

(Unadjusted $s) in Millions of $s

Domestic Box Office Revenues........ **$182.1**/($50.0)
Production Cost .... **$9.3**/($2.0)
Principal Photography............ **80** days estimated
Summer 1971

Director .... John Boorman

Producer .... John Boorman

Production Company .... Elmer Enterprises, Warner Bros.

Story by .... Based on the novel by
James Dickey

Screenplay by .... James Dickey

Cast .... Jon Voight, Burt Reynolds,
Net Beatty, Ronny Cox

Filming Locations ...... Tallulah Gorge in Tallulah Falls,
GA; the Chattooga River,
between Georgia and
South Carolina; Clemson,
SC

Genre................. Drama

Format................ Color (Technicolor)

Initial Release 7/30/1972

Rerelease.............. none

Running Time .... 109 minutes

MPAA Rating .... R

STANDING THE TEST OF TIME

ACADEMY AWARD Oscar Nominations and Wins

Best Picture: John Boorman, Producer

Directing: John Boorman

Film Editing: Tom Priestley

OSCAR TOTALS   Nominations 3   *Wins 0

AFI 100 YEARS 100 MOVIES SELECTION

2007 0   1997 0

TOP 300 FILMS POSITION ....none
All-Release Domestic Box Office in Equivalent 2005 $s

National Film Preservation Board Selection....none

OTHER AWARDS Best Picture Wins

	Year
Golden Globes .... none
New York Film Critics..................... none
National Board of Review.................. none
Film Daily Critics........................ none

*The picture was a tremendous struggle to make, but then it opened,
it became a monster hit, and it took everyone by surprise.*

—John Boorman

PLOT: Four Atlanta businessmen leave the city behind for a weekend canoeing trip in the wilds of Georgia, but their idyllic vacation soon turns dangerous as the locals, and nature itself, become more sinister.

PRODUCTION: Warner Brothers initially thought that James Dickey's dark and violent first novel, despite being a best seller, would have very limited appeal, so they capped the budget at $2 million, forcing the crew to mount the ambitious production with very limited funds. To save costs, they cast locals as extras. They even recruited some of the extras from a local jail: the prisoners were released during shooting, and went back to their cells at night when they wrapped. Perhaps the biggest challenge during pre-production was casting. Warner Brothers' John Calley gave John Boorman a shot at directing. Calley wanted big stars to play Lewis and Ed. After James Stewart, Marlon Brando, and Henry Fonda declined the role of Lewis because it was so dangerous, Boorman cast Reynolds, who he had seen on the *Tonight Show*. He said he liked how cool and in control Reynolds was. Also to cut costs, it was rumored that they did not insure the production, which Boorman denies. The actors performed their own stunts though, and author Dickey made an appearance as the Sheriff. No one except Ned Beatty (in his first on-screen role) had paddled a canoe before shooting, so they all learned for the film. The cast were all novices at archery, climbing and hiking, too. There were several injuries, but the actors never shied away from doing their stunts. Jon Voight fell nearly 20 feet when climbing a cliff and Burt Reynolds fractured his tailbone during one sequence: the pain in his face when he's injured in the film is real. Because the budget was so small, Boorman deferred part of his fee and they worked with a bare-bones crew. They battled poisonous snakes, insects, heat, and exhaustion and smashed six wooden canoes during the grueling shoot. Billy Redden, the boy who was cast as the banjo player, didn't actually know how to play, so they had another banjo-playing kid hide behind him and put his arm through Billy's shirt, so it looked as if he were playing. The night scenes with Jon Voight scaling the steep cliff were shot day-for-night. Boorman, and director of photography Vilmos Zsigmond, wanted a different look for the film so Zsigmond shot with Technicolor then used a dye transfer technique that later allowed him to increase the B&W levels to manipulate the mood. For the canoe scenes, they set up a stationary camera with a lens that panned just 4 or 5 inches above the water creating a chilling perspective and intensifying the fear.

DISTRIBUTION: *Deliverance* was one of the top domestic box office films of 1972, after *The Godfather* and *The Poseidon Adventure.* Oddly enough, the ratings board (and most critics) did not mention the rape scene. The year after *Deliverance* was released, thirty-one people drowned attempting to travel the stretch of river where the movie was shot. The royalties from the film's song "Dueling Banjos" made Warner Bros. more than the actual film cost to make. The two mountain men who rape and torture Beatty and Voight in the film were voted the number one movie villains of all time in 2005 by *Maxim* magazine. —*Dina Gachman*

THE POSEIDON ADVENTURE

20th Century-Fox, 1972

ALL-RELEASE EQUIVALENT 2005 $s

(Unadjusted $s) in Millions of $s

Domestic Box Office Revenues . . . . **$317.6**/($84.6)
Production Cost . . . .**$23.4**/($5.0)
Principal Photography . . . .**65** days estimated
4/3/1972–7/7/1972

Director . . . . Ronald Neame

Producer . . . . Irwin Allen

Production Company . . . . Irwin Allen Productions, Kent Productions

Story by . . . . Based on the novel by Paul Gallico

Screenplay by . . . . Stirling Silliphant, Wendell Mayes

Cast . . . . Gene Hackman, Ernest Borgnine, Red Buttons, Carol Lynley, Roddy McDowall, Stella Stevens, Shelly Winters, Leslie Nielsen

Filming Locations . . . . . . Shot primarily at 20th Century-Fox Studios with the exception of pre-capsize footage shot aboard the Queen Mary in Long Beach, CA

Genre . . . . Disaster

Format . . . . Color (DeLuxe)

Initial Release . . . . 12/12/1972 premiere (New York); 12/13/1972 general release

Rerelease 1974

Running Time . . . . 117 minutes

MPAA Rating . . . . PG

STANDING THE TEST OF TIME

ACADEMY AWARD Oscar Nominations and Wins

Actress in a Supporting Role: Shelley Winters

Art Direction: Art Direction: William Creber; Set Decoration: Raphael Bretton

Cinematography: Harold E. Stine

Costume Design: Paul Zastupnevich

Film Editing: Harold F. Kress

Music (Original Dramatic Score): John Williams

*MUSIC (Song – Original for the Picture):"The Morning After," Music and Lyrics by Al Kasha and Joel Hirschhorn

Sound: Theodore Soderberg, Herman Lewis

*SPECIAL ACHIEVEMENT AWARD (Visual Effects): L. B. Abbott, A. D. Flowers

OSCAR TOTALS Nominations **9** *Wins **2**

AFI 100 YEARS 100 MOVIES SELECTION
2007 0   1997 0

TOP 300 FILMS POSITION . . . . #94
All-Release Domestic Box Office in Equivalent 2005 $s

National Film Preservation Board Selection . . . . none

OTHER AWARDS Best Picture Wins

	Year
Golden Globes	none
New York Film Critics	none
National Board of Review	none
Film Daily Critics	none

There was the possibility of a star being badly hurt.

—Ronald Neame

PLOT: A luxury steamship making its last voyage across the Atlantic Ocean on New Year's Eve is struck by a tidal wave and capsizes at sea. A small group of survivors fight through fire, water, and explosions to find a way out.

PRODUCTION: Producer Irwin Allen, until then mostly known for his science fiction shows on television, conceived of the monster-budgeted disaster film after reading the best-selling novel by Paul Gallico. But the movie version almost sank before it was launched. Originally tagged with a then unheard-of budget of $5 million, Fox nearly pulled the plug two weeks before production as it sought to cut costs in the wake of several other flops. Fox management told Allen the movie was canceled, but Allen would not relent. He managed to convince the studio to guarantee half of the money needed and said he would provide the rest. Then he went across the street to a country club, where he found two of his friends, movie exhibitor Sherrill Corwin and indie producer Steve Broidy, enjoying an afternoon playing gin rummy. He got them to agree, on the spot, to invest $2.5 million in the film. And, just like that, the film was saved. While much of the pre-capsize footage of the luxury ocean steamer was shot aboard the *Queen Mary*, harbored off Long Beach, California, director Ronald Neame and his crew retreated to a soundstage at 20th Century-Fox studios to shoot the ship after it had been overturned by the wave. Actual photos and blueprints from the *Queen Mary* were used to design detailed sets that would need to be tilted with a forklift up to 35°, flooded with over 3.5 million gallons of water, and then flipped upside down. An excellent example of the incredible complexity involved in building these sets can be seen when looking at the Grand Saloon on the SS *Poseidon*. It was built in such a way as to be quickly and easily converted from upside down to right side up, and then back again. To accomplish this, the ceiling was carpeted on its reverse side and the floor was decorated with ceiling fixtures on its flip side. The film was mostly shot in sequence, so the cast became dirtier and showed more injuries as they went along. Many of the actors, all of whom did their own stunts, found themselves in incredibly dangerous situations as they moved about the intricate sets during filming. At times, shooting became so frightening for the cast that actor Red Buttons commented, "If true emotion counts for anything, we should all be up for Oscars next year."

DISTRIBUTION: The film Hollywood had initially dubbed "Irwin's Folly" went on to become a huge box office success, launching Irwin Allen as Hollywood's megaproducer of disaster movies. Although smaller, character-driven films such as *Easy Rider* and *The Graduate* were all the rage at the time, audiences turned out in record numbers to see *The Poseidon Adventure*. With $36.5 million in domestic rentals on its initial release, it was the second-highest-grossing film of 1972 after *The Godfather,* and although it didn't beat *Airport*'s $45 million in domestic rentals, Allen brought *The Poseidon Adventure* in at half the cost of that earlier disaster film. —*Mark D'Anna*

AMERICAN GRAFFITI
Universal, 1973

Director . . . . George Lucas

Producer . . . . Francis Ford Coppola

Production Company . . . . Lucasfilm Ltd., Coppola Company, Universal Pictures

Story by . . . . George Lucas

Screenplay by . . . . George Lucas, Gloria Katz, Willard Huyck

Cast . . . . Richard Dreyfuss, Ronny Howard, Paul Le Mat, Charlie Martin Smith, Candy Clark, Mackenzie Phillips, Wolfman Jack, Harrison Ford, Bo Hopkins

Filming Locations . . . . . . San Francisco Bay Area (San Rafael, Petaluma, Sonoma, Richmond, San Francisco, Novato, Mill Valley, Berkeley, Concord)

Genre . . . . Drama

Format . . . . Color (Technicolor)

Initial Release 8/1/1973

Rerelease 1978

Running Time . . . . 109 minutes

MPAA Rating . . . . PG

STANDING THE TEST OF TIME

ACADEMY AWARD Oscar Nominations and Wins

Best Picture: Francis Ford Coppola, Producer; Gary Kurtz, Co-Producer

Actress in a Supporting Role: Candy Clark

Directing: George Lucas

Film Editing: Verna Fields, Marcia Lucas

Writing (Story and Screenplay – based on factual material or material not previously published or produced): George Lucas, Gloria Katz, Willard Huyck

OSCAR TOTALS Nominations 5 *Wins 0

AFI 100 YEARS 100 MOVIES SELECTION
2007 . . . #62   1997 . . . #77

TOP 300 FILMS POSITION . . . . **#43**
All-Release Domestic Box Office in Equivalent 2005 $s

National Film Preservation Board Selection 1995

OTHER AWARDS Best Picture Wins

	Year
Golden Globes (Comedy)	1974
New York Film Critics	none
National Board of Review	none
Film Daily Critics	none

By God, I've got a movie here, and I'm going to get it made somehow.

—George Lucas

PLOT: Four pals cruise, eat at Mel's Drive-In, and listen to music while trying to figure out what to do with their lives. One of them finally goes off to college after a drag-race crash.

PRODUCTION: George Lucas doggedly shopped his semiautobiographical story to studios for a year. At one point, friends Willard Huyck and Gloria Katz helped him rewrite a fifteen-page treatment. Despite constant rejections, mounting personal debt, and other lucrative directing offers, Lucas stuck by his idea. He finally convinced United Artists' David Picker to invest $10,000 to develop a script. Richard Walters wrote a first draft, but Lucas rejected it and rewrote it himself. Picker promptly rejected that version, as did another round of studios. Producer Gary Kurtz finally brokered a deal with Universal's Ned Tanen when Francis Ford Coppola lent his recently hot *Godfather* name as executive producer. To secure even his minuscule $750,000 budget, Lucas had to relinquish final cut, agree to shoot without studio space, and pay his cast and crew scale. Huyck and Katz then helped him rewrite his final draft before shooting. Casting director Fred Roos led months of open cattle-call auditions at California high schools. He and Lucas plucked the cast of mostly young unknowns from thousands of hopefuls, including a carpenter named Harrison Ford. Shooting began on June 26, 1972, in San Rafael, California. After the very first day the crew lost their permit and had to shift the entire production to Petaluma. After a few more days, Lucas realized that he needed help with the cinematography. As a favor, Haskell Wexler flew up from L.A. every evening and assisted, then flew back down to work his day job making commercials. The production team averaged a healthy twenty setups a night despite wearying shoots that lasted from 9:00 p.m. to sunrise, constant equipment and automotive malfunctions, and a flat tire on the airplane in the final scene. They attempted the big car wreck finale three times without success before shooting ended on August 4. On an August 8 reshoot, the second unit finally got the car to roll over correctly. Verna Fields and Marcia Lucas helped Lucas edit the footage to a dizzying array of rock-and-roll songs and a Wolfman Jack radio show cut in by sound designer Walter Murch. While they labored to cut the film, Kurtz helped broker a deal to acquire the rights to more than forty popular songs for the bargain price of approximately $80,000.

DISTRIBUTION: The first public preview on January 21, 1973, was a hit with the audience, but Tanen hated it. After arguing with Coppola in the lobby, Tanen stalled the release and demanded cuts. Disliking even the title, Universal sent a list of more than a hundred alternatives they wanted Lucas to consider. Lucas refused. Subsequent successful previews finally induced Tanen and Universal to release the edited film. It opened in New York and L.A. on August 1, 1973, two weeks before general release. For a 1978 rerelease, Lucas restored cuts that had been forced upon him, changed Milner's postcredit date of death from June 1964 to December 1964, and added a Dolby stereo mix. The film went on to become one of the most profitable studio-financed films ever, earning more than $115 million in unadjusted domestic box office alone. For the DVD release in 1998, Lucas digitally added a dramatic sunset in the background of the opening shot. —*Scott Mazak*

THE STING

Universal, 1973

ALL-RELEASE EQUIVALENT 2005 $s
(Unadjusted $s) in Millions of $s

Domestic Box Office Revenues........**$605.6**/($169.0)
Production Cost ....**$24.2**/($5.5)
Principal Photography............**65** days estimated
1/22/1973–April 1973

Director	George Roy Hill
Producer	Tony Bill, Michael and Julia Philips
Production Company	Universal Pictures, Zanuck/ Brown Productions
Story and Screenplay by	David S. Ward
Cast	Paul Newman, Robert Redford, Robert Shaw
Filming Locations	On location: Los Angeles, CA; Chicago, IL; in studio Universal back lot, Universal City, CA
Genre	Crime
Format	Color (Technicolor)
Initial Release	12/25/1973
Rerelease	1977
Running Time	127 minutes
MPAA Rating	PG

STANDING THE TEST OF TIME

ACADEMY AWARD Oscar Nominations and Wins

*BEST PICTURE: Tony Bill, Michael Phillips, and Julia Phillips

*ACTOR: Robert Redford

*ART DIRECTION/SET DECORATION: Henry Bumstead/James Payne

Cinematography: Robert Surtees

*COSTUME DESIGN: Edith Head

*DIRECTING: George Roy Hill

*FILM EDITING: William Reynolds

*MUSIC (Adaptation Score): Marvin Hamlisch

Sound: Ronald K. Pierce, Robert Bertrand

*WRITING (Story and Screenplay – based on factual material or material not previously published or produced): David S. Ward

OSCAR TOTALS   Nominations **10** *Wins 7

AFI 100 YEARS 100 MOVIES SELECTION
2007 0   1997 0

TOP 300 FILMS POSITION .... **#13**
All-Release Domestic Box Office in Equivalent 2005 $s

National Film Preservation Board Selection.... 2005

OTHER AWARDS Best Picture Wins

	Year
Golden Globes	none
New York Film Critics	none
National Board of Review	1973
Film Daily Critics	none

Way before Guy Ritchie's polished bad-boy style and hugely complicated plot twists pulled in the punters, The Sting *pioneered the genre. [It] remains an entertaining way to spend a couple of hours—and unlike* Lock, Stock and Two Smoking Barrels—*it's more about charisma than greed.*
—Matt Ford, BBC

PLOT: Set in Depression-era Chicago, grifter Johnny Hooker seeks to avenge the murder of his partner on the orders of syndicate boss Doyle Lonnegan. He conspires with Harry Gondorff to drain Lonnegan of his money, power, and freedom.

PRODUCTION: Having scored a major triumph four years earlier with the western buddy film *Butch Cassidy and the Sundance Kid,* director George Roy Hill recruited the same highly charismatic stars—Paul Newman and Robert Redford—to ensure that *The Sting* would have star power to burn. It was the second of David S. Ward's projects to be filmed after *Steelyard Blues,* for which the writer researched pickpockets and other con artists. Ward had written the script with Redford in mind, but the actor required convincing. Hill, who routinely considered Newman for his action-adventures, found him to be an easy sell. Jack Nicholson was also considered before Redford climbed on board. Hill reportedly wanted to shoot in Chicago but got a chilly reception from Mayor Richard Daley, who felt the movie depicted his city negatively. Consequently, they shot there for only three days. Set designer Henry Bumstead created his version of the Windy City on the Universal City, California, back lot, where the rest of the movie was filmed while a few other shots were captured in downtown Los Angeles. Bumstead was able to create a highly believable "wire room," where the intricacies of the scam—which involved past-posting race results—could be choreographed. While the "long con" segments could be replicated with the usual Hollywood magic, close-hand card manipulation required the "stunt hands" of technical advisor John Scarne. Marvin Hamlisch's Oscar-winning score was dominated by interpretations of Scott Joplin's infectious ragtime music, which, while not of the period, added mightily to the film's appeal. Hill said he got the idea for using it after overhearing Gunther Schuller's *Scott Joplin: The Red Back Book* playing in his son's room. The period feel was also enhanced by "chapter headings" featuring vintage movie theater title cards and illustrations inspired by drawings in the *Saturday Evening Post.* The cinematography, which incorporated colors such as yellow, beige, and sepia, evoked a different era as well.

DISTRIBUTION: *The Sting* opened on Christmas Day, 1973, against *Magnum Force, The Exorcist, Don't Look Now,* and *Pippi Longstocking.* Julia Phillips became the first woman to win a Best Picture Oscar as co-producer. In 1974 author David W. Maurer filed suit, alleging that much of Ward's screenplay was adapted without credit from his book *The Big Con: The Story of the Confidence Man,* which described actual scams perpetrated by real-life 1920s Chicago grifters Fred and Charley Gondorf and a colorful cast of their associates. The case was settled out of court two years later. Although many moviegoers assumed incorrectly that Marvin Hamlisch wrote "The Entertainer" and other songs featured in the film, his arrangements did contribute to the sudden clamor for more ragtime music and opened the doors for a new appreciation of Joplin's work. Finally, Joplin's opera *Treemonisha* was being produced on Broadway and elsewhere, and he would be posthumously nominated for a Tony. In 1976 the composer would also win a special Pulitzer Prize for music. Ten years later, Universal tempted fate by releasing the sequel, *The Sting II,* which starred Jackie Gleason and Mac Davis. It did so poorly at the box office, the studio scrapped plans for a prequel. —*Gary Dretzka*

THE EXORCIST
Warner Bros., 1973

ALL-RELEASE EQUIVALENT 2005 $s
(Unadjusted $s) in Millions of $s

Domestic Box Office Revenues........**$722.9**/($232.7)
Production Cost ....**$53.9**/($13.0)
Principal Photography.......... **200** days estimated
8/14/1972–7/20/1973

Director .... William Friedkin

Producer .... William Peter Blatty

Production Company.... Hoya Productions

Story by.............. Based on the novel by
William Peter Blatty

Screenplay by .... William Peter Blatty

Cast .... Ellen Burstyn, Max von Sydow,
Lee J. Cobb, Linda Blair

Filming Locations ...... Except for prologue shot in
Iraq, film shot on location in
Boston for exteriors, in
New York, and in studio at
Warner Bros Studio, CA

Genre................. Thriller

Format............... Color (Metrocolor)

Initial Release 12/26/1973

Rerelease............ 1975, 1976, 1979 and longer
version 9/22/2000

Running Time .... 121 minutes; 132 minutes
9/22/2000 rerelease edition

MPAA Rating .... R

STANDING THE TEST OF TIME

ACADEMY AWARD Oscar Nominations and Wins

Best Picture: William Peter Blatty, Producer

Actress in a Supporting Role: Jason Miller

Actress: Ellen Burstyn

Actress in a Supporting Role: Linda Blair

Art Direction/Set Decoration: Bill Malley/ Jerry
Wunderlick

Cinematography: Owen Roizman

Directing: William Friedkin

Film Editing: Jordan Leondopoulos, Bud Smith,
Evan Lottman, Norman Gay

*SOUND: Robert Knudson, Chris Newman

*WRITING (Screenplay – based on material from
another medium): William Peter Blatty

OSCAR TOTALS Nominations **10** *Wins 2

AFI 100 YEARS 100 MOVIES SELECTION
2007..... 0   1997..... 0

TOP 300 FILMS POSITION .... #10
All-Release Domestic Box Office in Equivalent 2005 $s

National Film Preservation Board Selection....none

OTHER AWARDS Best Picture Wins

	Year
Golden Globes (Drama).....................	1974
New York Film Critics.....................	none
National Board of Review.................	none
Film Daily Critics.........................	none

Yes, I believe in exorcism. That's why the film's good. It's not made with cynicism.

—William Friedkin

PLOT: When twelve-year-old Regan's behavior begins to change, doctors tell her mother, "It's just nerves." But nothing they prescribe can tame the monster Regan soon becomes. The mother's last hope is a skeptical Jesuit priest who must conduct an exorcism.

PRODUCTION: In 1949 the *Washington Post* reported that a priest performed an exorcism on a fourteen-year-old boy whose behavior went beyond the explanations of science. William Peter Blatty, then a college student at Georgetown, remembered the story for twenty years before it inspired the novel that broke him out of comedy writing. But a best seller about demonic possession was not an easy sell at the studios. Executive producer Paul Monash, coming off the hit *Butch Cassidy and the Sundance Kid* (1969), scooped up the rights and parlayed his recent success to put *The Exorcist* on the fast track at Warner Bros. However, Monash did not remain on the picture for long. Blatty assumed control after a dispute over the story. While Warner queried directors Stanley Kubrick, Mike Nichols, and Arthur Penn, Blatty pushed them to hire William Friedkin, who had just won his Oscar for *The French Connection*. Friedkin disliked the 226-page screenplay adaptation Blatty had written, opting to return to the core story instead. Though Jack Nicholson and Roy Scheider lobbied to play Father Damian Karras, Friedkin picked playwright Jason Miller, who had just won a Pulitzer Prize. At first, Miller thought Friedkin wanted him to polish the screenplay, but Friedkin actually wanted the writer, a lapsed Catholic, to act. Rumors spread that the devil himself was trying to damn *The Exorcist*. Nine people associated with the film died during production. The set for the MacNeil house burned down. The crate carrying the demon statue of Pazuzu ended up in Hong Kong instead of its intended destination, Iraq. The shooting schedule nearly doubled, from 105 days to 200. When the practical effects didn't work, the budget skyrocketed, causing Warner Bros. executives to grow increasingly worried that this was their *Cleopatra*. But William Friedkin knew that everything had to look authentic for people to accept the girl's demonic possession, Chris Newman and the sound team mixed animal sounds with Mercedes McCambridge's raspy tones to create the demon's malevolent voice. Cinematographer Owen Roizman lit the scenes in high contrast to each other so that the editors could alternate from light to dark, good to evil. Special effects supervisor Marcel Vercoutere discovered that pea soup was the best substitute for vomit. Meanwhile, the cast and crew froze in the New York summer, as massive air conditioners blasted Regan's bedroom to make the actor's breath visible.

DISTRIBUTION: After seeing the final cut, one executive thought *The Exorcist* was so obscene that he recommended it never be released. The studio predicted *The Exorcist* would barely break even, and opened the film on the day after Christmas 1973 in only a handful of theaters. No one ever imagined lines forming around the block in cold weather for a ticket to meet the devil. But meet him people did, even against the advice of Billy Graham. Audience members screamed, most for more, a few for Jesus. Those who hadn't fainted departed the theaters in stunned silence. Appeals for exorcisms deluged local churches, and frightened "sinners" overwhelmed confessionals. *The Exorcist* possessed the box office of the early 1970s and continues to haunt popular culture today. After the fall of Saddam Hussein, Iraqi students in Mosul organized "The Exorcist Experience," a tour of famous sites captured in the film. —*Michael Kogge*

BLAZING SADDLES

Warner Bros., 1974

ALL-RELEASE EQUIVALENT 2005 $s

(Unadjusted $s) in Millions of $s

Domestic Box Office Revenues........ **$361.6**/($119.5)
Production Cost .... **$10.3**/($2.6)
Principal Photography................. not available
Summer 1973

Director .... Mel Brooks
Producer .... Michael Hertzberg
Production Company.... Warner Bros. Productions
Story by .... Based on the original story by Andrew Bergman
Screenplay by .... Mel Brooks, Norman Steinberg, Andrew Bergman, Richard Pryor, Alan Uger
Cast .... Gene Wilder, Slim Pickens, Cleavon Little
Filming Locations ...... Some shooting in Palmdale and in the desert; most at the Warner Bros. studio in Los Angeles
Genre................. Comedy
Format............... Color (Technicolor)
Initial Release 2/7/1974
Rerelease............. 1975, 1976, 1977, 1978, 1979, 1981, 1993
Running Time .... 93 minutes
MPAA Rating .... R

STANDING THE TEST OF TIME

ACADEMY AWARD Oscar Nominations and Wins

Actress in a Supporting Role: Madeline Kahn

Film Editing: John C. Howard, Danford Greene

Music (Song): "Blazing Saddles," Music by John Morris; Lyrics by Mel Brooks

OSCAR TOTALS Nominations **3** *Wins 0

AFI 100 YEARS 100 MOVIES SELECTION
2007 0   1997 0

TOP 300 FILMS POSITION .... #62
All-Release Domestic Box Office in Equivalent 2005 $s

National Film Preservation Board Selection.... 2006

OTHER AWARDS Best Picture Wins

	Year
Golden Globes	none
New York Film Critics	none
National Board of Review	none
Film Daily Critics	none

I had [Warner Bros. executive] John Calley's blessing to go all the way, so I went all the way.

—Mel Brooks

PLOT: The frontier town of Rock Ridge needs a new sheriff, but the state's scheming attorney general, who wants to run railroad tracks through the town, sends them a black man.

PRODUCTION: Producer, director, writer, and star Mel Brooks had directed two largely unseen movies and was having trouble getting a new screenplay greenlighted when agent David Begelman showed him *Tex X,* an outline by writer Andrew Bergman. Intrigued, Brooks put together a group of writers working together in the same room, much as when he wrote on Sid Caesar's *Your Show of Shows.* Warner Bros. executive John Calley felt *Tex X* sounded too much like a black exploitation picture, and the Warner board rejected Brooks's substitute title, *Black Bart.* Finally, coming out of the shower on the day before photography began, the final title struck him. Brooks lobbied hard for Richard Pryor to play the sheriff but was unsuccessful and hired Cleavon Little instead. He showed the script to John Wayne, hoping he might play the alcoholic gunslinger who becomes a deputy, but Wayne, who genuinely thought the script was funny, demurred because he thought the movie was too risqué for his image. Brooks was concerned about several scenes that might stretch the bounds of good taste, but Calley famously told him, "If you're gonna go up to the bell, ring it." The first day of production, a Friday, was disastrous. Brooks had hired Gig Young for the gunslinger part; the first scene called for him to hang upside down in a jail cell while talking with Little. Inverted, Young began to shake uncontrollably, and finally had to be taken by ambulance to the hospital. Desperate, Brooks called his friend Gene Wilder, who had read drafts of the script early on and wanted the role, but Brooks had felt he was too young. Wilder flew to California overnight, worked on wardrobe Saturday, practiced horse riding on Sunday, and was ready to shoot early Monday morning. Since Brooks had spent the previous Friday afternoon covering Little's angles after Young's departure and had managed to recast the second lead very quickly after the start of production, he lost just half a day. The picture remained on budget and on schedule for the duration of the production. Brooks shot *Blazing Saddles,* his first Hollywood movie, using two cameras rather than one, a method he continued from then on. He was particularly proud of an innovation he called "foreground music." This is when music is experienced first on a subconscious level before it is thrust into the action of a story on a very conscious level. One such example of this from *Blazing Saddles* is when Little rides in the desert to the tune of suitable background jazz music before suddenly stumbling upon Count Basie and his entire band happily playing "April in Paris."

DISTRIBUTION: After the initial screening for twelve Warner Bros. executives, the suits wondered aloud if it wouldn't be cheaper just to dump *Blazing Saddles* and avoid the marketing expenses altogether. Without telling the executives, producer Michael Hertzberg suggested running the film again that night, only this time in a theater that held 200 people. He and Brooks recruited less senior Warner employees. 300 people crammed into the theater, and this time the response was thunderous. To the surprise of the studio's dour dozen, *Blazing Saddles* was the talk of the Warner lot the next morning. The resulting general release came in the winter of 1974 and was modestly successful, but in 1975, when Warner had no big summer release, exhibitors clamored for another run with *Blazing Saddles. —Tom Dupree*

CHINATOWN
Paramount, 1974

ALL-RELEASE EQUIVALENT 2005 $s

(Unadjusted $s) in Millions of $s

Domestic Box Office Revenues. . . . .**$99.0**/($29.2)
Production Cost . . . .**$23.8**/($6.0)
Principal Photography. . . . .**44** days estimated
9/28/1973–November 1973

Director . . . . Roman Polanski

Producer . . . . Robert Evans

Production Company. . . . Paramount Pictures,
Long Road Productions,
Freedom Service Company,
Penthouse Productions

Story and
Screenplay by . . . . Robert Towne

Cast . . . . Jack Nicholson, Faye Dunaway,
John Huston

Filming Locations . . . . . . Los Angeles, Channel Islands,
Glendale, and Pasadena, CA

Genre. . . . . Crime

Format. . . . . Color (Technicolor)

Initial Release 6/20/1974

Rerelease. . . . . none

Running Time . . . . 131 minutes

MPAA Rating . . . . R

STANDING THE TEST OF TIME

ACADEMY AWARD Oscar Nominations and Wins

Best Picture: Robert Evans, Producer

Actor: Jack Nicholson

Actress: Faye Dunaway

Art Direction/Set Decoration: Richard Sylbert,
W. Stewart Campbell/Ruby Levitt

Cinematography: John A. Alonzo

Costume Design: Anthea Sylbert

Directing: Roman Polanski

Film Editing: Sam O'Steen

Music (Original Dramatic Score): Jeffy Goldsmith

Sound: Bud Grenzbach, Larry Jost

***WRITING** (Original Screenplay): Robert Towne

OSCAR TOTALS   Nominations **11** *Wins 1

AFI 100 YEARS 100 MOVIES SELECTION
2007 . . . #21   1997. . . #19

TOP 300 FILMS POSITION . . . . .none
All-Release Domestic Box Office in Equivalent 2005 $s

National Film Preservation Board Selection. . . . 1991

OTHER AWARDS Best Picture Wins

	Year
Golden Globes (Drama).	1975
New York Film Critics.	none
National Board of Review.	none
Film Daily Critics.	none

The picture's central metaphor is lack of knowledge: nobody knows what's going on and what the future holds for the city and the country. In Chinatown, *even the most seemingly innocuous of natural elements, water, become a political commodity, causing the most heinous and corruptive actions.*

—Emanuel Levy

PLOT: In 1937, during a drought, private detective Jake Gittes is hired to spy on the chief engineer of the city's water and power company, leading him into a murderous plot to control the destiny of Los Angeles.

PRODUCTION: Before writing *Chinatown*, Robert Towne was known primarily as a go-to guy for rewrites and revisions. In 1974 the Los Angeles native was offered $125,000 to write a screenplay for *The Great Gatsby*. Instead, based on a one-line pitch, Towne accepted $25,000 from producer Robert Evans to write a detective story. In his search for an appropriate crime for Jack Gittes to solve, Towne foresaw a trilogy that would put the wisecracking shamus at the center of scandals involving the city's very lifeblood: water, natural gas, and freeways. Evans, who had just switched from head of production at Paramount to producing his own projects, convinced Roman Polanski to return to Hollywood—where his wife, Sharon Tate, had been murdered five years earlier—to direct. Jack Nicholson was everyone's choice to play Gittes, while Evans had hoped to cast his wife, Ali McGraw. Her affair with Steve McQueen nixed that idea, and, after Jane Fonda turned down the job, the door opened for Polanski's first choice, Faye Dunaway. Casting John Huston as the evil Noah Cross not only worked artistically but also paid homage to the writer-director of *The Maltese Falcon* (1941), an early noir movie. Having that many high-voltage personalities collaborate on a major project doesn't always mean a masterpiece will be created. But when sparks flew on the set of *Chinatown*, the results were extremely positive. After a great deal of discussion, Polanski convinced Towne to change his happy ending to one far more tragic. Towne also revised the ending to have L.A.'s Chinatown play something other than a metaphorical role in the picture. Among other contributions, Nicholson named Gittes after his friend, producer Harry Gittes, and Dunaway suggested that Nicholson actually strike her during an argument between their characters. Contributions from Towne weren't nearly as welcome, though, and he was ultimately barred from the set. For his part, Evans fired composer Phillip Lambro at the last minute, giving Jerry Goldsmith only ten days to record a new score. Evans's decision to add a red tint to the film to give it more of a period feel angered Polanski, who demanded a look that more reflected Los Angeles's blistering sunshine.

DISTRIBUTION: Upon its release in June 1974, *Chinatown* was considered by the public and many critics to be a genre film, albeit one that featured outstanding acting, writing, and production values. The real-life conspiracy behind Noah Cross's monopoly of land and water rights in the film, which Towne saw as a crime equal to or greater than murder and incest, would become more relevant with repeated viewings. At its release, Gene Siskel wrote, "As much as I admire the work of both Polanski and Nicholson, I found *Chinatown* tedious from beginning to just before the end." Compared with other crime films in 2005 dollars, *Chinatown* would not make the top 15 when ranked by domestic box office. For example, the similarly budgeted *The Godfather* (which Towne had script-doctored and which was released two years prior to *Chinatown*) had done more than five times the business *Chinatown* did. The second installment of the planned trilogy, *The Two Jakes* (1990), was neither a critical nor commercial success. The third film has yet to be realized. —*Gary Dretzka*

THE TOWERING INFERNO

20th Century-Fox (domestic); Warner Bros. (foreign), 1974

ALL-RELEASE EQUIVALENT 2005 $s

(Unadjusted $s) in Millions of $s

Domestic Box Office Revenues . . . . **$362.4**/($107.1)
Production Cost . . . . **$56.5**/($14.3)
Principal Photography . . . .**64** days estimated
5/8/1974–8/7/1974

Director . . . . John Guillermin, Irwin Allen

Producer . . . . Irwin Allen

Production Company . . . . Irwin Allen Productions

Story by . . . . Based on the novels *The Tower* by Richard Martin Stern, and *The Glass Inferno*, by Thomas N. Scortia and Frank M. Robinson

Screenplay by . . . . Stirling Silliphant

Cast . . . . Steve McQueen, Paul Newman, William Holden, Faye Dunaway

Filming Locations . . . . . . 20th Century Fox Ranch, Malibu Creek State Park, CA; Hyatt Regency Hotel, San Francisco, CA; Bank of America Building, San Francisco, CA; 20th Century-Fox back lot Century City, CA

Genre . . . . Disaster

Format . . . . Color (DeLuxe)

Initial Release . . . . 12/10/1974 premiere (New York); 12/14/1974 general release

Rerelease . . . . none

Running Time . . . . 165 mintues

MPAA Rating . . . . PG

STANDING THE TEST OF TIME

ACADEMY AWARD Oscar Nominations and Wins

Best Picture: Irwin Allen, Producer

Actor in a Supporting Role: Fred Astaire

Art Direction/Set Decoration: William Creber, Ward Preston/Raphael Bretton

*CINEMATOGRAPHY: Fred Koenekamp, Joseph Biroc

*FILM EDITING: Harold F. Kress, Carl Kress

Music (Original Dramatic Score): John Williams

*MUSIC (Song): "We May Never Love Like This Again," Music and Lyrics by Al Kasha and Joel Hirschhorn

Sound: Theodore Soderberg, Herman Lewis

OSCAR TOTALS Nominations **8** *Wins 3

AFI 100 YEARS 100 MOVIES SELECTION

2007 0   1997 0

TOP 300 FILMS POSITION . . . . **#60**

All-Release Domestic Box Office in Equivalent 2005 $s

National Film Preservation Board Selection . . . . none

OTHER AWARDS Best Picture Wins

	Year
Golden Globes	none
New York Film Critics	none
National Board of Review	none
Film Daily Critics	none

We formed an amalgamation to create a single blockbuster script from the two books . . . I'm quite sure it is the first of many future films to be created in tandem by major companies.

—Irwin Allen, on the Fox and Warner Bros. co-financing deal

PLOT: High above the city of San Francisco, a gala event is under way to celebrate the opening of the world's tallest building. Meanwhile, fifty floors below, a fierce fire rages out of control. An architect and a fire chief must put out the fire and rescue the people trapped inside.

PRODUCTION: After the incredible success of *The Poseidon Adventure* (1972), Hollywood studios sought out the next big disaster epic. Producer Irwin Allen and 20th Century-Fox began an intense bidding war with Warner Bros. for rights to the soon-to-be-published novel *The Tower*. Warner Bros. eventually outbid Fox and went into production on a film about a deadly fire that breaks out in the world's tallest building. Allen, never one to be outdone, soon rushed into pre-production on his own movie, based on a very similar novel titled *The Glass Inferno*. As a race to complete the two movies seemed more and more inevitable, Allen began to realize that releasing such similar stories simultaneously would be tantamount to financial suicide for both parties. He therefore arranged a meeting with the heads of Fox and Warner and struck a historic deal, making *The Towering Inferno* the first-ever co-production between two major studios. 20th Century-Fox and Warner Bros. combined elements from the two novels into a single story, and split both the cost and any ensuing profits. With the power of two major studios behind him, Allen was given a budget of $14 million (nearly three times the cost of *The Poseidon Adventure*) to make the movie. Irwin Allen was one of the few producers prepared to bring a production this massive to the big screen. With a crew of thousands, he and co-director John Guillermin took over eight of the largest soundstages on the 20th Century-Fox lot in order to create the 138-story superstructure that would serve as the film's backdrop. The biggest challenge they faced on set was shooting the film's dangerous and complicated climax, in which the building's sprawling Promenade Room is flooded in a last-ditch effort to extinguish the rapidly encroaching fire. In order to shoot the scene, an impressive set covering more than 11,000 square feet with a 340-foot cyclorama of the San Francisco skyline surrounding it was built. It was constructed a full twenty-five feet above the ground so that the nearly 1 million gallons of water it was to be flooded with could easily run off without presenting a considerable threat for the actors. The flooding scene was the largest and most treacherous in the film, and serves as the best example of the incredible risks faced by both cast and crew on a daily basis. When filming finally wrapped on September 11, 1974, more than 200 stunts had been required, many actors had sustained injuries, and only eight of the film's fifty-seven sets were still intact.

DISTRIBUTION: Boasting the talents of two of Hollywood's biggest leading men in Paul Newman and Steve McQueen, *The Towering Inferno* was poised to be a box office hit. It was released on December 10, 1974, and although it received mixed reviews, the film was an immediate success. Audiences flocked to theaters in record numbers and, in a theatrical run that lasted nearly a year, the film went on to gross more than $48 million in domestic rentals. —*Mark D'Anna*

THE GODFATHER PART II

Paramount, 1974

ALL-RELEASE EQUIVALENT 2005 $s

(Unadjusted $s) in Millions of $s

Domestic Box Office Revenues . . . . **$161.2**/($47.5)
Production Cost . . . .**$56.3**/($14.2)
Principal Photography . . . .**180** days estimated
10/1/1973–6/19/1974

Director . . . . Francis Ford Coppola
Producer . . . . Francis Ford Coppola
Production Company . . . . The Coppola Company
Story by . . . . Based on the novel by
Mario Puzo
Screenplay by . . . . Francis Ford Coppola,
Mario Puzo
Cast . . . . Al Pacino, Robert Duvall,
Diane Keaton, Robert De Niro,
Talia Shire, Michael V. Gazzo,
John Cazale, Mariana Hill,
Lee Strasberg
Filming Locations . . . . . . On location in Manhattan, NY;
Washington D.C.; Lake Tahoe,
Los Angeles, CA; Trieste and
Sicily, Italy; Las Vegas, NV;
Miami, FL; Santo Domingo,
Dominican Republic
Genre . . . . Crime
Format . . . . Color (Technicolor)
Initial Release . . . . 12/12/1974 premiere
(New York); 12/20/1974
general release
Rerelease . . . . none
Running Time . . . . 200 minutes
MPAA Rating . . . . R

STANDING THE TEST OF TIME

ACADEMY AWARD Oscar Nominations and Wins

*__BEST PICTURE:__ Francis Ford Coppola, Producer;
Gray Frederickson and Fred Roos, Co-Producers

Actor: Al Pacino

*__ACTOR IN A SUPPORTING ROLE:__ Robert
De Niro

Actor in a Supporting Role: Michael V. Gazzo

Actor in a Supporting Role: Lee Strasberg

Actress in a Supporting Role: Talia Shire

*__ART DIRECTION/SET DECORATION:__ Dean
Tavoularis, Angelo Graham/George R. Nelson

Costume Design: Theadora Van Runkle

*__DIRECTING:__ Francis Ford Copppola

*__MUSIC__ (Original Dramatic Score): Nino Rota,
Carmine Coppola

*__WRITING__ (Screenplay adapted from other
material): Francis Ford Coppola, Mario Puzo

OSCAR TOTALS Nominations **11** *Wins **6**

AFI 100 YEARS 100 MOVIES SELECTION
2007 . . . #32   1997 . . . #32

TOP 300 FILMS POSITION . . . . .none
All-Release Domestic Box Office in Equivalent 2005 $s

National Film Preservation Board Selection 1993

OTHER AWARDS Best Picture Wins

	Year
Golden Globes	none
New York Film Critics	none
National Board of Review	none
Film Daily Critics	none

*It seemed to catch a greater spirit or dimension at least equal to the first film.
I think we achieved a movie that was a worthy successor to the first one.*

—Francis Ford Coppola

PLOT: The Corleone family moves west to support its new gambling interests. In a parallel story, young Vito Corleone arrives in America at the turn of the century and begins a fateful journey that will transform him into the Godfather.

PRODUCTION: *The Godfather* was so successful that Paramount became desperate for a sequel. But director Francis Ford Coppola's miserable experience on the first film made him loath to continue the story. He suggested that his friend Martin Scorsese do the film instead, but the studio declined. Finally persuaded by executive Charles Bludhorn to reconsider the assignment, Coppola made three demands: no studio involvement, a generous financial package, and the title: *The Godfather Part II.* The studio fought only the last point, but Coppola prevailed and introduced a numerical titling precedent that continues to this day. Coppola lost two key performers from the first film. Richard Castellano's negotiation to reprise the role of Peter Clemenza, a major figure in the upcoming story, ultimately broke down over Castellano's insistence on writing his own dialogue, a concession the director was unwilling to make. Coppola quickly reassigned Castellano's role to a new character, Frank Pentangeli. Playwright Michael V. Gazzo was cast the day before shooting began, and first appears in the film wearing a black armband memorializing Clemenza's death. Coppola had also hoped to lure Marlon Brando back for a flashback sequence at the end, but the actor was still smarting over the low payment for his services in the first film (he gave up a 10 percent profit participation for a total flat fee of $200,000), so Coppola was again forced to write out a character at the last minute. Director Elia Kazan was the first choice for mobster Hyman Roth but was unavailable, so, at Al Pacino's suggestion, the filmmakers cast legendary acting coach Lee Strasberg in his first film role ever. *The Godfather Part II* shoot was the polar opposite of the first film. The studio kept its word and left Coppola alone while the crew traveled across the United States, to Italy, and to the Dominican Republic, standing in for Batista-era Cuba. The production used the grounds and original buildings of the sumptuous 1939 Kaiser estate on Lake Tahoe as the Corleone family compound. Shortly after filming ended, the old main house was demolished so that condominiums could be built there. To recreate early twentieth-century Little Italy for the "young Vito" sequences, the crew transformed an entire New York City block: repaving it, removing lamps and air-conditioning units, and completely re-dressing both sides of the street. Eight years of movie time is depicted during the six-week shoot on the block, including the arrival of automobiles. The Ellis Island immigration center through which Vito enters America was built in a fish market in the Italian port city of Trieste, with the designers working from photographs of the period.

DISTRIBUTION: Paramount moved the release date on the *Godfather* sequel from March to December but maintained a similar release pattern, opening in five theaters before going wider. Nearly thirty minutes longer than its predecessor, the film played two fewer shows per day and brought in less than 40 percent of the first's total in worldwide box office. In November 1977, the *Godfather* saga was seen in another incarnation on NBC, when the network aired a combined, recut version of the two films over four nights in prime time, which told the story chronologically and added close to three-quarters of an hour of previously deleted material. —*Tom Dupree*

JAWS
Universal, 1975

ALL-RELEASE EQUIVALENT 2005 $s
(Unadjusted $s) in Millions of $s

Domestic Box Office Revenues....... **$802.9**/($260.0)
Production Cost .... **$44.1**/($12.2)
Principal Photography........... **159** days estimated
5/2/1974–9/15/1974

Director . . . . Steven Spielberg

Producer . . . . Richard D. Zanuck, David Brown

Production Company . . . . Universal Pictures, Zanuck/Brown Productions

Story by . . . . Based on the novel by Peter Benchley

Screenplay by . . . . Peter Benchley, Carl Gottlieb

Cast . . . . Roy Scheider, Robert Shaw, Richard Dreyfuss, Lorraine Gary, Murray Hamilton

Filming Locations . . . . . . Martha's Vineyard, Ma and Seal Rocks, Australia

Genre. . . . . Thriller

Format. . . . . Color (Technicolor)

Initial Release . . . . 6/20/1975 limited release; 7/25/1975 wide release

Rerelease. 1979

Running Time . . . . 124 minutes

MPAA Rating . . . . PG

STANDING THE TEST OF TIME

ACADEMY AWARD Oscar Nominations and Wins

Best Picture: Richard D. Zanuck and David Brown, Producers

***FILM EDITING:** Verna Fields

***MUSIC** (Original Score): John Williams

***SOUND:** Robert L. Hoyt, Roger Herman, Earl Madery, John Carter

OSCAR TOTALS   Nominations **4**   *Wins **3**

AFI 100 YEARS 100 MOVIES SELECTION
2007 . . . #56   1997 . . . #48

TOP 300 FILMS POSITION . . . . **#7**
All-Release Domestic Box Office in Equivalent 2005 $s

National Film Preservation Board Selection. . . . 2001

OTHER AWARDS Best Picture Wins

	Year
Golden Globes	none
New York Film Critics.	none
National Board of Review	none
Film Daily Critics	none

Spielberg didn't want to do [Jaws] at first. He said, "There are movies and there are films, and I want to make films." And we said, "Well, if this works, you can make films."

—David Brown

PLOT: A giant white shark terrorizes a New England resort during the height of the tourist season.

PRODUCTION: Peter Benchley's first novel spent forty-four weeks on the best-seller list, selling over 11 million copies. Producers Richard Zanuck and David Brown paid $150,000 for the film rights plus another $25,000 to Benchley for writing a script. Through several rewrites, extensive overtime, travel and accommodations, and a cameo appearance in the film, Benchley would eventually pocket about $250,000 (not including his 10 percent net profit participation, estimated to be worth $10 million). After Lee Marvin turned down Steven Spielberg's offer to play Quint, the director asked Sterling Hayden, who also had to decline: due to unpaid taxes, any income Hayden derived from the part would have been subject to a levy by the IRS. In the end, the part went to British actor Robert Shaw, who, coincidentally, was having tax problems of his own, and fled to Canada on his days off in fear of any contact with the IRS. *Jaws* had an initial budget of $3.5 million and a 55-day shooting schedule. However, there were so many misfortunes that the crew called the film "Flaws." For example, three animatronic sharks were built, each costing roughly $200,000, but none had been previously tested in the water. When the first "Bruce" (later nicknamed "the great white turd") made its debut off Martha's Vineyard, it sank thirty feet to the ocean floor, and a team of divers had to retrieve it. Another shark needed frequent repairs and was unavailable for certain shots. But the worst was yet to come. After the special effects team finished rigging Quint's Orca (a type of boat), it was so top-heavy that it was deemed unseaworthy. A large quantity of lead, which was needed as ballast, was rented at an exorbitant fee from a local dentist who was going to use it to shield his X-ray room. When actor Roy Scheider was trapped in Quint's sinking boat, it took seventy-five takes to get the shot right. While the on-screen boat was designed to sink, it proved more seaworthy than the film crew's Orca, which actually did sink. Divers managed to recover the camera and flew it, still submerged in seawater, to a Hollywood film lab, where, miraculously, technicians were able to save the film. The final cost exceeded $12 million and shooting ran 104 days over schedule. After two test screenings, Spielberg decided one last scream in the middle section was needed. The producers didn't want to pay for another day's shooting, so Spielberg footed the bill himself. The scene, involving Richard Dreyfuss, was shot in editor Verna Fields's swimming pool, with evaporated milk mixed into the water to make it look cloudy. The film was rushed to the next preview in Long Beach. The audience gave Spielberg the scream he wanted, but the day spent underwater gave Dreyfuss pneumonia.

DISTRIBUTION: Dreyfuss was quoted in *Time* magazine as saying that *Jaws* would be "the turkey of the year." But Universal liked the completed film so much that it began a TV advertising campaign that cost an unprecedented $700,000. The film opened on 490 screens, setting the standard for subsequent wide openings for Hollywood films. More than 67 million Americans went to see the movie (originally scheduled for a Christmas 1974 release), making it the first summer blockbuster. Spielberg stated that without John Williams's iconic score the film would have been only half as successful. —*Bob Canning*

THE ROCKY HORROR PICTURE SHOW
20th Century-Fox, 1975

ALL-RELEASE EQUIVALENT 2005 $s
(Unadjusted $s) in Millions of $s

Domestic Box Office Revenues........**$185.9**/($120.9)
Production Cost ....**$5.4**/($1.5)
Principal Photography............**44** days estimated
10/21/1974–12/19/1974

Director . . . . Jim Sharman

Producer . . . . Michael White

Production Company. . . . 20th Century-Fox Film Corp.

Story by . . . . Based on the rock stage musical
by Richard O'Brien

Screenplay by . . . . Jim Sharman, Richard O'Brien

Cast . . . . Tim Curry, Susan Sarandon,
Barry Bostwick, Richard
O'Brien, Jonathan Adams,
Nell Campbell, Peter Hinwood,
Meatloaf, Patricia Quinn,
Charles Gray

Filming Locations . . . . . . Shot at Bray Studios, Berkshire,
England

Genre. . . . . Musical

Format. . . . . Color (Eastmancolor)

Initial Release . . . . 8/14/1975 (UK); 9/26/1975 (U.S.)

Rerelease. . . . . Never out of theatrical release
in the U.S.

Running Time . . . . 100 minutes

MPAA Rating . . . . not rated

STANDING THE TEST OF TIME

ACADEMY AWARD Oscar Nominations and Wins
None

OSCAR TOTALS Nominations 0 *Wins 0

AFI 100 YEARS 100 MOVIES SELECTION
2007 0   1997 0

TOP 300 FILMS POSITION . . . . .none
All-Release Domestic Box Office in Equivalent 2005 $s

National Film Preservation Board Selection. . . . 2005

OTHER AWARDS Best Picture Wins

	Year
Golden Globes	none
New York Film Critics	none
National Board of Review	none
Film Daily Critics	none

*The Rocky Horror Picture Show would be more
fun, I suspect, if it weren't a picture show.*

—Roger Ebert, 1976

*Overall, however, most of the jokes that might
have seemed jolly fun on stage
now appear obvious and even flat.
The sparkle's gone.*

—*Daily Variety*, 1975

PLOT: When their car breaks down, newlyweds seek refuge in a mysterious castle, whose owner, an alien from the planet Transsexual, unveils his creation, a young man named Rocky Horror.

PRODUCTION: *Rocky Horror* first came to life as a stage production at the Royal Court Theatre Upstairs in London in June 1973. Written by English actor Richard O'Brien, the play is based on a combination of 1950s horror movies, pop musicals, and muscle movies. The show ran for months in London and was a smashing critical and commercial success, ultimately being named Best Musical of 1973 by the *London Evening Standard.* Producer Lou Adler saw the play and acquired American rights, opening it in Los Angeles, where it was a cult hit. Tim Curry, who had starred in London, was also the lead in L.A. That led to a deal with 20th Century-Fox to create a feature film version of the show. A stage version mounted on Broadway just before the movie was released was not successful and closed after a short run. The film was shot in and around Berkshire, England, with a minuscule budget that is more reminiscent of what one might expect to find on an independent film rather than a major studio release. The first set was a broken-down Victorian mansion at Oakley Court–Bray Studios. The production took about nine weeks and used sets that were often crude in appearance. There were campy performances by actors who were complete unknowns and a bizarre story line, which many critics felt was far better suited to musical theater than the big screen. Most of the original cast from London reprised their roles, including Tim Curry, Richard O'Brien, and Patricia Quinn. Newcomers Susan Sarandon and Barry Bostwick were cast as the newlyweds. When it was completed and a trailer for the film was screened by a high-ranking studio executive, he is rumored to have shouted, "Remove those lewd, lascivious lips mouthing the words 20th Century-Fox." History would, however, later reveal those lips to be among the most lasting and iconic images from a groundbreaking movie.

DISTRIBUTION: Initially released according to a very traditional strategy in mainstream movie houses, *The Rocky Horror Picture Show* was a critical and commercial failure. It wasn't until executive producer Lou Adler and Fox marketing executive Tim Deegan noticed that a small group of regulars were returning for multiple viewings of the film that the idea of staging midnight screenings was first presented. Introduced in New York City with little advertising, the midnight events and the word-of-mouth support they received made the film an underground cult sensation. Screenings have since evolved into a legitimate audience participation extravaganza, encompassing detailed props, sexually explicit costumes, a full-length audience script in which sarcastic retorts are shouted to characters on-screen, and even live action scene reenactments staged during viewings of the movie. It has now been playing continuously in theaters since 1975, making it the longest theatrical run in movie history. —*Mark D'Anna*

ONE FLEW OVER THE CUCKOO'S NEST

United Artists, 1975

ALL-RELEASE EQUIVALENT 2005 $s

(Unadjusted $s) in Millions of $s

Domestic Box Office Revenues........**$350.2**/($112.0)
Production Cost ....**$16.0**/($4.4)
Principal Photography............**60** days estimated
1/6/1975–March 1975
10 week shoot

Director	Milos Forman
Producer	Saul Zaentz, Michael Douglas
Production Company	Fantasy Films (The Saul Zaentz Company)
Story by	Based on the novel by Ken Kesey
Screenplay by	Lawrence Hauben, Bo Goldman
Cast	Jack Nicholson, Louise Fletcher, William Redfield, Danny DeVito, Will Sampson, Christopher Lloyd
Filming Locations	Shot entirely on location in Depoe Bay and Salem, OR
Genre	Drama
Format	Color (DeLuxe)
Initial Release	11/15/1975
Rerelease	none
Running Time	133 minutes
MPAA Rating	R

STANDING THE TEST OF TIME

ACADEMY AWARD Oscar Nominations and Wins

*__BEST PICTURE:__** Saul Zaentz and Michael Douglas, Producers

*__ACTOR:__** Jack Nicholson

Actor in a Supporting Role: Brad Dourif

*__ACTRESS:__** Louise Fletcher

Cinematography: Haskell Wexler, Bill Butler

*__DIRECTING:__** Milos Forman

Film Editing: Richard Chew, Lynzee Klingman, Sheldon Kahn

Music (Original Score): Jack Nitzsche

*__WRITING__** (Screenplay – adapted from other material): Lawrence Hauben, Bo Goldman

OSCAR TOTALS Nominations **9** *Wins **5**

AFI 100 YEARS 100 MOVIES SELECTION
2007 . . . #33   1997 . . . #20

TOP 300 FILMS POSITION . . . . #71
All-Release Domestic Box Office in Equivalent 2005 $s

National Film Preservation Board Selection. . . . 1993

OTHER AWARDS Best Picture Wins

	Year
Golden Globes (Drama)	1976
New York Film Critics	none
National Board of Review	none
Film Daily Critics	none

We'd borrow from the record company. There wasn't a record company making these pictures but the record company knew us 'cause we were—the record company.

—Saul Zaentz on how he got the money from Fantasy Records to make *One Flew over the Cuckoo's Nest*

PLOT: When he's sent to a mental institution after several stints in jail, the rebellious McMurphy bands the apathetic patients together and urges them to defy the strict routine of the institution and Nurse Ratched.

PRODUCTION: Ken Kesey's first novel was based on his experiences working the night shift at the Menlo Park Veterans' Hospital, where experiments with hallucinogenic drugs were carried out on volunteer patients. Kirk Douglas held the rights to the 1962 best seller for many years, and originally wanted to play McMurphy. Douglas sent the novel to Milos Forman, but the director never received the book, which was likely confiscated by Czech customs. Years later, Douglas passed the rights to his son, Michael, who teamed up with producer Saul Zaentz to get the film off the ground. Once again Forman was approached. When he agreed this time, it occurred to Douglas that the Czech director had never received the book sent to him ten years earlier. Finding a mental institution to shoot in proved difficult, as most facilities saw Kesey's book as a threat. In order to shoot in the Oregon State Hospital in Salem, the hospital director made a deal with the filmmakers: they could shoot in his hospital if they allowed actual inmates to be part of the crew (i.e., wrangling cable, cleaning, etc.). Since the major Hollywood studios were reluctant to finance a film about mental illness, Zaentz underwrote the project through his Fantasy Films Company. The projected budget was $2 million, but when Nicholson was cast, that number doubled. By self-financing the movie, Zaentz benefited from the 1971 Revenue Act, which allowed investment in films to qualify for a tax credit as long as they were produced in the United States. Like *Five Easy Pieces* and *Taxi Driver, One Flew over the Cuckoo's Nest* was financed using tax shelter money. Shooting began on January 6, 1975, in Oregon, and was Czech director Milos Forman's first English-language film. With the exception of a few scenes, the film was shot in sequence on location. During production, Forman made his lead actors shadow actual patients, many of whom were extras, because Forman thought it would add to the authenticity of the film. The director of the Oregon State Hospital, Dean R. Brooks, played the hospital director in the film. Many of his scenes with Nicholson were improvised.

DISTRIBUTION: The film swept the 1975 Academy Awards and was the second film (after *It Happened One Night,* 1934) to win in all major categories: Best Picture, Best Director, Best Adapted Screenplay, Best Actor, and Best Actress. *One Flew over the Cuckoo's Nest* was a critical and box office smash and was the Saul Zaentz Company's most profitable film, making over $15 million in net profits. Kesey was consulted on creating the movie, but he left two weeks into production over a dispute about the $20,000 he was paid for film rights. Kesey also strongly disagreed with the decision not to make the character of Chief Bromden the narrator, as he had been in the novel. When the movie opened, Kesey refused to see it and publicly criticized Forman for his interpretation of the story. A stage version was adapted for Broadway by Dale Wasserman in 1963. —*Dina Gachman*

TAXI DRIVER
Columbia, 1976

ALL-RELEASE EQUIVALENT 2005 $s
(Unadjusted $s) in Millions of $s

Domestic Box Office Revenues . . . . **$83.6**/($28.3)
Production Cost . . . . **$6.5**/($1.9)
Principal Photography . . . . **40** days
June 1975–September 1975

Director . . . . Martin Scorsese
Producer . . . . Michael and Julia Phillips
Production Company . . . . Bill/Phillips Production,
Columbia Pictures
Story and
Screenplay by . . . . Paul Schrader
Cast . . . . Robert De Niro, Cybill
Shepherd, Peter Boyle,
Albert Brooks, Leonard Harris,
Harvey Keitel, Jodie Foster
Filming Locations . . . . . . Around New York City,
including 13th St. between
2nd and 3rd Ave. in
Manhattan; 3rd Ave. between
13th and 14th St.; Ed Sullivan
Theater, 1697 Broadway;
brothel was at 226 13th St;
assassination attempt in
Central Park at Merchant's
Gate, 59th St. at Columbus
Circle
Genre . . . . Drama
Format . . . . Color (Metrocolor)
Initial Release . . . . 2/8/1976 premiere, Cinema I
(New York)
Rerelease 1996
Running Time . . . . 113 minutes
MPAA Rating . . . . R

STANDING THE TEST OF TIME

ACADEMY AWARD Oscar Nominations and Wins

Best Picture: Michael Phillips and Julia Phillips,
Producers
Actor in a Leading Role: Robert De Niro
Actress in a Supporting Role: Jodie Foster
Music (Original Score): Bernard Herrmann

OSCAR TOTALS Nominations **4** *Wins **0**

AFI 100 YEARS 100 MOVIES SELECTION
2007 . . . #52   1997 . . . #47

TOP 300 FILMS POSITION . . . . .none
All-Release Domestic Box Office in Equivalent 2005 $s

National Film Preservation Board Selection 1994

OTHER AWARDS Best Picture Wins
	Year
Golden Globes	none
New York Film Critics	none
National Board of Review	none
Film Daily Critics	none

*The metaphor of taxi cab occurred to me as
metaphor of male drifting loneliness . . . I was
not unlike Travis Bickle, a bundle of tightly
wrapped contradictions, driving around,
trying but unable to belong.*

—Paul Schrader

PLOT: Psychotic Vietnam vet Travis Bickle, a taxi driver who is disgusted not only by what he sees on the streets but by his own failure at romance and his inability to save a child prostitute, buys several handguns to assassinate a senator and to achieve true infamy.

PRODUCTION: With his career as a film critic stalled and his marriage broken, Paul Schrader found himself alone, depressed, homeless, and suffering from a bleeding gastric ulcer. As he lay in a hospital bed, the idea for *Taxi Driver* came to him. When he got out, he spent ten intense days writing two drafts of the script, which he later said "jumped out at me like an animal." Schrader was inspired by Dostoevsky's 1864 novella *Notes from the Underground,* a grim fable about an alienated man. He showed his script to Brian De Palma, who loved it and passed it on to producer Michael Phillips, who in turn passed it along to his wife, Julia Phillips, and Tony Bill, who optioned it for $1,000. (De Palma later received a point—a 1 percent net profit participation—as a finder's fee.) Within a few months, Bill and the Phillipses parted ways and the *Taxi Driver* project stayed with Julia and Michael Phillips. Marty Scorsese wanted to direct, but Julia Phillips refused until she saw *Mean Streets* and was instantly won over. She agreed under the condition that Scorsese get De Niro to star, which he did. Warner Bros. passed when the budget rose above $750,000. Columbia head David Begelman hated Schrader's script but okayed the picture after the Phillipses' movie *The Sting* became a huge hit and won a Best Picture Oscar and after the Phillipses agreed to also produce *Close Encounters of the Third Kind.* Both movies went into production at the same time, with Julia overseeing *Close Encounters* and Michael overseeing *Taxi Driver.* Scorsese later described the production schedule as "40 days and 40 nights." It was shot on a tight budget during a stifling heat wave in a crumbling city suffering a recession. De Niro prepared by actually driving a cab and interviewing U.S. soldiers and the mentally ill. Scorsese had previously cast Jodie Foster and loved her "Lauren Bacall voice." Her older sister was signed as a body double. Prior to shooting, Foster, then twelve, had to meet with a psychiatrist, who ruled her mentally fit to play the part. Harvey Keitel met with actual pimps and improvised his dance scene with Iris. De Niro improvised the scene where he looks in the mirror and asks, "Are you talkin' to me?" Scorsese later said he was influenced by Alfred Hitchcock in *The Wrong Man* when creating Bickle's POV. The Phillipses feared the movie would get an X rating (which meant Columbia wouldn't release it), mostly because of the bloody ending. Scorsese's solution was to wash out the bright color in the end sequence, especially the red blood. It worked. The MPAA ratings board gave the picture an R.

DISTRIBUTION: *Taxi Driver* opened in New York and broke first- and second-day box office records. There were lines around the block. It grossed nearly $12 million in domestic rentals in its first release. Major critics praised it as a contemporary masterpiece, despite concerns over violence. An unwanted homage came in 1981 when John Hinckley, obsessed with Foster, imitated Bickle and tried to assassinate President Ronald Reagan. The film has been paid homage in several other movies, including Quentin Tarantino's *Reservoir Dogs* and the British movie *Trainspotting,* about young English drug addicts. —*Alex Ben Block*

ALL THE PRESIDENT'S MEN
Warner Bros., 1976

ALL-RELEASE EQUIVALENT 2005 $s
(Unadjusted $s) in Millions of $s

Domestic Box Office Revenues . . . . **$212.5**/($70.6)
Production Cost . . . .**$29.2**/($8.5)
Principal Photography . . . . **96** days estimated
5/12/1975–November 1975

Director . . . . Alan J. Pakula
Producer . . . . Walter Coblenz
Production Company . . . . Wildwood Enterprises
Story by . . . . Based on the book by Carl Bernstein and Bob Woodward
Screenplay by . . . . William Goldman
Cast . . . . Dustin Hoffman, Robert Redford
Filming Locations . . . . . . On location: Washington D.C. exteriors; in studio: Maryland sound stage and several stages at Warner Bros. Burbank Studios, CA
Genre . . . . Drama
Format . . . . Color (Technicolor)
Initial Release 4/9/1976
Rerelease . . . . none
Running Time . . . . 138 minutes
MPAA Rating . . . . PG

STANDING THE TEST OF TIME

ACADEMY AWARD Oscar Nominations and Wins

Best Picture: Walter Coblenz, Producer

***ACTOR IN A SUPPORTING ROLE:** Jason Robards

Actress in a Supporting Role: Jane Alexander

***ART DIRECTION/SET DECORATION:** George Jenkins/George Gaines

Directing: Alan J. Pakula

Film Editing: Robert L. Wolfe

***SOUND:** Arthur Piantadosi, Les Fresholtz, Dick Alexander, Jim Webb

***WRITING** (Screenplay – based on material from another medium): William Goldman

OSCAR TOTALS   Nominations 8   *Wins 4

AFI 100 YEARS 100 MOVIES SELECTION
2007 . . . #77   1997 . . . 0

TOP 300 FILMS POSITION . . . . #227
All-Release Domestic Box Office in Equivalent 2005 $s

National Film Preservation Board Selection . . . . none

OTHER AWARDS Best Picture Wins

	Year
Golden Globes	none
New York Film Critics	1976
National Board of Review	1976
Film Daily Critics	none

Redford assured Woodstein that his devotion to the material was as serious as their own, and he didn't wish to be laughed off the screen . . . Redford promised there would be nothing in the film to which they could reasonably object.

—Jack Hirshberg, *A Portrait of* All the President's Men

PLOT: A true story about two *Washington Post* reporters who investigate a break-in at Democratic Party headquarters and then follow clues, secret sources, and hunches until they discover crimes that lead all the way to the White House.

PRODUCTION: During a media junket aboard a train full of reporters for the 1972 drama *The Candidate,* it was star Robert Redford asking questions. He wanted to know why only the *Washington Post* was writing about a recent break-in at Democratic national headquarters. The veteran reporters responded with cynicism that the coverage would all be whitewashed. That angered Redford. Shortly after Richard Nixon was reelected in November 1972, Redford contacted the two *Post* journalists, Bob Woodward and Carl Bernstein (dubbed "Woodstein"), but they were too busy to talk. In April 1973, Redford finally got Woodward to meet him for dinner, along with screenwriter William Goldman. Redford wanted to make a movie about him, but Woodward countered that they already had a book deal and suggested that Redford wait. Published in 1974, the book was a best seller. Soon after, Warner Bros. joined with Redford to acquire screen rights for $350,000. Warner CEO Ted Calley had to make a nervous phone call to Warner chairman Steve Ross for permission, since Warner was involved in many government-regulated businesses. Ross asked Calley if he loved it. When he said that he did, Ross wished him good luck. At first, Redford planned a modest $2 million budget, but when preproduction costs passed $800,000, he saw it would require more money and that he would have to star. Goldman did research in Washington, and six weeks later delivered his script. Some of the action, however, was improvised on the set. Because news of the movie had people at the *Post* nervous about how they would be portrayed, Redford and his wife, Lola, soothed the concerns of *Post* owner Katharine Graham at a tense breakfast. Redford recruited co-star Dustin Hoffman with a phone call in October 1974 and in December signed Alan Pakula to direct, based on his work on *Klute.* Goldman's script used the pursuit of truth as the key to drama and suspense. Pakula added realism by shooting in a near documentary style. It was impractical to film in the *Washington Post* building, so an exact replica of the newsroom was built for $450,000 on two soundstages in Burbank (with a thirty-five-foot-high wall torn down to accommodate the 240-foot-long newsroom set). Plans to shoot at Woodward's real apartment and the Watergate Hotel also became impractical, so they rented a warehouse forty-five minutes away in Maryland, where two sets that had been constructed in Burbank were shipped. There were problems securing permits to shoot exteriors, especially near the White House. The film quickly fell behind schedule, but the studio gave them unusual latitude. Pakula and editor Bob Wolfe trimmed 79 hours of film down to a releasable length. Some scenes were shot with dioptric lenses, creating a split-screen effect. Cinematographer Gordon Willis lit the newspaper office like a deep cavern. Even music was used sparingly. There is no music soundtrack, just the sound of people and the clacking of typewriters.

DISTRIBUTION: The anticipation was unparalleled. Six months before release, Warner had booked $15 million in exhibitor guarantees. The movie was an immediate hit with audiences and critics. It became the year's third-biggest hit in domestic box office after *Rocky* and *King Kong. —Alex Ben Block*

ROCKY
United Artists, 1976

ALL-RELEASE EQUIVALENT 2005 $s
(Unadjusted $s) in Millions of $s

Domestic Box Office Revenues........ **$352.8**/($117.2)
Production Cost .... **$5.5**/($1.6)
Principal Photography............ **20** days estimated
1/9/1976–February 1976

Director .... John G. Avildsen
Producer .... Robert Chartoff, Irwin Winkler
Production Company.... Chartoff-Winkler Productions
Story and
  Screenplay by .... Sylvester Stallone
Cast .... Sylvester Stallone, Talia Shire, Burt Young, Carl Weathers, Burgess Meredith
Filming Locations ...... In Philadelphia: 1818 E. Tusculum St., Kensington; Fairmount Park; City Hall; Museum of Art, Pat's King of Steaks Restaurant; in Los Angeles: Gym at 318 S. Main St.; LA Sports Arena; Olympic Auditorium; Resurrection Gym; skating rink in Santa Monica, CA; Shamrock Meats in Vernon, CA
Genre................. Drama
Format............... Color (DeLuxe)
Initial Release 11/21/1976
Rerelease............. none
Running Time .... 119 minutes
MPAA Rating .... PG

STANDING THE TEST OF TIME

ACADEMY AWARD Oscar Nominations and Wins

*BEST PICTURE: Irwin Winkler and Robert Chartoff, Producers

Actor in a Leading Role: Sylvester Stallone

Actor in a Supporting Role: Burgess Meredith

Actor in a Supporting Role: Burt Young

Actress in a Leading Role: Talia Shire

*DIRECTING: John G. Avildsen

*FILM EDITING: Richard Halsey, Scott Conrad

Music (Original Song): "Gonna Fly Now," Music by Bill Conti; Lyrics by Carol Connors and Ayn Robbins

Sound: Harry Warren Tetrick, William McCaughey, Lyle Burbridge, Bud Alper

Writing (Screenplay Written Directly for the Screen – based on factual material or on story material not previously published or produced): Sylvester Stallone

OSCAR TOTALS Nominations **10** *Wins **3**

AFI 100 YEARS 100 MOVIES SELECTION
2007 . . . #57   1997. . . #78

TOP 300 FILMS POSITION .... **#66**
All-Release Domestic Box Office in Equivalent 2005 $s

National Film Preservation Board Selection. . . . 2006

OTHER AWARDS Best Picture Wins

	Year
Golden Globes (Drama).....................	1977
New York Film Critics.....................	none
National Board of Review.................	none
Film Daily Critics.........................	none

[UA's PR execs] told [the UA cochairman] about how this myth was created. The underdog myth. This Sylvester Stallone story. And they said, "Is that where it started? You mean my people started it? . . . You devil. You devil. This is a lot of sh—!" I said, "Right . . . But this is one of the things that got us here."

—Gabe Sumner at a party the night before the 1977 Oscars

PLOT: In an inspirational saga, Rocky Balboa, a Philadelphia debt collector and club fighter, gets to box for the world heavyweight championship because the fighter scheduled to face the champ breaks his hand. Outmatched, Rocky never gives up.

PRODUCTION: In the mid-1970s, Sylvester Stallone was having lunch with Gene Kirkwood, an executive for producers Irwin Winkler and Robert Chartoff, in the MGM commissary, discussing ideas for a script Stallone would write. Kirkwood became interested when Stallone told him about Chuck Wepner, an unknown boxer who had gotten his shot at the championship fighting Muhammad Ali. Stallone went home obsessed and over the next few days wrote the story, dictating it while his wife, Sasha, typed. Less than a week later, Stallone returned with his eighty-page script, which Kirkwood loved and passed on to Chartoff and Winkler, who loved it as well. They then spent six months rewriting. It was the first movie under the producer's new output deal at UA, which gave them creative freedom to make any movie under $1 million. When told about it, UA executives said that a boxing picture starring an unknown would be box office poison, and they forced the producers to cross-collateralize with another movie, meaning if either movie became a hit, UA got paid back. UA approved director John Avildsen because he had brought in the 1970 hit *Joe* for just $300,000. The budget was $1,075,000 plus producer's fees of $100,000. Stallone was paid $35,000 for the script, $20,000 as an actor, and 6.75 percent of net profits (which earned him over $2 million). Avildsen cut his fee to $50,000 in return for a share of profits. Talia Shire got $7,500. UA executives screened *Lords of Flatbush* to see what Stallone looked like but mistook Perry King for him. They first saw Stallone when the movie was assembled. As the budget rose, UA complained, but after a screening it not only put up the extra money but also funded reshoots requested by Avildsen. The final cost was $436,000 over budget. The first test screening was before a jaded industry crowd at MGM. UA's head of marketing, Gabe Sumner, flew in to observe. The audience loved it and gave *Rocky* a standing ovation at the end. An amazed Sumner reported back to New York that they had a hit and could ride it all the way to the Oscars. The UA brass thought he was crazy.

DISTRIBUTION: UA's strategy was to open in a few theaters so it would play in packed auditoriums, for maximum reaction. The advertising costs were $4.2 million, slightly higher than the $4 million UA spent on ads for *One Flew over the Cuckoo's Nest* in 1975. UA execs called Stallone to New York and directed him to spin a story to the media that was essentially an underdog myth. Stallone went on tour and told the story to reporters and critics about how UA had wanted his script but he wouldn't sell it, despite being broke and the studio's offer of $150,000, unless he could star. Finally, UA let him star and paid him $18,000. It was baloney, but Stallone told it with heart and the media ate it up. The idea that *Rocky* might win an Oscar seemed absurd at first, but Sumner thought it would be good promotion. So UA pushed up the release to qualify for Oscar consideration, and the fantasy came true. Rocky received ten nominations, including acting and writing honors for Stallone. On Oscar night, Stallone was passed over, but like a true underdog, *Rocky* pulled out Best Picture at the end. Bill Conti's stirring theme music was a hit and became a standard anthem at sporting events and business meetings. —*Alex Ben Block*

ANNIE HALL
United Artists, 1977

ALL-RELEASE EQUIVALENT 2005 $s
(Unadjusted $s) in Millions of $s

Domestic Box Office Revenues . . . . **$110.0**/($38.3)
Production Cost . . . . **$10.5**/($3.3)
Principal Photography . . . . not available
5/19/1976–February 1977

Director . . . . Woody Allen

Producer . . . . Charles H. Joffe

Production Company . . . . Jack Rollins and Charles H. Joffe Production

Story and Screenplay by . . . . Woody Allen, Marshall Brickman

Cast . . . . Woody Allen, Diane Keaton, Tony Roberts, Paul Simon, Carol Kane, Janet Margolin, Shelley Duvall, Christopher Walken, Jonathan Munk

Filming Locations . . . . . . Manhattan, Coney Island, The Bronx, Long Island, Brooklyn, The Hamptons, in New York State; Beverly Hills, West Hollywood, Los Angeles, and Palos Verdes in California

Genre . . . . Romantic Comedy

Format . . . . Color (DeLuxe)

Initial Release 4/20/1977

Rerelease . . . . none

Running Time . . . . 93 minutes

MPAA Rating . . . . PG

STANDING THE TEST OF TIME

ACADEMY AWARD Oscar Nominations and Wins

*BEST PICTURE: Charles H. Joffe, Producer

Actor in a Leading Role: Woody Allen

*ACTRESS IN A LEADING ROLE: Diane Keaton

*DIRECTING: Woody Allen

*WRITING (Screenplay Written Directly for the Screen): Woody Allen, Marshall Brickman

OSCAR TOTALS Nominations 5 *Wins 4

AFI 100 YEARS 100 MOVIES SELECTION
2007 . . . #35   1997 . . . #31

TOP 300 FILMS POSITION . . . . none
All-Release Domestic Box Office in Equivalent 2005 $s

National Film Preservation Board Selection 1992

OTHER AWARDS Best Picture Wins

	Year
Golden Globes	none
New York Film Critics	1977
National Board of Review	none
Film Daily Critics	none

It was originally a picture about me, exclusively, not about a relationship. But sometimes it's hard to foresee at the outset what's going to be the most interesting drift. The guesses we started out with, many of them were wrong. But we wound up with the right guesses.

—Woody Allen

PLOT: Joke writer, stand-up comic, and intellectual Alvy Singer plods neurotically through New York City until he meets a ditzy, adorable midwestern girl named Annie Hall and discovers the pleasures and exasperations of true romance.

PRODUCTION: Woody Allen first conceived *Annie Hall* with writer Marshall Brickman after having just returned to America from making *Love and Death* in France and Yugoslavia. They first added the Annie and Alvy characters to a murder mystery plot that Allen had been long mulling, about a college professor's apparent suicide. (This character would find its way to the screen later, in *Crimes and Misdemeanors*.) They also considered it as a period farce set in Victorian England before settling on a contemporary setting. As the screenplay emerged, it emphasized the Alvy character, for whom free-form associations trigger memories and other diversions from reality. For months the film was named for the condition of being clinically unable to enjoy pleasure, "Anhedonia"—a title that United Artists executives hated. Allen had been away from his beloved Manhattan for two years, both on *Love and Death* and the earlier *Sleeper,* which was shot in Colorado and California. He was now determined to base his productions in New York City, and beginning with *Annie Hall,* for the better part of three decades he did just that. He enlisted the aid of master cinematographer Gordon Willis, who also shot the *Godfather* and Allen's black-and-white masterpiece *Manhattan.* Allen considered *Annie Hall* an artistic turning point in his career, because he learned much more about the technical craft as he worked with Willis, and also because he emerged from the period of "clowning around" in his previous films to a place where he could now include more serious themes alongside the comedy. *Annie Hall* characters would talk directly to the camera, transform into animated cartoons, and observe other actors playing themselves—all to illuminate Alvy's fragile psychological makeup in thoroughly unexpected ways. The carefully scouted New York locations would become a mark of Allen's work. He and Willis managed to celebrate the splendors of the city—despite the severe financial crisis New York was experiencing—while they told their story.

DISTRIBUTION: The first cut of the film, 2 hours 20 minutes, was vastly different from what we see today. That cut no longer exists. Allen had shot all the murder mystery footage, but only after initial test screenings did he realize that audiences were impatient to get back to the central love story. Years later, co-editor Ralph Rosenblum called the initial unedited footage a "chaotic collection of bits and pieces that seemed to defy continuity." Allen and his editing team jettisoned material unnecessary to the Alvy-and-Annie story. Reaction to the recut film was immediate and positive. Audiences responded so heartily that Ruth Morley's boldly casual costumes for Diane Keaton as Annie created a fashion trend, inspiring designers such as Ralph Lauren to market the "Annie Hall look" for years afterward. Because the Alvy character so resembled the public perception of Woody Allen, and because he was formerly romantically attached to Diane Keaton, whose real last name is Hall and who also went by the nickname "Annie," some have suggested that the film is at least partly autobiographical. The director denies this. *Annie Hall* made a net profit of $13 million on $29 million in worldwide rentals. —*Tom Dupree*

STAR WARS: EP IV A NEW HOPE

20th Century-Fox, 1977

ALL-RELEASE EQUIVALENT 2005 $s

(Unadjusted $s) in Millions of $s

Domestic Box Office Revenues...... **$1,085.1**/($461.0)
Production Cost .... **$41.9**/($13.0)
Principal Photography.................... **84** days
3/22/1976–7/16/1976

Director . . . . George Lucas

Producer . . . . Gary Kurtz

Production Company. . . . Lucasfilm Ltd.

Story and
Screenplay by . . . . George Lucas

Cast . . . . Peter Cushing, Carrie Fisher, Harrison Ford, Alec Guinness, Mark Hamill

Filming Locations . . . . . . 62 days EMI studio, UK; 8 days Shepperaton studio, UK; 14 days on location Tunisia

Genre. . . . . Sci-Fi

Format. . . . . Color (Technicolor)

Initial Release 5/25/1977

Rerelease. 1978, 1979, 1981, 1982, 1997

Running Time . . . . 121 minutes

MPAA Rating . . . . PG

STANDING THE TEST OF TIME

ACADEMY AWARD Oscar Nominations and Wins

Best Picture: Gary Kurtz, Producer

Actor in a Supporting Role: Alec Guinness

***ART DIRECTION/SET DECORATION:** John Barry, Norman Reynolds, Leslie Dilley/Roger Christian

***COSTUME DESIGN:** John Mollo

Directing: George Lucas

***FILM EDITING:** Paul Hirsch, Marcia Lucas, Richard Chew

***MUSIC** (Original Score): John Williams

***SOUND:** Don MacDougall, Ray West, Bob Minkler, Derek Ball

***VISUAL EFFECTS:** John Stears, John Dykstra, Richard Edlund, Grant McCune, Robert Blalack

Writing (Screenplay – written directly for the screen): George Lucas

***SPECIAL ACHIEVEMENT AWARD:** Benjamin Burtt Jr.

OSCAR TOTALS   Nominations **11** *Wins 7

AFI 100 YEARS 100 MOVIES SELECTION
2007 . . . #13   1997 . . . #15

TOP 300 FILMS POSITION . . . . #2
All-Release Domestic Box Office in Equivalent 2005 $s

National Film Preservation Board Selection. . . . 1989

OTHER AWARDS Best Picture Wins

	Year
Golden Globes	none
New York Film Critics.	none
National Board of Review	none
Film Daily Critics	none

I had visions of R2-D2 mugs and little wind-up robots, but I thought that would be the end of it.

—George Lucas

PLOT: Joining forces with a wise Jedi master and a space pirate, young Luke Skywalker sets off to rescue a kidnapped princess and overthrow an evil galactic Empire.

PRODUCTION: In 1973 George Lucas began shopping a thirteen-page treatment for a mythic sci-fi action adventure film called "The Star Wars," set in the thirty-third century and featuring a sixty-year-old Luke Skywalker. Universal and United Artists passed on it, but 20th Century-Fox's Alan Ladd Jr. offered Lucas $10,000 to develop the screenplay. As Lucas wrote for two years, he began pouring his own money into development by commissioning Ralph McQuarrie and Colin Cantwell to create preliminary artwork, founding Industrial Light & Magic (ILM) to produce the effects, and hiring Willard Huyck and Gloria Katz to polish the dialogue. At one point, Lucas passed up more points to retain ancillary rights, including sequels and merchandising. He had spent over $400,000 when final approval for the $8.2 million budget came in 1976. As shooting loomed, Lucas held months of casting sessions, part of them simultaneously with Brian De Palma for his horror film *Carrie*. Many of the actors were jointly up for parts in both films. Harrison Ford got the role of Han Solo by initially helping other actors read. Shooting began on March 22, 1976, in Tunisia, where sets were being built up to eight weeks prior. Searing heat, powerful winds and sandstorms, broken machines, unwieldy costumes, cast injuries, and a freak rainstorm slowed production. On April 7, shooting shifted to England's Elstree Studios, where a record heat wave, strict union crews, and Hamill's eye injury, which prevented close-ups until the final days of shooting, further derailed production. Rushing to meet deadlines, Lucas had three full crews working at one point. As production lagged, Fox shifted the original release from Christmas 1976 to summer 1977. By the end of principal photography, ILM had spent one year and half of its budget to produce an array of innovative technology, but little else. They were pushed to the limit to create more than 360 effects shots by the release date. Lucas fired his first editor, sparking Richard Chew and Paul Hirsch to work around the clock with Lucas and his wife, Marcia, to recut. The intense workload put Lucas in the hospital for hypertension, but he continued nonetheless. Reshoots back in America were complicated when Mark Hamill mangled his face in a car wreck, causing Lucas to film pickups with a double.

DISTRIBUTION: To pump up prerelease interest, Lucas and Charles Lippincott inventively tapped sci-fi conventions and released a comic book and a novelization. Despite positive preview screenings, Fox still tried to force exhibitors to book *Star Wars* in order to get *The Other Side of Midnight*. The film opened to long lines at 10:00 a.m. on May 25, 1977. A stunned Lucas first saw the lines snaking around Mann's Chinese Theater while eating nearby. Critics gushed enthusiastically, and audiences went virtually crazy—skipping work, trying to sneak in, holding picnics in line, and staying for repeat viewings. It played in some theaters for a solid year. The 1997 rerelease boasted enhanced digital sound and effects and new footage, including an originally incomplete scene between Jabba the Hutt and Han. —*Scott Mazak*

CLOSE ENCOUNTERS OF THE THIRD KIND

Columbia, 1977

ALL-RELEASE EQUIVALENT 2005 $s

(Unadjusted $s) in Millions of $s

Domestic Box Office Revenues . . . . **$424.1**/($156.6)
Production Cost . . . . **$62.8**/($19.5)
Principal Photography . . . . **100** days estimated
5 months starting May 1976
Reshoots April 1977

Director . . . . Steven Spielberg

Producer . . . . Julia and Michael Phillips

Production Company . . . . Columbia Pictures Corp.

Story and
  Screenplay by . . . . Steven Spielberg

Cast . . . . Richard Dreyfuss,
Francois Truffaut, Teri Garr,
Melinda Dillon

Filming Locations . . . . . . U.S. locations: Gillette, WY;
Mobile, AL; Mojave Desert, CA;
India location with 3,500 extras

Genre . . . . Sci-Fi

Format . . . . Color (Metrocolor)

Initial Release 11/16/1977

Rerelease . . . . 1980 (Special Edition)

Running Time . . . . 135 minutes (rerelease 132
minutes)

MPAA Rating . . . . PG

STANDING THE TEST OF TIME

ACADEMY AWARD Oscar Nominations and Wins

Actress in a Supporting Role: Melinda Dillon

Art Direction/Set Decoration: Joe Alves, Dan Lomino/
Phil Abramson

***CINEMATOGRAPHY:** Vilmos Zsigmond

Directing: Steven Spielberg

Film Editing: Michael Kahn

Music (Original Score): John Williams

Sound: Robert Knudson, Robert J. Glass,
Don MacDougall, Gene S. Cantamessa

Visual Effects: Roy Arbogast, Douglas Trumbull,
Matthew Yuricich, Gregory Jein, Richard Yuricich

***SPECIAL ACHIEVEMENT AWARD** (Sound
Effects Editing): Frank E. Warner

OSCAR TOTALS   Nominations **9**   *Wins **2**

AFI 100 YEARS 100 MOVIES SELECTION
2007 . . . 0   1997 . . . #64

TOP 300 FILMS POSITION . . . . #39
All-Release Domestic Box Office in Equivalent 2005 $s

National Film Preservation Board Selection 2007

OTHER AWARDS Best Picture Wins

	Year
Golden Globes	none
New York Film Critics	none
National Board of Review	none
Film Daily Critics	none

*Directing a movie with Truffaut on the set is like having Renoir around
when you're still painting by numbers.*

—Steven Spielberg

PLOT: While checking on a power outage one night, Roy Neary has a close encounter with UFOs, and becomes obsessed with finding out the truth about their existence.

PRODUCTION: *Close Encounters* began with a handshake in 1973 during production of Steven Spielberg's first feature, *The Sugarland Express,* when Spielberg and producers Michael and Julia Phillips discovered a shared interest in UFOs. Paul Schrader was among the writers who worked on the script. His version, called "Kingdom Come," was about an air force officer who is sent to prove UFOs don't exist, but he actually sees one and is abducted. Spielberg didn't like Schrader's script and fleshed out the story himself, using sketches and storyboards. Steve McQueen, Gene Hackman, Jack Nicholson, and James Caan were considered for the main role before Richard Dreyfuss was cast. The success of *Jaws* in 1975 catapulted Spielberg into the realm of Hollywood's top directors, allowing a then-troubled Columbia to take a chance on a big-budget film with a hot director. Spielberg spent a year working with an illustrator-conceptualist to come up with the look of the aliens and the spaceship. During preproduction location scouting, they settled on the Devil's Tower location in Wyoming as the perfect backdrop for the film's climax. J. Allen Hynek, an astronomer at Northwestern University, had originated the term "close encounters" in his book *The UFO Experience: A Scientific Inquiry,* and Spielberg invited him to serve as a technical consultant on the film. Columbia agreed to finance the project at $16 million. Cast and crew arrived in Mobile, Alabama, on May 30, 1976, to begin production, which stretched over the summer. The working title on the secretive set was "Watch the Skies," which was the last line of Howard Hawks's *The Thing.* The crew built the set for the film's climax with the mothership inside an airplane hanger. It was the largest indoor set ever made until that time. During the intense five-month shoot Spielberg lived in a Winnebago much of the time. Security was so tight that he was almost denied access to the set one day because he did not have his ID tag. The spaceships were all shot in post, and the special effects budget alone was approximately $3 million—a huge sum for the time. There were more than 200 shots that required special effects. The film came in over budget at $19.5 million.

DISTRIBUTION: Creating a marketing identity for *Close Encounters* was tricky, since no UFO movie had ever been attempted on this scale. Six months before the scheduled premiere, Columbia bought two-page "introductory" ads in twenty-seven major American newspapers. The campaign intensified as the premiere date neared, with ads appearing more regularly and long, mystifying trailers saturating theaters everywhere. The movie was one of the top films of 1977, bringing in $300 million at the box office worldwide. Because Spielberg had hurried through postproduction to make the 1977 release date set by Columbia, the cut of the film released to theaters didn't adhere to his initial vision of the film. In 1980 he reedited the film, giving audiences a chance to see inside the mothership, resulting in the 1980 special edition release and another $28 million in domestic box office. In 2003 the model of the mothership went on display at the Smithsonian Institution's National Air and Space Museum. —*Dina Gachman*

SATURDAY NIGHT FEVER

Paramount, 1977

ALL-RELEASE EQUIVALENT 2005 $s

(Unadjusted $s) in Millions of $s

Domestic Box Office Revenues . . . . **$435.0**/($159.8)
Production Cost . . . . **$10.3**/($3.2)
Principal Photography . . . . not available
3/14/1977–unknown

Director . . . . John Badham
Producer . . . . Robert Stigwood
Production Company . . . . Paramount Productions
Story by . . . . Based on a magazine article by Nik Cohn
Screenplay by . . . . Norman Wexler
Cast . . . . John Travolta, Karen Gorney
Filming Locations . . . . . . 100 percent on location in New York City
Genre . . . . Drama
Format . . . . Color (Movielab)
Initial Release 12/16/1977
Rerelease 1979
Running Time . . . . 119 minutes (R version); 113 minutes (PG version)
MPAA Rating . . . . R

STANDING THE TEST OF TIME

ACADEMY AWARD Oscar Nominations and Wins

Actor in a Leading Role: John Travolta

OSCAR TOTALS Nominations **1** *Wins 0

AFI 100 YEARS 100 MOVIES SELECTION
2007 0   1997 0

TOP 300 FILMS POSITION . . . . **#35**
All-Release Domestic Box Office in Equivalent 2005 $s

National Film Preservation Board Selection . . . . none

OTHER AWARDS Best Picture Wins

	Year
Golden Globes	none
New York Film Critics	none
National Board of Review	none
Film Daily Critics	none

*The brilliant thing about John Travolta is that he was able to make you
like a character who is basically unlikable.*

—John Badham

PLOT: Teenager Tony Manero is only a clerk in a Brooklyn hardware store, but whenever he visits the local disco, his dance moves make him a hero. Now he has to face the uncertain onset of adult responsibility.

PRODUCTION: A 1975 article in *New York* magazine, "Tribal Rites of the New Saturday Night" by Nik Cohn, reported on the underground disco scene, though Cohn later admitted he had almost completely fabricated the piece. Australian music mogul Robert Stigwood's assistant had gotten an advance look, and by the time the magazine was published, Stigwood already owned the film rights. John Travolta's manager noticed the piece as well and told his client it would be perfect for him, unaware that a movie was already in the works. Travolta had a huge following from the popular TV sitcom *Welcome Back, Kotter* but wanted to do movies. In winter 1976, Stigwood hired director John G. Avildsen, whose *Rocky* was receiving prerelease praise. Travolta, meanwhile, began an intense regimen under dance coach Denny Terrio and his personal trainer. Nine months later and twenty pounds lighter, Travolta had become such a superb disco dancer that *Saturday Night Fever* choreographer Lester Wilson incorporated many of the actor's moves. Travolta and Avildsen clashed over the script: the director wanted to soften the lead character, but the darkness swirling around Tony Manero was what attracted Travolta in the first place. Tension continued to rise until Stigwood fired Avildsen and brought in John Badham, who had only two and a half weeks to prep before the March 14, 1977, start date. The movie was shot by Ralf D. Bode in a real disco with filters, smoke, and other devices to augment the club's strobes and mirror ball. Four years before MTV, it established a new direction for the film musical, with images cut to the beat of the music. Huge crowds descended on the Brooklyn location to catch a glimpse of Travolta, forcing the production to shut down in frustration at noon on the first day because there was no way to avoid showing thousands of onlookers. The producers began putting out fake call sheets and rushing to the genuine location to get street shots before being inundated by Travolta's fans. Travolta also faced a personal tragedy as his beloved girlfriend, Diana Hyland, battled breast cancer. She passed away less than two weeks into the shoot. Travolta continued on by sheer force of will. When he saw the first rough cut, he was devastated: his solo dance in the disco, which he had worked on for nine months, had been cut in close-up. He successfully lobbied to reedit the scene to favor master shots that would show his footwork, producing one of the most arresting sequences in the film.

DISTRIBUTION: Paramount felt the picture was vulgar, with its nudity, swearing, and drug use. The filmmakers also feared a backlash was developing against disco itself. But when *Saturday Night Fever* was released in December, it became an immediate hit and ushered an iconic disco look and sound into the popular culture. Worldwide, it was the third-highest-grossing movie of 1977 after *Star Wars* and *Close Encounters of the Third Kind*. The soundtrack, featuring music by the Bee Gees, produced six number-one singles and sold 35 million copies worldwide. A PG-rated edit for broadcast TV was released the following year. —*Tom Dupree*

GREASE

Paramount, 1978

ALL-RELEASE EQUIVALENT 2005 $s

(Unadjusted $s) in Millions of $s

Domestic Box Office Revenues........**$520.5**/($207.3)
Production Cost ....**$18.0**/($6.0)
Principal Photography............**63** days estimated
June 1977–September 1977

Director . . . . Randal Kleiser

Producer . . . . Robert Stigwood, Allan Carr

Production Company . . . . Paramount Pictures

Story by . . . . Based on the original 1972 musical by Jim Jacobs and Warren Casey

Screenplay by . . . . Bronte Woodard, adaptation by Allan Carr

Cast . . . . John Travolta, Olivia Newton-John, Stockard Channing

Filming Locations . . . . . . Burbank, Huntington Park, downtown Los Angeles, Los Feliz, Malibu, and Venice, CA; Paramount Studios, Hollywood, CA

Genre . . . . Musical

Format . . . . Color (Metrocolor)

Initial Release . . . . 6/4/1978 world premiere, Grauman's Chinese Theatre (Hollywood, CA); 6/13/1978 premiere (New York); 6/16/1978 wide release

Rerelease 1980, 1998

Running Time . . . . 110 minutes

MPAA Rating . . . . PG

STANDING THE TEST OF TIME

ACADEMY AWARD Oscar Nominations and Wins

Music (Original Song): "Hopelessly Devoted to You," Music and Lyrics by John Farrar

OSCAR TOTALS   Nominations **1**   *Wins **0**

AFI 100 YEARS 100 MOVIES SELECTION

2007 0   1997 0

TOP 300 FILMS POSITION . . . . **#22**

All-Release Domestic Box Office in Equivalent 2005 $s

National Film Preservation Board Selection . . . .none

OTHER AWARDS Best Picture Wins

	Year
Golden Globes	none
New York Film Critics	none
National Board of Review	none
Film Daily Critics	none

We already have $15 million in advances and a sale to ABC. The '50s never went away, they just came back stronger than ever. Grease is the definitive '50s musical comedy. Boom. That's it. Thank you very much.

—Allan Carr

PLOT: Set in the late 1950s, a brief summertime romance between wholesome Australian exchange student Sandy Olsson and leather-jacketed gang leader Danny Zuko is unexpectedly rekindled as both start the new school year at Rydell High.

PRODUCTION: Jim Jacobs and Warren Casey's rollicking play focusing on teen romance, angst, and social status in high school in the late 1950s was first staged in 1971 in Chicago. In 1972, expanded into a full-blown musical, *Grease* hit New York and, propelled by glowing reviews, played its way through four different theaters over eight years before ending its 3,388-performance run in 1980. Talent-manager-turned-producer Allan Carr saw *Grease* on Broadway in the early 1970s and was able to snap up the option for $200,000 after animator Ralph Bakshi and producer Steve Krantz let it lapse. Carr hired writer Bronte Woodard to develop a story line faithful to the Broadway production, but with new songs and sequences. Early candidates for the film's lead roles included Henry Winkler, a popular TV presence via the 1950s-based sitcom *Happy Days,* and Susan Dey, who had starred on TV's *The Partridge Family.* But Winkler reportedly feared being typecast, and Dey and her agent were rumored to be apprehensive about the actress playing "another teen." Enter producer Robert Stigwood (*Jesus Christ Superstar, Tommy*), who had signed budding star John Travolta (TV's *Welcome Back, Kotter*) to a three-picture deal, the first of which was *Saturday Night Fever.* Travolta was ideal for Danny—he had appeared in *Grease* on Broadway in the lesser role of Doody. Stigwood felt that *Grease* would be perfect for Travolta and Carr concurred. Thus a co-producing partnership was formed, with Paramount now backing the project. The search for Sandy ended when Carr met pop singer Olivia Newton-John at a dinner party at Helen Reddy's house and, enthralled, offered her the role. Newton-John tentatively said yes but stunned Carr by insisting on a screen test to ensure that she was capable of the role. For a director, John Travolta suggested—and Stigwood and Carr agreed to—Randal Kleiser, a relative newcomer to feature films who had effectively guided the actor to an acclaimed performance in the 1976 TV film *The Boy in the Plastic Bubble.* The filming of *Grease* took place during the summer of 1977 at three local high schools doubling as Rydell High: Venice High School (early scenes), Huntington Park High School (dance contest), and John Marshall High School in L.A.'s Los Feliz district (graduation carnival and ending). Additional locations included the Los Angeles River channel near downtown (car race sequence) and the Pickwick Drive-In Theater in Burbank. The film's opening sequence was filmed at El Matador Beach in Malibu. The Frosty Palace hamburger stand was constructed on Paramount's back lot.

DISTRIBUTION: America in 1978, still riding a 1950s nostalgia wave, made *Grease* a giant hit. The film brought in $156 million in domestic box office on its initial release ($426.8 million in 2005 dollars), which made it Paramount's biggest hit since *The Ten Commandments* in 1956. As of 2007, it remained the third-highest-grossing musical of all time. A 1982 sequel, *Grease 2,* starring Maxwell Caulfield and Michelle Pfeiffer, came nowhere near duplicating its predecessor's success. —*Douglas Burns*

NATIONAL LAMPOON'S ANIMAL HOUSE

Universal, 1978

ALL-RELEASE EQUIVALENT 2005 $s

(Unadjusted $s) in Millions of $s

Domestic Box Office Revenues . . . . **$383.0**/($141.6)
Production Cost . . . . **$10.4**/($3.5)
Principal Photography . . . . **28** days estimated
10/24/1977–11/30/1977

Director . . . . John Landis
Producer . . . . Ivan Reitman, Matty Simmons
Production Company . . . . Universal Pictures
Story and
  Screenplay by . . . . Harold Ramis, Douglas Kenney,
Chris Miller
Cast . . . . John Belushi, Tim Matheson,
John Vernon, Verna Bloom,
Tomas Hulce, Karen Allen,
Martha Smith, Kevin Bacon,
Donald Sutherland
Filming Locations . . . . . . On location: at and around
the University of Oregon in
Eugene, Oregon; in studio:
University Studios,
Universal City, CA
Genre . . . . Comedy
Format . . . . Color
Initial Release . . . . 7/27/1978 premiere (New York);
7/28/1978 general release
Rerelease 1979
Running Time . . . . 109 minutes
MPAA Rating PG-13

STANDING THE TEST OF TIME

ACADEMY AWARD Oscar Nominations and Wins

None

OSCAR TOTALS   Nominations 0   *Wins 0

AFI 100 YEARS 100 MOVIES SELECTION
2007 0   1997 0

TOP 300 FILMS POSITION . . . . **#50**
All-Release Domestic Box Office in Equivalent 2005 $s

National Film Preservation Board Selection 2001

OTHER AWARDS Best Picture Wins

	Year
Golden Globes	none
New York Film Critics	none
National Board of Review	none
Film Daily Critics	none

We went further than I think Universal expected or wanted. I think they were shocked and appalled. Chris' fraternity had virtually been a vomiting cult. And we had a lot of scenes that were almost orgies of vomit . . . We didn't back off anything.

—Harold Ramis

PLOT: In 1962 a fraternity comprised of social outcasts, known as Delta, faces sanctions from the dean of Faber College, who enlists members of a more traditional fraternity to prod them into committing acts that would get them kicked off campus. Instead, they engage in a guerrilla war.

PRODUCTION: In the mid-1970s, the company that owned the irreverent humor magazine *National Lampoon* was looking to expand its brand. The multimedia company had already produced a live musical parody onstage in New York, a radio show, and the satirical off-Broadway revue *Lemmings,* while also contributing to *Saturday Night Live* (*SNL*) four of the original Not Ready for Primetime Players. *Animal House* was based on stories written for *National Lampoon* by Chris Miller, who in the early 1960s had been a member of Dartmouth's famously disruptive Alpha Delta Phi. The favorable reaction from readers inspired Doug Kenney and Harold Ramis to pursue the notion of a movie comedy about an "outlaw fraternity." Despite a dismissive response to their pitch, producers Ivan Reitman and Matty Simmons were able to talk Universal into giving them $3 million. Hamstrung by a tight budget, director John Landis was forced to improvise. College administrators who had read the script weren't anxious to open their doors to the filmmakers, but the president of the University of Oregon, who was still smarting over his decision to bar the production team of *The Graduate* from a school he had been at in California years earlier, agreed. For twenty-eight days, Landis and his crew had nearly open access to the college's facilities, including the dean's office. Landis asked the actors playing the Deltas to report to the Eugene campus five days early, so they could identify with each other as frat brothers in arms against Dean Wormer and the Alphas. John Belushi, the only *SNL* cast member who agreed to participate, made the commute between Eugene and New York City twice a week. Even so, Universal demanded that another name star be enlisted for marquee value. Landis talked his friend Donald Sutherland into playing a pothead professor. For two days of work, he was offered an up-front payment of $40,000 or a percentage of the gross. By taking the cash, Sutherland cost himself millions. For all the on-screen mayhem, including food fights and pranks involving horses, precious little damage was done to the sets and locations. The most notable exception was the hole Blutarsky put in the wall of the Delta house, using the guitar played by a young troubadour while serenading a group of sorority girls (including Belushi's real-life wife, Judith) during the toga party. Landis recruited family friend Elmer Bernstein to score the movie, which even he agreed was an odd choice. Most people's memories of the soundtrack are of such period-perfect songs as "Louie, Louie," "Shout," and "Money (That's What I Want)."

DISTRIBUTION: After testing positively in Denver, Universal and *National Lampoon* felt as if they might have a hit on their hands. It opened on twelve screens on July 28, 1978. On September 21, 1979, *Animal House* would be rereleased, ultimately bringing in over $140 million in domestic box office. This, despite reviews that acknowledged the humor in the film's antiestablishment posture but criticized it for not being as cutting-edge as the magazine. To this day, many observers consider *Animal House* the first example of "gross-out" comedy, and, as such, a precursor to the class acts *Porky's* and *American Pie.* —*Gary Dretzka*

MIDNIGHT EXPRESS

Columbia, 1978

ALL-RELEASE EQUIVALENT 2005 $s

(Unadjusted $s) in Millions of $s

Domestic Box Office Revenues......... $95.9/($35.0)
Production Cost .... $5.2/($1.8)
Principal Photography................ not available

Director . . . . Alan Parker

Producer . . . . David Puttnam, Alan Marshall

Production Company. . . . Casablanca Filmworks

Story by. . . . . Based on the book by William Hayes with William Hoffer

Screenplay by . . . . Oliver Stone

Cast . . . . Brad Davis, Randy Quaid, John Hurt, Bo Hopkins, Paul Smith, Mike Kellin, Norbert Wiesser, Irene Miracle

Filming Locations . . . . . . Fort St. Elmo, Malta; certain establishing shots taken in Istanbul

Genre. . . . . Drama

Format. . . . . Color (Eastmancolor)

Initial Release . . . . 5/18/1978 premiere (Cannes Film Festival); 10/6/1978 general release

Rerelease. . . . . none

Running Time . . . . 120 minutes

MPAA Rating . . . . R

STANDING THE TEST OF TIME

ACADEMY AWARD Oscar Nominations and Wins

Best Picture: Alan Marshall and David Puttnam, Producers

Actor in a Supporting Role: John Hurt

Directing: Alan Parker

Film Editing: Gerry Hambling

***MUSIC** (Original Score): Giorgio Moroder

***WRITING** (Screenplay – based on material from another medium): Oliver Stone

OSCAR TOTALS   Nominations **6**   *Wins 2

AFI 100 YEARS 100 MOVIES SELECTION

2007 0   1997 0

TOP 300 FILMS POSITION . . . . .none

All-Release Domestic Box Office in Equivalent 2005 $s

National Film Preservation Board Selection. . . .none

OTHER AWARDS Best Picture Wins

	Year
Golden Globes (Drama).	1979
New York Film Critics.	none
National Board of Review.	none
Film Daily Critics.	none

I saw Midnight Express *as a story about injustice. It wasn't about drugs. He could have been busted for carrying a pistol as far as I was concerned. The charge didn't really interest me; it was the miscarriage of justice.*

—Oliver Stone

PLOT: American Billy Hayes is arrested by the Turkish police for the transportation of hashish and sentenced to jail. When his appeal is overturned, his term is extended, and Hayes has only one hope of ending the unmitigated cruelty of life behind bars: escape.

PRODUCTION: After turning down *Platoon,* Columbia Pictures, undoubtedly moved by the intensity of Oliver Stone's screenplay, hired the burgeoning writer to adapt Billy Hayes's memoir, *Midnight Express*. In only six weeks, a first draft was complete. It was then that Stone and the film's director, Alan Parker, sat down together and went through the script page by page, equalizing their sensibility and developing its violent intensity. Their collaboration was formal, if not cold, but mutually respectful and, in creative terms, in sync. Meanwhile, the film's producers were put under a great deal of studio pressure to soften the violence that Stone and Parker believed was integral to the script. In its defense, Parker said, "I would like the audience to be shaken and shocked that such things happen almost to the point of disbelief—but never to lose them." The script took liberties with the real story, adding a girlfriend as a love interest, scenes of him being raped (Hayes had said the sex was consensual), and a scene of Hayes biting off a snitch's tongue. After a search spanning nearly a dozen countries, Parker decided upon Fort St. Elmo on Malta. From there, the crew set about converting the pristine Mediterranean fortress into a fearsome Turkish prison. Laboring in temperatures around 120 degrees, the film's carpenters, construction workers, and set designers committed an entire month to raising the structure's floor ten feet, and utterly reassembled its rickety roof. A handful of the fort's many interiors were converted into escape tunnels, courtrooms, and even a mental asylum; by the end of its reconstruction, St. Elmo had been transformed into a mini studio. Most of the cast was drawn from the local Maltese population, along with Greeks and Armenians who played the Turks.

DISTRIBUTION: The general rule for British productions until the mid-1970s was to spend an average of 10 percent of a film's budget on marketing. *Midnight Express* was a significant departure, being the first British production for which print and ad costs significantly exceeded the negative cost. The marketing and controversy were healthy for the box office. *Midnight Express* caused an uproar the moment it hit cinemas. The film's first public screening took place on May 18, 1978, at the Cannes Film Festival, prompting a statement of protest from the Turkish government. They branded it an unfair depiction of their penal system, and called for a boycott. The film subsequently broke records across Europe, drawing remarkable numbers from both England and France. By the time it reached the States, *Midnight Express* was already a legend. The real Billy Hayes complained about changes made in the script and later apologized to the Turkish people for the way they were portrayed, as did Stone, who years later said, "I think the Turks had a point . . . it's extreme. I think the humor in the screenplay might have softened it if some of it had made it into the movie, but it didn't. So, the Turks were right. It was rabid, but I was young." —*Sam Wasson*

SUPERMAN—THE MOVIE
Warner Bros., 1978

ALL-RELEASE EQUIVALENT 2005 $s

(Unadjusted $s) in Millions of $s

Domestic Box Office Revenues . . . . **$367.7**/($134.2)
Production Cost . . . . **$177.3**/($55.0)
Principal Photography . . . . **300 +** days estimated
19 months from
3/24/1977 to 10/1978
Filmed portion of Superman
II together with I

Initial Release 12/15/1978
Rerelease . . . . none
Running Time . . . . 143 minutes
MPAA Rating . . . . PG

Director . . . . Richard Donner
Producer . . . . Pierre Spengler
Production Company . . . . Dovemead Ltd. Production,
Alexander Salkind Presentation
Story by . . . . Mario Puzo based on characters
created by Jerry Siegel and Joe
Shuster
Screenplay by . . . . Mario Puzo, David Newman,
Leslie Newman, Robert Benton
Cast . . . . Marlon Brando, Gene Hackman
Filming Locations . . . . . . Pinewood Studios,
Buckinghamshire, England;
Shepperton Studios, Middlesex,
England; Alberta, Canada;
Red Rock State Park, NM;
San Francisco, CA;
New York City; Los Angeles,
CA; Hoover Dam, NV
Genre . . . . Action Adventure
Format . . . . Color (Technicolor)

STANDING THE TEST OF TIME

ACADEMY AWARD Oscar Nominations and Wins

Film Editing: Stuart Baird

Music (Original Score): John Williams

Sound: Gordon K. McCallum, Graham Hartstone,
Nicolas Le Messurier, Roy Charman

*SPECIAL ACHIEVEMENT AWARD (Visual
Effects):

OSCAR TOTALS   Nominations **4**   *Wins **1**

AFI 100 YEARS 100 MOVIES SELECTION
2007 0   1997 0

TOP 300 FILMS POSITION . . . . **#57**
All-Release Domestic Box Office in Equivalent 2005 $s

National Film Preservation Board Selection . . . . none

OTHER AWARDS Best Picture Wins

	Year
Golden Globes	none
New York Film Critics	none
National Board of Review	none
Film Daily Critics	none

*I had to fight [the producers] every step of the way,
because I knew if I didn't get it right, I was dead.*
—Richard Donner

PLOT: The classic comic-book hero is reinvented for the big screen in this adventure that recounts Superman's origins on Krypton, his coming of age in rural Smallville, and his efforts to thwart archvillain Lex Luthor in Metropolis.

PRODUCTION: In the early 1970s, father-and-son producers Alexander and Ilya Salkind won the nod to produce a Superman film from Warner Bros. (who controlled the character rights) on the condition that they assume the production costs. The Salkinds attracted financing by bringing aboard best-selling *Godfather* novelist Mario Puzo to pen the script and hiring two of the biggest stars of the decade—Marlon Brando and Gene Hackman—to star. (Brando earned $3.7 million plus a percentage to play Superman's father, Jor-El, a small role requiring only two weeks of filming.) Puzo's overlong script, submitted in 1975, prompted the Salkinds to bring in Robert Benton and David Newman (and Newman's wife, Leslie), writers of the flop Broadway musical *It's a Bird . . . It's a Plane . . . It's Superman,* to add punchier, comic beats. The Salkinds first choice to direct, Guy Hamilton (*Goldfinger*), could not work in England due to tax laws, so an offer went out to Richard Donner (*The Omen*). Donner deemed the script unsatisfying and at the last minute brought in his friend Tom Mankiewicz for another rewrite. Donner also enlisted his own production team (with designer John Barry brainstorming the crystalline Kryptonian sets) and took a chance on unknown Christopher Reeve to play the title role (over established actors, including Robert Redford and Nick Nolte). The Screen Actors Guild, to protest Salkind's producing two films simultaneously, created the "Salkind rule," which stipulates that producers must specify how many movies are being made. The Writers Guild didn't want more than four writers listed, so Mankiewicz was credited in the opening title sequence as "creative consultant." Filming began in March 1977, with studio work at England's Pinewood Studios and a second unit at nearby Shepperton Studios. The shooting dates for stars Brando and Hackman had already been set prior to Donner's hiring, and Mankiewicz's rewrites began to put the film behind schedule. The plan for *Superman* to be produced at the same time as its sequel (a trick they had performed on their 1973 production *The Three Musketeers*) was eventually scrapped as costs mounted, and Donner abandoned his work on *Superman II* to concentrate on finishing the first film. As many as eleven units helped deal with the frantic pace. Donner's careful, labor-intensive approach to filmmaking reportedly exasperated the bottom-line-focused Salkinds and their representative, co-producer Pierre Spengler. The working relationship between the director and the producers grew increasingly tense as filming and effects work stretched on, and by the end of the nearly nineteen-month production, it had grown toxic.

DISTRIBUTION: *Superman* was the number one film at the U.S. box office for eleven weeks in a row. Broadly praised by critics, it earned note for the manner in which it balanced three moods—somber Krypton, Rockwellian Smallville, and bright, busy Metropolis. The version released to theaters ran for 143 minutes. In the early 1980s, Alexander Salkind added nearly 45 minutes for international television and a special edition DVD in 2001, which ran 151 minutes. A 2006 release offered the original theatrical cut on DVD for the first time. —*Daniel Wallace*

ALIEN
20th Century-Fox, 1979

ALL-RELEASE EQUIVALENT 2005 $s
(Unadjusted $s) in Millions of $s

Domestic Box Office Revenues........ **$202.9**/($80.9)
Production Cost .... **$29.1**/($10.8)
Principal Photography...........**100** days estimated
7/5/1978–December 1978

Director .... Ridley Scott
Producer .... Gordon Carroll, David Giler, and Walter Hill
Production Company.... 20th Century-Fox Productions, Ltd. Brandywine Productions, Ltd.
Story by.............. Dan O'Bannon, Ronald Shusett
Screenplay by......... Dan O'Bannon
Cast .... Tom Skerritt, Sigourney Weaver, Veronica Cartwright, Harry Dean Stanton, John Hurt, Ian Holm, Yaphet Kott
Filming Locations ...... Shepperton and Bray Studios in the UK
Genre................. Sci-Fi
Format............... Color (DeLuxe)
Initial Release......... 5/29/1979
Rerelease............ 10/29/2003 (director's cut)
Running Time......... 124 minutes
MPAA Rating .... R

STANDING THE TEST OF TIME

ACADEMY AWARD Oscar Nominations and Wins

Art Direction/Set Decoration: Michael Seymour, Les Dilley, Roger Christian/ Ian Whittaker

*VISUAL EFFECTS: H. R. Giger, Carlo Rambaldi, Brian Johnson, Nick Allder, Denys Ayling

OSCAR TOTALS Nominations 2 *Wins 1

AFI 100 YEARS 100 MOVIES SELECTION
2007 0   1997 0

TOP 300 FILMS POSITION . . . . **#253**
All-Release Domestic Box Office in Equivalent 2005 $s

National Film Preservation Board Selection 2002

OTHER AWARDS Best Picture Wins

	Year
Golden Globes	none
New York Film Critics.	none
National Board of Review.	none
Film Daily Critics	none

The fact that the story happens to be set in space is really incidental . . . it's the story that matters. The actual setting could be practically anywhere at any time.

—Ridley Scott

PLOT: While investigating a distress signal on a distant planet, the crew of the spacecraft *Nostromo* stumbles upon a mysterious alien ship. Unknowingly, they bring an alien parasite back. It hatches, and the crew battles to stay alive.

PRODUCTION: After the relative failure of his first film, *Dark Star* (1974), screenwriter Dan O'Bannon wanted to write a serious and altogether more intense horror film. In 1976 O'Bannon wrote the original treatment for *Alien* with Ronald Shusett. Artist Ron Cobb created conceptual designs that captured the realistic approach. They sold the script to David Giler, Gordon Carroll, and Walter Hill of the Brandywine company, who had a production deal with 20th Century-Fox. Walter Hill was attached to direct, and Giler rewrote the script. However, production was forced to go into hiatus when 20th Century-Fox grew increasingly concerned over the prospect of committing to a new science fiction film, as the yet-unreleased *Star Wars* was still considered a substantial risk for the studio. While the film was on hiatus, Walter Hill stepped down and Ridley Scott was brought in to direct. Once *Star Wars* went on to become a box office hit, Fox's concerns were allayed and production on *Alien* moved forward. Actor Tom Skerritt had originally been cast as Ripley, but during development Ripley became a woman at the suggestion of studio head Alan Ladd Jr. To create the startling detail required for the close-up exterior shots of the *Nostromo,* director Ridley Scott brought in artists Chris Foss and Ron Cobb. Unhappy with their original drawings, Scott instructed them to design the ship to look more like an outer-space tugboat than a traditional spacecraft. Once they had designed the *Nostromo* to Scott's liking, effects supervisor Brian Johnson undertook the task of building the three miniature models that would be used during shooting. The largest such "miniature" was eight feet long and weighed over 800 pounds. Some of the models were even equipped with high-intensity quartz lights and internal plumbing so as to create the effect of exhaust during the ship's landing sequences. To create the alien and the unique landscape of the alien planet, Scott called upon the artistic talents of H. R. Giger. A set was built at Shepperton Studios in the United Kingdom based upon Giger's drawings, but upon seeing it Giger was so displeased that he had work immediately stopped. He requested new materials be brought in and, using bones, plasticine, cable, and small pieces of machinery, Giger and his team rebuilt the entire set to his specifications in time for the start of principal photography.

DISTRIBUTION: *Alien* was incredibly well received both by critics and the general public. Much of its initial success was due in no small part to the fact that it was released in the wake of the hugely successful run of *Star Wars*. Critics immediately embraced *Alien* as taking the *Star Wars* space opera model into a much darker, more terrifying place, in the tradition of horror classics such as *Halloween* and *Jaws*. One critic went so far as to label it "the scariest movie in history." Audiences responded positively as well. *Alien* was such a financial success that it spawned three sequels and the 2004 crossover *Alien vs. Predator.* It remains one of the more successful movie franchises to this day. —*Mark D'Anna*

APOCALYPSE NOW
United Artists, 1979

ALL-RELEASE EQUIVALENT 2005 $s
(Unadjusted $s) in Millions of $s

Domestic Box Office Revenues.........$205.7/($83.5)
Production Cost ....$83.4/($31.0)
Principal Photography...........**238** days estimated
3/1/1976–August 1977

Director .... Francis Ford Coppola

Producer .... Francis Ford Coppola, Gray Frederickson, Fred Roos, Tom Sternberg

Production Company.... Omni Zoetrope

Story by.............. Based on the novel *Heart of Darkness* by Joseph Conrad

Screenplay by......... Francis Ford Coppola, John Milius, with narration by Michael Herr

Cast .... Marlon Brando, Robert Duvall, Martin Sheen, Frederic Forrest, Albert Hall, Sam Bottoms, Laurence Fishburne, Dennis Hopper

Filming Locations ...... 100 percent on location in the Philippines and Napa Valley, CA

Genre................. War

Format............... Color (Technicolor)

Initial Release......... 8/15/1979

Rerelease............. 1987, 2001 *Redux* version

Running Time .... 153 minutes (202 minutes *Redux* version

MPAA Rating .... R

STANDING THE TEST OF TIME

ACADEMY AWARD Oscar Nominations and Wins

Best Picture: Francis Coppola, Producer; Fred Roos, Gray Frederickson, and Tom Sternberg, Co-Producers

Actor in a Supporting Role: Robert Duvall

Art Direction/Set Decoration: Dean Tavoularis, Angelo Graham/ George R. Nelson

*CINEMATOGRAPHY: Vittorio Storaro

Directing: Francis Coppola

Film Editing: Richard Marks, Walter Murch, Gerald B. Greenberg, Lisa Fruchtman

*SOUND: Walter Murch, Mark Berger, Richard Beggs, Nat Boxer

Writing (Screenplay – based on material from another medium): John Milius, Francis Coppola

OSCAR TOTALS   Nominations **8**   *Wins 2

AFI 100 YEARS 100 MOVIES SELECTION
2007 . . . #30   1997 . . . #28

TOP 300 FILMS POSITION . . . . #243
All-Release Domestic Box Office in Equivalent 2005 $s

National Film Preservation Board Selection. . . . 2000

OTHER AWARDS Best Picture Wins

	Year
Golden Globes	none
New York Film Critics.	none
National Board of Review.	none
Film Daily Critics.	none

More and more it seems like there are parallels between the character of Kurtz and Francis. There is the exhilaration of power in the face of losing everything, like the excitement of war when one kills and takes the chance of being killed.

—Eleanor Coppola

PLOT: Captain Willard travels up the Mekong River into Cambodia on a mission to assassinate a highly decorated American officer who has trained his own mercenary army. Along the way, Willard and the crew of a navy patrol boat find themselves wondering where sanity ends and madness begins in war.

PRODUCTION: George Lucas had originally created *Apocalypse Now* with his friend John Milius and was going to direct it as a documentary-style 16 mm multiple-camera movie. The film was one of the seven movies included in the deal Francis Coppola struck with Warner Bros./Seven Arts in American Zoetrope's early days. Once that deal blew up in 1970, the script was shelved until 1974–75. Lucas was busy then working on *Star Wars* and Milius was also tied up, so they told Coppola he could develop *Apocalypse Now* the way he wanted. Coppola decided to direct and finance it himself with profits from the *Godfather* movies. He guaranteed the budget with his personal property, which gave him complete creative control and ultimate ownership. Coppola wanted a big, visually exciting movie shot in both 70 mm and 35 mm and envisioned, a film more from the book *Heart of Darkness* than from Milius's original script though some notable sequences such as the helicopter attack (a purely Milius invention) remained. What began as a 14-week shoot on an approximately $13 million budget in the Philippines ended up being extremely difficult logistically, taking much longer and costing more than anticipated. Harvey Keitel, cast as Willard, was replaced two weeks into filming. Martin Sheen, who took his place, suffered a near-fatal heart attack in midproduction. Brando arrived in the Philippines overweight and unprepared for his scenes. Shooting was frequently interrupted when the Philippine military recalled helicopters lent to the production in order to fight real guerrillas. And a typhoon destroyed military sets, causing the film to shut down for three months. Back home, it took the film editors two years to edit the 1.35 million feet (250 hours) of exposed film, leaving approximately 247 hours of footage on the cutting room floor. It was the first film to use the 5.1 sound format, which is now standard for film soundtracks. During postproduction, the film was reconstructed around a voice-over by Captain Willard's character written by Michael Herr, a former war correspondent whose book *Dispatches* was also a source for the film, as was the Werner Herzog's 1972 film *Aguirre: The Wrath of God*. The first assembly ran over five hours. By the time it was screened at the 1979 Cannes Film Festival, where it won the coveted Palme d'Or, it was close to the final running time of 153 minutes.

DISTRIBUTION: Despite a mixed reaction from critics, *Apocalypse Now* became a hit in the United States, bringing in nearly $79 million in domestic box office in its initial release, although, with its $31 million negative cost and nearly $14 million in print and ad costs, it lost money. The seventeen 70 mm release prints distributed in the United States (and more for foreign versions) had no titles and were accompanied by a theatrical booklet with printed credits. The 35 mm release prints did have end credits and did not have booklets printed to accompany the showings. By 1981 the film had not yet made a profit, and Coppola still owed United Artists $7 million. He gave them U.S. TV rights to pay the balance. In 2001 Coppola did a reedit and released *Apocalypse Now: Redux* (Latin for "brought back"), which restored 49 minutes of scenes cut from the original. It drew unanimous praise from critics. —*Gary Dretzka*

KRAMER VS. KRAMER

Columbia, 1979

ALL-RELEASE EQUIVALENT 2005 $s

(Unadjusted $s) in Millions of $s

Domestic Box Office Revenues........**$253.2**/($106.3)
Production Cost . . . .**$21.5**/($8.0)
Principal Photography. . . . .**45 days estimated**
9/16/1978–October 1979

Director	Robert Benton
Producer	Stanley R. Jaffe
Production Company	Stanley Jaffe Productions
Story by	Based on the novel by Avery Corman
Screenplay by	Robert Benton
Cast	Dustin Hoffman, Meryl Streep, Jane Alexander, Justin Henry
Filming Locations	On location in Manhattan, NY
Genre.	Drama
Format.	Color (Technicolor)
Initial Release	12/17/1979 premiere (New York); 12/19/1979 general release
Rerelease.	none
Running Time	105 minutes
MPAA Rating	PG

STANDING THE TEST OF TIME

ACADEMY AWARD Oscar Nominations and Wins

*BEST PICTURE: Stanley R. Jaffe, Producer

*ACTOR IN A LEADING ROLE: Dustin Hoffman

Actor in a Supporting Role: Justin Henry

Actress in a Supporting Role: Jane Alexander

*ACTRESS IN A SUPPORTING ROLE: Meryl Streep

Cinematography: Néstor Almendros

*DIRECTING: Robert Benton

Film Editing: Gerald B. Greenberg

*WRITING (Screenplay – based on material from another medium): Robert Benton

OSCAR TOTALS   Nominations **9**   *Wins **5**

AFI 100 YEARS 100 MOVIES SELECTION
2007 0   1997 0

TOP 300 FILMS POSITION . . . . **#156**
All-Release Domestic Box Office in Equivalent 2005 $s

National Film Preservation Board Selection . . . .none

OTHER AWARDS Best Picture Wins

	Year
Golden Globes (Drama).	1980
New York Film Critics.	1979
National Board of Review	none
Film Daily Critics	none

I was surprised that teenagers went to the movie. I really thought it would be the kind of movie they would've stayed away from. But, in fact, either their parents were separated or divorced or their best friend's parents were separated or divorced, and they needed to know it was going to be all right, without reducing them to platitudes.

—Robert Benton

PLOT: When his wife leaves him, a self-absorbed ad exec must learn to care for his young son on his own, and then must fight for custody of him.

PRODUCTION: When producer Stanley Jaffe bought the rights to Avery Corman's 1977 novel, he saw only one actor in the lead role: Dustin Hoffman. François Truffaut was mentioned as the director of choice. However, screenwriter Robert Benton got the job. Hoffman, going through his own divorce at the time, refused the role at first. (James Caan was briefly considered, just in case.) Jaffe and Benson flew to London, where Hoffman was filming *Agatha*, to convince him to do the picture. After a series of twelve-hour meetings that bordered on group therapy, adding complexities of divorce not covered in the book and the first-draft screenplay, Hoffman agreed to play Ted Kramer. *Charlie's Angels* star Kate Jackson was the original choice to play Joanna Kramer, but she could not free herself from her grueling TV schedule. Jane Fonda was next on the list, but she turned it down. *Good Morning, America* host Joan Lunden was offered Ted's one-night-stand role in the film, but since it required nudity, she passed, opening the door to JoBeth Williams in her screen debut. Interestingly, this was the very role that was originally pegged for Meryl Streep. (To avoid an R rating, cinematographer Néstor Almendros would optically darken the nude scene.) No movie says more about truth and trust than *Kramer vs. Kramer*. Truth: Hoffman put so much of himself in the role by reliving his own painful feelings, dialogue, and experiences that Benton offered the actor a co-screenwriting credit (Hoffman refused). The famous ice cream scene between Hoffman and six-year-old Justin Henry, for instance, came from a real-life confrontation Hoffman had with his own young daughter. Another example was the seething anger the actor still harbored for his real ex-wife, which was exhibited in the unscripted smashing of the wineglass in the scene where the exes meet in a restaurant. Trust: Much of the dialogue was improvised, and, as Benton admits, improved. Streep, who was simultaneously filming Woody Allen's *Manhattan,* rewrote her own speech in the emotional divorce court scene, and lauded Benton for his trust in her, citing her experiences with Allen, who was much more dictatorial in style (Allen was known to say such things as "There's a reason for the comma in that speech"). Cinematographer Almendros faithfully realized Benton's vision by creating backgrounds that bring to mind the paintings of Italian masters such as della Francesca or Bellini, and for the exterior settings Almendros studied and approximated the look of artist David Hockney.

DISTRIBUTION: The film received ecstatic reviews and touched a nerve with moviegoers. To accommodate the demand during its first two weeks of release, theaters in Manhattan added 1:00 a.m. screenings. While many divorce law experts took issue with the movie's courtroom inaccuracies, the subject of divorce had long been suppressed by the Hays Code and the Production Code Administration (1934–68) and in the immediate post-Code era (1968–1980s). This was just one of a handful of motion pictures that broke the blockade, and is considered the classic among them, inaccuracies notwithstanding. The film came in number one at the domestic box office in 1979 against such summer release blockbusters as *Rocky 2* and *Alien*. Justin Henry was eight, the youngest ever, when nominated for the supporting actor Oscar. —*Bob Canning*

The 1980s

There are three movies that I am exceptionally proud of in my life, and I rarely commit to a list of films that I like, that I've made, . . . but these are the three films that I was passionately connected to. The first was ET, the second Schindler's List, and third is Saving Private Ryan.

—Steven Spielberg

TOP 10 ALL-RELEASE MOVIES DOMESTIC BOX OFFICE
By Initial Year of Release, 1980–1989

		Equivalent 2005 in Millions of $s
1	*E.T.: The Extra-Terrestrial*	$889.4
2	*Star Wars: Episode V The Empire Strikes Back*	$620.0
3	*Star Wars: Episode VI Return of the Jedi*	$597.6
4	*Raiders of the Lost Ark*	$554.7
5	*Ghostbusters*	$454.3
6	*Beverly Hills Cop*	$432.8
7	*Batman*	$403.5
8	*Back to the Future*	$374.7
9	*Tootsie*	$364.8
10	*Indiana Jones and the Temple of Doom*	$343.1
	Total:	**$5,034.9**

GENERAL U.S. STATISTICS, 1980

226,542,199
Total U.S. Population

42,486,828
U.S. Population
Age 15–24

19.6 Million
Average Weekly
U.S. Movie Attendance

DECADE OVERVIEW

If Hollywood demonstrated anything in the 1980s and early 1990s, it was a hunger for ideas; it didn't seem to know what to make. It wanted the lucid and the unexpected, material with a twist, a hook, a spin—in short, the simple-complex and the bold-subtle. Most consistently, Hollywood wanted the new old. It wanted sequels to documented hits (The Godfather Part III); it wanted updated remakes of classic (Heaven Can Wait) and Americanized remakes of overseas hits (Three Men and a Baby); it wanted revitalized genres (Body Heat and noir). The art of the sequel is one of repetition with variation . . . and the same can be said of the remake, the genre revival, and—according to conservative Hollywood—the aesthetics of the sure-fire investment.
—GERALD MAST AND BRUCE F. KAWIN, *A SHORT HISTORY OF THE MOVIES*

Firing Up the Franchises

The 1980s would see videocassette recorder (VCR) use in the United States rise from 1 percent in 1980 to 67 percent by 1990. Instead of destroying the movie business, the VCR reignited the American love affair with movies, especially for the baby boomers, the greatest moviegoing generation of all time. Now movie lovers could have a physical collection of films on tape to watch at their convenience. No more waiting for the Million-Dollar Movie on TV to see favorites. It provided a huge new source of revenue, most of which the studios kept. As a matter of course, studios took 80 percent of all video revenue off the top, as a cost of doing business, and placed the other 20 percent into a pool from which profit participants would draw an interest.

But despite this bit of good news for the studios, the larger picture looked pretty bleak. As the decade dawned, oil prices had soared due to an embargo, Jimmy Carter was president, Iran was holding Americans hostage, and there was a national economic malaise. The traditional movie exhibition business, along with other aspects of the film industry, was facing new challenges. The spread of cable as a way to watch movies was increasing rapidly, video stores were popping up everywhere, and pay TV services, led by HBO, grew in importance. As a result, many were predicting that there would no longer be a desire for the kind of movies Hollywood had made for years, or a need to go to theaters at all. They said the small screen would supplant the big screen. In time, however, Ronald Reagan became the first former movie actor to ascend to the White House, Iran released the hostages, and a new era of deregulation emerged. All of this was a shot of much-needed adrenaline for the economy. Business began to boom again.

Before 1976, movie investments were among the most interesting tax-shelter vehicles ever devised. Although changes in tax code laws between 1976 and 1986 (when the Tax Reform Act of 1986 took effect) made the rules less attractive, movies continued to be funded by limited partnerships, which were structured to allow various forms of tax shelter. One such partnership was Silver Screen's tie with Disney, which, through three separate partnerships (Silver

607

Screen II, III, and IV), raised nearly $1.1 billion to invest in such Disney films as *Down and Out in Beverly Hills* (1986), *Three Men and a Baby* (1987), and *Who Framed Roger Rabbit* (1988).

Movies still opened in theaters and built a marketing profile, but were then offered to consumers via pay per view and home video, supplanting network TV and local TV syndication in the order of release. The new home video revenue that was generated came at the perfect moment to feed Hollywood's newest trend—film franchises that set all kinds of box office records.

The marketing approach taken in the 1970s with *Jaws*—wide releases combined with saturation TV ad campaigns—became the new Hollywood business model in the 1980s. As revenues increased, production and marketing costs skyrocketed too. No matter how much money the original franchise movie made, each sequel generally cost more as the star actors, creators, and other contributors sought a bigger payday.

For some movies the rising costs were attributed to an increased number of special effects, including the use of miniatures, models, and sophisticated optics. George Lucas's special effects company, Industrial Light & Magic, set the standard for effects during the decade, as the company pushed the technology forward in new areas such as computer-generated images (CGIs).

Despite the high costs of making these tent-pole movies, the risk was more likely to pay off when that film opened in over 1,000 venues, most of which were new multiplex theaters that were being built at a record clip throughout the decade. For an increasing number of movies, the majority of their take would come during the first one or two weekends of release. This made it more difficult to show a profit from theatrical release alone, unless of course the film was a huge cash gusher. How well a movie did on opening weekend became the new measure of success for movies. Newspapers and television shows such as *Entertainment Tonight* soon began to track the number one picture at the box office each weekend. The benchmark for success in the Hollywood trade press was now grosses in excess of $100 million during the movie's initial domestic run. The increased revenue, along with improvements in movie production technology, also attracted new players into production and distribution, including Orion, which was founded by former executives at United Artists.

The rapid building of new multiscreen theaters throughout the decade made it easier to expand ticket sales by placing movies in several theaters at once when the demand was strongest. Theaters also benefited with the launch of the THX system by Lucasfilm, which set standards for theater sound and presentation. Early on in the 1980s, the U.S. Justice Department aggressively pursued exhibition companies over the practice known as splitting. By the end of the decade, however, under Republican president Reagan, the major studios returned to a vertical integration structure that included theater ownership—nearly fifty years after the U.S. government had filed for divorcement of studio-owned theaters in 1938 under Democratic president Franklin D. Roosevelt.

While many franchises produced sequels, they were not like the anticlimactic sequels of the past. This decade saw the birth of multiple franchises with sequels that were often as good or better than the original, reflecting the growing skill of the filmmakers and the special effects teams behind them. Building on the franchise films begun in the 1970s, the decade got off to a fast start with *Star Wars: Episode V The Empire Strikes Back* (1980) and a third *Star Wars* sequel, *Star Wars: Episode VI Return of the Jedi* (1983). George Lucas, who turned producer for the *Star Wars* sequels released in the 1980s, also produced the decade's other most profitable franchise: the Spielberg-directed *Indiana Jones* series, begun with *Raiders of the Lost Ark* in 1981. Steven Spielberg, by far the most successful director of the decade, had the highest-grossing movie with 1982's *E.T.: The Extra-Terrestrial,* which grossed over $664 million in worldwide box office on its initial release. It also helped propel the film's distributor, Universal Pictures, to the top ranks for the decade, alongside Paramount, Warner Bros., and 20th Century-Fox.

Other franchise films begun in the 1970s continued into the 1980s. Without Steven Spielberg directing, Universal Pictures' *Jaws 3-D* and *Jaws: The Revenge* dropped off dramatically in worldwide box office revenue. And even though Christopher Reeve continued on as Superman, each sequel in the 1980s made less than the one before. However, Sylvester Stallone continued to star in more *Rocky* films, which were very successful. The 1986 *Aliens* followed the popular *Alien* (1979), with Sigourney Weaver's salary increasing from $30,000 on the first film to $1 million on the second (with an $11 million payday coming on *Aliens 3* in 1997). Among the biggest franchise movie stars to emerge during the 1980s were Harrison Ford as Indiana Jones (while continuing to star in the *Star Wars* movies), Michael J. Fox in *Back to the Future,* Bruce Willis in *Die Hard,* Mel Gibson and Danny Glover in *Lethal Weapon,* and Eddie Murphy in *Beverly Hills Cop.* Once it hit, *Back to the Future* was the first franchise to shoot its sequels back to back. *Die Hard* (1988), featuring Bruce Willis as a cop caught in crisis, spawned three sequels spread over two decades. Mel Gibson and Danny Glover played buddy cops in the action thriller *Lethal Weapon* (1987), which generated a trio of sequels over the following decade. After becoming a sensation on *Saturday Night Live,* Murphy found blockbuster success with *Beverly Hills Cop* (1984) and *Beverly Hills Cop II* (1987). There was also Sylvester Stallone as Rambo in *First Blood* (1982), followed by *Rambo: First Blood Part II* (1985) and *Rambo III* (1988). The James Bond powerhouse, begun in the 1960s, continued with a new film released every two years in the 1980s, although the worldwide revenues in adjusted 2005 dollars were on the decline. Three films starred Roger Moore; then there were two with Timothy Dalton. *License to Kill,* in 1989, was the sixteenth film in the franchise and the lowest-grossing of them all (in equivalent 2005 dollars).

High-concept franchise movies also found a growing audience outside America, making foreign box office an increasingly important revenue source. American movie characters such as Darth Vader, Rambo, and the *Beverly Hills Cop* franchise's Axel Foley were icons around the globe. Most of these big-budget films grew out of traditional genres such as action, horror, and science fiction but distinguished themselves from earlier films in these categories through increasingly innovative, production values, and special effects. The invasion of these blockbusters and their box office domination in many countries dealt a huge blow to local industries, which had been revived after World War II. In Great Britain, there had been a renaissance earlier in the decade marked by the success of *Chariots of Fire,* but by the end of the 1980s the English industry, along with those in France and Italy, simply could not compete with the U.S.-produced blockbuster.

Another growing source of revenue was from extensive product and image licensing. Some of the blockbusters, such as *Star Wars,* brought in marketing partners and additional revenue through tie-ins with the fast food industry, soft drinks, and toys—considered to be the three biggest licensing categories. The merchandising campaigns often lived on beyond the theatrical release and even well into the home video launch.

The timing of a movie opening had also become much more crucial since the first weekend could either make or break a film. There were obvious key periods in which to open a big movie intended for a wider audience. The best period was summer, followed by Christmas, as both represented times of the year when audiences were most available. Kids were out of school, and one of the best holiday periods to emerge was the Fourth of July weekend.

E.T.: The Extra-Terrestrial
All-Release Domestic Box Office by Release Wave

Equivalent 2005 $s /(Unadjusted $s) in Millions of $s

Release Date	Release Wave	Domestic Box Office	Production Cost
6/11/1982	1	$777.1/($359.2)	$24.6/($12.2)
7/19/1985	2	$73.3/($40.6)	
3/22/2002	3	$39.0/($35.3)	
1982–2002		$889.4/($435.1)	$24.6/($12.2)

PRODUCTION SPOTLIGHT

Star Producers, Star Directors, and Star Actors Build Brands as Agents Exercise Increasing Clout

The blockbuster franchises that dominated the decade were created and controlled by a small group of players, led by George Lucas and Steven Spielberg, whose fantasy action-adventures consistently ranked among the top 5 highest-grossing movies. Spielberg worked at several studios but built his closest relationship at Universal, where his longtime friend, studio president Sidney J. Sheinberg, had first hired him to direct for Universal TV. Lucas built on his success in the San Francisco Bay area, where he located Industrial Light & Magic and several other divisions of his company, Lucasfilm. And Robert Zemeckis, a close ally of Spielberg, directed *Back to the Future* and *Who Framed Roger Rabbit,* both of which used ILM's special effects to enhance the magic of the storytelling. Other blockbuster creators included the team of Jerry Bruckheimer and Don Simpson, who coined the phrase "high concept" and produced *Top Gun* and *Beverly Hills Cop,* as well as Richard Donner and Joel Silver, who set off the *Lethal Weapon* series. There were also comedy franchises, such as Ivan Reitman's *Ghostbusters,* and the launch of the comic magazine franchise *Batman,* with Tim Burton directing the first in the series. Many of the decade's films often featured former stars from the TV show *Saturday Night Live,* such as Eddie Murphy, Bill Murray, Chevy Chase, Steve Martin, and Dan Aykroyd. Other top-grossing movies featured Sylvester Stallone competing against himself between *Rocky 3* and *Rambo: First Blood Part II.*

During this time, studios were investing millions of dollars in production, so having stars market their movie seemed like the best way to hedge their bets. Consequently, the salaries of high-profile actors soared. In the 1980s a new breed of talent agents and much more powerful agencies emerged with a virtual oligopoly on the market. For studios seeking stars, there were really only three places to find more name-brand talent—the William Morris Agency, which had been around since vaudeville; International Creative Management (ICM), which was pieced together after the government broke up agency powerhouse MCA in 1962; and the fast-rising Creative Artists Agency (CAA), which started when five agents splintered off from William Morris. Under the guidance of Michael Ovitz, who during the decade came to be called "the most powerful man in Hollywood," CAA became a major force in TV and especially movies. Ovitz guided the careers of numerous accomplished actors and used his leverage not only to get

---

1980s Movie Censorship: A Brief History

In 1984 the Motion Picture Association of America (MPAA) adjusts its ratings further: PG becomes PG and PG-13.

---

them high salaries but also to get some movies made that otherwise would never have reached a projector. For instance, he worked ardently to get *Rain Man* made for his client Dustin Hoffman after he had guided Hoffman to success in *Tootsie*.

By the mid-1980s, CAA had become the most powerful agency in Hollywood . . . CAA had Robert Redford and Debra Winger, plus director Ivan Reitman and the writing team of Jim Cash and Jack Epps Jr., working on the package deal that would eventually become the MCA film Legal Eagles. *Redford earned $5 million for the picture, Winger earned $2.5 million; Reitman approximately $2.5 million and the writers $750,000.*
In movie packaging, the agency does not collect a fee on the film's overall budget, as in TV packaging; it gets "just" a percentage of each client's take. By representing five key people in the Legal Eagles *package, CAA earned huge commissions, and its display of muscle in negotiating better deals for all of its clients raised the production costs of the move from the originally budgeted $25 million to $32 million.* Legal Eagles *was not a hit, and the additional $7 million was not recovered at the box office (although video rentals helped bail it, and many other films, out of the hole).*
—Stephen Singular, *Power to Burn: Michael Ovitz and the New Business of Show Business*

[Don] Simpson was the first producer to understand and exploit the significance of MTV. His action-packed, loud, flashy, simplistic, and tightly structured films brought crowds to the multiplexes every summer. His lowest-common-denominator films reflected the MTV generation, such as in his debut film Flashdance *(1983)—with its pop soundtrack and iconic "freeze-frame" ending. Other successes followed in the 80s:* Beverly Hills Cop *(1984) with its "fish-out-of-water" high concept, the sexy* Thief of Hearts *(1984), the high-flying* Top Gun *(1986)—the epitome of Simpson's technique, and the stock-car racing film* Days of Thunder *(1990) again with Tom Cruise. By the end of the 80s era as a result, most films were not designed for "thinking" adult audiences (such as* Driving Miss Daisy *(1989)), but were "low-brow" for dumbed-down teen audiences looking for sheer entertainment value or thrills.* —Tim Dirks

The most commercially popular genre in the American cinema of the 1980s has been the action-adventure film. This distinctly "masculine" form has featured no, or very few, parts for women. One fourth of the men became stars and/or specialized in action-adventure films, but only one woman has become a commercial star following an appearance in the action genre . . . In 1986 Sigourney Weaver was nominated for an Oscar Award for Aliens, *in which she played the head of a spaceship. Weaver thus became the first and only female, in the Oscar's sixty-two-year-history, to have been nominated for the lead award in an action-adventure film. No wonder Weaver's co-workers teased her on the set of* Aliens, *calling her "Rambolina"—in her screen heroics and weaponry she was the female counterpart of Sylvester Stallone.* —Emanuel Levy

"The only project that I ever did that anybody got was Raiders." —GEORGE LUCAS

Five of the Top 15 Action Adventure Films Are Released in the 1980s

Top 15 Action Adventure Films
All-Release Domestic Box Office
Equivalent 2005 $s /(Unadjusted $s) in Millions of $s

Rank	Film	Initial Release	Domestic Box Office	Production Cost
1	Raiders of the Lost Ark	1981	$554.7/($245.0)	$48.9/($22.8)
2	The Dark Knight	2008	$476.1/($533.4)	$229.4/($252.9)
3	Spider-Man	2002	$445.4/($403.7)	$190.0/($175.0)
4	Beverly Hills Cop	1984	$432.8/($234.8)	$26.3/ ($14.0)
5	Pirates of the Caribbean 2: Dead Man's Chest	2006	$414.3/($423.3)	$218.0/($225.0)
6	Batman	1989	$403.5/($251.2)	$84.3/($53.5)
7	Thunderball	1965	$395.2/($63.6)	$41.9/($6.8)
8	Spider-Man 2	2004	$385.4/($373.4)	$206.8/($200.0)
9	Superman—The Movie	1978	$367.7/($134.2)	$177.3/($55.0)
10	Smokey and the Bandit	1977	$364.3/($126.7)	$14.3/($4.4)
11	Goldfinger	1964	$352.1/($51.1)	$18.6/($3.0)
12	Indiana Jones and the Temple of Doom	1984	$343.1/($179.9)	$53.0/($28.2)
13	Pirates of the Caribbean: The Curse of the Black Pearl	2003	$324.7/($305.4)	$148.6/($140.0)
14	Indiana Jones and the Last Crusade	1989	$316.8/($197.2)	$87.2/($55.4)
15	Spider-Man 3	2007	$313.5/($336.5)	$243.0/($55.4)

Academy Award winner for Best Picture: none

U.S. INDUSTRY PRODUCTION STATISTICS, 1980s
Equivalent 2005 $s /(Unadjusted $s)

$45.0 Million ($24.9 million)
Average production cost of films featured in this chapter

$22.3 Million ($9.4 million)
Average production cost of all films released in the 1980s

Index of Top Feature Film Directors Included in This Chapter

1	Steven Spielberg	*Raiders of the Lost Ark*
		E.T.: The Extra-Terrestrial
		Indiana Jones and the Temple of Doom
		The Color Purple
		Indiana Jones and the Last Crusade
2	Irvin Kirshner	*Star Wars: V The Empire Strikes Back*
3	Robert Zemeckis	*Back to the Future*
		Who Framed Roger Rabbit
4	Richard Marquand	*Star Wars: VI Return of the Jedi*
5	Tony Scott	*Top Gun*
		Beverly Hills Cop II
6	Sydney Pollack	*Tootsie*
		Out of Africa
7	Ivan Reitman	*Ghostbusters*
8	Martin Brest	*Beverly Hills Cop*
9	Tim Burton	*Batman*
10	Peter Faiman	*Crocodile Dundee*

See Note to the Reader for selection criteria.

Top 10 Critically Acclaimed Lead Actors of the 1980s

Rank	Actor Name
1	Dustin Hoffman
2	Paul Newman
3	Michael Caine
4	Robert Duvall
5	Henry Fonda
6	Robert De Niro
7	Ben Kingsley
8	William Hurt
9	Michael Douglas
10	F. Murray Abraham

Rank	Actress Name
1	Katharine Hepburn
2	Meryl Streep
3	Shirley MacLaine
4	Geraldine Page
5	Sissy Spacek
6	Jodi Foster
7	Sigourney Weaver
8	Sally Field
9	Whoopi Goldberg
10	Cher and Jessica Tandy (tie)

See Note to the Reader for selection criteria.

High Box Office Does Not Always Mean High Profit

Even with *Who Framed Roger Rabbit*'s (1988) worldwide theatrical box office of $349 million, *Rain Man*'s (1988) $413 million, and *Batman*'s (1989) $411 million, all three films reported a loss to their net profit participants. As a general rule, fewer than 5 percent of released films show a profit for net profit participation purposes. With gross participations and other costs eating up the net participants' share, various lawsuits resulted, starting with Art Buchwald's against Paramount in 1989, which concerned net profits for the film *Coming to America* (1988); continuing with a suit by Winston Groom, author of the novel *Forrest Gump,* pertaining to his net share from that movie, released in 1994; and a suit against *My Big Fat Greek Wedding,* which was filed in Los Angeles in 2003 by Nia Vardalos, Tom Hanks, Rita Wilson, and Gary Goetzman. The bigger the budget, the more costly the ad campaign, and the greater the number of gross participants involved, the less likely big box-office movies will have positive net profits. Despite this, the 1970s and 1980s were a period of high profitability from theatrical releases. With rising production costs, rising print and ad costs, more gross participations, and more or less flat revenues, films released in future decades would be more and more dependent on video and other ancillary markets to break even, let alone make a profit.

PROFIT AND LOSS
Who Framed Roger Rabbit, 1988
Walt Disney Co. P&L as of 12/31/1990
Unadjusted $s in Thousands of Dollars

Description	Revenue and Costs	Percentage of Revenue
Domestic theatrical (box office)	$154,112	not available
Foreign theatrical (box office)	$195,000	not available
Total theatrical box office	$349,112	
Domestic theatrical (rentals)	$80,763	39%
Foreign theatrical (rentals)	$80,102	39%
Home video	$26,573	12%
Pay TV and nontheatrical	$11,996	8%
Consumer products and other	$5,686	2%
Subtotal gross receipts	$205,120	100%

Description	Revenue and Costs	Percentage of Costs
Distribution fees	$68,259	30%
Production cost (including overhead)	$58,166	26%
Advertising and publicity (worldwide)	$48,333	22%
Interest on production cost	$17,105	7%
Gross participations	$17,054	7%
Prints (worldwide)	$5,746	3%
Residuals	$3,415	2%
Other (checking, collections, conversion, trade dues, taxes, insurance, transportation, misc.)	$6,640	3%
Subtotal costs	$224,718	100%
Net profit (loss)	($19,600)	

Actors of the 1980s: Comparison of Salaries and Profit Participations
Equivalent 2005 $s /(Unadjusted $s)

Actor	Film	Initial Release	Salary
Sylvester Stallone	*Rocky IV*	1985	**$27.2 million** ($15 million)
	First Blood (AKA Rambo 1)	1982	**$7.1 million** ($3.5 million)
Michael Douglas	*Fatal Attraction*	1987	**$15.3 million including p/p*** ($8.9 million including p/p)
Eddie Murphy	*Beverly Hills Cop II*	1987	**$13.8 million** ($8.0 million)
	Beverly Hills Cop	1984	**$7.5 million** ($4.0 million)
Dustin Hoffman	*Tootsie*	1982	**$11.1 million** ($5.5 million)
	Rain Man	1988	**$9.6 million + gross p/p** ($5.8 million + gross p/p)
Jack Nicholson	*Batman*	1989	**$9 million excluding p/p** ($6 million salary + 15–20% gross p/p)
Bruce Willis	*Die Hard*	1988	**$8.3 million** ($5.0 million)
Michael Keaton	*Batman*	1989	**$7.9 million** ($5.0 million)
Tom Cruise	*Rain Man*	1988	**$5.0 million + gross p/p** ($3.0 million + gross p/p)
	Top Gun	1986	**$3.6 million** ($2.0 million)
Sigourney Weaver	*Aliens*	1986	**$1.8 million** ($1.0 million)
Arnold Schwarzenegger	*Terminator*	1984	**$0.1 million** ($75,000)

*Profit participation.

A Sampling of Director/Producer Salaries, 1980s
Equivalent 2005 $s /(Unadjusted $s)

Director/Producer	Film	Initial Release	Salary
Barry Levinson (director)	*Rain Man*	1988	**$4,127,219** ($2,500,000 + percentage of the gross)
Peter Guber and Jon Peters (executive producers)	*Rain Man*	1988	**$247,633/each** $150,000 + percentage of the gross/each

PROFIT AND LOSS
Batman, 1989
Warner Bros. Estimated P&L as of 1999
Unadjusted $s in Thousands of Dollars

Description	Revenue and Costs	Percentage of Revenue
Domestic theatrical (box office)	$251,189	NA
Foreign theatrical (box office)	$159,478	NA
Total theatrical box office	$410,667	
Domestic theatrical (rentals estimated)	$152,052	60%
Foreign theatrical (rentals estimated)	$71,765	28%
Other revenue	$29,583	12%
Subtotal gross receipts	$253,400	100%

Description	Revenue and Costs	Percentage of Costs
Distribution fees	$80,000	28%
Production cost (including overhead)	$53,500	19%
Advertising and publicity (worldwide)	$62,400	22%
Interest on production cost	$10,800	4%
Gross participations	$60,000	21%
Prints (worldwide)	$9,000	3%
Other (editing, dubbing, taxes, duties, customs, trade association fees, freight, handling and insurance, checking, collection, guild and union residuals)	$12,500	3%
Subtotal costs	$288,200	100%
Net profit (loss)	($34,800)	

Note: It was the gross participations, especially those paid star actor Jack Nicholson, that left net-profit participants with nothing. In addition to an "upfront" fee of $6 million, Nicholson also received 15 percent to 20 percent of the gross. Other participants had similar gross participations, which took $60 million of the film's income.

617

DISTRIBUTION OVERVIEW

Studios Morph to Keep Up with New Distribution Platforms

The growing number of ways to raise money for production and to exploit movies so that they result in much larger returns brought new attention to the movie industry from Wall Street investors and from media conglomerates looking to vertically integrate multiple businesses on a variety of global distribution platforms. The era when the movie business was first and foremost about the theatrical release was over. A movie could still be seen in theaters first, but now it could have a long life in ancillary media too. Because it took deeper pockets to pay for these expensive new productions and mass-marketing campaigns, significant changes in the ownership of the major studios through mergers and takeovers began to occur.

Columbia Pictures was a public company in 1982 when it was acquired for $692 million by Coca-Cola, the largest supplier of soft drinks to theaters and to the world. Coke also paid $445 million for TV and movie producer Embassy/Tandem, $200 million for Merv Griffin's television company *Wheel of Fortune,* and roughly $100 million for its Tri-Star investment. Although Coca-Cola was seeking synergy with its soft drink sales via these transactions, it racked up big losses instead and was soon embarrassed by management mistakes and bombs such as *Ishtar,* an inordinately expensive comedy with Dustin Hoffman and Warren Beatty. Coca-Cola did launch Tri-Star Pictures as a partnership with HBO and CBS, but never found the success it was looking for. After seven years of ownership, Coca-Cola sold Columbia and Tri-Star to the Sony Corporation, a sale that was controversial because it marked the first time a Japanese company owned a major U.S. studio.

Early in the decade Denver oil millionaire Marvin Davis and silent partner Marc Rich acquired 20th Century-Fox. After selling off many of the noncore assets, such as theaters in New Zealand, and buying out Rich's interests when he became a fugitive from U.S. justice, Davis sold Fox in mid-decade to Rupert Murdoch's News Corp., which found greater synergy with its TV, publishing, and satellite television interests. Murdoch in 1987 used Fox as a base to launch a fourth U.S. TV network.

Self-made Las Vegas gaming and transportation mogul Kirk Kerkorian first bought MGM in 1969. In 1981 MGM gobbled up United Artists, but Kerkorian still found little success in movies and sold MGM/UA to Ted Turner's Turner Broadcasting in 1986. However, Turner had even less success with the company. Kerkorian then acquired MGM/UA once again, only to sell it in 1990 to Giancarlo Parretti, the shady Italian financier who funded the deal with money borrowed from the French bank Crédit Lyonnais. Most of the bank's money was lost, and in 1996 Kerkorian bought MGM/UA a third time.

Late in the decade, Paramount Pictures was reorganized after the death of Charles Bludhorn, head of Gulf and Western, which had acquired the studio in 1966. Under new chairman

Martin Davis, who forced out the successful team of Barry Diller and Michael Eisner in 1984, Paramount sold off many of the old Gulf and Western assets and renamed the company Paramount Communications.

Walt Disney Studios, after a long decline following the death of its founder, was revived with new ownership and new management beginning in 1984, when Michael Eisner and Jeffrey Katzenberg arrived from Paramount and were joined by Frank Wells, a lawyer and longtime Warner executive. This triumvirate breathed new life into the Disney studio, business, and brand. Disney quickly emerged as a major player.

In March 1989, Warner Communications and Time, Inc., announced their intention to merge. Paramount subsequently launched a hostile bid for Time and filed suit to stop the merger. The formation of the new Time Warner company was finally completed in January 1990 and represented another effort at corporate synergy, with movies and magazines expected to boost each other. It also represented another example of how little synergy can be generated when a merger isn't a good fit.

The men who now occupy the ornate offices and enjoy the titles of chief executive officer or chief operating officer at the six major studios recognize that most of their industry's current convulsions are part of something larger—call it an evolution or a revolution, a transition or a take over—that will change the movie industry as dramatically as television did some 30 years ago. "This precise time, this historical moment, the actions we take in the next year, will dictate the make up of this industry twenty years from now," says Barry Diller, 41, chairman of Paramount Pictures. "In 20 years," Diller adds, "I don't believe all the same major movie companies that have been around for the last fifty years will still be here." —ALJEAN HARMETZ, ROLLING BREAKS AND OTHER MOVIE BUSINESS, 1983

Major Movie Distributors, 1980s

Buena Vista	Company is under new management beginning in 1984.
Columbia	Columbia is bought by Coca-Cola in 1982 then sold to Sony in 1989.
MGM/United Artists	Owner Kirk Kerkorian buys United Artists in 1981. MGM/UA is sold to Turner Broadcasting in 1986 and then bought for the second time by Kerkorian that same year.
Paramount Pictures	Martin Davis reorganizes and renames the company Paramount Communications in 1989.
20th Century-Fox	Fox is sold to Marvin Davis for $722 million in 1981 and then sold to Rupert Murdoch's News Corp. in 1985.
Universal Pictures	Continues under MCA ownership throughout the decade.
Warner Bros	Warner Communications announces its merger with Time, Inc., in 1989.

Spotlight on Orion Pictures

With new investor interest in movies, a handful of new movie distributors arose to take advantage of the growing capacity of the multiplex theaters. These companies benefited from the availability of funding but also ran into the usual problems posed by trying to make hit movies. Among the most noteworthy was Orion Pictures, which emerged in March 1978 when five executives who had left United Artists as a group, after winning three Best Picture Oscars in a row, started the company, taking as their symbol a constellation with five main stars. The founders were UA chair Arthur B. Krim, UA president Eric Pleskow, UA chair of the finance committee Robert S. Benjamin, UA head of business affairs William Bernstein, and UA head of production Mike Medavoy.

Orion began with a $100 million line of credit to finance films that would be distributed through Warner Bros., with Orion in theory controlling distribution and advertising. The plan was to have a studio, but no studio lot, to keep overhead costs low. The company was based in New York City, as was United Artists. Orion quickly made deals with actress-director Barbra Streisand, director-producer Francis Ford Coppola, and actor-producer John Travolta, among others. They paid high prices for top literary properties on which to base their movies, including $1 million for a new book by the author of *Coma*. They also agreed to distribute films from English entertainment conglomerate EMI. Within a year, Orion had more than fifteen films set in or nearing production. Among the first wave of films released in 1979, Orion's big hit was *10*, a romantic comedy starring Dudley Moore and Bo Derek. In late 1980, Woody Allen signed on to make movies.

After failures, such as the 1979 releases *The Great Santini* and *A Little Romance,* Orion's managers wanted to control their own distribution. So they acquired the assets of Filmways, a B-movie studio that had a 500-film library and a theatrical distribution apparatus in place, with an assist from HBO and a Wall Street bank. Orion's management quickly shed other Filmways subsidiaries that published books and made radio equipment, in order to focus on movies. The Filmways TV library included the former American International Pictures movies, as well as

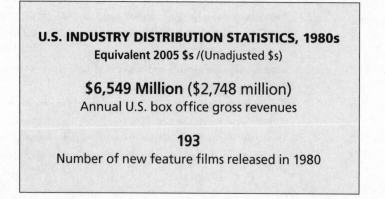

U.S. INDUSTRY DISTRIBUTION STATISTICS, 1980s
Equivalent 2005 $s /(Unadjusted $s)

$6,549 Million ($2,748 million)
Annual U.S. box office gross revenues

193
Number of new feature films released in 1980

such TV shows as *The Beverly Hillbillies, Green Acres, Mister Ed,* and *The Addams Family,* which provided syndication revenue and later fodder for remakes. Orion had the critically acclaimed Oscar winner *Amadeus* in 1984 but was off to a slow start despite the big expenditures. After six years, it still had only one big hit with *10,* which led the Wall Street banker to sell out its interest. Orion soon gained new investment first from Viacom and then from Metromedia and later National Amusements.

In February 1986, Orion finally had another hit when Woody Allen came through with one of his most successful films, *Hannah and Her Sisters.* That was followed in June by *Back to School,* a comedy starring Rodney Dangerfield, which took in nearly $100 million in domestic box office. In December *Platoon,* a Vietnam War film, was a critical and commercial hit. Orion also scored with the summer 1987 hits *Robocop* and *No Way Out.* As the decade ended, however, Orion films were doing poorly once again, with such disappointments as *Erik the Viking, The Package,* and the highly anticipated film about Jerry Lee Lewis, *Great Balls of Fire.* Within two years, despite the success of the 1990 release *Dances with Wolves,* Orion went down in flames, filing for bankruptcy. As it suffered through receivership, Orion's movie *The Silence of the Lambs* swept all five major Academy Awards. By the time of the Oscar party, however, most of the founders and key Orion employees were gone.

TECHNOLOGY SPOTLIGHT

Industrial Light & Magic, Visual Effects Magician

In May 1975, George Lucas gathered a group of special effects professionals in an old Van Nuys warehouse. Lucas challenged the new company, Industrial Light & Magic (ILM), to create the most dazzling special effects ever seen for his upcoming film, *Star Wars.* John Dykstra led the team in converting the warehouse into a studio, creating the ingenious Dykstraflex computerized motion control camera system and experimenting with innovative ways of filming miniature models. Their work earned them an Oscar in 1977 for Best Visual Effects. Lucas next launched ILM's computer division in 1979 with the specific directive of propelling the art of special effects into the realms of digital image processing, editing, and interactivity.

In the 1980s, ILM focused on improving computer effects software and advancing motion control systems. After scooping up their second Oscar for *The Empire Strikes Back,* the team developed the Empire Motion Picture Camera System and the "go-motion" animation blur system. As the decade progressed, it achieved a series of stunning digital milestones—the first all-digital sequence, the first computer-generated characters, the EditDroid nonlinear computer editing system, and Morf, an image manipulation software program for the film *Willow.*

Throughout the 1990s, ILM dominated the art of visual effects in modern big-budget filmmaking. Its work digitally replicating human skin and utilizing Morf in *Death Becomes Her,* employing digital compositing software and creating realistic life-forms in *Jurassic Park,* and

621

perfecting input scanning and image processing software for *Forrest Gump* helped it garner three Oscars in quick succession. Subsequent innovations included the interactive digital compositing and editing system SABRE, the VistaGlide dolly and camera motion control system for split-screen effects, Cari facial animation software, and Viewpaint for 3-D color and texture. It also set industry standards by creating the first completely CG main character in a feature film, developing software for photorealistic hair, fur, and skin, successfully compositing actors into a fully virtual set, perfecting the digital retouching of shots, and expertly mixing photorealistic cartoons with live action in *Mask*. By the close of the decade, ILM's digital advances enabled Lucas to realize his technologically daunting epic, *Star Wars: Episode I The Phantom Menace*. Ninety percent of that film utilized digital effects of some kind, including the second fully CG character and a number of completely CG scenes.

In the 2000s, ILM continued leading the pack in digital effects. It first developed the MARS motion and structure recovery system and the Creature Dynamics System. Then, in 2002, ILM helped Lucas create *Attack of the Clones,* the first major film shot completely on digital high-definition video. Most recently, ILM's development and use of the iMocap computer vision actor tracking system helped it win its fifteenth Oscar for the 2006 epic *Pirates of the Caribbean: Dead Man's Chest.*

ILM Achievements Through 2005

In 2004 President George W. Bush presents ILM with the National Medal of Technology.

ILM is the first (and only) entertainment company ever to receive this honor.

ILM has fifteen Oscar wins for Best Visual Effects and twenty-three nominations.

The company has received nineteen Scientific and Technical Achievement Awards.

The studio has worked on over 250 films.

THX and Dolby Raise the Bar for Theater Sound

The release of *Star Wars* and *Close Encounters of the Third Kind* marked the introduction of a new generation of sound in movies. Beginning in 1972, Dolby Labs offered a system to reduce extraneous noise. The public soon caught on. Many patrons would travel across town or pay more to attend movies with improved Dolby Noise Reduction.

In 1975 the first Dolby Stereo system for theaters allowed for the encoding of four channels of audio information on the movie strip (left, right, center, and surround). A home version, known as Dolby Surround, was offered after 1982, followed by an improved version, known as Dolby Pro-Logic, in 1987. Despite Dolby's advances in film surround formats, as the 1980s arrived many theaters still had antiquated sound systems. The loudspeaker systems that were placed behind the screen had been developed just after World War II. Theaters often had equipment that was mismatched, antiquated, or improperly positioned. The acoustics were often poor.

Filmmaker George Lucas was interested in exploiting all of the possibilities of the new film sound formats, so in 1980 he hired Tomlinson Holman, an audio equipment designer, to create a high-performance mixing stage. Holman's research led to a unified approach to theater design that became the foundation of the THX Sound System.

Lucas had long been unhappy that the sound created in postproduction was not what was ultimately heard in theaters. He applauded Dolby Laboratories and worked with them, but he saw that something more was needed. Lucas felt the public was cheated by not hearing movies the way the filmmaker intended. That led to the birth of the THX Sound System; the name THX was borrowed from Lucas's first feature, *THX 1138*. It was the first systematic approach to better cinema sound.

Lucas's *Return of the Jedi* was the first movie to be mixed on a THX mixing stage. The system's designs were applied to two commercial theaters in time for the film's opening day in 1983. Soon THX engineers were involved in every step of construction of new cinemas, which were being built at a record clip in the late 1980s. After construction, these engineers returned to test for acoustic and visual performance, to ensure that sound, music, and dialogue were evenly balanced and that background noise from nearby auditoriums, or even the candy counter and the lobby, would not distract from the presentation in that auditorium.

THX manufactured only one product to be used in a cinema installation. This was an electronic crossover used to divide the sound between speaker components. Manufacturers submitted products (amplifiers and loudspeaker components) to THX for testing, and those that passed were allowed to be used in THX-certified sound systems. One core focus of the system's design was the acoustic environment behind the screen. Holman developed the concept of the "baffle wall," which smoothed the sound coming from the screen speakers while absorbing the sound reflected from the screen itself. This concept was granted a patent. The core surround technologies behind THX remained Dolby Stereo and Dolby Stereo 70 mm. For his work at Skywalker Sound and Lucasfilm's THX division, Tomlinson Holman was given a Technical Achievement Award by the Academy of Motion Picture Arts and Sciences for "the research and systems integration resulting in the improvement of motion picture loudspeaker systems" in 2001.

TAP Takes It to the Next Level

With THX setting standards to address the major issues in cinema sound presentation, Lucas was also interested in ensuring that the variability of prints and their presentation was addressed. Along with the introduction of the THX Sound System, the release of *Return of the Jedi* also saw the creation of TAP, or the Theatre Alignment Program, as a service to the studios, filmmakers, and theaters. TAP was a comprehensive quality assurance program that reviewed release prints for image and soundtrack quality, provided exhibitors with technical facts about equipment alignment, oversaw on-site equipment alignment, and offered a toll-free phone number to report presentation problems.

On the printmaking front, TAP would have personnel at film labs around the world for several weeks before a movie was to premiere. They would check prints around the clock in some cases. In other instances, the TAP personnel would actually accompany the print to the theater. At the theater, other TAP engineers might be adjusting light levels and sound systems. In some cases they provided information from the director on how the film was to play (louder or softer, for instance).

By the end of the 1980s, both Dolby and THX were brands that meant better sound and visual presentation for filmgoers. That was one of the best forms of marketing for a theater. As new multiplexes were built they began to compete to see who could offer the best environment and presentation. That was good news for filmmakers and ticket buyers. The result was more improvements in movie presentation in the decade of the 1980s than in the entire preceding half century.

MARKETING SPOTLIGHT

Merchandising: The New Movie Mantra

There had been some licensed merchandise associated with movies over the years, from Shirley Temple dolls to the *Sound of Music* soundtrack, but the moguls didn't think the life cycle of a movie was long enough to translate into significant sales in a wide range of other merchandise categories. That bit of conventional wisdom began to change with *Jaws* in 1975 and even more so with *Star Wars* in 1977, its sequels in 1980 and 1983, and its prequels in 1999, 2002, and 2005, which together yielded licensing retail revenues of over $12 billion—a figure no other property in the realm of movie merchandising has come close to. There were action figures, lunch boxes, clothing, books, and much more. Curiously, George Lucas later said in an interview that he hadn't foreseen the licensing bonanza. Working together with Fox on the first film, Lucasfilm had set up the movie's release with a novel that predated the initial release by five months and a comic book that became an instant best seller and foretold the long lines at the box office, taking the rest of Hollywood by surprise. Because he held the sequel rights to his first film, Lucas had the leverage to get licensing rights back from the studio when making the deal for *The Empire Strikes Back.* He later said that he wanted those rights because he was unsure how much the studio would spend to market the movie, and he wanted to secure licensing partners to add further support and exposure.

With the licensing success of *Star Wars,* everyone in the movie business wanted in. It became a question of which movies would lend themselves best to toy, game, and merchandise sales. *Star Wars,* with its clear heroes and villains and uplifting themes, certainly had worked. That same formula would also work for *E.T.: The Extra-Terrestrial,* which sold lots of varied goods, including Reese's Pieces, a candy that saw its sales increase 80 percent after Mars turned down the opportunity to feature its M&M's candy in the film. But licensing also could have its downside. Because of the overproliferation of *E.T.* merchandise, Atari was nearly bankrupted and had to bury millions of units of unsold *E.T.* video games.

It was generally easier to license a sequel with an established profile and defined audience than a new, totally untested property. So every studio began looking for merchandising synergy. In the era of the franchises, franchising was in.

Unfortunately, the public didn't always follow the marketer's drumbeat. Although the John Huston–directed 1982 film *Annie,* a musical based on a long-running play, attracted large audiences in theaters, the movie lost money, as did the extensive merchandising efforts. That lesson came home again in the summer of 1984, which was a boom season at the box office but a merchandising bust for some. *Ghostbusters* was wildly popular in theaters, but its licensed merchandise didn't sell well in toy stores. It was only later on, after there was an animated TV series, *The Real Ghostbusters* (1986–91), that product sales would take off. The summer of 1988 included *Gremlins,* a hit for Warner at the box office but a dud for toy sellers, and *Who Framed Roger Rabbit,* which had a large tie-in program but only modest sales.

In 1989 a battle was waged between *Ghostbusters II, Indiana Jones and the Last Crusade,* and *Batman,* based on the comic book character, who was the subject of a campy 1960s TV series. All three movies performed well at the ticket window, but only one took off at retail—*Batman.* Its merchandising began months before the movie was released, with people wearing the *Batman* logo on a wide range of products, from T-shirts to pajamas. By the time the movie opened, there was full-scale Batmania. The endless merchandise focused largely on the Bat-Signal, the image of Jack Nicholson as the Joker, and the beefcake Michael Keaton dressed in the famed rubber suit. Warner Bros. took advantage of Batmania, selling product through its own stores as well as through the general retail marketplace with the help and expertise of Licensing Corporation of America. It didn't hurt that its wholly owned subsidiary D.C. Comics was the property owner and could support the program with an ongoing publishing program— something *Star Wars* did as well, with new stories that helped keep the saga alive between film releases.

Comparison of Five 1980s Films Initial Release
Equivalent 2005 $s /(Unadjusted $s) in Millions of $s

Film	Year	Domestic Box Office	Domestic Rentals	Foreign Rentals	Production Cost	Domestic Print and Ad Costs
Raiders of the Lost Ark	1981	$415.2 ($180.1)	$208.5 ($90.4)	$147.1 ($63.8)	$48.9 ($22.8)	$25.8 ($12.0)
Back to the Future	1985	$374.7 ($208.2)	$184.2 ($102.0)	$138.5 ($76.7)	$40.0 ($22.0)	$21.8 ($12.0)
Top Gun	1986	$305.4 ($176.8)	$137.6 ($79.6)	$130.6 ($75.6)	$33.9 ($19.0)	$21.4 ($12.0)
E.T.: The Extra-Terrestrial	1982	$777.1 ($359.2)	$457.5 ($209.8)	$284.2 ($130.4)	$24.6 ($12.2)	$20.2 ($10.0)
Rain Man	1988	$276.3 ($172.8)	$139.4 ($86.8)	$173.5 ($108.0)	$49.5 ($30.0)	$8.3 ($5.0)

EXHIBITION OVERVIEW

The Decade of Litigation

The 1980s began with the United States Justice Department declaring that exhibitors could not decide among themselves what theater was going to play a particular film. This practice was known as splitting. However, many exhibitors continued this practice despite the government's action in *U.S. v. Capitol*. These exhibitors looked to the *Greenbrier* decision in 1981 (*Greenbrier Cinemas Inc. v. Attorney General*), which held that splitting was not illegal. This decision, of course, was contrary to the decision in *U.S. v. Capitol*, as well as that in another case involving General Cinema Corporation in 1982 (*General Cinema Corp. v. Buena Vista*). The government pressed on despite the *Greenbrier* ruling, indicting exhibitors one by one. As legal bills soared, many decided to just pay fines or sign a declaration that they would never engage in splitting, rather than continue the fight. Still, some companies continued to split toward the latter part of the decade, and the government continued to prosecute: *U.S. v. Kerosotes* (1987), *U.S. v. Plitt Southern* (1987), *U.S. v. Cinemette* (1988).

The ongoing government litigation inspired some exhibitors to sue their exhibitor competitors. The results were mixed. The plaintiff was generally a smaller exhibitor that had been excluded from a split arrangement in a market shared with a larger exhibitor, which had been splitting with other larger theaters. The plaintiff's theater was generally inferior and did not produce box office results that were competitive with the defendant's. *Universal Amusements v. General Cinema* (1985), *Three Movies of Tarzana v. Pacific Theatres* (1986), and *Harkins v. General Cinema Harkins I* (1988) all ruled in favor of the defendant, while *7 Gables Corp. v. Sterling* (1987) ruled in favor of the plaintiff. Sterling Recreation Corporation operated the highest-grossing theaters in the greater Seattle area, while 7 Gables was a chain of smaller, much older theaters playing primarily art, foreign, and specialized films. 7 Gables claimed injury from the exclusive licensing of film by distribution to Sterling. The judge agreed with 7 Gables. That ruling, and its subsequent award, financially crippled Sterling, which eventually sold its Seattle theaters to Cineplex and its California theaters to Pacific.

Many believed the Justice Department's aggressive prosecution of theater exhibitors into the late 1980s had an ulterior motive. Some thought it was unusual for the Justice Department to pursue antitrust violations during a Republican administration, since such action was considered to be a Democratic Party agenda. Although the exhibitor lawsuits started under the Democrat Jimmy Carter's administration, they continued after Reagan became president in 1981. Once in office, President Reagan appointed William Baxter as his first antitrust boss. Baxter subsequently declared, " . . . Vertical mergers are never anticompetitive." There were whispers of MCA/Universal mogul Lew Wasserman's interest in seeing old antitrust law rewritten so that his company could enter the emerging pay TV market and also be able to own a movie theater company. Wasserman had been President Reagan's agent during his acting career and was still an important ally and confidant. By the end of Reagan's second term in office, ownership of movie theaters had changed dramatically. Although Wasserman had bought into the USA Network, he was denied permission by the Justice Department to enter into the merger of Showtime and The Movie Channel. He was not, however, denied ownership in a movie theater company.

In 1984 the Justice Department under Reagan revised its merger guidelines. On June 14 it issued a statement saying that it would continue to challenge harmful mergers but "seek to avoid unnecessary interference with that larger universe of mergers that are either competitively beneficial or neutral." The door of vertical integration had swung wide open.

In 1985 Columbia Pictures bought a controlling interest in the Walter Reade Organization's theaters. Columbia along with TriStar Pictures (Columbia had a one-third interest in TriStar) acquired the 230-screen Loews circuit. In 1985 Wasserman agreed to own 49.7 percent of Cineplex-Odeon. In 1986 Paramount acquired Mann, Festival, and Trans-Lux Theatres. And over the next two years, Warner Bros. became Paramount's partner in that acquisition. In 1988 Columbia continued its theatrical ownership expansion by acquiring the Boston-based USA Cinemas. In 1989 the Japanese electronics company Sony purchased Columbia. *Variety*, the industry trade publication, reported on January 7, 1987, that an estimated 4,357 screens changed hands during this transfer of ownership, at a cost of $1.62 billion.

After splitting finally ended, exhibitors returned to competitive bidding. This practice would eventually fade out in the 1990s, replaced by a process wherein distributors allocate film to theaters similarly to how exhibitors did it in the 1970s.

U.S. INDUSTRY EXHIBITION STATISTICS, 1980s
Equivalent 2005 $s /(Unadjusted $s)

$6.41 ($2.69–$3.99)
Average movie ticket price (1980–1989)

17,675
Number of U.S. screens, 1980
(14,171 indoor and 3,504 drive-in)

Franchise Films

Originating in the 1980s

Equivalent 2005 $s in Millions of $s

Rank	Franchise	Number of Films in Franchise	All-Release Worldwide Box Office
1	Batman	6	$3,176.9
2	Indiana Jones	4	$3,014.3
3	Back to the Future	3	$1,556.2
4	Die Hard	4	$1,467.3
5	Lethal Weapon	4	$1,446.6
6	Terminator	3	$1,401.7
7	Beverly Hills Cop	3	$1,254.7
8	Rambo	3	$1,110.2
9	Police Academy	6	$943.7

Indiana Jones

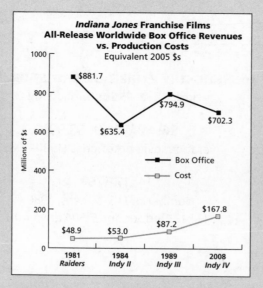

Batman

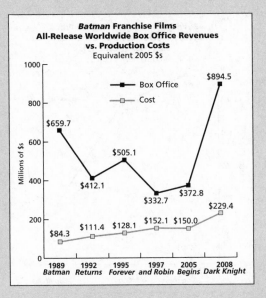

Batman Franchise Films
All-Release Worldwide Box Office Revenues
vs. Production Costs
Equivalent 2005 $s

- Box Office
- Cost

$894.5
$659.7
$505.1
$412.1
$372.8
$332.7
$229.4
$150.0
$152.1
$128.1
$111.4
$84.3

Millions of $s

1989 Batman | 1992 Returns | 1995 Forever | 1997 and Robin | 2005 Begins | 2008 Dark Knight

Back to the Future

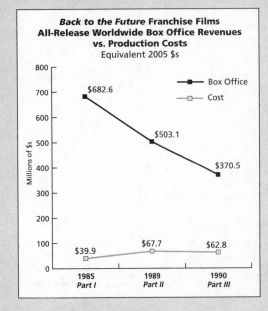

Back to the Future Franchise Films
All-Release Worldwide Box Office Revenues
vs. Production Costs
Equivalent 2005 $s

- Box Office
- Cost

$682.6
$503.1
$370.5
$39.9
$67.7
$62.8

Millions of $s

1985 Part I | 1989 Part II | 1990 Part III

Die Hard

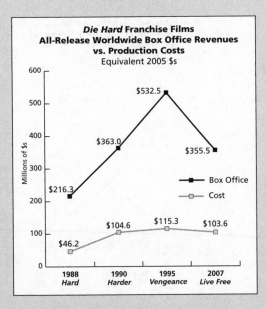

Die Hard Franchise Films
All-Release Worldwide Box Office Revenues
vs. Production Costs
Equivalent 2005 $s

$532.5
$363.0
$355.5
$216.3
$115.3
$104.6
$103.6
$46.2

- Box Office
- Cost

Millions of $s

1988 Hard | 1990 Harder | 1995 Vengeance | 2007 Live Free

Lethal Weapon

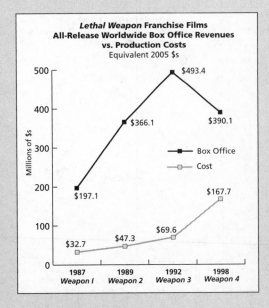

Lethal Weapon Franchise Films
All-Release Worldwide Box Office Revenues
vs. Production Costs
Equivalent 2005 $s

$493.4
$390.1
$366.1
$197.1
$167.7
$69.6
$47.3
$32.7

- Box Office
- Cost

Millions of $s

1987 Weapon I | 1989 Weapon 2 | 1992 Weapon 3 | 1998 Weapon 4

Terminator

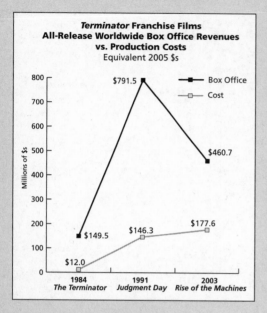

Beverly Hills Cop

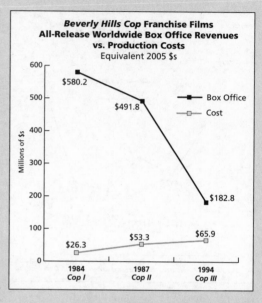

Rambo

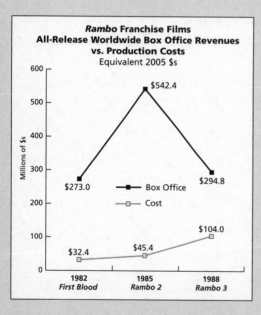

Police Academy

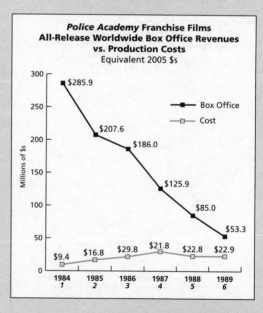

PROFIT AND LOSS
Police Academy Franchise
Warner Bros. P&L

Description	Revenue and Costs Unadjusted $s in Thousands of $s					
	1984	1985	1986	1987	1988	1989
Domestic theatrical (box office)	$81,199	$55,600	$43,579	$28,061	$19,510	$11,567
Foreign theatrical (box office)	$68,641	$59,393	$64,060	$48,758	$34,989	$21,623
Total theatrical box office	$149,840	$114,993	$107,639	$76,819	$54,499	$33,190
Domestic theatrical (rentals)	$37,140	$26,201	$19,929	$13,294	$9,017	$5,058
Foreign theatrical (rentals)	$30,889	$26,727	$28,827	$21,941	$15,745	$9,730
Home video	$4,348	$4,271	$4,263	$4,974	$4,256	$3,405
TV (worldwide)	$9,614	$7,559	$6,020	$3,212	380	0
Pay TV and nontheatrical	$11,378	$10,143	$10,203	$9,146	$7,238	$254
Consumer products and other (including accounts receivable)	$165	$12	$43	$5	$−41	$−970
Subtotal gross receipts	$93,534	$74,913	$69,285	$52,572	$36,595	$17,477
Distribution fees	$31,010	$25,086	$23,638	$18,136	$12,691	$6,220
Production cost	$5,005	$9,231	$12,239	$17,325	$13,858	$14,515
Advertising and publicity (worldwide)	$13,650	$11,307	$12,132	$11,419	$11,626	$12,406
Interest on production cost	$660	$893	$1,458	$4,592	$3,929	$2,542
Print (worldwide)	$2,879	$2,691	$2,999	$3,501	$2,921	$2,541
Residuals	$1,053	$2,184	$1,092	$1,213	$948	$607
Other (reprint, dubbing, subtitles, taxes, trade dues, freight, checking and collection costs, deferments, etc.)	$3,836	$3,008	$3,670	$2,558	$2,218	$1,715
Subtotal costs	$27,083	$29,314	$33,590	$40,608	$35,500	$34,326
Net profit (loss)	$35,441	$20,513	$12,057	($6,172)	($11,596)	($23,069)

Lower Box Office Does Not Necessarily
Mean Lower Net Profits

Although the *Police Academy* franchise is last in cumulative worldwide box office of the franchises begun in the 1980s, the first three movies in the series were very profitable, with producer Paul Maslansky taking in more than $14 million in net profits from the three films combined. Interestingly, Maslansky appeared as an expert witness for the plaintiffs—Art Buchwald and producer Alain Bernheim—in the lawsuit Buchwald levied against Paramount over net profits for the 1988 movie *Coming to America*. Maslansky defended the fairness of net profits in general but said that in certain circumstances net profit deals were unfair, particularly when less deserving gross participants ate up a net participant's profits.

> *On some pictures you have gross participants that are fairly paid a gross . . . and*
> *on other pictures you have gross participants that . . . are unfairly paid a gross*
> *participation . . . there are certain circumstances in which I feel the gross participants*
> *are undeserving because they, by themselves, do not in any way draw more*
> *customers into the theaters than, for example, the producer does,*
> *by virtue of (the) exploitation of his name or the writer's.* —PAUL MASLANSKY

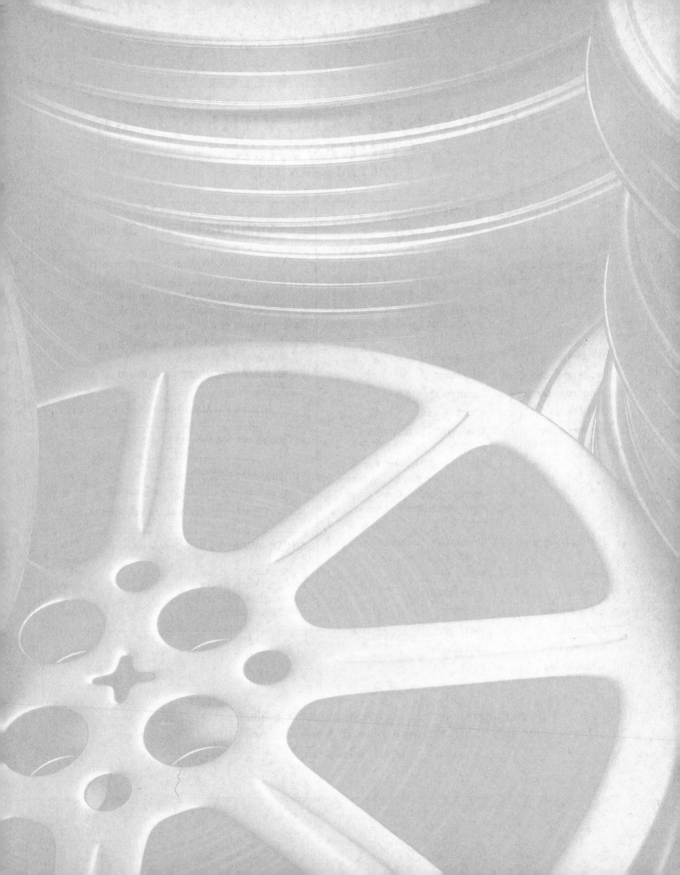

STAR WARS: EPISODE V THE EMPIRE STRIKES BACK

20th Century-Fox, 1980

ALL-RELEASE EQUIVALENT 2005 $s

(Unadjusted $s) in Millions of $s

Domestic Box Office Revenues....... **$620.0**/($290.3)
Production Cost .... 75.8/($32.0)
Principal Photography..................... **172** days
3/5/1979–6/25/1979
29 days (16 percent) on location
143 days (84 percent) in studio

Director .... Irvin Kershner
Producer .... Gary Kurtz
Production Company.... Lucasfilm Ltd.
Story by.............. George Lucas
Screenplay by .... Leigh Brackett, Lawrence Kasdan
Cast .... Mark Hamill, Harrison Ford, Carrie Fisher, Billy Dee Williams, Anthony Daniels, David Prowse, Kenny Baker, Peter Mayhew, Frank Oz
Filming Locations ...... On location: Finse, Norway; in studio: EMI Elstree, UK
Genre................. Sci-Fi
Format............... Color (DeLuxe)
Initial Release.......... 5/21/1980
Rerelease............. 1981, 1982, 1997
Running Time .... 118 minutes
MPAA Rating .... PG

STANDING THE TEST OF TIME

ACADEMY AWARD Oscar Nominations and Wins

Art Direction/Set Decoration: Norman Reynolds, Leslie Dilley, Harry Lange, Alan Tomkins/ Michael Ford

Music (Original Score): John Williams

*SOUND: Bill Varney, Steve Maslow, Gregg Landaker, Peter Sutton

*SPECIAL ACHIEVEMENT AWARD (Visual Effects):

OSCAR TOTALS   Nominations 4   *Wins 2

AFI 100 YEARS 100 MOVIES SELECTION
2007 0   1997..... 0

TOP 300 FILMS POSITION .... **#12**
All-Release Domestic Box Office in Equivalent 2005 $s

National Film Preservation Board Selection....none

OTHER AWARDS Best Picture Wins

	Year
Golden Globes	none
New York Film Critics......................	none
National Board of Review..................	none
Film Daily Critics......................	none

Nobody's ever going to let anybody make a movie. You have to go out and do it! And those who can figure out how to do it—do it. And nothing can stop them.

—George Lucas

PLOT: Pursued by the Empire's sinister agents, the Rebels flee across the galaxy. Luke Sky-walker continues his Jedi training, but must face a terrible truth during a confrontation with Darth Vader.

PRODUCTION: In a make-or-break move designed to gain independence from studio interference, George Lucas used his personal profits from *Star Wars* as collateral to finance its first sequel himself. He brokered a distribution deal with 20th Century-Fox, risking everything on his own ability to deliver a blockbuster film. With the clock ticking and his own money draining away, he first hired Leigh Brackett to try her hand at writing the screenplay. Tragically, she died of cancer shortly after delivering a draft in February 1978. Lucas then hammered out a second draft himself. When Lawrence Kasdan turned in his script for another pending project, *Raiders of the Lost Ark,* Lucas immediately snagged him to pump out a third draft of *The Empire Strikes Back.* Lucas and producer Gary Kurtz then launched a massive search for a director, finally selecting Irvin Kershner. Finally, with the core team set and the original cast returning, he was ready to thrust the production into principal photography. Before they began, Lucas made sure he had false script pages printed to preserve certain key plot secrets. Crews established their base camp in Finse, Norway, a few weeks before shooting commenced there on March 5, 1979. They were immediately besieged by bone-chilling temperatures and hazardous blizzard conditions that kept them virtual prisoners in their ski lodge. The problems continued at England's Elstree Studios. A fire and a delayed Stanley Kubrick production, *The Shining,* caused them to lose more time on constructing their sixty-four sets. For one in particular, the Dagobah swamp, crews covered an entire stage with a three-foot platform and flooded it. Once filming did begin on March 13, Mark Hamill suffered a battery of injuries, Alec Guinness endured an eye infection, and numerous machines and costumes malfunctioned. Then, on June 6, 1979, second-unit director John Barry died of infectious meningitis. Production halted for a half day for his funeral on June 11. By July, with the production ballooning into giant overruns, Lucas took decisive action. He sacrificed a percentage of his profits to Fox in return for their guarantee on a new loan with a new bank. It was another bold and risky move, but it paved the way for the film's release.

DISTRIBUTION: Lucas's instincts were validated when lines began forming outside theaters three days prior to the May 21 opening. It was an instant smash, raking in $9.6 million its first week in release and garnering heavy critical acclaim for its brooding tone, intense action, and shocking twists. In fact, the plot secrets had been so well guarded that most of those who had worked on the film first heard James Earl Jones's dubbed revelation that Vader was Luke's father when they watched the film in theaters with everyone else. Lucas's heavy financial risks were ultimately rewarded when the film went on to gross more than $538 million worldwide. One negative occurred when Lucas became briefly embroiled in a dispute with both the WGA and DGA over his film's unorthodox credits, which appear only at the end. Lucas begrudgingly settled with the two guilds to protect Kasdan and Kershner, and then he resigned from both organizations. —*Scott Mazak*

ORDINARY PEOPLE
Paramount, 1980

ALL-RELEASE EQUIVALENT 2005 $s
(Unadjusted $s) in Millions of $s

Domestic Box Office Revenues . . . . $130.5/($54.8)
Production Cost . . . . $14.2/($6.0)
Principal Photography . . . . **60** days estimated
10/9/1979–1/10/1980

Director . . . . Robert Redford

Producer . . . . Ronald L. Schwary

Production Company . . . . Wildwood Enterprises

Story by . . . . Based on the novel by
Judith Guest

Screenplay by . . . . Alvin Sargent

Cast . . . . Donald Sutherland, Mary Tyler
Moore, Judd Hirsch,
Timothy Hutton

Filming Locations . . . . . . Chicago, Fort Sheridan,
Highland Park, Lake Bluff,
Lake Forest, and Northbrook IL;
Apple Valley, CA; Paramount
Studios; Los Angeles, CA

Genre . . . . Drama

Format . . . . Color (Technicolor)

Initial Release 9/19/1980

Rerelease . . . . none

Running Time . . . . 123 minutes

MPAA Rating . . . . R

STANDING THE TEST OF TIME

ACADEMY AWARD Oscar Nominations and Wins

*BEST PICTURE: Ronald L. Schwary, Producer

Actor in a Supporting Role: Judd Hirsch

*ACTOR IN A SUPPORTING ROLE: Timothy
Hutton

Actress in a Leading Role: Mary Tyler Moore

*DIRECTING: Robert Redford

*WRITING (Screenplay – based on material from
another medium): Alvin Sargent

OSCAR TOTALS Nominations 6 ***Wins 4**

AFI 100 YEARS 100 MOVIES SELECTION
2007 0   1997 0

TOP 300 FILMS POSITION . . . . none
All-Release Domestic Box Office in Equivalent 2005 $s

National Film Preservation Board Selection . . . . none

OTHER AWARDS Best Picture Wins

	Year
Golden Globes (Drama)	1981
New York Film Critics	1980
National Board of Review	1980
Film Daily Critics	none

*I've been frustrated for many years in wanting to have total control of something.
It's like doing a painting. I started out to be an artist, and the one thing I always missed as
an actor was that when you painted a picture, it was yours. But directing comes about
as close as you can get to having it exactly as you want.*

—Robert Redford

PLOT: An upper-middle-class American family struggles to hold things together and love one another in the aftermath of one son's accidental death while sailing and the other son's subsequent suicide attempt prompted by guilt over what happened.

PRODUCTION: Originally a short story exploring the anatomy of depression, Judith Guest's 1976 novel *Ordinary People* was an instant best seller. Popular acting star, producer, and sex-symbol Robert Redford was interested in directing through his independent company, Wildwood Enterprises. When a staff member recommended *Ordinary People,* he decided it was the right material for his debut as a director. He felt it was time to do his own project. "I'd been interested in the challenge of keeping the family intact long before I read Guest's book, so I made this very low-budget film and finally I was able to say, this is the way I want to do it, this is my statement." The first draft screenplay took a year and a half, and the second draft another year, as Alvin Sargent meticulously adapted the novel's heavy dialogue into a brilliant screenplay. Redford was also keenly interested in design, seeking to contrast the nearly perfect home with the messy lives of the characters. For the role of Conrad, Redford conducted a nationwide search, finally casting Timothy Hutton, the nineteen-year-old son of the late actor Jim Hutton, in his feature film debut. To prepare, Hutton spent a week posing as an outpatient at a private psychiatric hospital. For the part of the psychiatrist, Judd Hirsch was cast (after Gene Hackman turned down the role), on the condition that he could film his scenes in eight days to accommodate his schedule for the TV show *Taxi.* The studio wanted Redford to play the father, but he cast more unconventional types: Donald Sutherland, known for playing off-the-wall characters, as the father, and Mary Tyler Moore, known primarily as the cheery career woman on TV, to play the cold, unsympathetic mother. Redford said, "I became interested in the dark side of Mary Tyler Moore." However, he worked intently to avoid having her be the villain. For instance, she is never seen in flashbacks like Conrad and Calvin, because Redford wanted to show her rigid self-control. He also wanted the viewer to experience the film on a visceral level. He succeeded in doing this by using silence more often than music, making Marvin Hamlisch's soft score even more poignant, framed by the gorgeous cinematography of John Bailey. Redford used unorthodox lighting techniques such as shooting the scenes at the doctor's office with increasingly darker lighting to re-create the effect of days getting dark progressively earlier through the autumn. Some scenes were shot at an abandoned laundry facility by Fort Sheridan, a sprawling, peeling army base on the North Shore that Redford refurbished as a soundstage, complete with a $200,000 reproduction of a fourteen-room traditional Lake Forest house.

DISTRIBUTION: After opening strongly to mostly critical raves in six theaters (with an average of $28,389 per screen), the movie widened, finishing in the top 15 highest domestic box office movies of 1980. Redford became the first major star to win the Best Director Oscar for his first film. His acceptance is one of the shortest ever: "Thank you very much." Judd Hirsch's portrayal drew praise from the psychiatric community as a rare instance when psychiatry is shown in a positive light. —*Hayley Taylor Block*

RAGING BULL

United Artists, 1980

ALL-RELEASE EQUIVALENT 2005 $s

(Unadjusted $s) in Millions of $s

Domestic Box Office Revenues . . . . **$55.9**/($23.5)
Production Cost . . . . **$42.7**/($18.0)
Principal Photography . . . . **100** days estimated
4/1979–10/1979

Director	Martin Scorsese
Producer	Irwin Winkler and Robert Chartoff in association with Peter Savage
Production Company	United Artists Films
Story by	Based on the novel by Jake La Motta with Joseph Carter and Peter Savage
Screenplay by	Paul Schrader, Mardik Martin
Cast	Robert De Niro, Cathy Moriarty, Joe Pesci
Filming Locations	Filmed on location in Manhattan, NY and Los Angeles and San Pedro, CA
Genre	Bio-Drama
Format	B&W & Color (Technicolor)— color used briefly in home movies sequence and the main title card
Initial Release	11/14/1980 (New York); 12/19/1980 general release
Rerelease	1990, 2005
Running Time	129 minutes
MPAA Rating	R

STANDING THE TEST OF TIME

ACADEMY AWARD Oscar Nominations and Wins

Best Picture: Irwin Winkler and Robert Chartoff, Producers

*ACTOR IN A LEADING ROLE: Robert De Niro

Actor in a Supporting Role: Joe Pesci

Actress in a Supporting Role: Cathy Moriarty

Cinematography: Michael Chapman

Directing: Martin Scorsese

*FILM EDITING: Thelma Schoonmaker

Sound: Donald O. Mitchell, Bill Nicholson, David J. Kimball, Les Lazarowitz

OSCAR TOTALS   Nominations **8**   *Wins **2**

AFI 100 YEARS 100 MOVIES SELECTION
2007 . . . . #4   1997 . . . #24

TOP 300 FILMS POSITION . . . . none
All-Release Domestic Box Office in Equivalent 2005 $s

National Film Preservation Board Selection 1990

OTHER AWARDS Best Picture Wins

	Year
Golden Globes	none
New York Film Critics	none
National Board of Review	none
Film Daily Critics	none

Raging Bull was seamless. It was perfect. We participated to a certain extent, but it felt as if we were being guided through it by this omniscient hand.

—Film editor Thelma Schoonmaker

PLOT: Talented boxer Jake LaMotta struggles toward his goal, the world middleweight championship, but his anger, jealousy, and paranoia conspire to alienate all those close to him, even the loyal brother who has managed his career.

PRODUCTION: When Robert De Niro discovered Jake LaMotta's autobiography while shooting *The Godfather Part II* in Sicily, he eagerly passed it on to Martin Scorsese. The director was skeptical: he was not a sports fan. But De Niro's "persuasion" over six years finally wore him down. They commissioned a script from Scorsese's college friend Mardik Martin, and then a rewrite from Paul Schrader, who simplified the story by combining LaMotta's brother and his manager into one character. Producers Irwin Winkler and Robert Chartoff, having recently won the Best Picture Academy Award for *Rocky,* were being urged to make a sequel, but they used their clout on *Raging Bull*'s behalf instead. Since five other boxing pictures were in the works at the time, they also convinced United Artists to allow Scorsese to shoot in black and white, arguing that this would make the film stand out from the crowd. The filmmakers found Joe Pesci working in a New York restaurant; De Niro had admired Pesci's only substantial film role, in *The Death Collector* (1976), and since then Pesci had largely given up on show business. Once cast as LaMotta's brother, Pesci in turn introduced them to Cathy Moriarty, a neighborhood girl who had never appeared in a film but had all the right natural qualities to play LaMotta's wife. Scorsese tackled the toughest logistical part first: the fight scenes. He was determined to make the audience feel as if they were inside the ring, so he used only one camera and captured shots that had been meticulously planned beforehand, effectively editing the scenes in advance. Each bout in *Raging Bull* is stylized in a different way, to help express LaMotta's emotional state at the time: for one, the ring is physically elongated; another restricts itself to handheld shots; a third places the camera above a flame bar to produce a disquieting shimmer. Such attention to detail stretched a planned five-week shoot to ten, for work that would total less than ten minutes in the finished film. To play the bloated LaMotta a quarter century later, De Niro insisted on actually gaining weight rather than using costume or makeup effects. After the "young Jake" wrapped, the production shut down for two months while the actor increased his girth from his fighting weight of 152 pounds to just over 210. When De Niro returned, Scorsese, concerned about his health, condensed a three-week schedule into ten days. Supervising sound effects editor Frank Warner used such outré sounds as a braying elephant to accentuate the boxing punches, supporting the suggestion that the audience was closer to the fighters than they had ever been before.

DISTRIBUTION: After early previews, Scorsese decided to abandon the flashback structure of Schrader's script, narrated by the LaMotta of 1964 as he prepares for a stage appearance. Instead, they restricted this setup to bookend scenes at the beginning and end. *Raging Bull* was not well received at first: a trade review even went so far as to warn distributors against booking the film. But today it is considered one of the outstanding films of its decade, and consistently ranks high on all-time lists. —*Tom Dupree*

NINE TO FIVE
20th Century-Fox 1980

ALL-RELEASE EQUIVALENT 2005 $s
(Unadjusted $s) in Millions of $s

Domestic Box Office Revenues . . . . **$246.1**/($103.3)
Production Cost . . . . **$29.4**/($12.4)
Principal Photography . . . . not available

Director . . . . Colin Higgins
Producer . . . . Bruce Gilbert
Production Company . . . . 20th Century-Fox Productions, IPC Films
Story by . . . . Patricia Resnick
Screenplay by . . . . Colin Higgins and Patricia Resnick
Cast . . . . Jane Fonda, Lily Tomlin, Dolly Parton, Dabney Coleman
Filming Locations . . . . . . On location: Los Angeles and San Francisco, CA; in studio: 20th Century-Fox, West Los Angeles, CA
Genre . . . . Comedy
Format . . . . Color (DeLuxe)
Initial Release 12/19/1980
Rerelease 1982
Running Time . . . . 110 minutes
MPAA Rating . . . . PG

STANDING THE TEST OF TIME

ACADEMY AWARD Oscar Nominations and Wins

Music (Original Song): "9 to 5," Music and Lyrics by Dolly Parton

OSCAR TOTALS   Nominations 1   *Wins 0

AFI 100 YEARS 100 MOVIES SELECTION
2007 0   1997 0

TOP 300 FILMS POSITION . . . . **#165**
All-Release Domestic Box Office in Equivalent 2005 $s

National Film Preservation Board Selection . . . . none

OTHER AWARDS Best Picture Wins

	Year
Golden Globes	none
New York Film Critics	none
National Board of Review	none
Film Daily Critics	none

I wanted to do this movie because the opportunity to work with those three women comes once in a lifetime. They are three distinct personalities in the film; they get to know each other and they like each other. It's the first buddy picture for women.

—Colin Higgins

PLOT: Three women feel abused and unappreciated by their boss, and fantasize about getting even with him. After a mix-up at the hospital involving a dead body, the women must kidnap their boss and hold him hostage if they hope to thwart his plans to blackmail them.

PRODUCTION: The original idea for the film came from Bruce Gilbert and Jane Fonda, who were very interested in doing a comedy about women in the workplace. Lily Tomlin and Dolly Parton were then approached about starring with Fonda in the as-yet-unwritten movie. Once they agreed, Gilbert brought the project to 20th Century-Fox, where they enlisted Patricia Resnick to write the screenplay, keeping in mind that it was to be specifically tailored for Fonda, Tomlin, and Parton. Resnick went undercover at an insurance brokerage office to research the lives of professional women before writing the quirky, offbeat comedy. Colin Higgins, who was fresh off the success of *Foul Play* (1978), which he wrote and directed, was then brought in to direct. Before going into production, Gilbert and Higgins went to the headquarters of the National Association of Office Workers in Cleveland, where they interviewed groups of women regarding their complaints about their status in the workplace. Higgins then reworked the screenplay based on what he had heard, and shortly thereafter production began on historic Stage 6 at 20th Century-Fox Studios. Following in the footsteps of screenwriter Patricia Resnick and director Colin Higgins, the three stars of *Nine to Five* relied heavily on their own research when the time came to bring their characters to life. For the role of Judy Bernly, a divorcee taking her first job in corporate America, Fonda met with numerous women who found themselves in similar professional situations. After learning of their problems and insecurities, she decided on the signature look of her character, which included conservative hair, oversized glasses, and a "prim but frilly" wardrobe. While preparing to play Violet Newstead, a long-term employee of the company who finds herself perpetually under the thumb of her inept, conniving boss, Lily Tomlin drew on her own experiences working as an assistant bookkeeper in New York City. It was an altogether different situation for Dolly Parton, however, who portrayed Doralee Rhodes, the boss's secretary. Never having worked on a film before, Parton was entirely unfamiliar with what was expected of her in terms of preparation. Thinking movies were shot entirely in order, word for word from the script, Parton not only memorized her lines but the lines of everyone else as well. "I knew the whole movie word for word before I ever came out here," Parton said, "which I found hilarious once I saw how movies were made."

DISTRIBUTION: Fox spent about $13 million on domestic advertising (about the same as the movie cost to make). *Nine to Five* was an immediate box office hit, grossing more than $179 million in worldwide box office. The film's immense success went far beyond the cinema, however. For example, the theme song "9 to 5" went on to be one of Dolly Parton's biggest, most recognizable hits. It held the number one spot on the Billboard Hot 100 for two weeks, was nominated for an Academy Award, and won two Grammy Awards (Country Song of the Year and Female Country Vocal of the Year). The film also inspired a TV sitcom, which aired from 1982 to 1983, and then again from 1986 to 1988. —*Mark D'Anna*

RAIDERS OF THE LOST ARK
Paramount, 1981

ALL-RELEASE EQUIVALENT 2005 $s
(Unadjusted $s) in Millions of $s

Domestic Box Office Revenues . . . . **$554.7**/($245.0)
Production Cost . . . . $48.9/($22.8)
Principal Photography . . . . **73** days
6/23/1980–10/3/1980
Second unit 8/21/1980–9/23/1980 (25 days)

Director	Steven Spielberg
Producer	Frank Marshall
Production Company	Lucasfilm Ltd.
Story by	George Lucas, Philip Kaufman
Screenplay by	Lawrence Kasdan
Cast	Harrison Ford, Karen Allen, Paul Freeman, Ronald Lacey, John Rhys-Davies, Denholm Elliott
Filming Locations	On location: Tozeur, Metlaoui, Kairouan, Sousse, Tunisia (20 days); on location: La Rochelle, France (5 days); on location: Kauai, Hawaii (4 days); in studio: EMI Elstree, Borehamwood, UK (44 days); second unit: Nefta, Tozeur, Metlaoui, Tunisia (25 days)
Genre	Action Adventure
Format	Color (Metrocolor)
Initial Release	6/12/1981
Rerelease	1982, 1983
Running Time	115 minutes
MPAA Rating	PG

STANDING THE TEST OF TIME

ACADEMY AWARD Oscar Nominations and Wins

Best Picture: Frank Marshall, Producer

*ART DIRECTION/SET DECORATION: Norman Reynolds, Leslie Dilley/Michael Ford

Cinematography: Douglas Slocombe

Directing: Steven Spielberg

*FILM EDITING: Michael Kahn

Music (Original Score): John Williams

*SOUND: Bill Varney, Steve Maslow, Gregg Landaker, Roy Charman

*VISUAL EFFECTS: Richard Edlund, Kit West, Bruce Nicholson, Joe Johnston

*SPECIAL ACHIEVEMENT AWARD (Sound Effects Editing): Ben Burtt, Richard L. Anderson

OSCAR TOTALS   Nominations **9**   *Wins **5**

AFI 100 YEARS 100 MOVIES SELECTION
2007 . . . #66   1997 . . . #60

TOP 300 FILMS POSITION . . . . **#15**
All-Release Domestic Box Office in Equivalent 2005 $s

National Film Preservation Board Selection 1999

OTHER AWARDS Best Picture Wins

	Year
Golden Globes	none
New York Film Critics	none
National Board of Review	none
Film Daily Critics	none

I mean, you can see certain similarities between almost any two movies. But coming up with a basic idea and developing it and making it work is very difficult and not to be underestimated.

—George Lucas

PLOT: Indiana Jones and his feisty ex-flame dodge booby traps, fight Nazis and stare down snakes in their worldwide quest for the Ark of the Covenant.

PRODUCTION: The idea for *Raiders of the Lost Ark* first popped into George Lucas's head as a loose homage to old serial cliffhangers. After cooking up the story of an adventurous archeologist grappling for the ark against Nazis with Philip Kaufman, he shelved it. Years later in 1977, flush from his *Star Wars* success, Lucas finally resuscitated it one day on a beach in Hawaii and pitched it to his friend Steven Spielberg. Soaking in the gripping details of the action-packed plot involving Indiana Smith (named after Lucas's dog), Spielberg instantly agreed to direct—provided Indy's last name became Jones. Lucas next hired Lawrence Kasdan to punch out a series of drafts while he and Spielberg began shopping their idea around for a distributor. Despite many studios passing due to budget fears, Michael Eisner at Paramount saw the huge potential in their offer and hammered out a deal. Rushing to cast the hero, they waded through a battery of screen tests before selecting Tom Selleck. When he proved unavailable due to his recently hot *Magnum PI* show on CBS, they hired Harrison Ford just three weeks prior to filming. To prepare for the shoot, Spielberg scoured elaborate cardboard miniature sets through his viewfinder to discover the best angles. He then compiled numerous detailed storyboards to guide him once the cameras were rolling. Now facing strict budget limits and a proposed 85-day shoot, the crew swooped into a submarine pen in La Rochelle, France, on June 23, 1980, and filmed scenes involving a submarine that had been constructed for another film, *Das Boot*. Regrouping back at England's Elstree Studios, they shot a series of giant set pieces, including the Well of Souls—complete with more than 6,500 live snakes slithering around on a sand-filled platform ten feet above the stage floor. The team then descended upon the oven-hot Tunisian desert. Filming where parts of *Star Wars* had been shot, the crew battled 130-degree heat, Ford's knee injury, dysentery, and general fatigue that prompted Spielberg and Ford to scrap a big fight scene and have Indy simply shoot an attacker to save time and precious energy. All in all, the shoot was a study in efficiency and economy. Lucas slashed costs by shrinking the Tanis dig site, excising vast swaths of unnecessary extras, trimming the size of a proposed Flying Wing German prop plane, and even helping to shoot some second-unit material. Spielberg answered the challenge by averaging forty setups a day on location, collaborating with a second-unit director, Michael Moore, to shoot some key action scenes and employing stock footage from *Lost Horizon* and *The Hindenburg* to cover certain shots. As a result of their efforts, filming wrapped ahead of schedule in 73 days.

DISTRIBUTION: Lucas and Spielberg previewed their rousing spectacle at Cannes, and then opened it on June 12, 1981. It was an instant hit, wowing critics, making the covers of *Time, Newsweek,* and *Rolling Stone,* and playing in some theaters for an impressive eighty-nine weeks. Including two rereleases, it went on to rake in over $386 million worldwide. The DVD, released in October 2003, sported digitally cleaned-up special effects. —*Scott Mazak*

SUPERMAN II
Warner Bros., 1981

ALL-RELEASE EQUIVALENT 2005 $s
(Unadjusted $s) in Millions of $s

Domestic Box Office Revenues........**$249.4**/($108.2)
Production Cost.....................**$153.9**/($54.0)
                  assumes 30 percent shot in 1977
Principal Photography...........**180** days estimated
                3/24/1977–late 1977 then
                from July 1979
      Filmed portion of *Superman—The Movie* (1978)
      and *Superman II* together

Genre................. Action Adventure
Format............... Color (Technicolor)
Initial Release......... 6/19/1981
Rerelease............. none
Running Time......... 127 minutes
MPAA Rating.......... PG

Director.............. Richard Lester
Producer............. Ilya Salkind, Pierre Spengler
Production Company.... Alexander and Ilya Salkind, International Films
Story by.............. Mario Puzo, based on characters created by Jerry Siegel and Joe Shuster
Screenplay by......... Mario Puzo, David Newman, Leslie Newman
Cast................. Christopher Reeve, Gene Hackman, Margot Kidder, Ned Beatty, Terence Stamp, Sarah Douglas
Filming Locations...... Pinewood Studios, Buckinghamshire, England; Calgary, Alberta, Canada; Niagara Falls, Ontario, Canada; Norway; Paris, France; St. Lucia

STANDING THE TEST OF TIME

ACADEMY AWARD Oscar Nominations and Wins

None

OSCAR TOTALS   Nominations 0   *Wins 0

AFI 100 YEARS 100 MOVIES SELECTION
               2007..... 0   1997..... 0

TOP 300 FILMS POSITION................... #163
All-Release Domestic Box Office in Equivalent 2005 $s

National Film Preservation Board Selection.... none

OTHER AWARDS Best Picture Wins

	Year
Golden Globes...........................	none
New York Film Critics.....................	none
National Board of Review..................	none
Film Daily Critics........................	none

Let me put it this way . . . all the good parts of Superman II *are mine.*

—Richard Donner, original director

PLOT: The sequel introduces a superpowered threat with three Kryptonian criminals who take over Earth. Superman is torn between his love for Lois Lane and his responsibility to protect his adopted home world.

PRODUCTION: Filming for *Superman II* began at the same time as the first film, with Alexander and Ilya Salkind intending to produce both films at once. This idea proved unworkable, and production on *Superman II* halted in late 1977 (though director Richard Donner had already shot roughly three-quarters of the sequel). Production was slated to resume in February 1979, but after the date came and went, Christopher Reeve signed on to the film *Somewhere in Time,* with the Salkinds filing a lawsuit in response. Reeve eventually agreed to begin work on *Superman II* in July. In March, the Salkinds informed Donner that his services would no longer be required on the sequel; the relationship between Donner and the Salkinds had soured during the making of the first film over budgets and differing creative visions. Richard Lester (*A Hard Day's Night*), who had worked on the first film as an arbiter between Donner and the Salkinds, stepped into the sequel's directorial shoes despite raw feelings from the cast over the circumstances of Donner's firing. David and Leslie Newman were brought back to revise the script, giving it a more lighthearted tone (particularly in scenes between Clark/Superman and Lois) that had been absent from the existing Tom Mankiewicz rewrite. *Superman* cinematographer Geoffrey Unsworth and production designer John Barry had died; in addition, Marlon Brando filed a lawsuit against the Salkinds over the percentage of profits owed him from the first film. In response, the Salkinds removed Brando's completed scenes from the sequel. Although Richard Lester refilmed many of the existing Donner scenes, Gene Hackman could not be coaxed back for additional filming as Lex Luthor. Thus approximately 30 percent of the theatrical version consisted of Donner-shot footage. Preserved Donner sequences included all of Hackman's footage, the introduction of the supervillains, and a diner confrontation between a powerless Superman and a bully. Lester's approach to filming proved looser than Donner's method, using three simultaneous cameras and static framing that marked a visual departure from the sweeping camera of the original cinematographer, Unsworth.

DISTRIBUTION: *Superman II* followed an unusual distribution pattern for a U.S. film, opening in Europe and Australia on December 4, 1980, but not seeing domestic release until the summer of 1981. The anticipation seemed to pay off, with a record-setting $24 million earned during the first weekend and a favorable critical reception. In 1983 Alexander Salkind released a version for international television distribution that ran 20 minutes longer, including cut scenes such as the destruction of the Fortress of Solitude. The existence of unseen footage prompted Internet fans to piece together their own version of "what might have been" had Donner not been replaced as director. These efforts fueled desire for an official release, and *Superman II: The Richard Donner Cut*—recut from the original negatives with the involvement of both Donner and screenwriter Mankiewicz—saw DVD release in 2006. Changes to this version included restored Brando footage, a new opening and closing, and new scenes between Lois and Clark/Superman (including one lifted from a screen test). —*Daniel Wallace*

CHARIOTS OF FIRE

20th Century-Fox (worldwide); Warner Bros. (foreign), 1981

ALL-RELEASE EQUIVALENT 2005 $s

(Unadjusted $s) in Millions of $s

Domestic Box Office Revenues . . . . **$128.6**/($59.0)
Production Cost . . . . **$12.1**/($6.0)
Principal Photography . . . . not available

Director . . . . Hugh Hudson

Producer . . . . David Puttnam

Production Company . . . . Allied Stars, Enigma
Productions Ltd.,
The Ladd Company,
20th Century-Fox

Story and
  Screenplay by . . . . Colin Welland

Cast . . . . Ben Cross, Ian Charleson,
Nigel Havers, Cheryl Campbell,
Alice Krige

Filming Locations . . . . . . The famous beach scenes
filmed at West Sands,
St. Andrews, Scotland; other
major locations include Eton
College and The Oval Sports
Centre at Bebington,
Merseyside

Genre . . . . Bio-Drama

Format . . . . Color

Initial Release . . . . March 1981 (UK); 9/25/1981
U.S. premiere (New York Film
Festival); October 1981 wide
release

Rerelease . . . . none

Running Time . . . . 123 minutes

MPAA Rating . . . . PG

STANDING THE TEST OF TIME

ACADEMY AWARD Oscar Nominations and Wins

*BEST PICTURE: David Puttnam, Producer

Actor in a Supporting Role: Ian Holm

*COSTUME DESIGN: Milena Canonero

Directing: Hugh Hudson

Film Editing: Terry Rawlings

*MUSIC (Original Score): Vangelis

*WRITING (Screenplay – written directly for the
screen): Colin Welland

OSCAR TOTALS   Nominations 7   *Wins 4

AFI 100 YEARS 100 MOVIES SELECTION
2007 0   1997 0

TOP 300 FILMS POSITION . . . . .none
All-Release Domestic Box Office in Equivalent 2005 $s

National Film Preservation Board Selection . . . .none

OTHER AWARDS Best Picture Wins

	Year
Golden Globes	none
New York Film Critics	none
National Board of Review	1981
Film Daily Critics	none

Sport is such a clean simple metaphor.

—David Puttnam

PLOT: A true story based on the lives of two British track athletes—Eric Liddell and Harold Abrahams—their involvement in the 1924 Summer Olympics in Paris, and the religious convictions driving them to win.

PRODUCTION: English film producer David Puttnam was flipping through a copy of *The Official History of the Olympics*—the only appealing book he could find in his newly rented L.A. home—when he got the idea to make a movie about British athletes of the 1924 Summer Games. Puttnam secured £17,000 in financing for the original screenplay from a small independent British company, Goldcrest. From there, screenwriter Colin Welland, began rigorous research, and emerged three months later with a script that Puttnam instantly delivered to the largely unknown actor Ian Charleson. Puttnam believed that new faces were essential to the film's credibility but he also knew that without a star, financing the production would be difficult. He had said, "In Hollywood, there's a constant, pervasive and—what is really dangerous—logical pressure to cast names." Nevertheless, he brought aboard director Hugh Hudson, who had never directed a feature film before. The project was eventually privately financed by Allied Stars, controlled by Mohammed Fayed, in partnership with 20th Century-Fox. After Fox put the movie into turnaround, meaning another studio could acquire the project by repaying Fox's costs, Alan Ladd Jr. picked it up at Warner Bros. for his production company, the Ladd Co. *Chariots of Fire* was now ready to run—albeit with a production headed by underdogs. Neither Ian Charleson or his costar Ben Cross were athletes so to prepare themselves, they began intensive training with an Olympic coach six weeks before shooting. On an average day, Charleson and Cross would run five miles in the morning, sprint the 100-meter dash in the afternoon, and jog a leisurely three miles at night. Puttnam knew he needed more than strong athletes. Before composer Evangelos Papathanassiou (aka Vangelis) saw the film's famous opening beach scenes, he was unsure about scoring the film. Having never written a film score in his life, he was reluctant to join Puttnam's menagerie of newcomers, but eventually was convinced by the producer's passion. In only one afternoon, Vangelis turned out the score that would take him to the top of the singles charts and solidify his status as the author of one of the most iconic musical phrases in film history.

DISTRIBUTION: Opening the film in London was key as the home market was likely to be more receptive to the film's narrative than, say, Los Angeles. If *Chariots* then spread west gradually, it could build the momentum it needed for major international box office. Word of mouth was worth more to the film's launchers than million-dollar promotional campaigns. As expected, Britishers cottoned to the film, but when it hit France and Italy, ticket sales waned. The picture's future looked grim. But once it was selected to open the New York Film Festival— the first time the honor was given to a British film—*Chariots of Fire* went on to pick up awards at major festivals everywhere. In America, TV commercials were abandoned in favor of modest newspaper ads and advance screenings, which only added to the air of quiet prestige surrounding the film. It is the number nineteen film on the BFI list of the top 100. —*Sam Wasson*

ON GOLDEN POND

Universal, 1981

ALL-RELEASE EQUIVALENT 2005 $s

(Unadjusted $s) in Millions of $s

Domestic Box Office Revenues . . . . **$273.7**/($118.7)
Production Cost . . . .**$20.4**/($9.5)
Principal Photography . . . . not available

Director . . . . Mark Rydell
Producer . . . . Bruce Gilbert
Production Company . . . . ITC Films, IPC Films
Story by . . . . Based on the play by Ernest Thompson
Screenplay by . . . . Ernest Thompson
Cast . . . . Katherine Hepburn, Henry Fonda, Jane Fonda, Doug McKeon, Dabney Coleman, William Lanteau
Filming Locations . . . . . . On location: Concord, Meredith, and Squam Lake, NH; on location: Los Angeles and Santa Monica, CA
Genre . . . . Drama
Format . . . . Color
Initial Release . . . . 12/4/1981 limited release in one theater each (New York and Los Angeles); 1/22/1982 general release
Rerelease . . . . none
Running Time . . . . 109 minutes
MPAA Rating . . . . PG

STANDING THE TEST OF TIME

ACADEMY AWARD Oscar Nominations and Wins

Best Picture: Bruce Gilbert, Producer

***ACTOR IN A LEADING ROLE:** Henry Fonda

***ACTRESS IN A LEADING ROLE:** Katharine Hepburn

Actress in a Supporting Role: Jane Fonda

Cinematography: Billy Williams

Directing: Mark Rydell

Film Editing: Robert L. Wolfe

Music (Original Score): Dave Grusin

Sound: Richard Portman, David Ronne

***WRITING** (Screenplay – based on material from another medium): Ernest Thompson

OSCAR TOTALS   Nominations **10** *Wins **3**

AFI 100 YEARS 100 MOVIES SELECTION
2007 0   1997 0

TOP 300 FILMS POSITION . . . . **#127**
All-Release Domestic Box Office in Equivalent 2005 $s

National Film Preservation Board Selection . . . . none

OTHER AWARDS Best Picture Wins

	Year
Golden Globes (Drama)	1982
New York Film Critics	none
National Board of Review	none
Film Daily Critics	none

I believed that in the role of Norman Thayer, Dad would win the Oscar that had eluded him for so long. I wanted to make that happen for him.

—Jane Fonda

PLOT: An elderly couple, who spend each summer near an idyllic rural pond, are visited by their daughter, the daughter's fiancé, and the fiancé's son, raising many of the unresolved relationship issues remaining between the father and daughter from years past.

PRODUCTION: Jane Fonda's producing partner Bruce Gilbert saw *On Golden Pond* on Broadway and immediately wanted to acquire movie rights as a vehicle for Henry Fonda and Katharine Hepburn. It had always been Jane's dream to do a movie with her father and brother Peter. She chose *On Golden Pond* even though it had no role for Peter and her part was small. She hoped her ailing seventy-six-year-old father would finally win a Best Actor Academy Award. Because her father had been in the hospital, production insurance was a problem. There was pressure to get the film shot that summer, before his health failed. Katharine Hepburn, despite her long career, had never worked with Henry, and almost canceled at the last minute after injuring her rotator cuff and tearing a tendon while playing tennis. To convince her, Jane recalled Hepburn's perfect dive in *The Philadelphia Story* and promised to do her own back flip dive in the movie's difficult stunt if Hepburn would remain. Equally challenging was financing a film with two elderly leads, which major studios doubted would do any business. Gilbert and Fonda finally got the money from ITC Entertainment Group, which released the film through Universal Studios in the United States (Universal contributed $2.5 million toward the $9.5 million budget). Cinematographer Billy Williams insisted on shooting at a lake that ran east to west, because it would give him a certain light. Location scouts visited more than 100 lakes from the Carolinas to Maine. The only one that met all conditions was Squam Lake in central New Hampshire, where they shot even though the original story was set in Belgrade, Maine, where screenwriter Thompson had spent summers. On the first day of production, Hepburn presented Henry Fonda with a "lucky hat" that had belonged to her love, Spencer Tracy. Fonda wore it in the film. Shortly after production began, so did a strike by screen actors, and production was shut down. Gilbert protested to SAG that they were not a studio film but part of a British independent. They got a waiver and resumed shooting. The house shown in the movie, rented from a local doctor, had to be modified, but the producers signed a contract promising to restore it to its original state after production. For the shoot, a second floor was added as a balcony. The owner liked it so much, he elected to keep it when production ended. Jane Fonda struggled secretly to perfect the back flip she had promised Hepburn she would do; even more trying were her efforts to get along with her father. Their real-life rift was quite similar to the plot of the movie. Hepburn later said, "There was a whole layer of drama in the scenes between [Jane] and Hank." Jane finally did her back flip for the cameras in July and it went well. She was relieved. Unfortunately, the footage was damaged by the lab and had to be reshot in September, when the water was freezing and she was out of practice.

DISTRIBUTION: The studios were proven wrong as *On Golden Pond* became one of the highest-grossing movies of 1981, and both Hepburn and Fonda won Oscars. Henry was too ill to attend the Academy Award's ceremony but watched on TV. Jane and her children brought him the Oscar statuette right after the show, and Henry's comment was, "I'm so happy for Kate." —*Alex Ben Block*

PORKY'S
20th Century-Fox, 1982

ALL-RELEASE EQUIVALENT 2005 $s
(Unadjusted $s) in Millions of $s

Domestic Box Office Revenues........ **$241.8**/($111.3)
Production Cost ....**$8.1**/($4.0)
Principal Photography............**42** days estimated
2/9/1981–4/6/1981

Director . . . . Bob Clark

Producer . . . . Don Carmody, Bob Clark

Production Company. . . . Astral Films

Story and
  Screenplay by . . . . Bob Clark

Cast . . . . Chuck Mitchell, Wyatt Knight,
Nancy Parsons, Scott Colomby

Filming Locations . . . . . . Ft. Lauderdale, Miami Beach,
Oleta River State Park, FL

Genre. . . . . Comedy

Format. . . . . Color

Initial Release 3/19/1982

Rerelease. . . . . none

Running Time . . . . 94 minutes

MPAA Rating . . . . R

STANDING THE TEST OF TIME

ACADEMY AWARD Oscar Nominations and Wins

None

OSCAR TOTALS   Nominations 0   *Wins 0

AFI 100 YEARS 100 MOVIES SELECTION
2007 0   1997 0

TOP 300 FILMS POSITION . . . . **#171**
All-Release Domestic Box Office in Equivalent 2005 $s

National Film Preservation Board Selection. . . . none

OTHER AWARDS Best Picture Wins

	Year
Golden Globes	none
New York Film Critics	none
National Board of Review	none
Film Daily Critics	none

*I was a football player and that was our universe.
We thought about nothing but football and sex.*

—Bob Clark

PLOT: A group of sexually charged high school students set out on a quest to lose their virginity. After being harassed and mocked by a sleazy nightclub owner named Porky, the students alter course and seek their revenge.

PRODUCTION: The idea for *Porky's* was something director Bob Clark began developing nearly fifteen years before the film actually went into production. It all started when Clark graduated from Hillsdale College in Michigan. Finding himself overtaken by nostalgia for his adolescence, as well as an intense determination to be a filmmaker, Clark began methodically collecting stories from his high school days as well as those of other students around the country. As Clark's career as a writer and director slowly gained momentum, he kept the idea for *Porky's* in mind, yet was never able to find a studio willing to finance the project. Finally, after the success of *Tribute* in 1980, 20th Century-Fox agreed to finance the film. Given a minuscule budget of $4 million, Clark assembled a cast of relative newcomers and headed to Florida to begin filming. However, two weeks before production was to begin, Clark received a call from 20th Century-Fox informing him that the studio had had a change of heart and was going to back out of the film. Determined, Clark kept the cast in Miami for nearly two weeks at his own expense until he was finally able to convince Fox's head of distribution to greenlight the film again. *Porky's* went into production on February 9, 1981. Because so much of the screenplay was inspired by actual events, Clark faced a number of difficult decisions during production. He found himself repeatedly questioning whether or not he should remain true to the actual stories or alter events to make them more palatable to a mainstream moviegoing audience. Many around Clark warned that the film's stark depiction of teenage sexuality, promiscuousness, and rampant anti-Semitism was too shocking and would be deemed offensive by both critics and the general moviegoing public. One scene for which Clark received considerable criticism involved the story of Jewish student Brian Schwartz (Scott Colomby). In the film, Schwartz must withstand abuse and ridicule from an anti-Semitic classmate. The two face off in a climactic fistfight, after which Schwartz, victorious, drives off in an expensive sports car. When Clark was asked why he wrote and shot the events as he did, especially since they risked inflaming Jewish stereotypes and anti-Semitic rhetoric around the country, his frank response was, "Because that's what happened." In the end, it was these shocking and risqué true-to-life scenes that made the film such a success.

DISTRIBUTION: *Porky's* was a smashing success for 20th Century-Fox, grossing over $235 million in worldwide box office. Many critics panned the film, labeling it as gratuitously vulgar and marginally obscene. But *Porky's* found support from some literary heavyweights such as Norman Mailer and Arthur Miller, who saw the film as a timely exposé of social mores. *Porky's* spawned two sequels and, following *National Lampoon's Animal House* in 1978, is considered another precursor to the more contemporary teen sex comedy *American Pie. —Mark D'Anna*

E.T.: THE EXTRA-TERRESTRIAL

Universal, 1982

ALL-RELEASE EQUIVALENT 2005 $s

(Unadjusted $s) in Millions of $s

Domestic Box Office Revenues........**$889.4**/($435.1)
Production Cost ....**$24.6**/($12.2)
Principal Photography.....................**61** days
9/8/1981–12/1981
Jan 1982–Feb 1982 retakes

Director .... Steven Spielberg
Producer .... Steven Spielberg, Kathleen Kennedy
Production Company.... Universal Pictures
Story and
  Screenplay by .... Melissa Mathison
Cast .... Dee Wallace, Henry Thomas, Peter Coyote, Robert MacNaughton, Drew Barrymore
Filming Locations ...... Tujunga, Northridge, Crescent City, Culver City, end other California locations
Genre................. Sci-Fi
Format............... Color (DeLuxe)
Initial Release.......... 6/11/1982
Rerelease............. 1985, 2002
Running Time .... 115 minutes
MPAA Rating .... PG

STANDING THE TEST OF TIME

ACADEMY AWARD Oscar Nominations and Wins

Best Picture: Steven Spielberg and Kathleen Kennedy, Producers

Cinematography: Allen Daviau

Directing: Steven Spielberg

Film Editing: Carol Littleton

***MUSIC** (Original Score): John Williams

***SOUND:** Robert Knudson, Robert Glass, Don Digirolamo, Gene Cantamessa

***SOUND EFFECTS EDITING:** Charles L. Campbell, Ben Burtt

***VISUAL EFFECTS:** Carlo Rambaldi, Dennis Muren, Kenneth F. Smith

Writing (Screenplay – written directly for the Screen): Melissa Mathison

OSCAR TOTALS   Nominations **9**   *Wins **4**

AFI 100 YEARS 100 MOVIES SELECTION
2007 . . . #24   1997. . . #25

TOP 300 FILMS POSITION .... **#4**
All-Release Domestic Box Office in Equivalent 2005 $s

National Film Preservation Board Selection.... 1994

OTHER AWARDS Best Picture Wins

	Year
Golden Globes	1983
New York Film Critics	none
National Board of Review	none
Film Daily Critics	none

It's about human values. It's about the understanding people have toward one another. It's about compassion and love. They share so much of what they know about their own environments with each other and they come to have a great understanding for each other's problems.

—Steven Spielberg

PLOT: An alien, abandoned on Earth, is befriended by ten-year-old Elliott. Taking his brother and sister into his confidence, Elliott hides E.T. from government agents while helping him contact his starship. The two form a bond, leading to a bittersweet farewell.

PRODUCTION: Stephen Spielberg, in collaboration with writer John Sayles, had attempted to develop a film called *Night Skies* about sinister aliens who terrorize a family. When Spielberg consulted screenwriter Melissa Mathison (*The Black Stallion*), she latched onto the script's subplot about Buddy, the only friendly alien, who developed a relationship with an autistic boy, and re-worked it into a screenplay called *E.T. and Me* in eight weeks. Spielberg was so impressed he felt he could simply shoot Mathison's first draft. When Frank Price, head of Columbia Pictures, turned it down, calling it a "wimpy Disney picture" Spielberg placed it with longtime mentor Sid Sheinberg at Universal Studios, on a $10.5 million budget. The titular alien got his unique look from Carlo Rambaldi—the designer of the aliens for Spielberg's *Close Encounters of the Third Kind*—who gave his new creation an extendible neck and a hint of Albert Einstein in his expressive eyes. Producer Kathleen Kennedy hired a woman at the famed Jules Stein Eye Institute to paint E.T.'s eyes, because Spielberg insisted they be absolutely believable. It took three months and cost about $1.5 million to make the creature. The script called for M&M's to be used as bait, enticing E.T. into Elliott's house; but when the candy maker decided E.T. might scare children, Hershey offered Reese's Pieces, which saw sales shoot up 65 percent after the movie's release. Spielberg had co-written and co-produced a supernatural movie set for release by MGM at the same time as E.T., and gave MGM the choice of the title *E.T.* or *Poltergeist*. MGM chose *Poltergeist*, leaving *E.T.* for the Universal movie. The actual E.T. existed in multiple forms, including an animatronic body, a close-up version used for facial expressions, and a full-body costume. A professional mime operated E.T.'s hands, a little person wore the full-body costume and a boy without legs (walking upside down in the costume on his hands) performed many of E.T.'s more athletic scenes, and Stephen Spielberg voiced E.T.'s dialogue on set. The film was shot in 61 days, under the cover name *A Boy's Life*. Said Spielberg, "I didn't want anyone ripping off the idea, turning it into a TV movie." Spielberg encouraged spontaneity from his child stars, and shot the film from such a low angle that the adult characters could rarely be seen from the waist up, preserving a child's-eye view of the world. Unlike most films, Spielberg abstained from using storyboards and shot the film in continuity, better preserving a linear and organic experience for his young actors.

DISTRIBUTION: The film premiered in May 1982 as the closing movie at the Cannes Film Festival and was then released in the United States on June 11, 1982. *E.T.* was a megahit, spending an extraordinary twelve consecutive weekends at number one, and quickly joining the short list of the biggest-grossing movies of all time. It was rereleased in March 1985, and then on home video in October 1988. In March 2002, *E.T.* returned to theaters with five minutes of new footage and updated special effects, sparking some controversy from purists (particularly controversial was the decision to digitally replace the guns of FBI agents with walkie-talkies). It made more than $792 million in all-release worldwide box office (more than $1.6 billion in 2005 dollars). —*Daniel Wallace*

TOOTSIE
Columbia, 1982

ALL-RELEASE EQUIVALENT 2005 $s
(Unadjusted $s) in Millions of $s

Domestic Box Office Revenues........**$364.8**/($177.2)
Production Cost ....**$50.6**/($25.0)
Principal Photography.....................**98** days
4/1/1982–8/28/1982

Director . . . . Sydney Pollack

Producer . . . . Sydney Pollack, Rick Richards

Production Company. . . . Mirage/Punch Production

Story by. . . . . Don McGuire, Larry Gelbart

Screenplay by . . . . Larry Gelbart, Murray Schisgal

Cast . . . . Dustin Hoffman, Jessica Lange, Teri Garr, Dabney Coleman, Charles Durning, Bill Murray

Filming Locations . . . . . . On location in New York City and the Columbia studio in California

Genre. . . . . Romantic Comedy

Format. . . . . Color (Technicolor)

Initial Release 12/17/1982

Rerelease. . . . . none

Running Time . . . . 116 minutes

MPAA Rating . . . . PG

STANDING THE TEST OF TIME

ACADEMY AWARD Oscar Nominations and Wins

Best Picture: Sydney Pollack and Dick Richards, Producers

Actor in a Leading Role: Dustin Hoffman

Actress in a Supporting Role: Teri Garr

***ACTRESS IN A SUPPORTING ROLE:** Jessica Lange

Cinematography: Owen Roizman

Directing: Sydney Pollack

Film Editing: Fredric Steinkamp, William Steinkamp

Music (Original Song): "It Might Be You," Music by Dave Grusin; Lyrics by Alan Bergman and Marilyn Bergman

Sound: Arthur Piantadosi, Les Fresholtz, Dick Alexander, Les Lazarowitz

Writing (Screenplay – written directly for the screen): Screenplay by Larry Gelbart and Murray Schisgal; Story by Don Mcguire and Larry Gelbart

OSCAR TOTALS   Nominations **10** ***Wins 1**

AFI 100 YEARS 100 MOVIES SELECTION
2007 . . . #69   1997. . . #62

TOP 300 FILMS POSITION . . . . #58
All-Release Domestic Box Office in Equivalent 2005 $s

National Film Preservation Board Selection. . . . 1998

OTHER AWARDS Best Picture Wins

	Year
Golden Globes (Comedy)	1983
New York Film Critics.	none
National Board of Review	none
Film Daily Critics	none

The most difficult part was figuring out how to keep it from being a one-joke movie.
—Sidney Pollack

PLOT: An actor whose reputation for being difficult makes him unemployable takes the role of a lead actress on a soap opera in desperation and soon falls in love with his female co-star.

PRODUCTION: Motivated by his experiences playing both father and mother in *Kramer vs. Kramer,* Dustin Hoffman took his glimmer of an idea to New York playwright Murray Schisgal, the first of many writers to work on the project. The final credit, after roughly ten complete script revisions, was sorted out by the Writers Guild, who named Schisgal and Larry Gelbart as the writers and gave story credit to Gelbart and Don McGuire. Elaine May also worked on the script for a reported $450,000 for three weeks' work, as did Barry Levinson, Valerie Curtin, and Robert Garland. Dick Richards (*Farewell My Lovely*) and Hal Ashby were both slated to direct the film, which had a working title of "Would I Lie to You?" Hoffman's choice, Sydney Pollack, thought the script was too simplistic, and agreed to helm the movie only if rewrites to flesh out a story and dialogue were completed. After Ashby left, Michael Ovitz of CAA created a "package" of talent for the movie that included Hoffman and Bill Murray. Hoffman gave Murray one of his gross profit participation points in the movie. Murray declined an up-front screen credit so people wouldn't think it was a Bill Murray movie. Pollack and Columbia felt that the film was timely, as society was beginning to take a closer look at gender and sexuality. In fact, *Tootsie* was released within a year of both *Victor/Victoria* (March 1982) and *Yentl* (December 1983), other pictures with men playing women and women playing men. Preproduction took approximately three months. Hoffman discovered that he sounded more feminine with a southern accent, and Meryl Streep, his co-star in *Kramer vs. Kramer,* coached him on feminine voice cadence as they ran lines from Tennessee Williams's play *A Streetcar Named Desire.* While Pollack did not want to appear in the film, he caved in after repeatedly receiving flowers from Hoffman, with the card reading, "Please be my agent . . . Love, Dorothy." The script revisions continued into production and are estimated to have added $2 million in cost to the production. Transvestite actor Holly Woodlawn came on board as a consultant to coach Hoffman on the intricacies of being a man acting as a woman. Word on the set was that the crew would give bad news to Hoffman only when he was in drag, acknowledging that he was "much nicer as a woman." Bill Murray improvised his lines on the set, confusing extras, but sending Pollack into hysterical fits of laughter. During production, it was Dustin Hoffman who came up with the title *Tootsie,* which was his mother's dog's nickname. The production ran 23 days over the budgeted 75 days, in part because of the changing scripts and Hoffman's illness during production. Editors Fredric and William Steinkamp sorted through 500,000 feet of footage to get the final 10,000 feet in roughly six weeks.

DISTRIBUTION: Released with the tag line "Desperate . . . he took a female role and became a star. If only he could tell the woman he loves," *Tootsie* was an immediate hit with holiday moviegoers. It became Columbia Pictures' biggest comedy (until the release of *Ghostbusters* in 1984) and was second for the year in domestic box office after *E.T. —Christine McDermott*

STAR WARS: EP VI RETURN OF THE JEDI

20th Century-Fox, 1983

ALL-RELEASE EQUIVALENT 2005 $s

(Unadjusted $s) in Millions of $s

Domestic Box Office Revenues........$597.6/($309.2)
Production Cost ....$83.7/($42.7)
Principal Photography.....................92 days
1/11/1982–5/8/1982
23 days (25 percent) on location
69 days (75 percent) in studio
26 days second unit

Director .... Richard Marquand
Producer .... Howard Kazanjian
Production Company.... Lucasfilm Ltd.
Story by............... George Lucas
Screenplay by......... Lawrence Kasdan,
George Lucas
Cast .... Mark Hamill, Harrison Ford,
Carrie Fisher, Billy Dee Williams,
Anthony Daniels, David Prowse,
Kenny Baker, Peter Mayhew,
Frank Oz
Filming Locations ...... On location: Yuma, AZ; and
Crescent City, CA; in studio:
EMI Elstree, UK
Genre................. Sci-Fi
Format................ Color (Rank; prints by DeLuxe)
Initial Release.......... 5/25/1983
Rerelease............. 1985, 1997
Running Time.......... 132 minutes
MPAA Rating .... PG

STANDING THE TEST OF TIME

ACADEMY AWARD Oscar Nominations and Wins

Art Direction/Set Decoration: Norman Reynolds, Fred Hole, James Schoppe/Michael Ford

Music (Original Score): John Williams

Sound: Ben Burtt, Gary Summers, Randy Thom, Tony Dawe

Sound Effects Editing: Ben Burtt

*SPECIAL ACHIEVEMENT AWARD (Visual Effects): Richard Edlund, Dennis Muren, Ken Ralston, Phil Tippett

OSCAR TOTALS   Nominations 5   *Wins 1

AFI 100 YEARS 100 MOVIES SELECTION
2007..... 0   1997..... 0

TOP 300 FILMS POSITION .... #14
All-Release Domestic Box Office in Equivalent 2005 $s

National Film Preservation Board Selection....none

OTHER AWARDS Best Picture Wins

	Year
Golden Globes	none
New York Film Critics	none
National Board of Review	none
Film Daily Critics	none

The whole emotion I am trying to get at the end of this film is for you to be emotionally and spiritually uplifted and to feel absolutely good about life. That is the greatest thing that we could ever possibly do.

—George Lucas

PLOT: Reunited, Rebel forces gather for a final offensive against the evil Galactic Empire, in a battle that will determine the fate of the galaxy.

PRODUCTION: To complete the final film in his original *Star Wars* trilogy, George Lucas needed to pluck a nonunion director from the ranks of hopefuls due to his own resignation from the DGA. To that end, he eventually settled upon Welshman Richard Marquand. Based on a first-draft script Lucas was calling "Revenge of the Jedi," Stuart Freeborn began developing creatures in September 1980 and Joe Johnston began storyboards in October. Lucas then gathered Marquand, producer Howard Kazanjian, and writer Lawrence Kasdan for story conferences in July 1981. Harrison Ford even got into the act, lobbying to leave his character, Han Solo, forever frozen in carbonite. Lucas rejected his idea and dispatched Kasdan to hammer out a series of drafts by the end of the year. Shifting to the casting process, Lucas employed four different men to bring Darth Vader to life—David Prowse and his stunt double, Bob Anderson, would fill Vader's famous costume during shooting, Sebastian Shaw would reveal his disfigured face, and James Earl Jones would dub his voice in post. Lucas also chose Kenny Baker, stuck inside R2-D2 for all three films in the series, to appear on-screen as an Ewok. Norman Reynolds had already been overseeing the construction of sets at England's Elstree Studios by the time shooting began on January 11, 1982. Problems arose almost immediately when technicians discovered scratches on footage shot during a sandstorm scene. To keep a close eye on potential problems during production, Lucas appeared on set as often as possible and even helped with some second-unit filming. He personally oversaw shooting when Sebastian Shaw came in for the secret revelation of Vader's face. Shaw appeared in the script only as "The Man" and completed his shooting and pickups in two days. When the production moved to the desert near the Arizona and California borders, Lucas strove for even more secrecy. He cloaked everything under a phony *Blue Harvest* horror film cover, erected guarded security fences around locales, and continued revealing dialogue and plot twists to actors only on the day of shooting, if at all. A series of problems nonetheless bedeviled the team in the desert, including Mark Hamill injuring his foot, a stuntman breaking his ankle, a fire damaging the Chewbacca costume, high winds halting production, and baking-hot temperatures steadily wearing them all down. After the crew traveled to Crescent City, California, to shoot the Ewok village sets, production wrapped on schedule in May. ILM then spent a full year polishing the effects.

DISTRIBUTION: Weeks before the initial release, Lucas changed the title to *Return of the Jedi*, rendering early promotional material useless. Long lines began forming outside theaters a full eight days prior to the film's May 25, 1983, release date—six years to the day after the original *Star Wars* opened. Critics' reviews were mixed, but the public flocked to it. In all-release worldwide box office, the film has grossed nearly $476 million. On the 2004 DVD release, Lucas digitally altered the face and ghost of Darth Vader to resemble Hayden Christensen, who portrayed young Vader in the subsequent prequels. —*Scott Mazak*

THE RIGHT STUFF
Warner Bros., 1983

ALL-RELEASE EQUIVALENT 2005 $s
(Unadjusted $s) in Millions of $s

Domestic Box Office Revenues . . . . **$43.1**/($21.2)
Production Cost . . . . **$54.9**/($28.0)
Principal Photography . . . . **72** days
3/8/1982–January 1983

Director	Philip Kaufman
Producer	Irwin Winkler, Robert Chartoff
Production Company	The Ladd Company
Story by	Based on the novel by Tom Wolfe
Screenplay by	Philip Kaufman
Cast	Charles Frank, Scott Glenn, Ed Harris, Lance Henriksen, Scott Paulin, Dennis Quaid, Sam Shepard, Fred Ward, Kim Stanley, Barbara Hershey, Veronica Cartwright, Pamela Reed
Filming Locations	On location in San Francisco Bay Area; Edwards Air Force Base, Lancaster, CA; aboard the USS *Coral Sea*; NASA facility, Ames, CA; Hamilton Air Force Base, Marin County, CA
Genre	Drama
Format	Color (Technicolor)
Initial Release	10/21/1983
Rerelease	none
Running Time	193 minutes
MPAA Rating	PG

STANDING THE TEST OF TIME

ACADEMY AWARD Oscar Nominations and Wins

Best Picture: Irwin Winkler and Robert Chartoff, Producers

Actor in a Supporting Role: Sam Shepard

Art Direction/Set Decoration: Geoffrey Kirkland, Richard J. Lawrence, W. Stewart Campbell, Peter Romero/Pat Pending, George R. Nelson

Cinematography: Caleb Deschanel

*FILM EDITING: Glenn Farr, Lisa Fruchtman, Stephen A. Rotter, Douglas Stewart, Tom Rolf

*MUSIC (Original Score): Bill Conti

*SOUND: Mark Berger, Tom Scott, Randy Thom, David MacMillan

*SOUND EFFECTS EDITING: Jay Boekelheide

OSCAR TOTALS   Nominations 8   *Wins 4

AFI 100 YEARS 100 MOVIES SELECTION
2007 0   1997 0

TOP 300 FILMS POSITION . . . . .none
All-Release Domestic Box Office in Equivalent 2005 $s

National Film Preservation Board Selection . . . . none

OTHER AWARDS Best Picture Wins

	Year
Golden Globes	none
New York Film Critics	none
National Board of Review	none
Film Daily Critics	none

I was in Chicago when the movie opened, and I went to a local theater there. I was shocked—I was the youngest guy in the audience. There wasn't a person under 30. They weren't getting them in, because there had been no real focus on 18-to-24-year-olds.

—Philip Kaufman

PLOT: When the Soviet Union shocked the Western world with the 1957 launch of the Sputnik satellite, the United States hastily begins a disorganized space effort, ultimately selecting seven astronauts for the Mercury program.

PRODUCTION: Producers Robert Chartoff and Irwin Winkler obtained the film rights for a reported $500,000, setting up the project at United Artists. Oscar winning screenwriter William Goldman doubted that a film could come from the material because of the wide structure of the book. At one point Winkler suggested omitting the legendary Chuck Yeager character, retaining a five-act structure focused on selection, training, Shepard, Grissom, and Glenn. After several drafts, directors came and went. Philip Kaufman was now aboard as director. However, Kaufman and Goldman had differing views on the script. Goldman then left the project and United Artists dropped it. The Ladd Company stepped in, keeping Kaufman as director. Kaufman then approached author Tom Wolfe to write the script. When Wolfe turned it down, Kaufman penned a version. To keep within the $28 million budget, it was decided that the entire film would be produced in California, with San Francisco substituting for the New York City and Washington, D.C., locations. With Chuck Yeager's saga (centering around the breaking of the sound barrier in 1947) now included, period aircraft from 1947 to 1963 would be used in the aerial sequences. Hundreds of antique cars and military uniforms from the era would be necessary for authenticity. Pancho Barnes's Fly Inn, the watering hole in the high desert, had to be built and then burned as it actually occurred near the same location. It was a hazardous and difficult shoot, beginning on March 8, 1982. Gus Grissom's reentry scene was filmed at Half Moon Bay, south of San Francisco. The crew was out in the ocean on a 100-foot barge surrounded by ten-to-twelve-foot swells and helicopters. The first day out the capsule slipped its hitch and went forty to fifty feet under the barge. The capsule then had to be pulled up and drained. In May, the cast and crew moved south to Edwards Air Force Base, in the Mojave Desert. Much of this filming was done at the old south base (formally Muroc Field), where Chuck Yeager first piloted the X-1 rocket plane on October 14, 1947. For the scene in which astronaut Gordon Cooper travels to Australia to communicate with John Glenn as he passes over the continent, six Aborigines were flown in and a number of kangaroos and wallabies were brought up from an animal farm in Los Angeles. In July the company returned to the San Francisco coast to film aboard the aircraft carrier USS *Coral Sea*. Cast and crew then moved to Hamilton Air Force Base for the complicated process work in the Mercury space capsules, the cockpit of the X-1, and the NF-104, where Yeager experienced his near-death flight, bailing out at 60,000 feet. Multiple Oscar winner John Barry was originally signed to score the film. He left during post-production and was replaced by Bill Conti, who was forced to work under a pressing deadline, writing the music during the day and recording it at night.

DISTRIBUTION: The film opened nationwide on 229 screens and grossed $1.6 million, ranking seventh in its first weekend. Reaction among critics was enthusiastic and favorable, but the final $21 million in domestic box office was disappointing. Nominated for eight Academy Awards, it lost out on Best Picture to *Terms of Endearment*. —*Frank McAdams*

TERMS OF ENDEARMENT

Paramount, 1983

ALL-RELEASE EQUIVALENT 2005 $s

(Unadjusted $s) in Millions of $s

Domestic Box Office Revenues . . . . **$212.6/($108.4)**
Production Cost . . . . **$16.7/($8.5)**
Principal Photography . . . . **80** days estimated
3/14/1983–July 1983

Director . . . . James L. Brooks

Producer . . . . James L. Brooks

Production Company . . . . James L. Brooks Production

Story by . . . . Based on the novel by
Larry McMurtry

Screenplay by . . . . James L. Brooks

Cast . . . . Shirley MacLaine, Debra
Winger, Jack Nicholson,
Danny DeVito, Jeff Daniels,
John Lithgow

Filming Locations . . . . . . Houston, TX; Lincoln, NE; New
York City, NY

Genre . . . . Drama

Format . . . . Color (Metrocolor)

Initial Release . . . . 11/20/1983 world premiere,
Coronet Theater (New York);
11/23/1983 limited release;
12/9/1983 wide release

Rerelease . . . . none

Running Time . . . . 131 minutes

MPAA Rating . . . . PG

STANDING THE TEST OF TIME

ACADEMY AWARD Oscar Nominations and Wins

*BEST PICTURE: James L. Brooks, Producer

Actor in a Supporting Role: John Lithgow

*ACTOR IN A SUPPORTING ROLE: Jack
Nicholson

*ACTRESS IN A LEADING ROLE: Shirley
MacLaine

Actress in a Leading Role: Debra Winger

Art Direction/Set Decoration: Polly Platt, Harold
Michelson/Tom Pedigo, Anthony Mondello

*DIRECTING: James L. Brooks

Film Editing: Richard Marks

Music (Original Score): Michael Gore

Sound: Donald O. Mitchell, Rick Kline,
Kevin O'Connell, Jim Alexander

*WRITING (Screenplay – based on material from
another medium): James L. Brooks

OSCAR TOTALS   Nominations **11**   *Wins **5**

AFI 100 YEARS 100 MOVIES SELECTION
2007 0   1997 0

TOP 300 FILMS POSITION . . . . **#226**
All-Release Domestic Box Office in Equivalent 2005 $s

National Film Preservation Board Selection . . . . none

OTHER AWARDS Best Picture Wins

	Year
Golden Globes (Drama)	1984
New York Film Critics	1983
National Board of Review	none
Film Daily Critics	none

*A heroic work of direction and adaptation. In one leap, Brooks has established himself
as a major presence, a film maker of humor, humanity and substance.*

—Sheila Benson, *Los Angeles Times*, 1983

PLOT: An eccentric mother and her only daughter share a combative, turbulent relationship, yet they are there for each other through various highs and lows in their lives—particularly when the daughter is stricken with cancer.

PRODUCTION: For his motion picture directorial debut, writer-producer James L. Brooks (*Starting Over,* TV's *The Mary Tyler Moore Show,* and *Taxi*) chose author Larry McMurtry's 1975 novel *Terms of Endearment.* The film rights were owned by Oscar-winning actress Jennifer Jones (*The Song of Bernadette*), who had envisioned the role of Aurora Greenway as a possible comeback vehicle. She relinquished rights to Brooks, however, when it was agreed that a younger actress was needed to portray the feisty and domineering Aurora. Brooks then got Paramount interested in the project and spent two years researching the picture and reworking McMurtry's story. Several actresses were considered for Aurora, including Anne Bancroft and Louise Fletcher, but Brooks immediately decided on Shirley MacLaine when "she was the only one who ever saw it as a comedy." Brooks also created the ex-astronaut character of Garrett Breedlove, Aurora's love interest, with Burt Reynolds in mind. Reynolds loved the part but was already committed to star in *Stroker Ace,* so Jack Nicholson won the role. Sissy Spacek was originally set to play Aurora's daughter, Emma, but lost the part to Debra Winger, a rising star with two Paramount hits—*Urban Cowboy* and *An Officer and a Gentleman.* The project was officially set into motion when Brooks received a message from Paramount executive Michael Eisner: "You have a 'go' movie, at $7½ million." Additional cast members were added: Jeff Daniels, a New York stage actor; Danny DeVito, a buddy from *Taxi*; and John Lithgow, snagged while on a three-day break from filming Paramount's *Footloose.* Shooting commenced in Houston's River Oaks neighborhood, then moved to Lincoln, Nebraska, and finally to New York City. Brooks's insistence on filming on location added an extra $1 million to the budget; the funds were finally obtained by a presale of the TV rights to NBC and from various investors. *Terms* became a high-profile production, primarily due to Debra Winger's romantic involvement with Bob Kerrey, the recently elected governor of Nebraska, and to rumors of a tumultuous relationship between Winger and MacLaine. MacLaine would later say: "She [Winger] marches to the beat of a different drummer than the rest of us." As for her role as Aurora Greenway, MacLaine reported that she based her character on the late Martha Mitchell, the outspoken, headline-making wife of John Mitchell, United States attorney general under Richard Nixon. "She was in my mind all the time," said MacLaine. "I always felt she was hovering while I was working."

DISTRIBUTION: James Brooks recalled: "Frank Mancuso, in charge of distribution at the time, found a weekend where other things weren't opening—the last available window, around Thanksgiving." Playing on 260 screens for its opening weekend, *Terms* culminated in a total domestic gross of $108 million during its run through April 1984—becoming the second-highest domestic-grossing film of 1983, behind *Return of the Jedi* (number three worldwide behind *Jedi* and *Octopussy*). In 1996 *The Evening Star,* based on a McMurtry novel that continued the *Terms of Endearment* story, was filmed by Paramount; it garnered indifferent reviews and mediocre box office. —*Douglas Burns*

SILKWOOD

20th Century-Fox, 1983

ALL-RELEASE EQUIVALENT 2005 $s

(Unadjusted $s) in Millions of $s

Domestic Box Office Revenues . . . . **$69.1**/($35.6)
Production Cost . . . . not available
Principal Photography . . . . not available

Director . . . . Mike Nichols
Producer . . . . Mike Nichols, Michael Hausman
Production Company . . . . ABC Motion Pictures
Story and
   Screenplay by . . . . Nora Ephron, Alice Arlen
Cast . . . . Meryl Streep, Kurt Russell, Cher
Filming Locations . . . . . . Albuquerque and Los Alamos, NM; Dallas, Howe, Texas City, and Tom Bean TX; Las Colinas Studios outside Dallas, TX
Genre . . . . Bio-Drama
Format . . . . Color (DeLuxe)
Initial Release 12/14/1983
Rerelease . . . . none
Running Time . . . . 128 minutes
MPAA Rating . . . . R

STANDING THE TEST OF TIME

ACADEMY AWARD Oscar Nominations and Wins

Actress in a Leading Role: Meryl Streep

Actress in a Supporting Role: Cher

Directing: Mike Nichols

Film Editing: Sam O'Steen

Writing (Screenplay – written directly for the screen): Nora Ephron, Alice Arlen

   OSCAR TOTALS   Nominations 5   *Wins 0

AFI 100 YEARS 100 MOVIES SELECTION
                              2007 0   1997 0

TOP 300 FILMS POSITION . . . . none
All-Release Domestic Box Office in Equivalent 2005 $s

National Film Preservation Board Selection . . . . none

OTHER AWARDS Best Picture Wins

	Year
Golden Globes	none
New York Film Critics	none
National Board of Review	none
Film Daily Critics	none

It was entirely about an awakening. And it turned out in my life to
be about me awakening also. I was galvanized by [Meryl] Streep. I was stunned by
what she brought, not only in terms of her part, but
what she brought to the others just by rearranging her soul a little bit.

—Mike Nichols

PLOT: The film recounts the true story of the life and death of Karen Silkwood, an employee at the Kerr-McGee plutonium plant in Oklahoma, who attempted to blow the whistle on the many safety violations at the plant but was instead killed in a mysterious car accident.

PRODUCTION: Executive producers Buzz Hirsch and Larry Cano first became interested in the story of Karen Silkwood upon reading of her death in the *New York Times.* Shortly thereafter they traveled to Nederland, Texas, where they met with Karen's father, Bill Silkwood. Eight months later Hirsch and Cano had come to an agreement with the Silkwood estate to produce a film that would focus on the mysterious circumstances surrounding Karen's death, as well as the alleged substandard working conditions at Kerr-McGee. They began investigating the story in depth, compiling a massive library of reports, transcripts of hearings, and taped interviews with family, friends, and co-workers. But the film hit a major snag when Hirsch was subpoenaed to appear in a lawsuit pitting the Silkwood estate against Kerr-McGee. When Hirsch refused to hand his research over to the court, citing protections afforded to him under the U.S. Constitution, a federal judge threatened to hold him in contempt of court and have him arrested. After a lengthy and costly legal battle, the U.S. Court of Appeals in Denver, Colorado, ruled in Hirsch's favor. In the spring of 1980 a deal was in place with ABC Motion Pictures, which had just been revived by the TV network, to produce the film. ABC had a deal to release its movies through 20th Century-Fox. Meryl Streep first became interested in the role of Karen Silkwood upon reading an early draft of the script in October 1979. This was the first film made at Las Colinas Studios in Texas. When it came time to start shooting, however, Streep found herself seriously wondering how to go about playing a character who wasn't a fictional creation, but rather someone who had once lived and still had friends and family around to judge her performance. Streep and director Mike Nichols went to work researching Karen's life, but they quickly agreed the best route for Streep to take was not to try to become Silkwood but rather to try to understand her. So they gathered a number of people who had known Karen personally, including her father and Drew Stephens, Karen's lover at the time of her death. Stephens was actually present on set during shooting so he could tell Streep what he remembered about Karen.

DISTRIBUTION: While *Silkwood* was well received by critics and was relatively successful at the box office, it wasn't without its share of controversy. After a particularly biting review from the *New York Times* in which the film was chided as not presenting "all facets of the case," William David, board member of the Karen Silkwood Fund, wrote an equally biting rebuttal. He said, "The irony is that a more complete documentary would have proved even more embarrassing for Kerr-McGee . . . a movie that is generally artistic, entertaining and accurate ought not to be relegated to the land of make-believe simply because it exposes aspects of reality that some would rather pretend are untrue." Cher's performance as a lesbian was Oscar-nominated and gave the singer credibility as a serious actress. —*Mark D'Anna*

INDIANA JONES AND THE TEMPLE OF DOOM
Paramount, 1984

ALL-RELEASE EQUIVALENT 2005 $s
(Unadjusted $s) in Millions of $s

Domestic Box Office Revenues........ **$343.1**/($179.9)
Production Cost .... **$53.0**/($28.2)
Principal Photography..................... **80** days
4/18/1983–8/26/1983
plus 16 days second unit

Director . . . . Steven Spielberg

Producer . . . . Robert Watts

Production Company . . . . Lucasfilm Ltd.

Story by . . . . George Lucas

Screenplay by . . . . Willard Huyck, Gloria Katz

Cast . . . . Harrison Ford, Kate Capshaw, Amrish Puri, Roshan Seth, Philip Stone, Ke Huy Quan

Filming Locations . . . . . . On Location: Kandy, Sri Lanka (13 days); in studio: EMI Elstree, Borehamwood, UK (67 days); second unit on location in the U.S.: Groveland, Cherry Creek, Tuolumne River, and Mammoth Mountain, CA

Genre . . . . Action Adventure

Format . . . . Color (Rank, prints by DeLuxe)

Initial Release 5/23/1984

Rerelease . . . . none

Running Time . . . . 118 minutes

MPAA Rating . . . . PG

STANDING THE TEST OF TIME

ACADEMY AWARD Oscar Nominations and Wins

Music (Original Score): John Williams

*VISUAL EFFECTS: Dennis Muren, Michael McAlister, Lorne Peterson, George Gibbs

OSCAR TOTALS Nominations **2** *Wins **1**

AFI 100 YEARS 100 MOVIES SELECTION
2007 0   1997 0

TOP 300 FILMS POSITION . . . . **#78**
All-Release Domestic Box Office in Equivalent 2005 $s

National Film Preservation Board Selection . . . . none

OTHER AWARDS Best Picture Wins

	Year
Golden Globes	none
New York Film Critics	none
National Board of Review	none
Film Daily Critics	none

I had to make this film different enough to make it worth doing, yet similar enough so it would attract the same audience. I had to satisfy myself creatively.

—Steven Spielberg

PLOT: Indiana Jones, his sidekick and a nightclub singer go in search of sacred stones stolen from a poor Indian village, encountering a diabolical cult and freeing enslaved children along the way

PRODUCTION: George Lucas started hashing out an outline for his highly anticipated sequel to *Raiders of the Lost Ark* in 1982. After developing the basic structure of a prequel idea, Lucas handed it off to Willard Huyck and Gloria Katz. They pumped it up by deftly integrating three major dropped bits from the original *Raiders* script—an escape from a violent melee behind a rolling gong, a frenetic mine-car chase, and a complex airplane escape and river-rafting action sequence. With his story growing increasingly dark, Lucas eventually decided to abandon the working title, "Indiana Jones and the Temple of Death," in an attempt to soften it. Before shooting could begin, a major hitch developed when the Indian government demanded a series of script changes before it would allow the team permission to film there. Executive producer Lucas refused and shifted his base to Sri Lanka, where he had a huge village set erected amidst the tea fields of the island country. He also hired a British construction company to build a 300-foot rope bridge over a nearby gorge for key shots. Principal photography began there on April 18, 1983, with the second-unit crew grabbing exterior action footage in Macau. The highlight of the Sri Lanka shoot was the nine-camera, one-shot destruction of the bridge, complete with explosives and flailing motorized dummies. Production then moved to Elstree Studios, where one scene called for bucketloads of various creeping and crawling bugs to be poured all over Kate Capshaw's body. Crews also constructed a huge mine set with what was essentially a working roller-coaster ride. Spielberg filmed the big mine-cart chase scene repeatedly from various angles and cut in the most dangerous shots from a miniature model in post. At one point while filming, child actor Key Huy Quan accidentally hit Kate Capshaw with a board and gave her a black eye. A more serious problem emerged when Harrison Ford suffered a severely herniated back. Although Ford gamely tried to work though it, Lucas eventually had to jet him back to America for papaya derivative treatments, delaying production for three weeks. ILM oversaw the effects work, including David Fincher, who provided some of the matte photography. For the lava pit scene, they built a half-scale thirty-foot set and then "sacrificed" three-foot-tall puppets in it.

DISTRIBUTION: The film opened on May 23, 1984, setting a then-record weekend haul of $25.3 million. Enhancing the experience for viewers, Lucas ensured that the film was the first to utilize the new THX Theatre Alignment Program, which required cinemas to meet strict technical standards. Critics were split, some lauding the film's humor and intensity while others attacked the dark and violent tone of the film, especially during a grotesque dinner scene and a human sacrifice. The complaints didn't stop there—angry parents deluged the MPAA with such a torrent of protests over the film's violence that a new PG-13 rating was introduced a short time later. Despite the controversy, or perhaps partly because of it, the film raked in over $333 million worldwide. —*Scott Mazak*

GHOSTBUSTERS

Columbia, 1984

ALL-RELEASE EQUIVALENT 2005 $s

(Unadjusted $s) in Millions of $s

Domestic Box Office Revenues....... **$454.3**/($238.6)
Production Cost .... **$58.3**/($31.0)
Principal Photography............ **75** days estimated
October 1983–February 1984
15-week shoot

Director .... Ivan Reitman
Producer .... Ivan Reitman
Production Company.... Columbia Pictures
Story and
 Screenplay by .... Harold Ramis, Dan Aykroyd
Cast .... Bill Murray, Dan Aykroyd,
Sigourney Weaver,
Harold Ramis, Rick Moranis,
Annie Potts
Filming Locations ...... On Location: Manhattan,
NY; Los Angeles and Beverly
Hills, CA; McCracken County,
KY; in studio: Warner Bros.
Burbank Studio Burbank, CA
Genre................. Comedy
Format............... Color (Metrocolor)
Initial Release.......... 6/8/1984
Rerelease............. 1985
Running Time .... 107 minutes
MPAA Rating .... PG

STANDING THE TEST OF TIME

ACADEMY AWARD Oscar Nominations and Wins

Music (Original Song): "Ghostbusters," Music and Lyrics by Ray Parker Jr.

Visual Effects: Richard Edlund, John Bruno, Mark Vargo, Chuck Gaspar

OSCAR TOTALS   Nominations **2**   *Wins 0

AFI 100 YEARS 100 MOVIES SELECTION
2007 0   1997..... 0

TOP 300 FILMS POSITION .... **#30**
All-Release Domestic Box Office in Equivalent 2005 $s

National Film Preservation Board Selection. . . .none

OTHER AWARDS Best Picture Wins

	Year
Golden Globes .... none	
New York Film Critics..................... none	
National Board of Review .... none	
Film Daily Critics .... none	

*When the first ghost appeared, the audience freaked out:
they both screamed and laughed at the same time.*

—Ivan Reitman

PLOT: Three parapsychologists, forced out of their university lab, decide to go into business catching ghosts—just as the gate to hell opens atop a Manhattan high-rise.

PRODUCTION: *Ghostbusters* began as a forty-page treatment by Dan Aykroyd, who had planned to co-star with his friend John Belushi. The story was set in the future, where there were many teams of ghostbusters. Producer-director Ivan Reitman had previously worked with both actors and was impressed with Aykroyd's treatment, but asked him to bring in writer Harold Ramis to streamline the story. Meanwhile, Columbia head Frank Price approved a $30 million budget, but only if Reitman, who had no script and no production team and had never managed a budget this large, could deliver the picture in one year. Reitman, Ramis, and Aykroyd worked feverishly for three weeks on Martha's Vineyard and finished the script with only two months to go before they had to roll film. The nebbish accountant part eventually taken by Rick Moranis was originally intended for John Candy, who had trouble imagining himself in the role the way Reitman and the writers intended. Most of *Ghostbusters* was filmed on studio sets, but to lend the zany film a geographical verisimilitude, the production spent four weeks on location in New York City. It stopped traffic on Central Park West (and thus throughout midtown Manhattan) for much of an entire day, and visited the New York Public Library, Lincoln Center, Tavern on the Green, and other New York landmarks. The joyous end-credit sequence, with hundreds of New York extras cheering the Ghostbusters on, benefits from this extra effort. Visual effects artist Richard Edlund's team contributed stunning optical effects, but just as impressive were the floor effects realized by supervisor Chuck Gaspar and his crew on the stage, including library cards eerily rocketing into the air and the levitation of star Sigourney Weaver. Predating sophisticated computer-generated effects technology, a remarkable portion of *Ghostbusters* was produced by hand. Edlund later noted that Hollywood expected the transition to digital effects to be a "slow dissolve," but it turned out to be a "hard cut."

Weaver, an experienced dramatic actress who was trying her hand at movie comedy for the first time, said she imagined it was like being in a Marx Brothers movie. Years later, Reitman acknowledged that some of his camera setups were inspired by Marx Brothers films. Production designer John DeCuir had constructed the famous New York street for *Hello, Dolly!* on the Fox back lot, and the elaborate sets for *Cleopatra*. His rooftop set for *Ghostbusters* was the largest ever built at Columbia.

DISTRIBUTION: Its jovial blend of spookiness and comedy made *Ghostbusters* an immediate smash hit. It brought in over $291 million in worldwide box office. Reitman says he knew the movie had struck a chord when, in only the second week of release, he saw New York street kiosks selling illegal T-shirts with catchphrases from the film. Two years before, Time, Inc., had entered into a joint venture deal with Columbia for exclusive rights for its HBO pay TV channel that required Time to pay extra when a movie exceeded its revenue targets. Because of the film's amazing success, Time was obliged to write a check for $36 million—more than the picture's actual production cost—and it immediately renegotiated its deal. —*Tom Dupree*

AMADEUS
Orion, 1984

ALL-RELEASE EQUIVALENT 2005 $s
(Unadjusted $s) in Millions of $s

Domestic Box Office Revenues . . . . $95.5/($52.0)
Production Cost . . . . $33.8/($18.0)
Principal Photography . . . . **120** days estimated
January 1983–July 1983

Director . . . . Milos Forman
Producer . . . . Saul Zaentz
Production Company . . . . Saul Zaentz Company
Story by . . . . Based on the play by Peter Shaffer
Screenplay by . . . . Peter Shaffer
Cast . . . . F. Murray Abraham, Elizabeth Berridge, Simon Callow, Roy Dotrice, Christine Ebersole, Tom Hulce, Jeffrey Jones, Charles Kay
Filming Locations . . . . . . Shot 100 pecent on location in Prague, Czech Republic, and Austria
Genre . . . . Bio-Drama
Format . . . . Color (Technicolor)
Initial Release 9/26/1984
Rerelease . . . . 4/5/2002 (director's cut)
Running Time . . . . 158 minutes (director's cut added 20 minutes back in)
MPAA Rating . . . . PG

STANDING THE TEST OF TIME

ACADEMY AWARD Oscar Nominations and Wins

*BEST PICTURE: Saul Zaentz, Producer

*ACTOR IN A LEADING ROLE: F. Murray Abraham

Actor in a Leading Role: Tom Hulce

*ART DIRECTION/SET DECORATION: Patrizia Von Brandenstein/Karel Cerny

Cinematography: Miroslav Ondricek

*COSTUME DESIGN: Theodor Pistek

*DIRECTING: Milos Forman

Film Editing: Nena Danevic, Michael Chandler

*MAKEUP: Paul LeBlanc, Dick Smith

*SOUND: Mark Berger, Tom Scott, Todd Boekelheide, Chris Newman

*WRITING (Screenplay – based on material from another medium): Peter Shaffer

OSCAR TOTALS Nominations **11** *Wins 8

AFI 100 YEARS 100 MOVIES SELECTION
2007 0   1997 . . . #53

TOP 300 FILMS POSITION . . . . none
All-Release Domestic Box Office in Equivalent 2005 $s

National Film Preservation Board Selection . . . . none

OTHER AWARDS Best Picture Wins

	Year
Golden Globes (Drama)	1985
New York Film Critics	none
National Board of Review	none
Film Daily Critics	none

The music is becoming the third character.

—Peter Shaffer during production

PLOT: Antonio Salieri, modestly talented court composer to the Holy Roman Emperor, is envious of Wolfgang Amadeus Mozart, whose breathtaking genius is embodied in a coarse, ribald personality. Salieri plots to right this "injustice" by destroying Mozart.

PRODUCTION: In 1980 the director Milos Forman called producer Saul Zaentz from New York and said, "There's a play here, and if you like it, we can make a picture out of it." Zaentz loved the play and agreed to finance the film. Forman worked with Shaffer on the screenplay, adding "more Mozart and more music." For four months at Forman's home in Connecticut—which Shaffer called "the prison"—the two men had many disagreements while turning a stylized play into a realistic film, but felt similarly humbled when they listened to Mozart's music each day. Although well-known actors coveted the two leading roles, Forman wanted lesser-known performers. More than a thousand auditions were held. F. Murray Abraham read for a small role and was helping Forman audition potential Mozarts by reading Salieri's lines when it struck the director that Abraham was the ideal Salieri. The distinguished Sir Neville Marriner agreed to conduct the score on the condition that not a single note of Mozart's music be changed. Meg Tilly was originally cast as Mozart's wife, Constanze, but tore a ligament playing soccer shortly before shooting began. After a whirlwind weekend casting in New York, and more screen tests on set, Elizabeth Berridge took over the role. Amadeus marked Forman's return to his native Czechoslovakia, still under Communist rule, after many years. Most of the production was filmed in Prague, which still featured eighteenth-century architecture. The *Don Giovanni* scene was filmed in the country's Tyl Theater, where two centuries earlier Mozart himself had conducted its world premiere. One of the only wooden opera houses still standing in central Europe, the structure was a potential tinderbox, but Forman's crew was still allowed to light the scene with hundreds of burning candles, to stunning effect. Secret police were placed among the production workers, a "secret" that everyone knew. Actors were followed wherever they went; performer Jeffrey Jones commented that it "felt like I was in a B-grade spy movie." At one point, Forman had a scene planned for 650–700 extras he felt were needed for a reaction shot, but Zaentz figured out a way to reduce that number to 50–100 extras without lessening the scene's impact. As a financier, Zaentz was a very hands-on producer, working creatively to help achieve quality within reasonable cost. This kind of commitment was shared by the entire cast and crew. For the "old Salieri" scenes, which were done at the beginning of the shoot, Abraham rose each day at 4:00 a.m. and endured four and a half hours of makeup by Dick Smith. After this procedure, he genuinely felt fatigued, which was ideal for his characterization. Actor Tom Hulce took piano lessons for the Mozart role, and even though he played silently to a pre-recorded score, Marriner later noted that he is never seen to strike the wrong key—not even during the scene in which he plays backward.

DISTRIBUTION: Against all odds, this period piece was an immediate success. At the 1985 Academy Awards ceremony there was a tense moment when Laurence Olivier, presenting the Best Picture award, failed to list the five nominees before announcing *Amadeus*'s award. Zaentz made sure to mention the other nominees in his acceptance speech. —*Tom Dupree*

BEVERLY HILLS COP

Paramount, 1984

<table>
<tr><td colspan="2">ALL-RELEASE EQUIVALENT 2005 $s
(Unadjusted $s) in Millions of $s</td></tr>
<tr><td>Domestic Box Office Revenues</td><td>$432.8/($234.8)</td></tr>
<tr><td>Production Cost</td><td>$26.3/($14.0)</td></tr>
<tr><td>Principal Photography</td><td>75 days estimated 5/14/1984–August 1984</td></tr>
</table>

Director . . . . Martin Brest

Producer . . . . Don Simpson

Production Company . . . . Don Simpson/Jerry Bruckheimer Production, Eddie Murphy Productions

Story by . . . . Danilo Bach and Daniel Petrie Jr.

Screenplay by . . . . Daniel Petrie Jr.

Cast . . . . Eddie Murphy, Judge Reinhold, John Ashton, Lisa Eilbacher, Ronny Cox, Steven Berkoff

Filming Locations . . . . . . On location in California: Beverly Hills, Los Angeles, Hollywood, Pasadena; on location in Michigan: Dearborn, Detroit

Genre . . . . Action Adventure

Format . . . . Color

Initial Release . . . . 12/1/1984 premiere (Los Angeles); 12/5/1984 wide release

Rerelease . . . . none

Running Time . . . . 105 minutes

MPAA Rating . . . . R

STANDING THE TEST OF TIME

ACADEMY AWARD Oscar Nominations and Wins

Writing (Screenplay – written directly for the screen): Screenplay by Daniel Petrie, Jr.; Story by Danilo Bach and Daniel Petrie Jr.

OSCAR TOTALS   Nominations **1**   *Wins **0**

AFI 100 YEARS 100 MOVIES SELECTION
      2007 0   1997 0

TOP 300 FILMS POSITION . . . . #37
All-Release Domestic Box Office in Equivalent 2005 $s

National Film Preservation Board Selection . . . . none

OTHER AWARDS Best Picture Wins

	Year
Golden Globes	none
New York Film Critics	none
National Board of Review	none
Film Daily Critics	none

That the film turned out to be coherent is a miracle.
That it is successful proves there is a God.

—Martin Brest

PLOT: A streetwise Detroit police detective goes to Beverly Hills to investigate the murder of his friend and finds himself thrown into a very different culture. Despite his questionable methods, the Los Angeles police department ultimately works with him to bring the murderer to justice.

PRODUCTION: In 1977 Danilo Bach wrote a script based on an idea he developed with Daniel Petrie Jr. in which an East L.A. cop transfers to Beverly Hills. Subsequent drafts changed the story to one of a tough Detroit cop who finds himself in southern California to solve a friend's murder. Mickey Rourke was signed to star but left after delays, and Sylvester Stallone was cast. When Stallone was unhappy with the script (woven together from six different drafts) he left the film. Al Pacino and James Caan were also considered, but producers Don Simpson and Jerry Bruckheimer turned to Eddie Murphy, then one of the hottest stars in Hollywood following his years on *Saturday Night Live,* his performances as a stand-up comic, and his role in the smash hit *48 Hrs.* (1982), which made him a movie star. With only two weeks left before shooting was to begin, Murphy was cast. Two of his co-stars, Judge Reinhold and John Ashton, won their roles when they set off on a comic riff during their audition. Another co-star, Gilbert R. Hill, was not an actor but a Detroit city commissioner. After David Cronenberg passed on directing the movie, Martin Brest flipped a coin to decide whether to accept the job. There was a great deal of worry that the movie wouldn't work. Murphy's last-minute casting forced another rewrite, which left some rough edges in the script. The character of Jenny was no longer a lover but just an old friend, and Mikey was no longer the lead's brother. But the star's stand-up experience helped smooth things out during photography: he often improvised, most notably in Foley's set piece at the Beverly Palms Hotel. He ad-libbed not only dialogue but entirely new scenes as well. Reinhold and Ashton also improvised jokes, so much so that they had to devise ways to keep themselves and the crew from laughing after several takes were ruined. Ashton would pinch his face hard and look down as if in frustration, although he was really laughing, while Reinhold would put his hand in his pocket and pinch his thigh hard to stay serious. The scene in which Murphy, Reinhold, and Ashton's characters explain the strip club arrest to Bogomil was entirely improvised. When location shooting in Detroit, local police would escort Brest around the city but not into certain dangerous neighborhoods. Undeterred, the director and his crew went on their own to get the shots they wanted. Murphy, who generally avoided caffeine, refused to have coffee despite being exhausted during the police station shoot, but once he was finally persuaded to drink some, he found the energy to ad-lib his "supercops" monologue. By the time the film wrapped, word at the studio was that Murphy had saved the troubled project.

DISTRIBUTION: The first movie to be shown on more than 2,000 screens, *Beverly Hills Cop* opened early in the Christmas season of 1984. Paramount's expectations of Murphy's box office power were on target: the movie was an immediate hit, with a $15 million opening weekend, and became the second-biggest smash of the year behind only *Ghostbusters,* grossing $316 million in worldwide box office (three-quarters of which was in the United States). The movie also commandeered radio, as the soundtrack album became a hit as well. —*Louis Burklow*

BACK TO THE FUTURE

Universal, 1985

ALL-RELEASE EQUIVALENT 2005 $s

(Unadjusted $s) in Millions of $s

Domestic Box Office Revenues . . . . **$374.7**/($208.2)
Production Cost . . . . **$39.9**/($22.0)
Principal Photography . . . . **75** days estimated
11/26/1984–4/20/1985

Director . . . . Robert Zemeckis

Producer . . . . Bob Gale, Neil Canton

Production Company . . . . Amblin Entertainment,
Universal Pictures

Story and
  Screenplay by . . . . Robert Zemeckis, Bob Gale

Cast . . . . Michael J. Fox, Christopher
Lloyd, Crispin Glover,
Lea Thompson

Filming Locations . . . . . . On location: Pasadena,
Hollywood, Burbank, Chino,
Los Angeles, and Whittier, CA;
in studio: Universal Studios,
Universal City, CA

Genre . . . . Comedy

Format . . . . Color (Technicolor)

Initial Release 7/3/1985

Rerelease . . . . none

Running Time . . . . 116 minutes

MPAA Rating . . . . PG

STANDING THE TEST OF TIME

ACADEMY AWARD Oscar Nominations and Wins

Music (Original Song): "The Power of Love," Music by
Chris Hayes and Johnny Colla; Lyrics by Huey Lewis

Sound: Bill Varney, B. Tennyson Sebastian II, Robert
Thirlwell, William B. Kaplan

*SOUND EFFECTS EDITING: Charles L. Campbell,
Robert Rutledge

Writing (Screenplay – written directly for the screen):
Robert Zemeckis, Bob Gale

OSCAR TOTALS   Nominations **4**   *Wins **1**

AFI 100 YEARS 100 MOVIES SELECTION
2007 0   1997 0

TOP 300 FILMS POSITION . . . . **#54**
All-Release Domestic Box Office in Equivalent 2005 $s

National Film Preservation Board Selection 2007

OTHER AWARDS Best Picture Wins

	Year
Golden Globes	none
New York Film Critics	none
National Board of Review	none
Film Daily Critics	none

It's a comedy adventure science fiction time travel love story.

—Robert Zemeckis

It's an action comedy adventure coming-of-age musical.

—Michael J. Fox

PLOT: A contemporary teenager travels thirty years back in time to 1955, when his parents were in high school. Once there, he has to encourage them to fall in love, or else he will cease to exist.

PRODUCTION: Just having finished *Used Cars* with screenwriting partner and director Robert Zemeckis, Bob Gale was visiting his parents in St. Louis when he happened upon his father's high school yearbook. He became fascinated with the fantasy notion of being able to know his parents when they were teenagers, and Zemeckis was equally enthusiastic. The script that emerged in 1980 was turned down by every studio in Hollywood; the reigning "teen comedy" style of the time was far raunchier, and the duo's two previous movies had met with only modest success. But then came Zemeckis's breakthrough hit *Romancing the Stone,* and suddenly everyone wanted another look at *Back to the Future.* Zemeckis brought it to the one person who had given him encouragement at first read: Steven Spielberg. Soon they had a deal with Universal, Spielberg's home studio. Michael J. Fox was the filmmakers' first choice for the lead, but he was starring in the popular television sitcom *Family Ties* at the time, so they cast Eric Stoltz instead. After initial shooting, it became evident to Zemeckis that although Stoltz was very talented and was giving his all, his performance wasn't producing the precise comedic tone the director intended. He went back to Fox, who agreed to work on the two projects simultaneously, producing extremely long days for the twenty-three-year-old actor. Christopher Lloyd based his classic mad-scientist character on the conductor Leopold Stokowski. The writers' first notion for the design of their time machine was an old refrigerator, but they quickly realized this might tempt smaller children to crawl inside a real one, and that the machine needed to be mobile. They decided instead to adapt the already futuristic appearance of the DeLorean car; three vehicles were used during filming, augmented with spare aircraft parts and electronics. To replicate a small town circa 1955, production designer Lawrence Paull studied contemporary printed material and screened movies of the period. Paull's team first dressed the "town square" on the Universal back lot for the pristine fifties, then dirtied it to give the effect of a town center that had gone to seed in the ensuing thirty years. Even with *Back to the Future*'s fantastic setting and science fiction concepts, the filmmakers kept the story closely focused on the human element: there are only about thirty visual effects shots in the film. Zemeckis asked composer Alan Silvestri for an "overblown fantasy old-fashioned movie score." Silvestri conducted a ninety-eight-piece orchestra, the largest ever assembled for a Universal project.

DISTRIBUTION: *Back to the Future* was an immediate smash hit, eclipsing even *Romancing the Stone,* and Zemeckis and Gale instantly became one of Hollywood's hottest writing teams. The "teaser" they had included at the end, implying a second story, became reality when Universal ordered not one but two sequels. They were shot back to back by virtually the same team (with the exception of the production and costume designers), with Zemeckis directing and Gale contributing screenplays from stories the two partners had worked out together. Universal parlayed the success of the franchise into rides at its theme parks in California and Florida, perhaps the best single testament to the film's enduring popularity. —*Tom Dupree*

THE COLOR PURPLE

Warner Bros., 1985

ALL-RELEASE EQUIVALENT 2005 $s

(Unadjusted $s) in Millions of $s

Domestic Box Office Revenues . . . . **$162.7**/($94.2)
Production Cost . . . . **$26.7**/($15.0)
Principal Photography . . . . not available
6/6/1985–August 1985

Director . . . . Steven Spielberg

Producer . . . . Steven Spielberg, Kathleen Kennedy, Frank Marshall, Quincy Jones

Production Company . . . . Warner Bros.

Story by . . . . Based on the novel by Alice Walker

Screenplay by . . . . Menno Meyjes

Cast . . . . Danny Glover, Whoopi Goldberg, Margaret Avery, Oprah Winfrey

Filming Locations . . . . . . On location: Ansonville, Charlotte, Lilesville, Marshville, and Wadesboro, NC; Newhall, CA; Kenya

Genre . . . . Drama

Format . . . . Color

Initial Release 12/18/1985

Rerelease . . . . none

Running Time . . . . 152 minutes

MPAA Rating PG-13

I want the audience to feel every color in Celie's rainbow, the rainbow she makes for herself and dives into headfirst.

—Steven Spielberg

STANDING THE TEST OF TIME

ACADEMY AWARD Oscar Nominations and Wins

Best Picture: Steven Spielberg, Kathleen Kennedy, Frank Marshall, and Quincy Jones, Producers

Actress in a Leading Role: Whoopi Goldberg

Actress in a Supporting Role: Margaret Avery

Actress in a Supporting Role: Oprah Winfrey

Art Direction/Set Decoration: J. Michael Riva, Robert W. Welch/Linda DeScenna

Cinematography: Allen Daviau

Costume Design: Aggie Guerard Rodgers

Makeup: Ken Chase

Music (Orignial Score): Quincy Jones, Jeremy Lubbock, Rod Temperton, Caiphus Semenya, Andrae Crouch, Chris Boardman, Jorge Calandrelli, Joel Rosenbaum, Fred Steiner, Jack Hayes, Jerry Hey, Randy Kerber

Music (Original Song): "Miss Celie's Blues"

Writing (Screenplay – based on material from another medium): Menno Meyjes

OSCAR TOTALS Nominations **11** *Wins 0

AFI 100 YEARS 100 MOVIES SELECTION
2007 0   1997 0

TOP 300 FILMS POSITION . . . . none
All-Release Domestic Box Office in Equivalent 2005 $s

National Film Preservation Board Selection . . . . none

OTHER AWARDS Best Picture Wins

	Year
Golden Globes . . . . none	
New York Film Critics . . . . none	
National Board of Review 1985	
Film Daily Critics . . . . none	

PLOT: The story focuses on two African American sisters growing up in an abusive family in the South during the early 1900s and the transformation of the eldest, Celie, as she finds her self-worth and evolves over the next thirty years.

PRODUCTION: Alice Walker spent a year writing her Pulitzer Prize–winning novel, *The Color Purple,* during a period of turmoil in her personal life (when she got divorced, left New York, and lived in a cottage while writing and taking care of her child). Walker wanted to honor the struggles of early twentieth-century African Americans (including her parents and grandparents). When the novel was published in 1982, there was a controversy over Walker's harsh depiction of African American men. Kathleen Kennedy, president of Steven Spielberg's Amblin Entertainment, sent the book to Spielberg because she thought his Jewish background and anti-Semitic experiences would help him understand the racism in the story. Spielberg met with Walker and they hit it off. This became his first venture into the world of adult drama. Spielberg asked Walker to write the screenplay, but she was unhappy with her effort and asked Spielberg not to use it. Menno Meyjes wrote the screenplay instead. Walker became a project consultant. Spielberg's first instinct was to shoot in black and white because he was afraid of sugarcoating the story, but he eventually decided on color, contrasting the harsh, heartbreaking scenes with a picturesque setting. For the leading role of Celie, Walker chose Whoopi Goldberg after seeing her stand-up act in San Francisco. It was her feature debut, as it was for Oprah Winfrey. Spielberg wanted singer Tina Turner to play Shug Avery, but she declined. Margaret Avery played the part, and Táta Vega provided the singing voice. Spielberg maintained Walker's epistolary format from the book by using voice-overs from Celie's letters. Walker insisted that 50 percent of the crew be persons of color, along with her all-black cast. This was one of the first and only times Spielberg worked without composer John Williams; instead he had Quincy Jones score the film. During filming, Spielberg had executive producers Peter Guber and Jon Peters banned from the set for offering "suggestions." Spielberg's son, Max, was born during production, and in the scene where Celie gives birth, the sound of the baby crying is the actual sound of the Spielbergs' baby crying. Allen Daviau's sweeping cinematography of the scene with the field of flowers was photochemically altered when the flowers didn't appear purple enough.

DISTRIBUTION: The film got mixed reviews but was a box office success. There was controversy about the adaptation. Some African American civil rights leaders were upset that Spielberg directed, and feminist and gay critics were unhappy that Spielberg interjected humor, reducing Celie's abuse to a battle of the sexes. They were also displeased that he had toned down the lesbianism into platonic female bonding. After it failed to win a single award among eleven Oscar nominations, some saw it as proof of racial bias in Hollywood. The film was the first to be released to VHS video entirely in the letterbox format. In December 2005, a musical adaptation of the novel opened on Broadway, co-produced by Oprah Winfrey. It was nominated for eleven Tony Awards in 2006 but only won for Best Leading Actress in a Musical. —*Hayley Taylor Block*

OUT OF AFRICA

Universal, 1985

ALL-RELEASE EQUIVALENT 2005 $s

(Unadjusted $s) in Millions of $s

Domestic Box Office Revenues . . . . **$152.0**/($87.1)
Production Cost . . . . **$54.5**/($30.0)
Principal Photography . . . . **80** days estimated
4/8/1985–7/27/1985

Director . . . . Sydney Pollack
Producer . . . . Sydney Pollack
Production Company . . . . Universal Pictures Ltd.
Story by . . . . Based on writings by Isak
Dinesen, Judith Thurman, and
Errol Trzebinski
Screenplay by . . . . Kurt Luedtke
Cast . . . . Meryl Streep, Robert Redford,
Klaus Maria Brandauer
Filming Locations . . . . On location: Shaba National
Game Reserve, Kenya; UK; in
studios: Shepperton Studios,
Surrey, England
Genre . . . . Drama
Format . . . . Color (Rank)
Initial Release 12/20/1985
Rerelease . . . . none
Running Time . . . . 150 minutes
MPAA Rating . . . . PG

STANDING THE TEST OF TIME

ACADEMY AWARD Oscar Nominations and Wins

*****BEST PICTURE:** Sydney Pollack, Producer

Actor in a Supporting Role: Klaus Maria Brandauer

Actress in a Leading Role: Meryl Streep

*****ART DIRECTION/SET DECORATION:** Stephen
Grimes/Josie MacAvin

*****CINEMATOGRAPHY:** David Watkin

Costume Design: Milena Canonero

*****DIRECTING:** Sydney Pollack

Film Editing: Fredric Steinkamp, William Steinkamp,
Pembroke Herring, Sheldon Kahn

*****MUSIC** (Original Score): John Barry

*****SOUND:** Chris Jenkins, Gary Alexander, Larry
Stensvold, Peter Handford

*****WRITING** (Screenplay – based on material from
another medium): Kurt Luedtke

OSCAR TOTALS Nominations **11** *Wins 7

AFI 100 YEARS 100 MOVIES SELECTION
2007 0   1997 0

TOP 300 FILMS POSITION .none
All-Release Domestic Box Office in Equivalent 2005 $s

National Film Preservation Board Selection . . . .none

OTHER AWARDS Best Picture Wins

	Year
Golden Globes	1986
New York Film Critics	none
National Board of Review	none
Film Daily Critics	none

People think it's an epic because it takes place over a period of 13 years.
It's not even shot in widescreen. Not only that, there is no story, it's a lot of conversations.
A woman goes to grow coffee and that doesn't work and her husband gives her syphilis and
she falls in love with a guy and he dies and that's the whole story.

—Sydney Pollack

PLOT: The story follows the memoirs of Danish author Karen Blixen during her years on a Kenyan coffee plantation during British colonial rule, including her marriage to a philandering baron and her love affair with a big game hunter.

PRODUCTION: Over the years, several noted directors had *Out of Africa* on their to-do lists, including David Lean, Nicolas Roeg (who saw Julie Christie and Ryan O'Neal as Baron and Baroness Blixen), and Orson Welles, who wanted Greta Garbo as his star. The head of Universal Pictures, Frank Price, was determined to see the film made by Sydney Pollack. It was based on the lyrical 1937 book by Isak Dinesen (Blixen's pseudonym). One of the first things Pollack had screenwriter Kurt Luedtke excise was Lulu, the bushbuck antelope Blixen rescued from the wild, much the way Joy Adamson did with Elsa the Lion in *Born Free*. He found the mental picture of Meryl Streep bottle-feeding a young animal too Disneyesque. Material from Judith Thurman's 1982 biography of Blixen was incorporated into the screenplay to enrich her character. Klaus Maria Brandauer impressed Pollack in *Never Say Never Again,* and he was the first actor to be cast. Initially, Audrey Hepburn was offered the role, but when she turned it down the part went to Meryl Streep, who perfected Blixen's accent by listening to actual recordings of the author reading her works. Production designer Stephen Grimes spent a year in a suburb of Nairobi, where they built a replica of the city, circa 1913. Local craftsmen erected two old-style hotels, the East African Standard Bank, government buildings, a church, a marketplace, and a full-scale railway station. An existing farmhouse on the Blixen estate was renovated to duplicate the original, and furniture belonging to Blixen was used by set designer Josie Mac-Avin. Robert Redford initially used a British accent, but Pollack found it distracting and had him drop it. Redford had to redub some early takes. While actual members of the Kikuyu ethnic group were used in the film, some who no longer practiced the ancient tribal custom of ear-stretching had to be fitted with custom-made drooping latex ears (at $15 a pair). Lions were imported from California, as they were trained to "act." In a night scene in which they attack an ox, a tethered lioness did not react as ferociously as hoped when Streep pretended to be whipping it. The actress maintains that Pollack ordered the lion untied so as to give it freedom to circle and snarl at Streep. Pollack duly disputes that scenario. In another scene, this one filmed during daylight hours, Streep comes within a few yards of a lion roaming free, while Redford, as Hatton, calmly tells her to keep her head. From the camera's perspective, the animal seems to be staring at its intended prey, but then it runs off. Out of camera range, the lion's trainer was offering the beast a tasty morsel.

DISTRIBUTION: A critical hit, *Out of Africa* was a solid performer at the box office as well, opening with $3.6 million in 922 U.S. theaters on its way to a worldwide gross of $128.5 million, with 67 percent of the gross coming from the domestic box office. Its length limited the number of plays each day, dampening the revenue potential. It was among the top 10 grossing movies of 1985 but did only 33 percent of the worldwide box office of summer blockbuster *Back to the Future* that same year. —*Bob Canning*

TOP GUN
Paramount, 1986

ALL-RELEASE EQUIVALENT 2005 $s
(Unadjusted $s) in Millions of $s

Domestic Box Office Revenues........$305.4/($176.8)
Production Cost ....$33.9/($19.0)
Principal Photography................not available
6/26/1985–unknown

Director .... Tony Scott
Producer .... Dom Simpson, Jerry Bruckheimer
Production Company .... Paramount Pictures
Story by .... Based on a *California* magazine feature by Ehud Yonay
Screenplay by .... Jim Cash, Jack Epps Jr.
Cast .... Tom Cruise, Kelly McGillis, Val Kilmer, Anthony Edwards, Tom Skerritt
Filming Locations ...... On location in California: Miramar Naval Air Station, San Diego Oceanside; Oakland; in studio: Paramount Pictures
Genre................. War
Format................ Color (Metrocolor)
Initial Release 5/16/1986
Rerelease............. none
Running Time .... 110 minutes
MPAA Rating .... PG

STANDING THE TEST OF TIME

ACADEMY AWARD Oscar Nominations and Wins

Film Editing: Billy Weber, Chris Lebenzon

*MUSIC (Original Song): "Take My Breath Away," Music by Giorgio Moroder; Lyrics by Tom Whitlock

Sound: Donald O. Mitchell, Kevin O'Connell, Rick Kline, William B. Kaplan

Sound Effects Editing: Cecelia Hall, George Watters II

OSCAR TOTALS   Nominations **4**   *Wins **1**

AFI 100 YEARS 100 MOVIES SELECTION
2007 0   1997 0

TOP 300 FILMS POSITION . . . . #102
All-Release Domestic Box Office in Equivalent 2005 $s

National Film Preservation Board Selection . . . . none

OTHER AWARDS Best Picture Wins
	Year
Golden Globes	none
New York Film Critics	none
National Board of Review	none
Film Daily Critics	none

Nobody really quite understood what it was going to be. They thought it was going to be
The Hunger *[my previous film] on an aircraft carrier. There was a lot of*
trepidation about whether it was gonna work or not work.
—Tony Scott

PLOT: The best of the best compete at the Top Gun School, for advanced navy fighter pilots.

PRODUCTION: Producer Jerry Bruckheimer saw an article by Ehud Yonay in the May 1983 issue of *California* magazine about the U.S. Navy's Top Gun School at Miramar Naval Air Station. There were also pages of aerial photography by Lieutenant Commander Charles "Heater" Heatley. Bruckheimer showed it to his partner Don Simpson, former head of production at Paramount, and purchased the screenplay rights. Several screenwriters passed before Paramount exec Jeff Katzenberg offered it to Jim Cash and Jack Epps Jr. It was important to the producers to have navy cooperation. Epps went to Miramar to do research, hear the jargon, and go on a flight. Cash and Epps compared it to a competitive sports movie. Retired Rear Admiral Pete Pettigrew was technical advisor. Among changes made at the navy's request was moving the opening dogfight to international waters (instead of over Cuba), eliminating most foul language, eliminating a crash on the deck of a carrier, and limiting the love interest to a contract employee, as navy rules prohibit fraternization between officers and regular sailors. Paramount executives gave the script a lukewarm reception and discussed selling off the project. Simpson and Bruckheimer pleaded their case and another draft was written, but the script was shelved. Frank Mancuso took over the job of chairman in 1984 from the departing Barry Diller, and brought in Ned Tanen to head production. With market share falling, the new regime gave the green light. Tony Scott was brought in as director. After casting was complete, the actors were scheduled for a navy survival course at Miramar. The male cast began hanging out with Miramar fighter pilots, with Cruise staying away because of character. A camaraderie began. A volleyball sequence was developed into the now famous montage. Two aircraft carriers were used, one for a dangerous night carrier landing. During a daylight shoot Scott asked to turn a ship to a certain angle for five minutes, to keep the sunlight. This particular maneuver cost $25,000, which Scott paid for by check on the spot. The special effects crew used a location in Oakland, California, to re-create shots intercut with real jet fighters. The crew shot from two and three camera positions. A pickup scene between Cruise and McGillis was later scheduled while Cruise was working on *The Color of Money*. Art Scholl, a noted aerobatic pilot, was killed when his plane failed to come out of a spin off the southern California coast. The film was dedicated to his memory.

DISTRIBUTION: The film went through ten weeks in postproduction after the first cut was deemed confusing. Film editors Billy Weber and Chris Lebenzon reedited, but the movie still got a mixed response at a test screening in Dallas. It was scheduled to open in June against two strong movies. Mancuso, whose background was in distribution, moved up the opening by a month to May 16, and established it in the market before the others arrived. Despite mixed reviews, it played in the top 10 for an extended period and was a huge hit, grossing almost $345 million in worldwide box office. Sales of Ray-Ban aviator sunglasses jumped 40 percent after the film's release. It also boosted pilot recruitment in both the navy and air force. The term "top gun" became ingrained in the American culture. —*Frank McAdams*

CROCODILE DUNDEE

Paramount (domestic); Hoyts Distribution and 20th Century-Fox (foreign), 1986

ALL-RELEASE EQUIVALENT 2005 $s

(Unadjusted $s) in Millions of $s

Domestic Box Office Revenues . . . . **$302.0**/($174.8)
Production Cost . . . . **$11.0**/($6.2)
Principal Photography . . . . not available
July 1985–February 1986

Director . . . . Peter Faiman
Producer . . . . John Cornell
Production Company . . . . Rimfire Films Ltd.,
Paramount Productions
Story by . . . . Paul Hogan
Screenplay by . . . . Paul Hogan, Ken Shadie,
John Cornell
Cast . . . . Paul Hogan, Linda Kozlowski
Filming Locations . . . . . . On location: Queensland,
Sydney; Kakadu National Park,
Australia; Manhattan, NY;
Newark Airport, Newark, NJ.
Genre . . . . Comedy
Format . . . . Color (Kodakcolor)
Initial Release . . . . 4/24/1986 (Australia);
9/25/1986 (U.S.)
Rerelease . . . . none
Running Time . . . . 102 minutes (U.S. version 98
minutes)
MPAA Rating . . . . PG-13 U.S. (Commonwealth
Censor rating: M)

STANDING THE TEST OF TIME

ACADEMY AWARD Oscar Nominations and Wins

Writing (Screenplay – written directly for the screen):
Screenplay by Paul Hogan, Ken Shadie,
John Cornell; Story by Paul Hogan

OSCAR TOTALS   Nominations **1**   *Wins **0**

AFI 100 YEARS 100 MOVIES SELECTION
2007 0   1997 0

TOP 300 FILMS POSITION . . . . **#106**
All-Release Domestic Box Office in Equivalent 2005 $s

National Film Preservation Board Selection . . . . none

OTHER AWARDS Best Picture Wins

	Year
Golden Globes	none
New York Film Critics	none
National Board of Review	none
Film Daily Critics	none

*[Dundee's] a mythical outback Australian . . . it's like the image Americans have of us,
so why not give them one? The Americans have been creating folk heroes for years.*

—Paul Hogan

PLOT: A cheerful outdoorsman from Australia's rugged Northern Territory is coaxed by a beautiful journalist into a visit to New York City, where the "fish out of water" teaches the citified natives a thing or two.

PRODUCTION: Australian actor-comedian Paul Hogan was very popular in his home country and becoming newly recognizable in America due to two successful advertising campaigns, for Australian tourism (during which he popularized the phrase "shrimp on the barbie") and for Foster's beer, when a long-gestating idea took hold. While fishing with Territorians in the great rivers of the north, Hogan had been struck by the fact that they disliked visiting even the smallest of towns: "If you took a few of those guys and carted them to New York, they would really think they're on another planet." An iconic character was thus born. Hogan and his manager-partner, John Cornell, secured private Australian financing for a modestly budgeted project that could still afford major talent such as cinematographer Russell Boyd (*Picnic at Hanging Rock*) and designer Graham Walker (*Mad Max*). The Australian Actors Equity originally opposed hiring an American actress for the second lead, but Hogan—supported by local interests as august as the *Sydney Morning Herald*—prevailed in his desire to avoid having an Aussie fake an American accent to play a character who was supposed to be a native New Yorker. Filming began in July 1985 in McKinlay, a settlement with a population of thirty in northwest Queensland, which doubled for the fictional Walkabout Creek, later becoming so popular as a tourist destination that one local business actually changed its name to Walkabout Creek Hotel. Desolate outback scenes were filmed at Kakadu National Park, home to thousands of species of plants and animals, as well as Aboriginal rock paintings dating back many millennia. A key crocodile attack was shot at Girraween Lagoon, chosen because it contained no real crocs: a $45,000 mechanical animal on a rail was used instead, powered forward by hydraulic rams. When the production moved to New York, it found the local authorities even more helpful than the Australians. Through fifteen-hour days from Times Square to SoHo, the only threat to the production schedule was the arrival of Hurricane Gloria, which forced one day off. While filming a subway scene involving 300 cheering extras, Hogan and Cornell each realized that the Dundee character could travel overseas.

DISTRIBUTION: Within days of its Australian release, *Crocodile Dundee* was breaking the country's all-time box office records. Cornell arranged two screenings for Hollywood industry, which ignited a ten-day negotiation. The U.S. rights were won by Paramount, which had been dogging the production even before it had rolled film, and which, victorious, vowed to spend more than the original production budget on promotion, to acclimate American audiences to the outback sensibility. Hogan personally crisscrossed the country to promote the film, granting some 300 interviews. Paramount insisted on adding quotation marks around Dundee's nickname "in case people thought it was a swamp movie," Hogan recalled. *Crocodile Dundee* was the number two domestic and worldwide grossing film, behind only *Top Gun* in 1986. It played in extended runs across the country well into the following year. Its U.S. video release sold 1.8 million units. —*Tom Dupree*

PLATOON
Orion, 1986

ALL-RELEASE EQUIVALENT 2005 $s
(Unadjusted $s) in Millions of $s

Domestic Box Office Revenues........**$226.7**/($138.0)
Production Cost.......................**$11.6**/($6.5)
Principal Photography............**54** days estimated
3/7/1986–May 1986

Director.............. Oliver Stone
Producer.............. Arnold Kopelson
Production Company.... Hemdale Film
Story and
 Screenplay by........ Oliver Stone
Cast.................. Tom Berenger, Willem Dafoe, Charlie Sheen
Filming Locations...... Philippines
Genre................. War
Format............... Color (CFI)
Initial Release......... 12/19/1986
Rerelease............. none
Running Time......... 120 minutes
MPAA Rating.......... R

STANDING THE TEST OF TIME

ACADEMY AWARD Oscar Nominations and Wins

*BEST PICTURE: Arnold Kopelson, Producer

Actor in a Supporting Role: Tom Berenger

Actor in a Supporting Role: Willem Dafoe

Cinematography: Robert Richardson

*DIRECTING: Oliver Stone

*FILM EDITING: Claire Simpson

*SOUND: John K. Wilkinson, Richard Rogers, Charles "Bud" Grenzbach, Simon Kaye

Writing (Screenplay – written directly for the screen): Oliver Stone

OSCAR TOTALS   Nominations 8   *Wins 4

AFI 100 YEARS 100 MOVIES SELECTION
2007...#86   1997...#83

TOP 300 FILMS POSITION................... #193
All-Release Domestic Box Office in Equivalent 2005 $s

National Film Preservation Board Selection....none

OTHER AWARDS Best Picture Wins

	Year
Golden Globes...........................	1987
New York Film Critics.....................	none
National Board of Review..................	none
Film Daily Critics........................	none

An English producer called John Daly ... actually read both scripts, Salvador *and* Platoon, *and asked which one I wanted to do first, which of course to a young filmmaker is like a dream. I picked* Salvador *first because I was so convinced that* Platoon *was cursed—it had been started so many times but not got made, so I thought it was not going to happen.*

—Oliver Stone

PLOT: Chris Taylor drops out of college and volunteers for Vietnam, where he undergoes a dramatic coming-of-age experience in a tragic combat situation. He soon finds himself caught between two sergeants, Elias and Barnes, reflecting the good and evil of war, respectively. Chris is able to relate his experiences in letters to his grandmother.

PRODUCTION: Oliver Stone went through a decade of rejections and disappointments with *Platoon*. The script came from his experiences as an army infantryman in 1967 along the Cambodian border. Stone was twice wounded and awarded a Bronze Star. By the time financing was in place ten years had passed. Hemdale lost money on Stone's previous film, *Salvador,* and was cautious about *Platoon*. By October 1985 the $6 million budget was in place with locations scouted in the Philippines, then under the shaky Ferdinand Marcos government. Line producer Alex Ho negotiated for military hardware and equipment. A massive crew of 250, many of whom were Filipino, was lined up. The U.S. military refused any cooperation, after the Department of Defense called the movie "totally unrealistic." This is partly because of the controversial drug sequence. Twenty-five black, white, and Hispanic actors had to be cast. Kyle MacLachlan and Keanu Reeves turned down the role of Chris Taylor. Charlie Sheen initially auditioned but was passed on. Several years later he reread for the role and got it. Retired marine Dale Dye trained the actors during fourteen days of living in the jungle, in an overgrown, insect-ridden tropical area, Camp Castenada, sixty miles south of Manila. They would be in the bush constantly, eating C-rations, sleeping in foxholes, and going on patrol with full gear and weapons. Dye even staged a "mortar attack" complete with special effects. The actors went by their character names in the script. Dye then had them rappel down a sixty-five-foot tower. As the days went on they became a platoon. The actors were then taken, tired and sweat-stained, right from the training area to the set for the first day of shooting. In the meantime, Corazon Aquino was swept into office as president. The cast and crew had to endure insects, jungle rains, and some dangerous moments in helicopters. Special effects with gasoline explosions were an added concern. In some instances Stone taunted the actors to get the desired angered effect. This was complicated by tensions and arguments between the Americans and Filipinos in the crew. Night shooting proved extremely difficult as the schedule wore on. Shooting ended the day before the rainy season began in full force.

DISTRIBUTION: Orion's initial plan was a limited late 1986 platform release in New York and Los Angeles followed by a slow building campaign into early 1987. When the film opened in six theaters in New York, Los Angeles, with Toronto added, on December 19 people were lining up around the block for a morning viewing. Orion was then forced to move quickly for a wider release as the film began attracting a strong female audience. In theaters across the country, audiences sat in stunned silence as closing credits rolled. Worldwide box office brought in $213 million. —*Frank McAdams*

BEVERLY HILLS COP II
Paramount, 1987

ALL-RELEASE EQUIVALENT 2005 $s
(Unadjusted $s) in Millions of $s

Domestic Box Office Revenues........ **$251.9**/($153.7)
Production Cost .... **$53.3**/($31.0)
Principal Photography............ **80 days estimated**
11/10/1986–late December 1986

Director . . . . Tony Scott

Producer . . . . Don Simpson, Jerry Bruckheimer

Production Company . . . . Paramount Productions, Eddie Murphy Productions

Story by . . . . Eddie Murphy, Robert D. Wachs, based on characters created by Danilo Bach and Daniel Petrie Jr.

Screenplay by . . . . Larry Ferguson, Warren Skaaren

Cast . . . . Eddie Murphy, Judge Reinhold, Jurgen Prochnow, Ronny Cox, John Ashton, Brigitte Nielsen, Allen Garfield, Gilbert R. Hill, Paul Reiser, Dean Stockwell

Filming Locations . . . . . . On location in California: Beverly Hills, Hollywood, Pasadena, Los Angeles, Sylmar, Baldwin Hills

Genre . . . . Action Adventure

Format . . . . Color (Technicolor)

Initial Release . . . . 5/19/1987 premiere (Los Angeles); 5/20/1987 wide release

Rerelease . . . . none

Running Time . . . . 102 minutes

MPAA Rating . . . . R

STANDING THE TEST OF TIME

ACADEMY AWARD Oscar Nominations and Wins

Music (Original Song): "Shakedown," Music by Harold Faltermeyer and Keith Forsey; Lyrics by Harold Faltermeyer, Keith Forsey, and Bob Seger

OSCAR TOTALS Nominations 1 *Wins 0

AFI 100 YEARS 100 MOVIES SELECTION
2007 . . . . . 0 1997 0

TOP 300 FILMS POSITION . . . . #159
All-Release Domestic Box Office in Equivalent 2005 $s

National Film Preservation Board Selection . . . . none

OTHER AWARDS Best Picture Wins

	Year
Golden Globes	none
New York Film Critics	none
National Board of Review	none
Film Daily Critics	none

If you're involved in something that's original, you know, you'll always go back and try to rehash it.
—Eddie Murphy

PLOT: Axel Foley returns to Beverly Hills to help Rosewood and Taggart investigate the shooting of Chief Bogomil and a connected series of crimes.

PRODUCTION: The huge financial success of *Beverly Hills Cop* helped establish the genre of action comedy and opened the way for a sequel. At first, however, Paramount was thinking of a television series rather than a second movie. This idea was quickly shot down by Eddie Murphy, who had no intention of returning to the grind of weekly television. He also understood there was more money to be made from a new movie than from a TV series. His insistence ensured that a sequel would be made and quickly. Murphy's base salary was $8 million. In 1983 producer Don Simpson met in his Paramount office with writer Larry Ferguson, then at work on the script for *Presidio*. On Simpson's desk sat a 9mm automatic pistol. Ferguson had heard about Simpson's brash style but was determined not to be intimidated. As they talked, Ferguson took apart the entire gun and put it back together, with not a word by either man about his actions. When he finished, Simpson said, "We want to be in business with you." Simpson forced Paramount to take Ferguson off *Presidio* to work on the cop sequel. Ferguson's script did not stray far from the flavor of Danilo Bach and Daniel Petrie's original. There had been talk of sending Axel to London and Paris, but Murphy did not want to film outside the United States. So he returned to southern California. Along with Axel, the characters of Rosewood, Taggart, and Bogomil were brought back; Bogomil would suffer a nearly fatal gunshot wound that would bring Axel back to California. At the same time, Rosewood's character was beefed up, showing more of his life away from work. Chris Rock made his film debut in a small role as a valet. When production commenced in 1986, Scott and his cast tried to recapture some of the improvisational quality that drove the popularity of the original. During one scene in Rosewood's apartment, for instance, Axel and Billy sing lyrics set to *The Dating Game*'s theme song. These lines were made up by Murphy and Reinhold on the set. More often, though, the film relied on the tried and true. Tony Scott had been chosen by Simpson and Bruckheimer to direct because of the success of *Top Gun*, and this movie reflected his action-oriented approach rather than Martin Brest's character-driven approach in the first. The set did not have the unsettled, disorganized feeling of the original; the cast was now familiar with each other and the shoot went very smoothly. The production went $4 million over budget, but Paramount approved the increases to cover extra music, an added chase sequence, and reshooting two scenes with more of Murphy's reaction.

DISTRIBUTION: Distributed even more widely than its predecessor, *Beverly Hills Cop II* was a hit, coming in at number three in domestic box office for 1987, behind *Three Men and a Baby* and *Fatal Attraction*. Like most sequels, though, its box office was not as large as that of the original, and the cost had doubled. Just as the first film's soundtrack was a fixture on radio three years before, the sequel's soundtrack introduced such hits as "I Want Your Sex" and "Shakedown," which won an Oscar nomination. —*Louis Burklow*

FATAL ATTRACTION
Paramount, 1987

ALL-RELEASE EQUIVALENT 2005 $s
(Unadjusted $s) in Millions of $s

Domestic Box Office Revenues........$256.8/($156.7)
Production Cost ....$24.1/($14.0)
Principal Photography............80 days estimated
July 1986–October 1986

Director . . . . Adrian Lyne

Producer . . . . Stanley R. Jaffe, Sherry Lansing

Production Company . . . . Paramount Pictures

Story by . . . . Based on the short story "Diversion" by James Dearden (later filmed as a short subject for the BBC in 1980)

Screenplay by . . . . James Dearden

Cast . . . . Michael Douglas, Glenn Close, Anne Archer

Filming Locations . . . . . . Manhattan, NY

Genre . . . . Thriller

Format . . . . Color (Technicolor)

Initial Release 9/18/1987

Rerelease . . . . none

Running Time . . . . 119 minutes

MPAA Rating . . . . R

STANDING THE TEST OF TIME

ACADEMY AWARD Oscar Nominations and Wins

Best Picture: Stanley R. Jaffe and Sherry Lansing, Producers

Actress in a Leading Role: Glenn Close

Actress in a Supporting Role: Anne Archer

Directing: Adrian Lyne

Film Editing: Michael Kahn, Peter E. Berger

Writing (Screenplay – based on material from another medium): James Dearden

    OSCAR TOTALS   Nominations **6**   *Wins 0

AFI 100 YEARS 100 MOVIES SELECTION
    2007 0   1997 0

TOP 300 FILMS POSITION . . . . #148
All-Release Domestic Box Office in Equivalent 2005 $s

National Film Preservation Board Selection . . . .none

OTHER AWARDS Best Picture Wins

	Year
Golden Globes	none
New York Film Critics	none
National Board of Review	none
Film Daily Critics	none

It was startling to go into a pharmacy and see myself on a magazine cover as "the most hated woman in America."

—Glenn Close

PLOT: A New York attorney has a brief extramarital fling while his family is away, but his lover turns out to be a dangerous psychotic who will stop at nothing to keep him for herself.

PRODUCTION: Producer Stanley Jaffe was in London scouting out new projects when he was presented with a short BBC film, *Diversion,* by writer-director James Dearden. It depicts the same situation as does *Fatal Attraction,* but ends when the mistress calls the protagonist's home and his wife reaches out to answer the phone. Jaffe and producing partner Sherry Lansing optioned the short and commissioned Dearden to extend it into a feature-length script. Every studio and twenty-six different directors turned the project down, finding that the story lacked a real hero, even after Michael Douglas was attached to play his specialty, what screenwriter William Goldman called "the flawed, contemporary American male." Finally Adrian Lyne expressed interest, and hired Nicholas Meyer to do some punch-up work on the script. No one involved expected the stunning audition that Glenn Close gave, as her prior wholesome screen image more closely resembled the wounded wife than the twisted femme fatale. *Fatal Attraction* was shot as much as possible in genuine New York locations, including nearly all interiors: Lyne had previously used the same location for Michael Douglas's apartment in *9½ Weeks.* The design department scouted more than 300 candidates before finding the Close character's loft. A reigning conceit during production was that the story had to be about anyone sitting in the audience. As Jaffe put it, it had to feel as if "it could happen to you." Years later, Douglas noted that he needed little preparation to portray his character, drawing most of it out of himself. The film went out for test screenings with Dearden's original ending, in which the Close character commits suicide and arranges it so that Douglas will be framed for the crime. But it was apparent that the audience craved a classic kind of closure, so the more operatic ending we see today is the product of a reshoot weeks later on a traditional constructed set. Close, who far preferred the original ending, finally relented after two weeks of persuasion.

DISTRIBUTION: *Fatal Attraction* hit a nerve in popular culture upon its general release, but the cautionary tale about the consequences of illicit sex—wincingly clear to many male audience members—was only part of its impact. The film appeared just as feminism was under siege, and though Close's character was clearly a fictional extreme, some feminists, including author Susan Faludi, perceived a subtext that single career women were dangerous to society—a notion that Lansing, the first woman to head a major studio, heatedly denied. But it was a must-see film and a topic of fervent international discussion, even making the cover of *Time* magazine. Later, Close was amused to learn that her most notorious scene had inspired a British expression for an aggressive woman who looks like potential trouble: "bunny-boiler." Its box office success became an issue in Art Buchwald's lawsuit against Eddie Murphy regarding Paramount's *Coming to America*: in an attempt to attack Hollywood's accounting system, attorney Pierce O'Donnell produced profit statements showing that while *Fatal Attraction* had made $166 million in worldwide rentals in two years, the picture showed a $100,000 deficit after expenses (including those for producers, director, and star) were deducted. —*Tom Dupree*

THREE MEN AND A BABY

Buena Vista (domestic); Warner Bros. (foreign), 1987

ALL-RELEASE EQUIVALENT 2005 $s

(Unadjusted $s) in Millions of $s

Domestic Box Office Revenues . . . . **$268.6**/($167.8)
Production Cost . . . . **$25.8**/($15.0)
Principal Photography . . . . **50** days estimated
4/20/1987–6/26/1987

Director . . . . Leonard Nimoy

Producer . . . . Ted Field, Robert W. Cort

Production Company . . . . Interscope Communications,
Silver Screen Partners III,
Touchstone Pictures

Story by . . . . Based on the screenplay for the
French film *Trois hommes et un
couffin* by Coline Serreau

Screenplay by . . . . James Orr, Jim Cruickshank

Cast . . . . Tom Selleck, Steve Guttenberg
and Ted Danson

Filming Locations . . . . . . Toronto, Canada, and
Manhattan, NY

Genre . . . . Comedy

Format . . . . Color (DeLuxe)

Initial Release 11/25/1987

Rerelease . . . . none

Running Time . . . . 102 minutes

MPAA Rating . . . . PG

STANDING THE TEST OF TIME

ACADEMY AWARD Oscar Nominations and Wins

None

OSCAR TOTALS   Nominations 0   *Wins 0

AFI 100 YEARS 100 MOVIES SELECTION

2007 0   1997 0

TOP 300 FILMS POSITION . . . . #138

All-Release Domestic Box Office in Equivalent 2005 $s

National Film Preservation Board Selection . . . . none

OTHER AWARDS Best Picture Wins

	Year
Golden Globes	none
New York Film Critics	none
National Board of Review	none
Film Daily Critics	none

*Luckily, there's enough of the domestic comedy to make the movie work,
despite its crasser instincts.*

—Roger Ebert

PLOT: Three swinging bachelors' lives are disrupted when a baby girl is left on their doorstep. Their initial ineptitude with the infant soon results in real affection for her, changing their lives forever.

PRODUCTION: After the success of *Revenge of the Nerds* in 1984, producer Ted Field took *Three Men and a Baby* to Disney's Touchstone division. It was an adaptation of Coline Serreau's 1985 French-language hit movie *Trois hommes et un couffin* (*Three Men and a Cradle*). In the mid-eighties, Touchstone was hesitant to "Americanize" another foreign film after several had failed. Still, with funding from the Silver Screen Partners III limited partnership, a $15 million budget was agreed for director Leonard Nimoy (marking his first non–*Star Trek* feature film directorial assignment). *Gentleman's Agreement* 1947 Oscar-winner Celeste Holm was cast as Ted Danson's mother, her first feature film in ten years. Nimoy also chose a pair of twins from over 400 babies to find the perfect Mary, eventually choosing Lisa and Michelle Blair for the role. Ted Danson, Steve Guttenberg, and Tom Selleck were cast as the three men. Filming began on April 20, 1987, in Toronto and New York. Ironically, the first scene was left on the cutting room floor. The shot intended to follow an extra into the raucous birthday party for Selleck's character, but after the extra bungled the scene several times, it was deleted. Also complicating production was the fact that the twins chosen for the role of Mary were gradually becoming more and more interested in the equipment on set rather than in interacting with their fellow actors. Nimoy, the set dressers, and the technicians had to devise clever ways to hide the audio setups from the savvy twins to prevent their constant distraction. Exteriors included Central Park and other recognizable locations in New York City. The bachelors' luxurious apartment was a Toronto-built set. The skyscraper designed by Selleck's character in the film was actually in the process of being built. It stands today as Scotia Plaza in Toronto.

DISTRIBUTION: Disney chose the tag line "They changed her diapers . . . she changed their lives" and were soon boasting a successful nationwide debut on November 25, grossing more than $10.3 million its first weekend. Most critics dismissed the remake as less entertaining than the original French version, but the public thought differently, as is evidenced in the rise from 1,006 screens on opening weekend to a wide release of 1,813 screens shortly thereafter. *Three Men and a Baby* was the biggest box office hit of 1987, surpassing even that year's thriller, *Fatal Attraction,* but was the only top domestic box office movie in the decade to garner zero Academy Award nominations. The home video debut (November 15, 1988) was as impressive as the initial theatrical release, perhaps spiked by an urban legend of a "ghost boy" appearing in a scene. Rumors of a young man's suicide in the bachelors' apartment (which, as noted, was actually a Toronto set built specifically for the movie) kept video sales growing. Some suspect that the studio started the rumor, but the actual "ghost boy" turned out to be a promotional standee of Danson that had been set aside behind a sheer curtain. The movie was the inspiration for the TV show *Full House,* which ran from September 1987 through May 1995. The movie's sequel, *Three Men and a Little Lady* (1990), garnered less than 50 percent of the domestic box office of the original. —*Christine McDermott*

WHO FRAMED ROGER RABBIT

Buena Vista, 1988

ALL-RELEASE EQUIVALENT 2005 $s
(Unadjusted $s) in Millions of $s

Domestic Box Office Revenues . . . . **$240.4**/($154.1)
Production Cost . . . . **$96.0**/($58.2)
Principal Photography . . . . **83** days estimated
U.S.: 12/1/1986–12/19/1986
UK: 1/5/1987–4/8/1987
Production Period (Animation) . . . . **239** days estimated
U.S.: 9/28/1987–5/21/1988
UK: 2/9/1987–5/14/1988

Rerelease . . . . none
Running Time . . . . 103 minutes
MPAA Rating . . . . PG

Director . . . . Robert Zemeckis

Producer . . . . Frank Marshall, Robert Watts

Production Company . . . . Amblin Entertainment, Touchstone Pictures, Silver Screen Partners III

Story by . . . . Based on the book *Who Censored Roger Rabbit?* by Gary K. Wolf

Screenplay by . . . . Jeffrey Price, Peter S. Seaman

Cast . . . . Bob Hoskins, Christopher Lloyd, Joanna Cassidy

Filming Locations . . . . . . Shot 2 weeks in Los Angeles, CA, then shut down and flew to London New Year's Eve with ILM's VistaFlex cameras, which would be used for the first time; shot in England at Elstree Film Studios, Borehamwood, England

Genre . . . . Animation/Live Action

Format . . . . Color (DeLuxe)

Initial Release . . . . 6/21/1988 New York City premiere; 6/22/1988 general release

STANDING THE TEST OF TIME

ACADEMY AWARD Oscar Nominations and Wins

Art Direction: Art Direction: Elliot Scott; Set Decoration: Peter Howitt

Cinematography: Dean Cundey

*FILM EDITING: Arthur Schmidt

Sound: Robert Knudson, John Boyd, Don Digirolamo, Tony Dawe

*SOUND EFFECTS EDITING: Charles L. Campbell, Louis L. Edemann

*VISUAL EFFECTS: Ken Ralston, Richard Williams, Edward Jones, George Gibbs

*SPECIAL ACHIEVEMENT AWARD: Richard Williams for animation direction

OSCAR TOTALS   Nominations **7**   *Wins **4**

AFI 100 YEARS 100 MOVIES SELECTION
2007 0   1997 0

TOP 300 FILMS POSITION . . . . **#175**
All-Release Domestic Box Office in Equivalent 2005 $s

National Film Preservation Board Selection . . . . none

OTHER AWARDS Best Picture Wins

	Year
Golden Globes	none
New York Film Critics	none
National Board of Review	none
Film Daily Critics	none

If done right, this could be something no one's ever seen before.

—Steven Spielberg

PLOT: In 1947 Hollywood, washed-up private eye Eddie Valiant is hired to investigate a murder by the hapless suspect, a cartoon rabbit. This leads him to visit hated Toontown, where a brutal crime ruined him years ago.

PRODUCTION: In Gary Wolf's 1981 source novel, human characters interacted with comic-strip-style cartoons; most "toons" spoke using word balloons, and the strips were produced by actually photographing them. Director Robert Zemeckis took this fanciful concept one step further: he wanted human characters to coexist with fully animated cartoons, in three-dimensional space, for the entire movie. There had been several previous attempts to achieve a similar effect, such as Gene Kelly dancing with cartoon stars Tom and Jerry in *Anchors Aweigh*. But unlike anything that had been done before, Zemeckis wanted his camera to move, change focus, and record animated figures affecting live-action props, just as if they were actually on the set. So *Roger Rabbit* would actually be three films in one: a period noir movie, an animated feature, and a special effects extravaganza. Zemeckis also wanted the animation to combine three different styles: Disney technique, Warner Bros. characterization, and the sense of humor of the zany Tex Avery. *Roger Rabbit* was a Disney co-production, but the producers wanted to include as many cartoon characters from other studios as possible, and to the audience's delight, they would be there in the dozens (a notable exception being Popeye and other characters from the Fleischer Studios). Disney and Warner Bros. contractually agreed to ensure their star characters, Mickey Mouse and Bugs Bunny, equal screen time. The ambitious project required two production units. On the soundstage, Zemeckis was filming the most elaborate "invisible man" movie ever attempted. He decided to shoot the live action just as he would have were there no cartoon characters involved, moving the camera as freely as he chose. The major actors had special mime training to help them simulate weight and mass in their nonexistent co-stars. Meanwhile, animation director Richard Williams's 300-person team was adding the cartoon characters to nearly every scene. Each cel was completely hand-drawn: there is no computer-assisted animation anywhere in the film. A typical shot required four animation plates: main character, matte for backlighting, highlights, and shadows. This quartet would be sent to the special visual effects artists at Industrial Light & Magic (ILM) for optical compositing with the live action. ILM realized 1,004 special effects shots on *Roger Rabbit*; its most elaborate "show" to that point had been *Return of the Jedi,* with fewer than 400 shots. The end credits were the longest ever for a feature up until that time; it took them ten minutes to roll.

DISTRIBUTION: An early preview of the nearly completed movie was not quite a triumph. The film broke toward the end, and when associate producer Steve Starkey returned from addressing the problem in the projection booth the theater was almost empty. This was not a good sign to the executives present. But Zemeckis, who had final cut of the picture, believed strongly in his project, and declined to change anything. Luckily, as the film came closer to completion, the preview reaction got better and better, and upon release, *Roger Rabbit* was an immediate blockbuster. Despite its box office success, as of December 1990, the film had a net loss of $19.6 million. —*Tom Dupree*

RAIN MAN
United Artists, 1988

ALL-RELEASE EQUIVALENT 2005 $s
(Unadjusted $s) in Millions of $s

Domestic Box Office Revenues . . . . **$276.3**/($172.8)
Production Cost . . . . **$49.5**/($30.0)
Principal Photography . . . . **18** Months
including **64** days estimated
on location 5/2/1988–7/28/1988

Director . . . . Barry Levinson
Producer . . . . Mark Johnson
Production Company . . . . Gubers-Peters Company
Story by . . . . Barry Morrow
Screenplay by . . . . Ronald Bass, Barry Morrow
Cast . . . . Dustin Hoffman, Tom Cruise, Valeria Golino
Filming Locations . . . . . . First four weeks of principal photography was based in Cincinnati, OH while also utilizing locations in Kentucky and Indiana. For two weeks, the company headquartered in Oklahoma City, shooting locations in Cogar, Hinton, Guthrie, and El Reno. Caesar's Palace in Las Vegas then hosted cast and crew for three weeks before a final move to Los Angeles.
Genre . . . . Drama
Format . . . . Color (DeLuxe)
Initial Release 12/16/1988
Rerelease . . . . none
Running Time . . . . 140 minutes
MPAA Rating . . . . R

STANDING THE TEST OF TIME

ACADEMY AWARD Oscar Nominations and Wins

*****BEST PICTURE:** Mark Johnson, Producer
*****ACTOR IN A LEADING ROLE:** Dustin Hoffman
Art Direction/Set Decoration: Ida Random/Linda DeScenna
Cinematography: John Seale
*****DIRECTING:** Barry Levinson
Film Editing: Stu Linder
Music (Original Score): Hans Zimmer
*****WRITING** (Screenplay – written directly for the screen): Screenplay by Ronald Bass, Barry Morrow; Story by Barry Morrow

OSCAR TOTALS   Nominations **8**   *Wins **4**

AFI 100 YEARS 100 MOVIES SELECTION
2007 0   1997 0

TOP 300 FILMS POSITION . . . . #125
All-Release Domestic Box Office in Equivalent 2005 $s

National Film Preservation Board Selection . . . . none

OTHER AWARDS Best Picture Wins

	Year
Golden Globes (Drama)	1989
New York Film Critics	none
National Board of Review	none
Film Daily Critics	none

Barry [Levinson] and I thought the Rain Man *script dealt with a fascinating subject, . . . and the opportunity to work with Dustin Hoffman and Tom Cruise was very enticing, but we had only nine weeks to put it together.*

—Mark Johnson

PLOT: Con man Charlie Babbitt kidnaps his autistic savant brother, Raymond, and takes him on a road trip after finding out that their father has left his multimillion-dollar estate solely to Raymond.

PRODUCTION: In 1984 writer Barry Morrow met real-life savant Kim Peek in Arlington, Texas, and was inspired to write *Rain Man*. Murrow's agent then sent the script to Dustin Hoffman, hoping he would agree to play Charlie Babbitt. After Hoffman was moved to tears watching a disabled savant play piano concertos by ear, he insisted on playing Raymond Babbitt instead. Hoffman had been looking to play a mentally challenged character ever since 1958 when he read Ken Kesey's novel *One Flew over the Cuckoo's Nest* while working at the Psychiatric Institute in New York and simultaneously studying acting. Hoffman fought for the movie even after director Martin Brest backed out. Spielberg's commitment to direct the third *Indiana Jones* movie resulted in his also turning down *Rain Man,* something he always regretted. While briefly involved, Spielberg convinced script doctor Ron Bass to do a rewrite with an autistic character, not a "lovable retard," as in Morrow's version. Hoffman asked his *Tootsie* director, Sydney Pollack to direct, but after writing a treatise about the film, Pollack said he didn't connect. Hoffman asked Barry Levinson to help convince Pollack. After Pollack passed, Levinson took the reins (although he had originally turned it down to make *Good Morning, Vietnam*). The delays caused United Artists to get antsy. It would have been shelved if Tom Cruise, a big box office draw, had not become attached. Hoffman, who had wanted Bill Murray as Charlie, said that even after it was greenlighted, the studio snidely called it "Two Schmucks in a Car." Hoffman spent two and a half years researching autism, meeting with Peek and other savants. Filming took eighteen months and was mostly on location, leaving scheduling loose, sometimes chasing the sun to capture the perfect "American" twilight moments. Hoffman and Levinson decided to play Raymond as blank, showing no emotion, so the audience would shape him into whatever they wanted him to be and be sympathetic. It took careful crafting to make sure that Cruise's transformation was noticeable. Hoffman fought the screenwriters to change the ending so Raymond wouldn't end up with Charlie, to maintain the movie's sense of authenticity. J. T. Walsh was going to play the psychiatrist, but when he couldn't, Levinson filled in (after Hoffman suggested it). Hoffman's son, Jake, played the boy at the pancake counter. *Rain Man* introduced German composer Hans Zimmer, who earned an Oscar.

DISTRIBUTION: The film opened with a disappointing $6 million box office gross. However, as word spread, the audience grew and *Rain Man* ended 1988 as the number one film in both domestic and worldwide box office. Levinson, who claims he can't remember actually accepting his Oscar, attributes the success to the relationship between Cruise and Hoffman, and to interest in the nature of autism, something relatively unknown at that time. When Morrow won the Academy Award, he gave his Oscar to Kim Peek, and when Hoffman won, he thanked Peek, who became an instant celebrity. Peek's father wrote a book, *The Real Rain Man,* and Peek was the subject of a full-length documentary and a NASA study on the brain. —*Hayley Taylor Block and Alex Ben Block*

INDIANA JONES AND THE LAST CRUSADE

Paramount, 1989

ALL-RELEASE EQUIVALENT 2005 $s

(Unadjusted $s) in Millions of $s

Domestic Box Office Revenues........**$316.8**/($197.2)
Production Cost ....**$87.2**/($55.4)
Principal Photography....................**63** days
5/16/1988–8/12/1988

Director . . . . Steven Spielberg

Producer . . . . Robert Watts

Production Company. . . . Lucasfilm Ltd.

Story by. . . . . George Lucas and Menno Meyjes, based on characters created by George Lucas and Philip Kaufman

Screenplay by. . . . . Jeffrey Boam

Cast . . . . Harrison Ford, Sean Connery, Denholm Elliott, Alison Doody, John Rhys-Davies, Julian Glover, River Phoenix

Filming Locations . . . . . . On location: various sites in Spain (16 days); in studio: EMI Elstree, Borehamwood, UK; Venice (44 days), Italy (3 days) second unit in Jordan and other U.S. locations

Genre. . . . . Action Adventure

Format. . . . . Color (Rank)

Initial Release 5/24/1989

Rerelease. . . . . none

Running Time . . . . 127 minutes

MPAA Rating PG-13

STANDING THE TEST OF TIME

ACADEMY AWARD Oscar Nominations and Wins

Music (Original Score): John Williams

Sound: Ben Burtt, Gary Summers, Shawn Murphy, Tony Dawe

*SOUND EFFECTS EDITING: Ben Burtt, Richard Hymns

OSCAR TOTALS   Nominations **3**   *Wins **1**

AFI 100 YEARS 100 MOVIES SELECTION
2007 0   1997 0

TOP 300 FILMS POSITION . . . . **#95**
All-Release Domestic Box Office in Equivalent 2005 $s

National Film Preservation Board Selection. . . . none

OTHER AWARDS Best Picture Wins

	Year
Golden Globes	none
New York Film Critics.	none
National Board of Review	none
Film Daily Critics	none

George Lucas and Steven Spielberg have created a new genre out of a very old one.

—Jeffrey Boam

PLOT: An adventurous archeologist and his father set out to find the Holy Grail before the Nazis. Despite being betrayed by a woman, they secure the Grail and prevent the Nazis from misusing it.

PRODUCTION: George Lucas started developing ideas for a third *Indiana Jones* sequel in 1985, throwing out a broad net in the hopes of zeroing in on an idea, or combination of ideas, that would inject the popular series with new vitality. He first turned to Diane Thomas. She wrote a haunted house script shortly before she died in a car wreck in October, but Lucas ultimately rejected it. Chris Columbus then penned an African adventure script, but Lucas also refused that. He next collaborated with Menno Meyjes on an idea about the Holy Grail. Lucas also continuously bandied about new ideas with director Steven Spielberg. Together they decided to depict Indiana as a young boy and to examine his relationship with his aging father in the film. Jeffrey Boam finally melded the swirl of ideas into a coherent final draft in late 1987. As shooting loomed, Spielberg and Lucas went straight to the source to cast Indiana's father. As the filmmakers had been partly inspired by James Bond when they dreamed up the Indy series, casting the original James Bond, Sean Connery, as Indy's father made perfect cinematic sense—despite the fact that Connery is only an improbable twelve years older than Harrison Ford. Cast and crew members began shooting on May 16, 1988, in Almeira, Spain. Using a slow, lumbering tank for a big chase scene, the team actually had to slow down Ford's pursuing horse and then shoot the whole scene undercranked. The production then shifted to England's Elstree Studios, the traditional home of Lucas's *Star Wars* and *Indiana Jones* trilogies. It would turn out to be Lucas's last major production shoot there, however, as shopping center developers were in the process of taking it over and partially divvying it up. The Venice catacomb set presented the team with their most daunting logistical hurdles. They spent months specially breeding thousands of disease-free rats for use in the shots, using hundreds of mechanical stand-ins for the critters for the most dangerous fire scenes. After leaving England, the crew captured some exteriors in Venice, closing down the Grand Canal for a few hours as Spielberg carefully framed his shots to avoid the countless TV antennas threatening to mar the film's 1930s authenticity. They also filmed at Petra in Jordan, using it as a stand-in for the temple that houses the Holy Grail, despite the fact that Petra possesses virtually no interior. The team finally returned to various locations in the American desert Southwest to shoot the opening train chase, and then filmed a later motorcycle sidecar chase pickup near Skywalker Ranch in California.

DISTRIBUTION: The film opened on May 24, 1989, raking in $29.4 million on its opening weekend. It became the first film in the series to receive a PG-13 rating. Critics generally acclaimed the film, mainly lauding its lighthearted sense of humor and compelling characterizations. The film went on to haul in over $494 million worldwide. It later spawned *The Young Indiana Jones Chronicles* TV series on ABC in 1992. The DVD release in October 2003 contained digitally polished effects. —*Scott Mazak*

DEAD POETS SOCIETY

Buena Vista, 1989

ALL-RELEASE EQUIVALENT 2005 $s

(Unadjusted $s) in Millions of $s

Domestic Box Office Revenues........**$154.0**/($95.9)
Production Cost ....**$25.8**/($16.4)
Principal Photography............**50** days estimated
11/14/1988–1/15/1989
10-week shoot

Director . . . . Peter Weir
Producer . . . . Steven Haft, Paul Junger Witt,
and Tony Thomas
Production Company . . . . Touchstone Pictures,
Silver Screen Partners IV
Story and
Screenplay by . . . . Tom Schulman
Cast . . . . Robin Williams
Filming Locations . . . . . . 100 percent on location in
Middletown, DE
Genre . . . . Drama
Format . . . . Color (Metrocolor)
Initial Release . . . . 6/2/1989 (limited); 6/9/1989
(wide)
Rerelease . . . . none
Running Time . . . . 128 minutes
MPAA Rating . . . . PG

STANDING THE TEST OF TIME

ACADEMY AWARD Oscar Nominations and Wins

Best Picture: Steven Haft, Paul Junger Witt, and
Tony Thomas

Actor In A Leading Role: Robin Williams

Directing: Peter Weir

*WRITING (Screenplay – written directly for the
screen): Tom Schulman

OSCAR TOTALS   Nominations **4**   *Wins **1**

AFI 100 YEARS 100 MOVIES SELECTION
2007 0   1997 0

TOP 300 FILMS POSITION . . . . .none
All-Release Domestic Box Office in Equivalent 2005 $s

National Film Preservation Board Selection . . . .none

OTHER AWARDS Best Picture Wins

	Year
Golden Globes	none
New York Film Critics	none
National Board of Review	none
Film Daily Critics	none

No matter what anybody tells you, words and ideas can change the world.

—John Keating (Robin Williams)

PLOT: Set at an all-boys prep school in 1959, *Dead Poets Society* is the story of a teacher who startles his students into an expanded awareness of life's possibilities through unconventional teaching methods.

PRODUCTION: Tom Schulman wrote the original story in 1985, inspired by the film *Goodbye Mr. Chips* and a teacher he had at his private high school in Nashville, Tennessee. This was his first feature-length script. At one point Liam Neeson was attached to star, and Dustin Hoffman and Bill Murray were considered. A year after it was written, producer Steven Haft optioned the script. With producing partners Paul Junger Witt and Tony Thomas, Haft thought of Robin Williams as the free-spirited teacher. Williams, who was still early in his movie career, has said he took the role because "Keating's essential credo about teaching—basically pushing the envelope and taking the chance, even though other people may disagree, to find a true and creative voice of your own . . . that's pretty much my own core philosophy about life." The producers wanted a director who could balance the intellectual aspects and extraordinary characters. Australian Peter Weir was known as an auteur director and had done only one other studio film (*Witness*). Weir says he "was in that kind of school, in that kind of classroom, in that year, 1959, at that age," so he related deeply. He was given the script by Jeffrey Katzenberg, head of Disney, and immediately wanted to do it. In the original draft was a scene that showed Keating in a hospital, dying of Hodgkin's disease. That was to be the motivation for his carpe diem life perspective. Weir convinced Schulman to cut the scene, saying the picture was about standing up for what you believe is right, not standing up for a dying man. Weir and cinematographer John Seale had worked together since 1975. This was composer Maurice Jarre's fourth collaboration with Weir. After scouting more than seventy private schools in the area, the filmmakers chose St. Andrew's school in Middletown, which is situated on 2,000 acres of farmland. To avoid disrupting the school, filming was mostly over the Thanksgiving and Christmas breaks. The production hired more than 3,000 extras. Weir and casting director Howard Feuer auditioned more than 500 boys. They gave upward of 5,000 haircuts and makeovers to extras to re-create the conservative styles of the late 1950s. During the shoot, the seven boys traveled as a pack and formed a bond like the one depicted in the story. Eighteen-year-old Ethan Hawke said, "The experience on that movie was, for lack of a better term, life-altering." Weir filmed in chronological order so that the cast could build history. Weir cautioned Williams not to be too much of an entertainer, but he did allow the star to improvise some scenes. Disney's notoriously thrifty studio had underscheduled the film, and Weir nearly drove himself to exhaustion to stay on schedule, averaging twenty-two setups per day over the 10-week shoot. At the end the studio gave him some extra time.

DISTRIBUTION: It was one of the first releases by Disney under its Touchstone banner, created to release more adult movies. Although it was risky to release a serious film in June against summer blockbusters, it was the sleeper hit of the summer. A novelization by Nancy H. Kleinbaum was published. —*Hayley Taylor Block*

BATMAN

Warner Bros., 1989

ALL-RELEASE EQUIVALENT 2005 $s

(Unadjusted $s) in Millions of $s

Domestic Box Office Revenues . . . . $403.5/($251.2)
Production Cost . . . . $84.3/($53.5)
Principal Photography . . . . 80 days estimated
10/10/1988–12/17/1988

Director . . . . Tim Burton
Producer . . . . Jon Peters, Peter Guber
Production Company . . . . Warner Bros.
Story by . . . . Based on characters created by
Bob Kane appearing in
magazines published by DC
Comics; story by Sam Hamm
Screenplay by . . . . Sam Hamm, Warren Skaaren
Cast . . . . Michael Keaton, Jack
Nicholson, Kim Basinger
Filming Locations . . . . . . London, UK; Bedfordshire, UK;
Hertfordshire, UK; Pinewood
Studios (Buckinghamshire)
Genre . . . . Action Adventure
Format . . . . Color (Eastman color)
Initial Release 6/23/1989
Rerelease . . . . none
Running Time . . . . 126 minutes
MPAA Rating PG-13

STANDING THE TEST OF TIME

ACADEMY AWARD Oscar Nominations and Wins

*ART DIRECTION/SET DECORATION: Anton
Furst/Peter Young

OSCAR TOTALS Nominations 1 ***Wins 1**

AFI 100 YEARS 100 MOVIES SELECTION
2007 . . . . . 0 1997 0

TOP 300 FILMS POSITION . . . . #42
All-Release Domestic Box Office in Equivalent 2005 $s

National Film Preservation Board Selection . . . . none

OTHER AWARDS Best Picture Wins

	Year
Golden Globes	none
New York Film Critics	none
National Board of Review	none
Film Daily Critics	none

*The first time you direct a movie on that scale it's kind of surreal.
You're not fearful because you don't know.*

—Tim Burton, on his first experience with a summer blockbuster

PLOT: Wealthy socialite Bruce Wayne lives a double life as the black-caped superhero Batman. He faces his greatest test, and avenges the murder of his parents, when the maniacal Joker menaces Gotham City.

PRODUCTION: The character Batman was created in 1939 for comic books by Bob Kane. It was serialized during the 1940s and was the basis for a campy 1960s TV series. Its trip to the big screen began in 1980 when screenwriter Tom Mankiewicz, co-writer of *Superman—The Movie,* penned a script that included characters such as the Penguin and Robin. That attracted producers Michael Uslan and Benjamin Melniker (who had obtained the character's film rights from DC Comics). Despite backing by producer Peter Guber, the project stalled for years. It eventually landed at Warner Bros., where Tim Burton (*Pee-Wee's Big Adventure*) signed to direct. Burton scrapped the Mankiewicz script, bringing in Sam Hamm to flesh out his own darker story concepts. A writer's strike temporarily froze progress, and Burton enlisted Warren Skaaren for an uncredited script polish (which included the removal of the Robin subplot). After the success of Burton's *Beetlejuice,* Warner Bros. greenlighted the production. The casting of Jack Nicholson as the Joker was met with praise, but the decision to fill the Batman role with Michael Keaton (then known primarily as a comic actor), raised the hackles of fans. Burton stuck by his choice. Sean Young earned a spot as Batman's love interest, Vicki Vale, but dropped out in favor of Kim Basinger after breaking her collarbone while filming a scene on horseback. Production designer Anton Furst, inspired by the darker reinterpretation of Batman in comics such as Frank Miller's *The Dark Knight Returns,* interpreted a gothic Gotham City that had been described in the script as "a random tangle of steel and concrete, as if Hell had erupted through the sidewalk and kept on growing." Shooting took place on location in England (using two historic homes as stand-ins for Wayne Manor) and at London's Pinewood Studios. In a production that was likened to a military operation, the *Batman* crew claimed the entirety of Pinewood's ninety-five-acre back lot, as well as most of its eighteen soundstages. Furst's Gotham City set became the biggest outdoor motion picture structure since 1960's *Cleopatra*. Keaton's restrictive costume weighed seventy pounds and was described by the actor as "fifty thousand rubber bands holding you down." Other characters in the film wore deliberately incongruous clothing, or, as costume designer Bob Ringwood put it, "how the year 2000 would look if somebody in 1945 had created it." Danny Elfman composed the film's moody score. A ninety-second teaser trailer released in January 1989 was a smash hit, with fans reportedly purchasing tickets to other films only so they could see the *Batman* preview.

DISTRIBUTION: *Batman* grossed a record-setting $42.7 million in its opening weekend, playing throughout the summer and finally closing on December 14. Its gross of $251 million ($411 million worldwide) made it the most successful film of 1989. Critics praised its dark, atmospheric look (the film won an Academy Award for Best Art Direction/Set Direction). *Batman*'s biggest windfall came in the realm of licensing—the movie is estimated to have pulled in an additional $750 million solely from tie-in items. —*Daniel Wallace*

LETHAL WEAPON 2

Warner Bros., 1989

ALL-RELEASE EQUIVALENT 2005 $s

(Unadjusted $s) in Millions of $s

Domestic Box Office Revenues........$236.6/($147.3)
Production Cost ....$47.3/($30.0)
Principal Photography............66 days estimated
11/2/1988–3/5/1989

Director . . . . Richard Donner

Producer . . . . Richard Donner, Joel Silver

Production Company . . . . Warner Bros., Silver Pictures

Story by . . . . Shane Black, Warren Murphy

Screenplay by . . . . Jeffrey Boam

Cast . . . . Mel Gibson, Danny Glover, Joe Pesci, Joss Ackland, Derrick O'Connor, Patsy Kensit

Filming Locations . . . . . . On location: Los Angeles, Century City, Culver City, and Santa Clarita, CA

Genre . . . . Action Adventure

Format . . . . Color (Technicolor)

Initial Release 7/7/1989

Rerelease . . . . none

Running Time . . . . 113 minutes

MPAA Rating . . . . R

STANDING THE TEST OF TIME

ACADEMY AWARD Oscar Nominations and Wins

Sound Effects Editing: Robert Henderson, Alan Robert Murray

OSCAR TOTALS Nominations 1 *Wins 0

AFI 100 YEARS 100 MOVIES SELECTION
2007 0   1997 0

TOP 300 FILMS POSITION . . . . #181
All-Release Domestic Box Office in Equivalent 2005 $s

National Film Preservation Board Selection . . . . none

OTHER AWARDS Best Picture Wins

	Year
Golden Globes	none
New York Film Critics	none
National Board of Review	none
Film Daily Critics	none

A lot of films are written for the special effects and stunts, and then the characters are made to fit the action. When we made Lethal Weapon, *we concentrated on the characters, and out of the insanity of the characters evolved the action pieces. The same thing happened in* Lethal Weapon 2.

—Richard Donner

PLOT: Two years after busting a gang of drug smugglers, police detective Roger Murtaugh and his crazy partner Martin Riggs must take down a South African crime ring before more Los Angeles cops are murdered.

PRODUCTION: Few at Warner Bros. contemplated a sequel to the original *Lethal Weapon* when it was released March 1987. But after a $120 million worldwide box office bonanza, executives had more than just a sequel in the works, they had a blockbuster franchise to exploit. Twenty-six-year-old *Lethal Weapon* scribe Shane Black, now one of the hottest pens in Hollywood, turned in a draft for the sequel that dug further into Riggs's dark past and culminated in his death. The studio did not want their franchise to meet such a premature end, so they hired writer Jeffrey Boam, straight off *Indiana Jones and the Last Crusade,* to tone down the edge and boost the buddy comedy. Joe Pesci's Getz, a minor character in Black's version, developed into the third wheel for Murtaugh and Riggs and spun much of the plot into motion. After having been fired from *Superman II* (1981), director-producer Richard Donner became increasingly possessive of the *Lethal Weapon* characters he had brought to life in the first picture. Warner Bros. nearly doubled Donner's budget from the original *Lethal Weapon* to ensure that the sequel's action sequences met blockbuster expectations. On a dusty road in the Hollywood Hills, Donner and cinematographer Stephen Goldblatt set up four cameras to film the tow-truck crash and grab from as many angles of impact as they could. Almost five nights were spent at the beach and more than 4,000 squibs were detonated to capture the three-minute scene when the helicopters open fire on Riggs's trailer. Even with all his experience directing big action moments, Donner had a difficult time figuring out the movie's money shot, in which Riggs brings down the house-on-stilts. He couldn't topple the actual John Lautner–designed "Rainbow House," which staked the cliffs off Mulholland Drive, and he didn't want to rely on miniatures, so he decided to build an identical model in nearby Valencia. City officials mandated that the building be structurally sound and potentially habitable. But no one ever lived there, for at fifteen past three one winter morning, the cast and crew cheered as the house-on-stilts came falling down for Donner's cameras.

DISTRIBUTION: Murtaugh and Riggs faced stiff competition that summer with *Indiana Jones and the Last Crusade, Batman, Ghostbusters II,* and *License to Kill,* necessitating unusual ploys to market *Lethal Weapon 2.* During a Lakers-Pistons game, CBS ran a spot that stated, "The magic is back," then cut to an injured Magic Johnson telling the camera, "And the magic is lethal." The Ramses condom commercial that played in one memorable scene inspired a cross-promotion that stamped the movie's title on more than 15,000 Ramses condoms for distribution in nightclubs. The strategy worked, with L.A.'s fearless cops finishing number three at the domestic box office in 1989 after *Batman* and *Indiana Jones.* But, like *Batman, Lethal Weapon* had a bigger U.S. audience than foreign, so it finished sixth in worldwide box office with $227.9 million, after *Indiana Jones* (number one worldwide with $474.2 million) and *Batman* (number two worldwide with $411.4 million). The appearance of a title-only opening in this film, which had also been used by *Star Wars* and a few others, soon became the standard for event movies. —*Michael Kogge*

701

DRIVING MISS DAISY

Warner Bros. (domestic); Majestic Films International (foreign), 1989

ALL-RELEASE EQUIVALENT 2005 $s

(Unadjusted $s) in Millions of $s

Domestic Box Office Revenues . . . . **$161.5**/($106.6)
Production Cost . . . . **$11.8**/($7.5)
Principal Photography . . . .**35** days
5/15/1989–7/5/1989

Director . . . . Bruce Beresford
Producer . . . . Richard D. Zanuck, Lili Fini Zanuck
Production Company . . . . Zanuck Co.
Story by . . . . Based on the play by Alfred Uhry
Screenplay by . . . . Alfred Uhry
Cast . . . . Morgan Freeman, Jessica Tandy, Dan Aykroyd, Patti LuPone, Esther Rolle
Filming Locations . . . . . . On location in Atlanta, GA
Genre . . . . Drama
Format . . . . Color (Technicolor)
Initial Release . . . . 12/13/1989 limited release; 1/26/1990 wide release
Rerelease . . . . none
Running Time . . . . 99 minutes
MPAA Rating . . . . PG

STANDING THE TEST OF TIME

ACADEMY AWARD Oscar Nominations and Wins

*BEST PICTURE: Richard D. Zanuck and Lili Fini Zanuck, Producers

Actor in a Leading Role: Morgan Freeman

Actor in a Supporting Role: Dan Aykroyd

*ACTRESS IN A LEADING ROLE: Jessica Tandy

Art Direction/Set Decoration: Bruno Rubeo/Crispian Sallis

Costume Design: Elizabeth McBride

Film Editing: Mark Warner

*MAKEUP: Manlio Rocchetti, Lynn Barber, Kevin Haney

*WRITING (Screenplay – based on material from another medium): Alfred Uhry

OSCAR TOTALS   Nominations **9**   *Wins **4**

AFI 100 YEARS 100 MOVIES SELECTION
2007 0   1997 0

TOP 300 FILMS POSITION . . . . .none
All-Release Domestic Box Office in Equivalent 2005 $s

National Film Preservation Board Selection . . . .none

OTHER AWARDS Best Picture Wins

	Year
Golden Globes (Comedy)	1990
New York Film Critics	none
National Board of Review	1989
Film Daily Critics	none

I just thought it was so superior to almost anything else I'd read. When we were having all those struggles trying to get the finance and Zanuck was struggling, I thought if we don't make this film, it's going to be a tragedy. It's gonna really break my heart, but we did make it.

—Bruce Beresford

PLOT: This movie follows a relationship that has formed over twenty-five years (beginning in 1948) between an elderly, strong-willed southern matron and her African American chauffeur as they come to realize that despite their different backgrounds, they have been friends and kindred spirits all along.

PRODUCTION: Alfred Uhry's play *Driving Miss Daisy* began as an off-Broadway production (starring Dana Ivey and Morgan Freeman) in a seventy-four-seat theater. It ended up having a successful three-year run in a much larger theater and winning Uhry the Pulitzer Prize (and an Obie for Freeman and Ivey). Uhry based the story on his grandmother Lena Fox and her chauffeur, Will Coleman, whom Uhry lived with when he was young. Lily and Richard Zanuck saw the play and bought the film rights in 1987. They were stunned when they had trouble finding financiers. Everyone they had spoken to expressed concerns that the public would not want to see a film about two elderly people. Even after paring down the budget, Warner Bros. was willing to finance only part of the project. Luckily, British producer Jake Eberts was passionate enough about it to finance the rest in exchange for international distribution. Australian director Bruce Beresford chose to shoot in a small town forty miles south of Atlanta, where things hadn't changed much in fifty years. They began preproduction, but it took so long for the deal to close that the Zanucks had to personally fund the prep. Shirley MacLaine and Elizabeth Taylor were considered for the lead role, but Beresford wanted someone in the real age range so the story could be portrayed as realistically as possible. Zanuck suggested Jessica Tandy, who was famous as a stage actress, to Beresford. Because insurers were worried about an octogenarian leading lady filming in the summer heat of the South, they made her pay for a completion bond out of her own pocket. They rented a house from an older lady in the town and shot the whole movie on location, in and around the house, to save money. They had a hard time finding a period house that didn't have a modernized kitchen, so they gutted the kitchen and built their own. The sets and costumes were very elaborate because the film spanned more than twenty-five years. Some real descendants of the chauffeur that Uhry based Freeman's character on were used as extras. Freeman developed his character as a composite of several people he knew, including his father, who had been a chauffeur while the family lived in Nashville. Hans Zimmer did the score electronically, using only synthesizers (no live instruments), all of which he played. During production, Tandy turned eighty years old.

DISTRIBUTION: The film was the third most successful domestic box office movie of the decade's ten Oscar-winning pictures after *Rain Man* and *Terms of Endearment* but made less than 30 percent of the domestic box office made by *E.T.: The Extra-Terrestrial,* the number one film of the 1980s. While it prompted much racial discussion, it also conveyed how people's thinking has changed and evolved over the years. Tandy won the Best Actress Oscar for her role, and at the age of eighty-one became the oldest winner of an Oscar, surpassing George Burns, who was eighty. Until 2005, this was the last film with an MPAA PG rating to win an Oscar for Best Picture. The film was nominated for nine Academy Awards but not for Best Director, which offended Zanuck, who said in his acceptance speech that the Oscar belonged to Beresford. —*Hayley Taylor Block and Alex Ben Block*

The 1990s

Titanic was a situation where I felt, I think, pretty much like the officer felt on the bridge of the ship. I could see the iceberg coming far away, but as hard as I turned that wheel there was just too much mass, too much inertia, and there was nothing I could do, but I still had to play it through.

—James Cameron

TOP 10 ALL-RELEASE MOVIES DOMESTIC BOX OFFICE

By Initial Year of Release, 1990–1999

		Equivalent 2005 $s in Millions of $s
1	Titanic	$824.8
2	Jurassic Park	$552.9
3	Star Wars: Episode I The Phantom Menace	$540.3
4	Forrest Gump	$505.6
5	The Lion King	$501.9
6	Independence Day	$444.0
7	Home Alone	$434.0
8	The Sixth Sense	$370.3
9	Twister	$350.5
10	Men in Black	$350.1
		Total: $4,874.4

GENERAL U.S. STATISTICS, 1990

248,718,302
Total U.S. Population

37,013,289
U.S. Population Age 15–24

22.9 Million
Average Weekly
U.S. Movie Attendance

DECADE OVERVIEW

Enter the Megabusiness

The event movies, franchise films, and instant blockbusters that drove the box office of the 1980s became more expensive, more high-tech, and more international in the 1990s, although profits became even harder to realize. As production and marketing costs soared, more and more movies opened with huge grosses only to fade after the first weekend, replaced by another big movie the following weekend. The number of days between the theatrical opening and availability of a film on home video and pay TV shortened during the decade from nine months to six months, and in some cases even less.

Seven Largest Countries in Terms of U.S. Motion Picture Piracy Losses, 1997

Country	Loss in Millions of $s
Russia	$312
United States	$250
Italy	$220
Japan	$149
China	$120
Brazil	$110
United Kingdom	$ 70

Total loss to the U.S. film industry in potential revenue from piracy
$2.3 billion

The theaters that had converted to more than one screen in the 1970s, and the boxy multiplexes built in the 1980s on the edges of a shopping center, gave way to a new generation of megaplexes, with dozens of screens, often attached to a food court or video game arcades. Many were part of huge indoor malls that served as community gathering places. During the decade the number of theater locations declined while the number of screens surged, reflecting a higher screen count at each location. By the end of the decade, however, many of the exhibitors would be in bankruptcy.

No picture was bigger during the decade than James Cameron's *Titanic,* which, in 2005 dollars, became the sixth-biggest-grossing movie of all time after *Gone with the Wind* (1939), *Star Wars* (1977), *The Sound of Music* (1965), *E.T.* (1982), and *The Ten Commandments* (1956). *Titanic* took in over $1.8 billion in worldwide theatrical box office, with over 65 percent coming from foreign markets. It was this success that gave momentum to wider, faster distribution of big movies abroad, which not only increased the global take but also was intended to help counter widespread movie piracy. The foreign distribution of movies was boosted as well by the fall of Communism, which opened up much of Eastern Europe and Russia as potential new markets. After a burst of initial enthusiasm, however, many of these markets were impacted deeply by the effects of piracy, with Russia accounting for the most motion picture piracy losses in 1997.

The huge grosses for successful blockbusters brought more demands from star performers and top filmmakers for a bigger share of the pie. Some stars like Bruce Willis, Tom Cruise, and Tom Hanks were able to command first-dollar gross deals, meaning that in addition to a substantial up-front salary, they received a percentage of almost every dollar taken in by the distributors. This was different from the profit participation deals of the past, in which a share of the box office came only after the studio made its costs back. Under this new arrangement, star actor Tom Hanks and star director Steven Spielberg each got 16.75 percent of the theatrical distribution revenues from *Saving Private Ryan* (1998), which made them more than $30 million apiece.

This decade also saw industry consolidation accelerate. By the end of the nineties bigger companies dominated the entertainment industry, and companies such as News Corp. (20th Century-Fox and Fox Broadcasting), Time Warner (Warner Bros. and New Line Cinema), and Viacom (Paramount, Blockbuster Video, and CBS) were changing the dynamics of ownership. Studios were no longer part of companies focused primarily on movies or TV shows. Many became divisions of larger, more diversified conglomerates with worldwide interests. These companies ushered in an era of more intense research, which was conducted at a higher cost. Everything was tested, from story concepts to TV commercials. These companies were also able to raise vast pools of funds from investors both in the United States and around the world. One major new studio, DreamWorks, was also formed during the decade and raised millions from investors and a trio of principals—director-producer Steven Spielberg, former Disney executive Jeffrey Katzenberg, and music and film entrepreneur David Geffen.

Movies were still shown on film, but there were signs that the end of the celluloid era was upon us as movies entered the electronic age. Digital technology was used first to store information, then to edit movies and TV shows, and later as a tool in special effects, leading ultimately to the beginning of digital cinema, which would transform production, distribution, and exhibition. The nineties marked the beginning of the Internet age, which had a profound effect on how movies were discussed, marketed, advertised, and distributed.

By the end of the 1990s, the VHS home video format, which had proven wildly lucrative for the movie industry, was starting to be replaced by the higher-quality DVD format, which offered greater capacity, was easier for consumers to use, and cost less to make than a cassette.

After a slowdown early in the decade, during a short national economic recession (July 1990–March 1991), cinema attendance and revenue steadily climbed through the rest of the decade. The number of theater admissions in the United States rose 23 percent, from 1.19 billion in 1990 to 1.47 billion in 1999. Ticket prices went from an average of $4.23 in 1990 to $5.08 by 1999. As a result, the total box office gross rose from $5.02 billion in 1990 to $7.45 billion in 1999.

The marriage of movies with digital and high-tech processes further advanced computer-generated visual effects, making it easier for a wide range of movies to take advantage of the new tools. These ranged from adding backgrounds to creating characters that never lived in the real world and to technology that could make frame-by-frame corrections or changes. Among

U.S. TV Households VCR vs. DVD Penetration, 1990s

	1990	1999
Percentage of U.S. households with VCRs	70.2%	85.1%
Percentage of TV households with DVDs	none	4.6%

the first films to showcase these new tools were Steven Spielberg's *Jurassic Park* in 1993 and George Lucas's *Star Wars: Episode I The Phantom Menace* in 1999, which featured Jar Jar Binks, the first character to be entirely digitally rendered.

The art of animation, which for many years had involved hand-painted cells, was revolutionized by the availability of computers that could take much of the drudgery out of the job, and at the same time produce new kinds of photorealistic characters. Pixar, first established by George Lucas, was spun off as a separate company in 1986 when it was purchased by Steve Jobs. Pixar went on to create a series of CGI movies, starting with *Toy Story,* that changed not only animation but also narrowed its differences with live action. Now artists were free to create whatever they could dream without ever going on location. These high-tech cartoons caught the imagination of the younger generation and led to an extraordinary boom in the licensing and merchandising of movies, with revenues soaring into the billions. They also drove a new generation of video games, many based on movies, that used high-tech methodologies to become ever more intriguing and realistic.

While the home video market became a huge revenue engine for movie distributors, it also provided an ideal platform for pirates. The theft and distribution of intellectual property, especially movies, became a billion-dollar business. It wasn't unusual for an illegal version of a movie to show up on the streets of China or in New York City as soon as it opened in the United States, often with a shaky copy shot with a camcorder from inside a movie theater. Jack Valenti, head of the Motion Picture Association of America, crusaded at home and abroad against a scourge that he likened to a cancer eating away at the business. Valenti pushed governments to toughen enforcement and treat piracy as a real crime. Beginning in the mid-1990s piracy also became an issue on the Internet, where technology allowed fans to swap files of everything from songs to movies.

Word of mouth among ticket buyers had always been a powerful force in movies, as friends swapped information or colleagues gossiped at the office. However, after the arrival of the Internet, gossip and rumors were distributed rapidly around the World Wide Web along with real information. One film showed how it could also be a powerful marketing tool. The low-budget independently produced movie *The Blair Witch Project* became a national sensation after false information was planted on the Internet that the murders shown on-screen were real, not staged by a filmmaker. Of course the events depicted in the movies weren't real, but the controversy they caused helped boost interest and ticket sales, and the Internet emerged as a powerful new force in movie marketing and distribution.

Summers and holidays were still filled with big-budget action, adventure, comedy, fantasy, and science fiction, with pictures premiering on the first weekend in thousands of theaters, but the decade also saw the rise of a new independent cinema. Using a more limited distribution model, often driven by reviews and word of mouth, specialty circuits developed to distribute these art and more serious films. The revival was led by Miramax Films, a maverick company that got its start in 1979 but was transformed when it won the distribution rights to the Steven Soderbergh film *sex, lies and videotape* after the movie's debut at the 1989 Sundance Film

Festival. In 1993 Miramax was acquired by the Walt Disney Company and then operated as a specialty film division. A new generation of filmmakers continued to gather at the Sundance Film Festival each January. Begun in 1978, the festival moved to Park City, Utah, in 1981 and in 1985 merged with actor, producer, and activist Robert Redford's Sundance Institute. By the 1990s interest in independent films was experiencing explosive growth, culminating with the midnight screening of *The Blair Witch Project* at the festival's twenty-first anniversary in 1999, which, together with its innovative Internet marketing campaign, launched that film into the top five independently produced and distributed films of all time in adjusted dollars, after *The Graduate* (1967) and *Duel in the Sun* (1947).

One particularly notable change that occurred during the decade related to the way Hollywood honors its own community. From the Golden Globes to the Oscars, the awards season was forever changed as voters were no longer required to go to a theater to see the movies they were voting for. Distributors pushing a picture for awards consideration began to send each legitimate voter a private copy of the movie on VHS or DVD for home viewing.

PRODUCTION SPOTLIGHT

Digital Takes a Big Leap Forward

For a century, 35mm strips of film had been the dominant media for production of movies, offering an international standard for exhibition and a high-quality image. However, the 1990s brought the digital age to Hollywood. Film clearly had drawbacks. The celluloid and cans were heavy, the film stock fragile and difficult to work with. To capture and deliver images, film required labor-intensive special handling and a high level of craftsmanship in the manufacture, chemical processing, editing, reproduction, and distribution processes. Even in the 1990s, the case could still be made that film was worth the trouble because it offered images with resolution four times better than the best analog broadcast TV of the era. It was also the standard worldwide. Put a movie on reels of film and ship them anywhere around the globe and

---

1990s Movie Censorship: A Brief History

In 1990 the Motion Picture Association of America (MPAA) adjusts its ratings further: X becomes NC-17, no children under 17.

No film rated NC-17 has been a box office success. While MPAA membership is voluntary, all major Hollywood studios submit their films to its rating board, and most theaters will only show films that are MPAA-coded.

they will be compatible with the local theatrical projection. That alone was a reason for theater owners and producers to reject change and stick with film. There were traditionalists who clung to film because of its heritage, including Steven Spielberg, who saw it as the medium of the great moviemakers of the past. It had served them well and it had served him well. Even after much of the industry converted editing from celluloid to digital using electronic systems such as those made by Avid, Spielberg made and edited all of his movies on film. But by the end of the decade, he was one of the few.

One of the first movies in the 1990s to showcase computer-generated special effects was *Terminator 2: Judgment Day* (1991), featuring a shape-shifting cyborg. The shape-shifting effect was created by Lucas's Industrial Light & Magic, improving on a technique they first used in a 1989 film, *The Abyss*, to make characters look like water in water. In *T-2*, as it was known, the effect made the actor look as if he were actually made of liquid mercury. This was done by a computer that simulated his movements, and then a computer paintbox program that added color and texture to the surface image. The computer combined the results with the live action, allowing the character known as T-1000 to turn from human form to liquid and back again on-screen.

In 1992 Lucasfilm illustrated how the new electronic tools could be used to deliver elements and complete work from multiple locations. During one project, a movie was projected at Skywalker Sound in Los Angeles by sound technicians as the soundtrack was being transmitted into the mixing theater at Skywalker Sound in Northern California. Digital got a boost as well with the global success of Pixar's *Toy Story* in 1995. Its CGI realism evidenced how the digital revolution was changing animation. It was the beginning of the end for a century of hand-drawn cartoons and animated features, almost all of which would be replaced by computer-generated imagery.

In 1999 Lucasfilm's *Star Wars: Episode 1 The Phantom Menace* became the first major movie to be exhibited to the public using digital cinema systems—one from Hughes/JVC and the other from Texas Instruments. The TI gear was the better of the two and remains a major player in digital cinema projection today.

Top 10 Critically Acclaimed Lead Actors of the 1990s

Rank	Actor Name
1	Jack Nicholson
2	Tom Hanks
3	Al Pacino
4	Tom Cruise
5	Geoffrey Rush
6	Anthony Hopkins
7	Robin Williuams
8	Leonardo DiCaprio
9	Kevin Spacey
10	Jim Carrey

Rank	Actress Name
1	Judi Dench
2	Jessica Lange
3	Jodi Foster
4	Susan Sarandon
5	Emma Thompson
6	Holly Hunter
7	Kathy Bates
8	Hilary Swank
9	Frances McDormand
10	Helen Hunt

See Note to the Reader for selection criteria.

Four of the Top 15 Special Effects, Special Visual Effects, and Visual Effects Oscar-Winning Films (1963–2008) Are Released in the 1990s

Top 15 Special Effects Oscar-Winning Films
All-Release Domestic Box Office
Equivalent 2005 $s/(Unadjusted $s) in Millions of $s

Rank	Film Title	Initial Release	Domestic Box Office	Production Cost
1	Star Wars: Ep IV A New Hope	1977	$1,085.1/($461.0)	$41.9/($13.0)
2	E.T.: The Extra-Terrestrial	1982	$889.4/($435.1)	$24.6/($12.2)
3	Titanic*	1997	$824.8/($600.8)	$243.4/($200.0)
4	Star Wars: Ep V The Empire Strikes Back	1980	$620.0/($290.3)	$75.8/($32.0)
5	Star Wars: Ep VI Return of the Jedi	1983	$597.6/($309.2)	$83.7/($42.7)
6	Raiders of the Lost Ark	1981	$554.7/($245.0)	$48.9/($22.8)
7	Jurassic Park	1993	$552.9/($357.1)	$94.6/($70.0)
8	Mary Poppins	1964	$538.8/($101.8)	$27.8/($4.4)
9	Forrest Gump*	1994	$505.6/($329.7)	$72.5/($55.0)
10	Independence Day	1996	$444.0/($306.2)	$93.4/($75.0)
11	Cleopatra	1963	$435.7/($57.8)	$280.8/($44.0)
12	Pirates of the Caribbean: Dead Man's Chest	2006	$414.3/($423.3)	$218.0/($225.0)
13	The Lord of the Rings: The Return of the King*	2003	$400.8/($377.0)	$276.0/($260.0)
14	Thunderball	1965	$395.2/($63.6)	$41.9/($6.8)
15	Spider-Man 2	2004	$385.4/($373.4)	$206.8/($200.0)

*Academy Award winner for Best Picture.

Pictures used to break [even] at three times negative cost, on average . . . but now they're breaking at five to six times negative costs. The old rules of thumb no longer apply.
—ENTERTAINMENT ATTORNEY PETER DEKOM

It seems that, like lemmings, we are all racing faster and faster into the sea, each of us trying to outrun and outspend and outearn the other in a mad sprint toward the mirage of the next blockbuster.
—JEFFREY KATZENBERG

Comparison of Two of the Top 10 Highest-Cost, Highest-Revenue Movies
All-Release Domestic Box Office, 1960–2005
Equivalent 2005 $s/(Unadjusted $s) In Millions of $s

Film	Initial Release	Domestic Box Office	Production Cost	Salary
Cleopatra	1963	**$435.7** ($57.7)	**$280.8** ($44.0) Actual cost net of insurance reimbursement **$198.6** ($31.1)	**Joseph L. Mankiewicz (writer, director) $1.0 million** (salary $150,000, Fox also paid him $1.5 million to buy out his production company + other fees) **Elizabeth Taylor (actress) $15.3 million** ($2.4 million salary + living expenses + overtime + participation net of lawsuit with Fox) **Richard Burton (actor) $4.8 million** ($250,000 salary + overages totalling $750,000)
Titanic	1997	**$824.8** ($600.8)	**$243.4** ($200.0)	**James Cameron (writer, director) $139.9 million** ($600,000 for screenplay plus $8 million salary + back end participation total $115 million) **Leonardo DiCaprio (actor) $48.7 million** ($2.5 million salary + gross p/p* total $40 million) **Kate Winslet (actress) $2.4 million** ($2.0 million salary)

*Profit participation.

Index of Top Feature Film Directors Included in This Chapter

See Note to the Reader for selection criteria.

The Number One Top Animation Film Is Released in the 1990s

Top 20 Animation Films
All-Release Worldwide Box Office
1930–2009
Equivalent 2005 $s/(Unadjusted $s) in Millions of $s

Rank	Film	Initial Release	Domestic Box Office	Foreign Box Office	Worldwide Box Office	Production Cost
1	The Lion King	1994	$501.9 ($328.5)	$698.1 ($455.2)	$1,200.0 ($783.7)	$104.5 ($79.3)
2	Snow White and the Seven Dwarfs**	1937	$760.9 ($160.6)	$268.6 ($9.7)	$1,029.5 ($170.3)	$20.2 ($1.5)
3	101 Dalmations	1961	$395.3 ($144.0)	$591.0 ($71.0)	$986.3 ($215.0)	$23.8 ($3.6)
4	Shrek 2	2004	$455.4 ($441.2)	$494.1 ($478.6)	$949.5 ($919.8)	$155.1 ($150.0)
5	Finding Nemo*	2003	$361.1 ($339.7)	$558.0 ($524.9)	$919.1 ($864.6)	$99.8 ($94.0)
6	Bambi	1942	$383.8 ($101.6)	$449.9 ($165.2)	$833.7 ($266.8)	$20.9 ($1.7)
7	Aladdin	1992	$336.2 ($217.4)	$445.5 ($287.7)	$781.7 ($505.1)	$39.0 ($28.0)
8	Shrek the Third	2007	$300.7 ($322.7)	$443.7 ($476.3)	$744.4 ($799.0)	$150.7 ($160.0)
9	The Incredibles*	2004	$269.9 ($261.4)	$370.0 ($370.0)	$639.9 ($631.4)	$95.1 ($92.0)
10	Ice Age: The Meltdown	2006	$188.4 ($192.5)	$405.9 ($294.2)	$594.3 ($486.7)	$77.5 ($80.0)
11	Toy Story 2	1999	$307.8 ($245.9)	$286.5 ($240.9)	$594.3 ($486.8)	$105.5 ($90.0)
12	Monsters, Inc.	2001	$289.8 ($255.9)	$299.3 ($271.3)	$589.1 ($527.2)	$126.8 ($115.0)
13	Pinocchio	1940	$465.2 ($84.3)	$116.3 ($4.3)	$581.5 ($88.6)	$36.8 ($2.6)
14	Rattouille	2007	$192.3 ($206.4)	$386.3 ($414.6)	$578.6 ($621.0)	$141.3 ($150.0)
15	Beauty and the Beast	1991	$251.1 ($171.4)	$314.6 ($203.7)	$565.7 ($375.1)	$40.1 ($28.0)
16	Kung Fu Panda	2008	$192.3 ($215.4)	$371.8 ($416.5)	$564.1 ($631.9)	$117.9 ($130.0)

Rank	Film	Initial Release	Domestic Box Office	Foreign Box Office	Worldwide Box Office	Production Cost
17	*Tarzan*	1999	**$215.9** ($171.1)	**$346.0** ($274.2)	**$561.9** ($445.3)	**$175.8** ($150.0)
18	*The Jungle Book*	1967	**$351.1** ($128.6)	**$206.6** ($42.2)	**$557.7** ($170.8)	**$22.6** ($3.9)
19	*Shrek**	2001	**$303.1** ($267.7)	**$245.5** ($216.7)	**$548.6** ($484.4)	**$66.2** ($60.0)
20	*Who Framed Roger Rabbit***	1988	**$240.4** ($154.1)	**$304.1** ($195.0)	**$544.5** ($349.1)	**$96.0** ($58.2)

*Academy Award for Best Animated Feature Film.

** Academy Special Achievement Award

*Note: Box office through June 2009 only.

Top 20 Animated Films, 1930–2009
All-Release Worldwide Box Office vs. Production Costs
Equivalent 2005 $s

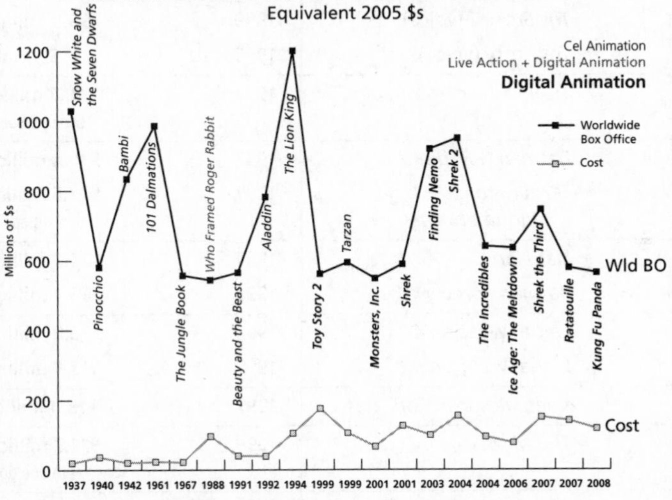

Note: 2009 box office through 6/16/2009 only.

Actors of the 1990s: Comparison of Salaries and Profit Participation

Equivalent 2005 $s/(Unadjusted $s)

Actor	Film	Initial Release	Salary
Bruce Willis	The Sixth Sense	1999	**$117.2 million** ($100,000,000 includes gross theatrical p/p* + video p/p) [Base salary $14 million + private jet ($450,000) + other allowance ($339,492) + p/p]
	Die Hard: With a Vengeance	1995	**$19.2 million/($15,000,000)**
	Die Hard 2	1990	**$11.2 million/($7,500,000)**
	Pulp Fiction	1994	**$1.1 million/($800,000)**
Tom Cruise	Mission: Impossible	1996	**$87.1 million** ($70,000,000 includes gross p/p)
Tom Hanks	Forrest Gump	1994	**$92.2 million** ($70,000,000 SAG scale + gross p/p)
	Saving Private Ryan	1998	**$48.0 million** ($40,000,000 includes gross p/p)
	Toy Story 2 (voice)	1999	**$5.9 million/($5,000,000)**
	Toy Story (voice)	1995	**$64,000/($50,000)**
Leonardo DiCaprio	Titanic	1997	**$48.7 million including p/p** ($40,000,000 including gross p/p)
Arnold Schwarzenegger	Batman & Robin	1997	**$30.4 million/($25,000,000)**
	Terminator 2: Judgment Day	1997	**$21.5 million excluding p/p** ($15,000,000 + gross p/p)
Jim Carrey	Liar Liar	1997	**$24.3 million/($20,000,000)**
	Batman Forever	1995	**$6.4 million/($5,000,000)**
Mel Gibson	Lethal Weapon 4	1998	**$36.0 million/($30,000,000)**
	Lethal Weapon 3	1992	**$13.9 million/($10,000,000)**
Sigourney Weaver	Alien: Resurrection	1997	**$13.4 million ($11,000,000)**
Keanu Reeves	The Matrix	1999	**$11.7 million excluding p/p** ($10,000,000 + 10% gross p/p)
Val Kilmer	Batman Forever	1995	**$9.0 million/($7,000,000)**
Tommy Lee Jones	Men in Black	1997	**$8.5 million/($7,000,000)**
Danny Glover	Lethal Weapon 4	1998	**$8.4 million/($7,000,000)**
Mike Myers	Austin Powers 2	1999	**$8.2 million/($7,000,000)**
	Austin Powers	1997	**$3.7 million/($3,000,000)**

Actor	Film	Initial Release	Salary
Al Pacino	*The Godfather Part III*	1990	**$7.5 million/($5,000,000)**
Jack Nicholson	*A Few Good Men*	1992	**$7.0 million/($5,000,000)**
Macaulay Culkin	*Home Alone 2: Lost in New York*	1992	**$6.3 million excluding p/p** ($4,500,000 + p/p)
	Home Alone	1990	**$0.1 million/($100,000)**
Will Smith	*Independence Day*	1996	**$6.2 million/($5,000,000)**
	Men in Black	1997	**$6.1 million/($5,000,000**
Michelle Pfeiffer	*Batman Returns*	1992	**$4.2 million/($3,000,000)**
Nicole Kidman	*Batman Forever*	1995	**$3.2 million/($2,500,000)**
Kate Winslet	*Titanic*	1997	**$2.4 million/($2,000,000)**
Julia Roberts	*Pretty Woman*	1990	**$0.4 million/($300,000)**
	Runaway Bride	1999	**$20 million/($17,000,000)**
John Travolta	*Pulp Fiction*	1994	**$0.2 million/($140,000)**

*Profit participation.

A Sampling of Director Salaries, 1990s
Equivalent 2005 $s/(Unadjusted $s)

Director	Film	Initial Release	Salary
James Cameron	*Titanic*	1997	**$139.9 million + p/p*** ($115 million total: $600,000 for screenplay, $8,000,000 salary + back-end p/p)
Steven Spielberg	*Saving Private Ryan*	1998	**$35.9 million + p/p** ($30 million from theatrical distribution + 16.75% of first dollar gross revenue)
Francis Ford Coppola	*The Godfather Part III*	1990	**$9.0 million + p/p** ($6.0 million + p/p)
M. Night Shyamalan	*The Sixth Sense*	1999	**$3.0 million** ($2.6 million)

*Profit participation.

General Corporate vs. Movie Business Salaries, 1995
Pretax* (1995 maximum individual tax rate 39.6%)
Equivalent 2005 $s/(Unadjusted $s)

Name	Job	Annual Earnings
Michael D. Eisner	CEO and chairman, The Walt Disney Company	**$11.2 million** ($8,774,707: $750,000 salary + $8,024,707 bonus)
Roy E. Disney	Vice chairman, The Walt Disney Company	**$1.1 million** ($850,000: $350,000 salary + $500,000 bonus)
Michael S. Ovitz	President, The Walt Disney company	**$1.3 million** ($1,000,000 annual salary) 5-year employment contract begun 10/1/1995 terminated 12/27/1996 with payout of **$49.8 million** ($38,869,000 including stock options for 3 million shares)
Edgar Bronfman Jr.	CEO, Seagram Co. Ltd.	**$2.1 million** ($1,634,420: $902,700 salary + $731,720 bonus)
Frank J. Biondi Jr.	Chairman and CEO, MCA (MCA Universal owned 80% by Seagram from 6/5/1995 until sold to Vivendi in June 2000. Salary from 4/23/1996 hire date through fiscal year end 6/30/1996)	**$1.3 million** ($1,043,590: $189,744 salary + $853,846 bonus)

*Note: See tax rate table in Note to Reader on page xi.

Salary + bonus does not include additional stock option compensation, taxed at a lower capital gains rate.

U.S. INDUSTRY PRODUCTION STATISTICS, 1990s
Equivalent 2005 $s/(Unadjusted $s)

$78.7 Million ($61.5 million)
Average production cost of films featured in this chapter

$40.0 Million ($26.8 million)
Average production cost of all films released in the 1990s

Films Winning Oscars for Both Art Direction and Best Picture, 1927–2005
Initial Release Domestic Box Office
Equivalent 2005 $s/(Unadjusted $s) in Millions of $s

Rank	Film	Initial Release	Domestic Box Office
1	Titanic	1997	$824.8/($600.8)
2	Ben-Hur	1959	$704.2/($74.7)
3	The Sting	1973	$568.2/($156.0)
4	My Fair Lady	1964	$457.4/($71.1)
5	The Lord of the Rings: The Return of the King	2003	$400.8/($377.0)
6	Lawrence of Arabia	1962	$263.8/($33.3)
7	Patton	1970	$255.4/($61.7)
8	Oliver!	1968	$182.7/($37.3)
9	Chicago	2002	$181.4/($170.7)
10	Gone with the Wind	1939	$161.9/($21.5)
11	The Godfather Part II	1974	$161.2/($47.5)
12	Out of Africa	1985	$152.0/($87.1)
13	Schindler's List	1993	$147.4/($96.1)
14	Gigi	1958	$145.9/($14.8)
15	How Green Was My Valley	1941	$129.1/($5.4)
16	Shakespeare in Love	1998	$127.2/($100.3)
17	The Apartment	1960	$125.6/($14.9)
18	Gandhi	1982	$115.0/($52.8)
19	The English Patient	1996	$114.1/($78.7)
20	An American in Paris	1951	$113.7/($8.3)
21	On the Waterfront	1954	$109.9/($9.6)
22	Hamlet	1948	$105.2/($7.2)
23	Amadeus	1984	$95.0/($52.0)
24	The Last Emperor	1987	$72.1/($44.0)
25	Cimarron	1931	$71.2/($2.4)
26	Cavalcade	1933	$62.2/($2.2)

Star Salaries Soar

Turning big-budget action movies, adventures, fantasies, and comedies into box office block-busters became the goal of major studios in the 1990s. The trend that started in the late 1970s and became more important in the 1980s is what truly drove the movie business in the 1990s—the elusive search for the next huge international hit.

No star was bigger than Tom Hanks, who starred in, or provided the voice for, thirteen films during the decade. Hanks was one of the more dependable performers in a business where the only sure thing was that costs were going to continue to rise. In the 1990s, along with bigger location budgets, came higher expenses for production (including special effects), as well as higher costs for marketing, research, and distribution. Amidst all of this, no single aspect rose more than salaries.

These "above-the-line" costs increased in proportion to the financial risks. The big corporations who owned the studios not only wanted research to show that the title, script, and concept were of interest to potential ticket buyers but also wanted a kind of insurance policy—big-name stars above the title. That way, even if the movie failed to draw an audience, the studio executives could say that it was actually the star who had failed, and they could still use the star's name and image to sell that movie in home video and to TV.

This change promised bigger revenues for hits and made it easier for stars deemed "bankable," meaning that their presence would help establish a movie in the marketplace, to reach a wider market. As attaching these big names to a movie became more essential, thus more expensive, the money available to other areas was reduced, including the salaries paid to lesser stars, who clearly did not benefit in the same way as their more famous counterparts.

This new brand-name formula was followed even though a number of studios found that only a handful of stars actually had any significant impact on a film's opening weekend box office during the 1990s, including Tom Hanks, Bruce Willis, Jack Nicholson, Tom Cruise, Julia Roberts, and Will Smith. And even among this group, there was no surefire correlation between their high salary and the success of the movie; some of their pictures proved to be big hits, while others were big disappointments.

Hanks was the most consistent of them all. His salary is a good indicator of how fast and how high salaries rose during the decade. His movies during this ten-year period had an astounding domestic box office of over $2.6 billion (in 2005 dollars; $1.8 billion unadjusted) with a global gross twice that. Compare that with $1.4 billion for nine Tom Cruise–starring films (in 2005 dollars; $1 billion unadjusted).

Hanks had grown up in a broken home, had two stepmothers over the course of his childhood and adolescence, and had lived in ten different houses in five different cities. Although he was a shy child, he showed an early sense of humor. He began working at various low-level jobs in high school, and then in college discovered his interest in drama. He quit college before graduating to begin his career in regional theater. He moved to New York City in 1980 and found a part in a slasher film before getting his big break when an ABC talent scout chose him to be one of the leads in a situation comedy called *Bosom Buddies,* in which he played a man pretending to be a woman much of the time. He soon had cameos on other shows, including *Taxi, Love Boat,* and *Happy Days,* where director Ron Howard invited him to audition for his movie *Splash,* as a man who falls in love with a mermaid. *Splash* was one of the top 10 films of 1984 and made Hanks a star.

Before *Forrest Gump,* Hanks was making roughly $5 million in salary per picture. Just before principal photography began on that film, Paramount insisted that Hanks and director Robert Zemeckis, among others, give back some of their up-front salary in return for a portion of profits. As a result, Hanks ended up making close to $70 million for his work. He also won the Oscar for Best Actor for *Forrest Gump,* following his win for *Philadelphia* the year before. By 1998 Hanks was making a base salary of $20 million per picture, which by then had become a standard of sorts for A-list movie stars who were in constant demand to front the studios' pictures. For Spielberg's epic World War II drama *Saving Private Ryan,* Hanks also received a share of the profits, which drove his final payday up to approximately $40 million.

High star salaries weren't a new concept. The idea that the public would pay to see the same performers over and over harks back to the era of Mary Pickford and the 1920s silent films. Beginning in the 1950s James Stewart, Kirk Douglas, and a few other stars found ways to get a percentage of profits from the studios to help pad their paydays. Still, as late as 1988, it caused a stir when Bruce Willis, then better known as a TV star than a movie star, was paid $5 million by 20th Century-Fox to star in *Die Hard.* At that time, the highest-paid actors such as Warren Beatty and Robert Redford got salaries that ranged from $2 million to $5 million. Dustin Hoffman had been paid $5.5 million to do *Tootsie* in 1982, and it took years for that figure to be topped. In 1988 Sylvester Stallone was paid a reported $12 million, possibly more, by Carolco, an independent company that needed his name attached to the film *Rambo III* to make significant international sales. Then came the 1990s, and it wasn't just Hanks who saw his compensation pop. Tom Cruise had made a $3 million up-front salary (plus a share of the gross) for *Rain Man* in 1988, but by 1992 he was commanding $13 million for the flop *Far and Away.* His up-front compensation rose to $15 million for *Interview with a Vampire* in 1994. For 1996's *Mission: Impossible,* he was a producer as well as star and ultimately made roughly $70 million. From then on he was a member of the $20 million club, his salary for such major roles as 1996's *Jerry Maguire* (along with a share of profits) and 1999's *Eyes Wide Shut.* In 1996 Jim Carrey became the first comedian to get a $20 million salary plus a share of profits for his role in *The Cable Guy,* which was a flop. That was the same year Demi Moore was paid $12.5 million to star in *Striptease,* another box office bomb.

The increased costs weren't just in salaries. These stars had retainers, publicists, favored producers, directors, and writers, who also saw their compensation rise. For Demi Moore's 1995 movie *The Scarlet Letter,* which had a budget of $50 million, *Variety* reported that Moore's support staff (assistant, chef, makeup artist, hairdresser, trainer, and three nannies) added more than $877,000 to the budget above and beyond her salary. *The Scarlet Letter* was also a box office disappointment.

By the second half of the 1990s, Hanks had also become a role model for successful actors as he segued into producing in addition to acting. He not only did some of his own theatrical films but also expanded into TV, most notably with the docudrama *From the Earth to the Moon*, a twelve-part series for HBO said to have cost $68 million. It won three Emmys and was named the best miniseries of that year. Hanks never seemed caught up in his success, though, unlike some other stars. His philosophy about what it takes to succeed was captured in a 1992 interview with CNN's Larry King: "There's no substitute for having a good movie. If we have a good story and we have told it in a good fashion, the audience will react. You can't fake them out; if it's no good, they'll find out very quick."

Tom Hanks Starring Films of the 1990s

Equivalent 2005 $s/(Unadjusted $s) in Millions of $s

Rank	Film	Initial Release	Director	Domestic Box Office
1	*Forrest Gump***	1994	Robert Zemeckis	**$505.6**/($329.7)
2	*Toy Story 2* (voice)	1999	John Lasseter	**$307.8**/($245.9)
3	*Saving Private Ryan**	1998	Steven Spielberg	**$292.8**/($216.2)
4	*Toy Story* (voice)	1995	John Lasseter	**$281.2**/($191.8)
5	*Apollo 13*	1995	Ron Howard	**$253.5**/($172.1)
6	*Sleepless in Seattle*	1993	Nora Ephron	**$196.1**/($126.7)
7	*The Green Mile*	1999	Frank Darabont	**$168.6**/($136.8)
8	*A League of Their Own*	1992	Penny Marshall	**$166.1**/($107.5)
9	*You've Got Mail*	1998	Nora Ephron	**$154.7**/($115.8)
10	*Philadelphia***	1993	Jonathan Demme	**$119.9**/($77.4)
11	*Joe Versus the Volcano*	1990	John Patrick Shanley	**$59.7**/($39.4)
12	*That Thing You Do!*	1996	Tom Hanks	**$37.5**/($25.9)
13	*The Bonfire of the Vanities*	1990	Brian De Palma	**$23.8**/($15.7)
	Total			**$2,567.3**/($1,800.7)

** Best Actor Oscar win.

* Best Actor Oscar nomination.

DISTRIBUTION OVERVIEW

Distributors Pay More for Market Share

In the summer of 1989, it seemed as if the hits would just keep on coming. This drove the production of a new generation of potential blockbusters, each supported by national saturation advertising campaigns. A year later, Disney set new marketing budget records for its version of *Dick Tracy,* which opened in June 1990 in 2,332 theaters, shelling out a reported $54.7 million in advertising worldwide on that film alone. Marketing spending sprees continued throughout the 1990s as the studio mantra became "get as much market share as possible." This often meant releasing as many big movies into the marketplace as possible in order to draw audiences away from competitors. Such thinking was, in part, a legacy of the 1980s, when Coca-Cola owned Columbia Pictures. Coca Cola firmly believed that high market share was a sign of success. What this belief didn't take into account, however, was the fact that spending more on marketing often meant smaller or nonexistent profits. Opening wide meant additional print costs and higher spending to service the exhibitors, but nothing soared more during the decade than the cost of marketing—an expense that included publicity activities, paid advertising, and promotion. Nevertheless, the market share race was on, and it seemed as if everyone was running in it. The increase in the number of big movies, and their concentration in the summer and end-of-year holiday period, created a traffic jam at the cinemas where three or four hugely

Top 5 Domestic Box Office Summer Tent Pole Films
Number of Theater Engagements at Release, 1989 vs. 1999

Rank	Film	Release Month	Number of Theater Engagements
	1989		
1	Batman	June	2,194
2	Indiana Jones and the Last Crusade	May	2,327
3	Lethal Weapon 2	July	1,803
4	Honey I Shrunk the Kids	June	1,371
5	Ghostbusters II	June	2,410
	1999		
1	Star Wars: Episode I The Phantom Menace	May	2,970
2	The Sixth Sense	August	2,161
3	Austin Powers 2	June	3,312
4	Tarzan	June	3,005
5	Big Daddy	June	3,207

expensive films might open all on the same weekend. The crowded marketplace forced distributors to spend even more on advertising, and to do it across more outlets.

In the 1990s, as the media outlets and distribution platforms proliferated, sophisticated new research made it possible to more carefully target desirable audiences for certain movies. In 1995–96, for instance, to open the James Bond movie *GoldenEye*, the studio spent $9.8 million on network TV advertising, $8.4 million on newspaper advertising, $4.2 million on spot TV ads, and lesser amounts on magazines, outdoor, syndicated TV, and cable TV, according to statistics compiled by the Competitive Media Reporting and Publishing Information Bureau. And all of this spending was in addition to the theatrical trailers they had paid to develop. Each year after that the cost of marketing rose, and the percentage that went to more traditional advertising vehicles, including national TV and newspapers, began to lessen as more and more money was spent on alternative marketing. At the same time, studios justified the increased investment and pursuit of high market share by pointing to the booming home video market, as well as other lucrative movie platforms such as pay TV (HBO, Showtime) and network and syndicated TV. Movie marketers were discovering that they could target different or more specific audience segments by advertising on different media outlets—using cable TV channels, for example—just as they had used specialty magazines for years.

The higher costs were also justified by the growth of the international market for American movies, especially the big blockbusters that often dominated foreign markets. As the economies of countries in Europe and Asia improved, discretionary spending by consumers there increased. These consumers often indulged on movies, although their money did not always go back to the film's producer because of rampant piracy. Late in the decade the efforts of the MPAA to curb piracy got a bit of a boost as the VHS tape format for prerecorded software was starting to be phased out in favor of the DVD. Various copy protection methods were applied in an attempt to make it difficult for pirates to copy the movies, with mixed success. The DVD also changed the revenue model for distribution of movies beyond theaters. Whereas studios had previously been able to charge video stores high prices for rental copies of a movie, the advent of the DVD brought with it new emphasis on selling directly to consumers at a lower price point. In other words, the studios would sell more units for less money per unit with the expectation that profits would be greater with the volume that a hit movie could provide.

U.S. INDUSTRY DISTRIBUTION STATISTICS, 1990s
Equivalent 2005 $s/(Unadjusted $s)

$7,609 Million ($5,021 million)
Annual U.S. box office gross revenues

385
Number of new feature films released in 1990

As Distribution Companies Morph, a New Full-Service Studio Is Formed

Throughout the 1990s, the consolidation of the major entertainment producers and distributors continued, with fewer and fewer companies controlling more and more brands and platforms on a global basis. The surge of revenue from home video and the growth of international markets had falsely convinced many on Wall Street and in the business community at large that the movie and TV industry was now more stable and predictable. MCA Universal, which had major interests in movies and TV and was considered one of the top studios, was sold in 1990 for roughly $6.1 billion to the Japanese electronics company Matsushita. This acquisition was recognized as Matsushita's bid to keep up with archrival Sony Corp., which in 1989 had bought Columbia Pictures from Coca-Cola for approximately $4.9 billion.

In 1990 Time, Inc., known for its magazines including *Time* and *Money,* completed its purchase of Warner Communications, parent company of Warner Bros. This merger of powerhouses created what was, at the time, the world's largest media conglomerate. New Line Cinema became part of that group when its founder, Robert Shaye, sold it to Ted Turner in 1994 for roughly $500 million and Turner Broadcasting was subsequently bought by Time Warner for approximately $7 billion in 1996.

In March 1994 Viacom, a TV producer and distributor that had been spun off from CBS years before due to antitrust concerns, acquired Blockbuster Video, which had emerged as the largest operator of retail video stories in the United States. Then in July of that year, Viacom won a bidding war against Barry Diller for Paramount Communications, which it took over in a cash-and-stock deal valued at $10 billion (including 50.1 percent of Paramount's stock), creating another major media player with interests in everything from exhibition to theme parks and cable TV channels such as MTV and Nickelodeon.

In 1995 Seagram Corp., a big Canadian liquor distributor, paid Matsushita $5.7 billion for Universal Studios after the Japanese suffered through a series of flop movies. That was also the year Westinghouse Electric bought the CBS television network, which would be acquired yet again at the end of the decade, this time by Viacom, joining it with Paramount Pictures and other assets in an even bigger entity.

Miramax, the company founded by Harvey and Bob Weinstein, was bought by Walt Disney Studios in 1993 for roughly $75 million. In 1996 the Walt Disney Company paid $19 billion to acquire the ABC television network, reshaping that company into a large entertainment conglomerate as well. The sale of TV networks had followed the 1992 decision to end rules limiting the networks' ability to produce the shows that they aired on their own stations.

This influx of new public and private investment fueled the boom in movie production, the increased cost of marketing, and the growth of the megatheaters. It also led to the creation of the first full-service studio in many decades, with the birth of DreamWorks in 1994. The company was founded and run by producer-director Steven Spielberg, the most successful moviemaker of his generation; Jeffrey Katzenberg, who had been forced to resign from Disney after a very public power struggle; and the wildly successful record producer and personal manager

David Geffen. The new studio was backed by the founders, who each put in $33 million, and Paul Allen, who invested over a half billion dollars. Allen, of course, had co-founded Microsoft with Bill Gates before taking major positions in cable TV, new media, and other areas.

DreamWorks began movie distribution on a steady basis in 1997 with *The Peacemaker,* and took on Disney/Pixar in animation beginning in 1998 with *Antz* [a Pacific Data Images (PDI) production], then with *The Prince of Egypt.* In 1999 it won the first of three consecutive Best Picture Oscars with *American Beauty,* followed by *Gladiator* (2000) and *A Beautiful Mind* (2001), with Universal sharing some of the distribution. DreamWorks acquired a majority interest in the northern California studio PDI prior to the release of *Shrek* in 2002. As a result, the Dream-Works animation division turned out to be the firm's most successful business and was spun off in 2004 to better compete with rival Pixar (who would be sold to Disney in 2006). The remaining live action group would be acquired by Viacom's Paramount Pictures in a $1.6 billion deal in 2006, before entering into another distribution agreement in 2009, this time with the Walt Disney Company.

Major Movie Distributors, 1990s

Buena Vista .The brothers Harvey and Bob Weinstein sell Miramax Films to the Walt Disney Company in 1993.

DreamWorks . . . . .The new company is founded in 1994.

MGM/United Artists . . . . .MGM/UA is sold by Kerkorian to Giancarlo Parretti in 1990 then bought back a third time by Kerkorian in 1996.

Paramount Pictures . . . . .Viacom takes control of Paramount Communications in 1994.

Sony . . . . .Columbia Pictures and TriStar Pictures are purchased from the Coca-Cola Company in 1989.

20th Century-Fox . . . . .Continues under News Corp. ownership throughout the decade.

Universal Pictures . . . . .Sold in 1990 to Matsushita, which sells an 80 percent share of MCA Universal to Seagram in 1995.

Warner Bros. . . . . .Time, Inc., completes its purchase of Warner Communications in 1990. The new company is called Time Warner. Time Warner acquires Turner Broadcasting in 1996, which includes New Line Cinema.

TECHNOLOGY SPOTLIGHT

The Pixar Story: Vision and Chance

In the 1990s, Pixar Animation Studios released three movies that featured the use of computer-generated images to create lifelike characters—*Toy Story, A Bug's Life,* and *Toy Story 2*—and won a total of nine Scientific and Technical Awards during the decade. These films were not only hugely successful; they also showcased new uses for digital technology, revolutionizing movie and animation production. Although it appeared to be an overnight success story for Pixar, these successes had been twenty years in the making.

Pixar's origin can be traced back to 1972, a time when computers could only form images with straight lines. That was when computer scientist Ed Catmull first began thinking about using computers to create animated movies. After earning his Ph.D. at the University of Utah, Catmull found his way to the New York Institute of Technology. A few months later Alvy Ray Smith, who had earned a Ph.D. from Stanford, found his way to NYIT and talked Catmull into hiring him. Catmull then began gathering together a larger team of early computer graphics pioneers, as director of the budding computer graphics research group.

In 1979 George Lucas was seeking people to develop computer graphics in movies. Lucas had three goals—to create processes for digital editing, to do the same for digital audio, and to create a scanner-printer to transfer images back and forth between video media and film. Raj Reddy, an artificial intelligence expert and visiting professor at Stanford from Carnegie Mellon, referred Lucas to Ralph Guggenheim, who had been a student of his. Guggenheim got together with Catmull and Smith and, after a visit to Lucasfilm, Catmull agreed to take a job there as head of a new division charged with advancing digital imaging. Catmull naturally brought many of his NYIT team with him.

The computer graphics group at Lucasfilm had the necessary talent, but the computers available at the time were too slow and the software they needed to create images that could be used in a 35 mm feature film had not yet been developed. Still, they were making progress and wanted to showcase some of what they had accomplished. Smith convinced their sister entity, Industrial Light & Magic, to give the team a chance to provide part of the effects for *Star Trek II: The Wrath of Khan.* Their contributions turned out to be the "Genesis Effect," stunning computer graphics experts who had never seen anything like it before.

By 1984 the graphics created by this group were greatly improving, but the storytelling quality was not keeping pace, which is where John Lasseter came in. Lasseter had attended Cal Arts, a school founded by the Walt Disney Company, studying character animation. After graduation he went to Disney, where he was able to work with some of the all-time great animators from the studio's past. Due to some management turmoil, the animation division there had fallen on hard times, but things looked up briefly when Disney produced the movie *Tron* using extensive computer special effects. The movie was visually dazzling, but the storytelling was lacking. As a result, the movie didn't perform as well as anticipated at the box office, which put a chill on the whole computer animation department, and Lasseter was fired in early 1984. However, during his time at Disney Lasseter had met the computer graphics team at Lucasfilm. That is when he and Catmull made a connection. Lasseter was soon hired on a project basis to work on a short film called *The Adventures of Andre and Wally B,* to be shown at an upcoming conference. This marked the entry of character (as opposed to effects) animation into the computer graphics world. After a short return to Disney, Lasseter came back to Lucasfilm to work on graphic elements for the movie *Young Sherlock Holmes.* Dennis Muren, an Oscar-winning visual effects supervisor at Industrial Light & Magic, was one of the few in his field who believed in CGI graphics and had asked the Pixar team to do the stained-glass sequence. The movie was later nominated for an Oscar for its visual effects.

In creating a scanner, the group had also developed a computer specially made to handle graphic images. That became the Pixar Image Computer. Over time various parts of the computer group were spun off, including Edit Droid, Sound Droid, and a games division known as Droid Works. That left the computer graphics group to function mostly as a research team, and soon they were caught up in budget cutting by executives at Lucasfilm looking to rein in costs. Rather than wait to see what their fate would be, Catmull and Smith approached Lucas about creating their own company. Lucas agreed, and they set off to seek funding. The business plan was to sell Pixar Computers while developing the CGI graphics capability to make digitally animated movies. They found their angel in Steve Jobs, a college dropout who had made a fortune as one of the founders of Apple Computer. After an earlier deal for financing by General Motors and Philips fell through, Jobs was able to acquire the computer division for $10 million in 1986. Half of that money went to Lucasfilm and the other half went to the capitalization of the new company, which was named Pixar after its major product, the Imaging Computer. Cofounders Catmull and Smith brought along with them thirty-eight employees from Lucasfilm, including, importantly, Lasseter.

Since computers were still too slow, Pixar's animation group was a sideshow at the new company, but that didn't stop the small team from tearing into their work. They decided to create the short film *Luxo Jr.,* which became a hit within the industry and went on to be the first 3-D CGI short film nominated for an Academy Award. The company made more shorts and developed the craft further but, not having sold as many computers as expected, they were bleeding red ink. Only Jobs's willingness to write checks to fund operations kept it afloat. The best thing that happened during these years was Pixar's development of a proprietary system for Disney called CAPS that revolutionized the making of 2-D cel animated films. Its success cemented a mutual admiration between the two companies.

Between 1986 and 1991, Jobs put almost $55 million into Pixar. To keep the animation division going, they went after work on commercials beginning in 1989. In 1990 Pixar was looking for the right property to turn into an animated feature when Disney approached Lasseter about directing a movie for them. Lasseter suggested that Pixar make the movie and Disney distribute it instead. For years, Disney had a rule: it did not distribute animated movies unless they were produced in-house. However, the new management at Disney agreed to a deal with Pixar for three animated features, starting with *Toy Story.* Disney president Jeffrey Katzenberg had a lot of input in the story development, but as the Pixar team incorporated those ideas with their own, the story went awry. After a year of work, Lasseter realized it was not working, and Katzenberg agreed. With Disney's blessing, and in record time, Lasseter led a reedit. Instead of the whole movie being scrapped, as the circumstances threatened, Pixar was finally on course. *Toy Story* was released in November 1995 and was not only a hit at theaters but also immediately recognized as a major move forward in computer animation. A week after the film's premiere, Pixar made an initial public stock offering, which provided extra funding. Shortly after that, a new deal was struck with Disney to share the cost and profits from future animated movies on a 50/50 basis.

Even before the release of *Toy Story*, Pixar had begun work on its second film, *A Bug's Life*. It was not an easy task. The second film was shot on Cinemascope, so the frame was bigger. There was a cast of literally thousands of characters. And unlike toy characters, which were easy to create on a computer, bugs and insects had many variations and lived in a constantly moving world of swaying grass blades, falling water, blowing smoke, and more. Pixar's goal was to achieve something beyond photorealism in animation: to achieve hyperrealism. Adding to the pressure was the threat of a competing film; Katzenberg had left Disney and formed DreamWorks with Steven Spielberg and David Geffen, and one of their first animated movies was *Antz,* a movie about an ant and his colony. Within the clubby computer graphics industry, this new competition changed the game for everyone, making it much more intense. Although *Antz* made it to the box office first in October 1998, *A Bug's Life,* released in November, brought in $191.6 million more in worldwide box office, with a total of $363.4 million.

Pixar's next film, *Toy Story 2,* was originally conceived as a made-for-video sequel. Lasseter developed the story, but a tight budget, personnel changes, and technical problems plagued the production. From early on in the process, the Pixar team had pushed for the sequel to get a theatrical release as well. A year before the scheduled release, Pixar executives decided that the made-for-video movie didn't work and that the movie would require a major creative overhaul for it to be a theatrical release. Disney still insisted on the same release date, so Pixar went into crash mode, remaking the movie in only nine months. It met the deadline, but at a cost. After that experience, Pixar determined that it would work only on films aimed at theatrical release. It also resolved never to work people that hard again.

Pixar sold approximately $2.8 billion worth in worldwide tickets on its first five features released through 2003, and made millions more on licensing, merchandising, and publishing spin-offs. While this proved profitable for Pixar, the leadership there chafed because Disney got to take distribution fees off the top before profits were equally split; and Disney owned the story and sequel rights. Negotiations became personal between Jobs and Disney chairman Michael Eisner, but the problem was solved when Eisner was replaced by Robert Iger, who oversaw a deal in 2006 for Disney to acquire Pixar for $7.4 billion in stock, making Steve Jobs the largest individual shareholder at Disney. Lasseter and Catmull took top executive positions overseeing both Pixar and Disney, as well as Walt Disney Imagineering, which builds theme park attractions.

MARKETING SPOTLIGHT

The average costs for P&A (prints and advertising) have been tracking double-digit increases every year since 1994. —HOLLYWOOD REPORTER, 2000

Year	MPAA Member Company Average Ad Costs of New Featured Films Millions of $s	Average Percentage Increase	Total U.S. Advertising Expenditures Across All Mediums Millions of $s	Average Percentage Increase
1990	10.20		129,968	
1995	15.38	51%	165,147	27%
2000	24.00	56%	347,472	50%
2001	27.28	14%	231,387	–7%
2002	27.31	0%	236,875	2%
2003	34.84	28%	245,477	4%
2004	30.61	–12%	263,766	7%
2005	32.36	6%	271,074	3%

Comparison of Five 1990s Films Initial Release
Equivalent 2005 $s/(Unadjusted $s) in Millions of $s

Film, Initial Release	Domestic Box Office	Domestic Rentals	Foreign Rentals	Production Cost	Domestic Print and Ad Costs
Titanic, 1997	$824.8 ($600.8)	$453.6 ($330.4)	$763.9 ($558.9)	$243.4 ($200.0)	$33.6 ($27.6)
Mission: Impossible, 1996	$262.5 ($181.0)	$135.0 ($93.1)	$187.7 ($129.6)	$99.6 ($80.0)	$37.3 ($30.0)
Independence Day, 1996	$444.0 ($306.2)	$257.0 ($177.2)	$328.3 ($226.4)	$93.4 ($75.0)	$36.1 ($29.0)
Twister, 1996	$350.5 ($241.7)	$193.6 ($133.5)	$165.0 ($113.8)	$114.5 ($92.0)	$34.5 ($27.7)
Men in Black, 1997	$350.1 ($250.7)	$192.6 ($137.9)	$211.8 ($151.7)	$103.4 ($85.0)	$33.0 ($27.1)

Note: Rentals estimated at 55 percent of domestic box office and 45 percent foreign box office; domestic ad costs from *Hollywood Reporter*. Domestic prints estimated based on $1,500/each print cost times the number of peak domestic engagements times two (to estimate the number of total screens)

EXHIBITION OVERVIEW

The Multiplex Problem

Blockbuster movies with big opening weekends produced the kind of cash flow that impressed Wall Street. Money from public and private sources became available to movie theater operators during the 1990s, and many theatrical exhibitors, such as United Artists and Edwards, used this revenue stream to invest heavily in building new, modern theaters.

The problem was that many of these new theaters were built prior to the advent of stadium seating, which came into favor when American Multi-Cinema (AMC) first introduced it in 1996. Newly built theaters with old-styled slope floors became instantly outdated. Many exhibitors were now stuck with twenty-year leases and construction costs for theaters that the American public was no longer interested in. Exhibitors needed to replace the theaters they had just built or their competitors would build against them. This created a huge dilemma for exhibitors, who could not afford to pay for both the old and new theaters.

The Edwards Theatre chain illustrates perfectly the plight of theatrical exhibition in the late 1990s. James Edwards had started with one theater in Monterey Park, California, which he purchased in 1930 during the Depression. Back then, the timing could not have been better, since talkies had been introduced just four years earlier. Over the next two decades Jim Edwards grew the chain to eighty screens. After selling his circuit, he retired to Orange County, in southern California, and quickly saw the opportunity this area offered to people who couldn't afford the rapidly rising Los Angeles home prices. Plus, this developing area had a new freeway, which offered an attractive alternative to the ever-increasing traffic problems in L.A. Given the enormous opportunities this presented, Jim Edwards's retirement did not last long. As new shopping centers were built, Edwards was there with his brand of multiscreen theaters. As developers saturated the landscape, so did his theaters. Edwards's screen count in Orange County rose to 207 by the mid-1990s. His continued building not only monopolized the area, effectively keeping serious competition out, but also cannibalized his own business. Ticket sales simply did not keep up with his rapid expansion. After Jim Edwards's death, his son James the third extended the expansion efforts outside of Orange County to other flourishing communities, but it was too late. In August 2000 Edwards Theatres would file for bankruptcy.

Many other theater operators were facing the same fate by the end of the decade. Carmike, General Cinema, AMC, Loews, Regal, and United Artists Theaters all had no choice but to file for bankruptcy as well.

Franchise Films
Originating in the 1990s
Equivalent 2005 $s in Millions of $s

Rank	Franchise	Number of Films in Franchise	All-Release Worldwide Box Office
1	*Jurassic Park*	3	$2,714.6
2	*The Matrix*	3	$1,808.8
3	*Mission: Impossible*	3	$1,718.8
4	*Home Alone*	3	$1,392.3
5	*American Pie*	3	$868.2
6	*Austin Powers*	3	$815.3

U.S. INDUSTRY EXHIBITION STATISTICS, 1990s
Equivalent 2005 $s/(Unadjusted $s)

$6.41 ($4.23 – $5.08)
Average movie ticket price (1990–1999)

23,814
Number of U.S. screens, 1990
(22,904 indoor and 910 drive-in)

Jurassic Park

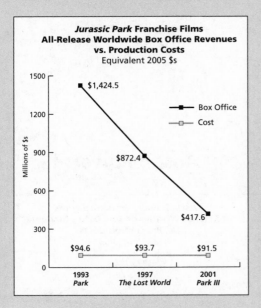

Jurassic Park Franchise Films
All-Release Worldwide Box Office Revenues
vs. Production Costs
Equivalent 2005 $s

The Matrix

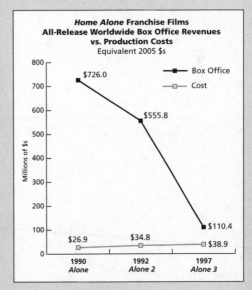

The Matrix Franchise Films
All-Release Worldwide Box Office Revenues
vs. Production Costs
Equivalent 2005 $s

Mission: Impossible

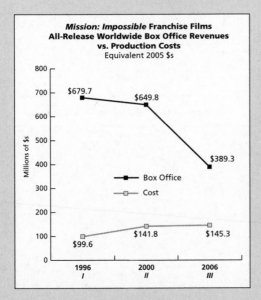

Mission: Impossible Franchise Films
All-Release Worldwide Box Office Revenues
vs. Production Costs
Equivalent 2005 $s

Home Alone

Home Alone Franchise Films
All-Release Worldwide Box Office Revenues
vs. Production Costs
Equivalent 2005 $s

American Pie

Austin Powers

American Pie Franchise Films
All-Release Worldwide Box Office Revenues
vs. Production Costs
Equivalent 2005 $s

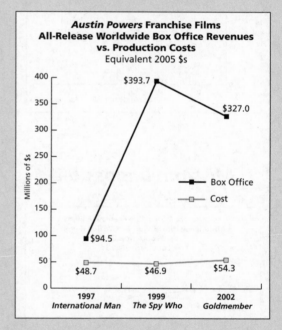

Austin Powers Franchise Films
All-Release Worldwide Box Office Revenues
vs. Production Costs
Equivalent 2005 $s

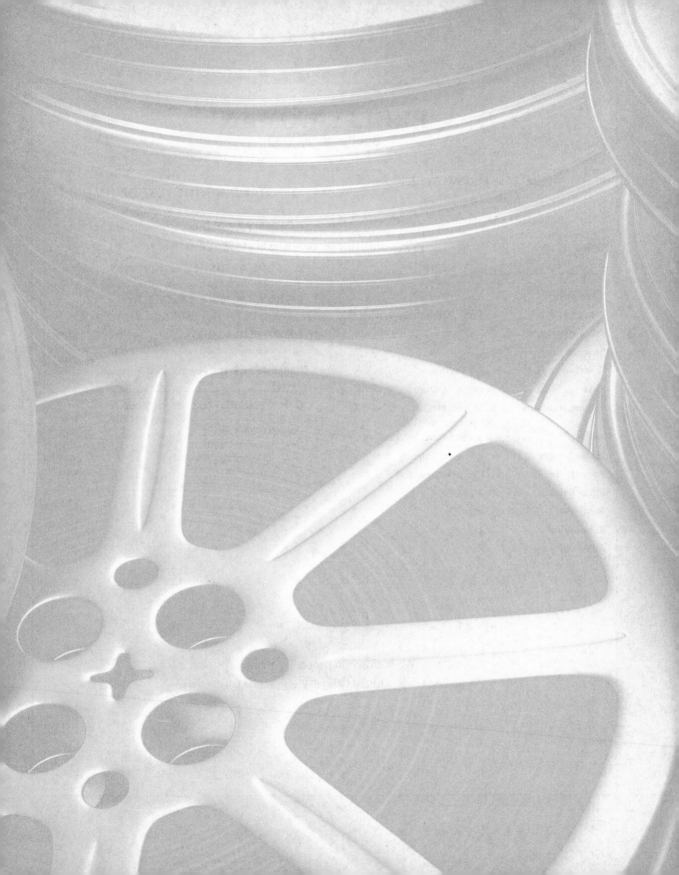

PRETTY WOMAN

Buena Vista, 1990

ALL-RELEASE EQUIVALENT 2005 $s

(Unadjusted $s) in Millions of $s

Domestic Box Office Revenues. . . . . . . **$270.4**/($178.4)
Production Cost . . . . **$34.4**/($23.0)
Principal Photography. . . . . **62** days estimated
7/24/1989–10/18/1989

Director . . . . Garry Marshall
Producer . . . . Arnon Milchan, Steven Reuther
Production Company. . . . Touchstone Pictures
Story and
  Screenplay by . . . . J. F. Lawton
Cast . . . . Richard Gere, Julia Roberts
Filming Locations . . . . . . Los Angeles, Beverly Hills, San
Francisco, CA; Walt Disney
Studios, Burbank, CA
Genre. . . . . Romantic Comedy
Format. . . . . Color (Technicolor)
Initial Release 3/23/1990
Rerelease. . . . . none
Running Time . . . . 117 minutes
MPAA Rating . . . . R

STANDING THE TEST OF TIME

ACADEMY AWARD Oscar Nominations and Wins

Actress in a Leading Role: Julia Roberts

OSCAR TOTALS   Nominations **1**   *Wins 0

AFI 100 YEARS 100 MOVIES SELECTION
2007 0   1997 0

TOP 300 FILMS POSITION . . . . **#133**
All-Release Domestic Box Office in Equivalent 2005 $s

National Film Preservation Board Selection. . . .none

OTHER AWARDS Best Picture Wins

	Year
Golden Globes	none
New York Film Critics.	none
National Board of Review.	none
Film Daily Critics	none

We both screw people for money.

—Edward Lewis (Richard Gere) to Vivian Ward (Julia Roberts)

PLOT: A modern-day Pygmalion meets *Cinderella* comedy about a successful corporate mogul in Los Angeles on business who hires a carefree prostitute to pose as his girlfriend for a week. During that time, he transforms her into a high-class lady and falls in love.

PRODUCTION: J. F. Lawton penned a dark script, originally titled "3000," about a drug-addicted prostitute hired for a week by a wealthy businessman. It borrows from the Pygmalion myth in George Bernard Shaw's play of the same name, which became the basis of the hit Broadway musical *My Fair Lady*. It also echoes the plot of Giuseppe Verdi's opera *La Traviata,* which was based on Alexandre Dumas's 1848 novel *La dame aux camélias*. Vestron Pictures bought the script and planned a low-budget ($3 million) production. A Vestron producer had seen Julia Roberts in *Mystic Pizza* and thought she'd be perfect for the lead. Roberts recalled the script as "a really dark, depressing, horrible, terrible story about two horrible people," but nevertheless was eager to prove she could carry a film. Then the project collapsed when Vestron went out of business. Producer Steve Reuther got the rights and teamed up with Regency's Arnon Milchan, and they stoked a secret bidding war between Universal and Disney's Touchstone for the rights to make it with them. Disney won but didn't want a downbeat ending for what was by then projected to be a $17 million film. Lawton rewrote the script twice to make it more of a love story, but Disney wasn't satisfied and fired him. They hired Stephen Metcalfe, who made the script even darker, then Robert Garland, and finally Barbara Benedek to rewrite the script. Meg Ryan was Disney's first choice, but she turned down the role, along with Molly Ringwald. After Julia held her own against several leading men in film tests, Roberts was cast, though Disney had doubts about whether she was a big enough box office attraction. Director Garry Marshall brought Roberts with him to New York to convince Richard Gere to do the film. Gere agreed to do it if Marshall beefed up his role. Then controversy began between Roberts and the producers over the nude scenes, which held up production for several weeks. Finally they agreed to keep the nudity discreet and filming began. The title was inspired by Roy Orbison's 1964 smash hit song "Oh, Pretty Woman," which was used on the soundtrack and became a hit all over again. The Regent Beverly Wilshire was the only hotel in L.A. that would grant Marshall permission to film its façade and re-create its lobby. He later recalled it was the only hotel that said, "Well, maybe [we've had a prostitute in here] a couple of times." Sets were built in Burbank to replicate the hotel interior and Edward's office. Roberts did research on the streets, approaching working girls on Hollywood Boulevard, who loosened up once she offered to buy them some food.

DISTRIBUTION: *Pretty Woman* was one of the most unexpected blockbusters, grossing more than $463 million worldwide and turning Roberts into one of Hollywood's most bankable actresses overnight. The iconic role would forever label her America's "pretty woman," even more than a decade later. Richard Gere hadn't had a hit since 1983's *An Officer and a Gentleman,* but this role won him national acclaim as the leading man of the nineties. —*Hayley Taylor Block*

GHOST
Paramount, 1990

ALL-RELEASE EQUIVALENT 2005 $s
(Unadjusted $s) in Millions of $s

Domestic Box Office Revenues . . . . **$329.8**/($217.6)
Production Cost . . . . **$32.9**/($22.0)
Principal Photography . . . . **97** days estimated
7/24/1989–12/5/1989

Director . . . . Jerry Zucker
Producer . . . . Lisa Weinstein
Production Company . . . . Paramount Pictures,
Howard W. Koch Production
Story and
Screenplay by . . . . Bruce Joel Rubin
Cast . . . . Patrick Swayze, Demi Moore,
Whoopi Goldberg,
Tony Goldwyn
Filming Locations . . . . Manhattan and Brooklyn, NY;
Paramount Studios, CA
Genre . . . . Romantic Fantasy
Format . . . . Color (Technicolor)
Initial Release 7/13/1990
Rerelease . . . . none
Running Time . . . . 127 minutes
MPAA Rating PG-13

STANDING THE TEST OF TIME

ACADEMY AWARD Oscar Nominations and Wins

Best Picture: Lisa Weinstein, Producer

*ACTRESS IN A SUPPORTING ROLE: Whoopi Goldberg

Film Editing: Walter Murch

Music (Original Score): Maurice Jarre

*WRITING (Screenplay – written directly for the screen): Bruce Joel Rubin

OSCAR TOTALS   Nominations 5   *Wins 2

AFI 100 YEARS 100 MOVIES SELECTION
2007 0   1997 0

TOP 300 FILMS POSITION . . . . #83
All-Release Domestic Box Office in Equivalent 2005 $S

National Film Preservation Board Selection . . . . none

OTHER AWARDS Best Picture Wins

	Year
Golden Globes	none
New York Film Critics	none
National Board of Review	none
Film Daily Critics	none

An impressive supernatural romantic drama in the vein of 1947's The Ghost and Mrs. Muir, Ghost *is a genre-bending blockbuster that turns mawkish sentiment into real emotional involvement through the skilled direction of Jerry Zucker.*
—Channel Four Film

PLOT: A romantic and haunting love story in which the ghost of a murdered Manhattan banker enlists a phony psychic to help serve justice for his death and save his girlfriend's life.

PRODUCTION: Inspired by a production of *Hamlet,* screenwriter Bruce Joel Rubin decided to "tell a story from the side of the ghost." Rubin's own journey took him from New York University, where he majored in motion picture production, to parts of Europe and South Asia, where he embarked on a spiritual quest that included time on the Greek isle of Paros and in a Tibetan Buddhist monastery in Nepal. In addition to exploring spirituality, he loved the idea of writing about a man avenging his own death. The two came together for him in this work. However, Rubin couldn't sell his idea. *Ghost* became one of the top 10 best unproduced scripts in Hollywood. Frustrated, he showed what he had written to friends, who suggested that it would be funny if the psychic was a fake. When Rubin rewrote and repitched the script, five producers were interested. He recalls that "Lisa Weinstein started crying when I told her the story, so I picked her. We took it to Paramount and Dawn Steele bought it." Producer Lindsay Duran suggested that Jerry Zucker direct. While Zucker was best known for his comedy *Airplane!* Duran knew that he was looking to direct a drama next. Rubin was unhappy because he thought Zucker wouldn't take the project seriously, but after the two had a great dinner meeting, he agreed. Rubin said, "I wrote nineteen drafts for Zucker, and somewhere around the tenth draft, the film began to turn into something I didn't care for. Yet I knew if I jumped ship, his version of the film would be made . . . So, I stayed aboard. . . . Interestingly enough, we began writing back down to where I had started and it was actually a better story because Zucker was now deeply invested in it." Rubin has said that the famed line "Ditto" came from his own life. He used to say it to his ex-girlfriend because he couldn't say he loved her. He had seen an interview of Patrick Swayze by Barbara Walters in which the actor had teared up while recalling memories of his late father, and Rubin thought he would be perfect to play the part of Sam Wheat. Zucker didn't see Swayze in the role but agreed he could audition (after fifteen other stars had turned down the part). When Swayze's six-scene reading left Zucker, Rubin, and Weinstein in tears, he was offered the job on the spot. Had Swayze not been right for the role, Zucker would have folded the project, as so many of his choices had turned down the part and he really wanted his first serious film to be great. Tony Goldwyn was cast from his audition tape after being recommended by his wife, who designed the set. Tina Turner auditioned for the role of Oda Mae Brown, but Whoopi Goldberg's comedic brilliance and chemistry with Swayze won her the part. Zucker (as he does in all his films) cast his entire family in the movie; he also allowed Rubin's mother to have a role, playing the part of the nun who gets the check for $4 million from Oda Mae Brown. The sounds made by the "shadow demons" are really the sounds of babies crying, played at extremely slow speed.

DISTRIBUTION: *Ghost* materialized as the summer of 1990's runaway hit. It was number two at the domestic box office behind *Home Alone* and, with foreign revenues outpacing domestic, number one at the worldwide box office for that year. Despite mixed reviews, it surpassed its blockbuster competitors, including *Total Recall* (with a cost of $80 million) and the money-losing *Bonfire of the Vanities* (with a cost of $47 million), among others. —*Hayley Taylor Block*

HOME ALONE
20th Century-Fox, 1990

ALL-RELEASE EQUIVALENT 2005 $s
(Unadjusted $s) in Millions of $s

Domestic Box Office Revenues . . . . **$434.0**/($285.8)
Production Cost . . . .**$26.9**/($18.0)
Principal Photography . . . . **66** days estimated
2/14/1990–5/16/1990

Director . . . . Chris Columbus

Producer . . . . John Hughes

Production Company . . . . Hughes Entertainment,
Twentieth Century-Fox

Story and
   Screenplay by . . . . John Hughes

Cast . . . . Macaulay Culkin, Joe Pesci,
Daniel Stern, Catherine O'Hara,
John Heard, Roberts Blossom,
John Candy

Filming Locations . . . . Chicago, IL

Genre . . . . Comedy

Format . . . . Color (DeLuxe)

Initial Release 11/16/1990

Rerelease . . . . none

Running Time . . . . 102 minutes

MPAA Rating PG-13

STANDING THE TEST OF TIME

ACADEMY AWARD Oscar Nominations and Wins

Music (Original Score): John Williams

Music (Original Song): "Somewhere in My Memory,"
Music by John Williams; Lyrics by Leslie Bricusse

OSCAR TOTALS   Nominations 2   *Wins 0

AFI 100 YEARS 100 MOVIES SELECTION
2007 0   1997 0

TOP 300 FILMS POSITION . . . . #36
All-Release Domestic Box Office in Equivalent 2005 $s

National Film Preservation Board Selection . . . . none

OTHER AWARDS Best Picture Wins

	Year
Golden Globes	none
New York Film Critics	none
National Board of Review	none
Film Daily Critics	none

I was mostly inspired by old David Lean films, particularly Oliver Twist *and*
Great Expectations, *both told from a child's perspective. No one has shown the terror of being
a child in an adult world better than Lean.*

—Chris Columbus

PLOT: As the McCallister family rushes off to Paris for Christmas, eight-year-old Kevin gets left home alone. Realizing crooks are about to rob his house, he cooks up a complicated scheme to thwart the bumbling burglars.

PRODUCTION: After his hit 1989 comedy *Uncle Buck,* director-writer John Hughes was encouraged to develop a new script with mass appeal to children and parents around the world. Hughes wrote the role of Kevin for Macaulay Culkin, having worked with him in *Uncle Buck.* However, director Chris Columbus auditioned hundreds of boys before agreeing on Culkin. As a huge fan of Joe Pesci from his roles in *Raging Bull* and *Goodfellas,* Columbus sought Pesci to play Harry. He was actually shocked when Pesci accepted. Originally, another actor was slated for Daniel Stern's role, but his asking salary was too high. Stern says he can't imagine not having played Marv. John Williams came onboard as musical director. With the principal cast and crew in place, Warner Bros. thought that the $18 million budget submitted by Hughes was still too high and demanded a $2 million reduction. Instead, Hughes took his project to 20th Century-Fox, where it was acquired by studio head Joe Roth. Approximately 10 percent of the budget went for sets in Chicago, which were used along with numerous Chicago-area landmarks. Production designer John Juto converted three gymnasiums to soundstages: a three-story Georgian house with a $50,000 kitchen and five upstairs bedrooms, a cluttered basement, and the first-class cabin of a 747. A school swimming pool hosted the flooded basement scene. A major set was created at O'Hare Airport's American Airlines Terminal 3. O'Hare also masqueraded as Paris's Orly Airport. Chris Columbus directed this Three Stooges–inspired film to be seen through a child's point of view. He added the character of Marley to provide a more emotional side. Columbus sought to make the film timeless and gave a sense of warmth and style to all elements, from wardrobe to cinematography. For Joe Pesci, the "family" material was a bit of a stretch from what he had previously done. The biggest problem was that his character's on-screen outbursts inevitably included the *F*-word. Columbus advised him to say the word *fridge* instead of "what came naturally." To compound matters, neither Pesci nor John Heard was pleased to be playing second fiddle to a nine-year-old boy. Both actors gave Columbus a difficult time about their place in the picture. In one of the scenes, where Marv and Harry hang Kevin up on a door hook, Harry threatens to bite off all of Kevin's fingers. As it happened, Pesci bit a little too hard, and to this day Culkin still has the "battle scar." Most of the film was shot in the Chicago suburbs of Winnetka and Wilmette, Illinois. Any other shots, such as those of Paris, are either stock footage or faked. John Candy's delightful supporting appearance was shot in one twenty-three-hour day.

DISTRIBUTION: The movie opened in 1,202 theaters and was the number one domestic box office film of 1990. It stayed in theaters well past the Christmas season and was in the number one spot at the box office from the weekend of November 16–18 through the weekend of February 1–3, 1991. It would remain a top 10 draw at the box office past Easter. —*Christine McDermott*

DANCES WITH WOLVES
Orion (domestic); Majestic Films International (Foreign), 1990

ALL-RELEASE EQUIVALENT 2005 $s
(Unadjusted $s) in Millions of $s

Domestic Box Office Revenues . . . . **$279.6**/($184.2)
Production Cost . . . . **$28.4**/($19.0)
Principal Photography . . . . **90** days estimated
7/17/1989–11/21/1989

Director . . . . Kevin Costner
Producer . . . . Jim Wilson, Kevin Costner
Production Company . . . . Tig Production
Story by . . . . Based on the novel by Michael Blake
Screenplay by . . . . Michael Blake
Cast . . . . Kevin Costner, Mary McDonnell, Graham Greene, Rodney A. Grant
Filming Locations . . . . Badlands National Park, Interior, Belle Fourche River, Black Hills, Fort Pierre, Rapid City, Pierre, Sage Creek Wilderness Area, Spearfish Canyon, and Triple U Standing Butte Ranch, SD; Jackson and Jackson Hole, WY; Fort Hays, KS
Genre . . . . Western
Format . . . . Color (DeLuxe)
Initial Release 11/21/1990
Rerelease . . . . none
Running Time . . . . 183 minutes
MPAA Rating PG-13

STANDING THE TEST OF TIME

ACADEMY AWARD Oscar Nominations and Wins

*****BEST PICTURE:** Jim Wilson and Kevin Costner, Producers

Actor in a Leading Role: Kevin Costner

Actor in a Supporting Role: Graham Greene

Actress in a Supporting Role: Mary McDonnell

Art Direction/Set Decoration: Jeffrey Beecroft/ Lisa Dean

*****CINEMATOGRAPHY:** Dean Semler

Costume Design: Elsa Zamparelli

*****DIRECTING:** Kevin Costner

*****FILM EDITING:** Neil Travi

*****MUSIC** (Original Score): John Barry

*****SOUND:** Jeffrey Perkins, Bill W. Benton, Greg Watkins, Russell Williams II

*****WRITING** (Screenplay – based on material from another medium): Michael Blake

OSCAR TOTALS   Nominations **12**   *Wins 7

AFI 100 YEARS 100 MOVIES SELECTION
2007 0   1997 . . . #75

TOP 300 FILMS POSITION . . . . #123
All-Release Domestic Box Office in Equivalent 2005 $s

National Film Preservation Board Selection 2007

OTHER AWARDS Best Picture Wins

	Year
Golden Globes (Drama)	1991
New York Film Critics	none
National Board of Review	1990
Film Daily Critics	none

This is a bonding film for all. You could put it anywhere in history—the Berlin Wall, Kuwait.
—Kevin Costner

PLOT: A Civil War hero, sent to a remote frontier outpost, becomes friendly with the local Native Americans, only to find himself trapped between two worlds.

PRODUCTION: In the early 1980s, Michael Blake wrote the script *Dances with Wolves* as a revisionist take on Indian-white relations. His Sioux characters were "noble savages" whose natural goodness was shown as superior to "civilized" white culture. There was little interest in the script when Kevin Costner received it in 1986. Costner urged Blake to turn the story into a novel. Pointing out that he had a slush pile of scripts being sent to him, he argued the story would have a greater chance of selling as a book. Blake wrote the novel, only to find it difficult to publish. The book was rejected several times before finally finding a publisher in 1988. Once this sale was made, Costner quickly acquired the film rights. Now a major star, Costner planned to produce and direct the film. After a brief plan to cast Viggo Mortensen as the title character, Costner realized that he would have to star in order to raise the necessary financing and for the film to have a chance at the box office. The rest of the cast was largely unknown, including Mary McDonnell, a recent Oscar nominee but hardly a big star, and several Native American actors. By the time Costner began shooting on the hills and plains of South Dakota, many in Hollywood viewed the project as troubled. Industry insiders laughed about "Kevin's Gate," a film that seemed destined to lose a fortune. Indeed, the film went way over budget. Costner made up the overages personally, giving him a financial stake in the film as great as his artistic one. In his determination to make the film as accurate as possible, Costner and his co-producers used extensive Lakota dialogue. The lines (25 percent of the script's dialogue) were simplified, using only feminine forms of speech. Although Costner would be saluted by Native American groups for his portrayal of the Sioux, many Lakota native speakers were amused to hear men in the film speak as though they were women. The film was shot entirely in sequence with the exception of the Civil War episode, which was shot last because the cornfield had to be grown for the production. The buffalo stampede also presented challenges for the crew because it could be shot for only ten minutes a day (the rest of the day was spent rounding up the herd). Despite all the overages, the film was completed without major incident.

DISTRIBUTION: The film was released on a platform schedule, growing from a handful of theaters to more than 1,600 screens in four months. The strategy was wildly successful and the film enjoyed strong word of mouth. By the Oscar ceremony, it was considered a foregone conclusion that *Dances with Wolves* would win multiple statuettes. Costner's belief in his project paid off financially as well. His practice of personally covering budget overages in exchange for greater participation allowed him to earn more than $40 million from the movie. The film's score, by John Barry, became quite popular. Barry also gained a famous fan: Pope John Paul II listed it as one of his favorite pieces of music. —*Louis Burklow*

ROBIN HOOD: PRINCE OF THIEVES

Warner Bros., 1991

ALL-RELEASE EQUIVALENT 2005 $s

(Unadjusted $s) in Millions of $s

Domestic Box Office Revenues . . . . **$252.0**/($165.5)
Production Cost . . . . **$81.7**/($57.0)
Principal Photography . . . . **77** days estimated
9/6/1990–12/22/1990

Director . . . . Kevin Reynolds
Producer . . . . John Watson, Pen Densham, Richard B. Lewis
Production Company . . . . Morgan Creek Productions, Warner Bros. Pictures
Story by . . . . Pen Densham
Screenplay by . . . . Pen Densham and John Watson
Cast . . . . Kevin Costner, Morgan Freeman, Mary Elizabeth Mastrantonio, Christian Slater, Alan Rickman
Filming Locations . . . . England locations: Northumberland, North Yorkshire, Hampshire, Buckinghamshire, Wiltshire, and East Sussex; France locations: Calvados, Aude, Moselle; Shepperton Studios, England
Genre . . . . Action Adventure
Format . . . . Color (Technicolor)
Initial Release 6/14/1991
Rerelease . . . . none
Running Time . . . . 138 minutes
MPAA Rating PG-13

STANDING THE TEST OF TIME

ACADEMY AWARD Oscar Nominations and Wins

Music (Original Song): "(Everything I Do) I Do It for You," Music by Michael Kamen; Lyrics by Bryan Adams and Robert John Lange

OSCAR TOTALS Nominations **1** *Wins 0

AFI 100 YEARS 100 MOVIES SELECTION
2007 0   1997 0

TOP 300 FILMS POSITION . . . . #157
All-Release Domestic Box Office in Equivalent 2005 $s

National Film Preservation Board Selection . . . . none

OTHER AWARDS Best Picture Wins

	Year
Golden Globes	none
New York Film Critics	none
National Board of Review	none
Film Daily Critics	none

Sometimes you just reach a point when you say, "I'm not going to go along any more. I think I've compromised enough."

—Kevin Reynolds on his struggles with the studio

PLOT: Robin of Locksley, returning to England from the Crusades, finds his castle destroyed and his father murdered by the villainous Sheriff of Nottingham. He leads a band of exiled outlaws against the sheriff while wooing the beautiful Maid Marian.

PRODUCTION: *Robin Hood* stories had been told on the silver screen for almost a century before writer Pen Densham decided to revive the genre in 1989. His outline, which he described as "Robin Hood à la *Raiders*," reimagined Robin Hood as a privileged fop redeemed by the horrors of the Crusades. Morgan Creek Productions snapped up the script for $1.2 million in 1990 and scrambled to line up a crew in order to beat out two other *Robin Hood* productions. Kevin Reynolds, who had given star Kevin Costner his first break in *Fandango,* was hired to direct, but confessed, "I'd done two pictures that hadn't made a dime, so I kind of knew they wanted me because of my connections with Kevin." Costner, riding high from *Dances with Wolves,* had turned down the part of Robin Hood once before, but reconsidered this time largely due to the involvement of his friend Reynolds. With deadlines looming, the stars moved double-time. Costner, Freeman, and Slater were given only a single script read-through. Alan Rickman (the Sheriff of Nottingham) and Mary Elizabeth Mastrantonio (Maid Marian) didn't sign on until just prior to the start of shooting—with Mastrantonio a sudden replacement to cover a pregnant Robin Wright Penn. Budgeted at an estimated $48 million, *Robin Hood: Prince of Thieves* was filmed on location in England and France, as well as at Shepperton Studios in Middlesex, England. Production designer John Graysmark aimed for a more "rugged, brutal look" than seen in previous versions of the story. Sean Connery was hired to appear in an uncredited cameo as Richard the Lionhearted. Shooting ran behind schedule, with complications from overhead jets roaring above the Sherwood Forest location on their way to London's Heathrow Airport, just ten miles away. Further trouble surfaced when test-screening audiences greatly preferred Rickman's sheriff to Costner's Robin Hood. Nervous producers demanded a recut that would boost Costner's screen time. Reynolds strenuously disagreed and was locked out of the subsequent edit. After viewing the new version and deeming it unsatisfactory, Reynolds walked off the film and abandoned the final cut. "You always start with a picture in your mind, and it is a compromise all the way from there," said Reynolds. The ordeal strained the friendship between Costner and Reynolds, since the latter felt the actor could have used his star clout to convince the producers to back off.

DISTRIBUTION: Released on June 14, 1991, *Robin Hood: Prince of Thieves* opened to mixed critical reviews but strong box office. Critics singled out Rickman's scene-chewing role as the Sheriff of Nottingham but chided Costner's on-again, off-again English accent. "He plays Robin as if the character were a movie star being gracious to his fans," said Vincent Canby of the *New York Times*. Ultimately, the film hauled in $390.5 million in worldwide box office. The movie was second in the 1991 domestic box office rankings behind *Terminator 2: Judgment Day*. Bryan Adams's ballad "(Everything I Do) I Do It for You" on the soundtrack and on his "Waking Up the Neighbors" album became a smash number one hit for about four months in the United States, the United Kingdom, and elsewhere. —*Daniel Wallace*

TERMINATOR 2: JUDGMENT DAY

TriStar, 1991

ALL-RELEASE EQUIVALENT 2005 $s

(Unadjusted $s) in Millions of $s

Domestic Box Office Revenues........**$311.9**/($204.8)
Production Cost ....**$146.3**/($102.0)
Principal Photography...........**120** days estimated
10/9/1990–3/28/1991

Director . . . . James Cameron

Producer . . . . James Cameron

Production Company . . . . Carolco Pictures, Inc.,
Lightstorm Entertainment,
Pacific Western

Story by. . . . . James Cameron

Screenplay by . . . . James Cameron,
William Wisher

Cast . . . . Arnold Schwarzenegger, Linda
Hamilton, Edward Furlong,
Robert Patrick

Filming Locations . . . . . . Fontana, Fremont, Lancaster,
Long Beach, San Jose, and
Los Angeles, CA

Genre. . . . . Sci-Fi, Action Adventure

Format. . . . . Color (CFI)

Initial Release 7/3/1991

Rerelease. . . . . none

Running Time . . . . 136 minutes

MPAA Rating . . . . R

STANDING THE TEST OF TIME

ACADEMY AWARD Oscar Nominations and Wins

Cinematography: Adam Greenberg

Film Editing: Conrad Buff, Mark Goldblatt,
Richard A. Harris

*MAKEUP: Stan Winston, Jeff Dawn

*SOUND: Tom Johnson, Gary Rydstrom, Gary
Summers, Lee Orloff

*SOUND EFFECTS EDITING: Gary Rydstrom,
Gloria S. Borders

*VISUAL EFFECTS: Dennis Muren, Stan Winston,
Gene Warren Jr., Robert Skotak

OSCAR TOTALS   Nominations **6**   *Wins **4**

AFI 100 YEARS 100 MOVIES SELECTION

2007 0   1997 0

TOP 300 FILMS POSITION . . . .#98

All-Release Domestic Box Office in Equivalent 2005 $s

National Film Preservation Board Selection. . . . none

OTHER AWARDS Best Picture Wins

	Year
Golden Globes	none
New York Film Critics	none
National Board of Review	none
Film Daily Critics	none

*There are things we are doing on this film that are extremely difficult,
from a filmmaking point of view, but I'm not steering away from them.
If it takes doing difficult things to make this movie, then we'll do difficult things.*

—James Cameron

PLOT: A shape-shifting cyborg is sent back into time to kill the future leader of the human resistance, but a reprogrammed terminator arrives to defend him.

PRODUCTION: *The Terminator* was one of Hollywood's most surprising successes of 1984. The small-budget sci-fi thriller gave writer-director James Cameron the clout to get movies green-lighted. But, Cameron didn't want to immediately use his newfound power for a sequel, saying that "Arnold [Schwarzenegger] always seemed more enthusiastic for a sequel than I was." After taking time to direct *Aliens* and *The Abyss*, he ultimately conceived of a sequel that would explore "a violent plea for peace." Schwarzenegger signed on immediately. A personal appeal from Cameron persuaded Linda Hamilton to reject another movie role and return to play Sarah Connor. With his stars back on board, Cameron and co-writer William Wisher wrote the first draft of the screenplay in just four weeks. The extensive special effects required were also prepped in whirlwind style by Industrial Light & Magic during preproduction. The story picks up thirteen years after the original. Cameron intended for the movie to have emotional resonance with viewers. In the sequel, the reprogrammed Terminator, Sarah, and John all bond as a unique nuclear family, something that the director believed was more vital in achieving a connection with viewers this time around than even the action was. Still, he maintained the fast-paced storytelling style that he had perfected in his earlier films. Despite his mantra "I'm not doing anything to get in the way of telling the story," Cameron never got in the way of the action either. He maintained such rigid control over his film that he earned the nickname "Iron Jim." While he believed that the emotional moments would form the bedrock of his story, he also knew that the film would stand or fall based on its special effects. This created a real challenge, as the swift pace of preproduction left little time for preparing FX. Cameron has said, "It was nobody's fault. There just wasn't enough time to design many things." Fortunately, he could rely on Stan Winston and Dennis Muren. A noted special effects man, Winston had a passion for creating artificial characters that still relied on solid stories and powerful acting. As a pioneer in computer animation, Muren was instrumental in creating the "liquid metal" aspect of the villainous T-1000. The revolutionary "morphing" technique, created by Muren, to depict one character changing into another combined with Winston's lifelike creations helped make Cameron's story become vividly alive, blurring the distinction between human actors and FX. The two special effects masters did not work alone. ILM employed thirty-five technicians, who produced five minutes of screen time at a total cost of $6.4 million. Their contribution to the film validated Cameron's belief that computer FX had reached maturity in terms of cost, time, and effort, as the film was completed on time and on budget.

DISTRIBUTION: The movie enjoyed a wide opening in one of the most lucrative times on the release calendar, the Independence Day holiday. It was number one at the 1991 worldwide box office with $519.8 million—$129.3 million more than second-place *Robin Hood*. ILM competed against itself for the best Visual Effects Oscar, obtaining nominations that same year for *Hook, Star Trek VI,* and *The Rocketeer* before winning for *Terminator 2*. —Louis Burklow

BEAUTY AND THE BEAST

Buena Vista, 1991

ALL-RELEASE EQUIVALENT 2005 $s

(Unadjusted $s) in Millions of $s

Domestic Box Office Revenues	**$251.1**/($171.4)
Production Cost	**$40.1**/($28.0)
Production Period	3½ years

Director	Gary Trousdale, Kirk Wise
Producer	Don Hahn
Production Company	Walt Disney Pictures, Silver Screen Partners IV
Story by	Based on the classic French fairy tale by Madame Le Prince de Beaumont
Screenplay by	Linda Woolverton
Cast	Paige O'Hara, Robby Benson, Richard White, Jerry Orbach, David Ogden Stiers, Angela Lansbury (voices)
Filming Locations	Disney Animation Studios, California and Florida
Genre	Animation
Format	Color (Technicolor)
Initial Release	11/15/1991
Rerelease	2002
Running Time	85 minutes
MPAA Rating	G

STANDING THE TEST OF TIME

ACADEMY AWARD Oscar Nominations and Wins

Best Picture: Don Hahn, Producer

*MUSIC (Original Score): Alan Menken

Music (Original Song): "Be Our Guest," Music by Alan Menken; Lyrics by Howard Ashman

*MUSIC (Original Song): "Beauty and the Beast," Music by Alan Menken; Lyrics by Howard Ashman

Music (Original Song): "Belle," Music by Alan Menken; Lyrics by Howard Ashman

Sound: Terry Porter, Mel Metcalfe, David J. Hudson, Doc Kane

OSCAR TOTALS   Nominations **6**   *Wins **2**

AFI 100 YEARS 100 MOVIES SELECTION

2007 0   1997 0

TOP 300 FILMS POSITION . . . . #162

All-Release Domestic Box Office in Equivalent 2005 $s

National Film Preservation Board Selection 2002

OTHER AWARDS Best Picture Wins

	Year
Golden Globes (Musical)	1992
New York Film Critics	none
National Board of Review	none
Film Daily Critics	none

It's kind of intimidating. You know whatever you come up with will be the definitive Beast. When Disney does a fairy tale, it's, like, forever.

—Beast supervising animator Glen Keane

PLOT: A musical retelling of the French fairy tale in which a beautiful young girl befriends and eventually falls in love with a once-heartless prince who has been transformed into a hideous beast by a witch.

PRODUCTION: Walt Disney had explored the possibility of animating *Beauty and the Beast* as far back as the 1930s, and again in the 1950s, but always reached an impasse: Belle imprisoned in the beast's castle for the entire second half of the story made it too claustrophobic. Then in 1987, a script was written that seemed to conquer the problem, and British animators Richard Purdum and his wife, Jill, were hired to develop and direct the project. In mid-1989 a small cadre of artists and animators flew to London for a ten-week period of development and preproduction, with a field trip to the Loire Valley in France and the beautiful provincial countryside. Art director Brian McEntee also studied French romantic painters such as Fragonard and Boucher for inspiration. The London session produced a well-crafted, serious drama with no music and very little humor, which concerned Disney execs. With *The Little Mermaid* showing strong legs, its songwriters, Howard Ashman and Alan Menken, got the call in December 1989 to write the songs. The Purdums objected, wanting "to do something that was not in the Disney mold." Disney responded by saying *au revoir* to the couple. When work began on the film it became Walt Disney Pictures' thirtieth full-length animated feature and its fifth movie to be based on a classic fairy tale, after *Snow White and the Seven Dwarfs, Cinderella, Sleeping Beauty,* and *The Little Mermaid*. Nearly 600 animators, artists, and technicians produced over a million drawings and 226,000 individually painted cels. Glen Keane, supervising animator for the Beast, visited the L.A. Zoo several times, and studied National Geographic videos, to create his character. The beast became a hybrid with the mane of a lion, the beard and head structure of a bison, the tusks and nose of a wild boar, the heavily muscled brow of a gorilla, the legs and tail of a wolf, and the bulky body of a bear. Robby Benson beat out Tim Curry to become the voice of Beast. Julie Andrews was considered for Mrs. Potts, but Angela Lansbury was hired for the role. David Ogden Stiers became Cogsworth after Patrick Stewart had to turn it down due to scheduling conflicts. CGI is used in several parts of the film, most notably in the three-dimensional ballroom dance sequence. It was the first computer-generated color background to be both animated and fully dimensional, giving the advantage of sweeping camera moves and perspectives, as well as theatrical lighting that would otherwise be impossible to achieve. The ballroom data were modeled using software by Alias Research, Inc., camera motion using Wavefront's Preview, and rendered with Pixar's Renderman software.

DISTRIBUTION: *Beauty and the Beast* is the only animated film ever to be nominated for the Best Picture Academy Award. (A Best Animated Feature Film category was used for animated features that followed *Beauty*'s release.) It is twelfth on the list of the top 20 animated films released through 2005 (in equivalent 2005 dollars). It also became Disney's first Broadway musical based on one of its own films, which ran an impressive 5,464 performances between 1994 and 2007. Disney released the direct-to-video anthology sequels *The Enchanted Christmas* (1997) and *Belle's Magical World* (1998). —*Bob Canning*

BATMAN RETURNS
Warner Bros., 1992

ALL-RELEASE EQUIVALENT 2005 $s

(Unadjusted $s) in Millions of $s

Domestic Box Office Revenues........**$251.5**/($162.8)
Production Cost ....**$111.4**/($80.0)
Principal Photography...........**100** days estimated
9/3/1991–2/20/1992

Director	Tim Burton
Producer	Denise Di Novi, Tim Burton
Production Company	Polygram Filmed Entertainment, Warner Bros. Pictures
Story by	Daniel Waters, Sam Hamm, based on characters created by Bob Kane and published by DC Comics
Screenplay by	Daniel Waters
Cast	Michael Keaton, Danny DeVito, Michelle Pfeiffer, Christopher Walken
Filming Locations	Pinewood Studios, Buckinghamshire; Universal Studios, Universal City, CA; Warner Bros. Studios, Burbank, CA
Genre	Action Adventure
Format	Color (Technicolor)
Initial Release	6/19/1992
Rerelease	none
Running Time	126 minutes
MPAA Rating	PG-13

STANDING THE TEST OF TIME

ACADEMY AWARD Oscar Nominations and Wins

Makeup: Ve Neill, Ronnie Specter, Stan Winston

Visual Effects: Michael Fink, Craig Barron, John Bruno, Dennis Skotak

OSCAR TOTALS   Nominations **2**   *Wins **0**

AFI 100 YEARS 100 MOVIES SELECTION
2007 0   1997 0

TOP 300 FILMS POSITION . . . . **#161**
All-Release Domestic Box Office in Equivalent 2005 $s

National Film Preservation Board Selection . . . . none

OTHER AWARDS Best Picture Wins

	Year
Golden Globes	none
New York Film Critics	none
National Board of Review	none
Film Daily Critics	none

For better or worse, I had more of an effect on this one.

—Tim Burton on his controversial reinterpretation of the franchise

PLOT: Batman is back for a sequel, this time wrestling with his feelings about the amorous Catwoman and thwarting the Penguin's plot to be elected mayor of Gotham City.

PRODUCTION: Impressed by the success of the first film, Warner Bros. largely gave Burton free rein on the sequel. "If I was going to do it, I had to do what I do," said Burton, who set about making a quirkier, gloomier, more gothic film. "What I had to offer was to make it feel fresh." Sam Hamm returned to write the script, but its plot was deemed unsatisfying by Burton, who commissioned a new version from Daniel Waters (*Heathers*), then brought in Wesley Strick for uncredited tweaks two months before the start of filming. All told, *Batman Returns* underwent eight script revisions, but Burton's focus on the characters left him with little interest in the story line ("Haven't you heard?" he joked to the press. "There is no plot"). Michael Keaton returned as Batman after a salary increase. Michelle Pfeiffer took the role of Catwoman, replacing Annette Bening, who bowed out due to pregnancy. Danny DeVito portrayed the sewer-dwelling Penguin ("I don't think there's anybody better at making the horrible acceptable," said Burton), and Christopher Walken signed on to portray corporate kingpin Max Schreck. None of the sets from the first film was reused. The majority of the production moved from London to Los Angeles, and the death of Batman designer Anton Furst necessitated a new look and feel courtesy of Bo Welch (*Edward Scissorhands*). Welch interpreted Gotham as a blend of "fascist art and architecture with World's Fair architecture, plus over-scaled decay." The redesigned city hinted at the extent to which Burton intended to reimagine the series, and the director flat-out stated that "*Batman Returns* is not a sequel to *Batman*." The Penguin's lair proved too big to be contained on the Warner soundstages, so Welch took over the fifty-foot-high Universal soundstage and refrigerated it to 35° as exterior temperatures topped 100°. Danny DeVito's heavy silicone makeup weighed twenty pounds and took two hours to apply, while Michelle Pfeiffer went through more than sixty Catwoman suits. The Penguin's flock of followers consisted of thirty penguin animatronics, four penguin suits worn by little people, a number of actual animals, and countless CGI penguin doubles.

DISTRIBUTION: Despite a mixed reception from critics, *Batman Returns* opened big, taking in $96.7 million in its first ten days. However, it quickly lost steam, dropping by 47 percent in its second weekend and setting off alarm bells among Warner executives. "It's too dark. It's not a lot of fun," an anonymous exec griped to *Entertainment Weekly* shortly after the release. The freak-show nature of the movie's characters made it unique among superhero films and a personal statement for Burton, but *Batman Returns* was viewed by some as inappropriate for children (the movie was promoted with McDonald's Happy Meals), and merchandise sales dipped. Theater operators also felt the pinch, having surrendered an estimated 65 percent of their take to Warner Bros. in exchange for what they had gambled would be a larger pie. Despite the controversy, *Batman Returns* was number three at the domestic box office in 1992 (behind *Aladdin* and *Home Alone 2*). Out of the five *Batman* movies released through 2005, *Batman Returns* would place third in worldwide box office (in equivalent 2005 dollars). —*Daniel Wallace*

UNFORGIVEN
Warner Bros., 1992

ALL-RELEASE EQUIVALENT 2005 $s
(Unadjusted $s) in Millions of $s

Domestic Box Office Revenues........ **$156.2**/($101.2)
Production Cost .... **$48.7**/($35.0)
Principal Photography............**57** days estimated
8/26/1991–11/12/1991

Director.............. Clint Eastwood

Producer .... Clint Eastwood

Production Company.... Malpaso Productions, Warner Bros. Pictures

Story and
 Screenplay by........ David Webb Peoples

Cast .... Clint Eastwood, Gene Hackman, Morgan Freeman, Richard Harris

Filming Locations ...... On location in Alberta, Canada, and Sonora, CA

Genre................. Western

Format............... Color (Technicolor)

Initial Release 8/7/1992

Rerelease .... none

Running Time .... 130 minutes

MPAA Rating .... R

STANDING THE TEST OF TIME

ACADEMY AWARD Oscar Nominations and Wins

*BEST PICTURE: Clint Eastwood, Producer

Actor in a Leading Role: Clint Eastwood

*ACTOR IN A SUPPORTING ROLE: Gene Hackman

Art Direction/Set Decoration: Henry Bumstead/Janice Blackie-Goodine

Cinematography: Jack N. Green

*DIRECTING: Clint Eastwood

*FILM EDITING: Joel Cox

Sound: Les Fresholtz, Vern Poore, Dick Alexander, Rob Young

Writing (Screenplay – written directly for the screen): David Webb Peoples

OSCAR TOTALS   Nominations **9**   *Wins **4**

AFI 100 YEARS 100 MOVIES SELECTION
2007 . . . #68   1997 . . . #98

TOP 300 FILMS POSITION ....none
All-Release Domestic Box Office in Equivalent 2005 $s

National Film Preservation Board Selection. . . . 2004

OTHER AWARDS Best Picture Wins

	Year
Golden Globes	none
New York Film Critics.....................	none
National Board of Review..................	none
Film Daily Critics.........................	none

I put it away, like a little tiny gem that you put on the shelf and go look at it and polish it and think, "Age is good for the character, so I'll mature a little bit."

—Clint Eastwood

PLOT: In 1880s Wyoming, an aging, widowed gunfighter who has tried to put his violent past behind him reluctantly accepts one last bounty-hunting job: to avenge a brutalized prostitute by killing once more.

PRODUCTION: David Webb Peoples completed a screenplay titled "The William Munny Killings" in 1976, but at the time several recent westerns, including *The Culpepper Cattle Co.* and *The Great Northfield Minnesota Raid,* had been box office disappointments, so the script kicked around Hollywood for years. Peoples sent it to Clint Eastwood as a sample of his work, and the director was impressed with the story's gritty evocation of the consequences of violence, etched in the face of one tormented man. But the script was owned by Francis Ford Coppola, who was trying unsuccessfully to get it off the ground. Later, Eastwood inquired about the writer's availability for another project, and learned that the rights to what was now called "The Cut-Whore Killings" had become unencumbered. He bought the script in 1983 and retained his option for nearly a decade. He envisioned playing the central character himself, but wanted to grow into the role so that both he and William Munny were of a similar age. During this long gestation period, Eastwood made one western, *Pale Rider,* but the genre as a whole was still out of favor in Hollywood when he finally decided the time was right to direct *Unforgiven.* Gene Hackman had already turned down the Peoples script when Eastwood asked him to star as the sadistic sheriff. Hackman felt he'd appeared in enough violent films, but Eastwood persuaded him to come around to his own view: not only was this story far from a tribute to violence, it would actually serve to deglorify carnage. Richard Harris's reaction was just the opposite when Eastwood called him to offer the role of the flamboyant British gunfighter. He was so delighted at the prospect of working with Clint Eastwood that he said yes immediately. The director had to insist that Harris read the script before committing. Most of *Unforgiven* was filmed in a pristine area of Canada southwest of Calgary. Eastwood deliberately chose a remote location and, from the start of shooting in August 1991, banned all modern vehicles from the set, to help provide the proper physical ambience for the actors. Other scenes were shot in the villages of Brooks, Drumheller, Stealer, and Longview, and at rodeos in Calgary and in Sonora, California. Eastwood later said that the violent saloon scene at the film's climax had particular resonance for him: while shooting it, he was keenly aware that he might be leaving the western genre forever, almost certainly as an actor. As with many of his productions, Eastwood took hands-on responsibility, even composing the main theme himself. Eastwood dedicated the movie to "Sergio and Don," a reference to Sergio Leone (*Man with No Name*) and Don Siegel (*Dirty Harry*), directors who provided him his most memorable characters.

DISTRIBUTION: *Unforgiven* was released in August, typically a down time for movie attendance. It immediately won critics, some of whom judged it Eastwood's masterpiece, and slowly built an audience. With a renewed interest in the western, aided by *Dances with Wolves* and the iconic nature of *Unforgiven*'s main character, the audience accepted this thoughtful, world-weary version of a classic Eastwood screen persona, and made *Unforgiven* an international success. —*Tom Dupree*

HOME ALONE 2: LOST IN NEW YORK
20th Century-Fox, 1992

ALL-RELEASE EQUIVALENT 2005 $s
(Unadjusted $s) in Millions of $s

Domestic Box Office Revenues....... **$268.8**/($173.6)
Production Cost .... **$34.8**/($25.0)
Principal Photography.......... **100** days estimated
12/9/1991–5/6/1992

Director .... Chris Columbus
Producer .... John Hughes
Production Company.... Hughes Entertainment, 20th Century-Fox Film Corp.
Story and
  Screenplay by .... John Hughes
Cast .... Macaulay Culkin, Joe Pesci, Daniel Stern, Catherine O'Hara, John Heard
Filming Locations ...... Chicago, New York, and Los Angeles
Genre................ Comedy
Format............... Color (Kodak)
Initial Relaease .... 11/15/1992 premiere (Los Angeles); 11/20/1992 general release
Rerelease .... none
Running Time .... 120 minutes
MPAA Rating .... PG

STANDING THE TEST OF TIME

ACADEMY AWARD Oscar Nominations and Wins

None

OSCAR TOTALS   Nominations 0   *Wins 0

AFI 100 YEARS 100 MOVIES SELECTION
2007 0   1997 0

TOP 300 FILMS POSITION .... **#136**
All-Release Domestic Box Office in Equivalent 2005 $s

National Film Preservation Board Selection....none

OTHER AWARDS Best Picture Wins

	Year
Golden Globes	none
New York Film Critics	none
National Board of Review	none
Film Daily Critics	none

I'm not sure there is anyone else in the business who can really get performances out of children the way he [Chris Columbus] can.

—Macaulay Culkin

PLOT: The McCallisters head for Miami, but Kevin gets on the wrong plane at O'Hare and ends up in New York, where hilarity ensues as he reunites with the escaped "wet bandits" from the original *Home Alone*.

PRODUCTION: As was his goal in *Home Alone*, director Chris Columbus once again sought to create a heartwarming holiday classic. In the first movie, the McCallisters' neighbor Marley brought out the emotional side of the film. In the sequel, it was the Central Park pigeon woman who provided the heartwarming Christmas element. Most of the original cast and crew returned, with a few new additions. Eddie Bracken was played by the owner of the toy store. Irish actress Brenda Fricker was chosen as the Central Park pigeon woman. Tim Curry was the smarmy hotel clerk, with Rob Schneider as a Plaza bellboy. Donald Trump had a cameo role, directing Kevin to the lobby in the Plaza Hotel. Actress Ally Sheedy appears as an airport clerk, and game show host Bob Eubanks has a cameo as a talk show host on *Ding, Dang, Dong*. For his role in this sequel, Macaulay Culkin was paid a reported $4.5 million plus a share of profits, after receiving only $100,000 on the first film. As in the first movie, there are elaborate booby traps to foil the robbers' plans. The robbers think they have outsmarted Kevin this time, but John Hughes's script puts Kevin on top with even more clever yet cartoonish violence. Some gags comically mirrored those from the original film, such as Harry once again setting his head on fire, except this time he attempts to put out the fire by sticking his head in a kerosene-filled toilet, which explodes. Marv, who was hit in the head with an iron the first time around, now gets pummeled with four bricks and a hundred-pound bag of concrete mix. *Home Alone 2* was filmed in Chicago, New York, and Los Angeles. (The scene where Kevin visits the World Trade Center was removed from U.S. TV broadcasts after 9/11; however some stations have been airing it again.) The sequel, with higher production values, ran a full two hours, whereas the original version was 102 minutes. In *Home Alone,* Kevin watches a movie called *Angels with Filthy Souls,* which was created especially for the film and pays homage to Cagney, O'Brien, and Bogart's *Angels with Dirty Faces*. In *Home Alone 2,* Kevin watches the film's sequel called *Angels with Even Filthier Souls*.

DISTRIBUTION: The film premiered in Century City, California, on November 15, 1992, then opened nationwide on November 20 in 2,222 U.S. theaters. On opening weekend it took in more than the original, despite critics who saw *Home Alone 2* as simply a remake, except with a change in venue. The film was also criticized for being gratuitously violent. Ultimately it did $359 million worldwide versus $478 million worldwide for the original, with a 40 percent higher production cost. The taglines used with this film were: "He's up past his bedtime in the city that never sleeps," "Yikes! I did it again!" and "First, he was home alone, now he's lost in New York." A real-life version of the Talkboy, the tape recorder Kevin plays with in the movie, was created by Tiger Electronics shortly after the film's release (along with its pink-and-purple counterpart, the Talkgirl). —*Christine McDermott*

A FEW GOOD MEN

Columbia, 1992

ALL-RELEASE EQUIVALENT 2005 $s

(Unadjusted $s) in Millions of $s

Domestic Box Office Revenues . . . . **$218.8**/($141.3)
Production Cost . . . . **$83.5**/($60.0)
Principal Photography . . . . **71** days estimated
10/21/1991–1/31/1992

Director . . . . Rob Reiner

Producer . . . . David Brown, Rob Reiner,
Andrew Scheinman

Production Company . . . . Castle Rock Entertainment

Story by . . . . Based on the play by
Aaron Sorkin

Screenplay by . . . . Aaron Sorkin

Cast . . . . Tom Cruise, Jack Nicholson,
Demi Moore, Kevin Bacon,
Kiefer Sutherland, Kevin Pollak

Filming Locations . . . . . . On location in California:
Culver City, Crystal Cove State
Park, Laguna Beach, San Pedro,
and Point Magu; on location in
Washington D.C.: Georgetown

Genre . . . . Crime

Format . . . . Color (Technicolor)

Initial Release 12/9/1992

Rerelease . . . . none

Running Time . . . . 138 minutes

MPAA Rating . . . . R

STANDING THE TEST OF TIME

ACADEMY AWARD Oscar Nominations and Wins

Best Picture: David Brown, Rob Reiner, and Andrew
Scheinman, Producers

Actor in a Supporting Role: Jack Nicholson

Film Editing: Robert Leighton

Sound: Kevin O'connell, Rick Kline, Bob Eber

OSCAR TOTALS Nominations **4** *Wins **0**

AFI 100 YEARS 100 MOVIES SELECTION
2007 0   1997 0

TOP 300 FILMS POSITION . . . . **#209**
All-Release Domestic Box Office in Equivalent 2005 $s

National Film Preservation Board Selection . . . . none

OTHER AWARDS Best Picture Wins

	Year
Golden Globes	none
New York Film Critics	none
National Board of Review	none
Film Daily Critics	none

*Where do you draw the line between being loyal and following orders,
and acting on your own when something is immoral or illegal. It's the same moral dilemma
the Nazis dealt with at Nuremberg, or Calley at My Lai.*

—Rob Reiner

PLOT: A military courtroom drama where the odds are stacked against two marines charged with the hazing death of a third. The defense team, led by an inexperienced navy JAG officer, ultimately prevails, bringing down the overbearing commanding officer.

PRODUCTION: Aaron Sorkin, a theater graduate from Syracuse University, already had two plays produced before *A Few Good Men* was staged on Broadway. He began as an actor and then felt his true talent was that of a playwright. His older sister, Deborah, a navy JAG officer, told him about a case that she was involved in at Guantánamo Bay, Cuba, where two marines were accused of killing another in a hazing incident. Sorkin spent a year and a half working on the script, beginning with notes on cocktail napkins while he worked as a part-time bartender. The play script went to twenty-three drafts and out-of-town tryouts before its Broadway opening. Producer-director Rob Reiner saw the play and immediately began negotiations with producer David Brown to acquire the screenplay rights, with Sorkin attached as the writer. Sorkin admitted screenwriting was a foreign form to him. William Goldman (*Butch Cassidy and the Sundance Kid, All the President's Men*) came in as a script consultant guiding Sorkin. Reiner was concerned with "plugging up some plot holes" from the play, such as the suicide of Lieutenant Colonel Markinson. Jack Nicholson was the first choice for the tough base commander, Colonel Nathan Jessup, earning about $5 million for two weeks of work. Demi Moore auditioned and got the part of Lieutenant Commander JoAnne Galloway. Tom Cruise was cast opposite Moore as Lieutenant (j.g.) Daniel Kaffee. Castle Rock was denied cooperation from the U.S. Marine Corps because of script content. The opening rifle drill sequence was then performed by the Texas A&M drill team. Shooting began on October 21, 1991, with most of the scenes coming right from the play. Lieutenant Colonel Markinson's (J. T. Walsh) suicide was more visually choreographed, as he dons full Marine Corps dress blues and then places an automatic pistol in his mouth. Reiner delayed filming a tension-filled confrontation scene between Cruise and Wolfgang Bodison, who played one of the accused, until the latter actor had sufficient time to prepare. The tension element had to mount as the defense team, led by Cruise, realizes the awesome challenge confronting them. An abandoned Los Angeles army barracks served as the interior of the Guantánamo base. Fort MacArthur, in San Pedro, now a state park, stood in for Colonel Jessup's base quarters. Crystal Cove State Park, in Laguna Beach, substituted for the base fence. Another confrontational scene between Walsh and Cruise in the latter's car proved extremely difficult, requiring four days and four nights of shooting, overcoming a plethora of production problems. The climactic testimony from Colonel Jessup required forty takes from Nicholson, with reaction angles from supporting characters.

DISTRIBUTION: The film premiered in Los Angeles on December 9, 1992, to qualify for the awards that year. It was met with largely impressive reviews, with a few critics suggesting contrivances. Under wide release the film was held as a stunning and powerful courtroom drama, echoing *The Caine Mutiny Court-Martial*. The military community was mostly silent given the film's success, aware that both play and film were based on a true incident. Worldwide distribution brought in $243 million at the box office. —*Frank McAdams*

JURASSIC PARK

Universal, 1993

ALL-RELEASE EQUIVALENT 2005 $s

(Unadjusted $s) in Millions of $s

Domestic Box Office Revenues........ **$552.9**/($357.1)
Production Cost .... **$94.6**/($70.0)
Principal Photography........... **70** days estimated
8/24/1992–11/30/1992

Director . . . . Steven Spielberg
Producer . . . . Kathlelen Kennedy
Production Company. . . . Universal Pictures, Amblin
Entertainment
Story by. . . . . Based on the novel by
Michael Crichton
Screenplay by . . . . Michael Crichton, David Koepp
Cast . . . . Sam Neill, Laura Dern,
Jeff Goldblum, Richard
Attenborough
Filming Locations . . . . . . Three weeks on Kauai, two
days in the Mojave Desert,
the rest on sound stages at
Universal and Warner Bros.
Genre. . . . . Sci-Fi
Format. . . . . Color (DeLuxe)
Initial Release 6/11/1993
Rerelease. . . . . none
Running Time . . . . 126 minutes
MPAA Rating PG-13

STANDING THE TEST OF TIME

ACADEMY AWARD Oscar Nominations and Wins

***SOUND:** Gary Summers, Gary Rydstrom, Shawn
Murphy, Ron Judkins

***SOUND EFFECTS EDITING:** Gary Rydstrom,
Richard Hymns

***VISUAL EFFECTS:** Dennis Muren, Stan Winston,
Phil Tippett, Michael Lantieri

OSCAR TOTALS   Nominations **3**   *Wins **3**

AFI 100 YEARS 100 MOVIES SELECTION
2007 0   1997 0

TOP 300 FILMS POSITION . . . . #16
All-Release Domestic Box Office in Equivalent 2005 $s

National Film Preservation Board Selection. . . . none

OTHER AWARDS Best Picture Wins

	Year
Golden Globes	none
New York Film Critics.	none
National Board of Review	none
Film Daily Critics	none

*If the movie is honorable, it can get people to say, "This is the first time
I've ever really seen a dinosaur. I think it's really happening as I'm watching."*

—Steven Spielberg

PLOT: An eccentric billionaire develops a means to clone dinosaurs as the main attraction of the ultimate theme park, but during its first preview, a powerful storm and a disgruntled embezzler combine to bring chaos.

PRODUCTION: Steven Spielberg and Michael Crichton were working together on a script when Spielberg idly asked the author about his next book. The subject thrilled Spielberg, whose fascination with dinosaurs had been lifelong. *Jurassic Park*'s publication in 1990 was an immediate sensation; Crichton had always wanted Spielberg to direct the movie version. For the only time in his career, Spielberg began storyboarding the novel even before a screenplay was completed, selecting scenes that he knew he wanted to translate to the screen. For the critical dinosaur effects, he engaged Phil Tippett, the master of "go-motion," frame-by-frame animation in miniature; Stan Winston, whose team would build full-size models; Michael Lantieri, to supervise the interaction between dinosaur models and live action; and Industrial Light & Magic's computer-savvy Dennis Muren, for combining the various elements in postproduction. Spielberg wanted the dinosaurs to be portrayed as animals, not monsters. To help achieve this performance, Tippett replicated the storyboards in 3-D stop-motion. The film's scientific advisor, paleontologist Jack Horner, is the leading exponent of the theory that dinosaurs' lineal descendants are birds, rather than reptiles. All creature designs conformed to this thesis, eschewing such former movie clichés as snakelike tongues. The shoot began with location work on the Hawaiian island of Kauai, which went well until the last day, when Hurricane Iniki devastated the island and stranded the filmmakers in a hotel ballroom for nearly eight hours. Aside from two days in the desert for archeological scenes, the rest of the film was shot on soundstages. As Tippett's crew did tests, Spielberg became concerned that "go-motion" movement, though skillfully executed, was not ideal. Muren, whose ILM had recently made significant digital effects breakthroughs on *Terminator 2* but had never attempted animating living creatures, asked to try some test footage. When Spielberg and Tippett watched the stunning result, the animator said, "I think I'm extinct." But as Tippett's 100 miniature shots were reassigned to ILM, his crew became invaluable in supervising movement and performance for the digital artists, and Spielberg referred to Tippett as the "director of dinosaurs" on the project. ILM artists took mime classes to help them focus on physical movement. An early scene involving a rampaging *T. rex* was so breathtaking that Spielberg changed the movie's ending to bring the creature back. Lantieri said the most difficult physical effect of the entire picture was answering the director's request to make the water in a glass vibrate with the huge beast's approaching footfalls. After weeks of agonizing, he finally stretched a guitar string under the glass and had a technician pluck it from below to create one of the film's most memorable shots.

DISTRIBUTION: *Jurassic Park* was a smash at the box office, bringing in $920 million in worldwide box office and spawning two sequels. Before the project began, Spielberg had been impressed with King Kong's majestic appearance during the Universal Studios theme park tram ride. Now his latest creation would not only dazzle the worldwide film audience but also join Kong as a new behemoth to thrill park visitors. —*Tom Dupree*

THE FUGITIVE
Warner Bros., 1993

ALL-RELEASE EQUIVALENT 2005 $s
(Unadjusted $s) in Millions of $s

Domestic Box Office Revenues . . . . **$284.7**/($183.9)
Production Cost . . . . **$59.5**/($44.0)
Principal Photography . . . . **70** days estimated
2/3/1993–5/16/1993

Director . . . . Andrew Davis
Producer . . . . Arnold Kopelson
Production Company . . . . Warner Bros. Pictures
Story by . . . . From a story by David Twohy based on characters created by Roy Huggins
Screenplay by . . . . Jeb Stuart and David Twohy
Cast . . . . Harrison Ford, Tommy Lee Jones, Sela Ward
Filming Locations . . . . . . On location primarily in Chicago, IL, and in North Carolina (Great Smoky Mountains, Blue Ridge Mountains, Bryson City, Tapoco)
Genre . . . . Crime
Format . . . . Color (Technicolor)
Initial Release 8/6/1993
Rerelease . . . . none
Running Time . . . . 127 minutes
MPAA Rating PG-13

STANDING THE TEST OF TIME

ACADEMY AWARD Oscar Nominations and Wins

Best Picture: Arnold Kopelson, Producer

*ACTOR IN A SUPPORTING ROLE: Tommy Lee Jones

Cinematography: Michael Chapman

Film Editing: Dennis Virkler, David Finfer, Dean Goodhill, Don Brochu, Richard Nord, Dov Hoenig

Music (Original Score): James Newton Howard

Sound: Donald O. Mitchell, Michael Herbick, Frank A. Montaño, Scott D. Smith

Sound Effects Editing: John Leveque, Bruce Stambler

OSCAR TOTALS   Nominations **7**   *Wins **1**

AFI 100 YEARS 100 MOVIES SELECTION
2007 0   1997 0

TOP 300 FILMS POSITION . . . . #117
All-Release Domestic Box Office in Equivalent 2005 $s

National Film Preservation Board Selection . . . . none

OTHER AWARDS Best Picture Wins

	Year
Golden Globes	none
New York Film Critics	none
National Board of Review	none
Film Daily Critics	none

*It's like a puzzle. The more a movie can be like a puzzle,
the more interesting it is to the audience.*

—Andrew Davis

PLOT: Chicago surgeon Richard Kimble, sentenced to death for the murder of his wife, sets out to find the real killer—a one-armed man—while staying one step ahead of U.S. marshal Samuel Gerard.

PRODUCTION: *The Fugitive* started life as a one-hour television drama. The series, created by Roy Huggins, aired on ABC from 1963 to 1967, and became a sensation in its day—its finale was the most-watched episode of any regular series in history at the time. Given the success of previous TV-to-movie transitions such as 1991's *The Addams Family,* the producers of *The Fugitive* used the TV show as a blueprint for approximately two-thirds of the script, according to producer Arnold Kopelson. Elements familiar from the original source included the harried lead character, Dr. Kimble, and his elusive one-armed nemesis. Harrison Ford, fresh from his success in *Patriot Games,* agreed to take on the lead role after Alec Baldwin dropped out. Tommy Lee Jones signed on as Kimble's dogged pursuer, Gerard, after Jon Voight and Gene Hackman both passed; Jones's performance would win him an Oscar and make him a breakout star. Working with an estimated production budget of $40 million, *The Fugitive* chronicled Kimble's roadtrip journey to clear his name, requiring extensive location shooting from Chicago (the film's primary setting) to the scenic countryside of North Carolina. One of the film's action sequences showcased a chain-hobbled Kimble running to escape a derailing freight train. Because the scene required an actual derailment—staged at the Great Smoky Mountains Railroad—Davis had only one chance to get his shot right. In *The Fugitive*'s signature sequence, Kimble plunges from a dam spillway rather than risk capture. Interior shots of the dam's inner workings took place in the Chicago freight tunnels, with the Cheoah Dam in Deals Gap, North Carolina, standing in for the structure's exterior. Stunt coordinator Terry Leonard planned the outside action and dropped numerous dummies of Harrison Ford from the dam's precipice over two days of filming (with each dummy costing an estimated $10,000). Davis, a Chicagoan, relished the chance to shoot again in his hometown (after his 1989 Gene Hackman vehicle *The Package*). In fact, it was Davis who suggested the location for the scene in which Kimble rents a flat on Chicago's Southeast Side. He had grown up in the Mexican-Serbian neighborhood, which he described as an "area gasping for breath," and knew it would perfectly echo the character's desperate straits. Principal photography ended May 16.

DISTRIBUTION: *The Fugitive* exceeded the expectations of nearly every forecaster, grossing $23.7 million to top the box office in its first weekend and remaining the number one film in the country for seven weeks. Roger Ebert called it one of the year's best films, stating, "Davis paints with bold visual strokes so that the movie rises above its action-film origins and becomes operatic." The movie received a rare A+ from audiences polled by CinemaScore, and received further validation with its Academy Award nomination for Best Picture (the only film based on a television series to be nominated for that honor). At its peak, *The Fugitive* played in 2,425 theaters, finally closing on March 24, 1994, with a gross of $183.9 million domestic ($368.9 million worldwide). *The Fugitive* inspired one sequel, 1998's *U.S. Marshals,* with Tommy Lee Jones returning as Gerard. —*Daniel Wallace*

MRS. DOUBTFIRE
20th Century-Fox, 1993

ALL-RELEASE EQUIVALENT 2005 $s
(Unadjusted $s) in Millions of $s

Domestic Box Office Revenues . . . . **$337.7**/($219.2)
Production Cost . . . .**$40.5**/($30.0)
Principal Photography . . . . **70** days estimated
3/22/1993–6/1/1993

Director . . . . Chris Columbus

Producer . . . . Marsha Garces Williams, Robin Williams, Mark Radcliffe

Production Company . . . . 20th Century-Fox, Blue Wolf Productions

Story by . . . . Based on the book *Alias Madame Doubtfire* by Anne Fine

Screenplay by . . . . Randi Mayem Singer, Leslie Dixon

Cast . . . . Robin Williams, Sally Field, Pierce Brosnan, Harvey Fierstein

Filming Locations . . . . . . San Francisco, Oakland, and various Northern California locations

Genre . . . . Comedy

Format . . . . Color (DeLuxe)

Initial Release 11/24/1993

Rerelease . . . . none

Running Time . . . . 125 minutes

MPAA Rating PG-13

STANDING THE TEST OF TIME

ACADEMY AWARD Oscar Nominations and Wins

*MAKEUP: Greg Cannom, Ve Neill, Yolanda Toussieng

OSCAR TOTALS Nominations **1** *Wins **1**

AFI 100 YEARS 100 MOVIES SELECTION
2007 0   1997 0

TOP 300 FILMS POSITION . . . .**#80**
All-Release Domestic Box Office in Equivalent 2005 $s

National Film Preservation Board Selection . . . .none

OTHER AWARDS Best Picture Wins

	Year
Golden Globes (Comedy)	1994
New York Film Critics	none
National Board of Review	none
Film Daily Critics	none

Ninety percent of parents who separate don't get back together again.
We don't want our audiences to see a dishonest film. We didn't set out to make The Parent Trap.
We're going to protect Mrs. Doubtfire. *We're keeping it honest.*

—Chris Columbus

PLOT: A divorced father of three disguises himself as an elderly British housekeeper to his ex-wife so that he can be close to his children.

PRODUCTION: In 1987, when *Alias Madame Doubtfire,* a British children's book, was brought to the attention of Elizabeth Gabler, then vice president of production at United Artists, she and her boss, Roger Birnbaum, both envisioned Robin Williams in the lead role. Unfortunately, the project went into turnaround when Kirk Kerkorian merged UA with MGM. Gabler followed Birnbaum to 20th Century-Fox, and they purchased the rights to the property. Randi Mayem Singer was hired to write the first draft of the screenplay, and it was given to Robin Williams's wife, Marsha. When she was informed that Chris Columbus, who had recently directed the first two *Home Alone* blockbusters, was available to direct, the Williamses were thrilled. Columbus did a rewrite, which was "brilliant," said Marsha, and Fox chairman Joe Roth told her, "It's a go!" That gave birth to Robin and Marsha Williams's new shingle, Blue Wolf Productions. Columbus envisioned a full-length Warner Bros.–type cartoon to open the film. Chuck Jones, the co-creator of Bugs Bunny and Daffy Duck, was hired to produce a cartoon about a pet bird and a hungry cat belonging to an old lady. Sound familiar? Jones came up with a green-feathered opera-singing parrot chased by a gourmet feline. Less than two minutes of the unfinished cartoon were ever used, but it was enough to establish Williams's character as a voice actor. Normally, cartoon voices are recorded before the animators draw the characters, but Williams's looping scene was done to completed visuals merely as a device to illustrate the process. Columbus defied the norm in other ways too. He asked Williams and Harvey Fierstein, who played Daniel's brother, to first do their scenes together as written on the page; then he gave them the luxury of an hour to improvise. For Williams especially, this was the equivalent of a kid playing with matches, as his trademark spontaneity could create sparks of brilliance as well as legal fires. For instance, when Williams ad-libbed an exchange with his ex-wife (Sally Field), complimenting her clothes as having a *Dances with Wolves* motif, the studio had to seek legal approval to reference the other movie in this way. Legal checks are traditionally done at script stage, so all of the impromptu references Williams made had to be cleared by the legal department after the scene was shot. The Oscar-winning makeup took about four hours to apply every day. The finished product was so realistic Williams tested it in public and got no second glances. He was even able to fool cast members when they saw him for the first time. Columbus wisely chose to photograph in the wide-screen anemographic process to avoid the staginess of the film's many interior settings. By doing so he created much more fluid and painterly on-screen compositions and was able to treat the eye to some of San Francisco's glorious vistas. The ending has TV star Mrs. Doubtfire comforting her young viewers who are separated from one parent by divorce. This was in direct response to then Vice President Dan Quayle's comments about family values in which he chided popular TV character Murphy Brown for having a child out of wedlock and for not involving the father in the baby's life, offending millions of single mothers.

DISTRIBUTION: The film was a big hit, coming in at number two for 1993 with worldwide box office of $676.6 million, behind *Jurassic Park*'s $920.1 million. —*Bob Canning*

SCHINDLER'S LIST
Universal, 1993

ALL-RELEASE EQUIVALENT 2005 $s
(Unadjusted $s) in Millions of $s

Domestic Box Office Revenues . . . . **$147.4**/($96.1)
Production Cost . . . . **$35.1**/($26.0)
Principal Photography . . . . **72** days
3/1/1993–5/26/1993

Director . . . . Steven Spielberg
Producer . . . . Steven Spielberg, Gerald R. Molen, Branko Lustig
Production Company . . . . Amblin Entertainment, Universal Pictures
Story by . . . . Based on the novel by Thomas Keneally
Screenplay by . . . . Steven Zaillian
Cast . . . . Liam Neeson, Ben Kingsley, Ralph Fiennes, Caroline Goodall, Jonathan Sagalle, Embeth Davidtz
Filming Locations . . . . . . Krakow, Poland; Auschwitz; Jerusalem
Genre . . . . War
Format . . . . B&W (DeLuxe)
Initial Release 12/15/1993
Rerelease . . . . none
Running Time . . . . 195 minutes
MPAA Rating . . . . R

STANDING THE TEST OF TIME

ACADEMY AWARD Oscar Nominations and Wins

*BEST PICTURE: Steven Spielberg, Gerald R. Molen, and Branko Lustig, Producers

Actor in a Leading Role: Liam Neeson

Actor in a Supporting Role: Ralph Fiennes

*ART DIRECTION/SET DECORATION: Allan Starski/Ewa Braun

*CINEMATOGRAPHY: Janusz Kaminski

Costume Design: Anna Biedrzycka-Sheppard

*DIRECTING: Steven Spielberg

*FILM EDITING: Michael Kahn

Makeup: Christina Smith, Matthew Mungle, Judy Alexander Cory

*MUSIC (Original Score): John Williams

Sound: Andy Nelson, Steve Pederson, Scott Millan, Ron Judkins

*WRITING (Screenplay – based on material previously produced or published): Steven Zaillian

OSCAR TOTALS   Nominations **12** *Wins 7

AFI 100 YEARS 100 MOVIES SELECTION
2007 . . . . #8   1997 . . . . #9

TOP 300 FILMS POSITION . . . . none
All-Release Domestic Box Office in Equivalent 2005 $s

National Film Preservation Board Selection 2004

OTHER AWARDS Best Picture Wins

	Year
Golden Globes (Drama)	1994
New York Film Critics	1993
National Board of Review	1993
Film Daily Critics	none

I interviewed survivors, I went to Poland, saw the cities and spent time with the people and spoke to the Jews who had come back . . . I spent more research time on this project than I had on any previous film.

—Steven Spielberg

PLOT: Oskar Schindler, a charming, roguish Austrian businessman, turns his enamel factory into a sanctuary for Jews during the Holocaust. His clandestine efforts saved 1,200 lives.

PRODUCTION: A chance encounter led to this memorable true story being told. Australian novelist Thomas Keneally, on a California trip, visited a Beverly Hills luggage store. The proprietor, Leopold Page, mentioned that he was a "Schindlerjuden," a Jew saved by Oskar Schindler. In the Holocaust years, Page was known as Poldek Pfefferberg. For more than three decades Pfefferberg had tried to interest any writer who would listen to the story of Oskar Schindler. When Keneally heard the story and saw the documents, he was hooked. It took two years to get the manuscript completed. Keneally's research included interviewing fifty Schindlerjuden in seven countries. Upon publication, in 1982, Sid Sheinberg stepped up and got Universal to purchase the screenplay rights, with Steven Spielberg to produce. Keneally wrote a lengthy draft. Billy Wilder then wrote a draft before retiring. Kurt Luedtke (*Absence of Malice, Out of Africa*) was hired by Spielberg and spent four years on the project. In the meantime, Spielberg was advised simply to make a donation rather than spend time and money on a depressing film. Martin Scorsese turned down a chance to direct, feeling that the project was a job for a Jewish director. Steven Zaillian was then brought in and eventually turned in a 130-page screenplay adaptation. Sidney Lumet also turned down the project, saying that he had already done a film about the Holocaust, *The Pawnbroker.* Finally, Spielberg decided that he should direct. Alan Thicke was his first choice for Schindler. Thicke turned the role down because of creative differences and scheduling conflicts. Swiss actor Bruno Ganz also turned down the lead, as did Stellan Skarsgård and Harrison Ford. Roman Polanski turned down the director's job because, as a Holocaust survivor, the script evoked bitter memories. After seeing Liam Neeson in a stage play, Spielberg decided on the Irish actor for Schindler. Costumes were needed for 20,000 extras for the Krakow sequences. Allan Starski's set of the labor camp at Plaszow was the largest ever constructed in Poland. Filming included the entire spectrum of weather conditions. Spielberg kept a copy of Keneally's book nearby during the entire shoot. Approximately 40 percent of the shots were handheld, to give the film a documentary feeling. Zaillian's 130-page screenplay went to 190 pages with Spielberg's additions. The Krakow liquidation sequence was lengthened from one to twenty pages based on "living witness testimony." Robin Williams came to the set for a few days of comedy relief to offset the feelings of a grim and depressing production. For the epilogue, at Mt. Zion Cemetery outside Jerusalem, all actors had to accompany the original Schindlerjuden they portrayed for the laying of the pebbles at Schindler's grave. (Schindler was denied U.S. immigration because of his membership in the Nazi Party. He died in 1974.) Shooting was completed in 72 days, four under schedule.

DISTRIBUTION: The film opened to largely impressive reviews despite the grim content, grossed $328 million in worldwide box office, and swept the Oscars. It reawakened many to the horrors of the Holocaust, in which the number of people lost has been placed between 17 million and 21 million. Spielberg used profits to create the Shoah Foundation, which preserved on video the testimony of many Holocaust survivors. —*Frank McAdams*

THE LION KING

Buena Vista, 1994

ALL-RELEASE EQUIVALENT 2005 $s

(Unadjusted $s) in Millions of $s

Domestic Box Office Revenues . . . . **$501.9**/($328.5)
Production Cost . . . . **$104.5**/($79.3)
Production Period . . . .**2 ½** years
Fall 1991–Spring 1994
Principal photograph commenced 6/15/1992
Final answer print 5/23/1994

Director . . . . Roger Allers, Rob Minkoff
Producer . . . . Don Hahn
Production Company . . . . Walt Disney Pictures
Story and
  Screenplay by . . . . Irene Mecchi, Jonathan
                                        Roberts, Linda Woolverton
Cast . . . . Rowan Atkinson, Matthew
                                        Broderick, Niketa Calame, Jim
                                        Cummings, Whoopi Goldberg,
                                        Robert Guillaume, Jeremy
                                        Irons, James Earl Jones, Moira
                                        Kelly, Nathan Lane, Cheech
                                        Marin, Ernie Sabella, Madge
                                        Sinclair (voices)
Filming Locations . . . . . . Created in studio at Walt
                                        Disney Pictures in Burbank, CA
Genre . . . . Animation
Format . . . . Color (Technicolor)
Initial Release . . . . 6/15/1994 premiere (New York
                                        and Los Angeles); 6/24/1994
                                        general release

Rerelease . . . . none
Running Time . . . . 87 minutes
MPAA Rating . . . . G

STANDING THE TEST OF TIME

ACADEMY AWARD Oscar Nominations and Wins

*MUSIC (Original Score): Hans Zimmer

*MUSIC (Original Song): "Can You Feel the Love
Tonight," Music by Elton John; Lyrics by Tim Rice

Music (Original Song): "Circle of Life," Music by Elton
John; Lyrics by Tim Rice

Music (Original Song): "Hakuna Matata," Music by
Elton John; Lyrics by Tim Rice

OSCAR TOTALS   Nominations **4**   *Wins **2**

AFI 100 YEARS 100 MOVIES SELECTION
2007 0   1997 0

TOP 300 FILMS POSITION . . . . **#25**
All-Release Domestic Box Office in Equivalent 2005 $s

National Film Preservation Board Selection . . . . none

OTHER AWARDS Best Picture Wins

	Year
Golden Globes (Musical)	1995
New York Film Critics	none
National Board of Review	none
Film Daily Critics	none

*The animal kingdom is a metaphor. A child loses a parent, goes out into the world,
tries to avoid responsibility, then faces it . . . I like the idea of animals.*

—Jeffrey Katzenberg

PLOT: Simba, son of the Pride Lands' king, is betrayed by his evil uncle, who kills the king and makes him feel responsible. Shattered, Simba leaves his home and begins his own personal odyssey.

PRODUCTION: The feature animation unit at Walt Disney Studios had undergone a dramatic renaissance with its 1989 release of *The Little Mermaid,* a classic fable set to a Broadway-style musical score and a worldwide smash hit. In 1990 Jeffrey Katzenberg, then chair of film production at Walt Disney Studios, was flying with other Disney executives from London to Paris to promote *The Little Mermaid* when they began talking about coming-of-age stories. On that flight, Katzenberg resolved to set such a story in Africa. Peter Schneider, president of Walt Disney Feature Animation and a fellow passenger on the fateful plane trip, put the project, then called "King of the Jungle," into development—but without the A-list talent. The studio was taking a risk. From *Snow White* on, all Disney animated hits had started as classics and featured humans. Katzenberg was doing an original story with talking animals. More than on any other Disney film, Katzenberg would take a hands-on role. To prepare to capture the beauty of Africa, six members of the creative team visited East Africa early on. More than 600 artists, animators, and technicians contributed to *The Lion King,* generating more than one million drawings, made up of 1,197 hand-painted backgrounds and 119,058 individually colored frames of film. *Mermaid* had been the first Disney production to use the Computer Animation Production System (CAPS), created jointly with Pixar. CAPS was a pioneering digital ink-and-paint system that made it far easier to color and manipulate traditional hand-drawn cels, and enabled stunning multiplane shots bestowing a three-dimensional effect. There was only one CAPS shot in *Mermaid,* but subsequent pictures used it exclusively, and by the time of *The Lion King*, Disney technicians were pushing the edges of its capability with spectacular results. Though it isn't readily apparent, there is computer animation in the film, notably in the wildebeest stampede sequence: the creatures were built in the computer and replicated hundreds of times, then shaded to look like handwork. *The Lion King* continued its uphill battle during production. It was considered a secondary film to *Pocahontas,* also in production at the time—so much so that many Disney animators chose to work on the latter film, feeling that it had greater commercial potential. They were mistaken.

DISTRIBUTION: *The Lion King*'s summer 1994 opening drew record-breaking crowds, though critical reaction was muted, some reviewers withholding the rhapsodic praise they had given *Beauty and the Beast* and *Aladdin.* Of all 1994 releases, it came in first in worldwide box office and second in domestic box office after *Forrest Gump.* While Katzenberg found gratuitous Elton John's song "Can You Feel the Love Tonight," which plays over the end credits, the audience disagreed. *The Lion King* soundtrack album went to number one—the first animated soundtrack ever to attain that position—and the song became a top 40 hit and went on to win the Academy Award. *The Lion King* was the most heavily merchandised picture in the studio's history, with hundreds of promotional tie-ins. By 1997 the total franchise had generated nearly $1 billion in profit and become the financial superstar of traditional Disney animation. —*Tom Dupree*

FORREST GUMP
Paramount, 1994

ALL-RELEASE EQUIVALENT 2005 $s
(Unadjusted $s) in Millions of $s

Domestic Box Office Revenues........$505.6/($329.7)
Production Cost ....$72.5/($55.0)
Principal Photography............**73** days estimated
8/27/1993–12/9/1993

Director .... Robert Zemeckis

Producer .... Wendy Finerman, Steve Starkey, Steve Tisch

Production Company.... Paramount Pictures

Story by.............. Based on the novel by Winston Groom

Screenplay by.......... Eric Roth

Cast .... Sally Field, Tom Hanks, Robin Wright, Gary Sinise

Filming Locations ...... Mostly in and around Beaufort, SC, with the bench scene shot in Savannah, GA; second unit photography for running sequences was filmed by second unit director Steve Starkey across the United States in approximately 50 days

Genre................. Drama

Format............... Color (DeLuxe)

Initial Release.......... 7/6/1994

Rerelease.............. none

Running Time.......... 142 minutes

MPAA Rating PG-13

STANDING THE TEST OF TIME

ACADEMY AWARD Oscar Nominations and Wins

*BEST PICTURE: Wendy Finerman, Steve Tisch, and Steve Starkey

*ACTOR IN A LEADING ROLE: Tom Hanks

Actor in a Supporting Role: Gary Sinise

Art Direction/Set Decoration: Rick Carter/ Nancy Haigh

Cinematography: Don Burgess

*DIRECTING: Robert Zemeckis

*FILM EDITING: Arthur Schmidt

Makeup: Daniel C. Striepeke, Hallie D'Amore, Judith A. Cory

Music (Original Score): Alan Silvestri

Sound: Randy Thom, Tom Johnson, Dennis Sands, William B. Kaplan

Sound Effects Editing: Gloria Borders, Randy Thom

*VISUAL EFFECTS: Ken Ralston, George Murphy, Stephen Rosenbaum, Allen Hall

*WRITING (Screenplay – based on material previously produced or published): Eric Roth

OSCAR TOTALS Nominations **13** *Wins 6

AFI 100 YEARS 100 MOVIES SELECTION
2007 ... #76   1997 ... #71

TOP 300 FILMS POSITION .... #24
All-Release Domestic Box Office in Equivalent 2005 $s

National Film Preservation Board Selection....none

OTHER AWARDS Best Picture Wins

	Year
Golden Globes (Drama).....................	1995
New York Film Critics......................	none
National Board of Review (tie)...............	1994
Film Daily Critics..........................	none

This breaks every rule of moviemaking that I know of. There's no quest, there's no bad guy, it's just the spirit of Forrest Gump that's the backbone of this movie.

—Tom Hanks

PLOT: An ordinary man gets involved in extraordinary situations in a story set during the Vietnam War years.

PRODUCTION: Producer Wendy Finerman loved Winston Groom's source novel from the first sentence—"Being an idiot ain't no box of chocolates"—when she read it in 1985. She was convinced it would make a wonderful movie, but it took years of unacceptable tries at a screenplay before it was ready. Finally, writer Eric Roth determined that the key to the project was the love story between Forrest and his childhood friend. Director Robert Zemeckis was soon attached, along with Tom Hanks, which in turn attracted other important creative personnel. Sally Field was the first choice for Forrest's mother, and Robin Wright was the only actress to read for Jenny, his girlfriend. Hanks was preparing the main character when an open casting call in Memphis yielded a Mississippi boy to play the young Forrest. His natural speaking cadence was so distinctive that Hanks imitated it for the role. Location work was done mostly in and near Beaufort, South Carolina, with the notable exception of a sequence in which Forrest runs across the country several times. The crew constructed the "Gump house" for exteriors and a nearby farm for Jenny's childhood home; not far away they found a location they could disguise as Vietnam for Forrest Gump's battle sequences. To train the actors playing Vietnam soldiers, Zemeckis hired military consultant Dale Dye, who put them through a strenuous "boot camp" that simulated what real veterans had to endure. Dye also helped the filmmakers depict a Vietnam firefight accurately, including what he called the "mass confusion" that surrounded such an event. For the remarkable sequences showing Forrest interacting with various historical figures, Zemeckis's team spent a year locating archival footage based on a general script guideline. They then fashioned dialogue to match, and the artists at Industrial Light & Magic blended in newly filmed live action, distressing the new footage to make it resemble the historical source. Later, Zemeckis ruefully said, "Digitally, you can create a flawless, perfect, moving lie." To achieve the illusion that actor Gary Sinise had become a double amputee, master illusionist Ricky Jay helped the crew devise a trick wheelchair, which was used in some of the shots. In addition, ILM artists filmed some of Sinise's scenes twice, removing obstacles that the actor's legs otherwise would have disturbed. Composer Alan Silvestri saw the completed film with a temporary music track and was so moved that he went home that very night and composed the main theme, which plays under the feather sequences that open and close the film; the former was the longest visual effects shot ever achieved by ILM.

DISTRIBUTION: The movie was a critical and box office success in the United States. Years later, Zemeckis said that at first he'd thought the picture would appeal only to those over thirty-five, and certainly only to Americans. But, despite some initial critical reservations, *Forrest Gump* became a mammoth international hit, bringing in $680 million in worldwide box office (more than $1 billion in 2005 dollars), as worldwide audiences seemed to focus on the human story. As an unusual testament to the film's popularity, the shrimping company founded in the movie by Forrest and a Vietnam buddy became a reality with the opening of a chain of Bubba Gump seafood restaurants, still operating today. —*Tom Dupree*

PULP FICTION
Miramax (domestic); Various (foreign), 1994

ALL-RELEASE EQUIVALENT 2005 $s

(Unadjusted $s) in Millions of $s

Domestic Box Office Revenues . . . . **$162.9**/($107.9)
Production Cost . . . . **$10.5**/($8.0)
Principal Photography . . . . **50** days estimated
9/20/1993–11/30/1993

Director . . . . Quentin Tarantino
Producer . . . . Lawrence Bender
Production Company . . . . A Band Apart, Jersey Films, Miramax Films
Story by . . . . Quentin Tarantino, Roger Avary
Screenplay by . . . . Quentin Tarantino
Cast . . . . John Travolta, Samuel L. Jackson, Uma Thurman, Harvey Keitel, Tim Roth
Filming Locations . . . . . . Southern California locations in Hawthorne, Pasadena, Los Angeles, Hollywood, and Riverside
Genre . . . . Crime
Format . . . . Color (DeLuxe)
Initial Release 10/14/1994
Rerelease . . . . none
Running Time . . . . 153 minutes
MPAA Rating . . . . R

STANDING THE TEST OF TIME

ACADEMY AWARD Oscar Nominations and Wins

Best Picture: Lawrence Bender, Producer

Actor in a Leading Role: John Travolta

Actor in a Supporting Role: Samuel L. Jackson

Actress in a Supporting Role: Uma Thurman

Directing: Quentin Tarantino

Film Editing: Sally Menke

*WRITING (Screenplay – written directly for the screen): Screenplay by Quentin Tarantino; Stories by Quentin Tarantino and Roger Avary

OSCAR TOTALS   Nominations 7   *Wins 1

AFI 100 YEARS 100 MOVIES SELECTION
2007 . . . #94   1997 . . . #95

TOP 300 FILMS POSITION . . . . .none
All-Release Domestic Box Office in Equivalent 2005 $s

National Film Preservation Board Selection . . . .none

OTHER AWARDS Best Picture Wins

	Year
Golden Globes	none
New York Film Critics	none
National Board of Review (tie)	1994
Film Daily Critics	none

In the movies, hit men usually murder and split. Here we don't leave; we hang out with them all morning. It's an old crime story, new take.

—Quentin Tarantino

PLOT: Three connected stories—about two hit men, an aging boxer, and a gangster's beautiful wife—are told out of sequence in an unusual mixture of banal conversation and sudden intense action.

PRODUCTION: Just off a worldwide festival tour for his first film, *Reservoir Dogs,* Quentin Tarantino became obsessed with a partially finished anthology script he and writing partner Roger Avary had struggled with while the script for *True Romance* was being shopped. He asked Avary for the use of his story "Pandemonium Reigns," about a fighter who refused to throw a bout. Tarantino rewrote the entire anthology over a frenzied three-month period in Amsterdam, during which time Avary came over to help him. Their respective writing credits have subsequently become a matter of dispute. Tarantino had a $1 million development deal with TriStar through Danny DeVito's Jersey Films, but because Avary needed income, he left the project to direct his own film, *Killing Zoe.* When TriStar turned the script down, producer Lawrence Bender sent it to Miramax and insisted upon a quick decision from Harvey Weinstein. *Pulp Fiction* became the first major film greenlighted by Miramax after its acquisition by Disney. Weinstein had a significant advantage when negotiating with agents since most actors loved Tarantino's work so much they were willing to accept less money to perform for the hot young director. They also knew *Pulp Fiction* was filled with juicy roles. Tarantino had written a leading character for John Travolta, who was then experiencing a career decline, but Weinstein wanted Daniel Day-Lewis. The director prevailed. Other roles were hotly contested too; Matt Dillon required a day to think about the boxer role, but by the time he called back to accept, Bruce Willis had been cast instead. Travolta and Willis both credit the film for resuscitating their careers, while the film also boosted Samuel L. Jackson and Uma Thurman to star status. Tarantino's set was effusive and electric, like the director himself. He insisted on rehearsals before shooting, to give the cast and crew a level of comfort. He used a handheld camera to film the dance contest scene with Travolta and Uma Thurman, rather than watching on a video monitor. The Weinstein brothers were so impressed after a visit to the set that they offered Tarantino and Bender a two-picture development deal on the spot.

DISTRIBUTION: *Pulp Fiction* was kept tightly under wraps before its debut at the 1994 Cannes Film Festival, having been shown in advance to only a few influential critics. It ended up winning the Palme d'Or, the festival's top prize, but not without some boos among the applause. This success utterly changed Miramax's release strategy: instead of giving the film a small summer release, the company decided to hold the U.S. premiere at the New York Film Festival in September, then open on more than a thousand screens a month later. At that premiere, a member of the audience passed out during one particularly intense scene. Weinstein and Bender had to assist him out of the theater. This incident became part of *Pulp Fiction* lore, a mythology that added to its reputation. *Pulp Fiction* was an instant hit and the highest-grossing film released by Miramax. Tarantino became a "rock-star" director, even appearing in a Broadway play and hosting *Saturday Night Live.* Because of the film's success, Weinstein has referred to Miramax as "the house that Quentin built." *—Tom Dupree*

BRAVEHEART

Paramount (domestic); 20th Century-Fox (foreign), 1995

ALL-RELEASE EQUIVALENT 2005 $s

(Unadjusted $s) in Millions of $s

Domestic Box Office Revenues........ **$111.4**/($75.6)
Production Cost .... **$92.3**/($72.0)
Principal Photography........... **100** days estimated
6/6/1994–November 1994

Director	Mel Gibson
Producer	Mel Gibson, Alan Ladd Jr., Bruce Davey
Production Company....	Icon Productions, Ladd Company Productions
Story and Screenplay by	Randall Wallace
Cast	Mel Gibson, Sophie Marceau, Patrick McGoohan, Catherine McCormack
Filming Locations	On location: Scotland, Ireland; in studio Ardmore Studios, Ireland
Genre.................	Action Adventure
Format................	Color (DeLuxe)
Initial Release	5/24/1995
Rerelease	none
Running Time	177 minutes
MPAA Rating	R

STANDING THE TEST OF TIME

ACADEMY AWARD Oscar Nominations and Wins

*BEST PICTURE: Mel Gibson, Alan Ladd, Jr. and Bruce Davey, Producers

*CINEMATOGRAPHY: John Toll

Costume Design: Charles Knode

*DIRECTING: Mel Gibson

Film Editing: Steven Rosenblum

*MAKEUP: Peter Frampton, Paul Pattison, Lois Burwell

Music (Original Dramatic Score): James Horner

Sound: Andy Nelson, Scott Millan, Anna Behlmer, Brian Simmons

*SOUND EFFECTS EDITING: Lon Bender, Per Hallberg

Writing (Screenplay – written directly for the screen): Randall Wallace

OSCAR TOTALS   Nominations **10** *Wins 5

AFI 100 YEARS 100 MOVIES SELECTION
2007 0   1997 0

TOP 300 FILMS POSITION ....none
All-Release Domestic Box Office in Equivalent 2005 $s

National Film Preservation Board Selection....none

OTHER AWARDS Best Picture Wins

	Year
Golden Globes	none
New York Film Critics.....................	none
National Board of Review..................	none
Film Daily Critics.........................	none

If you can't have fun making a picture, you shouldn't make it. We tried to be historically accurate, but half of what is known about William Wallace is legend anyway. Most of it comes from a poem by a blind poet known as Blind Harry, so why not put a little wit in it?

—Mel Gibson

PLOT: In thirteenth-century Scotland, clansman William Wallace avenges his wife's brutal murder by leading a ragtag army in revolt against the tyrannical King Edward I of England, using clever tactics to thwart Edward's better-equipped forces.

PRODUCTION: Tennessee-born writer Randall Wallace was eight when a relative returned from Scotland and told him that there were statues built there for the famous Wallace. In his forties, Wallace set out to turn that man's story into a script. There were few hard facts, but a public librarian found a 270-year-old reproduction of a book about Wallace by Blind Harry, written in 1477, 150 years after his death, that provided some real-life anecdotes. Wallace also got help from the Wallace Trust. He then sent his script to Mel Gibson, hoping that he would star. Gibson said that he didn't want to act in the film (he felt he was too old for the part), but he was interested in producing and directing it. However, Bruce Davey, Gibson's partner in Icon Entertainment, and producer Alan Ladd couldn't get the risky project financed until Gibson agreed to star as well. Icon and Ladd Company financed the picture, while selling U.S. distribution rights to Paramount and international rights to 20th Century-Fox. As a youth, Gibson had been inspired by *Spartacus, El Cid,* and other historical epics. He wanted his film to have a similar bigger-than-life scale. At times he directed 3,000 men on horseback, and the movie used 6,000 costumes. They used locations in Scotland and shot battle scenes in Ireland, where Gibson enlisted hundreds of extras from Ireland's army reserves, known for their military skills and fitness. The massive Battle of Stirling Bridge took six weeks to shoot. Gibson and his crew planned the battle scenes in part by positioning toy soldiers on a table. Nothing could be done about the weather in one of the wettest areas of Europe, so Gibson incorporated the overcast look into the movie. As is typical of Gibson, he created a relaxed atmosphere on the set by finding humor, initiating practical jokes, and directing some scenes in different voices, including impersonations of Elmer Fudd and Sammy Davis Jr. He also improvised bits that were comically ill-fitting, such as when he scampers away after borrowing an English soldier's uniform.

DISTRIBUTION: The brutality of thirteenth-century warfare in Gibson's first edit of the movie was so graphic it earned a NC-17 rating, which would make it difficult to distribute. So Gibson agreed to make cuts to secure an R rating. However, he refused to back off from a nearly three-hour running time, which was an issue among exhibitors, who wanted to fit in more performances. There was also some controversy about the many historical inaccuracies, but Gibson dismissed the criticism, saying that it was all just a legend anyway; Wallace commented that he was a dramatist, not a historian. Because of the spirit of the movie, it was widely embraced in Scotland and the United Kingdom. On its initial release in May 1995, *Braveheart* opened with $9.9 million in the United States, which was below expectations. It stayed in theaters for roughly eleven months, driven by word of mouth and repeat business, though it was on relatively few screens throughout that time. It grossed roughly $67 million in domestic box office before its ten Oscar nominations and five wins, which only added another $8 million to the total—a slim Oscar bounce. In domestic box office *Braveheart* brought in less than 40 percent of the number one 1995 film, Pixar's *Toy Story.* —*Tom Dupree*

BATMAN FOREVER
Warner Bros., 1995

ALL-RELEASE EQUIVALENT 2005 $s
(Unadjusted $s) in Millions of $s

Domestic Box Office Revenues. . . . . . . **$271.2**/($184.0)
Production Cost . . . . **$128.1**/($100.0)
Principal Photography . . . . .80 days estimated
10/15/1994–2/15/1995

Director . . . . Joel Schumacher

Producer . . . . Tim Burton, Peter Macgregor-Scott

Production Company . . . . Polygram Filmed Entertainment, Warner Bros. Pictures

Story by . . . . Lee Batchler, Janet Scott Batchler, based upon Batman characters created by Bob Kane and published by DC Comics

Screenplay by . . . . Lee Batchler, Janet Scott Batchler, Akiva Goldsman

Cast . . . . Val Kilmer, Tommy Lee Jones, Jim Carrey, Nicole Kidman, Chris O'Donnell

Filming Locations . . . . . . Carson, CA; Los Angeles, CA; Long Beach, CA; Portland, OR; Manhattan, NY; Long Island, NY; Warner Bros. Studios, Burbank, CA

Genre . . . . Action Adventure

Format . . . . Color (Technicolor)

Initial Release 6/16/1995

Rerelease . . . . none

Running Time . . . . 121 minutes

MPAA Rating PG-13

STANDING THE TEST OF TIME

ACADEMY AWARD Oscar Nominations and Wins

Cinematography: Stephen Goldblatt

Sound: Donald O. Mitchell, Frank A. Montaño, Michael Herbick, Peter Hliddal

Sound Effects Editing: John Leveque, Bruce Stambler

OSCAR TOTALS Nominations 3 *Wins 0

AFI 100 YEARS 100 MOVIES SELECTION
2007 . . . . . 0 1997 0

TOP 300 FILMS POSITION . . . . #132
All-Release Domestic Box Office in Equivalent 2005 $s

National Film Preservation Board Selection . . . .none

OTHER AWARDS Best Picture Wins

	Year
Golden Globes	none
New York Film Critics	none
National Board of Review	none
Film Daily Critics	none

I went back to the comic books I fell in love with.

—Joel Schumacher, contrasting his colorful take on the franchise with Tim Burton's brooding version

PLOT: Batman continues his crusade against evil doers who threaten the night, this time enlisting Robin as his partner in a bid to stop Two-Face and the Riddler from taking over Gotham City.

PRODUCTION: Stung by the disappointing box office take and off-putting tone of director Tim Burton's *Batman Returns*, Warner Bros. executives handed the directorial reins of the third film to Joel Schumacher (*The Lost Boys*), who made major changes in direction and cast. "Warner Bros. didn't want Tim to direct," said a source at the time. "He's too dark and odd for them." By all accounts the decision was mutual, though Burton remained on *Batman Forever* as a producer. Other changes included a new score (Elliot Goldenthal replaced Danny Elfman) and a new writing staff. But the biggest shock for some fans came in the title role, after Michael Keaton announced he would not return as Batman, forfeiting an estimated $15 million payday. "To lighten it up and brighten it up and be a cartoon was of no interest to me," said the actor. Val Kilmer (*Tombstone*) took over the role for his only time as the caped crusader. Rene Russo, already cast as Batman's love interest, was considered too old to play Kilmer's love interest, so she was replaced by Nicole Kidman. *Batman Forever* would finally introduce Robin to the franchise, telling his back story. Burton had cast Marlon Wayans as Robin, and he was even fitted with costumes. However, Schumacher wanted Chris O'Donnell (*Scent of a Woman*). Said Schumacher, "I didn't want to do a wide-eyes, cutesy, overly innocent Robin. Nor did I want an overly hip, street Robin." Wayans contract was paid off and he was dropped. *Batman Forever*'s script called for two villains: Two-Face (played by *The Fugitive*'s Tommy Lee Jones) and the Riddler, a role that went to *Ace Ventura*'s Jim Carrey after Robin Williams declined. "[Carrey's] physical capabilities seem to come from another universe," observed Schumacher. *Batman Forever* began filming in the fall of 1994 at the Warner Bros. Burbank studios, with exterior shooting on Long Island (where the Webb Institute for Naval Architecture became Wayne Manor), Alcatraz, and a California oil refinery. Production designer Barbara Ling created sets and props that burst with Day-Glo colors and neon tubing, which later put off some critics. "I think it was incumbent upon us to give our own version," said Schumacher, "trying to incorporate some of the things Tim started, but also to give it a never-before-seen look." The final film was subjected to tweaking by the studio, which cut more than 30 minutes to make it more family friendly (to encourage merchandising), including a subplot in which Batman obsesses on the death of his parents and recommits to remaining "Batman forever." The studio drummed up early buzz by partnering with U2 on a tie-in video for the song "Hold Me, Thrill Me, Kiss Me, Kill Me."

DISTRIBUTION: *Batman Forever* had a huge opening, raking in $52.8 million in its first weekend to smash the record held by 1993's *Jurassic Park*. Its total of $184 million ($336.5 million worldwide) made it the biggest movie of the summer and the second-highest grosser of 1995 behind *Toy Story*. More significantly, the film's box office revenues surpassed those of *Batman Returns*, earning Schumacher a "mission accomplished" validation from the studio for seemingly saving the franchise. —*Daniel Wallace*

APOLLO 13
Universal, 1995

ALL-RELEASE EQUIVALENT 2005 $s
(Unadjusted $s) in Millions of $s

Domestic Box Office Revenues........ **$253.5**/($172.1)
Production Cost .... **$89.7**/($70.0)
Principal Photography........... **82** days estimated
8/15/1994–12/9/1994

Director . . . . Ron Howard

Producer . . . . Brian Grazer

Production Company . . . . Universal Pictures, Imagine Entertainment

Story by . . . . Based on the book *Lost Moon* by Jim Lovell and Jeffrey Kluger

Screenplay by . . . . William Broyles Jr., Al Beinert

Cast . . . . Tom Hanks, Bill Paxton, Kevin Bacon, Gary Sinise, Ed Harris, Kathleen Quinlan

Filming Locations . . . . . . In Studio: Universal Studios, CA; on location: Houston, TX, including the Johnson Space Center; Florida, most notably the Kennedy Space Center in Titusville; Los Angeles and San Diego, CA

Genre . . . . Drama, Disaster

Format . . . . Color (DeLuxe)

Initial Release . . . . 6/22/1995 premiere (Beverly Hills); 6/30/1995 general release

Rerelease . . . . none

Running Time . . . . 140 minutes

MPAA Rating . . . . PG

STANDING THE TEST OF TIME

ACADEMY AWARD Oscar Nominations and Wins

Best Picture: Brian Grazer, Producer

Actor in a Leading Role: Ed Harris

Actor in a Supporting Role: Kathleen Quinlan

Art Direction/Set Decoration: Michael Corenblith/ Meredith Boswell

*FILM EDITING: Mike Hill, Dan Hanley

Music (Original Dramatic Score): James Horner

*SOUND: Rick Dior, Steve Pederson, Scott Millan, David MacMillan

Visual Effects: Robert Legato, Michael Kanfer, Leslie Ekker, Matt Sweeney

Writing (Screenplay – based on material previously produced or published): William Broyles Jr., Al Reinert

OSCAR TOTALS   Nominations **9**   *Wins **2**

AFI 100 YEARS 100 MOVIES SELECTION
2007 0   1997 0

TOP 300 FILMS POSITION . . . . **#154**
All-Release Domestic Box Office in Equivalent 2005 $s

National Film Preservation Board Selection . . . .none

OTHER AWARDS Best Picture Wins

	Year
Golden Globes	none
New York Film Critics	none
National Board of Review	none
Film Daily Critics	none

I think real life delivers better stories than anyone could possibly think up.

—Tom Hanks

PLOT: A docudrama based on Apollo 13's ill-fated 1970 mission. What was to be an ordinary lunar landing for astronauts Lovell, Haise, and Swigert, turned into a life-threatening mission: an extraordinary "successful failure."

PRODUCTION: Hollywood was already bidding on *Lost Moon: The Perilous Voyage of Apollo 13* after only one chapter had been written about an ill-fated American space mission to the moon. Co-author Jim Lovell was surprised to learn that Imagine Films had bought the rights. It was well known that Tom Hanks had always wanted to do something on Apollo 13, and so when Ron Howard decided to direct the film, Hanks was his first choice to play Lovell. Gary Sinise was asked to read the script, with no particular role in mind, and was drawn immediately to Ken Mattingly. Jim Lovell was given a role as the captain of the *Iwo Jima,* who shakes hands with Hanks on their return from space. Shortly into the project, Ron Howard saw mission control and realized that he wanted to tell its story too. He envisioned the film with three locations blending into one: the astronauts in space, mission control, and the loved ones at home. Everything really fell into place when NASA agreed to allow filming on their "Vomit Comet," a KC-135 aircraft used to create microgravity. Howard said he couldn't imagine what the film would have been like if they'd had to use wires. He wanted the film to be as exciting as it could be without compromising its integrity. The zero-gravity sequences were filmed in Ellington Field in Houston, where cast and crew flew between 500 and 600 arcs to achieve weightlessness. Each arc got them twenty-three seconds of zero gravity. It took thirteen days to complete these flights. When Kevin Bacon put on the pressure suit, it was the first real bout with claustrophobia he had ever had. All actors had to cope with the fatigue that came from wearing the suits. Howard strove to make the film as accurate as possible, though some details, such as the tension among the astronauts, were added for dramatic effect. To achieve technical accuracy, the dialogue between ground control and the astronauts was taken verbatim from actual transcripts. Howard used a considerable amount of archival footage from the networks and from NASA, but there were some things NASA could not have filmed. A great deal was created especially for the film. This newly created material was so realistic that astronaut Buzz Aldrin later assumed it was actual footage.

DISTRIBUTION: The film premiered in Beverly Hills on June 22, 1995, and across the United States on June 30, 1995. It immediately became a hit, bringing in $353 million in worldwide box office. Seven years later, on September 12, 2002, an IMAX version premiered with 24 minutes cut from the original version, including some language. It was the first 35mm film ever remastered for IMAX presentation. The film's tagline, "Houston, we have a problem," was voted fiftieth on AFI's 100 Years . . . 100 Movie Quotes list. Ironically, the words uttered by Jack Swigert were "Okay, Houston, we've had a problem here." Jim Lovell then repeated, "Houston, we've had a problem." Because Swigert's and Lovell's actual words suggested that the problem was already corrected, the quote was deliberately changed in the script. The film received wide critical acclaim as a compelling dramatization of an unprecedented catastrophe during the space race. The MPAA classification was PG because of the film's references to bodily functions in space. —*Christine McDermott*

TOY STORY
Buena Vista, 1995

ALL-RELEASE EQUIVALENT 2005 $s
(Unadjusted $s) in Millions of $s

Domestic Box Office Revenues........$281.2/($191.8)
Production Cost .... $38.4/($30.0)
Production Period .... 4 years
1991–1995

Director . . . . John Lasseter
Producer . . . . Bonnie Arnold, Ralph
Guggenheim
Production Company. . . . Pixar Animation Studios
Story by. . . . . John Lasseter, Pete Docter,
Andrew Stanton, Joe Ranft
Screenplay by . . . . Joss Whedon, Andrew Stanton,
Joel Cohen, Alex Sokolow
Cast . . . . Tim Allen, Tom Hanks, Don
Rickles, John Ratzenberger
(voices)
Filming Locations . . . . . . Pixar Studios in Pt. Richmond,
CA
Genre. . . . . Animation
Format. . . . . Color (Technicolor)
Initial Release 11/22/1995
Rerelease. . . . . none
Running Time . . . . 81 minutes
MPAA Rating . . . . G

STANDING THE TEST OF TIME

ACADEMY AWARD Oscar Nominations and Wins

Music (Original Musical or Comedy Score): Randy Newman

Music (Original Song): "You've Got a Friend in Me" Music and Lyrics by Randy Newman

Writing (Screenplay – written directly for the screen): Screenplay by Joss Whedon, Andrew Stanton, Joel Cohen, Alec Sokolow; Story by John Lasseter, Peter Docter, Andrew Stanton, Joe Ranft

*SPECIAL ACHIEVEMENT AWARD: John Lasseter for his inspired leadership of the Pixar *Toy Story* team, resulting in the first feature-length computer-animated film

OSCAR TOTALS   Nominations **4**   *Wins 1

AFI 100 YEARS 100 MOVIES SELECTION
2007 . . . #99   1997 0

TOP 300 FILMS POSITION . . . . #122
All-Release Domestic Box Office in Equivalent 2005 $s

National Film Preservation Board Selection. . . . 2005

OTHER AWARDS Best Picture Wins

	Year
Golden Globes	none
New York Film Critics	none
National Board of Review	none
Film Daily Critics	none

Toy Story *became the standard in the industry because it set a whole new precedent for the quality that people expect in an animated movie.*
—George Lucas

PLOT: Woody, a boy's favorite toy, feels neglected when he fears a new space hero toy (Buzz Lightyear) has replaced him, but despite their differences Woody and Buzz discover that they were meant to be friends.

PRODUCTION: While working at Disney as an animator, John Lasseter saw the short film *Tron* (1982) and immediately realized the potential of computer graphics. He wanted to use these new tools within the medium of animation, but he knew that story and characters were still needed to drive a full-length feature. Once at Pixar, Lasseter, Steve Jobs, and Ed Catmull shared a common goal: to make world-class computer animated films. After the success of their short film *Tin Toy,* which won an Oscar in 1988, Disney agreed to collaborate and produce three feature films with Pixar. John Lasseter got the green light for a full-length animated feature called *Toy Story.* The first computer animated feature ever made, it was a modern buddy story that ran contrary to the animation conventions of the time because it was neither a musical nor a fairy tale. Since computer-generated characters were such a new creation, there were doubts about whether audiences would even sit through this kind of full-length feature. To allay these concerns, the crew put together some textured and rendered characters. When they showed them to their Disney collaborators, they got the approval needed to proceed. John Lasseter's love of toys drove the film. He still treasures his beloved childhood Casper doll with its string-pull voice box. This toy was the inspiration for the character Woody. As part of the film's research, the creative team borrowed a company credit card and perused the aisles of a local toy store, filling their carts with all kinds of playthings. Making the first animated feature was not easy; the crew realized that they had to design all of the sets, hairstyles, and costumes. The world of *Toy Story* had to be created from scratch. When the film was presented in its rough form to Disney, the company was dissatisfied and promptly shut down the production only weeks before animation was due to start; Disney demanded that the story department move to L.A. so that the Pixar team could be supervised. Instead, Lasseter begged for two more weeks to make fixes. His animators then took all the Disney notes and made changes. The team turned the film around in the allotted time, and Disney loved it when it was screened again. They knew they were making something new, but nothing prepared them for the look of the film when it was rendered. The result was the beginning of a new genre of filmmaking.

DISTRIBUTION: *Toy Story* was an immediate success, opening to a $29.1 million weekend. It was the highest-grossing movie of 1995 in domestic box office. It went on worldwide to make $364.9 million and is in the top 20 of biggest worldwide grossing animation movies of all time. It also became a lucrative merchandising bonanza. This was not only a powerful return on a production budget of only $30 million but a phenomenal start for the nascent company. Pixar went public the same year, with 6.9 million shares offered at $22 per share. *Toy Story* was released in 2005 in a special edition tenth-anniversary DVD with a higher digital bit rate than any previous release. —*Rosaleen O'Byrne*

TWISTER

Warner Bros. (domestic); Universal (foreign), 1996

ALL-RELEASE EQUIVALENT 2005 $s

(Unadjusted $s) in Millions of $s

Domestic Box Office Revenues . . . . **$350.5**/($241.7)
Production Cost . . . . **$114.5**/($92.0)
Principal Photography . . . . **84** days estimated
5/1/1995–8/21/1995

Director . . . . Jan de Bont

Producer . . . . Kathleen Kennedy, Ian Bryce, Michael Crichton

Production Company . . . . Warner Bros., Amblin Entertainment

Story and

  Screenplay by . . . . Michael Crichton, Anne-Marie Martin

Cast . . . . Helen Hunt, Bill Paxton, Cary Elwes, Jami Gertz

Filming Locations . . . . . . Los Angeles, CA; Ames, IA; Oklahoma

Genre . . . . Disaster

Format . . . . Color (Technicolor)

Initial Release 5/10/1996

Rerelease . . . . none

Running Time . . . . 114 minutes

MPAA Rating PG-13

STANDING THE TEST OF TIME

ACADEMY AWARD Oscar Nominations and Wins

Sound: Steve Maslow, Gregg Landaker, Kevin O'connell, Geoffrey Patterson

Visual Effects: Stefen Fangmeier, John Frazier, Habib Zargarpout, Henry La Bounta

    OSCAR TOTALS   Nominations **2**   *Wins 0

AFI 100 YEARS 100 MOVIES SELECTION

                2007 0   1997 0

TOP 300 FILMS POSITION . . . . #70

All-Release Domestic Box Office in Equivalent 2005 $s

National Film Preservation Board Selection . . . . none

OTHER AWARDS Best Picture Wins

	Year
Golden Globes	none
New York Film Critics	none
National Board of Review	none
Film Daily Critics	none

*We were always trying to catch these weather windows and cut-and-pasting the script.
A lot of people were panicking and Jan had to keep his head. He held it together.*

—Bill Paxton

PLOT: A series of tornados are chased by rival teams of researchers, including an estranged couple who keep meeting at twisters.

PRODUCTION: Warner Bros. and Universal jointly purchased the *Twister* spec script, written by Michael Crichton and his wife, Anne-Marie Martin, for an estimated $2.5 million in 1994. Dutch cinematographer Jan de Bont's first directing effort, *Speed,* was one of the top 10 domestic box office films of 1994. He was looking for another project that would allow him to use the fluid camera movements for which he had become noted. *Twister* offered such a story. While script rewrites went on, the film was cast with recognizable actors rather than superstars, including Helen Hunt, known for the TV sitcom *Mad About You,* and Bill Paxton, who had recently performed supporting roles in James Cameron's *True Lies* (1994) and Ron Howard's *Apollo 13* (1995). Two writers, Joss Whedon and Steven Zaillian, had turned in rewrites of the script before production began, but de Bont was not satisfied. Uncredited screenwriter Jeff Nathanson was flown to the set two weeks into production, where he was kept very busy. The director would later say, "We were rewriting until the last day." The unfinished script contributed to a sense of constant turmoil on the set. The multiple cameras used by de Bont (who sought a documentary look to the action) had to compete with the constant noise of wind machines. Each shot had to be carefully planned to add special effects afterward. Stefen Fangmeier and his crew from Industrial Light & Magic created tornado shots using Dynamation's clip effects. Having to constantly experiment with the program to achieve the effects he sought, Fangmeier referred to *Twister* as "an incredibly satisfying learning experience on every level." That feeling was not shared on set. Hunt and Paxton suffered for de Bont's desire to have his actors as close to the action as possible. Both actors had to take hepatitis shots after filming a scene in a ditch full of bacteria. In another scene, Hunt sustained a concussion when she was hit in the head attempting to open a truck door as the vehicle sped past her in a cornfield. She called the experience "totally brutal." As the film fell behind schedule, the stress caused further problems. The original director of photography, Don Burgess, and other crew members walked off the set midway through the shoot. Jack N. Green, who got sole credit, was brought on as cinematographer. In the end, de Bont got the turmoil he wanted on film, even if it was accompanied by unwanted turmoil off camera.

DISTRIBUTION: *Twister* opened the summer movie season of 1996 on thousands of screens and was a hit. It was the number two film at both the domestic and foreign box office, coming in between *Independence Day* (first place) and *Mission: Impossible* (third place). Industrial Light & Magic was nominated for Best Visual Effects for its work by both the American and British Academies. Despite mixed reviews, some of which referred to the image of a cow flying across the screen as the movie's high point, the film was popular for its use of visually stunning special effects and the high energy of its cinematography. Its director had fused his filmmaking style with the script, allowing it to evolve into an entertaining summer popcorn movie. —*Louis Burklow*

MISSION: IMPOSSIBLE
Paramount, 1996

ALL-RELEASE EQUIVALENT 2005 $s
(Unadjusted $s) in Millions of $s

Domestic Box Office Revenues....... **$262.5**/($181.0)
Production Cost .... **$99.6**/($80.0)
Principal Photography...........**109** days estimated
3/13/1995–8/8/1995

Genre.................. Action Adventure
Format................ Color (Eastmancolor)
Initial Release.......... 5/22/1996
Rerelease .... none
Running Time.......... 110 minutes
MPAA Rating PG-13

Director .... Brian De Palma
Producer .... Tom Cruise, Paula Wagner
Production Company.... Cruise/Wagner Productions, Paramount Pictures
Story by.............. David Koepp, Steven Zallian based on the TV series *Mission: Impossible*, created by Bruce Geller
Screenplay by......... David Koepp, Robert Towne
Cast .... Tom Cruise, Jon Voight, Emmanuelle Beart, Henry Czerny, Jean Reno, Ving Rhames, Kristin Scott-Thomas, Vanessa Redgrave
Filming Locations ...... In studio: Pinewood Studios, Buckinghamshire, UK; Barrandov Studios, Prague, Czech Republic; on location: London, England; Annan and Cumnock rail line, Scotland; Prague, Czech Republic; McLean, VA; Washington, D.C.

STANDING THE TEST OF TIME

ACADEMY AWARD Oscar Nominations and Wins
None

OSCAR TOTALS   Nominations 0   *Wins 0

AFI 100 YEARS 100 MOVIES SELECTION
2007..... 0   1997..... 0

TOP 300 FILMS POSITION .... **#141**
All-Release Domestic Box Office in Equivalent 2005 $s

National Film Preservation Board Selection....none

OTHER AWARDS Best Picture Wins

	Year
Golden Globes	none
New York Film Critics	none
National Board of Review	none
Film Daily Critics	none

My first idea . . . was let's turn this whole thing upside down. In the first mission we'll do what never happens in Mission: Impossible: *We'll kill everybody.*

—Brian DePalma

PLOT: It is a mission that secret agent Ethan Hunt (Tom Cruise) has no choice but to accept: either ferret out the mole who murdered the members of his IMF team or face the CIA's justice as a suspected traitor.

PRODUCTION: The $270 million worldwide box office generated by Sydney Pollack's *The Firm* (1993) proved that Tom Cruise could open a movie. Now that Cruise had bankable power, he and partner Paula Wagner set up their new production company at Paramount to develop movie roles that played to Cruise's strengths. They discovered the perfect franchise vehicle in an old CBS TV show, *Mission: Impossible.* Paramount had long tried to turn the series into a motion picture, coming closest in 1985 with Peter Graves attached to star in his original role as Jim Phelps. Development took longer than anticipated, due to a complicated plot. Willard Huyck and Gloria Katz wrote the first draft of the screenplay; then a host of rewriters came aboard, including Steven Zaillian, David Koepp, and finally *Chinatown*'s Robert Towne. Veteran director Brian De Palma was hired for his ability to keep an audience on the edge of their seats. It would be the biggest box office movie of his career. When he wasn't breaking the story down with the writers, he was perfecting the action sequences with first-generation previsualization software. To keep the budget under control and win the studio greenlight, Cruise deferred his $20 million fee for a higher percentage of the box office. De Palma convinced Cruise to switch the story's opening mission from Vienna to Prague, which had invested heavily in a low-cost, state-of-the-art filmmaking infrastructure since the fall of Communism. But shooting in historic locations such as the Hotel Europa and the Charles Bridge posed lighting problems, as nailing fixtures to the walls was strictly prohibited. Fortunately, Stephen Burum, De Palma's longtime DP, stumbled across a company that produced helium-filled illumination globes, providing thousands of watts of light for the difficult locations. The stunt work at Pinewood proved equally daunting. While cabling down into the CIA vault, like the thieves in Jules Dassin's *Topkapi*, Tom Cruise kept smacking the floor and had to fill his shoes with sand to help keep his balance. He wanted to be whipped around during the film's climax on the train roof, but none of the wind machines, high-powered fans, or jet engines that the effects team tested generated a current strong enough to distort Cruise's face. They finally settled on a skydiving simulator, which hammered Cruise with a slipstream of 140 mph as he hung on for dear life.

DISTRIBUTION: Paramount released the film on 3,012 screens, making it the widest opening in cinema history as of that date. *Mission: Impossible* stayed in theaters well into December to gross the third-highest domestic box office of 1996 (behind *Independence Day* and *Twister*). Cruise's gambit to work for scale and take his monies off the back end more than doubled his usual payday. Paramount's $21 million domestic marketing campaign plastered a movie billboard on the Viacom building in Times Square and printed Cruise's profile on thousands of theater popcorn bags. Blockbuster played trailers for the film in their video stores. MTV put the music video for the soundtrack's U2 song in rotation. Apple spent $15 million for product placement of its computers in the film and ran *Mission: Impossible*–branded advertisements for its PowerBook that read: "After you see the movie, pick up the Book." —*Michael Kogge*

781

INDEPENDENCE DAY

20th Century-Fox, 1996

ALL-RELEASE EQUIVALENT 2005 $s

(Unadjusted $s) in Millions of $s

Domestic Box Office Revenues . . . . **$444.0**/($306.2)
Production Cost . . . .**$93.4**/($75.0)
Principal Photography . . . . **70** days estimated
7/28/1995–11/2/1995

Director . . . . Roland Emmerich

Producer . . . . Dean Devlin

Production Company . . . . Centropolis Entertainment,
20th Century-Fox Film Corp.

Story and

  Screenplay by . . . . Dean Devlin, Roland Emmerich

Cast . . . . Will Smith, Bill Pullman, Jeff
Goldblum, Mary McDonnell,
Judd Hirsch, Harry Connick Jr.,
Margaret Colin, Judd Hirsch

Filming Locations . . . . . . Los Angeles, CA; Blue Ridge,
GA; Colorado Springs, CO;
Dallas, TX, Fontana, CA; Grants
Pass, OR; Lakepoint, UT;
Manhattan, NY; Michigan City,
ID; Mount Kilimanjaro, Kenya;
Philadelphia, PA; Pittsburgh,
PA; Reykjavik, Iceland; Skull
Valley, UT; Stockhold, Sweden;
Sydney, Australia; Tooele, UT;
Washington D.C.; Wendover,
UT; West New York, NJ; White
Sands, NM; Windsor, CA

Genre . . . . Sci-Fi, Disaster

Format . . . . Color (DeLuxe)

Initial Release . . . . 6/25/1996 premiere; 7/3/1996
general release

Rerelease . . . . none

Running Time . . . . 145 minutes

MPAA Rating PG-13

STANDING THE TEST OF TIME

ACADEMY AWARD Oscar Nominations and Wins

Sound: Chris Carpenter, Bill W. Benton, Bob Beemer,
Jeff Wexler

*VISUAL EFFECTS: Volker Engel, Douglas Smith,
Clay Pinney, Joseph Viskocil

   OSCAR TOTALS   Nominations **2**   *Wins **1**

AFI 100 YEARS 100 MOVIES SELECTION
2007 0   1997 0

TOP 300 FILMS POSITION . . . . #33
All-Release Domestic Box Office in Equivalent 2005 $s

National Film Preservation Board Selection . . . . none

OTHER AWARDS Best Picture Wins

	Year
Golden Globes	none
New York Film Critics	none
National Board of Review	none
Film Daily Critics	none

*The most valuable thing Roland ever told me was "Look, Dean, you're not a genius.
I'm not a genius, and we're never going to be geniuses. But if we work really hard,
then hopefully, one day, we'll make a good movie."*

—Dean Devlin

PLOT: On July 4, aliens invade and all but obliterate the biggest cities on earth. A small group of survivors mobilize their forces, defeat the aliens, and save the world.

PRODUCTION: While promoting the surprisingly successful MGM science fiction drama *Stargate* in October 1994, producer and director Roland Emmerich was asked if he believed in aliens. When he said no, the reporter asked how he could then make a film like *Stargate*. Emmerich's response was, "I believe in the great 'what if?' What if tomorrow morning you walked out of your door and these enormous spaceships hovered over every single city in the world. Wouldn't that be the most exciting thing that could happen?" As *Independence Day* co-writer and Emmerich's producing partner Dean Devlin recalls, Emmerich then looked at him and said, "I think I have our next movie." They went to Mexico to write, and less than two months later, on a Thursday at noon, they were circulating the script for consideration, complete with a marketing plan. By Friday morning, 20th Century-Fox had purchased the screenplay, greenlighted the film, and agreed to pay Devlin and Emmerich $7.5 million plus a share of the profits. *Independence Day* went into preproduction the following Monday. Immediately thereafter, three conceptual artists began creating storyboards that included a conception of the alien monster. When built, the disgusting-looking eight-foot-long creature required frequent applications of low-tech K-Y jelly to maintain its sheen. A ten-by-four-foot model of the White House was constructed for $40,000 and blown up in a computer controlled explosion. The huge number of special effects was created by melding new techniques with the old, utilizing everything from the most modern computer-generated imagery to miniature models suspended by wires. More than 750 technicians toiled inside a former Hughes aircraft plant in west Los Angeles for nine months on the effects, both physical and computer-generated. It took thirty people four months to build a spacecraft that filled 52,000 square feet and weighed seventeen tons. To create the astonishing effect of massive fireballs shooting down the streets of New York City, the crew built a giant model encompassing dozens of city blocks. The model was hoisted onto its side with explosives at the bottom and a camera mounted at the top. When the explosives were ignited, the fire flashed upward through the model, creating the effect of fire shooting down city streets. However, when Emmerich and his team went to work creating the aerial dogfights between the human fighter jets and alien spacecraft, they relied exclusively on computers.

DISTRIBUTION: The pressure was on to get the movie finished not only for a Fourth of July release but also ahead of a similar sci-fi project at Warner Bros. directed by Tim Burton, *Mars Attacks!* To go along with the studio shots, the filmmakers mapped out a rapid tour of cities for exteriors, including New York, Washington, D.C., Utah, and parts of Los Angeles. When it was clear that the Fox film would be ready first, *Mars Attacks!* was moved to Christmas. When *ID4*, as it was known, opened at the end of June, it was an immediate hit despite mixed and even negative reviews from most major critics. It went on to become the highest-grossing film of 1996, bringing in nearly $817 million in worldwide box office. —*Mark D'Anna*

THE ENGLISH PATIENT
Miramax, 1996

ALL-RELEASE EQUIVALENT 2005 $s
(Unadjusted $s) in Millions of $s

Domestic Box Office Revenues......... **$114.1**/($78.7)
Production Cost .... **$54.8**/($44.0)
Principal Photography ....100 days estimated
9/4/1995–1/31/1996

Director .... Anthony Minghella
Producer .... Saul Zaentz
Production Company.... The Saul Zaentz Company, Tiger Moth Production
Story by.............. Based on the novel by Michael Ondaatje
Screenplay by .... Anthony Minghella
Cast .... Ralph Fiennes, Juliette Binoche, Willem Dafoe, Kristin Scott Thomas, Naveen Andrews, Colin Firth, Julian Wadham, Jürgen Prochnow
Filming Locations ...... Italy, North Africa
Genre................ Drama
Format............... Color
Initial Release 11/6/1996
Rerelease............. none
Running Time .... 160 minutes
MPAA Rating .... R

STANDING THE TEST OF TIME

ACADEMY AWARD Oscar Nominations and Wins

***BEST PICTURE:** Saul Zaentz, Producer

Actor in a Leading Role: Ralph Fiennes

Actor in a Supporting Role: Kristin Scott Thomas ·

***ACTRESS IN A SUPPORTING ROLE:** Juliette Binoche

***ART DIRECTION/SET DECORATION:** Stuart Craig/Stephenie McMillan

***CINEMATOGRAPHY:** John Seale

***COSTUME DESIGN:** Ann Roth

***DIRECTING:** Anthony Minghella

***FILM EDITING:** Walter Murch

***MUSIC** (Original Dramatic Score): Gabriel Yared

***SOUND:** Walter Murch, Mark Berger, David Parker, Chris Newman

Writing (Screenplay – based on material previously produced or published): Anthony Minghella

OSCAR TOTALS   Nominations **12** *Wins 9

AFI 100 YEARS 100 MOVIES SELECTION
2007 0   1997 0

TOP 300 FILMS POSITION .... none
All-Release Domestic Box Office in Equivalent 2005 $s

National Film Preservation Board Selection .... none

OTHER AWARDS Best Picture Wins

	Year
Golden Globes	1997
New York Film Critics......................	none
National Board of Review..................	none
Film Daily Critics	none

*It was a stamina issue of a strenuous location shoot. It was like being in purgatory.
I felt enormous pressure . . . It was very difficult.*
—Anthony Minghella

PLOT: As World War II ends, a Canadian nurse cares for an unidentified British pilot who was horribly burned in a plane wreck. The two are left in a ruined Italian monastery, where the nurse gradually learns her patient's back story, involving a tragic love affair.

PRODUCTION: Author Michael Ondaatje had based the central character in his 1992 novel *The English Patient* on Count Laszlo de Almasy, a Hungarian famous for exploring the Sahara Desert. The critically acclaimed book won the prestigious Booker Prize after it was published in the United Kingdom, where director Anthony Minghella read it in one sitting. Minghella, a writer of stage plays and television dramas whose first directing job was *Truly, Madly, Deeply*, a feature film financed by the BBC film division, pitched it as a movie to maverick American producer Saul Zaentz, who began pursuing it. Zanetz met with Minghella in Los Angeles to discuss how the complex story could be adapted for the screen. Zaentz then made a deal with 20th Century-Fox, who wanted Demi Moore to play Katherine, the upper-class Englishwoman, a part Minghella wanted to be played by Kristin Scott Thomas. After more casting conflicts emerged, Fox pulled out. As production neared, the film's future was in grave doubt. Then Miramax stepped in, with Zaentz putting up $6 million of his own money to win final cut. Zaentz brought in cinematographer John Seale and editor Walter Murch. Sean Connery read the script but was forced to pull out because of scheduling conflicts. In the meantime, Zaentz sent the book to Juliette Binoche, who loved it. Minghella revised the script numerous times, drawing on an actual journal left by Almasy about his 1930s expeditions in the Libyan desert. Minghella filled five notebooks with storyboards covering every shot in the film. To show different locations, Minghella used "palettes of color" to define the desert and places in Italy. The movie made significant changes from the book, which Ondaatje approved. Saul Zaentz assumed the role of "godfather" on the set. Everyone knew that he was taking a gamble on Minghella, who had never directed a film of such size and scope. It was a difficult production, but as filming progressed the cast and crew came together, believing in the project. "There was no star or someone fighting for screen position," said Zaentz. "Everyone was serious." Minghella and cinematographer John Seale had to rely on their judgment for angles and shots. They moved quickly, knowing that they wouldn't see the dailies until the locations were struck, which added more stress. The production design, by Stuart Craig, had a heavy logistical schedule involving German Afrika Korps uniforms and tracked vehicles for the brutal desert warfare scenes in North Africa. Walter Murch began editing on film but switched to the Avid video assist editing system to be at home with his son, who was suffering from a medical condition. The film took approximately five months to edit. "We knew we had something," said Zaentz.

DISTRIBUTION: The critics quickly acclaimed the film, which grew from an art house release into a major movie at the box office. It is fifty-fifth on the BFI top 100 list. At the sixty-ninth Academy Awards, on March 24, 1997, Zaentz was already being honored with the Irving G. Thalberg Award, and then added his third Best Picture Oscar for this movie. Juliette Binoche was a surprise winner, as the sentimental favorite was Lauren Bacall (*The Mirror Has Two Faces*). With nine Oscars, the film took its place among the most honored in Academy history. —*Frank McAdams*

LIAR LIAR

Universal, 1997

ALL-RELEASE EQUIVALENT 2005 $s

(Unadjusted $s) in Millions of $s

Domestic Box Office Revenues........**$253.3**/($181.4)
Production Cost ....**$79.1**/($65.0)
Principal Photography............**75** days estimated
7/8/1996–10/18/1996

Director	Tom Shadyac
Producer	Brian Grazer
Production Company	Universal Pictures, Imagine Entertainment
Story and	
Screenplay by	Paul Guay, Stephen Mazur
Cast	Jim Carrey, Maura Tierney, Justin Cooper
Filming Locations	On Location in California: Los Angeles International Airport, City Hall, Los Angeles City Jail, suburban Pasadena; in studio at Universal, Universal City, CA
Genre	Comedy
Format	Color (DeLuxe)
Initial Release	3/21/1997
Rerelease	none
Running Time	87 minutes
MPAA Rating	PG-13

STANDING THE TEST OF TIME

ACADEMY AWARD Oscar Nominations and Wins

None

OSCAR TOTALS   Nominations 0   *Wins 0

AFI 100 YEARS 100 MOVIES SELECTION
2007 0   1997 0

TOP 300 FILMS POSITION . . . . #155
All-Release Domestic Box Office in Equivalent 2005 $s

National Film Preservation Board Selection . . . . none

OTHER AWARDS Best Picture Wins

	Year
Golden Globes	none
New York Film Critics	none
National Board of Review	none
Film Daily Critics	none

*Jim plays a realistic character, which is what we both wanted to do.
It's the first time he shows up in a movie with his own hair.*

—Tom Shadyac

PLOT: A hard-charging defense attorney, who has let work interfere with his attention to his young son, becomes the victim of the boy's birthday wish: that he be unable to tell a lie for twenty-four hours.

PRODUCTION: Producer Brian Grazer had been actively trying to come up with a movie based on lying and truth-telling when a screenplay serendipitously landed on his desk, applying this concept to the legal profession (co-writer Stephen Mazur was himself a lawyer). Grazer gave the script to Jim Carrey, who shared it with Tom Shadyac, his director on *Ace Ventura: Pet Detective* (1994). Carrey had become a sensation not only in the two *Ace* films but also in *The Mask* and *Dumb and Dumber,* all of them based on a clowning, Jerry Lewis–like persona. But his most recent appearance, *The Cable Guy,* had featured a darker side that fans found more difficult to accept. As Shadyac put it, "His extreme success bred an expectation; people were just waiting to have that gut-wrenching laughter." *Liar Liar* was just what both men needed. "It was one of the few scripts where Jim and I laughed out loud reading it," recalled Shadyac. The filmmakers wanted *Liar Liar* to be more "reality-based" than any of the previous Carrey comedies. Though most of the film was shot on soundstages, they did extensive location work in the Los Angeles area. Exteriors were shot at city hall, and the crew was able to work inside the just-completed city jail. Most spectacularly, the production captured shots for the film's climax on the tarmac at Los Angeles International Airport. The summer of 1996 was very hot in southern California, so to maintain constant light levels without exposing the actors too directly to the heat of the sun, the production used a gargantuan 60-by-60-foot silk screen, anchored to a corrugated metal roof that, unfortunately, creaked with the slightest breeze, forcing an exercise in temper control. On scenes shot in suburban Pasadena, the sound crew also fought incessant airplane and bird noise, for unlike many directors, Shadyac disliked "looping," or lip-synching, favoring a clean audio track in postproduction for comedies. Carrey and Shadyac decided to play the character's enforced honesty as if it were Tourette's syndrome, as the director put it. The actor would go through comic convulsions as the unwanted, and almost always embarrassing, truth spewed out of his mouth. Shadyac, who was accustomed to Carrey's rich improvisational gifts, would regularly leave the camera running longer than necessary to catch all of his free-form spontaneity. He was careful to cast around Carrey a troupe of serious dramatic actors who, Shadyac said, "grounded" the manic performance.

DISTRIBUTION: The first test-screening audiences seemed happy enough to see Jim Carrey clowning once more, but Shadyac (known fondly as "Shady-Hack" for his cold-blooded eye in the editing room) realized almost instantly that the film had to be pared. He removed a subplot involving one of the Carrey character's early clients and tightened the pace of the action-filled ending sequences at the airport. The much brisker cut became an instant smash, as the film's simple concept—Jim Carrey as a lawyer who cannot lie—attracted Carrey's huge audience once again. Of the top 5 domestic box office hits of 1997 (*Titanic, Men in Black, The Lost World: Jurassic Park, Liar Liar,* and *Air Force One*), *Liar Liar* was the only film with no Oscar nominations. —*Tom Dupree*

MEN IN BLACK

Columbia, 1997

ALL-RELEASE EQUIVALENT 2005 $s

(Unadjusted $s) in Millions of $s

Domestic Box Office Revenues . . . . **$350.1**/($250.7)
Production Cost . . . . **$103.4**/($85.0)
Principal Photography . . . . **97** days estimated
3/14/1996–7/27/1996

Director . . . . Barry Sonnenfeld
Producer . . . . Walter F. Parkes, Laurie
MacDonald
Production Company . . . . Amblin Entertainment
Story by . . . . Based on the comic magazine
by Lowell Cunningham
Screenplay by . . . . Ed Solomon
Cast . . . . Tommy Lee Jones, Will Smith,
Linda Fiorentino,
Vincent D'Onofrio, Rip
Torn, Tony Shalhoub
Filming Locations . . . . . . New York, at Liberty State Park
in New Jersey, and in Los
Angeles
Genre . . . . Sci-Fi
Format . . . . Color (Technicolor)
Initial Release 7/2/1997
Rerelease . . . . none
Running Time . . . . 98 minutes
MPAA Rating PG-13

STANDING THE TEST OF TIME

ACADEMY AWARD Oscar Nominations and Wins

Art Direction/Set Decoration: Bo Welch/
Cheryl Carasik
*MAKEUP: Rick Baker, David LeRoy Anderson
Music (Original Musical or Comedy Score): Danny
Elfman

OSCAR TOTALS   Nominations **3**   *Wins **1**

AFI 100 YEARS 100 MOVIES SELECTION
2007 0   1997 0

TOP 300 FILMS POSITION . . . . **#73**
All-Release Domestic Box Office in Equivalent 2005 $s

National Film Preservation Board Selection . . . . none

OTHER AWARDS Best Picture Wins

	Year
Golden Globes	none
New York Film Critics	none
National Board of Review	none
Film Daily Critics	none

*Steven Spielberg called me and Barry Sonnenfeld said his wife sat up in the bed
after she read the script and screamed, "Will Smith!"*

—Will Smith

PLOT: While two federal agents, J and K, monitor all alien-related activity, they uncover an intergalactic plot and rush to foil it by tracking down the terrorist Edgar/Bug—hence saving the Earth from destruction.

PRODUCTION: The term "men in black" dates to the 1950s, when there were reports of men in black suits intimidating witnesses to UFO incidents. The name was adapted for a comic book series, *The Men in Black,* created and written by Lowell Cunningham and illustrated by Sandy Carruthers (for Aircel Comics, which was acquired by Malibu Comics and by Marvel Comics in 1994). Chris O'Donnell was first offered the role of J, but he felt the part was too much like his role as Robin in the *Batman* series. Then David Schwimmer turned it down, as did Clint Eastwood. Originally, Quentin Tarantino was offered the chance to direct the film, but when he passed it went to Les Mayfield. Mayfield left shortly before production began and was replaced by Barry Sonnenfeld. The original script took place in various locations throughout the United States (including Kansas, Nevada, and Washington, D.C.), but Sonnenfeld believed that if there were aliens, they would most likely be comfortable in New York. So the script was changed to centralize the story in the Big Apple. The MIB headquarters was based on the TWA terminal at JFK Airport. Sonnenfeld wanted to play the story as somewhat of a police procedural, such as *The French Connection,* except that when the agents were shaking a guy down, they were actually shaking down an alien. The first chase scene, in which J (Will Smith) shakes down a perp, was scheduled to be shot all around Lincoln Center, but when the New York Philharmonic wanted a $1 million fee, they switched locations to the Guggenheim Museum instead. For Rick Baker (alien makeup effects artist), this was the most challenging movie of his career, in part because Sonnenfeld changed direction during the production. At first he wanted aliens without human characteristics, but when he saw one with no eyes and wondered where it was looking, he changed his mind, asking that they all be altered to have more human qualities. Baker then had to get everything approved not just by Sonnenfield but by Steven Spielberg too. Compounding matters was the fact that the two did not always agree initially. The greatest amount of time was spent on the Edgar/Bug character. Sonnenfeld was becoming increasingly worried that the ending, a spoken debate between J and Edgar/Bug, was not what the film demanded. As a result, forty-five computer graphics shots never budgeted for were required. Each cost $100,000 to produce, adding $4.5 million to the total production cost. But when the shots were delivered, the film had just the action it had been missing. In retrospect, all agreed that it was the best money they had spent. Additionally, it was felt that the original plot was too complicated. Consequently, Sonnenfeld and his team cut an entire nation of aliens in postproduction. To alter the plot further, three scenes had to be redone. Luckily, one was subtitled, so only rewriting was required. The second was minimal too, entailing a change to what appeared on the big screen at MIB headquarters. The third scene involved reanimating the mouth of Frank, the talking pug dog.

DISTRIBUTION: The film, which opened July 2, 1997, was an immediate hit, grossing over $250 million in the United States and more than $587 million worldwide. It was followed by a sequel, *Men in Black II,* in 2002. —*Christine McDermott*

GOOD WILL HUNTING

Miramax, 1997

ALL-RELEASE EQUIVALENT 2005 $s

(Unadjusted $s) in Millions of $s

Domestic Box Office Revenues........**$189.4**/($138.4)
Production Cost ....**$12.2**/($10.0)
Principal Photography...........**100** days estimated
shot in 20 weeks in 1996

Director . . . . Gus Van Sant

Producer . . . . Lawrence Bender

Production Company . . . . Be Gentlemen Production,
Miramax Films

Story by. . . . . Matt Damon

Screenplay by . . . . Ben Affleck, Matt Damon

Cast . . . . Matt Damon, Robin Williams,
Ben Affleck, Minnie Driver

Filming Locations . . . . . . Toronto, Canada; Boston,
Cambridge, MA

Genre. . . . . Drama

Format . . . . Color

Initial Release . . . . 12/5/1997 limited release;
12/26/1997 expanded release;
1/9/1998 wide release

Rerelease. . . . . none

Running Time . . . . 126 minutes

MPAA Rating . . . . R

STANDING THE TEST OF TIME

ACADEMY AWARD Oscar Nominations and Wins

Best Picture: Lawrence Bender, Producer

Actor in a Leading Role: Matt Damon

*ACTOR IN A SUPPORTING ROLE: Robin
Williams

Actress in a Supporting Role: Minnie Driver

Directing: Gus Van Sant

Film Editing: Pietro Scalia

Music (Original Dramatic Score): Danny Elfman

Music (Original Song): "Miss Misery," Music and
Lyrics by Elliott Smith

*WRITING (Screenplay – written directly for the
screen): Ben Affleck, Matt Damon

OSCAR TOTALS   Nominations **9**   *Wins 2

AFI 100 YEARS 100 MOVIES SELECTION
2007 0   1997 0

TOP 300 FILMS POSITION . . . . **#299**
All-Release Domestic Box Office in Equivalent 2005 $s

National Film Preservation Board Selection. . . .none

OTHER AWARDS Best Picture Wins

	Year
Golden Globes	none
New York Film Critics.	none
National Board of Review	none
Film Daily Critics	none

We wrote it [the script] right out of frustration. It was like, Why are we sitting here?
Let's make our own movie. And if people come to see it, they come; and if they don't, they don't.
Either way it beats sitting here going crazy.

—Matt Damon

PLOT: Will Hunting, a mathematics prodigy from South Boston, works as a janitor at the Massachusetts Institute of Technology. Upon meeting Skylar, a Harvard premed student, Will has to overcome abandonment fears and learn to love.

PRODUCTION: Matt Damon began writing the script for *Good Will Hunting* in 1992 for a college class. He wrote roughly forty-five pages and shared them with his friend Ben Affleck, who joined the process. Together they embarked upon a five-year odyssey of ups and downs and turnarounds. The initial drafts were written as a thriller about a young South Boston man with a genius IQ who is recruited by the FBI. The script was submitted to Rob Reiner at Castle Rock, who suggested that the writers drop the thriller element and concentrate on character, particularly on how Will's genius is complicated by his anger and fears of abandonment. Reiner went to Oscar-winning screenwriter William Goldman, who validated Reiner's thoughts. Goldman has denied reports that he revised the entire script, writing, "When I read it and spent a day with the writers, all I said was this: Rob's dead right. Period. Total contribution: zero." Castle Rock placed the script into turnaround, where it was picked up by Miramax. Ultimately Damon and Affleck were cast in the film. The writers then convinced Miramax to hire Gus Van Sant to direct, and Robin Williams, Minnie Driver, and Stellan Skarsgård were cast in supporting roles. Writers Guild arbitration, although confidential, gave story credit to Matt Damon and screenplay credit to Matt Damon and Ben Affleck. *Good Will Hunting* was filmed on location in Toronto and the greater Boston area, with a twenty-week shooting schedule in 1996. The University of Toronto stood in for MIT and Harvard. The classroom scenes were filmed at McLennan Physical Laboratories in Toronto. The bar scenes were shot on location in South Boston and Cambridge. The constant rewriting resulted in a script that concentrated on Will's defense mechanisms. He is broken down and then rebuilt through the efforts of his therapist, who also learns something about himself in the process. Robin Williams ad-libbed much of the therapy scene where he talks about his late wife's idiosyncrasies, causing the crew to go into uncontrollable laughter. The film was dedicated to the memory of poet Allen Ginsberg and writer William S. Burroughs, both of whom died in 1997.

DISTRIBUTION: Despite an initial limited release, *Good Will Hunting* vaulted into the category of sleeper hit of the 1997 season, garnering enthusiastic reviews and surprising box-office numbers. With nine Academy Award nominations, it was primed for an upset in the Best Picture category. But it was the year of *Titanic*. Gus Van Sant later reflected that had he known just how successful the film would be, he would have left several more scenes in the final cut. —*Frank McAdams*

TITANIC

Paramount (domestic); 20th Century-Fox (foreign), 1997

ALL-RELEASE EQUIVALENT 2005 $s

(Unadjusted $s) in Millions of $s

Domestic Box Office Revenues....... **$824.8**/($600.8)
Production Cost .... **$243.4**/($200.0)
Principal Photography...........**160** days estimated
July 1996–March 1997

Director............... James Cameron

Producer .... James Cameron, Jon Landau

Production Company.... Lightstorm Entertainment

Story and
Screenplay by........ James Cameron

Cast .... Leonardo DiCapiro, Kate Winslet, Billy Zane, Kathy Bates, Frances Fisher, Gloria Stuart, Bill Paxton, Bernard Hill, David Warner, Victor Garber

Filming Locations ...... Fox Baja Studios, Rosarito, Baja California, Mexico; Halifax, Nova Scotia, Canada; Escondido and Malibu, CA

Genre................. Historical Drama, Disaster

Format................ Color (CFI)

Initial Release .... 1/01/1997 Tokyo International Film Festival (world premiere); 11/18/1997 London, England (London premiere); 12/14/1997 Los Angeles, CA (U.S. premiere); 12/19/1997 (wide release)

Rerelease............. none

Running Time .... 194 minutes

MPAA Rating PG-13

STANDING THE TEST OF TIME

ACADEMY AWARD Oscar Nominations and Wins

*BEST PICTURE: James Cameron and Jon Landau, Producers

Actress in a Leading Role: Kate Winslet

Actress in a Supporting Role: Gloria Stuart

*ART DIRECTION/SET DECORATION: Peter Lamont/Michael Ford

*CINEMATOGRAPHY: Russell Carpenter

*COSTUME DESIGN: Deborah L. Scott

*DIRECTING: James Cameron

*FILM EDITING: Conrad Buff, James Cameron, Richard A. Harris

Makeup: Tina Earnshaw, Greg Cannom, Simon Thompson

*MUSIC (Original Dramatic Score): James Horner

*MUSIC (Original Song): "My Heart Will Go On," Music by James Horner; Lyrics by Will Jennings

*SOUND: Gary Rydstrom, Tom Johnson, Gary Summers, Mark Ulano

*SOUND EFFECTS EDITING: Tom Bellfort, Christopher Boyes

*VISUAL EFFECTS: Robert Legato, Mark Lasoff, Thomas L. Fisher, Michael Kanfer

OSCAR TOTALS   Nominations **14** *Wins **11**

AFI 100 YEARS 100 MOVIES SELECTION
2007 ... #83   1997..... 0

TOP 300 FILMS POSITION .... #6
All-Release Domestic Box Office in Equivalent 2005 $s

National Film Preservation Board Selection....none

OTHER AWARDS Best Picture Wins

	Year
Golden Globes	1998
New York Film Critics....................	none
National Board of Review.................	none
Film Daily Critics..........................	none

A huge, thrilling three-and-a-quarter-hour experience that unerringly lures viewers into the beauty and heartbreak of its lost world. Mr. Cameron's magnificent Titanic *is the first spectacle in decades that honestly invites comparison to* Gone with the Wind.
—Janet Maslin, *New York Times*, 1997

PLOT: The "unsinkable" ocean liner RMS *Titanic* hits an iceberg and sinks during its 1912 maiden voyage, providing the backdrop for a shipboard romance between Jack, a scrappy, carefree steerage passenger, and Rose, a wealthy ingénue trapped in a loveless engagement.

PRODUCTION: The influences behind writer-producer-director James Cameron's *Titanic* were threefold. He happened to see *A Night to Remember*, the 1958 British film based on author Walter Lord's 1955 best-selling book that presents a minute-by-minute account of the *Titanic* disaster, then he read *Titanic: An Illustrated History*, by Don Lynch and Ken Marschall. Lastly, he caught a screening of the IMAX documentary film *Titanica and* decided that the epic sea disaster could also bookend an epic—albeit fictitious—shipboard love story. Cameron pitched his idea to executives at 20th Century-Fox, who "loved" the concept but not the estimated budget (in excess of $100 million.) To help close the deal, Cameron wrote an impressive 169-page film treatment. His first task was to visit the actual *Titanic* wreck, which had been located in 1985. Twelve dives were made to shoot footage, at a reported cost of $3 million. Fox, seeking a production facility with all the required stages, tanks, and support facilities, eventually decided to build one. Forty acres of a 100-acre seaside parcel were purchased near the coastal town of Rosarito in Baja California, Mexico. This facility included four stages: Stage 1, containing an eight-and-a-half-acre tank set adjacent to the Pacific Ocean; Stage 2, housing a smaller thirty-foot tank; and two additional stages for shooting interiors. A one-sided replica of the *Titanic*, built just 10 percent smaller than the actual ship, was constructed in the tank on Stage 1. A hydraulic cable system could "sink" the liner at a 6° angle (it could appear steeper by tilting the cameras). A smaller poop deck set, resembling a giant seesaw, could be rotated 90° vertically to simulate the ship's final plunge. While the Fox Baja facility was under construction (an effort completed in just 100 days), Cameron filmed the "present-day" scenes at a converted warehouse and aboard a ship at Halifax, Nova Scotia, Canada. Fox, meanwhile, concerned with escalating production costs, sought a partnership and eventually teamed with Paramount. Paramount's involvement contributed another $65 million—capped—to the budget, and gave the studio U.S. and Canadian release rights; Fox retained rights to the rest of the world. Later still, a beleaguered Cameron contributed his $10 million director's fee and profit participation points (estimated to be worth $25–$35 million) toward the film's stunning final cost of over $200 million.

DISTRIBUTION: Once in the editing room, the film could not be completed in time for the scheduled July 2 release date so Fox and Paramount reluctantly moved the date to December. But it was worth the wait. The film sailed to an astounding total worldwide box office gross of $1.8 billion, landed fourteen Oscar nominations and eleven Academy Awards. —*Douglas Burns*

ARMAGEDDON
Buena Vista, 1998

ALL-RELEASE EQUIVALENT 2005 $s
(Unadjusted $s) in Millions of $s

Domestic Box Office Revenues........**$275.5**/($201.6)
Production Cost ....**$167.7**/($140.0)
Principal Photography...........**120** days estimated
8/27/1997–2/18/1998

Director . . . . Michael Bay

Producer . . . . Jerry Bruckheimer, Gale Anne Hurd, Michael Bay

Production Company. . . . Touchstone Pictures, Bay Films, Jerry Bruckheimer Films, Pacific Western Productions, Valhalla Motion Pictures

Story by . . . . Robert Roy Pool, Jonathan Hensleigh; adaptation by Tony Gilroy, Shane Salerno

Screenplay by . . . . Jonathan Hensleigh, J. J. Abrams

Cast . . . . Bruce Willis, Billy Bob Thornton, Ben Affleck, Liv Tyler

Filming Locations . . . . . . Walt Disney Studios; South Dakota; New York; Texas; Washington, D.C.; Kennedy Space Center, Galveston, TX; Johnson Space Center, Houston, TX

Genre. . . . . Sci-Fi, Disaster

Format. . . . . Color (Technicolor)

Initial Release 7/1/1998

Rerelease . . . . none

Running Time . . . . 144 minutes

MPAA Rating PG-13

STANDING THE TEST OF TIME

ACADEMY AWARD Oscar Nominations and Wins

Music (Original Song): "I Don't Want to Miss a Thing," Music and Lyrics by Diane Warren

Sound: Kevin O'Connell, Greg P. Russell, Keith A. Wester

Sound Effects Editing: George Watters II

Visual Effects: Richard R. Hoover, Pat McClung, John Frazier

OSCAR TOTALS Nominations **4** *Wins 0

AFI 100 YEARS 100 MOVIES SELECTION
2007 0   1997 0

TOP 300 FILMS POSITION . . . . **#126**
All-Release Domestic Box Office in Equivalent 2005 $s

National Film Preservation Board Selection. . . .none

OTHER AWARDS Best Picture Wins

	Year
Golden Globes	none
New York Film Critics	none
National Board of Review	none
Film Daily Critics	none

An asteroid is pretty uninteresting; it looks like a big russet potato. But, because our asteroid is another character in the movie, we went all over the place in our design and left the reality behind.

—Michael White, production designer

PLOT: An asteroid is on a collision course with Earth. To save the world, a team is recruited by NASA and trained to fly to the asteroid, where they must drill into the surface and drop a nuclear device into its core.

PRODUCTION: In October 1996, screenwriter Jonathan Hensleigh called director Michael Bay with a "three-sentence idea" that intrigued him. Over the next two and a half weeks they fleshed out a treatment and pitched it to Disney. When Bay promised to deliver the studio's biggest movie of 1998, they gave him the green light without a script. An eight-man committee wrote the screenplay, counting uncredited contributions by Bay, Paul Attanasio, and Oscar winner Robert Towne. In May 1997, when producer Jerry Bruckheimer contacted NASA for its approval to shoot in classified areas of the Johnson and Kennedy Space Centers, he was given an immediate A-OK. After all, when he did *Top Gun* and *Crimson Tide,* the U.S. Navy enjoyed record recruitments. *Armageddon* followed three other films in rapid succession about the same subject: the destruction of Earth by a meteor. The TV movies *Asteroid* and *Doomsday Rock* debuted in February and August 1997, respectively, and in May 1998 Paramount released *Deep Impact,* with $353 million in worldwide box office. There were five special effects supervisors and 3,000 total scene setups for *Armageddon.* After three weeks at the Johnson and Kennedy Space Centers, cinematographer John Schwartzman recalled shooting a scene with Bruce Willis underneath a B-2, dangerously close to a certain piece of equipment. A NASA rep went pale, explaining, "That part his hand is next to is worth $60 million, and if he damages it, I could lose my job." Another hairy moment occurred on a launch pad when an unnamed actor, standing near a 100-foot-tall No Smoking sign, absentmindedly lit a cigarette within spitting distance of a tank of liquid nitrogen. On day 107 the team gathered on the Disney lot with Willis jumping and dodging the jagged holes and crevices caused by an asteroid quake, while 300 steam lines and three giant 100-mile-per-hour fans blew. The set required that production designer Michael White create rocklike buttresses, escarpments, and overhangs in a 30-foot-pit that was excavated below stage level. White would also take liberties with the spacesuits. The real ones were so bulky that he thought the cast would look like the Michelin Man, so he designed alternatives influenced by the combat gear won by Navy SEALs. His version was far more form-fitting that the real suits.

DISTRIBUTION: Aerosmith recorded several songs for the film, including "I Don't Want to Miss a Thing," which is to date their only number one hit since they began as a group in 1970. It stayed on top of the charts for four weeks and was nominated for a Best Song Oscar. Critical reviews were disparate, ranging from "It's an intensely visceral pleasure" (*Washington Post*) and a thumbs-up from the late Gene Siskel to its inclusion in perpetuity on Roger Ebert's Most Hated Films list. It won the science fiction fan group's Saturn Awards for Best Direction and Best Science Fiction Film of 1998, but also received seven Golden Raspberry (Razzie) nominations, with Bruce Willis winning Worst Actor honors. Among the top 15 disaster films, *Armageddon* ranks seventh in terms of domestic box office and second in terms of cost—after *Titanic. —Bob Canning*

SAVING PRIVATE RYAN

DreamWorks (domestic); Paramount (foreign), 1998

ALL-RELEASE EQUIVALENT 2005 $s

(Unadjusted $s) in Millions of $s

Domestic Box Office Revenues . . . . **$292.8**/($216.2)
Production Cost . . . . **$93.5**/($78.0)
Principal Photography . . . . **55** days estimated
6/27/1997–9/12/1997

Director . . . . Steven Spielberg
Producer . . . . Steven Spielberg, Ian Bryce,
Mark Gordon, Gary Levinsohn
Production Company . . . . DW Prods. UK Ltd.
Story and
  Screenplay by . . . . Robert Rodat
Cast . . . . Tom Hanks, Edward Burns,
Matt Damon, Tom Sizemore
Filming Locations . . . . . . On location in Ireland and
England
Genre . . . . War
Format . . . . Color (Technicolor)
Initial Release 7/24/1998
Rerelease . . . . none
Running Time . . . . 169 minutes
MPAA Rating . . . . R

STANDING THE TEST OF TIME

ACADEMY AWARD Oscar Nominations and Wins

Best Picture: Steven Spielberg, Ian Bryce, Mark
Gordon, and Gary Levinsohn, Producers

Actor in a Leading Role: Tom Hanks

Art Direction/Set Decoration: Tom Sanders/
Lisa Dean Kavanaugh

*CINEMATOGRAPHY: Janusz Kaminski

*DIRECTING: Steven Spielberg

*FILM EDITING: Michael Kahn

Makeup: Lois Burwell, Conor O'Sullivan,
Daniel C. Striepeke

Music (Original Dramatic Score): John Williams

*SOUND: Gary Rydstrom, Gary Summers,
Andy Nelson, Ronald Judkins

*SOUND EFFECTS EDITING: Gary Rydstrom,
Richard Hymns

Writing (Screenplay – written directly for the screen):
Robert Rodat

OSCAR TOTALS   Nominations **11** *Wins 5

AFI 100 YEARS 100 MOVIES SELECTION
2007 . . . #71   1997 0

TOP 300 FILMS POSITION . . . . **#109**
All-Release Domestic Box Office in Equivalent 2005 $s

National Film Preservation Board Selection . . . . none

OTHER AWARDS Best Picture Wins

	Year
Golden Globes	1999
New York Film Critics	1998
National Board of Review	none
Film Daily Critics	none

*Both the D-Day scenes and the last battle in the town of Ramelle were unlike anything
I've ever attempted, and therefore there was no instruction manual, no handbook that
would show me a precedent for how to do sequences like that.*

—Steven Spielberg

PLOT: Captain John Miller, of the 2nd Rangers, survives the Omaha Beach slaughter only to be sent on a special mission to find Private Ryan, whose three brothers have been killed in combat, so Ryan can return home to what is left of his family.

PRODUCTION: On a morning walk, with his newborn son in his New Hampshire town, screenwriter Robert Rodat looked at a memorial to local men lost dating back to the Revolutionary War. He noticed many names from the same families. Rodat felt that losing a son to a war is painful, but losing more than one is "inconceivable." He brought that story concept to producers Mark Gordon and Gary Levinsohn at the Mutual Film Company, who brought it to Steven Spielberg at DreamWorks. Spielberg had grown up listening to World War II stories from his father and watching war movies. The true story of the Niland family, which lost three of four sons in World War II, shaped Rodat's first drafts. The script was structured in bookend flashback, opening and closing in present time at the Normandy cemetery. Harrison Ford and Mel Gibson were considered for Captain Miller. While at Paramount, finishing work on *Forrest Gump,* Tom Hanks expressed interest in doing a "human war story." Spielberg decided on Hanks. Edward Norton turned down the role of Private Ryan. Scott Frank and Frank Darabont did rewrites on Rodat's draft, emphasizing the brutal elements in Stephen E. Ambrose's book *D-Day.* Art director Tom Sanders scoured locations in France, England, and Ireland. It was in the last that he found a perfect stretch of coastline similar to Normandy's. Spielberg turned to Dale Dye, retired marine captain, to prepare the actors. Dye's boot camp consisted of ten days of grueling military preparation: weapons training, close order drill, close combat, K-rations, individual maneuvers, and tactics along with World War II–era jargon and hand signals. Several actors resented the rigorous training and threatened to leave. Hanks persuaded them to tough it out. Matt Damon, as Private Ryan, was purposely excluded from boot camp so that the other actors would resent him in their character performances. Spielberg kept eight realistic war photos by photojournalist Robert Capa on the bulletin board of his office, and other copies at home. He stared at them relentlessly. He wanted to capture the same feel for the movie. It was the first time since *E.T.* that Spielberg shot in absolute continuity, including the 24-minute-long Omaha Beach sequence. He captured the invasion in three takes with two to five cameras. Spielberg told Gary Rydstrom and Gary Summers of Skywalker Sound to record real bullets and explosions for the soundtrack and not to use any stock footage. A section of Irish coastline was transformed into the German stronghold at Normandy, complete with Belgian gates and iron hedgehogs. The cliffs were dotted with pillboxes and mini-forts from which the Germans rained down their fire. Extras from the Irish Army were used. In England, forty-five miles north of London, a British aerospace facility served as a back lot. It was also used as the bombed-out French village and for the final "Alamo" battle sequence at the bridge.

DISTRIBUTION: Despite controversy over the level of violence portrayed, the film was a worldwide hit, grossing over $510 million at the global box office. The film inspired many media reflections. Many World War II veterans recalled not just Normandy but the entire European campaign. —*Frank McAdams*

SHAKESPEARE IN LOVE

Miramax (domestic); Universal (foreign), 1998

ALL-RELEASE EQUIVALENT 2005 $s

(Unadjusted $s) in Millions of $s

Domestic Box Office Revenues........ **$127.2**/($100.3)
Production Cost .... **$47.9**/($40.0)
Principal Photography........... **73** days estimated
3/12/1998–6/10/1998
Reshoots November 1998

Director............... John Madden

Producer.............. David Parfitt, Donna Gigliotti,
Harvey Weinstein, Edward
Zwick, Marc Norman

Production Company.... Universal Pictures, Miramax
Films, Bedford Falls Productions

Story and
  Screenplay by........ Marc Norman, Tom Stoppard

Cast.................. Joseph Fiennes, Gwyneth
Paltrow, Geoffrey Rush,
Judi Dench, Colin Firth

Filming Locations...... Barnes, London; Broughton
Castle, Banbury, Oxfordshire;
Eton College, Berkshire;
Hatfield House, Hertfordshire;
Holkham Hall & Estate, Norfolk;
Smithfield, Holborn;
Spitalfields, Shoreditch;
Whitehall, Westminster,
London; Shepperton Studios,
Surrey

Genre................. Romantic Comedy

Format................ Color (DeLuxe)

Initial Release......... 12/11/1998

Rerelease............. none

Running Time......... 122 minutes

MPAA Rating......... R

STANDING THE TEST OF TIME

ACADEMY AWARD Oscar Nominations and Wins

*BEST PICTURE: David Parfitt, Donna Gigliotti, Harvey Weinstein, Edward Zwick, and Marc Norman, Producers

Actor in a Leading Role: Geoffrey Rush

*ACTRESS IN A LEADING ROLE: Gwyneth Paltrow

*ACTRESS IN A SUPPORTING ROLE: Judi Dench

*ART DIRECTION/SET DECORATION: Martin Childs/Jill Quertier

Cinematography: Richard Greatrex

*COSTUME DESIGN: Sandy Powell

Directing: John Madden

Film Editing: David Gamble

Makeup: Lisa Westcott, Veronica Brebner

*MUSIC (Original Musical or Comedy Score): Stephen Warbeck

Sound: Robin O'Donoghue, Dominic Lester, Peter Glossop

*WRITING (Screenplay – written directly for the screen): Marc Norman, Tom Stoppard

OSCAR TOTALS   Nominations **13** *Wins 7

AFI 100 YEARS 100 MOVIES SELECTION
2007..... 0   1997..... 0

TOP 300 FILMS POSITION ....none
All-Release Domestic Box Office in Equivalent 2005 $s

National Film Preservation Board Selection. ...none

OTHER AWARDS Best Picture Wins

	Year
Golden Globes	1999
New York Film Critics......................	none
National Board of Review..................	none
Film Daily Critics...........................	none

PLOT: In a romantic period comedy of mistaken identities, mixed-up messages, and forbidden desires, Will Shakespeare looks for inspiration not only for his play but for his love life as well.

PRODUCTION: Writer Marc Norman got the idea when his son Zachary called from Boston University and suggested writing a story about Shakespeare as a young man in the Elizabethan theater. Norman knew that he couldn't write about this icon unless he had something new to say. He'd revisit this idea for nearly two years before he finally realized that Shakespeare was just a frustrated professional writer, very much like himself. After nine months of research, it became evident that once money entered Shakespeare's life, so too did backstabbing, lying, cheating, and lawsuits—all elements of present-day Hollywood. Norman recognized that in writing about Shakespeare he could potentially "satirize the movie business." He learned too that before *Romeo and Juliet,* Shakespeare was just a promising playwright who hadn't written anything better than the other writers of his day. But, according to Norman, "Shakespeare did something quite radical in *Romeo and Juliet* by starting out as a comedy and ending in tragedy." He began to wonder what exactly caused Shakespeare's creative breakthrough. As Norman relays the story, "I turned to the tried-and-true Hollywood theme that he met a woman who served as inspiration. By having him fall in love, Shakespeare goes from being a poet who can talk about love to somebody who has experienced love and can now write about it from his heart." It was a great idea, but historically women were not allowed to perform in the Elizabethan theater. The way to get around this challenge, of course, was to have a woman pretend to be a man. Norman finished the script in three months and in 1991 sold it to Universal, who sent it to writer Tom Stoppard. Norman said of Stoppard, "His name and playwright experience lent a legitimacy to Shakespeare and reassured those who may have questioned my ability." Stoppard added several characters, including Christopher Marlowe. Julia Roberts read the script and committed immediately. Roberts wanted Daniel Day-Lewis for the lead and flew to Dublin to meet him. However, Day-Lewis passed on the role and Roberts ultimately withdrew only a few weeks before production. The picture shut down. "When a picture collapses that close to production, it becomes damaged goods," Norman explained. "It creates a stigma in the industry that translates into 'there is something wrong with this picture.'" Also, Universal had already spent $4 million on set construction. Then, fortuitously, producer Donna Gigliotti gave the script to Harvey Weinstein, who fell in love with it. They spent 12–18 months on it before Universal sold the rights in 1997. John Madden was signed to direct and Gwyneth Paltrow to star. Several hundred actors read with Madden before he cast Joseph Fiennes. Producer Edward Zwick was initially set to direct but was unavailable by the time the film was made. However, his production company, Bedford Falls, remained involved. After initial test audiences had mixed reactions to the ending, a new version of Will and Viola's final scene was filmed in November 1998 (only weeks before release).

DISTRIBUTION: An immediate critical and commercial hit, the film became the first comedy to win Best Picture since 1977's *Annie Hall*. It is forty-ninth on the BFI top 100. Judi Dench won an Oscar even though she was only on-screen for roughly six minutes, making it the shortest performance ever to win an Oscar. —*Hayley Taylor Block*

THE MATRIX
Warner Bros., 1999

ALL-RELEASE EQUIVALENT 2005 $s
(Unadjusted $s) in Millions of $s

Domestic Box Office Revenues........ **$216.3**/($171.4)
Production Cost .... **$76.2**/($65.0)
Principal Photography........... **120** days estimated
3/14/1998–9/1/1998

Director .... Larry Wachowski, Andy Wachowski, Bruce Hunt
Producer .... Joel Silver, Zareh Nalbandian
Production Company.... Groucho II Film Partnership, Silver Pictures, Village Roadshow Pictures Entertainment
Story and
  Screenplay by .... Larry and Andy Wachowski
Cast .... Keanu Reeves, Laurence Fishburne, Carrie-Anne Moss, Hugo Weaving, Gloria Foster, Joe Pantoliano, Marcus Chong, Julian Arahanga, Matt Doran, Belinda McClory
Filming Locations ...... In studio: Fox Studios, Australia; on location: Sydney, Australia
Genre................. Sci-Fi
Format............... Color (Technicolor)
Initial Release 3/31/1999
Rerelease .... none
Running Time .... 136 minutes
MPAA Rating .... R

STANDING THE TEST OF TIME

ACADEMY AWARD Oscar Nominations and Wins

***FILM EDITING:** Zach Staenberg

***SOUND:** John Reitz, Gregg Rudloff, David Campbell, David Lee

***SOUND EFFECTS EDITING:** Dane A. Davis

***VISUAL EFFECTS:** John Gaeta, Janek Sirrs, Steve Courtley, Jon Thum

OSCAR TOTALS   Nominations **4**   *Wins **4**

AFI 100 YEARS 100 MOVIES SELECTION
2007 0   1997 0

TOP 300 FILMS POSITION .... **#218**
All-Release Domestic Box Office in Equivalent 2005 $s

National Film Preservation Board Selection.... none

OTHER AWARDS Best Picture Wins

	Year
Golden Globes	none
New York Film Critics......................	none
National Board of Review..................	none
Film Daily Critics	none

We just really want to see how the idea of an intellectual movie is received by the world. Because if audiences are sort of interested in movies that are made like McDonald's hamburgers, which do have value in our world, then we have to reevaluate our entire career.

—Larry Wachowski, before the release of *The Matrix*

PLOT: Hapless software coder Thomas Anderson (Keanu Reeves) discovers that true reality lies beyond the blinking cursor, where his Internet alter ego Neo might be the One chosen to lead the last bastion of mankind against the tyrannical forces of technology.

PRODUCTION: Brothers Larry and Andy Wachowski were discussing new comic book projects when they hit upon the seed that would become *The Matrix.* They scribbled their ideas of a vast Internet mythology in countless notebooks while they toiled day to day as carpenters. After landing an assignment to write the Sylvester Stallone vehicle *Assassins,* they showed their spec script for *The Matrix* to producer Joel Silver. Silver persuaded Warner Bros. to purchase it for $1 million, though the fusion of poststructuralism, quantum physics, kung fu, *Alice in Wonderland,* and Japanese anime befuddled executives. As the brothers reworked the screenplay, they made the low-budget, critically lauded thriller *Bound* to prove they could direct. But it was the 400-page graphic novel illustrated by comic book veterans Geof Darrow and Steve Skroce that finally convinced the studio. Actors were assigned philosophical tomes from Baudrillard to Schopenhauer for character study. The fight choreography involved more than four months of intense physical training on the wires with the famed martial arts master Yuen Wo-Ping. Every stage of production relied on computers, from previsualization of the action scenes to removal of the stunt wires. Green screens covered most of the walls of the thirty soundstage sets for later insertion of digitally rendered backdrops. Even the dimensions of time and space eventually submitted to the will of the almighty bit, a feat that gave *The Matrix* an Oscar in Visual Effects. Since the Wachowskis wanted to incorporate the kinetics of anime in the fights, John Gaeta's team invented a process called Bullet-Time. A rig of 120 still cameras and two motion-picture cameras captured the stunts at different frame rates and angles, while proprietary software interpolated the frames in between to create a 360° world inside the computer. This advancement expanded the toolbox of virtual cinematography to give filmmakers the ability to manipulate the speed and spatial coordinates of a shot the way they could lighting and focus. Nonetheless, the real world still had its more affordable advantages. Rooftops, office blocks, and other locations in Sydney doubled for the city of the Matrix, and the more than 15,000 liters of Super Slime that poured over Neo oozed better than any digital formulation could have.

DISTRIBUTION: The summer blockbuster season of 1999 started on the last day of March, as *The Matrix* rose to the top of the charts. Most critics viewed the film as an exercise of style over substance, where pop culture, Asian cinema, and postmodern philosophy are sampled for effect, not depth. Even the famous French theorist Jean Baudrillard, whose book *Simula and Simulacrum* is featured in a scene, considered *The Matrix* to be a complete misreading of his ideas. Critics be damned, because no one was listening. The Net finally had a narrative that pushed the buttons of its diverse users, from online gamers in China to chatting housewives in Indiana. Before long *The Matrix* expanded beyond its original programming to inspire philosophical best sellers, trench coat fashions, doctoral theses, copycat slo-mo effects, and two sequels. The film came in fourth at the worldwide box office for 1999 after *Star Wars: Episode I—The Phantom Menace, The Sixth Sense,* and *Toy Story 2.* —Michael Kogge

STAR WARS: EP I THE PHANTOM MENACE

20th Century-Fox, 1999

ALL-RELEASE EQUIVALENT 2005 $s

(Unadjusted $s) in Millions of $s

Domestic Box Office Revenues . . . . **$540.3**/($428.2)
Production Cost . . . . **$149.5**/($127.5)
Principal Photography . . . . **66** days
6/26/1997–9/26/1997

Initial Release 5/19/1999
Rerelease . . . . none
Running Time . . . . 133 minutes
MPAA Rating . . . . PG

Director . . . . George Lucas
Producer . . . . Rick McCallum
Production Company . . . . Lucasfilm Ltd.
Story and
  Screenplay by . . . . George Lucas
Cast . . . . Liam Neeson, Ewan McGregor, Natalie Portman, Jake Lloyd, Ian McDiarmid, Anthony Daniels, Kenny Baker, Pernilla August, Frank Oz
Filming Locations . . . . . . On location: Caserta, Italy; Chott El Gharsa, Tozeur, The Ksar-Medinine, and Hadada, Tunisia; Whippendell Woods, UK; in studio: Leavesden Studios and Pinewood, UK; pickups at Leavesden Studios: Fight Unit 5 days (9/1997–10/1997); 6 days (3/2/1998–3/7/1998) and additional days (August 1998)
Genre . . . . Sci-Fi
Format . . . . Color (DeLuxe)

STANDING THE TEST OF TIME

ACADEMY AWARD Oscar Nominations and Wins

Sound: Gary Rydstrom, Tom Johnson, Shawn Murphy, John Midgley
Sound Effects Editing: Ben Burtt, Tom Bellfort
Visual Effects: John Knoll, Dennis Muren, Scott Squires, Rob Coleman

OSCAR TOTALS   Nominations 3   *Wins 0

AFI 100 YEARS 100 MOVIES SELECTION
2007 0   1997 0

TOP 300 FILMS POSITION . . . . #17
All-Release Domestic Box Office in Equivalent 2005 $s

National Film Preservation Board Selection . . . . none

OTHER AWARDS Best Picture Wins

	Year
Golden Globes	none
New York Film Critics	none
National Board of Review	none
Film Daily Critics	none

Star Wars *comes out of my desire to make a modern fairy tale.*
—George Lucas

PLOT: Jedi Knights seek to uncover an evil which has been spreading throughout the galaxy. Along the way, they encounter a young boy with the potential to bring balance to the Force.

PRODUCTION: George Lucas decided to return to the director's chair for the first *Star Wars* prequel. He started transforming his idea into a draft in 1994, writing in longhand almost every day until 1997. Virtually from the outset, Lucas worked closely with design director Doug Chiang, who oversaw the creation of artwork for the many costumes, creatures, and storyboards. Together, they and producer Rick McCallum helped production designer Gavin Bocquet initiate set construction by the end of 1996. Lucas chose to finance the $127 million film himself and offer the eventual completed movie for distribution, risking his empire on its success and making it the most expensive independent film in history. Robin Gurland spent nearly three grueling years scouring the world for actors to flesh out the cast. Perhaps the trickiest role to fill was that of nine-year-old Anakin Skywalker. Gurland and Lucas sifted through thousands of hopefuls before they finally found their quarry—an unknown child actor named Jake Lloyd. Crews had already been constructing sets at England's Leavesden Studios a full year before filming began on June 26, 1997. As almost three-fourths of the scenes required bluescreen work, they built many of the set walls only high enough for the tallest actor. Shooting shifted to Italy in late July, and then to the baking 140-degree heat of Tunisia, where fifty tons of materials had been deposited in the middle of the desert. After the set of an entire village where 200 members of the cast and crew would work was erected, a huge storm with 120 mph winds ripped through and devastated everything. The tight-knit crew immediately pulled together to rebuild it all, ensuring they did not lose a single day of filming. Shooting wrapped on September 26, 1997, with postproduction work continuing for another eighteen months and eleven days of pickups occurring in the fall of 1997 and the spring of 1998. While Lucas ceaselessly refashioned various rough cuts from the footage, the ILM team polished off the 1,900 effects shots, digitally altering in some way almost 90 percent of the final film frames. The special effects highlights included a CGI Yoda for one shot and a completely CGI rendered character, Jar Jar Binks. Adding to the burgeoning digital atmosphere, Lucas successfully experimented with digital cameras for pickup shooting in August 1998.

DISTRIBUTION: It wasn't until April 1998 that 20th Century-Fox won the right to distribute the first prequel. By September 1998, the official title—*The Phantom Menace*—had been released, along with the official trailer. People were reportedly paying the full feature price for whatever film was carrying the trailer, watching just the trailer and then leaving before the movie began. The official Lucasfilm/Apple website recorded more than 3.5 million downloads in five days after the second trailer premiered on March 11, 1999. With anticipation growing to a fever pitch, lines began forming more than a month before the release at Mann's Chinese Theater. The film opened at one minute past midnight on May 19, 1999, raking in $28.5 million on opening day and eventually grossing more than $920 million worldwide. It became the first major feature to be digitally projected in public theaters on June 18, 1999. —*Scott Mazak*

THE BLAIR WITCH PROJECT
Artisan, 1999

ALL-RELEASE EQUIVALENT 2005 $s
(Unadjusted $s) in Millions of $s

Domestic Box Office Revenues........ **$177.3**/($140.5)
Production Cost .... **$0.04**/($0.04)
Principal Photography....................... 8 days
Fall 1997

Director . . . . Daniel R. Myrick, Eduardo Sanchez

Producer . . . . Robin Cowie, Gregg Hale

Production Company . . . . Haxan Films

Story and

  Screenplay by . . . . Daniel Myrick, Eduardo Sanchez

Cast . . . . Heather Donahue, Michael Williams, Joshua Leonard

Filming Locations . . . . . . Seneca Creek and Patapsco Valley State Parks, Maryland

Genre . . . . Horror

Format . . . . Color/B&W

Initial Release . . . . 1/25/1999 Sundance Film Festival; 5/1999 Cannes, France; 7/16/1999 U.S. limited release; 7/30/1999 U.S. general release

Rerelease . . . . none

Running Time . . . . 87 minutes

MPAA Rating . . . . R

STANDING THE TEST OF TIME

ACADEMY AWARD Oscar Nominations and Wins

None

OSCAR TOTALS   Nominations 0   *Wins 0

AFI 100 YEARS 100 MOVIES SELECTION
2007 0   1997 0

TOP 300 FILMS POSITION . . . . none
All-Release Domestic Box Office in Equivalent 2005 $s

National Film Preservation Board Selection . . . . none

OTHER AWARDS Best Picture Wins

	Year
Golden Globes . . . . none	
New York Film Critics . . . . none	
National Board of Review . . . . none	
Film Daily Critics . . . . none	

If we could wear down the actors physically and mentally, by the end, when really intense things are happening, they'd tap into part of the psyche they normally don't touch.

—Gregg Hale

PLOT: Three student filmmakers, working on a documentary project to explore the horrific local legend of the "Blair Witch," head into the Maryland woods, where an eerie and frightening presence gradually makes itself known.

PRODUCTION: Dan Myrick and Ed Sanchez developed the concept of *The Blair Witch Project*, with input from Gregg Hale, while they were all film students at the University of Central Florida in Orlando. Their innovative idea was to turn their lack of money and resources into a virtue. All images and sound would be recorded by unknown actors playing film students, who would naturally face the same limitations if the story were real. The resulting shaky, handheld footage would enhance the film's believability as a genuine documentary. Because most of the film would be improvised by the three leads, Myrick and Sanchez created a scenario mapping out the main plotline—keeping some of the details from their intrepid stars.

The Blair Witch Project was shot in eight days, six of them spent in the cold, remote Maryland woods. Once they were in the forest, there was almost no communication between the filmmakers and the actors, who relied on a GPS system to lead them each day to a "drop point" where they would find gear, food and water, and individual notes, and where they would leave behind the prior day's footage. With the exception of their tents and ground pads, which the crew readied for them in advance every day, the actors had to carry everything on their backs. Although the three had rehearsed together as much as possible, the filmmakers "massaged" them by planting unannounced props, or by giving one performer a piece of information or a stage direction the other two couldn't anticipate. By night, the crew created unsettling sounds; by day, they fashioned outré displays made of natural objects arranged in unnatural ways for the performers to stumble upon unawares. As the shoot wore on, the actors' genuine fatigue and disorientation became vital aspects of their portrayals, their tension clearly evident to audience members. The now-iconic off-kilter framing of star Heather Donahue near the end, when she tearfully "confesses" to the camera, was an accident.

DISTRIBUTION: Straining against a mass of material from two cameras, *Blair Witch*'s first cut ran 2 hours and 45 minutes. While it was being laboriously whittled down by half, the filmmakers, fascinated by the possibilities of the newly burgeoning Internet, created a website, built and designed by Sanchez, that went live in June 1998. Their masterstroke was to treat the "Blair Witch" legend as deadpan fact. Net surfers, many of whom weren't sure what to believe, descended on this provocative site. The filmmakers credit the site for the buzz that greeted them at the 1999 Sundance Film Festival, where their late-night screenings sold out instantly, and where Artisan won a hotly contested distribution auction. Artisan's subsequent marketing for the film, including an "official" website that drew 110,000 visitors during its first weekend, followed the initial recipe: the "Blair Witch" legend, including the eventual fate of the "student filmmakers," was real. They purposely deceived the public using the Internet. An elaborate superstructure and timeline were concocted to wrap around the material shown in the film, resulting in *Curse of the Blair Witch*, a metadocumentary placing the movie in its "historic context," complete with interviews with "friends and family" of the three main characters. —*Tom Dupree*

THE SIXTH SENSE
Buena Vista, 1999

ALL-RELEASE EQUIVALENT 2005 $s
(Unadjusted $s) in Millions of $s

Domestic Box Office Revenues . . . . **$370.3**/($293.5)
Production Cost . . . . **$46.9**/($40.0)
Principal Photography . . . . **38** days estimated
9/21/1998–11/13/1998

Director . . . . M. Night Shyamalan

Producer . . . . Frank Marshall, Kathleen
Kennedy, Barry Mendel

Production Company . . . . Hollywood Pictures, Spyglass
Entertainment

Story and
Screenplay by . . . . M. Night Shyamalan

Cast . . . . Bruce Willis, Haley Joel Osment,
Toni Collette, Olivia Williams,
Donnie Wahlberg, Glenn
Fitzgerald, Mischa Barton,
Trevor Morgan, Bruce Norris

Filming Locations . . . . . . On location in Philadelphia, PA

Genre . . . . Thriller

Format . . . . Color (Technicolor)

Initial Release 8/6/1999

Rerelease . . . . none

Running Time . . . . 107 minutes

MPAA Rating PG-13

STANDING THE TEST OF TIME

ACADEMY AWARD Oscar Nominations and Wins

Best Picture: Frank Marshall, Kathleen Kennedy, and
Barry Mendel, Producers

Actor in a Supporting Role: Haley Joel Osment

Actress in a Supporting Role: Toni Collette

Directing: M. Night Shyamalan

Film Editing: Andrew Mondshein

Writing (Screenplay – written directly for the screen):
M. Night Shyamalan

OSCAR TOTALS Nominations **6** *Wins 0

AFI 100 YEARS 100 MOVIES SELECTION
2007 0   1997 0

TOP 300 FILMS POSITION . . . . #56
All-Release Domestic Box Office in Equivalent 2005 $s

National Film Preservation Board Selection . . . . none

OTHER AWARDS Best Picture Wins

	Year
Golden Globes	none
New York Film Critics	none
National Board of Review	none
Film Daily Critics	none

There are spiritual questions that are really answered, about loss and loved ones and grief. These are universal themes, and that creates a great word of mouth that propels the movie forward.

—Frank Marshall

PLOT: A lauded child psychologist, depressed over failing one troubled patient, befriends a frightened little boy who is battling his own personal demons, and who leads the doctor toward his own self-awareness.

PRODUCTION: In September 1997, an agent for M. Night Shyamalan sent his script of *The Sixth Sense*—which had taken the writer five agonizing drafts to perfect—to David Vogel, chief of Disney's Hollywood Pictures unit. The agent required Vogel to read it over lunch that very day because of competing interest. Vogel was so impressed that he immediately offered $2 million and promised Shyamalan could direct, figuring on a midlevel star and modest budget. However, as part of his deal to star in *Armageddon* (1998), Bruce Willis had the right to consider every leading role in development at Disney. To everyone's surprise, and the studio's dismay, Willis selected *The Sixth Sense* instead of an action picture: "I raised my hand and asked to be included," he recalled later. Willis objected at first to Shyamalan directing, and his schedule delayed the start of production, but he eventually relented. Shyamalan used locations in his hometown, Philadelphia, as the backdrop for his cleverly constructed story, which depends upon a major plot twist at its climax that challenges viewers' previous assumptions. The budget estimated 16 weeks prep, 8 weeks principal photography, and 23.6 weeks post. Shyamalan and his crew achieved eerie effects through creative methods: for instance, a background track in every location is made up of human breaths, subliminally suggesting an unseen presence. The story's central conceit is visually emphasized at many points—the film never "cheats"—but most audience members require reflection, or even a second viewing, to notice. Willis, a natural lefty, helped preserve one secret by learning to simulate right-handedness. David Vogel had been the lone enthusiast for *The Sixth Sense* at Disney, where others felt he had spent too much for what they viewed as a modest film. When the shoot was about three-quarters completed, the studio sold foreign and domestic rights to independent producer Spyglass Entertainment, retaining only a 12.5 percent distribution fee.

DISTRIBUTION: *The Sixth Sense* opened in a summer that was dominated by *Star Wars: Episode I The Phantom Menace* (May) and the surprise hit *The Blair Witch Project* (July), which Shyamalan worried would siphon away some of his audience. His film finished its opening weekend at number one and, due to remarkably positive word of mouth, dropped only 2 percent the second week, remaining at number one for three more weeks. It ended the year in the number two domestic box office spot. At least part of the film's remarkable "legs" were aided by its subject matter: critics had played along with the filmmakers by keeping quiet about the central revelations, and nearly everyone who saw the film yearned for a second look because of its unique structure. Of all of Buena Vista's live-action releases to that time, *The Sixth Sense* was second only to *Mary Poppins* (1964) in adjusted domestic box office dollars—but, of course, the studio did not participate financially beyond its fixed distribution percentage, having sold away the rights to its biggest hit of the year. —*Tom Dupree*

TOY STORY 2
Buena Vista, 1999

ALL-RELEASE EQUIVALENT 2005 $s
(Unadjusted $s) in Millions of $s

Domestic Box Office Revenues.......$307.8/($245.9)
Production Cost ....$105.5/($90.0)
Production Period ....4 years
1995–1999

Director . . . . John Lasseter
Producer . . . . Helene Plotkin, Karen Robert Jackson
Production Company . . . . Walt Disney Pictures/Pixar Animation Studios Production
Story by . . . . John Lasseter, Pete Docter, Ash Brannon, Andrew Stanton
Screenplay by . . . . Andrew Stanton, Rita Hsiao, Doug Chamberlin, Chris Webb
Cast . . . . Tim Allen, Tom Hanks, Don Rickels, John Ratzenberger (voices)
Filming Locations . . . . . . Pixar studio in Pt. Richmond, CA
Genre. . . . . Animation
Format. . . . . Color (Technicolor)
Initial Release 11/24/1999
Rerelease . . . . none
Running Time . . . . 92 minutes
MPAA Rating . . . . G

STANDING THE TEST OF TIME

ACADEMY AWARD Oscar Nominations and Wins

Music (Original Song): "When She Loved Me," Music and Lyrics by Randy Newman

OSCAR TOTALS   Nominations 1   *Wins 0

AFI 100 YEARS 100 MOVIES SELECTION
2007 0   1997 0

TOP 300 FILMS POSITION . . . . #100
All-Release Domestic Box Office in Equivalent 2005 $s

National Film Preservation Board Selection. . . . none

OTHER AWARDS Best Picture Wins

	Year
Golden Globes (Comedy)	2000
New York Film Critics.	none
National Board of Review	none
Film Daily Critics	none

If you're having fun, and you love what you do,
then the work that ends up on the screen is gonna be great.

—John Lasseter

PLOT: Woody is kidnapped by a collector, and Buzz and the gang rush to rescue him. Woody must choose between the allure of his new life and the comfort of his former life with Andy.

PRODUCTION: The inspiration for *Toy Story 2* came from John Lasseter's children when they visited him in his office packed with collectible toys. Faced with the realization that a toy's real purpose is to be played with, Lasseter hit upon the idea of making a film about what it would be like to be a collectible toy. His decision to honor the integrity of the characters he and his team had created in the first film led to the inclusion of an idea cut from the original film: an action-packed Buzz Lightyear adventure. The crew also reused such models as door locks, sawhorses, and furniture from the original *Toy Story* cache; even a dog collar from *A Bug's Life* made its way onto the set. *Toy Story 2* was a challenging film because John Lasseter wanted the audience to revisit the familiarity of the first film while being introduced to new characters and environments that would broaden the film's scope. To build emotion into the 3-D animation, the film-makers used subtle lighting techniques and slow camera truck-ins to pull audiences into the story. Almost the entire voice cast returned from the first *Toy Story*, including Hanks and Allen, and new voices were added, including Kelsey Grammer and Joan Cusack. For the Oscar-winning Pixar short film *Tin Toy* (1988), Pixar had developed a new system for producing images to be used in motion pictures, from 3-D computer descriptions of shape and appearance. That system developed into a proprietary software known as Renderman, for which co-founder Ed Catmull and his team were awarded a Scientific and Engineering Oscar in 1992. This and other technical breakthroughs provided Pixar with new technology that could be used to apply details such as more realistic animal fur to Andy's dog. Despite this giant step forward, there were other technical challenges posed by the introduction of the new character Wheezy (an asthmatic toy penguin). In the film, when the character was placed on a dusty shelf, the technical crew discovered that dust was very hard to generate graphically. Two million dust particles were needed to create the effect. Also challenging was the decision to make a marionette show appear as though it were being broadcast on an old black and white TV. Nevertheless the resourceful team found solutions to these daunting problems. Composer Randy Newman wrote two new songs for *TS-2*.

DISTRIBUTION: *Toy Story 2*, the third Pixar movie distributed by Disney, was originally going to be a direct-to-video sequel. When the Disney executives saw the quality and story, they urged Pixar to expand it to feature length. They were right. In 2005 dollars, *Toy Story 2* brought in over $62 million more in worldwide box office than the first film. A major consideration for John Lasseter in the Disney/Pixar merger (2006) was retaining control over the *Toy Story* characters. —*Rosaleen O'Byrne*

The 2000s

Cinema is not truth twenty-four times a second, it is lies twenty-four times a second. . . . It's all illusion. . . . The characters, the dialogue, the production design, photography and visual effects must all strive to give the illusion that what you're seeing is really happening. . . . When you see a scene in 3–D, that sense of reality is supercharged.

—James Cameron

TOP 10 ALL-RELEASE MOVIES DOMESTIC BOX OFFICE
By Initial Year of Release, 2000–2009

		Equivalent 2005 $s in Millions of $s
1	The Dark Knight	$476.1
2	Shrek 2	$455.4
3	Spider-Man	$445.4
4	Pirates of the Caribbean: Dead Man's Chest	$414.3
5	The Lord of the Rings: The Return of the King	$398.4
6	Spider-Man 2	$385.4
7	The Passion of the Christ	$382.7
8	Star Wars: Ep III - Revenge of the Sith	$380.3
9	The Lord of the Rings: The Two Towers	$372.8
10	Finding Nemo	$361.1
	Total: $4,072.1	

Note: 2009 box office through 6/16/2009 only.

GENERAL U.S. STATISTICS, 2000

281,423,231
Total U.S. Population

41,995,000
U.S. Population Age 15–24

27.3 Million
Average Weekly
U.S. Movie Attendance

DECADE OVERVIEW

The Industry Slowly Adapts to the Twenty-First Century

The holy grail, as Hollywood entered the twenty-first century, was not just to have a successful movie but to have a "hit franchise." The studios pursued sequels and prequels, because conventional wisdom maintained that they were a way to reduce risk in a very risky business. These films had built-in marketing power as known brands, often generating significant additional income from ancillary markets via licensing. This was important to the big six companies, which had consolidated in the early 1990s into multinational distribution giants that dominated global entertainment—Warner Bros. (Time Warner), Disney, Sony, Universal (GE), Fox (News Corp.) and Paramount (Viacom)— and were now facing spiraling costs.

In 2000 the average studio movie cost $54.8 million to make and an additional $27.3 million for prints and ads, according to statistics compiled by the Motion Picture Association of America. By 2006 those costs had risen to $65.8 million to make an average studio movie plus $34.5 million for prints and ads. Blockbuster films, including franchise films, are naturally more expensive, with the production costs of the top 15 averaging $141 million, each not including interest and overhead. What is even more staggering are the marketing costs on these blockbusters: average ad costs on the number one franchise film between 2000 and 2005, *Lord of the Rings: Return of the King,* were $30.7 million in the United States alone, according to the *Hollywood Reporter.* With foreign ad costs running 125 percent above domestic costs, that brings worldwide ad costs to roughly $70 million. Add to that estimated worldwide print costs of $25 million and you have almost $100 million in print and ad costs on top of an estimated $260 million production cost.

Box office continued to rise as well, but mostly because of increasing ticket prices. The average ticket price jumped from $5.39 in 2000 to $6.55 in 2006. Thanks to that, box office gross rose from $7,661 million in 2000 to $9,488 million in 2006 even though the number of actual theater admissions rose less than 2 percent over that period, from 1,421 million in 2000 to 1,448 million in 2006.

To help manage their huge financial risk, the major companies investing $100 million or more in a single production looked to star power. If you were spending megamillions to create an event movie that would serve as a "tent pole," boosting the studio's entire slate of movies for that year, then spending $20 million or more in salary plus a share in the profits to the star helped to ensure that investment. For years the studios had been attacked for draining off all the profits from a movie before any could reach net profit participants (those who get paid only after the movie goes into profit). As stars became more powerful, often acting as producer as well as star, they got richer deals; and as big-budget movies proliferated, more stars were granted these big deals than ever before. What made the new star deals different, however, was that they tapped into gross profits instead of net profits. Some were called first-dollar gross deals because the star got a percentage of the revenue from the first money that the studio took in. This meant that the star got paid a big salary and then additional compensation, whether the movie was as big a hit as hoped or not. This put even more pressure on the distributor to make sure a movie brought in a lot of money its first weekend in release. The goal became to get as many of the people who were coming to see their favorite actor or actress into theaters early, before word of mouth about the quality of the movie or the competition impacted ticket sales. This led to ever wider releases. The strategy employed here is the direct inverse of the one used when the original *Star Wars* trilogy was released in the 1970s and 1980s. At that time, the prevailing theory was to release on a few screens first, then build. But by the time the prequel *Star Wars* trilogy films came out, blockbuster movies were being released into 3,000 theaters or more on opening day alone (which, with multiple screens in many theaters, meant twice that many prints).

The dominant entertainment distributors rationalized the soaring star compensation because they could make up almost all deficits from the home video market, where, through the first half of the decade, DVD sales rose steadily year after year. The revenue from DVDs, which cost far less to manufacture than the VHS tapes they replaced, was enormous, surpassing even theatrical gross box office. The number of DVD units sold rose from 188 million in 2000 to 1.3 billion in 2006. However, the real growth in DVDs was in the sell-through market, which barely existed in the VHS era. Now people bought rather than rented movies for their personal libraries. Sell-through rose from 174 million units (at an average price of $22.63 each) in 2000 to 1.1 billion units (at an average price of $22.40 each) in 2006. The market flattened out shortly thereafter, marking the end of the nonstop expansion of video sales, with most of the valuable library catalog of movies already released and with competition from new media encroaching.

For the first time, some movies were being electronically downloaded either to handheld devices such as Apple's iPod player or directly into a cable box or a home computer. There were ad hoc networks that traded movies electronically at high speed with little regard for copyrights or piracy laws. Despite efforts to fight this piracy by the studio's trade association, there was a change occurring, which meant that high-priced physical media were being displaced by lower-cost electronic delivery of the same movies and TV shows.

In the second half of the decade, as the lift from DVD decreased, the escalating costs of the big companies' infrastructure, demands for a return on investment from Wall Street, and the soaring star salaries began to take a toll. While these tent-pole movies had been a great source of continuing revenue ever since the beginning of the blockbuster era in the 1970s, many were ending their first sales cycle and going into film libraries still showing losses. In fact, some of them continued to bleed money even after they became library items because of the participations built into the initial deals. The cost of the star (whether writer, producer, actor, or director) often included long-term relationship deals under which the studio paid all the expenses and some salary in return for exclusive service, or at least a first look at what the talent might do next. In 2003 *Variety* reported that Sony led the studios with thirty-six such deals, including Adam Sandler's Happy Madison Productions, which made movies for the star as well as movies in which Sandler was only producer. These deals would soon come under greater scrutiny.

"After decades of seemingly unlimited star paydays, studios are fretting over declining audiences and rising production costs, and taking a hard new look at those eye-popping price tags," declared *Entertainment Weekly* magazine in a May 4, 2006, article about star salaries. That article singled out actor Tom Cruise, who, it reported, not only made a salary of about $25 million for *Mission: Impossible II* but also received participation of another $75 million. They also reported that he made another estimated $100 million from *War of the Worlds*. When *Mission: Impossible III* came along, Cruise's compensation and studio expectations were high, but the return was not as good as hoped. The movie opened in May 2006 with a $47.7 million weekend, a figure below the $65–$70 million expected for the opening. The movie went on to gross more than $397 million worldwide, in part because of strong international box office, but the hounds had been set loose. There was an outcry about the high cost of the star, production, and marketing, and about the ultimate low return on the studios investment. Cruise was ultimately forced out of the studio that had been his home for fourteen years amid messy publicity. The low point came when Sumner Redstone, chairman and controlling shareholder in Viacom, parent of Paramount, told the *Wall Street Journal* in October 2006 that he blamed Cruise for the low return, due to his behavior, including his public discussions of aspects of his religion, Scientology. Joining Cruise in having the clout to negotiate gross deals were a handful of directors, such as Steven Spielberg and Robert Zemeckis, as well as some of the most influential stars of the decade, including Tom Hanks, Julia Roberts, George Clooney, Brad Pitt, and Clint Eastwood, who also directed some of his movies.

A 2007 report by Global Media Intelligence of London, in association with Merrill Lynch, estimated that these gross participation deals produced income of $3 billion for the stars alone in 2006. By comparison, the residuals paid to all of the writers of movies and TV shows that year totaled only $125 million. This disparity was the subject of intense labor difficulties, including a 100-day strike in 2007–8 by the Writers Guild of America. The Global Media study also noted that despite eye-popping opening weekends and global grosses, most of the year's big movies were losing money because of the deals made by studios with top stars and filmmakers. According to the study's author, Roger Smith, Disney was the only major to report its annual expenses for these participations and residuals. Smith, a former movie executive, said if the other majors were spending at a similar rate, they were suffering losses of roughly $2 billion. Smith told the *New York Times* that the impact was enormous because participants "can easily be paid out on money-losing pictures."

Ironically, while their pay was going up, stars became less valuable. In the big franchise hit movies of the decade, a character such as Spider-Man or a concept such as *Star Wars* was more important than any one actor. In most cases, fans flocked to see *The Lord of the Rings* come to life or the *Harry Potter* books rise off the page more than they came to see a specific actor. "On the surface, movie stars are bigger than ever," wrote the *Hollywood Reporter* on May 1, 2008. "They're ubiquitous on magazine covers and late-night TV. Their every move is dissected on blogs and fan sites. But the box office reports tell a different story . . . Such comedic actors as Ben Stiller, Vince Vaughn, Jim Carrey and Will Ferrell have, in the past year or so, hit longtime or even career lows. Brad Pitt has slid from a career high of $478 million worldwide box office for *Mr. and Mrs. Smith* to a paltry $15 million worldwide for *The Assassination of Jesse James by the Coward Robert Ford,* low even by specialty standards."

By the middle of the decade, the studios began to slowly cut back on star salaries and other added compensations (such as vanity housekeeping deals, which provided studio offices and support staff, including a development executive, free of cost to select talent in exchange for the right to distribute any movie rights they may have bought or developed in that time). Disney reportedly made a deal that ensured the studio got most of its investment back on the two *Pirates of the Caribbean* sequels before star Johnny Depp and others got a rich slice of the profits. It wasn't only the stars who felt the squeeze. Many mid- and lower-range actors, who in past years commanded significant salaries, found that they were being paid less per role too. The huge sums of money that previously had gone to the stars now were putting a squeeze on everyone else who made, starred in, or worked around movies.

With more movies being financed outside the studio system, the studios no longer owned or controlled many of the films they distributed. This arrangement reduced their risk but also reduced their returns. Two of the biggest box office movies of 2008 were the Paramount-distributed films *Iron Man* (Marvel Studios) and *Indiana Jones and the Kingdom of the Crystal Skull* (Lucasfilm Ltd.). With the bulk of the profits going to the production companies on these films, the studio no longer had a cushion of megaprofits from their hit movies to help finance other films.

Once again the studios hoped that technology would rescue them. This time they sought to cut expenses by switching to digital production, which made significant advances throughout the decade as a technique for making movies, for doing special effects, and for postproduction. Digital was more cost-effective and gave producers greater control, since they could see what they shot more quickly and make changes and fixes more easily in postproduction using digital tools. With the second part of his *Star Wars* trilogy prequel, George Lucas had been among the first to shoot an entire movie using digital video cameras. Lucas was quoted by *Screen Digest* saying, "I can safely say that I'll never shoot another film on film." Nowhere were the benefits of digital more apparent than in the development of computer-generated images (CGI). These were images that never existed outside of the camera—images that were essentially programmed into existence. The process had been developed more than twenty years earlier but had reached new heights in the new century, with such animated hits as *Shrek* and such live-action movies as *The Lord of the Rings* films, for which whole new environments had been created using CGI. Pixar studios also used CGI technology to make a series of hit movies, releasing nearly one per year, including *Monsters, Inc.* (2001), *Finding*

U.S. Theater Admissions vs. Sales of DVDs and VHSs to U.S. Dealers, 2000–2006 in Millions		
	2000	2006
Total theatrical admissions	1,421	1,448
Total DVD units sold	188	1,325
Total cassettes sold	664	7
Sell-through DVD units sold	174	1,140
Rental DVD units sold	14	185
Sell-through cassettes sold	565	6
Rental cassettes sold	99	1

Nemo (2003), *The Incredibles* (2004), *Cars* (2006), *Ratatouille* (2007), *WALL-E* (2008), and *Up* (2009). These movies were so important to Disney, which held distribution rights, that when there was a disagreement during new contract negotiations in 2006, Disney resolved it by acquiring Pixar for approximately $7.4 billion in stock.

Some felt the arrival of digital and the growth of the Internet would finally challenge the dominance of the studio oligopoly that had run Hollywood for the past hundred years. After all, there were now lower-cost, high-quality digital cameras and editing tools available. There was no longer a need to make costly celluloid prints. Movies could be switched from one theater to another in an instant. But change came slowly for a variety of reasons. It was still costly to assemble the talent needed to make a movie, and it was still necessary to spend heavily on marketing and advertising to get an audience to show up at the right time to see a new movie. Also impeding rapid progress was the fact that conservative movie theater owners were calling on the studios to finance the switch from film to digital.

As the decade began, the key way to distribute movies was still via theaters, pay TV, home video, and TV. By the last half of the decade, the new mantra was multiplatform distribution that encompassed electronic media and Internet delivery as well.

PRODUCTION SPOTLIGHT

Studios Develop Fewer Star-Vehicle Original Movies

For every A-list actor making $20 million or more per movie, there are thousands pulling down SAG's minimum day-player rate of $655 a day. "If you are anything but the star, you only get what's left over," said Sally Kirkland, an Oscar nominee for the 1987 film *Anna* who has credits in more than ninety films. "Actors are finding themselves increasingly squeezed these days. I've had a great career so I can't complain much, but I feel awful for up-and-coming actors these days." "Scale plus 10"—the minimum plus 10 percent to cover agent commissions—is the reality for most of SAG's 98,000 members who are lucky enough to work. And fewer than 2,000 actors earn more than $100,000 annually.

2000s Movie Censorship: A Brief History

Jack Valenti retires as head of the Motion Picture Association of America (MPAA) and is replaced by Dan Glickman, former U.S. agriculture secretary during the Clinton administration. The MPAA's members include Paramount Pictures, Sony Pictures Entertainment, Inc., 20th Century-Fox Film Corporation, NBC Universal, Walt Disney Studios Motion Pictures, and Warner Bros. Entertainment, Inc.

As the strategy at the studios shifted toward putting more and more resources into fewer and fewer hugely expensive tent-pole movies in a quest to find the next blockbuster franchise, salaries and profit participations by stars who provided marquee value soared. Will Smith, Adam Sandler, Tom Cruise, Julia Roberts, Mel Gibson, and a handful of others were now routinely commanding $20 million a picture, sometimes with an additional big piece of the profits, often drawn from gross revenue. The making of midrange movies declined, and lower-budget filmmaking became part of the specialty film market, where the returns were usually much lower. The higher salaries were also pushed along by a powerful cadre of talent agents and personal managers who represented the stars, and often packaged them together with other talent and a high-concept property to justify their huge compensation packages. But as stars got more expensive, the return on movies in which their name appeared above the title remained unpredictable. Several studios focused on presold franchises rather than risk developing original ma-

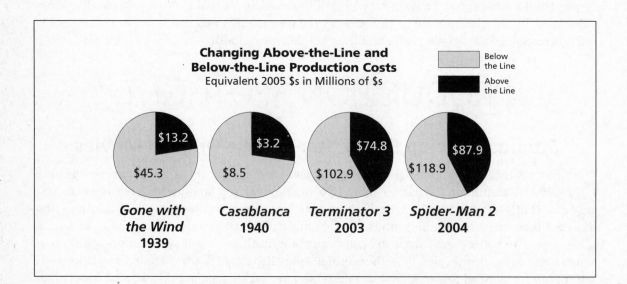

Changing Above-the-Line and Below-the-Line Production Costs
Equivalent 2005 $s in Millions of $s

Below the Line
Above the Line

$13.2 / $45.3 — **Gone with the Wind** 1939

$3.2 / $8.5 — **Casablanca** 1940

$74.8 / $102.9 — **Terminator 3** 2003

$87.9 / $118.9 — **Spider-Man 2** 2004

U.S. INDUSTRY PRODUCTION STATISTICS, 2000s
Equivalent 2005 $s /(Unadjusted $s)

$137.8 Million ($129.1 million)
Average production cost of films featured in this chapter

$60.0 Million ($60.0 million)
Average production cost of all films released in 2005

terial. Hit movies had always been a mix of original stories and adaptations of stories derived from magazine articles, books, comics, and Broadway plays. But originality was now taking a backseat. Of the eight movies with more than $500 million in worldwide box office released in 2007, 50 percent were franchise sequels and only one was based on an original story and script.

In the wake of the success of the *Lord of the Rings* and *Harry Potter* movies, the race was on not only to make big-concept movies, based on proven underlying material, but also to produce them so that they had appeal for both children and adults. This new emphasis on source material instead of a star's appeal pleased Wall Street, where for much of the decade huge sums of money were invested in movies, often by hedge funds that were involved in the buying and selling of many companies. What these number crunchers and stock market analysts valued was a source property of proven value, which they felt was a better indicator of whether a movie would succeed. The outside money had become increasingly important as studios looked to manage risk better. As a result, many of the outside investors were burned by pictures that probably never should have been made. These co-financing deals were typically put together at the stage where a movie got a green light, meaning it was approved to go into production. It was then that the studios were most likely to judge the risk and bring in partners before going forward.

There was concern that the highest-paid stars were reaching an age where they were less interesting to the youth market, which still accounted for the largest segment of active moviegoers. This stars-mean-less thinking was also pushed by the expansion of the international market, where only a handful of actors have any resonance at all. Foreign box office grew as a market for Hollywood movies throughout the decade even without star power. From 2002 to 2005 the domestic box office fell from $9.52 billion to $8.99 billion; however, the box office outside North America rose from $10.24 billion to $14.25 billion. Thus a new model was emerging that depended less on stars and more on proven source material.

Index of Top Feature Film Directors Included in This Chapter

1	Peter Jackson	*The Lord of the Rings* trilogy:
		The Fellowship of the Ring
		The Two Towers
		The Return of the King
2	Andrew Adamson	*Shrek 1*
	[with Kelly Asbury	*Shrek 2*
	and Conrad Vernon	*The Chronicles of Narnia:*
	(*Shrek 2*) and Vicky	*The Lion, The Witch, and*
	Jenson (*Shrek*)]	*the Wardrobe*
3	Sam Raimi	*Spider-Man 1*
		Spider-Man 2
4	George Lucas	*Star Wars: Episode II*
		Attack of the Clones
		Star Wars: Episode III
		Revenge of the Sith
5	Chris Columbus	*Harry Potter and the*
		Sorcerer's Stone
		Harry Potter and the
		Chamber of Secrets
6	Ron Howard	*A Beautiful Mind*
		Dr. Seuss' How the
		Grinch Stole Christmas
7	Mel Gibson	*The Passion of the Christ*
8	Andrew Stanton	*Finding Nemo*
	(with Lee Unkrich)	
9	Gore Verbinski	*Pirates of the Caribbean:*
		The Curse of the Black
		Pearl
10	Andy and Larry Wachowski	*The Matrix Reloaded*

Breakdown of a 2004 Production Dollar
Spider-Man 2, 2004
Unadjusted $s

Description	Production Cost	Percentage
Story	$20 million	10%
Screenplay	$10 million	5%
Producers	$15 million (Stan Lee, Grant Curtis, Laura Ziskin, Avi Arad, Joseph M. Caracciolo, and Kevin Feige)	7.5%
Director	$10 million	5%
Principal cast	$27 million (Tobey Maguire, $17 million; Kirsten Dunst, $7 million; Alfred Molina, $3 million)	13.5%
Other cast	$3 million	1.5%
Subtotal above-the-line	**$85 million**	**42.5%**
Production shooting costs	$45 million	22.5%
Visual effects	$65 million	32.5%
Composer and music costs	$5 million (Danny Elfman, $2 million)	2.5%
Subtotal below-the-line	**$115 million**	**57.5%**
Total	**$200 million**	**100%**

Top Five 2005 Worldwide Box Office Movies
Domestic vs. Foreign Splits
Unadjusted $s in Millions of $s

Film	Domestic Box Office	Percentage of Total	Foreign Box Office	Percentage of Total	Worldwide Box Office
Harry Potter and the Goblet of Fire	$290.0	32%	$606.0	68%	$896.0
Star Wars: Episode III—Revenge of the Sith	$380.3	44%	$469.7	56%	$850.0
The Chronicles of Narnia: The Lion, The Witch, and the Wardrobe	$291.6	39%	$453.1	61%	$744.7
War of the Worlds	$234.3	39%	$357.5	61%	$591.8
King Kong	$218.1	39%	$331.3	61%	$549.4

Franchises Dominate the Box Office
Comparison of Top Films in Ten-Year Increments (2007, 1997, 1987, 1977)
Worldwide All-Release Box Office (> $500 million)

Equivalent 2005 $s /(Unadjusted $s) in Millions of $s

Film	Initial Release	Worldwide Box Office	Description
Pirates of the Caribbean: At World's End	2007	**$894.8** ($960.4)	Franchise sequel
Harry Potter and the Order of the Phoenix		**$870.3** ($934.1)	Franchise sequel
Spider-Man 3		**$829.6**/($890.5)	Franchise sequel
Shrek the Third		**$744.4**/($799.0)	Franchise sequel
Transformers		**$654.1**/($702.0)	Based on Hasbro toy line
Ratatouille		**$578.6** ($621.0)	Based on original story by Brad Bird
I Am Legend		**$544.1** ($584.0)	Based on novel by Richard Matheson
The Simpsons Movie		**$483.8** ($519.3)	Based on Matt Groening comic and TV series
Titanic	1997	**$2,522.4** ($1,842.8)	Based on an original story by James Cameron
The Lost World: Jurassic Park		**$872.4**/($624.7)	Franchise sequel
Men in Black		**$820.9**/($587.8)	Franchise launch
Fatal Attraction	1987	**$511.8** ($320.1)	Based on an original story by James Dearden
Star Wars: Episode IV—A New Hope	1977	**$2,020.4** ($798.0)	Franchise launch
Close Encounters of the Third Kind		**$894.4** ($328.3)	Based on an original story by Steven Spielberg
Saturday Night Fever		**$826.5**/($302.7)	Based on a magazine article
The Spy Who Loved Me		**$533.0**/($185.4)	Franchise sequel

Information Industry's Contribution to Gross Domestic Product Rises Nearly 70 Percent While Manufacturing Declines 45 Percent and Finance Industry Grows 82 Percent from 1950 to 2000

Companies in the motion picture and sound recording segment of the information industry include producers and distributors of motion pictures (in theaters, on video, and on TV) and sound recordings. Sound recordings include music CDs, music videos, and other physical and digital albums. Also included are services that support filmmaking and sound recording.

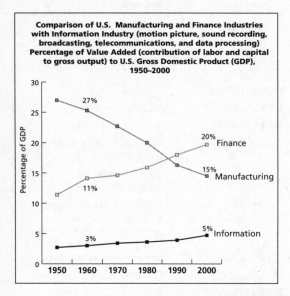

Comparison of U.S. Manufacturing and Finance Industries with Information Industry (motion picture, sound recording, broadcasting, telecommunications, and data processing) Percentage of Value Added (contribution of labor and capital to gross output) to U.S. Gross Domestic Product (GDP), 1950–2000

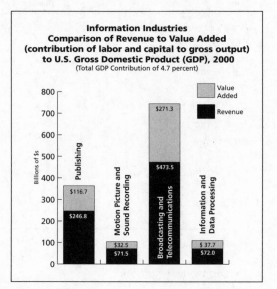

Information Industries
Comparison of Revenue to Value Added (contribution of labor and capital to gross output) to U.S. Gross Domestic Product (GDP), 2000
(Total GDP Contribution of 4.7 percent)

U.S. Motion Picture and Sound Recording Revenue Breakdown, 2000s

Unadjusted $s in Billions of $s

Motion picture and video production and distribution	$41.8
Motion picture and video exhibition	$9.7
Post production	$4.5
Subtotal	$56.0
Sound recording	$15.5
Total	$71.5

Increased Internet Use and Greater Dependence on Foreign Box Office Revenue Result in Increased Losses From Piracy

Losses to Major U.S. Motion Picture Studios From Piracy, 2005

$4.8 billion from foreign markets
$1.3 billion from the United States
$6.1 billion total lost
62% from hard goods piracy
38% from Internet piracy

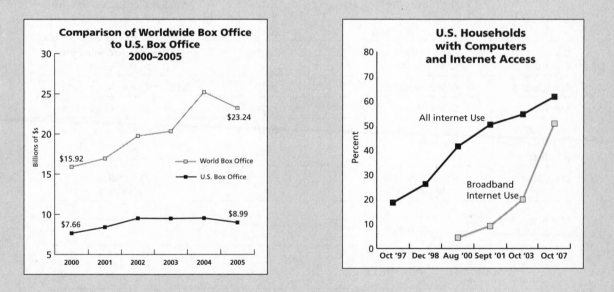

Comparison of Worldwide Box Office to U.S. Box Office 2000–2005

$15.92 ... $23.24
$7.66 ... $8.99

— World Box Office
— U.S. Box Office

U.S. Households with Computers and Internet Access

All internet Use

Broadband Internet Use

Oct '97 Dec '98 Aug '00 Sept '01 Oct '03 Oct '07

U.S. Media Usage, 2000–2005
Hours per Person per Year

	2000	2001	2002	2003	2004	2005
Television	1,502	1,553	1,572	1,615	1,620	1,659
Internet	100	125	138	155	165	172
Video games	65	66	71	76	78	73
Home video	43	47	57	60	67	63
Theatrical box office	12	13	14	13	13	12

A Sampling of Director Salaries, 2000s
Equivalent 2005 $s/(Unadjusted $s)

Director	Film	Initial Release	Salary
Peter Jackson	*King Kong*	2005	**$20 million excluding p/p*** ($20 million + 20% gross p/p— fee shared with wife and writing and producing partner Fran Walsh and the writer and co-producer Phillippa Boyens)
	The Lord of the Rings trilogy	2001 2002 2003	**$10.9 million excluding p/p** ($10.0 million + gross p/p for all three films)
Chris Columbus	*Harry Potter and the Sorcerer's Stone*	2001	**$11.0 million excluding p/p** ($10.0 million + gross p/p)
Ron Howard	*A Beautiful Mind*	2001	**$11.0 million/($10.0 million)**
Sam Raimi	*Spider-Man 2*	2004	**$10.3 million/($10.0 million)**
Andy and Larry Wachowski (Co-directors)	*The Matrix Reloaded* and *The Matrix Revolutions*	2003	**$4.2 million excluding p/p each** ($4.0 million + gross points each brother)
Mike Newell	*Harry Potter and the Goblet of Fire*	2005	**$1.0 million** ($1.0 million)

*Profit participation.

Producer/Directors/Actors in the Motion Picture and Video Industries Median Annual Earnings in 2002
Equivalent 2005 $s/(Unadjusted $s)

Salaried producers and directors	**$50,198/($46,240)**
Salaried actors	**$25,479/($23,470)**

Film Footage Comparison for Select Blockbuster Films

Film	Initial Release	Number of Feet of Film Exposed	Number of Days Principal Photography	Final Film Length in Minutes
The Hunchback of Notre Dame	1923	750,000	146	133
Greed	1924	446,103	198	114
Ben Hur: A Tale of the Christ	1925	752,000	120	143
Grand Hotel	1932	331,189	48	105
Mutiny on the Bounty	1935	668,005	84	132
San Francisco	1936	369,118	45	115
Gone with the Wind	1939	474,538	140	220
The Wizard of Oz	1939	129,529	86	101
The Bells of St. Mary's	1945	145,195	59	126
Quo Vadis	1951	580,000	129	171
Cleopatra	1963	633,600	200	243
Easy Rider	1969	127,000	30	94
The Wild Bunch	1969	333,000	81	148
The Godfather	1972	500,000	77	175
American Graffiti	1973	111,710	29	109
The Exorcist	1973	180,000	200	121
Jaws	1975	400,000	150	124
All the President's Men	1976	415,920	96	138
Star Wars Ep IV	1977	322,704	84	121
Superman: The Movie	1978	1,250,000	150	143
Apocalypse Now	1979	1,350,000	238	153
Star Wars Ep V	1980	602,194	172	118
Raiders of the Lost Ark	1981	318,755	73	115
Tootsie	1982	500,000	98	116
Star Wars: Ep VI	1983	578,600	92	132
Indiana Jones and the Temple of Doom	1984	440,360	80	118
Titanic	1997	1,300,000	160	194
*Star Wars: Ep I	1999	1,031,480	66	133
**Star Wars: Ep II	2002		61	143
** Star Wars: EP III	2005		58	140

Note:

Film footage shot in minutes is computed by dividing the number feet exposed by 90.

Average minutes of film shot per day is computed by dividing film footage minutes by the number of days of principal photography.

*Star Wars: Episode I feet of film exposed includes footage shot for special effects.

** Star Wars: Episode II and Episode III shot 100 percent digitally; conversion of digital tapes to minutes of film shot per day includes footage shot for special effects.

Actors of the 2000s: Salaries and Profit Participations
Equivalent 2005 $s/(Unadjusted $s)

Actor	Film	Initial Release	Salary
Keanu Reeves	*The Matrix Reloaded* and *The Matrix Revolutions*	2003	**$165.5 million including p/p*** ($156,000,000 including p/p from both films based on $30 million salary + 15% gross p/p)
Tom Cruise	*Mission: Impossible II*	2000	**$113.4 million including p/p** ($100,000,000 based on SAG scale + 30% gross p/p on box office and on TV licensing and 40% gross p/p on DVD and video)
	War of the Worlds	2005	**$100.0 million including p/p** ($100,000,000 including 20% gross p/p)
	Minority Report	2002	**$27.1 million excluding p/p** ($25,000,000 + % of gross)
Brad Pitt	*Ocean's Eleven*	2001	**$33.1 million including p/p** ($30,000,000 based on $10 million salary + $20 million p/p)
	Mr. & Mrs. Smith	2005	**$20.0 million excluding p/p** ($20,000,000 against 20% of gross p/p)
Arnold Schwarzenegger	*Terminator 3: Rise of the Machines*	2003	**$31.0 million excluding p/p** ($29,250,000 not including $1.5 million for perks + 20% royalty once gross passes $150 million domestic or $380 million worldwide)
Will Smith	*I, Robot*	2004	**$29 million excluding p/p** ($28,000,000 + 10% to 20% of gross)
	Bad Boys II	2003	**$21.2 million excluding p/p** ($20,000,000 + 20% gross p/p)
Adam Sandler	*Anger Management*	2003	**$26.5 million excluding p/p** ($25,000,000 against 25% of gross)
Mike Myers	*Austin Powers in Goldmember*	2002	**$27.1 million excluding p/p** ($25,000,000 against 21% of gross)

Actor	Film	Initial Release	Salary
Harrison Ford	*K-19: The Widowmaker*	2002	**$27.1 million excluding p/p** ($25,000,000 + 20% gross p/p)
Mel Gibson	*The Patriot*	2000	**$28.4 million/($25,000,000)**
	Signs	2002	**$27.1 million/($25,000,000)**
Julia Roberts	*Mona Lisa Smile*	2003	**$26.5 million/($25,000,000)**
	Erin Brockovich	2000	**$22.7 million/($20,000,000)**
Jim Carrey	*Bruce Almighty*	2003	**$26.5 million/($25,000,000)**
	Dr. Seuss' How the Grinch Stole Christmas	2000	**$22.7 million excluding p/p** ($20,000,000 + merchandising p/p)
Eddie Murphy	*Nutty Professor II: The Klumps*	2000	**$22.7 million excluding p/p** ($20,000,000 + 20% of gross)
Johnny Depp	*Charlie and the Chocolate Factory*	2005	**$20.0 million/($20,000,000)**
Tommy Lee Jones	*Men in Black II*	2002	**$21.7 million excluding p/p** ($20,000,000 + % of gross)
Cameron Diaz	*Charlie's Angels: Full Throttle*	2003	**$21.2 million/($20,000,000)**
Tobey Maguire	*Spider-Man 2*	2004	**$17.6 million/($17,000,000)**
	Spider-Man	2002	**$4.3 million/($4,000,000)**
Nicole Kidman	*Bewitched*	2005	**$17.5 million/($17,500,000)**
Reese Witherspoon	*Walk the Line*	2005	**$15.0 million/($15,000,000)**
Daniel Radcliffe	*Harry Potter and the Goblet of Fire*	2005	**$11.0 million/($11,000,000)**
	Harry Potter and the Chamber of Secrets	2002	**$3.3 million/($3,000,000)**
	Harry Potter and the Sorcerer's Stone	2001	**$0.1 million/($110,000)**
Angelina Jolie	*Mr. & Mrs. Smith*	2005	**$10.0 million/($10,000,000)**

*Profit participation.

General Corporate vs. Movie Business Salaries, 2005
Pretax* (2005 maximum individual tax rate 35%)
Equivalent 2005 $s/(Unadjusted $s)

Name	Job	Annual Earnings
E. Stanley O'Neal	Chairman and CEO, Merrill Lynch	**$35,500,335 including stock** ($700,000 salary + $14,100,000 bonus + $20,200,041 stock + $500,294 other)
Peter Cernin	President and COO, News Corp.	**$27,753,111 excluding stock** ($8,319,737 salary + $18,890,000 bonus + $543,374 other)
K. Rupert Murdoch	Chairman and CEO, News Corp.	**$23,635,946 excluding stock** ($4,508,694 salary + $18,890,000 bonus + $237,221 other)
Thomas E. Freston	President and CEO, Viacom	**$22,698,676 including stock** ($5,306,651 salary + $13,000,000 bonus + $4,298,700 stock + $93,325 other)
Kenneth D. Lewis	Chairman, president, and CEO, Bank of America	**$22,027,984 including stock** ($1,500,000 salary + $5,650,000 bonus + $14,630,099 stock + $247,885 other)
Reuben Mark	Chairman and CEO, Colgate-Palmolive	**$18,556,798 including stock** ($1,796,500 salary + $3,592,488 bonus + $12,873,800 stock + $294,010 other)
Louis C. Camilleri	Chairman and CEO, Altria Group (tobacco)	**$18,134,969 including stock** ($1,663,462 salary + $4,200,000 bonus + $7,730,000 stock + $4,541,507 other)
Summer Redstone	Exec chairman and founder, Viacom	**$17,351,383 including stock** ($5,806,651 salary + $7,125,000 bonus + $4,298,700 stock + $121,032 other)
Richard D. Parsons	Chairman and CEO, Time-Warner	**$16,004,074 including stock** ($1,500,000 salary + $7,500,000 bonus + $6,555,513 stock and options + 448,561 other)
S. J. Palmisano	Chairman, president, and CEO, IBM	**$12,396,337 including stock** ($1,680,000 salary + $5,175,000 bonus + $5,232,655 stock + $308,682 other)
Michael D. Eisner	CEO, The Walt Disney Company	**$10,272,988 excluding stock** ($1,000,000 salary + $9,111,806 bonus + $161,182 other)
Robert A. Iger	President and COO, The Walt Disney Company (replaced Eisner as CEO 10/2/2005)	**$9,813,448 including stock** ($1,500,000 salary + $7,739,941 bonus + $500,000 stock + $73,507 other)
G. R. Wagoner Jr.	Chairman and CEO, GM	**$5,479,305 including stock** ($2,200,000 salary + $0 bonus + $2,884,000 stock + $395,305 other)

Name	Job	Annual Earnings
Jeffrey R. Immelt	Chairman and CEO, GE	**$3,400,769 excluding stock**
		($3,225,000 salary + $0 bonus + $175,759 other. By contrast total compensation including bonus in 2006 was $17,863,452.)
Michael L. Campbell	CEO, Regal Entertainment Group (largest U.S. theater circuit in the United States)	**$1,649,062 including stock**
		($594,700 salary + $589,100 bonus + $465,262 stock)
Peter C. Brown	CEO and president, AMC Entertainment (second largest theater circuit in the United States)	**$1,142,332 excluding stock**
		($742,000 salary + $392,000 bonus + $8,332 other)

*Note: See tax rate table in Note to Reader.

Top 5 Critically Acclaimed Lead Actors, 2000–2005

Rank	Actor Name
1	Denzel Washington
2	Russell Crowe
3	Sean Penn
4	Philip Seymour Hoffman
5	Jamie Foxx

Rank	Actress Name
1	Julia Roberts
2	Nicole Kidman
3	Hilary Swank
4	Charlize Theron
5	Reese Witherspoon

See Note to the Reader for selection criteria.

827

A Sampling of Billion-Dollar
Unadjusted $s

Film	Initial Release	U.S. Box Office	Foreign Box Office	Worldwide Box Office
Harry Potter and the Sorcerer's Stone	2001	$318	$659	$977
Spider-Man	2002	$404	$418	$822
The Lord of the Rings: The Two Towers	2002	$342	$584	$926
The Lord of the Rings: The Fellowship of the Ring	2001	$315	$556	$871
The Lord of the Rings: The Return of the King	2003	$377	$742	$1,119
Harry Potter and the Chamber of Secrets	2002	$262	$617	$879
Finding Nemo	2003	$340	$525	$865
Pirates of the Caribbean: The Curse of the Black Pearl	2003	$305	$349	$654
Star Wars: Ep II Attack of the Clones	2002	$311	$338	$649
Star Wars: Ep I The Phantom Menace	1999	$428	$492	$920

Top 10 Blockbuster Movies
Highest Production Cost (>$150 million)
Highest Revenue Domestic Box Office (> $250 million)
All-Release Domestic Box Office, 1960–2009

Equivalent 2005 $s/(Unadjusted $s) in Millions of $s

Rank	Film	Initial Release	Domestic Box Office	Production Cost
1	Pirates of the Caribbean: At World's End	2007	$288.1/($309.2)	$282.6/($300.00)
2	Cleopatra	1963	$435.7/($57.7)	$280.8/($44.0)
3	The Lord of the Rings: The Return of the King	2003	$398.4/($377.0)	$276.0/($260.0)
4	The Lord of the Rings: The Two Towers	2002	$372.8/($341.7)	$255.1/($235.0)
5	Titanic	1997	$824.8/($600.8)	$243.4/($200.0)
6	Spider-Man 3	2007	$313.5/($336.5)	$243.0/($200.0)
7	The Dark Knight	2008	$476.1/($533.3)	$229.4/($252.9)
8	Pirates of the Caribbean: Dead Man's Chest	2006	$414.3/($423.3)	$218.0/($225.0)
9	Spider-Man 2	2004	$385.4/($373.4)	$206.8/($200.0)
10	The Chronicles of Narnia: The Lion, The Witch, and the Wardrobe	2005	$289.5/($291.6)	$200.0/($200.0)

Earning Movies, 1999–2004
in Millions of $s

U.S. Rentals	Foreign Rentals	Worldwide Video and DVD	U.S. TV	Foreign TV	Other Rights	Total
$259	$329	$436	$87	$86	$52	$1,249
$202	$209	$464	$80	$82	$60	$1,097
$170	$298	$484	$84	$90	$84	$1,210
$157	$276	$396	$88	$90	$86	$1,095
$183	$176	$500	$80	$80	$110	$1,129
$131	$304	$496	$90	$95	$88	$1,204
$170	$182	$500	$80	$80	$110	$1,122
$155	$180	$510	$85	$80	$112	$1,122
$155	$172	$480	$85	$95	$100	$1,087
$220	$240	$440	$90	$95	$100	$1,185

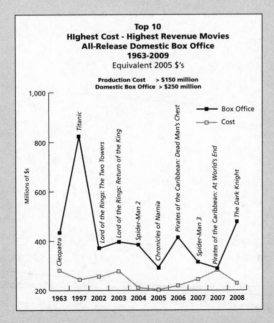

Top 10
Highest Cost - Highest Revenue Movies
All-Release Domestic Box Office
1963-2009
Equivalent 2005 $'s

Production Cost > $150 million
Domestic Box Office > $250 million

Terminator 3: Rise of the Machines, 2003
Budget Breakdown
Equivalent 2005 $s/(Unadjusted $s)

Story and rights	**$20.8 million**/($19,569,305)
Producer and staff	**$10.6 million**/($10,022,210)
Director and staff	**$5.3 million**/($5,006,294)
Talent and all fringes	**$38.1 million**/($35,878,092)
Subtotal above-the-line	**$74.8 million**/($70,475,901)
Production staff	($1,964,396)
Extra talent	($395,803)
Art department	($1,613,334)
Set construction	($6,854,816)
Set operations	($2,820,579)
Set dressing	($2,422,254)
Action props	($776,818)
Wardrobe	($1,638,379)
Picture vehicles and animals	($1,478,725)
Makeup and hair	($565,812)
Electrical	($2,578,571)
Camera	($2,419,866)
Sound	($358,865)
Transportation	($3,953,281)
Location	($4,361,743)
Film and lab	($1,036,505)
Videotape	($184,498)
Creature effects	($3,165,000)
Facility expenses	($1,877,450)
Tests	($60,000)
Second unit	($5,148,117)
Aerial unit	($256,751)
Special photography	($316,091)
Computer graphics	($203,793)
Total below-the-line fringes	($6,500,473)
Subtotal production	**$61.0 million**/($57,446,342)

Editing and projection	($2,512,563)
Videotape post	($288,552)
Music	($1,636,164)
Sound (postproduction)	($691,493)
Visual effects	($19,889,650)
Film, tape, and library	($301,683)
Titles and opticals	($142,500)
Total postproduction fringe benefits	($584,482)
Subtotal postproduction	**$27.7 million/($26,047,087)**
Publicity	($141,500)
Insurance	($2,000,000)
General expenses	($1,796,151)
Completion bond fee	($2,382,585)
Contingency	($7,000,000)
Other fringes	($30,668)
Subtotal other	**$14.2 million/($13,350,904)**
Total above-the-line	**$74.8 million/($70.5 million)**
Total below-the-line	**$102.9 million/($96.8 million)**
Total production cost	**$177.7 million/($167.3 million)**

Budget based on script dated 11/8/2001

100 days main unit photography (63 on location and 37 on L.A. stages)

60 day second unit photography

(45 days full and 15 days reduced)

7 days aerial unit

27 weeks postproduction

Films Winning Oscars for Both
Special Effects and Best Picture, 1927–2005
All-Release Domestic Box Office
Equivalent 2005 $s/(Unadjusted $s) in Millions of $s

Rank	Film	Initial Release	Domestic Box Office
1	*Titanic*	1997	**$824.8**/($600.8)
2	*Ben-Hur*	1959	**$754.3**/($85.8)
3	*Forrest Gump*	1994	**$505.6**/($329.7)
4	*The Lord of the Rings: The Return of the King*	2003	**$400.8**/($377.0)
5	*Gladiator*	2000	**$223.2**/($187.7)

PROFIT AND LOSS
Terminator 3: Rise of Machines, 2003
Warner Bros. Estimated P&L
Unadjusted $s in Thousands of $s

Description	Revenue and Costs	Percentage of Revenue
Domestic theatrical (box office)	$150,358	NA
Foreign theatrical (box office)	$283,000	NA
Total theatrical box office	$433,358	
Domestic theatrical (rentals)	$82,697	19%
Foreign theatrical (rentals)	$127,350	29%
Home video (worldwide)	$235,000	52%
Subtotal gross receipts	$445,047	100%

Description	Revenue and Costs	Percentage of Costs
Distribution fees	$146,249	28%
Production cost (excluding overhead)	$167,300	33%
Advertising and publicity (worldwide)	$75,600	15%
Interest on production cost	$10,400	2%
Gross participations	$89,000	17%
Prints (worldwide)	$24,000	5%
Other (editing, dubbing, taxes, duties, customs, trade association fees, freight, handling and insurance, checking, collection, guild and union residuals)	NA	NA
Subtotal costs	$512,549	100%
Net profit (loss)	($67,502)	

Notes:

Domestic theatrical rentals estimated at 55 percent of box office; foreign at 45 percent.

Home video estimated (high) at world average of top 10 billion dollar earning movies [$470 million retail (approximately 26 million units @ $18/each) × 50% to equal wholesale].

Distribution fees estimated at 30 percent domestic rentals, 40 percent foreign rentals, 30 percent home video wholesale.

Production cost per budget detail.

Domestic ads per *Hollywood Reporter* $33.6 million; foreign ads estimated at 125 percent of domestic.

Interest on production cost estimated (low) at prime + 25 percent from production start date until U.S. release.

Gross participations assume 20 percent paid Schwarzenegger after B/E

Domestic prints estimated at $1,500/each × peak U.S. engagements × 2 (to estimate number of screens); foreign estimated at 125 percent of domestic.

PROFIT AND LOSS
Mission: Impossible II, 2000
Paramount Estimated P&L

Unadjusted $s in Thousands of $s

Description	Revenue and Costs	Percentage of Revenue
Domestic theatrical (box office)	$215,409	NA
Foreign theatrical (box office)	$330,978	NA
Total theatrical box office	$546,388	
Domestic theatrical (rentals)	$118,475	23%
Foreign theatrical (rentals)	$148,940	30%
Home video (worldwide)	$235,000	47%
Subtotal gross receipts	$502,415	100%
		Percentage of Costs
Distribution fees	$165,619	28%
Production cost (excluding overhead)	$125,000	22%
Advertising and publicity (worldwide)	$83,700	14%
Interest on production cost	$15,800	3%
Gross participations	$169,264	29%
Prints (worldwide)	$24,766	4%
Other (editing, dubbing, taxes, duties, customs, trade association fees, freight, handling and insurance, checking, collection, guild and union residuals)	NA	NA
Subtotal costs	$584,149	100%
Net profit (loss)	($81,734)	

Notes:

Domestic theatrical rentals estimated at 55 percent of box office; foreign at 45 percent.

Home video estimated (high) at world average of top 10 billion dollar earning movies [$470 million retail (approximately 26 million units @ $18/each) × 50% to equal wholesale].

Distribution fees estimated at 30 percent domestic rentals, 40 percent foreign rentals, 30 percent home video wholesale.

Production cost per boxofficemojo.com.

Domestic ads per *Hollywood Reporter* $37.2 million; foreign ads estimated at 125 percent of domestic.

Interest on production cost estimated (low) at prime + 25 percent from production start date until U.S. release.

Gross participations assume 7.5 percent paid John Woo; 30 percent paid Tom Cruise (net of Woo).

Domestic prints estimated at $1,500/each × peak U.S. engagements × 2 (to estimate number of screens); foreign estimated at 125 percent of domestic.

DISTRIBUTION OVERVIEW

Wide Releases Cost Big Bucks

One of the most significant developments in distribution in the twenty-first century was the expansion of the number of theaters playing a single movie on its opening weekend. The concept of releasing movies in numerous theaters to take advantage of its high concept, big star, and massive national television advertising campaigns dates back to *Jaws,* which launched the era of the summer blockbuster in the 1970s. However, those releases opened in hundreds of theaters, not thousands, and were expected to build, not peak in one weekend.

By the 1980s and into the 1990s every weekend in the summer and around Christmas saw roughly half a dozen pictures released in a few thousand theaters upon opening. By the 2000s, with the advent of megacinemas, the number of theaters in which new releases opened climbed past 3,000, meaning that they were showing on approximately 6,000 screens altogether. On a list of the widest releases, compiled by the website Box Office Mojo as of May 2008, the first movie made before 2000 to open wide was *The Lost World: Jurassic Park,* in seventy-ninth place. It was released in 1997 into 3,565 theaters, a record at the time. This means that since then, there have been seventy-eight movies, all released after 2000, that opened in more theaters than that.

The trend to wider and wider releases hit a high on May 4, 2007, when *Spider-Man 3* opened in 4,324 theaters. It was out of release within sixteen weeks. That was followed by *Pirates of the Caribbean: At World's End,* which opened in 4,362 theaters on May 25, 2007. It ended its initial run after only nineteen weeks in release. Exhibitors were excited about these movies because they were considered presold, and because in both cases they released early enough in the season to ensure access to a large number of screens. This speaks to the issue of timing: some blockbusters open early to get as much playing time as possible, while others are timed to take advantage of special windows of opportunity such as the long Fourth of July weekend.

The question as to when a movie should open is also complicated by the kind of movie it is and who its likely audience is. Two movies can go into wide release at the same time and both do well if they attract different audiences, as is the case with an action movie and a romantic comedy. However, a number of studies have shown that when two similar

Comparison of *Indiana Jones* Franchise Films Opening Weekend

Film	Initial Release	Number of Theaters Opening Weekend
Jaws	1975	409
Raiders of the Lost Ark	1981	1,078
Indiana Jones and the Temple of Doom	1984	1,687
Indiana Jones and the Last Crusade	1989	2,327
Indiana Jones and the Kingdom of the Crystal Skull	2008	4,260

movies open against each other, at least one of them will not gross as much as hoped. Once a movie opens below par it rarely makes a comeback.

The risk of opening early is that if a film doesn't catch on quickly, it could be gone before the season even gets under way. Once it fails, the production price tag—in the hundreds of millions for summer or holiday movies—means nothing to its value going forward. If it fails theatrically, it almost always means it will garner lower revenue from all the aftermarkets including pay TV and DVD sales both domestic and foreign.

To facilitate the big openings, the studios increasingly avoided risky dramas and message pictures in favor of movies that appealed to a broader spectrum of ticket buyers. To cast the widest net, the studios aimed for a PG or PG-13 rating. G is viewed as a label that is just for kids. R means children are excluded without a parent, which means it is a nonstarter for revenue. In 2003 roughly 15 percent of movies were rated PG. By 2007 30 percent of movies were rated PG. At the same time movies with a restrictive R rating dropped from 20 percent of the total in 2003 to only 15 percent in 2007. G-rated movies remained constant at 5 percent of the total.

The point of these big openings was first and foremost to take in as much money as possible as quickly as possible before reviews, word of mouth, or a new competitive film release could kill them. There was also a side benefit. Being the number one movie inspired other ticket buyers to choose that movie. Conversely, a movie that didn't open as strongly as anticipated generated negative word of mouth that damaged its prospects.

The use of wide releases and saturation advertising was really an attempt to manufacture a blockbuster by using the distribution pattern to build momentum. The theory was that if you created enough noise about a picture and then got a big opening, that would bring in a whole other audience to see what it was all about. That is a method economists refer to as a "noninformative information cascade," which is a fancy way of saying that even in the face of negative reviews and downbeat word of mouth some will come to see a movie just because of advertising and because others are seeing it too. The problem was that while it was possible, to a certain extent, to manufacture a big opening weekend with enough marketing dollars and star power, it was not possible to ensure that it would be a sustained hit. That was especially true in the key summer and Christmas periods, when there might be seven or eight new films released in a single weekend. In 1993 a major movie earned roughly half its revenue in the first three weekends. By 2003 a big movie earned about three-quarters of its revenue in the same amount of time.

Research has shown that increasingly, the main factor determining the success of a movie after it opens is word of mouth, not advertising, promotion, merchandising, or even the momentum created by a big opening weekend. Since the 1980s, word of mouth has grown in influence on a movie's success, because most people trust the opinion of others they know or will follow the lead of those who regularly see movies early. The word-of-mouth phenomenon really took off in the 1990s with the advent of the Internet, which made it possible for self-appointed critics to reach much larger numbers of people. Online word of mouth grew even more crucial in the

2000s with the arrival of high-speed broadband, which gave rise to millions of bloggers who wrote their opinions about movies on the Internet to share with all.

This all hit home for distributors in the summer of 2005, when overall grosses fell approximately 5 percent from the prior year—the biggest drop since 1985—even though almost every major studio could claim at least one film that grossed more than $100 million. Accordingly, attendance was down too, falling by roughly 7 percent, which sent shock waves through the industry. The studios could see that things were changing, but they weren't quite sure how. Their parent companies were gobbling up Internet services and content providers, especially search engines and social networks, to hedge against this trend. This began a shift away from the use of expensive TV ads as the primary audience driver. TV advertising peaked early in the decade and actually began a decline as a percentage of a movie company's marketing expense was cut, including premium network buys on Thursday primetime, typically intended to catch audiences on the night before a movie opened.

In 2003 MPAA member companies spent 25.4 percent of their marketing money on network TV and another 16.9 percent on local, syndicated, and other forms of TV. That same year they spent 1.9 percent on Internet ads. By 2007 the use of network TV ads had dropped to 21.6 percent and other TV to 13.9 percent. Meanwhile, Internet advertising rose to 4.4 percent, and the use of other nontraditional media, such as viral marketing, outdoor, and event sponsorship, also rose significantly.

The summer of 2007 once again brought prosperity back to Hollywood for those who had the hits. However, there was a growing sense that things were not the same as they had been and movies, like all media, now had to have a strategy that included more distribution platforms beyond theatrical and TV, and marketing that reached busy people who did not watch much TV or go to movies unless they heard the buzz. What this all meant was that no matter how many marketing dollars were spent, no matter how presold a subject, star, or concept seemed to be, once a movie opened, the audience either created a buzz around it or spun negative reviews, and ultimately that was what decided the fate of a movie in the era of new media.

U.S. INDUSTRY DISTRIBUTION STATISTICS, 2000s
Equivalent 2005 $s/ (Unadjusted $s)

$9,110 Million ($7,661 million)
Annual U.S. box office gross revenues

458
Number of new features released

Major Movie Distributors, 2000s

Buena Vista . . . . The brothers Harvey and Bob Weinstein depart in 2005. Disney announces the retirement of their film distribution company name Buena Vista in 2007. Future Walt Disney Pictures, Touchstone Pictures, Miramax, and Pixar films will be distributed under the Walt Disney name.

DreamWorks SKG . . . . DreamWorks spins off DreamWorks Animation as a public company in 2004. DreamWorks SKG is sold to Paramount in 2006.

Paramount Pictures . . . . Viacom, owner of Paramount Pictures, completes its purchase of DreamWorks LLC in 2006 and enters into a seven-year exclusive agreement to distribute the films produced by Dreamworks Animation SKG. The DreamWorks film library is sold to a group headed by George Soros for $900 million in 2006. DreamWorks announces its intention to end its partnership with Paramount in 2008 and announces a multipicture distribution agreement with The Walt Disney Company in 2009.

Sony . . . . Sony, owner of Columbia and TriStar, acquires MGM/UA with a group of other equity partners in 2005.

20th Century-Fox . . . . Continues under News Corp. ownership throughout the first half of the decade.

Universal Pictures . . . . Universal Pictures and its owner Seagram are sold to Vivendi S.A. in 2000. Vivendi sells 80% of Universal to GE in 2004 where it becomes part of NBC Universal.

Warner Bros. Continues under Time Warner ownership throughout the first half of the decade.

TECHNOLOGY SPOTLIGHT

Cost Savings Filming Digitally

Star Wars: Episode II Production Cost (shot 100-percent digitally) vs. Star Wars: Episode I
Unadjusted $s

Description	Episode I	Episode II	Savings
Video equipment	$75,957	$17,675	$58,282
Film stock	$1,298,736	$0	$1,298,736
Tape stock	$0	$183,017	($183,017)
Negative processing	$323,865	$0	$323,854
Printing	$632,478	$0	$632,478
Telecine	$704,225	$0	$704,225
Location rushes (projection and transport)	$46,952	$0	$46,952
Scanning	$759,257	$0	$759,257
On-line for previews	$73,451	$0	$73,451
Shooting time (principal photography and effects labor costs savings)			$1,000,000
Total estimated production savings			**$4.7 million**
***Total estimated distribution savings**			**$21.4 million**
Total estimated savings by shooting and distributing digitally			**$26.1 million**

*Additional estimated savings if Star Wars: Episode II were distributed digitally in 2002 in all theaters rather than via physical prints [estimated domestic print costs at $1,500/each × peak number of domestic theaters (3,161) times two to get the number of screens/prints needed; estimated foreign print costs at 125 percent of domestic.)

Domestic distribution print costs	$9.5 million
Foreign distribution print costs:	$11.9 million
*Total estimated distribution savings	$21.4 million

MARKETING SPOTLIGHT

Consider the perverse logic of Hollywood: In 2003, the six major studios—Disney, Warner Bros., Sony, 20th Century-Fox, Universal, and Paramount—spent, on average, $34.8 million to advertise a movie and earned, on average, just $10.6 million per title. Even if the studios had made the movies for free—which, of course, they didn't—they would have lost $14.2 million per film on the theatrical run, or what the industry calls "current production." Given the fleeting attention span of the target audiences (mainly TV-watching teens) and the unmemorable nature of the ad copy, the studios believe they must show the same ad on the same programs at least eight times in order to draw an audience. As a result, the studios spend more to lure a teenager into a theater than they receive at the box office, which is reminiscent of the joke about the idiot in the garment business who "loses money on every sale but makes it up on volume." —EDWARD JAY EPSTEIN

"There is nobody I talk to in the business who isn't under pressure to defend what is being spent to market films," says Adam Fogelson, president of marketing and distribution for Universal. "There is more scrutiny and rigor in the financial process of how films are being marketed—and that is justified." —HOLLYWOOD REPORTER, 2008

Americans Age 12–39 Comprise 67% of Total Moviegoing Audience vs. 42% of Total U.S. Population

Motion Picture Theater Attendance by Age vs. U.S. Population by Age

Movie Attendance Age Range	Percentage of Total Movie Audience	Percentage of Total U.S. Population
12–24	38%	21%
25–39	29%	21%
40–59	24%	28%
60+	9%	17%

Comparison of Seven 2000s Films Initial Release Domestic Box Office
Equivalent 2005 $s/(Unadjusted $s) in Millions of $s

Film	Initial Release	Domestic Box Office	Domestic Rentals	Foreign Rentals	Production Cost	Domestic Print and Ad Costs
Shrek	2001	**$303.1** ($267.7)	**$166.7** ($147.2)	**$110.4** ($97.5)	**$66.2** ($60.0)	**$75.1** ($68.1)
Gladiator	2000	**$223.2** ($187.7)	**$122.8** ($103.2)	**$144.4** ($121.5)	**$116.8** ($103.0)	**$59.5** ($52.5)
Spider-Man 2	2004	**$385.6** ($373.6)	**$212.1** ($205.5)	**$190.5** ($184.6)	**$206.8** ($200.0)	**$59.4** ($57.5)
War of the Worlds	2000	**$234.3** ($234.3)	**$128.9** ($128.9)	**$160.9** ($160.9)	**$132.0** ($132.0)	**$58.2** ($58.2)
The Perfect Storm	2005	**$217.2** ($182.6)	**$119.4** ($100.4)	**$59.9** ($50.4)	**$158.8** ($140.0)	**$57.5** ($50.7)
The Chronicles of Narnia: The Lion, The Witch, and the Wardrobe	2002	**$291.6** ($291.6)	**$160.4** ($160.4)	**$203.9** ($203.9)	**$200.0** ($200.0)	**$51.6** ($51.6)
My Big Fat Greek Wedding	2002	**$266.4** ($241.4)	**$146.5** ($132.8)	**$63.2** ($57.3)	**$5.4** ($5.0)	**$21.4** ($19.7)

Note: Rentals estimated at 55 percent of domestic box office and 45 percent of foreign box office. Domestic ad costs from *Hollywood Reporter*. Domestic prints estimated based on $1,500/each print cost times the number of peak domestic engagements times two (to estimate the number of total screens).

EXHIBITION OVERVIEW

Bankruptcy, Consolidation, and the Emergence of Digital

One of the nation's largest exhibitors, Denver-based United Artists Theaters, was slow to react to the introduction of stadium seating. They continued to build new slope-floor theaters while their competitors changed gears and retooled. This, coupled with a large amount of decaying assets, made them a prime candidate for bankruptcy. Meanwhile, Philip Anschutz, a billionaire from Denver who had made his fortune in savvy oil and railroad investments, saw great opportunity in the new decade. Phil made a bold move purchasing and cobbling together three insolvent theater chains, United Artists (in 2000), Edwards (in 2001), and Regal (in 2002). The three circuits were consolidated under the Regal Theatres name.

In Kansas City, a struggling AMC Theatres, believing that "bigger is better," bought two circuits, Loews and General Cinema.

In 2006 the well-established Cinemark chain from Dallas bought a very solvent Century Theatres of Marin County for a reported $1 billion.

This consolidation of companies put nearly 60 percent of the entire U.S. box office in control of just three exhibition companies: Regal, AMC, and Cinemark. At the same time, it presented an opportunity to entrepreneurs looking for ways to survive against these behemoth theater chains. Niche theaters soon cropped up, including the Arclight in Hollywood, which opened in 2002 (attached to the iconic Cinerama Dome) and established itself as a high-end movie theater, attracting cinema intellectuals and discerning moviegoers willing to pay more for a first-class theatrical experience. Other examples include the Palace in Boca Raton, Florida, which is a traditional megaplex on the first floor while offering reserved luxury seating in the auditoriums on the second floor along with restaurants, a café, and meeting rooms. The wait staff at the Alamo Draft House in Austin, Texas, serves food and drinks to your table in the auditorium during movies. Landmark Theatres' Greenwood Village, south of Denver, Colorado, offers free popcorn and soda delivered to your seat. Not to be outdone, IMAX theaters began playing mainstream, high-budget blockbuster films. For the most part, these niche theaters have been successful, raising the bar for exhibition to keep up with the growing demands of the increasingly discriminating moviegoing audience.

By the middle of the decade there was also a long-awaited move toward digital exhibition, marking the beginning of the end of 35mm film as the main medium for shooting and showing movies, after roughly a hundred years of dominance. Film had provided a standard that was used worldwide, but it involved a lot of physical manipulation, was bulky to move around, and wore out after a number of runs in theaters. It had also become ever more costly as the number of theaters and screens requiring prints grew. Digital could be shown over and over without any physical degradation of the picture and, once antipiracy measures were developed, would allow the rapid electronic transfer of movies from one location to another and even from one screen to another within a multiplex at the touch of a key.

U.S. INDUSTRY EXHIBITION STATISTICS, 2000s
Equivalent 2005 $s/(Unadjusted $s)

$6.41 ($5.39–$6.41)
Average movie ticket price (2000-2005)

36,250
Number of U.S. screens, 2000s
(35,567 indoor and 683 drive-in)

Comparison of Top 5 Domestic Box Office Franchise Films
2000–2005

Film	Initial Release	Number of Theaters Opening Weekend	Number of Theaters at Peak Week	Total Number of Film Weeks in Release
Shrek 2	2004	4,163	4,223	21.3
Spider-Man 2	2004	4,152	4,166	22.7
The Lord of the Rings: The Return of the King	2003	3,703	3,703	24.3
Star Wars: Ep II Revenge of the Sith	2005	3,661	3,663	22.1
Spider-Man	2002	3,615	3,876	15.4

Star Wars Franchise Films Changing Release Patterns

Film	Initial Release	Number of Theaters First Week	Number of Theaters at Peak Week (screens, when known)	Weeks in Release	Total Number of U.S. Theaters	Total Number of U.S. Screens
Ep IV A New Hope	1977	32	Week #13 1,098 theaters	61	10,700	16,041
Ep V The Empire Strikes Back	1980	126	Week #11 1,279 theaters	63	9,400	17,675
Ep VI Return of the Jedi	1983	1,002	Week #11 1,764 theaters	52	9,400	18,884
Ep I The Phantom Menace	1999	2,970	Week #6 3,126 theaters (5,714 screens)	32	7,477	37,131 (12 digital, 4 showing Ep I)
Ep II Attack of the Clones	2002	3,161	Week #1 3,161 theaters (6,900 screens)	51	6,144	35,836 (124 digital, 63 showing Ep II
Ep III Revenge of the Sith	2005	3,661	Week #2 3,663 theaters (9,000+ screens)	22	6,114	37,740 (211 digital, 111 showing Ep III)

Note: The number of digital screens *Star Wars* films released into includes temporary facilities so may not agree with permanent digital screen totals.

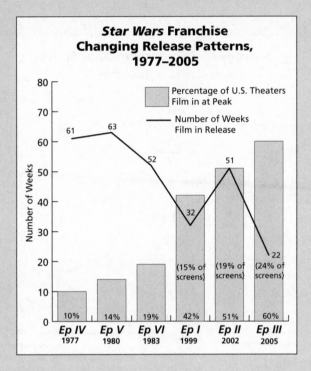

Star Wars Franchise Changing Release Patterns, 1977–2005

Legend:
- Percentage of U.S. Theaters Film in at Peak
- Number of Weeks Film in Release

	Ep IV 1977	Ep V 1980	Ep VI 1983	Ep I 1999	Ep II 2002	Ep III 2005
Percentage at peak	10%	14%	19%	42% (15% of screens)	51% (19% of screens)	60% (24% of screens)
Number of Weeks	61	63	52	32	51	22

Top 10 U.S. Theater Circuits as of 10/31/2005

Circuit	Number of U.S. Theaters	Number of U.S. Screens	Percentage of all Screens
Regal Entertainment Group	567	6509	18%
AMC Entertainment	209	3156	9%
Carmike Cinemas	309	2440	7%
Cinemark USA	198	2386	7%
Loews Cineplex Entertainment	134	1453	4%
National Amusements	89	1076	3%
Century Theatres	84	985	3%
Kerasotes Showplace Theatres	78	637	2%
Wallace Theatre Corp.	56	516	1%
Landmark Theatres	56	203	1%

Average Distributor/Exhibitor Splits
Unadjusted $s in Thousands of $s

	Regal 2005	AMC 2005	AMC 2000	AMC 1995
Admissions (box office revenues)	$1,662,200	$1,227,534	$763,083	$371,145
Film exhibition costs (film rentals and advertising costs)	$886,700	$649,891	$417,736	$182,669
Distributor/exhibitor average splits (rentals as a percentage of box office)	53%/47%	52%/48%	54%/46%	49%/51%
Average ticket price	$6.80			
Average concession per patron	$2.70			

Harry Potter

Franchise Films Originating in the 2000s
Equivalent 2005 $s in Millions of $s

Rank	Franchise	Number of Films in Franchise	Worldwide Box Office
1	Harry Potter	5	$4,598.7
2	The Lord of the Rings	3	$3,147.5
3	Pirates of the Caribbean	3	$2,633.7
4	Spider-Man	3	$2,545.2
5	Shrek	3	$2,242.5
6	X-Men	3	$1,232.9
7	Scary Movie	4	$896.2

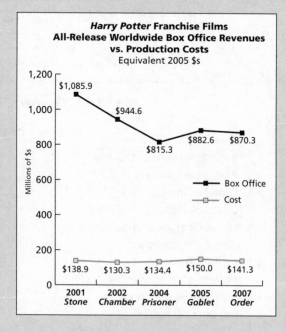

Harry Potter Franchise Films
All-Release Worldwide Box Office Revenues vs. Production Costs
Equivalent 2005 $s

The Lord of the Rings

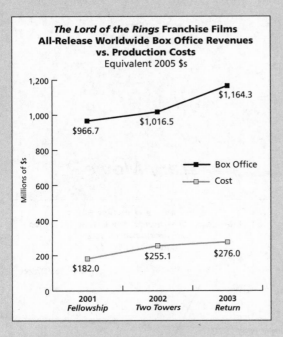

The Lord of the Rings Franchise Films
All-Release Worldwide Box Office Revenues
vs. Production Costs
Equivalent 2005 $s

Millions of $s

$966.7
$1,016.5
$1,164.3

- Box Office
- Cost

$182.0
$255.1
$276.0

| 2001 | 2002 | 2003 |
| Fellowship | Two Towers | Return |

Pirates of the Caribbean

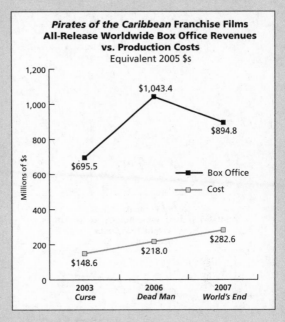

Pirates of the Caribbean Franchise Films
All-Release Worldwide Box Office Revenues
vs. Production Costs
Equivalent 2005 $s

Millions of $s

$1,043.4
$695.5
$894.8

- Box Office
- Cost

$148.6
$218.0
$282.6

| 2003 | 2006 | 2007 |
| Curse | Dead Man | World's End |

Spider-Man

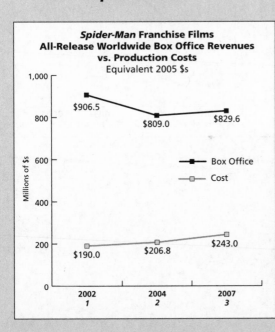

Spider-Man Franchise Films
All-Release Worldwide Box Office Revenues
vs. Production Costs
Equivalent 2005 $s

Millions of $s

$906.5
$809.0
$829.6

- Box Office
- Cost

$190.0
$206.8
$243.0

| 2002 | 2004 | 2007 |
| 1 | 2 | 3 |

Shrek

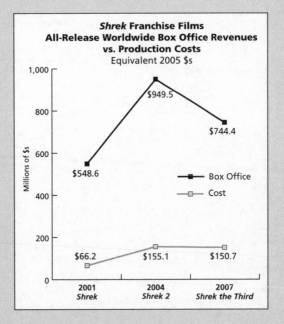

Shrek Franchise Films
All-Release Worldwide Box Office Revenues
vs. Production Costs
Equivalent 2005 $s

Millions of $s

$949.5
$744.4
$548.6

- Box Office
- Cost

$66.2
$155.1
$150.7

| 2001 | 2004 | 2007 |
| Shrek | Shrek 2 | Shrek the Third |

845

X-Men

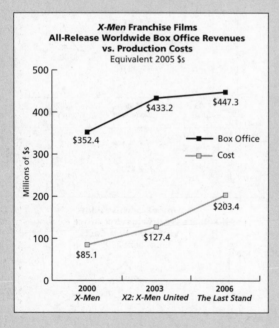

X-Men Franchise Films
All-Release Worldwide Box Office Revenues
vs. Production Costs
Equivalent 2005 $s

$352.4
$433.2
$447.3
$85.1
$127.4
$203.4

Box Office
Cost

Millions of $s

2000
X-Men

2003
X2: X-Men United

2006
The Last Stand

Scary Movie

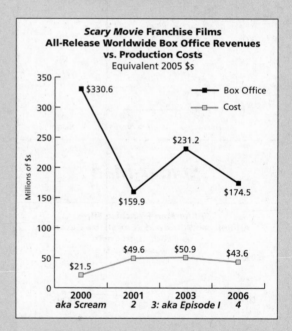

Scary Movie Franchise Films
All-Release Worldwide Box Office Revenues
vs. Production Costs
Equivalent 2005 $s

$330.6
$159.9
$231.2
$174.5
$21.5
$49.6
$50.9
$43.6

Box Office
Cost

Millions of $s

2000
aka Scream

2001
2

2003
3: aka Episode I

2006
4

GLADIATOR

DreamWorks (domestic); Universal Pictures (foreign), 2000

ALL-RELEASE EQUIVALENT 2005 $s

(Unadjusted $s) in Millions of $s

Domestic Box Office Revenues........**$223.2**/($187.7)
Production Cost ....**$116.8**/($103.0)
Principal Photography............**.89** days estimated
2/1/1999–6/4/1999

Director . . . . Ridley Scott

Producer . . . . Douglas Wick, David Franzoni, Branko Lustig

Production Company. . . . DreamWorks SKG, Universal Pictures, Scott Free Productions

Story by . . . . David Franzoni

Screenplay by . . . . David Franzoni, John Logan, William Nicholson

Cast . . . . Russell Crowe, Joaquin Phoenix, Connie Nielsen, Oliver Reed, Richard Harris, Derek Jacobi, Djimon Hounsou, David Schofield, John Shrapnel, Tomas Arana

Filming Locations . . . . . . Ait Benhaddou, Morocco; Malta; Tuscany, Italy; Bourne Woods, Farnham, Surrey, England; Alabama Hills, Lone Pine, CA

Genre. . . . . Action Adventure

Format. . . . . Color (Technicolor)

Initial Release 5/5/2000

Rerelease . . . . none

Running Time . . . . 154 minutes

MPAA Rating . . . . R

STANDING THE TEST OF TIME

ACADEMY AWARD Oscar Nominations and Wins

*BEST PICTURE: Douglas Wick, David Franzoni, and Branko Lustig, Producers

*ACTOR IN A LEADING ROLE: Russell Crowe

Actor in a Supporting Role: Joaquin Phoenix

Art Direction/Set Decoration: Arthur Max, Crispian Sallis

Cinematography: John Mathieson

*COSTUME DESIGN: Janty Yates

Directing: Ridley Scott

Film Editing: Pietro Scalia

Music (Original Score): Hans Zimmer

*SOUND: Scott Millan, Bob Beemer, Ken Weston

*VISUAL EFFECTS: John Nelson, Neil Corbould, Tim Burke, Rob Harvey

Writing (Screenplay – written directly for the screen): Screenplay by David Franzoni and John Logan and William Nicholson; Story by David Franzoni

OSCAR TOTALS Nominations **12** *Wins 5

AFI 100 YEARS 100 MOVIES SELECTION
2007 0   1997 0

TOP 300 FILMS POSITION . . . . #202
All-Release Domestic Box Office in Equivalent 2005 $s

National Film Preservation Board Selection. . . .none

OTHER AWARDS Best Picture Wins

	Year
Golden Globes (Drama).	2001
New York Film Critics	none
National Board of Review	none
Film Daily Critics	none

I studied his [Steven Spielberg's] technique [in Saving Private Ryan*] and the techniques that they used in the [photographic] process, and we nicked everything.*
—Ridley Scott

PLOT: A heroic Roman general is betrayed by the emperor's son, sold into slavery, and forced to fight as a gladiator, where he fights first for revenge and later to end the tyranny of the emperor.

PRODUCTION: In the 1950s and 1960s, as television cut into the audience for movies, one of the more effective strategies used by the studios to lure moviegoers back was the sword-and-sandals epic. This genre was used, much like science fiction, to address the contemporary world, its values and fears. David Franzoni drew upon the conventions of this genre to write *Gladiator,* the first script of his three-picture writing-producing deal with DreamWorks after his work on Steven Spielberg's *Amistad.* To reduce its risk on the $100+ million budgeted film, DreamWorks worked out an agreement with Universal to co-finance and distribute the movie overseas. Ridley Scott was approached to direct by executive producer Walter Parkes and producer Douglas Wick, who showed him a version of the 1872 painting titled "Pollice Verso" (Thumbs Down) by Jean-Léon Gérôme. Scott was immediately interested in the subject of ancient Rome but felt the script dialogue was too literal. He hired John Logan to rewrite it. Although Mel Gibson had been considered for the critical lead role, Wick said, "Russell Crowe's name came up pretty fast." The Australian actor had already established himself with American audiences in such films as *L.A. Confidential* and *The Insider.* He could bring to the role the physical vigor and brooding nature that the filmmakers had sought. The production began where the movie itself starts: with the battle sequence in Germania. As luck would have it, the British Forestry Commission had planned to deforest Bourne Woods, the area where the film was being shot, so Scott informed them that his crew would burn it down instead. That gave Scott free rein to shoot the battle scenes without concern for leaving the grounds as they were. Unfortunately, the rest of the film did not go as smoothly. Added to the challenge were the logistics of building a 52-foot-tall, full-scale replica of roughly one-third of the Roman Colosseum on the island of Malta. It took several months to construct at a cost of about $1 million. The rest was created utilizing CGI. Crowe, like Scott before him, had several problems with the script and made suggestions for changes. When the star believed his concerns were not being addressed, he walked off the set. Finally he reconciled himself to what he considered shortcomings in the screenplay, telling William Nicholson, a screenwriter brought in for rewrites, "Your lines are garbage but I'm the greatest actor in the world and I can make even garbage sound good." During the shoot on Malta, Oliver Reed suffered a fatal heart attack. His untimely death required a new and unplanned use of CGI. A body double was shot for Reed's remaining scenes (filmed in shadows) and a computer-generated image of Reed's face was superimposed over the double's face. This added more than $3 million in cost but allowed the producers to avoid recasting Reed's role and having to reshoot his scenes entirely.

DISTRIBUTION: *Gladiator*'s epic sweep and visceral battle sequences made it an immediate hit as soon as it opened in very wide release (2,938 screens, followed by 417 in Britain one week later). It was one of the biggest box office hits of 2000 and gave the fledgling DreamWorks studio its second consecutive Best Picture win, following *American Beauty. —Louis Burklow*

THE PERFECT STORM

Warner Bros., 2000

ALL-RELEASE EQUIVALENT 2005 $s

(Unadjusted $s) in Millions of $s

Domestic Box Office Revenues........**$217.2**/($182.6)
Production Cost ....**$158.8**/($140.0)
Principal Photography...........**100** days estimated
7/26/1999–12/23/1999

Director . . . . Wolfgang Petersen
Producer . . . . Paula Weinstein,
Wolfgang Petersen
Production Company. . . . Baltimore Spring Creek
Pictures, Radiant Productions
Story by . . . . Based on the book by
Sebastian Junger
Screenplay by . . . . Bill Wittliff
Cast . . . . George Clooney, Mark
Wahlberg, Diane Lane,
John C. Reilly, William Fichtner,
Bob Gunton, Karen Allen,
Mary Elizabeth Mastrantonio,
Allen Payne, John Hawkes
Filming Locations . . . . . . 17 days on location in
Gloucester, MA; 1 ½ weeks at
sea off Massachusetts and
California; balance on
soundstages at Warner Bros.
Studios, Burbank, CA
Genre . . . . Disaster
Format . . . . Color (Technicolor)
Initial Release 6/30/2000
Rerelease . . . . none
Running Time . . . . 129 minutes
MPAA Rating PG-13

STANDING THE TEST OF TIME

ACADEMY AWARD Oscar Nominations and Wins

Sound: John Reitz, Gregg Rudloff, Davaid Campbell, Keith A. Wester

Visual Effects: Stefen Fangmeier, Habib Zargarpour, John Frazier, Walt Conti

OSCAR TOTALS Nominations 2   *Wins 0

AFI 100 YEARS 100 MOVIES SELECTION
2007 0   1997 0

TOP 300 FILMS POSITION . . . . #216
All-Release Domestic Box Office in Equivalent 2005 $s

National Film Preservation Board Selection . . . . none

OTHER AWARDS Best Picture Wins

	Year
Golden Globes	none
New York Film Critics	none
National Board of Review	none
Film Daily Critics	none

We had people coming over and over again, just watching, because they had never, and I myself had never, seen anything like it. It was just spectacular.

—Wolfgang Petersen

PLOT: The crew of a fishing boat off the Massachusetts coast becomes trapped in the confluence of three intense weather patterns, creating the most terrifyingly powerful storm they have ever encountered.

PRODUCTION: Wolfgang Petersen was in postproduction on *Air Force One* when a sound mixer, knowing the director's interest in seafaring stories, gave him a copy of Sebastian Junger's best-selling 1997 nonfiction book about the fate of a fishing boat during a cataclysmic storm. Meanwhile, Warner Bros. acquired the film rights and only days later sought out Petersen to helm the picture. The book had been a publishing sensation, leading many actors to request a part. Petersen considered Mel Gibson and Nicolas Cage for the captain's role, but eventually gave it to George Clooney, who had originally auditioned for first mate, a part that ultimately went to Mark Walhberg. Cast members spent time in Gloucester, Massachusetts, real-life home of the storm-tossed fishermen, before principal photography began. Petersen understood that shooting at sea would be a logistical nightmare but one that was necessary for verisimilitude. Thus, he bought a sister boat to the film's *Andrea Gail*. It would spend only a week and a half at sea, but it was an essential week and a half. Three-fourths of *The Perfect Storm* was shot indoors. The key set was located on Stage 16 at Warner Bros., where *The Old Man and the Sea* had been filmed forty years earlier. The crew had built a seventy-foot replica of the *Andrea Gail* atop a massive tank. The replica was placed on a giant gimbal so its motion could then be computer-controlled. Wind machines, wave makers, water cannons, and two giant dump tanks simulated a terrifying storm and heaved drenched actors to and fro. Stunt men performed only the most dangerous moves; Clooney is replaced by a digital substitute for one perilous feat in the water. Most open-water ocean shots were created digitally by Industrial Light & Magic. Petersen's biggest concern was matching his water-tank live action with the digital effects that would be layered in later. Some live action was shot in Gloucester, where locals were suspicious that the Hollywood movie might not tell the story truthfully. Junger helped bridge that gap. Despite the realistic look of the fish-harvesting scenes, which impressed even the grizzled Gloucestermen, no actual fish were used; each one seen is either animatronic or made of rubber.

DISTRIBUTION: Early in the process, Warner Bros. marketing executives asked Petersen for a "jaw-dropping" image. While the production was still shooting, ILM's visual effects artists delivered a magnificent scene of the *Andrea Gail* riding up the face of an oncoming wave many stories tall. Petersen took advantage of the early footage, showing the scene and a first-cut trailer to the crew on the Warner Bros. lot while they were still toiling away on the film. The first full screening was in Gloucester before 1,500 audience members, including friends and family of the *Andrea Gail* crewmen. Their emotional and rousing response was echoed across the country and around the world. *The Perfect Storm* came in at number six in domestic box office in 2000 and is one of the top 15 highest-grossing disaster movies of all time. ILM nabbed an Academy Award nomination for Best Visual Effects on *The Perfect Storm* but lost out to *Gladiator*. However, it did win the visual effects award given out by the British Academy. —*Tom Dupree*

DR. SEUSS' HOW THE GRINCH STOLE CHRISTMAS

Universal, 2000

ALL-RELEASE EQUIVALENT 2005 $s

(Unadjusted $s) in Millions of $s

Domestic Box Office Revenues. . . . . . . **$309.0**/($260.0)
Production Cost . . . .**$139.5**/($123.0)
Principal Photography. . . . .**120** days estimated
9/7/1999–2/25/2000

Director . . . . Ron Howard
Producer . . . . Brian Grazer
Production Company. . . . Imagine Entertainment
Story by. . . . . Based on the book by Dr. Seuss
Screenplay by . . . . Jeffrey Price, Peter S. Seaman
Cast . . . . Jim Carrey, Jeffrey Tambor, Christine Baranski, Bill Irwin, Molly Shannon, Clint Howard, Taylor Momsen, Anthony Hopkins
Filming Locations . . . . . . Filmed entirely at Universal Studios and in Utah
Genre. . . . . Comedy
Format. . . . . Color (CFI)
Initial Release 11/17/2000
Rerelease. . . . . none
Running Time . . . . 105 minutes
MPAA Rating . . . . PG

STANDING THE TEST OF TIME

ACADEMY AWARD Oscar Nominations and Wins

Art Direction/Set Decoration: Michael Corenblith/ Merideth Boswell
Costume Design: Rita Ryack
*MAKEUP: Rick Baker, Gail Ryan

OSCAR TOTALS Nominations 3 *Wins 1

AFI 100 YEARS 100 MOVIES SELECTION
2007 0   1997 0

TOP 300 FILMS POSITION . . . .#99
All-Release Domestic Box Office in Equivalent 2005 $s

National Film Preservation Board Selection. . . .none

OTHER AWARDS Best Picture Wins

	Year
Golden Globes	none
New York Film Critics	none
National Board of Review	none
Film Daily Critics	none

Jim Carrey brought a level of passion and total belief in the story, its entertainment value, and a sense of just the hipness of this character.

—Ron Howard

PLOT: In the magical land of Whoville, the residents gleefully prepare for Christmas, except the Grinch, who is a bitter, secluded creature. But a compassionate child, Cindy Lou Who, befriends the Grinch and reminds everyone of the true meaning of Christmas.

PRODUCTION: Sought after by Hollywood for years, Theodor S. Geisel (Dr. Seuss) refused to license his books for movies. Because he had an unhappy experience in 1953 with *The 5,000 Fingers of Dr. T*, a fantasy he had written, he was reluctant to film any of his other works. When he finally acquiesced, releasing the animated version of *Grinch* in 1966, it proved so successful that he then refrained from other adaptations, believing that this last picture could never be outdone. After his death in 1991, his widow, Audrey, rejected all film offers until she realized that Seuss's unique version could now be fulfilled thanks to advances in computer technology. Studios sent their top producers to court her, but after director Ron Howard and producer Brian Glazer's second pitch, no other proposal had a chance. Because Grazer couldn't imagine anyone but Jim Carrey as the Grinch, Audrey Geisel visited the set of *Man on the Moon* to see if indeed Carrey was right for the part. (At one time, both Jack Nicholson and Eddie Murphy had been considered for the role.) Ron Howard secured Sir Anthony Hopkins as the narrator, and Max the dog was rescued from the pound only four or five months prior to filming. Cirque de Soleil performers were used for odd situations and characters. Intense preproduction included creating Whoville, its residents, and the town, while the Grinch had to be designed in such a way that the costume and makeup wouldn't limit Jim Carrey's wonderful facial and physical expressions. Carrey's makeup took two and a half to three hours to apply and one hour to remove. This regime lasted 92 days. Carrey compared wearing the suit and makeup to "being buried alive on a daily basis." His yellow contact lenses were so uncomfortable at times that he couldn't bear to wear them. Some shots of his eyes had to be filled in during postproduction. Oscar-winning makeup artist Rick Baker claims Carrey was a nightmare in the makeup chair, infuriating cast and crew with his complaining. The production stats are stunning: makeup appliances used during production (800); props created (more than 300); makeup designs created by Cinovation (225); snow used on sets (enough to cover nine football fields); number of ornaments (8,200); amount of crushed marble used to create snow for the Who suburbs' exterior set (152,000 pounds); outfits created by wardrobe (443); makeup artists used on busiest days (45); Styrofoam used to build sets (2 million linear feet). And all of this took place at Universal on eleven soundstages. Kevin Mack, as visual effects supervisor, managed more than 600 visual effects in the film, claiming 43 minutes of screen time, with more than 300 of those shots being major computer-generated effects. Yet Anthony Hopkins completed his narration in just one day.

DISTRIBUTION: In just thirty-three days, Universal's *How the Grinch Stole Christmas* surpassed *Mission: Impossible II* at the domestic box office and came in sixth in movies released in 2000 at the worldwide box office. Universal's distribution chief, Nikki Rocco, said, "*The Grinch* is a textbook example of a megahit: a film that's been so embraced by the public that everyone feels they have to experience it, and many people are experiencing it over and over again." —*Christine McDermott*

CAST AWAY
20th Century-Fox, 2000

ALL-RELEASE EQUIVALENT 2005 $s
(Unadjusted $s) in Millions of $s

Domestic Box Office Revenues . . . . **$264.6**/($233.6)
Production Cost . . . . **$102.1**/($90.0)
Principal Photography . . . . **114** days estimated
1/18/1999–4/26/1999 then
4/3/2000–end June 2000
Shot in two parts over 18 months,
with a one-year hiatus to allow for
Hanks's physical transformation

Director . . . . Robert Zemeckis
Producer . . . . Steve Starkey, Tom Hanks,
Robert Zemeckis, Jack Rapke
Production Company . . . . ImageMovers, Playtone
Productions
Story and
Screenplay by . . . . William Broyles Jr.
Cast . . . . Tom Hanks, Helen Hunt
Filming Locations . . . . . . Monuriki Island in Fiji with
additional footage in Texas;
Los Angeles, CA; Memphis, TN
(the homecoming scene at
FedEx); Moscow, Russia
Genre . . . . Drama
Format . . . . Color
Initial Release . . . . 12/7/2000 premiere; 12/22/2000
general release
Rerelease . . . . none
Running Time . . . . 143 minutes
MPAA Rating PG-13

STANDING THE TEST OF TIME

ACADEMY AWARD Oscar Nominations and Wins

Actor in a Leading Role: Tom Hanks

Sound: Randy Thom, Tom Johnson, Dennis Sands, William B. Kaplan

OSCAR TOTALS Nominations **2** *Wins 0

AFI 100 YEARS 100 MOVIES SELECTION
2007 0   1997 0

TOP 300 FILMS POSITION . . . . #140
All-Release Domestic Box Office in Equivalent 2005 $s

National Film Preservation Board Selection . . . . none

OTHER AWARDS Best Picture Wins

	Year
Golden Globes	none
New York Film Critics	none
National Board of Review	none
Film Daily Critics	none

That island becomes a really major character in the movie. In a way, after Tom, it was the next most important piece of casting.

—William Broyles Jr.

PLOT: A high-energy executive for Federal Express leaves his girlfriend to go on a business trip, but his plane crashes in the Pacific. For the next 1,500 days he must battle the elements as well as his own deteriorating mental stability to survive.

PRODUCTION: For years Tom Hanks and screenwriter William Broyles Jr. had been working with a story idea loosely based on *Robinson Crusoe*. Because Hanks had previously worked with director Robert Zemeckis on *Forrest Gump* to great success, he approached him first to gauge his interest in directing the film. While Zemeckis initially liked the idea, he was not satisfied with the film's ending, in which the castaway is eventually rescued by a group of tourists. He thought that if the film was to work philosophically, Chuck had to rescue himself. So Hanks and Broyles wrote a new ending which enticed Zemekis to direct. Most of the film was shot on a small island in Fiji, which presented a considerable number of challenges. Because the nearest inhabited island was almost ninety minutes away by boat, cast and crew had to be ferried at 4:30 a.m. daily to the island so that shooting could begin at 6:45 a.m. Producer Steve Starkey partially solved this obstacle by anchoring a cruise ship with roughly thirty-six berths off the island. This cut the commute for key cast and crew from 1½ hours by ferry to 5 minutes in a dinghy. To accommodate shooting while on the island, an extensive "production village" was built in the nearby forest. It included running water, a power plant, and individual "huts" for the various production departments with telephone, e-mail, and fax services. There were two prominent and highly publicized product placements in the film, one of which was paid in accommodation, the other in cash. The unpaid plug was for Federal Express, which had agreed to cooperate even though a plane crashes within the movie. Assuming correctly that it would not hurt the company's image, FedEx gave the production carte blanche to shoot at its headquarters in Los Angeles and Memphis, with use of its people, uniforms, and equipment at absolutely no charge. The CEO at the end of the movie was the real-life CEO of FedEx, Fred Smith. The other plug was for Wilson Sporting Goods, which provided the volleyball that the castaway paints with his own blood and aptly names Wilson. Wilson brilliantly serves as the castaway's man Friday—a surrogate confidant for him to talk to while alone on the island. In addition to the size of the production and the enormous complexity of shooting in a remote location, Zemeckis had to grapple with how to accurately portray the castaway's weight loss, too. It was decided midway through filming that the entire production would be shut down to allow Hanks time to actually lose the weight. Filming began in January 1999 in Moscow and continued from there to Los Angeles and Fiji through April. Zemeckis and team then left to film *What Lies Beneath,* returning to *Cast Away* in April 2000. By then Hanks had dropped nearly fifty pounds. The production reassembled on the island, where the remainder of the film was shot.

DISTRIBUTION: 20th Century-Fox's initial fears about distributing a movie in which nearly forty minutes pass with little dialogue or music were quickly allayed by the film's critical and commercial success. Wilson Sporting Goods ran its own campaign to promote the fact that it had provided the film with Hanks's "co-star." —*Mark D'Anna*

SHREK

DreamWorks, 2001

ALL-RELEASE EQUIVALENT 2005 $s

(Unadjusted $s) in Millions of $s

Domestic Box Office Revenues . . . . **$303.1**/($267.7)
Production Cost . . . . **$66.2**/($60.0)
Production Period . . . . **6 years**

Director . . . . Andrew Adamson, Vicky Jenson
Producer . . . . Jeffrey Katzenberg, Aron Warner, John H. Williams
Production Company . . . . PDI/DreamWorks
Story by . . . . Based on the book *Shrek!* By William Steig
Screenplay by . . . . Ted Ellion, Terry Rossio, Joe Stillman, Roger S. H. Schulman
Cast . . . . Cameron Diaz, John Lithgow, Eddie Murphy, Mike Myers (voices)
Filming Locations . . . . . . PDI Studios, Redwood City, CA
Genre . . . . Animation
Format . . . . Color (Technicolor)
Initial Release 5/16/2001
Rerelease . . . . none
Running Time . . . . 89 minutes
MPAA Rating . . . . PG

STANDING THE TEST OF TIME

ACADEMY AWARD Oscar Nominations and Wins

*ANIMATED FEATURE FILM: Aron Warner

Writing (Screenplay – based on material previously produced or published): Written by Ted Elliott, Terry Rossio, Joe Stillman, and Roger S. H. Schulman

OSCAR TOTALS   Nominations 2   *Wins 1

AFI 100 YEARS 100 MOVIES SELECTION
2007 0   1997 0

TOP 300 FILMS POSITION . . . . #104
All-Release Domestic Box Office in Equivalent 2005 $s

National Film Preservation Board Selection . . . . none

OTHER AWARDS Best Picture Wins

	Year
Golden Globes	none
New York Film Critics	none
National Board of Review	none
Film Daily Critics	none

Despite six years of effort involving the hopes, dreams and careers of hundreds of artists and technicians . . . you cannot create a hit. You can only make the best movie you and hundreds of other fellow artists are capable of making. And then, you hope for the best.

—Aron Warner

PLOT: An ogre who is forced to leave his home after it is invaded by banished fairy tale characters brokers a deal with Lord Farquaad to get his land back. The deal requires that he capture a beautiful princess who is to become the lord's bride and return her to the castle. After falling head over heels in love with the princess, however, the ogre simply cannot honor the deal.

PRODUCTION: Writer and illustrator William Steig, cartoonist for the *New Yorker* for more than six decades, wrote the children's storybook *Shrek!* in 1990. (The name is taken from the German and Yiddish word *shrek,* meaning "fear" or "terror.") The book caught producer John H. William's attention when he read it to his two young sons and found the story "iconoclastic, gross, and just a lot of fun." He brought the book to DreamWorks, where co-founder Jeffrey Katzenberg read it in 1994. Katzenberg loved the unusual fairy tale and decided it would be great to meld together the story of *Shrek* with state-of-the-art computer animation, using CG technology (a new art form at the time) to create a 3-D world. The film would be loosely based on the book, but with new aspects, such as characters from other fairy tales. In November 1995, DreamWorks acquired the rights to Steig's book. Andrew Adamson (from New Zealand) and Vicky Jenson agreed to direct. Chris Farley began work as the voice of Shrek, but in December 1997 his untimely death shut down production. His replacement, former *SNL* cast mate Mike Myers, brought a fresh perspective. By Christmas 1999, a storyboarded version was completed. Adamson's original plan was to use live-action miniature sets and backgrounds that would be animated. However, the PDI/DreamWorks artists convinced him that they could achieve the naturalistic lighting he wanted in CG. Although this had never been done before, Adamson agreed. They created thirty-six unique locations (more than any other CG animated film at that time), 1,250 props and environments, and thousands of characters (more than a thousand in Shrek's swamp alone). They were all part of what Katzenberg called "hyperreality." They also created the first realistic humans, able to express dialogue and emotion through a complex facial animation system (developed at PDI). Using special tools called shapers, the animators were able to create sophisticated movements of the face and body by applying interacting layers of fat, muscle, skin, hair, and clothing to their characters. There were also advances made in the creation of organic environments, such as clothing that wrinkles or moves. Production designer James Hegedus was given the difficult job of establishing that world, which ended up being greatly influenced by the detail of American realist painters such as Wood and Wyeth, and the coloring used by the impressionists (which, in this case, included a subtle palette with warm lighting, cool shadows, and complementary colors).

DISTRIBUTION: *Shrek* became the first animated film in competition at the Cannes film festival in eighteen years. It helped establish DreamWorks as a prime competitor to Walt Disney Pictures. *Shrek* was third at the domestic box office for films released in 2001, after *Harry Potter and the Sorcerer's Stone* and *The Lord of the Rings: The Fellowship of the Ring.* It won the first Academy Award exclusively for full-length animation, with Shrek and the Donkey appearing at the awards show. *Shrek 4-D* was created at Universal's theme park, which serves as a narrative link between *Shrek* and *Shrek 2.* —*Hayley Taylor Block and Alex Ben Block*

HARRY POTTER AND THE SORCERER'S STONE

Warner Bros., 2001

ALL-RELEASE EQUIVALENT 2005 $s

(Unadjusted $s) in Millions of $s

Domestic Box Office Revenues....... **$359.0**/($317.6)
Production Cost .... **$138.9**/($126.0)
Principal Photography .... **100** days estimated
9/1/2000–April 2001

Director .... Chris Columbus

Producer .... David Heyman

Production Company.... Warner Brothers Ltd.

Story by.............. Based on the novel by
J. K. Rowling

Screenplay by .... Steve Kloves

Cast .... Daniel Radcliffe, Rupert Grant,
Emma Watson, John Cleese,
Robbie Coltrane, Warwick
Davis, Richard Griffiths,
Richard Harris, Ian Hart,
John Hurt, Alan Rickman,
Fiona Shaw, Maggie Smith,
Julie Walters

Filming Locations ...... In England: Alnwick,
Northumberland; London; Iver,
Buchinghamshire; Oxford,
Oxfordshire; Durham;
Cloucestershire; Goathland,
North Yorkshire; Harrow,
Middlesex; Lacock, Wiltshire;
Bracknell, Berkshire; North
Yorkshire; in Scotland:
Highlands; West Highland
Railway Line

Genre................ Fantasy

Format............... Color (Technicolor)

Initial Release .... 11/4/2001 premiere (UK);
11/16/2001 general release
(U.S.)

Rerelease .... none

Running Time .... 152 minutes

MPAA Rating .... PG

STANDING THE TEST OF TIME

ACADEMY AWARD Oscar Nominations and Wins

Art Direction/Set Decoration: Stuart Craig/Stephenie McMillan

Costume Design: Judianna Makovsky

Music (Original Score): John Williams

OSCAR TOTALS   Nominations 3   *Wins 0

AFI 100 YEARS 100 MOVIES SELECTION
2007 0   1997 0

TOP 300 FILMS POSITION .... #65
All-Release Domestic Box Office in Equivalent 2005 $s

National Film Preservation Board Selection....none

OTHER AWARDS Best Picture Wins

	Year
Golden Globes	none
New York Film Critics....................	none
National Board of Review.................	none
Film Daily Critics.........................	none

*We made a decision to stay true to the book even if it meant being unconventional
as a movie and not fitting this into what Hollywood thinks a movie should be.*

—Steve Kloves

PLOT: Summoned by invitation to the Hogwarts School for Witchcraft and Wizardry from a life of drudgery as the orphaned nephew of the Dursley family, Harry Potter embarks on many magical adventures before returning home.

PRODUCTION: On a train ride from Manchester to London, England, in 1990, while her baby napped nearby, J. K. Rowling began writing *Harry Potter and the Philosopher's Stone.* The novel received rave reviews and soon became a bestseller in the United States but under the title *Harry Potter and the Sorcerer's Stone,* out of concern that the word *philosopher* would scare off young readers. Meanwhile, a friend of British producer David Heyman sent him an article about the book. He read a copy and began pursuing film rights the next day. Rowling met with Heyman, who at first envisioned a small British production. Instead, as book sales soared, the budget rose and together they found director Chris Columbus. With an estimated 100 million books in print, translated into forty-seven languages and circulating in 200 countries, the pressure to create a faithful cinematic representation of the first episode in the *Harry Potter* series was intense. The film was made by Columbus's 1492 Pictures and Heyman Films/Duncan Henderson Productions with Warner Bros. as the financier and distributor. The search then began for the right boy to play the role of Harry Potter. The director wanted the child actor (Daniel Radcliffe) who had starred in the BBC's *David Copperfield* but was told by the child's parents that they did not want him to do the film. At a chance encounter at a theater months later, the producer saw Radcliffe. He knew that this was the boy Columbus wanted. Despite the reluctance of the parents, and after several auditions, Daniel Radcliffe was invited to star in the film. The creative team then focused on casting the rest of the characters. Director Chris Columbus already had a feel for the world that he was trying to re-create. He had written *Young Sherlock Holmes* (1985), and the irony of the similarities in sets and characters was not lost on him. He said, "It was a sort of preparation for directing *Harry Potter.*" Columbus chose his production team with care, including Stuart Craig as the production designer, John Seale as director of photography, and Judianna Makovsky as the costume designer. Filming at the mostly British locations was not easy. It took a crew of 800 to make the movie. A big challenge for ILM, which did the visual effects, was the creation of the Quidditch stadium. Careful art direction was needed. Its cheering crowd suspended in the sky and two teams of flying Quidditch players zooming about on broomsticks had to appear seamless and realistic. Knowing that he could not include every detail of the book, Columbus endeavored to make a film that didn't sacrifice any of the story's complexity.

DISTRIBUTION: The film opened to a $90.3 million weekend, ranking it in the top 10 all-time box office openers on its release. With $976.5 million in worldwide box office, it outgrossed *The Lord of the Rings: The Fellowship of the Ring* ($871.4 million) and *Shrek* ($484.4 million), making it the number one movie of 2001. Warner Bros. was under pressure to produce a DVD worthy of the success of the film and book. The DVD-ROM was a milestone because for the first time it offered almost the entire content of a DVD in a computer-readable format. —*Rosaleen O'Byrne*

THE LORD OF THE RINGS: THE FELLOWSHIP OF THE RING

New Line, 2001

ALL-RELEASE EQUIVALENT 2005 $s

(Unadjusted $s) in Millions of $s

Domestic Box Office Revenues........$352.6/($314.8)
Production Cost ....$182.0/($165.0)
Principal Photography........... **274** days estimated
10/11/1999–12/22/2000
Trilogy shot together

Director .... Peter Jackson

Producer .... Barrie M. Osborne,
Peter Jackson, Fran Walsh,
Tim Sanders

Production Company.... Wingnut Films, New Line
Cinema

Story by.............. Based on the novel by
J. R. R. Tolkien

Screenplay by .... Fran Walsh, Philippa Boyens,
Peter Jackson

Cast .... Elijah Wood, Ian McKellen,
Liv Tyler, Viggo Mortensen,
Sean Astin, Cate Blanchett,
Orlando Bloom

Filming Locations ...... New Zealand

Genre................. Fantasy

Format............... Color (DeLuxe)

Initial Release .... 12/10/2001 world premiere
(London); 12/19/2001
U.S. release

Rerelease .... none

Running Time .... 178 minutes

MPAA Rating PG-13

STANDING THE TEST OF TIME

ACADEMY AWARD Oscar Nominations and Wins

Best Picture: Peter Jackson, Fran Walsh, and
Barrie M. Osborne, Producers

Actor in a Supporting Role: Ian McKellen

Art Direction/Set Decoration: Grant Major/
Dan Hennah

*CINEMATOGRAPHY: Andrew Lesnie

Costume Design: Ngila Dickson, Richard Taylor

Directing: Peter Jackson

Film Editing: John Gilbert

*MAKEUP: Peter Owen, Richard Taylor

*MUSIC (Original Score): Howard Shore

Music (Original Song): "May It Be," Music and Lyrics
by Enya, Nicky Ryan, and Roma Ryan

Sound: Christopher Boyes, Michael Semanick,
Gethin Creagh, Hammond Peek

*VISUAL EFFECTS: Jim Rygiel, Randall William
Cook, Richard Taylor, Mark Stetson

Writing (Screenplay – based on material previously
produced or published): Screenplay by
Fran Walsh, Philippa Boyens, and Peter Jackson

OSCAR TOTALS Nominations **13** *Wins **4**

AFI 100 YEARS 100 MOVIES SELECTION
2007 ... #50   1997..... 0

TOP 300 FILMS POSITION .... #67
All-Release Domestic Box Office in Equivalent 2005 $s

National Film Preservation Board Selection. ....none

OTHER AWARDS Best Picture Wins

	Year
Golden Globes	none
New York Film Critics.....................	none
National Board of Review.................	none
Film Daily Critics.........................	none

Imagine living in a country where the most important industry is making a film of The Lord of the Rings. *Isn't that a sign of a world you want to live in?*

—Ian McKellen

PLOT: In Middle Earth, a group of adventurers bands together on a dangerous and terrifying journey to destroy an enchanted ring whose power corrupts all those who come near it.

PRODUCTION: Bringing the *Lord of the Rings* trilogy to the screen was a task that had frustrated countless filmmakers since the late fifties. In 1969, after two years of negotiations, film rights were finally sold to United Artists, which at one point toyed with the idea of enlisting the Beatles as the stars. Impatient with various failed attempts, UA sold the rights to Saul Zaentz in 1976. Zaentz produced an animated feature in 1978 covering the first half of the trilogy, but it was widely viewed as a creative disappointment, and plans for further films lay fallow. New Zealander Peter Jackson had a distribution deal with Miramax, which had released Zaentz's *The English Patient*. Jackson had just founded Weta Ltd., his own special effects company, and was looking for an effects-heavy project. Jackson's original plan was to shoot the story as two films with a budget of $130 million. *Rings* spent about eighteen months in preproduction while Jackson and partners wrote the script and worked on design and effects. Before long, it became clear that the project would be far more expensive than Miramax and its corporate owner, Disney, had planned. They put *Rings* into turnaround causing Jackson to quickly put together a demo tape. During a presentation to New Line in summer 1998, founder and CEO Bob Shaye asked Jackson, "It's three books, isn't it? Shouldn't it be three films?" The production spent the next year expanding the length of the project accordingly. The astonishing scope and grandeur of the *Rings* films is the result of two key decisions: to make all three films simultaneously, doing away with duplicative startup costs and making efficient use of locations and costumes; and to produce in New Zealand, where there were favorable currency exchange rates, significant tax advantages and no film industry unions. Also, the breathtaking locations were brand-new to most of the world, adding to the sense of a remote, unseen fantasy land. Just before shooting began, Jackson replaced actor Stuart Townsend in the critical role of Aragorn, hiring Viggo Mortensen on two days' notice. On October 11, 1999, Jackson called "Action!" at long last.

DISTRIBUTION: The first indication that the movie would be a crowd pleaser came after an enthusiastic reception at the Cannes Film Festival to a 26-minute compilation of footage. Nevertheless, Tolkien fans, protective of their beloved trilogy, were complaining on the Internet about deletions from the book. After premieres in London, New York, Los Angeles, and Wellington, New Zealand, however, they turned out in droves and made the film a magnificent success. *Fellowship* came in number two of all 2001 film releases in worldwide box office with $871 million, after *Harry Potter and the Sorcerer's Stone*'s worldwide take of $976 million. The *Rings* film project was heavily documented for the hot new DVD aftermarket, leading to special extended editions that many viewers consider superior to the theatrical versions. *—Tom Dupree*

861

A BEAUTIFUL MIND

Universal, 2001

ALL-RELEASE EQUIVALENT 2005 $s

(Unadjusted $s) in Millions of $s

Domestic Box Office Revenues . . . . **$189.0**/($170.7)
Production Cost . . . . **$86.0**/($78.0)
Principal Photography . . . . .80 days estimated
3/26/2001–July 2001

Director . . . . Ron Howard
Producer . . . . Brian Grazer, Ron Howard
Production Company. . . . Universal Pictures, DreamWorks, Imagine Entertainment
Story by . . . . Based on the book by Sylvia Nasar
Screenplay by . . . . Akiva Goldsman
Cast . . . . Russell Crowe, Ed Harris, Jennifer Connelly, Paul Bettany, Adam Goldberg, Judd Hirsch, Josh Lucas, Anthony Rapp, Christopher Plummer, Austin Pendleton, Jason Gray-Stanford, Vivien Cardone
Filming Locations . . . . . . Locations in New York and New Jersey include Princeton University, most notable Manhattan College, Fordham University, and the Military Ocean Terminal in Bayonne
Genre . . . . Bio-Drama
Format . . . . Color (DeLuxe)
Initial Release 12/21/2001
Rerelease . . . . none
Running Time . . . . 134 minutes
MPAA Rating PG-13

STANDING THE TEST OF TIME

ACADEMY AWARD Oscar Nominations and Wins

*BEST PICTURE: Brian Grazer and Ron Howard, Producers

Actor in a Leading Role: Russell Crowe

*ACTRESS IN A SUPPORTING ROLE: Jennifer Connelly

*DIRECTING: Ron Howard

Film Editing: Mike Hill, Dan Hanley

Makeup: Greg Cannom, Colleen Callaghan

Music (Original Score): James Horner

*WRITING (Screenplay – based on material previously produced or published): Written by Akiva Goldsman

OSCAR TOTALS Nominations **8** *Wins **4**

AFI 100 YEARS 100 MOVIES SELECTION

2007 0   1997 0

TOP 300 FILMS POSITION . . . . .none
All-Release Domestic Box Office in Equivalent 2005 $s

National Film Preservation Board Selection . . . .none

OTHER AWARDS Best Picture Wins

	Year
Golden Globes (Drama)	2002
New York Film Critics	none
National Board of Review	none
Film Daily Critics	none

It's a movie about a mathematician with schizophrenia. Now, in retrospect that might seem like a commercial choice, but oh my God!

—Akiva Goldsman

PLOT: Princeton's star mathematician, John Nash, suddenly finds himself overcome by paranoid delusions involving secret government plots. Through the help of his wife, Nash struggles to overcome his mental illness and regain his foothold on reality.

PRODUCTION: The screenwriter Akiva Goldsman had a difficult job ahead of him. Adapting *A Beautiful Mind,* Sylvia Nasar's biography of Princeton's brilliant John Forbes Nash Jr., required that he dramatize a schizophrenic genius in an accessible but compelling manner. That meant no lofty mathematics or technical psychology—but what in its place? Drawing on his own experiences as the son of two psychologists, Goldsman, who grew up in close proximity to his parents' patients, devised a story that portrayed Nash's delusions not as hallucinatory but as indistinguishable from reality. There was more, however, to this decision than mere creative cunning. Brian Grazer, the film's co-producer, was concerned about marketability. "We gentrified it," he said, "and turned John Nash's life into more of a compelling thriller." So determined was Grazer to make *A Beautiful Mind* that he forfeited his normal producer fee in the hope that Universal would be won over by his conviction. And indeed it was. Once a first draft of the script was submitted, Ron Howard, fresh from *Dr. Seuss' How the Grinch Stole Christmas,* was ready to move it forward. Howard, it seems, was dedicated to authenticity—of a kind. Though his script was a clever combination of fact and imagination, the performances of his actors—especially that of Russell Crowe—wouldn't be. In order to better ensure the accuracy of Crowe's interpretation, Howard videotaped Nash (then seventy-two) discussing the ideas and events leading up to his Nobel Prize and presented it to the actor for him to study, but it wasn't until the mathematician visited the set with his wife that Crowe truly began to be fascinated by Nash. In fact, it was the mathematician's hands that were of particular interest to Crowe. When he saw that Nash had beautiful skin and polished nails, he expressly put that into the film. In addition, Howard insisted upon shooting his film in sequence, which proved not only costly but also utterly impractical from a production standpoint. Ultimately, though, it wasn't the director's production mandates that threatened the future of the film; it was, ironically, the Academy Awards.

DISTRIBUTION: Controversy swelled around *A Beautiful Mind* soon after the Oscar nominations were announced. Certain critics and journalists accused the filmmakers of suppressing John Nash's alleged bouts of anti-Semitism and homosexuality, claiming their whitewash of the subject rendered the film insincere and incomplete. Both Sylvia Nasar and Nash's wife denied his alleged homosexuality and claimed that whatever inflammatory statements he had made were spoken under the influence of his mental illness. To counteract the potential backlash against the film, Universal poured $15 million into positive pre-Oscar press and hired a public relations manager to counter negative campaigning by rival studios. Universal enlisted the support of the mental health community, who publicly defended the film on the basis of its honest depiction of schizophrenia; the studio PR people happily sent that around. *Newsweek* printed letters from those with personal experiences of the illness attesting to the picture's many merits. In the end, the extra efforts all paid off—in gold. On Oscar night, Academy voters sided with *A Beautiful Mind*—and so did moviegoers. —*Sam Wasson*

MY BIG FAT GREEK WEDDING

IFC (domestic); Various (foreign), 2002

ALL-RELEASE EQUIVALENT 2005 $s

(Unadjusted $s) in Millions of $s

Domestic Box Office Revenues . . . . **$266.4**/($241.4)
Production Cost . . . . **$5.4**/($5.0)
Principal Photography . . . . **36** days estimated
5/9/2001–6/30/2001

Director . . . . Joel Zwick

Producer . . . . Rita Wilson, Tom Hanks, Gary Goetzman

Production Company . . . . Gold Circle Films

Story by . . . . Based on play by Nia Vardalos

Screenplay by . . . . Nia Vardalos

Cast . . . . Nia Vardalos, John Corbett

Filming Locations . . . . . . Filmed in Chicago, IL; Ryerson Polytechnic University, Toronto, Ontario, Canada

Genre . . . . Romantic Comedy

Format . . . . Color

Initial Release 4/19/2002

Rerelease . . . . none

Running Time . . . . 95 minutes

MPAA Rating . . . . PG

STANDING THE TEST OF TIME

ACADEMY AWARD Oscar Nominations and Wins

Writing (Original Screenplay): Nia Vardalos

OSCAR TOTALS   Nominations **1**   *Wins 0

AFI 100 YEARS 100 MOVIES SELECTION
           2007 0   1997 0

TOP 300 FILMS POSITION . . . . **#139**
All-Release Domestic Box Office in Equivalent 2005 $s

National Film Preservation Board Selection . . . . none

OTHER AWARDS Best Picture Wins

	Year
Golden Globes	none
New York Film Critics	none
National Board of Review	none
Film Daily Critics	none

The fact that the movie got made, to me, is still a source of great amazement.

—Nia Vardalos

PLOT: A Greek woman falls in love with a non-Greek man and struggles to get her family to accept him while she comes to terms with her own heritage and cultural identity.

PRODUCTION: Nia Vardalos originally developed the story as a one-woman stage show while an actress with Chicago's Second City. She wrote the film about her courtship and marriage to another Second City player, Ian Gomez. Vardalos said, "In terms of my real life and my real marriage, everything that happened in the movie actually happened either to me, or a cousin, or happened to me 20 years before I even met Ian." She put the play up in Chicago originally, and then moved to L.A. Actress Rita Wilson, a Greek American herself, loved the play, and convinced her husband, Tom Hanks, to produce it as a movie along with his producing partner Gary Goetzman. Big studios were willing to back it only if the lead was a star. Vardalos was offered much more money to sell the screenplay and agree not to star. She refused, so the producers took a chance on her but made it a low-budget independent production. John Corbett, in Toronto making *Serendipity,* thought it was really funny and poignant. His agent mistakenly told him they had an offer out to someone else and told Vardalos that Corbett was out of the country shooting. They actually were both in Canada. Corbett happened to be in his hotel bar telling a crew member about the script one night, and Vardalos was at the same place with Gary Goetzman. Vardalos was thrilled. She'd had Corbett in mind since his role on *Sex and the City* and thought he'd be the perfect all-American guy. They talked with him for five minutes. The chemistry was evident, and they offered him the role. Vardalos was in on everything in the film, from the editing to the music. She filmed several scenes at her alma mater, Toronto's Ryerson University. Her husband, Ian Gomez, played the best friend, Mike, in the film, and her sister choreographed the dance scenes for the wedding. Most of those at the wedding were members of Vardalos's family, who flew in to help out. A lot of Greek restaurants in the area felt like it was their movie too, and would send over food to the set.

DISTRIBUTION: Released without much fanfare, *My Big Fat Greek Wedding* captured the hearts of mainstream moviegoers who aren't often exposed to smaller films. Nia Vardalos and John Corbett did weeks of promotion, and there was a great e-mail campaign that helped build word of mouth. Although there were no ad campaigns or commercials for the film at first, the movie went on to become the fifth-highest-grossing movie of 2002 in the United States and one of the highest-grossing romantic comedies of all time. It was a testament to the movie's word of mouth and popularity among audiences who went back to see it again and again. In unadjusted dollars, *Greek Wedding* surpassed *The Blair Witch Project* as the highest-grossing independent film of all time, until *The Passion of the Christ.* Vardalos's deal gave her 10 percent of profits, which reportedly paid her $35 million. The 2003 home video release, just before Valentine's Day, was the third-biggest rental debut in history. —*Hayley Taylor Block*

SPIDER-MAN

Sony, 2002

ALL-RELEASE EQUIVALENT 2005 $s

(Unadjusted $s) in Millions of $s

Domestic Box Office Revenues....... **$445.4**/($403.7)
Production Cost ....**$190.0**/($175.0)
Principal Photography...........**112** days estimated
1/8/2001–6/12/2001

Director	Sam Raimi
Producer	Laura Ziskin, Ian Bryce
Production Company....	Marvel Enterprises, Columbia Pictures, Laura Ziskin Productions
Story by..............	Based on the Marvel comic book by Stan Lee and Steve Ditko
Screenplay by.........	David Koepp
Cast	Tobey Maguire, Willem Dafoe, Kirsten Dunst
Filming Locations	New York City; Los Angeles; Sony Studios, Culver City, CA
Genre................	Action Adventure
Format...............	Color (DeLuxe)
Initial Release..........	5/3/2002
Rerelease.............	none
Running Time.........	121 minutes
MPAA Rating	PG-13

STANDING THE TEST OF TIME

ACADEMY AWARD Oscar Nominations and Wins

Sound: Kevin O'Connell, Greg P. Russell, Ed Novick

Visual Effects: John Dykstra, Scott Stokdyk, Anthony LaMolinara, John Frazier

OSCAR TOTALS   Nominations 2   *Wins 0

AFI 100 YEARS 100 MOVIES SELECTION

2007 0   1997 0

TOP 300 FILMS POSITION ....**#32**

All-Release Domestic Box Office in Equivalent 2005 $s

National Film Preservation Board Selection....none

OTHER AWARDS Best Picture Wins

	Year
Golden Globes	none
New York Film Critics.....................	none
National Board of Review..................	none
Film Daily Critics.........................	none

Who am I? You sure you want to know? If somebody told you I was just your average ordinary guy, not a care in the world . . . somebody lied.

—Peter Parker (Tobey Maguire)

PLOT: Teenager Peter Parker, bitten by a genetically altered spider, discovers he can shoot webbing and walk on walls. After his selfishness leads to the death of his uncle, Peter dedicates himself to fighting crime as Spider-Man.

PRODUCTION: *Spider-Man,* based on characters created by Stan Lee and illustrated by Steve Ditko for Marvel Comics, was an immediate hit when the character first climbed the walls in the 1962 comic *Amazing Fantasy #15.* Yet it took a tortuous four decades to reach the silver screen. In 1985 Canon Films acquired the film rights to the character from license holder Marvel for $225,000. Feisty independent movie distributor Canon, run by Israeli producers Menahem Golan and Yoram Globus, offered the film to *Poltergeist* director Tobe Hooper. However, the project stalled due to Canon's financial problems. In 1989 Golan scooped up the character rights for his new company, 21st Century Film Corporation, selling the theatrical rights to Carolco Pictures. Carolco then attached *Terminator* director James Cameron, only to shutter production for budget reasons in 1992. Lawsuits followed, with 21st Century suing Carolco over a producer credit, while Carolco sued other studios with interests in the character to obtain television and home video rights. In 1996 MGM picked up *Spider-Man* while Marvel Comics, Carolco, and 21st Century all entered bankruptcy, though MGM proved to be another temporary home. In 1998 a restructured Marvel won back the character's rights, settling any remaining lawsuits and selling *Spider-Man* to Sony in 1999. Sony Pictures hired David Koepp (*Jurassic Park*) to write the screenplay and took a risk on director Sam Raimi, whose biggest previous hit had been 1990's *Darkman.* Casting for the film's eponymous star touched on Leonardo DiCaprio and Freddie Prinze Jr. until Tobey Maguire (*The Cider House Rules*) agreed to portray Peter Parker for an estimated $4 million. The move triggered angst among Spider-Man fans, many of whom complained that Maguire looked too scrawny to play the part of a superhero. For his part, Maguire bulked up enough to convince his staunchest critics. "I was working out six days a week, two workouts a day. Sometimes I'd do an hour and a half of yoga, then hit the weight room. I also did gymnastics, martial arts, weights, and high-end cardio." Willem Dafoe signed on as the sinister Green Goblin, besting previous candidates such as Nicolas Cage and John Malkovich. With casting complete, filming began on January 8, 2001, on the Sony soundstages, working with an estimated production budget of $139 million. *Spider-Man*'s 2001 teaser trailer, which featured a helicopter snagged in Spider-Man's webbing between the twin towers of the World Trade Center, was pulled following the terrorist attacks of September 11.

DISTRIBUTION: *Spider-Man* debuted on May 3, 2002, in 3,615 theaters. It became a sensation right out of the gate, smashing box office records in its opening weekend with a gross of $114.8 million domestically. *Spider-Man* became the fastest theatrical release to reach $100 million (in three days) and took the crown of the highest-grossing domestic box office film of 2002, with a $403.7 million domestic haul and a worldwide gross of $821.6 million. The film also logged overwhelmingly favorable critical reviews to burnish its public acclaim. A. O. Scott of the *New York Times* said, "The filmmakers have succeeded in rejuvenating the character while staying faithful to his roots." —*Daniel Wallace*

STAR WARS: EP II ATTACK OF THE CLONES

20th Century-Fox, 2002

ALL-RELEASE EQUIVALENT 2005 $s

(Unadjusted $s) in Millions of $s

Domestic Box Office Revenues.......$342.4/($310.7)
Production Cost ....$130.3/($120.0)
Principal Photography.....................61 days
6/26/2000–9/21/2000

Format............... Color (DeLuxe prints); shot in
Cine Alta 24-frame HD digital
Initial Release......... 5/16/2002
Rerelease .... 11/1/2002 (IMAX)
Running Time......... 143 minutes
MPAA Rating .... PG

Director............... George Lucas
Producer .... Rick McCallum
Production Company.... Lucasfilm Ltd.
Story by............... George Lucas
Screenplay by......... George Lucas, Jonathan Hales
Cast .... Ewan McGregor, Natalie Portman, Hayden Christensen, Ian McDiarmid, Samuel L. Jackson, Christopher Lee, Anthony Daniels, Kenny Baker, Frank Oz
Filming Locations ...... On location: Lake Como and Caserta, Italy; Tozeur and MalMata, Tunisia; Seville, Spain (10 days); in studio: Fox Studios, Australia; Elstree Film Studios, London (51 days); pickups: Elstree Film Studios, Borehamwood, UK (2 days, 1/2002–2/2002) Ealing Studios, London (13 days, 3/2001); Ealing Green, London (5 days, 11/2001)
Genre................. Sci-Fi

STANDING THE TEST OF TIME

ACADEMY AWARD Oscar Nominations and Wins
Visual Effects: Rob Coleman, Pablo Helman, John Knoll, Ben Snow

OSCAR TOTALS   Nominations 1   *Wins 0

AFI 100 YEARS 100 MOVIES SELECTION
2007.....0   1997.....0

TOP 300 FILMS POSITION ....#79
All-Release Domestic Box Office in Equivalent 2005 $s

National Film Preservation Board Selection....none

OTHER AWARDS Best Picture Wins

	Year
Golden Globes	none
New York Film Critics.....................	none
National Board of Review.................	none
Film Daily Critics........................	none

I love this new digital world. We can just keep adding to it until it's right in the end.

—George Lucas

868

PLOT: Anakin Skywalker has grown into an accomplished Jedi apprentice, and he faces his most difficult challenge yet as he must choose between his Jedi duty and forbidden love.

PRODUCTION: George Lucas set out to make *Attack of the Clones* the first completely digital film in the *Star Wars* series. He started composing his screenplay in 1999, calling in co-writer Jonathan Hales to help with a final draft. While Lucas grappled with the script, Doug Chiang led the art department in creating more than 1,000 pieces of artwork and dozens of models. The countless designs were computerized for "animatics"—rough CGI moving storyboards— and the early creation of sets, costumes, and vehicles by the various production departments. Producer Rick McCallum went so far as to herald the endeavor as a new type of "virtual film-making." As shooting loomed, casting director Robin Gurland launched her massive, months-long search for an actor to flesh out Anakin Skywalker as a young man. Wading through some 1,500 submissions, she helped Lucas finally select Hayden Christensen to fill Darth Vader's formidable boots. To realize his digital vision for filming, Lucas and McCallum worked closely with Sony for five years to develop a new digital camera that sported high-quality Panavision zoom lenses. The state-of-the-art, high-definition camera recorded twenty-four progressive frames a second, just like a film camera. Rushing to meet deadlines, Lucas delivered the official cameras and final draft of his script to the crew only the week before the shoot began on June 26, 2000. By then, production designer Gavin Bocquet had overseen the construction of seventy digitally friendly sets at Fox Studios Australia, including a re-creation of the Sky-walker homestead from the original *Star Wars*. Despite the actors needing to adjust to the blue-screen sets and blank spaces where other actors or objects would normally appear, Lucas and his crew moved at a steady pace, averaging a healthy thirty-six setups per day. When shooting moved to challenging exteriors in Italy, Tunisia, and Spain, the new digital cameras proved themselves invaluable by handling both torrential rainstorms and 130-degree heat without a hitch. The technology enabled the team to view dailies with synchronized sound and begin ed-iting the footage almost immediately. Even before shooting wrapped on September 21, 2000, ILM was busy perfecting the almost 2,000 digital effects shots. While Lucas worked on various rough cuts of the film, four different supervisors oversaw the massive, eighteen-month visual effects enterprise, highlighted by the realization of a completely CGI Yoda dueling a stunt man with Christopher Lee's face digitally superimposed onto his body. The teams also utilized computer-generated digital doubles of actors for particularly difficult stunts.

DISTRIBUTION: Although digital technology aided the film immensely, digital piracy emerged as a major problem when bootleg copies started appearing and illegal uploads began proliferat-ing on the Internet. The film hauled in $80 million in its first North American weekend and went on to garner upward of $649 million worldwide. Sixty-three theaters digitally projected it in the United States and another thirty-one did so internationally, with audiences hailing its quality. Lucas reformatted and shortened the film for an IMAX exhibition in November 2002. The DVD release, also in November 2002, contained a few slight alterations to the dialogue and effects, as well as eight deleted scenes. —*Scott Mazak*

HARRY POTTER AND THE CHAMBER OF SECRETS

Warner Bros., 2002

ALL-RELEASE EQUIVALENT 2005 $s

(Unadjusted $s) in Millions of $s

Domestic Box Office Revenues . . . . **$288.7**/($262.0)
Production Cost . . . . **$130.0**/($120.5)
Principal Photography . . . . **100** days estimated
11/19/2001–7/26/2002

Director . . . . Chris Columbus
Producer . . . . David Heyman
Production Company . . . . Warner Bros. Productions, Heyday Films, 1492 Pictures
Story by . . . . Based on the novel by J. K. Rowling
Screenplay by . . . . Steve Kloves
Cast . . . . Daniel Radcliffe, Rupert Grint, Emma Watson, Kenneth Branagh, John Cleese, Robbie Coltrane, Warwick Davis, Richard Harris, Alan Rickman, Maggie Smith
Filming Locations . . . . . . In studio in the UK at Leavesden Studios, Hertfordshire; on location in England: Alnwick, Northumberland; London; Oxford, Oxfordshire; Durham; Cloucestershire; Goathland in Scotland: Glencoe and Glenfinnan, Highlands

Genre . . . . Fantasy
Format . . . . Color (Technicolor)
Initial Release . . . . 11/3/2002 premiere (UK); 11/15/2002 general release (U.S.)
Rerelease . . . . none
Running Time . . . . 161 minutes
MPAA Rating . . . . PG

STANDING THE TEST OF TIME

ACADEMY AWARD Oscar Nominations and Wins

None

OSCAR TOTALS   Nominations 0   *Wins 0

AFI 100 YEARS 100 MOVIES SELECTION
2007 0   1997 0

TOP 300 FILMS POSITION . . . . **#166**
All-Release Domestic Box Office in Equivalent 2005 $s

National Film Preservation Board Selection . . . .none

OTHER AWARDS Best Picture Wins

	Year
Golden Globes	none
New York Film Critics	none
National Board of Review	none
Film Daily Critics	none

Never trust anything that can think for itself if you can't see where it keeps its brain.
—J. K. Rowling

PLOT: Despite many obstacles, including a mischievous house elf named Dobby, transportation problems, and a family afraid of his talents, Harry Potter (Daniel Radcliffe) returns to Hogwarts to fight the dark force residing there, ultimately defeating it.

PRODUCTION: The second of seven planned movies based on J. K. Rowling's *Harry Potter* fantasy adventure series, took a darker turn. Director Chris Columbus went right from the first *Potter* production into *The Chamber of Secrets,* even beginning preproduction on some of the 950 shots requiring special effects while still in postproduction on *Sorcerer's Stone.* Things got off to a bumpy start when Hugh Grant, who was to play the celebrity wizard character Gilderoy Lockhart, dropped out due to scheduling conflicts. Instead, the part was played to rave reviews by Kenneth Branagh, one of three new characters. Equity, the actors' union, intervened when Daniel Radcliffe was offered only £125,000 (U.S. $181,500) for the role of Harry. They ultimately negotiated £2 million (U.S. $3 million) on his behalf. Production began at Leavesden Studios, Hertfordshire, on November 19, 2001, only three days after the release of *Harry Potter and the Sorcerer's Stone,* which was an immediate hit. The location manager, Simon King, coordinated the 450-person cast and crew as they built one of the biggest European film sets ever created by Warner Bros. Although the set for the book's *Chamber of Secrets* measured 250 by 120 feet, the set designers needed to create the illusion that it was even bigger. Because Leavesden Studios, situated in an old aircraft factory, had a height limitation of 28 feet, the sets were cleverly built downward, with only one foot of black-dyed water creating the illusion of depth needed for the flooded effect. Coupled with the CG-heavy art, set construction added to the rapidly increasing budget. Three hundred construction workers and twenty art directors and draftsmen, in addition to sculptors, portrait painters, and prop masters, built such sets as Dumbledore's office, the Burrow, the Dursleys' home, the Spider's Hollow, and the Whomping Willow. Harry's flying blue Ford Anglica required the acquisition of fourteen identical blue cars to make the visual effects work. All four of Columbus's children (Eleanor, Brendan, Violet, and Isabella) appear in small parts in the movie. Scheduling problems prevented composer John Williams from delivering a full score, so William Ross was hired to adapt Williams's work and conduct the orchestra during postproduction recording.

DISTRIBUTION: An immediate critical and commercial hit, the film grossed $88.3 million in its first weekend in the United States. It was not quite as big as the first *Potter* movie but still became second among 2002 releases worldwide, with nearly $879 million in box office. It was the final film for actor Richard Harris, who died October 25, 2002, shortly before the premiere. Of the first four *Potter* movies, it is the only one that did not get a single Academy Award nomination. It went on to set records with the home video/DVD release, and a version aired on ABC Family Channel in 2004 with scenes that had been deleted from the theatrical release fully restored. —*Rosaleen O'Byrne*

THE LORD OF THE RINGS: THE TWO TOWERS

New Line, 2002

ALL-RELEASE EQUIVALENT 2005 $s

(Unadjusted $s) in Millions of $s

Domestic Box Office Revenues........**$372.8**/($341.7)
Production Cost ....**$255.1**/($235.0)
Principal Photography.......... **274** days estimated
10/11/1999–12/22/2000
Trilogy shot together

Director	Peter Jackson
Producer	Barrie M. Osborne, Peter Jackson, Fran Walsh
Production Company	Wingnut Films, New Line Cinema
Story by	Based on the novel by J. R. R. Tolkien
Screenplay by	Fran Walsh, Philippa Boyens, Stephen Sinclair, Peter Jackson
Cast	Elijah Wood, Ian McKellen, Liv Tyler, Viggo Mortensen, Sean Astin, Cate Blanchett, Orlando Bloom
Filming Locations	New Zealand
Genre	Fantasy
Format	Color (DeLuxe)
Initial Release	12/5/2002 world premiere (New York); 12/18/2002 general release (U.S.)
Rerelease	none
Running Time	179 minutes
MPAA Rating	PG-13

STANDING THE TEST OF TIME

ACADEMY AWARD Oscar Nominations and Wins

Best Picture: Barrie M. Osborne, Fran Walsh, and Peter Jackson, Producers

Art Direction/Set Decoration: Grant Major/ Dan Hennah and Alan Lee

Film Editing: Michael Horton

Sound: Christopher Boyes, Michael Semanick, Michael Hedges, Hammond Peek

*SOUND EDITING: Ethan Van der Ryn, Michael Hopkins

*VISUAL EFFECTS: Jim Rygiel, Joe Letteri, Randall William Cook, Alex Funke

OSCAR TOTALS Nominations **6** *Wins **2**

AFI 100 YEARS 100 MOVIES SELECTION
2007 0   1997 0

TOP 300 FILMS POSITION . . . .**#55**
All-Release Domestic Box Office in Equivalent 2005 $s

National Film Preservation Board Selection . . . .none

OTHER AWARDS Best Picture Wins

	Year
Golden Globes	none
New York Film Critics	none
National Board of Review	none
Film Daily Critics	none

I just knew it was going to be an epic adventure.
The movie, yes, but also the making of the movie.

—Sean Astin

PLOT: *The Two Towers* is split into three parts: Frodo and Sam approach Mount Doom; Merry and Pippin are captured by Saruman's soldiers; and Aragorn, Gimli, and Legolas encounter the fabled Riders of Rohan.

PRODUCTION: About four months into the mammoth three-picture production schedule, and before anyone knew how *The Fellowship of the Ring* would be received, *The Two Towers* began principal photography. Director Peter Jackson insisted on as many actual locations as his design staff could manage, including a spectacular set carved out of a remote rock quarry that took more than seven months to create for the sprawling Battle of Helm's Deep. A major technological challenge for *The Two Towers* was to convincingly realize the character of Gollum, a skeletal, dwarfish being who was once human but had been corrupted by long exposure to Frodo's ring. Jackson hired actor Andy Serkis not only to perform Gollum's sibilant voice but also to move on set with the other actors, and again later by himself, in a motion-capture suit. The result is a stunning combination of computer-generated imagery and the natural movements of a physical performer. It was two years after Serkis's work before the filmmakers saw the finished composite. The Helm's Deep sequence was the largest battle scene yet filmed, but capturing it was torturous for the cast and crew. It required four straight months of night shooting in rain and cold, isolated from the rest of the production, which continued working in the daytime. Star Viggo Mortensen ruefully remembered the experience later as a "vampire life." On day 197 of production, catastrophe was narrowly averted when actor Sean Astin leapt into a river and stepped on a piece of glass, which pierced his foot. He was helicoptered to a hospital and required twenty stitches, but was back at work again the next day. The production also fought the quirky New Zealand climate: for a warm-weather scene in which Gollum captures a fish in a river, the crew arrived on location to find that it had snowed overnight. Using hot-air fans, fire hoses, and old-fashioned snow shoveling, the crew cleared the snow and deiced the riverbank in time for the 1:00 p.m. shoot, but Serkis remembered that when he dove in, he felt like he had been "punched in the chest" because the flowing river water was still near freezing.

DISTRIBUTION: *The Fellowship of the Ring* was an international pop culture sensation, quickly rising to a prominent spot on the all-time highest-grossing list. But by the time it was released, *The Two Towers* was already in the can. The sudden awareness that New Line was building an international blockbuster franchise produced more money for additional special effects shots as well as the budget to bring the cast and crew back together in 2002 for pickups on *Towers* and in 2003 for pickups on the third film, *The Return of the King*. It also motivated the go-ahead for Jackson to produce expanded-edition DVDs, restoring material he had reluctantly excised to minimize the running time. *Towers* was released the week before Christmas 2002 and stayed in active distribution for six months, until the release of the theatrical-edition DVD. Reviews were even more favorable than for the first picture, and *Towers* outperformed its predecessor at the box office, bringing in $926 million in worldwide box office, a favorable sign for the upcoming release of the final *Rings* film. —*Tom Dupree*

THE MATRIX RELOADED
Warner Bros., 2003

ALL-RELEASE EQUIVALENT 2005 $s
(Unadjusted $s) in Millions of $s

Domestic Box Office Revenues . . . . **$299.3**/($281.5)
Production Cost . . . . **$159.5**/($150.0)
Principal Photography . . . . **294** days
3/26/2001–6/2001
9/2001–8/21/2002
(production combined with
The Matrix Revolutions)

Initial Release 5/15/2003
Rerelease . . . . none
Running Time . . . . 139 minutes
MPAA Rating . . . . R

Director . . . . Larry Wachowski,
Andy Wachowski

Producer . . . . Joel Silver

Production Company . . . . Silver Pictures,
Village Roadshow Pictures
Entertainment

Story and
Screenplay by . . . . Larry and Andy Wachowski

Cast . . . . Keanu Reeves, Laurence
Fishburne, Carrie-Anne Moss,
Hugo Weaving,
Jada Pinkett Smith, Nona Gaye,
Daniel Bernhardt,
Matt McColm

Filming Locations . . . . . . In studio: Fox Studios,
Australia; on location: Sydney,
Australia and Oakland, CA

Genre . . . . Sci-Fi

Format . . . . Color

STANDING THE TEST OF TIME

ACADEMY AWARD Oscar Nominations and Wins
None

OSCAR TOTALS   Nominations **0**   *Wins **0**

AFI 100 YEARS 100 MOVIES SELECTION
2007 0   1997 0

TOP 300 FILMS POSITION . . . . **#108**
All-Release Domestic Box Office in Equivalent 2005 $s

National Film Preservation Board Selection . . . . none

OTHER AWARDS Best Picture Wins

	Year
Golden Globes	none
New York Film Critics	none
National Board of Review	none
Film Daily Critics	none

I've been doing this for 20 years and I've never seen anything like this. I've never been involved with a piece of entertainment that everyone wants a piece of. You dream of having a picture like this that means something to people.

—Joel Silver

PLOT: Neo, Trinity, and the rest of the rebel group led by Morpheus have seventy-two hours to prevent a quarter million Sentinels from wiping out Zion, the last human settlement.

PRODUCTION: Making a trilogy of films seemed like just a pipe dream while Larry and Andy Wachowski struggled for years to launch *The Matrix*. But after the release of that first film, it was apparent that their dreams were exactly what audiences around the world craved to see. *The Matrix* struck the Zeitgeist of the times, fixing itself as the movie experience of the Internet age. Soon Larry and Andy were headlining a multibillion-dollar franchise, overseeing comic books, producing nine Japanese-style animated shorts (*The Animatrix*), writing a 240-page script for a video game, and developing not just one but two films. At first, they contemplated making a prequel to *The Matrix*, then decided to shoot an epic sequel in two parts that Warner deemed the biggest project in its history. The combined production of *The Matrix Reloaded* and *The Matrix Revolutions* would be shot simultaneously in Australia for $300 million, with a third of the budget devoted to pioneering novel visual effects. The Wachowskis wanted the fights to outdo the original *Matrix* in every way, requiring Hong Kong choreographer Yuen Wo-Ping to spend six months with the actors to hone their moves and martial arts. Newcomer Jada Pinkett Smith (Niobe) jumped right into the training ring only a month after she gave birth to her daughter. The studio adopted a hands-off approach during production and let the Wachowskis work without interference. John Gaeta and the effects artists scrapped the original movie's still-camera Bullet-Time technology and devised a 180° Steadicam capture system that mapped actors and their movements onto computer models. Since camera, characters, and set became fully digital elements, the brothers could clone Agent Smith as many times as they desired in his "Burly Brawl" with Neo and have total freedom in selecting shutter speed and camera placement. The thrilling fourteen-minute car chase entailed a more conventional solution of computer previsualization and practical effects, later enhanced with CGI. Production designer Owen Paterson's team erected a complete 1.5-mile-long freeway with overpasses and walls at the decommissioned naval base in Alameda, California. Some takes demanded stunt drivers to synchronize their maneuvers in traffic of sixty cars at once. By the end of the 45-day freeway shoot, orchestrated collisions had wrecked more than 300 vehicles. Sadly, all the computer magic in *The Matrix* could not bring back Gloria Foster (the Oracle) and R & B singer Aaliyah (Zee), both of whom died during production.

DISTRIBUTION: Completion of the visual effects postponed the release of *The Matrix Reloaded* from 2002 to May 2003, with *Revolutions* following six months later. Warner advertised both films together until the Super Bowl, then put its muscle behind *Reloaded*. Merchandise provided great guerrilla marketing as Samsung sold Matrix-style cell phones and Coca-Cola hired a dozen "Agents" to attend a Los Angeles Dodgers baseball game drinking Powerade. Though these sequels didn't garner the international acclaim of the first film, both were in the top 10 in domestic and worldwide box office for the year. They are also among the top 10 most expensive movies ever released by Warner Bros. —*Michael Kogge*

FINDING NEMO
Buena Vista, 2003

ALL-RELEASE EQUIVALENT 2005 $s
(Unadjusted $s) in Millions of $s

Domestic Box Office Revenues........ **$361.1**/($339.7)
Production Cost .... **$99.8**/($94.0)
Production Period .... 3½ years
2000–2003

Director . . . . Andrew Stanton, Lee Unkrich

Producer . . . . Graham Walters

Production Company . . . . Pixar Animation Studios

Story by . . . . Andrew Stanton

Screenplay by . . . . Andrew Stanton, Bob Peterson, David Reynolds

Cast . . . . Albert Brooks, Ellen DeGeneres, Willem Dafoe (voices)

Filming Locations . . . . . . Pixar Studios, Emeryville, CA

Genre . . . . Animation

Format . . . . Color (Technicolor)

Initial Release 5/30/2003

Rerelease . . . . none

Running Time . . . . 100 minutes

MPAA Rating . . . . G

STANDING THE TEST OF TIME

ACADEMY AWARD Oscar Nominations and Wins

*ANIMATED FEATURE FILM: Andrew Stanton

Music (Original Score): Thomas Newman

Sound Editing: Gary Rydstrom and Michael Silvers

Writing (Original Screenplay): Screenplay by Andrew Stanton, Bob Peterson and David Reynolds; Original Story by Andrew Stanton

OSCAR TOTALS   Nominations 4   *Wins 1

AFI 100 YEARS 100 MOVIES SELECTION
2007 0   1997 0

TOP 300 FILMS POSITION . . . . #64
All-Release Domestic Box Office in Equivalent 2005 $s

National Film Preservation Board Selection . . . . none

OTHER AWARDS Best Picture Wins

	Year
Golden Globes	none
New York Film Critics	none
National Board of Review	none
Film Daily Critics	none

The thing we conquered the most was the cinematic trick of making you think you were underwater—something disappearing the in the murk, shafts of light, plankton in the water.

—Andrew Stanton

PLOT: Desperately looking for his missing son, Marlin, a neurotic fish, and Dory, his forgetful friend, encounter many obstacles before they are reunited with young Nemo, whose own adventures have led him across the ocean, through the perilous East Australian Current, and all the way to Sydney, where he landed in a scary dentist's aquarium.

PRODUCTION: With multiple projects in the pipeline, the need for additional space drove Pixar to build a new studio in Emeryville, California. Director Andrew Stanton's story started production in the old Point Richmond offices, then moved with the studio to the new building. This was the fifth feature-length film made at the Pixar studio under a distribution deal with Disney. There were nearly 200 crew members on the *Nemo* production alone. With so many films in production at the same time, the total number of employees at the studio had quadrupled and the emphasis had shifted from getting one film done at a time to getting every film done faster while still keeping costs under control. The new building was so much bigger than what everyone was used to that the teams of artists devised all kinds of crazy activities to promote a sense of unity. For example, all the men grew moustaches while all the women wore outrageous makeup. This exponential growth put pressure on Pixar to produce another hit. With Lasseter on board as executive producer for this film, Stanton invited Lee Unkrich (co-director on *Monsters, Inc.*) to be co-director on *Finding Nemo*. The original Pixar creative team of Andrew Stanton, Pete Docter, John Lasseter, Joe Ranft, and Lee Unkrich had all been dispersed to multiple projects, so Stanton was glad to have Unkrich back as a close collaborator. Set mostly underwater, *Nemo* provided an opportunity for the studio to raise the bar and make a compelling tale while incorporating complex visual effects never before done in CG animation. To accomplish this, Stanton sent his crew to the Great Barrier Reef in Australia and required them to get certified in scuba diving as part of their research observing and rendering water. After hours spent learning from oceanography professors and working with scans of dead fish in their computers, their first water test, according to Oren Jacob, the film's supervising technical director, "looked like a chlorinated swimming pool." Ultimately the studio tools group produced computer tests that were so good Stanton could not tell the difference between the live action and CG images. But making the footage look so real that it replicated undersea reality wasn't quite the goal either, so the effects were adjusted again to emphasize the cartoon world in which these events were taking place. Creating the water effects was an expensive task, but careful selection of key shots and the clever placement of other effects kept the budget down.

DISTRIBUTION: Pixar and Disney had another immediate hit. *Finding Nemo* opened to a $70 million weekend box office, setting a record (in unadjusted dollars) for the highest-grossing opening ever for an animated movie. The film brought in almost $865 million in worldwide box office. It remains, as of 2008, Pixar's highest-grossing movie, with *The Incredibles* coming in close behind. The film was released on DVD within six months of the movie's opening, in time for holiday sales in November 2003, making the DVD window, from its initial theatrical release to video, shorter than for any prior Pixar film. —*Rosaleen O'Byrne*

PIRATES OF THE CARIBBEAN: THE CURSE OF THE BLACK PEARL

Buena Vista, 2003

ALL-RELEASE EQUIVALENT 2005 $s

(Unadjusted $s) in Millions of $s

Domestic Box Office Revenues. . . . . . . **$324.7**/($305.4)
Production Cost . . . .**$148.6**/($140.0)
Principal Photography. . . . .**100** days estimated
10/2/2002–March 2003

Director . . . . Gore Verbinski

Producer . . . . Jerry Bruckheimer

Production Company. . . . Walt Disney Pictures,
Jerry Bruckheimer Films,
First Mate Production

Story by . . . . Ted Elliott, Terry Rossio, Stuart
Beattie, Jay Wolpert, based on
Walt Disney's "Pirates of the
Caribbean" attraction

Screenplay by . . . . Ted Elliott, Terry Rossio

Cast . . . . Johnny Depp, Geoffrey Rush,
Orlando Bloom, Keira Knightley

Filming Locations . . . . . . In studio: Walt Disney Studios,
Burbank, CA; on location: the
Caribbean islands; Los Angeles,
Long Beach, and Marineland in
Palos Verdes, CA

Genre. . . . . Action Adventure

Format. . . . . Color (Technicolor)

Initial Release 7/9/2003

Rerelease . . . . none

Running Time . . . . 143 minutes

MPAA Rating PG-13

STANDING THE TEST OF TIME

ACADEMY AWARD Oscar Nominations and Wins

Actor in a Leading Role: Johnny Depp

Makeup: Ve Neill and Martin Samuel

Sound Editing: Christopher Boyes and
George Watters II

Sound Mixing: Christopher Boyes, David Parker,
David Campbell, and Lee Orloff

Visual Effects: John Knoll, Hal Hickel, Charles Gibson,
and Terry Frazee

OSCAR TOTALS Nominations 5 *Wins 0

AFI 100 YEARS 100 MOVIES SELECTION
2007 0   1997 0

TOP 300 FILMS POSITION . . . . **#88**
All-Release Domestic Box Office in Equivalent 2005 $s

National Film Preservation Board Selection. . . . none

OTHER AWARDS Best Picture Wins

	Year
Golden Globes	none
New York Film Critics.	none
National Board of Review	none
Film Daily Critics	none

Everything that they say about water movies is true;
everything that can go wrong will go wrong.

—Gore Verbinski

PLOT: Jack Sparrow battles Captain Barbossa and his ghostly pirates to retrieve his vessel, the *Black Pearl*. Attempting to lift a curse from the pirates of the Caribbean, he finds and returns lost treasure.

PRODUCTION: Screenwriters Ted Elliot and Terry Rossio pitched an idea for a pirate movie to Disney executives in the early 1990s but were rejected. Steven Spielberg wanted to direct the film with stars Bill Murray or Robin Williams, but Disney still said no. Meanwhile, Jay Wolpert wrote a script based on the Disneyland ride, but it also was rejected, this time by producer Jerry Bruckheimer. Writer Stuart Beattie came on board, and later Elliot and Rossio. During that collaboration the theme of cursed pirates emerged. While the film was indeed inspired by the theme park ride at Disneyland, Bruckheimer was committed to making a film that could stand on its own. As the scope of the movie grew, with four writers feverishly working on what was fast becoming a swashbuckling epic, Disney executives Bob Iger and Michael Eisner considered shutting down the show due to increasing budgetary concerns. Bruckheimer helped convince them to continue by showing them animatics of the concept art. He also brought on Gore Verbinski to direct. Verbinski, who shared Bruckheimer's childhood love of pirate movies, wanted to make a film of epic proportion as homage to the swashbucklers made in the heyday of old Hollywood. Johnny Depp, then known for more obscure roles, was chosen for the lead role of Jack Sparrow, and Orlando Bloom was cast as Will Turner. Depp played Sparrow with a camp swagger and a pronounced swish that made the Disney executives nervous. When Michael Eisner claimed that Depp was ruining the film, Depp told Eisner that he had to either trust him or fire him. Bruckheimer and Verbinski had complete faith in Depp's choice of manner since the role of Will Turner had been written to read as an Errol Flynn–type hero. Because the lead characters' swordplay needed to be convincing on-screen, Bruckheimer employed Bob Anderson, a fight choreographer, who had trained Errol Flynn for *The Master of Ballintrae* (1953). Added to the complexities of dealing with the executives on the film, the director and the crew had an enormous challenge on their hands just trying to re-create pirate ships, film the open sea shots, and manage the water tank work. Dressing and directing a huge cast required a team of fifty makeup artists and forty hairdressers. A fire on set added to the increasing scope of the budget, incurring an additional $350,000 in costs.

DISTRIBUTION: These pirates won the opening weekend battle in style. *The Curse of the Black Pearl* was Disney's first PG-13 film to open in the United States. Despite Disney executive's fears that the film would flop, it scored a $46 million opening weekend and brought in over $654 million in worldwide box office overall. The world premiere of the film, staged at Disneyland in California, was the first such premiere to be held at the theme park. Disneyland is home to the original attraction that inspired the film. This attraction has now been updated to include the main characters from the movie. Disney quickly put into production not one but two sequels, both starring Depp again. —*Rosaleen O'Byrne*

THE LORD OF THE RINGS: THE RETURN OF THE KING

New Line, 2003

ALL-RELEASE EQUIVALENT 2005 $s

(Unadjusted $s) in Millions of $s

Domestic Box Office Revenues . . . . **$398.4/($377.0)**
Production Cost . . . . **$276.0/($260.0)**
Principal Photography . . . . **274** days estimated
10/11/1999–12/22/2000
Trilogy shot together

Director	Peter Jackson
Producer	Barrie M. Osborne, Peter Jackson, Fran Walsh
Production Company	Wingnut Films
Story by	Based on the novel by J. R. R. Tolkien
Screenplay by	Fran Walsh, Philippa Boyens, Peter Jackson
Cast	Ian McKellen, Elijah Wood, Viggo Mortensen, Liv Tyler, Sean Astin, Orlando Bloom, Ian Holm, Cate Blanchett, Sean Bean
Filming Locations	New Zealand
Genre	Fantasy
Format	Color (DeLuxe)
Initial Release	12/1/2003 world premiere (New Zealand); 12/17/2003 U.S. general release
Rerelease	none
Running Time	200 minutes
MPAA Rating	PG-13

STANDING THE TEST OF TIME

ACADEMY AWARD Oscar Nominations and Wins

*BEST PICTURE: Barrie M. Osborne, Fran Walsh, and Peter Jackson, Producers

*ART DIRECTION/SET DECORATION: Grant Major/Dan Hennah and Alan Lee

*COSTUME DESIGN: Ngila Dickson and Richard Taylor

*DIRECTING: Peter Jackson

*FILM EDITING: Jamie Selkirk

*MAKEUP: Richard Taylor and Peter King

*MUSIC (Original Score): Howard Shore

*MUSIC (Original Score): "Into the West," Music and Lyrics by Fran Walsh and Howard Shore and Annie Lennox

*SOUND MIXING: Christopher Boyes, Michael Semanick, Michael Hedges, Hammond Peek

*VISUAL EFFECTS: Jim Rygiel, Joe Letteri, Randall William Cook, Alex Funke

*WRITING (Adapted Screenplay): Screenplay by Fran Walsh, Philippa Boyens, and Peter Jackson

OSCAR TOTALS Nominations **11** *Wins 11

AFI 100 YEARS 100 MOVIES SELECTION
2007 0   1997 0

TOP 300 FILMS POSITION . . . . **#44**
All-Release Domestic Box Office in Equivalent 2005 $s

National Film Preservation Board Selection . . . . none

OTHER AWARDS Best Picture Wins

	Year
Golden Globes (Drama)	2004
New York Film Critics	2003
National Board of Review	none
Film Daily Critics	none

PLOT: The adventurers reunite as Frodo approaches the place where he will attempt to destroy the One Ring—but the evil Saruman has massed an awesome army, many times their number, against them.

PRODUCTION: The three *Rings* films were shot out of sequence, but actor Elijah Wood recalled a palpable sense of heightened excitement whenever the production turned to a scene from the final chapter. Director Peter Jackson had set himself a high bar with the Battle of Helm's Deep in *Towers,* but he fully intended to top himself in *Return of the King.* He introduced a terrifying new character held over from Tolkien's second book. The Helm's Deep battle had used computer-generated images and thousands of extras to depict an attack by 10,000 orcs. Now Jackson wanted to create a last stand at Pelennor Fields against 600,000 of the fierce creatures. Even considering the epic scope of the previous films, this would be the most spectacular sequence of all. Despite computer assistance, the human element was very much tasked. Before the production was over, it had required 15,000 garments, 48,000 pieces of armor, 10,000 arrows, and 12 million links of chain mail. Yet the props were so durable that only one sword was broken during the entire trilogy. The level of detail was so exacting that engraved on the inside of the breastplate worn by Bernard Hill as King Theoden was the motif of his House of Rohan—it could be seen only by the actor as he donned his costume. Shelob, a giant spider that guards the path to Mount Doom, actually enters in Tolkien's *The Two Towers,* but Jackson wanted to save the monster's appearance for the final film. This was one of the many alterations from the source material that the screenwriters made for dramatic effect. Andy Serkis was replaced digitally for his role as Gollum, but he had his moment in the sun during the film's first sequence, a flashback that showed audiences the actor himself as Smeagol, a Hobbit-like creature who was gradually transformed into Gollum by the Ring's corrupting power. A session of pickup shots in summer 2003 reunited the cast after two years apart, and would be their last work on the trilogy.

DISTRIBUTION: Jackson did and still does refer to his trilogy as "the film" and Tolkien's work as "the book," contending they are the serial telling of one long story. The author felt the same way and was disappointed that his original publisher divided the work into three parts. This was why Jackson resisted the studio's suggestion to include what-went-before prologues on the second and third films. It had been eight years since Jackson first inquired about the rights, but his long adventure was now complete. He had not only won over millions of skeptical Tolkien fans but also engaged and captivated viewers who had never before encountered the *Rings* story. New Line held *The Return of the King*'s world premiere in Wellington, New Zealand, before its earthshaking international release, which made it the second-highest-grossing movie of all time in worldwide box office (in unadjusted dollars) after *Titanic* and in the top 20 of worldwide box office movies in 2005 dollars. *Return* topped even the massive business of the first two films, earning more than $1 billion. It swept all eleven categories in which it was nominated for Academy Awards, which puts it in a tie with *Titanic* (eleven wins out of fourteen nominations) and *Ben-Hur* (eleven wins out of twelve nominations). It was the first fantasy film ever to win Best Picture. —*Tom Dupree*

THE PASSION OF THE CHRIST
Newmarket (domestic); Icon Productions (foreign), 2004

ALL-RELEASE EQUIVALENT 2005 $s

(Unadjusted $s) in Millions of $s

Domestic Box Office Revenues....... **$382.7**/($370.8)
Production Cost .... **$31.0**/($30.0)
Principal Photography........... **48** days estimated
11/4/2002–1/10/2003

Director . . . . Mel Gibson

Producer . . . . Mel Gibson, Bruce Davey,
Stephen McEveety

Production Company. . . . Icon Productions

Story by . . . . Based on the biblical story

Screenplay by . . . . Benedict Fitzgerald,
Mel Gibson

Cast . . . . Jim Caviezel, Monica Bellucci,
Claudia Gerini,
Maia Morgenstern

Filming Locations . . . . . . Matera, Italy; Cinecittá Studios,
Rome; Basilicata, Italy

Genre. . . . . Biblical Epic

Format . . . . Color (DeLuxe)

Initial Release 2/25/2004

Rerelease 2005

Running Time . . . . 126 minutes; 2005 release cut
version 120 minutes

MPAA Rating . . . . R

STANDING THE TEST OF TIME

ACADEMY AWARD Oscar Nominations and Wins

Cinematography: Caleb Deschanel

Makeup: Keith Vanderlaan and Christien Tinsley

Music (Original Score): John Debney

OSCAR TOTALS Nominations **3** *Wins 0

AFI 100 YEARS 100 MOVIES SELECTION
2007 0   1997 0

TOP 300 FILMS POSITION . . . . **#51**
All-Release Domestic Box Office in Equivalent 2005 $s

National Film Preservation Board Selection. . . . none

OTHER AWARDS Best Picture Wins

	Year
Golden Globes	none
New York Film Critics	none
National Board of Review	none
Film Daily Critics	none

A big dark force didn't want us to make this film.

—Mel Gibson

PLOT: Betrayed by Judas, Jesus is taken to Jerusalem and condemned to death. His slow, graphic, violent demise is depicted in minute detail during the last twelve hours of his life.

PRODUCTION: Mel Gibson attributes the concept to his personal struggle with self-destruction and despair. Spending $30 million of his own money to complete this project, Gibson produced, directed, co-wrote, and financed the entire venture. His rejection of the doctrinal changes made by Vatican II and his passion for a literal cinematic translation of the Gospels according to his own personal vision were the driving force behind the film. Gibson invested twelve years of his life in the project, culminating in his collaboration with screenwriter Benedict Fitzgerald. Together they set out to make the most authentic film about Christ. Rumors of the extreme violence in the script piqued the interest of global religious groups and fanned public anticipation to fever pitch. The film was shot on location at Mater, Italy, and at Cinecittà Studios, Rome. Latin and Aramaic were spoken throughout, making it a foreign-language film that required English subtitles. Caleb Deschanel, a Quaker, shot the film in a cinema verité style to bring the viewer directly into the drama, drawing inspiration from paintings by Caravaggio to set the tone. Gibson's decision to focus on the last twelve hours of Jesus's life was a controversial one, generating debate not only about the religious themes in the film but also about a line of dialogue considered too incendiary to remain in the first cut. The filmmaker ultimately kept the controversial line, which spoke of a potential curse on all Jews, but he placed it, spoken in Aramaic, in the sound mix under the ambient noise of the crowd. This controversy fueled the film's prerelease hype, as did all the buzz about the on-set incidents experienced by Jesus. Caviezel was plagued by accidents, culminating in a serious injury to his shoulder. In the makeup chair at 2:00 a.m. every day, Caviezel endured hours of application to make his skin appear flayed. He was struck by lightning during filming but was unharmed. After the lightning incident, he quipped, "I guess He didn't like that take."

DISTRIBUTION: Gibson and Bruce Davey's company, Icon Productions, Inc., partnered with Newmarket Films to distribute the movie in the United States. Newmarket, an independent company whose strengths lay in innovative marketing and distribution, set to work capitalizing on the film's controversial spin. Christian church groups in America, estimated to be 50 million to 80 million members strong, fanned prerelease hype by purchasing blocks of twenty thousand prerelease tickets, setting a record and making it the highest-grossing religious-themed film to date. It opened on Ash Wednesday 2004 and went on to become the highest-grossing R-rated film up to that time. Despite being banned in Israel and other countries, *Passion* earned $623 million in worldwide box office. In 2005 Gibson, in an effort to reach a wider audience, reedited the film, omitting five minutes of the most violent content. He acknowledged that *The Passion Recut* was still a "hard film." Already available on DVD, *The Passion Recut* was rereleased with an R rating on March 11, 2005, to 950 theaters in North America; it averaged only ten ticket buyers per screen. —*Rosaleen O'Byrne*

SHREK 2
DreamWorks, 2004

ALL-RELEASE EQUIVALENT 2005 $s
(Unadjusted $s) in Millions of $s

Domestic Box Office Revenues. . . . . . . **$455.4**/($441.2)
Production Cost . . . . **$155.1**/($150.0)
Production Period . . . . **3** years

Director	Andrew Adamson, Kelly Asbury, Conrad Vernon
Producer	David Lipman, Aron Warner, John H. Williams
Production Company. . . .	PDI/DreamWorks
Story by	Based on the book *Shrek!* by William Steig
Screenplay by	Andrew Adamson, Joe Stillman, J. David Stem, David N. Weiss
Cast	Julie Andrews, Antonio Banderas, John Cleese, Cameron Diaz, Rupert Everett, Eddie Murphy, Mike Myers, Jennifer Saunders (voices)
Filming Locations	PDI Studios, Redwood City and Glendale, CA
Genre.	Animation
Format.	Color
Initial Release	5/19/2004
Rerelease	none
Running Time	93 miniutes
MPAA Rating	PG

STANDING THE TEST OF TIME

ACADEMY AWARD Oscar Nominations and Wins

Animated Feature Film: Andrew Adamson

Music (Original Song): "Accidentally in Love," Music by Adam Duritz, Charles Gillingham, Jim Bogios, David Immergluck, Matthew Malley, and David Bryson; Lyrics by Adam Duritz and Daniel Vickrey

OSCAR TOTALS Nominations **2** *Wins 0

AFI 100 YEARS 100 MOVIES SELECTION
2007 0   1997 0

TOP 300 FILMS POSITION . . . . #29
All-Release Domestic Box Office in Equivalent 2005 $s

National Film Preservation Board Selection. . . .none

OTHER AWARDS Best Picture Wins

	Year
Golden Globes	none
New York Film Critics	none
National Board of Review	none
Film Daily Critics	none

The first film is a quest; we go A to B, and you kind of get to know the characters, who they are, what their fears are, et cetera. With the second film, we kind of wanted to mix up the story a little bit, make it a little bit more twisty and turny, give you a few surprises and see how these characters that we know react to these new situations.

—Kelly Asbury

PLOT: Newlyweds Shrek and Fiona, having returned from their honeymoon, must now tell Fiona's parents (the king and queen) that they are married, deal with the problems that ensue, and try to find their own "happily ever after."

PRODUCTION: *Shrek 2* was put into production before the first film was even completed. The producers didn't just want to make this film bigger; they also wanted a great story to sustain it. Ted Elliott and Terry Rossio, Oscar nominees (with Joe Stillman and Roger S. H. Schulman) for the first *Shrek* screenplay, opted out after disagreeing with the producers, who were insistent that this movie be a traditional fairytale. Andrew Adamson, one of the original *Shrek* directors, on board to direct this film too, added screenwriter to his credit. Significant lead time was required, but when the original film proved to be a hit, there was enormous pressure to move quickly. Since the team that knew *Shrek* well was still intact, they decided to go from outline to storyboard, skipping a completed screenplay, at least initially. Inspired by *Guess Who's Coming to Dinner,* Adamson decided to explore the theme of inverted expectations within the *Shrek 2* story, leading Shrek and Fiona to visit her parents. Co-directors Asbury and Vernon helped with the story structure. The fairy godmother, Dama Fortuna, originally created for the first *Shrek,* was featured in the sequel, along with new characters. The first year of the three-year production involved setting up all of the characters. Most sequences were storyboarded at least twenty times, with writing and rewriting occurring for all thirty-two sequences in the film. Seven artists in the art department were dedicated to generating the images needed to construct *Shrek*'s world in 3-D. Physical models were built for each location and lipstick cameras were installed within those models so they could be studied from every camera angle. It took animators an entire day just to complete one second on the screen. During most of the production, Vernon and Asbury were in northern California with animators, lighters, the surfacing department, and effects artists while Adamson was in the studio with actors at DreamWorks facility in Glendale, California. More than 300 Hewlett-Packard workstations were employed. Shrek's face was expressive because it had 218 working muscles. John Powell, co-composer of *Shrek,* dropped out of the second film due to a conflict. Jennifer Saunders, who had been turned down for a part in Disney's *The Little Mermaid,* was cast as the Fairy Godmother after Steven Spielberg heard her audition tape. Her vocal performance was recorded in England because she was in the midst of taping *Absolutely Fabulous.* For the "Hair Ball" sequence, actor Antonio Banderas, who was also appearing nightly in *9* on Broadway, strained his voice during the tedious three-hour recording, and the octave range for his musical had to be lowered accordingly. The film featured many inside references and allusions to pop culture, including the *New Yorker,* Garfield, Justin Timberlake, and *The Lord of the Rings.*

DISTRIBUTION: Bringing in over $920 million in worldwide box office and another $800 million in DVD and licensing revenue, *Shrek 2* was the fourth-highest-grossing animated film of all time (after Disney's *The Lion King, Snow White,* and *101 Dalmatians,* which all used cell rather than digital animation) when measured in 2005 dollars. Its success helped launch DreamWorks Animation as a separate public company in 2004. *Shrek the Third* was successfully released in 2007. —*Hayley Taylor Block and Alex Ben Block*

SPIDER-MAN 2
Sony, 2004

ALL-RELEASE EQUIVALENT 2005 $s
(Unadjusted $s) in Millions of $s

Domestic Box Office Revenues....... **$385.6**/($373.6)
Production Cost .... **$206.8**/($200.0)
Principal Photography...........**142** days estimated
4/12/2003–10/30/2003

Director . . . . Sam Raimi

Producer . . . . Laura Ziskin, Avi Arad

Production Company. . . . Marvel Enterprises,
Columbia Pictures,
Laura Ziskin Productions

Story by . . . . Based on the Marvel comic
book by Stan Lee and Steve
Ditko, and screen story by
Alfred Gough, Miles Millar,
Michael Chabon

Screenplay by . . . . Alvin Sargent

Cast . . . . Tobey Maguire, Kirsten Dunst,
James Franco, Alfred Molina,
Rosemary Harris, J. K. Simmons

Filming Locations . . . . . . New York City; Los Angeles;
Sony Studios, Culver City, CA

Genre. . . . . Action Adventure

Format. . . . . Color (DeLuxe)

Initial Release 6/30/2004

Rerelease. . . . . none

Running Time . . . . 127 minutes

MPAA Rating PG-13

STANDING THE TEST OF TIME

ACADEMY AWARD Oscar Nominations and Wins

Sound Editing: Paul N.J. Ottosson

Sound Mixing: Devin O'Connell, Greg P. Russell, Jeffrey J. Haboush, and Joseph Geisinger

*VISUAL EFFECTS: John Dykstra, Scott Stokdyk, Anthony LaMolinara, and John Frazier

OSCAR TOTALS Nominations **3** *Wins **1**

AFI 100 YEARS 100 MOVIES SELECTION
2007 0   1997 0

TOP 300 FILMS POSITION . . . . **#48**
All-Release Domestic Box Office in Equivalent 2005 $s

National Film Preservation Board Selection. . . .none

OTHER AWARDS Best Picture Wins

	Year
Golden Globes	none
New York Film Critics.	none
National Board of Review	none
Film Daily Critics	none

For the kids who come to see it, Spider-Man is their hero. So while the job of making this movie is to provide entertainment, it is also to create a story that shows them a moral character, someone who has to make tough choices and the right decisions in order to continue to be worthy of their admiration.

—Sam Raimi

PLOT: Peter Parker struggles to balance life as a superhero with the troubles of a young man. A new enemy, Dr. Octopus, uses his mechanical tentacles to wreak havoc throughout New York City, leading to a final showdown with Spider-Man at a waterfront pier. Mary Jane Watson learns Peter's secret, and the two come together as a couple.

PRODUCTION: Coming off the spectacular success of the first film, *Spider-Man 2*'s story came courtesy of four new writers, including Pulitzer Prize winner Michael Chabon. Having established the character, this time they wanted to show not just wall climbing and web shooting but also the character's "spider sense," which alerted him to potential danger. A casting squabble erupted when returning star Tobey Maguire requested revisions to the shooting schedule. The pressures of working on *Seabiscuit* had reportedly aggravated Maguire's back, leading him to express concerns over the sequel's stunt work. Outsiders called it a play for more money. A high-stakes face-off ensued, with the *Spider-Man 2* executives ultimately making an offer to Jake Gyllenhaal to star as Maguire's replacement. A contract renegotiation finally resolved the issue and netted Maguire a $17 million payday (up from $4 million for the first film). "I didn't have faith. I didn't think Tobey was going to be in it," confessed director Raimi to *Entertainment Weekly* magazine. The final film contains a wry line in which Peter Parker complains, "My back! My back!" after falling in an alleyway. Principal photography began April 12, 2003, in New York City. Much of the movie, including a particularly complicated wire shot that took place down the center of Wall Street, was filmed on location. "We executed one of the longest wire shots the Spydercam has ever done," executive producer Joseph M. Caracciolo said. "The Wall Street shot was around 2,400 feet." Alfred Molina, a self-professed *Marvel Comics* fan, wore an exoskeleton that weighed 75 pounds to portray Dr. Octopus, with offscreen puppeteers controlling his twitchy tentacles. The film's budget was estimated in the neighborhood of $200 million, with $20 million for story rights, $10 million on the screenplay, $15 million to the producers, $10 million to director Sam Raimi, $30 million on cast salaries (including Maguire's $17 million), $45 million on the shoot's below-the-line costs, $65 million to create the special effects, and $5 million on music. *Spider-Man 2*'s advertising was to have included logos on the bases in major league ballparks, but the plan was scrapped following an outcry from baseball purists.

DISTRIBUTION: *Spider-Man 2* debuted on June 30, 2004, in more than 4,000 U.S. theaters, making it the widest release up until that date. It set a record on its first day with a gross of $40.4 million, and its total weekend haul topped out at $88.1 million. It attracted near-universal critical acclaim, even besting the raves for the first film due to its focus on the emotional entanglements of its main characters and the complex performance of Alfred Molina as Dr. Octopus. By the time of its closing on December 19, 2004, *Spider-Man 2* had grossed $373.4 million in domestic box office, making it the second-highest of 2004 (after *Shrek 2*). Worldwide, the film took in over $783 million. *Spider-Man 2* became the first movie released in UMD format for the Sony PSP, and came bundled with the first one million PSPs for sale in the United States. An extended cut of the film, with 8 minutes of new footage, debuted on DVD in April 2007 under the name *Spider-Man 2.1.* —*Daniel Wallace*

MEET THE FOCKERS
Universal, 2004

ALL-RELEASE EQUIVALENT 2005 $s
(Unadjusted $s) in Millions of $s

Domestic Box Office Revenues . . . . **$283.1**/($279.2)
Production Cost . . . . **$82.7**/($80.0)
Principal Photography . . . . **70** days estimated
3/29/2004–June 2004

Initial Release . . . . 12/16/2004 premiere
(Universal City, CA); 12/22/2004
general release

Rerelease . . . . none

Running Time . . . . 115 minutes

MPAA Rating PG-13

Director . . . . Jay Roach
Producer . . . . Jane Rosenthal, Robert De Niro, Jay Roach
Production Company . . . . Tribeca Productions, Universal Pictures
Story by . . . . Jim Herzfeld, Marc Hyman
Screenplay by . . . . Jim Herzfeld, John Hamburg
Cast . . . . Robert De Niro, Ben Stiller, Dustin Hoffman, Barbra Streisand
Filming Locations . . . . . . On location in California: Universal Studios, Los Angeles County Arboretum and Botanic Garden, Queen Anne Cottage, Sepulveda Dam Basin, and Recreation Park in the San Fernando Valley
Genre . . . . Comedy
Format . . . . Color (Technicolor)

STANDING THE TEST OF TIME

ACADEMY AWARD Oscar Nominations and Wins

None

OSCAR TOTALS   Nominations 0   *Wins 0

AFI 100 YEARS 100 MOVIES SELECTION
2007 0   1997 0

TOP 300 FILMS POSITION . . . . #118
All-Release Domestic Box Office in Equivalent 2005 $s

National Film Preservation Board Selection . . . . none

OTHER AWARDS Best Picture Wins

	Year
Golden Globes	none
New York Film Critics	none
National Board of Review	none
Film Daily Critics	none

*All we had to do was just get everybody together and it felt like we were home.
It's like when you go home and it feels like you never left.*

—Jay Roach

PLOT: Greg Focker and his fiancée travel to Florida, where an outrageous first meeting takes place between his eccentric, perpetually horny parents and her traditionally conservative parents, all of them fiercely overprotective of their children.

PRODUCTION: Director-producer Jay Roach reunites the cast and crew of the 2000 hit film *Meet the Parents* for this sequel. Ben Stiller, who really wanted Barbra Streisand to play the role of his mother, called her from Europe to ask her. To his surprise, she agreed immediately. Streisand had produced and/or directed nearly all of her previous films, and so it was the first time since *All Night Long* was released in 1981 that Streisand was able to "just be an actress." James Brolin was originally approached to play Bernie Focker but declined. Roach then turned to Dustin Hoffman. He felt so strongly that Hoffman was the one to play the role that he fed the writers details about Hoffman to incorporate into the character. In essence, Roach was asking Hoffman to play himself. "And over all these years, no one had ever asked me to do that," Hoffman said. Streisand and Hoffman, who had been friends for four decades and had attended acting school together, had such terrific chemistry that they easily improvised on the set with Roach's encouragement. Not only did De Niro return to his character as Jack Byrnes, the semi-retired CIA agent, but once again he produced the film with Jane Rosenthal and Jay Roach. Blythe Danner and Teri Polo also returned as Dina and Pam Byrnes. The role of Little Jack, the toddler grandson of the Byrnes, required the character to perform sign language as taught to him by De Niro. Baby wrangler Rhonda Sherman was hired, along with twins Bradley and Spencer Pickren. The boys' mother was an occupational therapist, so the boys had actually learned to sign when they were only a few months old. De Niro spent time with them off camera so that their chemistry would work well on-screen. During production, the title was temporarily changed to "Meet the Fokkers" because the original title was deemed too vulgar, but changing the name would have upset the franchise's continuity. The MPAA would not allow the movie to use the original title unless they found an actual family with the name Focker. They did. While *Meet the Parents* had been shot on Long Island, this sequel was set in Miami, which was re-created in California at the Los Angeles County Arboretum and Botanic Garden. Roach discovered a 120-year-old Queen Anne cottage there that is one of the centerpieces of the grounds. The agreement with the arboretum stipulated that the house was not to be touched, so the production team placed a skin around it that made it look more like a home in Southern Florida. They also dressed the front of the structure with indigenous foliage.

DISTRIBUTION: *Meet the Fockers* premiered on December 16, 2004, in Universal City, California. It set a new record for the opening weekend of a comedy taking in $46.1 million. It was a global hit, grossing over $516 million worldwide ($186 million more in worldwide box office than *Meet the Parents*). It was the highest-grossing movie of Barbra Streisand's illustrious career. —*Christine McDermott*

STAR WARS: EP III REVENGE OF THE SITH

20th Century-Fox, 2005

ALL-RELEASE EQUIVALENT 2005 $s

(Unadjusted $s) in Millions of $s

Domestic Box Office Revenues	**$380.3**/($380.3)
Production Cost	**$101.4**/($101.4)
Principal Photography	**58** days
	6/30/2003–9/17/2003

Initial Release	5/19/2005
Rerelease	none
Running Time	140 minutes
MPAA Rating	PG-13

Director . . . . George Lucas

Producer . . . . Rick McCallum

Production Company . . . . Lucasfilm Ltd.

Story and

  Screenplay by . . . . George Lucas

Cast . . . . Ewan McGregor, Natalie Portman, Hayden Christensen, Ian McDiarmid, Samuel L. Jackson, Christopher Lee, Anthony Daniels, Kenny Baker, Frank Oz

Filming Locations . . . . . . In studio at Fox Studios Australia; pickups: Shepperton Studios, UK (11 days, 8/23/2004–9/3/2004); Elstree Studios, UK (1 day, 1/31/2005)

Genre . . . . Sci-Fi

Format . . . . Color (Deluxe prints); shot in Plus 8 HD digital

STANDING THE TEST OF TIME

ACADEMY AWARD Oscar Nominations and Wins

Makeup: Dave Elsey and Nikki Gooley

OSCAR TOTALS   Nominations **1**   *Wins 0

AFI 100 YEARS 100 MOVIES SELECTION

2007 0   1997 0

TOP 300 FILMS POSITION . . . . **#52**

All-Release Domestic Box Office in Equivalent 2005 $s

National Film Preservation Board Selection . . . . none

OTHER AWARDS Best Picture Wins

	Year
Golden Globes	none
New York Film Critics	none
National Board of Review	none
Film Daily Critics	none

And how does somebody who is normal and good turn bad? What are the qualities, what is it that we all have within us that will turn us bad?

—George Lucas

PLOT: Torn between loyalty to his mentor and the seductive powers of the dark side, Anakin Skywalker turns his back on the Jedi, thus completing his transformation into Darth Vader.

PRODUCTION: After twenty-eight years, George Lucas concluded his epic *Star Wars* series with the final prequel film of the second trilogy—*Revenge of the Sith*. Lucas began developing the screenplay in spring 2002, involving his art department at the earliest stages. They created a veritable avalanche of conceptual paintings to illustrate his ideas. The process was so dynamic and mutually inspiring that Lucas allowed the artists to feed his imagination with their creations, resulting in adjustments to planet and creature descriptions in the script. Emanating from that original approved art, production designer Gavin Bocquet began constructing sets while various artists and technicians created countless costumes, creatures, and models. By February 2003, the animatics department started utilizing the concept art to craft the crude digital storyboards that would serve as models for the final effects. Steven Spielberg helped previsualize some of the final duel. When the conceptual phase concluded in June, the team had churned out almost 3,000 artworks to aid in making the virtual film-before-the-film. Bocquet had been overseeing construction of the sets, including the Rebel Blockade Runner ship corridor set—an exact re-creation of the first set seen on-screen in the original *Star Wars*—before shooting finally began at Fox Studios Australia on June 30, 2003. Building on the success he had filming *Attack of the Clones,* Lucas chose to shoot the final prequel entirely with the next generation of high-definition digital cameras. The reappearance of Darth Vader's suit was one of the highlights of production. People from all departments rushed to the set to sneak a glimpse of actor Hayden Christensen wearing the iconic costume. When filming wrapped in September, five days ahead of schedule, work on the film actually intensified. Industrial Light & Magic oversaw the epic-scale effects project that had already started while Lucas was still writing and which would not finish until a few weeks before the film's release. As a series of rough cuts slowly took shape, Lucas directed virtual scenes on the computer, editing and retooling the rough animatics with Dan Gregoire and his team while simultaneously editing the overall film with Ben Burtt and Roger Barton. As animatics were completed, Lucas turned them over to ILM for photorealistic rendering. ILM ultimately labored for more than eighteen months on 90 animated minutes, digitizing an astounding 2,151 shots in some manner or another. Reshoots in 2004 and 2005 provided the final pieces in Lucas's grand digital mosaic.

DISTRIBUTION: Fans had begun lining up in some locations in North America over a month before the film's release date. The film premiered at Cannes on May 15, 2005, and then opened in the United States on May 19, 2005, six years to the day after *The Phantom Menace*. Critics hailed it as the best of the prequels. The film hauled in a whopping $50 million on opening day and went on to earn more than $850 million worldwide. It was the only movie in the *Star Wars* series to earn a PG-13 rating, and when Lucas released it on DVD on November 1, 2005, it became the only film in the series not released on VHS. —*Scott Mazak*

WAR OF THE WORLDS

Paramount (domestic); DreamWorks (foreign), 2005

ALL-RELEASE EQUIVALENT 2005 $s

(Unadjusted $s) in Millions of $s

Domestic Box Office Revenues....... **$234.3**/($234.3)
Production Cost .... **$132.0**/($132.0)
Principal Photography........... **72** days estimated
11/8/2004–3/7/2005

Director .... Steven Spielberg
Producer .... Kathleen Kennedy,
Colin Wilson
Production Company.... Amblin Entertainment,
Cruise-Wagner Production
Story by.............. Based on the novel by
H. G. Wells
Screenplay by......... Josh Friedman, David Koepp
Cast .... Tom Cruise, Dakota Fanning,
Miranda Otto, Justin Chatwin,
Tim Robbins, Rick Gonzalez,
Yul Vazquez, Lenny Venito,
Lisa Ann Walter,
Ann Robinson, Gene Barry,
Morgan Freeman
Filming Locations ...... On location: New York,
New Jersey, Virginia,
Connecticut, and California;
on California studio lots at
20th Century Fox Studios,
Century City; Sony Pictures
Studios, Culver City; Universal
Studios, Universal City; and
Warner Brothers Studios,
Burbank

Genre................. Sci-Fi, Disaster
Format............... Color (DeLuxe)
Initial Release......... 6/29/2005
Rerelease .... none
Running Time......... 116 minutes
MPAA Rating PG-13

STANDING THE TEST OF TIME

ACADEMY AWARD Oscar Nominations and Wins

Sound Editing: Richard King

Sound Mixing: Andy Nelson, Anna Behlmer, and
Ronald Judkins

Visual Effects: Dennis Muren, Pablo Helman,
Randal M. Dutra, and Daniel Sudick

OSCAR TOTALS Nominations 3 *Wins 0

AFI 100 YEARS 100 MOVIES SELECTION
2007 ..... 0 1997..... 0

TOP 300 FILMS POSITION .... #184
All-Release Domestic Box Office in Equivalent 2005 $s

National Film Preservation Board Selection....none

OTHER AWARDS Best Picture Wins

	Year
Golden Globes	none
New York Film Critics....................	none
National Board of Review.................	none
Film Daily Critics.......................	none

*This is the first film I really tackled using the computer to animate all the
storyboards . . . I got all the experts who had been working with
ILM [Industrial Light & Magic] on* Star Wars.

—Stephen Spielberg

PLOT: Invading aliens attempt to take over Earth with deadly force, causing havoc and mayhem, only to be thwarted by nature in the form of microscopic creatures—the common cold virus.

PRODUCTION: Encouraged by their success on *Minority Report* (2002), Stephen Spielberg and Tom Cruise decided to collaborate again on a retelling of the classic 1953 science fiction film *The War of the Worlds.* Mindful of paying homage to the cult classic, Spielberg also wanted to give a modern twist to the original story by making it a first-person account. His use of technology was a major factor in managing the complexities of planning the shooting of the film. George Lucas had introduced Spielberg to a method of filmmaking called Pre-Vis, the process of taking traditional hand-drawn storyboards and animating them to give a 3-D perspective. This powerful preproduction tool gave the director a blueprint for making the film. Actual location images were scanned into the computer, allowing for better interaction of CG effects with physical locations. Spielberg's experience with big-budget films drove the speed of preproduction, enabling principal photography to start in the fall of 2004 and end only 72 days later, half the time that a film of this scope normally takes. Shooting on both U.S. coasts began simultaneously with large CG-heavy sequences being prioritized and shot first to allow collaborators Industrial Light & Magic as much time as possible to create the creature effects. Visual effects guru Dennis Muren, a nine-time Academy Award winner, lent his considerable skill to bringing the multiple shots together. The production included the collation of live-action inserts shot in several locations, visual effects, practical sets, and underwater photography captured in a twenty-five-foot tank on the Universal Studios lot. Spielberg also purchased a 747 jet and had it disassembled on the lot to simulate a crash site. The film was shot on six stages spread out over three studio lots, with Spielberg simultaneously directing, approving creature effects, and editing. The aliens in this film were darker than in Spielberg's 1982 sci-fi film *E.T.: The Extra-Terrestrial.* Rather than descend from the sky, the aliens ascended from underground in their Tripod vehicles. A lot of attention was spent on creating the giraffelike motion of these creatures—their three-legged gait and the design of their walk cycles. The film was made for an estimated cost of $132 million, shooting in more than twenty-four locations, involving several thousand extras with sets constructed in five states throughout the United States. In 1953 the original *War of the Worlds* had been made for an estimated $14.6 million ($2 million in unadjusted dollars) but brought in only approximately $55 million in domestic box office ($4.4 million in unadjusted dollars).

DISTRIBUTION: The film opened to a $77 million box office weekend and continued to take in almost $592 in worldwide box office. It was the highest opening for a nonsequel film at that time, gaining entry to the elite group of only four films to top a $100 million opening weekend (*Star Wars: Episode III Revenge of the Sith*, $144 million; *The Lord of the Rings: The Return of the King*, $123.5 million; *The Matrix Revolutions*, $119 million; and *Harry Potter and the Prisoner of Azkaban*, $113 million). The DVD was released November 22, 2005. Paramount, who had also distributed the 1953 film, built interest in Spielberg's version of *War of the Worlds* by releasing a DVD of the original film on November 7, 2005. —*Rosaleen O'Byrne*

HARRY POTTER AND THE GOBLET OF FIRE

Warner Bros., 2005

ALL-RELEASE EQUIVALENT 2005 $s

(Unadjusted $s) in Millions of $s

Domestic Box Office Revenues....... **$290.0**/($290.0)
Production Cost ....**$150.0**/($150.0)
Principal Photography................not available
5/4/2004–unknown

Director . . . . Mike Newell
Producer . . . . David Heyman
Production Company . . . . Warner Bros. Pictures,
Heyday Films, Patalex IV
Productions Ltd.
Story by . . . . Based on the novel by
J. K. Rowling
Screenplay by . . . . Steve Kloves
Cast . . . . Daniel Radcliffe, Rupert
Grint, Emma Watson, Robbie
Coltran, Ralph Fiennes, Michael
Gambon, Brendan Gleeson,
Jason Isaacs, Gary Oldman,
Miranda Richardson, Alan
Rickman, Maggie Smith
Filming Locations . . . . . . Ashridge Estate, Hertfordshire;
Knebworth House,
Hertfordshire; Black Park,
Iver, Buckinghamshire;
Divinity School, Bodleian
Library, Oxford; Beachy Head,
Eastbourne; Glenfinnan
Viaduct, Fort William,
Highlands, Scotland; New
College, Oxford; Steall Falls,
Scotland; Virginia Water,
Surrey; Beckley Park,
Oxfordshire

Genre . . . . Fantasy
Format . . . . Color (Technicolor)
Initial Release . . . . 11/6/2005 premiere (London);
11/12/2005 premiere
(New York); 11/18/2005
general release (U.S.)
Rerelease . . . . none
Running Time . . . . 157 minutes
MPAA Rating PG-13

STANDING THE TEST OF TIME

ACADEMY AWARD Oscar Nominations and Wins

Art Direction/Set Decoration: Stuart Craig/Stephenie
McMillan

OSCAR TOTALS   Nominations **1**   *Wins 0

AFI 100 YEARS 100 MOVIES SELECTION
2007 0   1997 0

TOP 300 FILMS POSITION . . . . #112
All-Release Domestic Box Office in Equivalent 2005 $s

National Film Preservation Board Selection . . . . none

OTHER AWARDS Best Picture Wins

	Year
Golden Globes	none
New York Film Critics	none
National Board of Review	none
Film Daily Critics	none

PLOT: Harry Potter faces his greatest challenge when mysteriously selected to compete in the Tri-Wizard tournament, a contest in which competitors vie for the ultimate prize: eternal glory. Despite the return of Lord Voldemort, Potter must complete a series of dangerous tasks.

PRODUCTION: Translating the fourth *Harry Potter* book, a 734-page epic, into a coherent film presented an arduous task for the crew. The core team of author J. K. Rowling, producer David Heyman, and screenwriter Stephen Kloves chose TV-trained Brit Mike Newell (*Four Weddings and a Funeral*) as their director. Although there was talk of making two films to completely cover the story, Newell was persuaded by Alfonso Cuarón, director of the *Harry Potter and the Prisoner of Azkaban* (2004), to make one coherent film of the lengthy book. Careful selection was needed to whittle down the many subplots and remain true to the original story, something that fans had become accustomed to in the three previous installments. In this episode of the series, Rowling expands the Hogwarts world to include fantastic environments and events that make up the Tri-Wizard tournament. In order to complete the film's 1,400 effects shots, visual effects supervisor Jim Mitchell teamed up with the director, new to CG animation. With visual effects required throughout the film and groundbreaking techniques needed for underwater effects, nine companies spanning three continents were used to complete the shots. Newell was paid $1 million to direct, whereas Chris Columbus, who directed the first two films in the series, was reputed to have been paid $10 million (although the savings was not reflected in the higher total production cost). This film was the most complex of the series to date. The fantastic characters, unnatural environments, and special effects were incredibly ambitious and required careful planning. Newell later said he was least sure of himself directing the big set pieces and special effects. The look and design of the horntail dragon included a maquette with a fourteen-foot wingspan that was used as a reference for the 140 dragon shots needed. Roughly sixty blueprint drawings of the Quidditch World Cup arena were sent by the production to Industrial Light & Magic to refer to while building the visual effects for those incredible shots. Pyrotechnic effects were also needed to burn the tent city at the Quidditch stadium. To complete the effect, the crew had a hundred controlled fires on set, fueled by a propane pipe system. ILM embellished the shots by adding flying debris and flying fireballs. The underwater tasks were extensive, requiring the construction of a water tank with a blue screen lit from behind. The crew fitted a large Plexiglas panel on the side of the tank so that the director and actors could see each other. Daniel Radcliffe, who had to train for six months under water, spent forty-one hours and thirty-eight minutes over a period of three weeks in the tank. Other effects included mermaids, flying horses, and the digital removal of Lord Voldemort's (Ralph Fiennes) nose to make him appear snakelike.

DISTRIBUTION: With worldwide interest in *Harry Potter* at fever levels, *The Goblet of Fire* opened spectacularly, with a first weekend gross of $103 million boosted by its simultaneous release in IMAX. Encouraged by the *Prisoner of Azkaban* and its $14 million worldwide IMAX box office success, *Goblet* became Warner's seventh IMAX DMR release, and the second Potter film. The film went on to gross $896 million in worldwide box office. —*Rosaleen O'Byrne*

THE CHRONICLES OF NARNIA: THE LION, THE WITCH, AND THE WARDROBE

Buena Vista, 2005

ALL-RELEASE EQUIVALENT 2005 $s

(Unadjusted $s) in Millions of $s

Domestic Box Office Revenues........$289.5/($291.6)
Production Cost ....$200.0/($200.0)
Principal Photography.....................**124** days
6/28/2004–12/21/2004
9 days second unit in Prague, February 2005

Genre................. Fantasy
Format............... Color (Technicolor)
Initial Release......... 12/9/2005
Rerelease .... none
Running Time......... 139 minutes
MPAA Rating .... PG

Director .... Andrew Adamson
Producer .... Mark Johnson, Philip Steuer
Production Company .... Walt Disney Pictures, Walden Media
Story by.............. Based on the novel by C. S. Lewis
Screenplay by......... Ann Peacock, Andrew Adamson, Christopher Markus, Stephen McFeely
Cast .... Tilda Swinton, James McAvoy, Jim Broadbent, Liam Neeson (voice)
Filming Locations ...... In studio at Henderson Valley Studios, Auckland, New Zealand; on location in New Zealand: Auckland, Christchurch, Canterbury, Henderson, Hillsborough, Hobsonville; Czech Republic: Adrspach National Park, Trutnov, Purakaunui Bay; England: Shropshire, London; Poland, Tokarahi, Otago, Prague; California: Griffith Park, Los Angeles

STANDING THE TEST OF TIME

ACADEMY AWARD Oscar Nominations and Wins

*MAKEUP: Howard Berger and Tami Lane

Sound Mixing: Terry Porter, Dean A. Zupancic, and Tony Johnson

Visual Effects: Dean Wright, Bill Westenhofer, Jim Berney, and Scott Farrar

OSCAR TOTALS   Nominations **3**   *Wins **1**

AFI 100 YEARS 100 MOVIES SELECTION
2007 0   1997 0

TOP 300 FILMS POSITION .... **#113**
All-Release Domestic Box Office in Equivalent 2005 $s

National Film Preservation Board Selection....none

OTHER AWARDS Best Picture Wins

	Year
Golden Globes	none
New York Film Critics	none
National Board of Review	none
Film Daily Critics	none

As the movie starts to physically take place . . . it's always coupled with the attendant reaction of, "Oh my gosh, how are we going to pull this off?"

—Mark Johnson

PLOT: To escape the dangers of World War II, four children are sent to the English countryside, where they access a magical world, Narnia, through a wardrobe portal. Together they free Narnia from a wicked witch.

PRODUCTION: In the early 1900s, ensconced in a wardrobe, wrapped in an old coat, a young C. S. Lewis told stories to his brother, not knowing that eventually his fantasy tales would sell more than 100 million books. Walden Media optioned the series of seven *Narnia* books for film production in 2004. They collaborated with Walt Disney Pictures and chose Andrew Adamson (*Shrek 2*) to direct. No stranger to the complexities of CG technology, the director chose to use a combination of actors in prosthetic suits and CG characters in order to fabricate the diverse culture of Narnia. To keep costs under control, advance planning was important. Two years before the battle scene was shot, the director used Pre-Vis to map out the complex action. The director viewed 2,500 child actors on tape, met with 700, workshopped 400 of them, and dealt with 120 on an individual basis in order to choose the four children who would star in the film. Knowing that the child actors in the starring roles would change over the one-year production schedule, the director made the unusual decision to shoot the film in chronological order to capture the maturation of the young actors. Richard Taylor of Weta Workshop communicated with the director via videoconference several times a week to collaborate on conceptual design. The challenge lay in translating the numerous fantasy creatures into a realistic synthesis of human and animal-like movement. Howard Berger and his team at KNB FX Group, Inc., completed the full-size animatronics and prosthetics and had a parade of 170 monsters spanning twenty-three species for the director. Creating the thirty-plus types of creatures with various kinds of fur and skin was a huge task. Actors donned mechanical radio-controlled heads that were operated by as many as three puppeteers per actor. There were 1,600 visual effects shots created for the film, and in one sequence there were 4,920 creatures. Tempers flared on set when the director decided that he wanted radio-controlled heads on some of the character suits not designed for that. There were numerous other physical challenges too. For instance, the crew had to create snow, bring equipment into difficult terrain, deliver actors to the more remote locations by helicopter, feed 600 people on set, shelter them from the often wild weather, and protect their creature suits from the elements.

DISTRIBUTION: The movie was an immediate hit. With the support of its licensing partners, Disney's marketing push got a lot of play in Christian retail stores. The film made $23 million on its first day of release, going on to take $65 million at the box office its opening weekend and over $744 million in worldwide box office. The DVD was released April 4, 2006, just four months after the initial theatrical release, and sold four million copies on its first day. With MPAA-reported sales of 11.4 million sell-through units, it was the best-selling DVD in North America for 2006, passing *Harry Potter and the Goblet of Fire*. A special extended edition DVD was released for a limited time from December 15, 2006, through January 31, 2007. —*Rosaleen O'Byrne*

EPILOGUE

In the final years of the first decade of the twenty-first century, the movie business was impacted by a global economic meltdown that began in late 2008. These events not only redefined the kind of films that Hollywood was scrambling to make, but they also determined who would finance them. Studios from Sony to Warner Bros. announced layoffs in 2009, despite record box office results, as financing from banks and hedge funds quickly dried up. Not only was there no new money, but some previous commitments, including a large one to Paramount, were canceled, and the $500 million promised to United Artists under Tom Cruise was greatly scaled back too. These events led to a reassessment of many other deals made to date, with only a few showing a potential for profit, and the rest expected to lose money. As the stock market continued to sink, some of the debt was sold for 30 cents on the dollar, in return for which the new owner would get all the aftermarket and residual value from the movies.

Despite the economic downturn, however, moviegoing remained strong, with the first few months of 2009 showing increases in both box office returns and attendance. The popularity of 3-D helped drive this success, starting with the live-action movie *My Bloody Valentine 3-D* in January, followed by the animated films *Coraline* in February and the DreamWorks spoof of 1950s-style monster movies, *Monsters vs. Aliens,* in March, which broke records with a $59 million opening weekend. Although the rollout of digital 3-D had been slower than hoped, it was now heading toward its apex with James Cameron's *Avatar,* a live-action movie utilizing a combination of CG, real characters, and 3-D effects planned for release December 19, 2009, with a cost estimated in excess of $300 million.

While there had been much discussion about transitioning from film to digital for more than a decade, only a handful of filmmakers had actually begun using the new technology to make movies; starting with George Lucas, whose *Star Wars: Episode I The Phantom Menace* was the first movie to be projected digitally in the United States in 1999, when it was shown on four digital screens. Lucas was also the first to shoot an entire movie digitally with *Star Wars: Episode II Attack of the Clones,* which was released in the United States in 2002 on sixty-three digital screens. Although these movies paved the way for the new format, it was quite some time before the industry followed their lead.

It was actually the return of 3-D films that helped propel the overall movie business closer to digital projection, as the digital format is far superior to the analog format in which older 3-D films had been made. Among the first movies shown in digital 3-D was a version of *The Polar Express* that had been released in 2004 on IMAX. Given the choice, ticket buyers chose to see it in 3-D by a ratio of 14 to 1, which was a real wake-up call for the studios. As a result, in June 2005 the Mann Chinese 6 theaters in Hollywood, California, became the first commercial theaters to offer digital 3-D projection. The expansion continued in November 2005 when Disney and a number of technology partners rigged 100 theaters for a 3-D version of the animated comedy *Chicken Little,* which had been converted from 2-D by Lucasfilm's Industrial Light & Magic. This time the public elected to see the 3-D version by more than 3 to 1 over an available 2-D version. The theaters showing the movie in 3-D were also able to charge a premium price, which caught the attention of both distributors and exhibitors looking for ways to differentiate the theater experience from the rapid developments in home theater systems. In anticipation of the 3-D films coming in 2009, more than 14 percent of all U.S. screens became newly equipped for digital cinema by the end of 2008.

A myriad of other digital-related issues preoccupied Hollywood during the latter half of the decade as well. In November 2007, the movie industry ground to a near halt when the Writers Guild of America went on strike, primarily over DVD residuals and payments for distribution of film content via "new media," in particular the Internet, but also mobile devices including cell phones. The bitter strike lasted roughly 100 days, ending in February 2008 after the Directors Guild of America reached terms for a new contract, thereby creating a new-media template for other guilds to reference. Still, the Screen Actors Guild refused to follow the template and worked beyond an expired contract for months without reaching any settlement.

As the decade wound down, the film ranked as the number one biggest-domestic-grossing movie of the twenty-first century was the Warner Bros. release of *The Dark Knight,* the second in a new series of Batman movies directed by Christopher Nolan. *The Dark Knight* opened on Wednesday, July 18, 2008, on a record 4,366 screens in North America, and immediately broke the opening-day midnight-run record with $18.5 million, besting the $16.9 million take of *Star Wars: Episode III Revenge of the Sith* in 2005. Despite *The Dark Knight's* box office success, the *Star Wars* franchise remained number one in average worldwide box office per film, while the

six films in the *Batman* franchise (with a per film average of $530 million in worldwide box office and $143 million in cost in equivalent 2005 dollars) wouldn't even make the top five franchises. *The Dark Knight* does make the list of Top 10 Blockbuster Movies with domestic box office greater than $250 million and costs greater than $150 million in adjusted dollars. As of June 2009, nearly all of the films on that list were released in the 2000s decade with the exception of *Cleopatra* (1963) and *Titanic* (1997).

The financing of *The Dark Knight* also reflects the events of the decade in that it exemplifies the entry of Wall Street hedge funds as players in Hollywood. While Warner released the movie, half of the rumored $252 million cost of production was paid by Legendary Pictures, which had been founded by former venture capitalist Thomas Tull in 2005. For his multipicture deal with Warner Bros., Tull had

U.S. Theater Transition to Digital, 1999–2008

Year	Total Number of Theaters	Total Number of Screens	Digital Screens
1999	7,477	37,131	10
2000	6,992	36,250	14
2001	6,253	35,173	25
2002	6,144	35,836	75
2003	6,100	35,995	85
2004	6,031	36,652	93
2005	6,114	37,740	192
2006	5,939	38,426	1,916
2007	5,928	38,794	4,702
2008	5,786	38,834	5,600
			estimated

Top 5 Franchises
Average Worldwide Box Office per Film,
1970–2009
Equivalent 2005 $s/ (Unadjusted $s) in Millions of $s

Rank	Franchise	Number of Films in Franchise	Worldwide Box Office	Average Worldwide Box Office per Film	Production Cost	Average Production Cost per Film
1	Star Wars	6	$6,872.9 ($4,230.6)	$1,145.5 ($705.1)	$582.6 ($436.6)	$97.1 ($72.8)
2	The Lord of the Rings	3	$3,147.5 ($2,915.7)	$1,049.2 ($971.9)	$713.0 ($660.0)	$237.7 ($220.0)
3	Harry Potter	5	$4,598.7 ($4,475.4)	$919.7 ($895.1)	$694.9 ($676.0)	$139.0 ($135.2)
4	Jurassic Park	3	$2,714.6 ($1,913.6)	$904.9 ($637.9)	$279.8 ($230.0)	$93.3 ($76.7)
5	Pirates of the Caribbean	3	$2,633.7 ($2,680.9)	$877.9 ($893.6)	$649.1 ($665.0)	$216.4 ($221.7)

initially raised a pool of $225 million from a number of partners, including ABRY Partners, Bank of America Capital Investors, AIG Direct Investments, Columbia Capital, Falcon Investment Advisors, and M/C Venture Partners, most of which had never invested in movies before. The investment bank JPMorgan then added $250 million as a senior credit facility.

In addition to all of its other accolades, *The Dark Knight* was also the biggest hit in the history of IMAX, the large-screen format that increasingly had become a place where special versions of the most successful blockbusters were shown. IMAX was steadily expanding after having changed its economic model: instead of selling its big-screen theaters to exhibitors, IMAX began to finance new theaters too, so it could share in the revenue from each movie. In 2008 IMAX also began a major conversion to digital and digital 3-D. By the end of 2008 it had 51 digital theaters, up from zero the year before. In 2009 that number was on pace to grow to at least 150 domestic locations. At that time, IMAX CEO Greg Foster predicted that they would have 200 digital locations, all capable of playing digital 3-D, by 2010.

By the end of 2008, it was apparent that as big as the appetite for Hollywood films was in North America, it was even bigger overseas. Thanks to the success of various tent-pole movies that year, the major Hollywood distributors set a new record for international distribution of $9.9 billion, up approximately 4 percent from the year before. That meant that over the course of a two-year period, the foreign box office for Hollywood movies had risen roughly 15 percent. But as big-budget movies became more dependent than ever on international markets for revenues, those revenues came at a greater cost due to the international market's higher distribution fees and increased instances of piracy and currency fluctuations—a combination that made profits that much harder to obtain.

What's more, as the costlier international theatrical market widened over the domestic box office market, home video was beginning a slow decline. While the top 10 movies in 2008 took in 2.8 percent more at the box office, the top 10 DVDs released experienced a 15 percent decline in revenues, and the downward trend appeared to be ongoing. Upscale DVD users migrated to the high-def Blu-Ray format (which defeated HD DVD for category dominance), while the lower economic demographic stayed with DVDs or shifted to Internet delivery. But unit sales in the new format were not making up for the loss in the declining sales of the older format. As the cost of making movies escalated over the decade, the studios had looked to home video as an important source of additional revenue. Naturally, the unexpected erosion of this market became one more in a series of factors contributing to the studios' steep 2008–9 budget cuts and layoffs, even as the box office was booming.

As the decade came to a close, however, the good news was that movies were more popular than ever and were reaching consumers in more diverse ways: on big screens, on huge screens, on TV screens, and on cell phone screens. The most frequented theatrical venues were megaplexes averaging sixteen screens. These megaplexes were destination locations complete with food courts, video games, and shopping. And finally, after an astounding 100-year run, the era of celluloid film was ending, making way for the new and promising digital era that is upon us now.

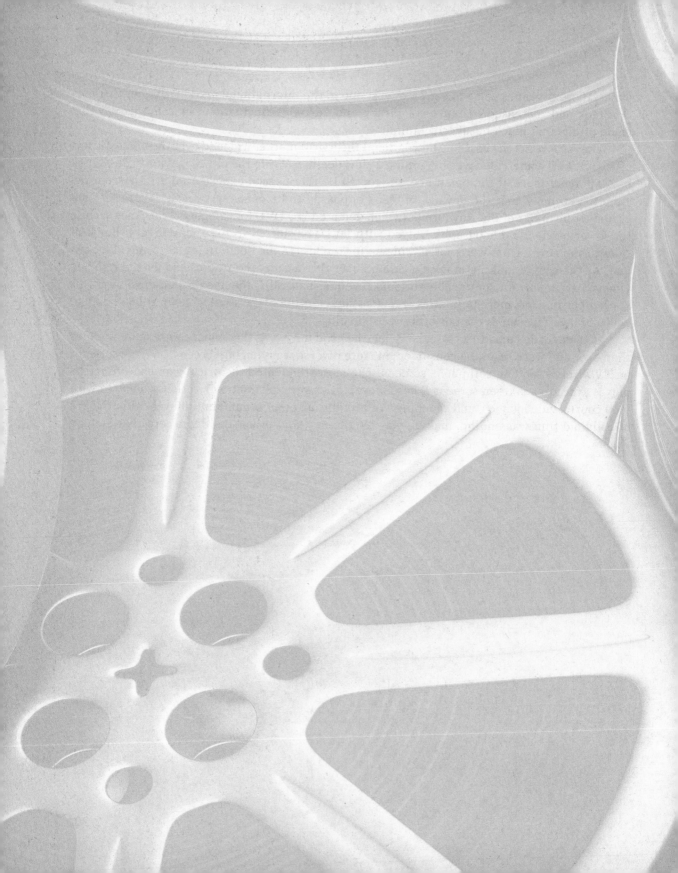

BLOCKBUSTING FILM SOURCES

Awards and Honors

Academy of Motion Picture Arts and Sciences Academy Awards (oscars.org)

American Film Institutes AFI Top 100 (afi.com)

Film Daily critics' awards from published annuals

Hollywood Foreign Press Association Golden Globes (goldenglobes.org)

Library of Congress National Film Preservation Board (loc.gov/film/)

The National Board of Review (nbrmp.org)

The New York Film Critics Circle (nyfcc.com)

Top 300 Films Position from the proprietary JAK Films database

Financial, Legal, and Statistical Reference

ABA Forum Committee on the Entertainment and Sports Industry (Volume 5, Number 3, Winter 1987) The Recent Acquisition of Theatre Circuits by Major Distributors by Gerald F. Phillips, American Bar Association (abanet.org)

American Civil Liberties Union, Film Censorship Timeline (aclu.org)

Entertainment Industry Economics—A Guide for Financial Analysis, 7th ed., by Harold L. Vogel

Film Daily Year Book, annual industry statistics (1915–68)

International Motion Picture Almanac (1969–)

Motion Picture Association Worldwide Market Research, U.S. entertainment industry annual MPAA market statistics reports

NATO Encyclopedia of Exhibition, annual National Organization of Theater Owners publications

Production Encyclopedia (1952)

Statistical Abstract of the United States: 2008, 127th ed., by the U.S. Census Bureau

Taxfoundation.org, Federal individual income tax rates (1910–2009)

Time, Inc., historical corporate salary surveys (time.com)

U.S. Bureau of Economic Analysis, Information Industry GDP (bea.gov)

Variety, annual rentals (1946–89)

Variety, annual All-Time Boxoffice Champs (1970–74)

Variety, annual Big-Buck Scorecard Rentals and Costs (1956–88)

Various Corporate Proxy Statements and Annual Reports

Various producer's statements from private sources

General Works

Adamson, Joe. *Groucho, Harpo, Chico, and Sometimes Zeppo.* Simon & Schuster, 1973.

Affron, Charles, and Mirella Jona. *Sets in Motion: Art Direction and Film Narrative.* Rutgers University Press, 1995.

Allvine, Glendon. *The Greatest Fox of Them All.* Lyle Stewart, Inc., 1969.

Altman, Diana. *Hollywood East: Louis B. Mayer and the Origins of the Studio System.* Birch Lane Press, 1992.

Ambrose, Stephen E. *D-Day*. Simon & Schuster, 1994.

Anderson, Lindsay. *About John Ford*. McGraw-Hill, 1981.

———. *Never Apologise: The Collected Writings*. Ed. Paul Ryan. Plexus, 2004.

Andrews, Nigel. *True Myths: The Life and Times of Arnold Schwarzenegger*. Carol Publishing Group, 1996.

Arkoff, Sam with Richard Trubo. *Flying Through Hollywood by the Seat of My Pants*. Carol Publishing, 1992.

Auiler, Dan. *Hitchcock's Notebooks*. Avon Books, 1999.

Avni, Sheerly. *Cinema by the Bay*. JAK Films, 2006.

Babas, Samantha. *The First Lady of Hollywood: A Biography of Louella Parsons*. University of California Press, 2005.

Bach, Steven. *Final Cut: Dreams and Disaster in the Making of Heavens Gate*. William Morrow, 1985.

Balio, Tino. *United Artists: The Company That Changed the Film Industry*. University of Wisconsin Press, 1987.

Balio, Tino, ed. *The American Film Industry*, rev. ed. University of Wisconsin Press, 1976.

Balshofer, Fred, and Arthur Miller. *One Reel a Week*. University of California Press, 1967.

Barrios, Richard. *A Song in the Dark: The Birth of the Musical Film*. Oxford University Press, 1995.

Bart, Peter. *Boffo: How I Learned to Love the Blockbuster and Fear the Bomb*. Hyperion, 2006.

Bart, Peter. and Peter Guber, *Shoot Out: Surviving the Fame and (mis)fortune of Hollywood*. Faber and Faber, 2004.

Baxter, Anne. *Intermission*. Putnam, 1976.

Baxter, John. *Stanley Kubrick: A Biography*. Carroll & Graf, 1999.

———. *The Cinema of John Ford*. A. S. Barnes, 1971.

——— *Sixty Years of Hollywood*. A. S. Barnes, 1973.

——— *The Hollywood Exiles*. Taplinger Publishing, 1976.

Beaver, Frank. *Oliver Stone: Wakeup Cinema*. Macmillan, 1994.

Behlmer, Rudy. *Inside Warner Bros. (1935–1951)*. Fireside, 1985.

———, ed. *Memo from Darryl F. Zanuck*. Grove Press, 1993.

Bell, Geoffrey. *The Golden Gate and the Silver Screen*. Cornwall Books, 1984.

Bengtson, John. *Silent Echoes: Discovering Early Hollywood Trough the Films of Buster Keaton*. Santa Monica Press, 2000.

Bengtson, John, and Kevin Brownlow. *Silent Traces: Discovering Early Hollywood Through the Films of Charlie Chaplin*. Santa Monica Press, 2006.

Berg, A. Scott. *Goldwyn: A Biography*. Alfred A. Knopf, 1989.

———. *Kate Remembered*. G. P. Putnam's Sons, 2003.

Bergan, Ronald. *Francis Ford Coppola, Close Up: The Making of His Movies*. Thunder's Mouth, 1997.

Bergreen, Laurence. *As Thousands Cheer: The Life of Irving Berlin*. Viking Press, 1990.

Bigelow, Albert. *Life and Lillian Gish*. Macmillan, 1932.

Birchard, Robert S. *Cecil B. DeMille's Hollywood*. Lexington: University Press of Kentucky, 2004.

Biskind, Peter. *Down and Dirty Pictures: Miramax, Sundance, and the Rise of Independent Film*. Simon & Schuster, 2004.

———. *Easy Riders, Raging Bulls: How the Sex, Drugs, and Rock 'n' Roll Generation Saved Hollywood*. Simon & Schuster, 1998.

———. *Godfather Companion*. HarperCollins, 1991.

Bitzer, G. W. *Billy Bitzer: His Story*. Farrar, Straus, and Giroux, 1973.

Black, Shirley Temple. *Child Star: An Autobiography*. McGraw-Hill, 1988.

Blake, Michael. F. *Lon Chaney: The Man Behind the Thousand Faces*. Vestal Press, 1993.

Blatty, William Peter. *The Exorcist from Novel to Film*. Bantam Books, 1974.

Blesh, Rudi. *Keaton.* Macmillan Company, 1966.

Block, Alex Ben. *The Legend of Bruce Lee.* Dell Publishing, 1974.

———. *Out-Foxed: The Inside Story of America's Fourth Television Network.* St. Martin's Press, 1990.

Blum, Daniel. *A New Pictorial History of the Talkies.* G. P. Putnam's Sons, 1973.

Bogdanovich, Peter. *John Ford.* University of California Press, 1978.

———. *Who the Devil Made It: Conversations with Legendary Film Directors.* Ballantine, 1997.

Bonderoff, Jason. *Brooke: An Unauthorized Biography.* Kensington Publishing, 1981.

Bosworth, Patricia. *Montgomery Clift: A Biography.* Harcourt Brace Jovanovich, 1978.

Bouzereau, Laurent, and Jody Duncan. *The Making of Star Wars, Episode I—The Phantom Menace.* Ballantine, 1999.

Bradley, Edwin M. *The First Hollywood Musicals: A Critical Filmography of 171 Features.* McFarland, 2004.

Brill, Lesley. *John Huston's Filmmaking.* Cambridge University Press, 1997.

Brode, Douglas. *The Films of Steven Spielberg.* Citadel Press, 2000.

Brody, Seymour. *Jewish Heroes and Heroines in America.* Lifetime Books, 1996.

Brown, Gene. *Movie Time: A Chronology of Hollywood and the Movie Industry from Its Beginnings to the Present.* Macmillan, 1995.

Brown, Jared. *Moss Hart: A Prince of the Theater.* Back Stage Books, 2006.

Brown, Karl. *Adventures with D. W. Griffith.* Farrar, Straus, and Giroux, 1973.

Brownlow, Kevin. *David Lean: A Biography.* St. Martin's Press, 1996.

Brownlow, Kevin. *The Parade's Gone By.* University of California Press, 1968.

———. *Hollywood: The Pioneers.* Alfred A. Knopf, 1979.

———. *Mary Pickford Rediscovered.* Harry N. Abrams, 1999.

Bruck, Connie. *When Hollywood Had a King.* Random House, 2003.

Buford, Kate. *Burt Lancaster: An American Life.* Alfred A. Knopf, 2000.

Burton, Hal, ed. *Acting in the Sixties.* London: British Broadcasting Corporation, 1970.

Call, Deborah, Vic Bulluck, and Valerie Hoffman. *The Art of Star Wars, Episode V—The Empire Strikes Back.* Ballantine Books, 1994.

Canby, Vincent, and Janet Maslin. *The New York Times Guide to the Best 1,000 Movies Ever Made.* Ed. Peter M. Nichols. St. Martin's Griffin, 1999.

Canham, Kingsley. *The Hollywood Professionals, Vol. 1: Michael Curtiz, Raoul Walsh, Henry Hathaway.* A. S. Barnes, 1973.

Capra, Frank. *The Name Above the Title, an Autobiography.* Macmillan, 1971.

Carnes, Mark C., ed. *Past Imperfect: History According to the Movies.* Henry Holt and Co., 1995.

Carringer, Robert L. *The Making of Citizen Kane.* Rev. ed. University of California Press, 1996.

Carroll, David. *The Matinee Idols.* Arbor House, 1972.

Cawelti, John G., ed. *Bonnie and Clyde: Tradition and Transformation.* Prentice-Hall, Inc., 1973.

Champlin, Charles. *George Lucas: The Creative Impulse.* Rev. ed. Harry N. Abrams, 1997.

Chandler, Charlotte. *Ingrid: A Personal Biography.* Simon & Schuster, 2007.

Chunovic, Louis. *Jodie: A Biography.* Contemporary Books, 1995.

Clagett, Thomas. *William Friedkin: Films of Aberration, Obsession and Reality.* 2nd ed. Beverly Hills: Silman-James, 2003.

Clarkson, Wensley. *John Travolta: Back in Character.* Overlook Press, 1997.

Cole, Lester. *Hollywood Red: The Autobiography of Lester Cole.* Ramparts Press, 1981.

Cohan, Steven and Ina Rae Hark. *Screening the Male: Exploring Masculinities in Hollywood Cinema.* Routledge, 1993.

Collier, Peter. *The Fondas: A Hollywood Dynasty.* Putnam, 1991.

Considine, Shaun. *Bette and Joan: The Divine Feud.* Dutton Books, 1989.

———. *Mad as Hell: The Life and Work of Paddy Chayefsky.* Random House, 1994.

———. *Barbra Streisand: The Woman, The Myth, The Music.* Dell Publishing, 1985.

Copetas, A. Craig. *Metal Men: Marc Rich and the 10-Billion-Dollar Scam.* G. P. Putnam's Sons, 1985.

Coppola, Eleanor. *Notes on the Making of Apocalypse Now.* Simon & Schuster, 1979.

Cowie, Peter. *Coppola: A Biography.* Scribner's, 1990.

———. *John Ford and the American West.* Harry N. Abrams, 2004.

Cripps, Thomas. *A Slow Fade to Black: The Negro in American Films 1900–1942.* Oxford University Press, 1977.

Cronin, Paul, ed. *George Stevens: Interviews.* University Press of Mississippi, 2004.

Crosby, Gary, and Ross Firestone. *Going My Own Way.* Fawcett, 1984.

Crowe, Cameron. *Conversations with Wilder.* Alfred A. Knopf, 1999.

Crowther, Bosley. *Hollywood Rajah: The Life and Times of Louis B. Mayer.* Holt, Rinehart, and Winston, 1960.

———. *The Lion's Share.* Dutton, 1957.

Curtis, Thomas Quinn. *Von Stroheim.* Farrar, Straus & Giroux, 1971.

Custen, George F. *Twentieth Century's Fox, Darryl F. Zanuck and the Culture of Hollywood.* Basic Books, 1997.

———. *Bio/Pics How Hollywood Constructed Public History.* Rutgers University Press, 1992.

Dalton, David. *James Dean: The Mutant King.* St. Martin's Press, 1974.

Dancyger, Ken. *The Director's Idea: The Path to Great Directing.* Focal Press, 2006.

Daniels, Les. *Batman: The Complete History.* Chronicle Books, 2004.

Dardis, Tom. *Keaton: The Man Who Wouldn't Lie Down.* Penguin Books, 1979.

Davis, Bette. *The Lonely Life.* Putnam's, 1962.

———. *This 'N' That.* Putnam's, 1987.

Davis, Ronald L. *John Ford: Hollywood's Old Master.* University of Oklahoma Press, 1995.

De Barbin, Lucy and Dary Matera. *Are You Lonesome Tonight?* Villard Books, 1987.

DeMille, Cecil B., and Donald Hayne. *The Autobiography of Cecil B. DeMille.* Facsimiles-Garl, 1985.

Deschner, Donald. *The Complete Films of Spencer Tracy.* Carol Publishing Group, 1993.

Dickey, Christopher. *Summer of Deliverance: A Memoir of Father and Son.* Touchstone, 1999.

Diner, Hasia. *In the Almost Promised Land: American Jews and Blacks, 1915–1935.* Johns Hopkins University Press, 1977.

Douglas, Kirk. *The Ragman's Son: An Autobiography.* Pocket Books, 1988.

Drazin, Charles. *In Search of the Third Man.* Limelight, 2000.

Duncan, Jody. *Mythmaking: Behind the Scenes of Star Wars: Episode II: Attack of the Clones.* Ballantine, 2002.

Dunne, John Gregory. *The Studio.* Limelight Edition, 1968.

Dunne, Philip. *Memo from Darryl F. Zanuck: The Golden Years at Twentieth Century-Fox.* Grove Press, 1993.

Durgnat, Raymond. *King Vidor, American.* University of California Press, 1988.

Eames, John Douglas. *The Paramount Story: The Complete History of the Studio and Its Films.* Additional text by Robert Abele. Simon & Schuster, 2002.

———. *The MGM Story: The Complete History of 50 Roaring Years.* Crown Publishers, 1975.

Eastman, John. *Retakes, Behind the Scenes of 500 Classic Movies.* Ballantine Books, 1989.

Fleming, Charles. *High Concept: Don Simpson and the Hollywood Culture of Excess.* Doubleday, 1998.

Ebert, Roger. *The Great Movies.* Broadway, 2002.

———. *The Great Movies Vol. II.* Broadway, 2006.

Edelson, Edward. *Great Movie Spectaculars.* Doubleday, 1976.

Eells, George. *Hedda and Louella.* Warner Paperback Library, 1973.

Eig, Jonathan. *Luckiest Man: The Life and Death of Lou Gehrig.* Simon & Schuster, 2006.

Eisner, Michael D. with Tony Schwartz. *Work in Progress.* Random House, 1998.

Eliot, Marc. *Walt Disney: Hollywood's Dark Prince.* Birch Lane Press, 1993.

Ellingson, Ter. *The Myth of the Noble Savage.* University of California Press, 2001.

Epstein, Edward Jay. *The Big Picture.* Random House, 2005.

Etulain, Richard W., and Glenda Riley, eds. *The Hollywood West: Lives of Film Legends Who Shaped It.* Fulcrum Publishing, 2001.

Evans, Robert. *The Kid Stays in the Picture.* Hyperion, 1994.

Everson, William K. *Love in the Film.* Citadel Press, 1979.

———. *American Silent Film.* Da Capo Press, 1998.

Ewbank, Tim, and Stafford Hildred. *Russell Crowe: The Biography.* London: Carlton Books, 2001.

Eyman, Scott. *Lion of Hollywood—The Life and Legend of Louis B. Mayer.* Simon & Schuster, 2005.

———. *Mary Pickford: America's Sweetheart.* Donald I. Fine, 1990.

———. *Print the Legend: The Life and Times of John Ford.* Simon & Schuster, 1999.

———. *The Speed of Sound: Hollywood and the Talkie Revolution*, 1926–1930. Simon & Schuster, 1997.

Faludi, Susan. *Backlash.* Three Rivers Press, 2006.

Farber, Stephen and Marc Green. *Hollywood Dynasties.* Fawcett Crest, 1984.

Ferber, Edna. *Giant.* Doubleday, 1952.

Fiegel, Eddie. *John Barry: A Sixties Theme: From James Bond to Midnight Cowboy.* Macmillan, 2002.

Finch, Christopher. *The Art of Walt Disney.* Harry N. Abrams 1995.

Finler, Joel W. *The Hollywood Story.* London: Wallflower Press, 2003.

Fisher, Lucy. *Sunrise: A Song of Two Humans.* British Film Institute, 2008.

Fishgall, Gary. *Against Type: The Biography of Burt Lancaster.* Scribner, 1995.

Flamini, Roland. *Thalberg: The Last Tycoon and the World of MGM.* Crown Publishing, 1994.

Fleischer, Richard. *Just Tell Me When to Cry: A Memoir.* Carroll & Graf, 1993.

Fleming, Alice. *The Moviemakers: A History of American Movies through the Lives of Ten Great Directors.* St. Martin's Press, 1973.

Fleming, Charles. *High Concept: Don Simpson and the Hollywood Culture of Excess.* Doubleday, 1998.

Flower, Joe. *Prince of the Magic Kingdom: Michael Eisner and the Re-Making of Disney.* John Wiley & Sons, 1991.

Fonda, Henry, and Howard Teichmann. *Fonda: My Life.* New American Library, 1981.

Fonda, Jane. *Jane Fonda: My Life So Far.* Random House, 2005.

Ford, Dan. *Pappy: The Life of John Ford.* Da Capo Press, 1998.

Fordin, Hugh. *MGM's Greatest Musicals: The Arthur Freed Unit.* Da Capo Press, 1996.

Forman, Milos. *Turnaround: A Memoir.* Villard, 1994.

Frascella, Lawrence, and Al Weisel. *Live Fast, Die Young: The Wild Ride of Making Rebel Without a Cause.* Simon & Schuster, 2005.

Fraser-Cavassoni, Natasha. *Sam Spiegel.* Simon & Schuster, 2003.

Frazer, John. *Artificially Arranged Scenes: The Films of George Méliès.* G. K. Hall, 1979.

Freedland, Michael. *The Warner Brothers.* St. Martin's Press, 1983.

Furia, Philip. *Irving Berlin: A Life in Song.* Schirmer Books, 1998.

Gabler, Neal. *An Empire of Their Own: How the Jews Invented Hollywood.* Crown, 1988.

Gallagher, Tag. *John Ford: The Man and His Films.* University of California Press, 1986.

Gardiner, Robin, and Dan Van Der Vat. *The Titanic Conspiracy: Cover-ups and Mysteries of the World's Most Famous Sea Disaster.* Birch Lane Press, 1995.

Gardner, Gerald. *The Censorship Papers: Movie Censorship Letters from the Hays Office, 1934 to 1968.* Dodd, Mead & Co., 1987.

Gatiss, Mark. *James Whale: A Biography, or James Whale the Would-Be Gentleman.* Cassell, 1995.

Geduld, Harry M., ed. *Focus on D. W. Griffith.* Prentice-Hall, 1972.

Gehring, Wes D. *Leo McCarey: From Marx to McCarthy.* Scarecrow Press, 2005.

———. *Leo McCarey and the Comic Anti-Hero in American Film.* Arno, 1980.

Gerstner, David A., and Janet Staiger. *Authorship and Film.* Routledge, 2003.

Gish, Lillian. *Dorothy and Lillian Gish.* Charles Scribner's Sons, 1973.

Gish, Lillian, and Ann Pinchot. *The Movies, Mr. Griffith and Me.* Prentice-Hall, 1969.

Goldberg, Victor. *Framing Contract Law, An Economic Perspective.* Harvard University Press, 2007.

Golden, Eve. *Vamp: The Rise and Fall of Theda Bara.* Emprise Publishing, 1996.

Goldman, William. *Adventures in the Screen Trade.* Warner Books, 1983.

———. *Which Lie Did I Tell? More Adventure in the Screen Trade.* Pantheon Books, 2000.

———. *Hype & Glory.* Villard Books, 1990.

Gomery, Douglas. *Shared Pleasures: A History of Movie Presentation in the United States.* University of Wisconsin Press, 1992.

———. *The Hollywood Studio System.* St. Martin's Press, 1986.

Goodman, Ezra. *The Fifty-Year Decline and Fall of Hollywood.* Simon & Schuster, 1961.

Goodwin, Michael, and Naomi Wise. *On the Edge: The Life and Times of Francis Coppola.* William Morrow, 1989.

Gottesman, Ronald, ed. *Focus on Citizen Kane.* Prentice-Hall, 1971.

Goudsouzian, Aram. *Sidney Poitier: Man, Actor, Icon.* University of North Carolina Press, 2004.

Gray, Beverly. *Ron Howard: From Mayberry to the Moon . . . and Beyond.* Rutledge Hill Press, 2003.

———. *Roger Corman: An Unauthorized Biography of the Godfather of Indie Filmmaking.* Renaissance Books, 2000.

Green, Stanely, and Elaine Schmidt. *Hollywood Musicals Year by Year.* Hal Leonard, 2001.

Griffith, Richard, ed. *The Talkies: Articles and Illustrations from a Great Fan Magazine 1928–1940.* Dover Publications, 1971.

Grobel, Lawrence. *The Hustons.* Charles Scribner's Sons, 1989.

Grossman, Gary H. *Superman Serial to Cereal.* Popular Library, 1977.

Gussow, Mel. *Darryl F. Zanuck: Don't Say Yes Until I Finish Talking.* Doubleday, 1971.

Halliwell, Leslie. *The Filmgoers's Companion*, 6th ed. Hill and Wang, 1965.

Hancock, Ralph, and Letitia Fairbanks. *Douglas Fairbanks: The Fourth Musketeer.* Henry Holt, 1953.

Haney, Lynn. *Gregory Peck: A Charmed Life.* Da Capo Press, 2005.

Harbinson, W. A. *George C. Scott: The Man, the Actor, and the Legend.* Pinnacle, 1977.

Harmetz, Aljean. *The Making of The Wizard of Oz.* Alfred A. Knopf, 1977.

———. *Rolling Breaks and Other Movie Business.* Random House, 1983.

Harris, Robert A., and Michael S. Lasky. *The Complete Films of Alfred Hitchcock.* Citadel Press, 2002.

Harris, Marlys J. *The Zanucks of Hollywood: The Dark Legacy of an American Dynasty.* Crown Publishers, 1989.

Haun, Harry. *The Cinematic Century: An Intimate Diary of America's Affair with the Movies.* Applause Books, 2000.

Hayes, Dade, and Jonathan Bing. *Open Wide: How Hollywood Box Office Became a National Obsession.* Miramax, 2006.

Henderson, Robert M. *D. W. Griffith: His Life and Work.* Oxford University Press, 1972.

Hepburn, Katharine. *Me: Stories of My Life.* Alfred A. Knopf, 1991.

———. *The Making of The African Queen, or How I Went to Africa with Bogie, Bacall and Huston and Almost Lost My Mind.* Alfred A. Knopf, 1987.

Herlihy, James Leo. *Midnight Cowboy.* Simon & Schuster, 1965.

Herman, Jan. *A Talent for Trouble: The Life of Hollywood's Most Acclaimed Director, William Wyler.* G. P. Putnam's Sons, 1995.

Herndon, Booton. *Mary Pickford and Douglas Fairbanks.* W. W. Norton, 1977.

Heston, Charlton. *The Actor's Life: Journals 1956–1976.* E. P. Dutton, 1976.

Highham, Charles. *Brando: The Unauthorized Biography.* New American Library, 1987.

Hill, Lee. *Easy Rider.* BFI Modern Classics, 1996.

Hirschhorn, Clive. *The Warner Bros. Story.* Crown, 1979.

———. *The Hollywood Musical.* Crown, 1981.

Hirshberg, Jack. *A Portrait of All the President's Men.* Warner Books, 1976.

Hitchcock, Susan Tyler. *Frankenstein: A Cultural History.* W. W. Norton, 2007.

Hopkins, John. *Shrek: From the Swamp to the Screen.* Harry N. Abrams, 2004.

Hopper, Hedda with James Brough. *The Whole Truth and Nothing But.* Doubleday & Co., 1963.

Horne, Gerald. *Class Struggle in Hollywood 1930–1950.* University of Texas Press, 2001.

Hotchner, A.E. *Doris Day: her Own Story.* William Morrow, 1976.

Huff, Theodore. *Charlie Chaplin.* Henry Shuman, 1951.

Hurst, Richard Maurice. *Republic Studios: Between Poverty Row and the Majors.* Scarecrow Press, 1979.

Huston, John. *An Open Book.* Alfred A. Knopf, 1980.

Jacobs, Diane. *Hollywood Renaissance.* Delta, 1980.

Jacobs, Lewis. *The Emergence of Film Art.* Hopkinson and Blake, 1969.

———. *The Rise of the American Film.* Harcourt, Brace, 1939.

Johnson, Nora. *Flashback: Nora Johnson on Nunnally Johnson.* Doubleday, 1979.

Johnson, Robert K. *Francis Ford Coppola.* Boston: Twayne, 1977.

Jordan, Richard T. *But Darling, I'm Your Auntie Mame.* Kensington, 2004.

Joyce, Aileen. *Julia: The Untold Story of America's Pretty Woman.* Windsor Publishing, 1993.

Kael, Pauline. *Movie Love Complete Reviews 1988–1991.* Penguin Books, 1991.

Kagan Research. *Media Trends: Actionable Metrics, Benchmarks & Projections for All the Major Media Sectors, 12th ed.* Kagan Books, 2006.

Karney, Robin, ed. *Chronicle of the Cinema: 100 Years of the Movies.* DK Publishing, 1995.

Kanin, Garson. *Garson Kanin's Hollywood.* Bantam, 1976.

Kashner, Sam, and Jennifer Macnair. *The Bad and the Beautiful: Hollywood in the Fifties.* W. W. Norton, 2003.

Katz, Ephraim. *The Film Encyclopedia.* 4th ed. Rev. Fred Klein and Ronald Dean Noeln. HarperCollins, 2001.

Kazan, Elia. *Elia Kazan, a Life.* Da Capo Press, 1988.

Kelley, Kitty. *Elizabeth Taylor: The Last Star.* Simon & Schuster, 1981.

Kelly, Louise. *Wichita County Beginnings.* Eakin Press, 1982.

Kennedy, Matthew. *Marie Dressler: A Biography.* McFarland, 1998.

Keough, Peter, ed. *Flesh and Blood: The National Society of Film Critics on Sex, Violence and Censorship.* Mercury House, 1995.

Kiehn, David. *Broncho Billy and the Essanay Film Company*. Farwell Books, 2003.

Kiern, Thomas. *Jane Fonda: The Candid Biography of the Controversial Superstar*. Granada Publiishing 1982.

Kim, Erwin. *Franklin J. Schaffner*. Scarecrow Press, 1985.

King, Tom. *The Operator*. Random House, 2000.

Kinnard, Roy. *The Lost World of Willis O'Brien*. McFarland, 1993.

Kinney, Jack. *Walt Disney and Other Assorted Characters*. Harmony Books, 1988.

Knapp, Laurence F. *Brian De Palma: Interviews*. University of Mississippi Press, 2003.

Knight, Arthur. *The Liveliest Art: A Panoramic History of the Movies*. New American Library, 1957.

Koszarski, Richard. *An Evening's Entertainment: The Age of the Silent Feature Picture, 1915–1928*. History of the American Cinema, vol. 3. University of California Press, 1994.

———. *The Man You Loved to Hate*. Oxford University Press, 1983.

Kotsilibas-Davis, James, and Myrna Loy. *Myrna Loy: Being and Becoming*. Knopf, 1987.

Kox, Donald. *The Magic Factory: How MGM Made An American in Paris*. Praeger, 1973.

Kozak, Jim, ed. *EOE: The 2001–2002 Encyclopedia of Exhibition*. National Association of Theater Owners, 2001.

Kracauer, Siegfried, and Leonardo Quaresima. *From Caligari to Hitler: A Psychological History of the German Film*. Princeton University Press, 1974.

Kramer, Stanley with Thomas M. Coffey. *A Mad, Mad, Mad, Mad World: A Life in Hollywood*. Harcourt Brace & Co., 1997.

Kreuger, Miles, ed. *The Movie Musical from Vitaphone to 42nd Street, as Reported in a Great Fan Magazine*. Dover Publications, 1974.

Lally, Kevin. *Wilder Times: The Life of Billy Wilder*. Henry Holt, 1996.

Lambert, Gavin. *GWTW: The Making of Gone with the Wind*. Little, Brown, 1973.

Landau, Diana, ed. *Gladiator: The Making of the Ridley Scott Epic*. Newmarket Press, 2000.

Lasky, Jesse L., with Don Weldon. *I Blow My Own Horn*. Doubleday, 1957.

Lassally, Walter. *Itinerant Cameraman*. London: John Murray, 1987.

Lavington, Stephen. *Oliver Stone*. London: Virgin Books, 2004.

Lawson, Valerie. *Mary Poppins, She Wrote: The Life of P. L. Travers*. Simon & Schuster, 2006.

Lax, Eric. *Woody Allen: A Biopgraphy*. Da Capo Press, 2000.

Leaming, Barbara. *Marilyn Monroe*. Three Rivers Press, 1998.

Leggett, John. *Ross and Tom: Two American Tragedies*. Simon & Schuster, 1974.

Leider, Emily W. *Dark Lover*. Farrar, Straus & Giroux, 2003.

Leigh, Janet, and Christopher Nickens. *Behind the Scenes of Psycho*. Pavilion Books, 1995.

Leish, Kenneth W. *Cinema*. Newsweek Books, 1974.

Lennig, Arthur. *Stroheim*. University Press of Kentucky, 1999.

Levitt, Theodore. *The Marketing Imagination*. Macmillan, 1983.

Litwak, Mark. *Reel Power: The Struggle for Influence and Success in the New Hollywood*. William Morrow And Co., 1986.

LoBrutto, Vincet. *Stanley Kubrick: A Biography*. Da Capo Press, 1999.

Long, Robert Emmet. *John Huston: Interviews*. University Press of Mississippi, 2001.

Lopate, Phillip. *American Movie Critics: An Anthology From the Silents Until Now*. Literary Classics of the United States, 2006.

Lord, Walter. *A Night to Remember*. Henry Holt, 1955.

Love, Bessie. *From Hollywood with Love*. David & Charles, 1981.

Lovell, Jim. *Lost Moon: The Perilous Voyage of Apollo 13*. Pocket Books, 1995.

Lukk, Tiiu. *Movie Marketing. Opening the Picture and Giving it Legs*. Silman-James Press, 1997.

Lumet, Sidney. *Making Movies*. Alfred A. Knopf, 1996.

Macnab, Geoffrey. *The Making of Taxi Driver*. Unanimous Ltd., 2005.

Madsen, Axel. *William Wyler: The Authorized Biography*. Thomas Y. Crowell, 1973.

———. *The New Hollywood: American Movies in the 70s*. Thomas Y. Crowell, 1976.

Mair, George. *Inside HBO: The Billion Dollar War Between HBO, Hollywood and the Home Video Revolution*. Dodd, Mead, & Co., 1988.

Maltin, Leonard, ed. *Leonard Maltin's Movie Guide, 2007*. Penguin Group, 2006.

Maltin, Leonard. *The Disney Films*. Crown, 1995.

Mann, William J. *Edge of Midnight: The Life of John Schlesinger—The Authorized Biography*. Billboard Books, 2005.

Manso, Peter. *Brando: A Biography*. Hyperion, 1994.

Marill, Alvin H. *The Films of Sidney Poitier*. Citadel Press, 1978.

Marner, Terence St. John, ed. *Directing Motion Pictures*. Tantivy Press and A. S. Barnes, 1972.

Marx, Harpo with Rowland Barber. *Harpo Speaks!* Freeway Press, 1974.

Marx, Samuel. *Mayer and Thalberg: The Make-Believe Saints*. Random House, 1975.

Masters, Kim. *The Keys to the Kingdom: How Michael Eisner Lost His Grip*. William Morrow, 2000.

Mathis, Jack. *Republic Confidential, Vol. 2: The Players*. Jack Mathis Advertising, 1992.

Mast, Gerald, and Bruce F. Kawin *A Short History of the Movies*. 6th ed., Prentice Hall College Division, 1996.

Matthews, Charles. *Oscar A to Z*. Main Street Books/Doubleday, 1995.

Mayo, Virginia with L.C. Van Savage. *The Best Years of My Life*. Beach House Books, 2001.

McAdams, Frank. *The American War Film: History and Hollywood*. Figueroa Press, 2005.

McBride, Joseph. *Frank Capra: The Catastrophe of Success*. Simon & Schuster, 1992.

———. *Searching for John Ford: A Life*. St. Martin's Press, 2001.

———. *Steven Spielberg: A Biography*. Simon & Schuster, 1997.

McBride, Joseph, and Michael Wilmington. *John Ford*. Da Capo, 1974.

McCarthy, Todd. *Howard Hawks: The Grey Fox of Hollywood*. Grove Press, 1997.

McCarty, John. *The Films of Mel Gibson*. Citadel Press, 2001.

McClintick, David. *Indecent Exposure: A True Story of Hollywood and Wall Street*. William Morrow and Co., 1982.

McDonald, Gerald D., Michael Conway, and Mark Ricci. *The Complete Films of Charlie Chaplin*. Citadel Press, 1965.

McDougal, Dennis. *The Last Mogul: Lew Wasserman, MCA, and the Hidden History of Hollywood*. Crown, 1998.

McGilligan, Patrick. *Yankee Doodle Dandy*. University of Wisconsin Press, 1981.

———. *Jack's Life: A Biography of Jack Nicholson*. W. W. Norton & Co., 1994.

Marcus, Alan. "Uncovering an Auteur: Fred Zinnemann." *Film History* 12, 1 (2000).

Meyers, Jeffrey. *Gary Cooper: American Hero*. William Morrow and Co., 1998.

Milano, Roy, Jennifer Osborne, and Forrest J. Ackerman. *Monsters: A Celebration of the Classics from Universal Studios,* Ballantine Del Rey, 2006.

Miller, Gabriel, ed. *Fred Zinnemann: Interviews*. Conversations with Filmmakers Series. University Press of Mississippi, 2005.

Miller, John. *Peter Ustinov: The Gift of Laughter*. Weidenfeld & Nicolson, 2002.

Mitchell, Glenn. *The Chaplin Encyclopedia*. B. T. Batsford, 1997.

Moldea, Dan E. *Dark Victory: Ronald Reagan, MCA, and the Mob.* Viking, 1986.

Mordden, Ethan. *The Hollywood Studios: House Style in the Golden Age of the Movies.* Alfred A. Knopf, 1988.

———. *The Hollywood Musical.* St. Martin's Press, 1981.

Mosley, Leonard. *Zanuck: The Rise and Fall of Hollywood's Last Tycoon.* Little, Brown, 1984.

Moss, Marilyn Ann. *Giant: George Stevens, A Life on Film.* University of Wisconsin Press, 2004.

Munn, Michael. *Charlton Heston.* St. Martin's Press, 1986.

Musser, Charles. *Before the Nickelodeon.* University of California Press, 1991.

———. *The Emergence of Cinema: The American Screen to 1907.* History of the American Cinema, vol. 1. University of California Press, 1994.

Nichols, Peter. *The New York Times Guide to The Best 1,000 Movies Ever Made.* Random House, 1999.

Nickson, Chris. *Will Smith.* St. Martin's Press, 1999.

Nielsen, Mike and Gene Mailes. *Hollywood's Other Blacklist: Union Struggles in the Studio System.* British Film Institute, 1995.

Noerdlinger, Henry. *Moses and Egypt: The Documentation to the Motion Picture The Ten Commandments.* University of Southern California Press, 1956.

Obst, Lynda. *Hello, He Lied and Other Truths from the Hollywood Trenches.* Little, Brown & Co, 1996.

O'Connor, Garry. *Paul Scofield: An Actor for All Seasons.* Applause, 2002.

O'Donnell, Pierce, and Dennis McDougal. *Fatal Subtraction: How Hollywood Really Does Business.* Doubleday, 1992.

O'Hara, Maureen. *'Tis Herself.* Simon & Schuster, 2004.

O'Leary, Liam. *Rex Ingram, Master of the Silent Cinema.* Academy Press, 1980.

O'Neil, Tom. *Movie Awards—The Ultimate, Unofficial Guide to the Oscars, Golden Globes, Critics, Guild and Indie Honors.* Berkley Books, 2003.

Oderman, Stuart. *Lillian Gish.* McFarland, 2000.

Oppenheimer, Jerry, and Jack Vitek. *Idol: Rock Hudson—The True Story of an American Film Hero.* Villard Books, 1986.

Osborne, John. *Almost a Gentlemen: An Autobiography, vol. II: 1955–1966.* Faber and Faber, 1991.

Osborne, Robert. *70 Years of the Oscar.* Abbeville Press, 1999.

———. *50 Golden Years of Oscar.* ESE California, 1979.

Osterholm, J. Roger. *Bing Crosby: A Bio-Bibliography.* Greenwood Press, 1994.

Paik, Karen. *To Infinity and Beyond! The Story of Pixar Animation Studios.* Chronicle Books, 2007.

Palowski, Franciszek. *The Making of Schindler's List: Behind the Scenes of an Epic Film.* Trans. Anna and Robert G. Ware. Carol Publishing Group, 1998.

Paris, Barry. *Audrey Hepburn.* Putnam, 1996.

Parish, James Robert, and Gregory Mank. *The Best of MGM: The Golden Years (1928–1959).* Arlington House, 1981.

Parish, James Robert. *Fiasco: A History of Hollywood's Iconic Flops.* Wiley, 2007.

———. *Pirates and Seafaring Swashbucklers on the Hollywood Screen.* McFarland, 1995.

Parisi, Paula. *Titanic and the Making of James Cameron: The Inside Story of the Three-Year Adventure That Rewrote Motion Picture History.* Newmarket Press, 1998.

Pearson, John. *The Life of Ian Fleming.* McGraw-Hill, 1966.

Peary, Danny. *Cult Movies 3.* Fireside, 1988.

Pedergast, Sara, and Tom Pendergast, eds. *St. James Encyclopedia of Pop Culture.* Gale Group, 1999.

———. *International Dictionary of Film and Filmmakers.* St. James Press, 2001.

Penzler, Otto. *101 Greatest Movies of Mystery and Suspense*. I Books, 2000.

Perry, George. *The Complete Phantom of the Opera*. Holt, 1991.

Phillips, Gene D. *Beyond the Epic: The Life and Films of David Lean*. University Press of Kentucky, 2006.

———. *John Schlesinger*. Twayne Publishing, 1981.

———. *Stanley Kubrick: A Film Odyssey*. Popular Library, 1975.

Phillips, Gene D., and Rodney Hill, eds. *Francis Ford Coppola: Interviews*. University Press of Mississippi, 2004.

Phillips, Jane. *Godfather: The Intimate Francis Ford Coppola*. University Press of Kentucky, 2004.

Phillips, Julia. *You'll Never Eat Lunch in This Town Again*. Random House, 1991.

Pickford, Mary. *Sunshine and Shadow*. William Heinemann, 1956.

Pierson, John with Kevin Smith. *Spike, Mike, Slackers & Dykes: A Guided Tour Across a Decade of American Independent Cinema*. Hyperion Miramax, 1995.

Place, J. A. *The Western Films of John Ford*. Citadel Press, 1974.

Plecki, Gerard. *Robert Altman*. Twayne Publishers, 1985.

Poitier, Sidney. *The Measure of a Man: A Spiritual Autobiography*. Harper Collins, 1998.

Poitier, Sidney. *This Life*. Knopf, 1980.

Pratley, Gerald. *The Cinema of David Lean*. A. S. Barnes, 1973.

Price, David A. *The Pixar Touch: The Making of a Company*. Alfred A. Knopf, 2008.

Pryor, Ian. *Peter Jackson: From Prince of Splatter to Lord of the Rings: An Unauthorized Biography*. St. Martin's Press, 2003.

Puttnam, David. *Movies and Money*. Vintage Books, 1999.

Puzo, Mario. *The Godfather Papers and Other Confessions*. G. P. Putnam's Sons, 1972.

Quigley, Martin S., ed. *First Century of Film*. Quigley Publishing, 1995.

Quinlan, David. *Quinlan's Illustrated Registry of Film Stars*. Henry Holt, 1991.

Quirk, Lawrence J. *The Films of William Holden*. Citadel Press, 1973.

Radovich, Don. *Tony Richardson: A Bio-Bibliography*. Greenwood Press, 1995.

Ramsaye, Terry. *A Million and One Nights: A History of the Motion Picture Through 1925*. Simon & Schuster, 1926.

Rebello, Stephen. *Alfred Hitchcock and the Making of Psycho*. December Books, 1990.

Rensin, David. *The Mailroom: Hollywood History from The Bottom Up*. Ballantine Books, 1993.

Reynolds, Debbie, and David Patrick Columbia. *Debbie: My Life*. William Morrow, 1988.

Rich, Sharon. *Sweethearts*. Donald I. Fine, 1994.

Richards, David. *Played Out: The Jean Seberg Story*. Random House, 1981.

Richardson, Tony. *The Long Distance Runner: A Memoir*. William Morrow, 1993.

Richie, Donald. *George Stevens: An American Romantic*. Museum of Modern Art, 1970.

Riley, Philip J. *Classic Silents: The Phantom of the Opera*. Magicimageg Filmbooks, 1996.

Ringgold, Gene, and DeWitt Bodeen. *The Films of Cecil B. DeMille*. Citadel Press, 1969.

Rinzler, J. W. *The Making of Star Wars: Revenge of the Sith*. Ballantine Books, 2005.

Riordan, James. *Stone: The Controversies, Excesses and Exploits of a Radical Filmmaker*. Hyperion, 1995.

Rittaud-Hutinet, Jacques, ed., Yvelise Denzter, coll. and Pierre Hodgson, trans. *LETTERS: Auguste and Louis Lumiere*. Faber and Faber, 1995.

Riordan, James. *Stone: A Biography of Oliver Stone*. Hyperion, 1995.

Robertson, James C. *The Casablanca Man: The Cinema of Michael Curtiz*. Routledge, 1993.

Robinson, David. *Chaplin: His Life and Art*. McGraw-Hill, 1985.

———. *Das Cabinet des Dr. Caligari*. British Film Institute, 2008.

Robinson, David, and Ann Lloyd, eds. *Movies of the Silent Years*. Orbis, 1985.

Robinson, Ray. *American Original: A Life of Will Rogers*. Oxford University Press, 1996.

Rogin, Michael. *Blackface, White Noise: Jewish Immigrants in the Hollywood Melting Pot*. University of California Press, 1996.

Rose, Frank. *The Agency: William Morris and the Hidden History of Show Business*. Harper Buxsiness, 1995.

Rosenblum, Ralph, and Robert Karen. *When the Shooting Stops . . . the Cutting Begins: a Film Editor's Story*. Da Capo, 1986.

Rosten, Leo C. *Hollywood: The Movie Colony, The Movie Makers*. Harcourt Brace, 1942.

Rubin, Steven Jay. *Combat Films, American Realism 1945–1970*. McFarland, 1981.

Ruth, Marianne. *Eddie: Eddie Murphy from A to Z*. W.H. Allen & Col, 1986.

Sarris, Andrew X. *The American Cinema: Directors and Directions 1929–1968*. Da Capo Press, 1996.

Schatz, Simon. *Boom and Bust: Hollywood in the 1940s*. Simon & Schuster, 1997.

Schickel, Richard. *D. W. Griffith: An American Life*. Simon & Schuster, 1984.

———. *Elia Kazan: A Biography*. HarperCollins, 2005.

———. *The Men Who Made the Movie*. Atheneum, 1975.

Schumacher, Michael. *Francis Ford Coppola: A Filmmaker's Life*. Crown, 1999.

Schwam, Stephanie, ed. *The Making of 2001: A Space Odyssey*. Modern Library, 2000.

Segaloff, Nat. *Hurricane Billy: The Stormy Life and Films of William Friedkin*. William Morrow, 1990.

Shaw, Don, and Jody Duncan. *The Making of Jurassic Park*. Boxtree, 1993.

Shindler, Colin. *Hollywood in Crisis: Cinema and American Society, 1929–1939*. Routledge, 1996.

Shipman, David. *The Great Movie Stars—The International Years*. A & W Visual Library, 1973.

———. *The Story of Cinema: A Complete Narrative History from the Beginnings to the Present*. St. Martin's Press, 1982.

Sibley, Brian. The Lord of the Rings: *The Making of the Movie Trilogy*. Houghton Mifflin, 2002.

Siegel, Scott and Barbara. *The Encyclopedia of Hollywood*. Facts On File, 1990.

Shone, Tom. *Blockbuster*. Simon and Schuster, 2004.

Sibley, Brian. *The Making of the Movie Trilogy (The Lord of the Rings)*. Houghton Mifflin Harcourt, 2002.

Sikov, Ed. *On Sunset Boulevard: The Life and Times of Billy Wilder*. Hyperion, 1998.

Silver, Alain, and James Ursini. *David Lean and His Films*. Silman-James Press, 1992.

Silverman, Stephen M. *The Fox That Got Away: The Last Days of the Zanuck Dynasty at Twentieth Century-Fox*. Lyle Stuart, 1988.

Simon, Charlotte Chandler. *Nobody's Perfect: Billy Wilder, A Personal Biography*. Simon & Schuster, 2002.

Sinclair, Andrew. *Spiegel: The Man Behind the Pictures*. Little, Brown, and Co., 1987.

Sinclair, Upton. *Upton Sinclair Presents William Fox*. Upton Sinclair, 1933.

Singular, Stephen. *The Rise and Rise of David Geffen*. Carol Publishing Group, 1997.

Slide, Anthony. *The New Historical Dictionary of the American Film Industry*. Scarecrow Press, 1998.

Singular, Stephen. *Power to Burn: Michael Ovitz and the New Business of Show Business*, Carol Publishing, 1996.

Sinyard, Neil. *Fred Zinnemann: Films of Character and Conscience*. McFarland, 2003.

Slide, Anthony, with Alan Gevinson. *The Big V*. Scarecrow Press, 1987.

Smith, Albert E., with Phil A. Koury. *Two Reels and a Crank*. Doubleday, 1952.

Snyder, Robert. *The Voice of the City: Vaudeville and Popular Culture*. Oxford University Press, 1989.

Solomon, Aubrey. *Twentieth Century-Fox: A Corporate and Financial History*. Scarecrow Press, 2002.

Sonnenfeld, Barry, Ed Solomon, Diana Landau, and Melinda Sue Gordon, eds. *Men in Black: The Script and the Story Behind the Film.* Newmarket, 1997.

Spada, James. *Peter Lawford: The Man Who Kept the Secrets.* Bantam Books, 1991.

Sperber, A. M., and Eric Lax. *Bogie.* William Morrow, 1997.

Spignesi, Stephen J. *The Complete Titanic: From the Ship's Earliest Blueprints to the Epic Film.* Birch Lane Press, 1998.

Spoto, Donald. *The Art of Alfred Hitchcock: Fifty Years of His Motion Pictures.* Anchor Books, 1992.

———. *Enchantment: The Life of Audrey Hepburn.* Crown Publishing Group, 2006.

———. *Notorious: The Life of Ingrid Bergman.* HarperCollins, 1997.

———. *Stanley Kramer: Filmmaker.* Samuel French, 1990.

———. *Madcap The Life of Preston Sturges.* Little, Brown & Co., 1990.

Squire, Jason E. *The Movie Business Book.* Prentice Hall, 1983.

Squire, Jason E. *The Movie Business Book* 3rd ed. Simon and Schuster, 2004.

Staggs, Sam. *All About "All About Eve."* St. Martin's Press, 2000.

———. *Close-up on Sunset Boulevard.* St. Martin's Griffin, 2002.

Stanley, Robert, Ph.D. *The Celluloid Empire: A Story of the American Motion Picture Industry.* Communication Arts Books, 1978.

Steinberg, Cobbett. *Film Facts.* Facts on File, 1980.

Stern, D. A. *The Blair Witch Project: A Dossier.* Onyk, 1999.

Stewart, James B. *Disney War.* Simon & Schuster, 2006.

Taubin, Amy. *Taxi Driver.* British Film Institute, 2000.

Taylor, John Russell. *The Life and Times of Alfred Hitchcock.* Da Capo Press, 1996.

Taylor, Robert Lewis. *The Life and Times of Hollywood Mogul Harry Cohn.* McGraw-Hill, 1990.

Thomas, Bob. *Golden Boy: The Untold Story of William Holden.* St. Martin's Press, 1983.

———. *King Cohn: The Life and Times of Hollywood Mogul Harry Cohn.* McGraw-Hill, 1990.

———. *Walt Disney: An American Original.* Simon & Schuster, 1976.

———. *Thalberg: Life and Legend of the Great Hollywood Producer.* Doubleday & Company, 1969.

Thomas, Tony, and Aubrey Solomon. *Films of Twentieth Century Fox.* Citadel Press, 1980.

Thompson, Douglas. *Clint Eastwood: Billion Dollar Man.* John Blake, 2005.

Thompson, Kristin. *The Frodo Franchise: The Lord of the Rings and Modern Hollywood.* University of California Press, 2008.

Thomson, David. *Showman: The Life of David O. Selznick.* Knopf, 1992.

———. *The Whole Equation: A History of Hollywood.* Knopf, 2005.

———. *Warren Beatty and Desert Eyes: Life and a Story.* Vintage Books, 1988.

———. *A Biographical Dictionary of Film.* William Morrow, 1976.

Tomas, Bob. *Thalberg: Life and Legend of the Great Hollywood Producer.* Doubleday, 1969.

Tomas, Bob. *Thalberg: Life and Legend of the Great Hollywood Producer.* Doubleday, 1969.

Tornabene, Lyn. *Long Live the Ring: A Biography of Clark Gable.* Putnam's Sons, 1976.

Tracy, Kathleen. *Morgan Freeman: A Biography.* Barricade Books, 2006.

———. *Matt Damon: Hollywood's Hottest Young Superstar.* St. Martin's Press, 1998.

Trakin, Roy. *Jim Carrey Unmasked!* St. Martin's Press, 1995.

Troyan, Michael. *A Rose for Mrs. Miniver: The Life of Greer Garson.* University Press of Kentucky, 1999.

Truitt, Evelyn Mack. *Who Was Who On Screen. 2nd ed.* R. R. Bowker, 1977.

Truffaut, François. *Hitchcock by Truffaut*. Simon & Schuster, 1966.

Turner, George E., ed. *The Cinema of Adventure, Romance and Terror*. ASC Press, 1989.

Ullman, S. George. *Valentino as I Knew Him*. Macy-Masius, 1926.

Vasey, Ruth. *The World According to Hollywood 1918–1939*. University of Wisconsin Press, 1997.

Valenti, Jack. *The Voluntary Movie Rating System*. MPAA, 1991.

Vaz, Mark Cotta. *Living Dangerously: The Adventures of Merian C. Cooper*. Villard Books, 2005.

Vaz, Mark Cotta, and Patricia Rose Duignan. *Industrial Light & Magic: Into the Digital Realm*. Ballantine Books, 1996.

Vertrees, Alan David, and Thomas Schatz. *Selznick's Vision: Gone with the Wind and Hollywood Filmmaking*. University of Texas Press, 1997.

Vidor, King. *A Tree Is a Tree*. Harcourt, Brace, 1953.

Viertel, Peter. *White Hunter, Black Heart*. Doubleday, 1953.

Vogel, Harold L. *Entertainment Industry Economics: A Guide for Financial Analysis*. Cambridge University Press, 1986.

Wachowski, Larry, et al. *The Art of the Matrix*. Newmarket Press, 2000.

Wagenknecht, Edward, and Anthony Slide. *The Films of D. W. Griffith*. Crown Publishers, 1975.

Walker, Alexander. *Audrey: Her Real Story*. Macmillan, 1997.

Walker, John, ed. *Halliwell's Film Guide*. 8th ed. HarperCollins, 1991.

Wallis, King. *King Vidor on Film Making*. David McKay, 1972.

Walsh, Raoul. *Each Man in His Time*. Farrar, Straus & Giroux, 1974.

Wansell, Geoffrey. *Haunted Idol: The Story of the Real Cary Grant*. William Morrow, 1983.

Watson, Coy, Jr. *The Keystone Kid*. Santa Monica Press, 2001.

Waxman, Sharon. *Rebels on the Backlot: Six Maverick Directors and How They Conquered the Hollywood Studio System*. Harper Perennial, 2005.

Wayne, Jane Ellen. *The Leading Men of MGM*. Carroll & Graf, 2005.

———. *The Life of Robert Taylor*. Warner, 1973.

Wellman, William. *The Man and His Wings: William A. Wellman and the Making of the First Best Picture*. Praeger Publishers, 2006.

———. *A Short Time for Insanity*. Hawthorn, 1974.

Whitfield, Stephen. *In Search of American Jewish Culture*. Brandeis University Press, 1999.

Wilkerson, Tichi, and Marcia Borie. *The Hollywood Reporter: The Golden Years*. Coward-McCann, 1984.

Williams, Pat, and Jim Denney. *How to Be Like Walt*. Health Communications, 2004.

Willis, John. *1987 Film Annual Screen World, Vol. 38*. Crown Publishers, 1987.

Winters, Shelley. *Shelley, Also Known as Shirley*. William Morrow & Co., 1980.

Wood, Tom. *The Bright Side of Billy Wilder, Primarily*. Doubleday, 1970.

Worrell, Denise. *Icons Intimate Portraits*. The Atlantic Monthly Press, 1989.

York, Michael. *Accidentally on Purpose: An Autobiography*. Simon & Schuster, 1991.

Young, Jeff. *Kazan: The Master Director Discusses His Films; Interviews with Elia Kazan*. New Market Press, 1999.

Youngerman, Joseph C., based on interviews by Ira Skutch and David Shepard. *My Seventy Years at Paramount Studios and the Directors Guild of America*. Directors Guild of America Publications, 1995.

Zierold, Norman J. *The Moguls*. Coward-McCann, 1969.

Zinman, David. *50 Classic Motion Pictures: Stuff That Dreams Are Made Of*. Crown, 1970.

Zinnemann, Fred. *A Life in the Movies: An Autobiography*. Charles Scribner's Sons, 1992.

Zolotow, Maurice. *Billy Wilder in Hollywood*. Limelight, 1987.

Film and Culture Magazines

American Cinematographer
American Film
Biograph Bulletin
Cineaste
Cinefantastique
Cinefex
Cinema Journal
Computer Graphics World
The Director
Dissent
Entertainment Weekly
Film Comment
Film Culture
Film History: An International Journal
Film Index
Film Quarterly
The Hollywood Reporter
Home Theater
Interview

Journal of Popular Film and Television
Locations Magazine (published by the Association of Film Commissioners International)
Los Angeles Business Journal
Motion Picture Herald
Moving Picture World
Photoplay
Quarterly Review of Film Studies
Theater Journal
Science Fiction Weekly
Screen Education
Screen International
Sight and Sound
Star Pulse
Starlog
Time Out London
Video
Wide Angle
Wired

Production Reports and Collections

American Graffiti shooting schedule, "As Shot" (1972) and production report (August 4, 1972)

Arthur Freed Collection at the University of Southern California Cinema-Television Library

Cecil B. DeMille Collection, Brigham Young University

The John Ford Papers, Lilly Library, Indiana University

Lucasfilm daily progress reports for *Star Wars* and *Indiana Jones* films

Studio records at the Academy of Motion Picture Arts and Sciences library (AMPAS files)

University of Southern California Cinema Television School Archives

Warner Bros. Collection, University of Southern California

Interviews

Frank McAdams telephone interview with E. M. Nathanson, June 7, 2007 (*The Dirty Dozen*)

Interview with Bob Rafelson, *Chicago Tribune*, by Gary Dretzka (*Five Easy Pieces*)

Interview with Arthur Hiller by Alex Ben Block, February 2, 2007 (*Love Story*)

Interview with William Friedkin by Michael Kogge, April 6, 2007 (*The French Connection, The Exorcist*)

Interviews with Gabe Sumner (UA head of marketing), Eric Pleskow (UA co-chairman), Gene Kirkwood (producer, production exec), Bob Chartoff (producer), Larry Kubik (Sylvester Stallone's first agent), and Lloyd Kaufman (UA head of PR), by Alex Ben Block (*Rocky*)

Interview with James Cameron by Academy of Achievement. Achievement.org, 1999 (*Titanic*)

Interview with Peter Benchley by Brian Handwerk, *National Geographic*, 2002 (*Jaws*)

Interview with Robert Wise by Harry Kreisler, Conversations with History: Institute of International Studies, UC Berkeley globetrotter.berkeley.edu/, 1998 (*The Sound of Music, West Side Story*)

DVD Extras and Documentaries

All About Eve, 20th Century-Fox Home Entertainment

Apocalypse Now, Bahr, Fax and George Hickenlooper. *Hearts of Darkness: A Filmmaker's Apocalypse*

Bambi, 2-disc Platinum Edition

The Best Years of Our Lives, Warner Bros. Home Video

The Bridge on the River Kwai, 2-disc Limited Edition

Cinderella, 2-disc Platinum Edition

Doctor Zhivago, DVD extras

Patton, 20th Century-Fox Home Entertainment, 2006

Dr. Strangelove, DVD extras, Columbia. 2001

Fantasia, 60th Anniversary Special Edition

Fiddler on the Roof

The French Connection, Five-Star Collection, DVD extras, 20th Century-Fox, 2001

From Here to Eternity

Giant, 2-disc Special Edition, Warner Bros. Home Video, 2005

The Greatest Show on Earth, Paramount Home Entertainment

How the West Was Won, Warner Bros. Home Video, 2002

Love Story, Deluxe DVD

Mary Poppins, 2-disc 40th Anniversary Edition

Mister Roberts, Warner Bros. Home Entertainment

Mrs. Miniver, Warner Bros. Home Video

Peter Pan, 2-disc Platinum Edition

Pinocchio: Gold Edition, Walt Disney Home Video

Singin' in the Rain, 2-disc Special Edition, Warner Bros. Home Video

Spartacus, DVD extras, Criterion Collection, 1998

Sunrise: A Song of Two Humans, John Bailey commentary, Fox Studio Classics, 2003

White Christmas, Paramount Home Entertainment

General Online Sources

allmovie.com

afi.com (American Film Institute)

americanlegends.com

bbc.co.uk/films

bfi.org (British Film Institute)

boxofficemojo.com

cinemasource.com

classicfilmguide.com

cobbles.com

combustiblecelluloid.com

digitalmediafx.com

dvdjournal.com

dvdtalk.com

dvdtown.com

dvdverdict.com

edison.rutgers.edu (Rutgers University Thomas Edison Papers)

emanuellevy.com

eopinions.com

fandango.com

filmcritic.com

filmeducation.org

filmhead.com

filmscouts.com

filmsite.org (AMC)

filmreference.com

filmthreat.com

flixter.com

fromscripttodvd.com

historyinfilm.com

imdb.com

hollywoodreporter.com

mi6.co.uk

mooviees.com

nytimes.com

oscars.org (Academy of Motion Picture Arts and Sciences)

reel.com

reelclassics.com

ropeofsilicon.com

rottentomatoes.com

scifi.com

screensource (amug.org)

silentera.com

slate.com

tcm.com (Turner Classic Movies)

thebigpicturedvd.com

the-numbers.com

thesmokinggun.com

thisdayindisneyhistory.com

totalfilm.com

tvguide.com

variety.com

wikipedia.org

widescreenmuseum.com

INDEX